THE OXFORD ENCYCLOPEDIA OF
AMERICAN LITERATURE

THE OXFORD ENCYCLOPEDIA OF

AMERICAN LITERATURE

Jay Parini

Editor in Chief

Volume 4

ANNE SEXTON – WRITING AS A WOMAN
IN THE TWENTIETH CENTURY

Topical Outline of Articles
Directory of Contributors
Index

OXFORD
UNIVERSITY PRESS
2004

OXFORD
UNIVERSITY PRESS

Oxford   New York

Auckland   Bangkok   Buenos Aires   Cape Town   Chennai
Dar es Salaam   Delhi   Hong Kong   Istanbul   Karachi   Kolkata
Kuala Lumpur   Madrid   Melbourne   Mexico City   Mumbai   Nairobi
São Paulo   Shanghai   Taipei   Tokyo   Toronto

Copyright © 2004 by Oxford University Press, Inc.

Published by Oxford University Press, Inc.
198 Madison Avenue, New York, New York 10016
http://www.oup.com

Library of Congress Cataloging-in-Publication Data

The Oxford Encyclopedia of American Literature / Jay Parini, editor-in-chief.
p. cm.
Includes bibliographical references and index.
ISBN 0-19-515653-6 (set: alk. paper)
ISBN 0-19-516724-4 (v. 1: alk. paper)
ISBN 0-19-516725-2 (v. 2: alk. paper)
ISBN 0-19-516726-0 (v. 3: alk. paper)
ISBN 0-19-516727-9 (v. 4: alk. paper)
1. American literature—Encyclopedias. I. Parini, Jay.
PS21 .E537 2003
810′.3—dc21
2002156325

Printing number: 9   8   7   6   5   4   3   2   1

Permission credits are on p. 517 of vol. 4, which constitutes
a continuation of the copyright page.

Printed in the United States of America
on acid-free paper

THE OXFORD ENCYCLOPEDIA OF
AMERICAN LITERATURE

ANNE SEXTON

by Ellen McGrath Smith

Anne Sexton is one of the most charged and memorable personalities in American literature. Her image as a taboo-breaking, glamorous New England housewife-turned-poet has made her a cultural icon for two generations in the United States and beyond. Her image has led many conservative critics to dismiss much of her work as extreme and sensationalistic while overlooking Sexton's incomparable flashes of imagery and insight. At the other extreme, her image has drawn many readers who admittedly read little poetry before Sexton's, expanding the audience for American poetry. In between these two extremes fall readers who, for many reasons, see Anne Sexton as a key player in the emergence at mid-century of a more personal and direct type of poetry, often referred to as confessional poetry, a term coined in 1959 by the critic M. L. Rosenthal in his review of Robert Lowell's groundbreaking collection of personal poetry, *Life Studies* (1959).

As a student of Lowell's, a major figure in American poetry from mid-century through the 1970s, Sexton initially followed his lead in blending personal subject matter and formal verse patterning. In this, she also followed the lead of another teacher and friend, W. D. Snodgrass, whose 1959 collection, *Heart's Needle*, dealt poignantly with the loss of a child through divorce. But although Sexton was influenced by these male poets' attention to family dynamics, intimate relationships, and individual emotional complexity, she significantly contributed in her own right to the confessional arena, writing from the perspective of an upper-middle-class woman raised to seek fulfillment solely through marriage, family, and home. The frustrations and conflicts experienced in this role are woven through her poetry; in this sense, she had her finger on the pulse of an entire generation of women who would demand more social,

Anne Sexton.
(*Courtesy of the Library of Congress*)

cultural, and civil equality during the second wave of the women's movement in the 1960s and 1970s. Her work pushed against unwritten boundaries of subject matter, voice, and attitude, a widening of the field also implemented by other women writers of the second wave, including Adrienne Rich, Carolyn Kizer, Kathleen Fraser, Grace Paley, Erica Jong, Marge Piercy, Judy Grahn, Nikki Giovanni, Maxine Kumin, and others.

Anne Gray Harvey was born on 9 November 1928 in Newton, Massachusetts, the youngest of three daughters in an affluent family with a history of prosperity and power in New England. Sexton's father, Ralph Churchill Harvey, ran a successful wool business but suffered from alcoholism and later lost most of his interest in the business. Sexton's mother, Mary Gray Staples Harvey, was a well-educated socialite whom Sexton would recall as distant and implacable. Both parents—in their real, distorted, and idealized forms—figure prominently in Sexton's poetry.

Educated in public and private New England schools, Sexton was never an academic standout, although she did write some poetry and was involved in theater during her school years. Following high school and a brief time at a finishing school, Sexton eloped at age nineteen with Alfred Muller Sexton II. This marriage lasted until 1973; they had two daughters together. Early in the marriage Sexton played the role of housewife, moving near her husband's college campus and, when he left college, relocating with him for duty in the naval reserves. With the birth of their first child, Linda, in 1953, the Sextons returned to the Boston suburbs, where both their families lived, and where Alfred Sexton, discharged from the navy, took a job in sales with his father-in-law's wool business.

After the birth of her first child, Sexton entered what would be a lifelong battle with depression. With her husband traveling frequently as a salesman, Sexton's psychiatric problems intensified when their second child, Joy, was born in 1955. In 1956 Sexton was admitted for the first time to a psychiatric hospital, and during the next three years she was largely unable to care for her children, who stayed for long stretches of time with relatives. At the same time, Sexton began treatment with Dr. Martin Orne, a Boston psychiatrist who encouraged her writing. Sexton continued to write and eventually, in 1957, she joined an adult education poetry workshop led by Tufts University professor John Holmes.

"THE BUSINESS OF WORDS": SEXTON'S EMERGENCE

Sexton's writing was quickly characterized by technical development, productivity, and success. Within four years of her venturing out to attend Holmes's workshop, her first book, *To Bedlam and Part Way Back* (1960), was published to numerous positive reviews. In a little over a decade's time, she received the Pulitzer Prize in poetry for her third full-length collection, *Live or Die* (1966). Throughout these years she continued to suffer from mental illness, which was exacerbated by her growing addiction to prescription medications and alcohol. Still, she received numerous awards, providing substantial income for her family, which was together under one roof by 1960. And although she was acutely agoraphobic, she traveled extensively as the demand and fees for readings of her work increased.

While the "confessional" label is the one most frequently given to Sexton and her work, it fails to account for the entire body and range of Sexton's poetry. In addition to the poems directly exploring interpersonal relationships, one can also identify poems of technical strength that are conscious of their part in a literary tradition; poems that mine the symbolic potential of the unconscious in the manner of Edgar Allan Poe and the French symbolist poets; and poems that undertake, from a woman's perspective, a more public critique of sociocultural practices and ideals. At times, these tendencies are present together within single volumes, even single poems, with one of the tendencies predominating. That is the case with *All My Pretty Ones* (1962), a book that deals primarily with loved ones and the death in 1959 of both of Sexton's parents. Recognizing these multiple tendencies is a way of seeing the work whole, without being overwhelmed by the poet's image as a confessional poet.

Sexton's fresh confessional voice sounded clearly in her first book of poems, *To Bedlam and Part Way Back*, which centered on the author's experiences as a psychiatric patient. Writing about such experiences had initially, in the mid-1950s, been encouraged by Sexton's psychiatrist as a therapeutic and confidence-building measure, but by the time the book was published, Sexton had become deeply involved in the craft and business of poetry, particularly through a poetry workshop that evolved out of Holmes's adult education class. Also in this workshop was Sexton's neighbor, Maxine Kumin, the Pulitzer Prize–winning author of *Up Country* (1972), and the two women established an ongoing working relationship, critiquing one another's poems daily while their children played in the background. Kumin has frequently attested to Sexton's relentless, arduous process of revision. *To Bedlam*, then, is a deeply private book, but tempered by Sexton's painstaking technical work—most of the book consists of poems written in patterned rhyme and meter.

To Bedlam opens with a poem addressed to Sexton's psychiatrist. *You, Doctor Martin*, written in the seven-line stanzas that are common in Sexton's work, sets the scene of "Bedlam," the psychiatric hospital, and celebrates the work of the psychiatrist, "an oracular eye in our nest," who

> twist[s] in the pull
> of the foxy children who fall
> like floods of life in frost.

What is striking about this and other poems in *To Bedlam* is the way in which Sexton credibly renders the patient's perspective while maintaining awareness of the expectations and assumptions of the "sane" world beyond the hospital, ironically referred to as "this summer hotel." This perspectival tension produces the paradox of the patient as a child in an adult's body—a paradox that haunts Sexton's confessional and symbolist poems as she traces the ego's search for parental love and, later, for divine love and mercy. For example, "Ringing the Bells," one of the most famous poems from *To Bedlam*, follows the rhythm of a child's verse while describing a music therapy workshop in the mental hospital. The playful rhythm, reminiscent of the nursery rhyme "The House That Jack Built," works in chilling counterpoint to the helplessness of the hospitalized, broken-down adults. Later in the book, the ambitious seven-part poem "The Double Image" looks at Sexton's relationship with her mother and her youngest daughter, following a seasonal structure and closing on the image of two portraits, one of Sexton and one of her deceased mother, eternally facing each other from opposite walls in the Harvey family home.

Sexton's more public, popular voice briefly materializes in *To Bedlam*. "Her Kind" became Sexton's signature poem at readings. It also was the name of the chamber rock group, Anne Sexton and Her Kind, that she formed in the late 1960s to provide musical accompaniment to her poetry. "Her Kind" invokes the idea of the woman poet as otherworldly, outside of the pale of social conventions. And in the poem "For John, Who Begs Me Not to Enquire Further," Sexton asserts her reasons for writing about personal matters, even though it makes others uncomfortable:

Not that it was beautiful,
but that, in the end, there was
a certain sense of order there;
something worth learning
in that narrow diary of my mind.

The confessional treatment of family dynamics, begun at the end of *To Bedlam* in poems like "The Double Image" and "The Division of Parts," is given full play in Sexton's second book, *All My Pretty Ones* (1962). Its title an allusion to a speech by MacDuff in Shakespeare's *Macbeth* upon learning that his wife and children have been murdered, this volume mainly examines familial relationships but also extends to relationships with other writers: W. D. Snodgrass in "To a Friend Whose Work Has Come to Triumph"; the Ohio poet James Wright in "Letter Written on a Ferry While Crossing Long Island Sound"; and "Love Song for K. Owyne." In this collection, Sexton frequently breaks into free verse, which was becoming much more common among American poets. At the same time, she began to delve into the complex associative image-making that give even her most autobiographical poems a more transcendent, mystical, and at times, surreal, aura. In this way, even as she lessened her dependence on patterned form, she employed image as a way of objectifying the private and forming a connection with readers.

"THE EXCITABLE GIFT": THE MIDDLE YEARS

In 1967, Sexton received the Pulitzer Prize for her most directly autobiographical collection to date, *Live or Die* (1966). In a note at the beginning of the book, whose poems are arranged chronologically by date of composition, Sexton acknowledges that the poems "read like a fever chart for a bad case of melancholy." Poems such as "Wanting to Die" and "Sylvia's Death"—this latter written in response to the 1963 suicide of the American poet Sylvia Plath, with whom Sexton was acquainted while studying with Lowell at Boston University—are personal reflections on mental illness and despair as well as an unflinching acknowledgment of these conditions among an alarming number of American poets. The poem "Flee

on Your Donkey," written in informal free verse with Sexton's characteristic use of unpatterned end and internal rhyme, appears early in the collection where, returning to the psychiatric hospital, the scene of Sexton's first book, the poem's speaker is anxious to get past it:

I have come back
but disorder is not what it was.
I have lost the trick of it!

Throughout, the author looks squarely at her struggle with suicidal impulses, finding uplift in the book's closing poem, "Live," written on the occasion of the birth of puppies in the Sexton household. "Today life opened inside me like an egg," the third stanza opens; the poem rises to a crescendo and a sense of resolve in the closing lines:

So I won't hang around in my hospital shift,
repeating The Black Mass and all of it.
I say *Live, Live* because of the sun,
the dream, the excitable gift.

Although it is predominantly a free-verse journal of inner turmoil, *Live or Die* also contains poems based on motherhood ("Little Girl," "My String Bean," "My Lovely Woman," and "A Little Uncomplicated Hymn").

In 1969 Sexton's *Love Poems* was published. This collection contains many of the Sexton poems that pushed boundaries and spoke frankly about sexuality, the body, and marital infidelity. Poems like "In Celebration of My Uterus" and "Moon Song, Woman Song" were also in step with the liberation of expression associated with the second wave of the women's movement. In *Love Poems*, the dynamics of real and imagined intimate relationships are tied to sociocultural issues of marriage and sexual politics, issues that feminism and the sexual revolution of the late 1960s had begun to scrutinize. Also in 1969, Sexton's play, *Mercy Street*, opened off-Broadway at the American Place Theater. Set in an Episcopal church, the play centers on the protagonist Daisy's efforts to use both psychology and theology as tools for healing the wounds of the past.

Sexton's growing interest in sociocultural critique was given full play in her 1971 book, *Transformations*, which revises in irreverent and updated terms seventeen fairy tales published in the nineteenth century by Jacob and Wilhelm Grimm. One of the collection's most anthologized pieces, "Cinderella," highlights the absurdity of the tale's details through graphic cause-and-effect statements and deadpan understatement, as with the elder stepsister's gruesome attempt to make her foot fit the gold slipper by slicing off her big toe:

The prince rode away with her until the white dove
told him to look at the blood pouring forth.
That is the way with amputations.

"Cinderella" ironizes the notion of marriage as a happy ending, as do other poems in *Transformations*, which is steeped in dark humor as certain middle-class norms are revealed, often through the piling up of unnerving similes, to be a veneer over insidious drives and desires, some rooted in Freudian psychology, others in American puritanical materialism.

"STILL ROWING": PERSONAL DECLINE AND FINAL WORKS

The 1970s brought a number of honors for Sexton, including a full-time appointment to teach creative writing at Boston University. But it was a short decade for the poet, whose continued depression, prescription drug addiction, and alcohol abuse took their toll; she committed suicide at home, alone, on 4 October 1974, a year after divorcing her husband and one month before her forty-sixth birthday. Her older child was in college at the time, her younger at a boarding school in Maine. Much of Sexton's posthumously published work bears traces of her emotional unraveling: *45 Mercy Street* (1976) includes "The Divorce Papers," a rough documentary of her brief life as a single woman, and *Words for Dr. Y* (1978) is part of a private file of poems Sexton viewed as strictly therapeutic and not to be published until after her death. Nonetheless, in addition to *Transformations*, Sexton published in her few remaining years two volumes of poetry—*The Book of Folly* (1972) and *The Death Notebooks* (1974)—and a third book, *The Awful Rowing toward God*, which, published in 1975, was for the most part finalized before her death.

In these works from the 1970s, Sexton ambitiously took on new subject matter, styles, and scope. *The Book of Folly* contains the multi-section poem "The Death of the Fathers," which marks Sexton's personal efforts to achieve closure with the past at the same time that it registers feminist anger and sadness over patriarchal oppression. The hold of patriarchal traditions is felt not only on the personal and social levels for Sexton in this volume; it also permeates her own investigations into Christianity in "The Jesus Papers," a sequence of nine poems closing *The Book of Folly*. Highly unorthodox, these poems portray Jesus in Freudian terms and highlight the sacrificial role of women, exemplified by Mary, to whom Jesus says, in "Jesus Suckles," "I am a truck. I run everything. / I own you." Born and raised Protestant (Congregational), Sexton did not practice as an adult, but in her last days she was receiving religious instruction from an Episcopal seminarian. Like many women at this time, Sexton sought creative ways to separate the spiritual sustenance from the sexism in organized religion.

The Death Notebooks was originally intended by Sexton to be published after her death but appeared in February 1974. Continuing the probing of theology begun in *The Book of Folly*, *The Death Notebooks* consists of poems that approximate prayer or chant, as the speaker builds through language a universe in which death and God are understood and accepted. It is, of course, a highly subjective—and at times, surrealistic—universe, full of anachronism, iconoclasm, doubt, and affirmation. For example, in "O Ye Tongues," Sexton finds soulmates in the Hebrew Psalmist and the eighteenth-century British poet Christopher Smart. In eight long-lined psalms, the speaker—at times playfully, at times in deadly earnest—moves through prayer, praise, rejoicing, lament, prophesy, and transcendence. Much in "O Ye Tongues" aligns Sexton with Walt Whitman and with Allen Ginsberg, the Beat poet who was Sexton's contemporary. That particular Beat blend of the sacred and the profane is seen in "The Furies," a sequence of fifteen poems in *The Death Notebooks* that vary in form and theme, from the sexual explicitness of "The Fury of Cocks" to the ontological reflectiveness of "The Fury of God's Good-bye."

This more public, incantatory voice is equally present in *The Awful Rowing toward God*, completed by Sexton before her death and published in 1975. "The Sermon of the Twelve Acknowledgments" is a prophetic guide to the months of the year, weaving idiosyncratic snippets of folk wisdom on a makeshift loom of Christian theology. The outcome of the "rowing" that frames the collection is a foregone conclusion; in the book's first poem, the speaker announces that "I know that that island [of God] will not be perfect" and that "this story ends with me still rowing." The rowing is also a metaphor for an isolated yearning for meaning that preoccupied Sexton's, especially during her last years.

[*See also* Confessional Poetry; Lowell, Robert; *and* Plath, Sylvia.]

SELECTED WORKS

To Bedlam and Part Way Back (1960)
All My Pretty Ones (1962)
Eggs of Things (1963)
More Eggs of Things (1964)
Live or Die (1966)
Love Poems (1969)

Joey and the Birthday Present (1971)
Transformations (1971)
The Book of Folly (1972)
The Death Notebooks (1974)
The Awful Rowing toward God (1975)
The Wizard's Tears (1975)
45 Mercy Street (1976)
Anne Sexton: A Self-Portrait in Letters (1977)
Words for Dr. Y: Uncollected Poems with Three Stories (1978)
The Complete Poems (1981)
No Evil Star: Selected Essays, Interviews and Prose (1985)
Selected Poems of Anne Sexton (1988)
Voice of the Poet: Anne Sexton (2000)

FURTHER READING

Bixler, Frances, ed. *Original Essays on the Poetry of Anne Sexton.* Conway, Ark., 1988. Includes work relating motherhood and poetry.

Colburn, Steven E., ed. *Anne Sexton: Telling the Tale.* Ann Arbor, Mich., 1988. Reminiscences by poets, critics, and friends of Sexton, as well as reprints of book reviews and essays on particular works, poems, and themes.

George, Diana Hume. *Oedipus Anne: The Poetry of Anne Sexton.* Urbana, Ill., 1987. Reads the poetry through a Freudian psychoanalytical lens.

George, Diana Hume, ed. *Sexton: Selected Criticism.* Urbana, Ill., 1988. Collection of critical perspectives, including psychoanalytical and feminist readings of Sexton's work.

Hall, Caroline King Barnard. *Anne Sexton.* Boston, 1989. Basic biographical and bibliographic overview, part of Twayne United States Authors Series.

McClatchy, J. D., ed. *Anne Sexton: The Artist and Her Critics.* Bloomington, Ind., 1978. The first essay collection on Sexton following her death, edited by a close friend and fellow poet.

Middlebrook, Diane Wood. *Anne Sexton: A Biography.* Boston, 1991. The biography, authorized by Sexton's literary estate, provides extensive personal and aesthetic details.

Morton, Richard E. *Anne Sexton's Poetry of Redemption: The Chronology of a Pilgrimage.* New York, 1989. Focuses on the spiritual aspects of Sexton's work.

Northouse, Cameron, and Thomas P. Walsh. *Sylvia Plath and Anne Sexton: A Reference Guide.* Boston, 1974. Brings together work on two important mid-century American women poets with complete bibliography.

Wagner-Martin, Linda, ed. *Critical Essays on Anne Sexton.* Boston, 1989. A range of essays on specific poems, books, and themes.

SAM SHEPARD

by Philip Parry

Sam Shepard is the best known, and has proved the most enduring, of those American dramatists who began their careers in the radical and alternative theater movements of the 1960s. Although his plays have become thoroughly mainstream, something of the aura of those early years still clings to his work.

Between 1964 and the mid-1970s, Shepard composed more than thirty short plays and sketches that take their chosen form to its practical limits. *The Tooth of Crime* (1972) brought this phase to an end; *Curse of the Starving Class* (1977), a very different kind of play, initiated a replacement phase. Curiously, both plays were given their world premieres in London, where Shepard lived for part of each year between 1971 and 1974. Despite a keen British following, however, he remains a distinctly American writer.

LIFE AND ART

Shepard was born Samuel Shepard Rogers in Fort Sheridan, Illinois, on 5 November 1943. A service child, he lived on army bases until he was eight, when his family moved to Duarte, California. He dropped out of formal education early, joined a group of repertory players in 1962, and the following year made his way to New York City at a time when off-off-Broadway theater was emerging. Shepard spent most of the next thirteen years serving his dramatic apprenticeship in radical and alternative theaters in New York City and San Francisco. This period of his life, when he could be certain of getting even his most experimental and least developed works performed by one makeshift company or another, was a playwright's heaven. These short plays contributed themes, images, and elements of stagecraft to the longer, less willfully experimental and more intricately plotted plays that were to develop out of them in the 1970s and 1980s.

Although there are powerful continuities between the work of Shepard's maturity and of his earlier apprenticeship, only one late play can be described as a throwback. *States of Shock* (1991), a "vaudeville nightmare" designed, as the pun in its title suggests, to show the disunity of the United States, both reads and—with its mad colonel,

Sam Shepard on a movie set, 1991. (© *Yves Forestier/Corbis Sygma*)

---

crippled veteran, shaky waitress, and masturbating white-suited white man—performs like a deliberate revival of the recklessly proliferating absurdism of his early work. This exception apart, Shepard has since 1977 emerged as a serious and weighty playwright who, in the tradition of Eugene O'Neill, chronicles dark family misfortunes. In *Buried Child* (1978), for example, beyond the door that leads "from the porch to the outside" are "the shapes of dark elm trees" that summon up *Desire under the Elms*, O'Neill's tragic tale of sexual passion and taboo that, like Shepard's play, is set on an isolated farmstead.

This second phase of Shepard's writing—unless *Simpatico* (first produced in 1994), a piece somewhat in the manner of David Mamet, proves an exception—has shown no sign of yielding to a third. Perhaps Shepard's growing involvement with filmmaking signals a shift in his interests and the end of his career as a productive dramatist. However, since he is just reaching his sixtieth birthday, there is time for further development. Nonetheless, it is likely that he will be principally remembered for four or five major plays of his second phase.

THE SHORT PLAYS

Viewed with hindsight—a privileged vision in Shepard's past-fixated world—his early playlets are his later plays in embryo. In each of the three scenes that compose *The Rock Garden* (1964), there is the imagistic germ of a much larger play. A man sits at the head of a table but does not speak to, or acknowledge the presence of, a teenage boy and girl who drink milk and exchange glances. The only action is the lifting up and setting down of their tumblers. Then, whether by accident or design (the text does not tell us which), the girl drops her glass, the milk spills, and there is blackout. Here, in silent symbolism, is an entire play. In the next scene the mother of the teenage boy lies in bed and talks to him. He is in his underwear. Step-by-step she compares him physically with his father: they share legs, feet, a torso. (In *Curse of the Starving Class*, Ella tells her son that his penis and his grandfather's are "almost identical in fact.") The boy responds by covering each bodily part as soon as it is mentioned; by the end of the scene he is fully dressed and is replaced by the man from scene 1, who now wears underwear. Through this pattern of dressing and undressing, father and son are mapped each upon the other (as are Wesley and his father in *Curse of the Starving Class*, where Wesley strips, washes, and puts on his father's soiled clothing). In the final scene man and boy, both in their underwear, do not look at one another but speak of their principal

interests. As the man tells of his gardening and domestic chores, the boy repeatedly falls off his chair. "It's always wet about the sprinkler heads," the man complains. (Martin's reply, when Eddie asks him in *Fool for Love* [first produced in 1983] what lawn maintenance involves, is "weeding around the sprinkler heads. Stuff like that." The repressed sexuality of the early play is reconstituted as sexual antagonism in the later.) But when, in his turn, the boy describes with extraordinary explicitness how he arouses women—"Actually girls really like fingers almost as well as a penis"—it is the man who falls over just as "the lights black out." The milk spilt in the first scene and the semen spilt in the third ("When I come it's like a river") are the play's symbolic offerings. Speaking without conversing, the grip of the past, family secrets, spilt seed and what grows from it: these are Shepard's ingredients, taken down from the shelf but not yet put together.

Cowboys #2 (1967) is another example of a recipe waiting to go in the oven. In it young actors in a piece of alternative theater (Gary Hanes and Philip Austin in the original production) impersonate Stu and Chet, young actors in a piece of alternative theater. Wielding "imaginary rifles" against "imaginary indians," they merely pretend to be cowboys. But their game is framed by intruders (members of the audience or rival players), who begin to replicate their speeches monotonously, and by the noises of modern, urban life. Playing at being cowboys, Stu and Chet are—with only a few adjustments here and there—Austin and Lee, the principal characters in *True West* (1980). Both pairs of men are self-conscious in their role-playing, and the connection between them is emphasized by a perhaps accidental, but still meaningful, coincidence: Philip Austin was an actor in the first play; Austin is a character in the second.

Role-playing is a common feature of Shepard's plays throughout both phases. One example is both more explicit and more mysterious than most. In *A Lie of the Mind* (first produced in 1985), Beth is a professional actress who reads her scripts to her pathologically jealous husband. His inability to recognize that acting is the job that actors do—"A job is where you don't have fun. You don't dick around tryin' to pretend you're somebody else" is his view—leads him to doubt her fidelity when she reads out love scenes in front of him and provokes him to a violent attack. Brain damaged from his blows, Beth near the end of the play dresses up "in a bizarre combination of clothing" in order to woo his brother. In short, by becoming once again an actress, she confirms the accuracy of his primitive suspicion: "That's why she wanted to become an actress in the first place. So she could get away from me." Perhaps the oddest feature of *A Lie of the Mind*, and further evidence of continuity between Shepard's two phases, is the way in which the play ends. After all the traumas that its characters have suffered, none of which has been explicitly cleared up, the play emblematizes the discovery of inner peace and restoration of harmony through the way in which Beth's parents fold up the American flag with military precision: "Now if everything works out right we should have all the stars on the outside and all the stripes tucked in." Short plays can perhaps afford to substitute images for arguments, but *A Lie of the Mind* is a very long play indeed, whose ending—like the flag—is too neat. Perhaps an effective dramatic resolution requires real neatness (whatever that might be) rather than a neat symbol; or perhaps neatness cannot adequately represent resolution, so that both the ending of the play and the flag might have been better if both had been allowed to flap around a bit more.

"Untethered" speech is the feature of Shepard's early plays that survives most memorably and most strangely into his later ones. (Speech-act theorists say that an utterance is "tethered at both ends" when it is directed by someone to someone as part of a fully contextualized speech-act exchange.) "In my experience [in writing plays]," Shepard has said, "the character . . . appears out of nowhere . . . and speaks. He doesn't speak to me because I'm not in the play. I'm watching it. He speaks to something or someone else, or even to himself, or even to no one" (Marranca, 1981, p. 214). Thus, Kent, the male lead in *La Turista* (1967), retreats from an active engagement with reality into "a world unrelated to anything on stage," and speaks from this world "even when he talks to the other actors." Since, in a play considered as an imaginative imitation of an external reality, characters speak to other characters, this stage direction is oddly phrased, as though Kent (like Stu and Chet) is an actor addressing other actors. Shepard thus anticipates the strange, occluded monologues with which characters throughout *Curse of the Starving Class* and *Buried Child* punctuate—while seeming to ignore—the plays in which they appear.

The Tooth of Crime is the last and longest of the first-phase plays. Once again its characters are performers: Hoss, an aging rock star, and Crow, the flashy young upstart destined to replace him. When they fight to the death, their chosen weapons are impersonation and improvisation, tools of the experimental actor's trade. Essentially, he will survive who shows the greatest mastery

of style. "Choose an argot," Crow insists, and speak in it: "Singles or LPs, 45, 78, 33 1/3." However, as this list of dated options suggests, *The Tooth of Crime* is itself severely dated. In a 1996 interview that prefaces a revised text of *Buried Child*, Shepard indicated both his affection for this play and a degree of dissatisfaction with it: "There's a strength to the play, [but] it doesn't go where I hoped it would go." The plays of his second phase are ones that go where he wants them to go.

THE LATER PLAYS

Three plays from Shepard's second phase contain moments so obviously connected that they map out for us the emotional territory that he has chosen to explore. In *Simpatico*, Simms tells Cecilia, an unwitting agent of blackmailers, that she is the innocent product of a past for which she is not responsible: "Not your fault. It's genetics. All in the genes. We've got nothing to do with it. It was all decided generations ago. Faceless ancestors." These words echo what Eddie tells May, his half sister and onetime lover, in *Fool for Love*: "You know we're connected, May. We'll always be connected. That was decided a long time ago." And, digging back a further five years, we encounter the speech in *Buried Child* where Vince describes seeing his face in a car's windscreen, and behind that face the faces of all of his ancestors, "clear on back to faces I'd never seen before but still recognized. Still recognized the bones underneath." (Behind this speech is glimpsed, however dimly, Macbeth's vision of eight kings: "What will the line stretch out to th'crack of doom? / Another yet? A seventh? I'll see no more. / And yet the eighth appears who bears a glass / Which shows me many more.")

Images of digging down and bringing up into the light abound; *Buried Child* is merely the most obvious and most fully worked out example. When Vince (whose name tells us he will win) returns to his grandparents' house in search of his roots, his father brings on stage an armful of carrots and a long-dead infant's corpse. If we halt the synopsis here and concentrate on these incidents (widely separated in performance time) we can see that Shepard has linked them through a deliberately bad joke. But behind the joke there is an image and a message: perfect carrots grow in perfect soil; carrots grown in stony soil develop roots that are crooked and branched; Vince and his rotted sibling are those branches. At the heart of this play, if we strip away its outer layers (Vince's father also brings on corn for husking), there is a little kernel playlet, working itself out through suggestive symbolism of the kind that Shepard was employing in the 1960s. What we need to add to this synopsis (explanation, context, and plot) to make it an accurate summation of *Buried Child* is what Shepard added to his dramatist's tool kit in the mid-1970s, when his mature plays began to emerge from their own burial ground and birthplace.

The set of *Curse of the Starving Class* provides an equally pure and even simpler example of how Shepard's plays represent the unfolding of a basic image or group of basic images. The curse of the play's title is, among many other things, the onset of Emma's menstrual bleeding. ("Never go swimming when that happens. It can cause you to bleed to death. The water draws it out of you.") This blood, by tradition both heavily tabooed and dangerously defiling, cannot—in even the most liberal modern theaters—be displayed directly but must be imaged. It is done by elements of the set ("a very plain breakfast table with a red oil-cloth covering it...two ruffled, red-checked curtains") and by displacement-substitution (when Wesley pisses over Emma's charts on the kitchen floor). This action—acceptable in one room, unacceptable in another—is itself displaced and, because it is so, exemplifies the family's more general habit of violating the limits of acceptable behavior by ignoring moral thresholds. Both their dysfunction and their breaching of boundaries are also imaged in the set by "four mismatched metal chairs...a working refrigerator and a small gas stove, set right up next to each other...a pile of wooden debris, torn screen, etc., which are the remains of a broken door."

Pictures, however, are always ambiguous, which is why one of them speaks a thousand words. Shepard, a dramatist who works through images rather than arguments, evades easy interpretation. *Curse of the Starving Class* begins with a heap of visual symbols and ends with the symbolic story of an eagle and a tomcat that are locked together in a mutually destructive embrace. The play's initial and terminal symbols, however, are simply alternative images for an unchanging reality. Shepard's plays are static because, the present being gripped by the past, all that can be managed is the illusion of movement. *True West* ends with Austin (a scriptwriter, a seller and teller of stories) and Lee (who sells a story that he can scarcely tell and will never be able to write down) frozen in an endless moment of mutual apprehension: "caught in a vast desertlike landscape, they are very still but watchful for the next, [as] lights go slowly to black." *Fool for Love*, arguably Shepard's finest play, perfectly illustrates—through its image of an old man sitting in

a rocking chair—the paradox of ceaseless movement that leaves one standing still. *Fool for Love* is, a stage direction tells us, "to be performed relentlessly without a break." Yet despite being packed with incident, its relentless activity merely revolves around itself. "I'm only gonna' be a second," Eddie says when the play's final version of his secret is told, "I'll come right back." But in that suspended and indefinitely extended second, the play ends. And when it begins again, at the next performance, we are back at the start. Of course, every play begins again at each performance, but most do not bite their tails in order to form a perfect circle. (Samuel Beckett's *Waiting for Godot* of 1955 is the most famous of those that do, and Beckett is an obvious influence on Shepard here and elsewhere.)

The unavoidable ambiguity of imagery can be both strength and weakness. *A Lie of the Mind* may end weakly with an enforced and merely symbolic closing, but *Buried Child* comes to a magnificently appropriate—and still open—ending. Halie exits up a spiral staircase, as though ascending to heaven, followed by her son, Tilden, who carries in his arms the bones of her murdered son-grandson-brother. What Halie's voice reports from above (when she is no longer visible) is a paradise of fertile crops, coaxed into abundance by the sun: "Maybe it's the sun. Maybe that's it. Maybe it's the sun." But, as Tilden, her "son," joins her in the "sun" with their "son," there is silence, the stage darkens, and the play ends. Here, Shepard deliberately pitches a play's conventional ending ("lights go to black") against Halie's final word ("sun"), so as to leave his audience with opposed and incompatible resolutions of the play's dark themes. When does a play end? When the words run out? Or when the lights dim? Plays are verbal occurrences that are also physical events, and this is a truth that Shepard has always recognized. "Sometimes theatre seems stuck in language and the physical body of the actor," he wrote to Joseph Chaikin, his friend and collaborator, in 1983. But then he immediately added that "it's those very limitations which also excite me about theatre."

[*See also* Theater in America.]

SELECTED WORKS

The Rock Garden (1964)
4-H Club (1965)
La Turista (1967)
Cowboys #2 (1967)
Me and My Brother (1968)
The Unseen Hand and Other Plays (1971)
The Mad Dog Blues and Other Plays (1971)

Geography of a Horse Dreamer (1974)
The Tooth of Crime (1972)
Action (1975)
Killer's Head (1975)
Angel City (1976)
Angel City, Curse of the Starving Class, and Other Plays (1977)
Buried Child (1978)
Hawk Moon (1981)
True West (1980)
Motel Chronicles (1982)
Fool for Love (1983)
The Sad Lament of Pecos Bill on the Eve of Killing His Wife (1983)
The War in Heaven (1986)
A Lie of the Mind (1985)
States of Shock; Far North; Silent Tongue (1991)
Simpatico (1995)
Buried Child (1995)
Cruising Paradise (1996)
When the World Was Green: A Chef's Fable (1996)
Eyes for Consuela (1999)
The Late Henry Moss; Eyes for Consuela; When the World Was Green (2002)

FURTHER READING

Bottoms, Stephen J. *Theatre of Sam Shepard: States of Crisis*. Cambridge and New York, 1998. A very thorough study that is the closest thing to a standard authority yet produced.

Chaikin, Joseph, and Sam Shepard. *Letters and Texts, 1972–1984*, edited by Barry Daniels. New York, 1989.

Cohn, Ruby. *New American Dramatists, 1960–1980*. London and Basingstoke, U.K., 1982. An account of Shepard's early experimental plays that puts them against the background of radical New York City theater of the 1960 and 1970s.

DeRose, David J. *Sam Shepard*. New York, 1992.

Dugdale, John. *File on Shepard*. London, 1989. A chronological listing of the plays with synopses and selections from early reviews.

Geis, Deborah R. *Postmodern Theatric[k]s: Monologue in Contemporary American Drama*. Ann Arbor, Mich., 1993. Chapter 3 ("Geography of a Storyteller: Monologue in Sam Shepard's plays") is especially relevant.

Malkin, Jeanette R. *Verbal Violence in Contemporary Drama*. Cambridge and New York, 1992. The section on Shepard is based on the belief, surely questionable in 1992, that *The Tooth of Crime* is "considered by many to be Shepard's best play."

Marranca, Bonnie, ed. *American Dreams: The Imagination of Sam Shepard*. New York 1981.

Reaves, Gerri. *Mapping the Private Geography: Autobiography, Identity, and America*. Jefferson, N.C., and London, 2001. Chapter 4 is titled "Sam Shepard's *Motel Chronicles*: A Microcosmic America."

Roudané, Matthew, ed. *The Cambridge Companion to Sam Shepard*. Cambridge and New York, 2002. A collection of seventeen specially commissioned essays, especially valuable for its discussion of Shepard's most recent—and unpublished—work.

Shepard, Sam. *Buried Child*. New York, 1997. This is a revised text of the play, prepared for Chicago's Steppenwolf theater company in 1995.

Tucker, Martin. *Sam Shepard*. New York 1992. A thorough survey up to *A Lie of the Mind*.

Tynan, Kenneth. *Oh! Calcutta! An Entertainment with Music*. New York, 1969. Contains a shortened version of *The Rock Garden*.

Wade, Leslie A. *Sam Shepard and the American Theatre*. Westport, Conn., and London, 1997. Especially strong on theatrical background and history.

THE SHORT STORY IN AMERICA

by Laurie Champion

Many critics agree with Frank O'Connor's 1963 assessment that "Americans have handled the short story so wonderfully that one can say that it is a national art form." Although the short story has received little critical attention compared with other genres such as poems or novels, it has flourished over the last century and a half to become an integral aspect of American letters. Washington Irving's "Rip Van Winkle" (1819) frequently is cited as the first American short story, or "tale," but the genre remained undistinguished until Edgar Allan Poe's well-known 1842 review of Nathaniel Hawthorne's *Twice-told Tales*. Since Poe's review, in which he distinguished short fiction from other genres, the American short story has evolved both in form and in content.

THE MID-NINETEENTH CENTURY

During the romantic period of American literature in the mid-nineteenth century, Edgar Allan Poe, Nathaniel Hawthorne, and Herman Melville contributed significantly to the development of the American short story. In form, style, and subject matter, their short fiction departed from early American sketches such as Washington Irving's "Rip Van Winkle" and "The Legend of Sleepy Hollow," tales generally made up of summarized narratives, episodic plots, and portraits of magical events. American romantic short fiction moved from a tale to a story with a unified plot, a protagonist, and a single effect.

Indicative of the title of one of Poe's collections of short fiction, *Tales of the Grotesque and Arabesque* (1840), his short stories are grotesque, blending elements of Gothic horror with cryptic settings filled with castles, tombs, labyrinth paths, and dark and gloomy rooms. The characters sometimes cross boundaries between the living and the dead and the situations question whether ghosts are more real than humans. Among Poe's most well-known gothic/grotesque stories are "The Premature

Charlotte Perkins Gilman (center). (© *Bettmann/Corbis*)

11

Burial," in which a man believes he is buried alive; "The Black Cat," in which the howling of a trapped cat leads to the discovery of a dead body; and "The Facts in the Case of M. Valdemar," in which the dying M. Valdemar agrees to be hypnotized and remains rigid yet semiconscious for seven months, until physicians attempting to awaken him transform him into a liquid mass. Perhaps Poe's most familiar story is "The Fall of the House of Usher." The story portrays Roderick Usher, who experiences mysterious feelings of dreariness, gloom, and terror that haunt him while he resides at the House of Usher. Roderick buries his twin sister, Madeline, and stores the coffin in a vault. At the end of the story, Madeline crashes through the walls and Roderick exclaims to his visitor that she has been buried alive. As Madeline, whose bloody body shows signs of physical struggle, stands in the doorway, the ensuing storm intensifies and the mansion crumbles and fades. Typical of Poe's themes and style, "The Fall of the House of Usher" is filled with cryptic descriptions of the Usher mansion and demonstrates psychological fear and terror.

Poe also wrote detective short fiction and is credited with inspiring the detective fiction genre that gave rise to later writers such as Arthur Conan Doyle, creator of the Sherlock Holmes character. Poe's series of detective short stories, which include "The Murders in the Rue Morgue," "The Mystery of Marie Rogêt," and "The Purloined Letter," depict Auguste Dupin as a shrewd detective able to unravel mysteries with his self-proclaimed ability to think like the perpetrator and examine evidence from his opponent's point of view.

Hawthorne's short stories also blur distinctions between reality and fiction, but with less grotesqueness than in Poe's short fiction. Hawthorne's best-known short story collection, *Twice-told Tales*, includes sketches and tales, most of which are allegories with moral messages. Many of Hawthorne's stories reveal early New England history and blend historical events with the supernatural. As in his longer works, Hawthorne's shorter fiction explores themes relevant to the Puritan conscience. "Young Goodman Brown," one of Hawthorne's most frequently anthologized short stories, illustrates techniques and themes found throughout his works. Typical of an allegory, the names of the characters reveal their traits. Goodman Brown sets out on a spiritual journey, in which he meets in the forest the devil and becomes distressed because his faith is gone. While running deeper into the forest, his wife, Faith, appears among both respected and disrespected members of the community. As he warns

Faith to resist, the vision disappears, and he awakens. The story criticizes Puritan doctrine that considers humans depraved beings who must constantly question whether they and members of their communities are worthy of salvation. Goodman Brown loses his faith, his wife, and respect for his community because he holds unattainable spiritual expectations for himself and others.

Three of Hawthorne's best-known stories reveal that science and intellect often conflict with concerns of the heart or soul. In "The Birthmark," the scientist Aylmer's wife dies during his attempt to remove a birthmark from her cheek. "Rappaccini's Daughter" concerns the plight of Beatrice, whose death is the result of an antidote her lover urges her to consume to counteract the poison her father has fed her as an experiment. "Ethan Brand" shows the downfall of Ethan, who spends eighteen years investigating humans in an attempt to find an unpardonable sin, only to discover that his own search has led him to commit the very unpardonable sin for which he has searched. These stories demonstrate the ironic dangers of searching for perfection, either physical or spiritual.

Compared with Hawthorne and Poe, Melville wrote a small body of short fiction, mostly essaylike stories. However, "Benito Cereno" and "Bartleby the Scrivener" remain among the finest pieces of short fiction written during this time period. "Benito Cereno" tells of Captain Delano, who joins a vessel inhabited by slaves, passengers, and crew, dwelling amidst hunger and disease. The twist in the story comes when the captain learns that the seemingly oppressed are really the empowered amongst the inhabitants of the vessel, which becomes a microcosm of society. "Bartleby the Scrivener" reveals the plight of Bartleby, who after three days of working as scrivener for a lawyer, begins to announce that he prefers not to perform his duties. The lawyer feels both angry and confused at Bartleby's behavior, and eventually invites him to live with him, an invitation Bartleby declines. When the lawyer moves his office and withholds from Bartleby the address, Bartleby becomes a vagrant and is consequently imprisoned. Further isolated and trapped within walls, Bartleby refuses to eat and eventually dies. Readers learn very little about Bartleby's history, but the story ultimately uses his plight to criticize ways intolerant societies treat nonconformists. Melville's short fiction moves closer to realism than does Hawthorne's or Poe's and provides a bridge between the romantic and the realist short story.

Among Poe, Hawthorne, and Melville, Poe contributed most significantly to the development of the American short story partly because of the body of stories he wrote, but more importantly because he first identified the genre in his well-known review of Nathaniel Hawthorne's *Twice-told Tales*. Although Poe does not use the term "short story," he refers to a work of short fiction as a "tale proper," a "prose tale," a "short prose narrative," and a "brief tale" and distinguishes tales from other genres such as novels or poetry. Arguing "unity of effect or impression" as having the utmost importance in composition, he offers concrete instructions:

> A skillful literary artist has constructed a tale. If wise, he has not fashioned his thoughts to accommodate his incidents, but having conceived, with deliberate care, a certain unique or single *effect*, to be wrought out he then invents such incidents—he then combines such effects as may best aid him in establishing this preconceived effect.... In the whole composition there should be no word written, of which the tendency, direct or indirect, is not to the one preestablished design.

Although much debated by contemporary literary theorists, many theories of literary criticism and many guidelines for writing short fiction rely at least in part on Poe's dictum.

LATE NINETEENTH TO EARLY TWENTIETH CENTURY

During the latter part of the nineteenth century and into the early twentieth century, American short stories became less like the essays or allegorical morality tales still somewhat apparent in the romantic period, and moved even more toward use of formal elements such as plot, character, and dialogue found in later short fiction. After the Civil War, American literature moved from romanticism to realism, and as the name "realism" suggests, the stories were told more realistically.

Building on Poe's initial definitions of the short story, Brander Matthews in 1901 published the influential essay "The Philosophy of the Short-Story," which alludes to Poe's "The Philosophy of Composition" and develops the principles that Poe outlines in his essay as well as in his review of Hawthorne's *Twice-told Tales*. Matthews says that more than mere length considerations distinguish the short story from other genres and that the short story differs from the novel "in its essential unity of impression" that "shows one action, in one place, on one day. A Short-story deals with a single character, a single event, a single emotion, or the series of emotions called forth by a single situation." Like Poe, Matthews offers guidelines for short-story writers, suggesting that, in addition to "originality and ingenuity," short fiction

should concisely display "symmetry of design." Elaborating upon Poe's and Matthew's ideas, many short fiction how-to books appeared during the first two decades of the twentieth century. Many of the formulas for writing fiction expounded in these books are still used to teach short-story writing.

Although William Dean Howells is considered a champion of American realism, his contribution to the short story rests more with his role as editor and his influence on realism in general than with his fiction writing. For example, as editor of the distinguished *Atlantic Monthly* and *Harper's*, he had considerable impact on the type of stories published. Similarly, Henry James, with his European ties and critically acclaimed novels, contributed to American letters in ways that shadow his short-story writings; however, he nevertheless produced a significant body of short stories. Many of James's stories question the purpose of art and the role of artists. Among these stories are "The Author of Beltraffio," "The Middle Years," "The Figure in the Carpet," "The Liar," and "The Real Thing." The last provides a good example of James's complex themes and subjects. In this story, an illustrator for popular magazines is able to depict Major and Mrs. Monarch as representative of the upper class to which they actually belong, yet despite repeated efforts, his renditions of them always look the same. Ironically, Miss Churn and Oronte, both from lower-class society, provide better models for depicting the upper class. The story suggests that renditions of reality do not always lead to artistic portrayals and conveys James's artistic philosophy that art need not imitate life but make an impression of life or truth.

During the 1890s, Stephen Crane produced a body of short fiction using techniques that inspired later writers. Like his masterpiece novel, *The Red Badge of Courage*, many of Crane's stories concern war: "A Mystery of Heroism," "An Episode of War," "The Price of the Harness," "Death and the Child," and "The Upturned Face." However, his most significant short stories are "The Open Boat" and "The Blue Hotel." While "The Open Boat" explores the subject of man against nature, "The Blue Hotel" concerns the notion of man against man. "The Open Boat" portrays four men who develop a strong camaraderie as they struggle against the forces of nature. "The Blue Hotel" concerns three men and reveals issues involving social responsibility. While the cowboy claims that the Swede's death is his own fault, the easterner assumes responsibility because he had refused to help the Swede fight for his convictions. While the easterner proclaims that the Swede's death is the result of all men's moral weaknesses, the cowboy only defends his own innocence. Both "The Open Boat" and "The Blue Hotel" suspensefully demonstrate relationships between groups of men who form a microcosmic society.

LOCAL COLOR

Paralleling realism, the local color tradition flourished in America during the latter half of the nineteenth century until the early twentieth century. Local color short stories reveal realistic images of lifestyles in specific regions of the United States. They portray commonplace scenes and characteristics of their chosen locales, representing character types, speech patterns, and social customs and beliefs. From Bret Harte's boisterous and ill-mannered westerners, to Edith Wharton's refined upper-class New Yorkers, to Kate Chopin's Creoles and Sarah Orne Jewett's New England villagers, these writers offer geographically specific portraits of America.

Southwestern humor describes the stories by writers such as Bret Harte and Mark Twain. Depicting Southwest frontiers, these stories often highlight the contrast between reality and appearance and frequently juxtapose a naïve southwesterner against an elite easterner. Additionally, these stories often consist of tall tales, told by a boastful narrator who exaggerates and sometimes performs pranks. They sometimes employ framing devices in which a narrator tells a story that contains an inner tale. Although many of Twain's best stories, including "The Story of the Old Ram" and "Buck Fanshaw's Funeral" are anecdotal and appear in larger works such as *Roughing It*, others, such as "The Man That Corrupted Hadleyburg" and "The Celebrated Jumping Frog of Calaveras County," represent fully developed stories. "The Man That Corrupted Hadleyburg" portrays a stranger who visits Hadleyburg and shows the greed and dishonesty of supposedly incorruptible citizens. "The Celebrated Jumping Frog of Calaveras County" is a framed narrative, in which the narrator, upon request from his eastern friend, approaches Simon Wheeler to inquire about Leonidas Smiley. Wheeler begins a rambling tale of Smiley and his frog, interjected with asides and digressive comments. Despite Wheeler's attempt to tell the narrator the tale of a one-eyed yellow cow, the narrator excuses himself. This story uses tall tale, exaggeration, trickery, digression, and humor, all elements of southwestern humor. Similarly, Harte's "The Luck of Roaring Camp" exemplifies local color in its lighthearted depiction of a group of miners. When a prostitute dies during childbirth, the rough, ill-mannered mining campers christen her child Thomas Luck. The presence of the infant among the men inspires them to become generous, compassionate, clean, and mannerly. The story humorously shows incongruity between the habits of the men before and after the infant arrives.

Southern plantation stories such as those by Joel Chandler Harris, Thomas Nelson Page, and George Washington Cable appeared in periodicals in the latter part of the nineteenth century, when the plantation literary tradition was in vogue. Although contemporary critics consider this type of fiction racist propaganda, Harris's series of Uncle Remus tales were immensely popular during this time and have become classics. The stories employ a framing device in which Uncle Remus, a wise old African American, incorporates wisdom and philosophy by telling allegorical tales about Br'er Rabbit, Br'er Fox, and other animal characters to entertain a young white boy. Charles Chesnutt, one of the most prominent late-nineteenth-century African-American short-story writers, also published stories in popular magazines, some of which are similar in structure to Harris's Uncle Remus tales. Chesnutt's stories, however, defy racism, as the African-American Uncle Julius outwits John, the white man to whom he narrates stories that reveal African-American myth and folklore.

Some of the most significant local color short-story writers during this time are women, many of whom characterize women who defy stereotypes. Sarah Orne Jewett's best-known short fiction concerns small northeastern communities such as Dunnet Landing, Maine, the setting of *The Country of the Pointed Firs* and related stories. In these stories, typically, the narrator is introduced to a resident of Dunnet Landing, who tells her a story that reveals regional folklore or history. These stories reveal lost loves, loneliness, and regret amidst a compassionate humanity that often makes heroes of ordinary people. The lives of women and their relationships with other women are central to Jewett's fiction. Jewett also contributed to the American short-story tradition by influencing other women local color writers such as Mary Wilkins Freeman, Kate Chopin, and Willa Cather, who dedicated her masterpiece *O Pioneers!* (1913) to Jewett.

Mary Wilkins Freeman's portraits of rural New England heroines represent independent and strong women. In "A New England Nun," Louisa, who learns that her fiancé is in love with another woman, releases his commitment to her so she can continue to live the solitary life she prefers. Through patience and persistence, Hetty, the protagonist of "A Church Mouse," becomes church sexton and establishes residency in the congregation's meeting hall. In "The Revolt of Mother," Sarah Penn unrelentingly demands that her husband keep the promise he made forty years ago to build a new house. Told humorously and tongue-in-cheek, "The Revolt of Mother" and "A Church Mouse" nevertheless describe strong women who defy oppressive societies.

Set mainly in New Orleans and rural Louisiana, much of Kate Chopin's fiction explores ways patriarchy restrains and oppresses women. Well known for her masterpiece novel *The Awakening*, Chopin also explores the plight of women in sexist societies in many of her short stories, of which the best known are "The Story of an Hour," "Desiree's Baby," "At the Cadian Ball," "The Storm," "Odalie Misses Mass," and "A Lady of Bayou St. John." In addition to showing white women as victims of sexism, Chopin is noted for her portrayal of the oppression of African-American women.

Well-known for her mockery of New York high society, Edith Wharton's stories such as "Souls Belated," "The Reckoning," "Autres Temps," "Bunner Sisters," "The Other Two," "The Long Run," and "Atrophy" often criticize the institution of marriage. In addition to the institution of marriage, Wharton examines society at large and shows the impact of oppression on women. In "The Rembrandt," for example, we see the plight of Mrs. Fontage, who ironically is victimized by her dignity and upper social class. Once wealthy, she now struggles to survive in a rented room because she lives in a society that has never encouraged women to care for themselves or tend to financial matters.

Writers such as Hamlin Garland and Willa Cather present the Midwest in their fiction. Many of Garland's works protest against the plight of exploited prairie farmers. In "Under the Lion's Paw," Garland's most anthologized story, the protagonist Tim Haskins endures and labors to turn a dilapidated piece of land into a productive farm. Haskins approaches the owner about buying the farm, only to be told that the value of the property as well as the rent has increased. Symbolically, Haskins is "under the lion's paw," in a no-win situation: if he relinquishes the farm, he forfeits his hard work and his source of income; if he buys the farm, he will be burdened with a high mortgage. Unlike Garland, Cather uses the midwestern prairie settings in the pastoral sense, in which her characters long for simple lives and feel close spiritual ties to the land. Although acclaimed for her novels, Cather also created a substantial body of short

stories, of which "The Sculptor's Funeral" and "Paul's Case" are best known.

EARLY TO MID-1900s

The early twentieth century marks a flourishing time in the history of the American short story. The time period embraces modernism, the most influential literary movement of the twentieth century. Short-story writers found many profitable markets for their work, and distinctions between commercial and literary short fiction were made. *The Best American Short Stories*, an annual collection of a guest editor's selection of the best American stories published each year, debuted in 1915, and in 1922 the first O. Henry Memorial Awards annual volume appeared. These annual collections continue to highlight the most esteemed American short-story writers. *The New Yorker* and *Story* magazines debuted in 1925 and 1931, respectively, and continue to publish the most distinguished short stories. During the 1930s, the New Criticism school of literary analysis began to influence both short-story writers and the ways critics looked at short stories. New Criticism focuses on the form and structure of literature and discourages using sources outside the text as considerations for interpretations. Both writers and critics began to pay more attention to formal elements of a text such as plot, setting, character, dialogue, tone, style, and theme, and the short story proved an ideal genre for this sort of analysis.

One of the most influential short-story writers of the early twentieth century is O. Henry (William Sydney Porter). His ironic, twisted endings have become synonymous with his name, and his formula for writing stories has influenced many writers, especially those writing for popular audiences. Whereas the novels of most writers overshadow their short stories, O. Henry continues to garner recognition for classics such as "The Ransom of Red Chief," "A Retrieved Reformation," "The Caballero's Way," and "The Hiding of Black Bill." Rare for a short story, "The Gift of the Magi" has become an international classic and is told around the world at Christmas. The story tells of young Della and Jim, who are very much in love but cannot afford to buy each other a Christmas gift. Della cuts and sells her hair to buy a chain for Jim's gold watch, while he sells his watch to purchase expensive combs for her hair. Representative of O. Henry's fiction, "The Gift of the Magi" represents ordinary people and uses sentiment to create entertaining, heartwarming stories that appeal to broad audiences.

Because of his influence on writers such as Ernest Hemingway, William Faulkner, and F. Scott Fitzgerald,

Sherwood Anderson is one of the most important short-story writers of the early twentieth century. Critically acclaimed for innovating the short story in structure, theme, style, and characterization, his stories have both entertained popular audiences and been hailed by literary critics. In addition to those included in his masterpiece *Winesburg, Ohio*, a short-story cycle that portrays individuals of the small town of Winesburg, Anderson's celebrated stories include "The Egg," "I'm a Fool," "I Want to Know Why," "The Man Who Became a Woman," and "Death in the Woods."

Southern women writers recognized as much for their contributions to the short story as for writings in other genres include Flannery O'Connor, Eudora Welty, Katherine Anne Porter, and Carson McCullers, often compared and contrasted with each other and cited as writers who have influenced contemporary southern women writers. O'Connor's stories usually explore Catholic and Christian ideologies, in which a character experiences an epiphany resulting from contact with an outsider. O'Connor blends humor and grotesqueness to the southern setting of her stories and gives them surreal and mythical qualities. Among well-known stories such as "The Life You Save May Be Your Own," "Good Country People," and "The Artificial Nigger," O'Connor's most anthologized short story remains "A Good Man Is Hard to Find." Exemplary of her short fiction, the story describes an epiphany the grandmother of a vacationing family experiences when encountered by The Misfit and two other men. The story represents the moment of grace O'Connor's characters experience through epiphanies.

Most of Welty's works take place in the Mississippi Delta and although realistically portraying southern mores and customs, they also allude to myths and folklore. Welty's stories embrace a variety of forms and themes. "Death of a Traveling Salesman" contrasts the loneliness of a salesman with the tightly bonded relationship between a couple that helps him after he drives his car into a ravine. Phoenix, the protagonist of "A Worn Path," demonstrates the same strength and triumph of her mythical name, while "Keela, the Outcast Indian Maiden" represents southern Gothic fiction, with its grotesque characterizations and descriptions of the unfortunate people exploited as circus freaks. Welty's best-known story, "Why I Live at the P.O.," is a humorous first-person account of Sister, who moves to the Post Office because she perceives that her younger sister's return has usurped her position in the family. Welty is known for the lyrical prose and poetic allusions to folklore and myth displayed in stories such as "Livvie," "The Wide Net," "A Still Moment," and those collected in *The Golden Apples* (1949) and *The Bride of the Innisfallen (1955).*

Unlike Welty and O'Connor, southern writer William Faulkner is better recognized for his novels than for his short stories, but he did produce a substantial body of short fiction. As in his novels, his short fiction chronicles southern history and reflects his complicated style, consisting of long complex sentences that often invite multiple interpretations. Among Faulkner's best-known stories—including "The Bear," "Red Leaves," "Barn Burning," "That Evening Sun," and "Dry September—"A Rose for Emily" remains Faulkner's masterpiece. It depicts Miss Emily Grierson, an aging southern belle, and juxtaposes the antebellum past of the South against two later generations of southern ideology.

Despite the fact that F. Scott Fitzgerald wrote short stories to support himself and that the quality and merit of his stories are uneven, he produced outstanding short fiction such as "May Day," "The Diamond as Big as the Ritz," "Winter Dreams," "The Rich Boy," "Babylon Revisited," "Last Kiss," and "Crazy Sunday." As in his novels, Fitzgerald's stories explore notions of loss of innocence and disillusionment of marriage. For example, in "The Rich Boy," although the young Anson deeply loves Paula, he finds excuses for marrying her and becomes a marriage counselor instead. Paula marries and divorces another man, but when Anson later encounters Paula, she is remarried and pregnant. After Paula dies during childbirth, the disillusioned Anson goes on a cruise, where he flirts with women in order to reaffirm his sense of self-worth.

Fitzgerald's contemporary Ernest Hemingway is one of the most significant and influential short-story writers of the twentieth century. Departing from short stories that focus on formal elements of literature and develop plot in classical ways, Hemingway's short fiction marks the beginning of the minimalist short story in America. Hemingway's often-quoted dictum that employs an iceberg analogy to say that seven-eighths of the meaning of fiction should take place under the surface level of the story has been the basis of many short-story guidebooks. Many of Hemingway's stories concern the protagonist Nick Adams, who usually undergoes an initiation experience. Best known among the Nick Adams cycle is "Big Two-Hearted River," in which Nick returns to the idyllic place of his youth only to find the land destroyed by fire. "Hills Like White Elephants," "A Clean, Well-Lighted Place," and "The Short Happy Life of Francis Macomber" are among Hemingway's most critically acclaimed minimalist stories. "Hills Like White Elephants" and "A Clean, Well-Lighted Place" consist almost entirely of dialogue that invites readers to interpret the situation as though eavesdropping. Typical of Hemingway's short stories and exemplary of his iceberg theory, the action in most of his stories occurs beneath the surface.

THE SECOND HALF OF THE TWENTIETH CENTURY

A large variety of short stories have appeared since the 1950s, when some writers continued to write stories in the traditional form and structure and others broke from that style. The 1950s and 1960s witnessed the civil rights movement, which paralleled the Black Arts movement, followed by the second wave of feminism in America. In addition to providing opportunities for women and ethnic short-story writers, short fiction by women and minorities was rediscovered. For example, since the rediscovery of Susan Glaspell's "A Jury of Her Peers" (1916) and Charlotte Perkins Gilman's "The Yellow Wallpaper" (1892), both stories have been reprinted in countless textbooks and anthologies and both have been the subject of many scholarly articles. In addition to publication of numerous African-American short-story anthologies and short-story collections by individual African-American writers, examples of the flourishing of the African-American short story during the 1960s and 1970s include the critical acclaim given to James Baldwin's "Sonny's Blues," which appears in his 1965 collection *Going to Meet the Man* and has since been reprinted in numerous anthologies and textbooks; the recognition of Toni Cade Bambara's *Gorilla, My Love* (1972), which continues to influence African-American women short-story writers; and the awarding of the 1978 Pulitzer Prize to James McPherson for *Elbow Room*. On the other hand, despite immense opportunity provided to women and minority writers during the 1960s and 1970s, it is interesting to note that the short stories of prominent Harlem Renaissance author Zora Neale Hurston were not collected as a volume until 1995; the seminal short-story collections of Native American Zitkala-Sa (*Old Indian Legends* and *American Indian Stories*) did not appear until 1985; Mourning Dove's short stories (*Coyote Stories*) were not rediscovered and reprinted until 1990; the groundbreaking stories by Chinese-American Sui Sin Far were not reprinted as the volume *Mrs. Spring Fragrance and Other Writings* until 1995; and Ralph Ellison's short stories were not collected

in a single volume until the 1996 publication of *Flying Home and Other Stories*.

Perhaps the most influential American short-story writer from the 1950s to the 1970s is John Cheever. Accolades for his short stories include a Pulitzer Prize, a National Book Critics Circle Award, an American Book Award, and the National Medal for Literature. He helped spur interest in the short story and contributed both to its commercial and literary successes. Told for the most part in a conventional form, Cheever's stories usually portray a male, white-collar protagonist. His characters are usually bored with marriage and desire personal fulfillment, although most are unable to articulate their concerns. Additionally, their material abundance contrasts with their spiritual emptiness. Among Cheever's best-known stories are "Goodbye, My Brother," "The Enormous Radio," "O Youth and Beauty!," "The Five-Forty-Eight," "The Country Husband," and "The Swimmer." Representative of Cheever's stories, "The Swimmer" presents Neddy Merrill's journey from a friend's house to his own home via swimming pools. He embarks upon this journey to celebrate the fine day's possibilities but the challenge begins to shake his confidence as he gradually becomes physically weaker and more disoriented. The story turns from a portrayal of reality to a surreal narrative as Neddy begins to remember events from his life and repressed memories emerge. The story suggests that whether Neddy's house really is empty as he finds it when he completes his journey or the image is a figment of his imagination, he comes to understand that his suburban lifestyle is empty. Instead of offering him a spiritual rebirth, as going into water might symbolize, Neddy's symbolic baptism exposes his shallow life.

Philip Roth, Saul Bellow, and Bernard Malamud dominated postwar Jewish-American writing. Whereas all three excelled in the novel, most critics agree that Malamud's artistic genius surfaces more in his short stories. Throughout his stories, he demonstrates hardships and despair to portray the plight of the contemporary American Jew. He employs a tightly woven, sparse, yet lyrical style and sometimes blends fantasy and allegory with realism. His best known stories include "The First Seven Years," "Idiots First," "Rembrandt's Hat," "The Jewbird," "A Choice of Profession," "Angel Levine," and "The Magic Barrel." Some of his stories, published individually but later collected in *Pictures of Fidelman* (1969), form a cycle that characterizes Arthur Fidelman, a failed painter. Malamud's reputation as a master of the short story began with the publication of *The*

Magic Barrel in 1958, and some of the stories in this collection are among the most anthologized stories in the American postwar canon. One of Malamud's most critically acclaimed stories, "The Magic Barrel" describes Leo Finkle, the lonely and isolated rabbinical student who seeks the services of a marriage broker. Although his motive for marriage is gaining a congregation, he falls in love with the picture of the marriage broker's daughter, a prostitute in whom he recognizes the hope of redemption. The story reveals irony because the broker is worried about his daughter, and although it is unlikely he really has a magical matchmaking gift, he indeed leads Leo to his ideal match. The experiences he encounters while searching for a mate change Leo from a person with superficial values to a spiritual human being.

Some of the most influential short-story writers of this period use postmodern techniques, especially metaphysical devices, in their short stories. The seminal postmodern short fiction writers John Barth, Donald Barthelme, and Robert Coover serve as good examples. Barth's short-story cycle *Lost in the Funhouse* (1968) consists of related stories depicting nameless characters, characters named from mythology, and the central character, Ambrose. The characters are storytellers, who personify intangible states such as love and art. The stories are metafictional in their thematic representations of the art of fiction writing, storytelling, or art in general. They are sometimes witty and almost always use language in a crafty manner so that the stories are about language itself. The stories are filled with nontraditional literary elements such as the use of italics and dashes.

One of the most influential writers since 1960, Donald Barthelme has written stories that are elliptical and use devices such as journal entries, diagrams, question-and-answer formats, and lists. Also exemplary of metafiction, Barthelme's short fiction frequently alludes to other writers, comments on art, and concerns the writing process. His stories play with language, as demonstrated in "Sentence," a story one sentence long but nevertheless packed with meaning.

Also representative of postmodernism are Robert Coover's short stories, many of which, like those of Barthelme and Barth, concern the art of fiction writing. In addition to many of the techniques found in the fiction of Barthelme and Barth, some of Coover's stories provide several beginnings or reveal several intertwined subplots. Throughout their short fiction, Barth, Barthelme, and Coover employ self-reflexivity in ways that allow the stories to comment about themselves. These stories defy plot summary and challenge description because the merit lies in the telling of the story, not the story itself.

John Edgar Wideman, one of the most significant contemporary African-American short-story writers, uses postmodern and metaphysical devices. Wideman explores a variety of themes and subjects, but much of his short fiction concerns personal and social relationships and criticizes racism. Wideman's complex writing techniques prevail in stories such as "All Stories Are True," "Signs," "Surfiction," "The Watermelon Story," "Doc's Story," and "Lizabeth: The Caterpillar Story." In "Surfiction," the title of which is a literary term that refers to a specific type of metafiction, Wideman creates levels of narratives that pay homage not only to Charles Chesnutt but also to the African-American short-story tradition. "Surfiction," as in many of Wideman's stories, reveals complex techniques that blur boundaries between fiction and reality.

Among the most prolific contemporary short-story writers is Joyce Carol Oates, a master of the short-story form. Aspects of Oates's short fiction include depictions of random violence (often grotesque), the sexual exploitation of women, and perverse obsessions. Her characters are frequently victims of both physical and psychological violence. Oates's most critically acclaimed short story, "Where Are You Going, Where Have You Been?," gives the suspenseful and chilling account of the psychological turmoil of the teenaged Connie, who is manipulated and seduced by Arnold Friend, who clearly plans to abduct her from her home and sexually torture and perhaps kill her. Although this story represents some of Oates's fiction, she uses a variety of styles and forms, both experimental and conventional.

It is no surprise that John Updike was chosen to edit the distinguished *Best American Short Stories of the Century* (1999), for he has been publishing short stories for half a century and is regarded as a master of style and form. Many of Updike's short stories reveal young men who experience some sort of initiation. His short fiction also addresses relationships between husbands and wives. Most of his fiction is set in urban Pennsylvania and addresses issues relevant to middle-class suburbia. Several of his fictional pieces make up cycles of stories, some involving the couple the Maples, others dealing with the character Henry Bech, and others portraying the young protagonist from "Pigeon Feathers." "A&P" and "Gesturing," among his most critically acclaimed stories, respectively depict a young male protagonist and a couple experiencing a troubled marriage, two of Updike's most common subjects. "A&P" depicts the plight of Sammy, a young clerk at the A&P grocery who defends three young girls the manager chastises. His heroic attempt and perhaps sexual desire inspire him to quit his job. Although uncertain of his decision, especially when the manager informs him that his attitude will haunt him throughout his life, Sammy nevertheless quits his job. In "Gesturing," Joan and Richard Maples have recently separated, leaving Richard no one for whom to perform his gestures, symbolic of the life force. Although both struggle to redefine themselves as individuals, the story ends with them eating together at a restaurant and laughing. Significantly, they continue to gesture together, suggesting that each has influenced the other in ways that have shaped their lives and that their long history of gesturing has not dissolved even though their marriage has ended.

Beginning in the 1970s, the American short story has experienced a renaissance. Creative writing classes have sprung up in universities across the nation, and well-known writers continue to teach these courses. A plethora of short fiction anthologies and manuals on writing fiction have appeared. Among the most influential was John Gardner's *The Art of Fiction* (1984), still considered the bible for college writing workshops. More literary journals—usually housed at universities—were developed, offering increased outlets for short fiction. The tradition developed by Anton Chekhov and started in America by Hemingway was termed "minimalism" and defined the sparse, terse style and the open-ended narratives of writers such as Frederick Barthelme, Amy Hempel, Ann Beattie, Bobbie Ann Mason, Mary Robison, and Tobias Wolff. Among this group of writers, Raymond Carver is the most influential. He is one of the few American writers whose reputation rests almost entirely on his work in the short-story genre. He usually writes of working-class people, many hopeless and desperate alcoholics. His better-known stories include "Where I'm Calling From," "Will You Please Be Quiet, Please?," "Feathers," "So Much Water So Close to Home," "Are These Actual Miles?," and "Errand." His most anthologized stories are "A Small, Good Thing" and "Cathedral." "A Small, Good Thing" concerns the parents of Scotty, a young child struck by a car on his birthday. During his hospital stay, his parents are taunted by phone calls that refer to him. After Scotty dies, the mother realizes the caller is the baker from whom she had ordered Scotty's birthday cake. She and her husband approach the baker and accuse him of insensitivity. Apologetically, he offers the couple bread, saying that eating is "a small, good thing." "Cathedral" concerns a visit by a blind man to visit his friend, a woman whose husband at first is jealous. At the end of the story, the blind man and the woman's husband bond through mutual understanding and respect that develops when they attempt to draw a cathedral. While in many of Carver's stories the characters remain hopeless, in both of these stories, characters experience some sort of spiritual awakening through connecting with another human.

THE FUTURE OF THE AMERICAN SHORT STORY

In addition to the multitudinous and delightful variety of stories being published at the beginning of the twenty-first century, the American short story received increased critical attention. Short-story collections were reviewed in both popular and literary magazines, and short fiction classes continued to be taught in higher learning institutions across the nation. More essays appeared about short stories, and more honors for American short stories were being awarded.

[*See also* Anderson, Sherwood and his *Winesburg, Ohio*; Baldwin, James; Barth, John; Barthelme, Donald; Carver, Raymond; Cather, Willa; Cheever, John; Chesnutt, Charles; Chopin, Kate; Crane, Stephen; Ellison, Ralph; Faulkner, William; Fitzgerald, F. Scott; Gardner, John; Garland, Hamlin; Gilman's "The Yellow Wallpaper"; Harte, Bret; Hawthorne, Nathaniel; Hemingway, Ernest; Henry, O.; Howells, William Dean; Irving, Washington; Jackson's "The Lottery"; James, Henry; Jewett, Sarah Orne; Malamud, Bernard; Melville, Herman and his "Bartleby the Scrivener"; Metafiction; Oates, Joyce Carol; O'Connor, Flannery; Poe, Edgar Allan; Twain, Mark; Updike, John; Welty, Eudora; Wharton, Edith; and Wideman, John Edgar.]

FURTHER READING

Current-Garcia, Eugene. *The American Short Story before 1850: A Critical History*. Boston, 1985. Provides valuable discussions of short-story writers such as Irving, Hawthorne, and Poe in relation to the beginning of the American short story.

Fagin, N. Bryllion. *America through the Short Story*. Boston, 1936. Reprints short stories categorized according to subjects and offers interesting discussions to introduce each chapter.

Gerlach, John. *Toward the End: Closure and Structure in the American Short Story*. University, Ala., 1985. Valuable for its examination of several American short stories in terms of their endings.

Lee, A. Robert, ed. *The Nineteenth-Century American Short Story*. Totowa, N.J., 1985. A collection of nine essays by different scholars, all of whom contribute valuable insights about specific nineteenth-century American short-story writers.

Levy, Andrew. *The Culture and Commerce of the American Short Story*. New York, 1993. Offers valuable interpretations of the short story as an American cultural project in works by authors ranging from Poe to Bobbie Ann Mason.

Lohafer, Susan. *Coming to Terms with the Short Story*. Baton Rouge, La., 1983. Offers short-story theory, but especially valuable for its interpretations of individual American classic short stories.

May, Charles E. *The Short Story: The Reality of Artifice*. New York, 1995. Provides an excellent analysis of the evolution of the short story genre.

May, Charles E., ed. *The New Short Story Theories*. Athens, Ohio, 1994. Although not limited to the American short-story tradition, this work offers a collection of essays that demonstrate various critical reactions to the short-story genre and show how it has evolved. Includes Brander Matthews's "The Philosophy of the Short Story" and Poe's "Review of *Twice-Told Tales*."

O'Connor, Frank. *The Lonely Voice: A Study of the Short Story*. New York, 1985. Valuable for its influential assessment of the protagonist of short fiction as being someone who stands outside of society.

Pattee, Fred Lewis. *The Development of the American Short Story: An Historical Survey*. New York, 1923. Important for its early assessment of American short-story writers from Irving to O. Henry.

Peden, William. *The American Short Story: Continuity and Change, 1940–1975*. Boston, 1975. Offers insightful essays about American short-story writers between 1940 and 1975.

Rhode, Robert D. *Setting in the American Short Story of Local Color, 1865–1900*. The Hague, 1975. Demonstrates the significance of setting in the American local color short story.

Voss, Arthur. *The American Short Story: A Critical Survey*. Norman, Okla., 1973. Gives overviews of American short-story writers through the 1950s, providing mostly summaries but some useful interpretations.

West, Ray B., Jr. *The Short Story in America, 1900–1950*. Chicago, 1952. Offers a valuable survey of the American short story beginning with the twentieth century.

LESLIE MARMON SILKO

by Amanda Fields

Born in Albuquerque, New Mexico, on 5 March 1948, Leslie Marmon Silko emerged in the late twentieth century to make her mark in a history of storytellers. Silko's work was recognized by the Native Writers' Circle of the Americas lifetime achievement award in 1994. In addition, she has been named a Living Cultural Treasure by the New Mexico Humanities Council, a title that befits the way her work strives for multiple perspectives while remaining true to the concept of storytelling embedded in her Laguna Pueblo ancestry.

In *Storyteller* (1981), a book of family photographs, poetry, and prose, Silko credits her Aunt Susie and her Grandma A'mooh (great-grandmother Marie Anaya Marmon) for passing on their avid love of the story. Indeed, Silko's storytelling roots are evident as she seeks to unfold and peruse the ways that the oral and the written can translate into new forms of preserving and valuing stories of the human condition.

Growing up on the Laguna Pueblo Reservation, Leslie Marmon Silko attended the Bureau of Indian Affairs school in Laguna, and after fifth grade, she continued her education at parochial schools in Albuquerque. In 1958 her fifth-grade class at Manzano Day School was assigned to create a story out of spelling assignment words, a task that influenced Silko's writing interest and subsequent development. After entrance into the University of New Mexico in 1964, marriage to Richard Chapman in 1966, and the birth of her first son, Robert William Chapman, she received a B.A. in English with honors in 1969. Upon entering the American Indian law program on a fellowship, she decided to leave the University of New Mexico law school and take graduate courses in English. "The Man to Send Rain Clouds," Silko's first published short story, appeared in the Winter–Spring 1969 issue of *New Mexico Quarterly*. In 1970 Silko left the university to teach at the Navajo Community College in Tsaile, Arizona, and she was awarded a National Endowment for the Humanities Discovery Grant. After a divorce from Richard Chapman, she married John Silko and gave birth to her second son, Cazimir Silko, in 1972.

With a Rosewater Foundation Grant, Leslie Marmon Silko moved to Ketchikan, Alaska, in 1973 to begin work on her first novel, *Ceremony* (1977). She won the Award for Poetry from the *Chicago Review* in 1974, the same year her *Laguna Woman: Poems* (1974) was published. In addition, during 1974 seven of her short stories were published, including the republication of the title story of Kenneth Rosen's anthology *The Man to Send Rain Clouds*. She received the Pushcart Prize for Poetry in 1977, the same year that *Ceremony* was published. In 1978 she began teaching at the University of Arizona. She also began her correspondence with James Wright, with whom she would develop a close writing rapport before his death from cancer in 1980. In 1981 Leslie Marmon Silko divorced John Silko and published *Storyteller*, for which she was awarded a five-year, $176,000 MacArthur Foundation Prize Fellowship. Silko went on to win the 1988 University of New Mexico Distinguished Alumnus Award. Over the next fifteen years five of her major works, including the novel *Almanac of the Dead* (1991) and a collection of essays called *Yellow Woman and a Beauty of the Spirit: Essays on Native American Life Today* (1996), were published.

CULTURE, RITUAL, AND IDENTITY

Silko's protagonists are often caught in a mixture of cultures and are engaged in pondering their identities within the arbitrary rankings of racial and ethnic hierarchy. In *Ceremony*, the character of Tayo is on a quest for personal and global healing through ritual and ceremony. He has grown up within the Laguna Pueblo culture, but he is often taunted for his absentee white father. After returning from World War II, he searches for an alternative method of healing from his exposure to a world in which he feels he has not found a place.

In addition, protagonists in Silko's work who are contemplating identity are undeniably tied to their homelands. For example, Indigo, in *Gardens in the Dunes* (1999), travels the world with the white woman and man who have chosen to care for her; however, her thoughts are always on getting back home to her Sand Lizard people, to her family from which she was taken. Yet Silko's writing clearly finds value and necessity in a multiplicity of cultures. Perhaps this multiplicity is reflected as well in her adept use of genre mixing and her effective slackening of the arbitrary lines between genres that have been defined and, subsequently, restricted by a Western literary canon and criticism. No character in Silko's work escapes the white world; no character escapes the United States government or the concept of socioeconomics. Food and land are taken, changed, destroyed, and often renewed. In *Gardens in the Dunes*, Indigo wonders how the white people she encounters on the East Coast obtain their food, and she subsequently wonders how the servants of the white people have time to grow and gather food for their own families. These telling thoughts from a little girl are indicative of an underlying argument for local economies that can be gathered from Silko's work. Silko's characters struggle with ecological concerns as they watch the land become barren under expansion and negligence. Her work, however, carries with it a grain of hope that lies, perhaps, in the promise of story preservation.

RETELLING AND PRESERVATION

In *Storyteller*, Leslie Marmon Silko combines prose, poetry, and photographs that meditate on the process of storytelling and create new spaces to see beyond the arbitrary boundaries of these genres. The physical book itself fits in one's hands lengthwise, neglecting the standard paperback measurements, which in itself calls attention to the fixed forms that the world of literature and the stories of life have appropriated. All of the segments or vignettes are connected to a larger thread, one that demonstrates the significance of valuing stories. In a fashion similar to *Storyteller*, Tayo's story in *Ceremony* connects to a myth that is retold in *Storyteller*. This embedded story is a retelling of a Laguna Pueblo clan tale, and it also appears in other works. It is important for these stories to reappear and be told in different ways, for no one version of a story is the only version, and this revelation is perhaps one of the most significant factors in critiquing Silko's work.

Silko has aptly demonstrated the importance of storytelling through various mediums, not only in her writing but also through the use of photography and film. Through the Laguna Film Project, which she founded, Silko filmed and produced *Estoy-eh-moot and the Kunideeyahs* (1980). In addition, Silko played herself, a Laguna storyteller, in a 1982 short film called *Running on the Edge of the Rainbow: Laguna Stories and Poems*.

Films are another method of telling the stories that continue to exist within a culture. By retelling, Silko preserves stories of the human condition, both within a certain clan or culture and more globally. Some critics question the publication of stories that draw strength from their oral presence. While Silko retrieves versions of stories told in the oral tradition, the publication of them is more of a preserving of those stories than a betrayal of the oral form. A reader or audience does not have to be present for the essence of a story to be saved, for it is evident in Silko's work that stories will continue to be told; they are necessary for human survival. A poignant example of this necessity is revealed in the short work, "Storyteller," from her book of that name. A young woman, who has been continuously molested by her deceased grandmother's husband, listens to the man as he dies, telling a story day after day. After the old man's death, the young woman begins to tell the story, for "it must be told, year after year as the old man had done, without lapse or silence." As an indication of the inner sanctity of the story within the individual, the young woman keeps telling the story long after anyone stays to hear it.

STORYTELLER

Leslie Marmon Silko's work cultivates a respect and concern for humanistic and ecological issues that need to be confronted more diligently. As human beings undergo the inevitable changes and crises of sustaining life, they might look to Silko's body of work for sincere meditations on the human condition in order to discover ways to create transitory, relevant forms of traditional stories and knowledge of ways of life that may otherwise be slowly destroyed. In addition, Silko's mastery of language evokes both physical and mental landscapes that grasp the implicit significance of story and its preservation. When examining her work, which springs forth from the American Indian literary renaissance of the 1960s and 1970s, it seems imperative to note her multifaceted contributions to American Indian, cultural, women's, and environmental studies. Most important, perhaps, readers might discover the ambiguity of defining identity as people and as individuals, the enduring telling of the stories within ourselves.

[*See also* Native American Literature *and* Writing as a Woman in the Twentieth Century.]

SELECTED WORKS

Laguna Woman: Poems (1974)
Ceremony (1977)

Western Stories (1980)
Estoyehmuut and the Gunnadeyah (1980)
Storyteller (1981)
*Running on the Edge of the Rainbow: Laguna Stories and
    Poems* (1982)
After a Summer Rain in the Upper Sonoran (1984)
Almanac of the Dead (1991)
Sacred Water: Narratives and Pictures (1993)
Love Poem and Slim Man Canyon (1996)
*Yellow Woman and a Beauty of the Spirit: Essays on Native
    American Life Today* (1996)
Gardens in the Dunes (1999)

FURTHER READING

Arnold, Ellen L., ed. *Conversations with Leslie Marmon Silko*. Jackson, Miss., 2000. Twenty-five years of
interviews with Silko that shed light on her writing
philosophies and can aid in an understanding of cultural knowledge in relation to her work. Interviewers
include Ray Gonzalez and Kim Barnes.

Barnett, Louise K., and James L. Thorson, eds. *Leslie Marmon Silko: A Collection of Critical Essays*. Albuquerque,
N.M., 1999. Critical essays, many of which cover the
nature of story and storytelling in Silko's work; includes
an extensive bibliography for further reference.

Graulich, Melody, ed. *Leslie Marmon Silko: "Yellow
Woman."* New Brunswick, N.J., 1993. A discussion
of the prevalent appearances of Yellow Woman in
Silko's work and in the Keres traditions, including
a background of Yellow Woman, an interview with
Silko, a collection of critical essays, and a selected
bibliography.

Jaskoski, Helen. *Leslie Marmon Silko: A Study of the
Short Fiction*. New York, 1998. Discussions by Silko
critics about uncollected short stories and those from
Storyteller; includes a bibliography.

Nelson, Robert M. *Place and Vision: The Function of
Landscape in Native American Fiction*. New York, 1993.
A discussion of Silko's *Ceremony*, N. Scott Momaday's
House Made of Dawn, and James Welch's *The Death of
Jim Loney* in relation to writing about landscape in the
Native American tradition.

Salyer, Gregory. *Leslie Marmon Silko*. New York, 1997. A
biography and criticism of Silko to 1997, including
a large bibliography. Salyer meditates on identity,
discusses several short stories, and focuses on the
process of storytelling.

Wright, Anne, ed. *The Delicacy and Strength of Lace: Letters
Between Leslie Marmon Silko and James Wright*. St. Paul,
Minn., 1986. Conversations between two poignant
writers in which they share personal thoughts about
writing and life.

CHARLES SIMIC

by Henry Hart

Charles Simic. (*Photo by Philip Simic*)

With his characteristic blend of whimsy and high seriousness, Charles Simic once remarked: "There are three ways of thinking about the world. You can think about the Cosmos (as the Greeks did), you can think about History (as the Hebrews did), and since the late eighteenth century you can think about Nature. The choice is yours. Where do you prefer to find (or not find) the meaning of your life? And do you include God on the menu? I myself fancy the cosmic angle. The brain-chilling infinities and silences of modern astronomy and Pascalian thought impress me deeply, except that I'm also a child of History. I've seen tanks, piles of corpses, and people strung from lampposts with my own eyes. As for Nature so-called, it's a product of Romantic utopias: noble savage, Rousseau, earthly paradise in the manner of Gauguin, the projects of Charles Fourier, our Transcendentalists, and so forth" (*The Unemployed Fortune-Teller*, 1994). Simic's qualifications and quips—"Until we resolve these questions, a nap in a hammock on a summer afternoon is highly recommended"—suggest that his three worldviews are tentative rather than dogmatic. While steeped in tradition, his own views, in fact, run counter to traditional assumptions about an orderly, meaningful, divinely created cosmos; a linear concept of history proceeding from genesis and fall to judgment and salvation; and a pastoral view of nature.

Much has been made of the "archaic" material in Simic's poems: the folklore, myths, riddles, fairy tales, proverbs, jokes, nursery rhymes, dreams, superstitions, and so on. Simic certainly explores these "archaic" or "primitive" forms of expression, raiding their structures and images for his poems, but he does so from a thoroughly modernist perspective. In his study, *The Myth of the Eternal Return; or, Cosmos and History*, Mircea Eliade, a writer Simic has read, argues: "The chief difference between the man of the archaic and traditional societies and the man of the modern societies with their strong imprint of Judaeo-Christianity lies in the fact that the former feels himself indissolubly connected with the Cosmos and the cosmic rhythms, whereas the latter insists that he is connected only with History." Eliade goes on to document how traditional cultures try to abolish or transcend history (the "profane time" of wars, plagues, and other calamities) through rituals that reenact the "sacred time" of the original creation of the cosmos. From the mythic perspective, the only "real" or "meaningful" historical events are those that ritualistically re-present the ideals, heroes, and gods that supposedly existed at or before the creation. Simic shares this urge to transcend history, but he has little of his ancestors' faith in a divine creator or a preexistent pantheon of eternal ideals and heroes.

If the Greeks and their pantheistic cousins believed they could repeatedly deliver themselves from the painful cycles of time by ritually following those cycles from destruction to re-creation, according to Eliade the Hebrew view of history was similarly hopeful, but different in its notion of a schedule for deliverance: "Since he can no longer ignore or periodically abolish history, the Hebrew tolerates it in the hope that it will finally end, at some more or less distant future moment. The irreversibility of historical events and of time is compensated by the limitation of history to time." In other words, history's bad times will end once and for all rather than every time you perform an antihistorical ritual, and one new beginning will follow this one apocalyptic end. Sooner or later, the Messiah will come again, ushering in a permanent new heaven and new earth.

The Judeo-Christian concept of a timeless utopia beyond history is little different from the romantic concept of nature that Simic mocks. Because his weltanschauung has been shaped by modern thinkers from Nietzsche and Emerson to Kafka and Heidegger, as well as his own experiences in Yugoslavia during World War II and its aftermath, Simic continually undercuts traditional worldviews with doggedly empirical ones. For Simic, cosmos, history, and nature are fundamentally one; they are all arenas of creative catastrophes, violent struggles, frightening voids, and magnificent re-creations. The drama, lyricism, and humor in his poems arise from the tensions between these archaic and modern perspectives.

THE LIFE BEFORE ART

Thinking of his early wanderings, Simic likes to joke that Hitler and Stalin were his travel agents. Born on 9 May 1938 to George and Helen Simic, he was initiated early into a knowledge of history's horrors. When he was three years old, Hitler's Nazis began bombing his native Belgrade. On 6 April 1941, the day the Germans began "Operation Punishment," a bomb set fire to a building across the street from his house, killing some of his friends; thousands were killed elsewhere. The Gestapo arrested his father, a successful engineer, and sent him to work in Germany, but he somehow escaped and returned home. In 1944, English and American planes targeted German strongholds in Belgrade but often destroyed residential neighborhoods. During the spring and summer, Simic regularly fled with his family to a grandfather's summer house in the countryside and then returned to the ruined city.

As if a world war weren't bad enough, national factions in Yugoslavia—royalists, communists, fascists, Nazi collaborators, and others—conducted a civil war, which made fleeing the city especially dangerous. On one occasion Simic found corpses in a ditch near his grandfather's house—the result of internecine fighting. On another occasion German soldiers, who were fleeing the advancing Russians, fired at him; a bullet whizzed by his ear. As soon as the Russians took control of Belgrade, he and his family went home. Undaunted by what he found, he happily played in the ruins with his friends, often collecting bullets and removing gunpowder to trade with older children for toys, food, and other desirables.

Simic started school in 1945, breezing through the first grades (his parents had already taught him to read). The real difficulty was finding a safe route to the schoolhouse through the gang-infested neighborhoods. For most of his adolescence, he had no father to advise and protect him. To escape the worsening situation in Belgrade, his father, George Simic, had traveled to Italy, where he had been arrested by the Germans as a spy. Americans liberated him from prison, but, fearing Stalin's iron-fisted communist rule and anxious about his deteriorating marriage, George did not go home. Instead, he stayed in Trieste until finally emigrating to the United States in 1950.

In Stalinist Belgrade, while locals hobbled about on crutches and Russians shot German prisoners, Simic survived as best he could. He joined a street gang, played hooky, fought other gangs, and stole things he needed (an ax-wielding man once chased him when he stole a bicycle pump). He fell in love with books: cowboy stories, mysteries, sea adventures, comic books, and then novels by Dickens, Zola, and Dostoyevsky. He also read Serbian epic ballads and folk poems, and on his many sleepless nights he listened to Duke Ellington, Count Basie, Billie Holiday, and other jazz musicians on the radio.

In order to join her husband in Trieste, Helen Simic took her two sons by train to Italy. Finding the border closed, they had to return to Belgrade. Later she tried to get to Italy by climbing through the mountains of southern Austria. They were rescued by the Austrian-American border patrol, handed over to the English, and deported to Yugoslavia, where guards escorted them to a series of prisons before they were allowed to go home. Although Stalin's communists promised to improve living conditions in Belgrade, they never did. In the late 1940s, the Simics were so destitute that on some days they had only onions and stale bread to eat. Their normal fare was a meatless stew concocted from potatoes, onions, and carrots. Their fortunes brightened when Helen, who had studied opera singing in Paris, began working again as a voice instructor. But Simic often got into trouble at school or simply skipped school to roam the streets (he once said that if he hadn't emigrated to the United States he would have ended up in reform school).

In 1953, the Simics managed to obtain passports that allowed them to leave Yugoslavia for Paris, where Helen's brother lived. For a year they lived in a run-down hotel, Simic's mother and younger brother sharing a bed while he slept on the hard floor. Simic struggled with the new language, failed all his courses except art and music, and made few friends. For entertainment he took to the streets again, wandering through the city at night like so many of the characters in his poems. If he scrounged together enough money, he went to movies; he had a taste for film noir and movie stars like Gene Tierney. Usually, however, he could only gaze at the glamorous people going to movie theatres, nightclubs, shops, and cafés, dreaming of the day he would be able to join them.

Having received U.S. visas in June 1954, the Simics bought tickets for a trip to New York on the *Queen Mary* with money generously provided by the World Church Service. After not seeing his father for ten years, Simic finally reunited with him at the port on 10 August. To introduce his family to America, George bought everyone hamburgers, french fries, milk shakes, and banana splits. Simic fell immediately in love with the beauty, ugliness, and ordinariness of New York. To better acclimate himself to the culture, he studiously watched television and read books he bought at shops with his father. He and his father gradually established a close bond because of their mutual passion for restaurants, movies, jazz, books, and talk. However, his relationship with his mother, who had no interest in American culture and little interest in his father's life in the United States, quickly soured.

In a Queens high school, Simic survived by keeping quiet (his foreign accent made him self-conscious) and doing his homework. He had little time to associate with his classmates, who tended to be hooligans, because he worked after school and on weekends. When his father was offered a job by the headquarters of the telephone company that employed him, the family moved to Chicago, living it up at the elegant Hotel Drake during the summer of 1955 before settling into an apartment in Oak Park, the suburb where Ernest Hemingway grew up. While his parents wrangled at home, Simic began to live the life of a typical American teenager, attending football games and hanging out at hamburger joints. He also made daily trips to the public library to satisfy his voracious appetite for books. At his high school he met sympathetic teachers and a few friends who wrote poetry. Inspired by their humble efforts, he tried his hand at a few poems. As he said in his memoir *A Fly in the Soup* (2000), his poetry writing "all began with my wanting to impress my friends, but then, in the process of writing, I discovered a part of myself, an imagination and a need to articulate certain things, that I could not afterward forget."

Simic also wrote in his memoir: "My greatest teachers, in both art and literature, were the streets I roamed." Drawn to both "high" and "low" culture, he adored the contradictions of his new home city: "Chicago gave a better sense of what America was than some small town or New York would have. Its mixture of being, at the same time, very modern and very provincial is a national characteristic. Add to that the realization that so much of our national prosperity depends on cheap labor. Immigrants and blacks kept Chicago humming." Chicago was the quintessential American melting pot and it became, for Simic, a surrogate college. Because of poor planning and lack of funds, he didn't go off to college like his other friends from Oak Park. Instead, like Hemingway, he left home and got a newspaper job. Tired of his parents' constant spats, he rented a room in a squalid tenement while working at the Chicago *Sun Times*. He also took night classes at the University of Chicago, painted, listened to jazz, read obsessively, and wrote poems, the first of which appeared in the winter 1959 issue of the *Chicago Review* (most of these poems, however, appalled him so much that he burned them in 1962).

Feeling restless, Simic decided to quit his job and move to New York in August 1958. Impoverished once again, he continued his diurnal and nocturnal walkabouts, studying all the tantalizing splendors of the city. A New Directions anthology of contemporary Latin American verse, which he found while browsing in a bookstore, gave him confidence in the kind of poetry he was writing. Jorge Luis Borges, Pablo Neruda, and their peers guided his attempts to incorporate folk surrealism, mysticism, and eroticism. He also learned to "cultivate [the] controlled anarchy" of avant-garde jazz musicians like Charlie Parker and Thelonius Monk.

To pay his rent and keep from starving, Simic sold shirts at Stern's Department Store on Forty-second Street, worked at the Doubleday Bookstore on Fifth Avenue, and filled out address labels at New York University Press. After a few years of scraping by, in 1961, to his great chagrin, he was drafted. For the routine humiliations of basic training he went to Fort Dix in New Jersey. Based on some aptitude exams he took, the army later sent him to Fort Gordon in Georgia to study military law enforcement and then shipped him to Kaiserslautern, Germany, to guard secret weapons as a military policeman. After three months in Germany he was transferred to France to work in a similar capacity.

His two-year tour of duty over, Simic returned to New York, married Helen Dubin in 1964, and studied for a B.A. degree in Russian at New York University (he received his degree in 1966). He took his first teaching job at California State University in Hayward. On the strength of his literary accomplishments, the Guggenheim Foundation awarded him a fellowship in 1972. After his year away from teaching, in 1973 he moved to the University of New Hampshire, where he has taught English ever since. His stature as one of America's most distinct and distinguished poets was duly recognized in 1990, when he won a Pulitzer Prize for his series of prose poems *The World Doesn't End* (1989) and several years later when he won a MacArthur fellowship. He has also won awards for his numerous essays on topics ranging from Emily Dickinson to Yugoslavian dictators, as well as for his many translations of Yugoslavian poets who have deeply influenced his work.

Although Simic isn't an overtly confessional writer, his life—especially his traumatic upbringing in Europe—left an indelible mark on his imagination. While poets tend to view childhood as an Edenic time of innocence, nostalgically celebrating their rambles among the daffodils and nightingales before the prison house of maturity descends, Simic finds little in his background that resembles a pastoral paradise. Far from Wordsworth's "clouds of glory," "intimations of immortality," and "meadow, grove, and stream . . . appareled in celestial light," as a child he witnessed corpses hanging from telephone poles, bombs incinerating buildings, enemy soldiers being shot, and guards leading him to real prison houses. The surreal, the grotesque, the horrendous were his "nature." His sardonic humor, dark urban settings, fondness for outcasts, obsessions with hunger and violence, and scorn for totalitarian utopias and intellectuals who support them all derive from his early years in war-torn Yugoslavia.

Simic's poetic strategy of defamiliarizing the ordinary through surreal imagery and narrative fragmentation originated in his fate as a displaced person. The ordinary and orderly lay in surreal fragments around his Belgrade home during the 1940s and 1950s. Junkyards and graveyards were his playgrounds. When he emigrated to France and the United States, he again encountered strange new worlds, often in silence and solitude because of his inability or hesitation to communicate. His geographical escapes and estrangements paved the way for his contemplative escapes from the nightmare of history. His gothic and comic surrealism, as he often acknowledges, is also a kind of realism—a documentation of the way things were and the way things continue to be in his native country and the rest of the world.

DARK NIGHTS OF THE SOUL

The central tension in Simic's work involves his contemplative quest for a divine Creator beyond history's carnage. To get beyond the afflictions he has suffered as a Serbian refugee, he repeatedly enters a "dark night" of mental purgation. But rather than meet a redemptive God, which is the traditional goal of the meditator's *via negativa*, Simic encounters the chilling silences and voids of the cosmos. In an essay published in *Orphan Factory* (1997), he admits: "I was always attracted to mystical and esoteric doctrines that propose the unknowingness of the Supreme Being, the ineffability of the experience of his presence and the ambiguity of our human condition. . . . If I believe in anything, it is the dark night of the soul. Awe is my religion, and mystery is its church." Simic refers to St. John of the Cross's famous treatise on meditation and contemplation, *The Dark Night*, in which the Spanish Renaissance divine charted the harrowing journey that "prepares the soul for the union with God through love by both purging and illumining it." What St. John prescribes is a radical realignment of the intellect, imagination, will, memory, and senses so that the humbled communicant can be infused with divinity.

Simic follows St. John's mystic way toward purgation and illumination, but, as he confesses right before his comment about the "dark night of the soul," he doesn't believe in a traditional God. On his many purgative retreats into silence, darkness, and solitude, he finds himself floundering in a meaningless, indifferent, and largely empty universe. His mood, however, is not so much despairing as surprised and uplifted by the sheer mystery of the universe, by the very fact that it exists. He identifies with Pascal, who wrote in the *Pensées*: "When I consider the brief span of my life absorbed into the eternity which comes before and after . . . the small space I occupy and which I see swallowed up in the infinite immensity of spaces of which I know nothing and which know nothing of me, I take fright and I am amazed to see myself here rather than there . . . , now rather than then." Brooding on the dark spaces and infinities of the cosmos, Simic feels the same sublime mix of terror and awe. If there is no God, there is certainly a mysterious origin and a mysterious cosmos to be celebrated—and decried—in poetry.

The best introduction to Simic's religious and historical preoccupations and to his deceptively simple style is "Butcher Shop," a poem in four quatrains that he regularly places at the beginning of his collections of selected poems. The poem starts with the colloquial matter-of-factness of Robert Bly's early poems, which greatly influenced Simic's. Like Bly, he interrupts and energizes his humdrum tone and colloquial vocabulary with Gothic imagery that expresses a wide range of feelings. One can imagine Simic on one of his nightly urban rambles stopping by the dimly lit butcher shop and remembering the times he went hungry, thought about stealing some meat, and worried about getting caught and imprisoned (he compares the shop to a jail in which "the convict digs his tunnel").

In the second stanza, Simic's persona establishes a more public context for the butcher shop, linking it with the battlefields of World War II and of other bloody wars. The butcher's apron is "smeared into a map / Of the great continents of blood." After his epiphany of a world full of butchery, the brooding nightwalker focuses on knives and their associations with ritual sacrifice and redemption. Faith and war, of course, go hand in hand in Yugoslavia and many other parts of the world, but Simic's speaker seems to be pondering the simple fact of sacrifice: that some die (whether animals, soldiers, heroes, or gods) so others may live. The sacrifice in his "dark church" may be noble because it heals "the cripple and the imbecile," but it also may be a sham if it only works for the most destitute and foolish.

The poem ends with more paradoxes. Staring at the butcher's block as if it were a torturer's block where bones are broken, the speaker notes that it is empty as a dry river bed but that it is specifically this corporeal absence that feeds him, that evokes a voice. He may be hearing the voice of a butchered animal or tortured human, or he may be hearing his own voice. Although he suggests, as he often does in his other poems about insomnia and late-night strolls through shadowy cities, that his "dark night" or "dark church" resembles the purgatorial "dark night" of the traditional Christian meditator, the voice and imagery here are more bodily and poetic than divine.

Despite his impatience with utopian visions of nature, many of Simic's early poems offer a pastoral paradise as a kind of substitute for the meditator's traditional concepts of divinity. "Summer Morning," which he included in *Dismantling the Silence* (1971), typifies his sacramental view of nature. Although the poem's narrator isn't wandering through a "dark night," he remains in bed with eyes closed, silent and solitary, listening and envisioning. "I know all the dark places / Where the sun hasn't reached yet," he says, and then imagines passing over the farmhouses and cornfields toward "Summer sky and eternal life." The figure he meets at the end of his contemplative journey is godly, transcendental, eerily quiet. Walking like Jesus over the waves of grass, he provides a model of holy simplicity to Simic's daydreamer.

Many critics have pointed to the plethora of references to silence, solitude, and darkness in Simic's poems, but few have shown that these conditions are part of a meditative continuum leading to voice, communion, and illumination. Even in his "object poems" in *Dismantling the Silence*—his fanciful discourses on forks, spoons, knives, shoes, and stones—Simic seems to be deliberately dying away from the temporal realm of historical calamity and courting a purgative "dark night of the soul" so that, in the end, he can reach some sort of sublimity or cosmic perspective. "Go inside a stone," he says in "Stone." "That would be my way. / Let somebody else become a dove / Or gnash with a tiger's tooth." Others can be political pacifists and warriors; he will be a hermit meditating in a stony cell that is cool and quiet. The humble constriction necessary to enter the dark stone leads to illumination and sublime texts—"The strange writings, the star-charts"—that, in turn, guide the initiate to an expansive vision of the cosmos.

One of Simic's most mysterious and moving early poems that also recapitulates a "dark night" is "Dismantling the Silence." Here Simic personifies and deifies silence as a corpse rather than as a living person or living god. The corpse might be a victim of history, but it plays a symbolic role as an avatar of the dead, indifferent, meaningless cosmos, of "the brain-chilling infinities and silences of modern astronomy" that Simic finds so frightening and enchanting. Acting as a kind of master mortician, Simic gives directions in his usual deadpan tone on how to preserve and bury the corpse. His embalming manual, as one might expect, is a highly eccentric one because it is also a "how-to" guide on communion and enlightenment. He tells his imaginary apprentice, who might as well be the reader, to cut open the body and empty it of ashes and water. The ritual cleansing is meant to be redemptive; the body, even though it's dead, can provide sustenance to "the root of a flower that hasn't drunk for a month." It can also sustain the communicant who is told to slip the dead man's bones under his skin. Having dismantled and reembodied "the silence" in this mordant ritual, the communicant is ready to proceed on his meditative *via negativa* to the heart of the mystery, which is the heart of the cosmos. Although there is no ordinary god waiting to carry on a colloquy at the conclusion of this "dark night," there is an intimation of something divine in the "empty heavens." Having dismantled and transcended death and silence, the meditator hears a mysterious, life-giving pulse: the universe's original "timeless" heart that continues to beat.

In other early poems, Simic plays the role of a contemplative apprentice trying to learn about the origin and evolution of the cosmos so that he can properly pay homage to its magnificent workings. "The ambition of literary realism is to plagiarize God's creation," he once wrote in a notebook. Simic's ambition is more complex—to imitate the Creation's baffling multiplicity through realism as well as surrealism. In "Elementary Cosmogony," collected in *Return to a Place Lit by a Glass of Milk* (1974), he offers a tongue-in-cheek portrait of himself as an initiate following a shadowy master he calls "the invisible"—a protean spirit who is part dadaist, part astrophysicist, and part God. His arduous apprenticeship culminates with a lesson on submitting to chance. Although Einstein used to maintain that God doesn't roll the dice, Simic's master believes otherwise: chance occurrences and random mutations govern the Creation and all subsequent creations, whether in nature or art.

If chance creates, chance also destroys. The parody of the fertile artist-god—the god who oversees destruction rather than creation—appears in many of Simic's poems, including "Charon's Cosmology," the title poem of a book he published in 1977. In Simic's version of the classical myth, Charon is the god of history's nightmare, of the grim temporal world, as well as the Greek god of the underworld who ferries souls of the dead over the rivers Styx and Acheron and who takes a coin placed in the mouths of the dead during burial as his fee. According to Simic, he is a dim brute whose "dark night" leads nowhere but to ignorant habit. Uprooted and confused, he cares only about picking the pockets of the dead to get his fee. If he finds "a mirror / Or a book / . . . he throws [them] / Overboard into the dark river." A mirror or a book might enlighten him about the monotony of his dismal trade. If "Charon's cosmology" revealed the magnificent cosmos around him, perhaps he would become a poet or mystic. His cosmos, unfortunately, is a diminished one, an underworld of death and silence. Charon is ultimately a pitiful creature. He isn't responsible for all the corpses piled by the river; he is merely the undertaker whose job it is to dispose of them. Although he doesn't strive to dismantle and transcend the deathly silence that enshrouds him like Simic's other mystical personae, he survives as best he can.

Simic's mystics and artists resemble Charon in the sense that they are also struggling to survive in a ghastly world. For them, books like St. John of the Cross's *Dark Night* are survival manuals that they adapt to their situations. They don't follow traditional meditational prescriptions to the letter; they don't completely purge—as St. John advised—"all the faculties, passions, affections, and appetites which live in its [the mind's] sensory and spiritual parts" and they aren't entirely "put to sleep and mortified in this night, which leaves them in darkness, that they may not be able to observe or experience anything in their lowly, natural way which would impede the soul's departure from itself and the house of the senses." Nevertheless, they repeatedly darken "the house of the senses," blinding themselves to historical realities and personal afflictions in order to live more intensely in the imagination.

One of Simic's most anthologized poems, "Prodigy," from *Classic Ballroom Dances* (1980), is another attempt to dramatize the boons of this meditational blinding. Again he recounts an apprenticeship to a master—in this case a chess player who is also a retired professor of astronomy. The action takes place around 1944 in a small house by a Roman graveyard. Outside, men hang from telephone poles. Planes and tanks shake the windows, distracting the players. Simic's boyhood persona concedes that he is playing war during the war, but his war against rickety chessmen is obviously quite different from the war against real men raging outside the house. "I remember my mother / blindfolding me a lot," he says, adding:

In chess, too, the professor told me,
the masters play blindfolded,
the great ones on several boards
at the same time.

The poem implies that to be an artistic prodigy, whether at chess or poetry or astronomy, one must enter a "dark night" of sensory deprivation so that the terrors of history don't confound the mind. The astronomy professor, who presumably has a cosmic perspective on things, is the ideal teacher for the prodigy. He teaches him to survive and flourish by transcending the horrors of history. He introduces him to chess, to the masters who resemble artist-gods, and perhaps to the supreme Artist who plays with the world with such reckless abandon.

For Simic, willful blindness is not a permanent escape from history so much as a stage in "the eternal return." His mystical personae free themselves from worldly menace, voyaging into Pascal's "infinite immensity of spaces" in search of a supreme being, only to return to earth so they can testify to reality's randomness, splendor, and evil in their cosmogonies and cosmologies. In the poems he collected in *Unending Blues* (1986) and following books, he increasingly emphasizes the worldliness of his mystics by inserting them—often hilariously—into mundane contexts. Emulating the example of traditional mystics by finding the sacred in the profane, the eternal in the temporal, Simic locates his fellow divines in the humdrum present even if they died centuries ago. In "First Frost," he envisages the seasonal death of the vegetation outside his New Hampshire house as a harbinger of a spiritual dying away from the world, as a stage in the meditative "eternal return" that leads to a union of time and timelessness. Gazing from his house, he observes that it is "The time of the year for the mystics. / October sky and the Cloud of Unknowing." In the anonymous fourteenth-century treatise *The Cloud of Unknowing*, the author envisions the meditator's "dark night" as a "cloud of forgetting" that obscures the world and a "cloud of unknowing" that obscures God. "The vigorous working of your imagination, which is always so active when you set yourself to this blind contemplation, must as often be suppressed," he says. Only love can penetrate what appears obscure to the intellect and reach God: "He may well be loved, but not thought. By love he can be caught and held, but by thinking never." In "First Frost," other medieval and Renaissance mystics make cameo appearances to lead Simic from his humble surroundings to the unknowable supreme being. Jakob Boehme sips tea in the kitchen and warns him "of the quiet / To which the wise must school themselves." Outside, in the honking of Canada geese, Simic hears: "Dame Julian of Norwich herself discoursing / On the marvelous courtesy and homeliness of the Maker." The poem's surreal way of blending the living and dead, the temporal and immortal, enacts what the mystics advocated and manages to incorporate some of their down-to-earth humor as well.

When mystics crop up in other settings, Simic invariably addresses them as masters introducing him to divine mysteries he adores but can't entirely believe. His ambivalence spurs his spiritual comedy, his meditative slapstick. At the beginning of "The Initiate" in *The Book of Gods and Devils* (1990), he recalls a nocturnal journey through New York City toward "Something supreme . . . / For which there will never be any words." St. Theresa of Avila, who is beautiful and grave, and her fellow countryman St. John of the Cross, who wears dark glasses presumably to make his "dark night" darker, lead the way. These sixteenth-century mystics, unsurprisingly, express disappointment with Simic's initiate. They remain distant in both time and attitude, enchanting him with their heroic faith that he can only emulate in a modern, quirky way.

Like many other modern poets, Simic has a powerful religious temperament without a God to fulfill it. His

enthusiasm for the sublime propels him on quests for divinity that ultimately collapse in skepticism and nihilism. Seeking God, he finds an ineffable mystery, an unknowable creator, and a cosmic void that scare him as well as astonish him. If he addresses God, he does so ironically, employing the language of orthodoxy only to subvert it. "You've been a long time making up your mind / O Lord, about these madmen / Running the world," he begins a late poem, "Psalm," from *A Wedding in Hell* (1994). Hoping for political justice, Simic knows all too well that history makes a mockery of justice and the sentimental pastoralism of religious utopias:

> I sought with my eyes, You in whom I do not believe.
> You've been busy making the flowers pretty,
> The lambs run after their mother,
> Or perhaps you haven't been doing even that?

Simic's religious skepticism arises from a more fundamental skepticism about the ability of language to embody and communicate reality. If biblical language seduces its readers into believing pastoral fictions in some namby-pamby never-never land, all language distorts reality to a certain degree. The philosophical questions Simic asks in his poems about being and nothingness spark other epistemological questions about what the mind can really know and articulate. How is one to distinguish truth from falsehood when the mind that processes reality and the language that expresses reality are so untrustworthy? Simic continually dramatizes these quandaries in poems that are as farcical as they are philosophical.

From his early poems to his latest in *Night Picnic* (2001), Simic dazzles by shifting between transcendental and mundane perspectives, examining the heavens from the earth and the earth from the heavens. The meditative moment in the title poem of *Night Picnic*, in which he mulls over his cosmic insignificance while sipping red wine, typifies his dialectic. As he ritually enacts an "eternal return" from the temporal to the infinite, from the historical to the cosmic, he does so like one of Shakespeare's fools whose zany wit exposes human stupidities and cruelties for what they are. The abrupt leaps between wisdom and buffoonery have unsettled and perplexed some readers. The critical consensus, however, is that Simic is one of our indispensable poets—a poet who has survived some of the worst experiences of the twentieth century with his head, heart, and sense of humor intact. His writing, as Seamus Heaney once remarked, "comes dancing out on the balls of its feet, colloquially fit as a fiddle, a sparring partner for the world." Human nature being what it is, Simic's lover's quarrel with the world shows no sign of abating. In book after book, he keeps teaching and entertaining us with his magnificent dancing and sparring.

WORKS

What the Grass Says (1967)
Somewhere among Us a Stone Is Taking Notes (1969)
Dismantling the Silence (1971)
White (1972)
Return to a Place Lit by a Glass of Milk (1974)
Charon's Cosmology (1977)
Classic Ballroom Dances (1980)
*Weather Forecast for Utopia and Vicinity: Poems,
    1967–1982* (1983)
Austerities (1982)
*The Uncertain Certainty: Interviews, Essays, and Notes on
    Poetry* (1985)
Selected Poems, 1963–1983 (1986)
Unending Blues (1986)
The World Doesn't End (1989)
The Book of Gods and Devils (1990)

*Wonderful Words, Silent Truth: Essays on Poetry and a
    Memoir* (1990)
Hotel Insomnia (1992)
The Unemployed Fortune-Teller: Essays and Memoirs (1994)
A Wedding in Hell (1994)
Walking the Black Cat (1996)
Looking for Trouble (1997)
Orphan Factory: Essays and Memoirs (1997)
Jackstraws (1999)
Selected Early Poems (1999)
A Fly in the Soup (2000)
Night Picnic: Poems (2001)

FURTHER READING

Stitt, Peter. *Uncertainty and Plenitude: Five Contemporary Poets.* Iowa City, Iowa, 1997. The chapter "Poetry in a Time of Madness" is a fine introduction to many of Simic's principal themes and some of the controversies that have attended his work.

Weigl, Bruce, ed. *Charles Simic: Essays on the Poetry.* Ann Arbor, Mich., 1996. Provides a good overview of reviews and essays.

WILLIAM GILMORE SIMMS AND ANTEBELLUM SOUTHERN LITERATURE

by John McCardell

Concluding his epic poem on the Civil War, *John Brown's Body* (1928), Stephen Vincent Benét perceptively defines the Confederacy as "the America we have not been." In that simple, telling turn of phrase Benet explains the central problem and challenge in attempting properly to understand and evaluate the literature of the Old South.

"The America we have not been" was fully a part of America in the years prior to 1860. The term "antebellum" would have elicited puzzled expressions in the streets of Charleston or New Orleans or in the cotton fields of Georgia or Mississippi. The South was not yet "the America we have not been." It thought of itself as American. Its newest states—Mississippi (1817), Alabama (1819), and Arkansas (1836)—joined the growing Union with; enthusiasm. Its people spoke the English language; read American newspapers, periodicals, and books; celebrated Independence Day; posted letters with American stamps; and weighed and measured in pounds and feet. Its families attended Baptist, Methodist, Presbyterian, and Episcopal churches. Its children studied American subjects instructed by American teachers, and its young men attended American colleges and universities. Its planters, farmers, merchants, and professionals tried to comprehend, if not to tame, the business cycle. Its soldiers fought side by side against Indians and Mexicans with other Americans under Old Glory. Its regularly amended or rewritten state constitutions broadened and extended political participation to an ever-wider circle of citizens. Its politicians belonged to the national Democratic and Whig parties and, within that American partisan framework, debated over banks, tariffs, and internal improvements (all parts of what Henry Clay, the great Kentuckian, called "the American System"). Its editors attacked and defended. Its philosophers pondered American constitutionalism and

William Gilmore Simms.
(*Courtesy of the New York Public Library*)

republican virtue. Its scientists studied American flora and fauna and geography.

And its writers chose American themes. Indeed, its writers were fully engaged in the effort to create a distinctive American literature, part of a broader quest for nationality that took on special urgency in the years after 1815. Conscious of their country's incompleteness culturally if not also geographically, a new generation of American writers took up the challenge posed by nationhood and expressed most vividly by Edward Tyrrell Channing in the address "Literary Independence," delivered at Harvard in 1818. America must establish, Channing declared, "a domestic literature upon what is peculiarly our own—our scenery, our modes of life, our history, and the antiquities of our country." The impulse to create a distinctively American literature was as acute in the South as it was in New England. The *Southern Review*, founded in Charleston in 1828, announced that its purpose was to "arrest the current [from abroad] which has been directed against our country generally and the South in particular." The *Southern Literary Messenger* began publication in 1834 with the intent of "building up a character of our own, and embodying and concentrating the neglected genius of our country."

American literary nationalism as propounded by Channing flourished in the Old South. The region's leading man of letters, William Gilmore Simms of South Carolina, wrote and lectured on the subject. "To write *from* a people, is to *write* a people—to make them live—to endow them with a life and a name—to preserve them with a history forever," Simms wrote in 1845. "We are rejoiced to behold," he continued, "symptoms of this independent intellectual working, simultaneously, in remote regions of the country; and flatter ourselves with the vision of a generous growth in art and letters, of which tokens begin to make themselves felt from the Aroostook to the Rio Brave."

A nation's writers, Simms believed, "must be born of her soil, and ardently devoted to its claims." Native genius must be shaped by "those natural objects which familiarly address themselves to the senses from boyhood." Its "whole soul must be imbued with sympathies caught from surrounding aspects within [its] infant horizon." The result will be a literature rich and diverse. "To any one who looks into the character of our people," Simms concluded, "and sees in what way the great popular heart beats in the several States of the confederacy—with what calm, consistent resolve in some—with what impatient heat in others—how cold but how clear in this region—how fiery, but how clouded in that;—there will be ample promise for the future, not only in the value of the material, but in its exquisite and rich variety."

Simms, who never traveled abroad, offered these thoughts in an essay entitled "Americanism in Literature," which was in fact a review of a lecture on the same topic delivered by Alexander B. Meek of Alabama before the Phi Kappa and Demosthenean Societies of the University of Georgia. Meek was a minor poet and historian, one of many writers of his generation who received encouragement from Simms and whose name and work have no memorial. "If our minds are only original," Meek had argued, "if we dare to think for ourselves, and faithfully picture forth, in our own styles of utterance, the impressions our minds shall receive from this great, fresh continent of beauty and sublimity; we can render to the world the most vigorous and picturesque literature it has ever beheld."

Originality, then, was to be pursued and prized. Yet Old World models were difficult to avoid. American writers read the works of their British counterparts and the criticism of those works by British critics. Measuring up to existing standards constituted a less difficult task than forming a new standard. Hence much American writing in the mid-nineteenth century was derivative, and for the most part that work has been neither highly regarded nor well remembered. The influence of Sir Walter Scott, in particular, held considerable sway. That influence might be understandable in a climate of literary nationalism, for no writer did more to create a history and populate it with heroic figures than Scott. His historical romances, wrote Simms in 1849, combined "the peculiar powers of the *raconteur* with those of the poet, painter, and the analyst of events and character" in a way "more perfect, more complete and admirable than any writer of his age." For Simms, as for other American writers, the challenge was to observe the conventional forms while meshing them with a distinctive American reality. At the same time, a national literature of merit would be the product of writings about the local and familiar.

Thus, Simms's statement in the introduction to *The Wigwam and the Cabin*, a collection of his best stories published in 1845, that "to be national in literature, one must needs be sectional," seemed to him a simple truth. "No one mind can fully or fairly illustrate the characteristics of any great country," he believed, "and he who shall depict *one section* faithfully, has made his proper and sufficient contribution to the great work of *national* illustration." Southern writers, like other American writers, wrote about scenes, people, events, and institutions that were immediate and familiar and had no reason to think their work anything other than American literature.

SOUTHERN THEMES

One of those institutions, of course, was slavery. Although slavery had been a major topic at the time the Constitution was written, and though southerners at that time had acquiesced in a variety of limitations on the growth of the institution, it was not until 1820, with the debate over Missouri statehood and the compromise that admitted it as a slave state but made its southern boundary the limit of slavery's national expansion, did it occur to southerners that slavery might be a peculiar sectional interest. And not until the crisis over the tariff in the 1830s, concurrent with the Nat Turner slave uprising in Virginia and the birth of the abolitionist movement in New England, did it occur to southerners that slavery was something that required defending. In the 1830s, however, beginning with Thomas R. Dew's published review of the debates over emancipation in the Virginia legislature, a systematic proslavery argument began to emerge. In 1837 Senator John C. Calhoun of South Carolina called slavery a "positive good." Dew, a young professor at the College of William and Mary, advanced both historical and scriptural arguments in laying the foundation for the defense of the South's peculiar institution. A reviewer of Dew's pamphlet for the *Southern Literary Messenger* in 1839 declared that "slavery is the great distinguishing characteristic of the southern states, and is, in fact, the only important institution which they can claim peculiarly as their own."

Yet the antislavery movement did not attract large numbers of adherents and in fact, into the 1850s, operated on the margins of politics and intellectual life. Though confined within a fixed territorial boundary, slavery remained an American institution that was protected, southerners believed, by constitutional and legislative compact. To write of slavery and plantations, then, was to write of American things. For the most part, therefore, it would be a mistake to try to distinguish southern writers from other American writers in the period before 1860, except to note the growing tension between their understanding of American things and that of Americans outside the South. Even then, the perceived differences between the sections was mostly a subtext for literary efforts that, like literature in other times and places, sought through the written word to find beauty or truth or insight in the felicitous expression of poetry or prose. Moreover, to begin to understand the work of southern writers before 1860, one must define literature more broadly and then meet with names and titles that are not instantly recognizable.

Some of that writing was quite specialized and directed toward a narrow audience. For example, Edmund Ruffin of Virginia was an agricultural reformer concerned over the exhaustive effect tobacco cultivation had on the soils of his native state. Ruffin experimented with marl, or fossil shells, and reaped a record corn harvest on his plantation. In 1818 he delivered a paper on new farming methods to his county agricultural society, thus launching a campaign for reform. In 1832 Ruffin published this paper, in expanded form, as *Essay on Calcareous Manures*, and in 1833 he founded the *Farmer's Register*, a monthly journal devoted to scientific agriculture. The journal survived nine years, perishing for lack of paying subscribers. Ruffin spent the year 1842 touring the state of South Carolina with Governor James Henry Hammond spreading the gospel of marl and broadening his understanding of both agricultural and political issues in the world beyond Virginia. In 1845 he declined appointment as the first president of the newly formed Virginia State Agricultural Society. In time he became an outspoken advocate of secession.

Some of that writing was done strictly for amusement, of author and of reader. William Elliott's *Carolina Sports*, for instance, published in 1846, describes hunting and fishing in and around Beaufort, South Carolina. Elliott, a well-educated member of the Beaufort planter elite, penned the essays that constitute the book over a period of almost twenty years. Of these by far the most interesting are "The Fire Hunter," which probes issues of race

and relationships between the several classes of whites, and "Incidents of Devil-Fishing," which describes the experience of harpooning giant rays along the Beaufort coast. Both stories are vivid accounts. Neither gets much below the surface of the event, leading critics to speculate that Elliott, unlike Melville or Faulkner, was disinclined to go beyond the superficial lest he come face to face with realities he would prefer not to confront.

Some of that writing was vigorously comical. Augustus Baldwin Longstreet, Johnson Jones Hooper, and Joseph G. Baldwin wrote tales of the southern frontier. In *Georgia Scenes*, published in 1835 by Harper and Brothers in New York, Longstreet, a Methodist minister, delighted a national readership with stories of an exotic Georgia frontier, where the militia drilled with umbrellas, the populace drank to excess, and the preferred form of public amusement was a "gander pulling." Hooper, of Alabama, introduced readers in the 1840s to Simon Suggs, whose motto, "it is good to be shifty in a new country," summarized the rough-and-tumble chaos of the southern frontier. The Virginia-born Baldwin wrote with genteel, urbane amusement of the *Flush Times in Alabama and Mississippi*, published in 1853, as a new society tried to establish itself while dealing with chicanery and buffoonery. Slavery was not a topic in these works. In later years, however, these writers turned from humor to polemic. Longstreet tried unsuccessfully to have the Harpers publish two anti-abolition pamphlets. Hooper attacked abolitionism in the Montgomery newspaper. Baldwin simply moved to California.

Some of that writing was of the highest and most imaginative quality. Edgar Allan Poe is not always considered a southern writer, perhaps because he was born in Boston, perhaps because he never threw down the sectional gauntlet, but more likely because he was so unconventional. In a time of intense literary nationalism, Poe believed art must necessarily be international and based his critical judgments on the "unity of effect" of a particular work. In a time when good poetry was synonymous with didacticism, Poe explored psychology and the supernatural and was a master of tone and meter. His tales of terror, his comic "grotesqueries," his detective stories all defined, if they did not indeed originate, the short story form. The most informed critical judgment of Poe's literary achievement must view him as neither southerner nor American but rather, as a recent critic has put it, "a citizen of the world, a status he would have considered entirely appropriate."

Much of that writing was of the most conventional, derivative, even pedestrian, sort. John Pendleton Kennedy of Maryland developed the cavalier legend in a series of unremarkable novels, the best-known of which was, and is, *Swallow Barn*, published in 1832, which idealized plantation life in Virginia and which imitates Scott. Equally unremarkable poets, including Thomas Holley Chivers, Richard Henry Wilde, and Philip Pendleton Cooke, "reverberate," writes a recent critic, "not so much in the mind as in the ear." In the 1850s a new generation of poets began to emerge, the best of whom was Paul Hamilton Hayne, whose major work was done during and after the Civil War.

Some of that writing explored problems of political theory, specifically the relationship of majority rule and minority rights. The eccentric, brilliant, Oxford-educated Thomas Cooper, who served as president of South Carolina College from 1820 to 1833, introduced the study of economics as a serious academic discipline and published *Lectures on the Elements of Political Economy* in 1826. These studies opposed the idea of protective tariffs and thus led Cooper to predict the day when the South would "be compelled to calculate the value of our union; and to inquire of what use to us is this most unequal alliance." Cooper became a spokesman for the doctrine of nullification as propounded by Senator John C. Calhoun. Calhoun, a young nationalist in 1815, devoted much of his public life and many of his public utterances to trying to solve the vexing question of minority rights. A sovereign state, he argued in 1828, was duty-bound to interpose itself between an unconstitutional act by the national government and the people upon whom such act would be inflicted. The doctrine of nullification, or state interposition, was hardly original with Calhoun; it had been advocated in the Virginia and Kentucky Resolutions of 1798 and 1799 and again by New Englanders opposed to the War of 1812. In later years, still seeking a means of preserving an increasingly diverse Union, Calhoun wrote *A Disquisition on Government* and *A Discourse on the Constitution and Government of the United States*, hoping, he stated, "to lay a solid foundation for political Science." These studies (both published in 1851), which viewed the Constitution as a compact entered into voluntarily by sovereign states, propounded novel remedies, including the idea of a "concurrent majority," by which a state or a section of the country would be required to give its assent to the making of federal laws.

Some of that writing was by African Americans. Slave narratives written, or at least dictated, by those who had escaped bondage, not only served a political purpose but also demonstrated the intellectual capabilities of the author. Of these, the best by far is the *Narrative of the Life of Frederick Douglass* (1845), which describes the degrading, dehumanizing effect of slavery even in its most humane setting and even on the Maryland periphery of the slave South. An equally important writer, William Wells Brown, escaped slavery in Missouri. His *Narrative* (1847), was probably the best-known account in his time. Of greater interest, however, is Brown's *Clotel*, the first novel by an African-American author, written and published in London in 1853. This work introduces the story of a liaison between Thomas Jefferson and a slave woman that produces two daughters, both of whom are auctioned off after their owner's death. One, Clotel, escapes the slave catchers only by jumping to her death from a bridge over the Potomac River in Washington. Brown, who spent the last twenty-four years of his life in Boston as a practicing physician, remained a persistently outspoken denouncer of slavery and also of racism, which he found present in white Americans North and South. Yet his vision remained one of integration of the races, a recurrent theme in his many writings over a long life.

Some of that writing was by women, even in the face of critical condescension. Writing professionally was no easier for the southern woman than it was for George Eliot or Emily Dickinson. In 1860 Mary E. Bryan wrote an article for the periodical *Southern Field and Fireside* entitled "How Should Women Write?" She noted that "those who seek to go beyond the boundary line are put down with the stigma of '*strong-minded.*'" Only a resolute woman would dare to overcome these obstacles. More often, as in the case of the highly intelligent South Carolinian Louisa Susannah McCord, wife of a prominent public figure, the irrepressible impulse to write, which she called "an absolute comfort, an almost necessity," found outlet only in private. "An effortless life is, to a restless mind," she confided in a letter, "a weary fate to be doomed to.... As to my productions being *closet dramas*, what else can a Woman write?"

Yet, also as in the North, there were some exceptions. Caroline Gilman, born in Boston, lived in Charleston. In 1832 she founded the *Rose Bud*, a children's magazine, which later became the *Southern Rose*, for adults. In addition to her editing duties, Gilman wrote fiction, poetry, and published *Recollections of a Housekeeper* in 1834 and *Recollections of a Southern Matron* in 1838. These two works describe life on a plantation and a young girl's coming of age. Caroline Lee Hentz wrote ten mostly forgettable, sensational, even melodramatic novels on a similar theme, with strong women on southern plantations as main characters. Her best-known work, *The Planter's Northern Bride*, published in 1854, contrasts the harmony, order, and paternalism of the plantation with northern "wage slavery" and offers a ringing justification of slavery.

Indeed, as time passed, more and more of that writing became part of an emerging proslavery argument. The earliest defenses of slavery had been based upon the Bible, history, and the Constitution and had contended that the existence of slavery, from time immemorial, had been central to social and political order. The emphasis was on class, not race, and the defense summoned the Greeks and the Romans as witnesses. As the abolitionist assault intensified, however, and as the principle of free soil, which would simply limit the extension of slavery, not interfere with it where it already existed, gained support, the proslavery argument began to invoke Negro inferiority and race control as the main justification.

Among the more forceful writers defending slavery were, in addition to Dew, James Henry Hammond and William J. Grayson of South Carolina and George Fitzhugh of Virginia. Hammond engaged in a correspondence with the British abolitionist Thomas Clarkson. Subsequently published in 1845, the Clarkson Letters put forth a scathing critique of the British industrial system, which Hammond contrasted with the paternalistic, hierarchical, deferential system of slavery. This argument reappeared in a long poem in heroic couplets by William J. Grayson, *The Hireling and the Slave* (1856), and more forcefully in George Fitzhugh's *Sociology for the South* (1854) and *Cannibals All! or, Slaves Without Masters* (1857). Taken together, these and a host of lesser writers, including Nathaniel Beverley Tucker, William Harper, and Henry Hughes, promulgated and over time developed a vision of a just and coherent social order that had slavery at its center and the slaveholder—beneficent, virtuous, civic-minded—as its moral exemplar. By 1860 this vision was so at odds with the vision of America as possessed by most of the rest of the country that secession and civil war resulted. But to the very end the slavery apologist's vision sought congruity with American nationality and claimed that that vision had been present from the beginning of nationhood. It was left to the poet Henry Timrod, in "Ethnogenesis," which celebrated the establishment of the Confederacy in 1861, to restate that vision in southern nationalist terms:

> For, to give labor to the poor,
> The whole sad planet o'er,
> And save from want and crime the humblest door,

> Is one among the many ends for which
> God makes us great and rich!

This writing appeared in books, pamphlets, and periodicals, the publication and distribution of which were seriously impeded by the geography of the region. Unlike compact New England, the South sprawled across 1,500 miles of varied terrain. The South never possessed a single urban center or cultural marketplace. Where nineteenth-century New England had Boston, the South had Baltimore, Richmond, Charleston, Savannah, Mobile, New Orleans, and Memphis. The potential for competition and diffusion was thus markedly greater. There was no single publishing center, no single literary community to which the aspiring southern writer might turn for the sort of automatic exposure that New England or New York City provided. Nor was there a sizable, concentrated market for published material. For all these reasons, though southern literary output was probably as varied in type as it was in quality—and in both cases more so than in other regions—it had constantly to struggle for recognition. Some writers, resigning themselves to this reality, cultivated northern audiences and publishers. Much of Simms's best-known fiction was published in New York. Perhaps it is only a coincidence that he has been regarded as the Old South's leading man of letters.

SOUTHERN LITERATURE AND THE CRITICS

For all these reasons, the literature of the Old South has to a large degree been overlooked or dismissed. Indeed, until quite recently the pre–Civil War South has been regarded, according to one critic, as "a region of literary reaction," in which little of merit and less of originality can be identified. This view began to take shape in the years following the war, during which the first serious attempts to write the history of American literature occurred. Inevitably the Civil War and its outcome influenced these efforts. Winning and losing mattered. To the victor went the privilege of defining the American literary tradition and the critical standards for evaluating past and present American authors. According to this emerging view, nation had triumphed over section, equality over slavery, right over wrong, North over South. The Old South represented "the America we have not been."

As a result, the definition of American literature, and the terms by which the stature of individual writers and works were to be determined, fell into the hands of scholars and publishers in a particular section of the country possessing a distinct point of view, who assumed the mantle of nationality. As a further result, the term "literature," which might have been more broadly understood, came instead to mean a particular kind of literature which, not surprisingly, had flourished in that part of the country that was defining the critical standards. The imaginative writer became the quintessential American writer. The writer of social or political commentary, the teller of frontier tales, the polemicist, received brief, barely polite attention. Meanwhile, poets or essayists had to meet the standard of Ralph Waldo Emerson, writers of historical fiction that of Washington Irving or James Fenimore Cooper, novelists Nathaniel Hawthorne, historians George Bancroft. In the 1890s, Charles Dudley Warner published the American Men of Letters Series, which fixed the canon and determined the rankings through a quite deliberate choice of authors and subjects. One southern writer, William Gilmore Simms, made the list. His biographer, the young, unknown but fully Reconstructed southerner William Peterfield Trent, delivered the uncompromising verdict: "It was a life affording few opportunities to talents that did not lie in certain beaten grooves. It was a life gaining its intellectual nourishment largely from abroad [hence in some way un-American],—a life that choked all investigation that did not tend to conserve existing institutions and opinions." For these reasons, Trent concluded, Simms's "place is not a high one; . . . When his environment is considered, the work he did will be deemed worthy of admiration rather than of fault-finding."

By about 1900, then, treatments of southern literary activity could thus be summed up by the Brahmin scholar Barrett Wendell: "Up to the Civil War, the South had produced hardly any writing which expressed more than a pleasant sense that standard models are excellent." Once critics, editors, and publishers had defined the terms, texts that did not fit disappeared. Even those few imaginative writers from outside New England went out of print, joining those of their contemporaries whose better work had been done in other fields of literary endeavor.

Succeeding generations, increasingly preoccupied with literature distinctively American, treated the South no differently. The reigning cultural mores in the heyday of New Deal liberalism, which tended to view the South as a persistent "problem," limited consideration of nineteenth-century writers. As late as 1941 this conventional critical wisdom echoed in the words of W. J. Cash in his influential *The Mind of the South*: "In general the intellectual and aesthetic culture of the Old South was a superficial and jejune thing." Summarizing a life's work given to arguing the South's place in American literary history, Jay B. Hubbell, trained by Trent, remarked in 1954 that "if circumstances had been more propitious, the literary achievement of the southern states would have been greater."

Only in the last third of the twentieth century have these critical standards begun to be questioned. More than one scholar has observed that the study of intellectual life in the Old South now stands where Puritan studies stood at the advent of Perry Miller. Numerous recent forays—biographies of Hugh Swinton Legaré by Michael O'Brien, of Simms by John C. Guilds (1992), of Hammond by Drew Gilpin Faust; a complete edition of Edmund Ruffin's diary; a collection of Louisa Susannah McCord's letters; assorted monographs on theology, education, and social thought; and the 1985 publication of *The History of Southern Literature*, edited by Louis D. Rubin Jr., Blyden Jackson, Rayburn S. Moore, Lewis P. Simpson, and Thomas Daniel Young, by far the best general survey of the subject—suggest that within another generation the critical landscape will have been transformed.

This latest scholarship makes a series of simple suggestions that are nonetheless audacious in the context of the past century. Perhaps, it urges, what southerners—who thought of themselves as Americans and who did not know a civil war would break out or that they would lose it—had to say about themselves and their world might be taken seriously and at face value. Perhaps the use of the tellingly ahistorical term "antebellum" to describe the South before 1861 might finally be abandoned. Perhaps the veil of defeat might be lifted, or at least pierced, and the burden of southern history, which more and more comes to resemble American history, might be borne more equitably. Perhaps the texture of southern literary life might then be seen in all its complexity, vitality, and substance and might look rather more like the rest of America than had once been supposed. Then and only then might intelligent and informed judgments be rendered concerning the stature of individual writers and the significance of southern literary achievement.

WILLIAM GILMORE SIMMS: THE CONTEXT

As the Old South's preeminent literary man, William Gilmore Simms offers the best case in point. Simms has not been especially well treated by literary historians or critics. In the main he has been viewed as an artist of realistic bent thwarted by conventions that preferred romanticism; as a gifted product of a slave society that cared little for literary accomplishment and thus denied his talents the freedom to range widely and to grow; as an undisciplined composer who wrote too much too quickly, never revised, and thus never produced a single truly great work; as a protean, indefatigable literary man whose efforts as poet, editor, essayist, dramatist, novelist, storyteller, and critic sought nobly but in vain to create and promote a distinctively southern literature. Indeed, critics have agreed with his own self-assessment, written in a moment of despondency, when he saw himself as "one who, after a reasonably long life, distinguished chiefly by unceasing labor, has left all his better works undone."

Trent's 1892 biography stood unchallenged for a hundred years. His conclusion echoed the opinions of Simms's close friend Paul Hamilton Hayne, who stated, "a really great author Simms emphatically was not." Wrote Trent, "there has never been a man whose development was so sadly hampered by his environment.... His place is not a high one.... When his environment is considered, the work he did will be deemed worthy of admiration rather than fault-finding." Trent's study received acclaim from northern reviewers but unmitigated criticism from the South. The Simms family took upon itself the protection of the writer's reputation from further potentially negative scrutiny. It placed the Simms papers off-limits indefinitely, until the *Letters* could be published and until an authorized biography could be written. Publication of the *Letters* began in 1952, with the fifth and final volume appearing in 1956 and a supplemental volume appearing in 1982. With the publication of the *Letters*, a small but zealous group of Simms scholars sought to compensate for what appeared to have been "long years of neglect" by reintroducing readers to many of Simms's works and by occasionally overstating his claims while seeking to raise his rank among American writers. Among the best of these studies, which have reached wide audiences, been reviewed in major journals, and not succumbed to the temptation to rank, are Joseph V. Ridgely's 1962 *William Gilmore Simms*, which looks chiefly at the author's effort to give his state and region a history of its own; *Long Years of Neglect*, a collection of essays on the current state of Simms scholarship edited by John C. Guilds in 1988; Charles S. Watson's 1993 *From Nationalism to Secession*, which, as its title suggests, traces Simms's changing orientation; and Mary Ann Wimsatt's 1989 *The Major Fiction of William Gilmore Simms*, which takes a fresh and insightful critical look. In addition, James E. Kibler Jr. in 1979 published a full, annotated list of *The Poetry of William Gilmore Simms*, and Kibler and Keen Butterworth published in 1980 the comprehensive *William Gilmore Simms: A Reference Guide*.

The long-awaited authorized biography, *Simms: A Literary Life*, by John C. Guilds, appeared in 1992. Comprehensive and workmanlike in its coverage of Simms's life and systematic in its assessment of Simms's "multifarious" talents, Guilds's biography modestly but predictably concludes that Simms "deserves place as a major American writer." In an unusual summary chapter that begins with Guilds encountering Simms's ghost, who asks "why have I been forgotten?" the author proceeds, much as did Trent, to rank Simms as a critic, where he "fares better than as a poet," as a dramatist "of considerably less significance," and finally as a writer of fiction where, "particularly as a *novelist*, Simms leaves his most enduring mark." Regrettably and undeservedly, Guilds's volume received less critical notice than might have been expected given Simms's enormous productivity and interesting life.

EARLY YEARS

Although critics may continue to debate Simms's literary merits, his life holds intrinsic interest, illuminates the work, and offers the least hazardous route to a proper estimation of Simms as a writer. Simms was born in Charleston on 17 April 1806. The childhood was father of the man. Simms's mother died in childbirth when young William was an infant. His father simultaneously went bankrupt and moved west, first to Tennessee, then to Mississippi, where he established a plantation. Simms was left in the care of his maternal grandmother, who had remarried a local grocer. The young boy was sickly, lonely, and an omnivorous reader. His grandmother would regale him with stories of Charleston at the time of the Revolution, under British occupation, when all of Carolina was caught up in civil war. Particularly vivid and memorable were accounts of the exploits of Thomas Singleton, Simms's maternal great-grandfather and a revolutionary war hero. Time and again in his revolutionary war fiction, Simms would give his hero the name of Singleton.

In 1818 a representative of his father returned to Charleston and, according to legend, attempted to kidnap young William and take him west. The grandmother contested the matter, and the case went to court. In an extraordinary moment, the judge asked the boy to decide whether to join his father or remain with his grandmother. Simms chose to remain in maternal Charleston, and the decision fixed him in place. Though on numerous occasions in later life opportunities for removal would present themselves, each time he would decide to remain in his native city.

Simms did travel west in 1825 to visit his father. The trip made a lasting impression. His journey took him through frontier Georgia, Alabama, and Mississippi. He spent several months traveling about the western South with his father, meeting frontiersmen, visiting Cherokee and Creek nations, and storing images and experiences that would find expression in his later writing. His father again urged Simms to leave Charleston and stay in Mississippi. Again the young man refused and returned to his native city.

In the summer of 1825, Simms took up the study of law in the office of Charles Rivers Carroll, who became a close friend. At the same time he helped found the *Album*, which called itself "a weekly literary miscellany" and which survived a year. He also met and became engaged to Anna Malcolm Giles, a grocer's daughter. The couple married in 1826 after Simms returned from a second visit west. Active in editing and contributing to the *Album*, in 1825 Simms also composed his "Monody, on the Death of Gen. Charles Cotesworth Pinckney," the revolutionary war hero. In 1827 he brought out a volume of poetry, *Lyrical and Other Poems*, containing his verses from the *Album*. These poems exhibited "blemishes," according to a reviewer, but also, wrote another, "the fire of true genius." Simms himself much later admitted that the volume "contained a great deal of very sorry stuff."

By the time he had turned twenty-one, Simms had been admitted to the bar and appointed a magistrate for Charleston. He had also become a father to Anna Augusta Singleton Simms, named in honor of her mother and her paternal grandmother. The young family now lived in Summerville, outside Charleston, less expensive and more conducive to the restoration of his wife's health after a difficult pregnancy and birth.

The nullification crisis precipitated by South Carolina's application of John C. Calhoun's theory of state interposition brought Simms back into the editorial fray. He first attempted, unsuccessfully, to found and sustain the *Southern Literary Gazette*. In 1829 he invested a small inheritance in the *City Gazette*, a newspaper, and served as its editor until June 1832. He became a vigorous critic of Calhoun and the nullifiers and suffered verbal and even physical abuse.

But the decision to lay down his editorial burdens was rather the result of a series of sharper blows in Simms's personal life. In 1830 both his father and grandmother died. Then, in February 1832, his wife succumbed to a long-lingering illness. Alone but for his beloved four-year-old daughter, Simms decided to visit the North. In the summer of 1832 he began his lifelong friendship with James Lawson of New York, a young Scottish immigrant, businessman, and occasional poet. Through Lawson, Simms would become acquainted with the New York publishing world and also with the city's literary and artistic community and would make almost annual visits to broaden and deepen these friendships.

THE CHOICE OF A PROFESSION

From this visit may be dated Simms's irrevocable decision to become the first American to try to make a living as a professional writer. Returning south, he took up his pen. Within the next three years he published *Martin Faber* (1833), a ghost story and his first work of fiction; *Guy Rivers* (1834), set on the Georgia frontier, the first of his border romances; *The Yemassee* (1835), a romance set in colonial South Carolina and telling the story of an Indian uprising in 1715; and *The Partisan* (1835), the first of his romances set in South Carolina during the Revolution. All four books were published in New York by Harper and Brothers and were noticed, thanks in part to the efforts of his friends, favorably and widely in New York newspapers and magazines. By 1836 Simms had established himself in the front rank of American writers, a position confirmed by an anonymous reviewer in the *American Monthly Magazine* who stated, "There is no author of whose abilities we deem more highly." Lest there be any doubt as to the extent of his reputation, a reviewer in the *New-York Mirror* commented that Simms "is now identifying himself with his native state by his truly American romances; but until he became the historian of Carolina fiction, he was scarcely spoken of as a Carolinian—we of the north claimed him—and proud enough we were to do so—for ourselves."

The successful young writer married into the plantation elite in November 1836 when he wed seventeen-year-old Chevillette Eliza Roach. His new wife's widowed father, Nash Roach, owned a Charleston town house and twin plantations of more than 6,000 acres on the Edisto River near Orangeburg, about fifty miles west of Charleston. To one of these estates, Woodlands, the newlyweds repaired, and for the rest of his days Simms would make Woodlands his beloved home.

Simms would know happiness there and also great sorrow. Chevillette would bear fourteen children, but only five would reach adulthood. Sickness would carry all the other Simms children away, one at birth, another after five days, several after a year or two, the rest by age six. Dividing his time among Woodlands from first frost until May, Charleston during the summer and fall, and New York for a month or two usually during the summer, Simms gave order and rhythm to his life even in the midst of tragedy. With his wife, who was never very long between pregnancies, he clearly had an intimate, if not always loving, relationship. While expecting their first child she accompanied him on a difficult trip by stage through western New England, complaining of sickness. For almost all his other trips, whether to the North or to the West, where he would often travel to read or to lecture, Chevillette stayed home.

Simms's relationship with his father-in-law is less well known. It is thought to have been amicable, though in his last will and testament Nash Roach pointedly willed Woodlands to his daughter and, after her death, to her husband if he should survive her, but, observing the ancient law of primogeniture, entailed the entire estate ultimately to their eldest surviving son. Any ambiguity in interpretation was resolved by the statement that Woodlands was "not to be subject in any manner to the debts, contracts, or engagements of [Chevillette's] present or any future Husband."

Some of the generational tension may have been caused by Nash Roach's reputation as a poor manager of his plantations. He was not inclined to scientific agricultural methods, was content to make whatever crop of cotton he could, and was a benign master of his seventy slaves. As Nash Roach neared death Simms took over management of the plantation and commented to a friend in late 1857 that he was undertaking "numerous and large reforms" by which he hoped to double his crop and halve his debt. In his writings Simms would celebrate the pastoral and romantic aspects of life at Woodlands, but he also well knew that operating it was a business.

Simms's primary business, however, was as a writer. He was always at work on several projects, and he viewed his time at Woodlands as primarily writing time. From 1836 to the outbreak of the Civil War, Simms was remarkably productive. His works are best approached within a framework shaped by the many forms of literary activity he practiced.

As a poet, Simms described himself as "frank, manly, and honest," and he held these qualities to be the mark of distinguished verse. He also believed his poetry to "exhibit the highest phase of the imaginative faculty which this country has yet exhibited." Most critics have found this claim exaggerated. Simms's best poetry treats those things he knew best. "The Lost Pleiad," uncharacteristically revised several times over the years, suggests his knowledge of mythology. "Maid of Congaree" and "Dark-Eyed Maid of Edisto" are good examples of Simms's ability to evoke the natural beauty of the South Carolina low country. "Chilhowee, the Indian Village" demonstrates the author's knowledge of Indian legend and his sense of the mystical charm of a vanished civilization. Simms wrote poetry all his life and encouraged promising young poets in their work. He was especially influential on the young Paul Hamilton Hayne, who was part of a small literary circle over which Simms presided in Russell's bookstore in Charleston in the late 1850s. Also noteworthy is Simms's collection and publication of *War Poetry of the South* (1867), the best collection of Confederate song and verse, uneven in quality but exceptionally valuable as an historical document.

As an editor Simms strove relentlessly to identify, encourage, and publish southern writers and to raise the level of literary consciousness among a southern readership. His efforts were mostly in vain. Yet he was never discouraged. In *Magnolia*, the *Southern Literary Messenger*, and the *Southern Quarterly Review*, among others, Simms tried but failed to sustain a magazine of quality. Too often too much of the content was supplied by the editor himself. Presciently in 1840 Simms described the plight of literary editorship in the South: "the editor feels his strength and his friends willingly promise theirs. His neighbors pledge their subscriptions, and the beginning of the work is made with considerable energy and éclat. But the progress of a few months soon undeceives the confiding." Contributors are dilatory, contributions mediocre, payments for subscriptions delinquent. As readership declines, "the editor discovers he has overtaxed himself," and "the general dissatisfaction of all the parties concerned,—the editor being among the first—soon leads to the early abandonment of an attempt in which nothing has been realized but discredit, annoyance, and expense."

Whether as editor or contributor, Simms could be an astute critic, and he clearly stated his view of the critic's role: "justly to discriminate, firmly to establish, wisely to prescribe, and honestly to award." He offered extended and candid reviews of the works of most contemporary English and American writers. His judgments were soundly based and gave no quarter. His review of *Moby-Dick* sternly submitted a "writ of *de lunatico*" against both the author and his "mad captain." Receiving highest praise was Poe, though Simms did think him "the most morally wretched of gifted men."

Simms was also a skilled essayist and commentator. Often his published essays began as public lectures, and he traveled widely throughout the South on speaking engagements. His favorite topics, and best essays, include "The Choice of a Profession," in which he describes how one is "called" to a certain kind of work, and "Poetry and the Practical," which seeks a middle ground between the polar opposites in the mind and in society. He was also a strong advocate of an international copyright law to protect literary property from piracy by unscrupulous foreign publishers.

Simms also had a wide-ranging correspondence. His published *Letters* have been described as a "raw biography." Simms was in regular communication with fellow planters, with writers North and South, with political leaders, and with his close New York friends James Lawson and the editor of the prestigious *Literary World* Evert A. Duyckinck. The letters convey a man of deep feelings about family, politics, society, and culture and no lack of candor in expressing those feelings. Whether reporting the death of a child, a too-frequent experience for Simms, advising a politician, commenting on the New York literary scene, sharing in the enthusiasm for territorial expansion with kindred spirits who called themselves "Young America," or simply describing the pleasures of plantation life, Simms is engaging and hearty. The *Letters* remain the best place for any student of Simms to begin.

DISCOVERING THE SOUTH

Simms's greatest achievement was his assembling, from native materials, a comprehensive view of a social, political, and moral order. The materials were necessarily southern, but the vision remained American. In his major fiction, Simms developed a theory of history and peopled it with characters that spanned the range of social "types." His sources, with which Simms was intimately familiar through his reading, were multiple. Scott, of course, provided a model for the use of local sources, an adaptable narrative form, and such plot devices as the love story, flight and pursuit, and mistaken identity. German romanticism encouraged probing of the mystical and spiritual. The Gothic novelists, especially William Godwin, introduced the themes of crime, villainy, and guilt. The Elizabethan and Jacobean dramatists, especially Shakespeare, informed Simms's sense of "decorum" in his characters and encouraged his use of history to comment on contemporary matters. From these sources Simms drew deeply, and to their forms he added research into historical documents, many of which became a part of his personal library, to produce a distinctive form, the historical romance. Simms defined the romance as "a poem in every sense of the word...the substitute which the people of today offer for the ancient epic." He was careful to distinguish the romance from the novel. Romances, Simms wrote, "are imaginative, passionate, metaphysical; they deal chiefly in trying situation, bold characterization, & elevating moral. They exhibit *invention* in large degree, & their progress is dramatic; the action being bold, salient, & with a regularly advancing convergence to the catastrophe."

In invention lay originality, which Simms prized. "In proportion as a man is imaginative is he *original*," he wrote, "and originality is the main secret of vitality." Indeed, originality mattered far more than good form. "Mere verbal correctness, good similes, and the simple exclusion of irrelevant matter do not constitute the only, or even the greater & more distinctive essentials," Simms declared. Rather, the elements of romance include "the felicity of moral, & natural painting in the description of scenes equally wild, wondrous & true." The romance "does not insist upon what is known, or even what is probable. It grasps at the possible; and, placing a human agent in hitherto untried situations, it exercises its ingenuity in extricating him from them, while describing his feelings and his fortunes in their progress."

These "human agents" comprised a whole catalog of character types, from the leader, or noble, through the yeoman or frontiersman or scout, to the lowest orders, white, red, or black. Intelligent, educated, natural leaders represent the traditional order of the South. The yeoman or scout is rough-hewn, the vanguard of advancing civilization: simple, direct, clear of thought, at home in the wilderness, supportive of the natural leader. The lowest order comprises two types: the poor whites (outlaws or reprobates; violent, self-centered, small-minded) and the slaves (dependent on the master, loyal, and grateful). In addition there are the Indians, primitive yet in their own way also noble, a race that must be supplanted and superseded as civilization advances.

Simms takes these character types through his historical romances, tales of the frontier, psychological studies, and short stories, and through them he seeks to realize the epic possibilities of a society that is still very much in a state of "becoming." The interdependence and mutual loyalty of "good" whites and slaves allows them to learn from one another as they seek to create and sustain an organic, deferential, coherent social order. Simms sees history unfolding through a series of phases up to the present moment. The first phase is the early colonial period, when Spain and France competed with England for power in the new world. *Vasconselos* (1857), for example, treats Spanish settlement in Florida and the interior, while *The Lily and the Totem* (1850) examines the French experience. The second period involves the history of British colonial settlement. In *The Yemassee* (1835), for example, Simms explores the theme of what would come to be called "manifest destiny" as English colonists engage and ultimately defeat the Indians. The third phase is the revolutionary period. In his cycle of revolutionary romances, Simms tells the story of the war in the South, treating it as the civil war it was and highlighting the courage and bravery of Francis Marion and the "partisans" who carried on guerrilla warfare against the British invaders. The final phase is the post-revolutionary period, during which westward expansion takes place and a distinctive American character begins to emerge. In *Guy Rivers* (1834) and *Border Beagles* (1840) for example, frontier types, anticipating Faulkner, predominate, and the challenges to fulfilling the idealized social order are clearly delineated.

By the mid-1850s, Simms was beginning to question whether the history he knew so well and had limned so imaginatively would be permitted a place in a country coming increasingly to be dominated by a northern majority. His 1852 revolutionary war romance *The Sword and the Distaff*, republished in 1854 as *Woodcraft*, was thought by Simms to be "as good an answer to Mrs. [Harriet Beecher] Stowe as has been published." Troubled by the growing Northern attacks on slavery and well aware of the impact of *Uncle Tom's Cabin*, Simms tells a tale of a planter, Porgy, who returns home to his ruined plantation after the Revolution. Simms's most memorable character, the witty, portly Porgy loves his food and drink and faces the prospect of rebuilding with dismay. He has little money, having exhausted his inheritance in pursuit of worldly pleasures. But he is determined to retain his ancestral home. With the advice and assistance of his one-armed Sergeant Millhouse, and through an advantageous marriage after a comical courtship to the Widow Eveleigh, Porgy finds wisdom and redemption. He discovers what is truly important. And yet he is not certain he can afford to keep his loyal cook, named, suggestively, Tom. But Tom will not allow himself to be released, and in a memorable reply to his owner he declines freedom: "Ef I doesn't

b'long to *you*, *you* b'longs to *me*! You hab for kep dis nigger long as he lib; and him for keep you . . . . I no guine to be free no way you kin fix it; so maussa, don't you bodder me wid dis nonsense t'ing 'bout free paper any more." In the ideal world of the southern plantation, everyone knows his place, and no one should attempt to disrupt the natural order.

In November 1856, Simms undertook a lecture tour in the North. His purpose was to tell the story of his state and region to a northern audience and to test the strength of the bonds holding the union together. His first lecture, in Buffalo, attracted an audience of 1,200 to hear him declaim on "South Carolina in the Revolution." Though his subject may have seemed appropriate, his text was partisan and his delivery offended. Simms recalled the bitter attack on Senator Andrew Pickens Butler of South Carolina by Senator Charles Sumner of Massachusetts in May 1856, for which Congressman Preston Brooks of the Palmetto State had physically attacked Sumner with a walking stick on the Senate floor: "neither Massachusetts, nor any other State, will gain anything of honour when they lend too eager a hand to the defamation of the Past of South Carolina." He repeated these views to dwindling crowds in Rochester and New York City, then abruptly canceled the remainder of the tour. Returning home, Simms concluded that only in a separate southern nation could the perfect social order he envisioned come to full flowering. He took up the cause of southern secession and became active in the cause of disunion.

SIMMS AND THE CIVIL WAR

When separation came and the Confederacy formed, Simms vigorously offered advice. From his knowledge of British movements in South Carolina during the Revolution he implored Governor Francis Pickens to fortify Port Royal Sound, the deepest channel in the whole South Atlantic, through which the British had entered Carolina in 1780 and toward which a Union naval expedition seeking to penetrate the Confederacy and create a strategic base for blockade operations would inevitably move. These urgings went unheeded. In November 1861 the predicted invasion, with the predictable results, occurred. Port Royal fell to the Union navy in hours, thus providing a coaling station for Union vessels and a beachhead from which the first experiments in Reconstruction could later be launched.

Simms suffered personally during the war. Long believing himself a man "marked for the scourge," in 1863 he lost his wife, weakened physically by the almost incessant demands of childbirth, to an early death at age forty-six from acute appendicitis. His beloved Woodlands suffered severe damage in a fire in March 1862, but a public subscription of funds enabled him partially to rebuild. Then, in February 1865, Simms hurriedly evacuated Woodlands as troops under the command of General William Tecumseh Sherman marched north from Savannah. Union troops burned Simms's house to the ground, and with it was lost almost the entirety of Simms's prized library, which may have been the largest and most valuable private collection of maps and historical documents anywhere in the South. He escaped with his family to Columbia in time to witness the burning of the city, which he describes vividly in his powerful *Sack and Destruction of the City of Columbia, S.C.* (1865).

After the war, physically enfeebled and financially prostrate, Simms tried valiantly to revive his prewar associations and return to the rigors of authorship while also seeking to restore Woodlands. He managed to produce two mediocre revolutionary romances and a serialized "mountain legend." He worked on, but never published, a "Southern Mother Goose." Of greatest value and merit was *War Poetry of the South*, published in New York in 1867. In May 1870, only a month before his death, Simms mustered the strength to rise from his sickbed to deliver an address, "The Sense of the Beautiful," to the Charleston County Agricultural Society. On 11 June 1870, the bells of St. Michael's Church "pealed forth," in the words of the *Charleston Courier*, "their requiem for the gifted Simms."

ASSESSMENT

"Mr. Simms's whole life has been one of public contribution," the *Courier* continued. "No man was more warmly attached to his native state, or defended, worked for, and served her more faithfully and constantly." The modern reader would not dispute. Indefatigably productive, Simms nonetheless wrote too much too quickly in a style that now seems dated and inaccessible. Still, his relentless impulse to order and explain, his unceasing effort to capture the beauty and history of his native South in prose and verse, his ambitious attempt to tell the epic story of his country, and his generous encouragement and promotion of literary activity together entitle him to the modern reader's attention. Though literary scholars will continue to quibble over Simms's placement in the hierarchy of nineteenth-century American writers, his life and work are probably of greater interest and value to the student

of history. His friend the poet Paul Hamilton Hayne found Simms "a man greater than his works." Hayne was correct. The life is intrinsically interesting; the work serves best to illuminate the life and the times. The judgment of Edgar Allan Poe in 1845 that Simms was "the best novelist which this country has, on the whole, produced" may be deemed extravagant. He was, however, without question the preeminent southern writer of his time. His works, and his name, remain today largely unknown. That, perhaps, is the fate of living in, and writing about, the "America we have not been."

But contemporary readers might also pay heed to the words of one who did not know that the times in which he lived would some day be called "antebellum." Willis Gaylord Clark, editor of the *Philadelphia Gazette*, had agreed to write a letter of introduction for Simms to take with him on his first visit to New York in 1832. "His mind is ever on the wing," the letter said, "and his heart, unless I greatly mistake it, is full of good feelings, genial juices, and the milk of human kindness." And, the writer concluded, "if you come to know him as well as I do, you will regret that you did not know him sooner."

[*See also* Autobiography: Slave Narratives; Autobiography: White Women during the Civil War; *and* Sentimental Literature.]

FURTHER READING

Butterworth, Keen, and James E. Kibler Jr. *William Gilmore Simms: A Reference Guide*. Boston, 1980. A complete compilation, from 1825 through the publication date, of everything written about Simms or his work. An essential reference.

Guilds, John Caldwell. *Simms: A Literary Life*. Fayetteville, Ark., 1992. The best biography of Simms, though preoccupied with establishing his claim to a higher rank among nineteenth-century writers.

Oliphant, Mary C. Simms, Alfred Taylor Odell, and T. C. Duncan Eaves, eds. *The Letters of William Gilmore Simms*. 6 vols. Columbia, S.C., 1952–1956, 1976. A magnificent collection, carefully edited and annotated, a "raw biography" that is the starting point for any serious student of Simms.

Ridgely, J. V. *William Gilmore Simms*. New Haven, Conn., 1962. Still the best treatment of Simms's effort to describe and order the progress of history and the place of the South in that history.

Trent, William P. *William Gilmore Simms*. Boston, 1892. Though dated and biased, still the most readable biography.

UPTON SINCLAIR AND THE MUCKRAKERS

by Erik Kongshaug

The muckrakers were mainly jour-nalists. It is historically ironic and philosophically appropriate that Upton Sinclair, a novelist, essayist, and pamphleteer, would come to most fully embody them through the quirk of his own exceptionalism in the matter of literary form.

As a historically bounded figure, the muckraker was freshly minted in the United States at the turn of the twentieth century, illegibly worn down before World War I, and swept out of circulation with the Dust Bowl and the Great Depression. But before even considering the muckraker's historical moment, we can most concisely understand her or his literary energy as emanating from the oxymoronic belief that an unaffiliated individual can create social reform and affect collective change through solitary, published activity. As literary praxis, muckraking may transcend its specific historical context. Looking backward in this broader, philosophical sense, the writings of an early American figure such as Thomas Paine exemplify muckraking. Looking forward, the writings of later American figures such as Malcolm X, Michael Harrington, Betty Friedan, Rachel Carson, and Ralph Nader exemplify muckraking as well. Muckraking is still being published today at the unincorporated edges of America's journalistic tradition and more rarely in the realms of essay and fiction. One can only hope we will still be able to find it in some literary form tomorrow.

Upton Sinclair.
(*Courtesy of the Library of Congress*)

A TWO-SIDED COIN

The term "muckraker" was coined by President Theodore Roosevelt in 1906 as an allusion to the Muck Rake Man in John Bunyan's *Pilgrim's Progress* (1678–1684), an allegorical character who could not see the Celestial City for looking down at his own activity. Roosevelt never actually referred to the muckraker as a discrete noun in his 1906 speech. The occupation was minted anew into its single, more scornful label on the following day by newspapermen aiming for easy periodical consumption and an emerging mass readership. Roosevelt, though, had taken some rather large literary liberties of his own. In recasting Bunyan's complex puritanical meaning into moral admonishment for a dangerous spirit rising among newspapermen—namely, the practice of what we now call investigative journalism—Roosevelt carefully elided at least the literal intent of Bunyan's allegory. Bunyan originally figured the Muck Rake Man to evoke the very sorts of plutocrats that these new investigative journalists were so busy going after.

In 1904, Roosevelt had ridden the cry for reform into his second term. Now his hobby horse was beginning to buck. The writers he named muckrakers continued to publish article upon article, marshaling mountains of facts, to expose the hegemony that was allowing Roosevelt to govern the country. They would continue to publish beyond Roosevelt's own presidency and well into the presidency of his hand-picked successor, William Howard Taft.

In addition to *The Jungle*, the 1906 novel that would launch Upton Sinclair's career and force Roosevelt to regulate the meatpacking industry, a few notable historical examples of muckraking stand out. Ida Mae Tarbell's serial publication of what would become *The History of the Standard Oil Company* in 1904 ultimately led to passage of antitrust legislation and the 1911 breakup of robber baron John D. Rockefeller's oil monopoly.

Lincoln Steffens's serial publication of what would become *The Shame of the Cities* (also published in 1904) investigated the cases of St. Louis, Pittsburgh,

Philadelphia, and Chicago in the already infamous light of New York political boss William Marcy Tweed. Steffens exposed municipal corruption as being enabled by ostensibly upstanding corporate citizens. His work would eventually prompt reform of not only city but state and federal government.

Working on ground broken by Frank Norris's 1901 novel *The Octopus* and excavated by the recent journalism of Charles Edward Russell, Ray Stannard Baker published a 1905 series of articles on discrimination in the railroads. The series built a case for government ownership that ultimately led to the railroads' federal regulation. It also led Baker to a subsequent groundbreaking series on race relations in the North and South, published as *Following the Color Line* in 1908.

Ida Tarbell. (*Courtesy of the Library of Congress*)

These and virtually every other collective cause the muckrakers introduced would be revisited by Upton Sinclair in his ninety published books and the countless pamphlets he would produce during his more than seven decades of activism.

LITERARY SUICIDE: THE BIRTH OF A PUBLIC INTELLECTUAL

Son of a long line of southern naval officers, son of a railroad magnate's daughter, Upton Beall Sinclair Jr., was born in a Baltimore boardinghouse on 20 September 1878. His mother focused his interests away from the unpleasant facts of history and onto literature. Ten years later the family moved north to New York City and more boardinghouses. He enrolled in City College at fourteen. New Yorkers Walt Whitman and Herman Melville had both died in the previous year. Sinclair first earned a way out of his alcoholic father's house by writing racially stereotyping jokes, at a dollar a pop, for the popular magazines of the day. He wrote his first story, about a young black boy who steals a bird, for $25. Turning to the hack fictional adventures of young men in the Naval Academy, he soon found himself living by his labor with words. He would never make a dime any other way.

Placing himself in the company of his three adolescent heroes—the romantic poet Percy Bysshe Shelley, William Shakespeare's Hamlet, and Jesus Christ—he took shelter in the idea of his own genius. Meta H. Fuller agreed. When they married, he was working on a self-described

literary masterpiece in a cabin in the woods. In 1901, after a series of rejections, he self-published *Springtime and Harvest*, and Meta gave birth to his only son, David. He discovered socialism the following year and came to the dismissive attention of the New York literary world through what amounted to a publicity stunt. Sinclair convinced a publishing house to release *The Journal of Arthur Stirling* in 1903 as if the narrator, who kills himself in the end, had actually written it. It was not merely a joke; in a very real sense Sinclair was psychologically exorcising his high romantic ambition. The press was not amused.

Some months before Roosevelt's second election, Sinclair published *Manassas*, an extensively researched novel of the Civil War. It drew the attention of the *Appeal to Reason*, a Kansas-based journal deeply rooted in the populist and socialist traditions of the radical, abolitionist "Free State" activists. After publishing Sinclair's series of articles on the unsuccessful 1904 Chicago meatpacking strike, the editor of the *Appeal* dared him to write a *Manassas* for wage slavery and gave him $500 for serialization rights. He took it, put a down payment on a New Jersey farm for his wife and new child and set off for the Chicago heartland. Once in "Packingtown," he put himself in the position of a meatpacking worker for seven weeks and investigated through observation.

The Chicago stockyards were the first fully realized manifestation of mass production the world had ever known. Sinclair, through a combination of journalistic acumen, political awakening, and personal despair, became its first poet. What he observed was hard for publishers to swallow at first. The novel, already appearing serially in the *Appeal*, had been accepted with a $500 advance by the Macmillan Company. When they saw the manuscript, though, Sinclair was told to cut out some of the bloodier details. He refused. Doubleday, Page and Company finally accepted it on condition that the "facts" be investigated. A reporter from the *Chicago Tribune* told them virtually every detail in the novel was false. After its own investigator discovered that the reporter had merely accepted a meatpacker's publicity department at its word, Doubleday agreed to publish *The Jungle* with the facts as Sinclair had presented them. The novel became an overnight best-seller, drew President

Roosevelt's attention, and provoked passage of the Pure Food and Drug Act of 1906.

Meat in *The Jungle* is also a metaphor for communicating the plight of the modern wage slave. The metaphor went largely unnoticed by the middle-class metabolism that consumed it. For the first and perhaps only time in his always class-conscious prose, Sinclair had allowed himself to personally and directly identify with America's subaltern laborer. His own wife had been ill in their unheated cabin during the previous winter, and their child had nearly died of pneumonia. Although written in the third person, the novel meticulously describes a series of concrete health and safety violations perpetrated by the corporate "packers" as recorded through the ingenuous eyes of the economic head of a peasant Lithuanian immigrant family, the uneducated, physically powerful Jurgis Rudkin. Jurgis and his entire family work harder and harder to stay afloat amid mortgage scams and environmental poisons. Accidents leave them crippled by misery and despair.

He winds up in jail on Christmas Day (the same day Sinclair began to write the novel), when his wife is about to give birth. In a midnight conversion, Jurgis, like Sinclair, discovers socialism. Although the political speaker is not Sinclair but an incidental character, the final lines of *The Jungle* are unambiguous: "—So spoke an orator upon the platform; and two thousand pairs of eyes were fixed upon him, and two thousand voices were cheering his every sentence . . . '—and Chicago will be ours! *Chicago will be ours!* CHICAGO WILL BE OURS!' " The Socialists felt a very real chance of winning in Chicago in 1906; Sinclair himself was running (nominally) as a Socialist for Congress in New York.

WESTERING LIGHTS

For the first time in his life, Sinclair had some capital of his own; he was twenty-eight years old, a public intellectual and the author of an international blockbuster. Days before that hope-filled 1906 election day (neither he nor the Chicago Socialists would prevail) Sinclair sunk his royalties into the foundation of a commune just across the Hudson River. Though it would burn down early the next spring and presaged the end of his first marriage, the commune experiment became the first step of a literary, spiritual, political, and physical migration west.

While Sinclair continued to write and publish (he never stopped, no matter his emotional state), the dysfunction of his marriage was consuming him. On the verge of nervous breakdown, he went to Carmel, California, to live temporarily with the poet George Sterling. In 1910, in an effort to find his health and balance through fasting, he went to a spa in Alabama where he met another writer and fellow southerner, Mary Craig Kimbrough, who would share his interest in health and much else. He sued for and obtained a divorce in Holland, remarried, and received legal custody of his son.

In 1914 he set his sites on the king of capitalism, John D. Rockefeller, as news of the Easter night Ludlow Massacre, at a coal mine in Colorado, drew his attention to the Colorado Fuel and Iron Company, part of the New York robber baron's Standard Oil Company. Sinclair and "Craig," as he called his wife, organized a New York picket against the parent company. Sinclair got himself arrested and locked up in the notorious Tombs, using the opportunity to fill in reporters on the details of the massacre. Craig bailed him out and Sinclair went west to Colorado. He arrived in the immediate wake of a class war that had raged for ten days after Rockefeller's men and state militia opened fire with machine guns on a striking mine workers' tent city, killing three women and eleven children. To finish the novel his Colorado visit inspired, he and Craig moved to southern California, where they would live until her death in 1961.

King Coal (1917), his second major literary work, carries unsung historical events through journalistically witnessed detail, as does *The Jungle* before it. It casts them into an aesthetically reflective form that resists elision and revision so long as the book is still being read. However, instead of directly identifying with the subaltern laborer, *King Coal*'s narrative follows Hal Warner, an upper-class college student on break who takes a summer job in the mine on a lark. Set on the Continental Divide, the novel straddles the great class rifts in America society and does not pretend to resolve them.

As with the Ludlow Massacre it was remembering, the novel never got the public attention it deserved. Even as it was being published, the country's attention was wandering outside of itself toward the events of World War I. The 1919 Bolshevik revolution in Russia would raise home front fears even higher. Red-baiting—public attacks on individuals and groups as communist—was on the rise.

LIBERTY HILL

By the time Sinclair got himself arrested in Los Angeles in 1923 for publicly reading from the First Amendment of the U.S. Constitution (an event that created that region's American Civil Liberties Union chapter), he had eighteen novels, nine works of nonfiction, and six plays in print (not to mention the pamphlets). Although a select handful of titles had been originally brought out by commercial publishing houses, all were now published and distributed primarily through his and Craig's own efforts. His newest titles were immediately translated into an assortment of languages. He sold his books very nearly at cost. Arguably he was the first major American literary figure to intentionally and successfully address his art to the masses.

That month the Los Angeles Police Department was staging mass arrests of Industrial Workers of the World, known as "Wobblies," under California's Criminal Syndicalism Act, which denied their right to assemble and speak in conjunction with a maritime and oil workers' strike that was underway in the port. The strike would ultimately fail. As with his direct intervention after the Ludlow Massacre, Sinclair's arrest on "Liberty Hill" in Los Angles would eventually provide the seed for a major novel. At the time he was still engaged in a noteworthy series of full-length nonfiction he called the "Dead Hand" books, a scornful reference to the "invisible hand" that guided Adam Smith's laissez-faire economic philosophy in *The Wealth of Nations* and possibly a direct allusion to the deathbed wills of the wealthy, so titled in George Eliot's great social novel *Middlemarch*. These six very readable self-published attacks on capitalist institutions were at the heart of Sinclair's status as a nationally important public intellectual amid the excesses of post–World War I America. In them, Sinclair muckrakes just about every institution—religion, journalism, education, and literature itself—whose auspices might have fostered his posterity as a writer beyond his lifetime. The Los Angeles maritime strike would find its literary home in 1927 in the hauntingly accurate, dramatically distilled denouement of his epic California novel *Oil!*.

First conceived in the heat of those events and deeply rooted in his firsthand experience with the local Los Angeles politics of the day, as documented and researched in the Dead Hand series, *Oil!* stands out as a great political novel. It resists the generic prescriptions of literary value that would too easily dismiss it as artless because of stylized, sometimes flat emotional relationships between characters. The deep emotion of *Oil!* functions primarily at the levels of historical reflection and place. Through powerfully meticulous oil industry detail, the novel unlocks the machinations of the Hollywood film industry and the antilabor, red-baiting press; Sinclair even transposes World War I to the 1920s with eerie

verisimilitude, as if history itself had made the error. "It was literally true," the narrator of *Oil!* notes simply, "that capitalist industry was a world war going on all the time."

LAYING DOWN THE MUCKRAKE

After one more major novel, *Boston*, published in 1928 in near-simultaneous historical response to the arrest and execution of the Italian immigrant anarchists Nicola Sacco and Bartolomeo Vanzetti, Sinclair found himself facing the Great Depression like the rest of the country that persisted in sharing his initials. His ideas began to sound mainstream to a swelling number of economically vulnerable lower- and middle-class Americans. After five decades of hopeful struggle, Upton Sinclair became a popular political figure. While continuing, as always, to write, Sinclair was nominated to run for governor of California on the Democratic ticket. His candidacy very nearly changed the face of American history and did change the face of California politics. It altered Sinclair's artistic relation to both. In August of 1934 Sinclair swept the Democratic primary in a landslide of nearly half a million votes. The newspapers and Hollywood launched an unprecedented campaign to defeat him through movie trailers and cartoons such as one depicting him as the crackpot counterpart of Stalin, Hitler, and Mussolini. President Franklin D. Roosevelt distanced his "New Deal" and himself from Sinclair's campaign. Sinclair was narrowly defeated by the Republican-machine politician Frank Merriam.

The American communists had opposed Sinclair's candidacy and ridiculed him for being too idealistic about class collaboration, and he partially blamed them for his defeat. In addition, Joseph Stalin's genocidal purges in Russia were contributing to a more general intellectual crisis in the American Left. By 1939 Sinclair was himself anticommunist as well as antifascist. His position was in closer accord with the majority mood of the country throughout World War II and into the Cold War beyond. At age sixty, Sinclair had what might be described as a second growth. Between 1938 and 1948 he interpreted and contextualized the international history of the period 1913–1946 for the pleasure and education of a popular audience through ten novels' worth of reflections by a lone, globetrotting sophisticate of his son's generation. The Lanny Budd novels, which came to be known as the World's End series, were commercially published bestsellers, one and all. (Although Sinclair kept the right to publish them himself, as always.) The third novel, *Dragon's Teeth* (1942), about the Treaty of Versailles, earned him a Pulitzer Prize.

He still wrote quite a few more books after that, including his autobiography and a play about the nuclear age. At age eighty-three, five months after Craig's death, he married Mary Hard Willis. He outlived her. Upton Sinclair died in a New Jersey nursing home on 25 November 1968, a year that would be remembered by the next wave of muckrakers, the New Left, who were just then beginning to be published.

SELECTED WORKS

The Jungle (1906)
King Coal (1917)
Oil! (1927)
Boston (1928)
The Autobiography of Upton Sinclair (1962)

FURTHER READING

Ahouse, John. *Upton Sinclair: A Descriptive, Annotated Bibliography*. Los Angeles, 1994. Invaluable for a synoptic overview of Sinclair's work. A pleasure to read in and of itself.

Bloodworth, William A., Jr. *Upton Sinclair*. Boston, 1977.

Brasch, Walter M. *Forerunners of Revolution: Muckrakers and the American Social Conscience*. Lanham, Md., 1990.

Harris, Leon. *Upton Sinclair: American Rebel*. New York, 1975.

Jensen, Carl. *Stories That Changed America: Muckrakers of the 20th Century*. New York, 2000. A clear, refreshing "best-of" anthology of muckraking in the broader sense with entries, including Sinclair, Steffens, and Tarbell, chosen and contextualized by the founder of Project Censored.

Mitchell, Greg. *The Campaign of the Century*. New York, 1992. The full story of Sinclair's 1934 gubernatorial bid.

Mookerjee, R. N. *Art for Social Justice: The Major Novels of Upton Sinclair*. Metuchen, N.J., 1988.

Sinclair, Mary Craig. *Southern Belle*. Oxford, Miss., 1999. This new edition of Craig's reminiscences, originally published in 1957, is of special interest because it revisits the work from a feminist perspective.

Starr, Kevin. *Endangered Dreams: The Great Depression in California*. New York, 1996.

Yoder, Jon. *Upton Sinclair*. New York, 1975.

ISAAC BASHEVIS SINGER

by James A. Lewin

What makes Isaac Bashevis Singer so exceptional? He is not only the sole writer working primarily in Yiddish to have won a Nobel Prize but also the only Yiddish writer included in the canon of American literature. Of course, Singer benefited from good, timely English translations. But he may have jumped out of the pack of acknowledged Yiddish masters of fiction because of a resonance in his work with ingrained American interests and values. His conjunction of spiritualism and sexuality definitely piqued the interest of readers of magazines ranging from *Commentary* to *Playboy*. On a deeper level, his commitment to conservative traditionalism also corresponds with an American yearning for basic moral clarity. Ironically, however, Singer's vision of ethical truth questions the assumptions of the tradition from which he developed. More of a muted reactionary than a homespun conservative, Singer responds to cultural and moral crisis with an aesthetic of storytelling. Singer reminds us that the pursuit of redemption, though heartbreaking and unrequited, cannot be abandoned.

The popularity of Singer's work may be compared to the attraction of the Holocaust Museum in Washington, D.C., for the millions of Americans who visit it every year. Beginning with a sense of having been displaced from the harmony of a primal home and cut off from the roots of spiritual identity, Singer reinterprets humanism for post-Holocaust humanity. He does not deal directly with the atrocities of war. Instead, he portrays the "before and after" of totalitarian inhumanity. Also, as the exponent of a lost world, his writing conjures up

Isaac Bashevis Singer.
(*Photograph by Jerry Bauer. Courtesy of the Library of Congress*)

an implicit protest against any and all literary, political, and religious authority not based on life itself. Isaac Bashevis Singer calls the reader to return, through his fiction, to a prophetic vision of human potential that challenges the living and resurrects the spirits—both holy and unholy—of the past.

The English translation of *The Family Moskat*, published in 1950, introduced Singer to American readers. A family epic, the novel paints a vast panorama of life in Jewish Warsaw during the years leading up to the Nazi invasion of Poland in 1939. Although it proved a critical success, receiving the Louis Lamed Prize for 1950, the author later complained that most of the financial rewards for the book went to the translators and publisher. His next novel in English was the translation of *Satan in Goray*, a book Singer had written and published in Yiddish in 1935, before he immigrated to the United States. The recipient of the Louis Lamed Prize for 1956, *Satan in Goray* (1955) deals with the phantasmagoric impact of the false Messiah, Shabbati Zevi, on a tiny Jewish community in seventeenth-century Poland. Based on these two works, Singer's stylistic range can be roughly defined. *The Family Moskat* is an old-fashioned novel, with a cast of characters stretching over generations. *Satan in Goray*, in contrast, is a collection of poetic vignettes portraying mass psychosis under a historical microscope. Much of Singer's work may be divided into either the psychological realism of *The Family Moskat* or the mystical surrealism of *Satan in Goray*. In addition, Singer wrote a number of works based on autobiographical experience, whether as first-person memoir or from the narrative point of view of a transparently fictionalized authorial alter ego.

He also used various pen names. His early literary works were published under the pseudonym Yitzchok Bashevis, the last name derived from his mother's first name. Memoirs and journalism appeared under the byline Warshawsky, or son of Warsaw, distancing the author from his higher literary aspirations. Eventually, his work came together under the name Isaac Bashevis Singer, which allowed the author to maintain his traditional roots while differentiating himself from his older brother, also a well-known Yiddish writer, Israel Joshua Singer, who died of a heart attack in 1944. In many places the author has referred to his brother as his spiritual and artistic master. Yet the younger Singer went on to attain heights of literary success beyond his older brother's recognized achievements. Among his many awards, I. B. Singer received the National Book Award for fiction in 1970 and 1974, and the Nobel Prize for Literature in 1978.

In 1990 he became the only author not writing primarily in English to be inducted into the American Academy of Arts.

GROWING UP IN JEWISH POLAND

Born on 14 July 1904 in Leoncin, Poland, Singer's earliest memories were of the tiny villages of Leoncin and Radzymin, where his father served as assistant rabbi. He was the third child of his parents, Pinchos Menachem and Bathsheba Zylberman. His sister, Hinde Esther, was thirteen and his brother, Israel Joshua, was ten when he was born. Another brother, Moyshe, was born some years later. In about 1908 the family moved to Warsaw. The father earned a meager income as the unofficial rabbi of a poor Jewish neighborhood. To receive official status, the author's father would have had to pass a rabbinical test in Russian, the language of the governing authorities in Poland at that time. But he never learned enough Russian to take the test. Like many Polish Jews, the author's family lived in an encapsulated world of colloquial Yiddish, biblical Hebrew, and Talmudic Aramaic. The author received his formative education at home. Later, he enrolled for a brief period in a rabbinical seminary, but his knowledge of European literature and philosophy came almost entirely from self-education.

The author describes, in the first-person vignettes of *In My Father's Court* (1966), the wonder and puzzlement of a small boy growing up in the big city. In his own home, "amidst the holy books, the peace of the Sabbath reigned," while outside the Warsaw streets were "full of shouting, turmoil, theft, robbery, war, injustice." His father, as the rabbinical authority for a strange parade of people, passes judgment on matters of love, marriage, and various business deals, as well as the standard issue of Jewish observance. A constant eavesdropper at the door of his father's study, the young Isaac gleans adult secrets of the battle of the sexes as well as insights into mystical lore. From his mother, the daughter of an anti-Hasidic rabbi, he learns to think as "a cold-blooded rationalist" who seeks the reason for every uncanny phenomenon. From his father, a softhearted idealist, he hears that "there is a particle of the divine in everything. Even the mud in the gutter contains divine sparks, for without them nothing could continue to exist." As food shortages increased during World War I, the author's mother took the thirteen-year-old Isaac and his younger brother to her family's village for refuge. In Bilgoray the author absorbed impressions he later used for his descriptions of the lost world of the timeless Jewish community.

By then, however, he had already begun to question the traditional path, delving into the philosophy of Spinoza and modern European authors. Following the example of his older brother, who had broken with religion and become a freethinker, the author returned to Warsaw. There he found a new intellectual home in the Writer's Club, where he could apply his intellectual curiosity and develop a new persona. In *Love and Exile* (1984) he depicts his transformation from a shy and stammering youth into a worldly sophisticate, serving the "idol of literature and the idol of love"—yet refusing to bow down, despite pressures from his peers, to the "idol of World Betterment."

With the world spinning toward another world war, Singer writes that he did not "have to be particularly prescient to foresee the hell that was coming." Relying on help from his elder brother, who never let him down, the author was able to obtain a visa to travel to America, where he remained. His mother and younger brother were not as fortunate, perishing along with millions of others in the Nazi Holocaust. His common-law wife and their son, meanwhile, escaped through the Soviet Union, eventually finding refuge in Israel. Spared his life, the author still needed to save his artistic soul.

REBORN IN POSTWAR AMERICA

Before Singer came to America, he had already established his talent as a writer, although he tended to be obscured by his more successful older brother's shadow. During World War II he almost stopped writing, except for a kind of believe-it-or-not column of strange facts for the Yiddish press. With the end of the war and the sudden death of his brother and mentor, he seems to have once again recreated himself. With a sudden urgency of purpose, Isaac Bashevis Singer emerged as the voice of a sole survivor dedicated to preserving the memory and meaning of a world that had been erased.

In *The Family Moskat* the decline and fall of one family represents a microcosm for the demise of Polish Jewry. The ambivalent relationship of the Poles and the Jews serves as the backdrop for the internal conflicts of the Moskats in their various branches. Through centuries of bare toleration, the Jews of Poland have maintained their distinctive identity, based on an unwavering religious faith, within the dominant Gentile culture. Even worldly Polish Jews, typified by Meshulam Moskat, cling to traditions of their ancestors. But this culture of devotion to the Torah is perishing. In its place, competing ideologies spawn a confusing array of individuals in pursuit of their own happiness. The death of Meshulam Moskat presages the end of an entire world.

The plot begins with Meshulam, against his better judgment, taking a third wife. Meanwhile, the aging children of his first two marriages, along with their spouses and offspring, are planning how to spend their anticipated inheritances even while insisting they wish only for the octogenarian patriarch to fulfill his measure of 120 years. The power behind the Moskat throne turns out to be Koppel Berman, the bookkeeper who runs the day-to-day business of the clan. The brothers and sisters—except for the youngest daughter, Leah—agree only on their enmity for Koppel. Eventually, Koppel pilfers the family fortune and persuades Leah to divorce her Hasidic husband and marry him instead. But these developments provide only the framework of the book.

The focus is on Asa Heshel, who marries into the Moskat family by a convoluted series of circumstances. Motivated by a desire to escape the provincial piety of his rabbinical family, Asa Heshel comes to Warsaw, the big city, where he is taken under the wing of Abram Shapiro, the wildly extroverted and pleasure-seeking son-in-law of Meshulam Moskat. Through Abram, Asa Heshel meets the beauteous, blonde, but sickly Hadassah, Abram's niece. Hadassah immediately falls in love with Asa Heshel. Despite her grandfather Meshulam's plan to order her destiny in the accepted manner of arranged marriages, Hadassah seems determined to follow her heart. Through a domino effect of dysfunctional family ties, Asa Heshel first marries Adele—daughter of Meshulam's third wife from her previous marriage—then abandons Adele for the love of Hadassah, who has in the meantime been married off as planned. But in Singer's world of tangled liaisons, a happy marriage defies the laws of nature. Inevitably, Asa Heshel also abandons Hadassah, though she remains loyal to him to the bitter end.

Just as Meshulam Moskat represents a last surviving vestige of Jewish integrity, Asa Heshel embodies the alienated Jew who can neither assimilate to non-Jewish culture nor remain Jewish. As prototype for a series of later Singer protagonists, Asa Heshel manifests an overwhelming sense of fatalism. His chief characteristic is utter passivity. He neither affirms nor resists the conflicting forces that push and pull him from one situation to the next. Though it is impossible to admire Asa Heshel, he has admirable qualities, including a sharp intelligence; a commitment to honesty, however painful to himself or others; and a determination not to be dependent on anyone else. Above all, he refuses to submit to false idols; iconoclasm seems his last connection to Jewishness.

Blessed with prodigious potential and an uncanny ability to inspire love in others, Asa Heshel neither fulfills his talents nor keeps his promises. He lets down everyone who has faith in him, because finally he has no faith in anything, least of all in himself. In the closing pages, his long-estranged first wife Adele perceives the central paradox of Asa Heshel's tortured soul. "He was one of those who must serve God or die. He had forsaken God, and because of this he was dead—a living body with a dead soul."

All the gargantuan yearnings and grotesque behaviors of the novel's characters appear under the shadow of the doom that, as the reader knows, historically awaits them. Yet when it comes, the German invasion of Poland catches everyone by surprise. The first victim is Hadassah, exemplar of innocence and true love. Only after she is dead does Asa Heshel realize what he has lost. Refusing to believe that time past exists only in present memory, shattered in spirit yet unable to mourn, Asa Heshel wonders why he is still alive. In this context, the novel wraps itself in minutely rendered historical realism in order to clothe the author's fictionalized confession of his own survivor's guilt.

Ending in apocalypse, inevitable death becomes the novel's grim answer to the vain hopes and dreams of life. And yet the hopes and dreams do not die. Refusing to escape to the east with his new lover, Barbara, though he is imbued with the dread of death, Asa Heshel determines to remain in Poland, even if it means his demise. Nevertheless, Asa Heshel returns to life in later Singer novels under various names. He is reincarnated as Hertz Dovid Grein in *Shadows on the Hudson* (1998) and again as Herman Broder in *Enemies: A Love Story* (1972), always portrayed as a former child prodigy and philosopher without a coherent philosophy except a vague mixture of Spinoza and Jewish mysticism, perpetually involved with three women simultaneously yet unsatisfied with any of them, the archetypal unassimilated non-Jewish Jew who yearns for the certainties of the faith of his ancestors but who finds no way to reconcile this longing with the requirements of intellectual consistency. Driven by an all-consuming need for love, this most unheroic lover and seeker of truth can certainly not be called a rationalist; yet he cannot give up the skepticism that rationalism assumes. Amazingly, women abandon themselves to him. But he can neither love nor allow himself to be loved. His sole redeeming trait is the utter honesty with which he admits his own hypocrisy.

From his published memoirs, parallels between the author's own life and the experiences of his protagonist become evident. Like Asa Heshel, Singer was the son of a rabbi, raised in a strictly observant home, who rebelled against the faith of his ancestors. Also like Asa Heshel, the author sought answers to his questions in the study of philosophy and the pursuit of romantic love. Finally, however, like Asa Heshel and his other alter egos, the author never closed the door on his lingering faith in providence. Belief of some sort in the deity of monotheistic religion remained the bedrock of Singer's worldview. But instead of worshipping this higher power, he chose to protest against it.

Vegetarianism was one manifestation of this protest. Singer became a strict vegetarian as a personal expression of his residual belief in a higher power and his stubborn refusal to participate in the cruelty of nature's drama of predator and prey. In a similar way, he protested against the cruelty of historical providence through the form of the confessional narrative that serves as both plea for forgiveness and refusal to accept easy answers of redemption. Protest against the cosmic silence may, in fact, explain the artistic bridge between his psychological realism and his fascination with the occult. On the one hand, he looks backwards at a lost innocence of piety and traditional values. On the other hand, he glances ahead at a brave new world of paralyzing terror that is coming unless we can learn the lessons of the past.

A PROPHETIC PROSE POEM

Written during the 1930s as the Nazis first came to power, *Satan in Goray* is both historical allegory and prophetic warning against the dangers of false ideology. Out of the depths of Jewish suffering, Singer reminds us that the Holocaust was not without precedent. In seventeenth-century Ukraine, followers of Bogdan Chmelnicki—a forerunner of Adolf Hitler—decimated the Jewish populations of eastern Europe. Whole communities were wiped off the map and the surviving remnant sank into despair. How could these horrors happen to the Children of Israel who yearned through long centuries for the Redemption? Perhaps, with all its horror, the nightmare of history had reached its climax and the darkest hours presaged the dawning of a new day? "The greatest cabalists in Poland and other lands uncovered numerous allusions in the Zohar and in antique cabalistic volumes proving that the days of the Exile were numbered. Chmelnicki's massacres were the birth-pangs of the Messiah." Such hope against hope served as the inspiration for the masses of eager disciples of Shabbati Zevi, the enigmatic leader of a movement that declared him to be the destined savior of Israel and the world.

Enthusiasm for the new teachings gathered momentum with the support of erudite scholars as well as ordinary folk. The bubble burst, however, when Shabbatai Zevi buckled under the pressure of the caliphate in Istanbul and converted to Islam. Nevertheless, many of his followers clung to the belief that even apostasy could be understood as part of the divine plan. This radical departure grew out of a belief that if purity and holiness could not bring the redemption, then perhaps degradation and profanity would. Esoteric texts were found to justify holy sins—"outwardly evil, inwardly virtuous"—that could raise the fallen sparks of the underworld. From this perspective, "the generation before redemption had to become completely guilty; consequently, they went to great lengths to commit every possible offense," including adultery, eating pork, and desecrating the Sabbath.

Based on thorough historical research, this novel is extraordinary in the way it portrays the effect of great events on otherwise anonymous individuals. With haunting verisimilitude, the narrative focuses on a typical yet vividly unique community emerging from the timeless mists of Jewish exile only to teeter over the edge of the historical abyss. Rather than attempting to pass judgment on the past, the author dramatizes the internal conflicts of the collective Jewish psyche. He focuses on the anguish, yearning, and religious hysteria of individuals caught up in the tides of developments beyond their comprehension or control. Obviously, the tragic fate of Goray reflects on the false messiahs of our own times. But the distinctive achievement of the book is to make believable the unbelievable phenomenon of ordinary people seized by the collective hypnosis of a cult mentality.

Structurally, however, the novel suffers from a lack of one central point of view. The narrative moves from one character to another, leaving the reader to put together the fragments of perception into a coherent pattern. Part of the difficulty in this mosaic approach is that the characters change in the course of the story. Reb Bainish, the head of the community and its spiritual guide, abandons his flock halfway through the plot. Mordechai Joseph, the leading opponent of Reb Bainish, begins as a self-serving rebel against authority and early follower of the false messiah, but he returns in the end, having learned the errors of his ways, to provide the antidote to the town's spiritual sickness. Reb Itche Mattes enters as a catalyst for change but proves both sexually and spiritually impotent.

The leading evildoer, Reb Gedalya, who appears after Reb Bainish has left the scene, never suffers the full consequences of his crimes. Instead, he escapes at the end, to mislead other innocents in other times and places.

Only Rechele, the disturbed daughter of one of the village's former leading citizens, embodies the tragic impact of both the external destruction and internal delusion of the community as a whole. Rechele represents the Shekhina, or the Jewish soul, in eternal Exile. With developing stages of horror upon horror, she becomes the central victim of the tale, possessed by the dybukk of an evil spirit determined to destroy her and hers. At the conclusion, the narrative adopts the voice of the eternal chronicler of the dead, declaring in solemn tones the doom of a woman, a village, and a people.

FURTHER ARTISTIC DEVELOPMENT

As strong as his first two novels were, the author continued to develop and refine his art with an array of novelistic triumphs. In 1960 the English translation of *The Magician of Lublin* blended the author's fascination concerning the world of the occult with the strongest tendencies of his psychological realism. Unified in its central point of view, it achieves a higher level of artistic consistency than his previous works. Also, it provides a metaphor for the author, who presents the artist as a kind of circus prestidigitator, apparently concerned only with pleasing the audience while behind the scenes he is deeply involved with pondering the deeper issues of time and eternity. And who can say if the magician's tricks are merely sleight of hand or, possibly, the result of hidden powers? Ultimately, however, Yasha the magician undergoes the most severe form of self-inflicted repentance for his proud mastery of the worlds of illusion.

In many ways *The Slave*, published in English translation in 1962, may be Singer's most accessible and satisfying accomplishment. For once Singer creates a wholly admirable protagonist. Even if Jacob sees himself as a sinner, all his sins are in the cause of true love. Set in the same historical context as *Satan in Goray*, Jacob also suffers the dire consequences of the Chmelnicki pogroms when he is literally sold into slavery to peasants. After he escapes, Jacob briefly becomes one of the deluded followers of the false messiah Shabbati Zevi. But as an anonymous individual, Jacob validates the contradictory teachings of the heretical movement. His love for the secret convert Wanda/Sarah, daughter of the primitive peoples of the Polish backcountry, raises the hidden sparks of holiness from the darkest recesses of pagan superstition to further the generations of ultimate redemption in the Holy Land.

In the two-volume saga consisting of *The Manor*, translated and published in 1967, and *The Estate*, which appeared two years later, the author returns to the epic novel of historical realism, going back to the middle of the nineteenth century, when the Jews of Poland caught their first glimpse of the glimmers of modernity on the horizon. With far greater mastery than he could summon up in *The Family Moskat*, the author weaves a multifaceted tapestry of interlocking stories and characters stretching across a span of generations reaching to America and Palestine as well as ancestral Jewish Poland and its environs. The sheer pleasure of reading this well-crafted, fast-moving saga is hardly diminished by what appears to be a somewhat stilted translation. But the reader should read both volumes in sequence. Together, they portray the author's vision of the causes for the disintegration of Jewish life in Poland, the consequences of which he had previously detailed.

The Manor and *The Estate* conclude, historically, where *The Family Moskat* begins, and they seem to have been written with less urgency than *The Family Moskat*. The multitudinous minor characters are clearly differentiated and major characters develop with more consistency. Instead of a grab bag of disparate individuals, the two-volume sequence suggests a well-organized plan covering the major possibilities of human development within the life and times of the novel's context. First, there is the Jewish entrepreneur, Calman Jacoby, who dares to capitalize on the failure of the Polish nobility to throw off the yoke of their Russian overlords. His material success leads to a spiritual decline that comes full circle when his worldly failings inspire a religious reawakening. His female counterpart, Clara, is clever and strong-willed enough to manipulate the men in her life, especially Calman, but her triumphs are hollow. In the end, Clara seems to outsmart herself and she perishes without the enduring love her soul desires. Calman and Clara's son, Sasha, is neither Jew nor Pole but a hybrid force of nature bent on exploitation and self-destruction. Lucian, the renegade Polish nobleman and the leading villain of the whole saga, provides a dose of pure evil and sheer criminality to offset the stumbling, well-intended, petty failings and venal sins of the other characters. Among these Ezriel, the Jewish psychiatrist, stands out as a more balanced and healthy version of Asa Heshel, weighed down with the same doubts and forbidden desires. Finally, Ezriel, unlike Asa Heshel, seems to resolve his inner conflicts and his dissatisfaction

with cosmopolitan European culture through a vaguely Zionistic return to his Jewish roots.

In *The Manor* and *The Estate*, the author presents an easily digested affirmation of Jewish tradition. Read without reference to his other works, these volumes convey the impression of a staunchly conservative writer who, though deeply troubled by the modern world, seems certain of the cure for the modern disease. Especially singled out for harsh treatment are all political radicals and would-be revolutionaries among the Polish Jews. Ezriel's sister serves a long sentence in Siberia after she has been betrayed by her comrade and lover, then returns to die a lonely and painful death. Ezriel's daughter, who also falls into the radical camp, similarly suffers a severe punishment for her crimes. But Ezriel's son, who quits school to join the pioneers in Palestine, serves as a beacon for his own father, suggesting a possible answer to the perpetual riddle of the Jewish question.

In contrast to the young radicals, traditional Hasidim never lose their otherworldly glow in *The Manor* and *The Estate*. Unlike the revolutionaries who aim at a materialistic redemption, the unenlightened Hasidic Jews in these novels still serve a higher spiritual redemption, though it remains unattainable in this world. While the radicals are willing to sacrifice themselves for the cause of humanity, they are doomed to oblivion by the forces of history. Singer's Hasidim retain purpose in both their lives and their deaths.

In subsequent novels, however, traditional Judaism as an answer to modern ills appears to become more problematic. In *Enemies: A Love Story* and *Shosha* (1978), Singer portrays the intellectual and moral alienation of Holocaust survivors who cannot adapt to contemporary life. In *The Penitent* (1983), the protagonist seeks repentance and return to tradition as the answer to moral relativism, yet the author confesses in an afterword that this answer is too simplistic for him, however much he recognizes the validity of the question. In all these works, Singer is in superb command of his narrative magic, developing one scene after another with both delightful suspense and deepest insight.

SHORT STORY MASTERPIECES

It is in his short stories, however, that the author's genius shines with most brilliance. As a selection of some—but far from all—of Singer's best efforts in the short story genre, *The Collected Stories* (1982) provides the best introduction and the most lasting testament to Singer's greatness. Many, including "Gimpel the Fool" and "The Spinoza of Market Street," have often been discussed and analyzed at length. Others, such as "Yentl the Yeshiva Boy," have been adapted, though without preserving the quality of their original genius, to stage and screen. But even those stories in this volume that have received less critical notice and popular acclaim can encapsulate the author's worldview with stunning effect. Readers must explore the stories for themselves, read and re-read their favorites, discovering nuances and insights they had previously missed.

Two of the stories, "Joy" and "Something Is There," summarize Singer's perspective on religion. Both begin in doubt and move through despair to an affirmation of an unconventional yet hard-won faith in a higher power. In "Joy," Rabbi Bainish of Komarov combines the suffering of Job and the defiance of the Kotzker Rebbe. Unable to carry on, he confesses to his leading disciple that he has decided "the atheists are right. There is no justice, no Judge." But the disciple does not leave his master, and Rabbi Bainish, facing his own imminent mortality, concludes that death, not life, is the real illusion. In his last commentary on the Torah, the rabbi declares that it is man's greatest blessing that the face of the deity remains concealed, like the moon on Rosh Hashannah. For unless the truth remained obscure, freedom of moral choice would not be possible. Finally, with his last breath, Rabbi Bainish murmurs: "One should always be joyous." Somehow, the charm of the story's narrative art makes these words believable.

Faced with a similar crisis of rabbinical faith in "Something Is There," Rabbi Nechemia from Bechev decides to express his "wrath against the Creator" by abandoning his post and wandering to Warsaw in search of "the real heretics" who believe in absolutely nothing. But the rabbi learns from freethinkers in a bookstore that "there are no unbelievers any more" since the "old ones have died," leaving a generation of impractical do-gooders. Meanwhile, the rabbi encounters the horrors of daily life on the streets of the big city, witnessing a violent robbery and barely escaping the clutches of a prostitute. Finally, a coal dealer invites the despairing rabbi into his apartment, providing hospitality and kind words of practical wisdom. No, the coal dealer admits, he cannot know if there is a Creator in heaven since he never met Him. Yet he feels that "Something is there."

The hidden face of an otherwise absent deity is, perhaps, the central paradox of Singer's work. But the forces of darkness are very much present and the devil or one of his legions often appears as the first-person narrator of Singer's short fiction. In "The Destruction of Kreshev" the narrator introduces himself as "the Primeval Snake, the Evil One, Satan," glorying in the downfall of innocence. Although news of the Enlightenment has barely reached Kreshev, hidden followers of the false messiah Shabbati Zevi undermine the tiny village and instigate the most savage cruelty against the townsfolk. Their victim, Lise, the beautiful and sophisticated daughter of one of the few prosperous families in town, suffers the "the forsaking of both this world and the next between the saying of a yes and a no." Similarly, in the gothic horror story "The Unseen"—also narrated by "the Evil Spirit"—the Seducer not only causes the unwary to sin, but also indicts his chosen victim in the hereafter, so that the old and foolish husband Nathan Jozefover becomes "a man who sees without being seen," consigned to eternal limbo for a fleeting moment of lechery. Both stories, invoking the terror of one naive betrayal leading to eternal perdition, conclude as Hasidic morality tales.

In "Zeidlus the Pope," the narrator—again identified as "the Evil One"—brags of undermining a righteous scholar impervious to all temptations except his own intellectual vanity. But in "The Last Demon" one of the more obscure agents of Asmodeus has to admit that he has fallen on hard times. What work is left for the demons "when man himself is a demon? Why persuade to evil someone who is already convinced?" Once, in the "godforsaken village" of Tishevitz where "Adam didn't even stop to pee," there lived a rabbi so sincerely pious that the demon had to give up his game. And now, since the holy rabbi died a martyr's death and the whole community has been wiped out, what remains to be done? "The generation is already guilty seven times over, but Messiah does not come. To whom should he come?" More optimistic, especially for an American readership, "The Little Shoemakers" condenses a saga of seven generations into a short story. In this tale, a living tradition of workmanship and family values survives the upheaval and transplanting of Abba Shuster and all his descendents from the village of Frampol to an unnamed town in New Jersey. The practical wisdom and way of life, symbolized by the knotted string he uses as a measuring tape for custom-made shoes, allows Abba and his sons to preserve their heritage and maintain their identity in the New World. Though moving and effective, most of Singer's stories steer clear of such exercises in sentimental self-congratulation.

More characteristic of Singer's worldview, "Grandfather and Grandson" depicts an aging Jew and his bomb-throwing progeny. Reb Mordecai Meir has lived all his life devoted to prayer and Torah study. Then, one morning, his grandson knocks on the door, beardless and in modern dress, looking for a hideout from the authorities. Though they are practically strangers to each other, the old Hasid and the young rebel come together, during the abortive 1905 revolution, in one unifying moment of apocalyptic doom. In their own very different ways, both are crushed by unfulfilled hope for redemption.

Well-known for his interest in the occult, Singer reserves a right to rational skepticism even as he exploits the paranormal for fictional effect. "Powers" attests to the reality of telepathic magic, yet the protagonist, with all his wizardry, cannot save his one true love from the Nazis. "The Séance" is a parody of the phony machinations of Mrs. Kopitzky, a charlatan posing as a spiritual medium, yet it gives her the last word: "We live forever and we love forever. This is the pure truth." "The Psychic Journey" begins on the Upper West Side of Manhattan. A chance meeting leads to a magical mystery bus trip in search of "clairvoyance, psychokinesis, and the immortality of the soul." The trip ends in Tel Aviv as an encounter with the reality of the 1973 Yom Kippur War.

Widely known and often criticized for his uninhibited portrayal of human sexuality, the author is distinctly unromantic on the subject of the relation between men and women. In his memoirs Singer describes his gradual realization that "love was no game. Love killed people." And in his stories he shows how both life and love can be killed by sheer devotion. "A Quotation from Klopstock" portrays a cynical womanizer, Max Persky, who seduces the virginal old maid Theresa Stein, about whom he says: "A time is coming when no one will believe that such women existed." Love, in Max Persky's lexicon, means total egoism or destruction of both lover and beloved. In "The Manuscript," a former actress of the Yiddish stage tells how she returned to Warsaw in the midst of the Nazi invasion to retrieve the one handwritten copy of her lover's novel. Then she returns with the manuscript only to find her "hero" in bed with another woman. In a single gesture, she destroys both the manuscript and her love.

The levels of virtuosity Singer achieved in his short fiction range across a spectrum of artistic mastery. Some of his efforts contain multiple stories within a story. In "Moon and Madness," for example, three narrators share tales on a common theme, the damage that can be done by misguided pity, concluding with a vision of cosmic evil as an illusion lost in the shining moonlight, "nothing but a coil of madness." Moreover, while *The Collected Stories* offers an accessible one-volume introduction to the author's work, it also leads, like the doorway of a mystical palace, into seemingly endless hallways with innumerable chambers of wonder. In "A Crown of Feathers," the author defines, by example, the quality of a masterpiece in the tale of the brilliant and beautiful Akhsa who rejects her chosen bridegroom, converts to Catholicism, and then suffers the most painful depths of self-inflicted penance to redeem her soul. At the same time, the story embodies a symbol of the inner truth "as intricate and hidden as a crown of feathers." Yet the wonder of the work is further enhanced in the 1974 National Book Award–winning collection in which it was the title piece; the collection is a series of stories that comment on each other, each a world in itself uniquely characteristic of the author's own individual style.

Singer writes out of a need to pose questions for which there may be no answers. His fiction turns eternal riddles into statements of conviction that compassion, humor, and ingenuity may somehow overcome the doom of false hopes. He transforms doubts of discredited faith into passionate belief in the right of individuals to pursue their doubts. He explores paranormal realms of spiritualism without sacrificing rational skepticism about occult phenomena. And he pushes the limits of sexual experimentation while remaining true to the longing of the soul for love from one other person. As a magician of imaginative prose, he always entertains and delights his readers. Much of his work is haunted by survivor's guilt, the ambivalent psychological debt that the living feel they owe to the dead. He suggests a strategy for the wise and courageous to "smuggle through" a world that he represents as a combination slaughterhouse and insane asylum. He warns us against the illusory claims made by false messiahs of ideological purity. Yet he also restores the status of the intuitive imagination as an antidote to despairing rationalism. What more can we ask from a master storyteller?

Isaac Bashevis Singer died on 24 July 1991.

[*See also* Jewish-American Fiction.]

SELECTED WORKS

The Family Moskat (1950)
Satan in Goray (1955)
Gimpel the Fool and Other Stories (1957)
The Magician of Lublin (1960)
The Spinoza of Market Street and Other Stories (1961)
The Slave (1962)
Short Friday and Other Stories (1964)
In My Father's Court (1966)

Mazel and Shlimazel; or, The Milk of a Lioness (1966)
The Fearsome Inn (1967)
The Manor (1967)
The Séance and Other Stories (1968)
When Schlemiel Went to Warsaw and Other Stories (1968)
The Estate (1969)
Elijah the Slave: A Hebrew Legend Retold (1970)
A Friend of Kafka and Other Stories (1970)
Joseph and Koza; or, The Sacrifice to the Vistula (1970)
Alone in the Wild Forest (1971)
The Topsy-Turvy Emperor of China (1971)
Enemies: A Love Story (1972)
The Wicked City (1972)
A Crown of Feathers and Other Stories (1973)
The Fools of Chelm and Their History (1973)
Why Noah Chose the Dove (1974)
Passions and Other Stories (1975)
A Tale of Three Wishes (1975)
*Naftali the Storyteller and His Horse, Sus, and Other
  Stories* (1976)
Shosha (1978)
Old Love and Other Stories (1979)
The Power of Light: Eight Stories for Hanukkah (1980)
The Golem (1982)
The Collected Stories of Isaac Bashevis Singer (1982)
The Penitent (1983)
Stories for Children (1984)
Love and Exile (1984)
The Image and Other Stories (1985)
Conversations with Isaac Bashevis Singer (1986)
The Death of Methuselah and Other Stories (1988)
The King of the Fields (1988)
Scum (1991)
The Certificate (1992)
Meshugah (1994)
Shadows on the Hudson (1998)
More Stories from My Father's Court (2000)

FURTHER READING

Alexander, Edward. *Isaac Bashevis Singer*. Boston, 1980. This volume introduces the reader to Singer's work in terms of his role as a chronicler of the Jewish people.

Allentuck, Marcia, ed. *The Achievement of Isaac Bashevis Singer*. Carbondale, Ill., 1969. This book offers a collection of previously unpublished essays by a variety of writers and critics on various aspects of Singer's work.

Biletzky, Israel Ch. *God, Jew, Satan in the Works of Isaac Bashevis-Singer*. Lanham, Md., 1995. Associating the author with Hassidic storytellers, this study analyzes how Singer both builds on and goes beyond the Jewish tradition that most inspired him.

Buchen, Irving H. *Isaac Bashevis Singer and the Eternal Past*. New York, 1968. An historical and aesthetic study of the author's relationship to both Jewish culture and European literary modernism, this was the first full-length critical analysis of Singer.

Farrell, Grace, ed. *Critical Essays on Isaac Bashevis Singer*. New York, 1996. Beginning with an editor's introduction that summarizes the reception of Singer's work during his lifetime, this volume includes some of the most influential reviews and critical articles as well as several previously unpublished essays on the author.

Friedman, Lawrence S. *Understanding Isaac Bashevis Singer*. Columbia, S.C., 1988. One of a series of volumes on Understanding Contemporary American Literature, edited by Matthew J. Bruccoli, this book introduces Singer to students and general readers.

Gibbons, Frances Vargas. *Transgression and Self-Punishment in Isaac Bashevis Singer's Searches*. New York, 1995. Using a psychoanalytic approach, this book applies a Freudian methodology to several of the author's novels and children's stories, analyzing problematic relationships in terms of male-female, human-deity, and author-fiction.

Hadda, Janet. *Isaac Bashevis Singer: A Life*. New York, 1997. An informative psychoanalytic biography of the author, this volume strenuously debunks his image as a grandfatherly sage.

Kresh, Paul. *Isaac Bashevis Singer: The Magician of West 86th Street*. New York, 1979. An intimate biography based on a close personal relationship with the author, this volume is structured as a series of interlocking flashbacks of the author's early development and vignettes of his daily life in the period leading up to and including his reception of the Nobel Prize for Literature.

Malin, Irving. *Isaac Bashevis Singer*. New York, 1972. This brief critical introduction to the author's early work emphasizes his artistry in short stories and closely structured novels as opposed to his longer historical epics.

Malin, Irving, ed. *Critical Views of Isaac Bashevis Singer*. New York, 1969. This valuable collection includes interviews with the author and influential critical essays on the impact of his early work, with a useful bibliography up to the date of publication.

Miller, David Neal, ed. *Recovering the Canon: Essays on Isaac Bashevis Singer*. Leiden, 1986.

Singer, Isaac Bashevis, and Richard Burgin. *Conversations with Isaac Bashevis Singer*. New York, 1986.

Telushkin, Dvorah. *Master of Dreams: A Memoir of Isaac Bashevis Singer*. New York, 1997. This poignant and moving first-person account by the author's personal secretary provides an intimate portrait of the author during the latter years of his life.

Tuszyanska, Agata. *Lost Landscapes: In Search of Isaac Bashevis Singer and the Jews of Poland*, translated from the Polish by Madeline G. Levine. New York, 1998. Using techniques of oral history, this ethnographic study returns to the conflicted contexts of Singer's fiction in post-Holocaust Poland, Israel, and the United States.

Wirth-Nesher, Hana. *City Codes: Reading the Modern Urban Novel*. New York, 1996.

Zamir, Israel, and Barbara Harshav. *Journey to My Father, Isaac Bashevis Singer*. New York, 1995. A first-person account by the author's estranged son, this memoir tells of a gradual and partially complete reconciliation during the last decades of Singer's life.

DAVE SMITH

by Kimberly Lewis

David Jeddie Smith was born on 19 December 1942 in Portsmouth, Virginia. He graduated from the University of Virginia, and was then educated at Southern Illinois University, where he earned an M.A. degree. He received a Ph.D. in 1976 from Ohio University, where he was able to write a creative writing dissertation. His poetry has earned him many awards and recognitions, including fellowships from the Guggenheim Foundation, the National Endowment for the Arts, and the Lyndhurst Foundation. He was a finalist for the Pulitzer Prize for both *Goshawk, Antelope* (1979) and *Dream Flights* (1981).

REGIONAL VISIONS

Although Smith has often lived outside of his native Virginia, his poetry remains steeped in its imagery—of the shore of the Chesapeake Bay, of the swamps, of the spruce trees, as well as of the inhabitants. The highly praised *Goshawk, Antelope* is a glaring exception to this regional fidelity, as in it Smith turned purposely toward the western landscape of Wyoming, only to return to his territory soon after. The stories of tough seaports, watermen and their women are especially frequent in early volumes such as *The Fisherman's Whore* (1974) and *Cumberland Station* (1976). Later volumes, including *The Wick of Memory* (2000), tend to draw heavily from scenes of Smith's own childhood that he brings to bear on more recent recollections of adult life and his own children.

Along with these tales of daily life and visions of Virginia is the constant affirmation of the state's inheritance of the history, the themes, and the literature of the American South. The ineradicable past—southern life and the Civil War—haunts the modern-day quotidian and personal memories:

> I've been posted west
> where birds the color of Union blue flare up
> and thicken the big sky, the widening circles—
> they make a kind of shadow you can't walk out of.
> Between us many states hurtle apart in the butternut sun.

Half-asleep our father stands, breath steaming, a streak
by the sycamore's exploding leaves, his face gone
black as our house where gray birds come to roost.

> *(Gray Soldiers*, 1983, p. 11)

Moving back and forth in time in his images and often in his verb tenses, the poet is witness to both his own and the region's history. Poetry, for Smith, is a romantic effort to reveal—if not to explain—what has surrounded him, bringing knowledge and understanding from the long-faded past to the present, and back again.

THE NARRATION OF EXPERIENCE

Smith shares his native state with Edgar Allan Poe, whom he considers to be the first important American poet, and to whom he addressed a volume of poetry. Regarding his major influences, however, he most often associates himself with James Dickey, Robert Penn Warren, and James Wright; with poets who combine lyrical inventiveness and a pure capacity for storytelling. Anecdote- or even prose-style narration is at the center of his poetic endeavors, as well as of his conception of the meaning and role of poetry. The poem is to tell a story of possibility, "create a little life," that is then altered and enhanced by the sound and the rhythm of the language in which the tale is told. "The beauty of lyric language could be employed with the rawness and ugliness of human experience," he articulates (Suarez, *Southbound: Interviews with Southern Poets*, 1999, p. 35).

A harsh critic of the apparently morally and socially vacuous nature of so-called language poetry, Smith has not swayed from narration of concrete human experience. In the remnants of the Civil War as in the memory of a hunting expedition with his grandfather, Smith's poetry attempts to approach, through images and the connections he creates between them, elusive mystery and universal significance. The poems of later volumes such as *Fate's Kite* (1995) do, however, venture into a new frivolity and immediacy. More often dwelling in the present tense, he has a playful familiarity with his reader, mentioning such popular subjects as Louis Farrakhan and Kirk Douglas. "Sometimes there's nothing to write about," he writes at the beginning of "A Map of Your Small Town." and yet he manages to bring a poem even out of the world's refusal of poetry.

FICTION AND CRITICISM

Smith's prose fiction is limited to two books. He wrote a single novel, *Onliness* (1981), that he describes as a zany parody of the southern gothic tradition with a shot-putter as protagonist. His volume of short fiction, *Southern Delights* (1984), on the other hand, does not stray far from the language-narration combination that characterizes his poetry. He relates such realistic tales as a death by motorcycle accident in the vaguely interiorized voice of a central character that rambles, laden with poetic description.

In addition to being a poet, Smith is also a prolific critic and devoted professor. He has edited *The Pure Clear World* (1982), a collection of essays on James Wright, and coedited *The Morrow Anthology of Younger American Poets* (1985) with David Bottoms. He has been a constant presence in American poetry journals as both contributor and editor, beginning in 1969 with the founding of the *Back Door*, a contemporary poetry magazine. Having taught English and creative writing in universities all over the country, and participated in numerous writing workshops and conferences, Smith is an outspoken proponent of creative writing programs. His collection of journal-style thoughts on poetry and essays on specific poets, *Local Assays* (1985), finishes with a section in defense of these programs that have often been attacked as a waste of time and money and as producers of mediocre poets. Despite the general acclaim for his own poetry, the poet has not escaped related criticism of his own deep roots in this creative writing establishment.

Smith resides in Baton Rouge, Louisiana with his wife Deloras and their three children. He teaches twentieth-century American poetry and creative writing at Louisiana State University and is coeditor of the *Southern Review*.

WORKS

Bull Island (1970)
Mean Rufus Throw Down (1973)
The Fisherman's Whore (1974)
Drunks (1975)
Cumberland Station (1976)
In Dark, Sudden With Light (1976)
Goshawk, Antelope (1979)
The Travelling Photographer (1981)
Dream Flights (1981)
Blue Spruce (1981)
Onliness (1981)
Homage to Edgar Allan Poe (1981)
The Pure Clear World: Essays on the Poetry of James Wright (1982)
In the House of the Judge (1983)
Gray Soldiers (1983)
Southern Delights (1984)
Local Assays (1985)
The Roundhouse Voices: Selected and New Poems (1985)
The Morrow Anthology of Younger American Poets (1985)
Cuba Night (1990)
The Essential Poe (1991)
Night Pleasures: New and Selected Poems (1992)
Fate's Kite: Poems, 1991–1995 (1995)
Floating on Solitude: Three Volumes of Poetry (1996)
The Wick of Memory: New and Selected Poems, 1970–2000 (2000)

FURTHER READING

Bawer, Bruce. "Dave Smith's 'Creative Writing.'" *New Criterion* no. 4 (December 1985): 27–33. A highly critical but interesting article on Smith's career, his poetry, *Local Assays*, and his defense of creative writing.

DeMott, Robert J. *Dave Smith: A Literary Archive*. Athens, Ohio, 2000. Decent biographical information in the introduction, and a list of personal letters and documents in the Dave Smith archives in Ohio.

Suarez, Ernest. *Southbound: Interviews with Southern Poets*. Columbia, Mo., 1999. One of the best interviews with Smith.

Weigl, Bruce, ed. *The Giver of Morning: On the Poetry of Dave Smith*. Birmingham, Ala., 1982. A few good essays on the early volumes of poetry.

GARY SNYDER

by Aaron K. DiFranco

In promoting a life close to nature and exploring the relation between the inner mind and the outer world, Gary Snyder falls into the tradition of American romanticism following Thoreau and Whitman. But whereas the transcendentalists perceived nature as symbolic and looked through it to find spiritual truths, Snyder emphasizes how the spiritual takes shape within the real, physical, and imaginative interactions between elements that make up the ecology of one's place. His engagement with the natural world and resistance to the monoculture of Western commercial industrialism have turned him toward environmental activism as well as philosophical meditations as lucid and penetrating as those of Emerson or John Muir. His work champions the idea of wilderness, where the multiplicity of nature and culture—inherently interconnected—can manifest itself in all its forms.

WEST COAST AND COUNTERCULTURE

Although his family was part of the European migration west through the early history of the United States, Snyder made a life of actively inhabiting the Pacific Coast and celebrating the cultures that merge there. Born in San Francisco on 8 May 1930, Snyder grew up with his sister on their parents' dairy farm in Washington State before the family moved to Portland, Oregon, in 1942. Much of his youth was spent ranging throughout the broad and relatively unsettled wilderness of the Pacific Northwest. His interest in his region took him on mountaineering and backpacking excursions in the Cascades and Sierra Nevada Mountains, where he came into contact with the Native American tribes of the region as well as the more recently established logging communities. Despite the differing cultural perspectives, Snyder began to notice how both groups responded to and formed their own cultural practices based on the particulars of place, that is, how the natural world established human lifestyles and attitudes.

These interests prompted him to study anthropology and literature when he entered Reed College in Portland in 1947. His senior thesis explored the stories of a local

Gary Snyder.
(Margaretta K. Mitchell Photography)

Native American tribe (published later as *He Who Hunted Birds in His Father's Village: The Dimensions of a Haida Myth* [1979]) and spurred his interest in how myth could be used to create cultural identity as well as shape reality. Snyder also studied East Asian art and aesthetics at Reed, coming in time to the works of Ernest Fenollosa and Ezra Pound. He maintained his ties to communities in the more remote parts of the region as well. This region was extensive: he worked summers variously with U.S. Forest Service trail crews, on U.S. Park Service archaeology projects, with timber companies on tribal reservations, and on a ship traveling to South America. His experiences in the backcountry exposed him to the life and lifestyles of distinct bioregions. The "text" of that reality would later inform the poems of *Myths and Texts* (1960), in which Snyder brings together Native American, Eastern, and Western traditions in presenting a reflexive self sensitive to and stimulated by the particulars of the environment. Not since Robinson Jeffers had a poet attempted to express such a comprehensive mind of the American Pacific coast; in contrast to the severe transport of Jeffers's "inhumanism," however, Snyder formulated his poems as ritual utterances. Processing sharp sense details, the poetry explores culture's basic forms of contact with nature, and Snyder's evocations in his "shaman's songs" make this natural world more palpable.

After completing his bachelor's degree in 1951, Snyder traveled to Indiana University to study linguistics, but he remained only one semester before returning to the West Coast and the political and cultural energies that would coalesce there as the San Francisco Renaissance. He lived briefly with the poet Philip Whalen, worked seasonally as a fire lookout for the Forest Service, and eventually enrolled as a graduate student in East Asian languages at the University of California, Berkeley, in 1952. A short-lived marriage to Alison Gass ended this same year. The San Francisco Bay Area already had a liberal poetic tradition with poets like Robert Duncan, Robin Blaser, Josephine Miles, Kenneth Rexroth, and Jack Spicer residing there, and Snyder's own life in the working-class hinterlands placed him against the mainstream values of the McCarthy era. The Beat sensibility building in the West at that time appealed to a younger generation weary and edgy from the Cold War climate and prevailing conservatism. On 7 October 1955, Snyder participated in the famous "Six Poets at the Six Gallery" reading along with Allen Ginsberg, Philip Lamantia, Whalen, Michael McClure, and Rexroth. The reading launched the Beat movement and challenged the reigning literary academicism. As evidenced by his fictionalization as Japhy Ryder in Jack Kerouac's *The Dharma Bums*, Snyder was solidly fixed as an exemplar for the developing social counterculture.

Snyder's *Riprap* (1959), perhaps because of the occasional quality of its poems, caught the kinetic exhaustion and exhilaration of American life, the local and the exotic, using clear, direct images and a colloquial tone like that advocated by William Carlos Williams. Not only do the poems show a developing awareness of how experience is rooted in the happening of a particular moment, but they also continue the exploration of how language constructs our perceptions of the world. These poems show, moreover, the influence of Snyder's studies at Berkeley, where he was translating the works of the misanthropic Chinese hermit Han Shan. These *Cold Mountain Poems*

(1958), in the same bearing as Taoist and Buddhist teachings, promulgate a release from the entanglements of an urbane, secular society and an attentiveness to the conditions of one's existence. Already exposed to the crisp imagism of the Japanese and Chinese poetic line through Rexroth's early translations, as well as through the work of Pound and Fenollosa, in these poems Snyder further developed an attention to phenomena in their relation to the poetic mind.

PACIFIC RIM REINHABITATION

Further contact with fledgling Buddhist groups in the Bay Area brought Snyder into contact with the Zen and "Pure Land" schools of Mahayana Buddhism and encouraged him, in 1956, to travel to Japan and begin his formal Buddhist training at the Zen Temple Shokoku-ji in Kyoto. This stay lasted only a year, after which Snyder left aboard the tanker S.S. *Sappa Creek* as an engine room worker. He stayed briefly in the San Francisco area after nine months at sea, then returned to Kyoto in 1959 to study at the Daitoke-ji monastery. This time he was accompanied by the poet Joanne Kyger, whom he married the following year. Based primarily in Japan, Snyder would spend the next decade exploring the regions around the Pacific, following his own wandering path of enlightenment and coming into contact with various Buddhist sects and their teachings. As part of his exploration of how communities develop and establish their local spiritual practices, Snyder performed circumambulation rituals with Mountain Buddhists—the Yamabushi—in Japan, encountered Vajrayana Buddhism in India and Nepal, met the Dalai Lama in Dharamshala, and fasted on an island in the East China Sea. With his poetic line already influenced by Asian aesthetics, the philosophies of the region now started penetrating deeper into his work: conceptions of existence as a unceasing state of flux were applied to the shifting circumstances of contemporary experience in *Six Sections from Mountains and Rivers without End* (1965), part of a long poem sequence he was writing. The Taoist and Buddhist apprehension of the universe as "empty" infusing the poems provided Snyder a means of rediscovering a life of value and resonant possibility.

After twelve years rambling along the Asian rim of the Pacific, Snyder returned to the United States. With him he brought a more practiced aesthetic and a social engagement nourished by his Buddhist training. He was accompanied by his third wife, Masa Uehara (Snyder and Kyger had divorced in 1965). Two books of poetry followed immediately, *The Back Country* (1968) and *Regarding Wave* (1969), which began to articulate imaginative yet vitally present alternatives to the mainstream industrial civilization whose ecological and economic imperialism was implicitly connected to the military escalation in Vietnam. Poems like "A Walk" and "Vapor Trails" blended Eastern philosophical awakening with Western lyrical epiphany while tracing out remote parts of consciousness, untamed yet accessible, that engaged fully with the natural world. Dealing with personal experience and acquaintances, yet public in their open engagement with contemporary events, they also seek to confront the quandaries of existence while constructing a symbiotic relationship with place. Moreover, Snyder's marriage and the birth of his sons, Kai and Gen, inspired a semi-confessional mode exploring new lyric possibilities for *Regarding Wave*. "Not Leaving the House," for example, expresses the creative possibilities in building a family life. Other poems, like "Song of the Taste," push the exploration of the erotic, domestic, and communal dimensions that a sensuous engagement with the world can develop.

Snyder also brought back to California a reinvigorated social engagement nourished by his Buddhist practice. His first book of prose, *Earth House Hold* (1969), collected essays that promoted alternative ways of conceiving one's relationship with the world—whether inspired by science, tribal worldviews, or poetry. Infused with countercultural idealism, the volume encouraged American social transformation. Snyder points to how, despite a dominant Western culture that dismisses them, Asian, Native American, and even Western cultures have continuously maintained "primitive" practices that express a more fundamental, archaic value system. Snyder connects the movement of the 1960s with a historical "Great Subculture" that stretches back to the Paleolithic and celebrates an active attentiveness to the natural world. *Earth House Hold* also includes journal selections from his time as a fire lookout and from his first time in Japan. Brief, musing, impressionistic, the journals represent Snyder's personal attempt to record the life of a particular place and serve as a more practical model of engaging with the world.

Though his writing promoted primitive values and wilderness, Snyder's insistence that escapism was rendered impossible by an awareness of humanity's broader interdependence with the rest of the globe's inhabitants undermined the romanticism implicit in the "back-to-the-land" movement and nature poetry. Instead, Snyder promoted a new sense of communal engagement sensitive to the geologic, biologic, and cultural forces shaping the life of a place. The informed understanding of one's individual bioregion, he proposed throughout his work, would help counter environmental devastation and promote stability. To put his ideals into practice, Snyder, with his family and friends, built a home with a balance of modern and archaic technologies on the San Juan Ridge in the California Sierra Nevada.

NATURE POETRY AND WILDERNESS ADVOCACY

Turtle Island (1974) united Snyder's pastoral sentiments and environmental politics and thrust him into broader public awareness. Reflecting his renewed contact with the West, the book embodies a sense of living at home in the world, of learning what it means to be a member of the larger ecological community, and emphasizes a focused commitment to that community. While tracing the natural and cultural history of the American landscape, his use of a Native American name for the North American continent as the title of his book prompted a reconsideration of the kinds of mythological, environmental, and social organizations with which American culture identified itself. The processes of the world that happen without function or purpose—"For Nothing," as one poem's title proclaims—are shown in the volume as sources of nourishment and spiritual possibility. The poems reexamine the virtues of wild nature by listening to the local residents, whether magpies or logging truck drivers. Snyder's ecocentric concern was further developed by the inclusion of the more programmatic manifesto "Four Changes," which outlines the kind of enterprises he believed the country needed in order to maintain ecological diversity and make salutary changes as a culture. The critically acclaimed volume was awarded the 1975 Pulitzer Prize.

With the success of *Turtle Island*, Snyder became a more publicly recognized spokesman for environmental issues, and his involvement with the West's politics increased. From 1974 to 1979, Snyder was a member of the Board for the California Arts Council. Organized by Governor Jerry Brown, the Arts Council explored ways in which the state could promote the work of artists for the greater social good. With the completion of his home in the Sierra, Snyder began other local projects, including the North San Juan School House and the Ring-of-Bone Zendo, a lay-Buddhist community center named after a book by his friend Lew Welch.

The following decade saw the continued publication of both poetry and prose. The appearance of *The Old Ways* (1977), a small collection of bioregionalist essays, and *The*

Real Work: Interviews and Talks, 1964–1979 (1980) constructs a context for his poetic practice while influencing the course of environmental activism and encouraging cultural critique. *Passage through India* (1983) provides journal entries—longer and more narrative than those of *Earth House Hold*—recounting his travels throughout Southeast Asia with Kyger and Ginsberg in the early 1960s. *Axe Handles* (1983), the first book of poetry since *Turtle Island*, reaffirms his commitments to family, region, work, and politics. The poems of this volume offer themselves as parables that encourage the finding of models for learning about the world. This was followed by *Left Out in the Rain* (1986), a collection of previously unpublished poems spanning the previous four decades.

In 1986, Snyder began teaching poetry and bioregional thought in the English department and Nature and Culture Program of the University of California, Davis. His popular poetic success and public activism had in some ways already brought him into mainstream culture as an icon of countercultural values, and he was able to use this new "institutional" position to push ecological thinking in new directions for new audiences. *The Practice of the Wild* (1990), more than a simple environmental treatise, explores the ethical and imaginative dimensions of wilderness. Snyder examines the roots of language along with past and contemporary cultural manners in order to articulate a lifestyle that engages with its surroundings in considered yet expansive ways. In voicing alternatives to the Western division between man and nature, he borrows frequently from the thirteenth-century Buddhist philosopher Dogen, asserting the uniqueness of all phenomena and simultaneously emphasizing how everything is ecologically interconnected. Another collection, *A Place in Space: Ethics, Aesthetics, and Watersheds* (1995), brings together new and old essays and presents a more cohesive picture of Snyder's own particular bioregional practices and principles. More locally oriented, the essays reflect on his life on the San Juan Ridge and the development of his personal aesthetics and interests.

The 1990s also saw the publication of two volumes spanning his poetic career. *No Nature: New and Selected Poems* (1992) arranges his poetry as an investigation of how language and perception structure human conceptions of and relations with "nature." This book was followed by the completion of Snyder's epic long poem sequence, *Mountains and Rivers without End* (1996). Poems from the sequence, written and published intermittently over the previous four decades, were finally brought together and structured according to the movements of

Japanese Noh drama in presenting a mythic journey of enlightenment through the landscapes of the Pacific Rim. The critically acclaimed sequence not only presents dazzlingly imaginative renderings of a reflexive consciousness, as in "Bubbs Creek Haircut," but also manifests visionary spiritual dimensions in poems like "An Offering for Tara" and "The Blue Sky." Expansive in scope, the book reflects a sense of life as momentary and cherishes the particulars of that life. Following the book's publication, Snyder was awarded the Bollingen Prize in 1997.

In 1991, Snyder married Carole Koda and lived with her and two stepdaughters in their home on San Juan Ridge. Though he retired from the University of California, Davis, in 2002, he remains an active advocate for poetry and the natural world.

[*See also* Beat Movement, The; Nature Writing: Poetry *and* Nature Writing: Prose.]

WORKS

Cold Mountain Poems (1958)

Riprap (1959)

Myths and Texts (1960)

Six Sections from Mountains and Rivers without End (1965)

The Back Country (1968)

Earth House Hold (1969)

Regarding Wave (1969)

Manzanita (1972)

The Fudo Trilogy (1973)

Turtle Island (1974)

The Old Ways (1977)

He Who Hunted Birds in His Father's Village: The Dimensions of a Haida Myth (1979)

Songs for Gaia (1979)

The Real Work: Interviews and Talks, 1964–1979 (1980)

Axe Handles (1983)

Passage through India (1983)

Left Out in the Rain (1986)

The Practice of the Wild (1990)

No Nature: New and Selected Poems (1992)

A Place in Space: Ethics, Aesthetics, and Watersheds (1995)

Mountains and Rivers without End (1996)

The Gary Snyder Reader: Prose, Poetry, and Translations, 1952–1998 (1999)

The High Sierra of California: Poems and Journals of Gary Snyder, Woodcuts by Tom Killion (2002)

FURTHER READING

Dean, Tim. *Gary Snyder and the American Unconscious: Inhabiting the Ground.* New York, 1991. Places Snyder's work in an American cultural context using a psychoanalytic approach.

Halper, Jon, ed. *Gary Snyder: Dimensions of a Life*. San Francisco, 1991. An extensive collection of personal reminiscences and critical pieces celebrating Snyder's life and work.

Molesworth, Charles. *Gary Snyder's Vision: Poetry and the Real Work*. Columbia, Mo., 1983. Begins to place Snyder's work in a political and social context.

Murphy, Patrick D. *Understanding Gary Snyder*. Columbia, S.C., 1992.

Murphy, Patrick D. *A Place for Wayfaring: The Poetry and Prose of Gary Snyder*. Corvallis, Ore., 2000.

Murphy, Patrick D., ed. *Critical Essays on Gary Snyder*. Boston, 1990. A strong collection of essays approaching Snyder's work from a variety of directions. It contains good bibliographic references and an interview with Snyder. Murphy provides sharp readings of Snyder's poetry.

Robertson, David. "Real Matter, Spiritual Mountain: Gary Snyder and Jack Kerouac on Mt. Tamalpais." *Western American Literature* 27 (Fall 1992): 209–226. An idiosyncratic but illuminating approach to Snyder's forms of practice and Buddhist thought.

Scigaj, Leonard M. *Sustainable Poetry: Four American Ecopoets*. Lexington, Ky., 1999. An academic study, this text attempts to place Snyder theoretically as an "ecopoet."

Steuding, Bob. *Gary Snyder*. Boston, 1976. One of the first studies on Snyder, it is still an excellent introduction to his early work.

GARY SOTO

by Steven P. Schneider

Born in Fresno, California, on 12 April 1952, Gary Soto is one of the most prominent Mexican-American writers of his generation. Soto's grandparents were born in Mexico, migrated to the United States, and worked in the fields and factories of Fresno. His father, Manuel Soto, was killed tragically in an accident at work when Soto was five years old. Soto's mother, Angie Trevino Soto, raised him, his older brother Rick, and his younger sister Debra in Fresno, located in the San Joaquin Valley, the setting of much of Soto's writing.

Gary Soto graduated from high school in 1970 and attended Fresno City College before moving on to California State University at Fresno. There he studied with the poet Philip Levine. In 1974 Soto graduated from California State magna cum laude. He married Carolyn Sadako Oda on 24 May 1975. They have one daughter, Mariko Heidi. Soto earned an M.F.A. degree in creative writing from the University of California at Irvine in 1976 and then began his career as a professor at the University of California at Berkeley, where he taught until 1992.

POETRY

Soto established his reputation as a poet with his first book, *The Elements of San Joaquin* (1977), and went on to publish numerous collections of poetry. Soto, however, has not limited his writing to the genre of poetry. He is also a prolific writer of nonfiction prose and young adult and children's fiction.

The Elements of San Joaquin is divided into three sections. The first presents a variety of characters and scenes from Soto's hometown. The reader is introduced to a harsh world of working-class people: factory workers, barbers, and abused and fearful women.

In the second section, Soto turns his attention to the fields and the Mexican migrant workers who hoe and harvest them. A sequence of eight poems evokes the essential elements of the valley where Soto was born and lived as a young boy. Two of the poems are titled "Wind," one "Sun," and two others "Fog" and "Rain" to suggest the strong influence of the weather upon the residents of the region. In "Field," the opening poem of the sequence, Soto recalls his experience after a day in the grape fields. Here the valley has become his identity:

> After a day in the grape fields near Rolinda
> A fine silt, washed by sweat,
> Has settled into the lines
> Of my wrists and palms.
>
> Already I am becoming the valley,
> A soil that sprouts nothing
> For any of us.

In the concluding section of his debut collection, Soto turns his attention to his family. "History" is a tribute to the poet's grandmother, who lit the morning stove at dawn and "sliced papas / Pounded chiles / With a stone / Brought from Guadalajara." She is portrayed as a pillar of strength with "A face streaked / From cutting grapes / And boxing plums." The figure of the *abuela* (grandmother) is central in Mexican-American poetry; she represents a connection to the family's Mexican roots.

The Elements of San Joaquin won the United States Award of the International Poetry Forum. The book was published at the beginning of a wave of interest in multicultural poetics that would bring to prominence Soto and other young writers of varied ethnic backgrounds. *The Elements of San Joaquin* was followed in quick succession by three more collections of poetry: *The Tale of Sunlight* (1978), *Where Sparrows Work Hard* (1981), and *Black Hair* (1985).

These early years in Soto's career as a poet were marked by increased critical recognition. Christopher Buckley, writing in the journal *Abraxas* in 1978, noted that Soto's first book had "something human and important to say, and this makes the craft worthwhile, and sets these poems above many." He won the Bess Hokin Prize for Poetry in 1978, a Guggenheim Fellowship in 1979, and a fellowship from the National Endowment for the Arts in 1981. In *Poetry* (March 1980), the poet and critic Alan Williamson compared Soto to both James Wright and Philip Levine in his review of *The Tale of Sunlight*: "At his frequent best,

Soto may be the most exciting poet of poverty in America to emerge since James Wright and Philip Levine."

Poverty is a subject Soto returns to again and again in *The Tale of Sunlight*. The first section is a narrative-lyric sequence about a character named Molina, Soto's childhood alter ego. Molina climbs chinaberry trees, draws bowls of soup out of hunger, and observes the migrating patterns of sparrows. The concluding section of poems is dramatic monologues told by a character named Manuel Zaragoza, who owns a cantina where strange events occur on a regular basis. In "The Vision," Manuel dreams of rising one morning "with the ability / to strum a guitar / and with a voice / To say, 'Hola, mi Novia.'" Zaragoza is a picaresque character who finds himself sleeping in a hammock among avocado trees, who knows "it is enough / To be where the smells / Of creatures / Braid like rope" and who keeps one eye on the moon in "The space / Between cork trees / Where the sun first appears."

In *Where Sparrows Work Hard* (1981), Soto continues to represent the harsh realities of the Chicano working-class communities in California. In these poems he hones his style of precise observation in clipped, enjambed lines.

Black Hair, Soto's fourth collection of poetry, marks a departure in several ways from his earlier collections. Here, Soto writes in a more relaxed manner about childhood. In the title poem, "Black Hair," he describes himself in the bleachers of a local playground where he admires Hector Moreno, "quick and hard with turned muscles." He writes, "I came here because I was Mexican, a stick / Of brown light in love with those / Who could do it." In "Oranges," one of Soto's best-known poems, he describes his first date at the age of twelve. He walks his girl "down the street, across / A used car lot and a line / Of newly planted trees" toward the drugstore. Inside, he offers to buy her a chocolate, only to discover that he is a nickel shy of the dime it costs. To make up the difference, he offers the woman behind the counter one of two oranges in his pocket. The concluding lines of the poem glow with his sense of accomplishment:

> I took my girl's hand
> In mine for two blocks,
> Then released it to let
> Her unwrap the chocolate.
> I peeled my orange
> That was so bright against
> The gray of December
> That, from some distance,
> Someone might have thought
> I was making a fire in my hands.

SOTO'S MEMOIRS

After the publication of *Black Hair*, Soto wrote four collections of memoirs: *Living up the Street: Narrative Recollections* (1985), *Small Faces* (1986), *Lesser Evils: Ten Quartets* (1988), and *A Summer Life* (1990). The first of these collections of autobiographical essays focuses on Soto's childhood experiences growing up in the neighborhoods and playgrounds of Fresno. These vignettes recall the meanness of Okie kids who referred to Soto and his siblings as "dirty Mexicans" and times he spent learning from his father how to hose the backyard or walking the streets looking for odd jobs in July.

In "Looking for Work," Soto writes that "we lived on an ordinary block of mostly working-class people: warehousemen, egg candlers, welders, mechanics, and a union plumber." Soto recalls watching *Leave it to Beaver* on television and thinking how different his own circumstances were: "Whereas the Beaver's family enjoyed dessert dishes at the table, our mom sent us outside, and more often than not I went into the alley to peek over the neighbor's fences and spy out fruit, apricot or peaches."

An essay in *Living up the Street*, "Baseball in April," became the title story of one of Soto's most popular books. In this essay, he describes the rejection he and his brother felt each year by not making the Little League team. He does eventually join a team with friends from school who played at Hobo Park near downtown Fresno. There he falls under the tutelage of a kindly coach named Manuel, "middle-aged, patient, and fatherly." Soto played catcher on a losing team, until one day "Manuel didn't show up with his duffle bag over his shoulder." In *Living up the Street*, Soto writes in a relaxed voice and captures the pathos of his Mexican-American boyhood. The book struck a popular chord with readers and won the 1985 American Book Award of the Before Columbus Foundation.

The three memoir collections that followed trace Soto's maturation into adolescence and adulthood, his marriage to his Japanese wife Carolyn, and the vicissitudes of their life together. In *Small Faces* he reflects: "Since we've been married—ten years—we've lived in twenty different places, two states, two countries, eight cities and five counties." This essay and the others in *Small Faces* chronicle the lives of friends and neighbors who make life an adventure for Soto, a man who looks "forward to what lies ahead, and . . . sorrow for what collects in memory."

Of Lesser Evils: Ten Quartets continues the writer's self-exploration and journey of discovery that began in *Living up the Street*. A review in *Booklist* (March 1988) notes that the "collection shows a writer who is becoming more reflective as he matures, making sober observations about women, marriage, pets, parenthood, teaching, writing, responsibility." With these three collections of essays, Soto effectively broadened his range as a writer and found in the essay a form congenial to personal reflection.

WRITING FOR YOUNG ADULTS

During the 1980s Soto published two collections of poetry and three collections of prose essays. He began the 1990s by publishing two more collections of his poetry, *A Fire in My Hands* (1990) and *Who Will Know Us?* (1990); a fourth autobiographical essay collection, *A Summer Life* (1990); and a collection of stories for young adults entitled *Baseball in April and Other Stories* (1990). With the writing of *Baseball in April and Other Stories*, Soto discovered a new audience for his writing. The eleven stories that compose the book portray the lives of Mexican-American young adults struggling with personal and social change. In *The New York Times Book Review*, Roberto Gonzalez Echevarria praised Soto: "Because he stays within the teenagers' universe . . . he manages to convey all the social change and stress without bathos or didacticism. In fact, his stories are moving, yet humorous and entertaining."

Baseball in April won the Beatty Award of the California Library Association. It also received recognition from the American Library Association as Best Book for Young Adults and sold more than eighty thousand copies. While Soto had developed a following for his poetry and autobiographical prose, he now was clearly tapping into a larger reading audience with this collection of baseball stories. Soto felt pride not only in the sales of this book but in the impact it had on young Mexican-American readers, from whom he began receiving fan letters. "I began to feel like I was doing something valuable," Soto says in *Ploughshares* (Spring 1985). "I thought I might be able to make readers and writers out of this group of kids." Soto's books for children and young adults represent a wide range of Hispanic experience and have sold over half a million copies.

Throughout his prolific writing career, Soto has maintained an abiding faith in the written word and taken special pride in his work as a poet. Even as he moved into the genres of memoir and children's writing, he continuously wrote and published collections of his poetry. In 1995 his *New and Selected Poems* appeared; it was nominated for the National Book Award and was a finalist for the Los Angeles Times Book Award. Since 1995 Soto has continued to publish in a variety of genres, including two

more collections of poems entitled *Junior College* (1997) and *A Natural Man* (1999), a play called *Novio Boy* (1997), and several more books written for children. Soto is considered one of the foremost interpreters of the experience of a generation of Mexican Americans, born in the 1950s, who have triumphed over discrimination and poverty. In his poem "Mexicans Begin Jogging," Soto expresses his attitude of defiance even as he is told to run from the border patrol by his factory boss, despite the fact that Soto is American:

What could I do but yell *vivas*
To baseball, milkshakes, and those sociologists
Who would clock me
As I jog into the next century
On the power of a great, silly grin.

[*See also* Nature Writing: Poetry.]

SELECTED WORKS

Entrance: 4 Chicano Poets; Leonard Adame, Luis Omar Salinas, Gary Soto, Ernesto Trejo (1975)
The Elements of San Joaquin (1977)
The Tale of Sunlight (1978)
Como Arbustos de Hiebla (1980)
Father Is a Pillow Tied to a Broom (1980)
Where Sparrows Work Hard (1981)
Black Hair (1985)
Living up the Street: Narrative Recollections (1985)
Small Faces (1986)
The Cat's Meow (1987)
Lesser Evils: Ten Quartets (1988)
Baseball in April and Other Stories (1990)
A Fire in My Hands: A Book of Poems (1990)
A Summer Life (1990)
Who Will Know Us? (1990)
The Bike (1991)
Home Course in Religion: New Poems (1991)
Neighborhood Odes (1992)
Pacific Crossing (1992)
The Skirt (1992)
Taking Sides (1992)
Local News (1993)
The Pool Party (1993)
Too Many Tamales (1993)
Crazy Weekend (1994)
Jesse (1994)
Novio Boy (1994)
Boys at Work (1995)
Canto familiar/Familiar Song (1995)
Chato's Kitchen (1995)
Everyday Seductions (1995)
New and Selected Poems (1995)

Summer on Wheels (1995)
Off and Running (1996)
The Old Man and His Door (1996)
Qué montón de tamales! (1996)
Snapshots from the Wedding (1996)
Super-Eight Movies: Poems (1996)
Buried Onions (1997)
Junior College: Poems (1997)
Novio Boy (1997)
Big Bushy Mustache (1998)
Chato and the Party Animals (1998)
Petty Crimes (1998)
Nerdlandia (1999)
A Natural Man (1999)
Jessie de la Cruz: Profile of a United Farm Worker (2000)
The Effect of Knut Hamsun on a Fresno Boy: Recollections and Short Essays (2000)
My Little Car (Mi Carrito) (2000)
Nickel and Dime (2000)
100 Parades (2000)
Poetry Lover (2001)
Scholastic Read (2001)
Fernie and Me (2002)
If the Shoe Fits (2002)
Amnesia in a Republican Country (2003)

FURTHER READING

De La Fuente, Patricia. "Ambiguity in the Poetry of Gary Soto." *Revista Chicano-Riquena* 11.2 (1983): 34–39.

De La Fuente, Patricia. "Entropy in the Poetry of Gary Soto: The Dialectics of Violence." *Discurso Literario: Revista de Temas Hispanicos* (Autumn 1987): 111–120.

Erben, Rudolf, and Ute Erben. "Popular Culture, Mass Media, and Chicano Identity in Gary Soto's *Living up the Street* and Small Faces." *Melus* (Fall 1991–1992): 43–52. An excellent treatment of Soto's depiction of Chicano identity conflict in the face of dominant, white, middle-class popular culture.

Manson, Michael Tomasek. "Poetry and Masculinity on the Anglo/Chicano Border: Gary Soto, Robert Frost, and Robert Hass." In *The Calvinist Roots of the Modern Era*, edited by Aliki Barnstone, Michael Tomasek Manson, and Carol J. Singley. Hanover, N.H., 1997. An insightful analysis of Soto's concern with heritage and community in resistance to the Puritan tradition of masculine self-reliance in American poetry.

Olivares, Julian. "The Streets of Gary Soto." *Latin American Literary Review* (January–June 1990): 32–49.

Rios, Alberto. "Chicano/Borderlands Literature and Poetry." In *Contemporary Latin American Culture: Unity and Diversity*, edited by C. Gail Guntermann. Tempe, Ariz., 1984.

Torres, Hector A. "Genre-Shifting, Political Discourse, and the Dialectics of Narrative Syntax in Gary Soto's *Living up the Street*." *Critica: A Journal of Critical Essays* (Spring 1988): 39–57.

JEAN STAFFORD

by Christopher Jane Corkery

West meets East in the work of Jean Stafford. In her characters and plots, privilege, too, meets deprivation, nature the world of human relations, and genius the world of the utterly ordinary. Jean Stafford was born into a family that had no inkling of her gifts and no aptitude for encouraging them. Born on 1 July 1915, Stafford lived with her family in Covina, California, until she was six. John Stafford, her father, who had inherited a large sum of money in his youth, took the family to San Diego when he tired of a walnut farming endeavor, and in the course of a year lost all of his money on the stock market. For the rest of her dependent years, Jean Stafford's family was to know poverty intimately, and she was to feel herself socially ostracized because of it.

Jean Stafford.
(© Oscar White/Corbis)

mother, Mary Ethel McKillop Stafford, kept the boardinghouse and was a genial woman, but seemed to have no idea of her youngest child's sense of displacement or of her genius, nor did she intervene in the instances when John Stafford was physically harsh with his children. Equally formative was Stafford's sense that she was alone among her siblings: two sisters, five and seven years older, and a brother, four years older. The two older girls made an early pair, living a separate life from their younger sister yet teasing her relentlessly and, on occasion, to Stafford's mind, brutally. Stafford maintained that her brother was the only family member with whom she was at ease. This brother, Dick, to whom she was close as a child, died in World War II. Her closeness to him gave substance to the primary relationship in her great novel *The Mountain Lion* (1947).

In her years at the University of Colorado, from which she received combined B.A. and M.A. degrees in 1936, after only four years, Stafford became friends with an older graduate-student group and entered a period of hedonistic living unusual in that town at that time. One from this group, Lucy McKee Cooke, whom Stafford would come to perceive as a completely negative influence, was smart, rich, and self-indulgent, and became Stafford's closest friend. At the time of Lucy's suicide by gunshot, Jean Stafford was standing in the same room with Lucy and her husband. Both the violence of that death and the wastefulness of it would influence many of Stafford's works. But Stafford was more angry at Lucy than mournful for her; Lucy's self-destruction mirrored too closely a wastefulness Jean Stafford feared in herself.

COLORADO

The Stafford family moved to Colorado in shame in 1921 after John Stafford's losses, settling first in Colorado Springs, but moving to Boulder in 1925; Stafford grew up in that city, where her mother would run a boardinghouse for university students, on whom Jean would wait at table. Her father rarely worked again at a paying job, spending most of his time in his basement, writing Western stories under the names of Jack Wonder and Ben Delight that rarely sold. John Stafford grew more and more eccentric in his middle age and gradually became mentally unstable. Jean Stafford's rage at her father for impoverishing their family was a formative emotion in her life, as were her always ambivalent feelings toward his idea of himself as a writer. Both scornful of it and yet conscious that his failure had something to do with her success and very existence as a writer, Stafford felt conflicted all her life at her sense of both his egotism and his isolation. Her

OBSTACLES

The tragedy of Jean Stafford's life may have been the disease of alcoholism, along with its concomitant depressions. Her father apparently had been a drinker for most of the years of his adult life. Her own drinking, begun in her college years, progressed quickly, and during the period of her depressing eight-year marriage to the poet Robert Lowell, became a serious threat to her health. Stafford met Lowell first at the University of Colorado's writers' conference in 1937. The difficulties of their marriage (out of which would come, much later, a story, "An Influx of Poets," that was to be a section of a partly written and unpublished novel, "A Parliament of Women") have been much written about, chiefly in terms of Lowell. For Stafford, however, her relationship with Lowell produced a signal event in her life that shaped her physically, and artistically, for the rest of her days. A passenger in Lowell's car when they were on an early date, she suffered massive facial injuries in 1938 when he crashed the vehicle into a brick wall in Cambridge, Massachusetts. Stafford, remarkably, never blamed Lowell for the accident, but suffered grievously as a result of it, enduring many painful surgeries throughout her life. The marriage was one of emotional disarray and conflict, yet also was undeniably formative in the development of both writers, who spent the first years of that marriage under the influence of Allen Tate and Caroline Gordon. They made lifelong friends in that time, too; for Stafford the most important of these was Peter Taylor.

BOSTON ADVENTURE

After her graduation from the University of Colorado in 1936, Stafford spent a fellowship year in Freiburg, Germany. The worst effect of this year was her probable contracting of gonorrhea, and the best, her acquisition of the German background for her first novel's main character. That novel is also much informed by Jean Stafford's perceptions of Boston's social world as seen in Robert Lowell's family. In *Boston Adventure* (1944) the realism of observed social detail is combined with a Proustian description of the minutiae of a young woman's consciousness and aesthetic development. Sonie Marburg comes from a poor island community, which may have been based on Nahant, a spit of land in Boston Harbor forty-five minutes from Boston, yet worlds away, in Stafford's conception of it. Chichester, Sonie's first home, has an unearthly and sometimes hellish quality. Sonie is the daughter of an émigré German cobbler who fancies himself superior to many, and of an unstable Russian mother who had thought she was coming to a better life in America and has found a worse one. A selfish, self-absorbed, and abandoning father and a neurotic mother

who is maniacally bitter over what she lacks and who is unconcerned with any aspect of Sonie's well-being are the useless guardians of Sonie's childhood.

Acting as parent to her mother and to her epileptic younger brother, Sonie works in the summers at a hotel where various ladies of Boston society come for the sea air. One of these women becomes Sonie's savior. In a fairy-tale manner, Miss Pride asks Sonie to come and stay with her in her Pinckney Street townhouse on Beacon Hill. It is to be a temporary arrangement, with Sonie assisting Miss Pride in typing her reminiscences; the stay lengthens, and though Sonie initially feels completely out of place, she realizes that this is the way not only out of her own depression and away from her mother's, but out of uncultured ignorance. Within the confines of an exclusive Boston salon, Sonie meets Dr. McAllister and his wife-to-be, Hopestill Mather, Miss Pride's niece. Boston society fascinates Sonie and she wants its pleasures, but she learns that it includes people, like Hopestill, as damaged as her mother. Hopestill, based largely on Lucy Cooke, functions as all that Sonie is not. Made bitter by the strictures of her own social environment, Hopestill dies of injuries caused by a deliberate fall from a horse to cause a miscarriage. Although the plausibility of much of the novel's action seems unlikely, and though its seriousness alternates—at times unexpectedly—with highly amusing satire, the novel is driven by the detailed attention Stafford gives to Sonie Marburg's perceptions: this author will pay heed to the development of a gifted young woman's mind, she lets us know, even if no one else will.

THE MOUNTAIN LION

Written during 1945 and 1946, chiefly while Stafford and Lowell were living in Damariscotta Mills, Maine, in a house Stafford had bought for them with her earnings from *Boston Adventure*, Stafford's second novel is markedly different from her first. Although Jean Stafford grew up long before the wave of feminism of the 1970s and though she distanced herself from that movement, *The Mountain Lion* describes with an acute feminist perception the childhood of Molly Fawcett, a girl in the western United States, such as Jean Stafford was. What Stafford embodies in this novel in an astonishingly vivid manner is the yearning of the lonely, intelligent child; the longing for belonging, which, in this case, never arrives; and the closeness to the world of nature born into one who is from the country—the comfort found there, and sometimes the defeat. What makes Stafford's story powerful is her ability to convey Molly's uncanny registering of so many things—gestures, tones, the rising or falling of affection contained in a phrase, the physical event of a grandfather's death, and the blossoming of a maturity that is confidently sexual. Molly's relationship with her brother Ralph, and its undoing as he moves away from her in his teenage years, is the central one of the novel. In some ways the story is tragic, yet the mountain lion that is its emblem is not hunted down and killed, but rather keeps her place close to the gods. Ralph, too, embodies Molly's other half, a half less sensitive—one that can make the crossing to adulthood and survive, though not without paying a great price for the experience. Stafford's style in *The Mountain Lion* is radically different than the more precious one of *Boston Adventure*. Although the focus in both is a young girl/young woman, the fog that surrounds Chichester and Beacon Hill in the first novel is replaced by the clear air of Colorado and by a prose that is plain and precise, yet capable of deeply moving description. Stafford considered her use of irony one of her chief virtues and felt that her principal model for it was Mark Twain; irony is at work in this novel in a way that allows the reader both distance and an uncanny, deep pity for its young protagonists.

THE STORIES

Some of Stafford's suffering as a result of her car accident with Lowell is described in her much-anthologized story "The Interior Castle." That work, constructs a splendidly isolated protagonist in whose mind we live while a surgeon delves deeply into her facial structure, and thus her identity, both past and future. The story is an exercise in the description of pain but also embodies the consciousness that we are alone in individual suffering and can survive it best by fully entering each room of our soul and psyche. As Jean Stafford understood the suffering of a child and of an artist manqué in *The Mountain Lion*, so too in her stories, the majority and best of which are in the Pulitzer Prize–winning *The Collected Stories of Jean Stafford* (1969). Here she depicts and lets us live the life of one who, often, is highlighted against her time in terms of what makes her or him feel apart from—not a part of—that world. In her arranging of *The Collected Stories*, Stafford chose geography as a defining line, placing stories based in Europe first in the book; these derive mostly from her experience as a young woman in Freiburg. The second section contains stories rooted in Boston "and other manifestations of the American scene"; these include "The Interior Castle" and "A Country Love Story," a harrowing story of a winter in Maine and a wife's sense of abandonment as her husband's depression deepens

and paranoia increases. The third section contains stories based in the West (one of these, the remarkable and tragic "A Summer's Day" [1947], was the first accepted of her *New Yorker* stories; another is one of Stafford's funniest stories of children and of Colorado, "The Healthiest Girl in Town"). The fourth section holds stories rooted in New York (among these, "Children Are Bored on Sundays" is another of her much-anthologized stories). Seven of Stafford's short stories won O. Henry Awards and many continue to appear in anthologies.

THE CATHERINE WHEEL

Stafford's third novel, *The Catherine Wheel* (1952), was written in less than a year, and during the time of her brief marriage (1950–1953) to Oliver Jensen, an editor-writer for *Life* magazine. *The Catherine Wheel* takes place in Maine and of its two main characters, the first, twelve-year-old Andrew Shipley, is like Molly Fawcett in the intensity of his character, his capacity for suffering, and his natural, and grievous, misunderstanding of adult realities. He suffers guilt at a secret desire to kill the older brother of his best friend, who is ignoring Andrew for the summer to focus on this brother, just returned from the navy. In his torment, Andrew is like the novel's other protagonist, his older cousin Catherine Congreve, who conceals a love affair with Andrew's father, and at whose house Andrew and his sisters summer while their parents are in Europe. What is remarkable about this story, as was true of *The Mountain Lion*, is Jean Stafford's evocative description of a child's mental wanderings and wondering, as well as of his anguish. Despite the somber themes and events, the novel is full, as are the other two, of lush description, both natural and social, and of the counterpoint of wit and humor that pervades most of Stafford's work.

Almost all of Stafford's major stories were first published in *The New Yorker*, where she had a strong and loving relationship with her editor, Katharine White. From 1959 to 1963 she was married to A. J. Liebling, a major figure in American journalism and a *New Yorker* writer of many years when Stafford met him. Liebling was Stafford's intellectual equal, and though the marriage had its flaws and ended with Liebling's death, it gave Stafford what friends deemed to be some of her happiest years.

Stafford produced a large amount of journalistic writing during the last decades of her life, including *The New Yorker*'s yearly "Christmas Books for Children" from 1969 to 1975. A sometime-recluse in her last years, and still an active drinker, Stafford—who continued to live in the house in Easthampton, Long Island, she had inherited from Liebling—suffered a stroke in November of 1976 and died on 26 March 1979. Although some critics regret what they viewed as the smallness of her *oeuvre*, the regret itself seems small-minded. Jean Stafford's three novels and masterful stories maintain their electric vivacity, and offer readers a provocative breadth of American experience. Her classical and subtle structures, her descriptions of landscape as an echo of individual loneliness, and her sense of the potency of human imagination (both author's and character's) for tragedy and for comedy, are richly satisfying and provocative.

[*See also* Lowell, Robert.]

SELECTED WORKS

Boston Adventure (1944)
The Mountain Lion (1947)
The Catherine Wheel (1952)
The Collected Stories of Jean Stafford (1969)

FURTHER READING

Goodman, Charlotte Margolis. *Jean Stafford: The Savage Heart.* Austin, Tex., 1991.

Hulbert, Ann. *The Interior Castle: The Art and Life of Jean Stafford.* Amherst, Mass., 1993.

WILLIAM STAFFORD

Robin Kemp

Born in Hutchinson, Kansas, in 1914, William Edgar Stafford moved frequently with his family during his childhood. The Great Depression bore heavily on the family; Stafford's biographer Judith Kitchen (1989) writes that young William's newspaper route was "at one point the family's only source of income" (p. 3). Despite these difficulties, the book-loving family remained close. Stafford completed high school and pursued further education at junior colleges, later working as a waiter to put himself through the University of Kansas.

Early on, Stafford developed a keen sense of right and wrong. His parents belonged to no particular organized religion, but the family attended church services from time to time. While at the University of Kansas, Stafford took action against racial segregation in the student cafeteria. When World War II broke out, he registered as a conscientious objector. Other poets who refused to fight on moral grounds were Robert Lowell and Brother Antoninus (William Everson), on whom Stafford would write extensively.

Stafford served his country in the Civilian Public Service from 1942 to 1946, doing backbreaking physical labor such as trail-blazing and firefighting in internment camp settings for $2.50 a month (in 2002 dollars, about 92 cents per day). What little time the conscientious objectors had left they filled with writing, art, music, and other creative endeavors. Stafford was encamped in Arkansas, Illinois, and California during the course of the conflict. Refusing to take part in what is now often referred to as "the Last Good War" put Stafford and other "C.O.s" at risk; Stafford wrote of an encounter with an angry mob in Arkansas. While in the work camps, he met his future wife, Dorothy Hope Frantz; the couple married in 1944. Stafford also worked for the Church of the Brethren and the interfaith group Church World Service as the war drew to a close.

During his four-year alternative service, Stafford could write for only an hour before work each morning, a seeming disadvantage that became a lifelong discipline. His record of his experiences in the camps became the core of his master's thesis at the University of Kansas, later published as *Down in My Heart* (1947). By the late 1940s, Stafford's work was appearing in popular magazines such as *The New Yorker*, *The Nation*, *Ladies' Home Journal*, and *Poetry*.

Stafford taught at Lewis and Clark College in Portland, Oregon, from 1948 until his retirement in 1980, taking time out to pursue a Ph.D. at the University of Iowa Writer's Workshop. Many great American writers of the twentieth century got their training from "the Workshop" during the time when Paul Engle was its director. While Stafford was there, along with fellow poets Donald Justice and W. D. Snodgrass, he had the chance to hear readings by Robert Penn Warren, Karl Shapiro, and Randall Jarrell. He received his doctorate in 1954.

His first book of poems did not appear until 1960, when Stafford was forty-six. *West of Your City* was put out by Newton Baird's and Robert Greenwood's Talisman Press, a small independent press that was active from about 1958 to 1969.

Harper and Row published Stafford's *Traveling through the Dark* two years later; it received the National Book Award in 1963. The title poem is perhaps Stafford's best-known piece; he worked on it at the Yaddo writers colony in 1956 and published it in *The Hudson Review*. It is a standard example in creative writing workshops. In this meditation on the thinness of the boundary between life and death, a driver stops to move a road-killed doe:

> Traveling through the dark I found a deer
> dead on the edge of the Wilson River road.
> It is usually best to roll them into the canyon;
> that road is narrow; to swerve might make more dead.
>
> By glow of the tail-light I stumbled in back of the car
> and stood by the heap, a doe, a recent killing;
> she had stiffened already, almost cold.
> I dragged her off; she was large in the belly.
>
> My fingers touching her side brought me the reason—
> her side was warm; her fawn lay there waiting,

alive, still, never to be born.
Beside that mountain road I hesitated.

The car aimed ahead its lower parking lights;
under the hood purred the steady engine.
I stood in the glare of the warm exhaust turning red;
around our group I could hear the wilderness listen.

I thought hard for us all—my only swerving—
then pushed her over the edge into the river.

Note how the car is portrayed as a "purring" living animal, whereas the doe is a "heap," a thing. Stafford plays this reversal of natural order against the emotional resonances of the dead deer and doomed fawn. He also creates tension by using casual diction within an eighteen-line heroic sonnet form; the effect is to contain emotions that could easily avalanche into pathos. Jonathan Holden sees the persona's voice as secondary to the poem's craftedness. Although it is in a sense "free verse," the ghost of meter moves through it: "the poem manages, while sounding conversational, to remind us of poetry, one reason being that the accentual prosody as deployed here by Stafford contains so many buried echoes of traditional prosody."

Even though this is Stafford's showpiece, widely taught and anthologized, other critics have been less than thrilled by it. Fellow Northwesterner Richard Hugo finds it somewhat inauthentic, griping in the *Kansas Quarterly*, "[S]top thinking hard for us all, Bill, and get that damned deer off the road before somebody kills himself." Ten years later, a group of poets savaged "Traveling Through the Dark" in the L = A = N = G = U = A = G = E journal *Hills* vol. 6–7 (1980): Bob Perleman dismisses it as "all persona in the worst sense" and "a typical neo-academic dirge for nature," while Ron Silliman calls it "didactic" and "smarmy," adding "all the language dissolves as you're reading it."

This difference of literary opinion has to do with both time and poetics. Perleman and Silliman are looking back at a nature poem steeped in primitivism (nostalgia for a less technological era) through the eyes of postmodernists, who see poetry and even language itself as a political construct. Hugo, a World War II veteran bombardier and technical writer for Boeing, necessarily views life and death, nature and technology, conquest and survival, in different terms from the pacifist poet's.

Stafford's antiwar poem "At the Bomb Testing Site" examines the dawn of the atomic age through the eyes of a lizard. Relying on a delicate balance of understatement and sense imagery (temperature, tension, sight, the lizard's grip on earth itself), Stafford neatly avoids the polemical trap that often awaits political poetry. The poem succeeds not because it tries to capture the apocalyptic moment of the bomb test, but because it remembers the preceding moment: life on this planet will never be the same. Portent drives the poem.

In his speech accepting the National Book Award in 1963, Stafford addressed the dual condition of the writer: that of creative ego balanced by respect for the art. The writer, he said, "has to be willing to stay lost until what he finds—or what finds him—has the validity that the instant (with him as its sole representative) can recognize—at that moment he is transported, not because he wants to be, but because he can't help it. Out of the wilderness of possibility comes a vine without a name, and his poem is growing with it." That statement encapsulates much of Stafford's belief about how writing, as a craft, is to be taught and learned.

In 1964, the Poetry Society of America chose Stafford for its Shelley Memorial Award; two years later, he would receive a Guggenheim Foundation grant. Meanwhile, as U.S. intervention in Vietnam and the antiwar movement heated up, Stafford's work found a new audience. Even so, Stafford was uncomfortable with the violent means that some antiwar protestors used; he was less interested in fighting back physically than in exercising peaceful resistance over the long term. In 1970, Stafford was named Library of Congress Consultant in Poetry, the equivalent then of today's U.S. poet laureate.

In 1993, the Poetry Society of America awarded Stafford its Robert Frost Medal. Later that year, he was injured in an automobile accident. He lived about two weeks, then died on 28 August 1993 at his home in Lake Oswego, Oregon. Today, Stafford's son and literary executor, Kim, an excellent poet and teacher in his own right, oversees the William Stafford Archives at Lewis and Clark College. Kim Stafford's analysis of his father's life and work, *Early Morning* (2002), is valuable not only for its biographical insights but also for its critical reading and background information about many of the poems.

[*See also* Nature Writing: Poetry.]

WORKS

Down in My Heart (1947)
West of Your City (1960)
Traveling through the Dark (1962)
Braided Apart (1976)

Stories That Could Be True: New and Collected Poems (1977)
Writing the Australian Crawl: Views on the Writer's Vocation
  (1978)
Segues: A Correspondence in Poetry (1983)
You Must Revise Your Life (1986)
An Oregon Message (1987)
Passwords (1991)
The Animal That Drank Up Sound (1992)
The Darkness around Us Is Deep: Selected Poems (1993)

FURTHER READING

Kitchen, Judith. *Understanding William Stafford*. Columbia, S.C., 1989. Excellent overall reference to Stafford's work, a good starting point for research.

Stafford, Kim. *Early Morning: Remembering My Father, William Stafford*. St. Paul, Minn., 2002. An insightful account of Stafford as husband, father, and poet, as told by his fellow poet, son, and literary executor.

WALLACE STEGNER

by Lani Wolf

Often called the "dean of Western writers," Wallace Stegner is remembered as a teacher, writer, historian, and conservationist who privileged the idea of place, particularly wilderness as place, in the formation of personal and national identity.

BIOGRAPHY

Born on 18 February 1909 on his grandfather's farm in Lake Mills, Iowa, Stegner spent the greatest part of his childhood in the last homestead frontier settlement in Saskatchewan, Canada, where his father tried unsuccessfully to farm. George Stegner then tried bootlegging, moving the family from place to place to avoid detection by the law. They stayed, for example, in Reno, Seattle, and Great Falls, Montana, before finally settling for a time in Salt Lake City. His family's mobility afforded Wallace the opportunity to

Wallace Stegner.
(Courtesy of the Library of Congress)

see still-pristine regions of the West—the Plains, the Rockies, the Sierras, the Great Basin, and the Colorado Plateau—and out of this grew his profound love of and awe for the land, his sensitivity to the relationship between humankind and the environment. As he said in *Wolf Willow: A History, a Story, and a Memory of the Last Plains Frontier* (1962), "I do not know who I am, but I know where I am from," and, "The world is very large, the sky even larger, and you are very small." We cannot understand ourselves, he felt, outside of the context of our surroundings.

Stegner finished high school in Salt Lake City and in 1930 graduated from the University of Utah. He received an M.A. degree (1932) and a Ph.D. degree (1935) from the University of Iowa, where he met his wife Mary, a fellow student, with whom he had one son, Page. In the following years he taught at Augustana University in Illinois and the

University of Utah, where he won a major literary prize for his first novel, *Remembering Laughter* (1937). Later, he taught at the University of Wisconsin, Harvard, and the Bread Loaf Writers' Conference in Vermont, where he met Robert Frost and Bernard De Voto, who were greatly to influence his thinking and writing. In 1946 he founded the Stanford University Creative Writing Program, serving as its director until his retirement in 1971. Many of his students have shared his connection with the land and strong sense of place, including Larry McMurtry in Texas, Wendell Berry in Kentucky, and Edward Abbey in New Mexico.

Throughout his long career, Stegner was the recipient of numerous awards. In the 1940s and 1950s, he became known as a short story writer, publishing seven stories in the *Best American Short Stories* series and five in the annual O. Henry volumes of prize-winning stories, including a first-prize winner, "The Blue-Winged Teal" (1954). His 1976 novel *The Spectator Bird* won the National Book Award, and his masterpiece, *Angle of Repose* (1971), the Pulitzer Prize. In 1992 he was given a PEN West Freedom to Write Award to mark his refusal of the National Medal for the Arts Award in protest of the politicization of the National Endowment for the Arts. He distinguished himself as a conservationist as well, serving for a time as a special assistant to Stewart Udall, President John F. Kennedy's secretary of the interior. Through his many years of work with the Sierra Club, the Wilderness Society, and the Committee for Green Foothills, he advanced the principle of wilderness preservation and the protection of lands in national parks. On 13 April 1993 Stegner—still a vibrant man—died in Santa Fe, New Mexico, at age eighty-four from injuries related to an auto accident.

FICTIONAL WORKS

Perhaps the greatest early influences on Stegner were his family's mobile lifestyle and the contrasting personalities of his father and mother. His father, a big, strong, violent man, conducted his life according to the acquisitive, exploitative, strike-it-rich mentality typical of western experience. His mother, on the other hand, espoused the virtues of steadiness, sacrifice, determination, family, social cooperation, and conservation. This conflict spurred his lifelong obsession with familial themes, his insistence on family as central to people's lives and a powerful shaping force on the land and institutions of the West and on western identity. In works such as *Mormon Country* (1942) and *The Gathering of Zion: The Story of the Mormon Trail* (1964), he shows that the West was settled by families rather than lone mountain men or miners. *The Big Rock Candy Mountain* (1943), his first popular and critical success, dramatizes his parents' incompatibility through the fictional characters Bo and Elsa Mason, wanderer versus nester, exploiter versus conserver; it also depicts his own search for stasis and meaning. The subject of both his last novel, *Crossing to Safety* (1987), and his masterpiece, *Angle of Repose*, is in large part marriage. Lyman Ward, the narrator, characterizes the relationship between his grandparents, Susan and Oliver Ward, thus: "What really interests me is how two such unlike particles clung together, and under what strains, rolling downhill into their future until they reach the angle of repose where I knew them. That is where the interest is. That's where the meaning will be if I find any."

His family's rootlessness and instability, the impermanence of any idea of "home," and the constant struggle, disillusionment, and relative poverty the family lived under contributed to his skepticism of the typical American Dream embraced by his father. In particular, he rejected its variation, the western myth of the lone cowboy, noble in his isolation and even violence, which he called a "national, indeed a human, fantasy." As the young boy Rusty in *Wolf Willow* learns after rescuing a cattle driver from a blizzard, the renegade folk hero typical of western myth is but an illusion:

> The Rusty Cullen who sat among them was a different boy, outside and inside, from the one who had set out with them two weeks before. He thought that he knew enough not to want to distinguish himself by heroic deeds: single-handed walks to the North Pole, incredible journeys, rescues, what not. Given his way, he did not think that he would ever want to do anything alone again, not in this country. Even

a trip to the privy was something a man might want to take in company.

WESTERN IDENTITY

As the critic Elliot West explains, Stegner finds meaning instead in our connection with the land and placedness within it, both physically and temporally. Westerners, he felt, do not have a "usable past," however. Authentic history and memory have been replaced with a timeless, mythical past that has made establishing temporal links difficult. In other words, westerners are historically "stuck" in an "amputated present," with no story to help them understand how things around them had come to be, or who in the world they were. He identified three reasons for this: the extremely varied western geography; diverse patterns of western settlement and the constancy of change; and the literary "fiction factories" that promoted a western mythology filled with antisocial wild men—cowboys and Indians; ranchers; land, cattle, and water barons; Wild Bill Cody; the Lone Ranger—depriving westerners of a sound literary tradition upon which to build. His "string of lariats" metaphor describes the remedy to the problem: like ropes tied from house to barn, tree to fence, to help people find their way in a blizzard, westerners need solid links between the past and present to move fully into the future. Individual and community links of history and memory are essential to a "possessed past," which integrates autobiography, family chronicle, geography, fiction, and history. Out of these stories a definition of "home" and a sound basis for identity will spring.

Stegner focused on these ideas in *Wolf Willow*, which chronicles his family's life in Saskatchewan, consciously stitching together history, memoir, and fiction in exploration of identity. *Angle of Repose*, too, is about the relations of man with his ancestors and descendants, built around patterns of conflict based on past versus present, Old West and New. To achieve this modulation between present and past, the narrator Lyman Ward examines the letters of his grandmother, Susan Ward, thereby coming to a greater understanding of his own tortured consciousness. History in this work is doubly important, for the principal characters, Susan and Oliver Ward, are based on real historical personages: Mary Hallock Foote, a popular illustrator and storyteller of the late-nineteenth-century West, and John Wesley Powell, a western land surveyor and early conservationist whom Stegner greatly admired and whose biography he wrote.

A writer of principle, Stegner felt that fiction was "dramatized belief," an arena for teaching ideas that he felt would better humankind—for example, the virtues of preservation and protection, the transformation of the rugged individualism of the West into partnership, tender caring for one another, and simple common decency between human beings. Often considered old-fashioned and more in tune with nineteenth-century writers than those of his own era, he was outside contemporary American fiction in that he focused on the concerns of families, friendship, and the humane qualities of characters rather than the despair, social criticism, and mythical nostalgia typical of his time. In response to criticism that *Angle of Repose* was very traditional and lacking in originality, Stegner said,

> I don't really aspire to write a novel which can be read backwards as well as forward, which turns chronology on its head and has no continuity and no narrative, which in effect tries to create a novel by throwing all the pieces in the bag and shaking the bag. . . . If you have to do *that* to be original, then I don't care about being original.

His writing style reflects the belief in simple sentence structure and diction; a plain style to highlight the story rather than the teller; and an emphasis on the details of ordinary places and lives in an effort to turn dailiness into transcendence.

LITERARY INFLUENCES

Stegner's literary influences are varied and many. Like Mark Twain, Stegner was a "disillusioned romantic," who in often bleak work expressed disappointment with humanity's foibles: self-centeredness, self-deceptions, and rapacious use of the land. Like Henry James, Stegner emphasized nuance of thought and emotion rather than plot in fictions that are less a complication resolved than a situation revealed internally. And both are masters of point of view, Stegner particularly so in *Angle of Repose*. In his fiction workshops Stegner often used the image of the garden hose, explaining, "you get more force with a nozzle." From Joseph Conrad he learned how to use a first-person narrator who could syncopate and unify the past and present, coming to understand the present through the past. With William Faulkner, he understood the importance of history, time, and the problematic, simultaneous existence of past and present. Like Anton Chekhov, his focus was on theme and the moral revelation of character. His most significant influence, however, was his mentor and longtime friend, Robert Frost. Both men took as their subject humankind's relationship to nature, which they saw as beautiful and mysterious, but also unforgiving

and threatening, reflecting the sinister depths of human nature. As realists, both believed in the essential hardness of life, its "coldness at the root," and in their writing sought a "momentary stay" against modernist confusion and despair. Indeed, Stegner seemed to pay conscious tribute to Frost by deriving the titles of two novels from his poetry, *Fire and Ice* (1941) and *Crossing to Safety*.

NONFICTIONAL WORKS

Historian and conservationist as well as fiction writer, Stegner wrote many nonfiction books, articles, and essays. In the essays of *One Nation* (1945), Stegner proved himself ahead of his time in terms of race relations, recognizing the "wall down the middle of America," white and Protestant on one side and all else on the other, deeming this one of America's biggest challenges. His biography, *Beyond the Hundredth Meridian: John Wesley Powell and the Second Opening of the West* (1954), advanced the idea that the West is not a New Eden, that its aridity will limit expansion. In often impassioned writing, Stegner brought attention to the environmental and human damage caused by blind adherence to frontier mythology, in many ways initiating the concept of the "ecological West." He honored Powell as a democrat, public servant, and searcher for useful knowledge who cared for the welfare of his country and its ordinary citizens rather than fame or reward. *Angle of Repose* fictionalizes the life of Powell through Oliver Ward, a participant in the Geological Survey of the 1870s who realizes the impossibility of bringing water to the high desert, mirroring Powell's groundbreaking but largely ignored *Report on the Arid Regions of the United States* (1878).

His biography of Bernard DeVoto, *The Uneasy Chair* (1974), memorializes the man who urged Stegner to write about environmental concerns, marking the turning point that made Stegner an activist; by urging Stegner, De Voto in large part shaped the body of Stegner's writing. With De Voto, Stegner pressed for the preservation of public lands and for constant public vigilance on behalf of their protection, believing that "we may love a place but still be dangerous to it." His famous "Wilderness Letter" (1960) set forth the "wilderness idea," the concept that wild places are not just physical but also spiritual sanctuaries necessary to humankind's mental and emotional health and psychic wholeness. "We need wilderness preserved," he wrote, "because it was the challenge against which our character as a people was formed. The reminder and reassurance that it is still there is good for our spiritual health, even if we never once in ten years set foot in it.

[It is] important simply because it is there—important, that is, simply as idea." Similarly, "We simply need that wild country available to us, even if we never do more than drive to its edge and look in. For it can be a means of reassuring ourselves of our sanity as creatures, a part of the geography of hope."

Without the land we are nothing, Stegner felt, a people without a future. He urged us to fulfill our potential as a "good animal," a familial and relative animal who will not destroy our habitat, who will live humbly with courtesy and restraint, who will renew ourselves in the wilderness, our greatest teacher.

[*See also* Nature Writing: Prose *and* Western Fiction.]

SELECTED WORKS

Remembering Laughter (1937)
The Potter's House (1938)
On a Darkling Plain (1940)
Fire and Ice (1941)
Mormon Country (1942)
The Big Rock Candy Mountain (1943)
One Nation (1945)
Second Growth (1947)
The Preacher and the Slave (1950)
The Women on the Wall (1950)
Beyond the Hundredth Meridian: John Wesley Powell and the Second Opening of the West (1954)
The City of the Living and Other Stories (1956)
A Shooting Star (1961)
Wolf Willow: A History, a Story, and a Memory of the Last Plains Frontier (1962)
The Gathering of Zion: The Story of the Mormon Trail (1964)
All the Little Live Things (1967)
The Sound of Mountain Water (1969)
Angle of Repose (1971)
The Uneasy Chair: A Biography of Bernard DeVoto (1974)

The Letters of Bernard DeVoto (1975)
The Spectator Bird (1976)
Recapitulation (1979)
American Places (1981)
One Way to Spell Man (1982)
The American West as Living Space (1987)
Crossing to Safety (1987)
Collected Stories of Wallace Stegner (1990)
Where the Bluebird Sings to the Lemonade Springs (1992)
Marking the Sparrow's Fall: The Making of the American West (1998)

FURTHER READING

Benson, Jackson J. *Down by the Lemonade Springs: Essays on Wallace Stegner*. Reno, Nev., 1995. Collection of essays by Benson on Stegner's oeuvre, dealing with, for example, his view of western identity, writing philosophy, environmentalism, and literary influences.

Hepworth, James R. *Stealing Glances: Three Interviews with Wallace Stegner*. Albuquerque, N.Mex., 1998. Collection of in-depth essays appropriate for those who seek a detailed view of Stegner's perspective.

Meine, Curt. *Wallace Stegner and the Continental Vision: Essays on Literature, History, and Landscape*. Washington, D.C., 1997. Excellent collection of essays addressing Stegner's career as writer, historian, and conservationist.

Rankin, Charles E. *Wallace Stegner: Man and Writer*. Albuquerque, N.Mex., 1996. Excellent collection of essays looking at Stegner's life and works from a variety of perspectives.

Stegner, Page, and Mary Stegner, eds. *The Geography of Hope: A Tribute to Wallace Stegner*. San Francisco, 1996. A collection in memoriam consisting of personal essays on Stegner as a man, a teacher, and a writer, edited by his son and wife.

GERTRUDE STEIN

by Dina Ripsman Eylon

Gertrude Stein, the expatriate American avant-garde author, poet, and playwright, was born in Allegheny, Pennsylvania, on 3 February 1874. During her lifetime she was known as the "American eccentric in Paris" who collected and supported postmodernist and cubist art. Although a prolific writer and speaker, her literary contribution was marginalized and seldom recognized. At the age of sixty, astounding her friends and foes alike, she achieved international acclaim when her book, *The Autobiography of Alice B. Toklas* (1933), became a sensational bestseller. Scholars later considered Stein one of the most influential writers of the twentieth century, often dubbed as "the Mother of Modernism." Stein's influence on a younger generation of writers like Ernest Hemingway, Sherwood Anderson, and Roger Wright has been underestimated and rarely explored. Known as "always a writer's writer," she continues to inspire original writing, testing and challenging traditional literary and linguistic forms.

Exceptionally versatile and innovative, Stein's writings attempt to convey cubist perspective in literary form. Her linguistic and stylistic experiments permeate into almost any known literary genre. She developed a personal relationship with parts of speech, phonetics, morphology, grammatical punctuation, and the innate meanings of plain English words. Furthermore, "sentences not only words but sentences and always sentences have been Gertrude Stein's life long passion." Driven by a desire to express herself in a new way, to break away from the literature of the nineteenth century, similarly to the newly forming visual art that was being created in Paris at the beginning of the twentieth century, she produced writings that were frequently unintelligible and "difficult." Consequently, many of her writings remained

Gertrude Stein, 1935.
*(Photograph by Carl Van Vechten.
Courtesy of the Library of Congress)*

unpublished at the time of her death in 1946 and some had to be self-published with the help of Alice B. Toklas, who established a small press, Plain Edition, specifically for that purpose.

During her early childhood Gertrude's parents, Daniel and Amelia (Keyser) Stein and their five children moved throughout Europe, subsequently settling in Oakland, California, in 1880. By the time Stein turned seventeen, she had lost both parents and had moved to San Francisco to live with her oldest brother, Michael. In 1892 Gertrude and her sister Bertha moved to Baltimore to live with their maternal aunt. A year later, following in the footsteps of her brother Leo, she entered the Harvard Annex (Radcliffe College) and studied under Hugo Münsterberg, William Vaughn Moody, and William James, her mentor and greatest influence. In 1896 Stein and Leon Solomons published the "Normal Motor Automatism" in *Psychological Review*. While at Radcliffe she failed her Latin exam and was refused her degree, which was ultimately awarded to her in 1898. On the advice of William James, she entered the Johns Hopkins School of Medicine in 1897, but failed four courses and did not receive a degree.

In 1903, Gertrude joined Leo in Paris, at 27 rue de Fleurus, and started working on the early drafts of *The Making of Americans: Being a History of a Family's Progress* (1925) and *Things As They Are: A Novel in Three Parts* (1950). Fascinated by Charles Loeser's collection of Cézanne's paintings in Florence, the Steins began collecting postimpressionist art works. In 1905 they purchased Henri Matisse's *La Femme au Chapeau* (1904–1905) and met Pablo Picasso, Gertrude's most admired friend and artist, who painted her illustrious portrait. In 1909 Stein published her first book, *Three Lives: Stories of the Good Anna, Melanctha, and the Gentle Lena*, and Alice B. Toklas, whom she had met in 1907, moved in with her. Their lesbian relationship lasted for thirty-nine years, until Stein's death. The couple kept a hectic literary and artistic salon in their apartment, frequented by prominent figures such as Matisse, Picasso, Guillaume Apollinaire, Georges Braque, Sherwood Anderson, Carl Van Vechten, and Ernest Hemingway. Remarkably, Stein and Toklas survived the two world wars, and the two decades between them were Stein's most productive and prolific years. (Altogether, according to the Yale Catalogue, Stein wrote 571 works between 1903 and 1946.) With the publication of *The Autobiography of Alice B. Toklas* in 1933, Stein attained celebrity status. In the mid-1930s Stein toured and lectured throughout England and the United States, promoting her writings and her modernist worldview.

EARLY WORKS

According to scholar Leon Katz (1963), Stein's first novella, *Q.E.D.*—completed in 1903 but not published during her lifetime—describes her love affair with May Bookstaver, a fellow student at the Johns Hopkins School of Medicine. After a short liaison, May Bookstaver favored another young woman over Stein. The love letters between Stein and Bookstaver were confiscated and destroyed by Alice B. Toklas. The manuscript itself—of which Toklas was unaware until 1932, when Stein uncovered it in a drawer full of unpublished manuscripts—was published posthumously as *Things As They Are* (1950) and in *Fernhurst, Q.E.D., and Other Early Writings* (1971). *Q.E.D.* as a work of lesbian fiction depicts a love lost triangle between three young women. Critics were eager to identify its characters with Stein and her former friends at the John Hopkins School of Medicine. Adele, "an unconventional woman" identified as Gertrude, is drawn to Helen Thomas, another middle-class, college-bred woman identified as May Bookstaver. Thereafter, an intense emotional and physical relationship develops between the two only to be disrupted by the third woman, Sophie Neathe. From a literary point of view, *Q.E.D.*, apart from its lesbian content, is Stein's "most conventional work. It has a plot, characters, a narrator, a beginning, a middle and an end" (*Three Lives*, 201).

Unsuccessful in her efforts to reconcile with Bookstaver, by 1903 Stein had decided to stay in Paris and moved in with her brother Leo. In Paris, Stein found a safe haven to write and cultivate her unique style. The following years were eventful and prolific as she was introduced to modern art and its founders. Leo and Gertrude and their oldest brother Michael began to purchase paintings by Paul Cézanne, Henri Matisse, Pablo Picasso, and other modernist artists.

In 1905, Stein commenced working on *Three Lives* (1909). In "A Transatlantic Interview 1946," she explained the means by which Gustave Flaubert's *Trois contes* (1877) and Paul Cézanne's painting, *La Femme au Chapeau*, influenced her work: "Cézanne conceived the idea that in composition one thing was important as the whole . . . it impressed me so much that I began to write *Three Lives* under this influence. . . . I was obsessed by this idea of composition, and the Negro story ["Melanctha" in *Three Lives*] was a quintessence of it." Stein wrote that "Melanctha," the second story in the book, "was the first step away from the nineteenth century and into the twentieth century in literature. However, the *Washington Herald* (12 December 1909) disagreed by calling the work a "peculiar exposition of the art of character delineation" and suggested that "she should attempt the same things with minds of a higher caliber" to achieve a more entertaining result. The *Kansas City Star* (18 December 1909) felt that the book was intended "for a strictly limited audience," requiring a slow pace of reading in order to grasp its ideas. Positively, other reviewers labeled it "a futurist novel" while almost unanimously sensing a need to unravel "the blur" it created.

Scrutiny for her work came also from her brother Leo, who described her fascination with language and form as "an abomination." Leo, who believed he was the Stein family's genius, dominated the discussions during their Saturday salons and would not support his sister's literary endeavors. Only in 1913, after he had left their apartment and moved to Italy, did Gertrude regain her self-confidence and, with the encouragement of her companion, Toklas, reestablish her literary career. Their apartment became "a literary Mecca," where Stein entertained and befriended young American writers such as Sherwood Anderson, Ernest Hemingway, Edith Sitwell, F. Scott Fitzgerald, Natalie Clifford Barney, and H.D. (Hilda Doolittle). Concurrently, Stein met the composer Virgil Thomson, who was instrumental in writing the music to her operas and staging them in England and the United States.

Stein and Toklas settled into a domesticity wherein Stein was the genius-writer, philosophizing with the male visitors in their sitting room, and Toklas assumed the role of the secretary, literary aide, and agent who entertained the wives of the male visitors in the kitchen. Bobby Ellen Kimbel has noted that Stein's writing "became more joyous, more rooted in the domestic scene which she experienced daily, and more openly erotic, as in 'Lifting Belly.'" Sometime before 1912 Stein wrote a portrait of Alice B. Toklas entitled "Ada." Stylistically, it follows Richard Bridgman's classification of Stein's early works in *Gertrude Stein in Pieces* (1970): "a simplified, abstract and repeated vocabulary, and utilizing participles, gerunds and impersonal pronouns moving with maddening deliberateness through diagrammatic sentences." Textually, the portrait depicts Ada, a young woman who lost her mother and lives with her father but later leaves home to find joy and happiness elsewhere, much like Alice herself. Upon examining the original manuscript, Bridgman claimed that Toklas "composed the major part of her first, brief autobiography." The piece ends with a confirmation of the union between Stein and Toklas, as their separate, individual entities become one: "Trembling was all living, living was all loving, some one was then the other one."

THE MAKING OF AMERICANS

From 1903 to 1911, Stein was intermittently engaged in the writing of her thousand-page book, *The Making of Americans: Being a History of a Family's Progress*, which was not published until 1925. In Stein's own admission, the book is about "the old people in a new world, the new people made out of the old," in a manner she confesses to have known very well: "We had a mother and a father and I tell all about that in *The Making of Americans* which is the History of our family...." In *The Autobiography of Alice B. Toklas*, Stein acknowledges "Henry James as her only forerunner" and alludes to *The Making of Americans* as a "monumental work which was the beginning, really the beginning, of modern writing."

Portrayed as the saga of three generations of the Hersland and the Dehning families, the book employs a number of Stein's early techniques of language and style and features a temporal form later known as continuous present. In the chapter "David Hersland," one finds a lengthy, repetitive, and superfluous rhetoric, "somewhat akin to the ultramodern 'stream of consciousness' school":

> Some are having a delicate feeling and they are ones that can be thinking and they are ones sometimes delightfully telling something, beautifully telling something, touchingly telling something, quaintly telling something, freshly telling something and they are ones dully telling something and flatly telling something and harshly telling something and telling and telling and not telling anything and something so that someone can be saying certainly that one was thinking that other one was not knowing anything and certainly the one was knowing that that one was certain that the one was not knowing anything.

> *(The Making of Americans, 1925, p. 790)*

Short of calling it a "linguistic murder," "a complete esthetic miscalculation," and "a tireless and inert repetitiveness which becomes as stupefying as it is unintelligible," as Conrad Aiken of *The New Republic* did in 1934, the *Literary Digest* in 1926 described the saga as "diffuse accounts of the mental and soul growth of each person, and digressions to include every individual that any one of them ever met. 'But now to make again a beginning' is a constantly recurring phrase throughout the first hundred pages; but one can never feel sure that a start has actually been made."

Yet not all reviews were as abrasive and unfavorable. Katherine Anne Porter of the *New York Herald-Tribune Books* noted in 1927, "It precedes *Ulysses* [by James Joyce] and *Remembrance of Things Past* [by Marcel Proust]." She raves about Stein's ability "to get at the roots of existing life, to create fresh life from them, give her words a stark liquid flowingness, like the murmur of the blood."

Thereafter, Stein began to be obsessed with words of "equal value." In her 1946 interview she said, "I was not interested in making the people real but in the essence or, as a painter would call it, value.... At this time I threw away punctuation.... it threw away this balance that I was trying to get." She concluded that words lost their meanings towards the end of the nineteenth century. Her mission, hence, was to "recapture" their meaning and value and "act within" each word. She also believed that Americans rearranged the English language by renewing its "word structure." This and the "idea of portraiture" occupied her work during what she called her "middle period," which began just after she finished writing *The Making of Americans* in 1911 and included *Tender Buttons* (1914), its climax.

FOUR SAINTS IN THREE ACTS
AND OTHER PLAYS

During World War I, Stein did not write much because of her relocation from Paris. After the war she found interest in the "play form" and wrote *Geography and Plays* (1922). Stein authored forty-seven plays between 1913 and 1920 and forty-three plays between 1920 and 1933. (Nineteen were produced in theaters in England and the United States.) *Four Saints in Three Acts* (1934), an opera composed by Virgil Thomson, ended this period of copious playwrighting. In her plays and skits,

Stein continued to experiment with words and forms. Plot, characters, and conventional dialogue are virtually nonexistent in her plays, which comprise phrases and linguistic structures cited by different actors, coming and going. The plays try to convey the "quality" of an "abstract painting," ignoring any conventional forms of dramatization. In *Gertrude Stein* (1961), Frederick J. Hoffman observes, "Stein adapts the play structure to her needs and to her conception of art. She said several times that there was something distressing about the pace of ordinary drama." Act 4 in *Ladies Voices* (in *Geography and Plays*) reads:

> What are ladies voices.
> Do you mean to believe me.
> Have you caught the sun.
> Dear me have you caught the sun.

Stein associated playwriting with landscapes. In her lecture "Plays," she comments, "I felt that if a play was exactly like a landscape then there would be no difficulty about the emotion of the person looking on at the play being behind or ahead of the play because the landscape does not have to make acquaintance." *Four Saints in Three Acts* became Stein's most elaborate and probably the most successful of her "play form" works. First performed in Hartford, Connecticut, in 1934, it featured an entirely African-American cast that was chosen for their "beauty of voice, clarity of enunciation, and fine carriage." Evidently, it became a smash. According to Joseph Wood Krutch of *The Nation*, "*Four Saints in Three Acts* is a success because all its elements—the dialogue, the music, the pantomime, and the sparkling cellophane *décor*—go so well with one another while remaining totally irrelevant to life, logic, or common sense." Krutch's review corresponded completely with the way Stein envisioned the opera in "Plays": "I think it did almost what I wanted, it made a landscape and the movement in it was like a movement in and out with which anybody looking on can keep in time. I also wanted it to have the movement of nuns very busy and in continuous movement but placid as a landscape."

THE AUTOBIOGRAPHY OF ALICE B. TOKLAS

After exhausting the dramatic form, Stein became involved again with the "form of narration." While working on *The Autobiography of Alice B. Toklas*, she "made a rather interesting discovery" that "other people's words are quite different from one's own, and that they can not be the result of your internal troubles as a writer." In writing *The Autobiography*, she explains, "I had recreated the point of view of somebody else. Therefore the words ran with a certain smoothness." As part of her narrative phase, she includes *Paris, France* (1940), *Wars I Have Seen* (1945), and *Everybody's Autobiography* (1937). The problem of narration is tightly coupled to the sense of time; great narrations, in her opinion, are devoid of historical time. In *Wars I Have Seen* she describes what she saw happening under her eyes "without a great sense of time." Her objective was to depict "an existence suspended in time." At the time of her interview with Robert Bartlett Haas (1973), six months before her death, she was still pondering the problem of time in the form of narration.

Over the years friends urged Stein to write about her life. She always said that Toklas is the one who ought to write it, as she was a witness to it all. However, as the years went by and Toklas showed no interest, Stein decided to write an autobiography using the narrative voice of Toklas. It was written at their summer residence in Bilignin, France, during a short period of six weeks. William Bradley, a literary agent who lived in Paris and could never find a commercial outlet for Stein's work, suddenly realized *The Autobiography*'s potential as a trade book. Additionally, he managed to sell serial rights to the *Atlantic Monthly*, a successful American literary magazine. The book turned into an overnight sensation. The American public became fascinated with Stein's colorful persona, with what she called the Lost Generation, and with the era of cubism and modernism. The short anecdotes, telling all in their legendarylike style, captured the imagination of a public infatuated with celebrities. Toklas's narrative voice allowed Stein to seize the center of the stage. She presented herself as a child prodigy, the favorite student of William James, the pioneer of the modernist literary genre, the one who discovered Picasso and many other artists in the art world of Paris, just to name a few.

Aside from Stein and Toklas, another major character in *The Autobiography* is the famous Spanish artist Pablo Picasso. The reader learns about Picasso's financial hardship and artistic struggle during the early period of his career. Stein recalls minute details and anecdotes about Picasso; his circle of friends; and even his mistress, Fernande Olivier. Ironically, Picasso had no command of the English language, and therefore could not read *The Autobiography*. In *Everybody's Autobiography* (1937), Stein recalls an evening she and Alice spent with Picasso and his wife, Olga, after they returned to Paris. Stein offered to read from *The Autobiography*, which by then was quite popular. As she translated passages from the book into colloquial French, Picasso, listening attentively, corrected some details, but his wife got up and left. Apparently, Olga was offended by the frequent mentioning of Fernande Olivier, Picasso's former lover. For two years afterwards, Stein did not see Picasso again. They resumed their friendship only after Picasso separated from Olga. The immense success of the book brought in a large income. For the first time, at the age of sixty, Stein earned substantial money. *The Autobiography* was soon translated into French by her friend Bernard Faÿ, bringing her acclaim in France. Fame and money made her a celebrity. She was invited everywhere as she recalled later in *Everybody's Autobiography*, the sequel autobiography: "Everybody invited me to meet somebody, and I went. I always will go anywhere once and I rather liked doing what I had never done before, going everywhere. It was pleasant being a lion, and meeting the people who make it pleasant for you to be a lion."

Shortly afterward, in February 1935, the "Testimony against Gertrude Stein" was published in *Transition*. This was a collection of responses to *The Autobiography* written by the actual artists portrayed in her anecdotes. Fuming with anger, they refuted her interpretation of the art world of Paris. *Transition*'s editor, Eugene Jolas wrote:

> These documents invalidate the claim of the Toklas-Stein memorial that Miss Stein was in any way concerned with the shaping of the epoch she attempts to describe. There is unanimity of opinion that she had no understanding of what really was happening around her, that the mutation of ideas beneath the surface of the more obvious contacts and clashes of personalities during that period escaped her entirely. Her participation in the genesis and development of such movements as Fauvism, Cubism, Surrealism, Transition [sic] etc. was never ideologically intimate and, as M. Matisse states, she has presented the epoch "without taste and without relation to reality."

Eugene Jolas was joined by Henri Matisse, Tristan Tzara, Georges Braque, André Salmon, and Leo Stein, Gertrude's brother, who was left out altogether from *The Autobiography*.

EXEGETICAL AND CRITICAL WRITINGS

Stein published her philosophy of writing and explained her literary techniques in quite a number of volumes and essays: *Descriptions of Literature* (1926), *Composition As Explanation* (1926), *How to Write* (1931), *Narration: Four Lectures* (1935), and *What Are Masterpieces and Why Are There So Few of Them* (1935). According to Shari Benstock and other feminist scholars, Stein's language

becomes tangible "if one is familiar with an essentially lesbian code." Such critics maintain that the modernist patriarchy can only decipher heterosexual texts written by heterosexual writers. Therefore, patriarchal critics misconstrued Stein's lesbian texts. In *Women of the Left Bank: Paris, 1900–1940* (1986), Benstock writes, "Stein's position as an alienated, misunderstood writer was due not only to her status as a woman writer in a highly patriarchal environment but also to her status as a *lesbian* writer." Stein's constant quest to re-create literature was propelled by her social setting and her lesbianism. Many critics see Alice Toklas's arrival in Stein's life as a catalyst, unleashing her hidden sexuality into her writings: "In accepting Alice's love, Stein learned a new language (or rather rediscovered a language she had known in childhood) and exchanged monologue for dialogue, preaching for joking. Her writing suddenly ceased imitating the patriarchy" (Benstock, 1986, 163).

Although it was obvious to all, Stein never admitted her lesbianism publicly. In an essay in *The Critical Response to Gertrude Stein* (1992), Catharine R. Stimpson discusses the lesbian lie ("No lesbians here") as part of an "unresolved problem" in feminist theory and as a source for groundbreaking style and original language. This unresolved predicament of denying lesbianism outwardly and having to live with it inwardly forced Stein to veil and disguise her sexual orientation in "an impenetrable" language, style, and to some degree, subject matter. If Stein ever wanted to be published, she had to acquire a mechanism of opaque writing, as it was not feasible to discuss homosexuality openly at the beginning of the twentieth century. This theory may also explain Stein's preoccupation with the equal value of words and equal parts of the whole. There was no right or wrong; there was no one way of loving. To justify her lesbian love as equal to heterosexual love in any respect, Stein had to restructure equality in words and meanings. She needed to re-create literature so that it would encompass and embrace a multiplicity of language and culture, manifested splendidly in her lyrical expression of lesbian sexuality, *Lifting Belly*. Furthermore, such critics argue, Alice's influence on Stein's writing is grossly underrated. In Alice, Stein found a critical reader, her other half, who could support and nurture her writing. Alice's role as a wife, lover, secretary, and housekeeper released Stein from all domestic responsibilities and enabled her to concentrate on her creative energy.

In her search for equal words and meanings, Stein "discovered inherent inequalities in linguistic principles that mirrored similar inequalities in the world in which she lived" (Benstock 1986, 186). These inequalities stem from the prevailing patriarchy in language and society. In her most appropriately titled poem, *Patriarchal Poetry*, published posthumously, she writes, "Patriarchal poetry makes no mistake makes no mistake in estimating the value to be placed upon the best and most arranged of considerations. . . . At a chance at a chance encounter it can be very well as appointed as appointed not only considerately but as it is use."

Based on Stein's "Arthur A Grammar," Benstock argues that Stein's linguistic pursuit centers on the relationship between the signifier and signified, the sum of which equals the term "sign." Stein, accordingly, saw these linguistic elements as equal, but her predecessors and contemporaries alike understood the signifier (the female element) as inferior and unreliable. Unlike her modernist contemporaries, she adopted this unstable signifier as her device to upend accepted patriarchal norms in the avant-garde literary movement of the twentieth century. Even when she apparently used the patriarchal meaning of signifier and signified, she overturned them completely. For instance, she used the word "Caesars" to signify female body parts in lesbian eroticism and "cows" to imply orgasms. ("Cows are very nice. They are between legs.") Indeed, if she were not to be published by the literary patriarchs of her time, nor to be included in their midst, she would rather re-create her own language away from patriarchy, "insisting not only that she was one of them, but that she had already outdone (and redone) their artistic efforts" (Benstock, 1986, 187).

Scholars, who comprehend Stein's language as closely related to her sexual orientation, can justify the fact that for more than sixty years the bulk of Stein's writings was elusive. Stein, they are now beginning to realize, used language as "a smoke screen," hiding "behind the language of her fictions, as she hid behind the 'male' persona she created for herself in her lesbian marriage" to Toklas (Benstock, 1986, 188). Moreover, she associated her genius with the predominant patriarchal genius of her male peers: "Pablo & Matisse have a maleness that belongs to genius. *Moi aussi* [me too], perhaps." This linguistic maleness pervaded her writings, particularly those she wrote after her union with Toklas. Nevertheless, despite what these scholars suggested, Stein vehemently denied any correlation between her sexual orientation and the ingenuity of her writings.

STEIN'S EXPATRIATION

After the success of *The Autobiography*, Stein was urged by her literary agent, William Bradley, to do a lecture tour in the United States. An American lecture tour could promote a sequel autobiography and boost Stein's popularity in America. Stein was getting increasingly curious about the country she had left thirty-one years earlier but decided to travel to America only after months of deliberations: "Before I came, before I began to come, while I was still in France, I wrote about meditating upon what would come, what would happen when I came." On 17 October 1934, Stein and Toklas embarked on the S.S. *Champlain* and arrived in New York Harbor seven days later. In *Everybody's Autobiography*, her account of the tour, Stein recounts that she would not have returned to America until she was in a position to become "a real lion a real celebrity." Amazingly, the tour was a hit: "Reporters thronged the ship, interviewers and photographers followed her everywhere, and her fans packed auditoriums to hear her talk."

In "I Came and Here I Am," Stein describes the manner in which everything in America appeared "strange," from "the shapes of the trucks" and the "little lights on top of the taxis" to the man-built roads and highways. It was also the first time Stein and Toklas saw the "high buildings," which made Toklas feel "very faint." Moreover, they were recognized everywhere and people addressed them by name. Newsreels and "talking cinema" fascinated her, as she had never seen them before. Astonished, she watched herself on film, talking and feeling so "natural." Of all the new technology Stein was exposed to in America, she best liked the medium of broadcasting, commenting that "in writing in *The Making of Americans* I said I write for myself and strangers and this is what broadcasting is." Apparently, despite Stein's constant affirmation of her American patriotism, her feelings for America were often ambivalent. In evaluating the grand lecture tour in America, she repeatedly mentions and compares France to the United States. Bluntly, she admits that

> Alice Toklas wanted to come back to live there. She wanted to come back to live not everywhere but in Avila and in New York and New Orleans and California, I preferred Chicago and Texas but I did not want to come back to live there. I like Paris and I like six months in the country but I like Paris. Everybody says it is not very nice now but I like Paris and I like to live there.

Six years before the tour, *Transition* surveyed a number of expatriate American writers who lived in Paris. In her response to the questionnaire, Stein praises the United States as "the oldest country in the world" and "the mother of modern civilization." But America, she adds, is somewhat behind Europe: it is "very early Victorian." "Rich and well nourished," America is fit to live in; yet, it is not "a place to work." Stein's circular retort to this intruding question reinforces the reader's suspicion concerning the real reason behind Stein's expatriation. It appears that the key to understanding her response is the word "Victorian." Indeed, several critics believe that it was Stein's sexual orientation that kept her from staying in the United States. She knew that she would not be accepted into society and would always remain marginalized as a writer. At any rate, in Paris among other lesbian artists of the Left Bank, she was neither excommunicated nor ostracized. She was one of many. She could write freely, preserving her identity and her creativity: "What has my life in America been, it has been the doing of everything that I never have done. Never have done, never could have done, never could have done again; that is the way my life in America began and is begun and is going on." While vacationing in southern France, Gertrude Stein collapsed on 19 July 1946 and was admitted to the American Hospital at Neuilly-sur-Seine, where she was to be operated on. On 23 July she managed to write a will, guaranteeing Toklas's control over her estate, donating her Picasso portrait to the Metropolitan Museum in New York City and her unpublished manuscripts to the Yale University Library, and entrusting her lifelong friend, Carl Van Vechten, with the funds to publish the entire corpus of her unpublished works. On 27 July, Stein died of cancer during the operation while still under sedation. Alice Toklas survived her by twenty years. Mournfully, she continued to live in Paris until her death in 1967, ensuring that Stein's will was executed to the dot. Gertrude Stein and Alice Toklas are buried side-by-side in Père Lachaise Cemetery in Paris.

[*See also* Anderson, Sherwood; Autobiography: General Essay; Fitzgerald, F. Scott; H.D.; Hemingway, Ernest; *and* Writing as a Woman in the Twentieth Century.]

SELECTED WORKS

Three Lives: Stories of the Good Anna, Melanctha, and the Gentle Lena (1909)
Geography and Plays (1922)
The Making of Americans: Being a History of a Family's Progress (1925)
The Autobiography of Alice B. Toklas (1933)
Four Saints in Three Acts: An Opera to Be Sung (1934)
Everybody's Autobiography (1937)
Things As They Are: A Novel in Three Parts (1950)

FURTHER READING

Benstock, Shari. *Women of the Left Bank: Paris, 1900–1940*. Austin, Tex., 1986. Contains a valuable analysis of Gertrude Stein's life and works.

Bloom, Harold, ed. *Gertrude Stein*. New York, 1986. Includes articles by Sherwood Anderson, Katherine Anne Porter, Thornton Wilder, Catharine R. Stimpson, and many others.

Bridgman, Richard. *Gertrude Stein in Pieces*. New York, 1970.

Curnutt, Kirk, ed. *The Critical Response to Gertrude Stein*. Critical Responses in Arts and Letters, no. 36. Westport, Conn., 2000. A collection of reviews and articles dated from 1909 to 1997.

Dictionary of Literary Biography. Vol. 86, *American Short-Story Writers, 1910–1945. First Series*. Edited by Bobby Ellen Kimbel. Detroit, Mich., 1989.

Haas, Robert Bartlett, ed. *A Primer for the Gradual Understanding of Gertrude Stein*. Los Angeles, 1973. Excellent starting point to Stein's works. Features the famous "Transatlantic Interview 1946."

Haas, Robert Bartlett, ed. *How Writing Is Written: Volume II of the Previously Uncollected Writings of Gertrude Stein*. Los Angeles, 1974. Includes essays on the writing of *The Autobiography of Alice B. Toklas* and Stein's lecture tour in America.

Haas, Robert Bartlett, and Donald Clifford Gallup. *A Catalogue of the Published and Unpublished Writings of Gertrude Stein*. Folcroft, Pa., 1971.

Hoffman, Frederick J. *Gertrude Stein*. Pamphlets on American Writers, no. 10. Minneapolis, Minn., 1961.

Hoffman, Michael. *Gertrude Stein*. Boston, 1976. Excellent analysis of Stein's works, arranged by genre.

Katz, Leon. "The First Making of 'The Making of Americans': A Study Based on Gertrude Stein's Notebooks and Early Versions of Her Novel (1902–1908)." Ph.D. diss., Columbia University, 1963. The first work to identify the connection between *Q.E.D.* and Stein's affair with Bookstaver.

JOHN STEINBECK

by Stephen K. George

John Steinbeck, author of such classics as *Of Mice and Men* (1937), *The Grapes of Wrath* (1939), and *East of Eden* (1952), remains firmly planted in the souls of his readers today. Ironically he is more popular with critics abroad than in his own country, yet he is read in more classrooms from Maine to California than any other American novelist. As Arthur Miller contends, no other author, "with the possible exception of Mark Twain, . . . so deeply penetrated the political life of the country" as Steinbeck did with the publication of *The Grapes of Wrath*. This epic novel, which even today registers number thirty-four on one list of America's fifty most banned books, continues to shape our view of the Great Depression, to enlarge our imaginations and social conscience concerning that era, and to provoke debate on our continued moral responsibilities toward the downtrodden. For many readers, John Steinbeck is not only the quintessential American, he is on the shortlist of authors whose work actually influences the way we live and see our world.

Yet just a few years removed from his centennial anniversary and in spite of a renaissance in critical appreciation, some academics continue to dismiss Steinbeck out of hand as sentimental, simple, too popular. Admittedly much of his prose and authorial manner is reassuring to beginning readers; *The Red Pony* (1937) and *The Pearl* (1947) continue to be classroom staples across the country. However, many of his works, including *Cannery Row* (1945), *East of Eden*, and *The Winter of Our Discontent* (1961), remain critically underappreciated for their stylistic complexity and layered meaning. Steinbeck's detractors also complain that his later work is uneven, that it declined in quality, and that he was out of touch with the literary and political issues of his day, particularly the

John Steinbeck.
(*Courtesy of the Library of Congress*)

Vietnam War. Perhaps what the author was really out of touch with were the expectations and whims of his critics, many of whom, as the biographer Jackson Benson (1984) observes, wanted him to write *The Grapes of Wrath* again and again.

If judged by his intended audience—as all writers ultimately should be—John Steinbeck stands in elite company in American letters. Steinbeck is one of a handful of writers (Emerson, Twain, William Faulkner, and Toni Morrison are others) who actually represent America in some significant way to the rest of the world. His best work, spanning a range from the critically underappreciated *The Pastures of Heaven* (1932) to the frequently misunderstood *The Winter of Our Discontent*, stands confidently alongside that of his artistic contemporaries. Acknowledged or not on the college syllabi of this nation, John Steinbeck remains a powerful current within the receding and advancing tide of American literary studies.

EARLY YEARS (1902–1935)

John Ernst Steinbeck was born on 27 February 1902 in the small farming community of Salinas, California, to John Ernst Steinbeck and Olive Hamilton. His father was largely of German ancestry, his mother Irish; his parents' combined influence might explain both John's studious work habits later in life as well his penchant for romance and sentiment. Olive Hamilton was a capable, energetic woman who taught in one-room schoolhouses in Monterey and King City before meeting John Ernst. More than anything she influenced her young son, the third child and only boy of four, in her cultivation of a household of reading and learning and in her clear Victorian standards of right and wrong, from which the young John often rebelled. John's father, a quiet, repressed man typical of many of the westerners later found in his son's work, was never as concerned with social status as Olive; indeed, he lacked a sense of fulfillment all his life, having failed in many business ventures and remaining afloat only by being appointed to the minor position of treasurer of Monterey County. Still, John senior played an important role in John's career by supporting, both emotionally and financially, his son's dreams, as when he sent John and his new wife, Carol, $25 a month while they lived in the family cottage at Pacific Grove.

John grew up in a large Victorian house on Central Street which the neighborhood kids referred to as the "Castle." Both his early reading of Sir Thomas Malory's Arthurian legends and the surrounding Californian mountains that looked so much like the towers of Camelot influenced him greatly, particularly in the themes of social decay and true nobility in works such as *Tortilla Flat* (1935) and *The Winter of Our Discontent*. John was also shaped by the natural beauty and mystery of central California's forests, valleys, rivers, and coast. Detailed descriptions of the landscape and connections of man to his environment, the two at times melded into one great whole, would become characteristic openings or themes of many of his most beloved works.

Although official records suggest an outgoing and active adolescence (senior class president, member of the track team and school play, editor of the school yearbook), John was often shy and usually an outsider, which might explain his empathy with such lonely characters as Jody in *The Red Pony* and George and Lennie in *Of Mice and Men*. After graduating from high school, John attended Stanford University off and on from 1919 to 1925, where (as an English major) he took courses in anything that he believed would help his writing, including a medical school class where they cut up cadavers; as John explained to a curious dean, he wanted to understand human beings. Intermingled with his Stanford education (he never did earn a degree) were a variety of manual labor jobs that gave him access to many of the people who would later inhabit his work. Often John would pay fifty cents or a dollar to a paisano (someone of mixed Spanish, Indian, Italian, and Portuguese heritage), hobo, or farmhand to tell him a story he could use later; the ending of *The Grapes of Wrath*, with Rose of Sharon giving her breast to save a starving man, came from just such a story. From a very early age John knew he was going to be a writer and that his focus (as with Twain, Langston Hughes, Raymond Carver, and others) would be the lives of ordinary, common folk.

Steinbeck's first novel, *Cup of Gold* (1929), falls short perhaps because it goes beyond what Steinbeck actually knew in its fictionalization of the life and adventures of the pirate Henry Morgan. Yet even in this first endeavor we see the writer to come: his interest in the Holy Grail and Arthurian legend as evidence of humanity's desire and potential for perfectibility; his personification of the land and holistic awareness of our connections to it, which are explored in depth in his next work, *To a God Unknown* (1933); his laconic wit combined with a focus on materialism's corrupting influence, to which he would return in his last novel, *The Winter of Our Discontent*. As apprentice works foreshadowing Steinbeck's future artistry, *Cup of Gold* and *To a God Unknown* deserve a great deal more critical attention, as do *The Pastures of Heaven* and *Tortilla Flat*, which are really short-story cycles bound by strands of place, theme, tone, and character. *Pastures*, one of Steinbeck's most lyrical novels, focuses on the inhabitants of a beautiful valley whose lives are affected, often negatively, by their contact with the well-meaning Munroe family. *Tortilla Flat*, the rollicking yet tragic tale of paisanos living on the edges of Monterey, was Steinbeck's first commercial success. Its exploration of the Arthurian legend through the carefree lives of Danny and his friends gave just a glimpse of what was to come from this small-town western writer.

DEPRESSION ERA (1936–1939)

Steinbeck's first wife, Carol Henning, had an impact on his best-known work, second only, perhaps, to that of Edward Ricketts. A tall woman described as "handsome" rather than "pretty," Carol met John in the summer of 1929 while he was working at the fish hatchery at Tahoe City, California. The two were immediately drawn to each other and after a passionate year-and-a-half courtship married on 14 January 1930. The penniless couple shifted back and forth from southern California to the Steinbeck family's Pacific Grove cottage, with Carol supporting John's writing by working a succession of temporary jobs, typing his almost indecipherable manuscripts, and generally curbing his emotional excesses and tendency for weak plot development. Carol was one of the very few readers during the author's life who could read his rough drafts, look him in the eye, and declare, "That's a load of crap—burn it." She was also a major influence in the development of Steinbeck's social conscience and consciousness. In November 1933 Carol began working for the Emergency Relief Organization, which aided those most affected by the Depression. At night she would tell her husband stories of starving children, migrant workers being paid slave wages, and the abuses of corporation and farm owners, all of which eventually found their way into John's fiction, from *In Dubious Battle* (1936) to *The Grapes of Wrath*. Indeed, *The Grapes of Wrath* is dedicated in part "To Carol who willed this book," with his wife providing the book's title from Julia Ward Howe's "Battle Hymn of the Republic." In both a practical and artistic sense, Carol made the work of Steinbeck's most productive period possible.

John and Carol's early years were the happiest of their marriage despite their relative poverty. Their life revolved around a tight-knit set of artists, intellectuals, and free spirits composed (at various times) of the mythologist Joseph Campbell, the writer Henry Miller, and the social critic Lincoln Steffens, as well as Richard and Jan Albee, Ritch and Tal Lovejoy, Bruce and Jean Ariss, Ellwood Graham, Francis Whitaker, and Virginia and Remo Scardigli. However, the most important member of this bohemian set and the greatest intellectual influence on Steinbeck throughout his life was his closest friend, Edward F. Ricketts, a slender, compact man with thick, dark hair whom Steinbeck met in October 1930 and knew for eighteen years until Ricketts's death in 1948. Ricketts was born in 1897 in Chicago and attended the University of Chicago from 1919 to 1922, where in his last semester he took a course in animal ecology from W. C. Allee, the biological theorist who proposed that all living organisms possess an innate drive to cooperate in the processes of reproduction and survival. Ricketts, a renaissance man of science who loved discussions of poetry, philosophy, and ethics, was also influenced by the holistic thinking of William Emerson Ritter and John Elof Boodin, ideas that in turn found expression in Steinbeck's work in the concepts of the "phalanx," "nonteleological thinking," and "breaking through." The "phalanx," a concept particularly important to Steinbeck's masterpiece *In Dubious Battle*, which explores the violence between strike organizers and landowners in California's apple orchards, is the idea that individuals also exist as part of a collective that can take on a life of its own. In what some critics have called the best strike novel ever written, the character Doc (the first of several Steinbeck characters to be patterned after Ricketts) observes how a "man in a group isn't himself at all; he's a cell in an organism that isn't like him any more than the cells in your body are like you," with each unit acting according to the principles of cognition and survival of the whole. The cost of this subsuming of the individual to the group is ultimately the brutal sacrifice of the idealistic Jim Nolan to promote the cause of the strikers. As the strike leader Mac says of Jim in an attempt to rally the demoralized strikers, "Comrades! He didn't want nothing for himself."

The ideas of "nonteleological thinking" and "breaking through" also surface in *In Dubious Battle*, as well as in *Of Mice and Men*, *The Grapes of Wrath*, and *Cannery Row*. Such thinking, also known as "is thinking," attempts to examine the world from a nonjudgmental perspective, asking first and foremost "what" something is rather than "why" it is, which to Ricketts—but not Steinbeck—was almost always irrelevant and would prevent a true "breaking through" to seeing reality, the truth of the whole, as it really was. Steinbeck, so much influenced by these concepts that he originally entitled *Of Mice and Men* "Something That Happened," was far too humanistic and socially conscious to give up on seeking the causes of and solutions to basic social problems of injustice. But he did find great sympathy with Ricketts's emphasis on treating human beings and their environment as part of one great tide pool whose whole was greater than the sum of its parts. The writer also realized that to many fundamental questions there may indeed be no absolute answers, no clear blacks and whites.

It was during this period that John Steinbeck wrote his two most famous works, *Of Mice and Men* and *The Grapes of Wrath*, for which he received the Pulitzer Prize in 1940. *Of Mice and Men*, the first of a new literary form described by Steinbeck as the "play-novelette," is thought by some to be the writer's purest work, with not a word wasted. It tells the story of two migrant workers, George Milton and Lennie Small, who are constantly forced to move from job to job because of Lennie's penchant for touching soft things, such as girls' dresses. With tragic undertones this novella explores how our desires for companionship, respect, and a home of our own are thwarted by forces and circumstances of which we are only vaguely aware. George and Lennie's dream of living "off the fatta the lan'" is really the American dream, which at the time of the Depression seemed more out of reach than ever for society's misfits. The reading public's reaction to this "little book" (as Steinbeck often called it) was overwhelming, with over 117,000 copies sold in the first two weeks of its release. Critics likewise were effusive in praise, with Ralph Thompson of *The New York Times* describing the book as "completely disarming" and Harry Hansen calling it "the finest bit of prose fiction of this decade."

However, no critic or reader could have predicted what would appear next. Drawing on the experiences described by Carol as well as his own in visiting the Okie migrant camps on journalistic assignment in 1936, Steinbeck began work on his "big book" in May 1938. In an intense period of writing that lasted until October and left the writer emotionally and mentally exhausted, John Steinbeck composed *The Grapes of Wrath*, thought by many to be *the* American novel of the twentieth century. This multilayered epic, a narrative of the Joad family interspersed with wide-angle expositions on man and the migrants in general, provoked such disparate reactions that Steinbeck was left both amazed and disheartened. Condemned in Congress and California as communist propaganda, lauded by Eleanor Roosevelt for its compassionate honesty, banned by school boards across the country for its "vulgarity" and "dishonesty," *The Grapes of Wrath* touched a national nerve as no novel had done since Harriet Beecher Stowe's *Uncle Tom's Cabin*. The novel grew out of the confluence of three great elements: a social catastrophe that staggered the country, a novelist at the peak of his artistic powers, and an audience in need of awakening. Immediately thrown into the national limelight as the most relevant writer since Mark Twain, Steinbeck's reaction when the book fell from the best-seller list the following year was to throw a party.

THE WAR PERIOD (1940–1948)

The next few years of Steinbeck's personal life would prove to be the hardest he would ever experience. He was drained from pouring his whole heart and soul into *The Grapes of Wrath* and from the death threats and charges of disloyalty to his community and country. (One small sample of the bitterness: when Steinbeck later tried to move back to Monterey and repair the family home, his gas supply was inexplicably cut off and the city denied his work permit.) He was at a crossroads artistically, feeling that he could do nothing more with the novel as a genre. And his marriage with Carol was falling apart; dealing with success did not come easily to either of them. Carol, who had been such a driving force in his life, was perhaps jealous of her husband's instant international fame, particularly since she had sacrificed a great deal to make it possible, a sacrifice to which John often seemed oblivious. On John's part, he had never handled attention well and was petrified that success might harm his craft, that he would never again be able to enter a room and quietly observe his favorite subject—ordinary people. For a writer who had moved within five years from the mostly local success of *Tortilla Flat* to becoming the leading figure in American literature, the transition was too much.

Motivated nearly as much by a desire for flight as by an interest in marine biology, Steinbeck turned to the romance of a scientific voyage (again, Steinbeck's paradoxical strains) by arranging a collecting trip to Baja California with Ed Ricketts on which Carol came along uninvited. With a crew led by Captain Tony Berry, they set off in March of 1940 to collect, label, and store samples of marine life found in the Sea of Cortez and then to write an account of their adventure, with Steinbeck primarily responsible for the narrative of their journey and Ricketts for the scientific data in its appendix. What resulted was Steinbeck's richest work of nonfiction, *Sea of Cortez* (1941), coauthored with Ricketts and released later with only the narrative portion as *The Log from the Sea of Cortez* (1951). In this book, which at its best waxes poetically philosophical, many of Steinbeck's major literary themes are explored, including his concern with ecology (decades before it became popular), his focus on the intertwining of all living things, and his quest to understand "what is" before jumping to "why" and "how" (nonteleological thinking). One of the most famous passages reads: "it seems apparent that species are only commas in a sentence, that each species is at once the point and the base of a pyramid, that all life is relational to the point where an Einsteinian relativity seems to emerge. . . . groups melt into ecological groups until the time when what we know as life meets and enters what we think of as non-life: barnacle and rock, rock and earth, earth and tree, tree and rain and air. . . . all things are one thing and that one thing is all things." Interspersing beautiful descriptions of coral life with lengthy treatises of interdisciplinary thought, *Sea of Cortez* implicitly argues that Steinbeck the novelist was also a serious philosopher.

Although his relationship with Carol may have temporarily improved because of some happy moments on the voyage, it quickly disintegrated upon their return. Earlier, in June 1939, Steinbeck had met a young singer, Gwyn Conger, through their mutual friend Max Wagner. Gwyn was pretty, talented, and greatly impressed with Steinbeck's writing, and though she was only twenty years old and John was thirty-eight, a covert romance began that was to last until the spring of 1941. After an unbelievable meeting in which John got Carol and Gwyn together, told them he didn't know what to do, and asked them to work something out, he and Carol were reunited. But this lasted only a week, and after their divorce on 18 March 1943, John and Gwyn were married in New Orleans on 29 March. However, even the wedding foreshadowed the stormy years ahead: Gwyn lost her ring, the minister arrived drunk, and two policemen burst in at the end claiming that Steinbeck had fathered an illegitimate child and that the woman was outside (a practical joke).

Fittingly, Steinbeck wrote his best-known works on war during his time with Gwyn, including *The Moon Is Down* (1942), a novel with somewhat flat, idealized characters that nonetheless proved inspiring to those in Nazi-occupied territories; *Bombs Away: The Story of a Bomber Team* (1942), an admitted piece of war propaganda that did work effectively as a recruiting tool; and war dispatches for the New York *Herald Tribune* which were later published in *Once There Was a War* (1958). Almost immediately after their honeymoon, Steinbeck at last received word from the War Department (some of whose members had questions about his patriotism) that he was cleared to serve overseas as a war correspondent. In total Steinbeck spent five months in Italy, North Africa, and England, writing on whatever took his fancy and giving a personal face to the war in the style of the New Journalism of the 1960s. He even went along incognito on PT boat raids, removing his journalist's identification and carrying a machine gun, for which offenses he would have been executed if captured. As he did his entire career, Steinbeck needed to be on the front lines, observing and reporting on the major events of his century: the Depression, World War II, the Cold War, Vietnam.

When he returned in October 1943 to New York, where he and Gwyn now lived in a brownstone apartment on East Fifty-first Street, he was a changed man—as one critic surmises, at the age of forty-one Steinbeck had been too old to go to war. He immediately set to work on one of his most beloved novels, *Cannery Row*, which is at once a tribute to Ed Ricketts (in the primary character of Doc) and Monterey as well as a stinging indictment of America's materialism and ruthless treatment of the defenseless. Governed by the theme of how our perspective shapes our reality, the book opens by listing the Row's denizens: "Its inhabitants are, as the man once said, 'whores, pimps, gamblers, and sons of bitches,' by which he meant Everybody. Had the man looked through another peephole he might have said, 'Saints and angels and martyrs and holy men,' and he would have meant the same thing." Unlike anything the author had written before or would ever write again (its 1954 sequel, *Sweet Thursday*, falls flat in comparison), it is, as Jackson L. Benson notes in *Looking for Steinbeck's Ghost* (1988), a litmus test for Steinbeck readers. When the book appeared, those who refused to see Steinbeck as anything but the "proletarian writer," a social realist, the man who exposed capitalism's dirty secrets and championed the working class, were flabbergasted at this apolitical work. Those who had suspected, and continued to suspect, Steinbeck's patriotism, could not believe that during the century's greatest upheaval, the writer had retreated to the confines of Ricketts's lab and the bums and prostitutes of the Row.

However, to those who honestly try to see what the author is saying, *Cannery Row* is one of Steinbeck's finest works. Loosely bound by a focus on two major parties (the first a failure, the second a qualified success), its thirty-two chapters are linked more in thought and tone than in plot. In his interweaving of the stories of Doc and the lab, Dora and the girls, Mack and the boys, Henri the artist and Frankie the misfit, *Cannery Row* is at once comic and tragic, sacred and profane, with a musical flow of snapshots of those on the Row that is poetically pulled together at the end with Doc's emotional reading from "Black Marigolds." Yet the book itself is not sentimental, dealing with the tender and tragic experiences of life from a distance, philosophically examining what is and leaving the reader on the doorstep of what could be. Called by Malcolm Cowley a "poisoned cream puff" for its veiled attack on middle-class hypocrisy and materialism, *Cannery Row* explores, more deeply than any other of Steinbeck's works, "Ed Ricketts's thesis that progress is specious, representing the destruction of nature and inevitably corrupting human nature as well" (Parini, 1995). In its very avoidance of the war then raging on all fronts, it draws attention to the battles fought daily within our own lives and communities, battles to be understood only by looking through the correct peephole. Steinbeck's novel of vision and perspective ends with the image of a rattlesnake staring back at the reader with "dusty frowning eyes."

Steinbeck completed *Cannery Row* just in time to win a wager with Gwyn on which would be finished first: the manuscript or her pregnancy. Thom, their first son, was born on 2 August 1944. After the mixed reaction from critics to *Cannery Row*, the writer immediately began work on *The Pearl*, an outwardly simple parable of a Mexican fisherman named Kino who finds the "pearl of world." For Kino, the gem represents economic and societal freedom, a chance for an education for his son Coyotito and a better life for himself and his wife, Juana. However, their dreams are destroyed when Kino slays an intruding thief and the dark ones of the village (symbolically the darkness within us all) drive the family from its home, with the couple desperately attempting to reach the faraway city and safety. Forced either to kill or be killed, Kino attacks his pursuers only to have a random bullet strike the baby. Kino and Juana return to their village carrying fear with them, having "gone through pain and . . . come out the other side," and with "a magical protection about them." Richly layered with Taoist strains of antimaterialism and embracing one's place within the universe, *The Pearl* is a minor jewel in the Steinbeck canon, often compared to Hemingway's *The Old Man and the Sea*. The novella also serves as the transition piece from Steinbeck's concern with "group man" and acceptance of life as it is to his later overriding concern—evident especially in *East of Eden* and *The Winter of Our Discontent*—with the lonely individual battling good and evil.

Although John and Gwyn had a second son, John IV, on 12 June 1946, their marriage continued to unravel. Gwyn, with some justification, felt her budding career as an actress and singer had been smothered by that of her husband and also resented that John's writing came first, even over the demands of raising the children, which Steinbeck left almost entirely to her. For his part, John had never particularly wanted children, and though he did his best as a father, he would never allow himself to be controlled by Gwyn's expectations. Neither of them saw the other clearly, and rather than having the open outbursts that punctuated his earlier marriage with Carol, conflicts were ignored and left to simmer. It was at this low point in their relationship that John learned that Ed Ricketts had been in a terrible accident, his Packard hit by a locomotive on its way into Monterey. John desperately tried to get to Ed, who lingered near death for four days, but because of flight delays didn't arrive in time; Ricketts died on 7 May 1948. After attending the funeral and taking care of his friend's personal things (including burning years of correspondence, which Steinbeck wanted to keep private), he flew back to New York only to receive a second bombshell—Gwyn wanted a divorce, immediately. Despite his failings in the marriage, Gwyn acted with pure cruelty, telling him that she had never really loved him and had been involved in numerous affairs during their marriage, and that little Johnny had been fathered by another man. Crushed both emotionally and artistically, John returned to the Pacific Grove cottage and began the task of rebuilding his life and work. Gwyn, however, would find her way back into her husband's life as the model in part for Steinbeck's most evil character, the sadistic prostitute Kate in *East of Eden*.

MATURE YEARS (1949–1961)

Shortly after leaving New York for California, Steinbeck met the woman who was to become his third wife and most loyal supporter. Elaine Anderson Scott was the daughter of a Texas oilman. She studied drama at the University of Texas and was one of the original stage managers of the Broadway hit *Oklahoma!* She was also the wife of the aspiring actor Zachary Scott, and they had a daughter named Waverly. However, the show-business lifestyle proved too much for their marriage, and by 1949 they had drifted apart. Elaine met John in the spring of 1949 through a mutual friend, the actress Ann Sothern, and over Memorial Day weekend he gave her a firsthand tour of "Steinbeck country." Attractive, outgoing, witty, Elaine was the woman John had waited for his whole life: strong enough not to be threatened by his fame but also a genuinely loving person who wanted him to succeed and who, as with Carol in the 1930s, made the work of his mature years possible. After meeting the approval of John's sister Mary and Elaine's family, the couple married on 28 December 1950 in the home of Harold Guinzburg, Steinbeck's publisher. Over the next two decades John and Elaine were inseparable.

With Elaine at his side, Steinbeck again began to flower artistically and in many directions, from the experimental drama *Burning Bright* (1950) produced by Rodgers and Hammerstein (which failed with audiences) to the screenplay *Viva Zapata!* directed by Elia Kazan and starring Marlon Brando, which was a huge success, earning over $3 million in the first month of its release in 1952. As with his contemporary Langston Hughes, Steinbeck was a prolific and varied artist, his work ranging from movies (Alfred Hitchcock's *Lifeboat*) to political speeches (for Adlai Stevenson) and modern translation (*The Acts of King Arthur and His Noble Knights*, 1976); about the only thing he didn't dabble in was literary criticism. Still, the project he had waited a lifetime to fulfill beckoned him: the autobiographical and biblical epic he once called "My Valley" and "The Salinas Valley" but wisely renamed *East of Eden*.

Steinbeck had begun preparation for his other "big book" long before, having written to the *Salinas-Californian* in January of 1948, while still married to Gwyn, to ask for the editor's help in doing research on the Salinas Valley from 1900 to the present. A curious and startling blend of family history (Steinbeck himself appears as a child in the novel, as does his mother's family, the Hamiltons) with the fictional story of Adam Trask and his twin sons Aron and Cal, *East of Eden* is a massive work exploring the corollary story of Cain and Abel. As Steinbeck puts it in the novel, "there is one story in the world, and only one. . . . Virtue and vice were warp and woof of our first consciousness, and they will be the fabric of our last. . . . There is no other story. A man, after he has brushed off the dust and chips of his life, will have left only the hard, clean questions: Was it good or was it evil? Have I done well—or ill?" In *East of Eden*, Steinbeck delves more deeply into the origin and nature of evil than in any previous work.

The novel's main story revolves around Adam Trask, who as a boy is nearly killed in a Cain and Abel–like quarrel by his brother Charles. Adam eventually leaves home and becomes involved with a battered young woman, Cathy Ames, who has just murdered her parents and fled her pimp, Mr. Edwards. Steinbeck's view of Cathy, later known as Kate, evolves as the novel progresses, a fluctuation for which many critics fault him as inconsistent. At first he posits her as a moral monster, born without conscience or feeling and thus beyond the ethical realm. Later, as the participating narrator, Steinbeck rethinks this position, and at the end, when Kate leaves her possessions to her son Aron and feels a pang of remorse upon remembering his face, the sadistic brothel proprietor does seem to be just within the moral realm. One of the most evil characters ever created in literature, Kate has been deplored by many feminists as a misogynist stereotype while simultaneously holding a fascinating appeal for the novel's readers. As a philosophical exploration of the vice of cruelty, Cathy Ames transcends any simple typing as a fictionalized Gwyn Steinbeck. Still, the horrific marriage with his second wife did shape the writer's concern that her genetic and environmental influence would permanently disfigure his own sons.

With this in mind, the novel pursues the idea of *timshel*, interpreted from the Hebrew by Steinbeck as "thou mayest," to suggest that no matter the circumstances, some moral choice is always possible. In the story this is elaborated, sometimes a bit artificially, by the wise Chinese servant Lee and Adam's closest friend, Samuel Hamilton (Steinbeck's grandfather). The theme is dramatized most powerfully in the conflict between Aron and Cal, with the latter representative of the strain of Cain present in all men. After a jealous Cal reveals to Aron that his real mother, Kate, is a whore and Aron subsequently enlists in the army only to be killed, Cal is presented with the choice to give in to guilt and self-hatred or to find forgiveness and understanding from his father and the novel's strongest female character, Abra. The epic's closing scene, reminiscent of Old Testament patriarchs passing on their blessing to the next generation, finds Adam releasing Cal from his sin with his final word: "Timshel."

Although Steinbeck felt *East of Eden* was the best book he ever wrote, critics have always been divided. He admitted that he tried to put every bit of wisdom he possessed into it, and undoubtedly he should have been more selective. The story line of the Trasks overpowers its foil of the Hamiltons in the end, some passages are overly wrought (as in *Cup of Gold*), and his final shedding of group man for the lonely individual in moral conflict left many critics wondering where the man who wrote *The Grapes of Wrath* had gone. Still, despite these flaws, *East of Eden* "remains a shockingly believable tale of family pathology" (Parini, 1995) as well as a forerunner, with its self-conscious style and narrative experimentation, of postmodernism. As Robert DeMott confesses, the novel's narrative voice "spoke to me and not at me. . . . [It] was the first book that gave me a handle on symbolic experiences, the first to make personal journeys, choices, and continuities seem like palpable endeavors" (George, 2002, p. 126). Beloved by readers and moviegoers alike (the powerful film version starring James Dean appeared in 1955), with some of the most beautiful prose descriptions of Steinbeck country ever committed to page, *East of Eden* continues to receive much-deserved critical attention.

From 1953 to 1959 Steinbeck and Elaine spent a great deal of time abroad, traveling (often with the boys) to the Virgin Islands, France, Italy, Denmark, Sweden, Japan, and England, with an extended period in Somerset doing research on Malory's *Le Morte d'Arthur* that Elaine remembers as their happiest time together. Steinbeck also began writing more nonfiction, including a travel series for *Collier's*, and he became more politically active, finding great sympathy with the worldview of Adlai Stevenson. The Steinbecks now had two homes, an apartment in New York on East Seventy-second Street and a summer cottage in Sag Harbor, Long Island, which sat on a little peninsula with its own boat dock. John renovated the house and built a small, six-sided writing haven he christened "Joyous Garde" after Lancelot's castle in Arthurian legend. Upon arriving home from England in October 1959, he was overwhelmed by the national scandal surrounding the nation's quiz shows, particularly Charles Van Doren and *Twenty-One*, all of which represented to him a pervasive moral decay that reached to the highest levels of society. In response to this and his inability to go forward with the Malory translation, Steinbeck began to work on his last piece of fiction, *The Winter of Our Discontent*.

Its title taken from Shakespeare's *Richard III*, *The Winter of Our Discontent* is the story of Ethan Allen Hawley, a man with a paradoxical heritage of pirates and Puritans who is now bankrupt and working as a clerk in the grocery store his family used to own. Set in New Baytown, a thinly veiled Sag Harbor, the novel follows "the disintegration of a man" as Hawley deliberately forsakes his moral principles and way of life in order to be a success in business. Ethan mistakenly believes that morals are relative, that he can change his way of being and then don his former self like replacing a shirt. He justifies his ruthlessness with an analogy of business to war, in which goodness and kindness are weaknesses, an idea the writer originally explored in *Sea of Cortez*. The new Ethan Hawley, both a fallen Christ as well as a Judas figure, ends up turning in his boss to immigration, enabling the death of the man he thought of as his brother, and playing with thoughts of infidelity with the town's temptress, Margie Young-Hunt. In all of this Steinbeck is exploring the theme of moral integrity and how such integrity is assaulted from all sides in the modern world. According to the novel's epigraph, "Readers seeking to identify the fictional people and places here described would do better to inspect their own communities and search their hearts, for this book is about a large part of America today."

Although *Winter* was endorsed by Lewis Gannett and Saul Bellow as the finest novel Steinbeck had written since *The Grapes of Wrath*, most of its reviewers lambasted the work for its cutesy language, inconsistent narrative point of view, and moralistic tone. Again, much of the academic and critical world, charging that Steinbeck had forsaken his earlier liberalism for the role of a moralist, lamented the decline of the writer. Put simply, these critics were wrong: although a flawed work, *The Winter of Our Discontent* is also Steinbeck's most postmodern, experimental, and underappreciated effort. Far from being inconsistent, the deliberate shift from first person to third person in each of the novel's two parts allows the reader to experience both the inner and outer Ethan Hawley, while the cacophony of voices in Ethan's head literally mirrors the divided consciousness he experiences as he sheds one way of life for another. Ethan becomes at once the American Everyman as well as one of the most richly wrought characters in the Steinbeck canon. The entire first volume of the *Steinbeck Yearbook* (2000) reassesses *The Winter of Our Discontent* as one of Steinbeck's most daringly complex works. At a time in his career when most other writers would have been content to mimic past successes, Steinbeck was breaking new artistic ground.

FINAL YEARS (1962–1968)

The decades of often personal attacks, many by critics who had little concern about the writer's intent, did finally break Steinbeck's creative will—he never published another word of fiction after *The Winter of Our Discontent*. However, he did give the public his final perceptions of the country in *Travels with Charley in Search of America* (1962) and *America and Americans* (1966). Based on a trip Steinbeck took in the fall of 1960, *Travels with Charley* represents the writer's last major effort to come to grips with the ever-changing landscape of America. Dubbing his camper-truck "Rocinante," after Don Quixote's trusty steed, and taking along his poodle Charlie as a companion and sounding board, Steinbeck traveled from Sag Harbor to Maine, across the Midwest and West to Washington state, down the California coast and over to Texas, and then through New Orleans and back to New York in eleven weeks. Containing some of his most beautiful descriptive passages and memorable anecdotes, the book attempts to explain the physical, spiritual, and cultural state of the nation, much of which Steinbeck finds disturbing. America, he concludes, has too much, wastes too much, and is in danger of becoming too homogenous. Most troubling is the racism Steinbeck finds in New Orleans, where he witnesses a group of women called the "Cheerleaders" harangue a black child as she enters a previously segregated school. The writer quickly retreated to Sag Harbor, overwhelmed by all he had seen and aware that his quest to rediscover his country had been impossible from the beginning. Yet one has to admire a man who in his late fifties and declining health would even undertake such a venture—it was typical Steinbeck. Despite its flaws, including an unbalanced structure and abrupt ending, *Travels with Charley* was almost uniformly praised, with *The New York Times* calling it "a pure delight, a pungent potpourri of places and people interspersed with bittersweet essays on everything from the emotional difficulties of growing old to the reasons why giant Sequoias arouse such awe."

On 25 October 1962, John and Elaine were having a quiet breakfast in their Sag Harbor home when John turned on the television for news concerning the Cuban missile crisis. The first words he heard were that he had just been awarded the Nobel Prize for literature. Their elation did not last long, however, as the East Coast establishment he had defied his whole life immediately turned on both him and the Nobel committee, with a brash editorial the very next day in *The New York Times* asking why a more influential and significant writer had not been chosen. Even more mean-spirited was Arthur Mizener's "Does a Moral Vision of the Thirties Deserve a Nobel Prize?," which appeared the eve before the Stockholm award ceremony on 9 December and trotted out the decades-old charges of sentimentality and irrelevance. The sheer vindictiveness of his critics' remarks—cheap shots on the field of literary criticism when the writer was at his most public and vulnerable—is an indirect measure of Steinbeck's powerful and abiding influence on American literature. Although deeply hurt by the barbs of his own countrymen, Steinbeck made clear in his acceptance speech that literature was and always would be for common readers and not emasculated critics, "the cloistered elect" and "tinhorn mendicants of low-calorie despair."

The last years of Steinbeck's life were largely happy, though as always he lived on the cusp of controversy. Friends with both John F. Kennedy and Lyndon B. Johnson, he enjoyed opportunities to serve his country and was eventually awarded the highest presidential honor, the Medal of Freedom. In 1963 John and Elaine went to the Soviet Union with Edward Albee and visited with various Soviet intellectuals, writers, and political representatives, many of whom were shocked that the author of *The Grapes of Wrath* so deeply loved his country. Steinbeck, informing one skeptic that he had never been a communist or a Puritan, explained that the America of the 1930s had changed radically and that the leaders of the Soviet Union did not want the Russian people to know this. In December of 1966 Steinbeck also made an intense visit to Vietnam as a correspondent for *Newsday*, visiting his sons Thom and John IV on his way. As during World War II, Steinbeck dressed in fatigues and dove right into the combat zone on foot and by helicopter. What he saw disturbed him greatly and began to change his perceptions of the war. However, the photos of him in military dress and his "Letters to Alicia" for *Newsday*, which gave a human face to the American GI, again made Steinbeck persona non grata for those in liberal academia. As the playwright Terrence McNally recalls, "I went to Columbia where you were forbidden to utter the words 'John Steinbeck.' American literature stopped with William Faulkner."

In October 1967, John checked himself into a New York hospital to undergo a five-hour back operation, not knowing how seriously ill he was. The next year he and Elaine alternated living in the New York apartment and Sag Harbor, with John wanting to be in the country and near the water but being forced back to the city for treatment of several minor strokes. That fall he actually felt a little better, though he was unable to write or work in his garden. But in November his breathing became labored, and he and Elaine moved back to New York. Having found out that the recent technique of heart bypass surgery was not an option, his body having given out on all levels, Steinbeck spent his last days looking out over the vistas of East Seventy-second Street with Elaine reading to him. John Steinbeck died at 5:30 P.M. on 20 December 1968. At his request the funeral service in St. James Episcopal Church in New York was conducted from the rites of the Church of England. A later service was held at Point Lobos in California; Steinbeck's ashes are buried in the family plot in Salinas.

LITERARY LEGACY

A small measure of John Steinbeck's literary impact may be seen in *John Steinbeck: Centennial Reflections by American Writers* (2002). This volume's nearly fifty contributors—who either claim to have been influenced by Steinbeck's work or who affirm his literary prominence—include Edward Albee, E. L. Doctorow, Barry Lopez, Norman Mailer, Arthur Miller, Kurt Vonnegut, and Terry Tempest Williams. Steinbeck moved his readers, inspired his fellow artists, and shaped his country's future as few other American writers have. The growing wave of Steinbeck scholarship likewise attests to his continuing relevance, with the appearance of groundbreaking works exploring his art (Robert DeMott's *Steinbeck's Typewriter*, 1997) and interdisciplinary possibilities (*Beyond Boundaries: Rereading John Steinbeck*, 2002), as well as a new academic journal, *The Steinbeck Review*, sponsored by Ball State University and appearing in the Fall of 2004. Steinbeck finally seems to be getting his critical due.

This activity seems appropriate given the sum of the writer's artistic achievement. In the three decades from 1932 to 1962, Steinbeck wrote one confirmed literary masterpiece, *The Grapes of Wrath*; four other classics in their own right, *In Dubious Battle*, *Of Mice and Men*, *Cannery Row*, and *The Log from the Sea of Cortez*; and several other works that shoulder well on the shelf with those of any of his contemporaries—*Pastures of Heaven*, *Tortilla Flat*, *The Long Valley*, *The Pearl*, *East of Eden*, *The Winter of Our Discontent*, and *Travels with Charley*. Far from declining in quality, the Steinbeck canon as a whole is remarkably consistent in representing one man's courageous attempt to explain the truth that he saw with clarity and compassion. The literary world would be poorer indeed without John Steinbeck.

[*See also* Proletarian Literature.]

WORKS

Cup of Gold (1929)

The Pastures of Heaven (1932)

To a God Unknown (1933)

Tortilla Flat (1935)

In Dubious Battle (1936)

Of Mice and Men (1937)

Of Mice and Men: A Play in Three Acts (1937)

The Red Pony (1937)

Their Blood Is Strong (1938)

The Long Valley (1938)

The Grapes of Wrath (1939)

The Forgotten Village (1941)

Sea of Cortez (with Edward F. Ricketts) (1941)

Bombs Away: The Story of a Bomber Team (1942)

The Moon Is Down (1942)

The Moon Is Down: Play in Two Parts (1942)

Cannery Row (1945)

The Wayward Bus (1947)

The Pearl (1947)

A Russian Journal (1948)

Burning Bright (1950)

The Log from the Sea of Cortez (1951)

East of Eden (1952)

Viva Zapata! (1952)

Sweet Thursday (1954)

The Short Reign of Pippin IV (1957)

Once There Was a War (1958)

The Winter of Our Discontent (1961)

Travels with Charley in Search of America (1962)

America and Americans (1966)

Journal of a Novel: The East of Eden Letters (1969)

The Acts of King Arthur and His Noble Knights (1976)

FURTHER READING

Astro, Richard. *John Steinbeck and Edward F. Ricketts: The Shaping of a Novelist.* Minneapolis, 1973. The best study available on Ricketts's impact on Steinbeck philosophically and as a writer.

Beegel, Susan, Susan Shillinglaw, and Wes Tiffany, eds. *Steinbeck and the Environment: Interdisciplinary Approaches.* Tuscaloosa, Ala., 1997. Essays from multiple disciplines (marine biology, philosophy, feminism) exploring how the author blended his art with his deep concerns for the environment.

Benson, Jackson J. *The True Adventures of John Steinbeck, Writer.* New York, 1984. The most complete biography (over 1,100 pages) to date and the starting point for any serious study of Steinbeck.

Benson, Jackson L. *Looking for Steinbeck's Ghost.* Norman, Okla., 1988.

Bloom, Harold, ed. The Grapes of Wrath: *Modern Critical Interpretations.* New York, 1992. Highly available collection of seven critical essays marred largely by a condescending and indecisive introduction.

Coers, Donald, Robert DeMott, and Paul Ruffin, eds. *After* The Grapes of Wrath: *Essays on John Steinbeck in Honor of Tetsumaro Hayashi.* Athens, Ohio, 1995. A defense of the writer's later work, it includes general essays on Steinbeck and Roosevelt, ethnicity, and movies, as well as a detailed 1993 interview with Elaine Steinbeck.

DeMott, Robert. *Working Days: The Journals of* The Grapes of Wrath, *1938–1941.* New York, 1989.

DeMott, Robert. *Steinbeck's Typewriter: Essays on His Art.* Troy, N.Y., 1997. Nine provocative essays exploring Steinbeck's own reading experience and the artistic creation of three of his major novels, including *The Grapes of Wrath.*

Fensch, Thomas. *Conversations with John Steinbeck.* Jackson, Miss., 1988.

French, Warren. *John Steinbeck's Fiction Revisited.* New York, 1994. A helpful reappraisal of the author's work during the 1930s, placing it in the ironic tradition of literary modernists.

George, Stephen K., ed. *John Steinbeck: A Centennial Tribute.* Westport, Conn., 2002. The most varied study of Steinbeck to date, it includes interviews, reminiscences, and critical essays by family, friends, fellow writers, and scholars.

George, Stephen K., and Barbara A. Heavilin. *The Steinbeck Review.* Berkeley, Calif., 2004. The foremost journal in Steinbeck scholarship, volume 1 focusing on Steinbeck and philosophy, volume 2 on teaching Steinbeck.

Hayashi, Tetsumaro, ed. *A New Study Guide to Steinbeck's Major Works, with Critical Explications.* Metuchen, N.J., 1993. An excellent student research tool; each chapter includes background information, a plot summary, discussion topics, and an annotated bibliography for the author's most commonly taught works.

Heavilin, Barbara A. *John Steinbeck's* The Grapes of Wrath: *A Reference Guide.* Westport, Conn., 2002. With chapters on content, context, themes, and narrative art, this is an essential reference work for Steinbeck's literary masterpiece.

Heavilin, Barbara A., ed. *Steinbeck Yearbook: The Winter of Our Discontent.* Vol. 1. Lewiston, N.Y., 2000. The predecessor of *The Steinbeck Review,* volume 2 focuses on the Arthurian tradition, volume 3 on Steinbeck's sense of place.

Lisca, Peter. *The Wide World of John Steinbeck*. New York, 1981. A new edition of the first major critical study of Steinbeck, with an updated afterword.

Meyer, Michael J. *The Hayashi Steinbeck Bibliography: 1982–1996*. Metuchen, N.J., 1998. The successor to the earlier Hayashi volumes, this is the newest and most thorough bibliography to date.

Meyer, Michael J., and Brian Raisback, eds. *Steinbeck Encyclopedia*. Westport, Conn., 2004. The preeminent reference work on the author, with entries by the leading Steinbeck scholars on every relevant topic.

Owens, Louis. *Steinbeck's Re-Vision of America*. Athens, Ga., 1985. Emphasizes the importance of four major California settings in Steinbeck's work while arguing for a reevaluation of the writer as an artist and philosopher.

Parini, Jay. *John Steinbeck: A Biography*. New York, 1995. Complimenting Benson's more scholarly work, this biography is especially insightful in exploring Steinbeck's creative process and reassessing his literary achievement.

Shillinglaw, Susan, ed. *John Steinbeck: Centennial Reflections by American Writers*. San Jose, Calif., 2002. An engaging collection of evaluative and personal pieces by forty-six contemporary writers.

Shillinglaw, Susan, and Kevin Hearle, eds. *Beyond Boundaries: Rereading John Steinbeck*. Tuscaloosa, Ala., 2002. A rich anthology of twenty-three essays exploring such interdisciplinary venues as "Steinbeck as World Citizen," "Steinbeck's Women," and "Steinbeck's Science and Ethics."

Steinbeck, Elaine, and Robert Wallsten, eds. *Steinbeck: A Life in Letters*. New York, 1975.

Timmerman, John H. *John Steinbeck's Fiction: The Aesthetics of the Road Taken*. Norman, Okla., and London, 1986. A chronological study of Steinbeck's novels with close attention to the development of his artistic premises.

See also the article on *The Grapes of Wrath*, immediately following.

JOHN STEINBECK'S
THE GRAPES OF WRATH

by *Jan Goggans*

"It means very little to know that a million Chinese are starving," John Steinbeck wrote in the preface to a 1941 script called *The Forgotten Village*, "unless you know one Chinese who is starving." That is the philosophy that served as the motivating force for Steinbeck's Pulitzer Prize–winning novel, *The Grapes of Wrath* (1939), the tenet on which he built, in numbingly intimate detail, the story of that singular Oklahoma family, the Joads, as they make their way across the United States during the Great Depression and on to California. While Steinbeck's focus on the Joads encourages readers to identify with this family—their strength, their frustration, their loss, and their resilient hope (to make them into the "one Chinese who is starving")—behind the method was a larger, grander purpose. The subject of Steinbeck's novel is not the suffering of a single family: it is the thousands of others like the Joads about whom Steinbeck wrote, the tragedy of large-scale suffering occurring in epic, biblical proportions among those on whom America so willingly turned its back in the 1930s.

BLACK DAYS IN AMERICA

After World War I, shifts in wheat prices created difficult financial times for farmers, and they saw little of the sudden wealth of the 1920s; correspondingly, they did not immediately feel the stock market crash on Black Thursday, 24 October 1929. As bread lines formed in the cities, they were perhaps glad to have their own stores of meat, eggs, and grain. Then the drought came. It began in the eastern United States, but by 1931, it had shifted to the Great Plains, and by 1935, it hit the southern plains as well. Crops failed in the searing heat, and there was neither water nor soil in which to plant new ones. Years of planting too often and planting the same kind of crop had depleted the soil, robbing it of nutrients and minimizing its ability to survive heat and drought. Dust storms began, black swells so forceful that skies darkened during the day and people wandered off, lost; they were found later, suffocated. On 14 April 1935, Black Sunday hit, darkening the skies from Oklahoma to Kansas. Just as city dwellers

had after the stock market crash, men and women on farms now faced the loss of everything they had worked their whole lives to create. Midwestern landowners, unable to coax any profits out of their property, began selling it at whatever price, forcing off families who had rented and farmed the land for generations. In the South, sharecroppers, families whose subsistence depended on as little as fifteen acres, were forced off the land, their work increasingly done by tractors bought by landowners with government loans.

From the South and the Midwest, the dispossessed families headed west, flooding into California at an unprecedented rate. Unlike their pioneering and gold rush predecessors, however, this wave of migrants was not glorified in either song or press. By 1933, the Great Depression had arrived in California, and in June 1934, more than one million Californians, of a population of six million, were on some form of public assistance. As the Depression wore on, the feeling intensified that there was not enough for all, partly out of prejudice and partly out of reality. More than 300,000 migrants arrived in California between 1930 and 1934 alone. Paul Schuster Taylor and his wife, the photographer Dorothea Lange, traveled up and down the state reporting on government camps, and published *An American Exodus* (1939), a book of essays and photographs they subtitled "A Record of Human Erosion."

Hindsight might point to a clear cause for the situation—a culture of unregulated capitalism in factories and on farms, a single-minded pursuit of profit at the expense of individual dignity that allowed those who owned the land and factories to exploit and disregard those who worked on and in them. In the 1930s, however, only a handful of intellectuals saw it that way. Many of them, moved to action by what they were witnessing, turned at least philosophically if not politically to Marxist and socialist theories, ideas about labor that sought to help the working class by ensuring, at the very least, a decent job for every human being, and at the most, a new society in which all men and women shared in the production of goods and their profits. John Steinbeck was one of these intellectuals.

Born in Salinas, California, a small agricultural town in the state's Great Central Valley, Steinbeck graduated from Salinas High School in 1919. After a year working odd jobs in New York City, he returned to his hometown to write, producing six novels from 1929 to 1937. Although his novels gained the immediate support of the East Coast and southern California socialists who were agitating for reform through theatrical productions and radio broadcasts, he was different than they were. For Steinbeck, the reforms were quite personal. "There are riots in Salinas and killings in the streets of that dear little town where I was born," he wrote in 1936, the same year he published *In Dubious Battle*, a labor and strike novel set in the California fruit country. The novel looks sympathetically at the needs of the workers, expressing a sense of outrage at the social injustice migrant workers faced in California. At the same time, it looks warily at the communist organizing of agricultural workers, showing how the political characters, Mac and Jim, manipulate the workers for communist purposes. It would not be until he wrote *The Grapes of Wrath*, published in 1939, that Steinbeck wrote clearly and powerfully in favor of government protection for union organizing and federal intervention on behalf of California's migrants and bitterly against the agricultural and financial monopolies that enabled worker exploitation.

HOPE WITHIN A HOPELESS TIME

In his analysis of the social literature that came out of the 1930s, *Hope among Us Yet* (1987), David P. Peeler argues that despite different themes or story lines, most novels shared certain similarities because they all responded to the Great Depression. Intellectuals viewed the stock market crash as a crisis in capitalism, one that however tragic was philosophically welcomed because of its clear indictment of capitalism and the corrupt conditions many writers felt accompanied it. Thus, despite the grim conditions the novels depict, their general tone is somehow hopeful. Emphasizing economic forces and social action over the individual's psyche, the novels generally attack America's social faults while at the same time denying that those faults are permanent; ultimately, they carry some idea for a solution. Thus, Peeler concludes, "If social art is to be effective, it must do two things. It must channel hope or anger toward some end, and not merely arouse emotions. Furthermore, it must at least hint of ways in which its hoped for ends can be achieved and maintained."

For Steinbeck, that hope is expressed in the collective power of men and women, in the present and future promise of their children, and in their combined ability to create not simply a new Eden but a wholly new kind of Eden. The strength of community is the message that prevails through even the grimmest of scenes in *The Grapes of Wrath*, and that is the theme Steinbeck sets out in a variety of situations, characters, and exchanges between characters. From the most hopeless of times comes the hope for the future. Dispossessed, reviled, starving—those who have been cast out of their old homes and turned back at the gateway to their dreams lead the way to a new type of community, from which the future springs: "They's stuff goin' on and they's folks doin' things," the former preacher Jim Casy, says:

> Them people layin' one foot down in front of the other, like you says, they ain't thinkin' where they're goin', like you says—but they're all layin' 'em down the same direction, just the same. An' if ya listen, you'll hear a movin', an' a sneakin', an' a rustlin', an'—an' a res'lessness. They's stuff goin' on that the folks doin' it don't know nothin' about—yet. They's gonna come somepin outa all these folks goin' wes'—outa all their farms lef' lonely. They's gonna come a thing that's gonna change the whole country.

The story of the Joads, the emblematic family whose journey west will, perhaps without their ever knowing fully how, "change the whole country," takes place over the course of a few months, moving from the family eviction from their home in Sallislaw, Oklahoma, to their first winter in California. Divided into three main sections, the novel covers the drought in Oklahoma, and its results, (chapters 1–11), the journey west (chapters 12–18), and their experience in California (chapters 19–30). Within that tripartite scheme, Steinbeck alternates the type of chapter, moving from specific narrative chapters about the Joads' experience to broadly painted, generalized excerpts of the American experience. It is an organizational scheme that bears the influence of John Dos Passos's experimental novel, *U.S.A.* According to the noted Steinbeck scholar Louis Owens (1989), the narrative chapters act like text, moving forward the plot of the novel, while the interchapters are like a wide-angle photograph, focusing on the general condition of the country. That shift in focus, from the specific to the general, reminds readers that the individual's tragedy is played out against a backdrop of ongoing humanity.

Fourteen of the thirty chapters are narrative. Those in the first section tell the story of the homecoming of the eldest son, Tom, and the family's departure for California, necessitated by the family's eviction off a forty-acre farm they have been "croppin" for "a long time," in Tom's words. The first ominous hint of the changes in store for Tom, who has been in prison for four years, comes in an early exchange between him and a truck driver who gives him a lift. "A forty-acre cropper and he ain't been dusted out and he ain't been tractored out?" the driver says, articulating the two forces behind the mass western exodus of the 1930s: drought and tractors. Finding the Joad farm abandoned, Tom hears his family has moved in with his Uncle John. When he finds them, they are loading up the truck that will take them west, and with little delay, Tom joins them: Ma and Pa Joad; Pa's brother John; Granma and Granpa; Tom's brothers Noah and Al; his pregnant sister, Rose of Sharon (Rosasharn), and her husband, Connie; and the two youngest children, Winfield and Ruthie. Along with them is Jim Casy, whom Tom met on his journey home from prison.

Alternating with the chapters that tell the story of how the Joads come to leave their home are the interchapters, what Steinbeck called the "intercalary" (or "inserted") chapters, which serve both to foreshadow what the Joads will soon face, and to put their isolated experience into the general framework of the western exodus. The opening of the novel, for example, moves the reader's eye from a panoramic view, one that emphasizes color, sound, and feel, to a single focus. "To the red country and part of the gray country of Oklahoma," the novel begins, "the last rains came gently." Slowly, the earth dries out, becoming "pale, pink in the red country and white in the gray country," and eventually it turns to dust. From this wide view, the novel moves in the next paragraph to a single field of corn, "each leaf tilted downward." In this opening, Steinbeck sets up the movement of the entire novel, the idea that what happens in the abstract affects something, or someone—that the large-scale view has a small-scale counterpart. At the same time, the novel insists upon the reverse of that idea. The dust from the cornfield collects, joins in with the dust from the roads, and finally does not settle back to earth at all, but disappears "into the darkening sky." Thus, in the opening chapter's insistent swing from narrow to wide focus, and back again, readers must see as well that the fate of the one is never isolated, that individuals collect, combine, commune.

Although the family's entrance onto Route 66—the "migrant highway"—does not occur until the second part of the novel, the trip starts at the very end of chapter 10, when, perched on top of their belongings, the family "look[s] back" and sees their home, "a little smoke rising from the chimney." Then, a hill cuts off their view. In that moment Steinbeck distills the novel's view of humankind's relationship to the environment. While Steinbeck never openly condemns the farmers, he does point to their practices as part of the problem. At the same time, he clearly sympathizes with the way humans shape their lives in response to place, particularly the places of their experiences. Early in the novel, Muley Graves, who refuses to leave Oklahoma, tells Tom that on his land is a gully with a bush under which he "laid with a girl" for the first time. Certainly not an environmentalist in the current meaning of the word, Steinbeck nonetheless emphasizes the value of land forms and landscapes for the cultural memories they preserve; at the same time, his novel insists that to a large extent, humans are powerlessness in the face of epic environmental forces, that the geography of the hill can "cut off" the entire cultural past.

The Dust Bowl was an ecological disaster that literally changed the country, and whether or not humans caused or contributed to that disaster, *it* changed *them*. This idea becomes increasingly important as the novel progresses, and it becomes clearer and clearer that the Joads' only hope in the West will be community. It is not simply the hostile cultural forces against which the Okies must band if they are to survive, it is also the land itself. Manipulated, plundered, carved, and reshaped, the California landscape still manages to exert its power over the landowners and agricultural workers who depend on it. The Joads learn this lesson early, in the second part of the novel. Driving along Highway 66, they must constantly seek shade, even driving at night sometimes to escape the heat. Despite their precautions, both Granma and Granpa die of heat-related causes—Granpa without ever making it out of Oklahoma. Granma, on the other hand, dies in the truck, and Ma, afraid the agricultural inspectors will not let them enter California with a corpse, hides it from them and the family. Thus, Granma is buried in California with the family's last $40, and their entrance into the land of their dreams is marked by loss, death, poverty, and, most of all, a pervasive sense of their powerlessness over the world they inhabit.

A DYING EDEN

In California, the Joads must face the reality of their shattered dreams. Noah has left the family at the Colorado River, and soon enough, Rose of Sharon's husband deserts her. After a brief stop at a Hooverville, where a fight breaks out, sending Casy to jail and Tom into hiding, the family moves on. In chapter 22, they find a government camp, Weedpatch, which Steinbeck modeled after a camp in Arvin, California. One of the many sections in the novel made vivid by Steinbeck's ability to translate his real experience into fiction, the chapters at Weedpatch include details and anecdotes taken straight out of camp manager Tom Collins's field reports for the Farm Security Administration. There are flush toilets, which scare Ruthie and Winfield, laundry facilities, and organized dances. Sadly, the Joads must leave the camp when they run out of money and work. They find work picking peaches, and Tom reunites with Casy, whose earlier philosophical musings about the "stuff goin' on" have sharpened into socialist actions and union organizing attempts. When deputies break in on a strike meeting, Casy is killed and Tom kills Casy's murderer. Tom must go into hiding and while there, he decides to take over where Casy left off. Coming to the conclusion that it may be as Casy said, that "a fella ain't got a soul of his own, but on'y a piece of a big one," Tom tells Ma he wants to devote his life to organizing the workers. In one of the novel's most famous speeches, lines that Woody Guthrie used to close his ballad, "Tom Joad," Tom says:

> I'll be ever'where—wherever you look. Wherever they's a fight so hungry people can eat, I'll be there. Wherever they's a cop beatin' up a guy, I'll be there . . . . I'll be in the way kids laugh when they're hungry an' they know supper's ready. An' when our folks eat the stuff they raise an' live in the houses they build—why, I'll be there.

With her son's decision to leave the Joad family and effectively enter the family of humankind, Ma is left as the heart and mind of the family. As the remaining family members struggle through the first winter rains, the strength she has displayed throughout the novel moves to center stage. Clearly, the new community, which Steinbeck envisions as springing from the migrant experience, is represented not only in Tom's speech, but also in Ma's actions, in her stoic ability to survive no matter what. That ability becomes crucial at the novel's highly symbolic ending. When Rose of Sharon finally gives birth, her baby is stillborn. The family must move from the boxcar they've inhabited because rains have finally threatened to flood it, and they find shelter in a barn, where a small boy is tending to his dying father. When Ma sees that the man is starving to death, she urges her daughter to feed him with the milk her breasts have made for her dead baby. Rose of Sharon, whose most consistent characteristic has been the mysterious smile that comes across her face whenever she

feels the baby within her, is left to carry the novel's hopeful meaning. As she offers her bared breast to the man, the mysterious smile returns to her lips—a smile that does not suggest so much the man's rebirth as a larger, more profound birth of a new society that actively helps one another and upon whom each member can depend.

THE BIBLICAL TRADITION

John Steinbeck looked at the social disasters of his day and turned them into epic art via the notion of biblical exodus. Throughout the novel abound the biblical references that are so much a part of the literature of American colonization—William Bradford, governor of Plymouth Colony, for example, compared the pilgrims to "Moyses and the Isralits when they went out of Egipte." Steinbeck's pilgrims are exiled from the Dust Bowl to a new Eden, which will not yield its material fruits but which does ultimately offer up a new "fruit"—the hope for community in and from the wilderness. Behind the novel's closing floods and single act of human nurturing lies the tradition, biblical and rich, of the inevitable human need to believe in a new beginning and a second chance.

FURTHER READING

Coers, Donald V., Paul D. Ruffin, and Robert J. DeMott, eds. *After* The Grapes of Wrath: *Essays on John Steinbeck in Honor of Tetsumaro Hayashi.* Athens, Ohio, 1995.

Davis, Robert Con, ed. The Grapes of Wrath: *A Collection of Critical Essays.* Englewood Cliffs, N.J., 1982. An intelligent and useful appraisal of the major criticism of *The Grapes of Wrath* to date, pointing to a shift from critical interest in the novel's ability to tell the truth of the situation to a concern for its artistic structure.

Ditsky, John, ed. *Critical Essays on Steinbeck's* The Grapes of Wrath. Boston, 1989. Includes a lengthy and specific introductory survey of nearly all the prominent articles and books published on *The Grapes of Wrath* to date, and nine critical essays by major scholarly figures, including some covering biographical explorations into Steinbeck's writing process, interdisciplinary pieces by cultural geographers and filmographers, and revisionist essays.

Donohue, Agnes McNeill. *A Casebook on* The Grapes of Wrath. New York, 1968. Divided into two main sections, "*The Grapes of Wrath* as a Social Document" and "*The Grapes of Wrath* as Literature," this collection is especially useful as an introduction to critical approaches.

French, Warren G., ed. *A Companion to* The Grapes of Wrath. New York, 1963.

Harmon, Robert B. The Grapes of Wrath: *A Fifty Year Bibliographic Survey*. San Jose, Calif., 1990.

Hayashi, Tetsumaro, ed. *Steinbeck's* The Grapes of Wrath: *Essays in Criticism*. Muncie, Ind., 1990. Eight essays, each focusing on a specific theme, such as community or communism; a metaphor, such as drinking or the Eldorado; or a motif, such as the quest motif or the journey motif.

Heavilin, Barbara A., ed. *The Critical Response to John Steinbeck's* The Grapes of Wrath. Westport, Conn., 2000. Through reviews, previously published essays, and original material, this book records the critical reception of *The Grapes of Wrath* up to the editions of the 1990s. Includes a chronology, bibliography, and extensive introductory essay.

Johnson, Claudia D. *Understanding* The Grapes of Wrath: *A Student Casebook to Issues, Sources, and Historical Documents*. Westport, Conn., 1999.

Owens, Louis. The Grapes of Wrath: *Trouble in the Promised Land*. Boston, 1989. Provides a lucid reading of the novel, emphasizing Steinbeck's handling of ecological themes. In addition, it provides readers with a clear understanding of both intent and technique.

Steinbeck, John. *The Harvest Gypsies: On the Road to* The Grapes of Wrath. Berkeley, Calif., 1988. Charles Wollenberg provides an excellent introduction to Steinbeck's research and the way it influenced the novel. The book is filled with quotations from Steinbeck's journals and letters; photographs by Dorothea Lange illustrate Steinbeck's words.

Wyatt, David, ed. *New Essays on* The Grapes of Wrath. New York, 1990. Four essays that divide Steinbeck criticism into three stages: the debate over Steinbeck's veracity, a phase of formal criticism, and the contemporary wealth of theoretical approaches to reading (feminist, new historical, deconstructive) to understand the novel.

See also the essay on John Steinbeck, immediately preceding.

GERALD STERN

by Kimberly Lewis

Gerald Stern was born in Pittsburgh in 1925. He graduated from the University of Pittsburgh in 1947 with a degree in English, and moved on to get a master's degree at Columbia University and to attend the University of Paris. He spent the next twenty years teaching high school and college, while writing but not publishing. He published his first poem, "The Pineys," in 1969, long after all of the literary movements of his own generation. It was not until 1977, however, with the award-winning *Lucky Life*, that Stern finally emerged onto the scene of American poetry. He has since received numerous awards and recognitions, including grants from the National Endowment for the Arts and the Guggenheim Foundation, and the National Book Award for Poetry for his more recent *This Time: New and Selected Poems* (1998).

MOVEMENT AND TRANSFORMATION

Stern is often compared to Walt Whitman, whose present-tense quest for self-definition, tone of exhilaration, and tendency to write primarily in the first person he shares. Unlike his critics, however, Stern prefers to associate his work with the enigmatic and metaphysical lyrics of Emily Dickinson. As Jane Somerville rightfully points out in *Making the Light Come* (1990), the voice of his first-person narrator is close to that of a fictional character or a performer, taking his reader along on his search for an understanding of himself and the world around him. This narrator is ever capable of transformation, during the course of a poem, into the objects in that world, into animals and trees, and into the role of beings with whom he so deeply relates as to share their experience. "Love for the Dog" illustrates this blurring transformation, as well as the humor that characteristically enlivens many of Stern's musings: "In the middle of his exhausted brain there rose a metaphor / of an animal, a dog with a broken spine sliding around / helplessly in the center of the slippery floor . . . . / He sat there proud of his metaphor, tears of mercy in his eyes, / unable in his dumbness to explain his pleasure, / unable now even to rise because of the spine." This sort of intimate interaction with the world around

him is a key element in Stern's movement toward the exhilaration and the truth he seeks. He most often finds it in solitary interaction with the natural world. It is in the country, "sitting in Raubsville, / the only Jew on the river, counting my poems" that he frequently wanders and speaks to his reader, while he imagines the rest of the literary universe convening in the cafés of the big city. Even in the poems that are set in the city (most frequently in New York), he remains with "one foot on 72nd Street, one foot in the river," dreaming and isolated from the crowds around him.

In both the city and the country, however, he is rarely still. Instead he moves constantly, walking through his transformations and his thoughts, in search of those "pockets" in the concrete universe where something unexpected may be revealed. "I'm back in Pittsburgh now," says the traveler, "it's only here / and maybe Detroit and maybe a little Chicago / that there are Joseph pockets where you can see / the dream turned around and the darkness illuminated, / some of the joy explained, some of the madness." He walks with his reader into such moments, presenting us not with the formal analysis of a discovery already made and digested, but rather with the enactment of thought, with the experience of encounters (more frequently human in later volumes) that redefine him. His voice tends to address us in informal and conversational tones. Inventive but rarely dwelling in convolutions of language for the sake of language, he balances on a thin line between lyric poetry and prose, reconciling the intellectual and the emotional extremes of the movements into which much of his generation of poets had polarized themselves.

MEMORY, JUDAISM, AND EXILE

Although the immediacy of experience is fundamental in Stern's poetry, his later work, in particular, attempts to bring the past, even a quotidian past, into the light of the present. He also makes numerous references to a more eternal history: that of the Bible, of the Holocaust, of his own Jewish upbringing, and of his sometimes-guilty distance from it. Featured in various collections of Jewish-American poets, Stern shies away from harsh classifications. Yet, with explicit sorrow and fraternity along with confusion, he addresses his Judaism most explicitly in poems like "Soap": "My counterpart was born in 1925 / in a city in Poland—I don't like to see him born / in a little village fifty miles from Kiev / and have to fight so wildly just for access / to books . . . . / I loved how he dreamed, how he almost / disappeared when he was in thought. For him / I write this poem, for my little brother, if I / should call him that . . . . " The artist, especially one like Stern who, in his "Self Portrait" likens himself to Van Gogh, sees himself sharing exile with the Jewish victims of the time of his adolescence.

In Stern's poetry, the wanderer seeking truth envisions himself more than once as a rabbi, living in the timeless margins of the world. In those margins, the chain of relation is elongated to include all manner of the exiled and the rejected, but specifically returns to images of animals and of the downtrodden. In his longest poem, "Hot Dog," he takes us with him into his life around Tompkins Square in Manhattan. A torrent of musings on religion, politics, and his own life accompany the descriptions of his surroundings, including Hot Dog, a homeless woman with whom he relates but cannot communicate. He finds her passed out in a cellar entrance one day, and in watching her he finds a religiousness that he has been seeking throughout the poem, perhaps throughout all of his poems. "I waited for some dark light / to turn bright in front of the Odessa, / I wanted to feel the light; I did it by stages, / with one eye then the other, I almost threw myself down on their bed . . . . / it was a kind of altar, half / cement, half steel; / . . . I couldn't tell whose mind they were in besides my own."

WORKS

Rejoicings (1973)
The Naming of Beasts (1973)
Lucky Life (1977)
The Red Coal (1981)
Paradise Poems (1984)
Lovesick (1987)
Two Long Poems (1990)
Leaving Another Kingdom: Selected Poems (1990)
Bread without Sugar (1992)
Odd Mercy (1995)
This Time: New and Selected Poems (1998)
Last Blue (2000)
American Sonnets (2002)

FURTHER READING

Moyers, Bill, and James Haba, eds. *The Language of Life: A Festival of Poets.* New York, 1995. Contains an interesting interview with Stern, addressing mainly the poems of *Lucky Life.*

Pacernick, Gary. *Meaning and Memory: Interviews with Fourteen Jewish Poets.* Columbus, Ohio, 2001.

Somerville, Jane. *Making the Light Come: The Poetry of Gerald Stern.* Detroit, 1990. A great book, and the only one devoted exclusively to Stern's work.

WALLACE STEVENS

by James Longenbach

There are two ways to describe the career of Wallace Stevens. One would be this: after having been born in Reading, Pennsylvania, in 1879, Stevens attended Harvard University and New York Law School; he began working in 1908 in the insurance industry, and in 1934 he was named vice president of the Hartford Accident and Indemnity Company, where he continued to work virtually until the day of his death in 1955. The other way of describing his career would be this: after publishing *Harmonium* in 1923, Stevens wrote no poems for almost a decade; but after his second book, *Ideas of Order*, appeared in 1935, he wrote consistently and in comparative obscurity for the rest of his life. His *Collected Poems* (1954) received the National Book Award and the Pulitzer Prize after his death in Hartford, Connecticut, in 1955.

Other great modern American poets had real jobs: T. S. Eliot worked as a banker and a publisher; Marianne Moore was an editor; William Carlos Williams was a doctor. What distinguishes Stevens is that he never gave the impression of feeling any tension

Wallace Stevens, 1952.
(*National Portrait Gallery, Smithsonian Institution/Art Resource*)

between the different aspects of his life. Instead, he thrived on their differences. He once quipped that "money is a kind of poetry," but he more often emphasized that his daily life was in no really meaningful way poetic. In an essay called "Surety and Fidelity Claims," he emphasized that his insurance work was above all else tedious: "You sign a lot of drafts. You see surprisingly few people. You do the greater part of your work either in your own office or in other lawyers' offices. You don't even see the country; you see law offices and hotel rooms." Stevens embraced tedium—the world of what he called, in his

poetry, the ordinary or the humdrum; in order to write poems at all, he needed to feel that his most fanciful poetic flights were balanced by a clear, no-nonsense engagement with the ordinary world. Depending on how we look at him, Stevens can seem like the most worldly or the most otherworldly of the modern poets.

You will never find Stevens sounding like Ezra Pound, who did Shelley one better by saying that poets should be the "acknowledged" legislators of their time. And you will not find in Stevens's poetry any of the aura of world-historical importance that clings to Eliot's *The Waste Land* (1922). For that reason, Stevens seemed during his lifetime to be out of step with most of the other moderns: his poems seemed too fanciful, too pretty, too unconcerned with the great questions concerning the fate of modern culture. But today, it has become clearer that Stevens was far from unconcerned with such questions; he simply did not address them in a style that carried with it the impression of cultural relevance.

PLAIN AND FANCY

As a poet, Stevens's entire effort was, as he put it in "Effects of Analogy," to press toward "the ultimate good sense which we term civilization." But Stevens rightly understood that it is not a simple task to arrive at that good sense; our ordinary world is not easy to apprehend, and we cannot take our common-sense apprehensions for granted. In his late poem "The Plain Sense of Things," he emphasizes that plainness is for him an achievement, the result of a never-ending struggle: "the absence of the imagination had / Itself to be imagined," he says, going on to offer a little parable:

> The great pond,
> The plain sense of it, without reflections, leaves,
> Mud, water like dirty glass, expressing silence
>
> Of a sort, silence of a rat come out to see,
> The great pond and its waste of the lilies, all this
> Had to be imagined as an inevitable knowledge,
> Required, as a necessity requires.

These final lines of the poem equate the recovery of the "plain sense of things" with the assumption of a rat's low perspective on the world. The rat sees muddy water for what it is; viewed from a higher point of view, the surface of the water would be clouded by reflections. Yet Stevens's construction of this earthbound point of view is itself a highly imaginative act: the poem both describes and enacts the paradoxical notion that the absence of the imagination must be imagined.

It is impossible to be plain, Stevens suggests over and over again, without being fancy, and even if his poems tilt at times to either of these extremes, the poems always contain the specter of the opposite quality. In an early poem called "The Snow Man," Stevens again emphasizes the difficulty of achieving a clear vision of the ordinary world. He says that "one must have a mind of winter" if one is to look at a bleak winter landscape and not attribute any human misery to the bleak natural world.

> One must have a mind of winter . . . not to think
> Of any misery in the sound of the wind,
> In the sound of a few leaves,
>
> Which is the sound of the land
> Full of the same wind
> That is blowing in the same bare place
>
> For the listener, who listens in the snow,
> And, nothing himself, beholds
> Nothing that is not there and the nothing that is.

Stevens is surely relying on a conventional literary topos here; Robert Frost reveals a similar interest in the wintery blankness of the natural world in poems like "Desert Places." But Stevens also suggests here in "The Snow Man," as he does in "The Plain Sense of Things," that the act of emptying the mind is a highly imaginative act: to "behold" nothing, rather than merely to "regard it," as the poems says, is to acquire some majesty. To distinguish a potent absence ("nothing that is not there") from a potent existential presence ("the nothing that is" there)

is to have achieved a kind of grandeur that Wordsworth would recognize.

"The Snow Man" is a well-known example of Stevens's quiet, meditative mode. At other times he can be extremely exuberant—playful to the point almost of seeming ridiculous (a quality whose positive function he wants us to consider). In "Tea at the Palaz of Hoon," a companion poem to "The Snow Man," Stevens writes with wild abandon not about the act of emptying the mind but about asserting that the mind is the source of everything—all perception, all value. The sound of this poetry is not plain.

> Not less because in purple I descended
> The western day through what you called
> The loneliest air, not less was I myself.
>
> What was the ointment sprinkled on my beard?
> What were the hymns that buzzed beside my ears?
> What was the sea whose tide swept through me there?
>
> Out of my mind the golden ointment rained,
> And my ears made the blowing hymns they heard.
> I was myself the compass of that sea:
>
> I was the world in which I walked, and what I saw
> Or heard or felt came not but from myself;
> And there I found myself more truly and more strange.

While "The Snow Man" is written in an oblique third person ("One must have a mind of winter"), "Tea at the Palaz of Hoon" is written in a regally assertive first-person voice. And in contrast to "The Snow Man," this poem says that in order fully to experience the world we must not let the world speak to us but must recognize that we speak for the world: our grand visions come exclusively from within, not from without.

Reading Stevens, it is crucial that we not limit him to either of these points of view. Both "The Snow Man" and "Tea at the Palaz of Hoon" were collected in Stevens's first volume of poems, *Harmonium* (1923), and not only throughout that book but throughout his career, Stevens oscillates between these perspectives, weaving what he once called "an endlessly elaborating poem" between the poles epitomized by these two poems. Sometimes, as in "Tea at the Palaz of Hoon," he emphasizes the mind's ability to fabricate elaborate metaphors or structures of belief, reminding us that all values are not naturally given in the world but are imposed on the world by human consciousness. At other times, as in "The Snow Man," he cautions us to remember that those structures of belief inevitably collapse in the face of events of which human consciousness can make no sense.

This endless elaboration is not systematic; Stevens offers no consistent program other than the need continually to challenge one perspective with another. Eventually, however, he offered three tentative prescriptions for a viable belief system in his great long poem, *Notes toward a Supreme Fiction* (1942): "It Must Be Abstract," "It Must Give Pleasure," and—most important—"It Must Change." However delightful the imagined palace of Hoon might be, we must not be allowed to grow accustomed to it. Sooner or later our most treasured metaphors, our most treasured beliefs, must be torn away, and we must begin again by distinguishing nothing from the nothing.

In many ways, the title of *Notes toward a Supreme Fiction* may stand for all of Stevens's poetry: throughout his career, Stevens was attempting to satisfy what the American pragmatist philosopher William James called the "will to believe." The supreme fiction was, for Stevens, something to which we assent while knowing it to be untrue. Like James and the other pragmatists, Stevens was interested in the usefulness of the stories we tell rather than in their singular truth. "The truth," said William James in a famous passage in *Pragmatism* (1907), "is what works," and like James, Stevens worked hard to delete the definite article so often placed in front of the word truth: his interest is not in "the" truth, but in our never-ending efforts to reformulate what might usefully be considered to be truth.

THE EARLY WORK

"Sunday Morning," one of the richest poems in *Harmonium*, is an early embodiment of Stevens's effort to formulate a supreme fiction—an idea or principle that might make provisional sense out of the chaos of experience. The poem consists of eight stanzas of fifteen blank verse lines and it moves, like most of Stevens's poems of middle or long length, by association and juxtaposition rather than by the unfolding of a linear argument or narrative (though the poem does contain bits of argument and of narrative). "In a skeptical age," Stevens once said, "in the absence of a belief in god, the mind turns to its own creations and examines them for the support they give." The eight sections of "Sunday Morning" offer differing perspectives on this proposition. The poem asks: How do we face our mortality without an assurance of some transcendental power? Where do we locate a sense of permanent value in a world that is exclusively finite and forever changing?

That is a topic common enough in nineteenth- and twentieth-century poetry; think of Matthew Arnold or Emily Dickinson. What distinguishes Stevens is that he does not spend much time wondering if there might be a world beyond us; he accepts that lack and transforms it into plenitude—a world of possibility. In the first stanza of the poem, there is no question of attending church on Sunday morning; we simply take pleasure in the sensual world around us.

> Complacencies of the peignoir, and late
> Coffee and oranges in a sunny chair,
> And the green freedom of a cockatoo
> Upon a rug mingle to dissipate
> The holy hush of ancient sacrifice.
> She dreams a little, and she feels the dark
> Encroachment of that old catastrophe,
> As a calm darkens among water-lights.
> The pungent oranges and bright, green wings
> Seem things in some procession of the dead,
> Winding across wide water, without sound.
> The day is like wide water, without sound,
> Stilled for the passing of her dreaming feet
> Over the seas, to silent Palestine,
> Dominion of the blood and sepulcher.

But notice what happens here as soon as the everyday quotidian world is embraced. Though the woman is luxuriating in the coffee and oranges, and though the uncaged cockatoo seems to be an image of her freedom, the woman is still troubled by the encroachment of that old catastrophe: change, mortality, death. Those lovely earthly things—the oranges and green wings—begin to seem (because they themselves are mortal) like things in a procession of the dead. We recognize that these pleasures will not last forever; we wonder how we will continue to be happy without them. So, as the final lines of the stanza suggest, we are tempted for a moment to think back to silent Palestine, to the religious consolation that the poem rejected even before it began.

But we are not tempted for long. "Why should she give her bounty to the dead?" asks the second stanza. Why cannot the woman simply continue to find solace in pungent fruit and green wings? And what good is an idea of a divinity if it is merely elusive and ethereal, coming to her only in shadows and dreams? To be satisfied, we need the concrete, sensuous realities of the earth—not the vague mythologies of a world beyond the senses. The last lines of the second stanza reaffirm that earthly things, "the bough of summer and the winter branch," will be the measures of the woman's soul. And yet the very way in which those earthly things are described once again raises the specter of their inadequacy: the full, weighted bough of summer becomes the barren branch in winter. The world fades; where then is our pleasure?

Having read only these two stanzas, we can see not only what the major preoccupations of "Sunday Morning" are but also how the poem works, how it moves. "Sunday Morning" offers not conclusions but a delicate interchange between doubt and affirmation: it is a potentially endless dialogue in which provisional assertions raise more questions in turn. The poem folds back on itself, revising, reconsidering. It forces readers to live in contingency, in change, and this formal principle will, at the end of the poem, be affirmed on the thematic level: change itself will become our only possible value.

The beginning of the fourth stanza restates the poem's dilemma.

> She says, "I am content when wakened birds,
> Before they fly, test the reality
> Of misty fields, by their sweet questionings;
> But when the birds are gone, and their warm fields
> Return no more, where, then, is paradise?"

The question is, once again, what do we do after the things we love die? The rest of the stanza provides one more provisional answer.

> There is not any haunt of prophecy,
> Nor any old chimera of the grave,
> Neither the golden underground, nor isle
> Melodious, where spirits gat them home,
> Nor visionary south, nor cloudy palm
> Remote on heaven's hill, that has endured
> As April's green endures; or will endure
> Like her remembrance of awakened birds,
> Or her desire for June and evening, tipped
> By the consummation of the swallow's wings.

These lines suggest that we must simply accept the idea that our earthly existence is all we have. Since there is no prophecy, no promise of eternal life, we must find permanence in nature: though summer turns to winter, April has a kind of permanence since it returns with the cycle of the seasons. The implication is that the earthly things we love—oranges, green wings—will always be returned to us.

But as the poem moves on, this answer is not good enough; it, too, must change. In the next stanza the woman says, "but in contentment I still feel the need of some imperishable bliss." The answer to this statement is pithy and severe: "Death is the mother of beauty," says Stevens, echoing Keats, who said in the "Ode on Melancholy," "she dwells with beauty—beauty that must die." Less pithily aphoristic, more beautifully inconclusive, is Stevens's explication of this traditional sentiment.

> She makes the willow shiver in the sun
> For maidens who were wont to sit and gaze
> Upon the grass, relinquished to their feet.
> She causes boys to pile new plums and pears
> On disregarded plate.

All these little things give pleasure, says Stevens, because we are aware of death. The oranges and bright green wings are important precisely because we know they are not permanent; death is the mother of beauty and of love. And the following stanza suggests that even if we could experience heaven, a perfect world in which nothing ever changed or died, then we could not possibly find anything beautiful. Only a sense of impermanence and change grants the human condition meaning.

Depending on our sensibility, we might find that wisdom either threatening or consoling. But as we might expect by now, Stevens feels both threatened and consoled. Given a choice, he will never choose between alternatives; he will always find a way of sustaining both alternatives at the same time. So in the penultimate stanza of "Sunday Morning," Stevens gives us a little desperation: he describes a kind of primitive ritual—a group of men attempting through ritual to lend, as Hart Crane said in *The Bridge* (1930), a myth to God.

> Supple and turbulent, a ring of men
> Shall chant in orgy on a summer morn
> Their boisterous devotion to the sun,
> Not as a god, but as a god might be,
> Naked among them, like a savage source.
> Their chant shall be a chant of paradise,
> Out of their blood, returning to the sky.

We are probably meant to find these lines a little exaggerated. That is, it is crucial that this desperation is registered in the poem, because otherwise the poem would run the risk of seeming smug—as if existential despair were merely for other, less enlightened people. Still, the poem does not end here. In the final stanza, Stevens calms down, pulling back from the frenzy of ritual. He brazenly redefines the terms of Jesus's immortality, suggesting that his life had value not because he is said to have risen from the dead, but rather because, like all human beings, he died. Here is the final stanza of the poem:

> She hears, upon that water without sound,
> A voice that cries, "The tomb in Palestine
> Is not the porch of spirits lingering.
> It is the grave of Jesus, where he lay."
> We live in an old chaos of the sun,
> Or old dependency of day and night,
> Or island solitude, unsponsored, free,

Of that wide water, inescapable.
Deer walk upon our mountains, and the quail
Whistle about us their spontaneous cries;
Sweet berries ripen in the wilderness;
And, in the isolation of the sky,
At evening, casual flocks of pigeons make
Ambiguous undulations as they sink,
Downward to darkness, on extended wings.

Like the opening lines of "Sunday Morning," these lines give us images of decline and decay; the difference is that now we have a reason not to be afraid. At the beginning, beautiful things became objects in a procession toward death; at the end, we take consolation in that procession—in change, in mortality—recognizing that we value those things because we will lose them.

Probably the most important thing about "Sunday Morning" is that it ends with images of change: the ripening fruit, the pigeons that sound so much like the swallows in Keats's ode "To Autumn." Stevens wants us to recognize the tenuousness or provisionality of his own conclusions. The American literary critic Kenneth Burke once said that true poems continually turn against "their own best discoveries," and Stevens's poems do this aggressively. No matter what he says, you can be sure of two things: first, that he will say it again, and second, that he will say the opposite somewhere else. The movement of both individual poems and the whole of his oeuvre is motivated by this logic: having offered a temptingly complete fiction, Stevens must again acquire (as he puts it in "The Snow Man") a "mind of winter," scraping away the fiction he has erected in order to face the cold, stark reality of a changing world. As a result, his poems seem constantly to rewrite themselves as they move forward; in addition, whole poems seem like rewritings of earlier poems. This is why the entire body of Stevens's poetry can sometimes seem of one piece: a giant, fluctuating poem about the attempt to formulate a supreme fiction about the human desire to attribute plausible meanings to the world.

THE MIDDLE PERIOD

After publishing *Harmonium* in 1923, Stevens wrote no poetry for almost a decade; the silence did not seem to bother him because other aspects of his ordinary life were just as fulfilling as the act of writing poems. When he began to write poems again in the early 1930s, however, he did seem somewhat chastened: while the poems continue to address elaborate philosophical themes, they also record Stevens's awareness of social conditions a little

more plainly. But the effect of this new sobriety is to make Stevens's fanciful side seem all the more crucial; Stevens could not honor the ordinary world by other than extravagant means.

In retrospect, consequently, even the well-known "Sunday Morning" does not give us the whole of Stevens. Its final lines are beautiful, echoing with the whole romantic tradition of poetry; reading them, we feel the shadows not only of Keats but of Milton, Whitman, and Tennyson. But seemingly we also feel that those lines are slightly in danger of seeming earnest; they lack the playfulness, the verbal exuberance that at other moments is an integral part of Stevens's worldview. "The Man on the Dump," first published in 1939 and then collected in *Parts of a World* (1942), offers a provocative adjustment: the poem registers the social conditions of the Great Depression but does not confuse seriousness with sanctimoniousness.

Throughout "The Man on the Dump," Stevens plays with the "waste land" imagery that for a long time seemed like such an integral part of Eliotic modernism: we live on the dump. But for Stevens, that is not such a bad place to live. He is not saying that our world has become a wasteland; he is saying that the dump is a good metaphor for what the world has always been. Here are the poem's opening lines:

Day creeps down. The moon is creeping up.
The sun is a corbeil of flowers the moon Blanche
Places there, a bouquet. Ho-ho . . . The dump is full
Of images. Days pass like papers from a press.
The bouquets come here in the papers. So the sun,
And so the moon, both come, and the janitor's poems
Of every day, the wrapper on the can of pears,
The cat in the paper bag, the corset, the box
From Esthonia: the tiger chest, for tea.

The freshness of night has been fresh a long time.
The freshness of morning, the blowing of days, one says
That it puffs as Cornelius Nepos reads, it puffs
More than, less than or it puffs like this or that.
The green smacks in the eye, the dew in the green
Smacks like fresh water in a can, like the sea
On a cocoanut—how many men have copied dew
For buttons, how many women have covered themselves
With dew, dew dresses, stones and chains of dew, heads
Of the floweriest flowers dewed with the dewiest dew.
One grows to hate these things except on the dump.

Stevens offers here a homeless man on a garbage dump. But we begin to sense right away that he means this figure to stand for all of us: the man on the dump has a name, Cornelius Nepos, who was not just anybody. Nepos was a Roman historian who wrote a vast history of the world in three volumes; the Roman poet Catullus dedicated his poems to Nepos. So by borrowing that name, Stevens suggests that this man on the dump is a kind of historian—someone who makes a record of the world for future generations, someone to whom poets look for records. He also suggests that the making of such records is precarious business; the work of Cornelius Nepos has by and large been lost.

It has been noted that the dump is not a negative image for Stevens, but notice that in the poem's opening lines, the dump does not seem to be particularly entrancing. It seems a bit dull, and yet it contains what Stevens calls "the janitor's poems of every day." Stevens suggests at least two things with that line: that all human endeavors are in some sense poetry and that the idea of poetry, in all its nobility, is contained within even the most mundane human effort. Even a list of things on the dump (the wrapper on the can of pears, the cat in the paper bag, the box from Esthonia) can be a kind of poetry. And Stevens seems to prefer this kind of poetry of everyday things to a gaudier kind of utterance; his repetition of the words "dew" and "dewy" make gaudy things seem silly:

> dew dresses, stones and chains of dew, heads
> Of the floweriest flowers dewed with the dewiest dew.
> One grows to hate these things except on the dump.

We need the dump, says Stevens. We need to be grounded in a world of necessity in order to appreciate fanciful things, just as in "Sunday Morning" we need to face our mortality in order to appreciate beauty—just as Stevens himself needed to go to work at the Hartford Insurance Company every day until he died.

But subsequent lines explain that this world of necessity, this world of everyday things on the dump, can seem ordinary in the worst sense of the word (dull, complacent) if we do not work to make something out of that world.

> Now, in the time of spring (azaleas, trilliums,
> Myrtle, viburnums, daffodils, blue phlox),
> Between that disgust and this, between the things
> That are on the dump (azaleas and so on)
> And those that will be (azaleas and so on),
> One feels the purifying change. One rejects
> The trash.
>
> That's the moment when the moon creeps up
> To the bubbling of bassoons. That's the time
> One looks at the elephant-colorings of tires.

> Everything is shed; and the moon comes up as the moon
> (All its images are in the dump) and you see
> as a man (not like an image of a man),
> You see the moon rise in the empty sky.

In contrast to "Sunday Morning," in which seasonal change offers real consolation, the return of spring seems here like nothing but dull repetition—azaleas and so on. Stevens wants the world to change, but he is insisting that to sit back and let the world change is not enough. Meaningful change must be worked for; it must be imagined, added to the dump. And we begin to do that, says Stevens, by rejecting the trash. The implication here is that not everything on the dump is trash; the good stuff must be sifted out and preserved. And by making this selection, by choosing to shape the dump, we cause more interesting changes to take place: the moon rises, and what once seemed to be a pile of tires now seems like an elephant. But notice that what has changed here is not so much the dump as such; what has changed is our way of perceiving it. We are able to see possibilities where before there was only trash.

The emphasis here is that Stevens means the man on the dump to be a representative for all humankind, and that becomes clearer in the poem's final lines. In the last stanza, Stevens no longer describes the individual actions of the tramp but describes what "one" does, what everyone does, on the dump. Here are the key lines, lines that resonate throughout all of Stevens's poetry: "One sits and beats an old tin can, lard pail. / One beats and beats for that which one believes."

Beginning with "Sunday Morning," as already noted, many of Stevens's poems are about the act of formulating something in which we might provisionally believe. "The Man on the Dump" is one of Stevens's most wonderfully profound poems about this problem because it is just a little bit ridiculous—it does not quite take itself seriously. In "Sunday Morning" we dance like savages in the sun for what we believe; Stevens moves away from that hysterical image in the poem's final lines. By contrast, in "The Man on the Dump" we beat a tin can for what we believe. This action makes "The Man on the Dump" feel like the grown-up version of "Sunday Morning." The poem is not only less earnest; it even tries to make the important work it describes seem a bit silly. It refuses to confuse the serious with the sanctimonious. It reminds us that at our moments of greatest power, we must remember most clearly our limitations. And in its final lines, "The Man on the Dump" offers a primal but slightly absurd image for poetic expression, for the making of supreme fictions.

Here is the poem's provocative last stanza, beginning with the lines about beating an old tin can:

> One sits and beats an old tin can, lard pail.
> One beats and beats for that which one believes.
> That's what one wants to get near. Could it after all
> Be merely oneself, as superior as the ear
> To a crow's voice? Did the nightingale torture the ear,
> Pack the heart and scratch the mind? And does the ear
> Solace itself in peevish birds? Is it peace,
> Is it a philosopher's honeymoon, one finds
> On the dump? Is it to sit among the mattresses of the dead,
> Bottles, pots, shoes and grass and murmur *aptest eve*:
> Is it to hear the blatter of grackles and say
> *Invisible priest*; is it to eject, to pull
> The day to pieces and cry *stanza my stone*?
> Where was it one first heard of the truth? The the.

We beat our old tin can, remaking and transforming the dump. And as we do so, we ask a sequence of questions. Does the nightingale, that traditional image for poetic inspiration, torture our ears? The implied answer is no, not really; the dump is not such a dramatic place. Then, the poem asks, is the dump a place of peace—a place for the philosopher's honeymoon, where all answers are given? The answer once again is no, not really; the dump is far from perfect. Nor is the dump the place of "aptest eve" or a place where grackles, those ugly little birds, become the voices of an "invisible priest." The poem's final line asks the question the poem has been approaching all along: "Where was it one first heard of the truth?" Where, in other words, do we discover value and permanence in this dump of a world? And the answer is one sentence, two words, two syllables that are the same syllable: "The the."

What are we to make of that? There are a number of ways to read that wonderful final sentence, but Stevens is probably suggesting that we only began to think of the truth as single and unchanging when we put the word "the," the definite article, in front of the word "Truth." Like the pragmatist philosopher William James, Stevens is saying that we diminish our world if we believe in a single-minded, exclusive concept of truth. If we do entertain such a notion, then our dump will, in fact, look like a wasteland—a falling away from some greater, more attractive state of existence. But if we conceive of truth as a plurality, a state of becoming rather than a state of perfection, then we will begin to feel at home in our world. Instead of lamenting its decline, we will pick up the never-ending task of change.

Stevens always published "The Man on the Dump" beside a poem called "On the Road Home," which begins with lines that help us to think about the phrase "the the."

> It was when I said,
> "There is no such thing as the truth,"
> that the grapes seemed fatter.
> The fox ran out of his hole.

Stevens emphasizes here that when we escape from "the" truth, when there is no longer any such thing as "the" truth, then we can accept the wonder of the world's trash; our pleasures seem fatter, more satisfying, and even wild animals (exemplars of our own wish for freedom) seem more exquisitely free. Our freedom hinges on our ability to redescribe the world—to throw over old descriptions, old doctrines, formulating new ones that will in time be rejected as well.

TOWARD THE FINAL ACHIEVEMENT

"The Man on the Dump" and "On the Road Home" were published side by side in *Parts of a World* in 1942, the same year that *Notes toward a Supreme Fiction* was first published as a chapbook. Five years later *Notes toward a Supreme Fiction* would appear as the final poem in *Transport to Summer* (1947), where it seems deceptively like a finale rather than the foundation on which Stevens's later poems rest. Building on the shorter poems of *Parts of a World* (and looking back to "Sunday Morning"), *Notes toward a Supreme Fiction* represents Stevens's best effort to describe what is valuable about ordinary experience; simultaneously—but not paradoxically—it is Stevens's most fancifully elaborate poem. It is the poem for which his earlier work seems in retrospect to prepare and the poem on which the many extraordinary poems of his prolific final years depend.

As has been mentioned, *Notes* is divided into three parts ("It Must Be Abstract," "It Must Change," and "It Must Give Pleasure"), each part consisting of ten cantos of twenty-one lines each. The supreme fiction must be abstract in the sense that it must be abstracted from experience—a constructed rather than a given thing. It must change because the world for which it accounts changes; a fiction that is useful at one historical moment may not be useful at another. Finally, the supreme fiction must give pleasure in the most profound sense of the word: it must make the human condition tolerable. The woman in "Sunday Morning" yearns for "imperishable bliss," but in *Notes*, Stevens speaks less desperately of "accessible bliss" and "expressible bliss": he wants to describe the pleasure that might be found even in the repetitive grind of our ordinary waking hours.

The first canto of "It Must Be Abstract" begins by instructing the "ephebe" or student to "become an ignorant man again," discarding all outmoded fictions. He must attempt to see the sun not as Phoebus Apollo but purely and simply as itself. "The Sun / Must bear no name," says Stevens, but as in "The Snow Man" and "The Plain Sense of Things," he also recognizes that it is difficult to achieve this purity of vision. In the second canto Stevens consequently acknowledges that "not to have is the beginning of desire": old fictions must be discarded only so that we may begin the task of constructing new ones. "From this the poem springs," says Stevens in crucial lines from canto 4: "that we live in a place / That is not our own and, much more, not ourselves." We need fictions in order to make our lives bearable, and much of the remainder of *Notes* proposes and discards various fictions, moving back and forth between what Stevens calls an "ever-early candor" (the willed state of ignorance) and a "late plural" (the fullness of the achieved fiction). One could also think of this vacillation occurring between the poles represented by "The Snow Man" and "Tea at the Palaz of Hoon."

In the eighth canto of "It Must Be Abstract," Stevens begins to propose a particular fiction. Like the poems of *Parts of a World*, *Notes toward a Supreme Fiction* was written during World War II, and for a time Stevens entertained the idea of heroism as the fiction necessary to a war-ravaged culture. But in *Notes*, Stevens insists that the heroic (or what he now calls the idea of "major man") cannot be divorced from ordinary experience. Major man is given an ordinary name ("MacCullough"), but Stevens describes him only generally and says that we must "give him / No names"—as if the act of identifying major man too clearly would compromise his usefulness as our supreme fiction. Yet the poem dramatizes our impatience ("Who is it?"), and Stevens finally offers us a glimpse of this great "rabbi" or "chieftain" in the final lines of canto 10. Expecting a figure of magnitude, we meet instead the man on the dump—a tramp "in that old coat, those sagging pantaloons," a single figure who unites "these separate figures one by one." Stevens makes the appearance of MacCullough seem like the Resurrection ("Cloudless the morning. It is he"), but this embodiment of the heroic ideal is simultaneously ordinary and extraordinary. Similarly, the poem itself must use extraordinary means, great flights of metaphor, in order to make us feel the wonder of the everyday world.

Having offered this fiction of the hero, however, Stevens immediately drops the idea, never to return to it: no fiction can be counted on to last forever and we must force ourselves to turn against our discoveries, testing them against a changing world. In canto 3 of "It Must Change," Stevens suggests that our hero could too easily become rigid and absurd, like the majestic statue of General Du Puy: "There never had been, never could be, such / A man." The general was "rubbish in the end," suggests Stevens, "because nothing had changed."

Throughout Stevens's poetry, statues often serve as emblems of fictions that need to be changed. But in *Notes*, as in "The Man on the Dump," even the changing world surrounding the statue does not change enough. The first canto of "It Must Change" rejects seasonal change as merely predictable: "It is a repetition . . . not broken into subtleties." Although the birdsong in canto 6 recalls Shelley's "Ode to the West Wind" ("Be thou me, said the sparrow"), the birdsong also yields the "granite monotony" of mere repetition. Once again, Stevens insists that meaningful change is something we do not merely observe but must help to enact; our fictions must be as rigorously dismantled as they are constructed.

The low points of *Notes toward a Supreme Fiction* are these moments in which our ordinary world seems incapable of sustaining us—of offering more than the repetition of the same old thing. "To sing Jubilas at exact, accustomed times," says Stevens in the first canto of "It Must Give Pleasure," is merely "a facile exercise." As a possible antidote to this vision of conventional piety, Stevens offers the Canon Aspirin, the supreme individualist, the man of extravagant imaginative power. In canto 5 the Canon consumes an elaborate meal of "lobster Bombay with mango / Chutney" but also takes note of the simple life of his sister and her daughters. Unlike the Canon, the sister lives in a world of other people; she holds her daughters "closlier to her by rejecting dreams." However attractive the Canon's extravagance may initially seem, he is finally an ineffectual dreamer—a fiction maker who is content to live within his imagination, refusing to test his dreams against the ordinary world. "He imposes orders" on the world rather than discovering them, says Stevens in canto 7; he "establishes statutes" instead of keeping his fictions malleable.

But having rejected ordinary repetition and extraordinary imaginative power, Stevens reaches the crisis point of *Notes toward a Supreme Fiction* in canto 8: he asks "What am I to believe?"—the same bald question that lies at the heart of "Sunday Morning" and "The Man on the Dump." His answer ("I have not but I am and as I am, I am") has several important connotations: he stands alone with poetry (the repeated "I am" embodying the rhythm of the iambs in the iambic pentameter line), with imagination (which Coleridge defined in the *Biographia Literaria* [1817] as "a repetition in the finite mind of the eternal act of creation in the infinite I AM") and also with the ordinary self ("as I am") in the ordinary world. In canto 9 of "It Must Give Pleasure," the climax of the entire poem, Stevens is now able to embrace mere repetition as the highest good. Once scorned as monotonous, birdsong now seems redeeming:

> These things at least comprise
> An occupation, an exercise, a work,
> A thing final in itself and, therefore, good.

Everyday experience that once seemed merely "common" is now treasured precisely because it is "common"—both ordinary and communal, a meal not eaten in solitude (like the Canon Aspirin's meal) but shared with other people.

> One of the vast repetitions final in
> Themselves and, therefore, good, the going round
>
> And round and round, the merely going round,
> Until merely going round is a final good,
> The way wine comes at a table in a wood,
>
> And we enjoy like men, the way a leaf
> Above the table spins its constant spin,
> So that we look at it with pleasure, look
> At it spinning its eccentric measure. Perhaps,
> The man-hero is not the exceptional monster,
> But he that of repetition is most master.

As these lines suggest, *Notes toward a Supreme Fiction* does not offer a vision of another world as our consolation. Instead, it goes to extraordinary lengths to reveal that the most ordinary experience is our highest value; the heroic state of mind is exceptional only inasmuch as it allows us to take pleasure in everyday experience. In these lines from canto 9, Stevens the poet and Stevens the insurance lawyer (who emphasized the dull routine of his work in "Surety and Fidelity Claims") have made each other possible.

In the final canto of "It Must Give Pleasure," the newfound pleasure of repetition is linked to the spinning of the planet—the "fluent mundo." But if these concluding lines make Stevens's supreme fiction sound dangerously whole and complete, the poem's coda jolts us back into the historical moment that provoked Stevens to write the poem in the first place: "Soldier, there is a war." We need to feel this line as an intrusion into the dangerously beautiful world that *Notes toward a Supreme Fiction* works to discover. "It is a war that never ends," Stevens continues, "Yet it depends on yours." Stevens wants to assert the importance of the poet's struggle with language in a time of war, yet he is careful not to equate the poet's struggle with the soldier's: they are

> parallels that meet if only in
> The meeting of their shadows or that meet
> In a book in a barrack.

Speaking here is the same Stevens who in 1939 responded to a *Partisan Review* questionnaire about the role of the writer in a time of social crisis by saying that a "war is a military state of affairs, not a literary one." This is not an aesthete's credo; Stevens knew that a socially responsible poet must acknowledge the limitations of poetry. As *Notes toward a Supreme Fiction* suggests, part of the strength of poetry is its ability to turn against itself, converting every certainty into an ambiguity.

LATER YEARS

After *Notes toward a Supreme Fiction* appeared as the final poem in *Transport to Summer*, Stevens would publish two more major books of poetry: *The Auroras of Autumn* (1950) and the final section of his *Collected Poems* (1954), called *The Rock*. These volumes contain both complicated long poems that build on the foundation of *Notes toward a Supreme Fiction* (*The Auroras of Autumn*, "An Ordinary Evening in New Haven," "The Rock") and an astonishing variety of shorter poems that continue to address the questions that had troubled Stevens even before he wrote "Sunday Morning."

In the very late "River of Rivers in Connecticut," for instance, Stevens speaks as a man who has seen the River Styx, the river that divides the world of the living from the world of the dead. But he hangs back, focusing our attention on a river "this side of Stygia," an ordinary river that is just as great as the mythic river.

> On its banks,
> No shadow walks. The river is fateful,
> Like the last one. But there is no ferryman.
> He could not bend against its propelling force.
>
> It is not to be seen beneath the appearances
> That tell of it. The steeple at Farmington
> Stands glistening and Haddam shines and sways.
>
> It is the third commonness with light and air,
> A curriculum, a vigor, a local abstraction . . .
> Call it, once more, a river, an unnamed flowing,
>
> Space-filled, reflecting the seasons, the folk-lore
> Of each of the senses; call it, again and again,
> The river that flows nowhere, like a sea.

In "Sunday Morning" a "procession of the dead" seems to wind across "wide water." Here, in contrast, the earthly river seems sparsely populated even when compared with the afterlife; there is no shadow on its banks, no ferryman to take us across. The force of the river could not be mastered by Charon (who ferries the souls of the dead across the Styx), suggesting that the earth cannot be encompassed by any myth. The river itself is a "commonness"; it has no metaphysical depth beneath its appearance. The things of this world (even our images of transcendence—the steeple) are merely reflected back to us in the river's shining surface. Yet the river is a wonder ("river of rivers") precisely because it holds us so firmly within our ordinary existence. Hanging on to a life that will soon end—his own life—Stevens finds the ultimate consolation in an image of meandering process, something that "flows nowhere." And he invites us to join in that process, a process that is at once the endless becoming of the earth and the endless project of his poetry; we must give the unnamed river its name "again and again."

"The final belief," said Stevens in a collection of aphorisms called "Adagia," "is to believe in a fiction, which you know to be a fiction. The exquisite truth is to know that it is a fiction and that you believe in it willingly." Speaking here is both a poet and an insurance executive who spent every day of his life attempting to fabricate the value of human property and life. Far from lamenting the partialness of his fabrications, Stevens celebrated it: "the imperfect is our paradise," he said in "The Poems of Our Climate." Far from being threatened by our inability ever to know for sure, he celebrated partial knowledge—what he called "flawed words and stubborn sounds." Stevens feared nothing more than he feared certainty, especially when he sensed it in his own poems. So if he is known as the poet who insists that we create the fictions by which we live, he must also be known as the poet who insists most bracingly that we must discard our most treasured formulas for living. "The poem must resist the intelligence," Stevens remarked on more than one occasion: "The poem must resist the intelligence / Almost successfully."

SELECTED WORKS

Harmonium (1923)
Ideas of Order (1935)
The Man with the Blue Guitar (1937)
Notes toward a Supreme Fiction (1942)
Parts of a World (1942)
Transport to Summer (1947)
The Auroras of Autumn (1950)
The Necessary Angel: Essays on Reality and the Imagination (1951)
The Collected Poems (1954)
Opus Posthumous: Poems, Plays, Prose (1957)
The Letters of Wallace Stevens (1966)
The Palm at the End of the Mind: Selected Poems and a Play (1971)
Collected Poetry and Prose (1997)

FURTHER READING

Bates, Milton. *Wallace Stevens: A Mythology of Self.* Berkeley, Calif., 1985. The best all-around introduction to Stevens's work and life.

Bloom, Harold. *Wallace Stevens: The Poems of Our Climate.* Ithaca, N.Y., 1977. A highly idiosyncratic but usually brilliant reading of all of Stevens's major poems.

Litz, A. Walton. *Introspective Voyager: The Poetic Development of Wallace Stevens.* New York, 1972. A detailed and attractively plainspoken account of the first half of Stevens's career.

Longenbach, James. *Wallace Stevens: The Plain Sense of Things.* New York, 1991. A reading of Stevens's major poems in relationship to the social and intellectual history of his time.

Poirier, Richard. *Poetry and Pragmatism.* Cambridge, Mass., 1992. An account of the relationship of Stevens (as well as Emerson, Frost, and Stein) to American pragmatist philosophy.

Vendler, Helen. *On Extended Wings: Wallace Stevens' Longer Poems.* Cambridge, Mass., 1969. A groundbreaking reading of Stevens's longer poetic sequences.

See also the article on *Notes toward a Supreme Fiction*, immediately following.

WALLACE STEVENS'S
NOTES TOWARD A SUPREME FICTION

by Philip Hobsbaum

Notes toward a Supreme Fiction is not a philosophic work, meditated and composed over many years. It is a poem about how we may employ poetry as a way of approaching reality. Poetry in this context is the "supreme fiction" and reality is the "first idea." This work was written rapidly, between mid-July and the end of August in 1942, and was first published as a chapbook in that year. It is not so much a summation of earlier writing by its author, Wallace Stevens, as a prefiguring of the major poems that were to come. It is not a single poem but, as the title word "Notes" might suggest, a collection of lyrics circling about a theme specific to them all. Behind it stands a source much frequented by Stevens in his earlier years: the notebooks of Matthew Arnold.

In form, *Notes toward a Supreme Fiction* is divided into three parts of ten cantos each. Each canto consists of twenty-one lines divided into seven tercets. A prolation precedes the three parts and an epilogue follows. The meter is blank verse—basically, lines of ten syllables each with five stresses. There is a tendency, characteristic of Stevens, to invert the first two syllables, so that a given line is likely to begin with a stress. Also, there are occasional rhymes, and a degree of internal assonance, that is, part-rhyming within the line. The work begins with a detached lyric, eight lines long.

This preliminary lyric, which begins "And what, except for you, do I feel love...?," is not addressed to the dedicatee of the poem, the staid Henry Church, Stevens's friend with whom he was never on first-name terms. It is addressed to poetry itself, or at least the mode of poetry, which, so Stevens feels, allows us to approach essential reality. As Thomas J. Hines suggests in his valuable book *The Later Poetry of Wallace Stevens* (1976), the vision of Stevens is akin to that of the German philosopher Martin Heidegger. Basically, it suggests that this planet, without human perception, is a barren rock, and that it is human perception that renders it a world. That perception, according to Stevens, is embodied in poetry.

What poetry perceives and re-creates is life as we ideally would know it. Several major poets have grappled with the problem of acquiring such knowledge. *Notes toward a Supreme Fiction* has as its predecessors *The Pleasures of the Imagination* by Mark Akenside, *The Task* by William Cowper, and *The Prelude* by William Wordsworth. Like them, it is an account—a cycle of accounts—of the way in which the imagination re-creates that which it experiences. *Notes* goes further than its predecessors, in saying that what we experience would not be experienced were it not for the enlivening effect of the imagination. The "you" of the preliminary lyric, the prolation, may be felt to stand for poetry in the sense that poetry is itself the creative spirit. This, for Stevens, has replaced the concept of God. But he has trouble in defining it, and that trouble is the occasion of his poem.

Wallace Stevens was raised as a Presbyterian. His mother was deeply pious, and she is commemorated in one of Stevens's autobiographical poems, "A High-Toned Old Christian Woman." In this poem Stevens suggests the imaginative possibilities outside her faith. But his attempt to embrace those possibilities was part of his abandoning his early religion. He became, so to speak, spiritually adrift. To a great extent, *Notes* ratifies this perception. Stevens rejects the deterministic notion of a universe created before man, with man as one of its devolved artifacts. Instead, he seeks to propose a universe whose raw material is rendered into an entity created by man—created through his perceptions.

PART ONE

The first part of *Notes toward a Supreme Fiction* is called "It Must Be Abstract." The "It" refers to the poetic process by which one approaches reality, or the "first idea." "Abstract," in this context, refers to the necessity to rid the mind of preconceptions. Stevens starts the first part and first canto of the work by addressing someone much younger than himself, a junior poet with a fresh mind. He addresses this junior poet by conferring on him the Greek word for a young man just attaining citizenship—especially one in (military) training:

Begin, ephebe, by perceiving the idea
Of this invention, this invented world . . .

The world is "invented" because, without the effort of invention, there would be no world. The supreme fiction, if it stands in place of God, must be abstract because it represents not the world but the world as it is conceived by him that perceives it. The supreme fiction, therefore, is a way in which we can get hold of the first idea—by stripping away prejudice and trying to reimagine reality as it is. In effect, the perceiver is the poet, since it takes the imagination of a poet to get any idea of the world. The speaker—Stevens, as it were—says to the ephebe, "Never suppose an inventing mind as source of this idea."

The world is not an objective entity devoid of human interference, nor is it a subjective entity evolved from the subconsciousness of the poet. Rather, it is an entity unfulfilled, unless perceived through the activity of the imagination. Crucial lines—crucial to the poem as a whole as well as to this first canto—are

How clean the sun when seen in its idea,
Washed in the remotest cleanliness of a heaven
That has expelled us and our images . . .

One cannot look directly at the sun; the sun, in that sense, has to be imagined. What we have to imagine is the sun without any intervening notion, be it clichéd concept, bad poetry, or personal dishonesty. Heaven "has expelled us and our images" because these are conceived aside from the entity that is the sun and are therefore tainted with other people's concepts, the configurations of a false world.

This expunging of prior concepts is, as it were, a mental operation killing all previous gods—much as Stevens, in order to write *Notes*, had to get rid of all vestiges of his early Presbyterian upbringing. In that sense, the statement "Phoebus is dead, ephebe" stands for all gods being dead, including the god of the Christian church. But such a god is necessarily "dead" because he "never could be named"; indeed, he was never properly alive. He was never properly alive because he was false. We have to cleanse our minds of cant. It is not enough even to name the sun, as "gold flourisher" or as anything else. We have to understand what the sun is, difficult though that may be.

This work does not proceed in a linear fashion, developing each point logically from the one preceding. Rather, it should be seen as a cycle of cantos (or lyrics), circling round a central problem, that of defining the supreme fiction that is to take the place of God. Canto 5 begins, "It is the celestial ennui of apartments." "Ennui" here means "the extreme boredom of inaction." There is a biographical point to be made. Before his marriage in 1910, Stevens had rented a flat in New York City, at 441 West 21st Street, where he and his wife lived until their move to Hartford, Connecticut, in 1916. His wife never settled happily in New York, which is one reason for the move to Hartford. Another may be that the flat had become for him a symbol of the dehumanizing city. Also, there may be a pun on "apartment," meaning "that which sets one apart." They were above the noise and clutter of the New York streets. "Celestial ennui" may be based on the not-wholly-unwelcome loneliness Stevens felt when left alone in the apartment during his wife's frequent absences revisiting their hometown of Reading, Pennsylvania. "Celestial" because it is not wholly unpleasant; "ennui" because the mood represents vacancy; nothing much is happening. The whole represents the effect of civilization that, in failing, sends us back to "the first idea"—that is, the notion of the sun as it might be perceived were we freed of contamination.

Such a process is difficult. Even one's turning into a hermit would not be sufficient. That could entail as much fuss of going and coming as living in a town. Therefore, even seeking the "first idea" can bring about ennui. The hermit ("the monastic man") may approximate to being an artist, and so, also, may the philosopher and the priest. But they have their human desires because of their wants and their needs: "not to have is the beginning of desire." Thus, the supreme fiction is embodied in what one desires and has not got. The analogy is with the way, at the end of winter, the cycle of nature discards past detritus and looks forward to the spring.

Canto 3 contrasts the candor with which poetry seeks to reaffirm this first idea with such dishonesty as is found in the uncertain play of moonlight. Moonlight is represented as an Arab performing meaningless music—"hoobla-hoobla-hoobla-how"—in a bedroom or study. That noise, derived from a hubble-bubble or hookah, is a distraction from more serious matters, in the same way false poetry is. We need to be critical of nature, whose wrong apprehension gives rise to so much bad art. Bad art, unlike the supreme fiction, is a contaminating process preventing us from approaching the first idea.

Stevens is thus the enemy of preconception. We are enjoined to scrape our minds clean as a means of approaching the first idea. Even Adam, in the Garden of Eden, had preconceptions. He exerted human reason, as philosophers have done since. Descartes, who famously said "I think, therefore I am," is a prime example. And Eve, instead of seeking the first idea, contemplated her own being, and that of her sons and daughters. Yet the first man and the first woman were not the first material entities. Even had they been able to cleanse their minds of preconceptions, they would still have had to work with the raw material of being: "there was a muddy centre before we breathed." It is from such raw material that "the poem springs": that poem which enables us to perceive and without which the material remains raw. In that sense, we are not creating but mimicking. Eve was wrong in thinking that the air is a mirror. It is more like the spaces in the side scenes of a stage in the theater. Stevens calls these "coulisses," a word perhaps found in the 1902 edition of *Webster's Dictionary* that he is known to have canvassed assiduously. We are liable to add to the meanings rather than open ourselves to them. Instead of the eternal music, we hear, as a result, the cacophony of a theater band.

Canto 5 warns us that we will not arrive at the first idea by a return to nature. The roaring lion and blaring elephant represent the anger of the animals, helpless to approach reality. The snarling bear—"cinnamon" is an allusion to the reddish-brown of its coloring—is in this regard of no more consequence than the playing of the lights on the surface of sunken reservoirs. All are phenomena of nature, and are not preferable to the lucubrations of a student in his lonely attic. He is compared with a sigil, a creature of the roofs looking out from his window as though he were a figure impressed on some arcane medallion. If such a student learned how to train the beasts, it would not bring him nearer to the first idea.

Canto 6 is a little like the third section of T. S. Eliot's "Ash Wednesday," in that it represents a struggle to find even the wherewithal to construct an approach to the first idea.

> Not to be realized because not to
> Be seen, not to be loved nor hated because
> Not to be realized . . .

This tendency of language epitomizes a struggle that is constant. The apparently more concrete tendency of language, to which it is opposed, in fact represents evanescence:

> . . . Weather by Franz Hals,
> Brushed up by brushy winds in brushy clouds,
> Wetted by blue, colder for white . . .

The weather may be felt as being changeable, and the artist Franz Hals was not noted for his landscapes but for his portraits. His weather may therefore be felt as especially changeable. However, the point of this particular canto, canto 6, is to impress upon the reader that the natural beauties upon which he depends—"the gay forsythia," "the fragrance of the magnolia"—are temporary and misleading. At least, they are so compared with the uncertainty with which the reader is surrounded:

> It must be visible or invisible,
> Invisible or visible or both:
> A seeing and an unseeing in the eye.

Of this uncertainty he must make something. It is necessarily a peculiar process to which Stevens gives a title that is famous: "an abstraction blooded." That is a way of saying that an apprehension of reality must be abstract, in that it is a classifying product of the mind, and also that it has to be brought physically down to earth in order to be understood. It is apparent that a paradox is involved. There the problem, around which these cantos circle, lies.

Canto 7 instances ways in which one can approach the first idea—a walk around the lake, a pause to see the plants grow. This is based on the walk that Stevens took daily to his office through Elizabeth Park in Hartford, Connecticut:

> A wait within that certainty, a rest
> In the swags of excellence bordering the lake . . .

Such moments of peace—James Joyce called them "epiphanies"—can clear the mind and boost the energies of perception.

Canto 8 considers whether it is possible to develop the ordinary person—MacCullough—into "major man," that is, a creature with supernormal propensities and powers. The conclusion is that the ordinary person remains ordinary because it does not follow that the "major man" is really a man. MacCullough is quite content to remain "lounging by the sea"—that is, immersed in the trivially sensual pursuits of life. He might achieve apprehension of "deepened speech" or "a leaner being," but it seems unlikely.

Canto 9 distinguishes the "romantic intoning," such as that of preset church services, from conceptual thought, which is here called "reason's click-clack." Neither of these approaches the discourse of the "major man." He is "the foundling of the infected part." That is to say, he is disowned from past preconceptions and should not be classified, as religions are, with a name.

Canto 10, the final canto of the first part, declares that only "major man" can achieve an approach abstract enough to apprehend the first idea, which is identified with reality. Such a man is neither a furious rabbi nor a disconsolate man of action; rather he is a figure somewhat disregarded, such as a tramp, outside conventional urban society. It is he who will be most likely neither to console nor sanctify but to propound. "Propound" in this context suggests a mode of approach amounting to a supreme fiction. It is to be remembered that, right through this first part of *Notes*, Stevens is suggesting ways of replacing the concept of "God."

PART TWO

The second part of *Notes* is called "It Must Change." This is a recognition that however permanent we may feel our present situation to be, it is in fact evanescent, altering all the time. There may be a moment, as told in the first canto of this part, when, for example, Italian girls enhance their beauty by wearing flowers in their hair, violets and hyacinths bloom, and bees go on their appointed rounds. But all will vanish in a universe characterized by inconstancy. The "old seraph" who observes them will transmogrify to a satyr, and the garden in which he has been sitting will deteriorate to "a withered scene." But in the seraph's view the change has not been sufficient, for, with the seasons, the garden returns. This is the earth; no subtlety here.

Canto 2 of this second part gives a concrete example. The president, who thinks himself all-powerful, cannot ordain a permanency. If the life of a bee is a joke not in the best of taste—a "blague"—he is unable to compel a repetition. He may order the arrangement of his curtains and banners; he cannot control the seasons. They may return, but in their own good time.

Canto 3 propounds an even more specific example. Nothing could seem more permanent than the statue of General Du Puy, the noble rider. Surrounding tombs might be removed, but the general remains, an inhuman bronze. Homage is paid to him by lawyers and doctors. Yet the general does not amount to major man. He may appear to transcend mortality, but the mortal man is already dead and is represented by a statue. And the statue has to come under the perception, "It Must Change." Sooner or later, it will collapse. Therefore, "the General was rubbish in the end."

Canto 4 tells us that apparent opposites depend upon each other—man on woman, night on day, winter on spring. This is the origin of change. Stevens here is anticipating some of the findings that were to manifest themselves in poststructuralism. One entity is defined by its difference from another entity. Thus, apparent unity is really disparity, and apparent disparity is really unity.

Canto 5 gives us a highly specific example of this. There was a planter, now dead, with a garden of wild orange trees that still persists. To some extent, the planter is a rehandling of Stevens's previous character, Crispin, protagonist of "The Comedian as the Letter C," and both have more than a little in common with Stevens. The planter had made his home on an island but thought wistfully of a further island that he would never visit and also of the island from which he had come. However, on dying, it was the island he had inhabited for most of his life that he regretted, even down to his banjo's twang. He sighed for his past life, as a more unaffected man "in a negative light" would not.

Other voices inhabit the garden. In canto 6 the sparrow invites us to empathy, calling "Bethou me," while other, more savage, birds bid us retreat: "K, k,-k," cry the bloody wren, the felon jay, the jug-throated robin: "So many clappers going without bells." The sparrow appears to be unchanging in its call, but, like the garden itself, it will end.

Canto 7 favors those who discount organized religion—"paradise" and "hymns"—in favor of "the easy passion, the ever-ready love." But such matters are of as "earthy a birth" as the accessible bliss for which the lover sighs. And this, in its turn, is equated with the courage of the ignorant man "who chants by book" and the heat of the scholar "who writes the book." All are of the preceding world and may be discounted as obstacles to the search toward the first idea.

Canto 8 is the down-to-earth fable of Nanzia Nunzio, whose name suggests a representative of female sexuality. She courts Ozymandias, who seems identifiable with Percy Bysshe Shelley's long-defunct and formerly powerful potentate in his sonnet of that name. Nanzia attempts to divest herself of every ornament and article of clothing, so that she may approach her lover as a pure bride. But this is impossible. Ozymandias says, apparently with the poet's approval, that a bride can never be naked. In order to perceive the bride, "A fictive covering / Weaves always glistening from the heart and mind." Nanzia is, ineluctably, a thing of earth.

Canto 9 addresses the problem of speech. Previously, what has been advocated is a refinement, a language peculiar to the task—in short, a mode of perception that will re-create the first idea. But anything the poet says may be adjudged gibberish, and certainly it has to relate to ordinary speech, or how else can it be understood? Yet, ordinary speech—"the gibberish of the vulgate" to use Stevens's phrase—brings in the very colloquialisms that the disinterested seeker after the first idea may wish to avoid. Is there a poem so refined that it can do without words, and would it not then be as imprecise an instrument as one that wastes time in "chaffer," that is to say, in bargaining with terms? It appears that, whatever form of speech one uses, there is a degree of compromise that tends to inexactitude.

The climax of this doctrine of compromise is reached in canto 10. Here, the poet sits like an old man on a bench in the park by a lake, contemplating change. The world is too volatile to be denied, yet it is created through its transformations. It is through transformations that it exists. Time will write these down, but, the implication is, by the time they are recorded they will have altered.

PART THREE

The third part of *Notes* is called "It Must Give Pleasure." Here we are up against the paradox: that to savor life is to block oneself off from the abstraction necessary to discover the first idea. Yet to eschew preconceptions savoring of earth is impossible. Canto 1 of this third part reiterates this problem, voiced again and again through *Notes*.

St. Jerome, a holy man who wrote the Latin version of the Bible known as the Vulgate, could not in his text help introducing such earthly and sensual instruments as tubas and strings, and his words were sung joyously by companies of voices. This is held to be "a facile exercise." It is akin to the natural phenomena—the sun rising, the sea clearing—which are not subject to rationalization but which nevertheless move us deeply. "We reason about them with a later reason." Yet is not this "later reason" nevertheless "reason"?

Canto 2 introduces "the blue woman." Like "the blue guitar" in an earlier poem, the color here indicates something beyond the normal parameters of being—an entity imaginative, decorated, romantic. She neither wishes that her silver jewelry ("argentines") should be coldly metallic, nor that the clouds should be merely foam, nor that blossoms should be merely decorative (rather than actively sexual), nor yet that her sensual dreams should be strengthened into actual sexual practice. There is a degree of contradiction here. The blue woman seems at once to wish desire to be ratified, and to unwish it. Possibly both conditions are resolved in her memory. Yet what she sees from her window is "real" and, at the same time, without intrusion—which would seem to indicate that what is seen is not, in reality, seen.

"Red" in canto 3 serves something of the same purpose in other poems by Stevens, in that it is usually associated with solidity and sensuality. Here it is the key attribute of an idol:

> An ancient forehead hung with heavy hair,
> The channel slots of rain, the red-rose-red,
> And weathered and the ruby-water-worn . . .

This idol could be variously interpreted and is not necessarily malevolent. The innocent children bring flowers in homage, not necessarily to the idol—the syntax is not clear upon the subject—but perhaps to the sheep grazing around it.

In canto 4 a further fable tells of the marriage of the exotic maiden Bawda to a great captain. There may be a sly reference here to Stevens's own marriage back in 1910: "puissant front" (he was a very large man) to "subtle sound" (she was a musician). In the canto there is some initial difficulty about the wedding, but it comes off because of the mutual love the bride and bridegroom have of the place Stevens styles "Catawba":

> It was neither heaven nor hell.
> They were love's characters come face to face.

There being no religious association with the place where they were married and in which presumably they were to dwell, it may be assumed that the marriage was happy. In this way, Stevens indicates that lack of a preconceived God can conduce to fulfillment.

Cantos 5, 6, and 7 are best taken together since they focus upon a figure called Canon Aspirin. Aspirin is a pharmaceutical product that gives the impression of curing headache by dulling one's sense of pain. It need not mean that the pain has been excised. A canon is a senior member of a Christian church, most markedly the Episcopal Church, which is in communion with the Church of England. This canon, it would seem, stands for a mode of perception that is an alleviant rather than a cure. He himself is thoroughly involved in sensual life:

> We drank Meursault, ate lobster Bombay with mango
> Chutney. Then the Canon Aspirin declaimed
> Of his sister, in what a sensible ecstasy
> She lived in her house . . . .

So the canon is a man of the world—our world, which would appear to prevent him from taking advantage of the clean-washed perceptions proposed in earlier cantos as a means of approaching the first idea. The canon's sister, a widow, is the mother of two children aged seven and four and, though not rich, maintains them in a state of decency. There are no dreams in her life. In other words, for the canon and his sister, what could be meaningful in life passes them by.

Here, Stevens is warring with his own nature, for he was an insurance lawyer earning a good salary, and was at ease with the delights of the table. This is life at a distance from the cultivating of a vision that washes away preconceptions in order to apprehend the first idea by means of the supreme fiction. The work never directly tells us what these are. However, Stevens seems to understand Canon Aspirin well enough. The canon imposes order, even though "to impose is not / To discover." In this way, as with his sister, the possibilities of being are denied him. Exploration is not the canon's strong point. He ought to have aimed at being stripped of every fiction except the necessary one: the fiction of an absolute. Alas, the senses of Canon Aspirin are too thickened by sensuality for him to hear "the luminous melody of proper sound."

The next two cantos, 8 and 9, also have to be taken together. Both are dominated by an angel; possibly identifiable with the seraph we have already seen in Part Two. Here, the angel seems to be the ideal observer we have been waiting for in the *Notes*. If the poet does not put himself forward in that role, at least he gives us some notion of what the angel sees:

> What am I to believe? If the angel in his cloud,
> Serenely gazing at the violent abyss,
> Plucks on his strings to pluck abysmal glory,
>
> Leaps downward through evening's revelations, and
> On his spredden wings, needs nothing but deep space,
> Forgets the gold centre, the golden destiny,
>
> Grows warm in the motionless motion of his flight,
> Am I that imagine this angel less-satisfied . . . ?

If the poet cannot divest himself of his earthly obligations, at least he can imagine the angel that will do this for him. The angel, it seems, is the poet's surrogate. The poet is able to imagine the angel, and also that which the angel enacts.

In any case, as canto 9 tells us, the poet can do all that angels can. He can, for instance, enjoy like them. This is more than the weedy wren and red robin—back again from canto 6 of the second part, and whistling—can do. Their song has no forward impulse; it is mere repetition. But this enjoyment is empathy with an angel's happiness. In the end, are men better than wrens—spinning round themselves, and watching a leaf above the table spinning? The human hero, it seems, is a master of repetition.

The third and final part of *Notes* ends in an unexpectedly familiar way, addressing the spinning world as "fat girl, terrestrial, my summer, my night." The poet has to be content with what he can find on earth. He has to lower his expectations. The phantom he sought, the supreme fiction, is the more than rational distortion of that which is before, behind, and around him. A philosophical lecture at the Sorbonne, famous French university that it is, can prove the rational to be irrational, until, that is, an unexpected flicker of feeling enables the poet to call the earth by name, "my fluent mundo." But at such a time the earth will have stopped revolving and will be an artifact—giving the impression of movement, but actually set in crystal.

That forms the end of *Notes* proper. An epilogue follows, addressed to a soldier and comparing his war with that of the poet. The poet finds opposition between the mind and the sky, between thought and day and night. He learns from the sun, symbol of life here as elsewhere, but patches together his poetry, symbolized by the moon, in his room. The poet's war never ends, but depends on the soldier's war. Indeed, the two are interdependent. The soldier writes lamely home, and finally comes home with such spoils as he has gained. But his exploits are poor except insofar as the poet has written—in no way lamely—about them. The fictive hero in the poet's discourse takes over from what had been thought the reality. This compensates for the hardships the soldier must necessarily suffer. It would seem that everything, even that which has been explored in this work, is a matter of words, especially words handled by a master.

There is no doubt that this particular poet is a master of words. *Notes toward a Supreme Fiction* abounds in charismatic phrases: "the celestial ennui of apartments," "Adam in Eden was the father of Descartes," "The lion roars at the enraging desert," "The glitter-goes on surfaces of tanks," "Bethou me, said sparrow." If the phrases seem a little less charismatic in the later stages of the work, this is an indication that they are more fully absorbed into the surrounding context.

However, the work does not proceed quite like that. It is not one cohesive text but a cycle of poems in what may well be Stevens's idiosyncratic version of the sonnet. In that sense, the separate cantos circle round a meaning, peck at it from different angles, and toward the end admit that a final meaning is not possible. The nearest Stevens can get to a supreme fiction is a degree of empathy with the experience of an angel that he himself, through his words, has created. The parallel is with the soldier of the epilogue. He does not exist except as the poet has perceived him.

[*See also* Long Poem, The.]

FURTHER READING

Bloom, Harold. "*Notes toward a Supreme Fiction*: A Commentary." In *Wallace Stevens: A Collection of*

Critical Essays, edited by Marie Borroff. Englewood Cliffs, N.J., 1963. A somewhat overstated and emotional but enthusiastic account of *Notes*.

Doggett, Frank A. *Wallace Stevens: The Making of the Poem*. Baltimore, Md., 1980. Much-quoted account of Stevens, taking due notice of his ideas.

Garraway, David R. *Wallace Stevens and the Question of Belief: Metaphysician in the Dark*. Baton Rouge, La., 1993. Relates Stevens's ideas to his poetry.

Hines, Thomas J. *The Later Poetry of Wallace Stevens: Phenomenological Parallels with Husserl and Heidegger*. Lewisburg, Pa., 1976. Lucid account of *Notes*, placing the poem in its intellectual context.

Leggett, B. J. *Wallace Stevens and Poetic Theory: Conceiving the Supreme Fiction*. Chapel Hill, N.C., 1987. Relates Stevens's theory to his poetic practice.

Leonard, J. S. *The Fluent Mundo: Wallace Stevens and the Structure of Reality*. Atlanta, Ga., 1988. Informed and inward discussion.

Patke, Rajeev S. *The Long Poems of Wallace Stevens: An Interpretative Study*. Cambridge, 1985. Painstaking account, with some illuminating insights.

Santilli, Kristin S. *Poetic Gesture: Myth, Wallace Stevens, and the Motions of Poetic Language*. London, 2002. Propounds a theory of poetic gesture, with especial reference to verbal patterings such as metonymy and synecdoche.

Vendler, Helen. *On Extended Wings: Wallace Stevens' Longer Poems*. Cambridge, Mass., and London, 1969. Rhetorical interpretation by a famous critic, but some readers could find a point-by-point account more helpful.

See also the article on Wallace Stevens, immediately preceding.

ANNE STEVENSON

by Emily R. Grosholz

Anne Stevenson.
(*Photograph by Anne Lennox*)

Anne Stevenson, like T. S. Eliot, W. H. Auden, and Sylvia Plath, is a poet whose literary life belongs both to the United States and to Great Britain. Born in Cambridge, England, on 3 January 1933 to American parents (Louise Destler Stevenson and the moral philosopher Charles Stevenson), she was raised in the United States and received her B.A. degree from the University of Michigan in 1954. But her first marriage (which produced her daughter) was to an English businessman, and her second (which produced her two sons) brought her to Oxford, where her husband was a distinguished Sinologist. She then lived with her third husband, a farmer-poet, in the Welsh border country. Subsequently, after several sojourns in Cambridge, she and her husband Peter Lucas, a Darwin scholar, have divided their time between a house in Durham and a seventeenth-century cottage in North Wales.

Long associated with the *Poetry Nation Review*, Stevenson is one of the most acclaimed poets in Great Britain. In 2002 she was awarded £60,000 as winner of the Northern Rock Literary Award, the largest annual literary prize granted in Great Britain. Her reputation as a poet in the United States has been steadily rising to that high standard after a number of years during which she was known in America more as a literary critic than as a poet. She published fifteen books of poetry between 1965 and the beginning of the twenty-first century, the last being *Granny Scarecrow* (2000), which followed *The Collected Poems, 1955–1995* (1996), superseding two earlier volumes of selected poems published in 1974 and 1987. Her prose works include two critical books on Elizabeth Bishop; a controversial biography, *Bitter Fame: A Life of Sylvia Plath* (1989); and *Between the Iceberg and the Ship: Selected Essays* (1998) in the University of Michigan Poets on Poetry Series.

THE SHADOW OF HISTORY

Anne Stevenson's poetry is formally compelling, as she moves with ease across a wide spectrum of poetic genres (from epistolary narrative to epigram) and of forms (from free verse to odes precisely rhymed and metered). The formal bravura is, however, always in the service of thought. As her mother's daughter, she broods over the meaning of history, of her two countries, and of her own braided life. As her father's daughter, she reflects on the philosophical conundrums of subject and object, nature and culture, thing and representation. As her own woman, she addresses eros and parenthood, ambition and letters, mutability and mortality.

The early book *Correspondences: A Family History in Letters* (1974) traces the fortunes of the fictitious Chandler family, whose members are transpositions of figures from her family tree as they move back and forth across the Atlantic Ocean over a period of 150 years. It is a meditation on both the experience of being Anglo-American and the constraints imposed by ordinary life upon talented and intelligent women. "Coming Back to Cambridge (England, 1971)" revisits her birthplace where the river and the streets are the same, where everything is familiar though she is, perennially, a stranger. The poem "A Summer Place (Vermont, 1974)" revisits the family retreat in Vermont, where the familiar in light of death and dispersal has become strange. The "Letter to Sylvia Plath (Grantchester, May 1988)" treats another woman's estrangement from life and within art; written from the village outside Cambridge where Stevenson was living at the time, it explores in imagination Plath's own lost Grantchester, which Stevenson knew very well from her research for Plath's biography. In "Waving to Elizabeth" (which is also tagged, but within the poem, 19 June 1983, Thornhill School, Sunderland), she looks up from the earth to the sky and back in time, to where she can see Bishop looking down, contemplating poetic geographies. For Stevenson, poems of history are poems of place, places both abandoned and reclaimed.

To visit is to revisit and then, with a shock of recognition, to measure the distance between then and now. *Granny Scarecrow* has another such poem, "Going Back (Ann Arbor, October 1993)," and its companion piece written a few years later, "Arioso Dolente," in which her father admonishes her—while playing Beethoven's piano sonata, opus 110—to "put all the griefs of the world in that change of key," and she herself exclaims,

> Consciousness walks on tiptoe through what happens.
> So much is felt, so little of it said.
> But ours is the breath on which the past depends.
> "What happened" is what the living teach the dead. . . .

"Going Back" observes both that the passage of time hazes and blurs and that fierce attachments (which must always be remembered) banish time, so much so that we can never be set quite free of them. This encounter with history at certain memorable places is also a haunting, a somber conclusion made especially clear in "The Unaccommodated (1995)."

THE TRACE OF PHILOSOPHY

Anne Stevenson's poetry is not exactly philosophical: it is not abstract or doctrinaire and it does not expound ideas. But it is—sometimes lightly and ironically, sometimes profoundly—informed by philosophical vocabulary and topics. *Minute by Glass Minute* (1982) contains the disquieting "Small Philosophical Poem," about an unlikely married couple: Dr. Animus, who likes to put things in order, and his wife Anima, who must always remind him of the insubstantiality of things, the vertigo of love and fear. To accompany a "square meal" of propositions, she always offers him "a small glass of doubt." This poem is flanked by "He and It (A Pathetic Fallacy)," "The Man in the Wind," "If I Could Paint Essences," and a sequence of five sonnets for Stevenson's philosophical father. In *Four and a Half Dancing Men* (1993), she considers the nature of time revealed, or obscured, in "Washing the Clocks," and in "Negations" she takes as her theme the growing absurdity of modern life in images that recall Jean-Paul Sartre's *Nausea* (1938).

But beside this brilliant surface play with philosophical words and themes, deeper philosophical concerns structure Stevenson's poetry from book to book. One is the relation between nature and culture, the world as

it runs on without us, as opposed to and implicated in human awareness. Many of Stevenson's stunning poetic seascapes are figures for this kind of meditation, where the beach, that changing and contested boundary between land and sea, stands for the boundary between thought and thing. "The sea is as near as we come to another world," she observes in "North Sea off Carnoustie," a poem in *Enough of Green* (1977). In the accompanying poem "Fire and the Tide," she analyzes the struggle of human life in these terms:

> As when the tide pulls the Tay out,
> scarring predictable mudscape—
> seawater's knifework
> notching quick runnel and channel.

Another concern is representation itself; when Stevenson treats it in a poem, the result is typically a kind of double vision. The representation becomes thinglike and stands like a latticework screen or a living mirror before us, along with what it offers to thought. "Resurrection," in *Enough of Green*, describes the green veil of early spring that half hides a chorus of birds, and then turns the birdsong into a silken overwriting, like the poem itself at the peak of its lyricism:

> That generous throat
> is a blackbird's. Now, a thrush.
> And that ribbon flung out,
> that silk voice, is a chaffinch's rush
> to his grace-note. Birds woo,
> or apportion the innocent air they're made for.
> Whom do they sing for?

Rivers, clouds, shadows, and smoke typically overwrite the landscape in Stevenson's poems, just at the moment when, poetically, she is self-consciously addressing her own representations, "a wordlife running from mind to mind" as she calls it in "Making Poetry."

Stevenson's poetry testifies that she has struggled not only to come to terms with her mother's history and her father's philosophy, but also to set them aside, in Husserlian brackets perhaps, in order to get on more clearly with life. The poems in which she asserts her own authority are among her most characteristic, conflicted, and eloquent. They are sometimes about eros, more often about writing. In the poems "Swifts," "To Write It," "Moonrise," and many others, she acknowledges that the burden of art is solitude. The creator must always pull something out of nothing (which entails facing the nothing), and that act is permanently unconsoled, unrecompensed, unaccompanied. The heartfelt empathy in her poems for Sylvia Plath, Elizabeth Bishop, Norman MacCaig, and Ted Hughes, are based on Stevenson's own experience of the rigors of constructing a poem:

> Axe the bole,
> plane the boards.
> Here is Art,
> the polished instrument,
> casket and corpse,

she writes in her "Poem for Henry Fainlight."

The epigrammatic poem "Vertigo" that begins *Granny Scarecrow* is at once a brief history, a meditation on mind and body, and an *ars poetica.*

> Mind led body
> to the edge of the precipice.
> They stared in desire
> at the naked abyss.
> If you love me, said mind,
> take that step into silence.
> If you love me, said, body,
> turn and exist.

Again and again, Anne Stevenson has decided in favor of the body, to turn and exist, while acknowledging the mind's romantic drift towards airy nothings, impossible flight. Thus, while piled high with speculation and verbal trapezing, her poems always in the end come down to earth, to the senses, to stubborn mortality, the pleasure—recorded in "A Present," written in 1999, of

> a lonely walker, cold
> but happy on the high ground, . . .
> The story in the marsh was a long memory
> retelling itself in a shower of gold.

If Darwin had been a poet, his poems would have had a family resemblance with those of Anne Stevenson.

[*See also* Auden, W. H.; Bishop, Elizabeth; Eliot, T. S.; *and* Plath, Sylvia.]

SELECTED WORKS

Elizabeth Bishop (1966)
Reversals (1969)
Correspondences: A Family History in Letters (1974)
Enough of Green (1977)
Minute by Glass Minute (1982)
Selected Poems (1987)
Bitter Fame: A Life of Sylvia Plath (1989)
Four and a Half Dancing Men (1993)
The Collected Poems, 1955–1995 (1996)
Between the Iceberg and the Ship: Selected Essays (1998)
Five Looks at Elizabeth Bishop (1998)
Granny Scarecrow (2000)
A Report from the Border (2003)

FURTHER READING

Goldstein, Laurence, ed. *Michigan Quarterly Review* 40, no. 4 (Fall 2001): 726–748. This section of *Michigan Quarterly Review* includes an essay by E. Grosholz, a review by J. Parini, and five poems by Stevenson.

Lucas, John, and Matt Simpson, eds. *A Collection of Essays on the Work of Anne Stevenson. Festschrift*, 2003.

ROBERT STONE

by Cates Baldridge

Robert Stone has written that "the first law of heaven is that nothing is free," and there are reasons enough to believe that he came by this hard truth early and ungently. He was born on 21 August 1937 in Brooklyn, New York, to a schizophrenic mother, Gladys Grant Stone, and an absent father, C. Homer Stone. By the age of six the young Stone found himself boarded in St. Ann's Marist academy—a quasi-orphanage, in his case—where physical and psychological brutality from both students and priests was daily fare. When his mother was well enough, Stone lived with her, taking trips to make "new starts" in various parts of the country, at least one of which ended with a stay in a homeless shelter. Despite, or perhaps in part because of such early dislocations of the spirit, the boy began to write stories that from the start garnered attention and praise, and which were obviously a welcome outlet for his stifled ambitions and for the active imagination that had hitherto served largely as a refuge.

Expelled from St. Ann's in his senior year for spreading atheism, Stone indulged his imaginative infatuation with the sea by joining the navy in 1955. He witnessed some combat during the Suez Crisis and did a journalistic stint in Antarctica before his hitch expired. Returning to civilian life in 1958, he began working for the *New York Daily News* while also attending classes at New York University, where he met his wife, Janice Burr, in a creative writing course. Married in late 1959, the newlyweds arrived in New Orleans soon after with no clear prospects, working various jobs and living from paycheck to paycheck. It was the era in the South of the budding civil rights movement as well as the violent backlash against it, both of which Stone observed at close hand and eventually transposed to his first novel, *A Hall of Mirrors* (1967).

While this initial work was slowly gestating, the author benefited from a stipend from Stanford University's writing program, from the encouragement of novelist Wallace Stegner, and from a Houghton Mifflin literary fellowship. Stone's unhurried and meticulous method of work is probably responsible for one of *A Hall of Mirror's*

signal strengths—that fact that it is not a snapshot of any particular year in the 1960s, but rather a surprising distillation of many of that decade's disparate elements, a compendium both of its early idealism and its later inebriated solipsism, of its sensual pleasures and its cold menaces. And thus, while the novel possesses some of the phantasmagoric aspects one often encounters in the fiction of the era's young writers, it tempers such extravagances with a more serious and tough-minded depiction of America's racism, economic exploitation, and spiritual emptiness than that delivered in the romps of, say, Tom Wolfe or Kurt Vonnegut.

In the seven years between the publication of *A Hall of Mirrors* and *Dog Soldiers* (1974), Stone's life was peripatetic but punctuated with genuine milestones of professional success. During the late 1960s he lived in England and engaged in freelance writing, including a stint in Vietnam that provided him with a raft of material for his next novel. Meanwhile, *A Hall of Mirrors* was awarded the William Faulkner Foundation Prize for the best first novel of 1967, and the author eventually garnered a Guggenheim Fellowship in 1971. During the early 1970s Stone also began a teaching career, serving as a writer-in-residence at Princeton University and later as a faculty member at Amherst College—a list of posts that would eventually grow to include Stanford, Harvard, the University of California at Irvine, and New York University, among others.

His long-awaited second novel was somewhat ahead of its time in that the American literary establishment did not seriously take up the Vietnam War as a subject until considerably later in the decade. While many of the Vietnam novels that followed Stone's play up the disconcerting voyage between an America of safe, unheroic normality and a war-torn "Nam" of psychedelic violence and perilous absolutes, *Dog Soldiers* makes the more provocative claim that the homeland is every bit as twistedly dangerous and amoral as the foreign battlefield, and that to a certain extent the former has been made so by our misguided involvement in the latter. Stone once wrote that "the early to mid-'70s still seem to me, in retrospect, like a creepy, evil time. A lot of bills from the '60s were coming up for presentation. *Dog Soldiers* was my reaction to that period." A reaction that many found true and instructive, apparently, for the novel won the National Book Award in 1975, and went on to find a place in Hollywood. The movie that resulted, *Who'll Stop the Rain* (1978), which featured Nick Nolte and Tuesday Weld, is well regarded—a bit more so than *WUSA* (1970), the film version of *A Hall of Mirrors*. Stone was involved in both screenplays, writing *WUSA* by himself and *Who'll Stop the Rain* in collaboration.

Stone's next novel, *A Flag for Sunrise* (1981), is a tale of disastrous conjunction—or rather, collision—of three very different Americans in the political maelstrom of the gothically sinister Central American nation of Tecan, where a reactionary kleptocracy is kept in power by the Tonton-like Guardia Nacional. There is, however, as much discussion of God's failings as there is of Caesar's in this novel, and the deity that seems to preside over Stone's fictional dictatorship is a figure out of both the Old Testament and meso-American mythology, enamored of blood offerings and inspiring antinomian fanaticism. Amid the backdrop of a failing revolution in which the trio have become involved, rare moments of excruciating epiphany are fleetingly available, but much more common is the negative realization of the main character, Holliwell, who, in a cosmic sense, "get[s] the joke now.... We're all the joke. We're the joke on one another. It's our nature." In the final analysis the novel's most disturbing implication is not that there exists "a world far from God, a few hours from Miami," but that the world at large lacks any redemptive spiritual dimension—that it stretches flat, monotonous, and blood soaked, all the way to the horizon.

A flood of official recognition came Stone's way in response to *A Flag for Sunrise*, including the *Los Angeles Times* Book Prize, the John Dos Passos Prize for Literature, and the American Academy and Institute of Arts and Letters Award. It is said that no prophet is honored in his own time, but appearing as it did at the beginning of a decade in which the tragic consequences of American meddling abroad would make frequent headlines, Stone's highly praised novel can be seen as that rarest of occurrences, the jeremiad that falls upon appreciative ears.

Like the protagonists of *A Flag for Sunrise*, those of *Children of Light* (1986), Stone's story of obsessive love amid the movie industry, seem to be on a collision course—though in the later novel there is something even more decidedly chosen about the smashup, something suicidally deliberate about the steerings toward disaster. Both main characters—the scriptwriter, Gordon, and the psychologically fragile yet brilliant actress, Lu Anne—share an assumption that despair is the natural default setting of all who see life clearly and who are not able to palliate it with relentless labors, aggressive egoism, or drugs. And yet there is one spot of blinding brightness amid the funereal gloom, for the most poignant aspect of this cocaine-smothered novel is that Lu Anne and Gordon's effect upon each other is very like that of an ecstasy-inducing drug, in both a beneficent and destructive sense. Their proximity endows them with a bliss that consumes, with a genuine high that is too intense to last. Thus, at the peak of his rapture Gordon thinks "that this [is] his golden girl and that she [is] in his arms and that they [can] never have peace or a quiet moment or a half hour's happiness." Frolicking upon this dubious height, Gordon realizes that "the philosophy whose comforts [Lu Anne] represented was Juggernaut," but also "that he was happy. That [this] was why he had come, to be with her in harm's way and be happy." As with Joseph Conrad and Graham Greene, so with Stone the evanescent happiness of life seems only to reveal itself in proximity to deadly menace.

Owen and Anne Browne, the couple at the center of *Outerbridge Reach* (1992), do not so much burn with passion as smolder with disappointment and claustrophobia. When a fluke provides Owen with the chance to compete in a round-the-world solo regatta, he quickly agrees to go. Anne, despite serious misgivings about both the man and the enterprise, supports his decision. For not the first time in Stone's novels, the lure of a life of absolutes—and escape from the nightmare of the ordinary—prove temptations too alluring to pass by. As Owen departs amid ambiguous portents, Anne—much to her own surprise—drifts into an affair with Strickland, the world-wizened and cynical filmmaker documenting the regatta. She is pushed toward adultery by the same smoldering discontents, broadening of horizons, and quickening of the senses that Owen is experiencing at sea, and thus shares an intimacy of imitation with her absent husband in the midst of her betrayal, feeling "more and more like going to sea herself.... The fact was they had been wasting their lives. She had been bored sick without knowing it. Owen had been right about the race. It had opened up life."

Since, however, "the first law of heaven is that nothing is free," this opening to possibilities comes only at the cost of physical and psychic peril, for out at sea the disintegration of craft and captain proceed in tandem. In Owen's mind, his boat's shoddy construction is a sign both of national decline and the absurdity of his own heroic pretensions. Too unwilling, though, to give up the idea of himself as one of life's winners, he succumbs to the temptation of filing false position reports while actually sailing back to New York City the short way around. Beset by shame, despair, self-loathing, and an attenuating sense of identity, he eventually commits suicide by stepping into the sea. The novel concludes a year or so later with Anne herself preparing to enter the next solo circumnavigation race—an act that will involve contrition, reparation, expiation, and, not the least of it, further personal and philosophical exploration.

In 1997 Stone brought out a collection of his short stories, titled *Bear and His Daughter* after one of the selections. The tales, only seven in number, are fine pieces of writing but do not represent any radical departure for Stone—indeed, their characters and plots will seem familiar to anyone who has read the novels. They are almost all marked by a looming sense of catastrophe—from the very first page the reader feels that the protagonists are in terrible danger, and the fact that this danger results from their own obsessions or omissions does not interfere with the anxious empathy that Stone always manages to evoke on their behalf. Also like the novels, the stories contain a number of truly funny passages cheek by jowl with the darker material. *Bear and His Daughter* makes it clear that if Stone has chosen to expend the vast majority of his efforts upon the novel, this has nothing to do with any slackening of power or acumen when he tackles the more compact genre of the short story.

Perhaps the most surprising aspect of Stone's novel *Damascus Gate* (1998) is its Dickensian plotting, in which a multitude of seemingly disparate souls collide with and carom off each other amid the frenetic and dangerous tides of modern-day Jerusalem. Stone makes a concerted attempt to paint the Holy City as, morally and politically, nothing less than the center of the world, the place where "religion . . . is something that's happening now, today," because "the monuments of Jerusalem [do] not belong to the past. They [are] of the moment and even the future." Thus, Stone depicts the fiercest and most ancient religious passions being confused with and compromised by the latest political expediencies (without the former loosing

their terrible power to alight the mind), all of which serves to evoke Jerusalem as a locale where the ancient and the postmodern are never far asunder, as a cauldron that has been uninterruptedly boiling over for a least three millennia and which always promises to explode tonight. The rather dizzying narrative revolves around the machinations of various zealot factions—Jewish and Christian—that are attempting to blow up the mosque atop the Temple Mount, an action that they believe will, according to their bent, either bring King Jesus back in glory or begin a war that will finally remove the Arabs from Israel. Involved either in league or in opposition to this conspiracy are various Israeli secret service agencies, the Communist Party, assorted soldiers of fortune, and various field operatives of the United Nations, all of which give rise to myriad complications and combustions. Although zealotry does not come off well in *Damascus Gate*, it is nevertheless the inexorable logic of all Stone's novels that our passionate longing to transcend our literally Godforsaken condition, to seek out sufficient meaning within a seemingly indifferent universe, drives us relentlessly toward those high ramparts of bliss and enlightenment whose admission fee is always reckoned in blood and regret.

[*See also* Vietnam in Poetry and Prose *and* War Literature.]

SELECTED WORKS

A Hall of Mirrors (1967)
Dog Soldiers (1974)
A Flag for Sunrise (1981)
Children of Light (1986)
Outerbridge Reach (1992)
Bear and His Daughter: Stories (1997)
Damascus Gate (1998)

FURTHER READING

Bloom, James D. "Cultural Capital and Contrarian Investing: Robert Stone, Thom Jones, and Others." *Contemporary Literature* 36, no. 3 (Fall 1995): 490.

Elliot, Emory. "History and Will in *Dog Soldiers, Sabbatical*, and *The Color Purple*." *Arizona Quarterly* 43, no. 3 (Autumn 1987): 197–217.

Finn, James. "The Moral Vision of Robert Stone: The Transcendent in the Muck of History." *Commonweal* 120, no. 19 (5 November 1993): 9–14.

Fredrickson, Robert S. "Robert Stone's Decadent Leftists." *Papers on Language and Literature* 32, no. 3 (Summer 1996): 315–334.

Garren, Samuel B. "Stone's 'Porque No Tiene, Porque Le Falta.'" *Explicator* 42, no. 3 (Spring 1984): 61–62.

Karagueuzian, Maureen. "Irony in Robert Stone's *Dog Soldiers.*" *Critique: Studies in Modern Fiction* 24, no. 2 (Winter 1983): 65–73.

Moore, L. Hugh. "The Undersea World of Robert Stone." *Critique: Studies in Modern Fiction* 11, no. 3 (1969): 43–56.

Parks, John G. "Unfit Survivors: The Failed and Lost Pilgrims in the Fiction of Robert Stone." *CEA Critic* 53 (Fall 1990): 52–57.

Pink, David. "An Interview with Robert Stone." *Salmagundi* 108 (Fall 1995): 119.

Sale, Roger. "Robert Stone." In *On Not Being Good Enough: Writings of a Working Critic.* New York, 1979.

Shelton, Frank W. "Robert Stone's *Dog Soldiers*: Vietnam Comes Home to America." *Critique: Studies in Modern Fiction* 24, no. 2 (Winter 1983): 74–81.

Solotaroff, Robert. *Robert Stone.* New York, 1994. The only book-length study of Stone.

Weber, Bruce. "An Eye for Danger." *New York Times Magazine* (19 January 1992).

HARRIET BEECHER STOWE

by Lorinda B. Cohoon

Harriet Beecher Stowe's reputation as an author of American literature is directly connected to *Uncle Tom's Cabin; or, Life among the Lowly* (1852), her first and best-known novel. With this text, Stowe gave American literature a novel that influenced the abolitionist movement, contributed to American iconography, and explored possibilities for women's involvement in political life. Stowe's text also offered fruitful material for puzzling over the quality of her writing and its peculiar power. During the nineteenth century, reviewers and critics debated Stowe's literary reputation, alternately praising her for her bold choices of subjects or criticizing her for her texts' artistic flaws.

Harriet Beecher Stowe.
(*Courtesy of the Library of Congress*)

As the nature and importance of American literature were established in the early part of the twentieth century, literary historians either neglected to mention Stowe or compared her unfavorably to nineteenth-century male writers such as Nathaniel Hawthorne and Herman Melville. These writers were seen as having written far superior material, especially in the areas of style and originality. In the late twentieth century and in the first few years of the twenty-first century critics have renewed their interest in Stowe's writing, focusing on her feminism, her talents as a regional writer, and the relevance of her travel narratives and other texts to cultural studies. Participants in ongoing discussions of representations of race in the nineteenth century continue to grapple with Stowe's characterizations of people of color. Whether celebrated or berated, Stowe's contributions to American literature cannot be ignored.

EARLY LIFE AND WRITINGS

Harriet Beecher Stowe was born on 14 June 1811 in Litchfield, Connecticut, to Lyman and Roxana Foote Beecher. Her mother having died in 1816, Stowe's writing was influenced by the education she received from her father and her older sister, Catharine. Stowe's father was a famous preacher and a devout Calvinist. Influenced by eighteenth-century New England theologian Jonathan Edwards and his ideas about inevitable punishment for human sinfulness, Lyman Beecher trained his children to believe that there could be no assurance of salvation. Stowe struggled to embrace her father's belief systems and she went through a conversion experience at age fourteen. As a result of her father's vocation and her early religious training, many of Stowe's texts examine the nature of faith and explore conversion experiences. In her fiction Stowe moves away from her father's fear-based beliefs and promotes a faith centered on love and forgiveness. Stowe's father noticed her talents early in her life and wrote that it was unfortunate that she was not a boy because she was a "great genius." Despite his lack of enthusiasm for the usefulness of talent in a daughter, Lyman Beecher provided an education for Stowe and did not attempt to prevent her from writing.

Stowe's formal education began in earnest with an 1824 move to Hartford, Connecticut, to attend Hartford Female Seminary, which was run by her sister Catharine. At the seminary Stowe began writing, and biographical accounts tell of Catharine discovering Stowe penning a tragedy titled "Cleon," about Nero's conversion to Christianity. Catharine discouraged Stowe's interest in writing epic dramas and suggested that her sister read Joseph Butler's *The Analogy of Religion, Natural and Revealed, to the Constitution and Course of Nature* as a model for serious, theological, nonfiction prose, which was supposedly more suitable for Stowe to emulate. In 1832 Stowe moved with the rest of her family from New England to Cincinnati, where she continued to work closely with her sister. In

Ohio, Catharine founded a new school for women, the Western Female Institute, and Stowe taught there from 1833 to 1836. During these years Stowe began writing for magazines, and in 1833 her first published writings appeared in *Western Monthly Magazine*. Publishing under her sister's name, Stowe also wrote a geography textbook titled *Primary Geography for Children* (1833). Afterward, Stowe and her sister were invited to join an Ohio writing group called the Semi-Colon Club, and the contact with other authors that it afforded seems to have encouraged Stowe to continue to write. Catharine's lasting influence can be seen in some of Stowe's later treatises on domestic life and child education.

MARRIAGE, FAMILY, FICTION, AND FAME

In 1836 Stowe married the theologian Calvin Stowe and gave birth to twin daughters in September of that year. Her family continued to grow and as it did she wrote to provide financial support. Stowe's early short story collection, *The Mayflower* (1843), contains regional details about New England habits and characteristics and uses the New England environment to convey the smallness and powerlessness of her characters as they face the forces of a large, unpredictable, and sometimes violent world. One of Stowe's young sons died in 1849, and for a while her writing pace slowed as she mourned his death.

In 1850 Stowe moved to Maine with her husband so that he could teach at Bowdoin College. In 1851 the first installment of *Uncle Tom's Cabin* appeared in the abolitionist *National Era* and in 1852 the book was published. In 1853 Stowe moved to Andover, Massachusetts, where her husband took a position at Andover Theological Seminary. The popularity of Stowe's book bought her more time to write, and in an answer to criticisms that *Uncle Tom's Cabin* was full of lies and inaccuracies, Stowe published *A Key to Uncle Tom's Cabin* (1853), which offered her sources for the text and supported it with newspaper accounts of slave sales and accounts from escaped slaves that corroborated her evidence about the horrors of slavery. Stowe continued to write steadily, even though the reception of her subsequent books never matched the instant popularity of *Uncle Tom's Cabin*. Stowe visited Europe in 1853 and described her visit in *Sunny Memories of Foreign Lands* (1854). Wishing to continue exposing the horrors of slavery, Stowe published *Dred: A Tale of the Great Dismal Swamp* (1856), another antislavery text. It drew inspiration from antislavery activist John Brown and from Nat Turner, who had organized a slave uprising in 1831. It featured a slave who is a half brother to his

mistress. The familial link that Stowe draws between the slave and the owner underscored the illogical nature of a slave system in which one family member might be the property of another solely on the basis of skin color.

Much of Stowe's writing investigates the culture of the New England region in which she came of age. *The Minister's Wooing* (1859) was one of her New England tales. It was followed by *The Pearl of Orr's Island* in 1861. Both of these combine commentary about how region and religion influence the choices women can and cannot make.

In her later books Stowe wrote on a variety of topics. *Oldtown Folks*, another volume about New England, was published in 1869. Stowe and her sister wrote a book about household organization and decoration titled *The American Woman's Home* (1869). In *Lady Byron Vindicated* (1870) Stowe told what she knew about Lord Byron's sexual relationship with his half sister. *Pink and White Tyranny* (1871) is a text about a sober young man whose wife wants a more exciting life than the one she finds herself living in a New England town. She never becomes a docile housekeeper, although she does repent her frivolous ways at the end of the novel.

In the 1870s Stowe spent winters in Florida and summers in Connecticut. These places influenced her book about Florida, *Palmetto-Leaves* (1873), and *Poganuc People: Their Loves and Lives* (1878), another New England novel. Stowe published less frequently in the 1880s, and stopped traveling to Florida in the winter. The *Atlantic Monthly* gave Stowe a party in honor of her seventieth birthday in 1881 that was attended by literary figures such as William Dean Howells, Thomas Bailey Aldrich, and Bronson Alcott. Stowe gradually withdrew from the activities of the literary world and near the end of her life she suffered from senility, becoming forgetful enough to require constant care. She died on 1 July 1896 in Hartford, Connecticut.

UNCLE TOM'S CABIN

Stowe's first novel began as a serialization in the *National Era*, an antislavery newspaper, on 5 June 1851 and ended on 1 April 1852. Stowe intended it to be a response to the Compromise of 1850, which left the western territories with the option of becoming slave states. The part of the Compromise that particularly infuriated Stowe, however, was the Fugitive Slave Act, which required free states to assist in returning runaway slaves to their southern owners. Stowe was inspired to write about the Fugitive Slave Act because of a letter from her sister-in-law, Mrs.

Edward Beecher. The letter told Stowe, "If I could use a pen as you can, I would write something that will make this whole nation feel what an accursed thing slavery is." According to accounts given by Stowe, the beginnings of the story that she used to awaken the nation came to her in a vision during communion in church. Stowe saw a black man being whipped, and during this treatment he continued to pray for his persecutors. Stowe saw Tom's unwillingness to be beaten into bitterness or vengeance as a victory over slavery, and she titled the chapter about Tom's death "The Victory." In Stowe's mind, Tom's prayers for the cruel slaveholders prove his humanity; no matter how harsh their treatment of him becomes, the slaveholders are not able to dispossess Tom of his kindness and forgiveness, attributes that give Tom a Christ-like transcendence over his physical circumstances.

As it combined the traditions of the sentimental novel and the abolitionist tract, *Uncle Tom's Cabin* captured the imaginations of thousands of readers. Part of its appeal was the mixture of stories about relations between North and South, men and women, and whites and blacks. Stowe moves between heartbreaking scenes with Little Eva, a beautiful, sickly girl, and scenes of horrifying cruelty that depict Simon Legree, a villainous plantation owner. Suspense is built into the episodes that detail how George and Eliza Harris use costumes and convincing stories to pass as white on their separate journeys to freedom. The stories of Eliza Harris and Uncle Tom figure prominently in the mixture of plotlines. In the opening scenes both Tom and Eliza live on a plantation in Kentucky owned by the Shelby family. When Mr. Shelby decides to sell Eliza's son to pay for his debts, Eliza decides to run away to Canada and take her son with her. Mr. Shelby sends Uncle Tom to New Orleans to be sold. On the journey "down the river" he meets Eva St. Clare. Eva's father, Augustine St. Clare, purchases Tom. Eva dies, but her goodness helps her to convince her father to free his slaves. He intends to do so but delays acting and then dies suddenly. His good intentions, combined with his lack of initiative, make St. Clare an important and complicated figure. His death shows what slavery does to slaves who have not been freed because their owners believe they are good owners and that their slaves are safe. St. Clare also has connections to New England; he grew up in there, and the consequences of his inaction indict northerners who give lip service to their belief in the evils of slavery but do nothing about them. Indeed, one of the most powerful aspects of Stowe's novel is that it does not excuse northerners from responsibility for the evils of slavery.

Stowe repeatedly emphasizes the North's involvement in slavery. She explores the racism of northern attitudes toward persons of color in her depiction of Miss Ophelia, a cousin of St. Clare who comes down from New England to stay with Eva. Miss Ophelia supports abolition, but her actions and attitudes are racist. She cannot bear to touch Topsy, and Stowe's text makes Miss Ophelia's hypocrisy clear. Simon Legree, whose name remained synonymous with calculated evil for over a century after the book was published, also comes from the North. Stowe's refusal to let the North remain blameless deepened her portrayal of slavery and encouraged her abolitionist readers to act. The text frequently addresses readers and asks them if they would be willing to break laws in order to enforce a greater moral right.

Stowe ends her characters' journeys in very different ways. Tom is sold to Simon Legree after St. Clare's death while Eliza makes her way to Canada. Under Simon Legree, Tom makes it his duty to protect Cassy, one of the other slaves, from taking her bitter anger toward Legree too far. Instead of murdering Legree or exacting vengeance in some other way, Cassy plans to run away, hiding in the house until it is safe to leave. Uncle Tom dies but never relinquishes his soul to Simon Legree, and Tom's unwavering faith softens Cassy's heart enough so that when she finds Eliza, who is her daughter, in Canada, she also finds faith. The end of the book depicts several family members reuniting in Canada and then moving to Africa. Aunt Ophelia takes Topsy back to Vermont, and when Topsy grows up she goes to Africa as well. Stowe's conclusions prove problematic because her story does not make a place for freed slaves to live in the United States: her black characters either go to Africa or they die. The troubling solutions that Stowe provides for her characters after they escape from slavery suggest that Stowe could not imagine economic livelihoods and peaceful domestic arrangements for persons of color in a postslavery world.

Despite its final descent into racist conclusions, Stowe's text makes powerful political statements about effecting social change. It is a feminist text, although Stowe did not clearly affiliate herself with women abolitionists who also were working to gain women's rights. The women in this novel are strong and many defy the men in their families to pursue a moral right. Mrs. Shelby resists the sale of Eliza's son and of Tom, and she insists that slavery is wrong. In the chapter titled "A Senator Is But a Man," Mrs. Bird tells her senator husband that she opposes the Fugitive Slave Act. Commenting on these domestic uprisings, Mr. Shelby tells his wife that she is getting to be an abolitionist and Senator Bird tells his wife that she is getting to be a politician. Eva uses persuasive rhetoric to convince her father to free the slaves. Eliza bravely enters the free world and meets social and physical challenges first by acting the part of a white traveler and then by escaping to freedom by crossing a river on chunks of floating ice. Cassy solves the problem of escaping from a cruel owner by cleverly haunting Simon Legree's plantation house. Aunt Chloe uses her cooking skills to feed fellow slaves and to stabilize her position with the Shelby family, while Dinah subversively disorders her kitchen in ways that allow her to maintain control of her space. These women exert what power they can over the domestic circumstances in which they find themselves. When she gives her women characters power, Stowe successfully complicates the notion that women's spheres were separate from those of men. Stowe's women practice politics in the parlor, abolition on the porches of plantations, and oratory from sick beds. With these descriptions of influence, Stowe explodes the idea that women's spheres incorporate only domestic or family issues.

In addition to questioning nineteenth-century ideas about separate spheres for men and women, Stowe also investigated the function of the law in maintaining slavery. Many characters in Stowe's novel break the laws regarding the return of runaway slaves, and Stowe actively encourages readers to participate in breaking the new Fugitive Slave Act by helping slaves to freedom. The laws that Stowe cares about the most are moral laws, and her text's premise is that slavery prevents slaves from learning and following God's laws. Stowe's text also indicates that faith can provide slaves with a legal contract with God that slaveholders cannot destroy. When Cassy tells Tom that he should quickly become hard-hearted like the rest of Simon Legree's slaves or else die slowly, Tom tells her that his soul is safe because it has been bought by God. Using her knowledge of religious beliefs and her understanding of the new laws that forced northerners to help slave owners, Stowe meditates on the power of law and calls on her readers to use all means necessary to resist the spread of slavery. Her text also contemplates what it means to be a citizen in a nation that claims all men are created equal at the same time that it writes laws that enforce a cruel inequality.

STOWE'S REPUTATION

After its initial publication, *Uncle Tom's Cabin* was both praised and criticized by Stowe's contemporaries. Henry James and Leo Tolstoy applauded Stowe's efforts while Charles Dickens criticized the novel's construction. Fellow abolitionist John Greenleaf Whittier supported all of Stowe's work even when subsequent books were criticized as much weaker than Stowe's best-seller. Stowe's use of dialect distressed some women writers. Sarah Josepha Hale insisted that there was no need for Stowe to have her southern characters talk as they did. Stowe recognized, as did the later authors Mark Twain and Rebecca Harding Davis, that dialect could give voice to the everyday needs, ideas, and political positions of characters from a variety of economic and educational backgrounds. Stowe enjoyed the success of the novel, and she began answering critics with the publication of *A Key to Uncle Tom's Cabin*. Although it sold over one million copies and was subsequently translated into many languages, Stowe did not make much money from *Uncle Tom's Cabin* because there was no international copyright law and because her contract with the publishing house that first produced the text did not protect her share of the profits. The lack of copyright control of the text actually helped to circulate it. Numerous dramatic versions of *Uncle Tom's Cabin* were produced and many cheap, unauthorized editions were published and circulated on both sides of the Atlantic.

The reputation and importance of *Uncle Tom's Cabin* continues to be a subject of debate. The characters of Tom, Topsy, and Little Eva have maintained a place in the popular imagination, but the critical attention and acclaim for Stowe's text has wavered. In 1949, James Baldwin argued persuasively that Stowe's text was subversively racist and damaging. Certainly, the use of the description "Uncle Tom" to describe a person of color who is absurdly subservient to oppressors has lingered, as have stereotypes of Mammy and Topsy. Others have criticized her writing style as insipid and unbearably sentimental. Frequently, Stowe's texts have been classified as popular fiction rather than literature. Recent attention has been given to Stowe's treatment of women, her use of dialect, and her use of the gothic, especially in her descriptions of Cassy. No matter how it is received, *Uncle Tom's Cabin* maintains its position as an antislavery text that sheds light on northern attitudes toward slavery before the Civil War.

STOWE'S NEW ENGLAND NOVELS

After *Uncle Tom's Cabin*, Stowe wrote several novels and sketches about life in New England. In these texts it is clear that Stowe was not particularly interested in writing about the courtship and marriage of young heroines; most of her women are very young, like Little Eva, or are already married. *The Minister's Wooing* examines family life, religious life, and the position of women who need to find livelihoods when they are left without any family or income. In this text three men are in love with one woman, who uses religious faith as a way to make a decision about a husband. *Oldtown Folks* also examines New England life and is similar in plot to *The Minister's Wooing*; its three suitors are a minister, a schoolmaster, and a less stable young man who is Aaron Burr's cousin. *Poganuc People* examines religious life in New England during Jonathan Edwards's Great Awakening. In this text, Stowe examines how Edwards's emphasis on the inescapability of sinfulness served to drive old New England families away from the church. Like *Uncle Tom's Cabin*, this text embraces a religion based on God's love rather than his wrath.

The Pearl of Orr's Island provides another example of Stowe's interest in New England. This novel is about how a young girl's love changes the ways of a rebellious youth. The text ends with the girl's death and the youth's ensuing conversion. The boy is an orphan descended from parents who are part Spanish and Catholic. Stowe endows the New England environment with powers of transformation and suggests that the love of a motherly girl, combined with the wholesome New England environment, will save this boy. This text's initial scenes of the Maine coast inspired Sarah Orne Jewett, another regional writer, and *The Pearl of Orr's Island* gained critical attention in the late twentieth century for its details about regional life and about women's lives.

TRAVEL COMMENTARIES

In addition to her antislavery texts and her New England novels, Stowe also published several books based on her travels. *Sunny Memories of Foreign Lands* was Stowe's first travel narrative, published after the popularity of *Uncle Tom's Cabin* permitted her to travel to England and France with a good deal of celebrity. Writing to an audience without travel experience, Stowe recounts famous people she has met and well-known places she has visited. These accounts say more about Americans' views of themselves and their use of the Old World to define their national identity than they do about life in England and France in the nineteenth century. Stowe's *Agnes of Sorrento* (1862), set in Italy, is a novel influenced by her travels to Europe. This book has a beautiful and kind heroine named Agnes. Agnes has three suitors, much like the characters in *The Minister's Wooing* and *Oldtown Folks*. Here, Stowe is interested in investigating the beliefs of the Catholic Church. In its tone and in direct statements, it conveys many anti-Catholic sentiments, while at the same time

Stowe praises some of the moral codes of Catholicism. Agnes adheres to the love-based religion Stowe explores in *Uncle Tom's Cabin* and *The Pearl of Orr's Island*.

During her later years Stowe bought a house in Florida, and her experiences there led her to write *Palmetto-Leaves*. This text, directed at northern readers, praises the warmth of the climate and the beauty of the foliage. It describes Florida as a kind of paradise, and as she does in her New England stories, Stowe depicts regional characters and scenes. She also describes race relations in the Reconstruction South and participates in post–Civil War racism by writing about African Americans with condescension and employing patronizing generalizations.

CHILDREN'S STORIES

While *Uncle Tom's Cabin* was written for adults, it found an immediate readership with children, and the plays and musicals based on it that were produced after its success also appealed to children. Stowe was aware of this audience, and while she produced her novels and essays for adults, she also wrote several pieces for children. She contributed to *Our Young Folks*, a children's magazine that began publication in 1865, as well as to other magazines for children and families. One of her novels, *Our Charley, and What to Do with Him* (1858), contains information about child rearing as well as stories for children. Other stories for children include *Queer Little People* (1867), *Little Pussy Willow* (1870), and *A Dog's Mission* (1881). These tales focus on animals, the daily lives of children, and children's relations to the natural world. They also address the differences between country and city life. Their appeal lies in the use of dialogue and details of everyday life and they make important contributions to the format of American children's literature, which became more realistic and less didactic in the 1870s and 1880s.

STOWE'S CONTRIBUTIONS TO AMERICAN LITERATURE

Uncle Tom's Cabin alone makes it necessary to reckon with Stowe when the nature of American literature is considered. Surrounded by controversy during its initial publication, this novel has continued to spark lively debates about race, gender, region, and national identity. Stowe's use of regional details and dialect must also be recognized as playing an important part in the history of the texts of the realist movement. Stowe's work provides rich material to scholars studying women's literature and lives, nineteenth-century sentimental fiction, and travel narratives. In addition, Stowe's characters and images continue to shape understandings of antebellum life in the United States.

[*See also* Children's Literature; Naturalism and Realism; Popular Fiction; *and* Puritanism: The Sense of an Unending.]

SELECTED WORKS

Primary Geography for Children, on an Improved Plan (1833)

The Mayflower; or, Sketches of Scenes and Characters among the Descendents of the Pilgrims (1843)

Uncle Tom's Cabin; or, Life among the Lowly (1852)

A Key to Uncle Tom's Cabin; Presenting the Original Facts and Documents upon Which the Story Is Founded. Together with Corroborative Statements Verifying the Truth of the Work (1853)

Sunny Memories of Foreign Lands (1854)

Dred: A Tale of the Great Dismal Swamp (1856)

Our Charley, and What to Do with Him (1858)

The Minister's Wooing (1859)

The Pearl of Orr's Island: A Story of the Coast of Maine (1861)

Agnes of Sorrento (1862)

Daisy's First Winter, and Other Stories (1867)

Queer Little People (1867)

The American Woman's Home; or, Principles of Domestic Science: Being a Guide to the Formation and Maintenance of Economical, Healthful, Beautiful, and Christian Homes (1869)

Oldtown Folks (1869)

Lady Byron Vindicated: A History of the Byron Controversy from Its Beginning in 1816 to the Present Time (1870)

Little Pussy Willow (1870)

Pink and White Tyranny (1871)

Palmetto-Leaves (1873)

Poganuc People: Their Loves and Lives (1878)

A Dog's Mission (1881)

FURTHER READING

Adams, John R. *Harriet Beecher Stowe, Updated Edition.* Boston, 1989. This biographical study provides a clear overview of her life and best-known texts. Also contains a helpful chronology and an annotated bibliography.

Ammons, Elizabeth, ed. *Critical Essays on Harriet Beecher Stowe.* Boston, 1980. This useful resource contains historical and more recent responses to Stowe's work that help to provide a context for changes in her reputation. Includes reviews and essays by George Sand, George Eliot, Henry James, and Langston Hughes, among others.

Baldwin, James. "Everybody's Protest Novel." *Partisan Review* 16 (June 1949): 578–585. Baldwin argues that *Uncle Tom's Cabin* has had a lasting negative effect because it promotes and proliferates racist stereotypes. An important resource for understanding the complexity and problems of Stowe's treatments of race.

Brown, Gillian. *Domestic Individualism: Imagining Self in Nineteenth-Century America.* Berkeley and Los Angeles, 1990. In a powerful exploration of household objects and self-ownership, Brown suggests that Stowe uses domestic details to expose gender- and race-based power structures. See pp. 13–60.

Fields, Annie. *Life and Letters of Harriet Beecher Stowe.* Boston, 1898. Fields was a friend of Stowe, and this text gives insight into contemporary views of Stowe's contributions to American literature.

Foster, Charles H. *The Rungless Ladder: Harriet Beecher Stowe and New England Puritanism.* Durham, N.C., 1934. This text traces the history of regional religious beliefs that are explored in Stowe's texts and places changes in Stowe's thinking about religion in the context of larger changes in religious life in New England.

Hedrick, Joan D. *Harriet Beecher Stowe: A Life.* New York and Oxford, 1994. This feminist study gives extensive attention to Stowe's everyday life and draws connections between her habits and interests and her writing. Offers extensive notes, a helpful index, and a bibliography to those interested in further study of Stowe's work.

Hildreth, Margaret Holbrook. *Harriet Beecher Stowe: A Bibliography.* Hamden, Conn., 1976. This bibliography provides information on texts by and about Stowe. Useful resource for researchers interested in tracking down musical and dramatic adaptations of Stowe's works.

Stowe, Charles Edward. *Life of Harriet Beecher Stowe Compiled from Her Letters and Journals.* Boston, 1889. Stowe authorized this biography, which was written by her youngest son. Publishes letters written by Stowe and provides invaluable insight into what Stowe wanted the public to know about her.

Tompkins, Jane P. *The Cultural Work of American Fiction, 1790–1860.* New York, 1985. Tompkins makes a powerful argument for *Uncle Tom's Cabin*'s importance to histories of American literature. See "Sentimental Power," pp. 122–146.

Wilson, Forrest. *Crusader in Crinoline: The Life of Harriet Beecher Stowe.* Philadelphia, 1941. This important biography won the Pulitzer Prize and has influenced all subsequent treatments of Stowe.

MARK STRAND

by Andrew Zawacki

Mark Strand was born in Summerside, Prince Edward Island, Canada, on 11 April 1934. Sandwiched between the celebrated generation of American poets born in 1927—John Ashbery, Adrienne Rich, W. S. Merwin, Galway Kinnell, James Wright, and Donald Hall, among others—and those of the 1940s, Strand once joked that he, Charles Wright, and Charles Simic comprise a "generation of three." Strand's parents left Canada when he was four, and he was raised and educated mainly in the United States and South America, returning to Nova Scotia for summers until he was twelve.

In midcareer Strand devoted a group of transparently autobiographical poems to his childhood memories. The "Poor North" section of *The Late Hour* (1978) and the new work appended to his *Selected Poems* (1980) indulge in nostalgia and a realism that, though uncharacteristically personal, are wedded to his more recognizable gnostic illuminations. The settings of Seabright, Wedge Island and Mosher Island, Fox Point, Hackett's Cove, and St. Margaret's Bay serve as backdrop for intensely lyrical poems in which the poet remembers "your mother before she was gray, your father before he was white," as the speaker witnesses himself inhabiting the past: "Now you invent the boat of your flesh and set it upon the waters / and drift in the gradual swell, in the laboring salt. / Now you look down. The waters of childhood are there." Despite the laconic sadness that permeates poems such as "Pot Roast" and "The House in French Village"—poems imbued with landscapes of snow, ice, rain, clouds with "the look of rags torn and soiled with use," soot-stained brick and gambrel roofs—the poet nonetheless claims that "for once I do not regret / the passage of time." While "Shooting Whales" employs passages from the Book of Job, spillages of moonlight manage to tear through the suffering, and in "A Morning," Strand offers a vision of hard grace as he recollects sailing in his uncle's boat: "I moved like a dark star, drifting over the drowned / other half of the world until, by a distant prompting, / I looked over the gunwale and saw beneath the surface / a luminous room, a light-filled grave, saw for the first time / the one clear place given to us when we are alone."

Educated at Antioch College, where he graduated with a bachelor's degree in 1957, Strand proceeded to Yale University to study painting. There he studied under Joseph Albers; befriended painter William Bailey, the subject of a monograph that Strand published in 1987; and met poet and novelist Robert Penn Warren, whose mentorship played an important role in fostering Strand's interest in writing poetry. Upon receiving a B.F.A. from Yale in 1959, Strand spent a year in Italy on a Fulbright Scholarship studying nineteenth-century poetry. His engagement with Italian poetry and art surfaces frequently, in poems such as "Leopardi"; the later villanelle "The Philosopher's Conquest," based on Giorgio de Chirico's 1914 painting; and "*Se la vita e sventura . . . ?*," in which an "unreachable sphere of light" is pitched against a night "Darkly inscribing itself everywhere," as the poet is "born into myself again and again."

Returning to the States, Strand enrolled in the University of Iowa's fledgling creative-writing program, where he studied under Donald Justice and presented a thesis of poems, "Walking Around and Other Exercises." After taking an M.A. in 1962, Strand taught a number of promising young poets, including Charles Wright, at the increasingly popular and prestigious Iowa workshop, before teaching at Columbia, Yale, Princeton, Brandeis, and elsewhere. He maintained a commitment to art and art criticism, publishing *Art of the Real* in 1983 and a study of Edward Hopper in 1994; he still promotes the work of contemporary artists, while painting, etching, and creating neosurrealist collages himself. Subsequent travels took him to Brazil, where he associated with American poet Elizabeth Bishop and translated the poetry of Carlos Drummond de Andrade. Having spent summers in Mexico as a teenager, in the late 1960s Strand began a long-standing friendship with writer Octavio Paz. Together the two edited *New Poetry of Mexico* in 1970, and the next year Strand published *18 Poems from the Quechua*. In 1973, Strand's translations of the poems of Spanish poet and artist Raphael Alberti appeared as *The Owl's Insomnia*, while 1976 saw the publication of *Another Republic: 17 European and South American Writers*, which he coedited with Simic.

Although his first poetry book, *Sleeping with One Eye Open* (1964), received little critical attention, his next two, *Reasons for Moving* (1968) and *Darker* (1970), along with his edited anthology *The Contemporary American Poets* (1969), earned Strand the praise of prominent critics such as Harold Bloom and Richard Howard, who argued that Strand's poems narrate the moment when he makes Rimbaud's discovery that *je est un autre* (I is an other). Strand received numerous honors, from Rockefeller and Ingram Merrill fellowships to a fellowship from the National Endowment for the Arts, and continued to publish in high-profile venues like *The New Yorker* and *Antæus*. If his presence in American poetry had become unmistakable, it was all the more remarkable for one whose work was haunted by absence.

EARLY ON

Strand's earliest poems begin from the premise of "moving to keep things whole." "In a field / I am the absence / of field," he writes in "Keeping Things Whole," the cornerstone of his debut volume: "Wherever I am / I am what is missing." Pursuing a secular version of the mystical or negative way, which claims that self-emptying is the first step toward achieving fullness, Strand presents foreboding scenes of "glassy air," vacant rooms, and a violent wind rattling the house, in which a sleepless, solitary listener waits, hoping that nothing will happen. "Oh, I feel dead," sighs the speaker of the title poem of *Sleeping with One Eye Open*, "Folded / Away in my blankets for good, and / Forgotten." In "Poem" the speaker notes that someone has entered the room to kill him, and in "The Tunnel," which bears an affinity to the bizarre, unnerving parables of Franz Kafka such as "The Burrow," someone tries to escape the gaze of a man who watches him ceaselessly from the front yard. Marked by a simplicity of language and spare diction, and indebted to symbolist iconography even as "The tree we lean against / Was never meant to stand / For something else," Strand's minimalist first poems are often as beautiful and elegiac as they are chilling. "We live unsettled lives / And stay in a place / Only long enough to find / We don't belong," claims the speaker of "Taking a Walk with You": "We are not here, / We've always been away."

A number of poems from Strand's debut were reprinted in *Reasons for Moving*, which opens with the darkly humorous "Eating Poetry," in which the speaker announces,

"Ink runs from the corners of my mouth. / There is no happiness like mine. / I have been eating poetry." Notwithstanding his bid to be a "new man," the speaker devolves into a canine figure, barking and licking the librarian's hand as he "romp[s] with joy in the bookish dark." Poems like "The Accident," "The Mailman," "The Suicide," and "Moontan" further Strand's preoccupation with the eerie, absurd, and illogical. The volume's closing poem, "The Man in the Mirror," tangentially recalls John Donne's "Sapho to Philænis"—"I remember how we used to stand / wishing the glass / would dissolve between us"—but is also a paradox in the manner of Jorge Luis Borges and Italo Calvino. The reader is finally uncertain whether the figure in the mirror is the speaker's lover, a muse, mere reflection, or some metaphysically alternative, ulterior double self. Deserted by the image that later returns, "I stand here," admits the speaker, "scared / that you will disappear, / scared that you will stay."

Enactments of absence are radicalized in *Darker* (1970), where Strand evinces a deep anxiety regarding the self's instability, combined with an assurance about rebirth. The speaker of "Giving Myself Up" gets rid of his body, his smell, his clothing, and "the ghost that lives in them," telling whomever is listening, "And you will have none of it because already I am beginning / again without anything." Likewise, in "The Remains" the speaker divests himself of his pockets and parents, his wife, even his own name and past, until "I change and I am the same. / I empty myself of my life and my life remains." Elsewhere he asks the "Guardian of my death" to "preserve my absence. I am alive." The diptych "My Life" and the seemingly posthumous "My Death" report that "I grow into my death" as a kind of "health," while their unresolved resolution, "My Life by Somebody Else," inquires, "Must I write *My Life* by somebody else? / *My Death* by somebody else?" Vanishing acts and doppelgängers are everywhere in this volume replete with strangeness and estrangement, yet the pair of psalmic poems, both titled "From a Litany," proclaim an elegant, lush praise for all of creation, while the wry "Courtship" is a tribute to procreation—or at least to the emotions and sexual motions that lead to marriage.

THE MIDDLE WAY

The seven-part title sequence of *The Story of Our Lives* (1973) is akin to a Möbius strip or an Escher drawing, on which the dynamics of living, reading, and going through the motions are inscribed. Two people, presumably husband and wife, read a Mallarméan "book" that supposedly contains their life story, clearly a tale of love up to the onset of their mutual fatigue and loneliness. The question of agency troubles the poem's subjects, who wish to author their own lives but instead end up reading the text that is writing them. The poem contains italicized passages from the couple's story—"The book says: *He put the pen down / and turned and watched her reading / the part about herself falling in love*"—so that the statement, "We say it is ideal. / It is ideal," resonates not only with what is edenic or perfect but also with the strictly theoretical. The poem highlights Strand's fixation on the perplexities of mimicry, inflection, and the way beginning and end confuse and confound one another, yet it does so through a series of narratives—a story as well as another story within—that are poignant and psychologically compelling, if not quietly tragic. Weighted by mortal gravity and bolstered by the levity of language and longing, the emotional balance of "The Untelling" is likewise inseparable from its seesawing, metanarrative form. Whereas spiritual desiccation had been one of Strand's foremost themes, the six-part "Elegy for My Father," in memory of Robert Strand (1908–1968), addresses a death that is quite literal. Through a litany of questions ("Are you tired and do you want to lie down? / *Yes, I am tired and I want to lie down*"), anaphoras ("You went on with your dying. / Nothing could stop you. Not your son. Not your daughter. . . . Not the wind that shook your lapels"), and simple declaratives whose repetition renders them vatic ("The hands were yours, the arms were yours, / But you were not there"), the son finally returns his burden. "Your shadow is yours," he tells his father, "I have carried it with me too long. I give it back."

A string of honors followed the volume, including the first Edgar Allan Poe Award and a Guggenheim Fellowship in 1974, a National Institute of Arts and Letters Award the following year, and, in 1979, a Fellowship of the Academy of American Poets for "distinguished poetic achievement." One award Strand was denied, however, was the Pulitzer. As poet, critic, and editor David Lehman recounts (2003), Strand nearly received the prize for his next book, *The Monument* (1978), but one of the three judges, Louis Simpson, objected to the volume because it was primarily in prose. Composed in fifty-two sections to parallel Walt Whitman's *Song of Myself*, which is given the last word in this playful, essayistic meditation on death and negative capability, *The Monument* is what Strand has called "a poem of self-assertion and self-erasure." Riddled with citations from Sir Thomas Browne, William Shakespeare, E. M. Cioran, Miguel de Unamuno, the Gospel according to Mark, and other sources enumerated in endnotes, the volume weathers the climate of poststructuralist "death of the author" theories so controversial at the time. "I too died once," the narrator admits, elaborating, "This poor document does not have to do with a self, it dwells on the absence of a self." An homage to subtraction, alterity, and "the *lux* of lack," and pitched between "adequate memorial" and anonymity, *The Monument* is both a "nougat of nothing" and a promise to the reader that "Through you I shall be born again; myself again and again . . . myself beyond death." The critic David Kirby (1990) considers the book to be the culmination of Strand's "program of self-effacement." Indeed, its dedication to a future translator—"*Siste Viator*," a popular Roman epitaph meaning "Stop, traveller"—may very well serve as a caveat: like the so-called author, the translator should refrain from asserting a personality at the expense of the text.

The Late Hour (1978), released the same year, represents a reprieve from loss. From its opening poem, "The Coming of Light," in which "Even this late the bones of the body shine / and tomorrow's dust flares into breath," the book breathes easier in images of wakefulness, whiteness, the dream of "clear sight." The poet and critic Linda Gregerson (2001) claims that its writing "follows the course of one who has decided to return from the brink of the grave to leave death to its own devices." While shadows and exile invade many of the poems, they also hold out the possibility of return and redemption. "All we lost in the night is back," praises the speaker of "Night Pieces," which closes the volume. And in "For Jessica, My Daughter," Strand imagines "a light / that would not let us stray too far apart . . . something you could carry / in the dark / when I am away."

THE LATER HOURS

The publication of Strand's *The Continuous Life* (1990) brought to a close about a dozen years of poetic silence. During the 1980s, while Strand was teaching at the University of Utah, he published translations, art criticism, three children's books, and a collection of short stories, *Mr. and Mrs. Baby and Other Stories* (1985). He was honored with a John D. and Catherine T. MacArthur Fellowship in 1987, and in 1990 he was named poet laureate of the United States. Exerting its author's wish to erase himself, *The Continuous Life* contains a cento after Virgil; a dialogue after Leopardi; a prose sestina after Chekhov; letters by Gregor Samsa and his sister Grete; a lost diary entry that speaks as though poets Goethe and Wordsworth and painters Corot and Raeburn were living friends; a conversation overheard at a supermarket between a man and a woman discussing narrative poetry; a bathtub dialogue with Borges about translation; a retelling of the Orpheus myth that speaks of a language "Where death is reborn and sent into the world as a gift"; and an anecdote about a subway station encounter between Jane, who lifts up her dress, and a married Princeton professor named John, who pulls down his pants. Other poems are as languorous and lyrical, informed by "the dark infinitive to feel," as these are fanciful and grotesque, making the volume Strand's most eclectic. "The Idea" depicts a cabin in the distance and a couple that determine "it was ours by not being ours, / And should remain empty. That was the idea," while "Luminism" reveals a "cry, almost beyond our hearing" that "rose / As if across time, to touch us as nothing else would, / And so lightly we might live out our lives and not know." "I had no idea," the poem closes enigmatically, "what it meant until now."

Strand received the Bollingen Prize for his follow-up volume, *Dark Harbor* (1993), a book-length poem in forty-five sections. Composed entirely in plaintive tercets that shuttle seamlessly between the florid, frozen clarities and obscurities of Wallace Stevens's poetry and the reticence, diminishment, and failure endemic to Samuel Beckett's prose, *Dark Harbor* is propelled by a desire that refuses the despair it negotiates. Its "Proem" inaugurates a pilgrimage on which the poet begins "to mark, almost as a painter would, / The passages of greater and lesser worth." Strand's romantic tendency to lean into transcendence achieves its zenith in this book, encroaching extinction and the quest for redemption forming parts of a single movement: "Tell me I have not lived in vain, that the stars / Will not die, that things will stay as they are, / That what I have seen will last . . . that what I have said has not been said for me." In the face of "terrible omens of the end," Strand seeks a vision of "how perfectly everything fits in its space," as he cultivates "a simplicity that turns being / Into an occasion for mourning, or into an occasion / Worth celebrating." The final canto affirms T. S. Eliot's certainty that the communication of the dead is tongued with flame beyond the language of the living, as an angel begins to sing "the silence of love, / Of pain, and even of pleasure."

After teaching at Johns Hopkins University from 1994 to 1997, Strand became a member of the Committee on Social Thought at the University of Chicago, where he currently teaches an array of seminars on poetry, fiction, drama, and philosophy. A former chancellor of the Academy of American Poets, he received the Pulitzer Prize for his 1999 collection, *Blizzard of One*. The book's most memorable lyric, "A Piece of the Storm," is a sublime account of "a solemn waking / To brevity, the lifting and falling away of attention, swiftly, / A time between times, a flowerless funeral," instigated by a lone snowflake, a "blizzard of one." The poem testifies to the half-quotidian, half-miraculous "feeling that this piece of the storm, / Which turned into nothing before your eyes, would come back, / That someone years hence, sitting as you are now, might say: / 'It's time. The air is ready. The sky has an opening.'" Another poem, "Morning, Noon, and Night," also envisages ghostly future selves, but its final image, if promising disclosure, offers a revelation rooted in narrowness, entrapment, finality, as the speaker dreams of floating "forgotten / On a midnight sea where every thousand years a ship is sighted, or a swan, / Or a drowned swimmer whose imagination has outlived his fate, and who swims / To prove, to no one in particular, how false his life had been." The book also features a comical suite of "Five Dogs," in which Strand incarnates himself as Spot.

Strand's collection of occasional essays on poetics spanning over two decades, *The Weather of Words* (2000), appeared the following year. Its quirky first selection, "A Poet's Alphabet," indicates that A is for "absence" ("die and you clear a space for yourself") while S is "for something that supplies a vacancy, which I might fill," and Y is for "why." The compendium reprints Strand's introduction to *The Best American Poetry 1991* anthology, where he claims that a poem is "language performing at its most beguiling and seductive while being, at the same time, elusive, even seeming to mock one's desire for reduction, for plain and available order." As he said in a 1998 interview in *The Paris Review*, "it's this language, the language of poetry, through which we're recognizably human."

WORKS

POETRY

Sleeping with One Eye Open (1964)
Reasons for Moving (1968)
Darker (1970)
The Story of Our Lives (1973)
The Sargentville Notebook (1974)
The Late Hour (1978)
Selected Poems (1980; 1990)
The Continuous Life (1990)
Dark Harbor (1993)
Blizzard of One (1998)
89 Clouds (1999)
Chicken, Shadow, Moon & More (2000)

PROSE

The Monument (1978)
Art of the Real (1983)
Mr. and Mrs. Baby and Other Stories (1985)
William Bailey (1987)
Edward Hopper (1994)
The Weather of Words: Poetic Invention (2000)

CHILDREN'S BOOKS

The Planet of Lost Things (1982)
The Night Book (1985)
Rembrandt Takes a Walk (1986)

FURTHER READING

Bloom, Harold, ed. *Mark Strand*. Philadelphia, 2003. An excellent, eclectic collection of Bloom's commentary, excerpted essays, and reviews of Strand's major work by various scholars; and brief biographical material pertaining to Strand's career.

Gregerson, Linda. "Negative Capability (Mark Strand)." *Negative Capability: Contemporary American Poetry*. pp. 5–29. Ann Arbor, Mich., 2001. An important essay that considers Strand's middle poems in terms of negation, narrative structure, and their built-in "clearing."

Howard, Richard. "The Mirror Was Nothing without You." In *Alone with America: Essays on the Art of Poetry in the United States since 1950*. pp. 589–602. New York, 1980. A definitive essay on Strand's early poetry, which is subtly contextualized by means of Howard's surrounding essays on other American poets.

Kirby, David. *Mark Strand and the Poet's Place in Contemporary Culture*. Columbia, Mo., 1990. A user-friendly, chronological, introductory book on Strand's life and work, from *Sleeping with One Eye Open* through *Selected Poems* and including brief references to Strand's art criticism, children's writing, short stories, anthologies, and translations.

Lehman, David, ed. *Great American Prose Poems: From Poe to the Present*. New York, 2003.

Shawn, Wallace. "The Art of Poetry LXXVII: Mark Strand." *The Paris Review* 148 (1998): 146–178. An accessible interview with Strand, conducted before the publication of *Blizzard of One*, in which he speaks about poetry, truth and meaning, emotion and monosyllables, "psychic space," reading and translating, the self, and "the proximity of the unknown."

WILLIAM STYRON

by Paul Sullivan

William Styron's best writing resonates with an emotional honesty that strives for a greater, universal truth. In his fiction Styron has relied on memories of his Virginia childhood and early adult life in New York City and Europe as starting points for broader novels. With his nonfiction, he has been more engaged in the political and social events of his time. Regardless of the form, his writing has always attracted attention—and often controversy.

FORMATIVE YEARS

Born on 11 June 1925 in Newport News, Virginia, William Clark Styron Jr. was the only child of William and Pauline Abraham Styron. His father worked for a defense contractor in the city's

William Styron.
(© *Bettmann/Corbis*)

shipyard, and his mother had been a music teacher before marriage. Until Styron reached age twelve, his childhood was uneventful. But in 1937 his mother's cancer, which had been in remission for ten years, returned. After two years of declining health, she died in 1939.

Until her death Styron had done well in school, but afterwards he seemed to lose interest. His father decided he needed to go away to prep school to broaden his worldview beyond Newport News. In 1940 Styron enrolled at Christchurch, an Episcopal school in northern Virginia, where he continued to be a mediocre student but began writing fiction. In the fall of his senior year his father married Elizabeth Buxton, a nurse; for the rest of her life, she and Styron barely tolerated each other.

Styron went to Davidson College in North Carolina in June 1942, but transferred the following June to Duke University, where he was part of a military training program during World War II. His interest in literature and writing deepened at Duke, and in the eighteen months he was there he published five stories in *The Archive*, the university literary magazine. At Duke he also met his mentor, William Blackburn, a professor of literature. Styron was called up by the marines in October 1944 and sent to San Francisco in July 1945 to await a posting to Japan. On 6 August, however, the atomic bomb was dropped on Hiroshima and three days later another one was dropped on Nagasaki. Japan surrendered on 14 August, and that December, Styron was discharged. He returned to Duke and graduated in June 1947.

Determined to become a writer, Styron moved to New York City. He took an editorial job at McGraw-Hill that lasted until October 1947, when he was fired. With a small inheritance and veterans benefits, however, Styron was able to write full-time. He began working on "Inheritance of Night," an early version of *Lie Down in Darkness* (1951). In this he was encouraged by Hiram Haydn, an editor who liked his stories and promised him an advance for a novel.

FIRST NOVEL

Lie Down in Darkness was published in September 1951, with Haydn as its editor. The twenty-six-year-old Styron became instantly famous. The novel, which takes place in Virginia over one day, cuts back and forth between the funeral of Peyton Loftis, an attractive and intelligent young woman, and the recollections of her parents, a family employee, and a priest. By using varying points of view, Styron created a pastiche that revealed the sordid family history that drove Peyton to kill herself. Peyton, for her part, was given the final word in a long, unbroken soliloquy from the grave—a speech reminiscent of that given by Molly Bloom at the end of James Joyce's *Ulysses* (1922). In addition to Joyce, Styron's other influence was William Faulkner, whose *As I Lay Dying* (1930) similarly revolved around a family trying to bury an aunt. Reviews of *Lie Down in Darkness* were remarkably positive, with several critics calling it the best novel of the year. Early the next year it won the American Academy of Arts and Letters' Prix de Rome, which subsidized a year in the Italian capital.

Styron left for Europe in March 1952. In April, after a month in London, Styron arrived in Paris. Almost immediately he fell in with a group of young American writers—Peter Matthiessen, George Plimpton, and Terry Southern—who were setting up what would become the *Paris Review*. Although all three would later become famous writers, Styron was then the only one with a reputation, and he lent his name to help start the journal. In June, Styron began to write *The Long March* (1953). The novella was based on a training march he had endured during his second stint in the marines in 1951 (worsening eyesight kept him out of the Korean War). Using the grueling march as the time frame, Styron wrote a parable of rebellion against the absurdity of the military. It was published in a new magazine, *Discovery*, in 1952 and as a paperback the next year.

Styron left Paris for Rome in October. While settling in, he became reacquainted with Rose Burgunder, a poet he had met the previous year. They were engaged in December, unengaged in January—because of pressure put on the relationship by her mother and his stepmother—but married on 4 May 1953. She was independently wealthy and they traveled together throughout Italy and France. Although he wrote little, these travels formed the basis for his second novel, *Set This House on Fire* (1960).

The Styrons moved back to New York City in December 1953 and he began writing his next novel. During six years of writing they moved to Roxbury, Connecticut, had three children—Susanna, Paola, and Thomas—and befriended and fell out with Norman Mailer, who considered Styron a rival. *Set This House on Fire*, which was published on 4 May 1960, followed a group of expatriate Americans living in Europe after World War II and through its narrator, Peter Leverett, was an indictment of America in the 1950s. Reviewers panned it, with most complaining it was long, boring, and preachy. This devastated Styron, even though the book's sales were strong. One consolation, however, was the novel's second life in France, which established his reputation among French readers.

PULITZER PRIZE

In the fall of 1960, Styron began research for *The Confessions of Nat Turner* (1967) and also started writing essays for *Esquire* magazine. This was the beginning of the most significant time in his writing career, and it lasted for the next two decades. As his biographer, James West (1998), has noted, Styron had been fascinated with Nat Turner since he was in high school. On a football trip in 1939, he spotted a sign marking where Turner's slave revolt had begun in 1831 and had been pondering a novel about it since. That fall and winter in 1960–1961, James Baldwin, a black author who had written *Giovanni's Room* (1956) in the voice of a white man, lived with the Styrons, and their talks convinced Styron he could write his third novel in the voice of an imprisoned black slave. During the early part of the decade, Styron researched what was then a little-known event. His primary source was Thomas Gray's *The Confessions of Nat Turner* (1832)—a pamphlet published after Turner was hanged—but Styron read widely about the period and the conditions of slaves in general. When he began writing he took liberties with events, added details, and gave Turner a more sophisticated idiom—that of the twentieth century. The end result, however, was a powerful, lyrical novel that brought universality to one man's struggle. He finished the novel in January 1967—a few months after the birth of his fourth child, Alexandria—and it was published in October.

Initial reviews were very strong, but soon—as it rose on the best-seller lists—Styron came under criticism. A white southerner whose grandmother had owned slaves writing from a black slave's perspective was more than many black nationalists could take. However, the book won the Pulitzer Prize and in 1970 the Howells Medal of the American Academy of Arts and Letters, awarded every five years to the best novel of the preceding period. However, angry debate, stoked by the publication of *William Styron's Nat Turner: Ten Black Writers Respond* in August 1968, remained bitter through the 1960s and early 1970s.

During the controversy, Styron was writing activist journalism for *Esquire*. His topics ranged from opposition to the death penalty—he took on the case of Ben Reid, who was facing the death penalty for murdering a woman—to the riots at the 1968 Democratic National Convention in Chicago. These and later pieces were collected in 1982 in *This Quiet Dust*.

In the 1970s, Styron was at the height of his fame and, in some circles, infamy. Struggling with an idea for another novel, he tried writing plays, encouraged by his neighbor, Arthur Miller. One of them, *In the Clap Shack* (1973), was performed at the Yale Repertory Theater. The play was based on a medical misunderstanding during his first stint in the marines; his trench mouth registered on military tests as syphilis, forcing his separation from other soldiers.

In the summer of 1973, the idea for *Sophie's Choice* (1979) came to him. Triggered by the recollection of a beautiful Polish woman he had met while living in Brooklyn in the spring of 1949, Styron wrote *Sophie's Choice* as a meditation on memory and the Holocaust. Through Stingo, the autobiographical narrator, the story ranges across the summer of 1947 in which he met Sophie Zawistowska and Nathan Landau, the intervening 30 years in which he has published several novels, and Sophie's recollections of Auschwitz, which change through the novel. As with *Nat Turner*, Styron researched the events he was writing about. He relied heavily on Olga Lengyel's *Five Chimneys* (1947)—a memoir of her time in Auschwitz—and Hannah Arendt's *Eichmann in Jerusalem* (1963). Because of the criticism over his writing about slavery, Styron made discussing Holocaust literature part of the narrative. Published on 11 June 1979, however, *Sophie's Choice* was Styron's greatest success with strong reviews, the American Book Award, and a movie option. The Academy Award–winning film, which opened in December 1982, increased interest in Styron in America, while the novel's translation solidified his reputation in France.

DEPRESSION

The 1980s, however, marked a painful shift in Styron's career. Without an idea for another novel and with enough money to live comfortably, Styron slipped into depression. In 1985 he was contemplating suicide until he was hospitalized. The cause of his depression then was a new type of sleeping pill, but he has suffered recurring bouts since. After his return home in the summer of 1986, he was able to write again, producing "A Tidewater Morning," a story about his mother that became the title story of a 1993 collection, and *Darkness Visible: A Memoir of Madness*. Published in shortened form in *Vanity Fair* magazine in 1989 and published as a book in 1990, *Darkness Visible* detailed Styron's depression, from his incapacitation during a visit to Paris to his first dream in years, which marked the beginning of his recovery. The piece won a National Magazine Award and the book served to elevate awareness of depression as a disease. In 1993 he was awarded the National Medal of Arts in recognition of his oeuvre. A decade later Styron said he was working on a novel about war.

[*See also* Autobiography: General Essay; Baldwin, James; Mailer, Norman; Matthiessen, Peter; *and* Miller, Arthur.]

SELECTED WORKS

Lie Down in Darkness (1951)
The Long March (1953)
Set This House on Fire (1960)
The Confessions of Nat Turner (1967)
Sophie's Choice (1979)
This Quiet Dust (1982)
Darkness Visible: A Memoir of Madness (1990)
A Tidewater Morning (1993)

FURTHER READING

West, James L. W. *William Styron: A Life*. New York, 1998. The only full-length biography of Styron. Hagiographic and uneven.

MAY SWENSON

by Joy Arbor

May Swenson was born on 28 May 1913 in Logan, Utah, to Dan and Margaret (Helberg) Swenson. She attended Utah State Agricultural College, not far from her home; her father was an assistant in the college's Woodwork Department. The eldest of a large Mormon family, she became skeptical of her faith while in college.

Wanting to write, she moved to New York City after graduation in the Depression years of the late 1930s. Until 1942 she had odd jobs; she edited, interviewed working-class people in New York City for a year for the Federal Writers' Project, and worked at a travel bureau. From 1942 to 1949 she worked her way up from typist to editor of two trade publications in the pharmaceuticals industry. Since

May Swenson. (© *Christopher Felver/Corbis*)

Swenson had saved her money, she took a year off to write poems and try to get them published. Her breakthrough came when she was published in *New Directions*, an annual produced by James Laughlin that focused on experimental and controversial work. She later became a part-time manuscript reader for *New Directions*.

While Swenson was sending her manuscript around to various publishers, she was invited to Yaddo, a residence and retreat for writers, artists, and composers. There, she met poet Elizabeth Bishop, with whom she maintained a lifelong correspondence. There and at MacDowell Colony, Swenson met other writers, artists, and composers. Between stays, she picked up odd jobs rather than career positions so she could focus on writing.

In 1954 *Another Animal* was published, and in 1958 *A Cage of Spines* appeared. Swenson went on the lecture and reading circuit to support her meager income. In 1959 she won a Guggenheim Foundation grant and in 1960 she received the Amy Lowell Traveling Scholarship. She spent a year traveling by car in Europe.

In 1963 *To Mix with Time* was published. In 1966 and 1967 Swenson served as writer in residence at Purdue University in West Lafayette, Indiana. There she met Rozanne Knudson, a fellow faculty member, who was to become Swenson's companion for the rest of her life. In 1967 Swenson and Knudson moved to the North Shore of Long Island in New York State. In the 1970s, Swenson took teaching stints that fit in with her schedule of camping trips; she taught at University of Lethbridge in Canada, the University of California at Riverside, the University of North Carolina at Greensboro, and several public schools in New York State. In 1973, Swenson and Knudson began to spend winters away from their cold North Shore cottage, fueling Swenson's work by going to warmer climes like Arizona and California.

In the 1980s Swenson was honored many times, participating in a gathering of poets at the White House, writing and delivering the Phi Beta Kappa poem at Harvard University's 1982 commencement, receiving Yale's Bollingen Prize for poetry in 1981, and serving as a chancellor of the Academy of American Poets from 1980 to 1989. In 1987 she received an honorary doctorate from Utah State University, published *In Other Words*, and won a MacArthur Fellowship. Swenson's poems about science were being included in anthologies such as *Science and the Human Spirit* (1989), putting her poems on pages next to Isaac Newton, the seventeenth-century scientist, and Robert Oppenheimer, the theoretical physicist credited with being the father of the A-bomb.

Knudson built them a winter house in Oceanview, Delaware. There, Swenson died on 4 December 1989 from a heart attack brought on by high blood pressure and asthma.

SCIENCE AND POETRY

Rather than informed by a religious or spiritual point of view as her Mormon background would suggest, Swenson's poetry is infused with an awareness of the world as seen by contemporary science. Certainly her poems are unusually observant about the world of nature. But Swenson's poetry also takes on the problems described by nuclear and theoretical physicists: that the observer affects the data she or he is trying to observe. Instead of a reality that can be recorded by impartial observer, there is interplay between the perceiver and the perceived. This is commonly known as the Heisenberg Principle. (Not only was Swenson well aware of contemporary scientific concepts, she quotes Heisenberg in her essay on science and poetics, "The Poet as Anti-specialist.") Swenson's poems are full of moments of interplay, where the observer and observed interact. The poem "Centaur" reveals a child riding her "horse," a stick she has cut and shaped with her knife. By the end of the poem, the child has become a centaur, the horse and rider in one, her mouth green from eating clover. In another poem, "Forest," the imagery of the forest environment is described as feline. The speaker feels "observed" by the forest even as she describes it, leaving the speaker and the reader with an entirely different concept of the usually peaceful forest. This forest pulses, watches, is ready to spring into action.

Her poems are also ones that do not just tell about animals and natural objects, as so many nature poems do, affirming their distance from what they describe. As readers, we are also imaginatively propelled into being cats, lions, bees, butterflies, a bull in a bullring, a bronco in a rodeo.

Swenson's poems take for granted the connections and distinctions between humans and other forms of life. In "Evolution" the speaker imagines similar yearnings among stone, lion, tree, and herself. Each admires aspects of the others' unique lives: the stone wishes to be alive; the speaker wishes for the lion's lawlessness and the tree's regenerative abilities; and the stone, lion, and tree marvel at human embracing and kissing. Swenson does not deny the too-human intellectual wish to transcend nature, but points out its absurdity by demonstrating it. "Out of My Head," the very title suggesting someone mentally disturbed, presents an intellectual speaker who wants to be in the world without the confines of the mind. Through a playful performance of self-questioning, the speaker notes how each mind thinks itself in the center of the world. Finally, the speaker acknowledges the impossibility of escaping the mind, and wishes to make the mind a

"vehicle," taking the speaker places that he or she cannot see from the center. Swenson both seriously engages mind/body dualism and pokes fun at its limitations.

RIDDLING POEMS

Swenson's rich and sensuous imagery shows her to be a poet in love with describing and imaginatively becoming the things of the world. Many poems demonstrate her appreciation of the material, tangible world, especially the world of nature. In "The Poet as Anti-specialist," Swenson describes a poet as someone who must describe the world but get beyond the names of things in order to get to things as they really are and are becoming. Since names are markers that prevent real understanding, it is not surprising that many of her poems resist naming their direct subject matter. Many are "riddling poems." Always interested in riddles and puns, in 1966 Swenson published *Poems to Solve*, a book of riddling poems appropriate for child and adult audiences alike. In 1971 *More Poems to Solve* was released. *The Complete Poems to Solve* was published posthumously in 1993.

CONCRETE POETRY

Another distinctive feature that relates to both Swenson's appreciation of the visual and, like the riddle, alludes to another way of knowing was her use of concrete poetry. Swenson rarely used regular stanza schemes and layouts for her poems. The shapes of her poems were often works of art themselves, laid out on the page in ways that suggested her subject matter. "Bleeding," for example, is a dialogue between an angry knife and a bleeding cut. Since the subject of the poem is the gash created by the knife and the space between the victimizer and the victim, the poem has a jagged blank edge running down the page. Another poem, "Women," compares women to rocking chairs ridden by men. The shape of the poem is actually in two rockers down the page joined by two lines that fit in with the poem whether one is reading the left or the right. Although Swenson's interest in visual form is clear from her earliest work, *Iconographs*, published in 1970, is a larger-format book that more easily contains these visual experiments. This concrete poetry invites the reader to read visually, as well as verbally.

SWENSON'S LEGACY

It is surprising that there is not more critical work on May Swenson. There are no critical biographies nor book-length collections of criticism. Swenson, like her lifelong friend, Elizabeth Bishop, was uncomfortable with the label "woman poet" or "lesbian poet," since she did not believe that there is a feminine poetic consciousness. Feminists have noted that poems by Swenson such as "Women" and "Bleeding" explore gender constructions, recuperating her poems for feminist lterary histories. But Swenson herself is rarely a topic for independent critical study, even as critical inquiry on Bishop has surged. As of the turn of the twenty-first century, gay and lesbian studies and queer theory have not seemed to yet claim Swenson for their own, despite Swenson's erotic love poems and the ambivalence about being "truthful" she presents in "The Truth Is Forced," a poem that could be read as embodying Swenson's own ambivalence about identifying herself as a lesbian in her poems.

Swenson has also been generally ignored by the burgeoning field of what has come to be called ecocriticism. Yet no one would deny that Swenson is a complex nature poet, combining science and empirical observation in new and innovative ways. One can only hope that the recognition of Swenson's contributions to these literary narratives is still in a "state of becoming."

[*See also* Nature Writing: Poetry.]

SELECTED WORKS

Another Animal (1954)
A Cage of Spines (1958)
To Mix with Time: New and Selected Poems (1963)
Poems to Solve (1966)
Half Sun Half Sleep (1967)
Iconographs (1970)
More Poems to Solve (1971)
The Guess and Spell Coloring Book (1976)
New and Selected Things Taking Place (1978)
In Other Words (1988)
The Love Poems (1991)
The Complete Poems to Solve (1993)
Nature (1994)
May Out West (1996)
Made with Words (1998)

FURTHER READING

Howard, Richard. "May Swenson." In *Alone with America: Essays on the Art of Poetry in the United States since 1950*. New York, 1969. A good critical essay examining Swenson's resistance to naming and its philosophical implications.

Knudson, R. R. *The Wonderful Pen of May Swenson*. New York, 1993. A biography that explores the poems for young readers.

Knudson, R. R., and Suzzanne Bigelow. *May Swenson: A Poet's Life in Photos*. Logan, Utah, 1996. Probably the best biography of May Swenson, coauthored by her companion and friend. Includes a foreword by Richard Wilbur, which is a good critical essay focusing on Swenson's appreciation and use of science in her poems.

Mitchell, Susan. "Foreword." In *Nature: Poems Old and New*, by May Swenson. Boston, 1994. Introductory and laudatory essay focusing on Swenson as a nature poet.

Ostriker, Alicia Suskin. *Stealing the Language: The Emergence of Women's Poetry in America*. Boston, 1986. An exploration of women's poetry, including May Swenson's, from a feminist slant.

BOOTH TARKINGTON

by Charles Robert Baker

The novels of Booth Tarkington were read by millions of Americans around the turn of the twentieth century, though today his name is known mostly to historians of American literature and to those of the oldest generation whose youthful reading included Tarkington's delightful series of the boyhood adventures of Penrod. His best-known adult novel, *The Magnificent Ambersons* (1918), has found readers through the decades as well.

EARLY LIFE

Newton Booth Tarkington was born on 29 July 1869 in Indianapolis, Indiana. His father, John Stevenson Tarkington, a graduate of Asbury College (now DePauw), was admitted to the Indiana bar in 1850 and served as private secretary to Indiana governor Joseph A. Wright. After Wright's term in office ended, John Tarkington established a law practice in the state capital, served as a captain of an Indiana infantry company in the Union Army, and returned to Indiana at the Civil War's end to serve a term as judge of the Marion County Civil Circuit Court. Tarkington was a well-established and highly respected lawyer when he married Elizabeth Booth. The couple's first child, Mary Booth Tarkington, was known by the nickname "Haute" or "Hautie" for Terre Haute, a city the girl loved visiting as a child.

Haute and her brother Booth, eleven years younger, enjoyed the advantages of growing up in a close-knit, financially stable, respected family. Their parents were devoted to literature and the arts and encouraged Haute and Booth in their artistic pursuits. The stability of the Tarkington household was briefly shaken during a national economic disaster, the panic of 1873. They lost their house in the most fashionable section of Indianapolis and moved into a two-family house in a less reputable

Booth Tarkington.
(*Courtesy of the Library of Congress*)

part of the city. Two years later, however, the economy began to recover, and the Tarkingtons, with the financial assistance of Elizabeth's brother, Newton Booth, were able to build a large brick house in a prosperous neighborhood.

Newton Booth was the "great man" of the family. Like his brother-in-law, he graduated from Asbury and was admitted to the Indiana bar. In 1850 he moved to California and made a fortune in the wholesale grocery and mercantile business. He was elected to the California state Senate in 1863, served as the governor of California from 1871 to 1874, and was a U.S. senator from California from 1875 to 1881. "Uncle Newton," who never married, shared his love and wealth generously with his sister's family and was instrumental in his nephew's becoming a writer.

Tarkington's elementary education began in the Indianapolis public schools; he was a well-read boy who at the age of six had dictated a story to his sister, and he quickly rose to the head of his class. In fourth grade, however, he ran afoul of his teacher, Miss Jameson, who persecuted him to the point that he became ill with a nervous disorder. His parents removed him from school in midyear. During his junior year at Shortridge High School, Tarkington developed a habit of truancy that, once discovered by his parents, resulted in his being sent to Philips Exeter Academy. Tarkington remained at Exeter during the summer following his graduation to complete work on the school's yearbook. He returned home in August 1889 with no immediate plans. During September and October, he took courses at a business college but soon lost interest. In November, he entered a recently opened art school to pursue his passion for drawing, planning to become a professional illustrator. He was encouraged in this by his friend and neighbor, the Indiana poet James Whitcomb Riley, who had accepted the teenager's cover illustration for Riley's 1886 collection, *The Boss Girl*.

Tarkington enrolled in Purdue University in September 1890 with the intention of continuing his art studies. After one year at Purdue, however, he transferred to Princeton, where he applied himself to having as much fun as possible without seriously damaging his academic standing. In addition to editing Princeton's three major student publications, the *Nassau Literary Magazine*, the *Tiger*, and *Bric-a-Brac*, Tarkington was president of the Dramatic Association and bass soloist in the Glee Club. In 1893, he wrote the book for that year's university musical, *The Honorable Julius Caesar*; acted the role of Cassius, trained the chorus, designed the costumes, and helped build the sets. Though academically brilliant, Tarkington chose to leave Princeton without taking a degree. He returned home to Indianapolis, determined, with the aid of a bequest from his recently deceased uncle Newton Booth, to become a freelance writer and illustrator.

APPRENTICESHIP, SUCCESS, AND DISSIPATION

For the next five years, Tarkington industriously sent numerous manuscripts and illustrations to magazine editors. Rejection slips arrived almost as quickly as works were submitted. In *Booth Tarkington: Gentleman from Indiana* (1955), James Woodress writes that Tarkington once stated, "I was for five years, and more, one of the rejected—as continuously and successively, I suppose, as any one who has ever written" (p. 60). Nonetheless, he persevered, and with the aid of his sister, Haute, he finally persuaded an editor to give his short novel *Monsieur Beaucaire* (1900) a serious reading. The editor, S. S. McClure, publisher of *McClure's Magazine* (an important vehicle for serialized fiction), did not like that period piece; a story of intrigue and duplicity among the nobility of eighteenth-century Bath, England; however, he agreed to read Tarkington's work in progress, *The Gentleman from Indiana*. Two weeks later he wrote to Tarkington offering both to publish the novel in book form and to serialize it in the magazine. Serialization would require cutting the manuscript almost by half, and McClure recommended that Tarkington come to the company's office in New York City. Tarkington, his long apprenticeship over, left Indianapolis on 13 January 1899.

The Gentleman from Indiana (1899) tells the simple, romantic, sentimental story of a young newspaperman, John Harkless, who comes from the East to Plattville,

Indiana, buys the city's run-down newspaper, and begins a campaign of civic improvement. The forces of evil that oppose him are the Whitecaps, hooligans resembling the Ku Klux Klan. In the end, the Whitecaps are routed, and Harkless wins the hand of the lovely Helen Sherwood. Although the story line is similar to hundreds of others popular in the early twentieth century, Tarkington's early command of realism distinguishes *The Gentleman from Indiana*. Its first lines alert the reader that Tarkington is no mere sentimentalist:

> There is a fertile stretch of flat lands in Indiana where un-agrarian Eastern travelers, glancing from car-windows, shudder and return their eyes to interior upholstery, preferring even the swaying caparisons of a Pullman to the monotony without. The landscape lies interminably level: bleak in winter, a desolate plain of mud and snow; hot and dusty in summer, in its flat lonesomeness, miles on miles with not one cool hill slope away from the sun.

This realistic depiction of their state did not please some of Tarkington's fellow Indianans, who felt that the new author might be sneering at small-town life and virtues. However, as the serial progressed, city newspapers throughout the state praised the work and chastised its detractors for being unable to face honest criticism.

The critical and commercial success of *The Gentleman from Indiana* brought editors and publishers to Tarkington's door. McClure, determined to not lose this talented newcomer, bought *Monsieur Beaucaire* for serialization and book publication. When Tarkington presented McClure with a small, satirical novel, *Cherry* (1903), however, McClure hesitated to accept it. F. H. Sears of Harper and Brothers quickly bought *Cherry* for the prestigious *Harper's Magazine*, serialized it in 1901, and published it in book form in 1903. That same year, *Monsieur Beaucaire* was dramatized, opening in Philadelphia on 7 October to a warm reception by audiences and critics. The play did not do well on Broadway, however, and Tarkington turned to writing a new novel, *The Two Vanrevels* (1902).

On 18 June 1902, Tarkington, now a socially sought-after celebrity, married the young, lovely, artistic, and sensitive Louisa Fletcher. She and the energetic author spent part of their honeymoon in a round of receptions and dinners in his honor in New York City. Tarkington added another dimension to their married life when he agreed to run for the Indiana House of Representatives on the Republican ticket. It is an indication of his fame that the voters of his home state elected him without his mounting anything resembling a political campaign. Nonetheless, he took his office seriously and was an effective representative, respected even by those who opposed his views.

When his legislative term ended, Tarkington took Louisa and his parents on a lavish eleven-month tour of Europe, enjoying the finest each country had to offer. He indulged his penchant for silliness by writing to his adored nephews, John, Donald, and Booth Jameson, about his travels—telling them that he had visited the Palatine Hill where "Romulus and Uncle Remus" founded Rome, sending them blackened pieces of art paper that he said were his sketches of the Catacombs, and promising them such disappointing gifts as calf-bound prayer books and woodcuts of the Apostle Peter.

On their return to America, Tarkington and his wife set up residence in New York City. He was swept into the New York literary scene, dining with Mark Twain and courted by publishers, but since he had not written anything of substance while abroad, he settled down to complete some unfinished projects: a dramatization of *The Gentleman from Indiana; The Beautiful Lady* (1905), a novella based on an incident in Paris; and a novel, *The Conquest of Canaan* (1905). Perhaps his most important work of this period is a collection of short stories, *In the Arena: Stories of Political Life* (1905). The stories had been published serially by *McClure's* and *Everybody's Magazine* from 1901 through 1905 and had drawn the attention of President Theodore Roosevelt, who, during a luncheon in Tarkington's honor at the White House in 1905, praised the stories and Tarkington's belief that all citizens should take an active role in politics.

At a literary dinner in 1905, Tarkington met Harry Leon Wilson. later to enjoy some fame as the author of *Ruggles of Red Gap*. At the end of a long, convivial evening, the men developed a plan to write plays together while living on the isle of Capri, which had enchanted Tarkington during his European travels. The next six years mark a low point for Tarkington. Although the collaborative effort produced ten plays, only one, *The Man from Home* (1908), was a success. The strain of travel between Capri, Rome, Paris, and New York, and the irritating presence of Wilson's wife, Rose O'Neil (an illustrator and the creator of the Kewpie doll), took a toll on Tarkington's marriage. Tarkington turned increasingly to alcohol to raise his spirits. In October 1911 Louisa charged him with mental cruelty and sued for divorce and custody of their daughter, Laurel, born in Rome in 1906.

RECOVERY

Tarkington moved back home to Indianapolis and began to pull himself together. In this effort he was aided by Susanah Robinson, from Dayton, Ohio, to whom Tarkington developed an intense attraction. The two were wed on 6 November 1912. At Susanah's insistence, Tarkington swore off alcohol and returned to prose fiction. Like an athlete, he went into training, avoiding everything that stood between him and his goal. He warmed up with a short story, "Mary Smith." Tarkington's painfully realistic portrait of its delusional and desperate young protagonist, Henry Millick Chester, recalls the bittersweet humor and crushing sadness of Willa Cather's 1906 masterpiece "Paul's Case." One of the best pieces he had ever written, it introduced a new style for him that emphasizes character development rather than ornate plotting and focuses on the adventures and misadventures of adolescence.

His next novel, *The Flirt* (1913), features the notorious Cora Madison, the prototype of a long line of selfish, egotistical young women characters who cause chaos in the lives of the men they encounter. But it is Cora's younger brother, Hedrick, who is of interest in this otherwise minor novel: he is the model for Tarkington's most famous character, Penrod Schofield.

Tarkington began writing his Penrod stories in 1913, but he had been gathering material for these tales, either consciously or subconsciously, all his life. Memories of his childhood and the lives of his nephews provided the ideas for these delightful stories of boyhood in Indiana of the late nineteenth and early twentieth centuries. Often compared favorably with Twain's *Tom Sawyer*, the Penrod stories are superbly comic, unidealized episodes of growing up. Penrod differs from Tom and Huck in that his adventures and interactions are confined to the relative safety of his small town. No Mississippi River beckons Penrod; no murderous Injun Joe or scheming Pap pursues him. He and three friends, Sam, Herman, and Verman, and his dog, Duke, spend their days dealing with more commonplace perils such as school pageants, dance lessons, maddening relatives, and pretty girls. Penrod was wildly popular among magazine readers, and editors battled to sign Tarkington. *Everybody's Magazine* published the first Penrod story, "Penrod and the Pageant," in June 1913, and the *Saturday Evening Post* published the second, "Talleyrand Penrod," the same month. But it was *Cosmopolitan* that won the bidding war by offering several thousand dollars for each story. The separate tales were collected in three volumes: *Penrod* (1914), *Penrod and Sam* (1916), and *Penrod Jashber* (1929). Tarkington continued his exploration of adolescence in *Seventeen* (1916), and the joys and tribulations of early childhood in *Little Orvie* (1934).

Tarkington turned his attention to the world his nephews and their fictional counterparts were growing up in and would eventually inherit a series of novels that began with *The Turmoil* (1915). As America struggled with immigration, industrialization, urbanization, and growing materialism during the Progressive Era, Tarkington chronicled the effects of these changes on his hometown and its citizens. *The Turmoil* begins bleakly, in an unnamed town clearly based on Indianapolis: "There is a midland city in the heart of fair, open country, a dirty and wonderful city nesting dingily in the fog of its own smoke." Bibbs Sheridan, a poetic young man who resists his father's demand that he enter the family's manufacturing business, sees that as the Sheridan wealth has grown, the Sheridan integrity has diminished. He is in love with Mary Vertrees, whose family maintains its nobility despite being impoverished. The tension between and within these two families produces a realistic view of the human misery that results from of an unbalanced pursuit of gain.

The Magnificent Ambersons continues the theme of *The Turmoil* but expands it to document the lives of three generations of the Amberson family as they descend from being the town's aristocracy to the city's working class. Isabel Amberson, only child of the founder of the family fortune, raises her son, George Amberson Minafer, in a way that makes him an arrogant snob incapable of dealing with the emotional, romantic, and financial crises that descend on the family. In the end, it is suggested that George will be able to achieve personal salvation through hard work and the love of a good woman.

Aside from its appeal as a story of love and loss, *The Magnificent Ambersons* is a faithful chronicle of American life during the Gilded Age and Progressive Era. Tarkington painstakingly depicted the smallest details of daily life—fashion, food, architecture, fine art—in a veritable museum of bygone style. Orson Welles filmed *The Magnificent Ambersons* immediately after his masterpiece *Citizen Kane*, and in 1998 the Modern Library selected it as one of the one hundred best novels published since 1900.

Alice Adams (1921) is often considered Tarkington's greatest achievement in presenting the rapid social and economic changes of the early 1900s. Alice aspires to a social status that her parents' economic circumstances prohibit, but her inventive, resilient spirit carries her through the tragedies that result from their pursuit of money. She alone emerges relatively unscathed and is able to live out Tarkington's recurring maxim that the acceptance of reality and hard work lead to happiness. The novel closes as Alice arrives at the steps of a business school, determined to forsake romantic fancy and make a new life for herself:

> How often she had gone by here, hating the obscurity of that stairway; how often she had thought of this obscurity as something lying in wait to obliterate the footsteps of any girl who should ascend into the smoky darkness above! Never had she passed without those ominous imaginings of hers: pretty girls turning into old maids "taking dictation"—old maids of a dozen different types yet all looking a little like herself.

Undeterred; she shows strength of character that makes her one of Tarkington's most admirable creations:

> Well, she was here at last! She looked up and down the street quickly, and then, with a little heave of the shoulders, she went bravely in, under the sign, and began to climb the wooden steps. Half-way up the shadows were heaviest, but after that the place began to seem brighter. There was an open window overhead somewhere, she found; and the steps at the top were gay with sunshine.

TRIUMPH, TRAGEDY, AND FINAL YEARS

Tarkington was awarded the Pulitzer Prize for *The Magnificent Ambersons* in 1919 and for *Alice Adams* in 1922. He received numerous honorary degrees, notably an M.A. and a Litt.D. from Princeton, and was honored by his peers with the National Institute of Arts and Letters' Gold Medal and the American Academy of Arts and Letters' Howells Medal. Tragedy intruded, however, when his daughter Laurel died on 13 April 1922, at age sixteen. The 1911 divorce allowed limited visitation between father and daughter, and that is thought to have been a factor in the girl's eventual mental breakdown. Laurel suffered from dementia praecox, now known as schizophrenia, and as her behavior became more erratic her remarried mother, fearing for her own safety and that of her newborn baby, sent Laurel to live with Tarkington and Susanah. They welcomed the unfortunate child, but Tarkington would not hear of her being hospitalized; he chose instead to hire a private nurse. Laurel managed to evade her nurse and stepmother and throw herself from a second-story window; the fall did not kill her, but she died from pneumonia that developed during her convalescence.

The economic disaster of the 1930s, the Great Depression, had little effect on Tarkington, who continued to enjoy life on a grand scale in his Indiana home and his summer place in Kennebunkport, Maine. His work continued to sell steadily, perhaps because stories of plucky young people determined to overcome adversity were just what the public wanted in those hard times. The depressed art market made it possible for Tarkington to amass a large collection of paintings, and he wrote humorously of his experiences in the art world in a series of stories first published in the *Saturday Evening Post* in 1936 and collected into a novel, *Rumbin Galleries* (1937). Entertaining, traveling, and collecting did not interfere with his writing, as prolific as ever; by his death, he had published a total of twenty-one novels, nine novellas, nineteen plays, and one hundred seventy-one stories. Even severe eye problems that afflicted him in the late 1920s and left him with only partial vision did not stall his literary projects; he merely hired a secretary to take dictation. He was dictating his final (unfinished) novel, *The Show Piece*, in his Indianapolis home when illness forced him to bed; he died two weeks later, on 19 May 1946.

Tarkington's writings exhibit craftsmanship, honesty, realism, and humor. His observations of the social and economic changes that challenged Americans during the late 1800s and early 1900s place him with more critically acclaimed writers such as William Dean Howells, Mark Twain, Sinclair Lewis, Henry James, Edith Wharton, and Willa Cather. But it is perhaps Tarkington's ability to entertain us, to make us laugh at ourselves and experience a seemingly simpler, happier time, to give us an appreciation of pleasures that are no less pleasurable because they are simple, that will ensure the endurance of his work.

WORKS

The Gentleman from Indiana (1899)
Monsieur Beaucaire (1900)
The Two Vanrevels (1902)
Cherry (1903)
In the Arena: Stories of Political Life (1905)
The Beautiful Lady (1905)
The Conquest of Canaan (1905)
His Own People (1907)
The Guest of Quesnay (1908)
The Man from Home (1908)
Beasley's Christmas Party (1909)
Beauty and the Jacobin (1912)
The Flirt (1913)
Penrod (1914)
The Turmoil (1915)
Seventeen (1916)
Penrod and Sam (1916)
Harlequin and Columbine and Other Stories (1918)

The Magnificent Ambersons (1918)
Ramsey Milholland (1919)
The Gibson Upright (1919)
Alice Adams (1921)
Clarence: A Comedy in Four Acts (1921)
The Country Cousin: A Comedy in Four Acts (1921)
The Intimate Strangers: A Comedy in Three Acts (1921)
The Ghost Story: A One-Act Play for Persons of No Great Age (1922)
Gentle Julia (1922)
The Wren: A Comedy in Three Acts (1922)
The Trysting Place: A Farce in One Act (1923)
The Fascinating Stranger and Other Stories (1923)
The Midlander (1924)
Tweedles: A Comedy (1924)
Women (1925)
Bimbo, The Pirate: A Comedy (1926)
Looking Forward and Others (1926)
Growth (1927)
The Plutocrat (1927)
The Travelers (1927)
Station YYYY (1927)
Claire Ambler (1928)
The World Does Move (1928)
Young Mrs. Greeley (1929)
Penrod Jashber (1929)
Mirthful Haven (1930)
How's Your Health? (1930)
Mary's Neck (1932)
Wanton Mally (1932)
Presenting Lily Mars (1933)
Little Orvie (1934)
Mister Antonio: A Play in Four Acts (1935)
Mr. White, The Red Barn, Hell and Bridgewater (1935)
The Lorenzo Bunch (1936)
Rumbin Galleries (1937)
Some Old Portraits (1939)
The Heritage of Hatcher Ide (1941)
The Fighting Littles (1941)
Kate Fennigate (1943)
Image of Josephine (1945)
The Show Piece (1947)
Your Amiable Uncle: Letters to His Nephews (1949)

FURTHER READING

Fennimore, Keith J. *Booth Tarkington*. New York, 1974. Includes a helpful chronology.

Mayberry, Susanah. *My Amiable Uncle*. West Lafayette, Ind., 1983. Enjoyable reminiscences by Tarkington's niece, with a moving account of Laurel's death and many photographs.

Russo, Dorothy Ritter, and Thelma L. Sullivan. *A Bibliography of Booth Tarkington*. Indiana, 1949. There is also a 1932 bibliography, complied by Barton Currie, with an interesting preface detailing Currie's painstaking work and Tarkington's contribution to it, but it does not cover Tarkington's late work.

Woodress, James. *Booth Tarkington: Gentleman from Indiana*. Philadelphia, 1955. The complete biography, with helpful bibliographical notes and many photographs.

Woodress, James. "The Tarkington Papers." *Princeton University Library Chronicle* 16 (Winter 1955): 45–53. Susanah Tarkington donated her husband's papers to Princeton in 1951; this is a detailed description of the holdings.

ALLEN TATE

by Edward Halsey Foster

Allen Tate—born John Orley Allen Tate on 19 November 1899 in Winchester, a rural town in Kentucky—was descended from old southern stock. A defender of the agrarian South against the urban, industrialized North, he was best known as a poet and a novelist, but he was also a distinguished editor, teacher, and critic, whose contributions to the New Criticism helped to make it the dominant American critical discourse at midcentury.

Tate's father was a businessman whose turbulent character was matched by his extravagant financial speculations. Tate's mother, in contrast, was a Virginia aristocrat, the descendent of genteel patrician families. The parents

Allen Tate. (Courtesy of the Library of Congress)

were very different temperamentally, and during Tate's childhood they separated. Tate's mother took charge of her shy, intellectually inclined son, even moving with him to college and keeping house there for him.

THE YOUNG POET

In 1919, Tate entered Vanderbilt University in Nashville, Tennessee, studying under John Crowe Ransom and sharing a room with Robert Penn Warren. He and Warren were asked to join a group of local intellectuals called "the Fugitives," including Ransom and Donald Davidson, who discussed poetry and founded one of the era's most famous literary journals, *The Fugitive* (1922–1925), generally considered to mark as the beginning of the Southern Renaissance. Tate, although only an undergraduate at the time, was a founding editor.

Tate read deeply in French symbolist poetry at this time, particularly works by Charles Baudelaire (Tate published a translation of Baudelaire's sonnet "Correspondence" when still an undergraduate), Tristan Corbière, Rémy de Gourmont, and Stéphane Mallarmé. He also immersed himself in the works of British and American poets

who carried the influence of the symbolists into English, notably William Butler Yeats and T. S. Eliot. Baudelaire above all seems to have set the model for Tate, who would devise a highly formal and traditional poetry that could deal with what to him was a world as tainted and corrupt as Baudelaire's Paris.

Tate graduated from Vanderbilt in 1923. Two years later he married Caroline Gordon, who was to become a successful novelist. He taught briefly in a rural school in West Virginia, then settled in New York, where he and Gordon became close friends with Hart Crane. Tate and Crane had earlier corresponded, finding in each other mutual enthusiasm for the work of Eliot (Crane had introduced Tate to Eliot's work), and the two men and Gordon decided to share a home outside New York. Problems ensued, however, for Tate was in many ways a conventional and conservative man, dismissive of Crane's homosexuality. Nonetheless, his regard for Crane's poetry remained high, and he wrote the introduction to Crane's first book, *White Buildings* (1926).

PRIVATE AMBITIONS AND PUBLIC DEMANDS

Tate's introduction is remarkable for its honesty. Commonly, when one poet sets out to introduce another, he passes over whatever would not seem positive, but although Tate rated Crane's work highly, he concluded his remarks with the statement that Crane's poetry "has its faults," which "lie in the occasional failure of meeting between vision and subject. The vision often strains and overreaches the theme"; but he added that this was not due to Crane's failings but was something that "appears whenever the existing poetic order no longer supports the imagination." The fault, then, lay ultimately with the culture, not the poet.

Tate's most famous work, one of the genuinely great poems of his generation, is "Ode to the Confederate Dead," written in 1925–1926 (but later much revised) when he was writing the introduction to *White Buildings*. Like the introduction, the poem is deeply concerned with the interdependencies of personal and political realities. It was initially called "Elegy for the Confederate Dead," but the poem is not really a lament (the modern connotation of "elegy") but rather a meditation, and Tate soon gave it the name by which it has become famous.

Davidson objected to the "Ode," believing that it reduced the Southern cause to Tate's private meditation, but the poem in fact is not a personal statement. The persona Tate created for the poem typifies, rather, a modern individual wholly caught up in his own worries and reality. The "Ode," Tate said in his essay "Narcissus as Narcissus" (1938), is " 'about' solipsism, a philosophical doctrine which says that we create the world in the act of perceiving it; or about Narcissism, or any other ism that denotes the failure of the human personality to function objectively in nature and society." For Tate, political and social awareness were supremely important, and poetry that encouraged the poet to display his wounds for its own sake was not worth much. Percy Bysshe Shelley, for example, was the very opposite of what Tate believed a poet should be.

For Tate, as for others of his generation, maturity meant functioning "objectively in nature and society." The term "objectively" can be problematic for postmodern readers who believe that the individual is "socially constructed" and that objectivity is, strictly speaking, a false notion. Although the ideal of an independent, self-willed individual may be untenable according to postmodern theory, it is central to Tate's beliefs. Tate accepted Eliot's definition of poetry, from "Tradition and the Individual Talent," as "not an expression of personality, but an escape from personality." Objectivity, Tate thought, was critical to the struggle to make poems become what he felt they should be.

In the "Ode," an individual passing a Confederate cemetery stops and reflects on what he sees. The dead soldiers remind him of human transience, their world flourishing now only in the observer's reveries. The observer is alone. There is no sense of his life or friends or ambitions beyond the present moment; his thoughts consume him entirely. He has severed himself from the concerns of the world and has spiraled, like the leaves falling on the graves, into an intellectual solitude that is ultimately as pointless to the world at large as the graves

themselves. The soldiers buried in the cemetery, however, did not pass out of the world in the privacies of their minds but rose heroically in defense of their culture. Their heroism is beyond the ambitions of the man who imagines them now. Asking what can be made of their valor and daring, the observer in the poem can only liken them to dying leaves. Nothing, in his vision, transcends death. Life for him is a self-absorbed speculation framed at its beginning and its end by oblivion. There is no spiritual salvation for him, only that oblivion, and there is no reason for him to struggle out of the chrysalis of his private ruminations.

Tate's "Ode" offers no solution to the dilemma it presents, nor would one expect a solution in a culture that, like the South at the time the poem was written, had abandoned its spiritual and cultural ideals, leaving individuals, like the observer in the poem, isolated with nothing but self-interest to define life. The lost world of the antebellum South, a world that the observer cannot recapture or even imagine, inspired ideals in its defenders, but it serves now only as a contrast to the spiritual catastrophe confronted by Tate's generation. The modern individual, as Wallace Stevens phrased it in his poem "Sunday Morning," is "unsponsored, free," but that, to Tate, was not enough. He wanted institutions, traditions, and culture, and these things had vanished, or were vanishing, from the modern world as he saw it.

Tate should be seen as, in certain ways, a modernist virtually against his wishes. His ideal was not to be "unsponsored, free" either as a person in the world or as a poet; poetry demanded mastery of traditional prosody—the skillful emulation of the accumulated discoveries, generation after generation, of the most delicate and rigorous ways to use the language. The modern individual, like the observer in the "Ode," was locked into perceptions that were his alone, but for Tate, tradition and cultural memory opened vastly richer possibilities. These he found in the formal properties of poetry, in the culture of the agrarian South, and eventually in the Roman Catholic Church, to which he converted in the 1950s.

A PUBLIC MAN

Tate became a prominent figure in literary communities in the late 1920s, counting among his friends Edmund Wilson, Kenneth Burke, Malcolm Cowley, E. E. Cummings, and other important figures in the New York literary world. During travels in Europe, he began friendships with Eliot and with Gertrude Stein. His public reputation at the forefront of American letters was confirmed with the publication of *Mr. Pope and Other Poems* (1928).

Although he was living in New York during the early years of his success, Tate remained a Southerner at heart, and in the late 1920s he embarked on a series of biographies of famous Civil War figures. Two volumes, one on Stonewall Jackson and a second on Jefferson Davis were published in 1928 and 1929, respectively. The third was to be a biography of Robert E. Lee, but this was abandoned midway to completion. In 1930, he returned to Tennessee, settling in an old house in the rural village of Clarksville. He contributed to the collection of essays *I'll Take My Stand* (1930), a rallying cry by the southern Agrarians against the industrialized, urban North. The contributors to this volume—among others, Warren and Ransom—believed, as the introduction to the book said, that "a genuine humanism was rooted in the agrarian life of the older South." Defending the South against the materialistic urbanized North, the Agrarians were utopians, but they could be critical of their own culture as well. Tate himself called the South to account for not having developed the spiritual and cultural ideal rooted in Christian humanism that he valued. *I'll Take My Stand* was followed in 1936 by *Who Owns America?*, which Tate edited with the journalist Herbert Agar, and which, like the earlier book, chastised big government and corporate America.

Tate's one novel is *The Fathers* (1938), a much admired book that draws on traditions and people from his mother's family. Tate's concern here is the deterioration of the aristocratic South, torn from within by violence—such as William Faulkner was describing in his own fiction at this time. As Tate saw it, the South was marred by self-contained individuals, too immersed in themselves, too solipsistic, to understand how tragically their actions affected others. In 1977, shortly before his death, he rewrote the ending of the novel, suggesting the history of his South in the postbellum era. Splendidly written, the book is one of the admired achievements of the Southern Renaissance.

At this time, Tate became a mentor to the new generation of poets. William Meredith (b. 1919) was among his students at Princeton. Others converts to his notions about poetry included Robert Lowell (1917–1977), John Berryman (1914–1972), and Randall Jarrell (1914–1965). Through Tate, a tradition from French symbolism through Eliot and Crane reached a younger generation and very largely defined what was best in American poetry by the late 1940s and early 1950s.

In 1937, when he was a college student, Lowell wrote to Tate asking permission to stay with him for a while. Tate politely answered no, excusing himself on the grounds of an already crowded household. Any further guests, he said, would have to live in tents. Lowell took him at his word, bought a tent, and pitched it on Tate's lawn. He stayed three months. Lowell's poetry owed much to Tate's example, and Tate considered "magnificent" Lowell's *Life Studies* (1959), which would have as substantial an effect on poetry as the "Ode" had three decades before.

Lowell and his generation learned to make poetry an embodiment of thought as it emerges inextricably from experience. They did not follow the romantics or transform poetry merely into an exercise in personality (that would be the work of younger confessional poets who did not grasp the traditions they thought they emulated). The result could be highly intellectual, but never simply that. Formidably cerebral though poetry like Tate's seemed to young writers in the 1960s, it is always emotionally grounded.

Tate's "Ode" is the poem by which he is best known, but the long meditative work "Seasons of the Soul" (1944) is more ambitious and perhaps greater. Its diction is unpretentious, even flat; no mere virtuosity in technique or diction distracts from the poem's implacable seriousness as a meditation on war. Divided into four sections, each concerned with one of the seasons, it ends brooding on "[i]rritable spring," which like Eliot's "cruelest month" in *The Waste Land* offers no sure solution to the angers of the world.

It is instructive to compare "Seasons of the Soul" with Lowell's somewhat more baroque and linguistically extravagant "The Quaker Graveyard at Nantucket." The energies Lowell projects are simply not in the more somber Tate, though the poems are closely related—the student and his teacher meditating on a violence that was inundating their lives—but Lowell can imagine at the end a religious epiphany, the possibility of spiritual salvation. Tate is never so sanguine, ending his poem with a vision of universal death and the suggestion that the mother or goddess of spring is "the mother of silences." It is not a poem of despair, though it comes very close to that, for the cycle of the seasons dominates, and the year ends with a struggle toward renewal. But for the agonies through which Tate's world was passing, this goddess can offer only forgetting.

From 1939 to 1942, Tate was an instructor at Princeton. From 1943 to 1944, he was the consultant in poetry at the Library of Congress (the position now known as poet laureate), the second to have that post. (His successor was his good friend and former Vanderbilt roommate, Robert

Penn Warren.) From 1944 to 1946, he edited the *Sewanee Review*. In 1951, he began teaching at the University of Minnesota, where he remained until his retirement in 1968. He was a member of the American Academy of Arts and Letters and the president of the National Institute of Arts and Letters. He received a Guggenheim Fellowship, an award from the Academy of American Poets, and the National Medal for Literature (1976).

Tate and Gordon were divorced in 1959, and he then married the poet Isabella Gardner, but that marriage, too, ended in divorce. In 1966, he married Helen Heinz, who had been one of his students. They moved two years later to Tennessee, where he died on 9 February 1979.

ART AS ICON

In "Narcissus on Narcissus," Tate defined poetry as

> merely a way of knowing something: if the poem is a real creation, it is a kind of knowledge that we did not possess before. It is not knowledge "about" something else; the poem is the fullness of that knowledge.... In a manner of speaking, the poem is its own knower, neither poet nor reader knowing anything that the poem says apart from the words of the poem.

That definition would surely have seemed sufficient to any of the New Critics—Ransom, Warren, Cleanth Brooks, and others. Various postmodern theories of language and poetry that have emerged during the past few decades, however, make it unlikely that Tate's definition would go unchallenged today. Tate wanted poetry to be the vehicle of transcendent and absolute "truths," free of the complexities and idiosyncrasies of individual perceptions. The poem's "truth" would not be inflected by the reader or the historical moment in which it was read.

Tate meant exactly what he said, and whether or not one accepts his definition of poetry, it is clear that he attributed enormous possibilities to a great poem. It could soar above the ordinary limitations and pursuits of the world. The claim is heroic, and whether it is true may well be irrelevant if, as in Tate's case, it leads to major work. The poem, his definition implies, cannot be solipsistic, and therefore it provided an escape from the labyrinths of a southern culture folded in on itself as much as an escape from isolations of the observer in the "Ode."

Tate's arguments for poetry are gigantic and demand the full seriousness of which he made himself a master. The postmodernist will say that Tate, defining poetry as he did, was telling himself a lie; but if one can accept that lie for the moment, one can enter the imagination of a writer who truly believed his poems allowed him to pass out of the solipsistic prisons decreed by his modern world.

As the social revolutions that marked the 1960s progressed, Tate gradually became irrelevant to younger poets like Allen Ginsberg, Charles Olson, Robert Duncan, and others represented in Donald Allen's *The New American Poets* (1960). He was now seen as an "academic" poet, transmitting dated ideas about poetic form. The new path for young poets to follow was suggested in Robert Creeley's statement, "Form is never more than the extension of content," which Charles Olson reported in his widely read essay "Human Universe" (1951). It did not follow that Tate's scrupulous attention to traditional prosody was a mistake, but that is how it seemed to many younger poets, and soon a major rift opened between the "academic poets," of whom Tate was now a principal spokesman, and the poets represented in Allen's anthology.

This was unfair to Tate, who, however one might fault him, was a master on his own ground. What should matter to the unbiased reader is that he was successful in meeting his own high demands about the nature of poetry. Tate's poems at their best have a fluidity and ease that may obscure the tremendous effort and conscientious control his poetics required. Younger writers such as those represented in Allen's anthology achieved a fluidity in their lines by utilizing the rhythms of spoken language. Tate avoided that solution—perhaps he found it too easy—and maintained in much of his work a cultured and learned, but also deeply human, tone that permitted the expression of certain extreme emotional states that have never been sympathetically conveyed through less formal and rigorous means. His work may be academic, but if so, it is academic in a good sense; it can at times be strict, cold, formal, and disciplined, but it also reveals, to those who give it the attention it requires, the craftsmanship, learning, and sensibility of a cultured and strongly sensitive person.

[*See also* Crane, Hart; Eliot, T. S.; Fugitives and Southern Agrarianism, The; Lowell, Robert; New Critics, The; Ransom, John Crowe; *and* Warren, Robert Penn.]

WORKS

Mr. Pope and Other Poems (1928)
Stonewall Jackson: The Good Soldier (1928)
Jefferson Davis: His Rise and Fall (1929)
Three Poems (1930)
Poems, 1928-1931 (1932)
Robert E. Lee (1932)
The Mediterranean and Other Poems (1936)
Reactionary Essays on Poetry and Ideas (1936)

Selected Poems (1937)

The Fathers (1938)

Reason in Madness (1941)

The Winter Sea (1944)

Poems, 1920–1945 (1947)

Poems, 1922–1947 (1948)

On the Limits of Poetry: Selected Essays, 1928–1948 (1948)

The Hovering Fly (1949)

Two Conceits for the Eye to Sing, If Possible (1950)

The Forlorn Demon (1953)

The Man of Letters in the Modern World (1955)

Collected Essays (1959)

Poems (1960)

Poems (1961)

Essays of Four Decades (1968)

The Swimmers and Other Selected Poems (1970)

Collected Poems (1970)

The Literary Correspondence of Donald Davidson and Allen Tate (1974)

Memoirs and Opinions, 1926–1974 (1975)

Collected Poems, 1919–1976 (1977)

The Fathers, and Other Fiction (1977)

The Republic of Letters in America: The Correspondence of John Peale Bishop and Allen Tate (1981)

The Poetry Reviews of Allen Tate, 1924–1944 (1983)

The Lytle-Tate Letters: The Correspondence of Andrew Lytle and Allen Tate (1987)

Cleanth Brooks and Allen Tate: Collected Letters, 1933–1976 (1998)

FURTHER READING

Bishop, Ferman. *Allen Tate*. New York, 1967. Concise introduction to Tate's work and reputation.

Carrithers, Gale H. *Mumford, Tate, Eiseley: Watchers in the Night*. Baton Rouge, La., 1991. Tate's opinions on industrialized, technological modernity.

Hammer, Langdon. *Hart Crane and Allen Tate: Janus-Faced Modernism*. Princeton, N. J., 1993. A study of their mutual indebtedness to T. S. Eliot and the radically different routes that they devised for themselves respectively.

Huff, Peter A. *Allen Tate and the Catholic Revival*. New York, 1996. Tate's Christian humanism as a background for his conversion of Catholicism and the implications of that conversion for his work.

Jancovich, Mark. *The Cultural Politics of the New Criticism*. New York, 1993. A study of Ransom, Warren, Tate, and the seeds of the New Criticism in their reactions against modern technological and industrial society.

Malvasi, Mark G. *The Unregenerate South: The Agrarian Thought of John Crowe Ransom, Allen Tate, and Donald Davidson*. Baton Rouge, La., 1997. The Agrarian ideology as variously developed by three of its principal defenders with particular attention to Tate's religious orientation.

Underwood, Thomas A. *Allen Tate: Orphan of the South*. Princeton, N. J., 2000. Exceptionally well documented biography covering the years 1899–1938.

JAMES TATE

by Arnold E. Sabatelli

James Tate is arguably one of the most influential poets of his generation. In 1967 he won the coveted Yale Younger Poets Award, one of the youngest writers ever to receive that honor. (He was a graduate student at the Iowa Writers Workshop at the time.) His book *The Lost Pilot*, published the same year, set the tone for the body of his poetry. Surreal, funny, irreverent, and at times almost wholly inaccessible, Tate's poetry has not strayed far from the approach and tone of his earliest work.

CAREER AND HONORS

Born in Kansas City, Missouri, in 1943, James Tate published a large body of work—poetry, fiction, and memoir—in the thirty-five years after the 1967 publication of *The Lost Pilot*, which was selected by Dudley Fitts for the Yale Series of Younger Poets. His *Selected Poems* (1991), won the Pulitzer Prize and the William Carlos Williams Award. *Worshipful Company of Fletchers* (1994) won the National Book Award. He edited *Best American Poetry*, which appeared in 1997. His honors also include a National Institute of Arts and Letters Award for Poetry, the Wallace Stevens Award, and fellowships from the Guggenheim Foundation and the National Endowment for the Arts. He is a chancellor of the Academy of American Poets. He has taught poetry at the University of California at Berkeley, Columbia University, and Emerson College. He teaches at the University of Massachusetts in Amherst, where he has worked since 1971.

OVERVIEW

Aside from the often impenetrable nature of the imagery, what makes the task of a concise overview of his work difficult is that unlike so many writers, Tate sustains the surreal and jarring rhetoric that made him famous with his first book, renewing it with each of his many volumes of poetry. This is not to say that they are all equally accomplished, but in each of them, he manages to reconnect with the eccentric voice that so captured the judge of the Yale Younger Poets Award in 1967. In other words, there are no overt shifts of focus, no ventures into different modalities, no obvious "moments" to help divide the body of work into component periods. Rather, one finds a continuum of tone, a unified, single body of work.

Feeding off the playfulness, irreverence, and illogic of writers like Theodore Roethke and Gertrude Stein, Tate turned away from the confessional poem and instead confronted readers with poetry that held fast to its own center. He creates a world in his poems, at once familiar and unfamiliar, and at times readers feel as if they are reading another language, a language they feel they may once have understood fluently, but have since forgotten. Tate forces us to realign our thinking in order to enter the world of the poem. We leave behind clear cause and effect, logic, coherence. We need to accept any and all juxtapositions of word and image, no matter how surreal, and allow them to take us down their own path toward an emotion. Even when meaning remains distant and wholly elusive, Tate's poems clearly take on all subjects, no matter how taboo or vulgar, and they are frequently laced with strange and poignant humor.

THE POETRY

The publication of *The Lost Pilot* dramatically altered the contemporary poetry scene. In its title poem, Tate offers perhaps the one clearly autobiographical or confessional note of his entire career, but even here the poem remains elusive and swiftly reaches beyond the autobiographical domain of the poem—the death of his father while flying a fighter mission over Germany when Tate was just five months old. The lost father of the poem is given features "hard like ebony" and is imagined as still orbiting forever in his own world, while the speaker is stranded in this world. The father still spins across the sky like some distant satellite, or a "tiny African God." When considering the lost pilot, the speaker feels dead himself, "the residue of a stranger." The intensity of emotion in the poem grows out of these charged, surreal images and observations. Ultimately, the speaker's inability to "get off the ground," to somehow reach beyond time to his lost father, speaks to Tate's poetic desire to lift off, to put his poems into orbit, visible and still bound to the world—though always distant, unreachable, and mysterious.

Throughout the 1970s, Tate published seven books, with numerous chapbooks and pamphlets thrown into the mix. His surreal yet mundane and even folksy voice had a great influence on creative-writing students. Schools of "surreal conversationalism" sprung up, and while he was only in his mid-twenties to mid-thirties, Tate's enigmatic imagery and approach was for a decade or more one of the primary influences on young student-poets. As the decade waned, his work began to be hit hard by the critics, who claimed it was monotonous, too inaccessible, and even self-indulgent. In part, they were responding to the furious pace, and in part to Tate's unflinching vision and approach. In the 1980s, Tate published only two complete volumes of poetry, staying the course of his earlier work, and in the early 1990s his *Selected Poems* received significant praise and several major awards.

In the *Selected Poems* it becomes clear just how unwavering Tate's poetic vision is. Take, for instance the opening lines of "The Last Days of April," from *The Lost Pilot*:

Through the ceiling comes
the rain to cool my lover
and me....

Then, compare them to the first lines of "Storm," from the volume *Reckoner* (1986):

The snow visits us,
taking little bits of us with it,
to become part of the earth....

In both poems the tone is quiet and intense, the weather intruding upon a muted romantic familiarity; and in each there is a foreboding—the "deep thirst" in the early poem, the snow that "falls far into the interior" in the latter poem. The poems feel almost as if they were written in the same moment in time. *Selected Poems* shows a poet who at age twenty-two (ironically, the age that his father was lost) creates a new contemporary surrealist poetry and who then nurtures and sustains that same voice and approach throughout over thirty years of writing. While some have regarded this as a failure to evolve poetically, it has later on been viewed as a positive aspect of his work—an example of his diligence and clarity as an artist. It is common for poets to move in and out of different approaches, often veering away from or toward formal constraints, rhyme, narrative, or even other genres. Denis Johnson, who published his first volume of poetry a few years after

The Lost Pilot, and whose early poetry bears a striking resemblance to Tate's, subsequently went on to become a celebrated novelist and story writer. James Wright, like many other modern and contemporary poets, moved away from formal, metered, rhymed poetry to image-rich free verse. But Tate continues to do what he has always done, certain and headstrong in his vision.

THE FICTION

While one is not altogether certain that it can be called fiction, Tate has published numerous short stories and collected them in two volumes, *Hottentot Ossuary* (1974) and *Dreams of a Robot Dancing Bee* (2002). He has also published a novel, *Lucky Darryl* (1977). Abandoning line and stanzas, Tate's fiction does not feel so much like a shift in genre as a more sustained and free-form approach to familiar themes and imagery. The latest of these volumes, *Dreams of a Robot Dancing Bee*, contains all of the absurdist, dark humor and imagery of his poetry. Some of the short story titles alone—"Traces of Plague Found near Reagan Ranch," "The Torque-Master of Advanced Video," "Beep"—give a sense of Tate's poetic sensibility merging with the fictional form. In these, as in his earlier pieces from *Hottentot Ossuary*, Tate never moves very far from poetry; in fact, selections from it were included in the *Selected Poems*.

ILLOGIC AND ILLUMINATION

Playfulness and intellectuality mix with an urgency to transcend cliché or anything that might be considered standard poetic discourse in the work of James Tate. The poems are often wholly impenetrable, so one sometimes has to sit back and merely enjoy the play of imagery, the collision of unexpected language, and the rich colors and sounds, as one might listen to free form jazz or look at abstract or surreal art. More often than not, his writing delivers us to a place where standard handholds—logic, coherence, causality—are not of much use. In their place we find compelling and unexpected juxtapositions of image and place where consistency of tone, recurring rhetorical and image patterns, and familiar objects and voices are all that anchor us. James Tate continues to add to his immense and singular poetic world.

SELECTED WORKS

The Lost Pilot (1967)
The Oblivion Ha-Ha (1970)
Hints to Pilgrims (1971)
Absences (1972)

Hottentot Ossuary (1974)
Viper Jazz (1976)
Lucky Darryl (1977)
Riven Doggeries 1979
Constant Defender (1983)
Reckoner (1986)
Distance from Loved Ones (1990)
Selected Poems (1991)
Worshipful Company of Fletchers (1994)
Shroud of the Gnome (1997)
The Route As Briefed (1999)
Memoir of the Hawk (2001)
Dreams of a Robot Dancing Bee (2002)
Lost River: Poems (2003)

FURTHER READING

Dooley, David. "The Life of Literature: Two Views." *Hudson Review* 45, no. 4 (Winter 1993): 534. Dooley compares Tate's surrealism of language with poet Linda Gregg's surrealism of the world.

McDaniel, Craig. "James Tate's Secret Co-pilot." *New England Review* 23, no. 2 (Spring 2002): 55. McDaniel shows how Tate integrates many elements from Fyodor Dostoyevsky's prose, especially *Crime and Punishment*.

Sadoff, Ira. "Transformation and Surprise: The Restoration of Imagination." *American Poetry Review* 24, no. 2 (March-April 1995): 24. Sadoff looks at how a number of poets, including Tate, emphasize imaginatively reinterpreting reality and experience rather than merely representing it.

Upton, Lee. *The Muse of Abandonment: Origin, Identity, Mastery in Five American Poets*. London, 1998. Chapter 4 offers a concise yet complex study of the origins of Tate's poetic approach.

EDWARD TAYLOR

by Adam Scott Miller

During his lifetime of eighty-seven years, Edward Taylor, a Puritan minister and poet, wrote more than forty thousand lines of verse. Much of Taylor's poetry is devotional and was composed during the course of frequent meditative exercises. As a result, he chose to keep his work private but left his manuscripts to his grandson, who eventually deposited them in the Yale University library. They remained there until their discovery in 1937. Subsequent critical attention has declared Taylor's verse to be colonial America's best poetry.

FAMILY AND EDUCATION

From his birth in Sketchley, Leicestershire, England, in 1642, Edward Taylor's life was circumscribed by the Puritan world of his parents. His strict Christian upbringing, combined with the concurrent dominance of Puritanism in England throughout his youth, moved his life toward the end that his parents intended: the life of a Puritan minister. Accordingly, Taylor received a solid education and may have briefly attended Cambridge University, but in 1660 Charles II was restored to the throne, and with his ascension came a decided impatience toward Puritanism. Taylor refused to compromise, and when he failed to subscribe to Charles's 1662 Act of Uniformity he lost a teaching position. At the age of twenty-six, his mind firmly set on pursuing a life of Puritan ministry, Taylor chose to leave England altogether, and he sailed for America on 26 April 1668.

Upon arrival in New England, Taylor enrolled at Harvard College. There he excelled in his studies and solidified his command of Hebrew, Greek, and Latin. For the rest of his life Taylor looked back at his time at Harvard with great fondness. He loved both the work and the sense of intellectual community. Such sentiments came naturally. Taylor was an incessant student with a wide variety of interests, and his inclination to scholarly work was magnified by the fact that his passion for knowledge was not simply a personal proclivity. Rather, his devotion to learning was representative of his devotion to God, and his love for one harmonized with his love for the other.

For Taylor, untangling mind from heart or theology from praise could not be done. Among a number of related factors, it was this very devotion to God that led Taylor to accept, though with some reluctance, an invitation in 1671 to leave Harvard and heed the call to serve as a minister in the recently incorporated frontier town of Westfield, Massachusetts. Taylor was willing to leave Harvard, but he also took every available book with him, and he spent the rest of his life collecting works for his personal library. In fact, when other means were denied him, Taylor would sit at night and copy out whole books by firelight. His library eventually contained more than one hundred such hand-copied volumes.

Although Taylor was something of a social and intellectual anomaly in Westfield, the congregation wanted him and they wanted him to stay. Taylor felt duty bound to remain, but he increasingly felt the weight of his intellectual and social isolation. Fortunately, this sense of loneliness was soon mitigated. In 1674, Taylor met, courted, and married Elizabeth Fitch. During their courtship they exchanged a number of love poems, one of which, written by Taylor, was a complicated rhymed acrostic that proclaimed his love for her in conjunction with his love for God. Feeling more at home as a married man, Taylor firmly resolved to stay in Westfield and set about the serious business of raising a family and tending to his congregation. Over the next fifteen years Elizabeth bore eight children, five of which died in infancy. On 7 July 1689, Elizabeth herself passed away, leaving Taylor the sole parent of three children. Taylor grieved the passing of his wife, as well as a number of his children, by composing elegies. In 1692, Taylor remarried. His second wife, Ruth Wyllys, bore six additional children.

MINISTRY

Taylor was an American Puritan through and through. His social and theological orthodoxy were the distinguishing features of his life, and at each turn his Calvinist heritage was everywhere apparent. The doctrines of total depravity, unmerited election, limited atonement, and irresistible grace determined the course of his life and the shape of his writing. But despite this backdrop of God's unaccountable grace and inscrutable wrath, the daily work performed by Taylor tended to be mundane. The work of a frontier minister, apart from preparing sermons and administering sacraments, consisted primarily of settling disputes, consoling families, maintaining civic order, and doubling as a physician. In short, Taylor's job was to be the glue that held the town together.

In 1679, after a number of setbacks, Taylor's Westfield congregation was at last formally organized. For the next thirty years Taylor struggled to shore up the church's foundation and to bring the large number of partially committed members completely into the fold. In these efforts Taylor employed every power traditionally available to him. In particular, Taylor chose to exercise his right either to give or withhold the Lord's Supper. To receive it, members of the congregation needed to demonstrate some sign that they were among the elect, such as a public confession of faith. A demonstration of election allowed an individual to become a full member of the congregation, enjoying the privilege of participating in the Lord's Supper. Taylor used this possibility for participation as an incentive to full conversion.

But by 1679 this practice of withholding the Lord's Supper had come under fire, and Solomon Stoddard, Taylor's powerful rival from nearby Northampton, openly advocated the innovative practice of admitting to the Lord's Supper anyone willing to consent to the church's articles of faith. Stoddard argued that because it is impossible to determine for certain in this life who has been destined for election and who has not, all should be admitted. Taylor saw this practice as an offense to God and an assault on the Puritan way of life. In his Foundation Day sermon in 1679, Taylor openly attacked Stoddard's position, and in 1693 and 1694 Taylor wrote a series of eight sermons, *A Treatise Concerning the Lord's Supper*, in which he passionately and systematically argued against Stoddard's liberal practice.

POETRY

Apart from a few assorted early poems and elegies, Taylor's poetry was a private endeavor, never published. His poetry tended to be deeply introspective and, hence, strictly personal. But the fact that Taylor's poetry was unintended for our eyes does not prevent us from appreciating it. Indeed, Taylor's verse is unparalleled in early modern American literature. Before the discovery of his poetry in 1937, it was generally assumed that in this period,

literature simply had nothing to offer. In this sense, Taylor is a pleasant and welcome surprise. In general, he is associated with England's metaphysical poets, such as John Donne and George Herbert. The primary point of identification is Taylor's use of metaphysical wit, in which unexpected analogies between apparently heterogeneous elements are elaborated and multiplied almost to the point of absurdity. Taylor's poetry is well known for its use of these elaborate and witty analogies between everyday items and spiritual matters.

That Taylor employed such techniques is no surprise. He had an eye for peculiar details and comparisons, and, moreover, these metaphysical tropes readily lent themselves to the production of the kind of devotional poetry that comprises the bulk of Taylor's corpus. One of Taylor's best-known poems, "Huswifery," illustrates the use of wit to a devotional end. In "Huswifery," Taylor uses his standard six-line stanza (rhyme scheme *ababcc*) and develops an extended comparison between God's work of grace and the work of a woman at a spinning wheel. He pleads with God to spin his conversion and weave his soul into a fine garment, and, with a shift of imagery, he then prays that God will one day clothe him with a glorious garment assuring him of salvation. "Huswifery" is an exceptional example of wit, but it also clearly demonstrates Taylor's dominant poetic concern: the nature of Christian conversion and the mystery of God's elective grace. Further, Taylor's poetry is especially concerned with obtaining that which his Calvinist heritage explicitly declares unobtainable: he yearns to experience God in a way that will absolutely assure him of his election. In this respect, Taylor's verse is a clear record of his failure to do so. But in itself, this does not detract from the overall effect. That he perpetually fails to obtain such an assurance of election from God is an indication of the deeply human fragility that makes his poetry so appealing.

Although it is clear that Taylor's poetry constantly borrows images and sensations from the mundane world of day-to-day life, it is also important to note that in the end his poetry fails to engage or address that commonplace world. This world is not his concern and he never uses its images for their own sake. The images used are images borrowed, images easily enough returned when their spiritual work is done. This sense of detached familiarity in which mundane images are briefly but gloriously united with spiritual concerns mirrors the relation of Taylor's public life to his private poetry. Taylor's poetry, though intimately related to his public ministerial life, is something that is ultimately different and detachable.

Taylor's poetry immerses itself in this world, but only in order to move beyond it to another.

MAJOR WORKS

Taylor's best-known poetic works are *God's Determinations Touching His Elect* (written around 1680) and *Preparatory Meditations* (written 1682–1725). *God's Determinations* is Taylor's only extended work of verse. It is apparently addressed to the half-way member of the Puritan congregation and it traces the various paths to salvation that the elect may follow. The poem is, in sum, a call to the uncommitted to believe and belong. Though *God's Determinations* suffers from a number of serious problems as a result of its inability to maintain a proper tone or create the needed coherence of dramatic structure, it nonetheless has brilliant moments. The plot of the poem consists primarily of an effort to get the elect to the wedding feast symbolic of their salvation. Along the way, personifications of Mercy and Justice pursue the elect and assist in gathering them into the congregation. Satan then rages at the gathered elect and Christ pleads with them to remain faithful. The poem concludes with a series of meditations in which elect souls carry out a process of self-examination.

Taylor's *Preparatory Meditations* contains his most compelling and respected work. At the age of forty, Taylor began composing these meditative verses of self-examination as part of a larger process of liturgical preparation. Many of the poems can be directly linked to accompanying sacrament-day sermons collected in Taylor's *Christographia* (1962) and *Upon the Types of the Old Testament* (1989), and many of them deal more or less directly with a specific passage of Scripture. It appears that in preparation for the Lord's Supper, Taylor would write a careful (and often dry) sacrament-day sermon and that these sermons then served as a kind of elaborate worksheet for the much more personal and emotional meditative verses that would follow. Taylor wrote the poems as part of an effort to examine his inadequate life, plead for grace, and praise God's perfection. In fact, the poems themselves become a kind of performative enactment of this process.

Many of the poems directly address Taylor's inability to write adequate poems and plead for the grace needed to praise God properly. For Taylor, it seems that the experienced effect of producing a poem (the meditative, devotional process that it demanded) was even more important than the finished product of the poem itself. The poems were a form of practical piety that allowed Taylor concurrently to reach out to God and measure his inability to do so.

Taylor composed the *Preparatory Meditations* over a period of forty years, until 1725. Through the final poem they manifest his peculiarly enflamed Puritan orthodoxy, and they never manage to hide his personality: sometimes monotonous and ill-tempered, sometimes intriguing and startling. Edward Taylor died 24 June 1729.

SELECTED WORKS

Diary (written 1668–1671)
God's Determinations Touching His Elect (written ca. 1680)
Preparatory Meditations (written 1682–1725)
A Treatise Concerning the Lord's Supper (written 1693–1694)
Christographia (1962)
Upon the Types of the Old Testament (1989)

FURTHER READING

Davis, Thomas M. *A Reading of Edward Taylor*. Newark, Del., 1992. A close reading of the *Preparatory Meditations* that takes into account their relationship with crucial events in Taylor's life.

Grabo, Norman S. *Edward Taylor*. Rev. ed. Boston, 1988. An account of Taylor's life and work that highlights the mystical elements of his poetic practice.

Keller, Karl. *The Example of Edward Taylor*. Amherst, Mass., 1975. An examination of Taylor's life and work to the end of assessing a Puritan understanding of art.

Rowe, Karen E. *Saint and Singer: Edward Taylor's Typology and the Poetics of Meditation*. New York, 1986. A treatment of Taylor's poetry focused on his use of typology.

Scheick, William J. *The Will and the Word: The Poetry of Edward Taylor*. Athens, Ga., 1974. Taylor's poetry examined in relation to his Puritan theology.

PETER TAYLOR

by Robert Wilson

Because he was born in Tennessee and much of his work is set there, Peter Taylor is unquestionably a southern writer. But his fiction differs from that of the other significant writers of the southern literary renaissance of the 1920s through the 1960s in its focus on urban and suburban settings of the Upper South rather than on the rural life of the Deep South. Taylor was younger than William Faulkner, the great master of southern and, indeed, of American fiction, and younger than the members of the South's two preeminent literary groups, the Fugitive poets and the Agrarians. As a result, the shadows of the Civil War and Reconstruction fall less boldly upon his work than on the work of those older writers, who had one foot in the nineteenth century and one in the twentieth. Taylor's sympathetic concern with the circumstances of blacks and women place him firmly in the twentieth century. (His other large theme of class shows up in almost every period and school of American literature.)

Although Taylor wrote three novels and ten plays, his greatest achievement was in the short story. His stories are realistic, psychologically complex, and deeply layered. Many of them focus on a world he knew well, that of upper-crust Tennessee families, mostly living in the cities of Nashville or Memphis or their suburbs, in the 1920s, 1930s, and 1940s. Such major stories from his sixty-year career as "A Long Fourth" (1946), "Venus, Cupid, Folly, and Time" (1959), and "The Old Forest" (1979) describe a genteel, moneyed way of life. Its characters belong to the country club set and live in big houses with servants; the fathers work in the professions and the mothers run their complicated households. Because this is the world of Taylor's parents and his own youth—his father was a lawyer and businessman; his mother was the daughter of

Peter Taylor.
(© *Bettmann/Corbis*)

a governor who was also a U.S. senator—he describes it from the inside.

On the surface he seems anything but alienated by this world's charming debutantes, big chauffeured cars, and social whirl. But often in a Taylor story the narrator is looking back upon his youth from middle age and evokes this upper-class world with something like his own youthful enthusiasm for it. But the plots of the stories show the naïveté of his youthful perspective, serving to undermine it, and reveal a more disillusioned and more complicated understanding in the grown-up narrator. Almost invariably the subject requiring this mature perspective has to do with class, race, the role of women, or the difficulty of living in families. This disjunction between the admiration of the youthful narrator and the disillusionment of the mature narrator is often a source of the story's richness and depth, and sometimes—for instance, when the narrator turns out to be unreliable—makes the stories yield their meaning with a satisfying reluctance.

EARLY LIFE AND WORK

Peter Matthew Hillsman Taylor was born on 8 January 1917 in the country town of Trenton, in the western part of Tennessee. His father had grown up on a farm near the town and his mother, who grew up in Nashville and Washington, D.C., also had roots in rural Tennessee. Peter was raised in Nashville and Memphis, as his father moved the family from city to city, and in 1926 the Taylors—Peter was the youngest of four children—moved to St. Louis, where his father became the president of an insurance company. The family returned to Memphis in 1932, and in 1935 Peter graduated from Central High School there. Perhaps two-thirds of Taylor's stories grow out of these few biographical facts. One persistent subject (in stories such as "What You Hear from 'Em" and "The Hand of Emmagene") is the transition from rural to urban life reflected in several generations of the Taylor family's own history. How Memphis and Nashville differ from each other is a point of interest in "The Captain's Son" and *A Summons to Memphis* (1986). Taylor's first book-length novella, *A Woman of Means* (1950), is set in St. Louis. His father's travails as a businessman figure in *A Summons to Memphis* and several of the stories. And the Washington connection that arose from his grandfather's election to Congress shows up in his last novel, *In the Tennessee Country* (1994), and in the late story "The Oracle at Stoneleigh Court."

But only a handful of his stories are overtly autobiographical. One story, "1939," begins with the sentence, "Twenty years ago, in 1939, I was in my senior year at Kenyon College." Taylor had ended up at Kenyon after first studying at Southwestern College in Memphis and Vanderbilt University in Nashville. At the former he had been a student of the poet Allen Tate and at the latter of the poet John Crowe Ransom. When Ransom went to teach at Kenyon in 1938, Taylor followed him, as did a young instructor named Randall Jarrell, who like Tate and Ransom would become one of the most eminent poets and critics of his time. Ransom established a program for writers at Kenyon and put them all together in the same house, apart from the other students. Taylor roomed there with another transfer student (from Harvard), Robert Lowell, who like Jarrell would become a lifelong friend and who would also become an important poet. "1939" tells about life for the writers at Kenyon, how separate they felt from the other students, who had "provincial manners" and "foppish, collegiate clothing." The main action of the story recounts a trip that Taylor and Lowell took to New York City at Thanksgiving break. Before the holiday they imagined that they might just leave college and begin their lives as writers, but after meeting two worldly girls in the city they realized that, as the train wheels told them on their trip home, they were "not yet, not yet, not yet" ready for that change.

When *The Collected Stories of Peter Taylor* appeared in 1969, it was dedicated to his mother, "the best teller of tales I know and from whose lips I first heard many of the stories in this book." Whatever the starting point is for his work—strict autobiography, a remembered milieu, or family tales—Taylor carefully chooses and arranges the elements of his fiction to create what he called "a second kind of truth" beyond the surface truth. His stories work toward psychological insight or a deeper understanding of experience than our unexamined lives generally present to us.

Virtually all of Taylor's stories are about families, that crucible in which we are both formed and tested. Relations between husbands and wives, fathers and sons, brothers and sisters, and country and city cousins, or between family members and the black servants who make up the larger household, are either the background against which the action in a story appears or the force that drives the action. In the title story of Taylor's earliest collection, *A Long Fourth and Other Stories* (1948), the family that has gathered for a Fourth of July weekend includes a Nashville doctor and his wife; two grown, unmarried daughters; and the only son, who is home visiting before entering the army and possibly going to war. When the family's longtime black cook, who lives in a shack behind the big house with her nephew, grows upset because the nephew is leaving town to work in an airplane factory, she tells the mother, "Miss Harriet, it's like you losin' Mr. Son." Harriet, who has been trying to console the cook, is deeply insulted by this remark, revealing her racial prejudice. When on the next night the cook and her nephew quarrel and Harriet declines to go comfort the black woman she has known for so long, her lack of sympathy draws an unsympathetic question from her husband, "Harriet, why should this be so hard for you?" The narrator observes that "he seemed to be making a larger and more general inquiry into her character than he had ever done before."

A later collection, *Happy Families Are All Alike* (1959), uses the famous opening line of Tolstoy's *Anna Karenina* (1875–1877) to show an even darker vision of family life. "Venus, Cupid, Folly, and Time," one of Taylor's most widely anthologized stories, appeared in this collection. In it an elderly brother and sister in a fictional city called Chatham give an annual party for all the "nice" children of the neighborhood. Never mind that the old couple behaves bizarrely and lives in the family's once-imposing home, which they have slowly been dismantling to lower their property-tax assessment. All the people of the town nonetheless long for the social distinction that an invitation suggests. When a brother and sister who have been invited to the party trick the old couple by substituting a lower-class boy for the brother, there is a climactic moment in which subtle hints about incest come explosively to the fore.

LATER LIFE AND WORK

After graduating from Kenyon, Taylor went briefly to graduate school at Louisiana State University, where

Robert Penn Warren and Cleanth Brooks were teaching and editing *The Southern Review*. Taylor continued to work at his fiction and began to publish it in literary quarterlies. He was drafted into the army in 1941 and spent nearly three years at an army post near Chattanooga before being sent to England in 1944, where he did not see combat. In 1943 he met a student of Allen Tate's named Eleanor Ross, who would become a highly regarded poet herself. They married within weeks and the union lasted more than fifty years, until Taylor's death. One of the most optimistic stories he ever wrote, "Rain in the Heart" (1945), draws its power from the early days of their marriage, when the main character travels from the army base where he is posted to visit his new wife for the weekend. In a world troubled by war and in a period of his life when army service draws him away from the social class in which he has always lived, the soldier feels grateful for the haven his marriage gives him.

After the army, Taylor spent most of his career teaching English and creative writing at a number of different colleges and universities; in the sixteen years before his 1983 retirement, he worked at the University of Virginia. He published stories steadily from the 1940s until his death, with a large number of them appearing in *The New Yorker* or in such literary quarterlies as *The Southern Review*, *Sewanee Review*, and *Shenandoah*. The publication of his *Collected Stories* in 1969 was a milestone in his career. Critics hailed Taylor as one of the greatest living American short story writers, the American Chekhov, but he did not become well-known to a wide range of readers until late in his career, when in 1986 he published *A Summons to Memphis*, his first full-length novel. The book won the Pulitzer Prize and the Ritz-Paris Hemingway Award.

A Summons to Memphis has a classic unreliable narrator and a structure familiar from many Taylor stories. The narrator looks back on his life from middle age, relating a series of family problems that seem to have stemmed from the family's move to Memphis from Nashville when he was young. The narrator, who lives in New York City, gets called back to Memphis by his sisters, first to prevent their father from remarrying two years after their mother's death and again when the father decides to become reconciled to the business partner whose betrayal years before had caused the family to move. Both the marriage and the reconciliation are thwarted, but the father and the son begin to renew their relationship until the father

himself dies. By the end of the story the reader sees how, without himself realizing it, the narrator has lived a life made barren by his estrangement from family and home.

Although Taylor's public acclaim came for this novel, he continued to write long, masterly stories late into his life, and in 1978 was awarded the prestigious Gold Medal for the Short Story by the American Academy and Institute of Arts and Letters. Probably the greatest of these late stories is "The Old Forest" (1979), as rich, complex, and satisfying a work as anything Taylor wrote in his career. In it, that familiar middle-aged narrator tells about the week before he is to be married to a society girl in Memphis in 1937. The groom spends the Saturday afternoon before the wedding with a former girlfriend, a young woman not of his class but of the new class of independent working women. There is a minor car accident and the girl runs off into the nearby woods and disappears. Much of the course of the story involves the groom's efforts to find her, because it becomes clear to everyone that the marriage cannot take place until he does. As the story unfolds it also becomes clear that the lost girl is being hidden by girls of her own class. Finally, the society bride realizes that only she can solve the mystery and does so by exhibiting the intelligence and independence of the working girls themselves. In the story, the Old Forest itself becomes a powerful symbol of chaos, mystery, and the need for freedom.

Taylor continued to write until the months of his final illness, telling his friends that "all I can do anymore is write." His last published work, a novel called *In the Tennessee Country*, appeared in the fall of 1994, only a few weeks after his death. In it an aging critic looks back on his life and regrets that he has not been an artist. Well into his own sixth decade as an artist, Peter Taylor was embracing the life that he had led.

[*See also* Fugitives, The, (and Southern Agrarianism); Jarrell, Randall; Lowell, Robert; Ransom, John Crowe; Short Story in America, The; *and* Tate, Allen.]

SELECTED WORKS

A Long Fourth and Other Stories (1948)
A Woman of Means (1950)
The Widows of Thornton (1954)
Tennessee Day in St. Louis (1957)
Happy Families Are All Alike (1959)
Miss Leonora When Last Seen and Fifteen Other Stories (1964)
The Collected Stories of Peter Taylor (1969)
Presences: Seven Dramatic Pieces (1973)

In the Miro District and Other Stories (1977)
The Old Forest and Other Stories (1985)
A Stand in the Mountains (1985)
A Summons to Memphis (1986)
The Oracle at Stoneleigh Court: Stories (1993)
In the Tennessee Country (1994)

FURTHER READING

Boatwright, James, ed. "A Garland for Peter Taylor on His Sixtieth Birthday." *Shenandoah* 28 (Winter 1977): 4–85. A collection of essays, memoirs, and poems by writers who knew Taylor.

Griffith, Albert J. *Peter Taylor*. Rev. ed. Boston, 1990.

Hamilton, Ian. *Robert Lowell: A Biography*. New York, 1982. Taylor figures heavily in this biography of his lifelong friend.

McAlexander, Hubert H. *Critical Essays on Peter Taylor*. New York, 1993. A helpful selection.

McAlexander, Hubert H. *Peter Taylor: A Writer's Life*. Baton Rouge, La., 2001. A biography by a scholar who knew Taylor in his last years.

McAlexander, Hubert H., ed. *Conversations with Peter Taylor*. Jackson, Miss., 1987. Interviews.

Stephens, C. Ralph, and Lynda B. Salamon, eds. *The Craft of Peter Taylor*. Tuscaloosa, Ala., 1995.

Warren, Robert Penn. "Introduction." In *A Long Fourth and Other Stories*. By Peter Taylor. New York, 1948. The first critical assessment of Taylor's work, and still the most perceptive.

Wright, Stuart. *Peter Taylor: A Descriptive Bibliography, 1934–1987*. Charlottesville, Va., 1988.

THEATER IN AMERICA

by Brenda Murphy

Historians of American drama and theater have long recognized the many obstacles to the profession of playwriting in America before the twentieth century. To begin with, a Puritan antitheatrical prejudice in the New England colonies resulted in laws that restricted the production of plays and "frivolous" entertainments well into the eighteenth century. Anyone who tried to make a living by producing or acting in plays in the cities of the colonial Northeast had a difficult time of it. The economic situation was even worse for playwrights because theatrical troupes preferred to rely on a proven repertoire of European plays imported from England rather than risk their capital on a new American play. The absence of copyright laws exacerbated the situation. Until 1865, any theatrical manager could produce a play without paying royalties to its author. A playwright could profit from a play only by producing it himself, by finding a manager who was willing to buy it outright on the hope that it would be a big success, or by publishing it. Once it was published, anyone could produce it without paying royalties. After 1865, American playwrights received royalties, but until the international copyright was established in 1891, a manager could pirate a British play without payment while having to pay for an American one. Naturally, then, it was chiefly American plays with potential for great popular success that were produced.

These conditions did not constitute a recipe for developing a great literary drama, but a uniquely American drama did emerge. In the eighteenth and early nineteenth centuries, American subject matter was adapted to the favored genres of sentimental comedy and romantic tragedy by playwrights such as William Dunlap, James Nelson Barker, and John Howard Payne. Although many states forbade drama during the American Revolution, heavy-hitting anti-Tory political satires, such as Mercy Otis Warren's *The Group* (Boston, 1775) and *The Block-heads; or, The Affrighted Officers* (Boston, 1776), also attributed to her by some historians, were popular. (Dates of plays are of first New York City production unless otherwise noted.) After the Revolution, Americanism suffused a series of plays in several genres, such as Susanna Rowson's romantic tragedy, *Slaves in Algiers; or, a Struggle for Freedom* (Philadelphia, 1794) and Royall Tyler's comedy of manners, *The Contrast* (1787), which celebrates America's plainspoken honesty and democratic values in opposition to European corruption, pretense, and hypocrisy.

MELODRAMA

The dominant dramatic genre of the nineteenth century in both Europe and America was melodrama. Viewed by recent critics and historians as a natural response to a deeply unsettled postrevolutionary political and social order, melodrama depicts a simplified moral universe in which good and evil are clearly recognizable traits of a hero and a villain who are locked in a struggle for dominance that is often violent and sensational. In melodrama, the forces of good usually win, affirming the established social order and assuring the audience that its moral values will triumph in the end, despite the unsettled times. A typical nineteenth-century American melodrama centers on an innocent and vulnerable female character who faces the threat of evil, usually sexual, from a villain, and is rescued, and often married, by a hero. This melodramatic paradigm is often used to address particular social and moral concerns. Among the most popular plays of the nineteenth century was George L. Aiken's *Uncle Tom's Cabin* (1852), one of the many adaptations of Harriet Beecher Stowe's novel that assuaged the country's anxieties about slavery, abolition, racism, and Christian values by containing them within the familiar melodramatic paradigm. Dion Boucicault's *Poor of New York* (1857) domesticated the increasingly disturbing issues of immigration and urban poverty. Many melodramas grew out of the temperance movement, the best known being W. H. Smith's *The Drunkard; or, the Fallen Saved* (Boston, 1844), which suggests that the hope for relief from the threats to society arising from alcoholism lies in reestablishing traditional religious and domestic values.

REALISM AND MODERNISM

Melodrama is by its nature a genre that lacks nuance. Its struggle between good and evil is depicted with bold strokes on a large canvas. There are no gray areas, and there is no room for depicting the complexity of moral dilemmas or the psychological complications of human characters. Partly out of dissatisfaction with the limitations of melodrama, and partly because they were intrigued by the possibilities of the new realism that was being practiced in the European theater by such playwrights as Henrik Ibsen, August Strindberg, and George Bernard Shaw and in American fiction by writers such as William Dean Howells and Henry James, a few playwrights toward the end of the nineteenth century began to apply the principles of realism to their own plays. Rejecting the simplistic moral worldview, the conventional plot, the flat characters, and the sensationalized staging of the melodrama, playwrights such as James A. Herne, Edward Sheldon, and Clyde Fitch worked at developing a realistic theater that represented "commonplace" middle-class American life directly and that invited its primarily middle-class audience to wrestle with moral and psychological complexity rather than to reaffirm traditional values. Howells, himself a playwright as well as a drama critic, articulated many of the principles of the realistic theater. The plays deemphasized plot and stressed character. They often integrated moral and social dilemmas into what Shaw called the "drama of discussion," so that the argument over a social issue became the action of the play instead of a tacked-on moral. In order to gain the audience's identification with the characters and the society they represented, the plays aimed at as complete an illusion of reality as was possible in the staging, a goal that was taken to extremes by playwright-producers such as Steele Mackaye, David Belasco, and William Gillette.

The first consciously realistic play on the American stage was Herne's *Margaret Fleming* (Boston, 1890), a play that reexamines one of the stock situations of melodrama: the wife's forgiveness of her errant husband. Rather than simply reaffirming the social order by reuniting husband and wife, Herne dramatizes his protagonist's psychologically believable reaction to her husband's breach of faith. Edward Sheldon's *Salvation Nell* (1908) is a realistic representation of the quintessential situation in American melodrama: the saving of a poor young woman's virtue. Clyde Fitch, the most popular American playwright at the turn of the twentieth century, used realistic social comedy to expose the corrupt values and social pretensions of America's upper middle class.

By the second decade of the twentieth century, realism was the choice of writers who wanted to write plays of literary quality for the American stage. In the era of Progressive politics, the drama of discussion had taken hold as a way of addressing social issues in which middle-class Americans, particularly in the large cities where theaters are concentrated, were keenly interested. Rachel Crothers addressed feminist issues such as the conflict between marriage and career in *He and She* (Poughkeepsie, New York, 1911) and the issue of the sexual double standard in *A Man's World* (1910), voicing a strong feminist position that was answered by the period's most successful male writer of serious plays, Augustus Thomas, in *As a Man Thinks* (1911). For the serious playwright, the theater had become the place to dramatize the effect of contemporary social and moral issues on middle-class life.

Because realism was somewhat late in arriving on the American stage, the introduction of modernism into both the writing and the staging of plays during the mid-1910s made for a unique aesthetic development, centered particularly in two semiprofessional Greenwich Village theater groups in New York City. The Provincetown Players, the primary goal of which was the production of new American plays, would generate two major playwrights in Eugene O'Neill and Susan Glaspell. The Washington Square Players was to evolve into the Theatre Guild, the most distinguished American production company for literary drama in the twentieth century. Since serious realistic plays were new to the American stage, both of these groups produced a number of plays in that mode as well as plays that reflected the effects of modernism, which had made an enormous impact on the bohemian, avant-garde artists and thinkers in Greenwich Village through the Armory Show of 1913, the first large-scale exhibition of modernist art in the United States.

The work of Glaspell and O'Neill illustrates well the aesthetic development in the American theater during these extraordinarily creative years. Glaspell, the older of the two, and an established fiction writer, had been one of the founders of the Provincetown Players, which was established to provide an avant-garde alternative to the commercial theater of Broadway. Glaspell's first play for the Players, the realistic one-act *Trifles* (1916), is now recognized as a classic example of both feminist drama and realist aesthetics. Although it deals with a gruesome murder, the play consciously avoids the sensational, focusing instead on the character of the woman who committed the crime and the gradual process of understanding that a group of women come to as they piece out her life and her motive from the "trifles" of her world—the kitchen that makes up the realistic set of the play. During the next five years, Glaspell's work increasingly exhibited characteristics of dramatic modernism—a move away from realistic situations that revealed a character's psychology and toward the direct representation of a character's subjective experience or consciousness on stage; an increasing abstraction and symbolism in the setting; and less realistic, more poetic dialogue. Glaspell's *The Verge* (1921), the culmination of this evolution for her, has a realistic framework, but it is essentially a symbolic drama about the condition of the female artist who is hampered in her quest to create art that is authentic and innovative by the public's limited expectations and the demands of men, children, and domestic life.

Like Glaspell, O'Neill began his time at the Provincetown Players with realistic one-acts, such as *Bound East for Cardiff* (1916) and *The Moon of the Caribees* (1918), but soon became interested in the aesthetics of modernism and the possibilities it opened up for the dramatization of psychological complexity. His own experiments in *The Emperor Jones* (1920) and *The Hairy Ape* (1922) coincided with the development of European expressionism as well as other American modernist experiments, such as Alice Gerstenberg's *Overtones* (1913). European expressionism focuses on the dehumanization of the "little man," the clerk or factory worker, by modern forces such as technology and capitalism. The plays are intended to represent the subjective reality of the character's consciousness by dramatizing the world not "as it is," but as the disturbed character perceives or experiences it. This is done through repetitive, robotic movement; staccato dialogue; subjective settings that reflect the distortions of nightmare or madness; and, usually, a progression from stability to madness or violence that ends in a "Schrei" or a shriek that signals the character's demise. O'Neill's early experiments with expressionism employ many of these techniques.

O'Neill quickly moved beyond this, however, pursuing his own deep interest in depicting the conflict between his characters' public personae and their private identities. He experimented with masks, most effectively in *The Great God Brown* (1926), and with dialogue, most notably in *Strange Interlude* (1928), an ambitious nine-act play with a dual dialogic framework that juxtaposes realistic dialogue with stream-of-consciousness dialogue in which the characters express their private thoughts to the audience.

While he was intrigued by the technical experiments for representing subjective experience on stage, O'Neill's most fundamental affinity with modernism was spiritual. Like many other modernists, O'Neill was appalled by the loss of faith in a sustaining religious myth and the lack of connection with the past in modern culture. He embarked on his own unsuccessful spiritual quest for what he called "God replacements" in plays such as *Lazarus Laughed* (Pasadena, California, 1928), *Dynamo* (1929), and *Days without End* (1934), but his larger project was an attempt to overcome this loss by remaking myth and mythicizing history. In *Desire under the Elms* (1924), O'Neill used the Phaedra and Hippolytus myth as a vehicle for understanding the attempt to transcend the characteristics that he saw enslaving human beings, modern and ancient, such as sexual desire, greed, and jealousy. In *Marco Millions* (1928) and *The Fountain* (1925), O'Neill used the historical figures of Marco Polo, the thirteenth-century Venetian merchant who traveled to China, and Ponce de Léon the Spanish explorer who searched for the Fountain of Youth in Florida, to represent the divided soul of the modern American. In *Marco* particularly, through satire akin to that of Sinclair Lewis's novel, *Babbitt* (1922), O'Neill represented a pragmatic man of action troubled by the need for romantic love and spiritual fulfillment. These characters figure the conflict that O'Neill represents most fully in *Strange Interlude*, a struggle among business, science, high culture, romantic myth, and traditional religion for the soul of America. O'Neill's most ambitious project, a cycle of plays called *A Tale of Possessors, Self-dispossessed*, of which only two plays are extant, was to address this theme fully in the context of American history.

It is *Mourning Becomes Electra* (1931) that most fully integrates O'Neill's modernist worldview with his aesthetic for the theater. He used a technique he called "unreal realism" in this play, discarding the aggressively antirealist techniques of the earlier experiments in favor of a realistic theatrical idiom that suggests a subjective perspective rather than emphasizing it. Instead of wearing masks, the Mannon family members have white, masklike faces that indicate the artificiality of their public personae. The dialogue is literary and symbolic, but it remains within the realistic frame. More fundamentally, O'Neill brings together his mythicizing and historicizing techniques to endow contemporary experience with transcendent meaning. The three-play cycle is a retelling of the classic Greek myth of Electra in the context of the American Civil War. While the Civil War evokes the essentially divided nature of the country, the Electra myth exposes the cracked foundation of the family.

BROADWAY BETWEEN THE WORLD WARS

After his apprentice years with the Provincetown Players, Eugene O'Neill's plays were all produced on Broadway, and with a great deal of success. This was partly because the Theatre Guild, with its strong base of regular subscribers for season tickets, was able and willing to put up the resources needed to mount his ambitious and demanding plays. But it is also a measure of the possibilities in the Broadway theater at the height of its productivity. In the 1925–1926 season, the peak year of activity, there were 255 new productions in the Broadway theater. This might be compared with 115 in 1915–1916 or 28 in 2000–2001. While many of these productions in the fun-seeking Jazz Age were unabashed entertainment with no literary ambitions, there was more opportunity at this time for plays with literary value to be produced than at any other time before or since. During the 1920s and 1930s, realism was the dominant aesthetic on the American stage. When one considers the dominance of Broadway over the rest of the country, and the predominance of the middle class in the Broadway audience, it is not surprising to see a number of playwrights representing the middle class to themselves and writing about concerns and issues in which they were invested. This middle-class realism embraced a wide spectrum of American life, from urban high society to the provincial small town. Within the mode of realism, there was the sparkling and witty society comedy by Philip Barry and S. N. Behrman, the slightly more earnest discussion-oriented comedy of Rachel Crothers, the satirical social criticism of George Kelly, the serious discussion plays of Sidney Howard and Lewis Beach, the pathetic character portraiture of Zona Gale, and a great deal more. This rich body of literature constitutes a *comédie humaine* for the American middle class between the two world wars, a revealing representation of values, conflicts, desires, and social forces.

During the 1920s, expressionism also appeared on the Broadway stage, with its avant-garde modernist techniques domesticated somewhat for middle-class consumption. The most typical American alteration of European expressionism is the addition of humor, which changed that form's worldview radically. Elmer Rice's *The Adding Machine* (1923), George S. Kaufman and Marc Connelly's *Beggar on Horseback* (1924), and John Howard Lawson's *Processional* (1925) make use of expressionistic techniques in their critiques of American society, but their tone is more satirical than the desperation of the German models or O'Neill's early plays. They suggest that America's obsession with money and business can be cured by a reawakening of the values of love, beauty, and personal fulfillment. Besides O'Neill's plays, Sophie Treadwell's feminist *Machinal* (1928), based on the notorious murder trial of Ruth Snyder, is the most significant expressionist piece produced on Broadway. Modernism made its way into American playwriting in a number of ways, as well, for example, in the antirealistic aesthetics in plays like William Saroyan's *The Time of Your Life* (1939) and Thornton Wilder's *Our Town* (1938) and *The Skin of Our Teeth* (1942).

The stock market crash of 1929 and the onset of the Great Depression had a significant effect on the theater, as they did on every aspect of American life. Coupled with the rising threat of fascism and world war in Europe, the Depression forced playwrights to address broader social concerns and to encounter the economic and political forces that threatened American well-being and security. In these unsettled times, melodrama once again emerged on the American stage, but in a more subtle form than in the nineteenth century. Lillian Hellman is a good example of the new social melodramatists. Her plays are informed by the deep structure of melodrama in that they represent reality as a battle between easily recognizable forces of good and evil. Unlike most of the earlier melodramas, however, her plays do not inevitably end with the triumph of good and the defeat of evil. Her first Broadway play, *The Children's Hour* (1934), which concerns a child's false accusation of lesbianism that eventually destroys her teachers' lives, exposes the evil that can come from a lie and the danger to the community of ignorance and prejudice. A staunch leftist and supporter of the Communist Party, Hellman used *The Little Foxes* (1939), a melodrama about a greedy family in the early-nineteenth-century South, to condemn both the capitalists who "eat the earth" and those who stand around and watch them do it. Hellman's antifascism is evident in *Watch on the Rhine* (1941), her most conventional melodrama, in which a hero of the resistance kills a would-be blackmailer—with the help and approval of his American in-laws—in order to carry on his work. It is a call for the United States to join the European war against fascism. Hellman kept her plays within the mode of realism with realistic settings, believable if rather sensational situations, and psychologically complex characters, thus implying that the struggle between good and evil was the underlying dynamic of human social order. A similar tactic was followed by playwrights such as Robert Sherwood in *There Shall Be No Night* (1940), Elmer Rice in *Judgment Day* (1934), and Clare Boothe Luce in *Margin for Error* (1939) to advance an antifascist political agenda.

The 1930s is also known for the development of a theater of direct engagement that is presentational, or directed outward to the audience and demanding involvement, rather than representational, or allowing the audience to observe the action on stage passively. The progenitor of this kind of drama is agitprop, or the agitation-propaganda play that was used by leftists in the labor movement to rally support for the cause during the Depression. It is a simple, direct form of theater that uses type characters and simple situations, songs, slogans, and direct challenges to the audience to incite involvement in the cause. Meant to be a portable theater, it makes little use of sets or props and can be put on in any available space. The techniques of agitprop were adapted in a number of ways, most notably in the Living Newspapers of the short-lived Works Progress Administration's Federal Theatre Project (1935–1939) that were meant to educate audiences about such issues as the housing shortage (*One-Third of a Nation*, 1938), the farm crisis (*Triple-A Plowed Under*, 1936), and public ownership of utilities (*Power*, 1937). A domesticated agitprop reached Broadway in the form of the Group Theatre's production of Clifford Odets's *Waiting for Lefty* (1935), a play that is set in a labor meeting where the rank and file wait for their representative, who turns out to have been murdered. Odets complicated the techniques of agitprop, introducing realistic scenes that dramatized the difficulties of the workers' lives and elicited understanding and sympathy from the audience before he ended with an actor rising from the audience and involving it in his call of "Strike! Strike! Strike!"

An unusual development on the American stage between the world wars was the resurgence of two seemingly outdated dramatic traditions, verse drama and the folk play. The use of verse, which was associated with the high-flown romantic tragedy of the early nineteenth century, had not been seen in a new play for some time when Maxwell Anderson wrote *White Desert* in 1923. While this play was not successful, Anderson's historical verse tragedies, *Elizabeth the Queen* (1930), *Mary of Scotland* (1933), and *Anne of the Thousand Days* (1948) met with popular as well as critical success. More interesting and original were his synthesis of the contemporary with the historical and colloquial prose with verse in *Joan of Lorraine* (1946), his play about Joan of Arc, and his verse treatment of the unjust executions in 1927 of the anarchists Sacco and Vanzetti, in *Winterset* (1935). Anderson's popular success opened the way for productions of verse plays like T. S. Eliot's *Murder in the Cathedral* (1936) and *The Cocktail Party* (1950). In the hands of such well-educated and talented playwrights as Langston Hughes, Zora Neale Hurston, Marc Connelly, and Paul Green, the so-called folk play of the period was a similarly literary endeavor, a manipulation of traditional folk materials to both express and mask contemporary attitudes and issues.

THE POSTWAR PERIOD

Despite the international respect accorded Eugene O'Neill, it was only after World War II that American drama emerged from its status as a footnote to the world repertoire and enjoyed a brief period of dominance on the world's stage. The development of a form of theater known as the "American style" is partly owing to the unique circumstance of the American theater's discovering realism and modernism at virtually the same time. It is evident that while realism was the dominant mode during the interwar period, these two aesthetics coexisted in the American theater throughout the twentieth century, with playwrights often using the techniques of one to enrich the other. In the 1940s several playwrights, notably Tennessee Williams and Arthur Miller, collaborated with director Elia Kazan and scene designer Jo Mielziner to create a true synthesis of the two in subjective realism. While the aesthetic framework is undeniably realistic, these artists drew freely on the techniques of expressionism to represent the subjective experience or perspective of the protagonist within the context of the realistic drama.

The first of these plays is Tennessee Williams's *The Glass Menagerie* (1945), which he characterized as a "memory play," the action framed by Tom's narrative and refracted through his memory. Through evocative lighting and scenery that became transparent, Mielziner made the contrast between past and present clear in the play, without resorting to the shattering of the "fourth-wall illusion" that the audience is eavesdropping on real people interacting in real situations on stage. Williams and his collaborators went further in *A Streetcar Named Desire* (1947), dramatizing Blanche DuBois's gradual retreat into psychosis as "desperate circumstances" close in on her through selective expressionistic techniques without losing the audience's belief in the overall illusion of reality. The technique reached its full development in Miller's

Death of a Salesman (1949), which uses a complex time scheme that juxtaposes the putative reality of stage present with the memory of past events that is running like a film in Willy Loman's head.

The accomplishment of this form of drama was the ability to retain realism's illusion of the fourth wall and still dramatize the consciousness or subjectivity of a character, a major modernist concern. The "American style," both of writing and of stagecraft, had an enormous impact on the theater, prompting Arthur Miller to call the 1950s "an era of gauze" because of the prevalence of transparent scenery and the drama's intense focus on the personal concerns and psychological problems of the individual rather than on the larger social issues that loomed in that decade, such as the McCarthyism that Miller and a few others attacked through the strategy of historical analogy in plays like *The Crucible* (1953). Besides Williams and Miller, playwrights such as William Inge, Robert Anderson, William Gibson, and Ketti Frings achieved great success in this vein during the 1950s. Although his autobiographical plays, written in the prewar period, represent a more straightforward realism, it is reflective of the times that the great posthumous success of Eugene O'Neill should come with the Circle in the Square's revival of *The Iceman Cometh* (1946) and the Broadway production of *Long Day's Journey into Night*, both in 1956.

ALTERNATIVES TO BROADWAY

The revival of *The Iceman Cometh* that is credited with reviving O'Neill's waning reputation took place off-Broadway, and it was in the late 1950s that the decentralization of the American theater from Broadway to off- and off-off-Broadway and regional theater began. During the 1940s, off-Broadway theaters like the Circle in the Square had shown the possibilities of fresh interpretations of older plays in small, intimate theaters. (Off-Broadway theaters must have 299 seats or fewer because of union regulations.) But it was the Living Theatre's 1959 production of Jack Gelber's experimental new play *The Connection* that was the beginning of what may be called the off-Broadway movement. This play about a group of drug addicts waiting for a delivery from their dealer, with its lack of a linear plot, its improvisational staging, and its jazz accompaniment, was a theatricalization of the Beat aesthetic. It ran for 768 performances and redefined the off-Broadway theater from a smaller Broadway to an alternative theater for experimental work on which Broadway producers were unwilling to risk their capital. Nearly all of the playwrights

who produced works of literary quality in the second half of the twentieth century began in the off-Broadway theaters, or the even smaller, more informal, and more experimental off-off-Broadway venues in New York City such as La MaMa and Caffe Cino, or in similar theaters in smaller cities.

Edward Albee, whose *Zoo Story* (1960) and *The American Dream* (1961) were produced in small Greenwich Village theaters, brought the new off-Broadway aesthetic onto Broadway. Heavily influenced by the absurdist theater of Samuel Beckett and Harold Pinter, which was heavily influenced by existentialist philosophy, Albee's early plays used modernist techniques to dramatize a worldview that had passed beyond the spiritual quest for "God replacements," and sought instead for ways to live in a world in which human life had no meaning. Instead of the rational argument of the discussion play, the chief technique for dramatizing the absurdity of human existence was to dramatize a metaphor for the human condition, such as pointless hope in Beckett's *Waiting for Godot* (Paris, 1953). Albee dramatized the basic animal nature of human beings and the impossibility of human communication in *Zoo Story*, and the myth of the happy family in *The American Dream*. Although his most successful plays, *Who's Afraid of Virginia Woolf?* (1962) and *A Delicate Balance* (1966), are written within a realistic aesthetic, they invite and reward interpretation from an absurdist perspective. Subsequent plays such as *Tiny Alice* (1964) and *Seascape* (1975) are unabashedly nonrealistic.

The off-off Broadway movement is perhaps best illustrated in the career of Sam Shepard, who began having his nonrealistic, highly imagistic, language-centered one-act plays with rock music produced in alternative venues such as Theatre Genesis and La MaMa in the mid-1960s and became a highly respected contributor to the world theater repertoire without having a premiere on Broadway. His early subjects were the quintessentially male mythic figures of twentieth-century American culture: the cowboy, the rock star, the gangster, the movie mogul. Shepard entered a new phase with his family trilogy, *Curse of the Starving Class* (London, 1977), *Buried Child* (1978), and *True West* (1980). Although they use a realistic theatrical idiom, it is an idiosyncratic one that some critics refer to as "hyperrealism," rendering some aspects of the setting in great detail while ignoring others and juxtaposing colloquial dialogue with extended poetic monologues. In these representations of wildly dysfunctional American families, connections to American myths and self-creations remain within a barely maintained framework of domestic realism. In subsequent plays such as *Fool for Love* (1983), *A Lie of the Mind* (1985), *Simpatico* (1994), and *The Late Henry Moss* (2001), Shepard continues to explore the mythic realm of the American psyche in the context of human relationships, particularly those of father and son. With his highly allusive, imagistic, and evocative language, he is one of the most poetic American playwrights.

Most of the serious playwrights in Shepard's generation began their careers as he did, in the off-off Broadway theater. This is particularly true for women, for whom the development of an alternative feminist theater movement during the late 1960s opened unprecedented opportunities for production as well as for the development of a consciously feminist aesthetic for drama. Playwrights such as Adrienne Kennedy, Maria Irene Fornes, Megan Terry, and Ntozake Shange consciously resisted what they considered to be male-gendered linear plots and psychologically integrated characters, creating instead a theater that relied on collaboration among the artists, improvisation, "transformational" characters with no fixed identity, open-ended action, and an eclectic mix of genres to express a feminist worldview. Although their aesthetic was not as pointedly articulated, most of the male playwrights of their generation, such as Arthur Kopit, John Guare, A. R. Gurney, and Lanford Wilson, also began in small, alternative venues with nonrealistic plays that tended to attack established middle-class values and institutions. One group that did have a clearly articulated agenda was the Black Arts Repertory Theatre, whose guiding spirit was Amiri Baraka (LeRoi Jones). Angry plays like *Dutchman* (1964) and *The Slave* (1964) expressed a revolutionary political agenda that rejected white liberalism and promoted black separatism.

During the 1960s and 1970s, the reputations of Arthur Miller and Tennessee Williams went into eclipse as they ventured away from Broadway and into nonrealistic dramaturgy. For Williams, who referred to this time as his "stoned age," this was a period of diminished craftsmanship because of drug and alcohol abuse. Although many of his plays from the period are weak on structure and coherence, the arresting imagery, the startlingly poetic use of language, and the postmodern structural experimentation in plays such as *The Gnädiges Fräulein* (1966), *The Red Devil Battery Sign* (1975), and *Clothes for a Summer Hotel* (1980) show the playwright's powerful imagination still at work. Miller's nonrealistic experimental plays, such as *After the Fall* (1964), *Elegy for a Lady* (1982), *Clara*

(1987), and *I Can't Remember Anything* (1987), continued his exploration of the human psyche, while *Incident at Vichy* (1964), *The Archbishop's Ceiling* (Washington, D.C., 1977), and the television adaptation of *Playing for Time* (1980) conducted a more characteristic exploration of the moral issues related to the contemporary social and political order. None of this work approached the broad public appeal of the two playwrights' earlier plays and it was considered increasingly obscure and irrelevant by influential theater critics.

END OF THE TWENTIETH CENTURY

The creation of American drama in the last two decades of the twentieth century is well illustrated by the career of David Mamet, perhaps the most versatile artist of the contemporary American theater. Mamet is an erstwhile actor and acting teacher, a respected director of both theater and film, and a writer of fiction, essays, and film scripts as well as plays. He began his playwriting career in regional theater with Chicago productions of such plays as the thirty-scene comedy *Sexual Perversity in Chicago* (Chicago, 1974). Beginning with *American Buffalo* (1977) and continuing with *Glengarry Glen Ross* (1984), *Speed-the-Plow* (1988), *Oleanna* (1992), *The Cryptogram* (1995), and *The Old Neighborhood* (1997), Mamet's major playwriting accomplishment has been the creation of a realistic idiom for the theater based on his unique dialogue that combines a consciousness of the power dynamics involved in the speech act with a highly artistic sense of the poetics of plain speech, profanity, and silences. Like O'Neill's and Shepard's, Mamet's focus became more personal and more domestic as he entered middle age; his dramaturgy became more realistic as he explored the effects of the dysfunctional family, particularly on children.

The literary playwright who enjoyed the greatest Broadway success during this period is another product of the regional theater, August Wilson, who profited from a long collaborative relationship with director Lloyd Richards at the Eugene O'Neill Theatre Center and the Yale Repertory Theatre in Connecticut. Wilson's major project, a play cycle that depicts the history of African Americans in each decade of the twentieth century, was nearly complete at the start of the twenty-first century. The first of his plays to reach Broadway was *Ma Rainey's Black Bottom* (1984), set in a Chicago recording studio in the 1920s. Like all of Wilson's plays, this one depicts black experience in the context of music, in this case the conflict between the rising generation of jazz musicians and the older generation of blues artists. Wilson's dramaturgy can be compared to the spiritual realism of Toni Morrison's fiction. Firmly anchored in a realistic framework in which psychologically complex characters interact in believable situations, his plays often introduce supernatural elements such as a ghost in *The Piano Lesson* (1990) and the Angel of Death in *Fences* (1987), which indicate that the reality of the supernatural world is as powerful a presence in his characters' lives as that of the natural world.

Working from the base of the feminist theater begun in the 1970s, a number of playwrights wrote plays about the issues and concerns of women from a feminist perspective. The dramaturgy of these playwrights ranges from the traditional tragedy of Marsha Norman's *'night Mother* (1983) and the "serious comedy" of Wendy Wasserstein's *The Heidi Chronicles* (1989) to the avant-garde experiments of Adrienne Kennedy, Tina Howe, and Emily Mann. A significant development for a younger generation of women playwrights is the application of many of the techniques of the feminist theater to other social issues, such as the treatment of racism in Anna Deavere Smith's *Fires in the Mirror* (1992) and Suzan-Lori Parks's *The Death of the Last Black Man in the Whole Entire World* (1990) and *Topdog/Underdog* (2001).

The 1990s may be remembered as the decade of identity politics in the American theater. It was a time when the politics of gender, sexual identity, and ethnicity informed the thinking of many theater artists and produced a number of memorable plays by such playwrights as José Rivera, David Henry Hwang, Paula Vogel, and Lee Blessing. The epitome of 1990s theater is undoubtedly Tony Kushner's two-play cycle, *Angels in America* (1992). This play uses an eclectic dramaturgy that Kushner called the "theater of the fabulous," combining realistic characters, sociopolitical commentary, humor, and sentiment with fantasy, myth, and epic. In the 1990s the epidemic of AIDS produced a subgenre of plays about the disease and its effects on both its victims and society. Kushner's play takes the occasion of a man dying of AIDS to write about identity politics in the context of a millennial conception of America's history and its future.

Like Kushner's play, the American stage at the turn of the twenty-first century was eclectic and open. It welcomed back its recognized giants in major revivals of the great plays of O'Neill, Miller, and Williams as well as productions of Miller's new work (*The Last Yankee*, 1993; *Broken Glass*, 1994; and *The Ride down Mount Morgan*, 1998 [London, 1991]) and Albee's (*Three Tall Women*, 1994, and *The Goat; or, Who Is Sylvia?*, 2002). It welcomed

Pulitzer Prize winners about AIDS and sexual abuse in Kushner's spectacularly produced *Angels in America* and Paula Vogel's minimalist two-character *How I Learned to Drive* (1997). Eve Ensler's taboo-shattering *The Vagina Monologues* (1998) was as popular off-Broadway as David Auburn's traditionally realistic family study *Proof* (2000) was on Broadway, and both were immediately produced in regional theaters. The consequence for dramatic literature was a creative juxtaposition of styles and theatrical idioms, an aesthetic of eclecticism that best characterizes American drama at the beginning of the twenty-first century.

[*See also* Albee, Edward; Eliot, T. S.; Hellman, Lillian; Hughes, Langston; Hurston, Zora Neale; Kushner, Tony; Mamet, David; Miller, Arthur, and his *Death of a Salesman*; Naturalism and Realism; O'Neill, Eugene, and his *Long Day's Journey into Night*; Hansberry's *A Raisin in the Sun*; Shepard, Sam; Wilder, Thornton, and his *Our Town*; Williams, Tennessee and his *The Glass Menagerie*, and *A Streetcar Named Desire*; *and* Wilson, August.]

FURTHER READING

Adler, Thomas P. *American Drama, 1940–1960: A Critical History*. New York, 1994. Part of Twayne's critical history of American drama, this is a useful overview, accessible to the general reader.

Bigsby, C. W. E. *A Critical Introduction to Twentieth-Century American Drama*. 3 vols. Vol. 1, *1900–1940*. Vol. 2, *Tennessee Williams, Arthur Miller, Edward Albee*. Vol. 3, *Beyond Broadway*. Cambridge, 1982–1985. The standard critical overview of twentieth-century American drama.

Bigsby, C. W. E. *Contemporary American Playwrights*. Cambridge, 1999. A critical overview of the work of ten American playwrights at the end of the twentieth century.

Bigsby, C. W. E. *Modern American Drama, 1945–2000*. 2d ed. Cambridge, 2000. A critical study of O'Neill, Williams, Miller, Albee, Shepard, Mamet, and others.

Bordman, Gerald. *American Theatre: A Chronicle of Comedy and Drama, 1869–1914*. New York, 1994. This and the two Bordman volumes below are part of Oxford's American Theater series. They discuss every Broadway production chronologically, providing plot summaries and production details.

Bordman, Gerald. *American Theatre: A Chronicle of Comedy and Drama, 1914–1930*. New York, 1995.

Bordman, Gerald. *American Theatre: A Chronicle of Comedy and Drama, 1930–1969*. New York, 1996.

Burke, Sally. *American Feminist Playwrights: A Critical History*. New York, 1996. Part of Twayne's critical history of American drama, this is a useful overview, accessible to the general reader.

Cohn, Ruby. *New American Dramatists, 1960–1990.* New York, 1991. A concise introduction to the playwrights of the period.

Demastes, William W. *Realism and the American Dramatic Tradition.* Tuscaloosa, Ala., 1996. A collection of critical essays that reflects the wide range of realism in American drama.

Demastes, William W., ed. *American Playwrights, 1880–1945: A Research and Production Sourcebook.* Westport, Conn., 1995. A useful source of information on plays, productions, and criticism for forty playwrights.

Goldstein, Malcolm. *The Political Stage: American Drama and Theater of the Great Depression.* New York, 1974. A good overview of political drama.

Grimsted, David. *Melodrama Unveiled: American Theater and Culture, 1800–1850.* Chicago, 1968. Offers the standard definition of the characteristics of American melodrama.

Hay, Samuel A. *African American Theatre: An Historical and Critical Analysis.* New York, 1994. A comprehensive historical overview in a theatrical context.

Hischak, Thomas S. *American Theatre: A Chronicle of Comedy and Drama, 1969–2000.* New York, 2001. A continuation of the series begun by Bordman.

McConachie, Bruce A. *Melodramatic Formations: American Theatre and Society, 1820–1870.* Iowa City, 1992. An influential study of the interrelation between melodrama and nineteenth-century American social forces.

Murphy, Brenda. *American Realism and American Drama, 1880–1940.* Cambridge, 1987. An overview of the emergence of realism as the dominant mode of drama on the American stage.

Murphy, Brenda, ed. *The Cambridge Companion to American Women Playwrights.* Cambridge, 1999. Part of the Cambridge Companions series, this volume of critical essays reflects the presence of women playwrights on the American stage from the beginning through the twentieth century.

Quinn, Arthur Hobson. *A History of the American Drama from the Civil War to the Present Day.* New York, 1936.

Quinn, Arthur Hobson. *A History of the American Drama from the Beginning to the Civil War.* 2d. ed. New York, 1943. This and the Quinn volume above constitute a two-volume history that was the standard for many years and is still useful, particularly for its extensive play publication and production information.

Roudané, Matthew C. *American Drama since 1960: A Critical History.* New York, 1996. Part of Twayne's critical history of American drama, this is a useful overview, accessible to the general reader.

Sanders, Leslie Catherine. *The Development of Black Theater in America: From Shadows to Selves.* Baton Rouge, La., 1988. A study of major black playwrights from the Harlem Renaissance through the late twentieth century.

Shafer, Yvonne. *American Women Playwrights, 1900–1950.* New York, 1995. This critical overview presents the work of thirty-five female playwrights in roughly chronological order.

Wilmeth, Don B., and Christopher Bigsby, eds. *The Cambridge History of American Theatre.* 3 vols. Vol. 1, *Beginnings to 1870.* Vol. 2, *1870–1945.* Vol. 3, *Post-World War II to the 1990s.* Cambridge, 1998–2000. This three-volume work by multiple authors is the standard history of American drama and theatre.

Valgemae, Mardi. *Accelerated Grimace: Expressionism in the American Drama of the 1920s.* Carbondale, Ill., 1972. An informative study of the impact of expressionism on the American theater.

HENRY DAVID THOREAU

by Thomas S. Hart

The facts of Henry David Thoreau's short life are simple enough. He was born David Henry Thoreau in Concord, Massachusetts, on 12 July 1817. He grew up in Concord and graduated at age twenty from Harvard, after what was by most accounts a fairly ordinary academic career. He briefly tried teaching, and then worked sporadically in the family pencil-making business and as a surveyor, while devoting most of his time to writing, which he considered his true career, despite its having brought him only modest success. He died of tuberculosis at age forty-four on 6 May 1862 in his family's home in Concord.

If people outside of Thoreau's circle of literary friends had been asked about him when he died, they might have described him as "that abolitionist," since his best-known writing during his lifetime was his speech and essay "Slavery in Massachusetts" (1854), which was widely distributed in William Lloyd Garrison's paper *The Liberator* and had also been picked up by Horace Greeley's *New York Tribune* and other papers. Although he had been working toward publication in book form of his other writing, only his self-published *A Week on the Concord and Merrimack Rivers* (1849) and the masterful but far from best-selling *Walden; or, Life in the Woods* (1854) were published during his lifetime. Soon after Thoreau's death, however, things changed. Not only did the Boston publisher Ticknor and Fields reissue *A Week* and *Walden*, they also published five new books: *Excursions* (1863), *The Maine Woods* (1864), *Cape Cod* (1865), *Letters to Various Persons* (1865), and *A Yankee in Canada, with Anti-Slavery and Reform Papers* (1866). Pieces of his journals were gathered in seasonal batches, edited by Thoreau's longtime correspondent H. G. O. Blake, appearing as *Early Spring*

Henry David Thoreau.
(*Courtesy of the Library of Congress*)

in Massachusetts (1881), *Summer* (1884), *Winter* (1887), and *Autumn* (1892). Publication of the complete journals in chronological order began in 1906—the same year in which Mohandas Gandhi, in South Africa, encountered Thoreau's essay "Civil Disobedience." Through the mid-twentieth century, Thoreau's reputation as a critically important writer and thinker on many fronts continued to grow. By 1965, when Walter Harding's *The Days of Henry Thoreau* appeared as the definitive biography, Thoreau had been granted the status of a major American literary figure. Throughout the late twentieth century, critical studies of Thoreau, many emphasizing his countercultural and scientific sides, proliferated. New works by Thoreau himself have actually grown out of this proliferation, including *Wild Fruits* (2000), edited by Bradley P. Dean and subtitled "Thoreau's Rediscovered Last Manuscript."

THOREAU'S MAIN WORKS

Walden is Thoreau's account of life and how to live it, based on the two years (1845–1847) he spent living in a small house he built himself near Walden Pond in Concord, Massachusetts. Unquestionably one of the classics of American literature, *Walden* is available in many editions, some containing useful critical commentary and other supplementary materials and others that include essays by Thoreau. Only a handful of Thoreau's essays are still popular and widely read. Generally, one can divide the essays into those in the natural history vein and those concerning political and reform issues. Two essays concerned with natural history are "A Winter Walk" (1843) and "Wild Apples" (first published in *Atlantic Monthly* in 1862). "Walking" (published in *Atlantic*

Monthly in 1862), the most often anthologized of the essays, is a plea for wildness, for living in the present, and for walking as pilgrimage. But Thoreau also brought nature into his political musings. "Civil Disobedience," first published as "Resistance to Civil Government" in *Aesthetic Papers* in 1849, contains Thoreau's thoughts on the relation of the individual to the state and was written after spending a night in jail for refusing to pay his taxes. Other issue-oriented essays include "Slavery in Massachusetts" (published in *The Liberator* in 1854) and "A Plea for Captain John Brown (1859). "Life without Principle" (1863) addresses how we waste ourselves in misdirected work and demeaning media and must "reconsecrate ourselves." Thoreau's usual method for writing essays was to bring together journal entries, then try the resulting product out as a lecture and check audience reaction before the piece was printed.

Thoreau's first book, written while at Walden Pond, was *A Week on the Concord and Merrimack Rivers* and is essential to an understanding of the man. In it, Thoreau describes how he and his companion (unnamed, but actually his brother John) meander on a canoe trip upriver and back. We are treated to comments on the actual trip, but even more to digressions of every sort on every subject. James Russell Lowell was the first of many to criticize these digressions, saying that they are "out of proportion and out of place and mar our Merrimacking dreadfully. We were bid to a river-party,—not to be preached at." Rambling, discursive, imperfect though it undeniably is, *A Week* is also delightful at many points, and certainly makes clear the person of its writer. It can be closely studied as a preparation for writing *Walden*, both structurally and stylistically. Without *A Week*, and without the difficult reception it received, it is not at all clear that Thoreau would have achieved his masterpiece, *Walden*: he learned much from writing *A Week* and seeing it through to its unsuccessful publication. Thoreau ended up having to subsidize the small press run of this first book, and then having to store himself some seven hundred unsold copies of the one thousand printed. Had *A Week on the Concord and Merrimack Rivers* struck a chord with readers, as it clearly did not, *Walden* would most likely have been a quick follow-up volume. Instead, and to excellent effect, the second book received another five years of careful honing.

Thoreau's journal is recognized today as an important literary document. Begun in earnest in the fall of 1838, it became, ultimately, the chief occupation of his life. Prior to his stay at Walden Pond, Thoreau wrote copiously, but

seemed to see the journal as primarily source material, tearing pages out at times to add to works in progress. By the late 1840s, this practice ceased, and from 1850 on the journal seems to have taken on a new tone, as though its author knew that this was not simply a conversation he was having with himself. Thoreau's other best-known works are *Cape Cod* and *The Maine Woods*. In each, three trips were made to the respective regions, and articles followed in magazines such as *Putnam's* and *Atlantic Monthly*. These articles, rearranged, became the books, published after Thoreau's death. For one so obviously concerned with a book's formal structure as Thoreau showed himself to be in both *A Week* and *Walden*, neither *Cape Cod* nor *The Maine Woods*, in whatever modified forms they appear today, could be considered, despite their attractions for lovers of Thoreau or the regions, completely satisfactory.

The Maine Woods is perhaps most notable for Thoreau's confrontation with nature at its rawest and least human in the "Ktaadn" section, as well as his expression of his dissatisfaction with hunting and killing—the entire ostensible purpose of one of his Maine ventures having been to accompany a companion on a moose hunt, an experience that Thoreau says, "suggested to me how base or coarse are the motives which commonly carry men into the wilderness." The book also features memorable portraits of some crusty Maine men, most notably of Joe Polis, a Native American guide who is clearly the book's central figure. Since his extensive note-taking, research, and journalizing about Indians never produced a full project (some scholars have thought Thoreau's unwritten "Indians" book would have been his real masterpiece), his writing about Polis is arguably his most sustained discussion of Native Americans. Finally, *The Maine Woods* is held by some to make a case—the first case, perhaps—for a system of national wilderness parks, as seen in the conclusion of the original "Chesuncook" section: "The kings of England formerly had their forests 'to hold the king's game,' for sport or food, sometimes destroying villages to create or extend them;...Why should not we, who have renounced the king's authority, have our national preserves...not for idle sport or food, but for inspiration and our true re-creation?"

Cape Cod, like *The Maine Woods*, also has its share of colorful characters, as well as glimpses of nature in a less-than-welcoming mode. It opens with Thoreau's examination of the aftermath of a shipwreck and his chilling descriptions of drowned bodies. Both of these books include large stretches of history and research on their respective subject areas, and both ultimately are, but in the most limiting sense, travel books. Thoreau's travel is always interior as well as exterior, but the interior shows up best as he travels his familiar Concordian grounds. The most noteworthy sections of *Cape Cod* are Thoreau's confrontations with the sea, and both books are read today as records of a vanished time. He concludes *Cape Cod* in a prophetic voice:

> The time must come when this coast will be a place of resort for those New Englanders who really wish to visit the sea-side. At present it is wholly unknown to the fashionable world.... What are springs and waterfalls? Here is the spring of springs, the waterfall of waterfalls. A storm in the fall or winter is the time to visit it; a light-house or a fisherman's hut the true hotel. A man may stand there and put all America behind him.

A COMPLEX ADVOCATE OF SIMPLICITY

Walter Harding opens the introduction to his 1965 biography, *The Days of Henry Thoreau*, by noting: "A hundred years ago Henry David Thoreau was looked upon as a minor disciple of Ralph Waldo Emerson. Fifty years ago he was thought of as an 'also-ran' who was rapidly and deservedly being forgotten. Yet today he is rated as one of the giants in the American pantheon and his fame is on an upward rather than a downward curve. It is universally agreed that he speaks more to our day than to his own." Nearly four decades later, Harding's words are still true. In fact, Thoreau—and his advocates—seem to be speaking today in so many voices that it is sometimes hard to make sense of them. For some, Thoreau is best understood as a hermit, an inveterate antisocial outsider. For others, it is his connection to nature that is of foremost importance. The political implications of Thoreau's work are uppermost for some readers, while others emphasize his scientific contributions. His spiritual and his philosophical statements are central to different groups. For some, consideration of Thoreau is inseparable from consideration of his relationship to his friend and mentor Ralph Waldo Emerson. And there are critics for whom any discussion of what Thoreau is saying is secondary to the way he is saying it: these critics focus on Thoreau as writer, as a master prose stylist. Each viewpoint has validity and can be useful in coming to terms with this complex writer; none is sufficient by itself.

THOREAU AS HERMIT. Thoreau wrote about and lived out his enjoyment of solitude, not only during his two years at Walden Pond, but on other occasions as well. He did not join up when utopian communities were formed, choosing not to participate, for example, in the Fruitlands experiment with Concord friends like Bronson Alcott. "As for these communities," he said, "I had rather keep bachelor's hall in hell than go to board in heaven." And there are Thoreau's words in the "Solitude" chapter of *Walden*, where he tells readers: "I find it wholesome to be alone the greater part of the time. To be in company, even with the best, is soon wearisome and dissipating. I love to be alone. I never found the companion that was so companionable as solitude."

But the same man wrote about society, went on companionable walks with friends, moved into the Emerson household, and seemed to feel himself connected to the issues of the day enough to lecture to his contemporaries about abolition or the Mexican War. The chapter following "Solitude" in Walden is "Visitors," which he begins by telling us that "I think that I love society as much as most." It is hard to make a case that a man who spent his entire adult life communicating to others through the written and, frequently, spoken word, was a true hermit. At the very core of all of Thoreau's thinking is a bedrock assumption that man is basically noble and good, in potential if not in actuality. This core belief is not that of an antisocial misanthrope. Most of Thoreau's life was not spent living alone in a cabin.

THOREAU AS NATURE LOVER. For transcendentalists, as for the romantics who preceded them, nature was crucially important, a source of inspiration and a reflection of truths about the universe around which one could build a life. Ralph Waldo Emerson articulated this at length in his first book, *Nature*, published in 1836. Records show that Thoreau checked this volume out of the Harvard library in both April and June of 1837, his final year at college, and by the fall of that year, he had formed the lifelong connection with Emerson that was of such importance to him.

Robert D. Richardson's 1986 biography *Henry Thoreau* notes:

> Most interesting of all for Thoreau is Emerson's insistence in *Nature* . . . that the individual, in searching for a reliable ethical standpoint, for an answer to the question of how to live one's life, had to turn not to God, not to the *polis* or state, and not to society, but to nature for a usable answer. . . . The laws of nature were the same as the laws of human nature and that man could base a good life, a just life, on those.
>
> (pp. 21–22)

What this suggests is that nature is not, as some think, understood by Thoreau to be a thing outside of ourselves, something to idealize and preserve, to build a movement around, to rally around and support. At the outset of "Walking," he says,

> I wish to speak a word for Nature, for absolute Freedom and Wildness, as contrasted with a Freedom and Culture merely civil,—to regard man as an inhabitant, or a part and parcel of Nature, rather than a member of society. I wish to make an extreme statement, if so I may make a emphatic one, for there are enough champions of civilization; the minister, and the school-committee, and every one of you will take care of that.

The man who, in discussing his departure from Walden Pond, made disparaging reference to having beaten a small path down to the shore from his house, making the path a metaphor for the well-beaten paths or mental ruts of our minds, would surely sigh at the signs everywhere on the many paths ringing the pond today urging visitors to "Stay on the Paths" to help preservation efforts. Thoreau saw the refreshing, the restorative, the divine in nature, but also (most notably in the "Ktaadn" section of *The Maine Woods*) understood nature's savage indifference:

> Perhaps I most fully realized that this was primeval, untamed, and forever untamable *Nature*, or whatever else men call it, while coming down this part of the mountain.... It is difficult to conceive of a region uninhabited by man. We habitually presume his presence and influence everywhere. And yet we have not seen pure Nature, unless we have seen her thus vast, and drear, and inhuman, though in the midst of cities. Nature was here something savage and awful, though beautiful.

So, for Thoreau, nature is finally analogous to, even identical with, ourselves. To "go back to nature" implies a retreat, whereas for Thoreau, nature was an encounter, most often with himself. Thus, to make of Thoreau what we would consider a "nature lover" today, or even an "environmentalist," is to risk seeing a part (however important) as the whole.

THOREAU AS POLITICAL THEORIST: THE MAN OF CONSCIENCE. Thoreau the political theorist was the man who rang the Concord town bell to summon townspeople to hear a lecture on abolition or to harangue them about the virtues of the dangerous John Brown. This is the Thoreau of "Civil Disobedience" and the man who urged listeners and readers, when a law was unjust, to break that law, and said directly, "Let your life be a counter-friction to stop the machine." This is the Thoreau who

influenced Martin Luther King Jr. and Gandhi, and who seems a perfect fit for the backpack of any countercultural radical. It was as an outspoken abolitionist that Thoreau was probably best known in his own day, because of the widely printed "Slavery in Massachusetts" speech. Talking of the Boston judge who is ponderously deciding the constitutionality of turning an escaped slave back over to his owner, he is splendidly scornful:

> Does any one think that Justice or God awaits Mr. Loring's decision? For him to sit there deciding still, when this question is already decided from eternity to eternity... is simply to make himself ridiculous. We may be tempted to ask from whom he received his commission, and who he is that received it; what novel statutes he obeys, and what precedents are to him of authority. Such an arbiter's very existence is an impertinence. We do not ask him to make up his mind, but to make up his pack.

Thoreau ends this diatribe with the image of his finding a pure and beautiful water lily, which reminds him of "the purity and courage which are immortal." And this is typical of Thoreau's political writings, for he returns to the concrete and the personal again and again, and we see that the political begins and ends there for him. As he puts it in "Civil Disobedience," in a key passage that may be read as excusing us from diving headlong into a life of complete and unrelenting activism:

> It is not a man's duty, as a matter of course, to devote himself to the eradication of any, even the most enormous, wrong; he may still properly have other concerns to engage him; but it is his duty, at least, to wash his hands of it, and, if he gives it no thought longer, not to give it practically his support. If I devote myself to other pursuits and contemplations, I must first see, at least, that I do not pursue them sitting upon another man's shoulders.

Even in his own less globally aware time, Thoreau knew how difficult was the act of getting off another's figurative shoulders; he understood how paying taxes in Concord could support a war with Mexico, and would surely have been disquieted by wearing shoes produced by workers exploited in a country halfway around the world.

THOREAU AS EMBODIMENT OF EMERSON'S THEORIES. Thoreau is sometimes cast in Ralph Waldo Emerson's shadow, but the reverse also takes place. Thoreau is praised as a "doer," while Emerson is reduced to a mere "thinker," a mentor without the ability to truly act on his own beliefs. Emerson preaches self-reliance, while Thoreau practices it. Emerson buys the wood lot on the pond, but Thoreau lives there. Whichever has the ascendancy, the two are inextricably intertwined. As Van Wyck Brooks put it in his classic 1936 study, *The Flowering of New England*:

> The two agreed on so many subjects, always with an edge of difference, that one might well have supposed the relation between them was that of master and pupil. Emerson was fourteen years the elder; and it was true that Henry had acquired some of his traits and mannerisms: his handwriting, his voice, even his nose seemed to have gone to school to Emerson.

Emerson's influence on Thoreau is undeniable, but the schema of one "doer" and one "thinker" is demeaning to both men. They were not master and pupil, but friends and colleagues. The better-established Emerson helped Thoreau make his way in the literary world, and, beyond publishing practicalities, offered him intellectual and philosophical challenges that helped him to grow. Not only was Thoreau's cabin at Walden Pond built on Emerson's land, it was to Emerson's house that Thoreau moved when his two years at the pond ended. But the two Concord transcendentalists had important dissimilarities as well as likenesses, and their friendship was not all smooth agreement.

In Emerson's largely loving biographical sketch of Thoreau, for example, he manages to put his friend down as he praises him, noting that "with his energy and practical ability he seemed born for great enterprise and for command; and I so much regret the loss of his rare powers of action, that I cannot help counting it a fault in him that he had no ambition." Emerson also noted that "A certain habit of antagonism defaced his earlier writings,—a trick of rhetoric not quite outgrown in his later, of substituting for the obvious word and thought its diametrical opposite."

The reality is that the relationship between Emerson and Thoreau was a complex friendship, marked by notable ups and downs, rather than either a simple master-disciple or a scenario of the pupil realizing the teacher's theories. And there is at least one critical stylistic difference between them. Both men make pronouncements about the human condition, and neither refrains from telling readers how to live. Thoreau's advice, however, always comes grounded in concrete experience and is developed from particulars of his life and specific observations on what is going on around him, while Emerson's pronouncements are proclaimed most often as basic self-evident truths. Emerson's chains of logic move from broad statement to broad statement; Thoreau's move from concrete example to broad statement, back and forth continually.

THOREAU AS SCIENTIST. Thoreau has always been recognized as a keen natural historian and observer and was elected a corresponding member of the Boston Society of Natural History. He sometimes worked with the foremost earth scientist of his day, Louis Agassiz. He read extensively, especially in his later years, scientific texts ranging from the ancients (Aristotle was a favorite) to groundbreaking works such as Charles Darwin's *Origin of Species*. Robert D. Richardson's biography makes a strong case for his having turned to a "great new project" of natural history in his later years that was to be "a culmination of lifelong concerns, but [which also] break[s] new ground.... Thoreau's interests have shifted to a profound new focus on production and dissemination, in generation and creative effort. The center of *Walden* is the desire to be free. The center of the late work is the desire to connect. The movement is from economy to ecology." Lest we believe that his science blossomed only in these later years, note that one of Thoreau's earliest published works was the 1842 essay (printed in *The Dial*) entitled "Natural History of Massachusetts." It is possible that had he lived to complete the vast project that had him, in the last years of his life, reshuffling his journals and envisioning clarifications of Agassiz, Darwin, and others, it might well be as a scientist that Thoreau is best remembered. He was excited and energized about his direction in 1860, but the following year he developed the tuberculosis that led to his death in May of 1862.

THE SPIRITUAL THOREAU. Thoreau turns, again and again, to spiritual concerns in his writing. The final chapter of *A Week on the Concord and Merrimack Rivers* is full of discussion of a better, more real world, one with a spiritual dimension:

> It is easier to discover another such a new world as Columbus did, than to go within one fold of this which we appear to know so well; ... and still history accumulates like rubbish before the portals of nature. But there is only necessary a moment's sanity and sound senses, to teach us that there is a nature behind the ordinary, in which we have only some vague pre-emption right and western reserve as yet. We live on the outskirts of that region.

Not long after this passage, Thoreau builds a lengthy analogy between astronomy and an internal exploration, in the crescendo of which he tells readers,

If we can reason so accurately, and with such wonderful confirmation of our reasoning, respecting so-called material objects and events infinitely removed beyond the range of our natural vision . . . why may not our speculations penetrate as far into the immaterial starry system, of which the former is but the outward and visible type? Surely, we are provided with senses as well fitted to penetrate the spaces of the real, the substantial, the eternal, as these outward are to penetrate the material universe. Veias, Menu, Zoroaster, Socrates, Christ, Shakespeare, Swedenborg,—these are some of our astronomers.

Thoreau was strongly attracted to the Eastern sages and Eastern works that were becoming available in translations in his day, and his journals are replete with references to mystical writers. His tendency toward paradox and contradiction was surely abetted by this attraction, and though it may seem at times an annoying writer's tic, Thoreau makes it work.

Thoreau, it is crucial to note, always reaches for the spiritual while solidly grounded in the material, the particular, and the actual. Heaven is under our feet as well as over our heads, he tells us in *Walden*, and he never stays at an ethereal, spiritual plane for too long. Thoreau always wed his most cosmic truths to durable material realities, as when he pulls back from a broad discussion of philanthropy and tells the reader, at the end of the first chapter of *Walden*, to "Rescue the drowning and tie your shoestrings."

THOREAU AS PHILOSOPHER. The approach to understanding Thoreau as a philosopher looks at the connection of transcendentalist ideas to German idealism and traces Thoreau's responses to major philosophies, whether in his rejection of the English utilitarian philosopher William Paley or his embracing of the philosophy of the German Immanuel Kant. Certainly, Thoreau was a well-educated man of his day, and aware of existing within a matrix of philosophical constructs. He considered himself a transcendentalist, even if he sometimes took that designation lightly, as when he begins the "The Succession of Forest Trees" (1860), by saying, "Every man is entitled to come to Cattle-Show, even a transcendentalist; and for my part I am more interested in the men than in the cattle."

Thoreau tells us early in *Walden*: "To be a philosopher is not merely to have subtle thoughts, nor even to found a school, but so to love wisdom as to live according to its dictates, a life of simplicity, independence, magnanimity, and trust. It is to solve some of the problems of life, not

only theoretically, but practically." Thus, while Thoreau was widely read in philosophy, it was not reading about philosophy but living a philosopher's life that attracted him.

There is a moving entry in his journal for 16 January 1852, about Bill Wheeler, a town drunk and ne'er-do-well. After encountering Wheeler one winter morning, asleep in what might best be called a "den," Thoreau says,

> I came away reflecting much on that man's life—how he communicated with none; how low he lived, perhaps from a deep principle, that he might be some mighty philosopher, greater than Socrates or Diogenes, simplifying life, returning to nature, having turned his back on towns; how many things he had put off—luxuries, comforts, human society, even his feet [he had lost these to frostbite years ago]—wrestling with his thoughts. I felt even as Diogenes when he saw the boy drinking out of his hands, and threw away his cup. . . . I was not sure for a moment but here was a philosopher who had left far behind him the philosophers of Greece and India, and I envied him his advantageous point of view. I was not to be deceived by a few stupid words, of course, and apparent besottedness. It was his position and career that I contemplated.

THOREAU THE MASTER PROSE STYLIST. Whatever one's vision of Thoreau, it is through his strong, pithy writing that the vision is received. Thoreau himself said in his young adulthood, "I have chosen letters as my profession," and wrote daily, scrupulously editing and recasting. He also wrote about his own writing a great deal in his journal, often being quite critical, condemning for example his compulsive use of contradiction, his need to express everything as a paradox. But critical or not, Thoreau's attitude toward his writing never varied in his conviction that this was a serious calling. He saw the act of writing as a lens through which one could measure a life. A journal entry for 28 February 1841 makes this clear: "Nothing goes by luck in composition. It allows of no tricks. The best you can write will be the best you are. Every sentence is the result of a long probation. The author's character is read from title-page to end. Of this he never corrects the proofs."

But Thoreau pored over the proofs of his own writing endlessly, working *Walden* through eleven major drafts, and recasting his other work right up to the day of his death. In an entry a couple of weeks earlier in the same year (22 January), he discusses the value of his journal as material to be groomed and combed, while also showing the link between one's writing and one's thoughts and one's very being:

> To set down such choice experiences that my own writings may inspire me and at last I may make wholes of parts. Certainly it is a distinct profession to rescue from oblivion and to fix the sentiments and thoughts which visit all men more or less generally, that the contemplation of the unfinished picture may suggest its harmonious completion. Associate reverently and as much as you can with your loftiest thoughts. Each thought that is welcomed and recorded is a nest egg, by the side of which more will be laid. Thoughts accidentally thrown together become a frame in which more may be developed and exhibited. Perhaps this is the main value of a habit of writing, of keeping a journal—that so we remember our best hours and stimulate ourselves. My thoughts are my company. . . . Having by chance recorded a few disconnected thoughts and then brought them into juxtaposition, they suggest a whole new field in which it was possible to labor and to think. Thought begat thought.

THE FINAL ASSESSMENT

Out of this multiplicity of viewpoints, then, how should one read Thoreau? In fact, there is no requirement to select any one way over another, and readers are advised to be inclusive rather than exclusive in their understanding of this complex advocate of simplicity. When one first comes to Thoreau, one is drawn to his pronouncements along the lines of that in the opening chapter of *Walden*, in which he claims that "I have yet to hear the first syllable of valuable or even earnest advice from my seniors." A reader will respond better to a claim such as that which opens the second *Walden* chapter: "At a certain season of our life we are accustomed to consider every spot as the possible site of a house." Thoreau can be understood as a man who did what he wanted to do, one whose life and art were merged into a harmonious whole.

When Thoreau declares, early in *Walden*, that "The mass of men lead lives of quiet desperation," that phrase has an unpleasant ring of truth to it, but Thoreau himself was emphatically not desperate. His anecdote of the Indian basket weaver, in the first chapter of *Walden*, is apposite: the Indian, who has woven baskets, is shocked that the white men to whom he goes to sell them do not buy them.

> Having seen his industrious white neighbors so well off,—that the lawyer had only to weave arguments, and by some magic wealth and standing followed,—he had said to himself; I will go into business; I will weave baskets; it is a thing which I can do. Thinking that when he had made the baskets he would have done his part, and then it would be the white man's to buy them. He had not discovered that it was necessary for him to make it worth the other's while to buy them, or at least make him think that it was so. . . . I too had woven a basket of a delicate texture, but I had not made it worth any one's while to buy them. Yet not the less, in my case, did I think it worth my while to weave them, and instead of studying how to make it worth men's while to buy my baskets, I studied rather how to avoid the necessity of selling them.

However one chooses to view Thoreau, it is this call to "weave your basket" that must excite a reader. Whatever its delicate or rough texture, whether or not it is valued by your neighbors, weave the basket of your life. In all of his guises, Thoreau can be seen as an empowerer. He tells us again and again that it is possible to live in a proper way. That was his mission: to discern the proper way to live, and then to get as close to that as he could. As he articulates that proper way to live, he empowers readers by insisting, and by demonstrating, that it is possible. To the degree that we fall short of an ideal existence, Thoreau is an uncomfortable companion, to be sure. In the end, labels and categories do not matter. Readers will continue to connect with Thoreau, finding in him a call to the best of themselves.

[*See also* Autobiography: General Essay; Emerson, Ralph Waldo; Nature Writing: Poetry; Nature Writing: Prose; *and* Transcendentalism.]

SELECTED WORKS
BOOKS

A Week on the Concord and Merrimack Rivers (1849)
Walden; or, Life in the Woods (1854)
Excursions (1863)
The Maine Woods (1864)
Cape Cod (1865)
Letters to Various Persons (1865)
A Yankee in Canada, with Anti-Slavery and Reform Papers (1866)
The Journal of Henry Thoreau (1906)
The Correspondence of Henry David Thoreau (1958)
Collected Poems of Henry Thoreau (1964)
Faith in a Seed (1993)
Wild Fruits (2000)
Essays of Henry D. Thoreau (2002)

MAJOR ESSAYS

"Natural History of Massachusetts" (1842)
"A Walk to Wachusett" (1843)

"A Winter Walk" (1843)
"Ktaadn and the Maine Woods" (1848)
"Resistance to Civil Government" (1849)
"Slavery in Massachusetts" (1854)
"A Plea for Captain John Brown" (1859)
"The Succession of Forest Trees" (1860)
"Walking" (1862)
"Life without Principle" (1863)

FURTHER READING

Brooks, Van Wyck. *The Flowering of New England.* New York, 1936. Brooks's magisterial account of the literary explosion in New England (especially Concord) in the mid-nineteenth century has two chapters devoted to Thoreau as well as countless other references to him.

Dean, Bradley P., ed. *Faith in a Seed: The Dispersion of Seeds and Other Late Natural History Writings.* Washington, D.C., 1993. A lovely volume that emphasizes Thoreau's scientific side.

Dean, Bradley P., ed. *Wild Fruits: Thoreau's Rediscovered Last Manuscript.* New York, 2000. Dean introduces and arranges journal entries, which Thoreau was working toward combining before he died. A beautifully produced book with illustrations by Abigail Rorer.

Harding, Walter. *The Days of Henry Thoreau.* New York, 1965. An examination of Thoreau's life by the man considered by many to be the dean of Thoreau scholars.

Hyde, Lewis, ed. *The Essays of Henry D. Thoreau.* New York, 2002. Thirteen major essays, with an excellent introduction and annotations.

Parker, Herschel. Introduction and notes to Henry David Thoreau section. In *The Norton Anthology of American Literature.* Vol. 1. New York, 1979. pp. 1506–1816. A masterful presentation of the most generous serving-up of Thoreau in any anthology.

Richardson, Robert D., Jr. *Henry Thoreau: A Life of the Mind.* Berkeley, Calif., 1986. Meticulous account of Thoreau's life from his graduation from Harvard in 1837 on. Beautifully designed and illustrated by Barry Moser.

Rossi, William, ed. *Walden and Resistance to Civil Government.* 2d ed. New York, 1992. A Norton Critical Edition, this work features helpful accompanying reviews and essays.

Shepard, Odell, ed. *The Heart of Thoreau's Journals.* New York, 1961. The best one-volume gathering of Thoreau's journals, arranged chronologically, with an insightful introduction and section prefaces by the editor.

Thoreau, Henry David. *A Year in Thoreau's Journal: 1851.* Introduction by Daniel Peck. New York, 1993. Peck's introduction, notes, and suggestions for further reading make this a very helpful volume.

See also the article on *Walden*, immediately following.

HENRY DAVID THOREAU'S
WALDEN

by Cornelius Browne

In 1845, Henry David Thoreau began building a small cabin in the woods near the banks of Walden Pond, just outside Concord, Massachusetts. He took up residence there on 4 July, and he remained until September 1847. While Thoreau's claim in *Walden, or Life in the Woods* (1854)—"I went to the woods because I wished to live deliberately, to front only the essential facts of life, and see if I could not learn what it had to teach, and not, when I came to die, discover that I had not lived"—is justly famous, he went to the woods not only "to live deep and suck out all the marrow of life," but also to write. The first project on his mind was *A Week on the Concord and Merrimack Rivers* (1849), a narrative of a boat trip Thoreau had taken with his brother John in 1839. To the pond he brought with him a stack of books and his voluminous, posthumously published *Journal*.

THE BOOK

While *Walden* contains many scenes of vivid immediacy and deftly explores an individual's intimate connection to the nonhuman world, it is important to keep in mind that this book is a highly crafted document that underwent no less than seven revisions over a period of eight years. So linked with the account of Thoreau's sensual and intellectual interface with the physical and social worlds around him is a record of his artistic development into one of the most important writers and thinkers in the American tradition. *Walden* is often cited as one of the seminal books in the lineage of American environmental writing, and it performs a still-essential chunk of cultural work. Thoreau, in *Walden*, insists not only that human beings, animals, trees, and ponds exist in an ecological complex, but that cultural artifacts such as texts and railroad cuts also participate in our perception of ecological relationships and are, therefore, overlooked parts of any particular ecology. Our relationships with not only the human but also the nonhuman world—and the expression of those relationships in language—are interlocked. *Walden* explores both, and therein lies its continuing relevance and its power to elicit fascination from generations of critics, scholars, students, and readers from all walks of life.

Walden is an act of re-creation on many levels. It condenses Thoreau's two-year experience at Walden Pond into one year, and the eighteen essays, or chapters, that make up the book are loosely structured by the seasonal cycle, beginning and ending in the spring. The penultimate chapter, "Spring," is the emotional apex of the book, coinciding with that time of year when the world renews itself. Thoreau drafted much of the first half of *Walden* while at the pond. He revised again in 1848 and 1849 and the final revisions, including most of the material onward from chapter 9, "The Ponds," were drafted between 1852 and 1854. Much of the content is drawn from his *Journal*, reworked and reexperienced through meticulous revision.

During the early stages of composition, Thoreau was lecturing in Concord to help subsidize his experiment at the lake. The earliest chapters of *Walden* have their origins in these lectures, partly because when Thoreau spoke, the townspeople proved more interested in why he was living alone at the pond and how he lived there than in anything else he happened to say. To most of them, his experiment in living was incomprehensible. Why would one forsake town life and commercial enterprise to live in a shack in the woods? Even Ralph Waldo Emerson, one of Thoreau's most influential friends and mentors, complained in his funeral eulogy for Thoreau that

> Had his genius been only contemplative, he had been fitted to his life, but with his energy and practical ability he seemed born for great enterprise and for command: and I so much regret the loss of his rare powers of action, that I cannot help counting it a fault in him that he had no ambition. Wanting this, instead of engineering for all America, he was the captain of a huckleberry party.

Not even Emerson could fully understand what Thoreau was trying to do at the pond and in *Walden*; he could not foresee the profound mark Thoreau's work—and primarily *Walden*—would leave on American thought and culture.

TENSIONS AND MEDIATIONS

The lasting power of the book derives from Thoreau's persistent plumbing of both the relationship between the individual and the American *socia* and the deeply conflicted relationship between America's culture and its physical environment. The articulation of these tensions in *Walden* continues to resonate in the American imagination. In the opening chapter, "Economy," Thoreau authorizes himself to speak from the position of an extreme individualist. He writes: "In most books, the *I*, or first person, is omitted; in this it will be retained; that, in respect to egotism, is the main difference. We commonly do not remember that it is, after all, always the first person that is speaking. I should not talk so much about myself if there were any body else whom I knew as well." From the outset of *Walden*, Thoreau insists upon a radical individuality that at first glance seems incongruous with the concern that *Walden* as a whole holds out for both society and the environment in which it is embedded. There are, of course, parallel—and productive—tensions in this book: tension not only between the individual and society, but also between the desire to articulate nature and the inability of language to do so, and especially between Thoreau's philosophical idealism, which privileges the human mind, and his profound respect for the tangible reality of the physical world. Though these tensions are never resolved, they incite deep contemplation, often through rich metaphoric figures that attempt a rapprochement between the ideal and the physical, as in this transformation of the simple act of fishing from a boat on the pond at night:

> It was very queer, especially in dark nights, when your thoughts had wandered to vast and cosmogonal themes in other spheres, to feel this faint jerk, which came to interrupt your dreams and link you to Nature again. It seemed as if I might next cast my line upward into the air, as well as downward into this element which was scarcely more dense. Thus I caught two fishes as it were with one hook.

Walden is concerned throughout with the torsion of fishing for two things at once: a rooting of experience in a well-known physical place and the grounding of thought in the relationships between the experiencing subject and the physical environment.

The foremost symbol of this experiential and philosophical fishing is the lake itself; Walden Pond is an interface: "Lying between the earth and the heavens, it partakes of the color of both." Standing on the frozen surface of the pond, Thoreau notices that "Heaven is under our feet as well as over our heads." As human beings, our primary way of perceiving relationships is visual, and in *Walden* the physical world is allowed to gaze back at us as the pond becomes an eye: "A lake is the landscape's most beautiful and expressive feature. It is the earth's eye; looking into which the beholder measures the depth of his own nature." Although Thoreau rarely abdicates the subject position, he gives serious consideration to the earth as possessed of its own ability to see and even speak—the pond functions as both intermediary and interlocutor. As the pond ice opens in the spring, Thoreau listens attentively: "The pond does not thunder every evening, and I cannot tell surely when to expect its thundering; but though I may perceive no difference in the weather, it does. Who would have suspected so large and cold and thick-skinned a thing to be so sensitive?" The pond is alive, it has a skin, it is sensitive, and it communicates. Thoreau next aligns the lake with a technological artifact: "The largest pond is as sensitive to atmospheric changes as the globule of mercury in its tube." Interestingly, although Thoreau allows the technological into his discussion, the nonhuman sphere exists on a larger scale than the human: the pond is "the largest" and the mercury in the thermometer is a mere "globule."

TEXT, TOOLS, ECOLOGIES

However, certain technologies become magnified at key places in *Walden*—especially the technology of writing. Writing comes to be seen as participating in an ecology that links the physical environment, the writer, the reader, the past, and the future. Walden Pond, *Walden*, and the twenty-first-century libraries all over the world that shelve the book can be understood to participate in a certain ecology. Take Thoreau's classic description of the melting sandbank at the end of the "Spring" chapter. First of all, Thoreau acknowledges that the effect and frequency of the phenomenon he observes are heightened by human manipulation of the land: "The number of exposed banks of the right material must have been greatly multiplied since railroads were invented." Both human culture and the sandy soil profile of the land surrounding Concord enhance the spectacle of the sandbank, but the most productive interface in this passage is not the boundary between the human railroad and the environment through which it cuts, but the one that exists between Thoreau's imagination and the material of the sandbank.

Thoreau gives us the composition of flowing materials that "overlap and interlace"—a mixture of sand and clay—and names it a "hybrid product," a gathering together of separate things. In that it is part mineral, part vegetable; it responds to a mutual influence, obeying "half way the law of currents and halfway that of vegetation." Thoreau introduces here a more complex conceptual interface. With a reasonable amount of effort, we have little trouble perceiving a transitional zone between a forest and a field or a forest and a railroad cut. Thoreau, however, takes the idea a step further. He insists upon an interpenetration of mineral and vegetable that begins to defeat our received categories. He calls our basic morphologies into question. Thoreau brings his imagination to bear on the flowing sand and clay, and he is reminded of lichens and "of coral, of leopard's paws or bird's feet, of brains or lungs or bowels, and excrements of all kinds." The movement shifts from simple life forms to more complex animals, and then, surprisingly, his focus narrows to the internal organs of beasts, then to excrement in this strange meditation. It is a shift from external to internal and then to the internal made external by animal excretion. We forget we are looking at a sandbank. All manner of boundaries are rendered permeable—animal, vegetable, mineral, internal, and external—and the flowing sand becomes a conglomerate of life, down to the viscera that sustain life, and life's more disagreeable processes. Thoreau stands awed and tells us that "I feel as if I were nearer to the vitals of the globe, for this sandy overflow is something such a foliaceous mass as the vitals of the animal body. You find thus in the very sands an anticipation of the vegetable leaf. No wonder that the earth expresses itself outwardly in leaves, it so labors with the idea inwardly."

He also finds the earth expressive of language. The inside of a book, of course, also consists of leaves, and Thoreau literally begins to read the earth, connecting mineral, vegetable, and animal worlds with a playful and idiosyncratic sound and typographical symbolism:

> The overhanging leaf sees here its prototype. *Internally*, whether in the globe or animal body, it is a moist thick *lobe*, a word especially applicable to the liver and lungs and the *leaves* of fat ($\lambda\epsilon\iota\beta\omega$, *labor*, *lapsus*, to flow or slip downward, a lapsing; $\lambda o \beta o \varsigma$, *globus*, lobe, globe; also lap, flap, and many other words), *externally*, a dry thin *leaf*, even as the *f* and *v* are a pressed and dried *b*. The radicals of lobe are *lb*, the soft mass of the *b* (single lobed, or B, double lobed) with the liquid *l* behind it pressing it forward.

Thoreau is obviously delighted by the sounds of human language. Language becomes the primary focus, and the liquid *l* pushing the lobe is an obvious reenactment of

the flowing sand and clay. He sees into the internal workings of the globe and finds the alphabet. The very basic structure of Western language and expression—the alphabet—finds itself embedded in the bowels of the earth in a powerful expression of how human culture, writing, and world interpenetrate.

This whole passage is remarkable because it posits the earth in clearly textual terms, yet those terms are to a large degree indecipherable, a mixture of alphabets and hieroglyphics awaiting some Champollion (who helped translate ancient Egyptian scripts) to decipher them. In order to emerge from the sandbank, the text demands the geomorphology of the railroad cut, a witnessing subject, and interpreters. Thoreau as witnessing subject in this passage submerges the narrating self as it approaches the "vitals of the globe" and implicitly calls upon the reader to perform Champollion's labor. In this sense, Thoreau's primary experience in nature becomes a virtual experience contained in a symbolic text, and once the text is read, the experience contributes to the ongoing aesthetic experience of the reader. Just as the flowing sand became language and thus permeated Thoreau's experience, the art of *Walden* permeates the reader's experience, and in this way functions as a negotiated site between the physical world, the text, and experience. It is a giving and receiving across time and space, and it is one of the rare texts that seems in this way to constitute an ecology wherever and whenever the book is pulled from the shelf.

Thoreau makes effective use of other technologies as well. In the middle of winter, Thoreau—who often worked as a surveyor—decided to map Walden Pond and sound its bottom. As should be clear by now, his plumbing the depths of Walden Pond becomes endowed in the retelling with deep metaphorical resonance. Thoreau describes in painstaking detail his measuring of the pond, and he discovers that "what I have observed of the pond is no less true in ethics." He feels he can "draw lines through the length and breadth of the aggregate of a man's particular daily behaviors and waves of life into his coves and inlets, and where they intersect will be the height or depth of his character." However, as Thoreau chops holes in the ice through which to drop his line, water flowing out causes an optical phenomenon that deeply troubles his claims to be able to graph the geometry of human character, especially his own. He sees reflected "a double shadow of myself, one standing on the head of the other, one on the ice, the other on the trees or hillside." Perhaps Thoreau perceives the basic doubleness of his urge to understand both himself and the nonhuman world. But perhaps even beyond that, he sees his double shadow as something universal—inhabiting the pond, the shore, and the flora. Any approach to ultimate knowledge, either of our own minds or of the universe, is inevitably reflected, turned on its head, or shadowed. This is the irony of romantic idealism—one seeks the ideal with the sense that what one seeks is ultimately elusive.

Although Thoreau is, at least on some level, clearly aware of this quandary, his awareness does not impede his relentless search for the meaning of his relationships to the social and physical environment. Engaging one of his wild neighbors, Thoreau enters into a game of hide-and-seek with a loon. Interestingly, Thoreau shares certain qualities with the loon. While Thoreau uses a weighted line to find the bottom of Walden Pond, the loon "had time and ability to visit the bottom of the pond in its deepest part." The loon is one of the most powerful symbols of the wild in *Walden*; its call, or as Thoreau puts it, "his looning," is "perhaps the wildest sound that is ever heard here, making the woods ring far and wide." To possess the ability both to plumb the depths and to utter the wildest call in the woods was certainly an element of Thoreau's desire, and he and the loon, so far, have much in common. However, the commonalty between human being and wild creature cannot finally hold up. In his rowboat, Thoreau chases the loon about the pond, and the loon consistently and with little effort eludes him, "looning" back at him: "I concluded that he laughed in derision of my efforts, confident of his own resources." The chase around the pond in pursuit of the symbol of wild nature is doomed to fail, as is the effort to plumb the symbolic depths of the pond and human character with a weighted line, with human tools.

SIMPLICITY AND COMPLEXITY

However, his failing is by no means a failure. The trajectory of the entire book is not a straight line as seen through the surveyor's transit. It is a cycling back upon itself—like the seasons—re-creating and reimagining its central problem over and over again. In a sentence the problem—answerable only through infinite questioning—Thoreau poses is, "Why do precisely these objects which we behold make a world?" The profundity of this question is often lost on us through our tendency always to simplify the question. Thoreau refuses to simplify thought, and therein lie both his success and the lasting value of *Walden* for us and for the future. *Walden* encourages readers to ask the unanswerable question, to approach it from various angles, to stand it on its head, to

ponder its double reflections and its shadow, to look for it both in ourselves and in our environment. The tools at our disposal are legion. Thoreau wonders, "Who knows but if our instruments were delicate enough we might detect an undulation in the crust of the earth?" Well, our instruments are now delicate enough, yet we are not much closer to knowing why precisely the things around us make a world. For Thoreau and for us, the instrument that demands the most delicate attention is language. It is through language that we may come to know our world, and the rich metaphorical texture of *Walden* comes much nearer an answer than Thoreau's chains and weights and lines, than our super accelerators and space shuttles. He would have us exercise our language.

Now, to claim that Thoreau refused to simplify difficult philosophical questions poses another problem. As a way of living, Thoreau advocated strongly for a more simple way of life, "for a man is rich in proportion to the number of things which he can afford to let alone." Here again is a short passage that cuts to the center of *Walden*. He achieves mental complexity through physical simplicity. Without the dross of commercial life, Thoreau created a place for himself from which he could observe the world around him and his deepest feelings and thoughts. By eschewing, at least as far as possible, the things of the town, Thoreau installed himself in a physical and mental place where "every morning was a cheerful invitation to make my life of equal simplicity, and I may say innocence, with Nature herself." In this way,

> We must learn to reawaken and keep ourselves awake, not by mechanical aids, but by an infinite expectation of the dawn, which does not forsake us in our soundest sleep. I know of no more encouraging fact than the unquestionable quality of man to elevate his life by conscious endeavor. It is something to be able to paint a particular picture, or to carve a statue, and so to make a few objects beautiful; but it is far more glorious to carve and paint the very atmosphere and medium through which we look, which morally we can do. To affect the quality of the day, that is the highest of the arts.

In order to affect the quality of the day, people must be awake, and one of the prerequisites for the kind of questioning Thoreau insists upon is a wide-awake and aware citizenry. He felt that Americans were sleeping their lives away, that for all their hustling and bustling toward the goal of getting a better living, they slumbered, unaware that their highest quality was to elevate themselves and their culture in ways transcending material wealth. It should come as no surprise that the morning holds immense significance in a book whose author claims, alluding to Coleridge and Chaucer, that he does not "propose to write an ode to dejection, but to brag as lustily as chanticleer in the morning, standing on his roost, if only to wake my neighbors up."

Thoreau also discovered neighbors in the woods: "I found myself suddenly neighbor to the birds; not by having imprisoned one, but having caged myself near them." However, he was deeply concerned with his human neighbors. Of course, Thoreau felt that he could better understand and exercise his concern by living away from Concord and the tumult of everyday life in nineteenth-century America. In so doing he could create a place on the shore of the pond that would grant him access to the mysteries of the physical world and the central philosophical problem of how human culture can best live with, not against, its environment. *Walden*'s powerful evocations of the natural world tend to overshadow the fact that Thoreau visited town periodically, and that in small, regular doses, the gossip and chatter of the town "was really as refreshing in its way as the rustle of leaves and the peeping of frogs. As I walked in the woods to see the birds and squirrels, so I walked in the village to see the men and boys; instead of the wind among the pines I heard the carts rattle." Physical nature and human culture participate in the same ecology, and Thoreau did not seal himself off from his culture. His act itself and the book that resulted are a direct engagement with his culture.

RETREAT AND ENGAGEMENT

Thoreau's alternating retreat and engagement is political action, and the example of his complex relationship with the larger culture is an antidote for the oversimplification of the citizen's role in a democratic culture. Thoreau talks of an Irish immigrant drawn to the dream of America as the land of the golden goose, where butter, bread, and money are plentiful. Although denied these things, he still dreams of potential access to material wealth, to things. Thoreau counters, "But the only true America is that country where you are at liberty to pursue such a mode of life as may enable you to do without these, and where the state does not endeavor to compel you to sustain the slavery and war and other superfluous expenses which directly or indirectly result from the use of such things." Thoreau's retreat into a life of physical simplicity and mental complexity is an act that has great potential to undermine the structures that he understands as threats to ways of living that exercise the mind and respect the integrity of all life within and around it. Americans'

insatiable appetite for material things, the culture of consumption, does not contribute to a richer life; on the contrary, it contributes to a government that condones slavery and wages a war of aggression on Mexico.

Thoreau takes his commitment to a better America beyond thought and into political action when, "One afternoon, near the end of the first summer, when I went to the village to get a shoe from the cobbler's, I was seized and put into jail, because, as I have elsewhere related, I did not pay a tax to, or recognize the authority of, the state which buys and sells men, women, and children, like cattle at the door of its senate-house." In his essay "Resistance to Civil Government" (1849), he calls for revolution against a government that condones slavery and invaded Mexico. But Thoreau's revolution is not one conducted with arms. His revolt was to withhold his participation in a government he considered unjust by refusing to pay taxes, a nonviolent protest, and he claims:

> I know this well, that if one thousand, if one hundred, if ten men whom I could name,—if ten *honest* men only,—aye, if *one* HONEST man, in this State of Massachusetts, *ceasing to hold slaves*, were actually to withdraw from this copartnership, and be locked up in the county jail therefor, it would be the abolition of slavery in America.

This is Thoreau's idea of passive resistance, embraced by advocates of freedom from Mohandas Gandhi to Martin Luther King Jr.

Thoreau's two-year retreat from society was not then a withdrawal from his culture but a contribution to it. If Thoreau's move to Walden Pond was initiated as a contribution to his culture, and if the structure of society, including its laws, sought to impede such an act, as Thoreau certainly thought it did, then it became time to exercise resistance to that society, which not only enslaved some human beings because of their skin color but also oppressed others because of their nationality. His experiment at the pond was an attempt to re-create and redefine the responsibilities of a citizen in a democracy. That citizen must remain aware, must think, must act, and, most importantly, hold sacred the integrity of individual beings, both white and black, American and Mexican, human and nonhuman. This citizen is the ideal member of a democratic community and the better community that would follow, in whatever manifestation, democracy. Thoreau was forward enough to see that democratic culture would not be the final form into which people organized themselves; it was a step in the evolution of human attempts to live in meaningful relationships with their social and physical environments. He felt that his government, and his community's unthinking support of it, had begun to impede that evolution.

It is at this juncture that the individual and the *socia* begin to approach each other. Though individuals may periodically be at odds with their culture, individuals of integrity and awareness are the only ones who can fully contribute to an improved collective life. This is not the individualism prevalent in his culture and down to our own, whose central concern is to gather and concentrate material wealth unto particular people. Thoreau, of course, redefines wealth to mean the potential that human beings possess to improve themselves and their culture—to affect the quality of the day—in ways immeasurable by material wealth. *Walden* calls for a wealth of understanding and awareness, a heightened perception of the connections between all things. *Walden* is an exercise in bridging boundaries, and in its "Conclusion," Thoreau shares insights he acquired at the pond:

> I learned this, at least, by my experiment; that if one advances confidently in the direction of his dreams, and endeavors to live the life which he has imagined, he will meet with a success unexpected in common hours. He will put some things behind, will pass an invisible boundary; new, universal, and more liberal laws will begin to establish themselves around and within him; or the old laws will be expanded, and interpreted in his favor in a more liberal sense, and he will live with the license of a higher order of beings. In proportion as he simplifies his life, the laws of the universe will appear less complex, and solitude will not be solitude, nor poverty poverty, nor weakness weakness. If you have built castles in the air, your work need not be lost; that is where they should be. Now put the foundations under them.

There is a recognizable pattern here of stripping down in order to re-create, and for Thoreau, to move inward was to enable oneself to expand out into the astonishing complexity of the universe. By embracing, if even for only two years, some of the conditions most despised and feared by American culture—solitude, poverty, and weakness—one may be able to dust off the trivial and unearth the key to the universe and one's own dreams.

LOCATION

But Thoreau's wake-up call was not only to think. It was to act. By situating himself in a cabin in the woods, Thoreau—through intense concentration on his physical surroundings—was able to locate himself, and his words speak eloquently to a global, twenty-first-century culture

whose displaced citizens are legion. Thoreau cried, "We know not where we are," and one of the most important lessons *Walden* has to teach is the value of learning where we are, both physically and metaphorically. In bemoaning the state of his culture, Thoreau describes ours: "There is an incessant influx of novelty into the world, and yet we tolerate incredible dulness." We live in a consumer culture in which novelty is the coin of the realm, and we search for instant gratification. In its questioning of this consumerist ethic may lie the greatest piece of cultural work *Walden* can exert. *Walden* is not only the record of Thoreau's two years at the pond. His thought developed over many years of revision, and one can read those thoughts forming, testing, questioning, and maturing in the text. *Walden* is a meticulous re-creation of the experience Thoreau underwent in the woods. Instead of offering clear-cut answers that turn readers into consumers, it presents questions that transform readers into thinkers. Walden also demands that we spend time with its complexity, and the book repays manyfold the effort put into its reading. Maybe the most important thing *Walden* might cause us to do is shut off the television for a few nights in a row, join Thoreau at Walden by pulling *Walden* off the shelf, and thereby follow Thoreau's model and strive really to understand where we are, how we can affect the day, and why the things around us constitute our world. That in itself could drastically change the culture.

[*See also* Emerson, Ralph Waldo; Nature Writing: Poetry; Nature Writing: Prose; *and* Transcendentalism.]

FURTHER READING

Adams, Stephen, and Donald A. Ross. *Revising Mythologies: The Composition of Thoreau's Major Works.* Charlottesville, Va., 1988.

Anderson, Charles R. *The Magic Circle of Walden.* New York, 1968. Anderson reads *Walden* as a work of art, drawing distinctions between autobiography, nature writing, and social commentary. Although we now see these categories as more fluid and are less likely to agree that time and nature are escapable through the "immortality of art," this is a valuable study of Thoreau's literary aesthetic.

Buell, Lawrence. *The Environmental Imagination: Thoreau, Nature Writing, and the Formation of American Culture.* Cambridge, Mass., 1995. This is a groundbreaking, encyclopedic study of environmental writing in the United States, using Thoreau, and particularly *Walden*, as a baseline.

Burbick, Joan. *Thoreau's Alternate History: Changing Perspectives on Nature, Culture, and Language*. Philadelphia, 1987. Focusing strongly on *The Journal*, this study takes a rhetorical and cultural approach to Thoreau's work, arguing that the naturalist and the poet were, for Thoreau, the same thing.

Cameron, Sharon. *Writing Nature: Henry Thoreau's Journal*. New York, 1985. Important study asserting that Thoreau may have considered *The Journal* his life's greatest work.

Cavell, Stanley. *The Senses of Walden*. San Francisco, 1981. Situates *Walden* as an early American philosophical text.

Golemba, Henry. *Thoreau's Wild Rhetoric*. New York, 1990. Rhetorical study of Thoreau's writing. Examines a crucial element in Thoreau's work, silence. Silences create textual moments the reader is obliged to fill.

Myerson, Joel, ed. *Critical Essays on Thoreau's* Walden. Boston, 1988.

Peck, H. Daniel. *Thoreau's Morning Work: Memory and Perception in* A Week on the Concord and Merrimack Rivers, The Journal, *and* Walden. New Haven, Conn., 1990. Provocative phenomenological reading of Thoreau's major work that draws extensively on the philosophy of Maurice Merleau-Ponty.

Sattelmeyer, Robert. *Thoreau's Reading: A Study in Intellectual History with Bibliographical Catalogue*. Princeton, N.J., 1988.

Schneider, Richard J., ed. *Thoreau's Sense of Place: Essays in American Environmental Writing*. Iowa City, Iowa, 2000. Recent collection of essays by a group of environmentally focused critics, engaging Thoreau and nineteenth-century understanding of place.

Shanley, J. Lyndon. *The Making of* Walden. Chicago, 1957. Landmark study of Thoreau's composition of *Walden*.

Walls, Laura Dassow. *Seeing New Worlds: Henry David Thoreau and Nineteenth-Century Natural Science*. Madison, Wis., 1995. Situates Thoreau in the context of nineteenth-century science and examines the importance of Alexander von Humboldt's work as Thoreau sought to heal the growing breach between science and poetry.

See also the article on Henry David Thoreau, immediately preceding.

JAMES THURBER

by Pegge Bochynski

James Grover Thurber (1894–1961), essayist, artist, short-story writer, and playwright, is generally considered the greatest American humorist of the twentieth century. Thurber was born in Columbus, Ohio, on 8 December 1894, to Charles and Mary Agnes Fisher Thurber. His mother was a high-strung, theatrical woman who had penchant for practical jokes. His father, a mild-mannered political clerk, was often out of work, and the family frequently depended on handouts from Mrs. Thurber's wealthy parents. Despite financial hardship, Thurber's early boyhood was a happy one, although it was not without challenges. When he was six, Thurber was accidentally shot in the eye with an arrow by his older brother, William. Because his injured eye was not removed promptly, his other eye became inflamed, eventually leading to total blindness when he was at the peak of his career. His injury isolated him from his peers and caused him to withdraw into a fantasy world.

When Thurber was a teenager, he told his younger brother, Robert, that nothing would stop him from pursuing his literary ambitions. At the time, however, he displayed little of the talent that would later win him worldwide recognition. In the fall of 1913, he matriculated at Ohio State University. Insecure, shy, and unkempt, he was friendless until he met Elliott Nugent, a "man about campus" who encouraged him to become involved in school activities. Thurber joined the staff of the university newspaper, *The Ohio State Lantern*, as well as *The Sun-Dial*, a monthly student publication of which he became editor in chief. Thurber was also deeply influenced by Joseph Russell Taylor, an English professor, who instilled in Thurber a lifelong admiration for Henry James.

James Thurber.
(Courtesy of the Library of Congress)

During World War I, Thurber left college without taking a degree and became a code clerk at the American embassy in Paris from 1918 to 1920. Upon his return from France, he worked as a reporter for the Columbus *Dispatch*, where he wrote the Sunday half-page, "Credos and Curios." A mixture of humor, literature, and editorial opinion, the column allowed Thurber to experiment with parody, satire, and other literary forms. During his tenure at the *Dispatch*, he also wrote five plays for the Scarlet Mask Club at Ohio State, where he met his first wife, Althea Adams. Althea was very much like his mother—assertive, aggressive, and self-confident—and became a prototype for what was later termed the "Thurber woman."

After he and Althea were married in 1922, Thurber worked as a freelance writer. Ambitious for her husband, Althea encouraged Thurber to reach beyond the limited career opportunities Columbus offered, suggesting that they go to Paris. There Thurber worked on a novel, which he never finished. Eventually he obtained a job as a reporter for the Riviera edition of the *Chicago Tribune*. In 1926, his marriage on shaky ground and his future as a writer uncertain, Thurber returned to the United States alone. His homecoming marked an upswing in his career.

TALK OF THE TOWN

At a cocktail party in 1927, Thurber met E. B. White, who became a valued mentor, friend, and coworker. White introduced Thurber to Harold Ross, founder of the struggling *New Yorker* magazine, who hired Thurber to be the Sunday editor. Thurber wanted to write, not edit, and he did everything he could to undermine his editorial position. Finally Ross realized that he was misusing

Thurber's talent and "demoted" him to writer. Thurber began to thrive, as did *The New Yorker*. His humorous essays and short stories, along with his contributions to the "Talk of the Town" column, won him and the magazine much acclaim. In 1929, Thurber and White collaborated on what would be the first book for both of them, *Is Sex Necessary?* A spoof on the sex manuals of the day, the book parodies Freudian psychoanalysis and highlights the tension between the sexes. Thurber also unintentionally debuted as an illustrator in *Is Sex Necessary?* He was fond of doodling, and during the day he would fill his wastebasket with penciled drawings. White retrieved them, inked them in, and persuaded the publisher to include them in the book.

The tension between men and women portrayed in *Is Sex Necessary?* escalates into an all-out war in *The Owl in the Attic and Other Perplexities* (1931). Eight stories chronicle the marital missteps of Mr. Munroe, a timid, ineffectual, mechanically inept daydreamer, and Mrs. Munroe, his competent, self-assured wife. To an extent, the Munroes' contentious relationship mirrored the Thurber's deteriorating marriage. After an extended separation, James and Althea reconciled long enough to become parents of their daughter, Rosemary, but continued to live apart after her birth in 1931. They were divorced in 1935. During his marriage to Althea, Thurber developed the character of the beleaguered male in several short stories, until the "Thurber man" finally crystallized in "The Secret Life of Walter Mitty." Henpecked by a domineering wife and flummoxed by mechanical devices, Mitty retreats into a fantasy world where he can be anything he wants to be—the commander of a Navy hydroplane, a world-renowned surgeon, or a man fearlessly facing a firing squad. But by the time "The Secret Life of Walter Mitty" was published in 1939 in *The New Yorker*, Thurber had been happily married to Helen Wismer for four years. Although he continued to parody male-female relationships, the theme became less prominent in his later work.

With the publication of *The Seal in the Bedroom and Other Predicaments* in 1932, Thurber firmly established his career as an illustrator and cartoonist. In this collection of drawings, Thurber portrays the battle between the sexes visually instead of verbally. Women appear large, intimidating, and hostile, while men are small and wear bewildered, fearful expressions. Because of their surreal and primitive style, his drawings were often compared to the work of Henri Matisse and Pablo Picasso. Thurber became widely recognized as an accomplished humorist

a year later when he published *My Life and Hard Times* (1933). Based on his early years in Columbus, Thurber's mock autobiography is peopled with eccentrics, practical jokers, and other unconventional characters who are caught up in a fantastic, bizarre, chaotic world. The success of *My Life and Hard Times* enabled him to quit his job at *The New Yorker* and write full time.

As a successful author and illustrator, Thurber continued to produce best-sellers, including *The Middle-Aged Man on the Flying Trapeze* (1935), a collection of short stories that reveal a darker side of his humor; *Let Your Mind Alone!* (1937), a satire on popular psychology, intellectualism, and mechanization; and *The Last Flower* (1939), a parable in pictures about global devastation after World War XII. In 1939, Thurber also collaborated on play with Elliott Nugent, who had become a successful playwright, actor, and director. A domestic comedy with a serious twist, *The Male Animal* is the story of a college professor who jeopardizes his marriage and his job when he decides to read to his students a letter written by political radical Bartolomeo Vanzetti. The play was a resounding hit when first produced in 1940, made into a movie in 1942, and revived in 1952 during the McCarthy era when the right to free speech was under attack.

BLINDNESS AND FAME

Thurber's eyesight continued to worsen, and in 1940 he had five operations to improve his vision. The surgery was unsuccessful, and he became blind, which caused him to suffer a nervous breakdown in the summer of 1941. During his recovery, he composed first by laboriously handwriting his stories and later by dictation. For a while, he continued to draw with the aid of a Zeiss loop, a special magnifying lens, but was forced to give up illustrating in 1951. Despite his handicap, he published *My World—and Welcome to It* (1942), *Men, Women, and Dogs* (1943), and *The Great Quillow* (1944). *The Thurber Carnival*, published in 1945, was his most successful artistic and financial achievement. An anthology of his best short stories and cartoons over a fifteen-year period, the book won him universal critical acclaim and cemented his reputation as a masterful comic artist. *The Beast in Me and Other Animals* (1948), Thurber's first new collection of stories and sketches after he became blind, and *The Thurber Album* (1952), a nostalgic memoir of his life in Columbus, earned him further praise. In 1950, Thurber turned down an honorary degree from Ohio State University because the college had imposed a gag rule on visiting speakers. He did, however, accept similar honors from Williams

College in 1951 and Yale University in 1953. In 1956, *Further Fables for Our Time* was published and a year later earned the Liberty and Justice Award from the American Library Association. In 1958, Thurber was the first American writer since Mark Twain to be "called to the table" by the editors of *Punch*. When his stage adaptation of *The Thurber Carnival* opened on Broadway in 1960, he fulfilled a lifelong dream and debuted as a professional actor. He played himself for eighty-eight performances in the Tony Award–winning play before his health deteriorated and the show closed. *Lanterns and Lances* was published in 1961; Thurber died from a stroke on November 4 of the same year. His reputed last words were "God bless . . . God damn," a phrase that aptly sums up a life marred by tragedy and graced by success.

WORKS

Is Sex Necessary? (1929)
The Owl in the Attic and Other Perplexities (1931)
The Seal in the Bedroom and Other Predicaments (1932)
My Life and Hard Times (1933)
The Middle-Aged Man on the Flying Trapeze (1935)
Let Your Mind Alone! and Other More or Less Inspirational Pieces (1937)
The Last Flower (1939)
The Male Animal (1940)
Fables for Our Time and Famous Poems Illustrated (1940)
My World—and Welcome to It (1942)
Men, Women, and Dogs (1943)
Many Moons (1943)
The Great Quillow (1944)
The Thurber Carnival (1945)
The White Deer (1945)
The Beast in Me and Other Animals (1948)
Thirteen Clocks (1950)
The Thurber Album (1952)
Thurber Country (1953)
Thurber's Dogs (1955)
Further Fables for Our Time (1956)
Alarms and Diversions (1957)
The Wonderful O (1957)
The Years with Ross (1959)
Lanterns and Lances (1961)
Credos and Curios (1962)
Vintage Thurber (1963)
Thurber and Company (1966)
Selected Letters of James Thurber (1980)

Collecting Himself: James Thurber on Writing and Writers, Humor and Himself (1989)
Thurber on Crime (1991)
People Have More Fun Than Anybody: A Centennial Celebration of Drawings and Writings by James Thurber (1994)
Thurber: Writings and Drawings (1996)

FURTHER READING

Bernstein, Burton. *Thurber: A Biography*. New York, 1975. A thorough presentation of Thurber's life drawn from private papers and firsthand interviews. Quotes extensively from Thurber's letters.

Fensch, Thomas. *The Man Who Was Walter Mitty: The Life and Work of James Thurber*. The Woodlands, Tex., 2000. A personal perspective that draws on the work of biographers Holmes, Kinney, Grauer, and Bernstein. Addresses discrepancies in other biographies that the author claims to correct.

Grauer, Neil. *Remember Laughter: A Life of James Thurber*. Lincoln, Nebr., 1994. An accessible, candid account that demonstrates how Thurber's early life in Columbus, Ohio, profoundly shaped his later work.

Holmes, Charles. *The Clocks of Columbus: A Literary Career of James Thurber*. New York, 1972. An authoritative portrait that reveals the devastating effect of Thurber's blindness on his philosophy, behavior, and writing.

Holmes, Charles, ed. *Thurber: A Collection of Critical Essays*. Englewood Cliffs, N.J., 1974. Features articles on every phase of Thurber's literary career, including differing evaluations of his work. Includes helpful chronology and short bibliography.

Kinney, Harrison. *James Thurber: His Life and Times*. New York, 1995. The most exhaustive treatment of Thurber's life and work to date. Thoroughly researched, this study includes detailed appendices, notes, and a chronology.

Morsberger, Robert. *James Thurber*. Boston, 1964. The first full-length treatment of Thurber's literary output, quoting extensively from his works and putting them in thematic context.

Toombs, Sarah Eleanora. *James Thurber: An Annotated Bibliography of Criticism*. New York, 1987. Comprehensive survey of criticism from the 1940s to the 1980s.

ALEXIS DE TOCQUEVILLE

by Kathryn W. Kemp

The two-volume work *Democracy in America* (1835, 1840) grew out of a nine-month trip to the United States early in the career of a distinguished French statesman and writer, Alexis de Tocqueville. Convinced that democracy in some form would soon replace the old authoritarian systems of administration, he saw the United States as a case study of this new form of government. He wrote for a French audience, which he hoped would draw useful lessons from his observations of Jacksonian America. Tocqueville's book has become a standard resource for students of American history and government and has inspired many other works, including a documentary television series.

Alexis de Tocqueville.
(*Courtesy of the Library of Congress*)

EARLY LIFE

Tocqueville's aristocratic parents narrowly escaped execution while imprisoned during the French Revolution. This period of fear and uncertainty marked the psychological life of Tocqueville's family, particularly that of his mother, and probably contributed to his usually serious demeanor. The influence of the Jansenists, rigorously pious Catholics, also is evident in some of his thinking. Born in Paris on 29 July 1805, Tocqueville became a gifted scholar. After completing his education, he became a magistrate in April 1827. Three years later, when Louis-Philippe supplanted Charles X on the French throne, Tocqueville continued to serve in his post, but only reluctantly did he swear the required oaths of allegiance to the new monarch. He felt pessimistic about his future in the new regime, as did his close friend and colleague, Gustave de Beaumont. To avoid the turmoil of politics, the two jurists found it expedient in 1831 to seek a leave of absence. They would spend some months examining the innovative penitentiaries of the United States, institutions that employed full or partial solitary confinement in their attempt to reform inmates. In May, Tocqueville and Beaumont arrived in New York City. They stayed in America until the following February, not only looking at prisons, but also examining American culture as they toured through seventeen of the twenty-four United States.

TRAVELING IN AMERICA

Tocqueville and Beaumont spent a large part of their time in the cities of the North and East. But wherever they went—New York City, Boston, Philadelphia, Baltimore, Cincinnati, or New Orleans—"society" received them enthusiastically. They met many prominent people, including the former president, John Quincy Adams, and the sitting chief executive, President Andrew Jackson. Despite Tocqueville's often fragile health, the two men also traveled into wilderness areas around the eastern Great Lakes. They saw Niagara Falls, and a Chippewa guide took them as far as the settlement of Saginaw, Michigan. They also made a side excursion to Canada.

Travel in the 1830s presented huge difficulties, so their plan to go by riverboat from Cincinnati to New Orleans during the winter months of 1831–1832 required constant revision. Ice blocked the rivers, boats ran aground, and overland detours involved walking through deep snow or riding in rickety conveyances of all sorts. En route, Tocqueville became ill and the two travelers accepted the rough hospitality of a drafty log postal station at Sandy Bridge, Tennessee, where water froze in the cup before it was consumed. In spite of these difficulties, Beaumont nursed his friend back to health and they completed the journey to New Orleans. Arriving on the first day of the new year, they spent three days before beginning the return leg of the trip. In another twelve days they had arrived at Norfolk, Virginia, having bypassed important southern cities such as Charleston, South Carolina. They immediately sailed for Washington, D.C., where they called on President Andrew Jackson before sailing for Europe in February 1832.

WRITING *DEMOCRACY*

Very shortly after their return to France, Beaumont was dismissed from his position for political reasons. Tocqueville, who already had begun to contemplate a change in careers, resigned in protest. The two had coauthored a report on American prisons—*Du système pénetentiare aux Etats-Unis et de son application en France* (The U.S. penitentiary system, 1833)—that was well received, winning the 14,000 franc Montyon Prize of the French Academy (Académie française), and they evidently had planned to collaborate on a general study of the United States. However, their differing interests and literary styles soon led them to work on separate projects. Beaumont's novel, *Marie, ou l'esclavage aux Etats-Unis* (Marie, or slavery in the United States, 1835), explored race relations in America. For his part, Tocqueville decided to analyze the expansion of democracy in the light of American government, politics, and a few other, closely related topics. First, he made a brief visit to Great Britain to observe the beginnings of the Great Reform, which seemed to confirm his thesis on the inexorable expansion of democracy. He then retired to an attic in his parent's home to write the first volume of *Democracy in America*, employing two young Americans to translate and summarize documents. In the process, he referred to *The Federalist*, the classic essays supporting ratification of the U.S. Constitution, among other American works. When the first volume of *Democracy in America* appeared in 1835, its immediate success led to publisher to exclaim, "Well, it seems you've written a masterpiece!"

DEMOCRACY, VOLUME 1

Despite his aristocratic origins, Tocqueville had come to believe that democracy would supplant the older European systems. He wrote to enlighten the French, whose recent experiments with representative government had sometimes produced disastrous results. America was a testing ground for the new system, with important lessons to teach those who would hear them. His goal was to find those lessons and convey them to the people of his native land.

With a lawyer's attention to detail, *Democracy in America* begins by examining closely the mechanisms of the American governmental system. Jared Sparks, a noted American scholar of the day, introduced Tocqueville to the idea that American government has its foundation at the local level. Having spent a large part of his visit in the Northeast, he begins with the New England township and then moves his analysis up to the county and finally to the state and federal levels of government. Readers who are not enthralled by these details might prefer to move on to the second part of this volume, with its descriptions of American political culture in the era of Andrew Jackson. Most chapters or sections begin with a summary of contents, a practice now out of fashion, but very helpful to the reader. Among other topics, *Democracy* treats political associations, freedom of the press, and the "omnipotence of the majority."

Tocqueville agreed with James Madison, who had identified the "tyranny of the majority" as a great stumbling block for democracy in *The Federalist* number 51. Americans believe, Tocqueville wrote, "that there is more enlightenment and wisdom in a numerous assembly than in a single man....It is the theory of equality applied to brains." Although a majority is capable of error, Tocqueville observes that no obstacles "can retard, much less halt, its progress and give it time to hear the wails of those it crushes as it passes." He applied this theory to state governments and concluded, "If ever freedom is lost in America, that will be due to the omnipotence of the majority driving the minorities to desperation and forcing them to appeal to physical force."

The eighteenth and last chapter of this volume is "The Present and Probable Future Condition of the Three Races That Inhabit the Territory of the United States." A few of his observations seriously err, for example: "the Negro has no family; for him a woman is no more than the passing companion of his pleasures." Had Tocqueville and Beaumont's final swing through the South been less hasty, the author of *Democracy in America* might have observed that slaves did form strong family units in spite of the oppressive conditions of their lives. In another case, he states that Indians have not "borrowed one idea or one custom" from the whites, but goes on to report a few pages later that the Cherokee Nation enjoyed constitutional government and a newspaper published in its own language.

These shortcomings are insignificant in the face of Tocqueville's many penetrating observations of American society. For example, his pessimistic views on the future of the Indians were confirmed in the immediately ensuing years. The government had recently begun a program of

Indian removal. A footnote quotes some of the documents relating to the intrusion of whites into Cherokee territory in the Southeast, which was to end in Andrew Jackson's refusal to enforce U.S. Supreme Court rulings favorable to the Indians.

In this concluding chapter, Tocqueville points out that the presence of slavery seems to drag down the development of any place where it exists. He offers as evidence a voyage down the Ohio River. On the right bank, or northern side, all is flourishing, while on the left bank of the river sparse population and indolence dominate. Furthermore, the white southerner learns habits of command from birth, and as a result is less tolerant of frustration than his northern counterpart. Slavery, "so cruel to the slave was fatal to the master." However, having committed to the system, southerners cannot easily extricate themselves from it. Tocqueville doubted that the institution could last: "Either the slave or the master will put an end to it. In either case, great misfortunes are to be anticipated."

Although Tocqueville sees the obstacles facing the progress of democracy to be considerable, he is not without hope. In the face of various problems such as the tyranny of the majority or the effects of slavery, he sees reason to hope that the religious scruples of Americans, their tendency to form associations for mutually useful ends, and the presence of a free press will allow American democracy to meet its challenges.

BETWEEN VOLUME 1 AND VOLUME 2: MARRIAGE

In 1835 Tocqueville and Beaumont returned to Britain and Ireland, again observing the progress of democracy against the old, aristocratic system of rule. When he returned to France, Tocqueville ignored the preferences of his family to wed an Englishwoman, Mary Motley. Although she was neither aristocratic nor beautiful, she and Tocqueville had shared an intimate relationship for several years, and he was deeply attached to her. For the sake of the marriage, she became a Catholic.

In 1836 Tocqueville again received the Montyon Prize, this time for *Democracy in America*. The death of his mother in the same year put him in possession of the family estate of Tocqueville. The new Mme. de Tocqueville took a major role in managing the property and making a comfortable home there. Tocqueville and his wife, who had no children, divided their year between this country estate and Paris. Now, Tocqueville began to write the second volume of *Democracy*.

DEMOCRACY, VOLUME 2

Reflecting Tocqueville's own interests, the second volume has more to say about democracy in general than about America in particular. He expands on his theories, using the United States to provide illustration. For example, in a chapter titled "Some Reflections on American Manners," he ascribes the manners of the Americans to their democratic culture and then expands on those of the vanishing aristocracy: "The principal characteristics of the aristocracy remain engraved in history after its destruction, but the slight and delicate forms of its manners are lost to memory almost immediately after its fall." With typical realism he goes on to observe, "One should not attach too much importance to this loss, but it is permissible to regret it."

Volume 2 continues Tocqueville's argument that while democracy is the trend of the future, it is a future full of risk. In its concluding chapter he writes, "I am full of fears and hopes. I see great dangers which may be warded off and mighty evils which may be avoided and kept in check." He asserted his belief that democratic nations could be virtuous and prosperous if they had the will to be so.

Tocqueville reiterates his warning against the tyranny of the majority but adds to this the danger of other forms of tyranny taking hold. He contends that the old aristocratic system produced public spirited leaders, whereas democracy, by inducing citizens to pursue individual interests first, exposes the state to domination by unscrupulous groups and individuals. He also reemphasizes the importance of religious sentiment, associations, and the free press as bulwarks against such threats.

This volume of four sections examines intellectual movements, sentiments, mores, and political society over a span of seventy-seven chapters. Each chapter is a concise essay bearing a descriptive title, and essays with related topics are clustered together. All of this makes browsing by topic convenient.

TOCQUEVILLE AFTER *DEMOCRACY*

In 1841, a year after the publication of the second volume of *Democracy*, Tocqueville was elected to the Academy of Moral and Political Sciences, and after some intense politicking was voted membership in the French Academy in December. Although his second volume of *Democracy* aroused somewhat less enthusiasm than the first, Tocqueville was well launched into a public career.

He also continued to write on history and government and a good part of his works are preserved.

Tocqueville had been elected to the Chamber of Deputies in 1839, and soon spoke out in favor of the abolition of slavery in all French possessions. However, the author of *Democracy* also defended the pursuit of national greatness by means of conquest. After visiting Algeria, he wrote *Travail sur l'Algerie* (1841), in which he expressed his approval of the French colonization of Algeria while deploring the venality and incompetence of its colonial administration. He also stated his rejection of Islam as inferior to Christianity. (His sentiments on Hinduism were similar.) He believed that these colonized people should not enjoy the full rights of French citizens.

After the Second Republic fell in 1848, Tocqueville won a seat in the Constituent Assembly, where he served on the committee to write a new constitution. He was elected to the new Legislative Assembly in 1849 and within a month was appointed minister of foreign affairs, an office he held for five months. At this time he began to suffer seriously from tuberculosis. When he opposed Louis-Napoleon's coup in December 1851, the new regime imprisoned him as one of a large group of representatives who had opposed the change. Writing in the *London Times*, he anonymously condemned the new government. He resigned from a local elected office rather than take the oath of allegiance required by Louis-Napoleon. Deprived of an active political role, he turned again to writing. *Souvenirs*, his memoir of the revolution of 1848, investigated the events that had transformed the French government as well as Tocqueville's personal career and pointed out continuities that survived the changes.

As his health continue to deteriorate, Tocqueville continued to write. In 1856 he published, simultaneously in French and English, his last major work, *L'Ancien Régime et la révolution*. This account of the coming of the French Revolution succeeded and he began to research a sequel. However, his health, always poor, now became seriously impaired. He went to Cannes for reasons of health in 1858. On 16 April 1859 he died there only a few days after a final visit from his lifelong friend and traveling companion, Gustave de Beaumont. He is buried in Paris.

ENDURING INFLUENCE

In the United States, translations of *Democracy in America* continue to enjoy a prestige only slightly less than that of the actual founding documents of the nation. Politicians, jurists, clergymen, and educators all turn to its pages for explanations of how America works, or at least for arguments to bolster their various political and social positions. So respected is its reputation that it has generated at least one apocryphal quotation, "America is great because it is good; if it ceases to be good it will cease to be great." Even presidential speechwriters have invoked this pious phrase, attributing it to the man who never wrote it. His actual words and thoughts remain as valuable tools for a deeper understanding of the nature of democracy in America and throughout the world. *Democracy* has been in print since the appearance of its first volume in 1835, and translations may be purchased in volumes of all qualities, from elegant, leather-bound editions to thrifty paperbacks. His other major works have been translated into English, although some may not always be found. Publication of his complete works has added up to about thirty volumes and is still in progress.

FURTHER READING

Jardin, Andre. *Tocqueville, a Biography*. Translated by Lydia Davis with Robert Hemenway. New York, 1988. A thorough and readable biography that assumes a modest knowledge of French history on the part of the reader.

Pitney, John J., Jr. "The Tocqueville Fraud." *The Weekly Standard* (13 November 1995). Traces the history of the spurious quotation about American goodness and greatness.

Tocqueville, Alexis de. *Journey to America*. Translated by George Lawrence. Westport, Conn., 1981. A revised edition of Tocqueville's notebooks from his American journey.

TRANSCENDENTALISM

by Peter Coviello

In September 1836, the same month Harvard celebrated its second centennial, several men assembled in the Boston home of George Ripley, a Unitarian minister, the publisher of *The Christian Examiner*, and a Harvard graduate. Gathered with him were other youngish men, affiliated in some fashion with Unitarianism or Harvard or both: Frederick Henry Hedge, Convers Francis, James Freeman Clarke, Orestes A. Brownson, Amos Bronson Alcott, and another Harvard Unitarian who had only four years earlier resigned his pulpit, Ralph Waldo Emerson. The group, which went on to meet intermittently and informally over the next years, would later include among its participants Theodore Parker, Christopher Pearse Cranch, William Henry Channing, Henry David Thoreau, Nathaniel Hawthorne, and Jones Very, as well as Margaret Fuller, Sophia Ripley, and Elizabeth Peabody. (The inclusion of women was, in its time, notably progressive.) It was, as Alcott described it, "a company of earnest persons enjoying conversations on high themes and having much in common." Though Emerson always referred to the group as the Hedge Club—convened when Hedge was in to Boston from his parish in Bangor, Maine—it would come to be known, more lastingly, as the Transcendental Club.

Transcendentalism was in certain respects the first indigenously American intellectual movement of any heft—the first, at least, to inspire directly succeeding generations of American intellectuals and any number of literary monuments. (Writers as diversely inclined as Thoreau, Whitman, and Hawthorne, and later Wallace Stevens, Marianne Moore, and John Ashbery, might all be seen to work in and upon a tradition whose point of origin is Emersonian transcendentalism.) It is entirely appropriate too that the transcendentalist movement should have begun in a setting as unstructured and informal as a discussion group. To the degree that transcendentalism can properly be called a "movement" it was so only briefly (its heyday was 1836–1850) and perhaps then only retrospectively. The varied salvos of its participants followed no systematized program, took up a great diversity of concerns, and were coordinated with each other only loosely. The transcendentalist cause itself sprang from primarily religious crises, though it branched out quickly to include matters of philosophy, education, social and political organization, and aesthetic practice. The coherence attributed to an entity as untidy as transcendentalism is in large part a function of the unity of its cumulative effect: whatever else it may have done, transcendentalism revolutionized American literary endeavor.

RELIGION AND PHILOSOPHY

The year 1836 was catalytic, the transcendentalists' oft-cited *annus mirabilis*. The ferment of the previous years—wracked soul-searching by a handful of young Unitarian ministers who found themselves increasingly uneasy with the creed they were meant to profess—realized itself at last in a veritable torrent of writing. No less than five major manifestos appeared in 1836: Ripley's *Discourses on the Philosophy of Religion*, William Henry Furness's *Remarks on the Four Gospels*, Alcott's *Conversations with Children on the Gospels*, Brownson's *New View of Christianity, Society, and the Church*, and Emerson's *Nature*. These works confronted matters of theology, religious orthodoxy and institutional structure, art, aesthetics, education, and epistemology. A number of journals were established as well with editors sympathetic to the New Thought: most famously, the *Dial*, edited by Emerson and Margaret Fuller, but also the *Boston Quarterly Review*, *Western Messenger*, *Massachusetts Quarterly Review*, *Spirit of the Age*, and others. Compared with this great and varied outpouring the proceedings at Harvard's centennial were, to the transcendentalists who observed them, pitiably sterile.

Though resistant by design to formulae and creeds, transcendentalism could nevertheless claim for itself a core set of presumptions. At its root transcendentalist thought was defined by its turn away from the strictures of both eighteenth-century rationalism and New England Calvinism toward a contrary belief in the limitless indwelling potential of individual human nature—a potential not only for good but for expansive knowledge and revelation, a direct experience of divinity itself. As against the skeptical empiricism of John Locke, which tended to view the human self as but a compendium of its empirical impressions, transcendentalism postulated a self of boundless interior depth and expanse, alive to whole worlds beyond the merely empirical. They believed in "the infinitude of the private man," in Emerson's ripe phrase. For the transcendentalists, the ever-unfolding world was bathed in the light of God's creative grace; human nature was not fallen from that grace but an integral part of it, an extension and functioning microcosm of the divine structuring of the world. The ravishing self-renovations of divinity (which had been so important to Calvinism and the First Great Awakening) were in this sense not only available to but, in the transcendentalist view, immanent within human nature. A full acknowledgment of this fundamental truth would work revolutions, the transcendentalists believed, in the religious as well as artistic, social, and political order of things.

Transcendentalism was thus a species of imported romanticism: a means of denouncing both the narrow empiricism of Locke and the unbending Calvinist doctrine of humankind's natural depravity. Tellingly, it was a philosophical romanticism first given wide hearing in America through the work not of any philosopher but of a poet. In 1829 a Calvinist intellectual from Vermont named James Marsh brought out an edition of Samuel Taylor Coleridge's *Aids to Reflection* of 1825. Here Coleridge labored through categories derived from Immanuel Kant to produce a vision of human faculties at once broader than empiricism seemed to allow and more amenable to experiences of vision and inspiration. At the center of Coleridge's argument was a distinction between two intellectual faculties: the "understanding," taken to be a perceptive faculty that responds to and processes phenomena of an observable, empirical kind; and "reason," which enabled the mind to apprehend intuitively the extra-empirical, the universals that underlie and give structure to the phenomenal world. ("Man is conscious of a universal soul within or behind his individual life," Emerson wrote in *Nature*. "This universal soul, he calls Reason: it is not mine, or thine, or his, but we are its; we are its property and men.") Though initially employed mostly as a term of abuse, meant to disparage the obtuseness and airy abstraction of Emerson and his circle, the very designation "transcendental" comes from Kant's 1788 *Critique of Practical Reason*, in which he considers the question of these extra-empirical universals and our mode of knowing them: "I call all knowledge *transcendental* which is concerned, not with objects, but with our mode of knowing objects so far as this is possible *a priori*." Coleridge adapted the Kantian belief in a world of knowledge beyond that of the brute senses—Kant's idealism—and used it to defend against the aridity of empiricism: its tendency toward bloodless rationalism, an increasingly mechanistic worldview, and a cold reduction of the human to its accumulated sense data.

It was through Marsh's edition of Coleridge's text that many future transcendentalists came to Kant and, through Kant, to Goethe, Fichte, and Schelling. The provenance of these ideas—their arrival in America in the work of an English poet—is consequential, though not (as is often suggested) because the American philosophical efforts that would follow were therefore pedestrian or shallow, merely second-hand. Rather, the influence of the literary, of an essentially aesthetic disposition toward intellectual concerns, was to be among the primary distinguishing marks of transcendentalist thought throughout its course. Kantian idealism, and specifically the belief in a human faculty responsive to phenomena beyond the strictly empirical, undoubtedly prompted the transcendentalist revolution. But these ideas did not arrive from the Continent without significant refraction.

Part of what refracted such philosophical matters was their embeddedness, for the transcendentalists, within more local ecclesiastical disputes. It is often said that transcendentalism was a fundamentally religious movement, and that its origins lay more in the conflicts of early nineteenth-century Protestantism than in the history of philosophy. Perry Miller, a seminal and revered scholar of the movement, contended in 1950 that "the Transcendental movement is most accurately to be defined as a religious demonstration." The issue is complicated, though, by the fact that the doctrinal conflicts of the early part of the century were not solely institutional but were instead deeply entangled, in the minds of the transcendentalists, with the specifically philosophical dilemmas into which Kant and others had granted them fresh insight. In a more narrow sense, the religious derivation of transcendentalism is clear: it stands as one major response to the steep post-Enlightenment decline of Calvinism. Without injustice one could describe transcendentalism, at least in its early stages, as a reform movement within the Unitarian church of New England. Unitarianism was itself already a reform movement of sorts, a creed at whose core was a faith in the improvable, fundamentally benevolent moral nature of humankind, a belief directly at odds with the orthodox Calvinist view of the innate moral depravity of the individual. The decline of Calvinist authority in New England, and of the forbidding God and demon-haunted worldview of Calvinist theology, was precipitous, and Unitarianism was part of that declension. As Orestes Brownson put it, "Unitarianism has demolished Calvinism, and made an end in all thinking minds of everything like dogmatic Protestantism."

By the early 1830s, many younger Unitarians were eager to push the reformist impulse further and to carry into the future the spirit of the work of William Ellery Channing, an early spokesman for New England Unitarianism whose eloquent defense of the amplitude of human possibility, and of the strength of individual insight and intuition over programmatic institutional dogma, made him a figure of heroic proportions among thinkers of Emerson's generation even when they would depart from him. (Emerson famously called Channing "our bishop.") To that later generation, Unitarianism had grown stale and ossified, bound by its own invidious codes and strictures. "It is negative, cold, lifeless," Brownson said. Philosophically the younger generation thought Unitarian doctrine remained too tightly in the grip of an outmoded and delimiting empiricism. Unitarians had initially distanced themselves from what they took to be the superstition and demagoguery of Calvinism by turning to John Locke and the rationalist faith in the world of empirical phenomena he professed. Locke, for the forward-thinking Unitarians, promised a way to bring Christianity out of the dark ages and into step with the great intellectual advances of the Enlightenment. By the 1830s the transcendentalist turn to Kantian idealism was thus also a way of restoring to Unitarian belief an element it had lost in its progressivist break from Calvinism: it spoke to the individual's capacity for intuitive revelation and a direct experience not merely of the empirical but of the divine. The transcendentalists, we could say, returned to the Calvinist ideal of an individual soul ravished by the in-flooding of God's immediate presence—an ideal made newly accessible by the popular revivalism of the Second Great Awakening—while attempting to strip away all the institutions or doctrinal systems that might mediate between the individual and his or her direct experience of divinity. Armed with the tools of Kantian idealism and anti-Calvinist optimism, the new generation hoped to separate themselves at last from what Emerson called "the corpse-cold Unitarianism of Brattle Street and Harvard College."

Of course, the details of these controversies can seem quite remote to readers of Emerson or Thoreau or Fuller, and even to readers of their more contemporary commentators. In the work of Theodore Parker especially, but also William Henry Channing (W. Ellery's nephew) and William Henry Furness, debates over matters of theology and the face of modern Protestantism were indeed given more direct consideration than in many of the writings that are today more widely renowned. More recent scholarship too has tended toward an interest in the social and political extensions of the transcendentalist cause, emphasizing the often knotty relations of its participants to abolitionism, feminism, and a proto-Marxist communitarianism, perhaps as a corrective to the long-standing critical preoccupation with what Perry Miller insisted was the movement's "inherently religious character." But the concerns of religion and philosophy, of politics and aesthetics, were in the 1830s not so removed from each other, and it was in fact one of the signal strengths of the transcendentalist generation to see in these apparently separate spheres an elemental confluence. If the individual was indeed a microcosm of God's creative divinity, if the extent of human possibility was truly limitless, and if the individual possessed within herself or himself the faculties to know the world's divinity firsthand, then what was most needed, the transcendentalists believed, was a sweeping away of all the inherited vocabularies and calcified forms of order that ran contrary to these facts and which impaired any individual's access to revelation. Such an upheaval necessarily would be at once religious, philosophical, and political.

LITERATURE AND POLITICS

And, as it proved in the event, it would be literary. To be sure, many of the members of the transcendentalist circle involved themselves in more or less direct social action and would not have thought of themselves as mere literati or aesthetes. Theodore Parker, author of *A Discourse of Matters Pertaining to Religion* (1842) and an unapologizing firebrand, was not alone in worrying over Emerson's relative political timidity, nor was Margaret Fuller (though she revered him) in thinking that Emerson "always seemed to be on stilts." Considered apart from the works now taken as most representative—*Nature*, *Walden*, and later Whitman's *Leaves of Grass*—the transcendentalist movement might fairly be placed among the 1830s collection of stridently reformist "causes." Parker and James Freeman Clark sought to replenish Protestantism and argued passionately for institutional as well as doctrinal reform within Unitarianism. Reformist ambitions of still broader reach were nurtured at Brook Farm in the 1840s, an experiment in a kind of agrarian communitarian living directed by George Ripley, which for all its high-flown utopianism was more successful than tends to be remembered. Hawthorne modeled the unhappy commune of *The Blithedale Romance* (1852) after Brook Farm, and his mordant portraits, along with a later reminiscence by Emerson and the utter failure of a similar venture at Fruitlands, have obscured the fact that, before the major fire that caused its ruin, the enterprise at Brook Farm lasted a full six years (1841–1847), even after its sharp turn to the doctrines of Fourierism under Albert Brisbane in 1843. Nor were more immediately contentious issues brushed aside. As Thoreau's essays in defense of John Brown eloquently and angrily testified, transcendentalism, though habitually wary of organized philanthropy, could indeed make common cause with abolitionism, especially as the latter sought to disparage the corrupt authority of governments and political parties in favor of the preeminence of individual moral conscience. It was on these terms that Emerson himself came, slowly but decisively, to the antislavery cause.

There was more. Lifelong reformers of American education, Bronson Alcott and Elizabeth Peabody came into the transcendentalist circle as founders of an experimental school in Boston, where the pedagogical program made ampler room for the child's intuitive intellectual gifts and right to unrestricted inquiry than was elsewhere allowed. Margaret Fuller too could be counted as a reformist educator, though this would be to narrow the scope of her prodigious intellect. Her crowning achievement, *Woman in the Nineteenth Century* (1845), brought the freshness and rigor of transcendentalist thought to the still-protean arena of American feminism, arguing for a vision of women's intellect as unbounded and vast with potential as men's and against the customs of education and social life that would deny women such equality. Abolitionism, education reform, feminism, communitarianism, utopian agrarianism: if transcendentalist thinkers were not at the defining center of all these movements—if they were not indispensable to their operation—still it is undeniable that they played an important part in matters

of considerable moment in nineteenth-century America. These lived commitments were more than sufficient to temper, at the very least, accusations of a political quietism or apathy endemic to transcendentalist thought.

Such accusations, though, are not entirely without cause. They emerge largely in relation to two basic facts. First, it is clearly in the realm of the literary that transcendentalism's mark was ultimately the deepest, that its influence has been the most pronounced and its thought the most enduringly incisive. That the first great realization of American literary ambitions occurred directly on the heels of transcendentalism (in the works of Hawthorne, Melville, Whitman, Dickinson), and was in no small measure inspired by it, did much to solidify the movement's reputation as an essentially literary enterprise. Perhaps more consequentially, though, in much of the work itself there is a vein of real ambivalence with respect to many types of explicitly civic action—a wariness and suspicion that are difficult to separate from the works' more unwavering positions of aesthetic advocacy. What transcendentalist writing tended at crucial moments to reveal was not a seamless coincidence but rather an unresolving tension between literary or aesthetic principles and the imperatives of the broader social world. In works whose declared intentions were often otherwise, transcendentalist authors found themselves again and again underlining the potentially poor fit between aesthetic and political ideals. Transcendentalist thought was from the first shaped by literary sensibilities and ambitions, as we have seen, and Emerson's were chief among them. This did not in any way prevent transcendentalists from venturing formidable speculation upon ethics, epistemology, religion, politics, and much else. It meant only that those speculations were given shape—some would say enlivened, others disfigured—by minds schooled in and tending to aesthetic preoccupations. The cognitive tensions inhering in this approach are among transcendentalism's most difficult and potent legacies to American intellectual life.

The literary disposition of the movement makes sense at several levels. Most obviously, the transcendentalist circle relied immensely, for its real-world effects, upon persuasive language. Their primary formats were the printed word

Elizabeth Peabody.
(*© Oscar White/Corbis*)

and the lyceum address, both avenues in which formal mastery and a capacity to dazzle with eloquence were at a high premium. And in the post-Calvinist climate of antebellum New England, where the moral authority of the individual was coming more and more to eclipse that of any collective or external regulatory body, the inspired utterance of the lone individual was itself ripe for elevation to new and exhilarating levels of prestige. Compounding this was the newly prominent romantic ideal—on clear display in Coleridge—of the artist as solitary genius, inspired by private vision and possessing a unique access to revelation and its quicksilver truths. Finally, a key element of transcendentalist thought itself involved the unceasing evasion of the doctrines of the past. "God himself culminates in the present moment," Thoreau wrote in *Walden*, suggesting an intellectual project that demanded the fashioning not only of new thought but of new modes of expression, a language uncaptured by the static vocabularies of the past and therefore more alive to inchoate possibilities and new emergences. "Every new relation," Emerson wrote in "The Poet," "is a new word," and it was the poet's task to slip free of the world's established usages and give expression to that glimpse of the unperceived. ("The sign and credentials of the poet are," according to Emerson, "that he announces that which no man foretold.") If the transcendentalist project was initially to renovate American religion—and, along with it, a whole host of political and social institutions—the terms of its own argument dictated that it could do so only by refusing to speak in the hardened trade languages of religion, philosophy, or politics. The language of art, by its nature unpredetermined and constantly self-transforming, was an ideal vehicle.

MAJOR TEXTS

For all of this, the most significant transcendentalist achievements proved to be in neither fiction nor poetry (nor, for that matter, in music or painting). There were in the circle several able poets: Christopher Cranch, William Ellery Channing II, Thoreau and Emerson themselves, and most notably Jones Very, a composer of striking lyrics of religious ecstasy and devotion and a man many thought demonstrably insane, who was embraced by the transcendentalists for the very madness that to them seemed only to corroborate his genius. But the poetry of Whitman—clearly inspired by Emersonian principle but energized by far too diverse a range of impulses to be called strictly transcendentalist—would soon overshadow all this work. Hawthorne was easily the most successful writer

of fiction within the circle, but as his sardonic, skeptical, and witheringly anti-utopian works kept demonstrating, he would not have considered himself a practicing transcendentalist by any means. As it transpired, the strongest transcendentalist work was accomplished in nonfiction prose: in the essay, the article, the address. All the practitioners were capable of eloquence, but the movement's most lasting achievements were authored by Emerson, Thoreau, and Fuller.

The essays of Emerson and Thoreau, so long set beside one another because of the close attachment between the two men, do indeed make a revelatory pairing. In matters of style and even of intellectual temperament, the two were significantly different writers. Far more confidently than his mentor Emerson, Thoreau was at home in the pace and pattern of narrative; he could be anecdotal as well as polemical. His style is elegant and learned, dense with classical reference, but also plainspoken and, for all his satirical barbs, strikingly genial and familiar. Even with his fondness for classical allusion, his exacting descriptions of all manner of natural phenomena, and his penchant for extended metaphor, Thoreau presented himself in prose that is notably low in indirection and ornament. An amiable accessibility invests even the preachier moments of *Walden*, his triumphant narrative memoir of 1854. In contrast, Emerson's writing can seem somewhat prickly: it followed more circuitous routes, shifted more precipitately between the registers of the literal and the figurative, and tended to accelerate away from objects and toward abstract thought with disorienting rapidity. His prose could be every bit as compact and lucid as Thoreau's, and his gift for aphorism is without parallel in American letters; but in the darting movements of thought, the paratactic turns and abrupt contractions between expansiveness and compression, Emerson's prose set itself apart from that of his peers. Beginning with the essays that *Nature* comprises, and equally in his first and second series of *Essays* (1841, 1844), Emerson's work persistently traced the movement of a mind working everywhere to evade the settled thought: his arguments refused to be orderly and, despite their density, proceeded with an unhurried indirection. He explored an idea by worrying it, often from a quick succession of perspectives. These practices did not aim at obscurity—though Emerson was frequently accused of it—but constituted instead a kind of tactic. They came together as part of his attempt to fashion a mode of expression nimble enough to capture movements of thought *away* from certainty and formula: in Emerson's own terms, to make language itself move at the speed of nature.

In the differences of style between Emerson and Thoreau we see also real differences of disposition: most elementally, the difference between Thoreau's patient and close-grained approach to nature and the example of its particular objects, and Emerson's more insistently abstracting vision of nature as vast unfolding metaphor, the analogue to and ideal of human thought. But these differences do not displace the essential points of congruence between them. In form and content, the shared aim of their works was individualist, utopian, and expressivist: a truer self-relation, enabled both by a keener understanding of the conventionalities and habituated practices that stand between ourselves and the world and by the cultivation of a mode of address to that world that is unconstrained, vital, new. "Whoso would be a man must be a nonconformist," Emerson wrote, and it is a sentiment that echoes throughout the defiant postures and sly satire of *Walden*. But for both Emerson and Thoreau nonconformity was not, as it tends now to be perceived, a matter of displaying the proper badges and attitudes of disaffection. What nonconformity demanded, above all else, was a principled refusal to speak in the world's languages: an unwillingness to adapt oneself to agreed-upon usages and established forms of knowing, to the orders of the past which, through no custom more than its language, the present constantly inherits. In *Walden*, Thoreau spoke of "the inadequacy of residual statement," revisiting on his own terms Emerson's oft-spoken "objection to conforming to usages that have become dead." For Emerson this meant a revision of the conventional languages of public address, be they religious, philosophical, or literary; for Thoreau it required an upheaval in the most immediate language of all—the language of daily action, the lived life.

In Emerson's essays as in *Walden* (and in Thoreau's other works, especially *The Maine Woods*, 1864, and *Cape Cod*, 1865, both published posthumously) nature is the primary model for this project of self-realignment. For nature recurs, but is ever new; to Emerson, the natural world stood before human eyes as a ceaseless unfolding—"What we call nature," he wrote, "is a certain self-regulated motion, or change"—a system whose immense and instantaneous transformations constantly outstrip our modes of knowing it, embalmed as they must be in the slower-moving element of language. Here too, for both Emerson and Thoreau, art was of paramount importance, inasmuch as the task of the artist was imagined to be essentially one of renovation. Great monuments of art were inspiring to both men, less for what they said individually than for their thrilling display of the artist's ability to make new that which had grown stale, to replenish those things that for too long had been smothered under the deadened, habituated terms of their description. And finally, though it remained a largely implicit contention, for both authors America itself seemed an ideal—if at present horribly flawed—landscape in which the individual might accomplish such a bold project. "The centuries," Emerson wrote, "are conspirators against the sanity and authority of the soul." Born in a moment of definitive break from its ancestry, and consequentially as unburdened by the inheritance of centuries of ritual and belief as any nation could be, America promised an especially congenial atmosphere in which to pursue the jettisoning of all things tired and calcified in favor of a tireless elaboration of the new.

It would be foolish to deny that these were works of real social, political, and philosophical consequence—or that they were intended as such. But they are nevertheless more truly literary works than anything else, and not simply because of the eloquence or fineness of their construction. Rather, the ideal they so passionately pursue—an ideal of the self perpetually shedding its intellectual inheritances and reinventing its languages of apprehension—is an essentially formal one, dependent finally upon what we might call an aesthetics of the expressive self. Political meaning can surely be drawn from the elaboration of such an aesthetic. Thoreau's case against the nation's emerging market economy, its cycles of needless labor for superfluous commodity, is a strong one, and very directly made, as were his arguments in defense of abolitionism. Though Emerson was the more esoteric of the two, his distaste for the degradation of language itself into a "municipal speech" used only "to expedite the affairs of our pot and kettle" speaks as well to a trenchant critique of the dangers to American democracy of rituals of consensus: the danger that in our hurry to agree upon the terms we might use in conversation with one another—a hurry expedited in large part by the demands of commerce—we might accede to a great and debilitating calcification of our view of the world, a terrible stifling of emergences and possibilities.

Still, whatever the potency of these critiques, they are each explicitly tied to a formal aesthetic of the self that, for good or ill, delimits their pragmatic political applicability. In the first place, to the degree that political engagement involves a recognition of the legitimacy of attachments among, and the needs of, a multitude of other people, the ideal of the unfettered self, constantly divested of its constraints, would be problematic. As Orestes Brownson understood more clearly than most, both Emerson and Thoreau had difficulty imagining other people—even people dear to them—as much other than obstacles, hindrances to the self's capacious mutability. (Thoreau advised his readers to "live free and uncommitted," and in "Experience," his most anguished effort to grapple with the matter of the self's human attachments, Emerson warned more bitingly of "the importunate frivolity of other people.") To speak to the centers of power and the perpetrators of injustice is, moreover, almost necessarily to speak in a vocabulary that originates with someone else: to seek redress of grievance, equal representation, fair treatment before the law, and so forth. To refuse on principle to speak these conventional languages on the ground that they are derivative and made lifeless by cant is, as many have remarked, to cede much of the ground of political contestation. In all, the ideal of a perpetual overturning of established languages, making way for the previously unseen or unspoken, does offer real purchase on certain kinds of civic and institutional malady. And it is without question an ideal that since 1850 has shaped American literary practice—particularly American poetry—more profoundly than any other principle. The formalism of Emerson and Thoreau should not, then, lead us to consider their works consequential solely in literary terms. But it does invest even their keenest political ideals with an intransigence and an impracticability that cannot be pretended away.

The work of Margaret Fuller is, at least partially, the exception to all this. Though it is often remarked that her eloquence in conversation, dazzling as it was, exceeded the fluency of her prose, she nevertheless left behind an impressive and varied body of work: essays in literary and art criticism, memoirs, some footling verse, journalism, and several books, including her major intellectual achievement, *Woman in the Nineteenth Century*. She was early on drawn to Emerson (who was himself particularly impressed by her insistent, impulsive, difficult presence) and the two went on to edit the *Dial* together from 1840 to 1844. Like Emerson, she was absorbed by the problem of the self and its internal relations. She too longed for the possibility of a truthful self-relation, a mode of being in which the full extent of her intellectual passion might

express itself undistorted. It was a major point of *Woman in the Nineteenth Century* that the lives of contemporary women were circumscribed more cruelly and needlessly, the vitality of their selves assailed more wantonly, than any thinking person with a desire to live amply should be made to bear. But the writing of this work was in part catalyzed by Fuller's removal from Boston to New York in the mid-1840s, and her installment as a journalist for Horace Greeley's *Herald Tribune*. Here, her work took a pointed turn. She continued to write literary criticism, as she had done for the *Dial*, but she produced as well impassioned, focused, and often incendiary pieces on prisons, slavery, the status of women and immigrants, and the abuse of the nation's expanding laboring classes. By 1847 Fuller was in Italy, and instead of pursuing any genteel literary sojourn she found herself heatedly involved in the idealist struggles of Mazzini's Italian Republic. (She gained notoriety for her liaison with Angelo Ossoli, whose child she bore in 1848; all three died on the return voyage to America, in a shipwreck just off the coast of Fire Island in 1850.) The critic Ann Douglas (1977) describes Fuller's career suggestively as a movement "from literature to history," and though Fuller never abandoned the astute and combative idealism she had nurtured in the transcendentalist circle, in the end injustice and oppression more than kept pace in her work with falsity and cant as the most dire enemies of freedom.

MODERN INHERITANCES

The tension between aesthetic ideals and political commitment—in Emerson and Thoreau, the often strained belief that a genuinely progressive art would necessarily embody progressive thought; in Fuller, the growing suspicion that it need not—comes down to us in a number of forms. We see it, in fact, wherever transcendentalism left a lasting mark—and in the last 150 years of American life, that influence has been widely distributed. Beyond the revered generation of writers who followed hard upon the movement's heyday, transcendentalist thought has informed a great wealth of American intellectual enterprises. Most enduringly, the Emersonian ideals of ceaseless renovation, and of the necessary provisionality of all expressive forms, have been of defining importance to the practice of American poetry, from Whitman down to today. (Emerson's wisest critics have always been poets, and it is immensely revealing, in our own moment, to read his work back through the lens of his inheritors: Hart Crane in *White Buildings*, A. R. Ammons in *Corson's Inlet*, John Ashbery in "The Skaters" and *A Wave*.)

The transcendentalists' combined skepticism, with respect to the timelessness of institutions, and optimism, with respect to human possibility, also helped inspire a later generation of intellectuals that would include such luminaries as William James, Oliver Wendell Holmes Jr., and John Dewey—the architects of a tradition of American social and philosophical thought known today as pragmatism. And as pragmatism came to shape American social thought in the 1920s, and authors of that era turned increasingly for inspiration to the literary monuments of the mid-nineteenth century, transcendentalist principles found refracted expression yet again in the work of high modernists like Wallace Stevens, Jean Toomer, William Carlos Williams, William Faulkner, and T. S. Eliot. For these modernist writers, as for the pragmatists, the transcendentalist belief in the provisionality of ideas and of forms was essential. But on equally clear display in their works—especially those written after the devastation of World War I—was an explosive tension between a faith in the clarity and sheltering power of achieved aesthetic form, and the necessity of acknowledging the chaotic, disordering violence of the historical world. What resulted was modernism's habitual struggle to shore up fragments of perfected creative order against the ruins of industrial civilization.

If modernism too inherits, along with other transcendentalist impulses, something of the movement's signature uneasiness around the collision of art and history, we are today no less the recipients of that defining tension. We see it given renewed expression in a multiplicity of contexts, as much in the contemporary rifts among academics between "theory" and "literature" as in the broader divisions within modern environmentalism—still another reformist movement with important transcendentalist origins. For ourselves, finally, these are among the defining paradoxes of the ongoing transcendentalist legacy and as such ought not to be brushed away, either by pious condemnation or complacent hagiography. The relation of selves to history, of art to politics, of language to life: these are matters which transcendentalism, by the unsettled quality of its thought, encourages us to sustain as unendingly open questions, permanently available to refinement and reconfiguration.

And it is worth recalling too, at the end of a survey such as this, that the dilemmas of transcendentalist thought were lived through in infinitely particular ways, by writers who agreed on much but disagreed on more. The Transcendental Club, James Freeman Clarke recalled, was known as "the club of the like-minded; I suppose because no two of us thought alike"—so much so that a too narrow interest in "transcendentalism" as such threatens to flatten out the idiosyncrasy of individual participants' contributions and potentially to obscure, rather than illuminate, the contours of particular works. Emerson was beyond doubt the guiding force of American transcendentalism. But just as surely as his works influenced other transcendentalists, those works do not of themselves explain the mysticism of Jones Very, the socialism of Orestes Brownson, or the iconoclasm of Theodore Parker—nor for that matter do they account for the variations in transcendentalist thought that accompany its migrations around New England and into New York, Cincinnati, St. Louis, and beyond. We remember transcendentalism as a movement because of what it inspired: most immediately, the great quickening of literary expression called, for convenience, the American Renaissance. But the transcendentalists themselves, and the works they produced, are more profitably understood in the grain of each author's tenacious individuality. Though he boasted never to have acquired a disciple, in this last matter Emerson did sound the clarion call, to which many around him responded: "Absolve you to yourself," he wrote, "and you shall have the suffrage of the world."

[*See also* Emerson, Ralph Waldo; Essay in America, The; Hawthorne, Nathaniel; Nature Writing: Prose; Thoreau, Henry David and his *Walden*; *and* Whitman, Walt.]

FURTHER READING

Buell, Lawrence. *Literary Transcendentalism: Style and Vision in the American Renaissance*. Ithaca, N.Y., 1973. An astute updating of Matthiessen and Miller, with an eye toward the interplay of aesthetic and historical ambitions.

Douglas, Ann. *The Feminization of American Culture.* New York, 1977. An account of the ascension of sentimentalism in post-Calvinist America, with an especially fine chapter on the career of Margaret Fuller.

Matthiessen, F. O. *American Renaissance.* New York, 1941. The seminal, pathbreaking account of the generation of antebellum writers that included Emerson, Thoreau, Hawthorne, Melville, and Whitman.

Menand, Louis. *The Metaphysical Club: A Story of Ideas in America.* New York, 2001. An exploration of the emergence of pragmatism in late-nineteenth-century American intellectual life, which notes the strong influence of Emerson and transcendentalism on the postbellum generation.

Miller, Perry. *The Transcendentalists: An Anthology*. Cambridge, Mass., 1950. The most thorough introduction to the movement, containing original documents from a multitude of participants, each introduced and situated by Miller, as well as Miller's powerful essay on transcendentalism's religious origins and significance.

Myerson, Joel. *The Transcendentalists: A Review of Research and Criticism*. New York, 1984. A useful and extensive bibliography of work on transcendentalism.

Poirier, Richard. *The Renewal of Literature: Emersonian Reflections*. New York, 1987. An incisive and theoretically informed meditation on the consequences, for literature and literary thought, of Emersonian premises about language and the act of writing.

LIONEL TRILLING

by Sanford Pinsker

In an autobiographical lecture originally delivered at Purdue University in 1965 and later published in *The Last Decade: Essays and Reviews 1965–75* (1979), Lionel Trilling recalled that the "great word in the College [Columbia] was INTELLIGENCE" and that he had early adopted the motto "THE MORAL OBLIGATION TO BE INTELLIGENT" from his teacher there, John Erskine. For Trilling, moral values coupled with an acute intelligence were at the center of what he did as a literary critic, cultural commentator, and educator. One could see these preoccupations as early as his dissertation on Matthew Arnold, which became a great success when it was published as a book in 1939. Trilling's

Lionel Trilling.
(© *Bettmann/Corbis*)

study revealed much about Arnold's writing, and also about his thoughts as they related to the society in which he lived. As Trilling put it in the volume's preface: "I have undertaken in his book to show the thought of Matthew Arnold in its complex unity and to relate it to the historical and intellectual events of his time." The result, Trilling concludes, "may be thought of as a biography of Arnold's mind."

Matthew Arnold was clearly one of the strongest influences on Trilling, especially with regard to duplicating in twentieth-century America what Arnold had done for nineteenth-century England: to understand, value, and conserve what was important from the past, and to be a proponent of the free play of the critical intelligence on the present. Another abiding presence in Trilling's thought was Sigmund Freud, especially as his work provided a landscape of the mind and a portrait of modern civilization's neurotic discontents. The joining of these powerful forces, Arnold and Freud, led to a complicated understanding of what "culture" means as each age in its turn measures the requirements for a virtuous person and society.

"Magisterial" is the adjective that often precedes the name Trilling, not only because his wide-ranging moral criticism dominated the literary-cultural scene in the years between the publication of *The Liberal Imagination* in 1950 and his death in 1975, but also because Trilling carried himself with a dignity approaching the regal. As a teacher, he was revered by generations of Columbia undergraduates (including the poets John Hollander and Allen Ginsberg, as well as the literary-political essayist Norman Podhoretz) not only for his courses in modern literature or the romantics, but also for the justly famous sequence of required humanities survey courses he team-taught with Jacques Barzun. English majors and nonmajors alike hung on every word of his polished lectures, and many waited for their later appearance in journals and then between hard covers. As a member of what would come to be known as "the New York Intellectuals," Trilling could not only range freely through the world of ideas but could also apply the lessons he learned about the noble and the base to the contemporary situation. Finally, as an academic who transcended academia, Trilling was one of the few intellectuals of whom the general public might have heard. He was something of a celebrity, famous as fame was defined for intellectual types in the days before television talk shows and popular gossip magazines.

LIFE

Lionel Trilling was born in New York City on 4 July 1905 to David W. and Fannie Cohen Trilling. His parents were eastern European immigrants who suffered a series of financial reversals in the New World. Trilling's father became a tailor when it was clear that a career in the rabbinate was not possible, and he later made an ill-fated switch to the wholesale fur business. A series of bad marketing decisions and the stock market crash of 1929 wiped out whatever money the Trillings had, and in later years Lionel and his wife, Diana, struggled to support them.

Trilling began his assimilation to the culture of Western humanism in 1921, when he entered Columbia University as a sixteen-year-old freshman. There he received his B.A. in 1925, his M.A. in 1926, and his Ph.D. in 1938. At the beginning of his career, Trilling taught briefly at the University of Wisconsin at Madison (1926–1927) and Hunter College (1927–1930), but it was Columbia University with which he is most associated. In his autobiographical lecture, Trilling remembered his college years as a time of "intense and pervasive questioning of the prevailing way of doing things—that is to say, of the majority's way of doing things, and of the business community's way of doing things." The questioning continued throughout the early years of Trilling's career, fueled by the crises of modernity brought about by World War I and the economic turmoil that pitted capitalism against communism. His unease with the culture swirling around him led Trilling to declare, in *Beyond Culture* (1965), that "It is a belief still preeminently honored that a primary function of art and thought is to liberate the individual from the tyranny of his culture in the environmental sense and to permit him to stand beyond it in an autonomy of perception and judgment." Small wonder, then, that Trilling should find himself attracted to an oppositional figure such as Matthew Arnold. He represented, often in nagging, preachy ways, the proposition that literature had replaced religion in the twilight region between the death of firm Victorian shibboleths and the uncertainties of modernism.

Trilling's dissertation was a bold, ambitious project, and had Trilling not been the son of immigrant Jews, the granting of tenure to him would have been a certainty. But it was decidedly not, for this was a world in which Ivy League colleges invoked quotas to restrict the number of their Jewish students and to bar even the brightest Jewish professors. The tenured members of the English department felt that Trilling, a "Freudian, a Marxist, and a Jew" (their words), was not entirely comfortable at Columbia, nor would he ever be. He lacked the proper credentials, which is to say, he was not a white Anglo-Saxon Protestant. Trilling's notebooks detail just how nerve-wracking his battle for tenure was, and how many of his senior colleagues felt that someone with his background would never properly master the rhythms of American prose.

Add to these woes the fact that Trilling had always hoped to make his mark as a novelist, and the ingredients for inner torment, often expressed in long bouts of writer's block, are in place. Outwardly, Trilling carried himself with supreme confidence, but—if his wife's testimony in *The Beginning of the Journey: The Marriage of Diana and Lionel Trilling* (1993) can be believed—internally he was riddled with self-doubt. Diana Trilling was not shy about taking credit for freeing her husband from his woe, although many readers have not been convinced of this; Trilling, they felt, would have found a way of fulfilling his destiny with or without Diana.

A LIBERAL IMAGINATION

Trilling's work on Matthew Arnold was followed, in 1943, by an equally seminal work on the modern British novelist E. M. Forster. In the study's introduction, "Forster and the Liberal Imagination," Trilling made a sharp distinction between the critical mind of liberalism and classic liberalism's tendency toward the dogmatic and uncritical. What a novelist such as Forster shows, Trilling argued, is an "unremitting concern with moral realism...not the awareness of morality itself but of the contradictions, paradoxes and dangers of living the moral life."

Contradictions and paradoxes were the touchstones of formalist criticism, in Trilling's day known as the New Criticism. For critics such as John Crowe Ransom and Cleanth Brooks, close reading of a lyric poem meant bringing to the surface its verbal tensions (usually expressed as ironies, paradoxes, or verbal contradictions). Writing about Forster in particular, but foreshadowing what he would later explore in novelists such as Mark Twain, Henry James, and F. Scott Fitzgerald, Trilling insisted that "the liberal mind is sure that the order of human affairs owes it a simple logic: good is good and bad is bad.... Before the idea of good-and-evil its imagination fails; it cannot accept the improbable paradox." Trilling's purpose, unlike that of the New Critics, was not to confine himself to the aesthetic niceties of the page. Instead, he insisted that reading fiction had, above all else, a moral purpose and that it dealt, above all else, with "the dangers of living a moral life."

For Trilling, Forster was at war with the liberal mindset, just as Trilling himself was. Classical liberalism had become a "loose body of middle class opinion which includes such ideas as progress, collectivism and humanitarianism." The modern world was a more complex and morally difficult place that only the literary imagination at its best could fully explore. Criticism had to be conducted in the same spirit: passionately engaged with the past as well as the present, willing and able to avoid middle-class shibboleths, and perhaps most important of all, independent of mind. As one of Forster's characters puts it, one must be equipped to see the world "steady and whole."

The analyses offered up in *E. M. Forster* make it clear that Trilling was neither a clumsily doctrinaire Freudian nor an easily reductive Marxist. Writing about *Howard's End*, a novel in which property ownership and class consciousness play a large role, Trilling argued that "on the one hand class is character, soul and destiny," but on the other hand, "class is not finally determining." Instead, class struggle is interiorized as "moral struggle in the heart of a single person."

Trilling's study of Forster, at that time the greatest living British novelist, was widely praised; it would also be his last sustained scholarly study. Hereafter he would spend his time writing articles, reviews, lectures, prefaces, and even fiction. In the last category, Trilling wrote two short stories—"Of That Time, of That Place" (1943) and "The Other Margaret" (1947)—that are by any standard highly successful efforts, but no more stories followed. Instead, Trilling's only novel, *The Middle of the Journey*, appeared in 1947. As a novel of ideas that explores a variety of intellectual responses to late capitalism, it remains a period piece. The intellectual grappling that goes on across the political spectrum may be interesting, but the characters are not. John Laskell, the novel's protagonist and Trilling's mouthpiece, visits friends and there discovers the shallowness embedded in stereotypical liberals, the treachery of those who idealistically cling to communism, and what happens when a true believer on the left turns abruptly around to join the far right.

The Middle of the Journey did not harm Trilling's reputation, but the knotty, demanding paragraphs of the novel needed a way to breathe that clearly he could not supply. His essays, however, were another matter. *The Liberal Imagination* made Trilling famous and sold more than one hundred thousand copies. No literary critic, then or now, can claim such success; and the reason for this lies not only in "Freud and Literature" or "Art and Neurosis," but also in the appeal of the collected essays to a large middle-class audience that still shared the goal of participating in a national debate about culture.

CULTURE WARS

One example of cultural debate in the years immediately following World War II was what is now widely regarded as the most famous conference ever held by a "little magazine." The *Partisan Review* assembled an impressive group of New York writers and intellectuals, including Trilling, Irving Howe, and Norman Mailer, to explore whether a sea change had occurred during the postwar period. The year was 1952, and the conference was called "Our Culture and Our Country." Philip Rahv and William Phillips, the magazine's editors, strongly suspected that the pressing concerns that had once rallied them around their typewriters no longer existed, or at least had been significantly altered by the collapse of Europe. America was once commonly thought of as a place hostile to art and culture, but, they wondered, did that formulation—and the "alienation" it created among intellectuals—still apply?

Lionel Trilling minced no words when he announced that "an avowed aloofness from national feeling" could no longer be considered the "first ceremonial step into the life of thought." Rather, America now offered an intellectual the "not inconsiderable advantage of a whole skin, a full stomach, and the right to wag his tongue as he pleases." As legions of commentators have since remarked, it was the word "our" in the conference's title that told the whole story. America had emerged from the war as the world's preeminent power, and there were signs, Trilling argued, that the new affluence nearly everywhere in evidence might yet benefit the arts and intellectual life generally. There were Fulbright grants, more university teaching positions, and other indicators that, as he put it, "we are notably better off." These pronouncements differed markedly from those of the younger Trilling, who had been suspicious of business culture and who had once dabbled, however briefly, in the far left and other enterprises of what he now called "the adversary culture."

Norman Mailer, arguably America's most important young novelist, could hardly contain his disagreement with the questions posed by the *Partisan Review* editors. "I think I ought to declare straightaway that I am in an almost total disagreement with the assumptions of this symposium," he began, making it clear that he was not about to number himself among the sellouts. Irving Howe felt much the same way as he held fast to memories of the 1930s, when the only good capitalist was a thoroughly disgraced one. Two years later, Howe and Mailer launched a new magazine whose name, *Dissent*, made clear their position with regard to accommodation (or as they preferred to call it, "conformity"); and Howe published "The Age of Conformity," a stinging attack on accommodation that many thought was directed at Trilling.

Two subsequent collections of essays—*The Opposing Self* (1955) and *A Gathering of Fugitives* (1956)—confirmed Howe's suspicions that Trilling was taking undue satisfaction in the relatively benign politics of the Eisenhower era, and that Trilling believed that those politics promoted the kind of stability congenial to good literature. Trilling would continue to embrace versions of cultural conservativism for the rest of his life, although it was a conservatism that had been with him since the time he had chosen Matthew Arnold and E. M. Forster as objects of study.

Trilling's association with the *Partisan Review* circle was built partly on his sympathy for their anti-Stalinism, and partly on his own belief that the radical politics of the adversarial left were not conducive to cultural health. By contrast, Trilling believed that Freudianism made the tragic imagination possible to understand, and in *Freud and the Crisis of Our Culture* (1955), he both extended and reworked the various ways in which Freud had influenced his approach to literary texts. As Joseph Shoben points out in his study *Lionel Trilling* (1981), "no set of ideas so consistently, so dominantly, preoccupied Lionel Trilling's throughout his career as those formulated by Sigmund Freud in *Civilization and Its Discontents*. . . . In a number of ways, his familiarity with Freud increasingly shaped and gave a language to some of Trilling's most intimate experiences and lent a distinctive color to some of his central values."

The 1960s were a time of countercultural turmoil, and Columbia University was one of the places where "the days of rage" against the war in Vietnam ended in buildings being taken hostage and faculty offices being looted. The riots and the anarchy they spurned deeply saddened Trilling, who was often singled out for special abuse as a venerable professor who had been instrumental in propping up what the student revolutionaries regarded as a suspect Western tradition. Much of what would happen in the streets was prophesied in *Beyond Culture: Essays on Literature and Learning* (1965) and was much on Trilling's mind as he delivered the Charles Eliot Norton lectures at Harvard (published in 1972 under the title *Sincerity and Authenticity*). The adversary culture that Trilling had once associated with 1930s radicalism was with us once again, albeit in a slightly altered form. Trilling used the occasion to trace in some detail the conflict between the socialized personality and the autonomous individual. It was a distinction he had made many times before, but on this occasion Trilling invoked passing references to a whole new cast of critical-theoretical characters: Raymond Williams, Claude Lévi-Strauss, Lucien Goldman, Walter Benjamin, Nathalie Sarraute, Michel Foucault, and Jacques Lacan. Many regard *Sincerity and Authenticity* as Trilling's most sustained effort since the Forster book.

LAST YEARS

Trilling's last years were filled with honors, not least of which was being chosen to deliver the first Thomas Jefferson Lectures in the Humanities (published in 1973 as *Mind in the Modern World*). *The Last Decade: Essays and Reviews, 1965–1975*, edited by Diana Trilling in 1979, demonstrates how wide-ranging Trilling's interests were: he wrote on James Joyce's letters, Whittaker Chambers (a former communist turned FBI informant), and Jane Austen. In the same year, Diana Trilling also edited *Prefaces to the Experience of Literature* and, as part of a twelve-volume Uniform Edition of Trilling's works, *Of This Time, Of That Place and Other Stories*. A year later she edited *Speaking of Literature and Society*.

Diana Trilling may have been the most protective of Trilling's reputation in the years following his death, but she was hardly the only keeper of the flame. The first round of obituaries were filled with praise of Trilling's lifelong career as a literary critic and cultural analyst, but there are good reasons to believe that Leon Wieseltier's edition of Trilling's posthumous essays, *The Moral Obligation to Be Intelligent* (2000), will be both more lasting and more valuable. "Even when he spoke for no one but himself," Mark Shechner wrote in the pages of *The Nation*, "he was looked upon as a spokesman and came, in time, to be something of a standard source." Trilling's work will last as long as there are people who care deeply about the complicated business of living a moral life amid everything that militates against high culture.

SELECTED WORKS

Matthew Arnold (1939)
E. M. Forster (1943)
The Middle of the Journey (1947)
The Liberal Imagination: Essays on Literature and Society (1950)
The Opposing Self: Nine Essays in Criticism (1955)
Freud and the Crisis of Our Culture (1955)
Beyond Culture: Essays on Literature and Learning (1965)
Sincerity and Authenticity (1972)

The Moral Obligation to Be Intelligent: Selected Essays (2000; edited by Leon Wieseltier)

FURTHER READING

Chace, W. M., ed. *Lionel Trilling: Criticism and Politics.* Stanford, Calif., 1980. Especially good at placing Trilling within the larger context of literary criticism.

Krupnick, Mark. *Lionel Trilling and the Fate of Cultural Criticism.* Evanston, Ill., 1986. Remains the best book-length study of the Trilling canon.

O'Hara. Daniel T. *Lionel Trilling: The Work of Liberation.* Madison, Wis., 1988. Reads Trilling's career as a single, completely comprehensive work of self-fashioning.

Shoben, Edward Joseph. *Lionel Trilling.* New York, 1981. A useful introduction for beginning students.

Trilling, Diana. *The Beginning of the Journey: The Marriage of Diana and Lionel Trilling.* New York, 1993. Remains the best source for information about Trilling's childhood and early career.

MARK TWAIN

by Ron Powers

Mark Twain is the fountainhead to the great winding waterway of America's native-born literature, a literature that finds profundity in the personal experience and everyday speaking habits of its people; in their typically wry humor in response to pretense, oppression, and sorrow; and in their founding democratic ideal that rebukes all forms of tainted privilege and power, including the deep American strain of racism. No other single author is as closely identified with shaping a voice that propelled the young nation toward its final break from the rigid dictates of European literary forms. No other nineteenth-century writer remains as readable at the dawn of the twenty-first, nor as strikingly prophetic of contemporary themes and concerns. And no figure ever did more to romanticize the experience of American boyhood.

These distinctions are all the more remarkable considering that Mark Twain was no child of a lettered lineage and was never trained in the academic disciplines that enriched such other great writers of his age as Ralph Waldo Emerson and Henry David Thoreau, who attended Harvard College, and Henry James, who went to Harvard Law School. Experience was his academy, and its most sacred text was the Mississippi River. "A wonderful book," he called the water's surface in *Life on the Mississippi* (1883), "which told its mind to me without reserve . . . and it was not a book to be read once and thrown aside, for it had a new story to tell every day."

The river was an influence both real and metaphorical throughout his life. He was born Samuel Langhorne Clemens on 30 November 1835, between the forks of one of its tributaries, the Salt River, in the hamlet of Florida, Missouri. He was the sixth of seven children born to John Marshall Clemens, a dour, self-educated Virginian with aspirations to the law, and the former Jane Lampton, a small, vivacious Kentuckian whose red hair and exploding,

Mark Twain.
(Courtesy of the Library of Congress)

opinionated wit she passed along to Samuel.

The family was poor despite John Marshall's earlier accumulation of some seventy thousand acres of rich Tennessee woodland for a total of only around $500. John was never able to resell this bounty in his lifetime, and the frustration of this "prospective wealth" spawned Mark Twain's lifelong obsession with making money. A few months before Samuel's birth his parents, questing for prosperity, had immigrated to Missouri from Tennessee to join the family of Jane's brother-in-law, John Quarles, who owned a farm near a village of one hundred people.

Sickly and frail, Samuel passed his first four years at the Quarles farm, exploring its precincts as soon as he was old enough to walk. He returned for summer visits throughout his boyhood. His experiences there—specifically, his close mingling among the few dozen black slaves kept by John Quarles—formed the essential foundation from which he grew his literary imagination. Wandering freely among their quarters, Samuel stored up intensely detailed memories of the epic stories the slaves told one another, the densely encoded spirituals they sang day and night, and most importantly, the distinct rhythms, diction, and figures of speech that the African-American dialect comprised as it had been refining itself over two centuries. The voices of Mark Twain's two enduring Negro characters, Jim in *Adventures of Huckleberry Finn* (1884) and Roxana in *The Tragedy of Pudd'nhead Wilson* (1894), were gestated in these encounters. Along with this sense of inflected language, Samuel developed an enlightened perception of black people as fellow human beings. This acceptance, radically at odds with much of white American opinion throughout his lifetime (and beyond it), would lend moral fervor to Mark Twain's most accomplished novels and essays and would motivate him as a financial patron of black Americans long before such efforts became politically fashionable.

THE HANNIBAL BOYHOOD YEARS

In 1839 John Clemens moved his family to Hannibal, about forty miles east of Florida. The elder Clemens's long quest for prosperity would end there in failure; but for Samuel the ensuing fourteen years later proved golden. Here, on the Mississippi's western shore, lay the town-and-wilderness venue for a boyhood that fueled his "mortal nostalgia," as the biographer Dixon Wecter called it in *Sam Clemens of Hannibal* (1952). Clemens would revisit this "heavenly place" in stories throughout his life, commingling memory and imagination to craft a national ideal of boyhood under his pen name, Mark Twain.

In pre–Civil War Hannibal, the high-strung and impressionable young boy lived out the last years of the Arcadian America as Thomas Jefferson had conceived it. He explored the great river, the hills and woods and cemeteries near its banks, and the vast cave system that lay three miles below the town. He relished the stimulation of the minstrel shows, "mesmerizers," and circuses that came to town, and worked their themes into his fantasies. He formed friendships with the vivid children whom he would later enshrine in his most popular literature as Tom Sawyer, Huckleberry Finn, Joe Harper, and Becky Thatcher, and he observed the grown-ups who would be distilled into Aunt Polly, the Widow Douglas, Pap Finn, Muff Potter, and the evil Injun Joe—the model for whom apparently was a gentle man named Joe Douglas, partly of Osage extraction, who lived peacefully in the town until his death at age 102.

But not everyone in the town was gentle. Cruelty, violence, and sorrow formed a vast dark side to his Arcadia—and thus deepened the wells of his literature. Before entering adolescence Samuel had discovered the corpse of a stabbed man that had been laid out in his father's law office; witnessed the first fatal shooting in Hannibal; seen a townsman bludgeon one of his slaves to death with a lump of iron ore; stood by as a widow fired a shotgun round into the chest of a man who had been harassing her daughter; and, while picking berries with friends in the slough of a Mississippi island, come upon the body of a murdered runaway slave.

Nature itself sometimes seemed monstrous: the creek waters where he loved to frolic claimed two of his friends in drowning accidents, and disease struck down an older sister and brother before Samuel had turned ten years old. At age eleven he saw his father, stricken with pneumonia, die nearly penniless, encumbered still by the unsold Tennessee land. John Clemens left behind a nearly destitute household that included his widow and four surviving children: elder siblings Orion and Pamela; Samuel; and the youngest, Henry.

These and other traumas burned themselves deeply and permanently into Samuel Clemens's restless psyche. (Mark Twain gives hints in his journals that he watched, through a keyhole, as the doctor opened his dead father's chest for the autopsy.) The odd feeling of personal guilt he later expressed over many of them might have been enhanced by the severe brand of dogma handed down in the Presbyterian church he attended with his mother. Images of an affronted and punishing God sending fiery vengeance down upon fallen humankind found their way into much of Mark Twain's late novels and essays.

Ironically (given his later antipathy toward it), it was the Bible that facilitated Clemens's passion for words. His formal education was episodic, brief, and largely against his will. He attended a series of small schools in and around the town and he skipped classes—"played hooky"—whenever the urge took him. His academic career was essentially behind him by the age of ten. But thanks largely to a woman named Mary Ann Newcomb, a spinster associate of one of his "dame school" teachers, Clemens received a thorough immersion in the discipline of reading. Chief among his learning texts was the Bible. Over his lifetime he grew familiar with more than half its sixty-six books, and made more than four hundred allusions to it in his writings. Along with the works of Shakespeare, Sir Walter Scott, and Tom Paine, the Bible formed the core of his self-administered education. Symptomatic of the pessimism that overtook him in his last years, the Bible also became a chief target of his bitter satire. In 1909, a year before his death, he wrote a series of essays mocking the Christian faith with such vitriol that they were suppressed by his daughter Clara and published only after her own death, in 1962, as *Letters from the Earth*.

PRINTER'S APPRENTICE

Clemens's involvement with words took a palpable turn soon after his father's death. In the fall of 1847, the family resources depleted, Jane Clemens sent him to the offices of a newspaper called the *Hannibal Gazette* to help out in any way he could. He would not be paid, but his meager meals and board there would relieve a little of his family's strain. When the *Gazette* was purchased by Joseph Ament in the spring of 1848 and renamed the *Missouri Courier*, Clemens stayed on, sweeping the floor and fetching water. Soon he learned to set type and became a printer's apprentice. In 1850 Orion returned from St. Louis, where he had been dabbling in Whig politics, and opened up a small weekly newspaper of his own, the *Hannibal Journal* (soon the *Hannibal Journal and Western Union*). He took on Clemens as an unpaid assistant the following January. Samuel's typesetting prowess was a boon to his dreamy, chronically inept brother. More significantly, though, the job gave Samuel many chances to experiment with his own writing impulses. The results were often bombastic. During Orion's frequent business trips out of town (usually to try, in vain, to unload the Tennessee land), Samuel liked to set some of his own compositions into type—often a satiric broadside aimed at some rival editor or town character. At other times he indulged himself in pure whimsy, as in this "item":

TERRIBLE ACCIDENT!
500 MEN KILLED AND MISSING!!!

We had set the above head up, expecting (of course) to use it, but as the accident hasn't happened yet, we'll say (To Be Continued.)

STEAMBOAT PILOT

Yet his emerging local fame was hardly enough. Weary of his brother's failure to turn a profit and his family's lack of prospects, in June 1853 the seventeen-year-old Clemens fled Hannibal on a downstream packet, the first leg of the national and global wanderings that would occupy the rest of his life. He worked for a while setting type in St. Louis, then made his way to New York City, Philadelphia, and Washington, D.C., taking similar jobs and sending letters describing his travels back to Orion's newspaper. Returning briefly to the Mississippi Valley in 1855, he dabbled at some satirical newspaper essays, then declared himself headed southward for the Amazon River in Brazil to make a fortune in the coca trade.

Along the way, though, he rediscovered his boyhood enchantment with the Mississippi River. Booked as a passenger on the steamboat *Paul Jones*, destined for New Orleans, in early 1857, the twenty-one-year-old Clemens talked the pilot into letting him steer a little. By the time the boat docked, Clemens had wheedled the pilot, a master steamboat man named Horace Bixby, into taking him on as an apprentice. Thus began another phase of exalted experience that would flavor Mark Twain's literature, most notably in one of his greatest works, *Life on the Mississippi*.

He perfected his piloting skills and his vast knowledge of the river over the next four years. He later wrote that under Bixby, he achieved the feat of committing the Mississippi and its landmarks to memory—or at least the 2,600-mile round-trip stretch of it between St. Louis and New Orleans. He was equally attentive to the vast and colorful array of human characters that flowed along this watery world, noting the language they spoke, the songs they sang, the many ways in which they revealed themselves. They included the rough itinerant raftsmen, the deckhands, the gamblers and con artists, the visiting Europeans, the fetching young women, the wealthy southern planters with their slaves and servants in tow. "When I find a well-drawn character in fiction or biography I generally take a warm personal interest in him," he observed in *Life on the Mississippi*, "for the reason that I have known him before—met him on the river." He would deeply tap these imprinted memories—of the water, the land, the people, and their talk—for his fictional and nonfictional portraits of American life.

The young pilot found time, as well, to further his self-education and his evolving political sensibilities. The fervently populist, anti-aristocratic works of Tom Paine consumed many of his idle hours on board.

Clemens left the river in April 1861 at the outbreak of the Civil War, when a Union blockade halted commercial river traffic. His Mississippi idyll was marred by a devastating loss of the kind that had struck at him twice before and would recur with cruel regularity during his life. In February 1858 he had secured a menial job on the steamboat *Pennsylvania* for his younger brother Henry (whom he cast as Sid in *The Adventures of Tom Sawyer* [1876]). Samuel had hoped to offer the excitements of his new world to the bookish boy. But on 13 June—Henry's twentieth birthday—the *Pennsylvania*'s boilers burst on an upriver run from New Orleans to St. Louis and it exploded. Henry was mortally scalded. Samuel, traveling on a trailing steamer, arrived at his brother's bedside in a makeshift hospital at Memphis, but Henry died on 21 June. In his old age Clemens claimed that he had caused the death by telling a doctor to administer morphine to Henry—a botched dosage, in the old writer's unreliable recall.

Henry was the third sibling whose death Samuel had witnessed. His sister Margaret had died of a fever while the family was still in Florida, Missouri, and his adored brother Benjamin succumbed to a sudden illness when Samuel was seven. Perhaps influenced by his mother's histrionics (he recalled that she made him kneel and place his hand on the dead brother's still-warm forehead), Samuel would forever blame himself for these deaths, as well as others, including Henry's. "Dead brother Ben. My treachery to him," ran a cryptic entry in one of Mark Twain's journals.

The morbid intensity of this guilt, together with the corrosive pessimism toward humankind that emerged in his late writings, is at odds with the abiding popular (and reductive) perception of Mark Twain, which is that of a humorist. It has fueled a pervasive scholarly emphasis on Mark Twain's "divided" or "dual" personality and on the psychic "wound" and the "anxieties" that, some critics maintain, both influenced and limited his literary career. From the 1920s onward, critics and biographers have been bemused by the paradoxes, the double identities, and the theme of "twinning" that preoccupied Samuel Clemens–Mark Twain and that also seem to express his central personality. This focus has given a Freudian tone to much of what has been written about him. But perhaps Mark Twain himself most succinctly reconciled the paradox. "Everything human is pathetic," he wrote in one of the Calendar entries in *The Tragedy of Pudd'nhead Wilson*. "The secret source of humor itself is not joy but sorrow. There is no humor in heaven."

NEWSPAPERING OUT WEST

His piloting vocation shut down by the impending war, Clemens, now twenty-five, tried to sort out his sympathies. They were as yet unformed. He drifted back toward Hannibal and joined a ragtag collection of young Confederate irregulars in Marion County—more from a sense of adventure than out of any strong secessionist beliefs. The youths made fitful gestures toward drilling, cadged meals from nearby farmers, and panicked at rumors that Union troops commanded by Ulysses S. Grant were tracking them. Clemens soon left the unit. A quarter-century later he fictionalized the experience in "The Private History of a Campaign That Failed," a haunting story whose central, invented action had Clemens and his friends gunning down a lone, unarmed traveler whom they believed to be a Union soldier.

An astonishing stroke of good luck handed Clemens the itinerary for his next adventure—and a chance to escape the carnage of the Civil War. In March 1861 President Abraham Lincoln, acting on the suggestion of his attorney general, the St. Louisan Edward Bates, had appointed Orion Clemens territorial secretary, or provisional governor, of the Nevada Territory. (Orion had campaigned for Lincoln in St. Louis.) Samuel, in turn, got Orion to appoint him "secretary to the secretary" in exchange for financing the westward trip for both of them. In July 1861 the brothers set forth on a cross-country stagecoach journey to the West, from where Samuel would enjoy the first blaze of national reputation as a comic writer under the pen name Mark Twain.

Samuel spent a few weeks helping Orion line up a territorial legislature and steering his naïve brother through political conflicts. But his deep-seated dream of quick, great wealth soon drew him to the mineral mines then snaking through the silver-rich Comstock Lode near Virginia City. He plunged into the rough world of speculators and miners, drinking hard and gambling with them as he tried to capture a share of the riches they were extracting.

Fortunately for American letters, Samuel Clemens proved a hopeless miner-speculator. Frustrated and broke, he turned to the moneymaking talent that he still regarded as merely a sideline. He began sending written sketches, under the pen name Josh, to the *Virginia City Territorial Enterprise*. Soon he was a staff reporter on the best newspaper between St. Louis and the West Coast. In the midst of a turbulent, nearly lawless boom town, he had stumbled into an enclave of gifted young bohemian writers who (while covering the news with dutiful accuracy) enlivened the *Enterprise*'s pages with madcap hoaxes, mock feuds, tall tales, and satires. Soon Clemens was a central figure among them, carousing and writing with equal combustive force. He formed friendships with such established writers as Bret Harte and Artemus Ward. In February 1863, at age twenty-seven, he began signing his dispatches "Mark Twain." The words have a riverboat referent—they are the "two-fathom" call of the "leadsman" with his pole, constantly probing the water depths beneath the boat. The writer claimed later to have taken the pseudonym from a Mississippi steamboatman named Isaiah Sellers, who published brief river items under that name.

In any event, the new signature liberated Clemens from obscurity and heralded his embrace of the writing life. True, he would constantly move back and forth between the two personas—between Clemens the middle-class fortune seeker, family man, and social climber and Twain the wild satirist, travel writer, platform speaker, and literary lion. Furthermore, "Mark Twain" did not prove a shield that would insulate him from his inborn grief, rage, and depression. But never again would he be just Samuel Clemens. He had begun his ascent into the mythic.

As Mark Twain he wrote sketches for newspapers in Nevada and San Francisco and for the *New York Sunday Mercury*. He toured the Sandwich (later Hawaiian) Islands in early 1866 and sent travel letters to the *Sacramento Union*. Returning to California, he gave a talk in San Francisco on his island experiences that enthralled the house, prompted several more speaking engagements around the state, and formed the contours of a comic lecture hall persona that would compete in popularity throughout his life with his written work. And as Mark Twain he wrote his first nationally celebrated humorous story, "The Celebrated Jumping Frog of Calaveras County," a reworking of a tale he had heard in a California mining cabin. First printed in the New York–based *Saturday Press* as "Jim Smiley and His Jumping Frog," it earned him an instant reputation in the East as The Wild Humorist of the Pacific Slope. Twain was thrilled to hear that the literary eminence James Russell Lowell declared it to be "the finest piece of humorous writing ever published in America." In 1867 it was republished as the title piece in Twain's first book, a collection of his western sketches.

EXCURSION TO THE HOLY LAND; MARRIAGE TO LIVY

In 1867 Mark Twain signed on as a working journalist aboard the steamship *Quaker City*, bound for the Mediterranean with some seventy passengers en route through several European countries and on to the Holy Land. The travel letters that he sent back to the *San Francisco Alta California* and other newspapers formed the first draft of one of his masterworks, *The Innocents Abroad* (1869). A descriptive account of the excursion, Twain's fellow passengers, and the indigenous characters they encountered, *Innocents* broke from staid and romantic travel book tradition. It shocked and delighted readers with its richly satirical point of view, boldly showcasing its narrator's barbed irreverence for Old World landmarks, works of art, legends, and sacred relics.

> I wish to say one word about Michael Angelo Buonarotti. I used to worship the mighty genius of Michael Angelo—that man who was great in poetry, painting, sculpture, architecture—great in everything he undertook. But I do not want Michael Angelo for breakfast—for luncheon—for dinner—for tea—for supper—for between meals. I like a change, occasionally. In Genoa, he designed every thing; in Milan he or his pupils designed every thing; he designed the Lake of Como . . . in Florence, he painted every thing, designed every thing, nearly, and what he did not design he used to sit on a favorite stone and look at, and they showed us the stone. In Pisa he designed every thing but the old shot tower, and they would have attributed that to him if it had not been so awfully out of the perpendicular . . . he designed St. Peter's, he designed the Pope . . . the eternal bore designed the Eternal City, and unless all men and books do lie, he painted every thing in it! . . .

> I never felt so thankful, so soothed, so tranquil, so filled with a blessed peace, as I did yesterday when I learned that Michael Angelo was dead.

The impact of this capering, comic jaundice, more or less sustained over 650 pages, helped liberate Americans from a reflexive obsequiousness toward all things European or "biblical" in origin (as distinct, of course, from the Bible as a text). Peddled door-to-door by subscription salesmen—a strategy that Mark Twain vastly preferred to the more genteel method of bookstores—it sold more than 100,000 copies in its first two years.

By that time Twain was married. He had first seen Olivia Langdon's image in an ivory miniature carried by her brother Charles, a passenger on the *Quaker City*. Enchanted by her beauty, he secured an invitation to dine with the Langdon family during their visit to New York City shortly after Christmas 1867 and on New Year's Eve escorted her to Steinway Hall to hear a reading by Charles Dickens. But he won her only after a long courtship, during which time he labored to validate his respectability in the estimation of her father Jervis, a wealthy coal-mining magnate who presided over society in Elmira, New York. In time, Twain's charm overcame his reputation as a hard-drinking, loose-living westerner, and the two were married in the Langdon home on 2 February 1870.

Twain idolized the frail "Livy" Clemens (she had suffered a spinal disease as a girl) through their thirty-four years of marriage and she returned his deep affections. He strove to abandon the habitual smoking, cursing, and hard drinking that affronted her refined upbringing and to adopt her Christian piety. He was less than successful, though his problems with drink abated. He allowed her to proofread the drafts of nearly everything he wrote for publication and accepted her occasional criticisms of taste and propriety. But despite their mutual love, the misfortune that darkened Twain's life set in almost at once. Their first child, Langdon, was born prematurely and died eighteen months later, in June 1872, probably of diphtheria. Twain, as he had with other losses, blamed himself: he had neglected to replace the baby's blanket when it slipped off during a carriage ride on a cold morning.

Despite this bereavement, Twain's marriage to Livy propelled him into prosperity and what became a happy, productive eighteen-year interlude. Livy's inheritance enabled them in October 1871 to rent a house in Nook Farm, an exclusive region of subdivided land beside a river in West Hartford, Connecticut. Among the writers who lived in the close-knit community were Harriet Beecher Stowe and Charles Dudley Warner. In early 1873 the couple bought a tract nearby, on Farmington Avenue, and commissioned the great house where they lived and entertained lavishly until 1891. Their first daughter, Olivia Susan, was born in 1872; known as Susy, she was Twain's favorite child and began writing a biography of him at age thirteen. Clara followed in 1874 and Jane Lampton (Jean) in 1880.

THE EARLY NOVELS

Beginning in 1871 the Clemenses spent their summers near Elmira at Quarry Farm, owned by the husband of Livy's sister. In a small, octagonal, vine-covered study on a hilltop there, Twain produced some of his most significant works.

His output (and income) grew prodigious. He published *Roughing It*, a freewheeling account of his Nevada and California years, in 1872, and churned out sketches and columns for several newspapers. By 1874 his national popularity as a lecturer had reached its peak—he would take the stage nearly a thousand times during his life—but by then the royalties on his books allowed him to suspend his grueling travel regimen.

At dinner one night, Twain and his novelist-neighbor Charles Dudley Warner began complaining about the low state of contemporary novels. Their wives, listening in amusement, challenged the two men to do better. Soon Twain and Warner began collaborating on *The Gilded Age*, a rambling novel, by turns satirical, melodramatic, and turgid. Its meandering plotlines dealt with post–Civil War greed and mendacities in Washington, D.C. (Warner's purview), as filtered through the fortunes of a Missouri clan grasping for wealth (Twain's, as he borrowed liberally from his own family saga). Published in 1873, *The Gilded Age* drew enthusiastic reviews and sold briskly for a time despite its wildly veering tone and structural awkwardness. It introduced one character of comic-heroic proportions, the silver-tongued promoter Colonel Beriah Sellers, who inspired a stage dramatization, revised by Twain, that toured for ten years and generated higher revenues than the book.

Twain's next work of fiction was entirely his own. Only a modest success upon its publication, *The Adventures of Tom Sawyer* grew to be the most popular of all his books and bestowed on America its canonical image of boyhood. Shortly after his wedding he had confided, in a letter to his Hannibal childhood friend Will Bowen, that "the old life

has swept before me like a panorama. . . . [T]he old faces have looked out of the mists of the past." In June 1874, ensconced at Quarry Farm, he began immersing himself in that reverie. The larking Tom Sawyer, Twain's alter ego, lived in the river town of St. Petersburg, a stand-in for Hannibal. Twain launched the boy on a series of escapades drawn from memory, narrating the tale in the voice of an educated adult man.

He put the manuscript aside in the fall of that year to begin a series of magazine essays that took up his life as a young steamboat apprentice and pilot. "Old Times on the Mississippi," printed serially in 1875 as seven articles in the *Atlantic Monthly*, was an exquisitely detailed (but selectively sunny) portrait of river life and river denizens in the peak years of the steamboat age. The work combined comedy and rich historic detail, always refracted through Twain's improving imagination. On their completion, the author then returned to *Tom Sawyer*. The book was published the following year in England and America.

SOCIAL LION; MEETING HOWELLS

By now the once-impoverished Samuel Clemens of Hannibal, Missouri, not only had found acceptance in an elite eastern community; as Mark Twain, he presided over it. He and Livy filled their nineteen-room gingerbread Gothic house with luxurious furniture and appointments and constantly entertained guests with dinners and parties. Twain's social circle included the nationally prominent minister Henry Ward Beecher and his sister, the author Harriet Beecher Stowe; the Reverend Joseph H. Twichell, a frequent traveling companion; the Ulysses S. Grants; and many others.

None of these acquaintances reached as deeply into Twain's affections as did the novelist, critic, and editor of the *Atlantic Monthly*, William Dean Howells. A mild-mannered, self-made intellectual from Ohio, Howells had painstakingly worked himself into the inner circles of Boston literary culture. He thus made an unlikely comrade to the profane and flamboyant young refugee from the wide-open West. Yet even before the two met, Howells had conferred enormous legitimacy on Twain in 1869 by generously praising *The Innocents Abroad* in the *Atlantic Monthly*'s august pages. A little stunned by this notice, Twain paid an uninvited call at the magazine's offices to meet the author of the unsigned piece. The fastidious Howells never forgot his first glimpse of Twain, with his unruly thatches of red hair and mustache and his outlandish sealskin coat.

But the two young men were drawn to one another, and their intense thirty-nine-year friendship was among the few pleasurable constants in Twain's life. Howells read most of Twain's draft manuscripts, offering editorial suggestions about them—often raising a cautionary note about coarse language or shocking narrative—and boosting the major books with unfailingly positive reviews. Just as valuable, though, was their extraordinary personal rapport. Twain's quick temper, which could terminate friendships in a flash, never surfaced in his dealing with Howells. The two men laughed together, enjoyed rich and probing conversations on their customary long walks, attended baseball games, and were regular visitors in one another's households. Howells portrayed all of this in his 1910 reminiscence, *My Mark Twain: Reminiscences and Criticisms*, which stands as one of the tenderest and most unbounded celebrations of nineteenth-century male friendship on record.

MONEY ANXIETIES

The cost of Twain's extravagant social displays inevitably began to eat deeply into both his revenues and Livy's inheritance. The financial pressure was reflected in a waspish, bitterly denunciatory social-political tone that crept into his magazine and newspaper pieces—a tone that would utterly overtake him in his final years.

As his financial worries deepened, he began to shift his attention from purely literary ideas to a series of moneymaking projects and schemes. In 1878 he took his wife and daughters on a sixteen-month tour of Germany and other countries. Twain had contracted to write a travel book. *A Tramp Abroad*, published in 1880, focuses on the narrator's wanderings in the Swiss Alps with a shadowy "agent" named Harris—in reality Joseph Twichell, who had joined him there. Discursive, jocular, and overtly commercial, it remains a minor part of his oeuvre.

More significant was *The Prince and the Pauper*, published in 1882. Set in sixteenth-century England, it imagined a thirteen-year-old Prince Edward caught in a mixed-identity fiasco with his look-alike friend, the commoner Tom Canty, who ascends the throne in the prince's place. The novel illuminated some of Twain's central obsessions: switched identities, outcast claimants to royalty, the picaresque wanderings of young boys.

TWO MASTERWORKS

These works, however, paled in literary majesty beside two new manuscripts fitfully in progress during this period. Immediately upon publication of *The Adventures of Tom Sawyer*, Twain had plunged into a sequel boys' book and had written several chapters by the end of 1876, switching the narrator's voice from his own to that of Tom's illiterate vagabond friend, Huckleberry Finn. Twain's writing, while precise and purposeful from sentence to sentence, never adhered to a preconceived thematic structure. As a result, he frequently lost his sense of direction with a work-in-progress (this had happened with *Tom Sawyer* as well as the "Old Times" sketches) and either abandoned it or, as in this case, laid it aside. It languished for three years. Then he wrote five more chapters and abandoned it again. During this time, Twain took up another of his ambitions: to write a book about the Mississippi River. In the spring of 1882, accompanied by his publisher James R. Osgood and a stenographer named Roswell Phelps, he returned to the river to gather fresh notes and impressions. At St. Louis the three boarded the first of several steamboats that would take them to New Orleans and then north as far as St. Paul, Minnesota. Back at Quarry Farm, Mark Twain yoked his new material to the "Old Times" essays from the *Atlantic Monthly* and unleashed the whole as a great shifting prose torrent, by turns memoir, travel narrative, history, portraiture of people and places, humorous set pieces, mythic stories, and dreamlike musings. (He also poured in a few discarded sections from other works, most notably the so-called Raft Chapter from his novel-in-progress about Huckleberry Finn.)

Life on the Mississippi, published in 1883, is placed highly among Twain's works, though some critics have disparaged its frequent use of secondhand source material and its eccentric shifts of theme and even genre from chapter to chapter. Its main virtue, besides the varied richness of its language, is as a magnificently detailed time-lapse photograph of "interior" America during two vital phases of the nineteenth century: the mid-century era of steamboat commerce and culture and the post–Civil War era of rapid change, ushered in by the railroad, electric lighting, and manufacturing.

Life on the Mississippi enjoys one additional claim to literary merit: the experience of researching and writing it reignited Twain's imaginative connection to the boys' book he had set aside. He retrieved it and completed its second half in 1882 and 1883, working alternately on the Mississippi manuscript and other projects.

Twain lived twenty-six more years after the publication of *Adventures of Huckleberry Finn* in 1885, but not long enough to comprehend what a cornerstone of world literature the novel would become. Indeed, the first significant reaction to it was its banishment from the shelves of a library in Concord, Massachusetts, as "inelegant, rough, ignorant . . ."—a reference to Huck's coarse vagabond dialect as he narrates his long downriver flight on a raft in the company of the runaway slave Jim. ("That will sell 25,000 copies for us sure," Twain wrote in a sardonic letter, and he was essentially right; spurred by this whiff of the forbidden, sales of the novel topped 50,000 within three months.) For many years, *Huckleberry Finn* was reviewed and read as another boys' adventure novel. Reviewers liked the humor and the series of predicaments the two companions faced. They disapproved of Huck's indecorous speech and his chronic fibbing (to would-be captors and other threatening adults) and they puzzled over the last twelve chapters: the attenuated and needlessly outlandish schemes hatched by Huck and Tom Sawyer, newly arrived from St. Petersburg upriver, to free Jim from captivity on the Phelps farm in the Deep South. These escapades, torturous to Jim, seem especially gratuitous given the revelation that Tom knew all along that Jim's owner, Miss Watson, had granted Jim his freedom in her will.

DEEPER APPRECIATION OF *HUCKLEBERRY FINN*

By the 1890s a new wave of critics began to appreciate the book's sharp observations of manners and morals along the great Mississippi waterway. But not until the mid-twentieth century did scholars begin to plumb its astonishing depths of social, linguistic, political, and allegorical suggestiveness; its masterful use of irony to highlight the evils of racial bigotry; and the instinctual gallantry toward Jim that lay half buried under Huck's naïve ramblings about his "nigger" companion. Huck's cathartic conversion in chapter 31—in which he tears up a letter he has written in the throes of perceived sinfulness that discloses Jim's whereabouts and vows to himself, "All right, then, I'll go to hell!"—was identified as the moral turning point of the novel, if not of American literature. Later in the twentieth century, the problematic final twelve chapters—dismissed by T. S. Eliot and others as the book's imaginative failure—were exonerated as a brilliantly subtle allegory of the tribulations imposed on technically freed black Americans through the lingering racism that permeated the Reconstruction years. Huck's "inelegant" voice, far from a corrupting influence, has been seen as the liberating model for all the American masters of vernacular who followed Twain, from Ernest Hemingway to Flannery O'Connor to J. D. Salinger to Russell Banks. As for the sheer quality of the writing, the distinguished critic Harold Bloom has speculated in *Mark Twain* (1986) that Huck's

joyful "sunrise" passage at the beginning of chapter 19 is "the most beautiful prose paragraph yet written by an American."

"The first thing to see, looking away over the water, was a kind of dull line," is Huck's muted observation that begins the key aria in this passage, which then builds with all the controlled drama and color of the dawn itself:

> that was the woods on t'other side—you couldn't make nothing else out; then a pale place in the sky; then more paleness, spreading around; then the river softened up, away off, and warn't black any more, but gray; you could see little dark spots drifting along, ever so far away—trading scows, and such things; and long black streaks—rafts; sometimes you could hear a sweep screaking; or jumbled up voices, it was so still, and sounds come so far; and by-and-by you could see a streak on the water which you know by the look of the streak that there's a snag there in a swift current . . . and you see the mist curl up off of the water, and the east reddens up, and the river, and you make out a long cabin in the edge of the woods, away on the bank on t'other side of the river, being a wood-yard likely . . . then the nice breeze springs up, and comes fanning you from over there, so cool and fresh, and sweet to smell, on account of the woods and the flowers . . . and next you've got the full day, and everything smiling in the sun, and the song-birds just going it!

All of the posthumous praise for *Huckleberry Finn* would have been news to Twain himself. Influenced by the early critical scoldings and the disapproval of his adored daughter Susy, he regarded the book with detached resignation—as a beloved effort but a mild failure.

Twain would have been even more astonished at the charge of racism directed at the book in the twentieth century's latter half. In 1957 the National Association of Colored People charged that it was laced with "racial slurs" and "belittling racial designations," chiefly, Huck's oft-repeated use of the toxic term "nigger" in reference to Jim. In the early 1980s African-American activists succeeded in having *Huckleberry Finn* removed from many schools and public libraries, famously including the Mark Twain Intermediate School in Fairfax, Virginia. An equally impassioned counterargument from scholars, including several black intellectuals, held that *Huckleberry Finn* was conspicuously antiracist. Twain, speaking ironically through the received language of a mid-nineteenth-century southern boy, was illuminating the viciousness and the absurdity of racism, as in this exchange between Huck and Aunt Sally in chapter 32, as Huck relates a steamboat mishap:

"We blowed out a cylinder head."

"Good gracious! anybody hurt?"

"No'm. Killed a nigger."

But the money worshipper in Twain would have been most enthralled by the book's escalating popular success. Through the end of the twentieth century, *Adventures of Huckleberry Finn* never went out of print, selling more than twenty million copies in some fifty languages worldwide. One can almost hear Twain's ghost enviously muttering that this posthumous windfall is "tainted": " 'Tain't yours, and 'tain't mine."

DECLINE AND BANKRUPTCY

Huckleberry Finn was the nineteenth among the forty-six books (many of them tracts or collections of sketches) that Twain issued during his lifetime. It marked the apex of his literary achievements. (With typical myopia regarding his own genius, he prized the *Personal Recollections of Joan of Arc*, a stilted historical romance published in 1896 with the refined Susy as its primary audience, as his best.) His personal fortunes were by then at the beginning of a long decline. An incorrigible speculator in dubious get-rich ventures, he had begun in 1880 to pour money into the most catastrophic of them all: a machine under development by James Paige that, the inventor claimed, would end centuries of compositing drudgery by setting type automatically. Twain's memories of laboring manually in a series of print shops, combined with his lifelong obsession with great riches, made Paige's project an irresistible lure.

The problem, though, was that Paige could never get the machine to work for very long without breaking down—not surprising, perhaps, in view of its eighteen thousand parts. Twain could not wean himself from the fantasy that someday the contraption would work and make him a multimillionaire. In a steady stream of investments from 1880 until the machine's final failure in 1894, he subsidized Paige's futile tinkerings with more than $150,000 of his and Livy's money. These losses vitiated other assets, most notably Twain's own publishing company, which had successfully brought out *Huckleberry Finn* and then, in 1886, scored an enormous success with *Personal Memoirs of U. S. Grant*. The firm, called Webster and Company, declared bankruptcy in 1894 after Twain diverted a large part of its assets to Paige.

The trauma of these reverses darkened Twain's lifelong jaundiced view of humankind, and of his faith in his own prowess, particularly as a provider for his family. The metaphor of "Man's mind" as "a mere machine: an automatic machine" took root in his consciousness and flavored the bitter essays and half-finished manuscripts of his old age. A novel published in 1889, *A Connecticut Yankee in King Arthur's Court*, prefigured this gloomy assessment. Framed as a time-travel adventure back to the chivalric era in England, the story veers from Twain's familiar madcap comedy contrivances to a newer, utterly disjunctive motif: violent combat, clinically and coldly rendered. The book concludes with the grisly Battle of the Sand Belt, a mass slaughter of an army of medieval knights by the time-traveling protagonist Henry Morgan, who unleashes on them the weapons of modern industrial technology. The scenes amount to an eerily accurate prophecy of the mechanized warfare that would engulf western Europe a generation later.

> I touched a button and set fifty electric suns aflame on the top of our precipice. . . .
>
> I shot the current through all the fences and struck the whole host dead in their tracks! *There* was a groan you could *hear!* It voiced the death-pang of eleven thousand men. It swelled out on the night with awful pathos. . . .
>
> Stand to your guns, men! Open fire!
>
> The thirteen gatlings began to vomit death into the fated ten thousand. They halted, they stood their ground a moment against that withering deluge of fire, then they broke, faced about and swept toward the ditch like chaff before a gale. A full fourth part of their force never reached the top of the lofty embankment; the three-fourths reached it and plunged over—to death by drowning.
>
> Within ten short minutes after we had opened fire, armed resistance was totally annihilated, the campaign was ended, we fifty-four were masters of England! Twenty-five thousand men lay dead around us.

The collapse of assets that helped fuel these apocalyptic visions forced the Clemens family to spend most of the 1890s in self-imposed exile from America. Living frugally in Germany, Italy, and France from 1891 through early 1895, Twain furiously churned out essays and book manuscripts and made eight transatlantic crossings to seek American investors for his disintegrating business ventures. He produced *The Tragedy of Puddn'head Wilson*, a strange hybrid of a novel published in 1894 that joined a wild farce of mixed identity with a strong investigation of aristocratic decadence and racism in a small, Hannibal-like river town. The chief virtue of this novel is the character Roxana, condemned to a slave's life because of her one-sixteenth strain of black blood. Roxana is by far the most compelling and complete female character Twain ever rendered; her suffering, indignation, and many arias of soulful speech place her virtually on a par with Jim in *Huckleberry Finn.*

AROUND THE WORLD, AND MORE SORROW

In 1895, having secured the services of Standard Oil executive Henry Huttleston Rogers in shoring up his imperiled finances, Twain at age sixty made perhaps the most heroic gesture of any literary figure of the century. With Livy and daughter Clara in tow, he embarked on an around-the-world, hundred-city lecture tour for the avowed purpose of earning enough money to pay the $100,000 he owed his creditors. His daughters Susy and Jean remained in America. In the span of twelve months, he made appearances in Hawaii, Australia, New Zealand, Ceylon, India, Mauritius, South Africa, and other locales. His final travel book, *Following the Equator,* published in 1897, was a fairly straightforward account of his itinerary. The book's royalties and the yield of Henry Rogers's investments in his behalf allowed Twain to pay his creditors in full, as he had promised to do. But by that time the author had suffered another bereavement, the most devastating yet of all his losses.

He had disembarked from his tour in England and rented a house in Guildford to recuperate when, on 18 August 1896, he received a cable from America: Susy was dead at twenty-four of meningitis. Stupefied with grief, rage, and self-blame, Twain entered into a protracted dreamlike existence. He pronounced himself "never quite sane in the night" and came to regard the world as a version of hell.

The final years of Twain's life were a poignant mixture of public lionization and private misery. Remaining in Europe after Susy's death, he hobnobbed with Sigmund Freud; Emperor Franz Josef of Austria-Hungary; and the Polish inventor Jan Szczepanik, who had devised a rudimentary forerunner of television. He returned to a joyously receptive America in 1900 and became an instantly recognized figure on boulevards and trains and at public events. He introduced the young Winston Churchill to his first American lecture audience and received a series of honorary degrees—from Yale, the University of Missouri, and Oxford University. In 1906 he began wearing the white serge suit that became part of his iconography.

Privately, his despair worsened as Livy's health began to fail in 1902 and the two spent long periods apart as she deteriorated. In 1904 Livy died; the epileptic seizures that had plagued Jean began to worsen, and Clara entered a sanatorium to recover from a nervous breakdown.

THE GREAT DARK

Most of his writings from the mid-1890s onward were either frankly commercial attempts to resuscitate the figures of Tom and Huck (*Tom Sawyer Abroad* [1894] and *Tom Sawyer, Detective* [1896]) or dark private screeds intended for posthumous publication. Obsessively exploring the indifference of God to man's suffering, Satan's active presence in the world, the ironclad laws of the individual's nature, and many dreamlike permutations of dual personality, these included "The Chronicle of Young Satan," *The Mysterious Stranger* (1916), *What Is Man?* (1906), "The Great Dark," and *Letters from the Earth* (1962). He also dictated segments of his autobiography (published in 1924 as *Mark Twain's Autobiography*) and sat for interviews with his designated biographer, Albert Bigelow Paine.

Mark Twain died on 21 April 1910 at Stormfield, his home near Redding, Connecticut. He died swathed in renown and with the affection of the American people securely lodged, but at a limited level—as a humorist, an author of boys' books. His countrymen had not yet come to grips with the full scope and the more dangerous radiance of his literary vision. He died without comprehending the profound degree to which he had placed his imprint on the voice, the stance, or the democratic and moral concerns of American letters in the new century just unfolding.

And yet he died not entirely unappreciated for his enduring greatness. In *My Mark Twain,* Howells bade farewell to his friend with this eulogy: "Emerson, Longfellow, Lowell, Holmes—I knew them all and all the rest of our sages, poets, seers, critics, humorists; they were like one another and like other literary men; but Clemens was sole, incomparable, the Lincoln of our literature."

[See also Children's Literature; Howells, William Dean; *and* Stowe, Harriet Beecher.]

SELECTED WORKS

The Celebrated Jumping Frog of Calaveras County and Other Sketches (1867)
The Innocents Abroad (1869)
Roughing It (1872)
The Gilded Age (1873)
The Adventures of Tom Sawyer (1876)
A Tramp Abroad (1880)
The Prince and the Pauper (1882)
Life on the Mississippi (1883)
Adventures of Huckleberry Finn (1885)
A Connecticut Yankee in King Arthur's Court (1889)

Tom Sawyer Abroad (1894)
The Tragedy of Puddn'head Wilson and Those Extraordinary Twins (1894)
Personal Recollections of Joan of Arc (1896)
Tom Sawyer, Detective and Other Stories (1896)
Following the Equator (1897)
What Is Man? (1906)
The Mysterious Stranger (1916)
Mark Twain's Autobiography (1924)
Letters from the Earth (1962)

FURTHER READING

Bloom, Harold, ed. *Mark Twain.* New York, 1986. An anthology of critical essays.

Brooks, Van Wyck. *The Ordeal of Mark Twain.* New York, 1920. An influential debunking of Twain's literary stature, informed by Brooks's application of Freudian theories to the author's early family life and cultural origins.

Cardwell, Guy. *The Man Who Was Mark Twain.* New Haven, Conn., and London, 1991. An investigation of Twain's emotional complexities.

Cox, James M. *Mark Twain: The Fate of Humor.* Princeton, N.J., 1966. An examination of the structure of American humorous writing in Mark Twain's lifetime.

DeVoto, Bernard. *Mark Twain's America.* Boston, 1932. A rebuttal to Van Wyck Brooks's thesis by a Twain historian and editor.

Emerson, Everett. *The Authentic Mark Twain.* Philadelphia, 1984. A life of Twain.

Fishkin, Shelly Fisher, ed. *The Oxford Mark Twain.* New York and Oxford, 1996. A twenty-nine-volume republication of Twain first editions with interpretive essays by late-twentieth-century scholars and writers.

Howells, William Dean. *My Mark Twain: Reminiscences and Criticisms.* New York, 1910. A memoir by the author's longtime friend, reviewer, and editor.

Kaplan, Justin. *Mr. Clemens and Mark Twain.* New York, 1966. Generally regarded as the standard biography.

Lauber, John. *The Making of Mark Twain: A Biography.* New York, 1985. Twain's life through his wedding with Olivia Langdon.

Lynn, Kenneth S. *Mark Twain and Southwestern Humor.* Boston, 1959. An analysis of the ways in which political and social currents were expressed through humorous conventions during the author's formative years.

Mack, Effie Mona. *Mark Twain in Nevada.* New York, 1938. The author's western years.

Paine, Albert Bigelow. *Mark Twain, a Biography: The Personal and Literary Life of Samuel Langhorne Clemens.* 3 vols. New York, 1912. The first full-scale biography of Twain, written with the author's active participation.

Rasmussen, R. Kent. *Mark Twain A to Z.* New York, 1995. An encyclopedic compilation of information about Twain and his works.

Steinbrink, Jeffrey. *Getting to Be Mark Twain.* Berkeley, Calif., and Los Angeles, 1991. Twain's life from 1867 through 1871.

Wecter, Dixon. *Sam Clemens of Hannibal.* Boston, 1952. A reconstruction of the author's boyhood and hometown.

See also the article on *Adventures of Huckleberry Finn*, immediately following.

MARK TWAIN'S
ADVENTURES OF HUCKLEBERRY FINN

by Pauls Toutonghi

It has been more than a century since Mark Twain's own publishing company printed *Adventures of Huckleberry Finn* (1885) in Hartford, Connecticut. Over the decades since its publication, *Huckleberry Finn* has become one of the most cherished novels in the canon of American literature. Students of all ages have found their interest kindled by discussion of the novel's plot, characters, and captivating narrative voice. Frequently quoted by scholars, Ernest Hemingway's statement that "All modern American literature comes from one book by Mark Twain called *Huckleberry Finn*" should not be overlooked. Indeed, this single text has inspired numerous writers. The roster of novelists who owe allegiance to it is too long to enumerate fully. Traces of this book can be seen in many of the most significant volumes in the American literary canon.

Formally, *Huckleberry Finn* combines elements of realism, the pastoral, and the drama of the open road. Few novels can match its exuberance of language. Twain's remarkably entertaining vocabulary—allegedly issuing from the point of view of a young boy—constantly surprises the reader. Its vulgarities can be shocking; occasionally they have sparked critical distaste and disapproval. However, though critics initially gave the book a mixed reception, the body of critical thought on Twain has evolved to consider *Huckleberry Finn* a classic of American prose form. It stands as Twain's most important work and will be read far into the twenty-first century.

INITIAL CRITICAL RECEPTION

It is important to remember that Twain published *Huckleberry Finn* in a literary environment vastly different from the marketplace of today. In 1885, advertising had not yet evolved into a nationwide industry. Sales were fueled primarily by the serialization of a novel in a magazine. Major works by many eighteenth- and nineteenth-century American authors, including Harriet Beecher Stowe, Henry James, and James Fenimore Cooper, appeared in serialized form before they were released in single editions. But

until *Huckleberry Finn*, Twain had rejected this method of publication for his own work.

From 1869, when *The Innocents Abroad* was a nationwide best-seller, until 1884, Twain sold his books through subscription publication, a type of marketing that reached its height in the years after the Civil War, when armies of traveling salesmen moved across the country, selling a widening array of consumer goods from door to door. Subscription agents hawked brooms, bromides, and books. Depending mostly on his or her charisma, and armed with only brief excerpts and a sales pitch, a subscription agent would sell thousands of advance orders for a novel slated for publication. The heyday of subscription publication was clearly the decade from 1869 to 1879. By 1885, however, it was losing its adherents as the national distribution of magazines grew and became more efficient.

In *My Mark Twain* (1910), the noted editor William Dean Howells quoted a letter from Twain in which the author wrote, "Anything but subscription publication is printing for private circulation." Private circulation, in this case, can be interpreted as small-number sales. In 1884, however, following an extensive courtship by Richard Watson Gilder, editor-in-chief of the *Century Magazine*, Twain agreed to release small sections of his novel in successive issues of the *Century*. Excerpts from *Huckleberry Finn* appeared in the December 1884, January 1885, and February 1885 issues. This method of publicity was seemingly quite successful. In its first two months of publication, *Huckleberry Finn* sold 57,000 copies, a remarkable number even by today's standards.

In order to cater to the tastes of the *Century*'s more genteel readers, Twain eliminated much of the vulgarity from the serialized sections. However, once he made the uncut version of the book available, certain segments of the American public raised objections. In March 1885, the Public Library of Concord, Massachusetts, banned *Huckleberry Finn* from its shelves. On the day following this ban, the *New York Herald* published an article that summed up the decision of the library's administrators: "Another committeeman perused the volume with great care and discovered that it was couched in the language of a rough, ignorant dialect." The *Herald* added that the committee members of the library had found that "all through [*Huckleberry Finn*'s] pages, there is a systematic use of bad grammar and an employment of inelegant expressions." This criticism fueled sales of *Huckleberry Finn*, however, and provoked media reports in newspapers across the country.

Critical consideration for the book grew rapidly. In 1920, Van Wyck Brooks, one of America's leading cultural critics, published *The Ordeal of Mark Twain*. In this critical milestone, Brooks put forward a strong argument against Twain's work, based in part on the very crudity that some initial reviewers found offensive. Brooks's text is fairly convoluted, however, in that it argues that Twain was a victim of circumstance rather than a literary opportunist. Brooks believed that the "greatness" of Twain's novels had been "thwarted" by the uncouth nature of his subject matter, combined with the difficulties caused by censorship by his family and editors. Though this vein of criticism would not be taken up by many critics, *The Ordeal of Mark Twain* would serve as a starting point for book-length studies of Twain's work, especially those that engaged in "close reading" of his fiction and nonfiction texts.

American interest in this novel proved inexhaustible, and the Brooks work can be seen as early evidence of the ways in which the novel galvanized the literary community. Reactions were frequently split between competing newspapers in a single city. Typical of the reaction to *Huckleberry Finn* is its critical reception in San Francisco, where Twain had worked as a news reporter early in his literary career. The *San Francisco Chronicle* pronounced the novel "the most amusing book Mark Twain has written for years." The *San Francisco Daily Examiner*, however, published a brief, scathing review, saying that the book was, "without a motive, a moral, or a plot." This negative assessment was just one brand of criticism that *Huckleberry Finn* endured. Reviewers of the book often objected to Huck himself, whom they found to be amoral—if not gleefully, then at least obliviously so. Of course, this critique has faded over time. Huck now seems fairly innocent. In the twentieth century, much of the controversy over *Huckleberry Finn* has focused on the question of racism in the text, discussed later in this article.

HUCKLEBERRY FINN AS A CHILDREN'S BOOK

In another note to William Dean Howells, this one collected by Charles Neider in *The Selected Letters of Mark Twain*, Twain described his work with the character of Tom Sawyer:

> If I went on now, and took him into manhood, he would just lie, like all the one-horse men in literature, and the reader would conceive a hearty contempt for him. It is not a boy's book at all. It will only be read by adults. It is only written for adults.

Tom Sawyer also figures in the plot of *Huckleberry Finn*, if only at the book's beginning and end. Indeed, Twain frequently implied that *Huckleberry Finn* was also intended for a mature audience, and that because of this he had infused the text with narrative complexity. Although Twain did intend to write a book that dealt with the innocence of childhood, and with the ways in which children interpret the world's most cynical problems, there is little evidence that he imagined it evolving into a common text in elementary school classrooms.

Yet this is how many readers encounter the book for the first time. Teachers have utilized *Huckleberry Finn* in classrooms because of its appeal to young audiences. What are the reasons for this broad appeal? Chief among them are Huck's fierce resilience and his independence from social conventions. This is, in fact, a humorous irony: many schoolchildren are reading a text in which the central character is a child who rejects schooling. Critics too have noted *Huckleberry Finn*'s appeal to the young imagination. The adventure story at its heart and its easy-to-read, plain-speech narrative style are perhaps further explanations for the novel's broad appeal.

Beneath this pleasing façade, however, there is a much darker story line that seethes with some of the most serious questions that faced nineteenth-century America. Slavery plays a pivotal role in the book. The condemnation of slavery, furthermore, is only implied, as Twain allows the action of the novel to speak for itself. Perhaps in part because Huckleberry Finn seems not to be a very sophisticated narrator, Twain refrains from issuing broad abolitionist statements through Huck's voice. This is a difficult quandary for a young reader. The student of *Huckleberry Finn* must quickly learn to understand implicit, rather than explicit, condemnations of social ills such as slavery. Moreover, Huck and his companion, Tom Sawyer, are perpetually faced with thorny moral dilemmas. Huck, especially, must continually struggle with life in a world that seems on the brink of wholesale moral bankruptcy. Theft, the slave trade, and the application of unjust laws through force—this is the world of *Huckleberry Finn*.

AN APPEALING ADVENTURE STORY

The story itself is a blur of motion. It opens with Huck Finn isolated in the home of the Widow Douglas, a genteel southern woman whose predictable morality strains Huck's boyish exuberance. She has agreed to adopt him and provide him with a home because Huck's own father is a landless alcoholic who drifts in and out of society. There is immediate conflict between Huck's desire to be free of social restraints and the Widow Douglas's attempts to constrain his behavior. Huck, of course, relays this conflict in an informal, breezy tone. His words are ingratiating and casual:

> The Widow Douglas, she took me for her son, and allowed she would sivilize me; but it was rough living in the house all the time, considering how dismal regular and decent the widow was in all her ways; and so when I couldn't stand it no longer, I lit out.

The misspellings, double negatives, and humorous objections to the very things that most Americans take for granted add up to an appealing narrator. The subject matter, however, also draws the reader into the story. After the first few pages, which serve as an introduction of sorts, the plot begins to move quite rapidly. One night, Huck sneaks out of the Widow Douglas's home—surely these are the elements of boyhood fantasy—and he and his friends hold a clandestine meeting in a nearby cave. They form a secret society, vowing to become a band of ruthless robbers tormenting the town of St. Petersburg for the rest of their lives.

Predictably, this plan goes awry. The boys are not criminals, and so they are unable to commit any of their planned crimes. Though they meet at night in the caves and establish elaborate rituals and bylaws that must be signed in blood, their association amounts to little more than a group of friends gathering beyond the purview of adults. If this atmosphere sounds strangely familiar, it is because of the rough similarity to the plot of *Tom Sawyer*. The gang does not come to fruition, and even as it is collapsing, Huck's father suddenly resurfaces. Mr. Finn kidnaps Huck to a dilapidated cabin on the banks of the Mississippi River.

Any consideration of the story line of *Huckleberry Finn* will stretch to a breathless length, carried away by the manner in which the plot brings episode after episode before the reader's attention. It is perhaps more fruitful to the scholar—or the casual reader—of the text of *Huckleberry Finn* to consider its specific language. Though the following passage comes later in the book, it

gives a good sense of the vigor and gusto with which Huck narrates. Describing a moment of surprise at the dinner table, Huck relates:

> My heart fell down amongst my lungs and livers and things, and a hard piece of corn-crust started down my throat after it and got met on the road with a cough and was shot across the table and took one of the children in the eye and curled him up like a fishing-worm. . . .

There is an unwillingness to use clichés in this passage, but Twain crafts this unwillingness as simply the guileless voice of a youthful narrator. This passage, then, is a careful artifice. It is quite humorous as well, and gives the reader the flavor of the rambunctious narration that characterizes Huck.

Yet Huck is not always so energetic. His captivity at the hands of his father dismays him, and it is only after some time that he manages to escape. Huck fakes his death by drowning and flees to a small island in the middle of the river, where he takes refuge while the residents of St. Petersburg search for his body. Also on Jackson Island, by coincidence, is the slave Jim. Jim has escaped from his captivity in the Douglas household. Predictably, the two runaways find each other. Following a brief moment of suspicion, during which Jim fears that Huck will return to town and betray the runaway slave, the older man trusts Huck with the location of his camp. Huck pledges his fealty to Jim, but not because of any overarching sense of the evil of slavery. "People would call me a low down Ablitionist and despise me for keeping mum," Huck says, "but that don't make no difference. I ain't agoing to tell, and ain't agoing back there anyways." He simply accepts Jim; Huck decides further to spurn the town from which he has come and to reject the prevalent morals of a racist society, which demand that he turn in the runaway slave.

From this point, the man and the boy are bound together. They embark on a river voyage, setting out onto the Mississippi on a raft. They intend to make it to the mouth of the Ohio, whence Jim will be free to take a steamboat into the North. They never make it. In the tradition of the American picaresque, Huck and Jim have numerous entertaining yet darkly tinted adventures. They find a cabin cut loose from its foundation and floating on the Mississippi. In the cabin is only the body of a man, shot dead, so Huck and Jim loot his home. Jim learns the identity of the body but will not allow Huck to look at the dead man's face. Later, the reader discovers that the dead man was Huck's father.

Within days, Huck and Jim again manage to go astray. They stumble into a long-running feud between two southern families, reminiscent of the legendary battle between the Hatfields and the McCoys. After a few dangerous moments, Huck and Jim extricate themselves from this situation, only to be swept up by two opportunistic con men, the Duke and the King. The Duke and the King force Huck and Jim into a mad swirl of confidence schemes. These schemes culminate with Jim's abduction and with the two con men attempting to sell him back into slavery. Huck is unaware of the planned kidnapping until it occurs, and afterward he assiduously tries to track Jim down and free him. The trail leads Huck to Silas and Sally Phelps, Tom Sawyer's uncle and aunt. Shockingly, they are the ones who have purchased Jim.

The end of the novel is an intricately plotted melodrama. After the coincidental appearance of the Phelps family, Twain uses more coincidence to advance the story line. Huck sneaks onto the Phelps property, where he finds Jim confined in chains. As Huck plots to free Jim, Tom Sawyer suddenly appears, bringing his exuberance and love of mischief. The two friends concoct an elaborate plan to free Jim—a plan that fails spectacularly, nearly getting all three of them killed.

At the pinnacle of the story, when the action has reached its most dire state and Tom Sawyer has just been shot in the leg, Twain plays a trump card. Tom reveals that Jim is actually a free man because the younger Douglas sister has died two months earlier, stipulating in her will that Jim be liberated. "Turn him loose! He ain't no slave; he's as free as any cretur that walks this earth!" When Huck furiously accosts Tom, demanding to know why he failed to reveal this news immediately, Tom maintains that he merely craved the excitement of the escape. The slave-hunters relent, and Jim is granted his freedom. Huck decides that he will go west, into the American frontier, the unexplored territories. He does not want to return to St. Petersburg. "But I reckon I got to light out for the Territory ahead of the rest," Huck concludes, "because Aunt Sally she's going to adopt me and sivilize me and I can't stand it. I been there before." His tone brings a circular sense of completion to the novel's conclusion. This is the same voice that began the book, and it promises an unbroken vista of potential future misadventures. Of course, this can be brought into question, since *Huckleberry Finn* does in fact read as an autobiography, and autobiography can be seen as the highest form of the very "sivilizin" that Huck hopes to reject.

THE PERSONALIZATION OF SETTING

The town of St. Petersburg can be taken as a caricature of Twain's boyhood home, Hannibal, Missouri. For this and *Tom Sawyer*, Twain chose to set the action in a small town on the Mississippi River in the 1840s, corresponding to the years of his own boyhood. Indeed, Twain intended *Huckleberry Finn* as a sequel to *The Adventures of Tom Sawyer*. Set in the same milieu and featuring many of the same characters, the two books have significant similarities. Twain originally planned to structure the plot of *Huckleberry Finn* much like that of *Tom Sawyer*. There was to be a murder trial in which Jim, the innocent victim, would be unjustly accused. Huck Finn, with the help of Tom Sawyer, would save Jim at the last possible moment, providing irrefutable evidence of his innocence.

Critics have often pointed out that the writing of *Huckleberry Finn* took Twain eight years. These were difficult years for Twain, during which he endured the death of his youngest son and the prolonged illness of his wife, Olivia. What perhaps began as an adventure story and sequel ended as a grim reminder of the difficulties facing American society during Twain's time. The book is not merely an adventure story; it is a catalogue of racism, scheming opportunism, and the trials of innocence in the modern era. Huck's difficult moment of moral choice—the moment when he must decide whether to help Jim or turn him in—ranks with any of the key moments of decision in the novels of Sarah Orne Jewett or William Dean Howells.

MARK TWAIN AND THE MOVEMENT TOWARD REALISM

Though Twain's work is often infused with an appreciation of journalistic style, his twists of plot are worthy of any nineteenth-century English Gothic novel. Why, then, is there widespread academic insistence that Twain ranks among the founders of American realism? In a fascinating introductory essay to *Huckleberry Finn*, John Seelye writes, "Literary realism was a movement that placed heavy emphasis on materials drawn from the author's own experiences." Seelye admits that although the adventures of Huck and Jim are based on no principle other than "pure chance," the style in which they are relayed is almost journalistic in its tone. Though the book cannot be accused of an overwhelming devotion to realism, its tone has all the hallmarks of a realistic work: an easy and conversational voice, an unwillingness to extrapolate broad theoretical concepts from the small matters of life, and a devotion to detail. As Kathryn Van Spanckeren (1999) writes, "Twain's style, based on vigorous, realistic, colloquial American speech, gave American writers a new appreciation of their national voice." Indeed, many authors have argued that Twain's rise was fueled by the uniquely American difficulties of Reconstruction and post–Civil War expansion to the west. To a nation buoyed by the potential of manifest destiny, a book of adventures that concludes with the youthful narrator setting out for the unclaimed western territories must have been powerfully appealing.

Ten years after his publication of *Huckleberry Finn*, Twain had the bulk of his writing life behind him and had become a popular speaker on the international lecture circuit. He viewed his own work as iconoclastic, and he was not willing to identify with the school of realism or the school of romantic literature. He was, however, willing to share his opinions about the faults of each. In his now famous essay "Fenimore Cooper's Literary Offenses," published in the July 1895 issue of the *North American Review*, Twain wrote, "If Cooper had been an observer his inventive faculty would have worked better; not more interestingly, but more rationally, more plausibly." Twain also established nineteen rules for fiction and humorously cited Cooper for violation of eighteen of them. Clearly, these rules were written with *Huckleberry Finn* in mind. From one to eighteen, they correspond to the approach Twain took in that novel. Here is an author struggling with the significant figures of the age, hoping to establish his position in the history of American literature.

A number of characters in contemporary American fiction trace directly to *Huckleberry Finn*. The openings of J. D. Salinger's *The Catcher in the Rye* and Ernest Hemingway's "Nick Adams" stories display marked affinity with Twain's fiction. The influences of Twain's particular brand of realism can be seen in the subtle realism of Raymond Carver, or in the exuberant realism of such writers as Ann Beattie, Richard Ford, and even Saul Bellow. Without doubt, his inheritors are numerous. Yet the questions that arise from *Huckleberry Finn* have proved more lasting and complex than perhaps even Twain could have imagined.

HUCKLEBERRY FINN AND RACE

In *Monteiro* v. *Tempe High* (19 October 1998), the Ninth Circuit Court of Appeals ruled against the plaintiff, Kathy Monteiro, who had petitioned the court urging that *Huckleberry Finn* be removed from her daughter's high school reading list. Chief among her objections to the book was its repeated use of the word "nigger," which Monteiro found offensive and degrading. Monteiro's attorney argued that the use of this term in a classroom environment led to racist taunting and created an environment that was not conducive to instruction. Writing for the majority, Judge Stephen Reinhardt rejected the request to remove the book from the curriculum. He did say, however, that this was a difficult and intricate decision. "In this case," wrote Reinhardt, "the competing interests are the First Amendment rights of high school students to receive information or ideas—even when contained in literary works that may in today's world appear to have racist overtones—and the rights of those same students to receive a public education that neither fosters nor acquiesces in a racially hostile environment." Reinhardt considered the question of whether *Huckleberry Finn* "fosters a racist environment in the classroom" to be subordinate to the First Amendment rights of students to read any given work of literature.

Is racism embedded within the text of *Huckleberry Finn*? As is frequently the case with questions in literary studies, there can be no definitive or simple answer. The issue of race, however, certainly has become one of the major points facing any contemporary reader of *Huckleberry Finn*. In her excellent introduction to the Oxford edition of *Huckleberry Finn*, the Nobel Prize–winning novelist Toni Morrison (1996), an African American, writes that her initial encounters with the novel were deeply disturbing, not because of the derogatory term "nigger" but rather because of what she deems the "over-the-top minstrelization" of Jim. Morrison feels insulted by the ways in which Twain paints the character of Jim, making him clownish and "relentlessly idiotic." She believes that the explanation for this choice is complex. "In addition to accommodating a racist readership, writing Jim so complete a buffoon solves the problem of...how to effectively bury the father figure underneath the minstrel paint." Twain disguised Jim in the idiot's clothes in order to make him a less threatening character.

Indeed, this is the deeper truth of *Huckleberry Finn*. During their time together on the raft, Jim and Huck establish a deep bond that in many respects transcends the racial barriers that society has set between them. Jim's meditative good humor serves as the antithesis of the disposition of Huck's biological father, who is prone to drunken rage and abuses Huck at the novel's beginning. Yet there can be no doubt that Twain intended this novel for the broad American market. America in the mid-1880s was a troubled nation burdened with the failures of Reconstruction. There is no documentary evidence to support the idea that the American reading public was prepared to accept a book in which a white child was given succor by an older, black father figure. The masking that Twain gives to Jim serves only to deepen the sorrow at the center of this book. The reader longs for Jim to speak from the center of his own deep compassion for Huck, and to take his rightful place in Huck's mind as a moral tutor. But this speaking never occurs.

As Shelley Fisher Fishkin (2000) points out in her significant essay, "Was Huck Black? Mark Twain and African-American Voices," many of Twain's contemporaries launched significant attacks against racism in America. However, as she also points out, Twain did not: "Twain's attacks were more subtle, less risky, less courageous. They are also more lasting." Do the complexities of the novel, she wonders, limit the power of its social critique? Or can its condemnation of racism be inferred from the great gulf between the way that Jim deserves to be treated and the way in which society treats him? The bond between Huck and Jim cannot be questioned, nor can its importance in the text be doubted.

Immediately before the novel's conclusion, Jim reveals to Huck that the corpse they found in the cabin was actually Huck's father. It is a powerful moment, partly because Huck's father has been such a force of violence, whose abuse has overshadowed Huck throughout the book:

> "Doan' you 'member de house dat was float'n down de river, en dey wuz a man in dah, kivered up, en I went in en unkivered him and didn' let you come in? Well, den, you k'n git yo' money when you wants it; kase dat wuz him."

This is an excellent example of both the minstrelization of Jim and the intimacy of the bond between the two central characters. Jim has kept this knowledge to himself throughout, worrying that despite Huck's dislike for his father, the boy would be overwhelmed by learning the truth of his death. It is a deeply caring act, and one that implies fatherly stewardship. Yet Jim's voice is cloaked in an eye-dialect that denigrates him. The reader cannot help but pause over his words, struggling for a moment just to make sense of them. Jim's words are robbed of their dignity. This, then, is the anguish of slavery—the dehumanization of the slave—and its ether hangs just beyond the visible world of the printed page.

LOVE AND LEGACY

A catalogue of the adventures and misadventures in *Huckleberry Finn* would be quite lengthy. As in any good picaresque or adventure novel, the episodes of action form a formidable part of the text. Yet what remains with the reader after the book has been closed? A remembrance of an organizing environment—the Mississippi River and its placid waters—and a sense of two characters journeying together toward a broader goal, taking a trip of the most profound sort. Toni Morrison identifies one particular moment of "journeying" as the emotional center of *Huckleberry Finn*. In chapter 24, Jim and Huck exchange stories from their lives while moving slowly over the waters of the Mississippi. Much has happened up to this point. The two characters are mulling over the events thus far, reprising the action and offering anecdotes from their own pasts. Jim relates a moment when, in a fit of anger, he hit his own daughter. He relays the intense shame that he felt afterward:

> "Oh, Huck, I bust out a-cryin' en grab her up in my arms, en say, 'Oh, de po' little thing! The Lord God Amighty fogive po' ole Jim kaze he never gwyne to fogive hisself as long's he live!' "

This revelation of a fault, a moment when Jim was an abusive parent, contrasts powerfully with the gleeful way in which Huck's father has taken to violence. Huck's father has been unrepentant; contemporary readers cannot help but note that his abuse must have left deep scars on Huck's personality. Yet, as Morrison points out, there is a silence after this confession. Huck does not speak. Chapter 24 ends, and chapter 25 begins with a burst of action as the Duke and the King bring Huck and Jim to the brink of another disastrous adventure. Morrison notes that this is the text's most significant silence. Jim's essential goodness has been displayed, but Huck has not offered a reply. What could he say that wouldn't interfere with Jim's voice? Here, the older man is allowed primacy in the text, and humanity, and resonance.

Even in its silences, then, *Huckleberry Finn* manages to paint a subtly eloquent portrait of its characters. There can be little doubt that the immediate surface of the text has overt tones of racial discrimination. Yet when the characters are quiet—when they are not enmeshed in their historical context—they betray their affinity for one another, as well as Twain's attention to them as human beings. Though critical response to *Huckleberry Finn* has been hostile at times, it remains a vitally important book. The way that this novel can engender debate even among casual readers ensures that it will hold its position as one of the foremost documents of American literary realism.

FURTHER READING

Beaver, Harold. "Run, Nigger, Run: *Adventures of Huckleberry Finn* as a Fugitive Slave Narrative." *Journal of*

American Studies 8 (1974): 339–361. An excellent early study of the intricacies of race in the book. One of the best on the topic.

Bloom, Harold, ed. *Mark Twain*. New York, 1986. One of America's widest-ranging critics draws together an impressive and varied array of essays.

Brooks, Van Wyck. *The Ordeal of Mark Twain*. New York, 1920. A classic text, one of the first book-length critical studies of Twain. Some ideas are outdated.

Budd, Louis J. *A Listing of and Selections from Newspaper and Magazine Interviews with Samuel L. Clemens, 1874–1910*. Arlington, Tex., 1977. A very informative bibliography.

DeVoto, Bernard. *Mark Twain's America*. Lincoln, Nebr., 1997. A classic study originally published in 1932 but surprisingly fresh.

Duncan, Dayton, and Ken Burns. *Mark Twain*. New York, 2001. The companion to the 2001 Public Television series about Twain's life. Colorful, engaging format, ideal for younger readers.

Fishkin, Shelley Fisher. "Was Huck Black? Mark Twain and African-American Voices." In *The Adventures of Huckleberry Finn*, edited by Susan K. Harris. Boston, 2000. Thinks about race in *Huckleberry Finn* in a new and thought-provoking way.

Gillman, Susan Kay. *Dark Twins: Imposture and Identity in Mark Twain's America*. Chicago, 1989. Elegant and thoroughly modern examination of Twain's work, including a lengthy section on Huck and Jim.

Howells, William Dean. *My Mark Twain*. Boston, 1910. One of the classics of Twain scholarship; details the relationship between Howells and Twain.

LeMaster, J. R., and James D. Wilson, eds. *The Mark Twain Encyclopedia*. New York, 1993. Though the subject matter varies widely, an excellent introduction to a number of topics in Twain, with a solid index.

Morrison, Toni. Introduction. In *Adventures of Huckleberry Finn*, The Oxford Mark Twain, edited by Shelley Fisher Fishkin. London, 1996.

Pinsker, Sanford. "*Huckleberry Finn* and the Problem of Freedom." *Virginia Quarterly Review* 77.4 (Autumn 2001). Very persuasive, and a good place to start any critical essay.

Powers, Ron. *Dangerous Waters: A Biography of the Boy Who Became Mark Twain*. New York, 1999. Probably the best biography of Twain; Powers is an elegant writer who has exhaustively researched the topic. Covers mostly Twain's boyhood, directly relevant to the climate in which *Huckleberry Finn* takes place.

Seelye, John. Introduction. In *Huckleberry Finn*. New York, 1985. A strong introduction, written in a conversational style.

Stephens, George D. "*Huckleberry Finn* as a Journey." *Mark Twain Journal* 13.2 (1966): 11–15. A good source of information about the actual journey that Huck and Jim take.

Tatham, Campbell. "'Dismal and Lonesome': A New Look at *Huckleberry Finn*." *Modern Fiction Studies* 14.1 (1968): 47–55. A reconsideration of Huck, instrumental in reshaping the landscape of critical debate about humor in *Huckleberry Finn*.

Van Spanckeren, Kathryn. "The Rise of Realism: 1860–1914." Washington, D.C., 1999. A comprehensive look at the literary milieu in which Twain played a big part.

See also the article on Mark Twain, immediately preceding.

JOHN UPDIKE

by Patricia B. Heaman

John Updike is perhaps America's most versatile, prolific, and distinguished man of letters of the second half of the twentieth century, having created a literary oeuvre that includes fiction, poetry, essays, criticism, a play, children's books, memoirs, and other prose. His first published short story and poem appeared in *The New Yorker* in 1954; he joined the staff in 1955 and has continued to publish in that magazine throughout his career. Since his first book in 1958, few years have gone by in which he has not published at least one volume, as well as an impressive number of book reviews, short stories, poems, art reviews, and topical and personal essays. His reputation rests largely on his fiction, for which he has won numerous prestigious awards, prizes, and recognitions. His subject matter is closely linked to his personal experience of small-town, middle-class life in America from the time of World War II through the beginning of the twenty-first century. Much of his early work is based on memories of people, places, and events associated with his childhood and youth in southeastern Pennsylvania, and works of his mature period focus largely on the themes of marriage, adultery, religious faith, and family life. Despite occasional forays into non-American settings and past and future time frames, Updike's fiction for the most part reflects the culture, conflicts, and concerns of his readers' American time and place. His recent work often deals with a return to or reflection on the personal, historical, or literary past as it has created the present and is interpreted and transformed by a contemporary consciousness.

John Updike.
(© *Christopher Felver/Corbis*)

few miles from Shillington, the small town where he lived with his parents, Wesley and Linda Hoyer Updike, and his maternal grandparents for his first thirteen years. In Shillington, he could walk to school, to the Lutheran church that fostered his religious beliefs, to the playground where he spent long summer days, to the neighborhood movie theater he avidly attended several times a week, and to the trolley that took him and his mother to the shops and public library in Reading. He felt dislocated by his family's move in 1945 to a farm near Plowville, eleven miles away, that had been his mother's birthplace. Although he and his father, who taught mathematics at Shillington High School, drove to school daily, he felt isolated at the sandstone farmhouse and spent much of his adolescence in the welcome company of pen, pencil, and blank paper, writing and drawing cartoons, interests encouraged from an early age by his mother, who had literary ambitions of her own. Growing up among adults, Updike was a precocious child and exceptional student whose emotional life and aesthetic sensibilities were deeply rooted in the family and environment that nurtured him. His first ambition was to be an animator for Walt Disney; later he hoped to become a cartoonist for a magazine like *The New Yorker*.

THE IMPRINT OF TIME AND PLACE: THE EARLY YEARS, 1932–1950

John Hoyer Updike was born on 18 March 1932, in Reading, the urban hub in southeastern Pennsylvania a

BREAKING AWAY: 1950–1957

After graduating as class president and co-valedictorian of Shillington High School in 1950, Updike attended Harvard on a scholarship. He left southeastern Pennsylvania at eighteen, but the people, places, and memories of his early years had left strong impressions that drew him back repeatedly and have remained a permanent source of inspiration for his writing.

At Harvard, he majored in English literature and drew cartoons and wrote for the *Harvard Lampoon,* of which he was elected president and editor in his senior year. In Boston, he met Mary Pennington, a fine arts student at Radcliffe; they were married in 1953. The following year, Updike wrote his senior thesis on Robert Herrick, a sixteenth-century English poet; sold his first poem and story to *The New Yorker;* and was graduated summa cum laude. He won a Knox Fellowship to the Ruskin School of Drawing and Fine Art at Oxford, where he lived with Mary in 1954 and where their first child, Elizabeth, was born in 1955. He returned to the United States in 1955 to accept a staff position at *The New Yorker,* for which he wrote poems, short stories, and essays, and contributed to "The Talk of the Town" section for the next two years.

Having achieved rather early and easily a good measure of the professional success he had dreamed of as a youth, Updike went through a period of spiritual crisis during which he "read a lot of theology because I needed to. I was kind of despairing or at least felt very hollow" (Plath, 1994, p. 75). The writings of Søren Kierkegaard and Karl Barth had an especially lasting influence on his work. The New York literary scene had become "unnutritious and interfering" (Plath, p. 24) for him shortly after the birth of his second child, David, in 1957, when Updike decided to leave the security of his position to take his chances as a freelance writer by moving his family from Manhattan to Ipswich, Massachusetts, where they would make their home for the next seventeen years.

THE USES OF MEMORY:
EARLY WORK, 1958–1965

Updike told an interviewer for *The Paris Review* in 1968 that "Nothing that happens to [writers] after twenty is free from self-consciousness because by then we have the vocation to write. Writers' lives break into two halves. At the point where you get your writerly vocation you diminish your receptivity to experience" (Plath, p. 28). Updike took up his writerly vocation in a small-town setting, albeit one more solidly middle-class and sophisticated than Shillington, and quickly set about recording the time of "receptivity to experience" that inspired most of his work from 1958 to 1965. He drafted a long autobiographical novel, "Home," which he chose not to publish, instead reshaping much of the material into other work of this period. He continued contributing poems, reviews, and short stories to *The New Yorker,* and published his first book, *The Carpentered Hen and Other Tame Creatures,* a collection of poems, in 1958.

In the same year, he wrote a novel, *The Poorhouse Fair,* published in 1959 by Alfred A. Knopf, the publishing firm he has been associated with ever since. A third book, *The Same Door,* a collection of short stories, was also published in 1959. These three books clearly justified his decision to leave New York. More important, along with *Assorted Prose,* a collection of early nonfiction published in 1965, they introduce the genres that he would master over time and announce the subject matter, persistent themes, even recurring characters that define Updike's work as it develops over nearly fifty years.

The autobiographical essay from *Assorted Prose* (1965), "The Dogwood Tree: A Boyhood," provides the best entrée to Updike's early work by evoking vividly the people, places, and events sealed in his memory, attesting to the habit of close observation that is a hallmark of his writing, and suggesting the many ways in which his imagination transformed early impressions into art. The essay re-creates the patterns of life in small-town, middle-class America between the Depression and the end of World War II, a period when so little changed in Updike's family and surroundings that this time and place came to represent a stable world shaped by close relationships and endowed with strong feelings of identity and belonging, a world to which he could return repeatedly, in his life and his writing, to measure the loss that time inevitably brings, a theme that dominates much of his fiction.

"The Dogwood Tree" inscribes Shillington as "the center of the world" for young Updike, and Reading as "the master of cities, the one at the center that all others echo." The essay also captures a child's earliest intimations of "Three Great Secret Things"—sex, religion, and art—mysteries that will be explored repeatedly throughout Updike's work. The piece ends with thirteen-year-old John regretfully leaving the house in Shillington with his parents to move to the farm. On leaving his boyhood home, he turns abruptly from the shadow of the dogwood tree planted at the time of his birth, now playing against the side of his empty house in the moonlight: "so it is," he writes, "that my shadow has always remained in the same place."

Between 1957 and 1965, Updike published two volumes of poetry: *The Carpentered Hen and Other Tame Creatures* and *Telephone Poles and Other Poems* (1963). The title of the first volume evokes a homely version of William Butler Yeats's exquisitely crafted golden bird of "Sailing to Byzantium" as Updike's emblem of the artist's gift for transforming ordinary things of the fleeting world into permanent objects of art. The poems, which Updike has described as "light verse, a kind of cartooning in print" (Plath, p. 39), forecast Updike's delight in the malleable properties and magical power of language, which through rhythm, metaphor, wordplay, and the paradoxical reassurance and surprise of unexpected rhyme can make us experience with fresh joy objects of the familiar world around us. A poem like "Player Piano" mimics the rhythm and timbre of the mechanical instrument, which in turn mimics, with unapologetic artificiality, a human performance. The delight is in the artifice. "Ex-Basketball Player" poignantly sketches the scaled-down life of a former small-town athletic hero reduced to pumping gas, a prototype of Rabbit Angstrom. The second volume, *Telephone Poles*, assumes a more serious tone in its tributes to the world of memory and everyday objects. "Shillington, " for example, reflects on inevitable change in the world of time and on the subjective images locked in memory that cannot be preserved in photographs.

Also between 1957 and 1965, Updike published three volumes of short stories, a genre he suggested in 1978 "may be what I do best" (Plath, p. 126). Many stories in *The Same Door* feature a youthful protagonist who, under various names, shares qualities and experiences of the adolescent Updike, or present characters more fully fleshed out in subsequent works: the high-school athlete in "Ace in the Hole" anticipates the protagonist of the Rabbit novels; and "Snowing in Greenwich Village" introduces Richard and Joan Maple, the married couple whose life Updike returns to in later stories to work variations on the theme of the vulnerability of married love and the temptations of adultery. *The Same Door* was praised for its treatment of ordinary people and events in the understated manner of James Joyce and Anton Chekhov. A second volume, *Pigeon Feathers* (1962), confirmed Updike's mastery of this form in classic stories like "A&P," "Pigeon Feathers," and "Lifeguard," which are widely anthologized in high-school and college texts and introduce Updike to new generations of readers. Other stories in this collection, like "Wife-Wooing" and "The Blessed Man of Boston, My Grandmother's Thimble, and Fanning Island," demonstrate his versatile use of voice and mood as well as his innovative use of form to create a range of emotional and aesthetic effects. A third volume, *Olinger Stories* (1964), collects stories set in Olinger, Updike's fictionalized version of Shillington, and conveys a strongly felt sense of place reminiscent of Sherwood Anderson's *Winesburg, Ohio* and James Joyce's *Dubliners*. Of this volume, Updike said, "if I had to give anybody one book

of me it would be the . . . *Olinger Stories*" (Plath, p. 28). These three collections in themselves would assure Updike a distinguished place in the tradition and development of the American short story.

It is as a novelist, however, that Updike is best known, and it is the novels that have made him the subject of more than twenty-five book-length critical studies. After he left New York in 1957, "full of Pennsylvania things I wanted to say" (Plath, p. 25), Updike wrote four novels published between 1958 and 1965, all based on material drawn from memories of Pennsylvania, the time of Updike's "receptivity to experience."

The Poorhouse Fair locates the old people's home of the title in New Jersey; nonetheless, it is clearly based on the "poorhouse" at the end of the street where Updike grew up in Shillington, and the leader of the residents who rebel against a dehumanizing system, John Hook, is based on memories of Updike's grandfather. As his first published novel, *The Poorhouse Fair* is noteworthy for several reasons. Unlike first novels of thinly veiled autobiography recalling a recent past in which a series of initiatory experiences has brought the youthful protagonist to the threshold of a future yet to be discovered, *The Poorhouse Fair* is set in a not-so-distant future of the late 1970s and portrays people between the ages of seventy and ninety, fully aware of their mortality but determined to preserve their identity and integrity in the face of growing dependency and approaching death. On the single day of the annual fair, on which the home opens its grounds to the public to display and sell the residents' handiwork, Updike dramatizes a characteristic theme: the loss of human freedom and agency with the passage of time. The resistance to such loss is led by Hook, a former schoolteacher, who champions religious faith, pride in craftsmanship, and meaningful work against the dehumanizing policies of impersonal institutions based on rationalism, secularism, and efficiency. The latter are represented by Conner, the well-intentioned but bureaucratic manager of the Diamond County Home for the aged. The largely positive reception of the novel, for which he received the Rosenthal Foundation Award in 1959, earned Updike recognition as a promising young author. *Rabbit, Run* (1960), his second novel, discussed below in the context of the other Rabbit novels, fulfilled this promise.

Two other Pennsylvania novels, *The Centaur* (1963) and *Of the Farm* (1965), pay tribute to Updike's parents. Memories of his father inspired *The Centaur*, an ambitious and complex novel about a father-and-son relationship that won the National Book Award and demonstrated Updike's ability to complement the realism of his earlier fiction with modernist techniques. He experiments here with a layered narrative by employing what T. S. Eliot referred to the "mythic method" of James Joyce's *Ulysses*, through which the naturalistic elements of the plot reverberate mythic echoes. Narrated retrospectively by Peter Caldwell, who has left his hometown to become a painter in New York, the novel sets the story of George Caldwell, the tired and sick teacher who sublimates his own desire for death and peace for the sake of his son's future, in the context of the myth of Chiron, the centaur divided between his divine and animal natures, who gives up immortality to expiate the crime of his pupil and protégé, Prometheus, who stole fire from the gods for humanity. George's daily sacrifices of work and care in a situation that will surely be the death of his spirit are recognized retrospectively by his son as the equivalent, on the mundane level of Olinger life, of Chiron's heroic sacrifice. Surrealistic dream sequences, the fluid integration of past and present time, and the use of cubistic juxtapositions and multiple perspectives suggest the ways in which Peter, through Updike, transforms the methods of modern visual art into a narrative that enables him to understand his past and articulate his love for his father. Following the popular success of *Rabbit, Run*, the largely positive critical reception of *The Centaur* assured Updike's place in the top rank of contemporary American novelists.

Of the Farm returns to the setting of the sandstone farmhouse of Updike's adolescence to deal with the effects of love, ambition, jealousy, and possessiveness in the relationships of a mother, her son, and his wife. Like *The Centaur*, it is a revisiting of the past by an artist, Joey Robinson, a once-aspiring poet now working in advertising in New York, who returns to introduce his second wife and her son to his mother and the home of his youth, which his mother has made into a shrine memorializing his past and which she hopes he will eventually make his home. During the weekend visit, the subtle psychological interactions among the characters mix memory and desire as Joey is caught between the pull of the natural world of the farm, his mother, and the past, and the vision of the future he hopes to find with his new wife in the city.

THE RABBIT SAGA, 1960–1990

Undoubtedly, the novel that established Updike's fame and made him a central, though controversial, figure

for critics was *Rabbit, Run*. Updike set his second novel firmly in the immediate present of the American 1950s by narrating it in the present tense, a technique not common at the time. The novel introduced readers to Harry C. "Rabbit" Angstrom, Updike's best-known character and the protagonist of three subsequent novels. Through the four novels, published at roughly ten-year intervals, Updike takes his former basketball star turned car salesman, a representative of middle America, through the years from 1959 to 1990, tracing along with his protagonist's life a history of American culture from the Eisenhower years to the presidency of George Herbert Walker Bush. Updike has in fact claimed that his "fiction about the daily doings of ordinary people has more history in it than history books" (*Picked-Up Pieces*, 1975, p. 501).

As the first novel in the series and Updike's best-known work, having sold more than 2.5 million copies (Schiff, 1998, p. 33), *Rabbit, Run* explores, against the background of the material progress of the postwar Eisenhower era, his characteristic subject matter: marriage, family relationships, adultery, and the longing for the religious certainty and moral direction that seem to elude characters enmeshed in a secular culture. Caught between the emerging egocentric morality of following one's instincts to maximize the intensities of life and the more altruistic morality of a communal social and religious order, Rabbit at twenty-six regrets the loss of grace and skill that made him special as a high-school basketball star, and he tries to escape the downward turn of his life by leaving his pregnant wife, Janice, and their two-year-old son, Nelson, to pursue what Updike has called an "escapist, have-it-my-way will to live" (Plath, p. 98). He runs away from his hometown outside Brewer, Updike's fictionalized version of Reading, where he feels trapped in a troubled marriage, a meaningless job demonstrating kitchen gadgets, and a disorderly and depressing apartment, to search for "something that wants me to find it." His quest takes him on an all-night drive south as far as West Virginia and back again. He begins an affair with a woman named Ruth, and moves into her Brewer apartment. The Reverend Jack Eccles, as the voice of social responsibility, is enlisted by Rabbit's in-laws to persuade him to return to his family, and Rabbit does go home when his wife gives birth to their daughter, Becky. But he leaves again shortly after they return from the hospital, and Janice, distraught and drinking heavily after this second abandonment, accidentally drowns the baby while trying to bathe her. This novel, with its flawed hero and shocking catastrophe, created a stir as critics and readers divided between partisans of Rabbit's search for freedom and self-fulfillment and those who saw him as a callow, selfish antihero whose philandering and irresponsibility led to the tragic death of his daughter. The book, now a classic text in American literature, made a strong impression on early readers, who became avid fans not only of subsequent installments in the life of Rabbit Angstrom, but of Updike's fiction in general.

The mythic appeal of Rabbit as an Everyman attempting to cope with the pressures of American life in the second half of the twentieth century and the ambiguous ending of the novel that leaves him undecided about returning to his family or continuing his quest made readers eager to know what happened to him. Updike published a sequel in 1971, *Rabbit Redux*, the darkest novel in the series, which shows thirty-six-year-old Harry back home with Janice and Nelson, in a ranch house in a sterile new suburb outside Brewer, working in a print shop as a Linotyper, a blue-collar job that technology is making obsolete. He is bewildered by the issues and events that troubled America in the 1960s: the Vietnam War, racial unrest and violence, youth rebellion, the sexual revolution, the drug culture, women's liberation, and the attempt to conquer space by sending explorers to the moon—the kinds of contemporary issues that Updike's critics had accused him of avoiding in his earlier treatment of white, middle-class, small-town America. Harry initially takes his stand in this cultural confusion by placing an American flag decal on the rear window of his Ford Falcon, announcing his identification with white, working-class America and rejecting the criticism of an emerging counterculture of youthful dropouts, war protesters, black radicals, and liberal intellectuals sympathetic to these disaffected groups.

His acceptance of guilt for his past lapses has left Harry in the condition of stasis he had so dreaded in *Rabbit, Run*. He has lost interest in sex, which he now associates with guilt and death. Harry finds the tables turned when Janice leaves him and Nelson to live with her Greek-American lover, Charlie Stavros, who works at her father's car dealership. But the spark of desire to discover the meaning of his life that made him run in the past has not been altogether extinguished, and Rabbit pursues freedom again by becoming involved with Jill, a teenage runaway flower child who has rejected the wealth and privilege of her upper-middle-class family, and Skeeter, a black revolutionary, Vietnam veteran, and drug dealer. Representing aspects of American life Harry fears, Jill and Skeeter move into his house and initiate him into

the 1960s version of freedom: rejection of the traditional family and its pursuit of the American Dream; disregard for the authority of laws and moral conventions that inhibit the pursuit of personal gratification through drugs and sex; and contempt for the state that sends its young, mostly black and poor, to die in a war that has neither a clear goal nor a foreseeable end. Harry's openness to new experience allows him to join the turned-on teach-in and love-in they conduct in his home. But he again learns the cost of freedom as the victims in this novel multiply to include Nelson, the disturbed product of the broken family; Jill, who dies in a fire apparently set by Harry's indignant neighbors to show that they will not countenance the spectacle of interracial sex and drug use they witness as peeping Toms; and by implication all the victims of race crimes and riots, of a war whose body count is recorded nightly on the evening news, indeed all the young no longer protected by competent adults confident of the values they live by. Against Harry's search to find meaning in the midst of personal and national confusion and violence, Updike contrasts the cool, rational, scientific quest to reach unexplored space through the moon shot. This graceful conquest of the unknown, however, yields little more than a blurred television image of gray blankness on a body long dead. It opens no new frontier in which to create the world anew, and Rabbit and Janice come together at the end of the novel, weary, sadder, and wiser, to make the best of the world they have inherited and helped to create.

Rabbit Is Rich (1981), the most widely acclaimed novel of the series, is also the happiest, showing that the Angstroms have survived their personal crises, and America has survived its decade of war, assassinations, racial conflict, and generational tension. Despite the energy shortage that creates long lines at gas pumps and the double-digit inflation of the 1970s, Harry and Janice discover themselves in 1979 as inheritors of the good life when Harry becomes manager of his deceased father-in-law's Toyota agency, of which Janice and her mother are co-owners. In a mood that often sparkles with the ebullience of Shakespearean comedy dancing on the brink of tragedy, the content, middle-aged Angstroms join the country-club set, take Caribbean vacations with other couples, invest in gold as a hedge against inflation, and experiment with partner-swapping, their economic and sexual freedom reassuring them that "life is sweet." But Harry's midsummer night's dream is shadowed by the nagging existential dread of *Rabbit, Run*, and he fears the disturbing undercurrents in a nation "running out of gas."

He wonders what has become of Ruth and the child she was carrying when he left her. His longing for lost daughters intensifies when Nelson, sullen and angry, moves back home without finishing college. Nelson, who has none of young Rabbit's charm, grace, or optimism, repeats his father's youthful pattern by abandoning the woman he has made pregnant while carrying on an affair with another. The shallowness of the American Dream is revealed in the Toyota slogan: "You asked for it; we got it," suggesting that the heart's desire can be bought. Nonetheless, the novel moves through a delightful parody of a Shakespearean comic ending in the celebration of Nelson's shotgun wedding and ultimately modulates into the miraculous tone of Shakespeare's late romances when Rabbit takes into his arms his true heart's desire, the granddaughter whose new life seems to restore the lost innocents of the past: his drowned daughter, Becky; the daughter he suspects Ruth may have borne after he abandoned her; and Jill, whose young life was immolated in the fire of *Rabbit Redux*.

The final novel in the series, *Rabbit at Rest* (1990), published thirty years after *Rabbit, Run*, concludes the series in an elegiac mood with the premature death of Harry, a fifty-six-year-old overweight junk food addict, who has worn out his heart. He now spends part of each year in Florida while Nelson is supposedly managing the Toyota dealership, but is actually driving it into bankruptcy by embezzling profits to support his cocaine addiction. Ignoring hints about Nelson's problem as he ignores the signals his heart has been sending him, Harry spends his time eating, golfing, and reading history, uncannily disturbed by the image of sudden, unexpected death visited on the passengers of Pan Am Flight 103 when it exploded over Lockerbie, Scotland. The meaning of the image becomes clear to him when he suffers a heart attack while Sunfishing with his dearly loved nine-year-old granddaughter, who nearly drowns as a result of his carelessness. The fact that he was able to rescue her from the same fate as Becky, even while his own heart seemed to be giving out, restores some of the feeling of the heroism of his youth. But Harry has been granted a brief reprieve, not a new life. He cannot resist the temptation of the opportunity to make love to his son's wife. In disgrace with his family, he drives south to Florida, completing the journey he had abandoned in *Rabbit, Run*. There he makes a last attempt to recapture his youth and grace in a one-on-one game with a black boy he calls Tiger on a dirt basketball court. The massive heart attack he suffers as he takes a shot "he can't miss" sends him

to the hospital, where he accepts his life and his death with the ambiguous word he can't bring himself to utter: "Enough."

Recognizing the centrality of the Rabbit novels to his oeuvre, Updike published all four novels together in 1995 under the title *Rabbit Angstrom: A Tetralogy*. Many critics have called this Updike's greatest achievement, the work on which his reputation as a major American writer will rest. Rabbit Angstrom, whom Updike has described as the part of himself that stayed in Pennsylvania, has joined the list of American seekers that includes Huck Finn, Nick Adams, Jay Gatsby, Ike McCaslin, and Holden Caulfield.

THE MIDDLE YEARS: 1957–1990

By 1965, when his achievements were recognized by his election to the American Academy of Arts and Letters, Updike was firmly established in his "writerly vocation," having created a significant body of work from the "Pennsylvania things" that he felt the urgent need to write about when he left New York in 1957. Following the move to Ipswich, two more children were born—Michael, in 1959, and Miranda, in 1960—and throughout the 1960s the Updikes were involved in the town through the family's participation in church, school, local government, and cultural activities. Updike had established a pattern of writing daily at an office he rented downtown, and he and Mary joined the social life of other young couples with children. This immersion in family life in the early 1960s provided subject matter for Updike's mature fiction, as did the troubled time for his nation and his marriage in the late 1960s and early 1970s. New sources of inspiration came from travel and from the extensive reading Updike did, much of it for the book reviews he published regularly. In 1964, he visited Russia, Bulgaria, Romania, and Czechoslovakia for the State Department. He lived with his family in London in 1968, when the rancorous domestic debate over the Vietnam War so disturbed him that he felt he had to leave the country. In the 1970s, he traveled to Japan, Korea, South America, and Africa, but Ipswich remained home for the Updikes until the failure of their marriage of twenty years led to separation in 1974. Updike lived in Boston for a year, then moved in with Martha Ruggles Bernhard and her three sons, who lived in Beverly Falls, Massachusetts. When the Updikes' no-fault divorce became final in 1976, he and Martha were married and moved to Georgetown, Massachusetts, where they lived until 1982. They have lived since then in Beverly Farms,

Massachusetts. Despite difficult and life-changing events, these were professionally productive years for Updike, culminating in the many recognitions and awards he received for his work in the 1980s and 1990s, when he had become a commanding figure in American letters.

THE MATURE WORK: 1968–1990

This phase of Updike's career is framed by two autobiographical works: the title poem of *Midpoint and Other Poems* (1969) and *Self-Consciousness: Memoirs* (1989). "Midpoint," a philosophical poem written when Updike was thirty-six, looks back over his life, articulates his beliefs, and recognizes the literary tradition he has inherited. Beginning in the celebratory style of Whitman with Wordsworthian recollections of childhood, ruminating in the manner of Auden on the structure of solid matter, paying tribute as Yeats does to people and memories that shaped his adult years, echoing the religious meditations of T. S. Eliot, he concludes in the couplets of Pope and the tone of Byron with a summation and a resolve: "Born laughing, I've believed in the Absurd, / Which brought me this far; henceforth if I can, / I must impersonate a serious man." The poem heralds Updike's mature work, in which his experience and memories, his awe in contemplating the solidity of material reality, and his faith in a nonmaterial world are placed in the context of an inherited literary tradition. Continuing the central theme of individual freedom and social constraints in works dealing with love, sex, marriage, adultery, and faith, Updike's work of this period reflects an increasing self-consciousness of its connection to intellectual, historical, and literary traditions.

The novel that begins this period, *Couples* (1968), reached the top of the best-seller list and remained on the list for eight months, making Updike famous as the chronicler of "the post-pill Paradise" of the 1960s sexual revolution whose picture appeared on the cover of the 26 April issue of *Time*. In an almost sociologically realistic and explicit treatment of the morals and manners of marriage and adultery in a small New England town, ten couples serve as a collective protagonist to portray people no longer bound by traditional religious beliefs or social restraints attempting to create a new kind of community based on a shared social life. Enjoying the blessings of upper-middle-class economic security and leisure, these characters nonetheless sense something central missing from their lives, a gap they fill by maintaining a pattern of social activities, oiled by alcohol and gossip, that lead to adulterous relationships. The group's behavior is foregrounded through one of the couples, Piet Hanema and Foxy Whitman, who discover that even the most permissive social order limits individual freedom. Their affair, begun when Foxy is ripely pregnant, tests the limits of the group's tolerance when soon after the birth of her son, Foxy becomes pregnant by Piet and has an abortion, arranged by a member of the group in exchange for a night with Piet's wife, Angela. Their recklessness in breaking the unspoken rules is articulated by Foxy's husband, Ken, who demands a divorce: "Simple infidelity could be gotten around, even a prolonged affair, but with my *child* in her belly—." The expulsion of Piet and Foxy from "Paradise" when they leave Tarbox signals the failure of the group's experiment.

Updike's later and less sociological exploration of group sexual practices as a substitute for the congregational bond once provided by traditional Christianity, *The Witches of Eastwick* (1984), provides a delightfully dark comic revisiting of the premise of *Couples* by focusing on "un-coupled" divorced women. This foray into magical realism, which won high praise even from critics who had previously shown at best grudging recognition of his talent, allowed Updike to assimilate cosmic and natural forces precluded by the social realism of *Couples* into the novel: he brings the devil in the person of Darryl Van Horne into twentieth-century New England to surround himself with a coven of modern witches eager to experiment with the magical creative power unleashed by their sexual freedom, which, as in *Couples*, turns destructive when it threatens the lives of their neighbors and the social fabric of the community. Like *Couples*, the novel ends with a cleansing apocalyptic fire when the town's church is struck by lightning.

The theme of marriage and adultery is also the subject of a trilogy inspired by Updike's careful rereading of the works of Nathaniel Hawthorne, especially *The Scarlet Letter*. Reflecting Updike's deepening consciousness of his "writerly vocation" and his literary ancestry, *A Month of Sundays* (1975), the first novel of the trilogy, "writes back" to Arthur Dimmesdale, the minister who is Hester Prynne's secret partner in adultery in *The Scarlet Letter*, through the postmodern, self-reflexive voice of Reverend Tom Marshfield, who consciously deploys language to seduce readers. When his affairs with members of his congregation are revealed, Marshfield is sent for rehabilitation to a motel in the Arizona desert for clergymen whose lapses have rendered them unseemly shepherds for their flocks. There he composes a diary, which his "keepers" hope will serve the therapeutic functions of confession and repentance by articulating his failures as a husband, father, and pastor. A writer who, like Updike, delights in the doubleness of language, Marshfield produces a journal that becomes a multilayered allegory of desire in its sexual, religious, psychological, and literary permutations. *Roger's Version* (1986) and *S.* (1988) complete the trilogy from the perspectives of narrator-protagonists suggested by the other two characters in Hawthorne's masterpiece: the betrayed husband, Roger Chillingworth, and his adulterous wife, Hester Prynne.

Another tale of marriage and adultery, *Marry Me*, was written mostly in the early 1960s but not published until 1976. It reflects, like many of his other novels of marriage and adultery, Updike's longtime fascination with Denis de Rougemont's analysis of the Tristan and Isolde myth in *Love in the Western World*. Labeling his fiction a romance, Updike plays with the conventions of medieval romance and with Hawthorne's distinction between the romance and the novel to develop De Rougement's thesis that romantic love cannot survive the everyday domestic routines of marriage and that only forbidden love, which thrives on exquisite longing and suffering for an absent or unattainable love object, can sustain itself. Romance, comedy, pathos, and irony make this light treatment of marriage and adultery a work that gives full range to the playfulness of Updike's genius as he offers multiple endings to invite the reader to help resolve the dilemma of Jerry Conant, the protagonist who lacks the will to choose between staying with the wife he is reasonably happy with and losing the deliciously self-indulgent sensations of illicit desire and guilt by making his mistress just another wife.

In 1977, Updike, perhaps in response to criticism that his fiction was limited to white, Protestant, middle-class, suburban American subject matter treated in a retro-realistic mode, created something of a tour de force with *The Coup* (1978), whose protagonist, Colonel Hakim Felix Ellelloû, the rabidly anti-American Islamic former dictator of Kush, a mythical African nation, attempts to write his memoirs from exile in the south of France. He shifts between the first- and third-person perspectives from which he views his divided self as he tells the story of his failed attempt to manage both his country's problem and his personal relationships with his four wives and a mistress. Although its fantastic Third World setting and protagonist represent departures, Updike's delight in verbal play, retrospective narration by a writer-protagonist, and the theme of the inextricability of the personal from the political/social context have been apparent since his earliest work.

Updike continued to write poetry through his middle years, publishing *Tossing and Turning* in 1977 and *Facing Nature: Poems* in 1985. He also published several distinguished collections of short stories, including *The Music School* (1966), *Museums and Women and Other Stories* (1972), *Problems and Other Stories* (1979), and *Trust Me* (1987). A collection of linked stories, *Too Far to Go: The Maples Stories* (1979), parallels the dissolution of the Updikes' marriage in the breakup of Richard and Joan Maple, and contains one of his best-known stories, "Separating," about a family's pain and confusion when marriage fails. Two books of loosely related tales, *Bech: A Book* (1970) and *Bech Is Back* (1982), based on the adventures and trials of his alter ego, the Jewish-American writer Henry Bech, provide wry commentary on the contemporary construction of the "writerly vocation" and the critical enterprise in America. The extensive reading and research that Updike did on James Buchanan refused to be shaped into the novel he had planned on the one U.S. president from Pennsylvania; it became his only attempt at playwriting, *Buchanan Dying* (1974).

Updike reached the height of critical success in the 1980s and 1990s when the acclaim he had received over the last decades culminated in his winning, among many other recognitions, the American Award for Fiction, the Pulitzer Prize, and the National Book Critics Circle Award for *Rabbit Is Rich*, and the Pulitzer Prize, the National Book Critics Circle Award, and the Howells Medal of the American Academy of Arts and Letters for *Rabbit at Rest*. His journalistic writing and his deepening body of critical prose, which included by this time essays on European, African, and classic and contemporary American writers, is represented in *Picked-Up Pieces* (1975) and *Hugging the Shore: Essays and Criticism* (1983), which received the National Book Critics Circle Award for Criticism. A new direction was taken in *Just Looking* (1989), a collection of essays on art and art exhibits, a genre that has increasingly occupied Updike's interest. Critical recognition for his extensive body of work has made Updike not only one of America's foremost living novelists, but arguably its most venerable and versatile man of letters.

Self-Consciousness, memoirs published in 1989, when Updike was fifty-five, suggests his readiness to sum up his life and career in the reflections of "a serious man" who since childhood has been fascinated by the mystery of his unique consciousness, of "something intrinsically and individually vital that must be defended," persisting through time even as it assumes and sheds its various selves. Updike traces the origins of this consciousness by reviewing his ancestry and early shaping experiences; he acknowledges his awareness of legacy as well as ancestry in the letter he writes to his two grandsons, to pass on the inheritance he has uncovered. As age makes the prospect of death more real, he ends by speculating on the possibility of "being a self forever," affirming his faith in "the very realm where we exist and where all things precious are kept—the realm of emotion and conscience, of memory and intention and sensation," and by announcing, "I have the persistent sensation, in my life and art, that I am just beginning."

LOOKING BACK: SINCE 1990

The reflective tone of *Self-Consciousness* is apparent in much of Updike's work since 1990, a time for collecting and "a terminal phase of tidying-up" (*More Matter*, 1999, p. 812). *Collected Poems 1953–1993* brings together works in a genre that Updike has practiced with pleasure since the 1940s. *Odd Jobs: Essays and Criticism* (1991) and *More Matter* collect the growing body of nonfiction prose.

Although Rabbit was put to rest in 1990, Updike made corrections and revisions to the four novels in 1995 for the Everyman edition of *Rabbit Angstrom: A Tetralogy*. If Updike found in Rabbit the part of himself that never left Pennsylvania, he invented in Henry Bech another alter ego, the part of himself that writes, whose tales were collected in *The Complete Henry Bech: Twenty Stories* (2001).

Updike still surprises readers with new directions and welcome revisitings. Some of the historical material from his research on James Buchanan finds a place in the 1992 novel about the problems of reconstructing the past, *Memories of the Ford Administration*. *The Afterlife and Other Stories* (1994) returns to the Pennsylvania settings of Updike's early work, the Tristan and Isolde theme, and the Maples after their divorce. *Licks of Love: Short Stories and a Sequel* (1999) updates readers on the surviving members of the Angstrom family. The Tristan and Isolde legend is boldly reworked in a new setting in *Brazil* (1994), his second novel to use non-American characters and settings. The research into family history recorded in *Self-Consciousness* yielded material for *In the Beauty of the Lilies* (1996), Updike's longest and most ambitious novel to date, which some critics have called his finest novel. Both panoramic and encyclopedic, the novel follows four generations of an American family, along with the history and culture of the American century, as it seeks a moral center in the tension between two powerful myths: religion and the movies. The theme of ultimate endings and loss is treated in *Toward the End of Time* (1997), in which Updike returns to the kind of futuristic setting of his first novel, to present the last days of a protagonist diagnosed with prostate cancer, of an America broken by war, and of a planet depleted and poisoned by the inventiveness of its inhabitants.

Even in the face of the end of time, Updike's imagination is inexhaustible and his love affair with the printed word continues. *Gertrude and Claudius* (1999) writes back to Western literature's best-known story of adultery and its consequences, *Hamlet*, to interpret it with brilliant psychological and historical verisimilitude from the point of view of the adulterous lovers. *Americana and Other Poems* (2001) revives the subject matter that has remained central to Updike's work; no other writer has made the second half of the American century more completely his own and more recognizable to his readers. A new novel, *Seek My Face*, appeared in 2002, his seventieth year. For nearly half a century John Updike has pleased, provoked, amused, informed, surprised, and delighted many readers. His vision of American life and the elegance of his writing have made an important and enduring contribution to American letters.

WORKS

NOVELS

The Poorhouse Fair (1959)
Rabbit, Run (1960)
The Centaur (1963)
Of the Farm (1965)
Couples (1968)
Rabbit Redux (1971)
A Month of Sundays (1975)
Marry Me (1976)
The Coup (1978)
Rabbit Is Rich (1981)
The Witches of Eastwick (1984)
Roger's Version (1986)
S. (1988)
Rabbit at Rest (1990)
Memories of the Ford Administration (1992)
Brazil (1994)
Rabbit Angstrom: A Tetralogy (1995)
In the Beauty of the Lilies (1996)
Toward the End of Time (1997)
Bech at Bay (1998)
Gertrude and Claudius (1999)
Seek My Face (2002)

SHORT STORY COLLECTIONS

The Same Door (1959)
Pigeon Feathers (1962)
Olinger Stories (1964)

The Music School (1966)
Bech: A Book (1970)
Museums and Women and Other Stories (1972)
Problems (1979)
Too Far to Go: The Maples Stories (1979)
Bech Is Back (1982)
Trust Me (1987)
The Afterlife and Other Stories (1994)
Licks of Love: Short Stories and a Sequel (1999)
The Complete Henry Bech: Twenty Stories (2001)

POETRY

The Carpentered Hen and Other Tame Creatures
    (1958)
Telephone Poles and Other Poems (1963)
Midpoint and Other Poems (1969)
Tossing and Turning (1977)
Facing Nature: Poems (1985)
Collected Poems, 1953–1993 (1993)
Americana and Other Poems (2001)

ESSAYS AND CRITICISM

Assorted Prose (1965)
Picked-Up Pieces (1975)
Hugging the Shore: Essays and Criticism (1983)
Just Looking (1989)
Odd Jobs: Essays and Criticism (1991)
Golf Dreams: Writings on Golf (1996)
More Matter (1999)

DRAMA

Buchanan Dying (1974)

MEMOIRS

Self-Consciousness: Memoirs (1989)

FURTHER READING

Bloom, Harold, ed. *John Updike: Modern Critical Views.* New York, 1987. Includes an introduction by Bloom and reprinted essays by John W. Aldridge, Richard H. Rupp, David Lodge, Tony Tanner, Joyce Carol Oates, Cynthia Ozick, and others.

Boswell, Marshall. *John Updike's Rabbit Tetralogy: Mastered Irony in Motion.* Columbia, Mo., 2001. A reading of the formal structure of the individual novels and the tetralogy as a whole in the context of the existential thought of Kierkegaard and Barth.

Broer, Lawrence R., ed. *Rabbit Tales: Poetry and Politics in John Updike's Rabbit Novels.* Tuscaloosa, Ala., 1998.

A collection of essays on the tetralogy by such major interpreters of Updike's work as Campbell, Greiner, Ristoff, Wood, and others.

DeBellis, Jack. *John Updike: A Bibliography, 1967–1993.* Westport, Conn., 1994. The most comprehensive bibliographic resource.

DeBellis, Jack. *The John Updike Encyclopedia.* Westport, Conn., 2000. A comprehensive volume with entries on the works, major characters, themes, biographical data.

Detweiler, Robert C. *John Updike.* Rev. ed. Boston, 1984. A comprehensive study of the fiction through 1982.

Galloway, David. *The Absurd Hero in American Fiction: Updike, Styron, Bellow, Salinger.* 2d rev. ed. Austin, Tex., 1981. A reading of the early fiction in the existential context of Camus's notions of the absurd, particularly *The Myth of Sisyphus.*

Greiner, Donald J. *The Other John Updike: Poems, Short Stories, Prose, Plays.* Athens, Ohio, 1981. Valuable addition to studies that focus primarily on the novels.

Greiner, Donald J. *John Updike's Novels.* Athens, Ohio, 1984. A close reading of the novels through *Rabbit Is Rich,* with particular attention to critical reception.

Greiner, Donald J. *Adultery in the American Novel: Updike, James, and Hawthorne.* Columbia, S.C., 1985. A reading that uses primarily Updike's essays and reviews to establish links between Updike and his predecessors in the canon, focusing on the religious and social treatment of adultery.

Hamilton, Alice, and Kenneth Hamilton. *The Elements of John Updike.* Grand Rapids, Mich., 1980. An important early study of religious themes in Updike's work.

Hunt, George W. *John Updike and the Three Great Secret Things: Sex, Religion, and Art.* Grand Rapids, Mich., 1980. An analysis of the early work in the context of Kierkegaard, Barth, and Jung.

Macnaughton, William R., ed. *Critical Essays on John Updike.* Boston, 1982. Essays by Kazin, Tanner, Hunt, Detweiler, Oates, Theroux, and others, along with a survey of criticism.

Modern Fiction Studies 20 (Spring 1974) and 37 (Spring 1991). Both issues devoted entirely to critical essays on Updike's fiction.

Neary, John. *Something and Nothingness: The Fiction of John Updike and John Fowles.* Carbondale, Ill., 1992. A comparative study of religious and philosophical themes in the works of the two authors.

O'Connell, Mary. *Updike and the Patriarchal Dilemma: Masculinity in the Rabbit Novels.* Carbondale, Ill.,

1988. A feminist reading of the first three Rabbit novels.

Plath, James, ed. *Conversations with John Updike*. Jackson, Miss., 1994. A collection of thirty-two interviews, including those for *The Paris Review, Life*, National Public Radio, and *The Harvard Crimson*, arranged in chronological order and intended for a range of audiences. Valuable commentary by Updike on his life and work.

Pritchard, William H. *America's Man of Letters*. South Royalton, Vt., 2000. Excellent study of Updike's achievement.

Schiff, James A. *John Updike Revisited*. New York, 1998. An excellent, comprehensive evaluation of Updike's work that updates earlier critical overviews to demonstrate the growth of his reputation.

Tanner, Tony. *Adultery in the Novel*. Baltimore, 1979.

Taylor, C. Clarke. *John Updike: A Bibliography*. Kent, Ohio, 1968. Covers work from 1949 to 1967.

Thornburn, David, and Howard Eiland, eds. *John Updike: A Collection of Critical Essays*. Englewood Cliffs, N.J., 1979. Essays by Oates, Steiner, Lodge, Markle, and others.

Trachtenberg, Stanley, ed. *New Essays on* Rabbit, Run. New York, 1993. An introduction by Trachtenberg and four essays on the novel.

Wood, Ralph C. *The Comedy of Redemption: Christian Faith and Comic Vision in Four American Novelists*. Notre Dame, Ind., 1988. A comparative theological study focusing on the Rabbit novels, *Couples*, and *Midpoint*.

Yerkes, James, ed. *John Updike and Religion*. Grand Rapids, Mich., 1999. A collection of essays by theologians as well as literary critics.

JONES VERY

by Gerry Cambridge

Jones Very's claim on literary posterity comes mainly from a brief period between September 1838 and the spring of 1840 when, in a burst of unprecedented creativity, he wrote the three hundred poems, mainly sonnets, that constitute that claim. During that period, Very believed, spectacularly so, that he had "seen the light" in religious terms. Whatever else it achieved—which wasn't much—this spell of religious exaltation was good for his poetry. Most of the rest of the roughly eight hundred seventy poems he composed, from the early 1830s, when he was in his early twenties, to 1880, the year of his death, was tepid stuff by comparison, mainly of interest these days to scholars wishing to see what "the proud full sail" of his best work had developed from and would molder into. Very was for a time associated with the transcendentalist movement headed by Ralph Waldo Emerson, which emphasized personal intuition as a major source of spiritual truth. The Very scholar Helen R. Deese has argued convincingly, however, that the Very of the so-called "ecstatic" period, at least in his best work, was "essentially a mystic" outside classification.

EARLY LIFE AND WORK

Very was born in Salem, Massachusetts, on 28 August 1813, the eldest son in a family of six, to Jones Very Sr., a ship's captain, and his first cousin, Lydia Very. His mother from all accounts was an atheist. By comparison, her studious son became decidedly spiritual in bent, as well as a gifted scholar: he went to Harvard in September 1833 and while there broke a record by becoming the first student to win the Bowdoin essay prize twice. In 1836, the year he graduated, he was appointed a tutor in Greek at Harvard. A lecture he gave in December 1837 on epic poetry led to an acquaintance with the transcendentalist Elizabeth Palmer Peabody, who introduced him to Emerson. Very would impress both him and his wife, Lydian; Emerson would later refer to him as "our brave saint." The force of his presence was such that, after one visit, he left them, Emerson's wife, Lydian, wrote, "rejoicing." Very wasn't seen that way by others, however. By fall 1838 his increasingly erratic behavior was becoming the butt of gossip for students, behind his back. On 14 September he announced in his classroom to his students that they should "flee to the mountains, for the end of all things is at hand." He was sacked at once by the president of Harvard College, Josiah Quincy, returned to Salem, and, after continuing to pronounce himself as the Second Coming (he visited Elizabeth Peabody and tried to convert her on the spot), was sent to the McLean Asylum in Charlestown. He was there for a month; released, he returned to Salem. His academic career was, of course, finished. His brief life as an inspired poet, however, was only beginning.

THE "ECSTATIC" PERIOD

The effect his religious mania—or "sania," as one wit commented—had on his writing, as Helen R. Deese, editor of *Jones Very: The Complete Poems* (1993) has pointed out, was dramatic. Whereas the pre-mania Very had written scrupulously and laboriously, often rewriting, we know from manuscript sources that the reincarnated poet wrote quickly with almost no changes, often cramming sheets of paper with numerous sonnets written in pencil. Most of the poems would remain sonnets, though toward the end of the "ecstatic" period Very began using quatrains as well.

The new phase of work begins, appropriately, with "The New Birth," an urgent sonnet of spiritual rebirth full of a hectic crowding of images; it continues with "The Journey": only God knows Very's path in his spiritual exaltation, Very asserts; addressing the reader, he closes his poem: "And canst thou tell then where my journeying lies? / If so thou treadst with me the same blue skies." The poem achieves liftoff in that remarkable closing line of ten assertive monosyllables: Very as skywalker, as a traveler in a placeless place. Many of the poems of this period, however, simply restate conventional Christian doctrine or are exhortations to the reader to follow Christ, couched in sonnet form. For instance, in "The Coming," Very can announce, with an enthusiasm unlikely to be shared by skeptical contemporary readers, "He comes! The Son of

Man is glorified!" Though the stringent poet-critic Yvor Winters claimed him in 1936 as a devotional poet, "one of the finest...in English," in most of the devotional poems the doctrine oppresses the poetry. They read like mere versified theology. There are exceptions: in "Enoch" the biblical imagery is complementary to Very's main message—that however fine the places of worship built by men, men have left themselves "unfinished and in ruins"; yet, they are "the only temple [God] delights to fill." And "The Removal" is a fascinating dialogue sonnet, ostensibly spoken at the outset by God, who, as the owner of a house, asks the occupant—the will of the individual addressed—to leave, so that he, God, may "restore" for the occupant "a better house."

The Very of these poems looks out at his fellows and calls them "The Dead" in a sonnet of that title; Earth is a cemetery of living dead over which he broods in "The Graveyard." The poet also praises physical poverty for its foregrounding of spiritual matters: in "The Thieves," a five-stanza piece in rhyming quatrains, the narrator is burgled. His neighbors rally round and replace, with "far more" material goods, what the thief took. The narrator responds that by encouraging him to value what they give, they too are thieves—they "rob [him] more the more they give." What they steal is his indifference to earthly wealth. In "The Pilgrim," a sonnet, the traveler, "infirm and grey," seems unsustained by food given by the kind citizens; the poem's narrator asks him why. He says nothing but simply points "to heaven." The narrator concludes: "And then I knew the food they gave away, / And home they offered were but for a day." These are not quite good enough. For "The Pilgrim," and by implication for Very, the eternal reality is the absolute.

While a poem such as Very's "The Pilgrim" could be accused of dangerously devaluing earthly existence for the sake of a hypothetical afterlife—an argument used by detractors of religion in general—there is nothing programmatic about Very's aesthetic. In "The Day Not for Gain," like an American Wordsworth he argues for pure being as opposed to the psychological equivalent of "getting and spending." He asserts that anyone unprepared to welcome the morning sun and notice the flowers, merely full of their own selfish thoughts, has made "the sovereign day" "a slave." Meanwhile, in "The Bunch of Flowers," a stately and sonorous poem in quatrains somewhat in the manner of George Herbert, Time, personified, "with withered hand," holds out a rose exemplifying his "gifts" to a young child, a youth, a mature man, and an old man, in turn. The child, who

resembles the rose itself for the narrator, soon strews the flower's petals; the youth keeps it a little longer, admiring it before dropping it; the mature man keeps it longest, values it most, and, rather than discarding it, has it wither on his heart; the old man takes it sadly and soon drops it because of weakness. At the poem's close the narrator, on being offered the rose yet knowing that "none could bear away the flower," refuses to accept it. Very here propounds a pure cynicism; as one can't keep the rose, which is the gift of Time and presumably emblematic of the richness of life, he would rather not have it in the first place. No traditional Christian doctrine is posited as consolation; there is no guarantee of "salvation" at all. The narrator finally exists, rather eerily, in the realm of pure spirit.

Very's period of religious exaltation seems to have halted, quite suddenly, in early 1840. It would be as much as eight months before, scholars assert, he wrote another poem. But the period of his finest work was over.

VERY AND POSTERITY

Modern thought has, predictably, tried to explain Very's "ecstasy." Edwin Gittleman, in his *Jones Very: The Effective Years, 1833–1840* (1967), pointed to Very's complex feelings for his reputedly atheist mother; there is some evidence relating to a psychosexual crisis in the mid-1830s that led Very to be wary of women; he also had some of the symptoms of temporal lobe epilepsy which could account for aspects of his behavior. What cannot be doubted, though, is Very's genuineness. In practical terms, at least, his brief "exaltation" cost him dearly.

Unlike some other poets of extreme vision, Very achieved publication in his lifetime. *Essays and Poems* (1839), however, edited by Emerson, was distinguished mainly by its rather bland selection of poems. It would be the only collection of Very's work he would see in print.

Jones Very died on 8 May 1880 at age sixty-six, after some forty years of relative reclusion and obscurity, which he occupied by sporadic preaching as a Unitarian and in writing unremarkable verse. When *Poems by Jones Very* (1883) appeared three years later with a memoir by William P. Andrews, the anonymous reviewer in the *Atlantic Monthly*, who had met the poet around 1850, described him as "quiet, reserved, silent, serene"; he was a man who "looked as if he belonged to another sphere." In poems such as "Day," "Night," "The Journey," "Enoch," "The Dead," "Morning," "The Removal," "The Eye and Ear," "Yourself," "Thy Better Self," "The Day Not for Gain," "The Pilgrim," and "The

Bunch of Flowers," Very had brought back sometimes troubling insights from that "other sphere" of the spirit he had briefly visited. The small body of inspired work he produced deals with spiritual concerns unlikely to date. It was penned by a poet, as the *Atlantic Monthly* observed over a century ago, "singularly out of keeping with this age of worldliness." That this is even truer today does not diminish the best work's considerable power.

[*See also* Transcendentalism.]

SELECTED WORKS

Essays and Poems (1839)
Poems by Jones Very (1883)
Poems and Essays (1886)
Jones Very: Selected Poems (1966)
Jones Very: The Complete Poems (1993)

FURTHER READING

Bartlett, William Irving. *Jones Very: Emerson's "Brave Saint."* Durham, N.C., 1942. Historically valuable not just for its basic biography but for printing seventy-one poems previously unpublished in 1942, the majority from the "ecstatic" period.

Deese, Helen R., ed. *Jones Very: The Complete Poems.* Athens, Ga., 1993.

Gittleman, Edwin. *Jones Very: The Effective Years, 1833–1840.* New York, 1967. A readable psychological study, not without dry wit, which makes bold assertions as to the possible causes of Very's "ecstasy."

GORE VIDAL

by Jay Parini

Gore Vidal is a novelist, essayist, playwright, and provocateur whose career has spanned six decades, beginning in the years immediately following World War II and continuing into the early years of the twenty-first century. In addition to a major sequence of seven novels about American history and such satirical novels as *Myra Breckinridge* (1968) and *Duluth* (1983), he has written dozens of television plays, film scripts, and even three mystery novels under the pseudonym of Edgar Box. He has also written well over one hundred essays, gathered in numerous volumes published between 1962 and 2001. Taken as a whole, this seemingly varied work has an uncanny unity, exhibiting a tone of easy familiarity with the world of politics and letters, an urbane wit, and a sense of supreme self-confidence on the part of the writer. Vidal's lineage in American literature may be traced back to Henry James, the sophisticated American from the upper echelons of society who mingles with European sophisticates, and Mark Twain, the raw humorist and critic of American empire.

Gore Vidal. (© *Corbis*)

EARLY LIFE AND WORK

Vidal was born on 3 October 1925 at West Point, New York, with high political and social connections. His father, Eugene Luther Vidal, held a subcabinet-level position in the Roosevelt administration as director of the Bureau of Air Commerce from 1933 until 1937. Gore's maternal grandfather was Senator Thomas Pryor Gore of Oklahoma, a Democrat who played an important role in his party's politics for many decades. Senator Gore's daughter and Gore Vidal's mother, Nina Gore Vidal, was divorced from Eugene in 1935, when Vidal was ten, and married Hugh D. Auchincloss, a wealthy financier, who in

turn divorced her and married Jacqueline Kennedy's mother, thus establishing a connection between Vidal and the Kennedy clan that persisted through the presidency of John F. Kennedy.

In the fall of 1940, having attended for some years a prep school called St. Albans in Washington, D.C., Vidal entered the Phillips Exeter Academy in New Hampshire and graduated in 1943, at which point he entered the Reserve Corps of the U.S. Army. After a brief training period at the Virginia Military Institute, he joined the Army Transportation Corps as an officer and was sent to the Aleutian Islands. He wrote much of his first novel, *Williwaw* (1946), during a run between Chernowski Bay and Dutch Harbor. Suffering from serious frostbite and arthritis, he was sent back to the States, where he finished the novel while recuperating in a military hospital. *Williwaw* focused on a rivalry between two naval officers. In its tight-lipped, minimalist style, it reflects Vidal's reading of Hemingway and Stephen Crane. For a writer barely out of his teens, the book was an extraordinary achievement. It seemed absolutely authentic and put Vidal on the map of young postwar novelists that included Norman Mailer, John Horne Burns, and Truman Capote.

Having little money despite his patrician roots, Vidal moved to Guatemala, where the living was cheap. There he shared a house (as a friend) with Anaïs Nin, who wrote about Vidal in her diaries of that period. By any standard, the postwar years were productive ones for the young Vidal, who published eight novels between 1946 and 1954. These include *The City and the Pillar* (1948), *The Judgment of Paris* (1952), and *Messiah* (1954).

The City and the Pillar is notable for reasons that go beyond its aesthetic qualities. Vidal's hero is Jim Willard, who as the story opens slumps in a New York City bar recalling the years from 1937 to 1943. What he visualizes through an alcoholic haze is the time he first made love to Bob Ford—an American as prototypical as his name. The pursuit of Ford by Willard gives the novel its mythic shape, though Vidal is ever the satirist, ready to send up literary and social conventions. Jim's quest takes him through the homosexual demimonde of California, which Vidal writes about with reportorial cool. His dizzying quest ends in a reconciliation scene that turns unexpectedly nightmarish. In the 1948 version of the novel, Jim strangles Bob. In a 1965 revision, Vidal eliminates that melodramatic ending, transforming the murder into a rape—a more believable conclusion. In all, *The City and the Pillar* counts among the first explicitly gay novels in the history of American fiction.

Vidal suffered the consequences of bringing a gay novel before a wide audience in 1948. Indeed, his next five novels were dismissed by the mainstream press. Among the best of these was *Messiah*, a prophetic novel that makes deft use of the modernist technique (pioneered in the twentieth century by André Gide in *The Counterfeiters*, 1926) of the journal within the memoir—a form that Vidal would exploit to good effect in later novels. Vidal's narrator is Eugene Luther, who considers the 1950s from a vantage of half a century, recalling the spread of a peculiar religious cult based on the figure of John Cave, who preaches the goodness of death and encourages suicide among his followers. Yet Cave himself is hardly willing to practice what he preaches; though murdered in the end, his ashes are spread across the country, giving him a mystical presence in the cultural air. Soon Cave becomes a commodity, like everything else in America, and his followers merchandise him with relish. The religion that evolves in Cave's wake is fiercely hierarchical and bound to the literal Cavesword created by his Pauline apostles. The whole is wittily satirized by Vidal.

BY THE HUDSON RIVER

After a period in Europe when he traveled with his friend Tennessee Williams and met both André Gide and George Santayana, Vidal settled along the Hudson River in a mansion called Edgewater with his companion, Howard Austen. Among the many projects that occupied him during this period was *The Judgment of Paris*, one of his most compelling early novels. The ghost of Henry James hovers over this work, set largely in Europe, although its style looks forward to the later Vidal, being dryly witty and deeply ironic. But *The Judgment of Paris* is a fine work in its own right, describing the European sojourn of a young man who must choose among three women. Each

represents a different tack for Vidal's hero: a political life, an intellectual life, and a sensual life. (The story is founded on the Greek myth in which Paris was forced to choose among Hera, Athena, and Aphrodite.)

With single-mindedness, Vidal set out to free himself from economic worries, having made little from his five novels in the wake of *The City and the Pillar*. Writing as Edgar Box, he published three mystery novels: *Death in the Fifth Position* (1952); *Death before Bedtime* (1953); and *Death Likes It Hot* (1954). These clever fictions, which play off the conventions of the mystery novel with considerable gusto, did not solve their creator's financial problems. Like William Faulkner and F. Scott Fitzgerald before him, he turned to writing scripts. Vidal took naturally to the new medium of television, producing dozens of scripts in the course of the next decade, which has been called the golden age of television. Among his large number of adaptations were Faulkner's "Barn Burning" and Henry James's *Turn of the Screw* (1898). Perhaps his best original teleplay was "Visit to a Small Planet," televised on 8 May 1955.

The success of this teleplay prompted Vidal to turn the script into a full-dress Broadway play. With considerable fanfare, *Visit to a Small Planet* opened in 1957 and ran for 338 performances. The plot centers on a visitor from outer space who arrives in Virginia with the hope of witnessing the Battle of Bull Run in 1861. Having come about a century too late, he establishes himself as the guest of a family called Spelding. When the government learns that this visitor, named Kreton, would like to start World War III, pandemonium ensues. Yet Kreton is actually an innocent creature at heart. He believes that war is the greatest achievement of the human race, so it follows that humans should be allowed to destroy themselves.

Just in time, a group from Kreton's native planet arrives to take him home. They explain, rather apologetically, that poor Kreton is mentally retarded—a mere child, in fact. Vidal's play, in its whimsy and scathing satire, recalls Oscar Wilde and George Bernard Shaw, though it reverberates with Vidal's idiosyncratic tone. It remains a minor masterpiece of the period, one permeated with the tones and particular cultural histrionics of the period.

The 1950s was, of course, a great age for drama. Tennessee Williams, Arthur Miller, and others were producing their masterpieces. In fact, Vidal never devoted himself to writing plays as he might have; consequently, he did not develop as a dramatist. He did, however, manage another fine play, *The Best Man*, which beginning in 1960 ran on Broadway for 520 performances and was successfully revived in 2000. It was also made into a successful 1964 film starring Henry Fonda, with a screenplay by Vidal. Two other plays for Broadway were *Romulus* (produced in 1962), adapted from Friedrich Durrenmatt's *Romulus der Grosse* (1949), and *An Evening with Richard Nixon and . . .* (produced in 1972). Neither of these attracted much of an audience or met with critical success.

Screenwriting was lucrative, then as now, and Vidal devoted considerable energies over five decades to the genre. His early credits include *The Catered Affair* (1956), *I Accuse!* (1958), and *Suddenly, Last Summer* (1959). He also worked on the script of *Ben Hur* (1959) and doctored a number of other screenplays. Decades later he wrote a television version of *Dress Gray* (1986; based on a novel by Lucian K. Truscott IV) that received an Emmy nomination. In an unexpected turn, he also acted in several films, including *Bob Roberts*, where he played a worn-out American politician to great effect.

THE POLITICIAN AS NOVELIST

Vidal observed the political world from the sidelines for many years, but this vantage did not satisfy him. Hoping for a more active role, he ran for the U.S. House of Representatives in 1960 as a Democrat-Liberal in New York State's highly Republican 29th District. In his public speeches he supported many controversial ideas, including the recognition of the People's Republic of China, shrinking the Pentagon's budget, and putting more federal money into education. Given the conservative nature of the region and, more generally, the times, he was defeated, though he won more votes in his district than John F. Kennedy, who headed the Democratic ticket. In 1982, more on whimsy than anything that seemed based in reality, he ran in the Democratic primary for the U.S. Senate in California; to the surprise of many, he finished second in a crowded field behind Jerry Brown, a well-known political figure in the state.

One can hardly imagine a man of Vidal's literary ability feeling content to endure the grind of daily work in the House or Senate. One nevertheless must admire a writer so engaged in the issues of his day that he would run for public office. The experience of practical campaigning can only have helped him when he began the chronicle of American history and politics that started with *Washington, D.C.* (1967) and continued through *Burr* (1973), *1876* (1976), *Lincoln* (1984), *Empire* (1987), *Hollywood: A Novel of America in the 1920s* (1990), and *The Golden Age* (2000). This body of work has a ring of authenticity missing in most American political fiction.

THE MOVE TO ITALY

After the failed run for office in 1960, Vidal chose to focus again on his main career, that of novelist. Early in the decade he moved to Italy, where he has remained, though with many short intervals of residence in the United States. In Rome, the library of the American Academy proved useful. There he worked on *Julian* (1964), the first novel in which he became a mature writer of fiction with his own style and manner. In every way, *Julian* represents the first fruit of Vidal's reinvention of himself as a Roman. Like a ventriloquist, he enters into the mind of Julian, following the noble Roman as he renounces Christianity and embraces paganism, then moves from philosopher-soldier to emperor. The historical details are fascinating, enhanced by Vidal's shrewd embellishments.

A huge commercial success, *Julian* ranks high among Vidal's creations, a novel equal in quality to *Burr*, *Lincoln*, and *Myra Breckinridge*. As an historical novel about the ancient world, it rivals anything by Mary Renault or Robert Graves; in fact, Vidal as a writer is generally more sophisticated than Renault and less cranky than Graves. He writes with massive authority about the ancient world, much as he does when he writes about the American past. It is this authority for which he is probably most valued by his readers.

Novels by Vidal have often come in pairs. *Messiah* could be seen as a prelude to a later apocalyptic novel, *Kalki* (1978). *Myra Breckinridge* has a sequel, *Myron* (1974). And *Julian*, in its way, gestures toward *Creation* (1981). The latter novel purports to be the memoirs of a retired diplomat, Cyrus Spitama, who is half Persian and half Greek. Spitama offers a panoramic view of life in the fifth century B.C., taking in the Persian-Greek wars as well as visits to India and China. Over thirty years of service to the Persian Empire, Spitama has seen it all. He just happened to be present when Zoroaster was assassinated, met the Buddha as well as Confucius, and even (almost accidentally) bumped into Socrates, whom he engages to rebuild a masonry wall. Only a writer of Vidal's audacity would dare to attempt a novel with such scope.

Creation entertains and enlightens, but it lacks the aesthetic tightness of *Julian* (a tightness borne of Julian's own idiosyncratic voice, which is pure Vidal). Spitama is just too global, and his voice often seems too much the disembodied voice of History, devoid of personal inflection. Spitama is knowledgeable and world-weary. One inevitably marvels at the amount of information Vidal has assimilated and transformed into fiction in the course of *Creation*. Even when Spitama is being painfully didactic, telling us more than we might really want to know about Democritus or specific protocols at the court of Darius, there remains the suppleness and sharpness of the prose itself. The surface glimmers as the old narrator surveys the world as he found it with an eye for the exact and memorable detail.

SATIRES

Vidal's satirical novels include *Myra Breckinridge, Myron, Duluth, Live from Golgotha* (1992), and *The Smithsonian Institution* (1998). *Myra Breckinridge* is surely the high point of the author's work in this vein. Like many previous works, it is written in the form of a memoir. This time the speaker is Myra, formerly (before a sex change) Myron, and the nephew of Buck Loner, a retired horse opera star. Myra has come back to Hollywood to claim her inheritance, owed by Buck to Myron, who appeases her by giving her a position as teacher at the Academy of Drama and Modeling—an astute appointment since Myra is, among other things, a movie buff of the first order who (like Vidal himself) adores "celluloid, *blessed* celluloid." She is also a protofeminist who repeatedly warns, "No man will ever possess Myra Breckinridge." One of the kinkiest, funniest, and most shocking scenes in any Vidal novel is Myra's seduction of a strapping young student called Rusty Godowsky, who is anally raped with a dildo by the triumphant Myra.

As sequel to *Myra, Myron* picks up the story about five years later. A novel of restoration, even a parody of restoration, it completes the portrait of a fractured ego, fusing the split figure of Myra-Myron. Hopping about in time, blending celluloid reality with everyday reality, *Myron* pushes beyond the mock realism of *Myra Breckinridge* into something even more peculiar. *Myron*'s rhetoric, so weirdly flat and colloquial, presents a deeply amusing contrast to Myra's decadently baroque ebullience. The two novels cannot, in fact, be separated without a loss to either.

Never one to ignore the reality of politics behind the imaginary world he creates, Vidal teases out links between Hollywood-style fantasy and American politics as Richard Nixon appears in various guises. At one point, for example, Nixon arrives at MGM on the back lot, asking if 1948 has an extradition treaty with the future. This link between the twin capitals of Washington and Hollywood becomes a dominant theme in two of the later novels of Vidal's American sequence, *Empire* (1987) and *Hollywood*, where these connections are explicitly and (as opposed to *Myron*) realistically explored.

Duluth is certainly Vidal's bleakest work, though it might also be considered his funniest. A Swiftian rant against what life in America had become by the 1970s, *Duluth* ("Love It Or Loathe It, You Can Never Leave It Or Lose It") was regarded by some critics as the author's most subversive, most bitter, novel. The conceit is postmodern: a narrative purportedly the property of one Rosemary Klein Kantor, the Wurlitzer Prize winner who, like the infinite number of monkeys in a room who manage to type out *Hamlet* by accident, creates this novel (as well as the TV series *Duluth*) out of a word processor that contains the plots of ten thousand previously published novels. Full of wordplay, a variety of gags, sleights of thought, and baroque fictional whirligigs, *Duluth* constitutes Vidal's most open assault on the excesses of American mass culture.

Live from Golgotha emerges from the same netherworld as *Duluth, Messiah,* and *Kalki* (the latter a novel in the vein of *Messiah*, featuring a messianic figure bent on destruction). This insane burlesque of the Gospels takes place at the end of the second millennium. Science and technology by now command the world, making it possible for holograms, even people, to be shifted around in time with ease. NBC is present at the Crucifixion, filming away, and the first bishop of Ephesus, Timothy, has been hired as anchorman. There is a glitch, however; a ruthless computer hacker has sent a virus to corrupt the extant Gospels, so that Timothy must get the "true" story, whatever that might be. St. Paul, Shirley MacLaine, Oral Roberts, and Mary Baker Eddy are among the gathering who witness the Crucifixion, further confusing everyone. In the end, there is no true story; there are only fictions, each crazier than the next one. It seems possible that Timothy is himself, like a character from Jorge Luis Borges, merely a dreamer himself, dreaming the universe.

The Smithsonian Institution arrived in 1998, a slender novel in a similarly fantastic vein as the earlier satires, although this work has a tender side absent from the previous satires. Vidal lavishes affection on T., a thirteen-year-old boy lost in that venerable Washington institution and wandering the corridors of history as the figures of various exhibitions come to life at night, after the museum closes. Set in 1939, when Vidal himself was an adolescent, this novel cannot help being drenched with personal history as well as public history. The development of the atomic bomb forms a kind of eerie backdrop to the novel, which is part science fiction, part historical romance, and part satire. As a narrative it is fantastic, sweet, and exceptionally droll, but it lacks the ferocious bite of the earlier satires and seems to gesture wanly in the direction of Vidal's more realistic fictions of history. It might be considered a superior amusement, though not one of Vidal's finer works.

THE AMERICAN CHRONICLE

Vidal's canny exploration of American history that begins with *Washington, D.C.* and ends with *The Golden Age* may be seen by future critics as his principle achievement in fiction. Though not originally conceived as a sequence, the series starts with a fairly conventional novel that opens in 1937 at a party where the defeat of President Franklin Roosevelt's cynical effort to enlarge the U.S. Supreme Court finds cheerful support among a group of political insiders. The two main families whose lives are chronicled over a decade of national events are those of Senator James Burden Day and Blaise Sanford, who owns the *Washington Tribune*. Clay Overbury, who regards Senator Day as his mentor, serves as a link between the two families by marrying Enid Sanford, daughter of the newspaper baron. Vidal's plot turns on a bribe that ultimately serves to destroy the senator's career.

Washington, D.C. remains a competent narrative, but nobody could have foreseen how the American chronicle would unfold from this modest beginning. *Burr* comes next in the sequence, and it stands out as one of the richest of Vidal's works, a novel that brings handsomely into play the author's various talents, including an intimate sense of history and an understanding of political motivations. The novel was finished about the time Vidal moved from Rome to Ravello, a remote town perched on a cliff side overlooking the Mediterranean Sea between Salerno and Naples.

Charlie Schuyler, a young law clerk and journalist who works for Aaron Burr, narrates the novel. Burr, of course, was the man who killed Alexander Hamilton in a duel in 1804 and who, two years later, initiated a secessionist conspiracy that challenged many assumptions of America's constitutional architects. Writing in the immediate wake of the 1960s, Vidal presents a challenging counternarrative of American power, one that would grow into a marvelous exploration of American imperial aspirations in future sequels. In *Burr* he draws a vivid portrait of the Founders, writing about Washington and Jefferson, among others, as though they were friends and neighbors. The effect remains fresh and startling.

The story of Charlie Schuyler continues in *1876* (1976). Schuyler returns to New York on the eve of his country's centennial. Vidal summons a vision of the Gilded Age,

scanning that gaudy and energetic period in American history with an eye for the kind of idiosyncratic detail that marked *Creation*. He writes about the construction of new churches in Brooklyn, about livestock trotting down East Twenty-fourth Street, and about the origins of Chinatown and Central Park. Like the author himself, Schuyler is the panoptical observer, taking in everything from a discreet distance. He sees but is rarely seen—the ideal Vidalian hero.

Ideally, historical novels generate a feeling of resonance with contemporary affairs, and *1876* achieves that. (Indeed, it was published in America's bicentennial year of 1976—a remarkably well-timed publication.) Vidal cleverly aligns his echoes between present and past, so that Samuel J. Tilden reminds one of the well-meaning but ultimately ineffective George McGovern, while Rutherford B. Hayes recalls the bumbling Gerald Ford. Mark Twain (in his white suit) comes off as a Tom Wolfe figure, the satirist as gadfly, a precursor of Vidal himself, who often quips in public like a latter-day Twain. The Vietnam War and the Civil War are drawn into parallel rows of absurdity and cruelty, while the Lincoln assassination reminds one inevitably of President Kennedy's demise in Dallas. The Babcock break-in might be taken as a dry run for Watergate. And so the comparisons unfold.

The next novel in the sequence, *Lincoln*, is perhaps the least typical. Vidal's prose is less self-consciously fluent and attractive here, and the subject itself, for once, occupies center stage. The astonishing weight of the material—a nation pushed to the limit because of a bloody and divisive civil war—soon takes control of the narrative, and Vidal wisely steps aside and allows the story to find its own realistic contours. Writing in the *New York Review of Books*, the critic Harold Bloom characterizes Vidal as "a masterly American historical novelist, now wholly matured, who has found his truest subject, which is our national political history during precisely those years when our political and military histories were as one, one thing and one thing only: the unwavering will of Abraham Lincoln to keep the states united." He discusses *Lincoln* in the context of Vidal's developing career, musing on "the still ambiguous question of Vidal's strength or perhaps competing strengths as a novelist." Adamantly, Bloom concludes: "*Lincoln*, together with the curiously assorted trio of *Julian*, *Myra Breckinridge*, and *Burr*, demonstrates that his narrative achievement is vastly underestimated by American academic criticism, an injustice he has repaid amply in his essayist attacks upon the academy, and in the sordid intensities of *Duluth*."

An important element of *Lincoln* is the contrast between Salmon P. Chase and Lincoln. Chase was the archetypal Republican abolitionist writhing with jealousy over the president; he was mean-spirited and deceptive as well as crudely pious. In Vidal's rendering, Lincoln is single-minded, ready to sacrifice anything—including the Constitution and human rights—to preserve the Union. Chase, by contrast, appears genuinely concerned about the slaves, while Lincoln has no real interest in their freedom. Indeed, he uses abolition simply as a useful tool in winning support for the war at a critical juncture. At the core of the novel is Lincoln's determination to use all means to support one end.

The last three novels in the chronicle, *Empire*, *Hollywood*, and *The Golden Age*, offer a panorama of the first half of the twentieth century, a time when the American Empire became a global enterprise. The latter novel comes full circle, revisiting (quite literally) the key moments and the characters of *Washington, D.C.*, which is focused on the Sanford family. As usual, real characters (including Theodore Roosevelt, William McKinley, William Jennings Bryan, Henry James, Henry Adams, and Franklin Roosevelt) mingle with fictitious ones. Fact and fiction become, once again, permeable; the world, recast by Vidal, is given the kind of unity that only fiction can generate.

The convergence of various worlds, such as Hollywood and Washington, the twin capitals of the American Empire, occupy Vidal in these later novels. In *The Golden Age*, Vidal in magisterial fashion ties together the various strands of the chronicle, offering a pageant of the national experience in the years from the entry of the United States into World War II through the end of the Korean conflict. It is all familiar material for Vidal, who lived through these tempestuous years. In *The Golden Age*, Vidal's distrust of Roosevelt and Harry Truman is typical of his attitude generally toward those who pluck the strings of history. He is cynical and savvy, mistrusting those in control, always interested in how—through the propagandistic use of Hollywood films and journalism—consent is manufactured by the ruling class.

AN AMERICAN MONTAIGNE

Although the novel has preoccupied Vidal and offered a main stage for his writerly activity, he has been an essayist from the mid-1950s to the present. This vein of his work opened with numerous short reviews for various journals, such as *The Reporter*, the *New York Times Book Review*, and *Esquire*. These assignments led to larger essays and reviews, many of which became large ruminations on the state of the nation itself. In the 1960s he became a leading writer for the newly established *New York Review of Books*, in whose pages he would address a wide range of cultural and political topics. His sharp and scolding manner, with a tonal range from the highly formal to the sharply colloquial, became a kind of trademark, separating his incidental prose from that of other writers. Numerous volumes that collected his incidental pieces appeared at regular intervals, including *Rocking the Boat* (1962), *Reflections on a Sinking Ship* (1969), *Matters of Fact and Fiction: Essays, 1973–1976* (1977), *The Second American Revolution and Other Essays (1976–1982)* (1982), *At Home* (1988), and *The Last Empire: Essays, 1992–2000* (2001).

In a sense, Vidal's career in the essay culminated in 1993 when he won the National Book Award for *United States: Essays, 1952–1992* (1993). That massive volume unearthed a whole continent of brilliant writing about literature and politics. Over a hundred essays were gathered there, showing off Vidal as a shrewd, uncompromising observer of American political history, cultural history, and world culture. He wrote about homosexuality, about French fiction, about such important American figures as William Dean Howells, F. Scott Fitzgerald, Orson Welles, Eleanor Roosevelt, and Tennessee Williams. As readers of his entertaining memoir, *Palimpsest* (1995), would discover, he had actually known most of the people he was writing about. His unique presence on the scene of history gives to his essays a feeling of authority and intimacy. Indeed, they often begin with a personal anecdote about the person whose work or career lies at the center of the essay and then move into a more discursive vein.

Though cool, elegant, and witty, the essays comment harshly on American politics and foreign policy. Vidal became, in the 1960s, a leading spokesman for the New Left, an iconoclast who was willing to debate William F. Buckley on television and write scathing essays about Richard Nixon. In "Pink Triangle and Yellow Star," he drew stunning parallels between the persecution of homosexuals and Jews. In "The Holy Family" he burst the bubble of awe and admiration that had kept the Kennedy family free of criticism for many years. He poked fun at any number of American icons, from Theodore Roosevelt (whom he called "an American sissy") to Edmund Wilson, the most revered man of letters in the twentieth century. In "Rabbitt's Own Burrow" he surveyed the career of his contemporary, John Updike, with a ferocious eye. Perhaps more importantly, he singled out neglected writers for praise, raising their profile in the world of letters. Among those he helped to reach a wider audience were Italo Calvino and Dawn Powell, both of whom he knew as friends.

In recent years he has waged a continual war on those who would attempt to diminish freedom. In "Shredding the Bill of Rights," for example, he says:

> It has always been a mark of American freedom that unlike countries under constant Napoleonic surveillance, we are not obliged to carry identification to show to curious officials and pushy police. But now, due to Terrorism, every one of us is stopped at airports and obliged to show an ID which must include a mug shot (something, as Allah knows, no terrorist would ever dare fake).

As usual, his ability to say what everyone knows and to make it unsettling is a particular gift. He simply tells the truth as he sees it, without worrying about the implications, for himself or his reputation. This habit has won him many admirers and numerous enemies as well. It might be argued that Vidal, as a writer and perpetual didact, is at his best in his essays, and that a century from now he will be remembered mostly for this work.

A MAN OF LETTERS

It almost seems a put-down to call someone a man of letters. The term smacks of amateurism and antiquarianism, although it has been applied with dignity to many noble figures of the past, such as William Dean Howells and Edmund Wilson. Yet there is nothing about the concept that deserves scorn. A man or woman of letters is someone who ranges widely over the field of literature and life, who attempts to write in various forms, and who becomes one of the stable, central voices of his or her generation.

It could easily be argued that no American since Mark Twain has performed in this role so ably as Gore Vidal. His American chronicle itself represents a vivid counternarrative of American history and politics. The satirical novels are unique, and add a vein of Swiftian humor to American literature unlike anything that preceded them. His workmanlike achievements as a dramatist and screenwriter were, at least in their time, notable. Finally, his essays and reviews have earned him a permanent place in American letters and politics. In his memoirs, *Palimpsest*, he has left a remarkably entertaining record of his life and times, which are also the life and times of the nation. Although the quality of the work has varied, the total effect of his presence in American literary culture has been considerable.

[*See also* American Essay, The; Capote, Truman; Gay Literature: Poetry and Prose; James, Henry; *and* Williams, Tennessee.]

SELECTED WORKS

Williwaw (1946)
In a Yellow Wood (1947)
The City and the Pillar (1948)
The Season of Comfort (1949)
A Search for the King (1949)
Dark Green, Bright Red (1950)
Death in the Fifth Position (as Edgar Box) (1952)
The Judgment of Paris (1952)
Death before Bedtime (as Edgar Box) (1953)
Death Likes It Hot (as Edgar Box) (1954)
Messiah (1954)
A Thirsty Evil (1956)
Visit to a Small Planet (1957)
Suddenly, Last Summer (1959)
The Best Man (1960)
Rocking the Boat (1962)
Romulus (1962)
Julian (1964)
Washington, D.C. (1967)
Myra Breckinridge (1968)
Weekend (1968)
Reflections upon a Sinking Ship (1969)
Two Sisters (1970)
An Evening with Richard Nixon and . . . (1972)
Burr (1973)
Homage to Daniel Shays (1974)
Myron (1974)
1876 (1976)
Matters of Fact and of Fiction: Essays, 1973–1976 (1977)
Kalki (1978)
Creation (1981)
The Second American Revolution and Other Essays (1976–1982) (1982)
Duluth (1983)
Lincoln (1984)
Armageddon? (1987)
Empire (1987)
At Home (1988)
Hollywood: A Novel of America in the 1920s (1990)
A View from the Diners' Club (1991)
Live from Golgotha (1992)
Screening History (1992)
United States: Essays, 1952–1992 (1993)
Palimpsest: A Memoir (1995)
The Smithsonian Institution (1998)

The Golden Age (2000)
The Last Empire: Essays, 1992–2000 (2001)

FURTHER READING

Baker, Susan. *Gore Vidal: A Critical Companion*. Westport, Conn., 1997.

Dick, Bernard F. *The Apostate Angel: A Critical Study of Gore Vidal*. New York, 1974.

Kaplan, Fred. *Gore Vidal: A Biography*. New York, 1999.

Kiernan, Robert F. *Gore Vidal*. New York, 1982.

Parini, Jay, ed. *Gore Vidal: Writer against the Grain*. New York, 1992.

Stanton, Robert J. *Gore Vidal: A Primary and Secondary Bibliography*. Boston, 1978.

White, Ray Lewis. *Gore Vidal*. Boston, 1968.

VIETNAM IN POETRY AND PROSE

by Joseph Duemer

The American literature of the Vietnam War, even at so short an historical distance from the end of the war (1975), can seem exotic to the contemporary reader, who might be excused for thinking of it as a species of travel writing, providing an imaginative tour of an exotic place and a turbulent historical period, but depicting a fundamentally different order of reality. This view, paradoxically, represents an important truth even while making it difficult to come to an understanding of this body of writing. Travel writing imposes a double burden on writers: first, to understand for themselves what they have seen so far from home, and, second, to bring at least some of that experience home to their countrymen. That is exactly the burden that many writers who served in Vietnam—as soldiers, journalists or civilian advisers—take up. In her book *Travel Writing: The Self and the World* (1997), Casey Blanton describes the problem with precision: "Melville's Ishmael, sole survivor of an epic journey...discovers the central dilemma of travel literature when he begins to tell the reader of *Moby-Dick* about Queequeg's home: 'It is not down on any map. True places never are.' Ishmael's attempts to represent the exotic island homeland of his friend are frustrated by the inherent difficulty of rendering the foreign into familiar terms." Melville's great novel (1851) and Joseph Conrad's *Heart of Darkness* (1902), both concerned with venturing into the unknown regions of the world and the self, provide important points of reference for many of the American writers who have taken the American war in Vietnam as a subject. Along with Graham Greene's short novel *The Quiet American* (1955), these texts provide a stylistic point of departure for many writers going to or coming from Vietnam.

The "inherent difficulty" of bringing home intelligence is confronted, directly or indirectly, by writers whose work has been shaped by their participation in—or in some cases their opposition to—the American war in Vietnam. One response is what anthropologists have called "thick description," but long in use by imaginative writers. Bruce Weigl's poem, "Temple Near Quang Tri,

Not on Any Map" (*The Monkey Wars*, 1985) adopts this strategy:

> Dusk, the ivy thick with sparrows
> Squawking for more room
> Is all we hear; we see
> Birds move on the walls of the temple
> Shaping their calligraphy of wings.
> Ivy is thick in the grottos,
> On the moon-watching platform
> Ivy keeps the door from fully closing.

What often motivates the American writers who encountered Vietnam directly is the desire to produce some kind of report of their experience of the true places they have seen that are not on any map. In Weigl's poetry and in Robert Olen Butler's fiction, for example, the beauty of the Vietnamese landscape becomes a fundamental, almost erotic, element of meaning, particularly as it contrasts with the violence of battle. Vietnam, paradoxically, becomes both a true place in this sense and a hellish zone beyond reality, not on any map. When their tour was up, American soldiers spoke of returning to "the world." For writers who did not go to Vietnam, but who confront the war in their work, the problems are different, consisting often of a need to understand what appears beyond comprehension, to find historical and moral contexts for a new kind of war. Denise Levertov, Robert Bly, and Robert Stone (who did travel briefly to Vietnam as a journalist during the war) figure prominently among this group.

As literary eras are usually measured, the Vietnam War period is brief. The war is usually said to have lasted from 1965, when the first U.S. Marine Corps battalion came ashore to protect the American airbase in Da Nang, until 1973, when the last U.S. combat troops left South Vietnam. There had been a substantial American military presence advising the Army of the Republic of Vietnam (ARVN) since 1963, however, and the last marine guards were not evacuated from the roof of the U.S. Embassy in Saigon until April 1975, when the government of South Vietnam fell to the invading army of the Democratic Republic of Vietnam (North

Vietnam). Whether it lasted eight or twelve years, the Vietnam War remains the longest in American history. The primary phase of the Vietnam period of American literature is brief, but it is followed by a second phase that extends well beyond the end of the war itself—poems, novels, essays, biographies, stories, and memoirs continue to appear as American writers, both combatants and noncombatants, keep working to digest the historical, personal, and moral effects of the war. Interestingly, a third phase has developed, in which writers like John Balaban, Bruce Weigl, W. D. Ehrhart, Martha Collins, and Dana Sachs seek to produce an American response to the postwar realities of contemporary Vietnam.

There are a number of ways to schematize the work of American writers who have dealt with the subject of Vietnam. The most obvious is chronological, but many studies and anthologies, such as Stewart O'Nan's *The Vietnam Reader* (1998), take a thematic approach within a broader chronological organization. It is also useful to distinguish among the subjects and themes characteristic of different literary genres.

THEMES

The central theme of American literature from the Vietnam War is the loss of idealism, a loss figured most often by descriptions of chaos and disintegration that function as the guiding metaphors around which many texts from the Vietnam War are structured. Paradoxically heightening the sense of irony, such disillusionment is often represented against the backdrop of Vietnam's stunning physical beauty. Along with the disintegration of individual lives and ordinary interpretations of reality, language itself begins to turn inside out. This is a fact that soldiers were acutely aware of themselves. No one took seriously the replacement of the word "retreat" with the phrase "tactical redeployment," or of the descriptive and accurate term "free fire zone" with the official "pre-cleared firing area." In a defense against military euphemism, a now anonymous writer produced the satire "What the Captain Means," which purports to be a news conference in Vietnam. The piece has been reprinted anonymously many times; the excerpt quoted here is from John Clark Pratt's *Vietnam Voices* (1984):

CORRESPONDENT: What do you think of the F-4?
CAPTAIN: It's so fuckin' maneuverable you can fly up your own ass with it.
INFORMATION OFFICER: What the captain means is that he has found the F4C Phantom highly maneuverable at all

altitudes and he considers it an excellent aircraft for all missions assigned.
CORR.: I suppose, Captain, you have flown a certain number of missions over North Vietnam. What did you think of the SAMs used by the North Vietnamese?
CAPT.: Why those bastards couldn't hit a bull in the ass with a base fiddle. We fake the shit out of them. It's no sweat.
IO: What the captain means is that the surface-to-air missiles around Hanoi pose a serious problem to our air operations and that our pilots have a healthy respect for them.

Satire cuts both ways, distancing even as it reveals the truth. "What the Captain Means" concludes:

CORRESPONDENT: One final question. Could you reduce your impression of the war into a simple phrase or statement, captain?
CAPTAIN: You bet your ass I can. It's a fucked up war.
IO: What the captain means is . . . it's a FUCKED UP WAR.

The language of patriotic idealism comes under close scrutiny in Vietnam writing. Near the beginning of Ward Just's novel *A Dangerous Friend* (1999), Sidney Parade, a young man recently recruited into "the effort" in Vietnam, comes to a realization: "As . . . [he] spoke, he felt the power of the logic. Of course he was describing an illusion, but men died for illusions, at Thermopylae or Antietam, or Verdun. Illusion was another word for ideal, something serious and altruistic, neither heartless nor selfish." This theme of idealism's failure directly affects the narrative and even lyric structures American writers have employed to embody the American experience in Vietnam. During the war, the poet James Wright, who served in the army just after World War II, published a poem titled "Ars Poetica: Some Recent Criticism" (*Two Citizens*, 1973), in which he remarks, "Reader, we had a lovely language. / We would not listen." The poem concludes with an address to those who have destroyed the language with violence: "Ah, you bastards, / How I hate you."

Idealism has two different meanings, each of which bears on our reading of the literature from the war. On one hand, there is the simple, patriotic idealism of the American marines who went ashore at Da Nang in 1965 described in Philip Caputo's memoir *A Rumor of War* (1977)—an idealism that did not last more than a few patrols and firefights for the soldiers, but which persisted back in "the world" as part of the politics of the war. And there is the wider-ranging intellectual idealism of the policymakers—chronicled in David Halberstam's still-sobering *The Best and the Brightest* (1972)—whose moral and political certainty led to miscalculation after miscalculation, political as well as military. This sort of political or philosophical idealism created, in the gestalt of Vietnam combat, a radical break between the soldiers' own experiences and the official version of the war. This break between experience and narrative haunts the American literature of Vietnam, particularly that written by veterans, though it was also felt among the reporters who covered Vietnam from 1963 on. In addition to David Halberstam's work, Neil Sheehan's *A Bright, Shining Lie* (1988) explores in savage detail the competing narratives of the brass in Saigon and Washington and the infantrymen and their officers slogging through the Mekong Delta. "Of course there was not a straight story in the sense of a narrative that began in one place and ended in another," Ward Just's narrator remarks at the beginning of the *A Dangerous Friend.*

POETRY

John Clark Pratt, the leading critic of the American literature of the Vietnam period, divides the American poetry dealing with the Vietnam War into three basic types: "political protest poems, usually written by established poets who had not been to Vietnam; verse novels, in which chronologically linked poems depict one person's experiences at war; and the hundreds of usually short, personal lyrics that present individual scenes, character sketches, or events." To these must be added a substantial body of work produced by American poets after the end of the war that, while not dealing directly with combat or experiences in Vietnam, has been influenced by what could be termed a Vietnam aesthetic—descriptive realism combined with situational extravagance, irrationality, and absurdity.

The earliest published poetry dealing with the Vietnam War came from established poets such as Robert Bly, Denise Levertov, Muriel Rukeyser, W. S. Merwin and Allen Ginsberg. In Ginsberg's long poem *Wichita Vortex Sutra* (1966), which takes place as the poet drives across the United States listening to the radio and drinking in the landscape of America, he makes use of Ezra Pound's "ideographic method" in order to juxtapose bits of history, literature, and popular culture into the vortex of the poem's title. In section 2 the poet mentions the Republican Senator George D. Aiken of Vermont, who is quoted as saying that American involvement in Vietnam began with a "bad guess." The poet then notes that "in 1954, 80% of the / Vietnamese people would have voted for Ho Chi Minh." Secretary of Defense Robert McNamara and Senator John C. Stennis are also called

to testify in Ginsberg's epic. By placing his "vortex" in Wichita, Ginsberg locates it in the literal and figurative heart of the country; by making it a "sutra," or prayer, he seeks to find some spiritual cleansing or at least coherence through language.

If Ginsberg adopts the bardic, historically engaged voice of Walt Whitman and Pound, W. S. Merwin and Robert Bly assume a voice that barely whispers. Bly's "Counting the Small-Boned Bodies" and Merwin's "When the War Is Over" and "The Asians Dying" exemplify this mode. Denise Levertov and Muriel Rukeyser represent a more politically engaged point of view. Rukeyser, in fact, went to Hanoi in North Vietnam during the war. In her poem, "Flying to Hanoi," she writes,

> I thought I was going to the poets, but I am going to
> the children.
> I thought I was going to the children, but I am going to
> the women.
> I thought I was going to the women, but I am going to
> the fighters.
> I thought I was going to the fighters, but I am going to the
> men and women who are inventing peace.
> I thought I was going to the inventors of peace, but I am
> going to the poets.
> My life is flying to your life.

Rukeyser's poetry comes to Vietnam out of her empathy for the poor and marginalized in her own country; that is, she sees the Vietnamese as one more community being exploited by American interests. Other established literary figures who took the war as a subject such as Bly, Merwin, and Levertov would have been even more keenly aware of the ongoing cultural discourses invoked by their work. These more "literary" poets often explicitly tie their treatment of the war to larger historical and cultural narratives. In her poem "Resistance Meeting: Boston Common," Jean Garrigue writes,

> April in the Public Garden.
> Also glittering are the hides of horses
> That the policemen sit on like Order and Reason
> Which is not unlike the order and reason of superior
> fire power,
> The order of Poseidons and nuclear umbrellas....

Other poets, like George Oppen, approach the war indirectly. Oppen's poem, "Power, the Enchanted World," written in the 1960s, is saturated with the violence of American foreign policy, characteristically knitting that concern to the domestic facts of poverty and social isolation. Among the most consistent opponents of the war among American poets has been the anarchist Hayden

Carruth. As both poet and editor he produced a body of work that stands in opposition to violence of all kinds, but especially of state violence. In his poem "The Birds of Vietnam," he begins by invoking Asian birds he has never seen before shifting to the "endangered species" of his own country and finally to the endangered country of Vietnam:

> And why, in my image of that cindered country,
> should I waste my mourning? I will never have
> enough. Think of the children there,
> insane little crusted kids at the beckoning fire,
> think of the older ones, burned, crazy with fear,
> sensible beings who can know hell, think
> of their minds exploding, their hearts flaming.

Although these and other established poets were the first to publish poems dealing with the Vietnam War, their poems were not the first to emerge from the war. The first American poetry of the war was written by soldiers in the field. A sizable collection of this work can be found in *Carrying the Darkness* (1985), an anthology edited by W. D. Ehrhart, himself a poet who served in Vietnam. A majority of the poets represented in *Carrying the Darkness* did not sustain literary careers after the war. Paradoxically, this is what makes the book so valuable to the contemporary reader: many of the poems possess the intensity of folk poetry. It is a folk poetry of combat, as even the titles indicate: "Night Flare Drop: Tan Son Nhat," "50 Gunner," and "A Black Soldier Remembers" which begins:

> My Saigon daughter I saw only once
> standing in the dusty square
> across from the Brink's BOQ/PX
> in the back of the National Assembly
> next to the ugly statue of
> the crouching marines facing
> the fish pond the VC blew up
> during Tet....

A few of these soldier-poets did go on to establish themselves as writers after the war. Among the most significant of these are Bruce Weigl, Yusuf Komunyakaa, W. D. Ehrhart, Kevin Bowen, and the conscientious objector John Balaban, who worked in a hospital in South Vietnam helping to evacuate injured children from the war zone. Balaban's "In Celebration of Spring" borrows the literary trope of the green man to mourn the war dead. All of these poets have dealt directly with the war as subject matter, but have also sought to knit their experience of the war into their later lives and to the American culture

they inhabit. This group of poets represents a collective memory that is as important to American history as the British poets of World War I were and are to that tradition.

FICTION

If the American poetry of the Vietnam War begins in self-expression and ends in despair, Vietnam War fiction begins and ends in complexity, irony, and ambiguity. The inevitable movement of characters from innocence to experience is marked by the development of a sense of absurdity and contradiction. Rostok, a character in Ward Just's *A Dangerous Friend*, tells Sydney on his first day in Vietnam, "You'll get used to it, Syd. It takes a minute. Of course you need a lust for complexity. You need ambiguity in your heart." And in his earlier story, "The Congressman Who Loved Flaubert," Just considers the nature of political language: A group of academics is ushered into Congressman LaRuth's office. They are there to urge the congressman to present a sense-of-the-Congress resolution "denouncing imperialism." As he reads over the text, LaRuth is impressed by its "eloquence," though he is also aware of its futility. Just's use of the word "eloquence" seems designed to evoke an earlier anti-imperialist story, Conrad's *Heart of Darkness*, in which Marlow discovers the manuscript that Kurtz had been preparing for the Society for the Suppression of Savage Customs. Marlow remarks upon the "eloquence" of the document. The reader of Just's story is certainly intended to recall Kurtz's fanciful and empty rhetoric, as well as the phrase scrawled across the final page: "Exterminate the brutes!" The American fiction of the Vietnam War—much of it profoundly eloquent—is deeply distrustful of eloquence, especially the eloquence of politics.

In addition to Melville and Conrad, the shadow of Graham Greene's *The Quiet American* hangs over much fiction taking the war as subject. Political innocence is at once dangerous and protective. More than anything else, though, it provides a way of seeing the world that ignores ambiguity, paradox, complexity, and confusion. Greene's novel—that of an outsider—presents the American Alden Pyle as dangerous not only to himself, but especially to those principles and people he loves. And yet his innocence protects him from the madness, despair, and cynicism of the other characters. Greene's novel was denounced by many American critics when it first appeared in 1955; those denunciations now appear "innocent" in exactly the sense that Greene's novel undertakes to explore. A. J. Liebling trashed the book in a 7 April 1956 essay, the tone of which now strikes the reader not as disdainful, as Liebling intended, but merely embarrassing. After Vietnam, Americans were disabused of their innocence, none more than American writers.

Stylistically, this is a body of work that ranges from the Hemingway-like plain descriptions in David Halberstam's novel *One Very Hot Day* (1967) to the more experimental motions of Jayne Anne Phillips's *Machine Dreams* (1984). It is predominantly a naturalistic fiction, however, relying on clear narrative lines and description to evoke the incomprehensible nature of the conflict. It is a naturalism haunted by the surreal, a point Beidler makes effectively in his study *American Literature and the Vietnam Experience* (1982).

The fiction of the Vietnam War can be divided for convenience into combat and noncombat narratives. The great majority of the combat narratives are authored by participants in the war, though not necessarily by combatants. For instance, David Halberstam worked as a journalist in Vietnam. The usefulness of the distinction between participants in the war and those who consider it from a greater distance has formal consequences, marking important differences of perspective and narrative point of view. Briefly, writers who took part in the war directly have a greater commitment to naturalistic description and straightforward narrative. This is particularly true of the first wave of novels to come out after the war: Larry Heinemann's *Close Quarters* (1977), Wayne Karlin's *Lost Armies* (1988), and even Tim O'Brien's *Going after Cacciato* (1978), though this latter book presents a more complex formal design.

Halberstam's *One Very Hot Day* can stand for much of the early fiction from participants in the war. The novel evokes, without actually re-creating, the Battle of Ap Bac, which took place in the Mekong Delta in 1963 and in which U.S. advisers played an important, though ultimately futile, role. Five American helicopters were shot down by massed small-arms fire. It was a battle that demonstrated the strength and discipline of the Viet Cong and the weakness and poor morale of ARVN troops. Neil Sheehan gives a detailed account of this battle in the first one hundred pages of *A Bright, Shining Lie*, his biography of John Paul Vann. It is useful to read Sheehan and Halberstam together. *One Very Hot Day* presents the war from the point of view of an ARVN infantry unit and its American advisers. The language of the novel forms a taut structure for the containment of anger. In a disciplined and clear prose, Halberstam captures the sudden violence of war as well as its tedium. The novel is the fictional

enactment of the ideas contained in Halberstam's nonfiction *The Making of a Quagmire* (1965), published two years earlier. The central thrust of both Halberstam books is the courage of soldiers and the moral failure of politicians, both American and Vietnamese. Because it reflected their experiences and frustrations so effectively, *One Very Hot Day* became popular with Americans fighting in the Mekong Delta in the mid-1960s and into the 1970s, a sort of inoculation against complete cynicism—someone, at least, understood the soldier's life.

Halberstam spent time with combat units in the Mekong Delta, but he was a journalist, not a soldier. His perspective is more detached than writers who served in the armed forces. Tim O'Brien brings the infantryman's perspective to writing about the war. Even in his *Going after Cacciato*—a novel about a fanciful journey across continents from the rice paddies of Vietnam to the boulevards of Paris led by Specialist Fourth Class Paul Berlin—a journey to find Cacciato and bring him back to his unit—there is an emphasis on realistic detail even while the frame of the story is allegorical. Perhaps the only example of magic-realism to come out of Vietnam, *Going after Cacciato* is an imaginary journey that makes the daily reality of war not just bearable, but meaningful. Before he wrote *Going after Cacciato*, O'Brien published a memoir called *If I Die in a Combat Zone, Box Me Up and Ship Me Home* (1973), and a fair amount of the material from the earlier book finds its way into the fictional world of the later one. By putting the ordinary reality of war in a heroic narrative frame, O'Brien manages to balance the contradictions experienced by those fighting the war. Later, O'Brien brings these materials into even finer focus in his novel-in-stories *The Things They Carried* (1990).

Frustration with politicians and headquarters officers became a central political theme in war fiction from the mid-1960s onward—and not only in fiction, but in the political discourse in general. In the decades since the war, this natural cynicism has hardened into the argument that the American military "could have won the war" had they been allowed to fight it on their own terms. It is an argument that takes the fact that the American and South Vietnamese bureaucracies often put ordinary soldiers' lives at risk for strictly political objectives and expands it into a myth to rationalize a defeat that remains largely incomprehensible, especially to many of those who fought in Vietnam. But such an argument ignores the historical realities of the conflict, specifically, the cost in lives and treasure that would have been expended in order to invade North Vietnam and defeat the communist government.

Jeffrey Record effectively refutes the myth in his study *The Wrong War: Why We Lost in Vietnam* (1998).

The Vietnam War was a consuming reality for Americans between 1965 and 1973, so it is not surprising that writers who did not go to Vietnam, or who visited there briefly, would also undertake the war or at least its historical and social context as subjects. Norman Mailer's *Why Are We in Vietnam?* (1967) narrates a hunting trip to Alaska to shoot big game from a helicopter and only mentions Vietnam in the last two sentences, yet because of the title a kind of dread expectation hangs over the text. It is a typically brilliant Mailer trick, but one that resonated deeply at the time the novel was published.

DRAMA

Leaving aside film, which is beyond the scope of this survey, there is not an extensive dramatic literature from the Vietnam War; the drama that does exist, however, is among the most provocative and experimental work of the period. Among the traditional dramatists, David Rabe is preeminent. Beidler's *American Literature and the Experience of Vietnam* mentions plays by George Tabori (*Pinkville*), Adrienne Kennedy (*An Evening with Dead Essex*), and Tom Cole (*Medal of Honor Rag*), but then comments: "Surely the most important development in dramatic literature of the war (and one of the most important developments in Vietnam writing at large) was the production of two plays [both in 1971] by David Rabe, *The Basic Training of Pavlo Hummel* and *Sticks and Bones*. These, along with *Streamers* in 1977, would form a body of work so sustained and continuous as to be thought of as a major Vietnam trilogy."

Near the beginning of Rabe's *Sticks and Bones*, a character named Sergeant Major knocks on the door of the home of characters named Ozzie and Harriet. He is leading a character named Dave:

OZZIE: Dave...?
SGT. MAJOR: He's blind.
OZZIE: What?
SGT. MAJOR: Blind.
OZZIE: I don't...understand.
SGT. MAJOR: We're very sorry.
OZZIE, *realizing*: Ohhhhhh. Yes. Ohhhhh. [*Realizing*] I see ...sure. I mean, we didn't know. Nobody said it. I mean, sure, Dave, sure; it's all right—don't you worry. Rick's here too, Dave—Rick, your brother, tell him "Hello."
RICK: Hi, Dave.
DAVID: You said "Father."
OZZIE: Well...there's two of us, Dave; two.

DAVID: Sergeant, you said "home." I don't think so. [...] It doesn't feel right.
[*Ozzie calls to Harriet, who is upstairs. When she comes down and sees Dave, Ozzie begins to explain, his speech filled with pauses:*]
OZZIE: Harriet...don't be upset...they say...Harriet, Harriet...he can't see...Harriet...they say—he can't ...see. That man.
HARRIET, *standing very still*: Can't see? What do you mean?
SGT. MAJOR: He's blind.
HARRIET: No. Who says? No, no. [...]
SGT. MAJOR, *with a large sheet of paper waving in his hand*: Who's gonna sign this for me, mister? It's a shipping receipt. I got to have somebody's signature to show you got him. I got to have somebody's name on the paper. [...]
OZZIE: Fine, listen, would you like some refreshments?
SGT. MAJOR: No.
OZZIE: I mean while I do this. Cake and coffee. Of course you do.
SGT. MAJOR: No.

In addition to the dark wit of having Ozzie and Harriet's son returned to them as a piece of freight that must be signed for, the power of this passage in the play derives from the silence that is built into the language. And while Dave has been returned to his family, he knows he has not returned home. "It doesn't feel right," he tells the Sergeant Major, speaking for many veterans returning from Vietnam.

Three experimental theater companies made important contributions to the social discourse of the Vietnam period: the Living Theatre, the San Francisco Mime Troupe, and the Bread and Puppet Theater. These companies continue to produce socially engaged, experimental theater. The Living Theatre's current promotional materials offer the following description of the company's development during the 1960s:

Founded in 1947 as an imaginative alternative to the commercial theater by Judith Malina, the German-born protégée of Erwin Piscator, and Julian Beck, an abstract expressionist painter of the New York School, The Living Theatre has staged more than 80 productions.... During the 1960s, the company began a new life as a nomadic touring ensemble. In Europe, they evolved into a collective, living and working together toward the creation of a new form of nonfictional acting based on the actor's political and physical commitment to using the theater as a medium for furthering social change. The landmark achievements of this period include *Mysteries and Smaller Pieces, Antigone, Frankenstein* and *Paradise Now*.

The San Francisco Mime Troupe's aesthetic has remained consistent. The group's Web site (http://www.sfmt.org/) offers this by way of history and approach:

> Our artistic history has been a series of experiments with popular theater forms. Founding director R. G. Davis began in 1959 with avant-garde performance events in lofts and basements; when he discovered commedia dell'arte (Italian Renaissance marketplace comedy) he began a nearly 40-year tradition of free shows in the parks. Since becoming a collective in 1970, we have done melodramas, spy thrillers, musical comedies, epic histories, sitcoms, cartoon epics. Our trademark style draws from all these genres and is based on their common elements: strong story line, avowed point of view, larger-than-life characters, fantasy, live music.

The Bread and Puppet Theater was founded in 1962 by German sculptor Peter Schumann. Using puppets to reinterpret folk tales as well as classic works of literature, the group moved steadily toward greater social engagement as the sixties progressed. As the company's political commitments grew, so did the size of their puppets, growing to human scale and beyond. During the Vietnam War, the puppets became part of many anti-war marches and demonstrations. The Bread and Puppet Theater's influence can still be clearly seen in the large puppets carried by American and European protesters in contemporary demonstrations.

Two additional plays—one from the period of the war, the other from the postwar period—need to be mentioned: Barbara Garson's *MacBird* (1967), a seriously flawed satirical adaptation of *MacBeth* that casts Lyndon Johnson as the heavy; and the hit musical *Miss Saigon* (1990), a sentimental and revisionist adaptation of Puccini's opera *Madama Butterfly*, in which the Japanese heroine is replaced by a Vietnamese bargirl. Both plays say a great deal more about their authors and audiences than they do about Vietnam.

CONTINUING NARRATIVES

Nonfiction reportage such as Norman Mailer's *The Armies of the Night* (1968) began appearing during the war, and Philip Jones Griffiths's *Vietnam, Inc.* (1971) also deserves mention. Griffiths is a photographer and his book is primarily a photographic record of the effects of the American on Vietnamese society; the photographs, however, are interspersed with a highly polemical prose that goes well beyond the role of captions. Together, the photographs and writing make a whole in the same way as James Agee and Walker Evans's *Let Us Now Praise Famous Men* (1941).

The postwar period, however, has been marked by an explosion of memoirs and meditations on the personal and historical meaning of the war. Philip Caputo's *A Rumor of War* is representative of one subgenre of this large and diverse body of writing—the first-person account by a participant. Caputo served as a marine first lieutenant with the first American combat forces sent to Vietnam in 1965. Also recalling wartime experiences are the memoirs of conscientious objector John Balaban, *Remembering Heaven's Face* (1991), and those of the Quaker activist Lady Borton, *After Sorrow* (1995). These books share with Caputo's work a passionate though plainspoken prose style drawing on literary influences ranging from Melville and Conrad to the poet Robert Lowell.

Other memoirs deal with the broader context of the war. Employing the first-person narrative voice in order to tease out the strands of individual lives from the fabric of history, Duong Van Mai Elliott's *The Sacred Willow: Four Generations in the Life of a Vietnamese Family* (1999) provides the American reader with a panoramic view of Vietnamese culture and society unavailable in any other single work. On a smaller scale, Margot Adler's *Heretic's Heart* (1997) presents a picture of the American antiwar left from the inside. Among the virtues of both books is that they explode the easy generalizations and clichés that have become part of the postwar discourse on Vietnam. Dana Sach's *The House on Dream Street* (2000), which tells the story of a young American woman's life in Hanoi well after the end of the war, perhaps represents the beginning of a new American vision of Vietnam—that of a country rather than a war.

That war, as Americans know, is still being contested. The battle for control of the continuing narrative of the war is enacted by two works published in the 1990s. The first is Robert McNamara's pair of political retrospectives *In Retrospect: The Tragedy and Lessons of Vietnam* (1995) and *Argument without End: In Search of Answers to the Vietnam Tragedy* (1999); the second is Paul Hendrickson's *The Living and the Dead* (1996), which begins with a short biography of McNamara and then offers brief descriptions of the lives of six Americans affected by his policies while he was secretary of defense: a door gunner who saw action and was injured in Vietnam, an army nurse, an artist who as a young man attempted to throw McNamara off the deck of the Martha's Vineyard ferry, an upper-class Vietnamese, and an American Quaker, who, in imitation of the monk Quang Duc and other Vietnamese Buddhists, immolated himself at the Pentagon in order to register his opposition to the Vietnam War.

TRANSLATION AND THE VIETNAMESE DIASPORA

The Vietnamese diaspora has already begun to produce a literature of its own. John Balaban's masterful translation of the eighteenth-century Vietnamese poet Ho Xuan Hung, *Spring Essence* (2000), draws on the scholarship of expatriate Vietnamese as well as his own skills as a translator and poet. Nguyen Ba Chung and Kevin Bowen's *Six Vietnamese Poets* (2002) brings six important twentieth-century Vietnamese poets into English for the first time. Mong-Lan's first book of poetry, *Song of the Cicadas* (2001), combines a contemporary American poetic sensibility with an immigrant's awareness of what has been lost. The young Vietnamese poet Linh Dinh, who has lived in Europe and Vietnam and who has been influenced by American and French poetic models, is beginning to publish important work in several genres, including stories. "Make it new!" Ezra Pound exhorted his modernist friends at the beginning of the twentieth century; with the Vietnam War now long over, the historical connection forged by the violence of that conflict has begun to create a new literature out of strands of the old.

[*See also* O'Brien, Tim, and his *The Things They Carried.*]

FURTHER READING

Balaban, John. *Vietnam: A Traveler's Literary Companion.* San Francisco, 1996. A pocket-sized edition of beautifully translated short stories by modern Vietnamese writers.

Bates, Milton J. *The Wars We Took to Vietnam: Cultural Conflict and Storytelling.* Berkeley, Calif., 1996. A comprehensive and elegant study of the ways that race, class, sex, and age has shaped the narratives Americans have constructed to understand the war.

Bates, Milton, et al. *Reporting Vietnam.* 2 vols. New York, 1998. These two volumes collect the most important American journalism about the Vietnam War. Many of the pieces are of high literary quality.

Beidler, Philip D. *American Literature and the Experience of Vietnam.* Athens, Ga., 1982. The best short overview of the American literature of the Vietnam era.

Bowen, Kevin, Ba Chung Nguyen, and Bruce Weigl, eds. *Mountain River: Vietnamese Poetry from the Wars.* Amherst, Mass., 1998. Excellent translations, mostly by American poets and veterans, of Vietnamese poetry from the war. Bilingual.

Duiker, William J. *Ho Chi Minh: A Life.* New York, 2000. A patriot, a revolutionary strategist, and finally a kind of deity, the character of Ho Chi Minh pervades the American experience in Vietnam. This is a meticulously researched and richly textured portrait of the man and his times.

Elliott, Duong Van Mai. *The Sacred Willow.* New York, 1999. A family history spanning three generations that is also a history of modern Vietnam. The narrative provides the American reader with an understanding of Vietnamese reactions to the wars of the twentieth century from within Vietnamese society.

Greene, Graham. *The Quiet American.* Viking Critical Edition. New York, 1996. Greene's novel portraying the earliest stages of American involvement in Vietnam was loudly denounced by American critics when it was first published in 1955. This edition collects documents and commentary that contextualize the wide effect this British novel has had on American literature of the Vietnam period.

Huyen, Sanh Thong. *An Anthology of Vietnamese Poetry: From the Eleventh through the Twentieth Centuries.* New Haven, Conn., 1996. The most comprehensive collection of Vietnamese poetry in English; supersedes in scope if not quality of translation the out-of-print *A Thousand Years of Vietnamese Poetry.*

Isserman, Maurice, and Michael Kazin. *America Divided: The Civil War of the 1960s.* New York, 2000. A useful overview of the social and political scene in the United Stated during the Vietnam War.

Jamieson, Neil L. *Understanding Vietnam.* Berkeley, Calif., 1993. Literary analysis of Vietnamese literature as a way of understanding the modern history of Vietnam. Such understanding is crucial to a full understanding of the American literature of the war.

Karlin, Wayne, Le Minh Khue, and Truong Vu. *The Other Side of Heaven: Postwar Fiction by Vietnamese and American Writers.* Willimantic, Conn., 1995. Representative short fiction dealing with the war, with an emphasis on personal narrative.

Marr, David G. *Vietnam 1945.* Berkeley, Calif., 1995. Focusing on a single year in twentieth-century history and a single country, Vietnam, this work has the forward motion and detailed intensity of a novel.

Nelson, Cary. *Modern American Poetry.* New York, 2000. This general anthology is supplemented by a useful collection of resources on the poetry of the Vietnam War, available on-line at http://www.english.uiuc.edu/maps/vietnam/vietnamwar.htm. Includes John Clark Pratt's essay from *The Encyclopedia of the Vietnam War,* "Poetry and Vietnam."

O'Nan, Stewart, ed. *The Vietnam Reader*. New York, 1998. A comprehensive anthology of American literature from the war. Includes fiction, nonfiction, drama, poetry, and popular songs.

Page, Tim, Doug Nivin, and Chris Riley. *Another Vietnam: Pictures of the War from the Other Side*. Washington, D.C., 2002. Surprisingly serene photographs from the war period by mostly anonymous North Vietnamese photographers.

Pratt, John Clark, comp. *Vietnam Voices: Perspectives on the War Years, 1941-1982*. Athens, Ga., 1984. A running account of the Vietnam War in documents, poems, stories, journalism, and commentary. Arranged chronologically.

Templer, Robert. *Shadows and Wind: A View of Modern Vietnam*. New York, 1998. Essays on many aspects of contemporary Vietnam by a reporter long resident in the country. Useful background, especially for contemporary literature.

Tucker, Spencer C., ed. *The Encyclopedia of the Vietnam War: A Political, Social and Military History*. 3 vols. New York, 1998. Comprehensive and authoritative coverage of the Vietnam War in all its aspects.

Young, Marilyn B., John J. Fitzgerald, and A. Tom Grunfeld. *The Vietnam War: A History in Documents*. New York, 2002. A useful account of the war based on documents reproduced in the text.

KURT VONNEGUT

by Jerome Klinkowitz

Kurt Vonnegut is a novelist who came to prominence during the cultural turmoil of the American 1960s, but whose work dates back to the 1950s, addressing popular concerns of that era as well. In subsequent decades he has remained at the forefront of both narrative innovation and social concern, making his more than half-century career in letters a valuable index to artistic and more broadly cultural issues.

BIOGRAPHY

Until 1976, Vonnegut signed his work "Kurt Vonnegut, Jr." He was born on 11 November 1922 in Indianapolis, Indiana, the third child of Kurt Vonnegut Sr. (an architect in practice with the family firm) and Edith Lieber (the daughter of a prominent brewer and patron of the arts). If these antecedents imply wealth and social status, one should also note that most of such trappings were lost to the Vonneguts during the financial catastrophe of the Great Depression. As a result, young Kurt had to forgo the private education his brother Bernard and sister Alice had received, in favor of a public schooling he has always referred to as a cornerstone of his egalitarian sense of civics.

Regarding the work he would publish, including novels, short stories, essays, and occasional dramatic works, Vonnegut says that "I myself find that I trust my own writing most, and others seem to trust it most, too, when I sound like a person from Indianapolis, which I am" (*Palm Sunday*, 1981, p. 79). His most characteristic form of expression in all these genres is the American vernacular—like Mark Twain's tone of voice a century earlier, a solid, middle American perspective rooted in the basics of democratic experience. That the author would use it as a foundation for radically innovative fiction, an undertaking usually reserved for the avant-garde, is no less significant than the fact that his egalitarian manners were learned and adopted as treasured values even as his family's wealth was lost.

Vonnegut spent three years at Cornell University, studying the sciences with plans to become a biochemist,

Kurt Vonnegut. (*Photograph © Jill Krementz*)

262

a "useful" occupation his father found preferable to the economic uncertainties of the arts. The young man's heart, however, was in the extracurricular activity that had made his high school years such a joy: student journalism. Here was his exposure to good writing and training in it—not via the lofty canons of the English department, but among the real world tasks of working reporters. Here, too, was another anchor in the day-to-day nature of life as lived by common people and another pull in the opposite direction from any possible cultural elitism.

Army service in World War II interrupted this education. Captured as an infantry scout during the Battle of the Bulge in December 1944, Vonnegut was put to prisoner-of-war work in Dresden, Germany, where on the night of 13 February 1945 he experienced the Allied firebombing of the city, the largest loss of life (over seventy-five thousand persons) from a single event in European history. Surviving only because his group of POWs was sheltered in a meat locker several stories underground, Vonnegut emerged to find this architectural treasure of a city almost totally destroyed. For weeks afterward he served as a corpse miner, exhuming burned and asphyxiated bodies from their shallow basement shelters and heaping them on pyres to be cremated.

Repatriated following the German surrender in May, Vonnegut spent the summer of 1945 recuperating at home. In September he married his childhood sweetheart, Jane Cox, and began graduate study in anthropology at the University of Chicago. After two years he left without a degree, his thesis topics rejected for being too far ahead of their time (involving the parallel study of primitive and civilized groups, a technique then considered improper). Thanks to his brother Bernard, by now an internationally prominent atmospheric physicist, a job awaited him writing news copy for the General Electric Corporation's research laboratory in Schenectady, New York. Here he produced publicity extolling GE's philosophy that progress was their most important product, but evenings and weekends were devoted to writing short stories questioning these same ideals. By 1950, when enough of these pieces had been accepted for a year's salary to be banked, Kurt left with his wife and growing family (and with the draft of his first novel as well) to live on Cape Cod, Massachusetts, and pursue fiction writing full time.

Except for brief supplements of income through temporary work in the 1950s and a few short-term creative writing professorships afterward, Kurt Vonnegut has supported himself through the second half of the twentieth century and into the twenty-first by writing.

With his wife, Jane, he raised six children—three of their own plus three nephews adopted when Kurt's sister and brother-in-law died within a day of one another in 1958. In 1970, with the relatively late onset of fame thanks to the best-seller status of his novel *Slaughterhouse-Five* (1969) that was published the year before, he moved to Manhattan, separating from his wife and eventually divorcing to marry the literary photographer Jill Krementz at decade's end.

In addition to publishing novels, Vonnegut has distinguished himself as a spokesperson on social and cultural topics by means of essays and speeches.

FUTURISTIC FICTION WITH FAMILIAR VALUES

For the first two decades of his professional writing career, Kurt Vonnegut worked as a salable but critically unheralded author of short stories for family magazines and of novels that reached an essentially paperback market. Though respectably published, his works were not received as highbrow material. Instead, he spoke to commonly shared concerns, using popular formats that met middle-class audiences on their own terms—in the copies of *Collier's* magazine and *The Saturday Evening Post* resting on side tables, in barbershops, and in doctors' waiting rooms, and in paperbacks purchased at bus stations or from a drugstore's rack.

The themes of Vonnegut's work of these years involve new realities being tested against familiar values and practices. Sometimes the material is futuristic, but rarely is it ever strictly science fiction. Instead, stories such as "The Euphio Question" and "EPICAC" explore such scientific interests as extraplanetary radio waves and the new world of computers by running them through the gamut of middle-class American manners. The radio waves, for example, prove as popular (and as hazardous) as too much free alcohol, while the computer, programmed to write love letters, falls hopelessly in love itself. Even more, of Vonnegut's stories, appearing in *Cosmopolitan*, *Ladies' Home Journal*, and *Redbook* as well, concern thoroughly domestic issues, tested not against new science but rather against the emerging ethic of corporate life. In one, a wife struggles against the confining perfectionism her high-tech husband attempts to design for her. In another, a husband feels compelled to fabricate a career based on phony expertise to balance his wife's status as a celebrity. Throughout these five dozen stories that Vonnegut wrote throughout the 1950s and into the early 1960s runs a familiar message: that material wealth and intellectual pretension are less sustainable (and of far less practical value in producing happiness) than are the common virtues of simple middle-class life—just what readers of *Collier's* and the *Post* wanted to hear, living this way as they did.

Kurt Vonnegut's short stories are collected in *Welcome to the Monkey House* (1968) and *Bagombo Snuff Box* (1999). As volumes, their success follows his fame as a novelist, because such pieces as "Poor Little Rich Town" and "The Foster Portfolio" were never intended as more than passing entertainments for the readers of weekly magazines. Yet their status in the author's canon is significant, reflecting as they do his own immersion in the vernacular aspects of common American life and providing evidence of his strong command of narrative form. One of his rejected theses in the University of Chicago's anthropology program involved tracing the fluctuations between good and evil in simple tales. Here the young graduate student had discerned not just a different pattern between stories from primitive and from civilized peoples, but was able to spot identifying profiles that distinguished modern short stories according to the different magazines that published them. Hence, to his anthropologist's experience with human types is added a storyteller's proficiency with form. Both would prove important for his novels written over these same years.

Player Piano (1952) is Vonnegut's first novel, though more readers of the time would know it by the title of its 1954 paperback edition, *Utopia 14*. Drawing heavily on Vonnegut's experience writing publicity for General Electric's research laboratory, it envisions a future in which high technology and corporate refinement have managed to streamline human existence. The result is an unhappy one, for with no meaningful work to do, people find their lives, though physically easier, to be without purpose. As for the human soul, corporate groupthink would extinguish everything personal about it, leaving even the engineers of this new society no more individualistic than the cogs in the automated machines they design.

One engineer, Dr. Paul Proteus, revolts, joining a movement led by a minister trained in anthropology, the Reverend James Lasher. Between Dr. Proteus's standards of practicality and Reverend Lasher's spokesmanship for human ideals, readers get a clear picture of how progress as an end in itself is a defeating proposition. Yet *Player Piano* stops short of being shrill dystopian protest, for Vonnegut winds up showing how it is the very human need to tinker and devise improvements that inevitably sets people against themselves. Without the interference

of a science that takes itself too seriously, the author suggests, these tendencies eventually balance each other out, a theme prominent in so many of his short stories of the time, in which spiritual and material elements must strive for a workable coexistence.

Player Piano is a typical first novel, the kind any intelligent person might write, addressing issues its author finds complicating his life as he sets out to make a place for himself and his family in the world. Given how little money its publication earned him, Vonnegut might never have written another novel, had not his principal means of support, the family magazine short story, seen its market severely contract at the end of the 1950s. With commercial television taking an increasing share of advertising, magazines such as *Collier's* and *The Saturday Evening Post* cut back on the number of items they could publish, and in some cases went out of business altogether. Vonnegut's response was to fill in for declining sales by taking up a new form for him, that of the paperback original. *Player Piano* had sold so few copies in hardcover (less than five thousand) that the cloth-binding stage might for now be skipped completely. For a short outline he would be paid the price of a *Post* story ($2,700) and mass sales of even a thirty-five-cent pulp edition could earn the difference between this and the other $5,000 the author might have received from another three or four sales to such secondary venues as *Argosy* and the science fiction journals. Paperback originals became his mainstay for the next several years.

With its lurid cover and almost campily suggestive pitch to readers, *The Sirens of Titan* (1959) mocks the mass market form that the author's second novel takes, that of space opera (a term derived from the pulp Westerns known derisively as "horse operas"). In fact, Vonnegut is continuing with an approach begun with *Player Piano* and running through this and his next three novels, all of them written without any hope of great literary fame (or of even serious critical response). In each, he would let matters of form take care of themselves by adopting a tried-and-true favorite of popular readers—first futuristic dystopia, now space opera, and in coming works the comfortably familiar formats of the spy thriller, the apocalypse of military science gone mad, and the prince-and-the-pauper story adapted to contemporary society. Developed from the author's first novel is his theme of human purpose. People need to be useful for something if their lives are to have meaning. But amid all the deliberately comic claptrap of flying saucers and transgalactic aliens in this new work is a serious message: that in devising a purpose for their lives, people should not resort to claiming Divine responsibility for what is in fact their own creation of meaning. Once again, Vonnegut's anthropological orientation gives the work direction, informed as it is by an understanding of cultural relativism.

Mother Night (1961) addresses issues of human purpose on an individual basis. Its protagonist, Howard Campbell, is an American living in prewar Berlin, enjoying great success as a playwright in the German language. As war looms, he is talked into being an American spy whose propaganda broadcasts for the Nazis will contain coded information essential to the Allied cause. He seeks refuge in love and in art, hoping to keep his self secure while letting his work for Hitler's Reich become too ludicrous to be believed. To his great dismay, German listeners believe him, while his coded messages remain unintelligible to himself. The fact that he broadcasts news of his beloved wife's death without even knowing the fact, let alone that he is transmitting it, serves as his ultimate loss of integrity. After the war, he is given a new life, equally empty, that fifteen years later lets him become a pawn once again for international politics, this time as waged by Soviet, Israeli, and neo-Fascist interests. What the corporate state would do to Dr. Paul Proteus, any number of modern nation-states do quite handily to Howard Campbell.

On the eve of his execution by Israel for presumed crimes against humanity, Howard Campbell—with incontrovertible proof of his innocence in hand—executes himself, for crimes against himself. As a spy thriller, *Mother Night* thus pushes readers' expectations beyond the usual limits of this subgenre's form, all the while exploiting its format to the fullest. Like *The Sirens of Titan*, it takes a familiarity with form and uses it to examine less familiar issues, yet ones perfectly resolvable within the givens of convention. Indeed, the conventions themselves—of espionage, divided loyalties, and the hope of hiding a true self safely away from the world's intrusions—make possible much of what the author wants to say.

In *Cat's Cradle* (1963) Vonnegut dramatizes a writer's compulsion to express himself on a topic that outgrows his initial intention. Planned as another paperback original and published as a hardcover novel instead because its acquiring editor changed firms, this variation on the tale of Armageddon works its theme into a premise for composition. Its narrator-protagonist has planned to write a book about the creation of the world's first atomic bomb as exploded over Hiroshima on 6 August 1945. His working title is a metaphor for this moment in history:

The Day the World Ended, he plans to call his completed work. However, as with Vonnegut's first three novels, its action soon exceeds the form's usual limits—in this case most apocalyptically so, as the world quite literally does come to an end in the process of the book's completion.

The culprit is "ice-nine," a substance that reformulates the freezing point of water to a temperature so high that everything turns frigidly solid, ending all forms of life on Earth. It is the irresponsible creation of the same scientist who devised the atomic bomb, blithely unconcerned with the effects of what is for him simple intellectual ingenuity. To this extent he is innocent, though the author is quick to brand such moral insouciance as criminal. Others in the novel are more obviously guilty, but only of such familiar human frailties that the reader can hardly condemn them. Instead, Vonnegut once again repeats the wisdom expressed at the end of his first novel, *Player Piano*: that once having evolved beyond the simplicity of great apes, humans seem quite brilliant at engineering the means for their own hapless destruction.

In *God Bless You, Mr. Rosewater* (1965), the author presents a character who would change all this by redistributing his billion-dollar fortune ten or twenty dollars at a time. What is the absolutely least amount of money you'd take not to kill yourself right now, he bargains with despondent callers on a help line, and usually buys them a happier existence for less than the price of a fancy dinner. Eliot Rosewater's philanthropy succeeds at the grassroots level, where Vonnegut is fond of locating so much of his fiction's action. Eliot has left the princely surroundings of his foundation's Park Avenue offices to work among the paupers of Rosewater County, Indiana, a region whose paltry assets have been monopolized and exploited by his family since Civil War days.

Written at the economic low point of Vonnegut's career, this novel presents the most bitter satire he would ever write, fixated as the narrative is on the destructive but irresistible power of money. Characters are alternately pathetic and despicable. Eliot himself refuses to romanticize them; his philanthropy seems motivated less by altruistic love than by a desire to shame his parents and break down the family fortune into units so small that none can have the power to corrupt human life. Although the novel is omnisciently narrated, its voice is unrelentingly sarcastic, expressing both Eliot's disgust with wealth and Kurt Vonnegut's demoralization at his own paltry earning power. Its brightest moment, so to speak, is the introduction of the character Kilgore Trout, a washed-up science fiction writer whose dire view of existence articulates the need for valuation better than money provides.

Darkest moments come before the dawn. In 1965, with his author's advance from *God Bless You, Mr. Rosewater* insufficient to support his family and with no prospects for magazine sales, Vonnegut took temporary leave from his home on Cape Cod to accept a faculty appointment at the University of Iowa's Writers Workshop. Here, as the lowest salaried instructor on campus, he could at least equal what had been his earnings for selling three short stories a year to the no longer existing *Saturday Evening Post*. More important, it gave him the time to begin work on a much more challenging novel, his narrative inspired by the bombing of Dresden he had witnessed twenty years before. It was a book he'd wanted to write since being repatriated, but a workable form had always eluded him. Although existing subgenre formats had proved useful for his first five novels, the conventions of a war story were inadequate to capture the special experience Vonnegut had in Dresden. Now he would have the chance to invent a new way of expressing such material.

INNOVATIONS IN THE NOVEL

"I would hate to tell you what this lousy little book cost me in money and anxiety and time" (p. 2), Vonnegut complains to readers in the first chapter of *Slaughterhouse-Five*, the novel he had wanted to write for almost twenty-five years but couldn't, because a proper form for it had eluded him. He also spends time in these opening pages apologizing to his publisher for turning in a manuscript "so short and jumbled and jangled" because "there is nothing intelligent to say about a massacre" (p. 17), which is what the firebombing of Dresden had been.

By articulating the nature of his problem, Vonnegut is taking the first step toward solving it. Apologizing for one's self is considered a poor form of introduction, and talking about one's involvement in the writing of a novel in its own first chapter is even less conventional. Speaking this way in a preface or an introduction would have been radical enough. But by placing himself squarely in the first chapter of such a work, Vonnegut announced that *Slaughterhouse-Five* would be anything but a conventional novel. For two hundred years traditional fiction had expected readers to suspend their disbelief and receive narrative details as if they were represented actions, actions that could have taken place in the outside world. Only recently had avant-garde writers undertaken experiments with the metafictive properties of this form by making an author's composition of his or her work its own subject.

Because there is a small dose of space opera to it, some readers consider *Slaughterhouse-Five* a work of science fiction. As in *The Sirens of Titan*, Vonnegut employs life from outer space to put earthling conditions in better perspective. There the lesson had been the futility of anything other than contrived purpose to human history. Here the perspective is more philosophical, derived from the Tralfamadorian concept of time, which is that all moments exist simultaneously. Hence the protagonist, Billy Pilgrim, experiences what the novel calls "time travel," moving with apparent randomness among periods in the past, present, and future. The technique has its psychological and physical equivalents, but for a precise explanation, Billy's Tralfamadorian host uses the example of what novels are like in this transgalactic civilization:

> each clump of symbols is a brief, urgent message—describing a situation, a scene. We Tralfamadorians read them all at once, not one after the other. There isn't any particular relationship between all the messages, except that the author has chosen them carefully, so that, when seen all at once, they produce an image of life that is beautiful and surprising and deep. There is no beginning, no middle, no end, no suspense, no moral, no causes, no effects. What we love in our books are the depths of many marvelous moments seen all at one time. (p. 76)

This description fits *Slaughterhouse-Five* itself and indicates the effect Vonnegut wants to achieve. In the way that it skips from time to time and from topic to topic, the narrative resists a sense of linear accumulation, striving instead for a more spatially oriented understanding of Billy Pilgrim's wartime and postwar experiences. It is the identity he is able to find between instances of time in 1964, for example, and 1944 (and, for that matter, childhood memories from the 1920s) that lets him make sense of the person he is. Not by any means of oversight does the firebombing of Dresden appear. It is by means of its anticipation and aftermath—a long aftermath running the course of Billy Pilgrim's life—that Vonnegut is able to write about such an event that defies transcription.

Kilgore Trout appears in *Slaughterhouse-Five* to act once more as a spokesperson for certain values—this time not socioeconomic but artistic. In Vonnegut's next novel, *Breakfast of Champions* (1973), the first he would write in the spotlight of cultural fame, Trout is a major character active from the narrative's start, which puts him on a course to intersect with the book's other central figure, Dwayne Hoover. As always, Trout is a science fiction writer wasting away in neglect. But in Hoover he finds a person he never dreamed existed: a reader of his work. This reader's misfortune, however, is that his own sense of depression leads him to take Trout's fiction the wrong way, letting himself be convinced that the writer's metaphorical rendition of human life is true. The results are disastrous, and stand as a corrective to any overly literal readings of a book like *Slaughterhouse-Five*. Yet the power of art to capture the meaning of human existence is demonstrated by another character introduced here, the painter Rabo Karabekian, whose abstract art (in the manner of Barnett Newman and Mark Rothko) speaks for the prime human value of self-awareness.

After writing in obscurity for twenty years, Vonnegut found the belated onset of fame a challenge. Received critically as an important innovator in fiction and read by many as a moralist rather than for entertainment, he responded by adopting a spokesperson's tone in much of his work. Three volumes of essays—*Wampeters, Foma, and Granfalloons* (1974), *Palm Sunday* (1981), and *Fates Worse Than Death* (1991)—flavor social, cultural, and political commentary with the mannerisms of artistic fancy, while novels of this period—*Slapstick* (1976), *Jailbird* (1979), and *Deadeye Dick* (1982)—feature narrators who hold special positions in their society and can speak for larger values as naturally as doing anything else in character. The protagonists of these three novels are respectively president of the United States (during a future in which the nation has crumbled), former adviser to President Richard Nixon (just released from a Watergate-related jail sentence), and heir to the artistic prominence of a once respectable family. Each of these novels addresses questions central to public concern, such as how social welfare is less effective than the mutual care provided by extended families and how civic idealism must struggle to maintain its integrity. Each also gives its author prominence in the work itself, by beginning with an autobiographical statement in which Vonnegut associates himself with the fictive narrative to come. Originally a metafictive technique in *Slaughterhouse-Five*, where the impulse was to emphasize the book's constructed nature, this personalized way of beginning a novel now identifies the novel as a work of public spokesmanship. Yet in making sense of the great social issues of his time, Vonnegut would inevitably return to himself as a point of reference—how he had lived his life and how he had written his books.

INNOVATIONS IN THEME

With his novel *Galápagos* (1985) Vonnegut undertook an experimentation with theme that equals the technical innovations in his earlier fiction. Having addressed important issues of his time as both an essayist and a self-confidently discursive novelist, he now turned to the novel's storytelling powers in order to craft narratives that expressed his ideas in fresh new ways. Since *Player Piano* Vonnegut had understood how machines that steal human dignity not only are made by humans but are made in a way that they cannot resist. In similar manner his subsequent works regretted that only when humans had yet to evolve beyond the simplicity of great apes were they not disposed to create so much trouble for themselves and for others. *Galápagos*, narrated by Leon Trout, Kilgore's son, takes this same idea but makes a story of it in a quite different way: by tracing human evolution another million years forward. Two simple devices let this story be told. The materials for this next million years of human history are provided by a small group of people whose tour to the islands Charles Darwin made famous is isolated there, thanks to an international economic collapse and the global warfare that follows. Here, as untouched by other influences as were the properties of nature Darwin had studied so many years before, the humanity they share takes an interesting evolutionary course, as survival skills slowly fashion a human being with a much smaller brain, much less dexterous hands and feet, and much less encouragement to harm itself. To cover the million years of history, a special narrative posture is required; by being a ghost who has refused passage into the afterlife when he is killed in a shipyard accident during the building of the travelers' cruise ship, Leon is able to remain on duty to see how the whole affair turns out, so many years later.

Bluebeard (1987) devises another kind of history—a retelling of modern art history with an eye toward explaining the celebration of human self-awareness that Vonnegut finds central to the work of abstract expressionism. The narrator is Rabo Karabekian, in character from his role in *Breakfast of Champions* but fully developed as a protagonist with a history of his own. His career progress, from apprenticeship to a popular illustrator (for the same family magazines in which Vonnegut's short stories had appeared, albeit a generation later) to wartime service (including, like Vonnegut, a period as a POW) and eventual success as an innovative painter (helping pioneer the triumph of American art as abstract expressionist action painting, just as Vonnegut had contributed to innovations that characterized 1960s American fiction), comprises the story of American art in the twentieth century. As with Vonnegut's fiction, that story involves the maker's attempt to engage the central issues of humanity without resorting to elaborate representation. Karabekian's triumph, after his initial success and then technical failure with the materials of abstract art, is to devise a style of figuration that, in its grandness of scope, suggests the richness of human experience, based as that experience is on the ability people have to be analytically aware of their own being. It is no accident that this scheme reflects the progress of literary history through the half-century Vonnegut has participated in it.

The author looks forward as well, writing his next novel, *Hocus Pocus* (1990), in a manner responsive to lives being lived by those a full generation younger than himself. Its narrator is Eugene Debs Hartke, an Army officer whose career has ended with his inability to accept his country's reaction to those who fought the war. The action is set in the year 2001, eleven years ahead of the time this novel was published—nothing like the million-year span that gives *Galápagos* so much room to revolutionize humanity, but plenty of time for certain trends of the American 1980s to develop, including privatization of certain government responsibilities (such as the running of prisons) and the selling off of assets to foreign investors. A professor at a small private college, Hartke seems happy enough, although his experience with the school's history and its standard curriculum gives him occasional doubts. Eventually his outspokenness gets him fired, but he happily takes a new job teaching in the nearby state penitentiary. Conditions there strike him as much closer to the realities of life than those being experienced at the college, and he has sympathetic understanding for the prisoners who have been channeled here by those same forces—a sympathy akin to that expressed by his namesake, Eugene Debs, the social reformer who a century earlier had looked at the constraints of modern life and said, "While there is a lower class I am in it. While there is a criminal element I am of it. While there is a soul in prison I am not free." These famous lines are what Vonnegut chooses for the novel's epigraph, and are tested against conditions the author sees in the world his children's generation has inherited.

With *Timequake* (1997) Vonnegut takes the opportunity to draw on all his various strengths as a novelist, including talents as diverse as social comment and metafictive experiment. Structurally, it is as innovative as *Slaughterhouse-Five*, and for the same reason: its author has had trouble writing the book, and has elected to let those difficulties determine its form. In this case it has

meant not so much junking a first draft as recycling parts of it into a new manuscript that centers not just on the writer's compositional act but also on his life as it is being lived during the process. By this means Vonnegut is able to combine his penchant for autobiography with some very real technical concerns, formal matters that eclipse the personal, while at the same time giving himself the opportunity for the public spokesmanship at which he excels. This authorial activity parallels the original novel's plot, involving the "timequake" of its title, in which the universe stops expanding and instead jumps back to a period ten years before, meaning that a decade will repeat itself. This is the narrative from which the author salvages parts, offering them to the reader in the context of both his compositor's task and his life as being lived at the moment. Those moments themselves can have their own complexities of space and time, such as when he learns that his older brother is dying, news that prompts long memories. By the end, readers can enjoy the timequake story, which is full of wry examples of how free will is a style of behavior that has to be learned, and also can appreciate the artistic and moral source of it, a person whose wealth of experience and richness of character make him more interesting than any possible fictive creation.

[*See also* Metafiction.]

WORKS

Player Piano (1952)
The Sirens of Titan (1959)
Canary in a Cat House (1961)
Mother Night (1961)
Cat's Cradle (1963)
God Bless You, Mr. Rosewater (1965)
Welcome to the Monkey House (1968)
Slaughterhouse-Five (1969)
Happy Birthday, Wanda June (1971)
Breakfast of Champions (1973)
Wampeters, Foma, and Granfalloons (1974)
Slapstick (1976)
Jailbird (1979)
Palm Sunday (1981)
Deadeye Dick (1982)
Galápagos (1985)
Bluebeard (1987)
Hocus Pocus (1990)
Fates Worse Than Death (1991)
Timequake (1997)
Bagombo Snuff Box (1999)

FURTHER READING

Allen, William Rodney. *Understanding Kurt Vonnegut.* Columbia, S.C., 1991. A reliable basic introduction.

Boon, Kevin A. *Chaos Theory and the Interpretation of Literary Texts: The Case of Kurt Vonnegut.* Lewiston, N.Y., 1997. A sophisticated analysis of antecedants for Vonnegut's themes and methods in physics.

Boon, Kevin A., ed. *At Millennium's End: New Essays on the Work of Kurt Vonnegut.* Albany, N.Y., 2001.

Broer, Lawrence R. *Sanity Plea: Schizophrenia in the Novels of Kurt Vonnegut.* Ann Arbor, Mich., 1989.

Klinkowitz, Jerome. *Keeping Literary Company: Working with Writers since the Sixties.* Albany, N.Y., 1998. A memoir of working with Vonnegut.

Klinkowitz, Jerome. *Vonnegut in Fact: The Public Spokesmanship of Personal Fiction.* Columbia, S.C., 1998. A study of Vonnegut's nonfiction prose.

Leeds, Marc. *The Vonnegut Encyclopedia.* Westport, Conn., 1995. Cross-referenced characters, locales, and themes in Vonnegut's work.

Leeds, Marc, and Peter J. Reed, eds. *Kurt Vonnegut: Images and Representations.* Westport, Conn., 2000. A collection of original essays on Vonnegut's work.

Merrill, Robert, ed. *Critical Essays on Kurt Vonnegut.* Boston, 1990. Mostly reprinted material.

Mustazza, Leonard. *Forever Pursuing Genesis: The Myth of Eden in the Novels of Kurt Vonnegut.* Lewisburg, Pa., 1990. The most complete investigation of Vonnegut's beliefs.

Mustazza, Leonard, ed. *The Critical Response to Kurt Vonnegut.* Westport, Conn., 1994. New and reprinted essays.

Pieratt, Asa B., Jr., Julie Huffman-klinkowitz, and Jerome Klinkowitz. *Kurt Vonnegut: A Comprehensive Bibliography.* Hamden, Conn., 1987.

Reed, Peter J. *The Short Fiction of Kurt Vonnegut.* Westport, Conn., 1997.

Reed, Peter J., and Marc Leeds, eds. *The Vonnegut Chronicles.* Westport, Conn., 1996. Original essays.

Scholes, Robert. *The Fabulators.* New York, 1967. The first and still essential treatment of Vonnegut's fiction, from the standpoint of its self-conscious storyteller's art.

See also the article on *Slaughterhouse-Five*, immediately following.

KURT VONNEGUT'S
SLAUGHTERHOUSE-FIVE

by James P. Austin

Has Billy Pilgrim gone mad? Or has this protagonist of Kurt Vonnegut's classic novel *Slaughterhouse-Five* truly "come unstuck in time"? The text itself offers two possible explanations. It could be true that Pilgrim was abducted by aliens from the planet Tralfamadore, who see time not as fleeting and linear but as something that always already exists, that life's moments are accessed in any order. Or it could be true that Pilgrim had gradually lost his mind after surviving the Allied bombing of Dresden, Germany, in World War II and a plane crash in Vermont years later. The injuries sustained in these places may have slowly warped Pilgrim's mind, causing him to believe that the alien abduction story written by an obscure science fiction writer, Kilgore Trout, had in fact happened to him.

But Vonnegut never explicitly informs us which version of events is actually true. This is significant because it opens a window into some of the prevailing themes Vonnegut innovatively develops in *Slaughterhouse-Five*. This "undecide-ability" of the narrative, as well as its refusal to adhere to a traditional structure, seem deliberate decisions on Vonnegut's part. Traditional structure, with its tight organization and eventual resolutions, cannot effectively tell the story of the firebombing in Dresden, or of the effects it had on the people who survived the bombing. Like the atomic bombings in Hiroshima and Nagasaki, the firebombing of Dresden does not simply end for the people involved; it is ongoing, never ending, and always present. Billy Pilgrim is Vonnegut's example of a man dislodged from time by his experience in and survival of one of the twentieth century's worst atrocities—the near-total destruction of a German city at the end of the war, a destruction for which United States and British bombers are responsible.

The open space between the truth or fiction of Pilgrim's story also creates a tone that does not match the sobering reality of the massacre Pilgrim survived. The bombing was total, nondiscriminate, leaving over seventy-five thousand people dead; the novel, by contrast, is often silly and funny, the narrator himself almost a comedian. But within this discrepancy lives the biting satire of the novel: Billy Pilgrim was a survivor of a horrific and largely forgotten atrocity, delivered at the hands of his own government. His survival was more luck than it was anything else. And when he returned from war, his family and friends seemed largely uninterested in the miraculous fact that Pilgrim was alive. Everybody, it seems, missed the point. His aberrant survival of the war goes unnoted.

"SO IT GOES"

Vonnegut himself, it seems, takes us aside in the first chapter of *Slaughterhouse-Five*, sharing with us his troubles in writing a war book about Dresden. He wants to, of course, but claims to have written thousands of pages on the matter and thrown them all out. It is not traditional for a writer to include a chapter in a novel detailing his ongoing problems with the writing of the novel we are reading. But at his first opportunity, Vonnegut has transgressed that boundary, indicating that what we are reading is a much different type of book. It is somehow significant that we understand Vonnegut's ongoing difficulties, how he couldn't seem to encapsulate his own, real-life survival of the Dresden bombing within the pages of traditional storytelling conventions. This helps us recognize Vonnegut's own need to tell the story in a nontraditional manner, which is exactly what occurs in subsequent chapters. Storytelling can stifle the experience, tidying it up for our consumption. But Vonnegut finds a way, after thousands of discarded pages and over two decades, to forge ahead with a novel that he terms "a failure," possibly because even the innovations he employs cannot possibly convey the scenes of destruction and death in Dresden, and the subsequent disorientation from normal life that a survivor like Vonnegut himself felt.

If nothing else, this first chapter does indicate a strong departure from traditional narrative. Like so many postmodern texts, *Slaughterhouse-Five* is purposely self-aware. The text mentions itself, discussing problems between form and meaning, and how sometimes the two do not match. Such texts do not typically seek to render the novel invalid by exposing its traditions and machinations to the reader, or questioning the ability of narrative to convey something meaningful, but to use this self-awareness to generate a different layer of meaning, one that might inch closer to communicating something about experiences like the one Vonnegut endured as a prisoner of war in Dresden.

With this in mind, we approach the story of Billy Pilgrim, which starts in the second chapter of the novel. The first thing we learn about Pilgrim is that he is "unstuck in time," and that he has just leaped from being an elderly man to being a groom on his wedding night years earlier, and that, these days, this is how Billy has come to exist. He visits the events in his life randomly, since they all exist simultaneously. But Vonnegut makes an important note here, which is that all of this is only according to Billy Pilgrim himself. The actual narrator of the book makes no real claim to the truth of Pilgrim's claims.

Pilgrim's life is also quickly summarized. We learn about his birth, his upbringing, and are also told about his service in World War II, though this remains undeveloped until later in the chapter. In this summary, we are told two important things that indicate Billy Pilgrim suffers from post-traumatic stress disorder. Not long after his return from the war, Pilgrim returned to school, married, and suffered a "mild nervous collapse," as if the return to normalcy was what brought him over the edge. Second, we learn that, years later, Pilgrim is the sole survivor of a plane crash in Vermont, and that he suffers a head injury. When he returns home, Pilgrim begins writing letters to the local newspaper, claiming to have been abducted by aliens, and as a result has come unstuck in time, that he visits past and future events of his own life all the time. It is only much later that we learn Pilgrim is mimicking a science fiction novel by a man named Kilgore Trout.

These facts are powerful indicators that the jumbled sequence of Pilgrim's life, as well as his claim of being imprisoned on the planet Tralfamadore in an alien zoo, reflect his deteriorating mental state. The two jarring events that he has miraculously and randomly survived have finally broken him. But again, Vonnegut's narrator expresses only occasional doubt about the validity of Pilgrim's claims, and does follow Pilgrim through his time travel, allowing a narrative of sorts to slowly emerge from the random play of events.

Vonnegut punctuates the scenes involving death with the near-mocking phrase "So it goes." At first, this phrase nearly offends, dealing with death in the apparently flippant manner that it does. But like so many elements in *Slaughterhouse-Five*, the phrase represents upended

expectation. Instead of being severe and sober, the phrase is breezy and darkly comedic. But the phrase does correspond to the very presence of a non-soldier like Billy Pilgrim in the world's largest war ever, and to the random fact of his survival. In the second and third chapters, we learn how Pilgrim falls in with two trained Allied scouts and Roland Weary, all stuck behind enemy lines and trying to return to the relative safety of their own side. Roland Weary is a big, clumsy man, just the sort to bully Pilgrim; he also envisions an alliance with these "real" soldiers of war, the scouts, and that the three of them would save Pilgrim's skin together and go by the hilariously clichéd name The Three Musketeers.

Eventually, the scouts abandon Pilgrim and Weary, who are too slow, and advise them tersely to "find somebody to surrender to" before disappearing into the woods. Pilgrim and Weary, who seem equally inept, fight briefly before they are located by German soldiers patrolling the area. As the Germans decide what to do about Pilgrim and Weary, three shots ring out in the distance, and the narrator informs us that the two trained scouts have been ambushed and killed by Germans. Pilgrim and Weary survive, however, and are taken to a POW camp.

This exchange is significant because it represents a strong example of just how miraculous and random Pilgrim's survival was. The scouts, conditioned to move quickly in rough terrain and to thrive behind enemy lines, were the ones found and killed by trained German soldiers. Pilgrim and Weary, on the other hand, were discovered by German farmers and adolescents, pressed into duty as soldiers. Pilgrim and Weary are quintessentially bumbling soldiers, and yet they were the ones who survived. The fact of who survives and who does not is randomly determined, just as Billy Pilgrim later experiences the events of his life in an equally random manner. The randomness of Pilgrim's survival is developed further in subsequent chapters.

DANCING BETWEEN MOMENTS

This one "scene"—of Pilgrim being stuck behind enemy lines, of finding Weary and the scouts, of being dumped by the scouts, and yet somehow still surviving—is actually a part of a montage with other scenes, which all take place at different points in Pilgrim's life. While Pilgrim is enduring his survival and entrance into a POW camp, he is also much older, an optometrist, and also giving a speech even later in life, and doing many other things in other parts of his life. What becomes evident here, then, is that Pilgrim's fractured existence—either real or imagined—always brings him back to the war, back to his experience as a POW, back to his survival of the Dresden bombing. He may have to relive it at any moment. This reinforces the notion that surviving the hardship of this bombing is not a singular experience, not something one does and then finishes doing. It is not tidy or linear. Instead, the experience is ongoing and jagged, as Pilgrim's fractured life illustrates.

The journey to the POW camp amounts to a long train ride, with prisoners herded into cars moving at a snail's pace for days. Weary and Pilgrim are separated, and during the ride, Weary dies from gangrene in his deeply wounded (and untreated) feet. Before he dies, Weary extracts a promise from some men to have revenge upon the one responsible for his death: Billy Pilgrim. This scene is significant because it leads to some of Pilgrim's problems within the camp, but it also illustrates, once more, how two equally inept soldiers can have such different fates. Weary dies from an injury Pilgrim himself never sustained, but easily could have. In fact, despite his ineptitude, Pilgrim has suffered no significant injuries. He survives a train ride many other POWs did not, and he arrives at the camp.

At the camp, Pilgrim meets Paul Lazzaro, who has promised his full vengeance upon Pilgrim to Weary, and Edgar Derby, a nice enough man, old for a soldier, who is among the most reasonable men in the novel. We are told from early in the novel that Derby will be killed by firing squad after the Dresden massacre for looting a teapot. Lazzaro, identified as the only man in camp with a body less soldierly than Pilgrim's, survives, even though he steals valuable jewelry from the destroyed homes of the dead residents of Dresden.

During the train ride, Pilgrim is zapped forward in time—if, indeed, such a thing as "forward" exists in Pilgrim's mind—to the night he was abducted by aliens. We are told about the long trip to Tralfamadore, and how, during the journey, Pilgrim asks to read an alien text. This moment proves significant to understanding the text in our own hands. An alien explains to Pilgrim that Tralfamadorian texts have "no beginning, no middle, no end, no suspense, no moral, no causes, no effects." The alien also explains to Pilgrim that no human could ever understand a Tralfamadorian book, because the human mind has not been trained to think that way. The effect is not linear and partial, but full and instantaneous.

In fact, *Slaughterhouse-Five* itself seems structured in a way alien to the linearity of our expectations, very much like the texts from Tralfamadore. Despite our efforts to read the text as Vonnegut has structured it, we often

latch on to any semblance of coherence. This is a sly and chilling reminder to the reader that we do, in fact, read the world like a text, with stable beginnings and ends, with tidy morals, with cause and effect. Our reality is constructed in this manner. But the dirty presence of a war, and of massacres and survival, do not adhere to the normal rules of the text. Vonnegut knows it, and uses the Tralfamadorian text to illustrate the limits of traditional narrative, while also striking out with a new one of his own.

After several other jumps, Pilgrim is returned to the war. One of these jumps involves the circumstances of his own death, which occurs in 1976, when Lazzaro finally does get the vengeance he promised Roland Weary during the war. He shoots Pilgrim just after Pilgrim has finished a speech, and so Pilgrim experiences death, for a while. But even death is not final; it is simply another of the simultaneous moments of Pilgrim's life, and from his own death he is returned to the war. The Americans leave the camp because they have been sold off for their manual labor to Germans in Dresden, an open city, undefended, known by both sides to have no significant part of the war effort.

The narrative of Pilgrim's survival at Dresden is gradually revealed, interspersed between other events in Pilgrim's life, including the plane crash he survived in Vermont years after World War II, his time in the hospital after the crash, and more revelations about his time spent on Tralfamadore. Pilgrim and other American POWs in Dresden were kept at night in a slaughterhouse near the city; their slaughterhouse was designated with the number five, and existed deep within the ground. When Allied bombers level Dresden, Pilgrim, the other POWs, and a few German guards are deep within the slaughterhouse while the rest of the city burns—including a group of young female prisoners Pilgrim, Derby, and Lazzaro had spied on while the women were showering only days before. The women were kept underground, too, but their space was too close to the surface, and theirs were among the deaths at Dresden that day.

This revelation of Pilgrim's survival—and indeed, of Vonnegut's, as this aspect of the novel is true to the author's life—completes a cycle of random luck and irony that characterizes the novel. Pilgrim survived because, quite by luck, he and the other Americans were kept in a deep vault usually reserved for slaughter. In this context, however, the slaughterhouse is their saving grace, reversing its intended function. And they could have been stored *anywhere* at night. Instead, without realizing it, the

German soldiers housed their prisoners at the safest place in Dresden.

The danger, though, is not over. When the survivors emerge the day after the bombing, the narrator describes Dresden, which had only the day before been the most beautiful place most prisoners had ever seen, as resembling the surface of the moon. They are marched to an inn near the edge of the destruction, which had remained open in anticipation of massive numbers of refugees. But the American POWs and the German soldiers were the only ones to emerge from Dresden. Eventually, the Americans return to Dresden to dig for bodies. This is when Derby is shot for stealing a teapot and when Lazzaro gets away scot-free with pocketfuls of valuable gems.

CONCLUSIONS

Slaughterhouse-Five is, at many points, a disorienting novel to read. It was considered innovative when first published, and as a modern classic today. Vonnegut purposely reverses or even dismisses several traditional narrative devices, as well as our own expectations for linear narrative, of the steady passage of time, of stable meaning. But he writes, according to his own style, a novel fitting both the subject matter and the times in which *Slaughterhouse-Five* was written. In the final chapter, Vonnegut bemoans, in the darkly comedic tone characterizing the novel, the recent deaths of Robert Kennedy and Martin Luther King Jr., as well as the bygone death of his own father. He also mentions the "count of corpses created by military science in Vietnam," which at the time was America's latest war. He punctuates each rumination with the now-familiar "So it goes."

We can conclude that the situation in the world, according to Vonnegut, was severe. Still troubled by his own survival of the Dresden bombing, by the deaths of significant public figures like Kennedy and King, by America's foray into a disastrous conflict in Vietnam, and by "plain old death," Vonnegut writes a novel befitting the times. Plain old narrative will not do the trick. As with so much work produced during this era, Vonnegut alters narrative tradition to suit what he feels are dire times.

And what can we learn from Billy Pilgrim? Has he gone mad, or has he become unhinged in time? The question is never satisfactorily answered by the narrator; he only expresses doubts as to Pilgrim's sanity, nothing more. Crazy or true, Pilgrim's story indicates that, for many, the process of survival is lifelong. He is always being brought back, physically and psychologically, to the site of his miraculous survival.

The survival is miraculous because Pilgrim was not qualified to serve in war, and had no skills that contributed to his survival. There was no rhyme or reason to his survival and Edgar Derby's death. Staples of American life—free will and justice, for example—recede in this context. There is no justice is Dresden, no justice for Edgar Derby, and none, ultimately, for Billy Pilgrim. Just random luck and irony. Considering this, how could Billy Pilgrim's story be told in any other way? *Slaughterhouse-Five* may not be a mad book about a mad man, but it does express its own doubt in stable narrative to tell a story of war and survival.

[*See also* Metafiction.]

FURTHER READING

Allen, William Rodney. *Understanding Kurt Vonnegut.* Columbia, S.C., 1991. Critically analyzes some of Vonnegut's most popular works.

Bloom, Harold, ed. *Kurt Vonnegut.* Philadelphia, 2000. An interpretation of Vonnegut's major works, with an introduction by Bloom, one of America's foremost literary critics.

Giannone, Richard. *Vonnegut: A Preface to His Novels.* Port Washington, N.Y., 1977. Prefaces Vonnegut's novels with criticism and interpretation.

Klinkowitz, Jerome. Slaughterhouse-Five: *Reforming the Novel and the World.* Boston, 1990. Considers the manner in which *Slaughterhouse-Five* redefined traditional literary conventions; includes bibliographical references.

Petterson, Bo. *The World According to Kurt Vonnegut: Moral Paradox and Narrative Form.* Abo, Finland, 1994. Explores Vonnegut's use of moral paradox in relation to innovations in narrative structure.

See also the article on Kurt Vonnegut, immediately preceding.

DEREK WALCOTT

by Gerry Cambridge

In "Crocodile Dandy," an essay about the Australian poet Les Murray, which amusingly begins with "the barbarians" approaching "the capital" with their rambunctious and superbly learned bards in tow, Derek Walcott provides a witty shorthand for the surprise of Empire at finding its former colonies' poets more *au fait* with its civilization's great art than it is itself. Walcott, as a son of the former colony of the British Empire, St. Lucia, is a perfect example—a poet from the margins, greatly learned in English literature, who has been widely feted both in Britain and America.

BACKGROUND

The experience of being raised in a last outpost of Empire was not the end of the complications in Walcott's childhood, however. Born on 23 January 1930 in Castries, St. Lucia—he became of such fame there that its former Columbus Square was in 1993 renamed Derek Walcott Square—Walcott was unusual in other ways. He had two white grandfathers, of Dutch and English origin, and he was born into a middle-class, genteelly poor, mixed-race Methodist family in a mainly black, Catholic, island community. English was the language of its elite. French Creole was the language of its country peasants. His father, Warwick Walcott, a local civil servant and a man of artistic temperament, died at age thirty-four when he and his twin brother, Roderick, were just one year old. His resourceful mother, Alix, a teacher, brought up the twins and their older sister and saw to it they were involved in local community dramatics, which for the twins led to a lifetime interest in theater. (Though best known in the United States as a poet, Walcott has written numerous plays in a long career as a playwright.) At age eleven Walcott won a St. Lucia government scholarship to St. Mary's College in Castries, an institution renowned

Derek Walcott. (© *Corbis*)

throughout the region for high educational standards. He received the equivalent of an English public school education, studying the classics of English literature as well as Latin.

As a poet, this gave him a respect for his craft that he has never lost; he has resolutely refused, sometimes controversially, to prefer a racially motivated aesthetic to a regard for the art of poetry. Indeed, he has said that such regard is ultimately more revolutionary—that a writer of genuine maturity subtly assimilates even the literary tradition of a colonizer, subverting it to his or her own ends. Walcott has therefore been unapologetic about the strong influences on show in his early poetry; as a painter of talent, an art where being schooled with a master is a commonplace idea, he had no problem accepting the notion of serving a conscious apprenticeship in verse. Thus, he "went to school" with masters such as W. H. Auden and Dylan Thomas, strong early influences, yet used the new subject of the Caribbean for material. In a sense, this enabled Walcott to have the best of both worlds. His material was new, but he wrote of it, in the poetry at least, using time-honored forms which quickly established him as a considerable presence, initially in England, where he was taken up in the 1960s by the influential editor of the *London Magazine*, Alan Ross. This established his early reputation and also explains English poet Philip Larkin's early awareness of his work. When the professedly xenophobic Larkin compiled *The Oxford Book of Twentieth-Century English Verse* (1973), he included several of Walcott's distinguished early poems.

EARLY WORK

Walcott was precocious. With $200 borrowed from his mother, he self-published his first book of verse, *25 Poems* (1948), at the age of eighteen; at age twenty his first play, *Henri Cristophe* (1950), was staged. By the time his first trade collection of verse, *In a Green Night: Poems, 1948–1960*, appeared in 1962 from the British publisher Cape, followed quickly in 1964 by an early *Selected Poems*, published in New York City, Walcott had graduated from University College of the West Indies in Mona, Jamaica, with a B.A. degree in 1953 in Latin, French, and English. He had also married and divorced Faye Moyston—the marriage lasted from 1954 to 1959—and fathered a son, Peter, in 1955. He had, moreover, studied theater in New York City on a Rockefeller Foundation fellowship in 1958 and moved to Trinidad in 1959, where he had founded the Little Carib Theatre Workshop—a finally unsuccessful attempt to establish a professional theater for the Caribbean—which he would run until 1976.

In a Green Night contained "A Far Cry from Africa," Yeatsian in tone and one of Walcott's best-known early poems. It also included marvelous pieces which Walcott has seldom bettered, including *Tales of the Islands,* ten anecdotal sonnets luminous with Caribbean atmosphere; *Letter from Brooklyn,* a portrait of a genteel old Christian lady writing to the poem's narrator about his dead father; and the beautiful incantatory lyric, *Sea Chantey,* which showed an early awareness not only of the gorgeousness of pure sound as exemplified by place names in the Antilles, but of how form could focus and complement content. These were pieces which spoke lucidly in a distinctive voice. They embodied triumphantly the poet's desired aesthetic in *Islands*: to write a verse "clear as sunlight," and as "ordinary / as a tumbler of island water." These early poems are self-sufficient. They admit a reader ignorant of the writer's complicated background; they foreground aesthetic pleasure, something not always to be said of the later Walcott. The reader quickly finds that the poet does not always stick to his expressed desire for lucidity. At times the elevated register in some of the work—a register one critic complained would not be out of place in Jacobean drama—seems overly rhetorical. The English poet Gerard Manley Hopkins coined the name "Parnassian" for a poet's achieved style, a language unique to each considerable poet which he or she could produce at will. Walcott has written considerable quantities; his eloquence can be a poetic liability. The best work—which can be magnificent—tends to be the plainest.

MIDDLE PERIOD

In *The Castaway and Other Poems* (1965), *The Gulf and Other Poems* (1969)—its title a barbed pun on the water separating St. Lucia from America—and the autobiographical sequence *Another Life* (1973), the poet begins to examine themes of isolation and exile. The figure of Robinson Crusoe finds an artistic equivalent in the isolated poet, and America begins to appear in poems like "The Glory Trumpeter" and "A Village Life," an elegy set in New York City, as was "God Rest Ye Merry Gentlemen," an ironic Christmas poem set on Sixth Avenue. In contrast against these are poems such as "Homecoming: Anse La Raye," in which Walcott as outsider returns to his home island—a theme he would revisit often in later books. Meanwhile, the book-length autobiography of childhood and youth, *Another Life*, written between 1965 and 1972, is a remarkable poem, not least for some of its vibrant characters, many delineated in a list (like characters in Dylan Thomas's *Under Milk Wood*) in section 2 of chapter 3 but also including Anna, representing Andreuille Alcée, the poet's first love and muse, who gives rise to some of Walcott's loveliest lyrical writing, and Gregorias, representing Dunstan St. Omer, a renowned Caribbean artist whose rambunctiousness is vividly depicted. When his friend opens the window and exhorts the poet to "Listen!" it is as if "the thunderous Atlantic / Were a record he had just put on." Similarly, formalizing in art the raw matter of the Caribbean would be a constant Walcott endeavor.

Themes of exile and return continued in Walcott's books of verse through the late 1970s and early 1980s, which included *Sea Grapes* (1976), *The Star-Apple Kingdom* (1979), and the somewhat ironically titled *The Fortunate Traveller* (1981), published the same year Walcott began his long-standing association as a teacher, later professor, of creative writing at Boston University. The period's outstanding poems include the eleven-part dramatic monologue "The Schooner, Flight" of *The Star-Apple Kingdom*, spoken by a sailor-poet nicknamed Shabine, "the patois for / any red nigger," gone to sea and still in love with his estranged wife, Maria Concepcion. The narrative is engagingly written in an elevated English mingled with touches of patois which briskly evoke the character's speech pattern; unlike elsewhere, when Walcott's thematic preoccupations can become tedious, issues of exile and postcolonial life are enlivened here by being enacted through the narrative of the sailor's life, his unsatisfied yearning for an island that "heals with its harbour / a guiltless horizon."

The Fortunate Traveller, meanwhile, seemed Walcott's first American book, reflecting his increased involvement, as a teacher, with the United States. It showed, unusually for a writer entering his fifties, the occasional echo of Robert Lowell, a close friend whom he had first met in Trinidad in June 1962. (Lowell would prove instrumental in introducing Walcott to New York literary society.) It contains outstanding pieces such as "North and South," Walcott's narrative meditation on race in America and his own position as "a colonial upstart at the end of an empire," and "Early Pompeian," a moving extended elegy for a baby daughter stillborn at seven months to his third wife, Norline Metivier. Walcott's preference for an elevated address, however, still reigned in some of the volume's poems. One of them, "The Season of Phantasmal Peace," which one critic, Mervyn Morris, says offers a "vision of universal love," seems for other readers to show that the high poetic style, uncontrasted with a lower vernacular to ground it, is obsolete.

The best poems in Walcott's next collection, *Midsummer* (1984), however—a sequence of fifty meditations set variously in Rome, London, rural England, Chicago, and his native Caribbean—form an at times stunning mosaic of impressions and considerations. Here, Walcott's wonderful visual sense—with Anthony Hecht and Richard Wilbur he must be among the most painterly of living poets, a master at visual evocation—and his memories and main themes of his divided background meet in a diction at once dignified, sonorous, and yet plain speaking. When Walcott does not overwrite, his work achieves a singular power, the effortless fluency of a master working at the height of his abilities. That is the case in numbers 23, 28, 30, 49, 50, 52, and 53, the last of which is a superb condensed memoir of a Syrian incomer to Walcott's home town of Castries when he was young; the marginality of Walcott, the colonized outsider, is relative.

The quality achieved there is at times one Walcott would maintain in his next book, *The Arkansas Testament* (1987), which is divided into two sections, the perhaps hopefully titled "Here," St. Lucia, and "Elsewhere"—everywhere else. Many of the book's pieces are in a trim, three-beat quatrain, including the volume's opening five poems, among them the beautiful "The Villa Restaurant," an affecting paean to the restaurant's "terra-cotta waitress"—Walcott praises magnificently when he has a mind to—and the book's opening poem, "The Lighthouse." The latter is a three-section narrative that evokes emotions known to everyone returning to a loved place made strange by absence. The poet wanders his home town, Castries, meets an old friend, "a lovely actor" once, who has languished as a postal worker. He contrasts himself implicitly with his unachieving friend.

The contrast is by no means unironic, however: the poet is cut off from "the heat of home." Perhaps the volume's strongest poem, "The Light of the World"—signifying beauty—continues this Walcottian tradition of poems featuring the return of a wanderer. The poet falls instantly in love with a woman he sees on a sixteen-seat bus in which they're both traveling. She and her beauty—which, if he won, he says he would "never leave"—become the symbol for the people and island life he has left. When he is dropped off outside his lodgings, the ironically named Halcyon Hotel, he fears to say goodnight because the word would be "full of inexpressible love." The van stops and a man holds out of the window for him a packet of cigarettes he had dropped in disembarking. All that the poet can give them is "this thing," he tells us, his poem of complicated regret. Intellectually, the poem may be judged sentimental. It has, however, a convincing emotional veracity. The book's other highlights include the twenty-four-section title poem, which narrates an overnight stay in an Arkansas motel and the narrator's discomfiture in the racist South—written not long before Walcott decided to take a St. Lucian rather than an American passport; "For Adrian," an affecting elegy spoken in the persona of a dead child; an account of a love affair in "Summer Elegies"; and "Fame," a bleak little portrayal of the barrenness of eminence.

AS A PLAYWRIGHT

Though theater had been central to Walcott's artistic endeavor from the outset, his biographer Bruce King (2000) has called the poet as dramatist "uneven," albeit with "a few real classic plays to his credit." These include *Dream on Monkey Mountain* (first performed 1967), perhaps Walcott's most famous play. In the mythopoetic style of Walcott's early manner, it is a dream-set investigation of West Indian identity via an old charcoal burner, Makak, which examines issues of colonialism and ethnic difference and delineates the fantasy of returning to a "pure" African heritage. *Pantomime* (first performed 1978), in Walcott's later, more realist manner, is a sardonic investigation of racism and colonialism probed via Harry Trewe, a retired white actor and hotel owner, and his employee, a black Trinidadian, Jackson Phillip. To entertain guests Trewe decides that he and Phillip will stage a comic reworking of the Crusoe–Man Friday story. This play within a play allows the playwright to investigate the complexities of the two characters and their cultural situation. In its uneasy switching of roles, the piece rapidly becomes the "Pantomime" of the play's somewhat ironic title.

OMEROS, NOBEL FAME, AND THE LATE POETRY

When Walcott was awarded the Nobel Prize in 1992, it was ostensibly for *Omeros* (1990)—the modern Greek word for "Homer"—his massive, three-hundred-page chronicling of contemporary Caribbean life in all its complexity. Walcott's heroes are ordinary men and women: his Hector and Achille have worked as island fishermen; his Helen, gorgeously depicted, has worked as an island waitress and as a headstrong maid for Major Dennis Plunkett and his Irish wife, Maud, characters who enable Walcott to investigate issues of colonialism and history. At the center of *Omeros* is the love triangle between Hector, Achille, and Helen, but the poem extends beyond the personal into wider relevance. While not a conventional narrative—it jumps between several stories, in cinematic fashion, and its narrator establishes his postmodern credentials by having a walk-on part at odd moments—in its concurrent episodes *Omeros* is a multilayered, colossal work, huge in sweep and ambition. A technical tour de force, it employs some 2,500 three-line stanzas in loose terza rima, separated into seven books, using a rangy, expansive hexameter line. It is widely regarded as one of Walcott's major achievements.

However, *The Bounty* (1997) and *Tiepolo's Hound* (2001), show the poet mainly writing a relatively relaxed Parnassian. *The Bounty*, which begins with a powerful elegy for the poet's mother, Alix, concludes with thirty-seven meditations; lacking the pressure of significant external event, they founder in Walcott's effortless eloquence. It is a verbosity often shared by *Tiepolo's Hound*, ostensibly a narrative about the life of Camille Pissarro, who lived in St. Thomas for five years in childhood before leaving to paint in Paris, never to return. While it contains numerous touches of Walcott's characteristic gorgeous description, the sequence seems too long and self-indulgent. In a review, the Australian poet-critic John Kinsella suggested with some justification that it could have been cut by half without losing anything significant.

Derek Walcott is undoubtedly a major voice in contemporary letters, and certainly the major poet of the Caribbean. The brilliant clarities of diction found in some of the earlier poems, and the more imaginatively achieved delineations of his own complex background—which stand in microcosm for the cultural complexities of the Caribbean—seem sure to be lasting. Even an outsider to the cultural experiences depicted can read such works out of delight rather than duty, to paraphrase what Walcott once wrote regarding Robert Frost. When one reads such poems as these, Robert Graves's remark (used on the dust jacket of Walcott's *Selected Poems* [1964]) that the Caribbean poet had more awareness of "the inner magic" of English than his "English-born" contemporaries, seems decidedly modest praise.

SELECTED WORKS

25 Poems (1948)
Epitaph for the Young (1949)
Henri Christophe: A Chronicle in Seven Scenes (1950)
Poems (1951)
Harry Dernier (1952)
The Sea at Dauphin (1954)
Ione: A Play with Music (1957)
Ti-Jean: A Play in One Act (1958)
In a Green Night: Poems, 1948–1960 (1962)
Selected Poems (1964)
The Castaway and Other Poems (1965)
The Gulf and Other Poems (1969)
Dream on Monkey Mountain and Other Plays (1970)
Another Life (1973)
Sea Grapes (1976)
The Joker of Seville and O Babylon! (1978)
The Star-Apple Kingdom (1979)
Remembrance and Pantomime: Two Plays (1980)
Selected Poetry (1981)
The Fortunate Traveller (1981)
The Caribbean Poetry of Derek Walcott, and the Art of Romare Bearden (1983)
Midsummer (1984)
Collected Poems, 1948–1984 (1986)
Three Plays: The Last Carnival; Beef, No Chicken; and A Branch of the Blue Nile (1986)
The Arkansas Testament (1987)
Omeros (1990)
Poems, 1965–1980 (1992)
The Bounty (1997)
What the Twilight Says: Essays (1998)
Tiepolo's Hound (2000)

FURTHER READING

Baer, William, ed. *Conversations with Derek Walcott*. Jackson, Miss., 1996. A gathering of some of the most significant interviews with the poet by the editor of the *Formalist* magazine. Though often contradictory, Walcott is at his best in interviews. His written prose can often seem turgid and divagatory by comparison.

Brown, Stewart, ed. *The Art of Derek Walcott*. Bridgend, Wales, 1991. A dozen essays by various authors on central themes of, and books by, Walcott. Useful as an introduction, with a good bibliography.

Hamner, Robert D. *Epic of the Dispossessed: Derek Walcott's "Omeros."* Columbia, Mo., and London, 1997. The definitive guide to Walcott's most significant long poem, exhaustive in detail. Hamner sets Walcott's epic in context and examines the poem in the context of Walcott's career to date.

King, Bruce. *Derek Walcott and West Indian Drama: "Not Only a Playwright but a Company": The Trinidad Theatre Workshop, 1959–1993.* Oxford, 1995. Detailed account of Walcott and Trinidadian theater.

King, Bruce. *Derek Walcott: A Caribbean Life.* Oxford, 2000. The standard biography. Though somewhat hamstrung by its subject's still being alive and too often focusing on practical minutiae of little real significance, it also gives an exhaustive overview of Walcott's life and work, with a fine and detailed bibliography.

ALICE WALKER

by Stefanie K. Dunning

Alice Walker, perhaps best known for her Pulitzer Prize–winning novel *The Color Purple* (1982), has always been committed to social and political change. This was nowhere clearer than in *The Color Purple*, which brought to light questions of sexual abuse and violence in the black community, while demonstrating the liberatory possibilities inherent in every life. *The Color Purple* tells the story of Celie, who is the victim of systematic gender oppression, at the hands of first her stepfather and then her husband. Despite the severe abuse Celie endures, she is a triumphant character who ultimately achieves a free and comfortable life. The principal male character—Celie's husband, Albert—is also redeemed and so transcends his abusive past. Many critics have argued that *The Color Purple* is Walker's best work, noting its inspired epistolary style (i.e., written in the form of letters) and the dynamic voice of its protagonist.

Although *The Color Purple* was an enormous success, it sparked considerable controversy. Some black men, who felt that her portrayals of them reinforced animalistic and cruel stereotypes about black masculinity, condemned Walker for her complexly drawn male characters. These unfair criticisms coincided with the premiere of the film *The Color Purple*, which did not depict domestic abuse in the complicated ways the book did. This iniquitous criticism obscured the significance of the novel, which exposed aspects of black female struggle unfamiliar to a mainstream American readership. Yet long before *The Color Purple* drew the attention of popular audiences, Alice Walker's work had already established her as an accomplished artist and activist. Her work explores race, gender, sexuality, and class, building on Walker's observations and experiences as a child and young adult in the rural South.

CHILDHOOD AND YOUTH

Alice Walker was born on 9 February 1944 in Eatonton, Georgia. She was the youngest of eight children. Walker's

Alice Walker. (© *Bettmann/Corbis*)

parents were sharecroppers, which meant that they farmed land belonging to someone else in exchange for living there. The system of sharecropping was one of cruel inequity; black workers were often exploited for their labor and rarely were paid what the crop they produced was worth. Because of this, Walker has often said that the system of sharecropping was worse than slavery because unlike slavery, sharecropping masqueraded as paid labor when in reality it was not. Walker was a hard worker and applied these lessons to her studies. Walker was an excellent student and valedictorian of her high school class; for her academic achievements she won a scholarship to Spelman College and ultimately completed her education at Sarah Lawrence College.

After graduating from college, Walker participated in various progressive movements. Never content simply to wait for an injustice to disappear or be rectified by someone else, Walker was active in the civil rights movement of the 1960s and worked in the voter registration drives. She had the opportunity to meet Martin Luther King Jr., and she attended the March on Washington. Embodying the feminist adage that "the personal is political," Walker was married to a Jewish civil rights lawyer, Mel Leventhal, and they became the only legally married interracial couple in Mississippi at the time. She was also among the first people in the United States to teach a women's studies course, which she instituted at Wellesley College. That these events had quite an impact on the young Walker is evident in her writing.

ART AS ACTIVISM

Just as her experience growing up in the rural South in a sharecropping community would influence and shape her later work, so too did her experiences with activism during the civil rights movement. In Walker's work, the relationship between her activism and her art is clear, as she repeatedly examines and exposes oppression. Walker does not simply draw back the curtain on injustice; she also imagines the transcendence of that injustice in her work. For this reason, it has often been said that all of Walker's novels have "happy endings." What this suggests about Walker is not that she is unrealistic but rather that she is interested in ways people who have been marginalized can overcome oppression.

Her first novel, *The Third Life of Grange Copeland* (1970), clearly draws on her experiences as a child in a sharecropping community and offers not only a critique of gender and race relations under that system but also a vision of what is possible through change. *The Third Life of Grange Copeland* depicts the family of Grange, his wife, Mem, and their son, Brownfield. Sharecropping renders Grange abusive and neglectful of his family; he leaves them and goes north. When his mother commits suicide, Brownfield decides to go in search of his father but never makes it farther than a few miles from home. Slipping into the same cycle of sharecropping and abuse that characterized his parents' relationship, Brownfield becomes far more abusive than his father and ultimately ends up in jail for murdering his wife. Grange returns, largely reformed during his time in the North, to lovingly raise his granddaughter, Ruth, who, as the heroine, anticipates the strong female protagonists that characterize Walker's work.

Like all of her heroines, Alice Walker is herself an agent of change. Walker once said that the best role model is someone who is always changing. Instead of desiring a long shelf life, Walker asserts that she wants to remain fresh. This commitment to fluidity and evolution characterizes both her life and her work. This is especially clear in her novel *Meridian* (1976). Walker's experiences at Spelman College may have provided her with the setting for *Meridian*, the story of a young woman of the same name who attends a college, much like Spelman, for young black women and becomes a daring activist, willing to die in order to protect black people from injustice. It is a book that also draws on many themes in Walker's own life, specifically her Native American heritage. In the novel, Meridian's father educates her about the Native Americans who occupied the land before they did and shows her their ancient burial grounds, which are eventually destroyed in the course of the novel. *Meridian* also articulates Walker's notion of "womanist" politics, in that it features a female protagonist evolving through the pain of gender and racial inequity.

WOMANISM AND BEYOND

The term "womanist," coined by Walker in 1983, asserts that not only gender oppression but also race oppression must be confronted, which affects and shapes gender in inexorable ways. Furthermore, the term "womanist" conjured a conception of blackness and womanness that feminist theory had been unable to represent; it not only provided the meaning of these intersecting identities but also connoted something of the spirit of them. Womanism enabled black women to articulate their commitment to gender liberation while not requiring them to forsake their struggle for race liberation as well. In womanism, Walker synthesized various liberation ideologies that have often been at odds. Womanism has repeatedly been invoked to describe the complicated interplay between race and gender faced by African-American women and represents another of Walker's major contributions to the study of literature and feminism.

In keeping with her womanist politics, Walker continued to engage difficult issues in her later works. Her novel *Possessing the Secret of Joy* (1992) focuses on a character who was featured minutely in *The Color Purple*, Tashi. Tashi, an African woman married to Celie's son in *The Color Purple*, subjects herself to the practice of female circumcision. In *Possessing the Secret of Joy* Walker explores her physical and emotional pain around this "traditional" African practice. This novel drew less mainstream controversy but engendered some academic controversy. Many scholars, especially scholars working in the area of Africa, saw Walker's novel as an Americanized condemnation of African culture, arguing that she was an outsider interfering in a culture she knew nothing about. Walker, however, felt that she was able to understand what it means to be physically maimed because when she was eight years old her brother blinded her in one eye with a BB gun. In Walker's view, a lifetime of partial blindness provided a fitting metaphor to help her understand the burden of going through life with a part of your body violently excised by a society that does not take seriously the pain inflicted on the bodies of girls. Walker referred to her blinded eye and the wounds born by the women who endured circumcision as "warrior marks" in a film of the same name she made about female genital mutilation with Pratibha Parmar. Despite the criticism engendered by Walker's discussions of female genital mutilation, what remains indisputable is that Walker's concern for young women was the impetus for the creation of the film and her book *Possessing the Secret of Joy*.

Like *Possessing the Secret of Joy*, much of Walker's work is characterized by a thematic interest in cultures and people outside the American context. These themes are fully developed in her novel *The Temple of My Familiar* (1989). This novel features characters from a range of cultural backgrounds, including South American, African American, and Native American. Walker's interest in Latin-American culture, which was first articulated in *The Temple of My Familiar*, can also be seen in her novel, *By the Light of My Father's Smile* (1998). In another work, Walker focused on questions of interpersonal and communal healing. Titled *The Way Forward Is with a Broken Heart* (2000), this work is a semifictionalized account of her relationship with her former husband and chronicles other important relationships in her life. She also wrote *Sent by Earth: A Message from the Grandmother Spirit after the Bombing of the World Trade Center and Pentagon* (2001), which proposed peace, love, and healing as antidotes to tragedy and tyranny.

Walker's work demonstrates a remarkable grasp of the political realities of systematic oppression. Walker is such a prolific writer that it would be impossible to discuss all of her work; she has written in almost every form and genre. Her first published work, in fact, was a book of poems called *Once* (1968). Her poetry embodies some of her most profound insights. Walker's legacy of activism is to be found not only in her work but also in her contribution to the lives of emerging writers and in her homage to the black writers who preceded her. Because of Walker's interest in Zora Neale Hurston, Hurston's book *Their Eyes Were Watching God* is now considered an essential African-American text. Walker has also written about Langston Hughes, another figure important in her life, and established a scholarship for emerging writers in the name of Hughes and Hurston at Spelman College. In this way, Walker has unambiguously contributed to the art of writing, both on and off the page. Like her work, which always offers the unexpected but necessary commentary, Alice Walker is an artist who has succeeded at remaining fresh.

[*See also* Hurston, Zora Neale.]

WORKS

Once: Poems (1968)
The Third Life of Grange Copeland (1970)
In Love and Trouble: Stories of Black Women (1973)
Revolutionary Petunias and Other Poems (1973)
Langston Hughes, American Poet (1974)
Meridian (1976)
Good Night, Willie Lee, I'll See You in the Morning (1979)
You Can't Keep a Good Woman Down (1981)
The Color Purple (1982)
In Search of Our Mothers' Gardens: Womanist Prose (1983)
Horses Make a Landscape Look More Beautiful: Poems (1984)
Living by the Word (1988)
To Hell with Dying (1988)
The Temple of My Familiar (1989)
Her Blue Body Everything We Know (1991)
Finding the Green Stone (1991)
Possessing the Secret of Joy (1992)
Warrior Marks: Female Genital Mutilation and the Sexual Blinding of Women (1993)
The Same River Twice: Honoring the Difficult (1996)
Anything We Love Can Be Saved: A Writer's Activism (1997)
By the Light of My Father's Smile (1998)
The Way Forward Is with a Broken Heart (2000)
Sent by Earth: A Message from the Grandmother Spirit after the Bombing of the World Trade Center and Pentagon (2001)

FURTHER READING

Bloom, Harold, ed. *Alice Walker*. Philadelphia, 2002. A review of modern critical perspectives on Alice Walker's work.

Gates, Henry Louis, Jr., and K. A. Appiah. *Alice Walker: Critical Perspectives Past and Present*. New York, 1993. One of the most sustained and useful treatments of Alice Walker's life and work.

Howard, Lillie P., ed. *Alice Walker and Zora Neale Hurston: The Common Bond*. Westport, Conn., 1993. An interesting and insightful collection of essays exploring Alice Walker and the influence of Zora Neale Hurston in her work.

Lauret, Maria. *Alice Walker*. New York, 1999. This is a more contemporary treatment than the Gates and Appiah volume of Alice Walker. An in-depth consideration of Alice Walker's activism and an analytical discussion of several of her major novels.

Tuzyline, Jita Allen. *Womanist and Feminist Aesthetics: A Comparative Review*. Columbus, Ohio, 1995. An engaging discussion comparing feminist versus womanist texts, with a full discussion of Walker's definition of womanism in chapter 3.

Van Dyke, Annette J. *The Search for a Woman-Centered Spirituality*. New York, 1992. An excellent consideration of Alice Walker's spirituality can be found in chapter 3.

WAR LITERATURE

by Pauls Toutonghi

What text epitomizes the literature of war? A battle-field account by an American soldier? A work of fiction written at the time of a war? Or fiction written after a war, but set in a remembered zone of conflict? The poetry of the battlefield? The poetry of those left out of the battle? What about the literature of the interned? The literature of the violated? The literature of the displaced, of the indigenous peoples of America? The literature of the immigrants who arrived in the United States in the wake of foreign wars? The choices are innumerable.

What about the Cold War, a war that had no quantifiable beginning or end? It could be argued that the anxiety of the nuclear arms race was reflected, quite substantially, in twentieth-century American fiction and playwriting. Finally, the reader cannot forget great works of scholarship, such as Modris Eksteins's *Rites of Spring: The Great War and the Birth of the Modern Age* (1989), works that defined, in clinical and expository prose, the realities of fighting a modern, mechanized battle.

THE EARLY COLONISTS AND THE WAR WITHIN

The experience of war—and its singular trauma and absurdity, its pathos and its brutality—has touched every generation of American writer. The earliest literature, produced as a result of experiences within America, was often printed in Europe. As returning colonial entrepreneurs, writers of North American experiences were often quite successful in their home countries. Arguably, the first of these was the Spanish envoy Alvar Nuñez Cabeza de Vaca, who was captured and imprisoned by Indians in 1528. After he returned safely to Spain, Cabeza de Vaca published an account of his disastrous experience as a part of the Spanish Crown's expedition to Texas and Florida led by Pánfilo de Narváez. This book, *The Journey of Alvar Nuñez Cabeza de Vaca and His Companions from Florida to the Pacific, 1528–1536* (1542), was the first to describe the indigenous peoples of the North American continent, and among the first to construct a narrative of war and imprisonment.

Indeed, Cabeza de Vaca's book would be the first of dozens of captivity narratives, books that formed the backbone of what could be considered early American literature. These stories were important for a variety of reasons, and typically featured the inhumane treatment of the author during his or her imprisonment after a Native American raid. Perhaps most critically, they established the indigenous peoples of the North American continent as an "other," as irredeemably savage and fully fit for the colonial enterprise. Books ranging from John Smith's *A True Relation of . . . Virginia* (1608) to Mary Rowlandson's *A True History of the Captivity and Restoration of Mrs. Mary Rowlandson* (1682) to John Williams's *The Redeemed Captive Returning to Zion* (1707) marginalized Native populations and fueled the land-grab opportunism of early settlers.

THE RISE OF AMERICAN NATIONALISM

In the eighteenth century, works of journalism were the primary medium in which writers expressed their sentiments regarding war and warfare. At the beginning of the century, newspaper publishers had to contend with the censorship of the British Crown, which dictated what could and could not be published within America's colonial borders. James Franklin, Benjamin Franklin's brother, was among the first to defy this rule of law. In 1721 he established the *New-England Courant*. Although the *Courant* was banned two years later, it led to important publications such as the *New-York Weekly Journal* (1733). The *Weekly Journal*'s publisher, John Peter Zenger, was acquitted of charges of seditious libel in 1735 with the help of young attorney Alexander Hamilton.

From 1735 through the American Revolution, news-papers such as *Weekly Journal* played a critical role in the dissemination of politically motivated calls for a war of independence. The first of John Dickinson's famous twelve letters opposing Britain's colonial legislation, collected as *Letters from a Pennsylvania Farmer* (1768), appeared in the *Boston Chronicle* on 21 December 1767. The *Letters* was a strident document, and helped spur readers toward the looming war for separation from the British Empire.

THE REVOLUTIONARY WAR AND NATION BUILDING

The latter decades of the eighteenth century saw a flowering of American imaginative literature, and an expansion of the ways that it dealt with the idea of war, and the need for independence. Although literacy was not predominant among the early colonists of America, the written word played a significant role in the Revolutionary War. Dramatic literature—widely read if not necessarily widely produced—fueled the push toward independence. Mercy Otis Warren's plays *The Adulateur* (1773) and *The Group* (1775) are barely disguised parodies of Thomas Hutchinson, royal governor of the Massachusetts colony, and express thinly veiled sentiments in favor of rebellion and American nationhood.

Thomas Paine's pamphlet *Common Sense* (1776) helped fuel the fervor toward battle. It was widely and illegally distributed and read at town meetings and to the militia who assembled to overthrow the rule of the British colonial government. *Common Sense* asserted that British rule amounted to the "laying of a Country desolate with Fire and Sword, declaring War against the natural rights of all Mankind." Paine's work became a rallying point for a young American identity.

Importantly, the Declaration of Independence (1776) and the United States Constitution (1787) were also written documents. The act of writing these treatises has been historically interpreted as the most important act of American statehood, as the definitive midpoint and conclusion of the war with Britain. Thus, the salient act of American nationality is a written one; the Constitution can be viewed as a set piece of literature written in response to war.

This literary approach to the necessities of governing continued in the early days of the new Republic. Between October 1787 and May 1788, Alexander Hamilton, John Jay, and James Madison published a series of anonymous essays in New York newspapers, essays commonly referred to as *The Federalist Papers*. These essays argued for the ratification of the Constitution, and were instrumental in convincing readers of the *New York Packet* and

John Dickinson by John B. Forrest.
(© *Stapleton Collection/Corbis*)

the *Independent Journal*—two of New York's largest newspapers—to support ratification.

It is possible, then, to read these early works of the literature of war as primarily ones concerned with the why of war, and not with its specifics. There are some exceptions, of course. Predominantly, however, the face of battle—or the faces of those whose lands were destroyed in some way by the rampaging armies—were largely absent from the war literature of the time. Even as a few years passed, significant publications only celebrated the glory of the war's patriotism or the biographies of its generals and founders. John Marshall's significant biography *The Life of George Washington* (1805–1807) celebrated the war exploits of the nation's first president. Another celebratory work, Joel Barlow's epic poem *The Columbiad* (1807) was printed and distributed with widespread success. Though Barlow had first published it in 1787 as *The Vision of Columbus*, the edited version of this poem about the American Revolution had a stridently nationalistic tone.

THE WAR AGAINST SLAVERY

Perhaps the most critical battle in the history of American literature is the battle for the end of slavery, for the enfranchisement and human rights of the nation's African-American population. The degree to which the fight over the end of slavery influenced the unfolding of the Civil War remains a question of much scholarly debate.

What cannot be argued is the way in which the issue of slavery—and the efforts to eradicate it—brought war to the lives of numerous Americans. The question of whether Kansas would be admitted to the Union as a free or slave state touched off some of the bloodiest battles on American soil before the Civil War. The abolitionist John Brown's doomed raid of the arsenal at Harpers Ferry, Virginia, in 1859 has fascinated writers for more than one hundred fifty years, inspiring notable books as recent as Russell Banks's *Cloudsplitter* (1998). Nat Turner's slave rebellion—catalogued in his widely publicized memoir, *The Confessions of Nat Turner; Leader of the Late Insurrection in Southampton, Va.* (1831)—was one of many bloody battles in the attempt to rid the nation of slavery's yoke.

The literature of this struggle for freedom—its memoirs, novels, and newspaper reports—demonstrated to Americans of the mid-nineteenth century that their country was a nation torn by clashing ideologies. The abolitionist movement was spearheaded by William Lloyd Garrison, whose newspaper, *The Liberator* (1831–1865), advocated any social action that could bring about the end of slavery. Newspapers were the sole mass media of the Civil War era. As such, they fulfilled all of the functions of literature: sparking the passions and imaginations of readers, *The Liberator* was an important means of circulating social and political ideals.

Another critical form in this fight was the slave narrative. Although the slave narrative existed as an American literary form throughout the eighteenth and nineteenth centuries, the form's widespread acceptance can perhaps be traced to 1845, when Frederick Douglass published his *Narrative of the Life of Frederick Douglass, an American Slave, Written by Himself*. A close collaborator with numerous New England abolitionists, Douglass traveled the nation giving lectures about his life experiences. He was in the vanguard of a surge in publication of slave narratives. Among the most powerful are the self-written works of the fugitive slaves Leonard Black (1847), Henry Watson (1848), and Henry Box Brown (1849).

The Narrative of Henry Box Brown, Who Escaped from Slavery Enclosed in a Box 3 Feet Long and 2 Wide. Written from a Statement of Facts Made by Himself, With Remarks upon the Remedy for Slavery was edited by Charles Stearns, a prominent Boston publisher and abolitionist. This text is uniquely important partly because of the physical torment and trauma that its author was forced to endure. It is also notable, however, for the remarks included by the volume's editor, remarks that stress the necessity of the end of slavery, even if the end is not achieved through peaceful means.

Narratives of slavery's trauma and the war to escape from its dominion were also written by women. Harriet Ann Jacobs's *Incidents in the Life of a Slave Girl* (1861) was published during the Civil War. It detailed her life in slavery, which was a chronicle of depravity and sexual assault, as well as fear of the Fugitive Slave Act of 1850, which allowed slave owners to pursue escaped slaves into "free" states. Jacobs's work was used as a rallying point for the efforts to raise armies of enlisted men in the North, and to fight against the ideas represented by the fugitive slave legislation.

The novel—with its power to give dramatic weight and staging to the violent events of a conflict—was also influential in the history of the literature of the war to end slavery. Traditional interpretation of literary history cites Harriet Beecher Stowe's *Uncle Tom's Cabin; or, Life among the Lowly* (1852) as perhaps the most critical book in the struggle toward nationwide emancipation. Though the book has been treated quite poorly by recent critical work, it remains one of the best-selling novels of its time. It brought the conditions of slavery into the public view and prompted widespread concern for slavery's end. Further, it served as ammunition for those who would fight for its end, and oppose—with violence—the armies of the American South.

POETRY AND FICTION OF THE CIVIL WAR

While the most widely read piece of Civil War literature is undoubtedly Abraham Lincoln's Gettysburg Address (1863), numerous other printed works influenced the literary environment of this time. In his introduction to *The Norton Book of Modern War* (1991), Paul Fussell writes that:

> It could be said that the American Civil War was the first modern one, for it was the first mass war fought in the industrial age, the first to rely on railroads and telegraph, armored battleships, fast-firing ordinance, and mass-produced, machine-made weapons, uniforms and shoes.

The modernity that he notes, of course, was also responsible for an accompanying rise in battlefield casualties. Battles increased in intensity as the mechanized slaughter of thousands of men could suddenly be concentrated into a meager number of hours. These hours, and their aftermath, were ably chronicled by numerous journalists and poets. Among these, however, perhaps none has achieved the widespread critical recognition and appreciation of Walt Whitman.

In his collection of poems *Drum-Taps* (1865), Whitman eulogizes the armies of young men flung into battle by the necessities of political conflict. It is in these poems that the brutalized soldier first stands as an individual, his torn and bloody body fully visible to the reader. In poems such as "The Wound-Dresser," Whitman describes his journey through the hospital tents of the Union army. "As an old man bending I come among new faces," he writes, and then catalogs the "clotted rags and blood," the "stump of an arm," "the amputated hand," the "yellow-blue countenance" of the soldier dying from a deep wound in the side.

Although Whitman famously held, in his collection of journalism *Specimen Days* (1882), that "the real war will never get in the books," his poetry and prose worked to imprint—indelibly—the legacy of the war in the American imagination. He is, without doubt, the best-known poet of the Civil War, and his outlook on its disastrous consequences has helped shape the way the American reading public considers the notion of war. Indeed, numerous historians have held that the Civil War has changed over the course of time, changing along with its historiography—along with the way the war was written.

Another major writer who wrote a key Civil War text was Herman Melville. Better known for his tale of whale hunting, *Moby-Dick*, Melville also wrote a collection of poems, *Battle-Pieces and Aspects of the War* (1866), which dealt with the war and its composite elements. Though it was not tremendously successful, *Battle-Pieces* was a significant statement on the war by one of the country's foremost writers. It stands among numerous other poems that sought to describe and illustrate the specifics and issues of the Civil War.

A work that has been noted by critics since its publication is John William De Forest's *Miss Ravenel's Conversion from Secession to Loyalty* (1867). Reviewed in the *Atlantic Monthly* by William Dean Howells, De Forest's novel is considered a precursor of American realist texts. It presents a measured and detailed analysis of the path of a wealthy family that moves, because of business interests, from the South to the North. Its refusal of sentimentality has been noted by critics seeking to establish the book as an influence on the later work of John Dos Passos, Theodore Dreiser, and Ernest Hemingway.

However, the power of the Civil War on the American literary imagination can perhaps be illustrated by the fact that two of the most famous works written about the war were not published until the 1890s. Ambrose Bierce's *Tales of Soldiers and Civilians* (1891) was written at a time when Bierce was well known as a journalist and wit. The book consists of piquantly observed character sketches and cynical musings on the hypocrisy of power.

Moreover, Stephen Crane's *The Red Badge of Courage* was not composed and published until 1895. A staple of elementary and high school literature studies, *The Red Badge of Courage* follows a volunteer soldier in his first battle. It thus mirrors the experience of many readers, who approach the book without having lived through battle. Its images are wholly violent and visually traumatic; the soldier watches the slaughter of his comrades, then flees. Much was made both of the book and of the adversarial

relationship between Crane and Bierce, who feuded in the prominent periodicals of the day.

CIVIL WAR MEMOIRS

The period immediately following the Civil War also saw a swell in the number of published memoirs. Soldiers and civilians flooded the market with the accounts of their lives. These accounts frequently focused on the battles in which the men had fought; more often than not, these were patriotic accounts, accounts that failed to emphasize the brutality of war. Among these numerous books, noteworthy is Thomas Wentworth Higginson's *Army Life in a Black Regiment* (1870). Higginson was a well-known journalist. Throughout the war, he published articles in the *Atlantic Monthly* about subjects ranging from the specifics of battle to the rebellion of Nat Turner. His account of commanding the First South Carolina Volunteers contains a careful assessment of the racial questions of the period.

Other significant recollections include J. B. Jones's *A Rebel War Clerk's Diary at the Confederate States Capital* (1866), Daniel G. Crotty's *Four Years Campaigning in the Army of the Potomac* (1874), and the memoirs of William Tecumseh Sherman (1875), one of the Civil War's most controversial soldiers. Sherman—infamous for his scorched-earth campaign through the South to the Gulf of Mexico—reflects on the mistakes he made as a general and warns the future of the danger of war's escalating mechanization and brutality.

This surge in memoirs did not subside for a number of years. Ulysses S. Grant published his memoirs in 1885, shortly before his death. By this time, he had served as president of the United States (1869–1877), and his administration had been excoriated for its corruption in the Whiskey Ring scandal. His memoir was a national best-seller, and used a stoic wit and close attention to detail to describe Grant's career in the Civil War.

The publication of Civil War memoirs extended into the early years of the twentieth century, when the last survivors of the era began to die. Susie King Taylor's *Reminiscences of My Life in Camp with the 33rd United States Colored Troops, Late 1st S.C. Volunteers* (1902) has only recently taken its rightful place among the Civil War's great memoirs. It deals with a range of complex issues, and still enlivens academic debate of the ways in which race was treated in the militias of the North.

A final salvo, perhaps, came from Mary Chesnut, the wife of a prominent figure in the government of South Carolina during secession. What is now known as *Mary*

Chesnut's Civil War was first published as *A Diary from Dixie* (1905). This work is an intensely literary text, to which Chesnut—the author of several novels—gives a lush and fictive tone.

MANIFEST DESTINY

The question of whether or not to include the story of the U.S. Army's forcible expansion westward—as well as the story of the violent warfare thrust upon the indigenous inhabitants of the North American continent—should not even be debated. Without a doubt the bloodiest and most protracted war in American history, the struggle to displace the Native Americans is cataloged in a long literature of warfare. What are the salient aspects of this particular war literature? In this case, the war became a micromanaged war, in which the tyranny of power brought its violence down upon a people solely because of their ethnic heritage. The locus of the war, then, became the Native American individual.

The literature of this war for land can be considered in the scope of its various struggles and fights. The Trail of Tears—the forced removal of the Cherokee people from their homes in Georgia, North Carolina, and Tennessee to Oklahoma Territory—occurred from 1838 to 1839, and inspired a range of writing. Documents referring to this component of the war are chronicles of failed peace, of government deception, and of genocidal legislation, such as the Indian Removal Act of 1830, which provided a legal basis for the violent confiscation of lands controlled by Native peoples.

From this era, some voices raised literary protest over the violence forced upon the natives. William Apess wrote *Indian Nullification of the Unconstitutional Laws of Massachusetts, Relative to the Mashpee Tribe* (1835), which was a direct protest of state law. Apess was also involved in the Boston literary and political scene, working with William Lloyd Garrison on the staff of *The Liberator*. It has also been a setting for contemporary writers who wish to look back and reconsider this era—among the first violent struggles of the Indian wars. Diane Glancy's novel *Pushing the Bear: A Novel of the Trail of Tears* (1996) is set in this warlike milieu.

THE INDIAN WARS

After the Civil War, the Indian wars began in earnest, and federal troops initiated a systematic program of extermination, culminating with the massacre of the Sioux at Wounded Knee on 29 December 1890. In the intervening twenty-five years, numerous Native American leaders spoke out against the process of white settlement on Indian lands. In various interviews with the press, leaders such as Sitting Bull, Chief Joseph, and Crazy Horse argued that the land of America was being unjustly seized from their stewardship.

Once of the most mythologized battles of the Indian wars occurred at the Little Bighorn River in Dakota Territory on 25 June 1876. General George Armstrong Custer and his men were all killed during the course of this battle, and the popular media seized upon this battle, turning it into further ammunition in the war to subdue Native American resistance. Long before the battle, Custer had been sending dispatches to New York from the frontier, dispatches that were originally published in *Galaxy* magazine, and subsequently collected in his book *My Life on the Plains* (1874). After his death, Custer was lauded as a hero, and his friends and relatives published numerous accounts of his life, accounts such as Elizabeth Bacon Custer's *"Boots and Saddles"; or, Life in Dakota with General Custer* (1885).

Assessment of the warrior whom Custer harassed and who ultimately took Custer's life—Crazy Horse—took some more time to reach the history books. Widely vilified until the latter half of the twentieth century, Crazy Horse has emerged in more recent literature as a heroic figure. Peter Matthiessen's *In the Spirit of Crazy Horse* (1983) ponders the influence of Crazy Horse's story on Leonard Peltier, the imprisoned Native American Rights activist. The noted historian Stephen E. Ambrose wrote a balanced consideration of both men, *Crazy Horse and Custer: The Parallel Lives of Two American Warriors* (1986). Also, Larry McMurtry has written a definitive biography, *Crazy Horse* (1999).

Another critical figure of the period who has received a great deal of attention is Chief Joseph. Joseph was the leader of the Nez Percé tribe of Idaho, Oregon, and Washington, and defeated U.S. Army troops in several engagements during the Nez Percé War of 1877 before his surrender. The speech he made at his surrender, which ended with the statement, "From where the sun now stands, I will fight no more forever," decreed an end to his fight against the U.S. government and was reprinted in an 1879 interview with the *North American Review*. Included in Merrill D. Beal's book *"I Will Fight No More Forever": Chief Joseph and the Nez Perce War* (1963), Chief Joseph's speech is a stunning, and weary, indictment of the hostile government policies.

Finally, consideration must turn to the battle at Wounded Knee, at which more than three hundred Sioux

Indians, many women and children, were massacred by U.S. Army troops on 29 December 1890. The incident has animated the imaginations of numerous writers. Dee Brown's *Bury My Heart at Wounded Knee: An Indian History of the American West* has received a great deal of critical attention since its publication in 1971. Another notable work, Reneé Sansom Flood's *Lost Bird of Wounded Knee: Spirit of the Lakota* (1995), uses the massacre as the point of departure for a moving and interesting work of biography. In *Lost Bird*, Flood catalogs the life of one of the few Sioux survivors of that battle—an orphaned girl.

A chronological digression that must be mentioned is James Fennimore Cooper's *The Last of the Mohicans* (1826), which is set during the French and Indian War (1754–1763). Although it could be included in the literature of nation building—it stratifies and codifies the imagined Indian as an "other"—*The Last of the Mohicans* is especially powerful if the reader keeps in mind the intense slaughter and exile that followed its publication by only a few years.

THE SPANISH-AMERICAN WAR AND THE PHILIPPINE INSURRECTION

The role of the media in the Spanish-American War, and its successor, the Philippine Insurrection (also known as the Filipino-American War), cannot be underestimated. Both William Randolph Hearst's *New York Journal* and Joseph Pulitzer's *New York World* profited directly from publishing sensational accounts of the situation in Cuba. Columnists for both papers embellished stories of valiant Cuban resistance against the colonial powers of Spain, and when the battleship USS *Maine* was sunk in Havana's harbor on 16 February 1898, Hearst ran unproven headlines blaming forces loyal to the Spanish government. Public outcry in the United States led to a declaration of war. The United States invaded Cuba and Puerto Rico in the Caribbean and the Philippines in the Pacific, where its forces quickly defeated the forces of the Spanish navy. A good historical consideration of this period is Charles Brown's *The Correspondents' War: Journalists in the Spanish-American War* (1967).

In the United States, public sentiment largely supported the war against Spain. However, President William McKinley indicated that, under the newly ratified Treaty of Paris (6 February 1899), he intended to maintain the Philippines as an American colony. In Manila, Philippine forces were hostile to the American occupation, leading to an insurrection that lasted until 1902 and was America's first protracted war in Asia.

A small group of writers and intellectuals rose up against this occupation. Mark Twain was at their forefront, and he wrote numerous newspaper articles and speeches advocating a return of the Philippines to Filipino forces. On commission for a women's magazine, Twain wrote "The War Prayer," an antiwar short story that was not published until it was collected into the volume *Europe and Elsewhere* in 1923. "The War Prayer" deals with complex issues of religion and war, criticizing the official role that churches played in the sanctification of battle. "The War Prayer" is an eloquent statement against war, written by one of the nation's most notable writers.

WORLD WAR I

Although the United States would not become involved in the continental war in Europe until 1917, the violence experienced by many of the nation's young writers in 1917 and 1918 shaped the work of a generation. This Lost Generation of writers is known for work haunted by an awareness of brutality, and the senseless nature of organized violence. One of the first voices to describe the despair of the mechanized war experience was John Dos Passos. His work *Three Soldiers* (1921) raised numerous objections to the sufferings of war.

The Lost Generation consisted of American expatriates living abroad in Europe. Though the war does not often appear directly in their work, its influence can be traced; it haunts the texts, an ephemeral background. Ernest Hemingway's novel *A Farewell to Arms* (1929), for example, is based on his own experiences as an ambulance driver on the battlefields of Europe during World War I. Like Hemingway, the main character of *A Farewell to Arms* is wounded in battle. Hemingway's book speaks eloquently of the senseless nature of armed conflict.

Before World War I, much American writing was steeped in the language of patriotism. The idea of the soldier was an idea steeped in the perceived glories of combat. Combat was, for early American writers, the physical expression of the willingness to fight for an ideal, and thus a worthy end for those who died in it. But with World War I, much of this changed. Fictional characters of this time period can be seen struggling with the meaning of the death and destruction that they witness. Poets pick up on Walt Whitman's description of the carnage of battle and extend it—expanding the poetic vocabulary to include the falsity of the war in which war has been depicted in the literature of the past.

Plays dealt explicitly with this subject matter. Maxwell Anderson and Laurence Stallings collaborated on the well-received work *What Price Glory?* (1924), which cast a caustic eye on governments willing to send their young men into battle. Anderson would later write *The Eve of St. Mark* (1942), a significant World War II play. Women writers also had an important role, with poets such as Amy Lowell writing several key antiwar poems. Many of these voices are collected in Margaret Higonnet's anthology *Lines of Fire: Women Writers of World War I* (1999).

The alienation of the narrator, the loneliness of the individual before the required experiences of social life—experiences such as conscription into the army and battle—these are similarities shared by modern literature and modern warfare. Ezra Pound's long poem *Hugh Selwyn Mauberly, Life and Contacts* (1920) turns at one point to contemplation of the war that has just passed:

> There died a myriad,
> And of the best, among them.
> For an old bitch gone in the teeth,
> For a botched civilization.

The acerbic, caustic narrative voice is steeped in bitterness as a "botched" civilization that would willingly butcher so many of its best young men. American poetry of the battle—all attempts at describing the war in a poetic sense—was influenced by T. S. Eliot's remarkable *The Waste Land* (1922), one of the hallmarks of modernist literature. Eliot worked as a contemporary to Pound and E. E. Cummings, whose poem "next to of course god America i" (1922), which declares, with stinging irony:

> why talk of beauty what could be more
>   beautiful than these heroic happy dead

Like many college-age Americans, Cummings volunteered to serve in the Norton-Harjes Ambulance Corps. His experiences embittered him toward both war and standard poetic diction; like many Lost Generation writers, he struggled with his experiences in the trenches. His novel based on his wartime days, *The Enormous Room* (1922), was one of the most significant works of the period. William Faulkner also had critical works about the war—*Soldiers' Pay* (1926) and *A Fable* (1954)—though he was an inveterate liar and tale-teller about his own armed service.

THE SPANISH CIVIL WAR

Ernest Hemingway would also play an important role in the Spanish civil war, a war that, though it was not fought on American soil or with U.S. troops, nonetheless attracted a fair number of American combatants. Hemingway's novel *For Whom the Bell Tolls* (1940) is the story of an American who dies in this conflict, and it is a sprawling, dramatic work in support of the then-defeated Loyalist armies. The roster of American writers who traveled to Spain to issue journalism reads like a roster of the form's luminaries: Lillian Hellman, Archibald MacLeish, William Faulkner, Theodore Dreiser, John Steinbeck, Sherwood Anderson, John Dewey, and Martha Gellhorn. Most of these writers supported the Loyalist cause, a cause that ultimately failed in 1939, resulting in the dictatorship of General Francisco Franco.

THE FICTION OF WORLD WAR II

Until the attack on Pearl Harbor in December 1941 spurred the American imagination into the fray of World War II, there were numerous advocates of nonintervention in what was perceived as a mostly European war. The publishing world had saturated Americans with images of the traumatic fighting of World War I, and few of its citizens believed that intervention was necessary. With the economy only sluggishly beginning to recover from the Great Depression, there seemed to be numerous arguments against war. The America First Committee—an organization that opposed to the deployment of U.S. troops abroad—counted such prominent citizens as Charles Lindbergh among its members. Once the United States was attacked, however, the country was soon on a war footing, in both Asia and Europe.

The literature of World War II is detailed and voluminous. Streamlined techniques of production and distribution contributed to the issue of a breadth of writings unparalleled in any previous conflict. Immediately after the cessation of hostilities in 1945—and the lift of wartime limits on the consumption of goods such as paper—the literature of war began to come out of the publishing houses. There were the usual memoirs of soldiers, as well as memoirs written by those left behind. There was war poetry. Indeed, the American publishing industry embraced all aspects of the war experience with vigor.

Numerous important works of fiction have dealt with questions raised by World War II. Saul Bellow's slender first novel, *The Dangling Man* (1944), relates the story of a young man who is waiting, with some degree of agony, for his draft notice. Gore Vidal's critically important first novel, *Williwaw* (1946), tells an elegant adventure story set within the broad spectrum of the armed conflict. John Horne Burns's novel *The Gallery* (1947) tells of the experiences of an American GI in postwar Italy. Even writers who normally wrote light fictions applied themselves to the World War II, such as Irwin Shaw with his melodrama *The Young Lions* (1948).

Perhaps the largest-selling book was Norman Mailer's *The Naked and the Dead* (1948). Told from the perspective of a veteran returning to America, this book follows the exploits of a marine platoon deployed in the Southeast Asia theater. It does not comment on war, but simply presents the war in gritty, foul detail, and thus issues a commentary through implication.

Mailer's work can be considered the midpoint between the popular fictions that sought, as their primary goal, to entertain their audiences, and the serious stylistic experiments that came from more literary writers. John Hawkes wrestled with his time as an ambulance driver in Germany to create the novel *The Cannibal* (1949), published when he was just twenty-three. Gertrude Stein, in *Wars I Have Seen* (1945) and *Brewsie and Willie* (1946) also confronted war with her unique literary perspective.

The novels did not stop with the end of the 1940s. James Jones's *From Here to Eternity* (1951) was a romantic sprawl of a war novel, simultaneously sad and violent and couched in the tradition of gritty war reporting. He also wrote *The Thin Red Line* (1962), which was published in the same year as Joseph Heller's *Catch-22* (1962), which has sold over eighteen million copies. Indeed, the fiction of the war has accumulated steadily, with many of the writers who experienced the war still alive and willing to write about it. Notable among these fictional representations of warfare is *Slaughterhouse-Five* (1969) by Kurt Vonnegut, which is based on his experiences as a survivor of the fire bombing of Dresden. *Gravity's Rainbow* (1973), a work by experimental American author Thomas Pynchon, as well as *Ceremony* (1977), Leslie Marmon Silko's dramatic work about the readjustment of a Native American soldier who has endured great trauma in World War II, are also important.

The market for war fiction shows no signs of relenting. As recently as 2002, James McBride published a critically lauded war-based novel, *Miracle at St. Anna*, which follows the exploits of an all-black regiment trapped in the mountains of Italy, cut off from their incompetent generals and pinned down by two fascist armies. It is a riveting and elegantly written war novel.

However, much of the fiction written since the end of World War II lacks the record of scholarship that marks the writing produced concomitant with or immediately after the war. Which of these myriad works will have a lasting impact on the American literary environment? That remains to be seen. What can be expected is that works such as John Okada's *No-No Boy* (1976)—that deal with previously neglected subjects such as the Japanese internment during the war—will last and undergo a large volume of critical reading.

THE POETRY OF WORLD WAR II

The American poetry of World War II is somewhat more epigrammatic than the fiction. Whereas war novels were frequently over six hundred pages, the American poems of World War II tend to be short and precise. Randall Jarrell's "The Death of the Ball Turret Gunner" (1968) is perhaps the best known of the poems, with its haunting final line, "When I died they washed me out of the turret with a hose." Jarrell's poems about the war are frequently written from the perspective of the dead; for this reason they have a haunting immediacy that makes their language quite memorable.

Frequently, individual poems, such as Robinson Jeffers's "Fantasy," Thomas McGrath's "Crash Report," Muriel Rukeyser's "Poem (I lived in the first century of world wars)," or Denise Levertov's "Life at War," have achieved widespread fame. Richard Eberhart's "The Fury of Aerial Bombardment" is one of the most vivid and lyrically intricate poems to come out of any conflict, and place itself in the canon of American literature. Collections of poems focused around the war, however, have been somewhat rare. Equally short—but powerful—are the Japanese-American internment camp haiku, which have been collected in numerous volumes, including the *Oxford Book of War Poetry* (1984), edited by Jon Stallworthy.

THE MEMOIRS OF WORLD WAR II

On the eve of American involvement in World War II, Bob Hoffman published his memoir, *I Remember the Last War* (1940), in an attempt to dissuade the populace of the United States from going into battle again. He warned against the physical danger into which American boys would be forced to go.

Following the pattern of all American wars up until this point, however, the years during the war saw a surge in the patriotism of the general populace. From 1941 to 1945, the stories circulated about the war were primarily news reports from the peripheries of combat; even these were frequently edited and censored. In the years immediately following the war, there were numerous memoirs written about wartime. The experience of war—throughout American history—has typically prompted an exhaustive written response. War has convinced thousands of writers of the noteworthy nature of their lives. This is part of the allure of the experience; its power to build identities can frequently serve as a mask for its more insidious and sorrowful dimensions.

The genre of reportage—carefully imagined nonfiction writing from everyday life—was widely practiced during World War II. The war correspondents published their writings in numerous stateside publications, and some, like Ernie Pyle, died in battle. Others, like William L. White, survived, and continued to write for years following the conflict.

When approaching the autobiographical writing of World War II, however, the reader is best served by consulting one of the numerous recent anthologies, anthologies grouping many different types of first-person memoir. The recollections of soldiers, as always, are in plentiful supply. Resources such as *The Two World Wars: A Selective Bibliography* (1964) or Gwyn M. Bayliss's comprehensive volume *Bibliographic Guide to the Two World Wars: An Annotated Survey of English-Language Reference Materials* (1977) are quite helpful. For slightly more uncommon perspectives on the war, a number of resources are available. Yvonne Klein edited the helpful volume *Beyond the Home Front: Women's Autobiographical Writing of the Two World Wars* (1997). C. Tyler Carpenter and Edward H. Yeatts coauthored the dual memoir *Stars without Garters: The Memoirs of Two Gay GIs in World War Two* (1996).

THE AMERICAN LITERATURE OF THE HOLOCAUST

Perhaps no literature of war bears a heavier burden than the literature of the Holocaust, a burden fraught with the difficulty of expressing a mechanized brutality that has no precedent in world history. Although most accounts of the Holocaust were written by survivors (with a few notable exceptions), these survivors were also predominantly European Jews, and published their memoirs in languages other than English. Among American writers who grappled with the Holocaust, however, few are as noted as Elie Wiesel, who was awarded the Nobel Peace Prize in 1986. His novel *Night* (1958) can be read as a hybrid of memoir and fiction. Originally written as *Un di velt hot geshvign* ("And the World Remained Silent"), Wiesel's text was somewhat longer and based more on factual representation, *Night* was an abridgment. Born 30 September 1928 in Romania, Wiesel is a death camp survivor—of Auschwitz, Buna, Buchenwald, and Gleiwitz. He has been in the United States since 1956 (naturalized in 1963), and teaches at Boston University and other colleges. He shares with some other Holocaust survivors the experience of immigrating to America after World War II, establishing a place in the nation's consciousness and literature.

Factual collections of Holocaust literature belong to the history of the voiceless, the nameless dead, and the testimony of witnesses. Numerous American scholars have tried, with varying degrees of success, to reassemble and recreate a literature of the six million dead. Basic factual resources are important to this segment of American literature. Lucy S. Dawidowicz's *The War against the Jews* (1975), as well as Martin Gilbert's *The Holocaust: A History of the Jews of Europe during the Second World War* (1986) and Mindy Weisel's edited volume *Daughters of Absence: Transforming a Legacy of Loss* (2000), are critical texts. *Still Alive: A Holocaust Girlhood Remembered* (2001), written by Ruth Kluger, besides being a harrowing personal memoir also references other key texts of survival.

An excellent resource for students who seek to grasp the complexities of the literature of the Holocaust is Daniel Schwarz's readable and carefully reasoned *Imagining the Holocaust* (1999). Schwarz surveys the imaginative literature of the Holocaust, including such important works as John Hersey's *The Wall* (1950), Jerzy Kosinski's *The Painted Bird* (1965), Leslie Epstein's *King of the Jews* (1979), Thomas Keneally's *Schindler's List* (1982), Cynthia Ozick's *The Shawl* (1989), and even Art Spiegelman's critically acclaimed graphic novel *Maus: A Survivor's Tale* (1986). Hersey's book, written from his perspective as a non-Jewish observer of the Holocaust, followed closely after his other critically acclaimed works about war, *A Bell for Adano* (1944), and *Hiroshima* (1946). This is, of course, only a partial list of the fiction.

Numerous important questions—such as what it means for a voice that is not that of a survivor to tell a story about the Holocaust—orbit around this literature. Poetry still is being written and collected, both about the Holocaust itself as well as about the legacy of having parents or grandparents who survived or lost their lives. Anna Rabinowitz's collection of poems *Darkling* (2001), circles these very themes. The American poetry of the Holocaust is capably represented in the volume edited by Charles Fishman, *Blood to Remember: American Poets on the Holocaust* (1991). This wartime genocide also continues to be considered and recast by contemporary American literature. Jonathan Safran Foer's *Everything Is Illuminated* (2002) was among the best-selling volumes of literary fiction in its year of publication.

THE WARS IN ASIA

The Korean and Vietnam wars were obviously quite different, and the impulse to group them together in one subheading can be questioned. However, they do represent two military involvements on the continent of Asia, separated by just over ten years. From the perspective of warfare, the Korean War was much more conventional—featuring opposing armies of troops, engaged in open battle in a traditional sense. In fact, it could be argued that this was the last American war of this type in modern history. The Vietnam War was an exercise in guerrilla combat, with the battlefield more fluid, and located most solidly in the minds of individual soldiers.

The literatures of these wars differed vastly as well. The Korean War was a short war (1950–1953). Although its chief military figures—Dwight Eisenhower and General Douglas MacArthur—both wrote memoirs, far more interesting are the stories written by the soldiers on the ground or Korean-Americans in the United States. These works range across the limits of perspective and emotion.

Two notable works of fiction have appeared partly from the Korean War, and are widely divergent in their approach to the ideas of conflict, war, and perspective. James Salter's *The Hunters* (1956) and Susan Choi's *The Foreign Student* (1998) are interesting counterpoints for study of the war's resultant literature. Numerous surveys of literature and remembrances also have been issued over the years. An excellent starting point is either Philip West and Suh Ji-moon's volume *Remembering the "Forgotten War": The Korean War through Literature and Art* (2001) or Carina Del Rosario's *A Different Battle: Stories of Asian Pacific American Veterans* (1999).

Vietnam was a much more prolonged conflict, and involved more American soldiers. The casualties of Vietnam extended beyond the battlefield: scarred veterans, unable to adjust to life after guerrilla warfare, and a divided populace, many of whom did not support the conflict. It can be argued that the residual effects of Vietnam on the general public were as significant as the American Revolution or Civil War. A panoply of voices arose from Vietnam, both during and after the conflict.

Among the most successful voices is that of Tim O'Brien, whose novels and short fiction—particularly the work of the interrelated stories in *The Things They Carried* (1990)—catalog the senseless brutality and unpredictable trauma of this jungle-based conflict. They also consider questions of return to society, and whether or not this experience was possible after the war. Some of his stories capture the anguish of drafted young men, who must choose between evading the draft by leaving family and country, or going to fight in a war in which they do not believe.

Other voices deserve recognition. Daniel Lang's 1969 *New Yorker* article "Casualties of War" was published in book form and made into a film (1989) directed by Brian De Palma. Two critical works have great importance: Philip H. Melling's *Vietnam in American Literature* (1990) and Philip D. Beidler's *Re-writing America: Vietnam Authors in Their Generation* (1991). The dauntingly titled *Vietnam Reader: The Definitive Collection of American Fiction and Nonfiction on the War* (1998), edited by Stewart O'Nan, is indeed comprehensive, though perhaps not definitive.

CONTEMPORARY TERRORS: THE COLD WAR AND 11 SEPTEMBER

The ironic opening of Stanley Kubrick's 1964 film *Dr. Strangelove, or How I Learned to Stop Worrying and Love the Bomb* is quite telling:

> For more than a year, ominous rumors have been privately circulating among high level western leaders, that the Soviet Union had been at work on what was darkly hinted to be the ultimate weapon, a doomsday device.

With the demise of the Soviet Union in 1991, the popular media made much of the idea that the United States was now the sole superpower in the world, and that this would ensure the safety and stability of human society into the future. Yet, as the conflicts in the Persian Gulf and Yugoslavia have illustrated, as long as the nation maintains a standing army, its forces will be ensnared in conflicts around the world.

Furthermore, with the 11 September 2001 attacks on the World Trade Center and the Pentagon, American soil has once again become the locus of war. This war shares numerous similarities, psychologically, with the conflict in Vietnam. Its battlefields and combatants are largely invisible, largely unknown. *The New Yorker* has already devoted an entire issue to the response of America's writers to the terror attacks (2001). Beyond this, however, the literature of this new war remains unwritten.

[*See also* Autobiography: White Women during the Civil War; Crane's *The Red Badge of Courage*; Hemingway, Ernest;

Jarrell, Randall; Mailer, Norman; O'Brien, Tim, and his *The Things They Carried*; Vietnam in Poetry and Prose; Vonnegut's *Slaughterhouse-Five*; and Whitman, Walt.]

FURTHER READING

Clarke, George Herbert, ed. *The New Treasury of War Poetry: Poems of the Second World War*. New York, 1968. Numerous sources. Very insightful.

Fussell, Paul, ed. *The Norton Book of Modern War*. New York, 1991.

Klein, Yvonne, ed. *Beyond the Home Front: Women's Autobiographical Writing of the Two World Wars*. New York, 1997. Accurate and sharply observed.

Schwarz, Daniel R. *Imagining the Holocaust*. New York, 1999. One of the best recent studies of the Holocaust and what it means to read or write about such a difficult event.

Sperber, Murray A., ed. *And I Remember Spain: A Spanish Civil War Anthology*. London, 1974.

Stallworthy, Jon, ed. *Oxford Book of War Poetry*. New York, 1984.

ROBERT PENN WARREN

by John Burt

The breadth of Robert Penn Warren's work over a sixty-year publishing career is matched by no other major American writer of the twentieth century. First poet laureate of the United States, three-time winner of the Pulitzer Prize (twice for poetry, once for fiction), he is the author of eighteen books of poetry and ten novels, including *All the King's Men* (1946), probably the most important novel of American politics. He also wrote several books and essays about race and segregation that helped the white South to come to terms with racial integration, coauthored *Understanding Poetry* (1938), a textbook that shaped how literature was taught in the United States for forty years, and was a beloved teacher.

Robert Penn Warren, ca. 1970. (*National Portrait Gallery, Smithsonian Institution/Art Resource*)

EARLY LIFE AND EDUCATION

Robert Penn Warren was born on 24 April 1905 in Guthrie, Kentucky, a small railroad town on the Tennessee-Kentucky boundary. His father, Robert Franklin Warren, was a small businessman who ran a number of ventures. His mother, Anna Ruth Penn Warren, was a schoolteacher. Although Robert Franklin Warren's own education had been interrupted, and his circumstances reduced, by the death of his mother, the Warrens raised their two sons and daughter in a middle-class and well-read household. The young Robert Penn Warren excelled in school, skipping two grades and graduating from high school at the age of fifteen. He spent many of his childhood summers in Cerulean Springs on the farm of his maternal grandfather, Thomas Gabriel Penn, who had served as a Confederate cavalry officer under Nathan Bedford Forrest during the Civil War. A brooding but larger-than-life figure who appears repeatedly in Warren's poetry, Gabriel Penn shared with his grandson his interest in European and

American history. He also told Robert stories about his own experiences, such as the hair-raising incident in which he and his soldiers summarily executed a party of "bushwackers" (nominally guerrillas, in fact merely predators) in Civil War Tennessee, a story Warren retold in his 1957 poem "Court-martial."

Like many ambitious young men of his generation, Warren sought admission to the U.S. Naval Academy, spending a postgraduate year at Clarksville High School in Tennessee to prepare himself. Shortly before he was to depart for Annapolis he lost the use of one eye in a freak accident and was at risk of developing sympathetic blindness in the other. A naval career now being out of the question, his parents arranged for him to attend Vanderbilt University in the fall. It turned out to be a fortunate improvisation, for there Warren had John Crowe Ransom for a teacher and Allen Tate for a friend, and became associated with the literary circle later known as the Fugitive group.

ASSOCIATION WITH THE FUGITIVE GROUP

The Fugitives began informally as a group of young professionals, some of them veterans of the World War I, some of them associated with Vanderbilt, who came together to discuss philosophy in the living room of Sidney Mttron Hirsch, the eccentric polymath who drew them all together. Gradually their interests shifted in the direction of poetry, which they both wrote and studied intensely. Although the tastes of the older members of the group—Ransom most especially—favored the poetry of Thomas Hardy and A. E. Housman, the young members, Tate most passionately but Warren as well, were fascinated by the poetry of T. S. Eliot and Ezra Pound that was just coming into circulation. Even before the publication of *The Waste Land* (1922), the young Warren, fresh out of a Tennessee high school, was writing poetry of a startlingly Eliotic kind. The end product of all this passionate investment in poetry was *The Fugitive*, a little magazine that—like *Secession, Broom, The Double Dealer,* and *The Dial*—made a mark in the history of poetry far out of proportion to its limited circulation and its short life span, publishing poems of Warren, Tate, Ransom, Donald Davidson, Merrill Moore, and Laura Riding. The example and the enthusiasms of the poets who published in *The Fugitive* both taught a later generation of writers what writing is, and also bound them to a heritage they would have to resist in order to become themselves. These poets shaped, both positively and negatively, the literary careers of writers as diverse as Hart Crane, Stark Young, Andrew Lytle, Robert Lowell, Randall Jarrell, Peter Taylor, Flannery O'Connor, and Reynolds Price.

Upon graduation from Vanderbilt, Warren attended graduate school at the University of California at Berkeley and at Yale and won a Rhodes Scholarship to Oxford, but he found the world of literary scholarship dull and indeed less literary, less attuned to the making and serious reading of poetry, than his circle of semiamateurs in Nashville. The best parts of his education at these great universities being extracurricular, Warren never did finish his doctoral work. While at Berkeley, Warren met Emma Brescia, the brilliant but unstable daughter of the composer and conductor Domenico Brescia, whom he married secretly before leaving for his term at Oxford. While at Oxford, Warren published the first of his more than forty books, *John Brown, the Making of a Martyr* (1929). This debunking popular biography, ironic and defensive in tone, was one of a series of Confederate-slanted historical works produced by writers associated with the Fugitives, such as Allen Tate's biography of Stonewall Jackson and Andrew Lytle's biography of Nathan Bedford Forrest. Men driven to bloodshed in the name of high ideals were to become something of a key subject for Warren; one can see John Brown in Warren's darkest protagonist, Jeremiah Beaumont of *World Enough and Time* (1950). Through such figures of cruel idealism, Warren is led to brood on the deep problem at the heart of much of his political fiction, the problem of the inner connection between our deepest values and the heart of darkness, the logic that connects our most central moral motivations with our least moral acts, making nothing more dangerous to us and to our world than our own virtues. But John Brown in Warren's biography is only intermittently such a figure; more often he is a pure con artist and humbug, whose financial double-dealing and shady business practices are more out of Mark Twain's world than Joseph Conrad's.

During his time at Oxford, Warren also wrote "The Briar Patch," his contribution to *I'll Take My Stand* (1929). This volume, by a group of twelve southerners whose membership overlapped that of the Fugitive circle, was the manifesto of the Agrarian movement, which argued that industrialization, urbanization, and modernization generally would cost the South much of what was valuable about its traditional culture. As an economic program, the book's defense of Jeffersonian yeoman agriculture is sentimental nonsense, but literary people were often attracted to economic nonsense in the late 1920s, and were even more attracted to crank theories like Social Credit in the 1930s. Next to Social Credit, fascism, and Stalinism, Agrarianism seems like a mere hobbyhorse. Agrarianism is in any event best understood as a literary rather than a political or economic movement. Most of the Agrarians, after all, were and remained professors, not farmers or politicians, and many were creative writers, not social scientists. What seems to have been most on their minds was the distaste for modern culture they saw in figures like Leo Tolstoy and William Butler Yeats, and it is a long slide from there down to Action Française and Mussolini.

Warren was in England while the movement was being organized, and he does not seem to have been very much invested in the Agrarians' actual program. "The Briar Patch," however, is a foolish essay, and Warren regretted writing it to the end of his days. Its main argument is that industrial development of the South, such as had been proposed by Henry Grady in the 1890s as the chief engine for modernization of the South's economy and culture, would not solve the problem of race hatred, because the factory owners would whip up racial antagonism to keep the unions out. Warren wrote this essay from the standpoint of someone who opposes race hatred (as expressed in such things as lynchings) but supports racial segregation. To some extent the defense of segregation in "The Briar Patch" is mere protective coloration, designed to make its principal argument palatable to southern readers, but the essay also reflects the unexamined loyalty many decent-enough white southerners gave to segregation. In the essay's defense, though, one should point out that Warren also argued that if the South were going to adopt the separate but equal position, it would have to do rather more to ensure the realization of the "equal" part (an argument that offended Donald Davidson, one of the Twelve Southerners), and that any white man who fails to treat the black man with respect fails also to respect himself. The main argument of the essay itself, for that matter, is one that no fully committed racist would have made.

Warren's convictions about race changed over the years. Even while writing "The Briar Patch," he felt that his defense of segregation was strained, and his struggles with making southern culture come to life in the writing of his first novella, *Prime Leaf* (1930), persuaded him that much of his defense of southern politics would have to go by the boards. Warren's convictions on racial segregation changed slowly but thoroughly, and in such later works as *Segregation: The Inner Conflict in the South* (1956) and *Who Speaks for the Negro?* (1965), Warren emerged as an important, if sometimes cautious, southern integrationist. Segregation had gathered around itself all of the hysteria of threatened cultural loyalty; Warren's work in these years was to argue that the South could accept integration without becoming merely another version of the North. (indeed, since even under segregation there was a great deal more social intimacy between white and black in the South than in the North, an integrated South might have a few lessons to teach the North), and that to accept integration was not to abandon one's southernness but to become a better kind of southerner. *Who Speaks for the Negro?* contains interviews with dozens of significant figures of African-American political and cultural life, from Ralph Ellison (one of Warren's closest friends) and James Baldwin through Martin Luther King Jr. and Malcolm X. Warren was one of the last journalists to speak with Malcolm X. To the surprise of both, they got along famously and set up further meetings, which were aborted by Malcolm's assassination. Warren caught Malcolm in the midst of his movement away from the racist theology of Elijah Muhammad, and he caught the public intellectuals of the African-American community at the moment when integrationism was beginning to give way to a much harder-edged nationalist separatism. Few writers could have caught all the nuances of these transformations with Warren's sensitivity.

YEARS AT LOUISIANA STATE UNIVERSITY

After Warren returned to the United States in 1930, he took short-term positions in the English departments of Vanderbilt and Southwestern College in Memphis before landing a position at Louisiana State University (LSU) in Baton Rouge. Although by that time Huey Long had left the governorship in the hands of his subordinate, O. K. Allen, he was still the dominant presence in the state and LSU was very much his creation, an institution he was very much concerned to put on the map. Long interfered a great deal in everything he ran: he deposed the editor of the student newspaper for criticizing him, and not only wrote all the football team's marching songs but also called plays from the stands. He left the English Department alone, however, and he never insisted that the *Southern Review*, the distinguished literary quarterly edited by Warren and Cleanth Brooks, follow his party line. (Indeed, although it was traditional then to consider the *Southern Review* a right-wing periodical, the *Partisan Review*, then a distinctly left-wing periodical, published many of the same authors.)

Warren's own feelings about Long were ambivalent. He saw the urgent human needs that gave Long power and which Long did in fact do something to address, but he also saw Long's power hunger and his disregard for the rule of law. Long's daughter took his Shakespeare course, and Warren remembered that when he lectured about *Julius Caesar*, the usual background noise of knitting needles was not to be heard: the students all knew what that play was about. Warren's poetry took on a harder, more formal quality during this period, seeking—as did the work of many others at this time—a dark and lapidary style under the tutelage of John Donne, Andrew Marvell, and other Elizabethan masters. For Warren, this effort culminated in *Thirty-Six Poems* (1935), a volume issued by the same small press that published Wallace Stevens's *Ideas of Order* (1935), and in the even darker and somewhat phantasmagoric *Eleven Poems on the Same Theme* (1942), published by New Directions.

Warren's most influential work of this period was a series of textbooks, *An Approach to Literature* (1936), *Understanding Poetry* (1938), *Understanding Fiction* (1943), and *Modern Rhetoric* (1949), all written with Cleanth Brooks. Because *Understanding Poetry* was associated with New Criticism, and because New Criticism has fallen out of favor, it is altogether too easy to see that book as part of an attempt to treat poetry as detached from its political and historical context and to promote a habit of purely aesthetic reading that might serve the purposes of a politically conservative quietism. This view of New Criticism certainly does not describe what Warren actually practiced, especially in his later works on Dreiser and Melville. (Indeed, the anthology of American literature that Warren, Cleanth Brooks, and R. W. B. Lewis published in 1973, *American Literature: The Makers and the Making*, was easily the most historically literate anthology of its day, and considerably more historically literate than most competing anthologies even decades later; it was also, with its interest in folksongs, tall tales, spirituals, political oratory, and Native American speeches, invested in a broad idea of the American literary canon before broad ideas of that canon were a popular concern.) The best way to think about *Understanding Poetry* is to remember that it began life as a pile of mimeographs under the title "Sophomore Poetry Manual" and that it was designed for use at the public university of the poorest state in the Union in the depths of the Great Depression. The purpose of the book is to give a craftsman's inside view of the making of poetry to students who might otherwise not think of poetry as part of their intellectual world; it aims at sharpening the reader's poetic sensibility in the same way that all those evening conversations in Sidney Hirsch's living room sharpened the young Robert Penn Warren's. It provides those things the intellectually hungry young man from Guthrie got from the amateurs in Nashville and did not get from the professionals at Berkeley, Yale, and Oxford.

EARLY NOVELS

Warren's first novel is also the fruit of his years at LSU. *Night Rider* (1939) concerns the attempts during the first years of the twentieth century of the mostly poor tobacco farmers of Kentucky and Tennessee to organize a collective in order to counteract the power of the great buyers, which resulted in an upheaval known to historians as the Black Patch War, the major turning point of which took place in Guthrie two years before Warren's birth. The novel should be seen in the context of other novels of social conflict, such as Frank Norris's *The Octopus* (1901) and the protest novels of the 1930s, but as with Warren's other political fictions, it is Conrad's combination of irony and compassion that seems to underlie Warren's practice. Warren brings to the novel of social protest a morally complex sensibility, what he called, in an essay about Katherine Anne Porter, "irony with a center." He is aware of the tragic inner contradictions of the movements he describes, and while unable to resolve them, he is also unwilling to retreat into sterile cynicism.

Perse Munn, the protagonist (whom the narrator always refers to derisively as "Mr. Munn"), finds himself almost by accident in a position of leadership in the farmer's Association. Like many Warren protagonists, Mr. Munn is a detached figure, aware of a kind of inner emptiness, someone who hopes that strenuous political commitments might yield him a deeper identity; indeed, what moves him to eloquence at the Association meeting where he first makes his mark is his reflections upon the sight of some of the suffering people before him. His eloquence is the product of his longing for their kind of integrity, but longing does not of itself produce integrity. (One can see him as a distant descendant of Henry James's John Marcher or of Hawthorne's Wakefield.) Early in the novel he defends a poor farmer named Bunk Trevelyan from a murder charge because he is convinced that somehow Trevelyan's wife seems to be more at the heart of life than he is, and in the service of this quest for life he (only half realizing what he is doing) frames an innocent African American. In the end Trevelyan does the dirty work for the Association, and ultimately—after trying to blackmail the organization—is killed by Munn himself. The Trevelyan subplot partly turns on what comes of an unthinking idealization of people whom one thinks of as victimized. Munn is very slow to see exactly what Trevelyan is because he has a moral investment in not seeing him accurately; idealizing Trevelyan is a way he can silence his doubts about his own moral authority. Trevelyan draws Munn, or rather, through Trevelyan, Munn draws himself, deeper and deeper into a snarl of discrediting complicities, which his ultimate murder of Trevelyan does not cut through but only further tangles. At each step Munn seems passive, almost sleepwalking, even when he involves himself centrally in the novel's violent action.

The movement itself, faced with resistance from the growers, descends in a self-destructive spiral of violence. The "Night Riders" of the title are the Association's enforcers, who seek to keep the farmers who have refused to join the Association from cutting separate deals with the buyers—first by threats, then by scraping their beds of young plants, then by burning their barns. Finally, the Association's acts unleash a storm of racist intimidation, not because the Association's aims have any obvious racial angle, but because the atmosphere of violence the Association fosters lets the genie of racist ugliness out of the bottle. The increasing violence of the Association ultimately plays into the buyers' hands, since it forces the authorities to bring in soldiers to restore order. Warren's treatment of this descent, however, is nuanced and sensitive, since the Association does not start out as a sinister organization and each step appears in its immediate context to be an at least plausible response to the exigencies of a very fallen world. Therefore, although it is clear that the Association completely loses its way, it is not clear at what point it crosses the line, and the narrator's sympathies, for all his criticism of the

Association's acts, are always with the farmers, never with the buyers. Kenneth Burke summed up Warren's stance in the novel very well in describing *Night Riders* as a work of "tragic liberalism."

Munn's moral disintegration parallels that of the Association, but takes an even darker turn. In tandem with his political descent is his sexual descent, his grubby affair with Lucile Christian and ultimately his rape of his own wife, whom he has been subjecting to an escalating series of small cruelties in the apparent belief that through cruelty he may somehow burn through his inner numbness. Ultimately, he stops short of his one final planned act of violence, the murder of Senator Tolliver, who had backed the Association to begin with but lost his nerve as the struggle turned ugly. Munn faces his own death, at the hands of the soldiers who have been called in to restore order, with a combination of resignation and indifference.

Like all of Warren's first four novels, *Night Rider* includes an inset short story, the story of Willie Proudfit. These inset stories—the narrative of Ashby Windham in *At Heaven's Gate* (1943), the Cass Mastern episode in *All the King's Men*, and the story of Munn Short in *World Enough and Time*—work through a moral economy that contrasts with the situation of the protagonists of the larger novel. The protagonists of the inset *exempla* have all committed unrightable wrongs, but by facing themselves unflinchingly, by acknowledging their involvement in a vast network of complicity in which it is never possible to be morally pure, they are able to work through an experience of soul-destroying evil to gain a kind of redemptive knowledge. While unable to extricate them from their crimes, it nevertheless saves them from the sense of despair and meaninglessness to which knowledge of complicity might lend itself.

If *Night Rider* demands to be seen as a social-realist novel, *At Heaven's Gate* (1943) demands to be seen as a high modernist novel, with highly stylized narration and multiple points of view. Although in embracing the cause of the farmers against the buyers *Night Rider* in some way embodied Agrarian values, it was also in some ways a devastating critique of Agrarianism, not only in that the Association's own methods bring it to grief, but also in that the novel's most fallen characters are not actual small farmers, but sympathetic town folk like Mr. Munn, whose attraction to Agrarian values is uncomfortably like that of the Agrarians themselves—intellectuals from a small city who yearn for a more authentic life close to the soil. *At Heaven's Gate* is a novel of the city, of Nashville, but its values are more straightforwardly Agrarian than

the values embodied in *Night Rider*, since it critiques the urban values of the New South.

At Heaven's Gate turns on the machinations of a corrupt financier, Bogan Murdock, who promises development and modernization (now we might say "globalization") and whose misadventures are based on the real doings of an actual Nashville financier, Rogers Clark Caldwell. We see Murdock's empire through the eyes of his young protégé, Jerry Calhoun, who—enticed by the older man's charisma—entangles himself further and further in moral toils, going so far as even to dispossess his own father. Like Mr. Munn, Calhoun is something of a sleepwalker, and does not so much choose his acts as discover himself already in the midst of doing them. As he is drawn further into Murdock's corrupt schemes, he is also drawn into a relationship with Sue Murdock, the boss's doomed, rebellious daughter. (Sue Murdock, in her combination of sexual vulnerability and sexual cruelty, in her predatory crassness that somehow never fully undoes the idealized emotional investment the novel has in her, stands in a long line of doomed heroines of southern fiction. She is a darker, but also more victimized Candace Compson, and Peyton Loftis of William Styron's *Lie Down in Darkness* [1951] is her literary daughter.)

Jerry's affair with Sue is at once a kind of proxy affair with her father and an Oedipal transgression against him. Seeing through Jerry as she does, Sue alternately manipulates and scorns him, which increases her magnetism for him. To mortify her father, she goes on to affairs with Jason Sweetwater, a labor organizer who has just led a turbulent but failed attempt to organize Murdock's coal miners on Massey Mountain. Sue then leaves Sweetwater for Slim Sarrett, a poet, boxer, literary critic, and closeted homosexual whose romantic lies about his earlier life (he had claimed that his father had been killed in a steamboat explosion), and whose sexual identity, are both exposed in a humiliating way. Sarrett ultimately murders Sue and escapes to a new life in the North (while a black servant is implicated in his crime). Public sympathy for Murdock in the wake of his daughter's death ironically keeps Murdock's corrupt dealings from destroying his empire and Jerry Calhoun is left to go to jail in Murdock's place.

ALL THE KING'S MEN

Warren began thinking about a text on the rise and fall of Huey Long as early as 1937, when he began work on the verse drama *Proud Flesh*. Although *Proud Flesh* was produced for the stage in Minnesota after Warren left LSU in 1942 (LSU having diverted the money for his promotion into extra feed for the mascot, Mike the Tiger), by 1943 Warren had become dissatisfied with the drama, and was reworking the material into a novel.

When *All the King's Men* appeared in 1946, it was widely taken as a commentary on the possibility that European-style totalitarianism might arise also in the United States. While it was natural at that time to see Warren's book as a cousin to Sinclair Lewis's *It Can't Happen Here* (1935), and while other books, such as Hamilton Basso's *Sun in Capricorn* (1942) and Adria Locke Langley's *A Lion Is in the Streets* (1945), had seized upon Huey Long as the prototype American totalitarian, *All the King's Men* is best seen as a novel about populism, not totalitarianism. The novel turns on the conflict between upland Populists and lowland Bourbons that had been a theme of southern politics since Reconstruction. Willie Talos overturns the power of lowland aristocrats who have ruled the state for sixty years in their own interest and who have always clothed themselves in the trappings of disinterestedness, virtue, and noblesse oblige. His willingness to transgress the law is a reflection of his sense that where law does not serve human need it lacks moral authority, and any law that stands in the way of urgent human need is made to be broken. Willie's views do not quite reduce to the Stalinist claim that one must break eggs if one is to make an omelette, a view that could justify almost anything. His view is that law is the servant and not the master of an ideal of justice that is best embodied in the human flourishing of the poor, and that one does not understand the meaning of the law if one allows legal technicalities to stand in the way of feeding the hungry. But that argument is one reason why Willie gets into trouble, for if one's vices are motivated by one's virtues, one does not recognize one's vices as vices until it is too late to free oneself from them.

Willie portrays himself as a figure that is willing to break law to serve justice, and so long as he is making his case against those whose sense of their own uprightness has a large measure of self-interest, he holds his own very well. But when he himself begins to doubt whether he really does ultimately serve justice, he finds himself in trouble. When the state auditor, Byram White, is caught with his hand in the till, Willie humiliates him, but—fearful of giving his opponents an opening—lets him off the hook. This moves Willie's upright attorney general, Hugh Miller, to resign in protest. Miller's resignation seems to cause Willie to feel a crisis of confidence, to which he responds by promising to build a large free hospital that he can leave as a legacy.

The hospital project becomes the focus of a kind of moral hysteria, as if Willie were using the project to prove his own moral worth to himself. Willie is very eager to keep certain corrupt contractors (who are tied to his political enemies but will betray them for a price) out of the hospital project. Willie's rigidity about making this deal at first seems strange, because one might have thought that the good of building the hospital would outweigh the bad of a few greased palms. After all, as Willie had said to Adam Stanton, his candidate for chief surgeon at the hospital, you have to make the good out of the bad, because there is not anything else to make it from. But Willie had gotten his own political start fighting a corrupt construction contract, and in his moment of self-doubt his seizing upon this issue is a way of proving to himself that he is really morally different from his enemies, which is why his normally loose-jointed pragmatism will not serve him in this crisis.

Ultimately, it is Willie's own desire to prove that he really was on the right side after all that undoes him. He is driven by a blackmail attempt against his wastrel son to make a deal with the contractor Gummy Larson in an arrangement brokered by his oleaginous lieutenant governor, Tiny Duffy. While Willie is still fuming over that concession, his son dies in a football accident, which moves him to repudiate the deal. Tiny Duffy, enraged over Willie's act, sets in motion the machinery that results in Willie's assassination by tipping off the tense, vindictive, puritanical Adam Stanton about Willie's affair with Adam's sister, Anne Stanton, knowing that this will drive Adam into killing Willie.

Willie's story is not that of a politician who goes bad because he is tempted by power into corruption. It is a story of the unresolvable contradiction between law and justice, where law functions with sterile and mechanical ferocity (and serves the interests of the powerful) while justice, by motivating the breaking of law, invites a descent into chaos. The lament of *All the King's Men* is not that absolute power corrupts absolutely, but that good and the means of good are irreconcilable.

All the King's Men is also the story of Jack Burden, who was merely a walk-on character in *Proud Flesh* but is the protagonist of *All the King's Men*. Jack is the alienated son of a well-to-do Gulf Coast family with strong political connections and a long history in the state. He is revolted by the shallowness and materialism of Burden's Landing, the family's home town. But he is at a psychological and sexual impasse as much as at a political and moral one. Jack is offended by the sexual predaceousness of his mother, who cast off his father and has since collected husbands and furniture with the same avidity. And he is unable to accept the life of a Burden's Landing aristocrat, partly because of an inability to settle on a calling and partly out of a genuine moral revulsion against that life. He has a failed romance with his neighbor, Anne Stanton, and a close but vexed relationship with her brother, the remote, intense, puritanical Adam Stanton. He also has a strong tie to an elderly neighbor, a retired judge named Montague Irwin. Casting off his Burden's Landing life, and unable to complete his dissertation in history, he puts his research skills to work for Willie, digging up dirt on his opponents.

The crisis in Jack's career comes when he is asked to investigate Judge Irwin, whose hidden, corrupt past he discovers. As the tangled plot concerning the hospital project unfolds, he is dispatched to put pressure on Judge Irwin, who evades the threat by shooting himself. Jack is told by his mother the next morning that the judge was actually his father. Jack is probably the only character in the Western canon whose moral redemption is worked by causing his father's death. Understanding that the judge could have saved himself by telling Jack of their relationship, Jack comes to the conclusion that in a way his suicide was an act of moral courage. What Jack learns from this is that the moral life is a quest not for purity but for understanding the meaning of one's complicities and for reaching past complicities to a sad wisdom. It is this wisdom of complicity that ultimately is the political and the moral burden of the novel.

The wisdom of complicity with which *All the King's Men* concludes is a reflection on the political events of the late 1940s, not of the middle 1930s. Like Ralph Ellison's *Invisible Man* (1952), Jack Burden revises his political enthusiasms of the 1930s, but does not really repudiate them; he has been chastened, tempered in the fires of irony, but he has not turned his coat. And the wisdom of complicity, the recognition that all human beings, as human beings, have a share in the human darkness, is a lesson specifically of the postwar era. That is because World War II had shown all people how vulnerable to that darkness, and how close to it, we all are, and had offered us the temptation, which only sad wisdom can keep one from disastrously embracing, to view ourselves as exempt from human fallenness.

WORLD ENOUGH AND TIME

Warren's next novel, *World Enough and Time* (1950), marks the close of Warren's best period as a novelist. Warren began to think about the novel as early as 1944 when—while he was serving as poetry consultant to the Library of Congress—the novelist Katherine Anne Porter gave him a copy of a pamphlet called *The Confessions of Jeroboam O. Beauchamp* with the remark that the story was "exactly up his alley." The Kentucky Tragedy, as the story of the 1826 murder of Kentucky politician Solomon Sharp by his former protégé, Jeroboam Beauchamp, is called, had been told several times in the nineteenth century, in novels by Thomas Holley Chivers and William Gilmore Simms and in Edgar Allan Poe's play, *Politian* (1835). Warren's version, the darkest novel in his oeuvre, is a meditation on the fatality of a certain kind of idealism and on the kinship between idealism and sadism.

Jeremiah Beaumont, the novel's protagonist, is educated as a lawyer by Colonel Cassius Fort, whose probity and rectitude he admires. Hearing that his benefactor had seduced and abandoned a woman in a distant county, Beaumont—feeling a revulsion against the advantages he had gained by being Fort's protégé—spontaneously resolves to marry the woman and murder her seducer. The woman in question, Rachel Jordan, is not at first enthusiastic about this scheme, but Beaumont manages through persistence and sheer force of will to extort her into demanding revenge from him. Beaumont wants to see himself as a revenge seeker, but he is also aware that unless Rachel really does want revenge, then he is only a bullying madman. He is perceptive enough to see that Rachel is reluctant and clever enough to argue that her reluctance may be failure of nerve and self-betrayal (and therefore a further indictment of Fort) rather than plain sanity. As with each person whose desire to serve others involves overriding their wishes in favor of his or her own conception of their true interests, the line between serving others and dominating them cannot be easily drawn.

For the same reasons, it is hard to distinguish in Beaumont's case between eros and cruelty and between sexual repression and a highly refined form of sadism in which revulsion against sexuality itself takes on a sexual thrill. Beaumont himself has moment of anguished self-doubt about his own motives, and indeed his cruelest acts are not so much the product of direct fanaticism so much as of his attempts to shout down his own doubts about his project. Characteristically, he treats his own moments of self-doubt as moments of weakness rather than of sanity, as moments of betrayal of Rachel rather than as moments in which he might discover what in fact she really wants. (As the story unfolds, however, Rachel becomes so swept up in Beaumont's dark enthusiasm that it is hard to say what she really desires; neither she nor the reader any longer has a clear idea what she wants in her own right.)

At this point a political crisis intervenes. The economy of Kentucky collapses and a shortage of specie makes it impossible for debtors to meet their obligations. The legislature passes a replevin bill, allowing for debtor relief. The bill unleashes a violent conflict between Relief and Anti-Relief groups, with both Beaumont and Fort finding themselves on the Relief side. The state supreme court rules that the replevin bill is unconstitutional but the legislature responds by replacing the court with a more compliant one. (In interviews about this book, Warren has pointed out how much these events resemble the national court-packing crisis of 1937.) This last step is too much for Colonel Fort, who comes out against the new court. Fort and Beaumont run against each other for the state legislature, and in the course of the campaign a pamphlet appears accusing Fort of having fathered Rachel Jordan's long-dead child. Another pamphlet appears, saying that that child was in fact begotten by one of Rachel Jordan's slaves. This accusation finally provides Jeremiah with the pretext for murdering Fort, which he rather clumsily does just as Fort is preparing to announce a solution to the court crisis that he thinks will satisfy everyone. (In the Beauchamp case, as in the novel, the second pamphlet was apparently the work of members of Beauchamp's own party, attempting to provoke him into the murder he went on to commit.)

In a tangled and byzantine trial, Beaumont is convicted. He and Rachel botch a suicide pact in their underground cell. Then they manage (unlike Beauchamp) to escape execution, finally taking refuge in the swampy country between the Cumberland and Tennessee Rivers with a degenerate bandit called La Grande Bosse. There they succumb to despair and Rachel dies; Jeremiah atones for his sins, and as he is returning to turn himself in to the authorities he is jumped by bounty hunters and beheaded.

For all of Beaumont's folly and violence, Warren can never treat him with the irony with which he treats Mr. Munn or Jerry Calhoun, because in some hard-to-define way he retains a kind of nobility and even eloquence despite everything, and if he is maddened, at least he is maddened by justice. But the novel leaves the reader no safe place to stand. Beaumont and the New Court faction stand for the people, yet their politics can produce only chaos. The Old Court group stands for order, but the order is unjust and venal. Beaumont's quest for a more than human moral perfection makes him demonic. But as the narrator keeps cautioning us, we cannot jeer at him without becoming small, contemptible, and self-pitying, because we jeer at him for embracing ambitions we were always too shallow to entertain for ourselves. If his idealism is illusion and vanity, our realism is self-pity and cowardice. The novel ends in a moral impasse of which it can make us more deeply aware but which it cannot solve.

The period of Warren's greatest fame as a novelist was a time of personal crisis. Warren reports that after he finished his long narrative poem *The Ballad of Billie Potts* in 1943, he could not finish another poem for ten years. Warren, like Thomas Hardy, always thought of himself as a poet who wrote novels, so despite the success of Warren's fiction during this period, he described it as a kind of dark age. The poetic impasse may have had a biographical origin. These are the years of the disintegration of his first marriage, and Warren's poetry began coming again almost immediately after he married the novelist and travel writer Eleanor Clark in 1952. But the impasse could also have arisen from Warren's sense of having exhausted the resources of the tensely formal, darkly impersonal, morally bleak style he brought to perfection in *Eleven Poems on the Same Theme* in 1942. Once Warren's poetry began to revive in what became the book-length *Brother to Dragons* (1953), his novels moved away from the center of his mind. Still, in *Band of Angels* (1955) Warren produced perhaps the classic instance of the "tragic mulatto" story, and in *The Cave* (1959) (a novel loosely based on the Floyd Collins case, about the commotion and upheaval surrounding the failed attempt to rescue a trapped spelunker from a Kentucky cave) and *Flood* (1964) (a novel that turns on an alienated writer's return to his hometown to make a film about its last days before its obliteration by a Tennessee Valley Authority dam), Warren captured something of the deracination and shallowness of a modernized South.

REVIVAL OF WARREN'S POETIC CAREER

Warren's poetic career came back to life in two very different books. The breakthrough volume was *Brother to Dragons*, a tale in verse and voices concerning the murder of a slave by two of Thomas Jefferson's nephews, Lilburne and Isham Lewis, in Smithland, Kentucky, on the evening of the great New Madrid earthquake of 1811, a murder to which the historical Jefferson never seems to have responded. Warren began work on it in the early 1940s, planning a narrative poem in a balladic style much like *The Ballad of Billie Potts*. He quickly grew impatient with what he derisively called the imitation of folk simplicity, and the failed poem gnawed at him until it was finally published in 1953. Even after its initial publication it remained an obsessive concern, and Warren republished it as a two-act play in 1976 and as an extensively rewritten narrative poem in 1979. He was at work on yet another version as late as 1987. For all of its manifest imperfections—its hyperbolic language, its lack of architectonic control, its relentlessly extreme emotionalism—*Brother to Dragons* is the most intellectually ambitious and original work in Warren's oeuvre. *Brother to Dragons* is called "a tale in verse and voices." Set in "no place" and in "no time," its various characters—Thomas Jefferson, the Lewis brothers, the murdered slave, George, and Warren himself—seem to appear out of darkness and to return to it, not always aware of each other's presence. The center of the poem is a long confrontation between Jefferson and Warren in which they argue about the meaning of the murder.

The Thomas Jefferson who speaks in the poem does not much resemble the historical president. The fictional Jefferson has become embittered by the failure of his Enlightenment faith in human nature and by the shortcomings of the United States, the embodiment of the Enlightenment ideals that Jefferson himself wrote into the Declaration of Independence. In a figure of speech quite shocking in its rage, Jefferson compares the relationship between his vision of human possibility and actual human nature to the relationship between Pasiphae and the bull, comparing the elaborate artificiality of his philosophy to the mechanical bull, the "infatuate machine of her invention," in which Pasiphae waited "laced, latched, thonged up, and breathlessly ass-humped / For the ecstatic stroke." Warren could hardly make a harsher case against idealism and against American exceptionalism than his Jefferson does here. But in Jefferson's revulsion against all things human, one last and most destructive vice still lingers, the hope of purifying one's self through rage, even through rage directed against the self.

Jefferson's sister Lucy, the mother of the Lewis boys, intervenes. Perhaps without much justification she feels some complicity in the murder. That is because Lilburne—unable to resolve his grief over her death (since he, rightly, believes that his own alcoholic sadism, particularly toward his slaves, had something to do with causing it)—murdered his slave George (John in the 1979 revision) in a rage after the young boy had accidentally

(or perhaps not) broken a pitcher once belonging to Lucy. (In some way the whole story has to do with the boys' unresolved guilt about Lucy. Once their crime is discovered—the chimney into which they had bricked the remains of the slave George having been thrown over by the New Madrid earthquake that evening—the brothers attempt to shoot each other over Lucy's grave. But Lilburne, perhaps deliberately, misfires his pistol, tricking the weaker Isham into killing him and taking the rap for the murder. Isham, however, escapes, later becoming one of the few American casualties at the Battle of New Orleans.) Lucy sees the whole story as being somehow about the failure of love, her love especially, to redeem her children from their own cruelty. Jefferson sees it instead as being about how love is itself inseparable from narcissist cruelty (being in essence a form of it), comparing love to the act of kissing a mirror already slimed with one's own saliva.

The moral crisis of the poem comes when Lucy insists that Jefferson take Lilburne's hand and acknowledge him, which Jefferson sternly refuses to do. Lucy, acutely noticing that Lilburne's cruelties are actually effects of his revulsion against his own inner darkness (as with Ahab or Roger Chillingworth, nothing makes one demonic so much as a fanatical revulsion against the demonic), argues that Jefferson's revulsion against Lilburne is a version of Lilburne's own crime. Jefferson's ultimate acknowledgement of Lilburne turns the poem toward its conclusion, in which a recognition of our complicity in human fallenness is the basis of a kind of wisdom that enables us, if not to be redeemed, at least not to be mastered by that fallenness.

Warren's notes to himself while he was writing *Brother to Dragons* are full of citations to Hannah Arendt's *The Origins of Totalitarianism* (1951). *Brother to Dragons*, obliquely, is Warren's holocaust book, and in it he wishes, in the manner of Reinhold Niebuhr, to turn the encounter with the worst human nature can do into an occasion through which, by a mutual recognition of human fallenness, human beings can stop torturing each other. *Brother to Dragons* is also Warren's Cold War book, warning the victorious United States of the dangers of a vindictive self-righteousness that might destroy the world in order to save it. And, coming as it does in the year preceding the decision in the case of *Brown v. Board of Education of Topeka* (1954), it is his civil rights book, possibly the most harrowing book about race written by any white southerner.

Warren's other breakthrough poetic book is *Promises* (1957). One of the repeated stories of 1950s poetry (the same story is told of Robert Lowell and of Adrienne Rich) is that of the rejection of a taut, impersonal, stylistically formal and tonally cold poetic ethos learned from Eliot in favor of a stylistically looser and more personal, even confessional ethos that became the poetic idiom of the 1950s and 1960s. Warren is moved by his new marriage and the births of his two children to reflect upon his history, his family, and his region. The result is a volume of two long poetic sequences that brood on the ways in which his children will have to come to terms with history (and with him) and make their own way in an imperfect world, perhaps with more wisdom than their father had, working out if not a way of healing that world at least a way of continuing a human life in the face of its darkness. The confessional style is said to have originated with W. D. Snodgrass in *Heart's Needle* (1959) and with Robert Lowell in *For the Union Dead* (1964). But in numerous ways *Promises* anticipates many of the strengths (and not many of the weaknesses) of that movement.

Warren's works over the next decade are concerned in large measure with the problem of working a pragmatic accommodation with a world that, for all its harshness, one has to come to love, with all one's own limitations and vices, and which one must somehow see as it is, without illusions but also without bitterness. This movement in Warren's poetry culminates in the complex but tender elegies he wrote for his father ("Mortmain," in 1960) and for his mother ("Tale of Time," in 1966).

LATE POETRY

With the volume *Incarnations* (1968), Warren's poetry took a fascinating turn. What is novel in *Incarnations* is the sequence of fifteen poems titled "Island of Summer," which is an extended meditation on the nonhuman inner ferocity of nature (and of human nature). Set on the isle of Port Cros in the Mediterranean, the first poem of the sequence, "What Day Is," reflects how the different waves of human habitation on the island all seem to have worn themselves down to nothing over time, leaving only the brilliant, dazzling emptiness of unfended sunlight, glittering everywhere like metal grit.

In the poem "Natural History," the poet sees human history as amoral and cruel in the way natural history is. The principal effect of the waves of bloody conquest of the island is that the root of the laurel has profited and the leaf of the live oak has achieved a new luster. The

poet's son finds a Nazi helmet with a neat, circular hole in one temple and a raw, jagged gash out the other. That dusk he observes a missile test, the missile exploding with a chilly but unearthly beauty in which there is a kind of truth, but a truth in which the human has no place at all.

The sequence concludes with a phantasmagoric subsequence called "The Leaf." The speaker seeks refuge in the shade of a fig tree whose hand-like leaves—their fingers broad, spatulate, stupid, ill-formed, and innocent—both conceal and reveal the shame of human living and human grief. The speaker remembers climbing to a hawk's nest, finding in the hawk's fierce perspective the point of view of absolute nature, bearing a kind of truth beyond knowledge and beyond survival. Ultimately, the speaker is folded into the whirl of natural process, but it is a natural process of which he cannot grasp the secret, and which he can behold but not master.

Audubon: A Vision (1969) works out the relationship between this apprehension of a nonhuman ferocity at the heart of nature, poetic sublimity, and what the poet is capable of knowing and bearing. "The Dream He Never Knew the End of," the long early narrative section of the poem, is a retelling of the story of the near murder of the naturalist and artist James Audubon by a weird innkeeper and her two loutish sons. The story, which Audubon himself told in "The Prairie," a chapter of his *Ornithological Biography* (1831–1839), is cast as a kind of initiation. Audubon lies awake under the bearskins, listening as the woman's oafish sons sharpen their knives, but he makes no move to prepare for his confrontation. Indeed, he imagines himself to be in the power of a fairy tale witch, and thinks that if he allows her to kill him, he will come into possession of an indefinable metaphysical secret. Just before the woman and her sons make their move, a party of hunters arrives, discovers the murder in prospect, and summarily lynches the would-be killers. Audubon watches, rapt, transfixed, but also oddly disappointed that now he will not grasp the secret that death would have vouchsafed him.

What Audubon discovers from this incident, and what seems to be the secret of his art, is "walking in the world," a way of holding death and truth before one all the time, not surrendering to it but allowing it to center and ground one's perception. Audubon is for Warren a model of artistic heroism, able to face the human darkness, and to understand that that darkness is also the darkness of the sublime, without being destroyed by it.

Warren's next three volumes—*Or Else* (1974), *Can I See Arcturus from Where I Stand* (1974), and *Now and Then* (1978)—show Warren at the height of his powers, working a dark and bleak vein of poetry worthy of Hardy with a demonic, and sometimes hilarious and manic, energy. These poems frequently center upon some moment of charged stillness, in which time stops and eternity breaks through and in which a sublime urgency reduces the poem to silence. Moments of charged stillness ground such poems as *Chain Saw at Dawn in Vermont in Time of Drouth*, where the insistent "*now! now!*" of the chain saw opens the poet's heart both to darkness and to compassion for those who, in their turn, must face that darkness. In poems like *Forever O'Clock*, a dazzle of no-time overwhelms the speaker in vertigo, but also marks a moment where language has been deformed by something beyond language. And in *Evening Hawk* the poet imagines a point of view beyond himself but accessible only to poetry, although poetry of a nonhuman kind, the point of view of a stern and clear eternity, imagined here as a hawk soaring in the last light of sunset, visible in the flash from the point of view of a speaker in darkness below.

Warren continued to write poetry of power and depth through his last volumes: *Being Here* (1980), *Rumor Verified* (1981), *Chief Joseph of the Nez Perce* (1982), and *Altitudes and Extensions* (1985), a remarkable harvest for a man reaching his eightieth year. Warren died in September of 1989. Yet it is "Heart of Autumn," the last poem of *Now and Then*, that seems to represent not only a final poetic testament, but a kind of self-elegy and palinode as well.

[*See also* Fugitives and Southern Agrarianism, The.]

SELECTED WORKS

John Brown: The Making of a Martyr (1929)
"The Briar Patch" (1929)
Prime Leaf (1930)
Thirty-Six Poems (1935)
An Approach to Literature (1936)
Understanding Poetry (1938)
Night Rider (1939)
Eleven Poems on the Same Theme (1942)
At Heaven's Gate (1943)
Understanding Fiction (1943)
All the King's Men (1946)
Modern Rhetoric (1949)
World Enough and Time (1950)
Brother to Dragons (1953)
Band of Angels (1955)

Segregation: The Inner Conflict in the South (1956)
Promises (1957)
The Cave (1959)
The Legacy of the Civil War (1961)
Wilderness (1961)
Flood (1964)
Who Speaks for the Negro? (1965)
Incarnations (1968)
Audubon: A Vision (1969)
Meet Me in the Green Glen (1971)
Or Else (1974)
Can I See Arcturus from Where I Stand (1974)
A Place to Come To (1977)
Now and Then (1978)
Being Here (1980)
Rumor Verified (1981)
Chief Joseph of the Nez Perce (1982)
Altitudes and Extensions (1985)

FURTHER READING

Bedient, Calvin. *In the Heart's Last Kingdom: Robert Penn Warren's Major Poetry*. Cambridge, Mass., 1984.

Blotner, Joseph. *Robert Penn Warren: A Biography*. New York, 1997.

Burt, John. *Robert Penn Warren and American Idealism*. New Haven, Conn., 1988.

Burt, John. *The Collected Poems of Robert Penn Warren*. Baton Rouge, La., 1998.

Casper, Leonard. *The Blood-Marriage of Earth and Sky: Robert Penn Warren's Later Novels*. Baton Rouge, La., 1997.

Clark, William Bedford, ed. *Critical Essays on Robert Penn Warren*. Boston, 1981.

Clark, William Bedford. *The American Vision of Robert Penn Warren*. Lexington, Ky., 1991.

Clark, William Bedford, ed. *Selected Letters of Robert Penn Warren*. Baton Rouge, La., 2000.

Conkin, Paul Keith. *The Southern Agrarians*. Nashville, Tenn., 1985.

Corrigan, Lesa Carnes. *Poems of Pure Imagination: Robert Penn Warren and the Romantic Tradition*. Baton Rouge, La., 1991.

Donohue, Cecilia. *Robert Penn Warren's Novels: Feminine and Feminist Discourse*. New York, 1999.

Ferriss, Lucy. *Sleeping with the Boss: Female Subjectivity and Narrative Pattern in Robert Penn Warren*. Baton Rouge, La., 1997.

Grimshaw, James A. *Understanding Robert Penn Warren*. Columbia, S.C., 2001.

Grimshaw, James A., and James A. Perkins, eds. *Robert Penn Warren's* All the King's Men: *Three Stage Versions.* Athens, Ga., 2001.

Guttenberg, Barnett. *Web of Being: The Novels of Robert Penn Warren.* Nashville, Tenn., 1975.

Hendricks, Randy. *Lonelier Than God: Robert Penn Warren and the Southern Exile.* Athens, Ga., 2000.

Justus, James H. *The Achievement of Robert Penn Warren.* Baton Rouge, La., 1981.

Koppelman, Robert S. *Robert Penn Warren's Modernist Spirituality.* Columbia, Mo., 1995.

Rubin, Louis D. *The Wary Fugitives: Four Poets and the South.* Baton Rouge, La., 1978.

Runyon, Randolph. *The Taciturn Text: The Fiction of Robert Penn Warren.* Columbus, Ohio, 1990.

Stewart, John L. *The Burden of Time: The Fugitives and Agrarians.* Baton Rouge, La., 1965.

Strandberg, Victor. *The Poetic Vision of Robert Penn Warren.* Lexington, Ky., 1977.

Walker, Marshall. *Robert Penn Warren, a Vision Earned.* New York, 1979.

Watkins, Floyd C. *Then and Now: The Personal Past in the Poetry of Robert Penn Warren.* Lexington, Ky., 1982.

Watkins, Floyd C., and John T. Hiers, eds. *Robert Penn Warren Talking: Interviews, 1950–1978.* New York, 1980.

See also the article on *All the King's Men*, immediately following.

ROBERT PENN WARREN'S
ALL THE KING'S MEN

by John Burt

All the King's Men (1946), by Robert Penn Warren, is the most important novel of American politics. Warren's novel broods upon the issues raised by the rise and fall, in the late 1920s and early 1930s, of the Huey Long regime in Louisiana. Although there are many parallels between the careers of the two ruthless southern governors, Warren always denied that Willie Talos (Willie Stark in published editions before 2001, when the typescript name was restored) was based in any very exact way upon Long himself. Warren explained that he knew Willie from the inside, as he did not know Huey.

Warren borrowed from current events a great deal more than the general themes and political history of the Long regime, so that many of the small details of Willie Talos's life and character are unmistakably Long's. But Warren drew most of the key plot devices from his own creativity, not from history.

When the novel appeared only months after the end of World War II, it was inevitably seen as recounting the story of a potential American totalitarian leader and as admonishing American readers about the ease with which the United States might have gone the way of the Soviet Union or Germany in the 1930s. It was later taken as a cautionary tale about the corrupting influence of political power on leaders with idealist convictions, a warning about how absolute power corrupts absolutely even when the aims which that power desires to serve are good ones.

Neither of these views quite describes the novel. Willie is by no stretch of the imagination a totalitarian leader, although he certainly does practice a great deal of political intimidation (chiefly by blackmailing his opponents with evidence of their genuine misdeeds) and spends a great deal of energy investigating the financial and sexual doings of his opponents. Despite his impressive bodyguard and his ability to whip up frenzied crowds, actual political violence, or for that matter even the credible threat of violence—whether mob violence or thug violence—is no part of his practice. Nor does Willie ever have so much control over the state's political institutions that he need not fear opposition at the polls. Furthermore, the key intellectual hallmarks of a truly totalitarian regime, as opposed to rule by bosses or thugs, are precisely those absent from Willie's regime. Nowhere does Willie claim, as Hitler and Stalin did, to be driven by a new vision of the human prospect, a world-transforming ideology that licenses him to use violence in the service of a transvaluation of values. Nowhere does he offer his supporters a new kind of political consciousness and the chance to become a new kind of human being. Nowhere does he offer them the opportunity to be magnetized by great abstractions that transcend the world of ordinary interest politics. Willie Talos is not the leader of a healthy democratic state, but neither in means nor in ends does his regime resemble the great tyrannies of the mid-twentieth century.

Nor is Willie Talos merely a charismatic politician undone by the corruptions that attend upon the use of power. In Robert Rossen's Oscar-winning 1949 film, Willie is tempted by his position to accept bribes, and he finally sells out to the economic interests he came to power to oppose. But nothing remotely like this happens in the novel. Willie serves the same class interests at the moment of his assassination that he had served from the beginning, and although there is a great deal of shady business in his government (not including, however, financial corruption of its chief), Willie's death is not caused by a succumbing to the temptations of power. He is not undone by evidence of corruption, but by the deep contradiction between means and ends that attend all urgent political questions, a contradiction that only becomes the deeper when one concedes that those who experience it probably actually seek to serve the values they say they do.

POLITICAL BACKGROUND

The state in which *All the King's Men* takes place may or may not be Louisiana. The political geography of the state is familiar to the entire South, turning on a conflict, best described in C. Vann Woodward's *The Origins of the New South* (1951), between very poor white farmers in the upland regions and a better-off Bourbon aristocracy in the lowlands. This conflict is one of long standing in southern culture and politics, and literary treatments of it date all the way back to William Byrd's *History of the Dividing Line* (written around 1728, published in 1866), and continue through William Faulkner's *Absalom, Absalom!* (1936) to Charles Frazier's *Cold Mountain* (1997), but it particularly characterized southern politics in the decades following the Populist revolt of the 1890s. The wave of Populist revolution was driven by the economic grievances and cultural resentments of small upland farmers, and brought to prominence a series of famous racist demagogues, including "Pitchfork" Ben Tillman, Tom Watson, James K. Vardaman, and Theodore Bilbo. The somewhat anticapitalist resentment politics of the Populist demagogues, in which racist hostility and class hostility were intertwined, persisted in the South through the era of George Wallace, after which a new generation of politicians, exemplified by Jimmy Carter and Bill Clinton, transformed the political culture of the South so that the contest between Bourbon and Populist was no longer at its core.

Given how strongly Populist politics depended upon race baiting, Populist demagogues like Huey Long, who did not depend upon race baiting very much, stand out. Like Long, Willie Talos is not a race baiter. Indeed, it is his opponents who play the race card most effectively. When at the beginning of his career Willie was an assessor back in upland Mason City, he had chosen to give a school construction contract to the low bidder rather than to the contractor who had curried favor with kickbacks to the local courthouse gang. The courthouse gang, whipping up hysteria with the claim that Willie's contractor would employ African-American bricklayers, managed to override Willie's choice and drive him from office. The pet contractors, however, did such a poor job that the fire escapes collapsed during a fire drill, injuring many students and returning Willie to public life.

Although the Cass Mastern episode crucially turns on race, the main political plot of *All the King's Men* turns on class conflict, not racism. Warren gives priority to class in *All the King's Men*, one suspects, because had he given priority to race; northern readers might have thought it was a book only about benighted southerners, and not about themselves or their own politics as well. Books about southern politics that did turn on race tended to the view that racism was a disease of the ignorant poor and that racism could be kept in check by keeping political power in the hands of the decent folk. (*To Kill a Mockingbird*, 1960, is an instance of this kind of book.) That kind of

argument is drawn directly from the Bourbon storehouse, and it is hard to see how it could be deployed without inflaming the class resentments that so energized Populist racism. This is perhaps a second reason why Warren's novel is invested so much more in class conflict than in racial conflict.

Long himself, the most formidable of the Populist demagogues, came to power in 1928 in the poorest state of the Union, which then had only two hundred miles of paved road, not a single bridge over the Mississippi River, and a requirement that schoolchildren buy their own textbooks. When Long became governor, Louisiana's economy was essentially a colonial one, with out-of-state corporations, principally Standard Oil, extracting tremendous wealth from the local oilfields but returning very little to the people of the state. It was not a poor state, as Willie Talos was to remark in *All the King's Men*, but a rich state full of poor people. Long taxed the oil companies, broke the power of the Bourbon aristocracy that had ruled the state since the end of Reconstruction, provided free textbooks for the public schools, built a phenomenal number of roads and bridges, and made a great university of the agricultural and mechanical college that William Tecumseh Sherman had founded just before the Civil War. He also engaged in a great deal of blackmail and intimidation, and several times the state militia and the New Orleans police (the latter ruled by Long's enemies) faced each other with drawn weapons.

When Long went to the U.S. Senate in 1932, he reluctantly gave up the governorship to O. K. Allen, a disciple so complaisant he was said to have signed a leaf that blew across his desk. Once in the Senate, Long embraced crank economic doctrines, such as his famous Share Our Wealth plan, and adopted a paranoid, anti-Semitic rhetoric not far removed from that of Father Charles Coughlin, becoming finally a sinister enough figure so that President Franklin Roosevelt remarked that if the New Deal were to fail, he would face either a right-wing coup led by Douglas MacArthur or a left-wing coup led by Huey Long. The Share Our Wealth movement did not survive Long's assassination in 1935, although his successors were not thrown out of Baton Rouge until 1942.

WILLIE TALOS'S STORY

The plot of *All the King's Men* runs in two major streams, one of them the story of the rise and fall of the governor, Willie Talos, the other the story of his press secretary, confidant, and blackmailer-in-chief, Jack Burden. The first is a story about politics—not merely about idealism and corruption or about power and ruthlessness, but about the inevitable tension between law and the concept of justice that ought to underlie law, between means and ends, between human needs and established rules. The second is a story about different views of the relationship between knowledge and moral identity, about whether the recognition that human nature is fallen is capable of motivating only cynicism and despair. The two threads are closely related to each other: first, in that the sensibility chastened by the recognition of our mutual complicity is meant to be the foundation for a political morality that is capable of serving a strenuous moral project with generosity and pragmatism, without self-righteousness, vindictiveness, or self-deceit; and second, in that the full understanding of the unavoidable but painful contradiction between good and the means of good that haunts all politics brings in its train the generous recognition of a common fallen humanity.

We first see Willie at the height of his power, wheedling and threatening an elderly judge, Montague Irwin, who has decided to endorse an opposition candidate. Although there is no question that Willie is practicing the politics of coercion, it is also clear that the upright hauteur of the judge has more to do with snobbery than with rectitude, and is largely self-serving, protecting the economic and social dominance of his class. The judge, defending his endorsement, argues that he is turning his coat because his conscience demands it, but Willie snaps that the judge and his conscience have been messing in politics a long time, with the implication that his noblesse oblige is simply the way he and his class have justified controlling the state in their own interests for the generation or two before Willie displaced them. When Willie guesses that some political operative has shown the judge some dirt reflecting on Willie's candidate, Willie proposes waving "a shovelful of the sweet-smelling" under the nose of the judge's conscience, so that the judge can tell the newsmen all about him and his conscience, after which the judge and his conscience can "go off arm in arm together, telling each other how much they think of each other."

Willie's phrase is devastating, because it captures the undercurrent of vanity so common in practitioners of unhand-me-sir political uprightness. Willie then launches a disquisition about dirt, noting that "a diamond is only a piece of dirt that got awful hot" and that God Almighty took a piece of dirt and blew on it and created "you and me and George Washington and mankind blessed in faculty and apprehension." It does not persuade the

judge, and it really is not meant to, but it does make Willie's case: that the measure of a law is whether it serves a sense of justice that is deeper than law, and that no law can be deeper than urgent human need. "You have to make the good out of the bad," Willie will argue later to the equally unresponsive Adam Stanton, "because there's nothing else to make it from."

Willie's appeal here is twofold. First, he has the credibility of superior candor. Against the background of the high-sounding bad faith mouthed by the Burden's Landing plutocrats, Willie's frank transgressions have at least the virtue of being carried out without pretense. But Willie is actually aiming higher than mere candor, and this is the second and deepest appeal of his position, for his claim is that he represents an immanent higher morality through which the pervasively rotten structure of Bourbon self-regard can be criticized and replaced. His willingness to transgress is not, or not chiefly, the sign of his mere will to power, but the sign of a transforming moral purpose that can only be taken seriously because it disguises itself as cynicism and amorality.

Willie's position is formidable, but only so long as he believes it himself, for certainly it is open to any rascal to treat what he does as merely the breaking of eggs without which no omelettes are made. If Willie were to doubt the ultimate purity of his own motives, he could not distinguish himself from his own enemies. It is precisely this kind of doubt that sets the machinery of the plot in motion. The state auditor is caught with his hand in the till, but rather than fire him and give his enemies an opening, Willie chooses to terrify him.

This pragmatic compromise, defensible if only barely so, is the last straw for Hugh Miller, Willie's upright and somewhat stiff attorney general (whom Jack Burden, with conscious envy of his rectitude, always mocks as "Hugh Miller, clean hands, pure heart, Harvard Law School, Lafayette Escadrille, Attorney General"). Miller's resignation moves Willie to prove to himself that his pragmatic compromises really were intended to serve a moral purpose after all.

One of the problems with boundless moral self-confidence is that people can acquit themselves of just about anything by seeing it pragmatically as the price of effectiveness. But one of the problems with moral self-doubt is that individuals cannot do anything to reestablish their belief in their own good faith, since anything designed for that purpose is ipso facto manipulative, and the defense of necessity that they offer for their moral compromises is something they have seen through and discredited in advance. That is why there is an air of hysteria to everything Willie says about the project he launches at this moment as a way of redeeming himself to himself: the Willie Talos Hospital, which he seeks to make the greatest hospital imaginable. To make his hospital great, Willie seeks to attract the surgeon Adam Stanton; Stanton, however, the child of a former Bourbon governor, despises Willie, who cannot—with all his argumentative resources—persuade him to join the staff. Unbeknownst to Willie, Jack Burden persuades Adam to take the position by showing him evidence of his father's corruption, so that Adam's agreement is really an act motivated by despair, not by the idealism that, strangely, Willie is asking for from him.

Naturally, the various unsavory elements that gather around Willie whenever he has to do business—led by his gargantuan lieutenant governor, Tiny Duffy—want a piece of the hospital. But uncharacteristically for someone who might be expected to see the good of building the hospital as outweighing the bad of the graft it would require, Willie wants them to have no part of it. That the hospital will do good is important to Willie, but it is also important that it be a kind of good he does not have to make out of the bad; he entered political life by opposing a corrupt construction contract, and he does not want his final testament to be a construction contract not much different from the ones his enemies were capable of. He has to prove to himself that he was, despite appearances, not only after power and money after all.

Circumstances, however, conspire to force Willie into making a deal. His loutish college football star son, Tom, may or may not have impregnated an incautious young woman, but Willie's opponents are ready to seize on that possible fact for the advantage it gives them. Willie first tries to wriggle free by blackmailing Judge Irwin, but the judge's suicide closes out that possibility. Driven into a corner, Willie agrees to deal with Tiny Duffy's pet contractor, one Gummy Larson, and almost immediately Tom Talos is injured, and sent into a fatal decline, in a football accident. In an frantic attempt to purify himself, Willie breaks the deal with the contractor, dismisses his mistress, Anne Stanton, and plans to return to his estranged wife. Tiny Duffy is enraged enough by Willie's act to set in motion Willie's assassination by making an anonymous call to Adam Stanton, telling him that his sister is the governor's mistress (and that is why the governor offered him the position at the hospital).

Willie's story is not a story about the corruptions of power. It is the story of a transgressive quest for justice. If one is willing to transgress the law in order to serve justice, one enters into a world in which it is no longer possible to tell whether one is serving justice or a will to power. If one does not want to serve only a will to power and does not want to be self-deceptive about one's own hunger for justice, these moments when law and justice are at odds with each other threaten to give one over to confusion. Willie's problem is not that his immoral means have put his moral ends out of reach, but that the irreconcilability of good and the means of good leave it impossible to tell what good ultimately is.

JACK BURDEN'S STORY

If Willie's story is one about politics and justice, Jack Burden's story is one about ethical psychology. If Willie's realpolitik ultimately seems to disguise an intense but nervous idealism, Jack's cynicism—reflected in a tough-guy narrative stance such as one might find in Dashiell Hammett or even Mickey Spillane—has an almost wholly negative purpose, that of repudiating the thoroughly inauthentic society of his class and of his immediate family.

The chief thing that moves Jack to his position in Willie's entourage is his disgust with the world of his upbringing. To some extent this disgust is purely psychological, reflecting his quite legitimate disgust with his own family, and most specifically with his mother. She has discarded Jack's ineffectual father (or, one should say, the man whom Jack thinks is his father), and since then married and drained an assortment of husbands, accumulating different kinds of spouses with the same zest she brings to collecting different sorts of furniture. There is also something disconcertingly sexualized about the spell she keeps trying to weave over Jack, as if the pressure she keeps applying to him to take what she thinks of as a decent job and to settle down were also a demand to be yet one more of her erotic pets. Jack's apparent father, Ellis Burden, whom Jack refers to as "The Scholarly Attorney," has—in the aftermath of the failure of his marriage—become a wandering evangelist caring for "unfortunates."

Jack's revulsion against the world of Burden's Landing is not merely a revulsion against his mother, however, for there really is something aimless and alienated about the lives of all of the Burden's Landing characters. Judge Irwin, whom we later learn to be Jack's father, seems always to be adrift in a life that looks like a hobby; although he is a distinguished former civil servant; we see him avidly building a model of a Roman ballista, with which he launches a ball of bread into a chandelier. Adam

Stanton, Jack's best friend, seeks to give his life meaning by throwing himself into saving lives as a surgeon, but there is always something askew about him, as if he has to try too hard to prove to himself that he is not in some sense already dead. Anne Stanton, Jack's youthful romantic interest, also tries hard to prove her reality to herself with charitable works, and drifts into an affair with Willie, attracted by the illusion of his more intense moral reality.

Jack's job with Willie is to dig up discrediting information about Willie's opponents. It is a natural job for someone who seeks to purify himself through repudiation, and it is also a job for someone with research skills, which Jack—as a failed Ph.D. in history—has in abundance. It is his desire to purify himself through repudiation that had led to his failure to complete his dissertation, because Jack's central conviction is that if one knows anyone thoroughly, what one knows is the specific reason that makes that person despicable. Like secret knowers in Hawthorne such as Roger Chillingworth or Ethan Brand, Jack believes that what you know when you know someone is the secret crime that individuates them.

The crime that individuates the subject of Jack's dissertation research—Ellis Burden's great-uncle, Cass Mastern—is hardly a secret one, or at least is not one that he seeks to conceal. Mastern, a gawky, earnest youth coming up from Mississippi to attend Transylvania College in Lexington, Kentucky, is seduced by his best friend's torrid wife, Annabelle Trice. The friend shoots himself, apparently accidentally, while cleaning his pistol. But he has left his wedding ring on his wife's pillow so that she, if nobody else, will know the real cause of his death. By chance, Annabelle's slave Phebe notices the ring and Annabelle fears that Phebe will gossip. Even more, she fears the gaze of her slave's eyes, full of their knowledge, and so sells her down the river. This shocks Cass, who futilely tries to rescue Phebe and then, equally futilely, frees his own slaves. When the Civil War breaks out, Cass, although he opposes slavery, stands with his people, albeit refusing to carry a weapon and serving as a kind of medic until he is mortally wounded during the Atlanta campaign.

The Cass Mastern episode, an inset short story so vivid that William Faulkner wondered why Warren had not chosen it, rather than the Long dictatorship, as the subject of his novel, is a puzzle to Jack; he cannot see how a fallen person can attempt to come to terms with his fallenness without becoming foolish. What Jack cannot understand is that one can gain a kind of wisdom from recognizing one's inevitable complicity in the darkness of the world, a wisdom that, while not redemptive, at least makes it possible for one to behave with moral generosity despite everything—which is the big lesson he is himself about to learn.

When Willie has to subject Judge Irwin to political pressure, he assigns Jack the task of finding out what there is to find about him. (One sign that Jack perhaps did not want to entirely repudiate Burden's Landing is the shock he feels when he learns dark truths about Judge Irwin.) Jack indeed discovers a kickback in the judge's past, one in which an attempted whistle-blower had been driven to suicide. When Jack confronts Judge Irwin about these events, the judge will not be intimidated. Later that evening he commits suicide, and the following morning Jack learns from his distraught mother that the man he has driven to destroy himself is in fact his father.

This shocking recognition has an unexpected effect on Jack. First, it presents him with a new picture of his mother, whom he had always seen as a cold-hearted user of men. Second, it gives him a new picture of Judge Irwin, for all his faults. The judge could easily have taken himself off the hook by telling Jack that he is his father, and that he chooses not to do that in the crisis shows that he at least has the integrity not to take the easy way out. The political plot of the novel, the catastrophe setting in motion Willie's death, seems to roll on without Jack from this point as he ponders the meaning of what he has learned. But he does learn the important lesson, the lesson of the recognition of complicity that underlies the moral lives of fallen but not ultimately despicable people.

Jack's lesson bears fruit in two final acts, each morally ambiguous in its own way. The first is his rejection of the opportunity to revenge himself upon Tiny Duffy. When he confronts Duffy with evidence of his role in Willie's murder, Jack feels a moment of high moral satisfaction. But confronting himself in the mirror that evening, he feels that satisfaction grow sour, as if he sees that it is another form of his old desire to purify himself through repudiation. Ultimately, given a chance to kill Tiny by telling what he knows to Sugar-Boy, Willie's driver and bodyguard, Jack lets the opportunity drop. Tiny may not exactly deserve Jack's mercy, but by his act Jack at least frees himself from a self-defeating ethos. Jack's second act is more ambiguous. Although Judge Irwin's suicide enabled Jack's mother to find herself, she is still troubled about it, and asks Jack if the judge had been in some kind of trouble the night before his suicide. Jack tells her, in a lie obviously modeled upon the one Kurtz tells to Marlow's Intended at the end of *Heart of Darkness* (1902), that he was not. Jack's lie is not totally self-serving. His mother already knows that Jack is somehow responsible for Irwin's death. But what she does not know is whether Jack had found out something truly disgraceful about him, so in telling this lie to his mother, Jack behaves generously toward the judge, and insofar as he restrains himself from rubbing his mother's face in ugly truths, toward her as well.

All the King's Men is not a book about the great mid-century tyrannies, but this concluding turn marks it as a book of the years immediately after World War II. As in Ralph Ellison's *Invisible Man* (1952), Warren's detached narrator sees his convictions of the 1930s at a distance, having had a harrowing experience of the ironies of politics. Like Ellison's narrator, Warren's does not rest in irony and withdrawal (as do later protagonists of the 1950s and 1960s, from Holden Caulfield to Captain Yossarian) but returns to a chastened version of his earlier commitments. (Jack goes so far as to work to make Hugh Miller the next governor.) These late-1940s writers are forced to take a step back from their 1930s commitments. But they do not leave those commitments completely behind and indeed have most of the same political allegiances at the end that they did at the beginning, however chastened their expectations now might be. The ethos that values a recognition of complicity also marks *All the King's Men* as a book of the late 1940s. Having faced a vision of the worst things human beings can do to each other, and facing also a political confrontation between enemies who had new powers of destruction at their disposal, the novelists of those years saw the danger of soaring and crusading political ambitions and of vindictive self-righteousness. In light of this, they sought, by comprehending human nature with all its faults, at least to hold themselves back from doing the worst acts in the name of the best aims, and perhaps to do a little better than that.

FURTHER READING

Clark, William Bedford. *The American Vision of Robert Penn Warren*. Lexington, Ky., 1991.

Clark, William Bedford, ed. *Critical Essays on Robert Penn Warren*. Boston, 1981.

Gray, Richard J. *The Literature of Memory: Modern Writers of the American South*. Baltimore, 1977.

Gray, Richard J., ed. *Robert Penn Warren: A Collection of Critical Essays*. Englewood Cliffs, N.J., 1980.

Grimshaw, James A. *Understanding Robert Penn Warren*. Columbia, S.C., 2001.

Guttenberg, Barnett. *Web of Being: The Novels of Robert Penn Warren*. Nashville, Tenn., 1975.

Holman, C. Hugh. *The Immoderate Past: The Southern Writer and History*. Athens, Ga., 1977.

Justus, James H. *The Achievement of Robert Penn Warren*. Baton Rouge, La., 1981.

Ruppersburg, Hugh M. *Robert Penn Warren and the American Imagination*. Athens, Ga., 1990.

Warren, Robert Penn. *Robert Penn Warren's* All the King's Men: *Three Stage Versions*. Edited by James A. Grimshaw and James A. Perkins. Athens, Ga., 2000.

Woodward, C. Vann. *Origins of the New South*. Baton Rouge, La., 1951.

See also the article on Robert Penn Warren, immediately preceding.

EUDORA WELTY

by Wendy Martin and Sharon Becker

In her autobiography, *One Writer's Beginnings* (1984), Eudora Welty reflects on the complicated relationship between literature, literary criticism, and authorial intention: "The story and its analyses are not mirror-opposites of each other. They are not reflections, either one. Criticism indeed is an art, as a story is, but only the story is to some degree a vision; there is no explanation outside fiction for what the writer is learning to do." This observation goes to the heart of the difficulty regarding the categorization of Welty's writing. Though a proud daughter of the South, Welty resisted the label of "regionalist," observing that everyone was from someplace, so that every writer was, essentially, a regionalist.

Eudora Welty.
(Courtesy of the Library of Congress)

mundane and extraordinary circumstances. These stories are simultaneously funny and thoughtful, straightforward and profound, focused on the South yet encompassing the greater American experience.

Eudora Welty published her first short stories and entered the literary world toward the final decades of the American modernist movement; her early work is influenced by the literary experiments of modernist writers such as William Faulkner, Ernest Hemingway, and even Gertrude Stein. Welty incorporates mythic structure, irony, and symbolism, and demonstrates an extraordinary command of language, both of the written word and of the spoken within the written, that allows for a complex expression of character without losing simplicity of style. Thus, she was able to balance the edicts of modernism with the tradition of domestic fiction practiced by southern women writers from the 1920s through the 1940s. This combination of high literary style with the quotidian details of ordinary lives often confused early critics of Welty's work, who looked either for the former, in order to declare the work serious fiction, or for the latter, to mark the work as enjoyable but not serious.

Similarly, she wrote compelling portraits of women, and forged a path for other women writers, but she refused to wear the mantle of "woman writer" or "feminist." For Welty, the most important accomplishment was to create compelling characters and a well-crafted narrative rather than a public persona as a famous author. Details outside of that process, such as finding the meaning of, or the symbolism, in her stories were not as important to Welty as the writing itself.

Although in *One Writer's Beginnings*, Welty describes her life as "sheltered," she produced works of an extraordinary range: whether she wrote of sharecroppers or disillusioned spinsters, she trained her eye on the panorama of life in the South and wrote what she saw and heard. Eudora Welty talked about the nature of short stories in a 1991 interview, observing, "I'm not any kind of prophet, but I think it's in our nature to talk, to tell stories, [to] appreciate stories." Her own novels and short stories are engaging and often extremely humorous; her work is populated with finely drawn characters, men and women from all walks of life who are faced with both

Even in her earliest works, Welty eschewed traditional views of gender, making critics and readers uncomfortable with her often visionary approach to American life, both in and outside of the South. It is this radical restructuring of gender codes, experiences, and expectations, however, that has allowed Welty's work—from the earliest to the most recent—to resonate with generations of readers of both sexes. Her work feels contemporary and alive; her trademark humor and her shoot-from-the-hip style are timeless constructions regardless of whether Welty's characters are mid-1800s pioneers or young women pining for lives in the big world beyond their small town. Sensitive to the nuances of gender politics, Welty doesn't limit her viewpoint to the feminine—she is as dedicated to exposing the difficulty in traditional expectations for American men as for women.

Throughout her career, Eudora Welty described herself primarily as a short-story writer, but her novels garnered her as much, or more, critical acclaim. The publication of her novel *Losing Battles* in 1970 caused such a critical stir that Welty was soon praised as a novelist of the first rank. The publication in 1972 of *The Optimist's Daughter*, a novel most often viewed as an interpretation of Welty's life in Jackson, Mississippi, solidified her reputation in the literary world. It is important to note that although Welty's stylistic and narrative technique was considerably refined in these later works, her subject matter—women rejecting traditional gender roles, men looking for a place in the world, and men and women struggling with relationships both beginning and ending—didn't change, and her artistic explorations reflected the preoccupations of critics and readers who were themselves trying to come to grips with the changing roles of men and women in the wider world.

A WRITER'S BEGINNINGS

Welty's father, Christian Welty, was raised on a farm in Ohio and met Eudora's mother, Chestina Andrews, when both were schoolteachers in West Virginia. They moved to Jackson, Mississippi, so he could make new start, and fortune, as a businessman. Eudora Alice Welty was born in Jackson, Mississippi, on 13 April 1909—she was the firstborn of the Welty family's three children, and the only girl. Though Eudora and her siblings were native-born Mississippians, the "outsider" status of her parents is often cited as the reason Eudora was able to observe southern culture and write about it with such a clear, concise eye. Additionally, Chestina's large, gregarious southern family provided her daughter with a wealth of characters on whom to base her stories.

Storytelling and reading played a central role in Eudora Welty's childhood and gave her a profound respect for the rich world of the written word. In *One Writer's Beginnings*, Welty fondly recalls the sound of her parents' voices reading their favorite books to one another in the evenings. Coupled with this love for reading was Welty's appreciation of the raucous storytelling as well as the gossip of Jackson's citizens, who enjoyed gathering on porches and store steps to catch up on the day's news. Her writing is infused with this spirit of folktales and anecdotes, of stories invented to scare children into doing good and

to explain away the world's idiosyncrasies, of inventive language and regional vernacular. Even as a young girl, Welty was writing, and one of her earliest stories was published in the children's magazine *St. Nicholas*, which was certainly early validation of her literary talent.

After attending high school in Jackson, where she worked on the student paper, Welty moved to Columbus, Mississippi, in 1925 to attend Mississippi State College for Women. She studied there for two years before transferring to the University of Wisconsin, where she received her B.A. in 1929. Her studies focused primarily on art history and English literature, and she discovered that she especially loved the poetry of W. B. Yeats. While at college, Welty wrote stories, sketches, and poems for student publications.

In 1930, following her father's advice, Welty entered the Columbia University Graduate School of Business in New York to study advertising. She thoroughly enjoyed the frenetic world of New York, especially plays, museums, and dancing all night with her friends. The Harlem Renaissance was in full flower at the time, and there was vibrant artistic energy in Manhattan that belied the early years of America's Great Depression. To her great regret, Welty had to leave her exciting, cosmopolitan life to return to Jackson to care for her father during his illness. After his death in 1931, she took part-time jobs with local newspapers and wrote ad copy for DJDX, the radio station her father owned, in order to support herself and help her family. During this unusually demanding time, she rededicated herself to a passion ignited in college: writing short stories.

In 1933, Welty became a junior publicity agent for the Works Progress Administration (WPA). For three years, she traveled around the eighty-two counties of Mississippi to promote local WPA projects, such as the building of roads and airstrips as well as canning facilities and other projects designed to bring economic solvency to poor and rural areas. Welty interviewed the people she met while working, and these encounters left an indelible impression in her mind of what it was to live through the Depression in the South. More so than even her time in New York City, the experience of learning about people from all walks of life in her own state was the spark for her "wanting to become a real writer, a true writer." Though Welty later lived within the prescribed boundaries of Jackson, Mississippi, her experiences with the WPA gave her access to a vast storehouse of knowledge on the human condition.

In addition to interviewing the residents of rural Mississippi counties, Welty photographed them, their homes, and the countryside. When she was a young woman, Welty's father gave her a camera, and she became dedicated to photography as well as to writing; in fact, her photography influenced her writing. As she explains in *One Writer's Beginnings*, "Life doesn't hold still. Photography taught me that to be able to capture transience, by being ready to click the shutter at the crucial moment, was the greatest need I had."

Using her inexpensive Brownie camera, Welty took photographs that were not just poignant testaments to the spirit of the American people during the Great Depression but also encapsulated stories of individual lives. Her subjects varied widely, from "Tomato Packers Recess (Copiah County)," a portrait of a group of men and boys gathered around a young man with a hat pulled low over his eyes and playing the guitar, to "Home with Bottle Trees (Simpson County)," which depicts a stark, dilapidated shack surrounded by spindly trees whose branches are topped with glass bottles. The bottles were thought to trap evil spirits before they could get inside the house, a superstition that later played a large role in Welty's story "Livvie."

Developing and printing the photos in her own kitchen, Welty nuanced the images of her casual, unposed subjects and the quiet power of rural towns and buildings. This close attention to her photography served a purpose; in her view, her photographs and stories were extensions of one another. She developed a manuscript around her photographs that she titled *Black Saturday*; it contained text and photos of African Americans who lived in Mississippi. At the time, books such as *Roll, Jordan, Roll* (1932), a sentimental photo essay of the "Old South," were popular; even so, there was little interest in her book. However, Welty did manage to find a space to display her photographs, and in 1936 she had a one-woman show in the Lugene Gallery in New York City. Much later in Welty's life, two collections of her photographs were published: *One Time, One Place: Mississippi in the Depression; A Snapshot Album* (1971), based on the *Black Saturday* photo essay, and *Photographs* (1989), a larger collection of all the photographs Welty took in the 1930s.

The year of her gallery showing, 1936, was also the year Welty published her first story, "Death of a Traveling Salesman," in *Manuscript* magazine. Soon she was receiving offers from New York publishers expressing interest in a novel. However, when she indicated that she was committed to the short story, interest in her work flagged—major publishers thought that a collection of short stories by an unknown, "regionalist" writer was too risky. At this time, Welty came to the attention of the highly influential publishers of the *Southern Review*, Robert Penn Warren and Cleanth Brooks, who rejected "Petrified Man" but did accept "A Piece of News" and "A Memory." Within a few years, her stories were appearing in the *Atlantic* and were championed by such well-respected modernist writers as Ford Madox Ford.

THE WRITER'S CAREER BEGINS

In the spring of 1940, literary agent Diarmuid Russell offered his agency's services to Welty. Because she was anxious to get her stories published in the "slicks," high-profile magazines such as *Saturday Evening Post, Collier's,* or *Good Housekeeping*, Welty accepted Russell's offer. Russell felt that if Welty's stories could be placed in respected national magazines, publishing houses would be more likely to accept a manuscript of short stories from her even though she was an unknown writer. By December 1940, Welty's stories "Powerhouse" and "A Worn Path," both collected in *A Curtain of Green* (1941), were sold to *Atlantic Monthly*, one of the most prestigious and longest running of the national magazines. In 1941, Doubleday published *A Curtain of Green*, Welty's first a collection of short stories, with an introduction by Katherine Anne Porter. Its seventeen stories reflected a variety of styles and subjects, from local color grotesque to classical mythology. In addition to the publication of her first book, in 1941 Welty won a second prize O. Henry Award for "A Worn Path." She would win first prize the following year for "The Wide Net," and again in 1943 for "Livvie."

The most famous story of *A Curtain of Green*, "Why I Live at the P.O.," is the best example of Welty's developing sense of narrative and humor. Told in comic monologue, the story involves the postmistress in China Grove, Mississippi, and the events that have fractured and reconvened her family circle. Her sense of outrage at these events is so complete that she packs up all of her possessions and moves to her post office. The narrator, Sister, pours out the story, in high comic mode, of her sister, Stella Rondo, who ran off with Sister's boyfriend, Mr. Whitaker, and returned two years later with a two-year-old child. The family is full of neurotic and eccentric characters who are as unreliable as the narrator.

In 1943, Welty's next collection of short stories, *The Wide Net, and Other Stories*, was published. The previous year Welty had expanded a short story into a novella, *The*

Robber Bridegroom (1942). *The Wide Net* was a group of eight stories, all of them displaying a mythical complexity not found in *A Curtain of Green*. *The Wide Net* marks Welty's coming of age as writer during the height of American modernism. The collection also represents the influence of the Fugitives, a group of southern writers, such as John Crowe Ransom, Robert Penn Warren, and Allen Tate, who championed southern regionalism but fought against the stereotypes of the antebellum South while rejecting encroaching northern, urban cultural values. Although Welty's work embraced similar concerns, unlike the Fugitives she wrote about women and African Americans, and she did not think that agrarianism was an effective antidote to contemporary urban society.

Like William Faulkner, Welty creates characters who are particularly attuned to the flux and pull of time, especially the looming presence of "the Southern Past." This struggle with time is often revealed to the reader through an interior monologue. The stories also reflect a modernist understanding of narrative, including the fracturing of time and a stream-of-consciousness technique featuring nonlinear logic. The stories of *The Wide Net*, in particular the title story, contain characters who often spiral inward toward a greater understanding of themselves; this understanding is, in turn, applied to the world and people around them. Therefore, the husband of a pregnant wife in "The Wide Net" must descend to a netherworld run by "the King of the Snakes" before returning to the earth with a greater understanding of life. The protagonists of all the stories in this collection must battle the primitive, and complete a regression, before coming to wholeness in the world. Thus, though the stories are set in the South, it is clear that Welty's intention was to use this location as a microcosm of the greater world and of the struggles all people confront when faced with an often confusing and unsettling modern world.

The Robber Bridegroom prefigures Welty's eventual career as a novelist. The novella is set in the Mississippi River end of the Natchez Trace, an area once home to the Natchez Indian tribe, where settlers like Clement Musgrove, a pioneer cotton planter, his second wife, Salome, and his daughter, Rosamond now live. This novella reflects American tall tales and legends as well as the classical myth of Psyche and the traditional Grimm Brothers story "The Fisherman and His Wife." Though by no means a best-seller, this novella firmly established Welty as writer interested in simultaneously invoking the innocence associated with the American past and the more complicated struggles of individuals in the American

present. Welty, then, repeatedly returns to the application of myth upon the landscape of America in order to uncover a character's individual truth. As she simultaneously uses the landscape of the small town as well as the wilderness, both the home and the adventurous spirit become sites of mythic proportion and monumental discovery.

There is a shift in focus between the stories of *The Wide Net* and *The Robber Bridegroom* and the narrative of Welty's first novel, *Delta Wedding* (1946). Though Welty continues to use classical mythology in her stories, she shifts away from the dreamlike quality of the writing in *The Wide Net* and focuses on the ordinary details of a Mississippi family planning a wedding. Critics often compare the text of *Delta Wedding* to Virginia Woolf's novel *To the Lighthouse*. Indeed, Welty deeply admired the British modernist Woolf, whom she acknowledged as one of the greatest influences on her. Both novelists celebrate the multifaceted abilities of a traditional mother with a large family, and both narratives are told from multiple points of view—in Welty's novel, all of them female. *Delta Wedding* is set in 1923, after World War I and before the Great Depression. The narrative focuses on the dynamics of the Fairchild family and the effects of not a wedding, but of the saving, by the bride's uncle, George Fairchild, of a cousin almost killed by a train. The family is buffeted by stormy tensions as turbulent crosscurrents push and pull against each aunt and uncle, each child and adult. In this complex familial ecology, Ellen Fairchild, an outsider who becomes an insider through marriage, provides the life raft of harmony. *Delta Wedding* attracted a larger readership than Welty's previous work, thus establishing her career as a novelist as well as a short-story writer.

In 1949, *The Golden Apples* followed *Delta Wedding* with a closely knit collection of short stories. This collection embodies the experimental approach of the stories of *The Wide Net*; each of the stories in *The Golden Apples* was primarily published in various magazines and journals before Welty arranged them in rough chronological order, revised them, and crafted them into a narrative that is both enhanced by the strength of the individual stories and clarified by their placement within the story cycle. The stories trace the developmental arc of a group of families living in Morgana, Mississippi, as they follow different paths in the search for the golden apples of fulfillment. Through the stories of Miss Eckhart, the town's piano teacher, who is not originally from Morgana, and Virgie Rainey, a poor girl who is Miss Eckhart's star pupil, readers see the provincial and utilitarian nature of Morgana from the outsider's point of view. Though Virgie has a passion and talent for music, the pursuit of music as a dream is far out of her family's realm. In a grotesque interlude, the family's goats are allowed into the parlor, where they dine on Virgie's practice piano. Virgie's isolated life in Morgana, painful as it is, is seen by Welty as an adequate preparation for life in the larger world: Virgie's isolation has fostered a rich and full inner world of the mind and a strong sense of defiance that allow her to forge an individualism that others in the small town will never have.

Welty's novel *The Ponder Heart*, published in 1954, achieved popular and critical success. It shifts focus away from southern womanhood to southern manhood with a comic exploration of the life and loves of a southern gentleman. The story of Uncle Daniel Ponder is told through the eyes of his unmarried niece, Edna Earle Ponder. Edna looks on with increasing dismay as Uncle Daniel woos and marries a series of inappropriate women; somehow, he even inadvertently kills one of his wives by tickling her to death during a thunderstorm. In spite of this preposterous event, the narrative and the narrator remain loyal to Uncle Daniel, and the novel functions as a tragicomic examination of the absurd and sometimes disconcerting path people travel toward love. In this novel, Welty questions the traditional configuration of gender roles and responses in the unsettling quest for love and marriage. This inventive narrative of Uncle Daniel's comic heart, told in a southern idiom, received the William Dean Howells Medal of the American Academy of Arts and Letters for to the best work of American fiction between 1950 and 1955. In 1956, Jerome Chodorov and Joseph Fields made *The Ponder Heart* into a play that had a successful run on Broadway.

In her next collection of short stories, *The Bride of the Innisfallen, and Other Stories* (1955), Welty moves away from her southern setting in several of the stories. Written mostly while Welty was in Ireland visiting the Anglo-Irish author Elizabeth Bowen, the stories in this collection anticipate aspects of postmodernism and magical realism. The stories, characterized by a skillful use of repetition and an elastic sense of time, are structured variations on Homer's tale of Circe. Welty retells the original story from Circe's point of view, thereby liberating her from being a mere interlude in the story of a male wanderer. Circe's journey serves as the central metaphor for all the stories. The bride in "The Bride of the Innisfallen" and Gabriella in "Going to Naples" are actively involved with

journeys, and like Welty's Circe, they are women who have adventures of their own.

The years between 1955 and 1970 were difficult for Welty. Though she published a few stories and completed a story for children, *The Shoe Bird* (1964), these years were consumed with the many demanding responsibilities of caring for her aging mother as well as dealing with the deaths of her two brothers. Nevertheless, Welty managed to work on and complete her novel *Losing Battles*, which was published in 1970. Originally conceived as a novella, *Losing Battles* is a wry, funny look at a family reunion in the hill country of northeastern Mississippi during the Great Depression. In addition to ushering in the second half of Welty's career, this novel contained the subtext of Welty's life as an unmarried writer who lives in her mother's house. Exploring a spinster schoolteacher's unflagging dedication to her community and the struggles of the Renfro family to reunite under difficult personal circumstances, this novel represents both a personal and a larger cultural struggle for familial and societal harmony at a time when America itself was deeply unsettled. Welty's narrative technique does not rely on extensive description and interior examination of the character's hearts and minds, as it does in much of her earlier work. Instead, narrative gives way here to what Welty described in an interview as doing "something altogether in action and conversation and still show the same thing."

In *Losing Battles*, written from an interior perspective, an extended family gathers to celebrate Granny Vaughn's ninetieth birthday as well as Jack Renfro's homecoming from prison. While members of the Vaughn-Beecham-Renfro family each tell a story, the past interpenetrates the present, and the reader is allowed a comic glimpse into the lives of the families over six generations. However, as Welty stated in an interview later in her life, Julia Mortimer, the spinster schoolteacher, is the "heroine" of the novel. Julia's battle with the closed-minded attitudes and country ways of a small town, and her resistance to the institution of marriage and family, stand as a heroic counterpoint to the vainglorious actions and reception of the returned "hero," Jack Renfro. In an effort to escape from the penitentiary fields on a mule, Jack is a mock hero, an absurd savior whose actions don't succeed. However, Welty doesn't utterly condemn the Renfro clan for their excited reception of Jack. Though Julia Mortimer is the heart of the novel, she has lived a life without connections to other people, and it is the Renfro family as a group, not as flawed individuals, that collectively embodies the deepest human emotions. Ultimately, just as Julia Mortimer loses her battle to be buried alone under the steps of the schoolhouse, and is instead interred in the community graveyard, Welty's final message is one of accepting, or in Julia's case submitting, to the ties that bind.

In 1973, Welty won the Pulitzer Prize for her novel *The Optimist's Daughter* (1972). Again, the story includes autobiographical elements as it focuses on a family that is reunited when a daughter returns to Mississippi to care for her ill father. In her examination of marriages over the generations—including her parents' marriage, her father's second marriage to an unsavory younger woman, and her own, which ended in widowhood—Laurel McKelva Hand comes to a deeper understanding of both her past and her present self. The symbolic return to home, and to her father, helps Laurel unite her fractured identities—the childhood self that was left behind in her parent's home and the adult self she has created. Recapitulating Welty's own life, Laurel's homecoming allows her to anchor herself in the present while accommodating herself to her past. Another important autobiographical dimension of this novel is the portrait of Laurel's mother, which is based on Welty's own mother's childhood in West Virginia; however, the larger story is really a complex narrative of the relationship between parents and children as well and, once again, of the powerful, consuming, and difficult emotion of love.

Welty's reentry into the literary world rekindled interest in both her writing and her life. Responding to her increasing popularity, Welty accepted numerous requests for interviews and speaking engagements, making a concerted effort to keep her carefully protected home life private in order to continue to write. During the rest of the 1970s, she concentrated on nonfiction works, such as *The Eye of the Story* (1978), and edited *The Collected Stories of Eudora Welty* (1980).

In 1983, Welty gave a series of lectures about her life as a writer at Harvard University that was published as *One Writer's Beginnings* in 1984. This literary autobiography is not intended to be a total revelation of her "real life," but instead foregrounds the love of books and stories in the Welty household; it also provides a sensitive examination of the importance of the Mississippi landscape and its people to Welty's writing. The book is neither a personal memoir nor a manual of writing technique; rather, it is a meditation on Welty's development as writer. The sections, titled "Listening," "Learning to See," and "Finding a Voice," delineate the growth of Welty's ability to develop and craft a story; the growth of these techniques is directly related to her experiences in the world, and are not simply limited to the pragmatic advice of most writers to "write every day" or "read more." *One Writer's Beginnings* appealed to a wide audience and was on *The New York Times* best-seller list for forty-six weeks. In general, its popularity increased the sales of *The Optimist's Daughter* and renewed interest in all of Welty's works.

THE WRITER CONTINUES

In the final decade of Welty's life, two volumes of her photography were released and numerous editions of her previous works were published. She was frequently the subject of interviews, and her work received considerable attention from scholars of American literature and culture. In 1999, Welty was the first living writer to be included in the prestigious Library of America series. This honor was yet another in a line of numerous fellowships, prizes, and honors including two Guggenheim Fellowships (1942–1943 and 1949–1950), three O. Henry Awards (1942, 1943, 1968), and the National Institute of Arts and Letters award for fiction in 1944. She also received the William Dean Howells Medal from the American Academy of Arts and Letters for *The Ponder Heart* (1955), the Edward McDowell Medal (1970), the National Book Award for fiction for *Losing Battles* (1971), the National Medal for Literature (1980), and the American Book Award for *The Collected Stories of Eudora Welty* (1981) and *One Writer's Beginnings* (1984). In 1987, Welty won one of France's highest civilian awards, Chevalier de l'Ordre des Arts et Lettres; in 1996 she received the Chevalier de la Legion d'Honneur. She was also awarded the Presidential Medal of Freedom (1980), the P.E.N./Malamud Award for excellence in the short story (1991), and the National Endowment for the Humanities Frankel Prize (1992).

Much of Welty's fiction, including *The Robber Bridegroom, The Ponder Heart,* and *The Shoe Bird,* have been adapted for Broadway, off-Broadway, community theater, and television movie productions. Her short stories "Why I Live at the P.O," "A Piece of News," "Lily Daw and the Three Ladies," and "Petrified Man," have been adapted in various forms as stage productions. Welty was also a literary critic and theorist, a recipient of numerous honorary degrees, and a subject of many interviews (she enjoyed cooking traditional southern meals for those assigned to interview her). She continued to live and work in Jackson, Mississippi, until her death at the age of ninety-two on 23 July 2001.

In the introduction to *One Time, One Place*, Welty comments on the "living relationship" between the outside world and the inner self. Her aim was "not to point a finger of judgment but to part a curtain" that veils other people's inner lives. Through humor and southern sensibilities; through mythological figures and eccentric small town denizens; through the concentrated narrative of a short story and the extended text of a novel, Eudora Welty created a body of work that will continue to part that curtain for generations of readers.

[*See also* Fugitives and Southern Agrarianism, The.]

WORKS

A Curtain of Green, and Other Stories (1941)
The Robber Bridegroom (1942)
The Wide Net, and Other Stories (1943)
Delta Wedding (1946)
Music from Spain (1948)
The Golden Apples (1949)
Short Stories (1950)
The Ponder Heart (1954)
The Bride of the Innisfallen, and Other Stories (1955)
The Shoe Bird (1964)
A Sweet Devouring (1969)
Losing Battles (1970)
One Time, One Place: Mississippi in the Depression; A Snapshot Album (1971)
The Optimist's Daughter (1972)
A Pageant of Birds (1974)
Fairy Tale of the Natchez Trace (1975)
The Eye of the Story: Selected Essays and Reviews (1978)
Women!! Make Turban in Own Home! (1979)
Acrobats in a Park (1980)
Bye-bye Brevoort (1980)
Moon Lake and Other Stories (1980)
Twenty Photographs (1980)
White Fruitcake (1980)
Retreat (1981)
One Writer's Beginnings (1984)
Four Photographs by Eudora Welty (1984)
In Black and White: Photographs of the 30's and 40's (1985)
The Little Store (1985)
Photographs (1989)
The Norton Book of Friendship (1991)
A Writer's Eye: Collected Book Reviews (1994)
Welty: Collected Essays and Memoirs (1999)
Welty: Collected Novels (1999)

FURTHER READING

Binding, Paul. *The Still Moment: Eudora Welty, Portrait of a Writer.* London, 1994.

Bloom, Harold. *Eudora Welty: Comprehensive Research and Study Guide.* New York, 1999. An examination of four of Welty's short stories: "Death of a Traveling Salesman," "Why I Live at the P.O.," "The Wide Net," and "No Place for You, My Love," each followed by a selection of critical responses from a variety of viewpoints.

Carson, Barbara H. *Eudora Welty: Two Pictures at Once in Her Frame.* Troy, N.Y., 1992. Examines Welty's use of the concept of reality in her fiction.

Champion, Laurie, ed. *The Critical Response to Eudora Welty's Fiction.* Westport, Conn., 1994. Provides a representative selection of criticism of Welty's fiction from the 1940s to the 1990s.

Gretlund, Jan Nordby. *Eudora Welty's Aesthetics of Place.* Newark, Del., 1994. A close reading of Welty's works emphasizing her technique of using the southern landscape and architecture.

Gretlund, Jan Nordby, and Karl-Heinz Westarp, eds. *The Late Novels of Eudora Welty.* Columbia, S.C., 1998. A collection of fourteen essays centered on Welty's last two novels, *Losing Battles* and *The Optimist's Daughter*. The editors privilege these novels as being the best of Welty's writing, in both technique and vision.

Gygax, Franziska. *Serious Daring from Within: Female Narrative Strategies in Eudora Welty's Novels.* New York, 1990. Emphasizes an exploration of Welty's use of language and narrative techniques that indicate "female writing."

Harrison, Suzan. *Eudora Welty and Virginia Woolf: Gender, Genre, and Influence.* Baton Rouge, La., 1997. The author applies the theories of Mikhail Bakhtin to the paired novels of Woolf and Welty. A useful analysis for readers interested how Welty reflects Woolf's concerns.

Johnston, Carol Ann. *Eudora Welty: A Study of the Short Fiction.* New York, 1997.

Kreyling, Michael. *Understanding Eudora Welty.* Columbia, S.C., 1999.

Manning, Carol S. *With Ears Opening like Morning Glories: Eudora Welty and the Love of Storytelling.* Westport, Conn., 1985. Detailed examination of Welty's use of the oral tradition as a narrative technique and theme.

Mark, Rebecca. *The Dragon's Blood: Feminist Intertexuality in Eudora Welty's* The Golden Apples. Jackson, Miss., 1994. A close examination of the stories in Welty's *The Golden Apples*, valuable for readers interested in Welty's application of myth.

Marrs, Suzanne. *One Writer's Imagination: The Fiction of Eudora Welty*. Baton Rouge, La., 2002. A chronological and comprehensive reading of Welty's works focusing on the intersection of biography and fiction.

McHaney, Pearl, ed. *Eudora Welty: Writers' Reflections upon First Reading Welty*. Athens, Ga., 1999.

McHaney, Pearl, ed. *Eudora Welty: The Contemporary Reviews*. Cambridge, Mass., 2003.

Mortimer, Gail L. *Daughter of the Swan: Love and Knowledge in Eudora Welty's Fiction*. Athens, Ga., 1994. A skillful examination of Welty's works based on Welty's use of evocative images to reflect human consciousness.

Pingatore, Diana R. *A Reader's Guide to the Short Stories of Eudora Welty*. New York, 1996.

Polk, Noel. *Eudora Welty: A Bibliography of Her Work*. Jackson, Miss., 1994.

Pollack, Harriet, and Suzanne Meyers, eds. *Eudora Welty and Politics: Did the Writer Crusade?* Baton Rouge, La., 2001.

Prenshaw, Peggy Whitman, ed. *More Conversations with Eudora Welty*. Jackson, Miss., 1996. A collection of interviews and profiles of Welty, especially of interest to beginning scholars of Welty's life and fiction.

Schmidt, Peter. *The Heart of the Story: Eudora Welty's Short Fiction*. Jackson, Miss., 1991. Focuses on Welty's fiction through the lens of historical and social context.

Trouard, Dawn, ed. *Eye of the Storyteller*. Kent, Ohio, 1990. A collection of essays aimed against the traditional view of Welty as a writer within a strictly southern context.

Waldron, Ann. *Eudora: A Writer's Life*. New York, 1998. An unauthorized biography that gives a solid overview of Welty's life. Waldron, however, does not include a critical approach to any of Welty's works.

Weston, Ruth D. *Gothic Traditions and Narrative Techniques in the Fiction of Eudora Welty*. Baton Rouge, La., 1994. Weston both examines and redefines Welty's use of the Gothic by applying it specifically to Welty's repeated trope of trapped women.

NATHANAEL WEST

by Jane Goldman

The satiric genius Nathanael West was born Nathan Weinstein and died, aged thirty-seven, before his work met with the kind of critical acclaim it deserved. "Do I love what others love?," a motto from the German poet Johann Wolfgang von Goethe, is inscribed below the drawing of a man hugging a mule in the bookplate that his friend, the writer S. J. Perelman, designed for West while they were still at college. In fact, West, in his brief life, did not, it seems, love what most others loved.

His posthumous reputation rests on four short and devastatingly funny, bleakly surrealist, satirical novels. His debut novel, *The Dream Life of Balso Snell* (1931), is a virtuoso satiric parody of the cult of high modernism, whose techniques he refines to powerful effect in the anticapitalist, antifascist satires *Miss Lonelyhearts* (1933), *A Cool Million* (1934), and *The Day of the Locust* (1939). Edgar Allan Poe and Charles Baudelaire were his muses. West scorned what he called the "muddle-class" realism of Sinclair Lewis and Theodore Dreiser and championed the formally experimental, short lyric novel that he recognized as a potently "distinct form," particularly appropriate for American use.

"Forget the epic, the master work," he advises in "Some Notes on Miss L." (1933), a defense of his second novel, *Miss Lonelyhearts*: "In America fortunes do not accumulate, the soil does not grow, families have no history. Leave slow growth to the book reviewers, you only have time to explode. Remember William Carlos Williams's description of the pioneer women who shot their children against the wilderness like cannonballs. Do the same with your novels."

West's characters are often alarmingly portrayed without psychological depth and appear grotesquely dehumanized or objectified, but West nevertheless mined

Nathanael West. (*Courtesy of the New York Public Library*)

and recommended psychology as a kind of mythic resource: "Psychology has nothing to do with reality nor should it be used as motivation. The novelist is no longer a psychologist. Psychology can be something much more important. The great body of case histories can be used in the way the ancient writers used their myths. Freud is your Bulfinch; you cannot learn from him."

In West's writing, European modernism combusts with the violence of the American comic strip. His skilled avant-garde style harnessed to a coruscating social and political critique seems to have nonplussed many of his contemporaries in the 1930s, when to perpetuate a modernist style was to go against the dominant left-wing political doctrine of socialist realism prescribed by the Soviet Writers' Congress. "Somehow or other I seem to have slipped in-between all the 'schools,' " he confided to F. Scott Fitzgerald in 1939: "My books meet no needs except my own, their circulation is practically private and I'm lucky to be published." In his 1934 preface to a reissue of *The Great Gatsby*, Fitzgerald identified West as a young writer indeed "being harmed . . . for lack of a public." Fitzgerald, who considered him "a potential leader in the field of prose fiction," died the day before West, and this loss to American letters all but eclipsed reports of West's death in the newspapers. The press reports of the motor accident that killed West focused mainly on the more publicly significant death of his wife, Eileen, the famous model for Ruth McKenney's highly successful *New Yorker* sketches and the 1938 novel *My Sister Eileen*, which became a play in 1941.

But while he struggled for wider public recognition, West was during his lifetime a much admired and internationally respected writer's writer. In American circles his talent deeply impressed and was endorsed by Fitzgerald. He was also a close friend and colleague to William Carlos Williams, with whom he coedited *Contact* magazine and in whose epic experimental poem, *Paterson* (1946–1958), appear risqué moments from West's life. And he was a lifelong friend to the writer S. J. Perelman (who became his brother-in-law). He was greatly admired by Edmund Wilson. West was equally *au fait* with the European avant-garde. He met a number of French surrealists on his formative trip to Paris in 1926; he also knew the exiled German dadaist George Grosz and contributed to Grosz's short-lived magazine *Americana*. Like many of his contemporaries, West served in Hollywood as a screenwriter, which gave him a second education in the production of fantasy and escapism for mass consumption and the material for his last novel, *The Day of the Locust*, a satire on the Hollywood dream factory. Eventually, Hollywood also gave him some financial stability to support his art.

EARLY YEARS AND EDUCATION

Perelman's magnificent surrealist portrait of his friend, which appeared in *Contempo* magazine in 1933, endorsed the publication of West's second novel, *Miss Lonelyhearts*. It remains one of the most helpful introductions to West, who is pictured as, among many other things,

> an intellectual vagabond, a connoisseur of first editions, fine wines, and beautiful women...a dweller in the world of books...equally at home browsing through the bookstalls along the Paris quais and rubbing elbows in the smart literary salons of the Faubourg St. Honore, a rigid abstainer and non-smoker...rarely leaving his monastic cell, an intimate of Cocteau, Picasso, Joyce and Lincoln Kirstein, a dead shot, a past master of the foils, dictating his novels, plays, poems, short stories, epigrams, aphorisms, and sayings to a corps of secretaries at lightning speed, an expert judge of horseflesh, the owner of a model farm equipped with the latest dairy devices—a man as sharp as a razor, as dull as a hoe, as clean as whistle, as tough as nails, as white as snow, as black as the raven's wing, and as poor as Job. A man kind and captious, sweet and sour, fat and thin, tall and short, racked with fever, plagued by the locust, beset by witches, hagridden, cross-grained, a fun-loving, serious-minded dreamer, visionary and slippered pantaloon. Picture to yourself such a man, I say, and you won't have the faintest idea of Nathanael West.

This bizarre portrait, which continues with another entirely contradictory depiction, does nevertheless give a pretty clear idea of West, who did briefly in the 1920s live the life of an American flâneur (idle) writer in Paris and who was, from early youth, steeped in the hyperaesthetics and sartorial elegance of a fin-de-siècle (late-nineteenth-century) bibliophile, sensualist, and flâneur. He was also an enthusiastic hunter and a "damned good shot," according to no less than William Faulkner, and he did in fact at one time have a share in a farm (with the Perelmans).

The young West experimented with a number of different names and personae before settling on Nathanael West. Nicknamed "Pep" and sometimes known as Nathaniel, he adopted various permutations of his family names, the most extravagant of which was Nathaniel Von Wallenstein Weinstein. He was born Nathan Weinstein in New York City on 17 October 1903 to Russian-Jewish immigrant parents. He was the first child of Anna Wallenstein and Max Weinstein. His father made his fortune in the construction and real-estate business, but it was largely wiped out in the stock market crash of 1929. (Like many, he went from shirtsleeves to shirtsleeves in a lifetime.) West made good use of his family's wealth, while it existed, to educate himself in literature and art. Knowledgeable in classical and contemporary literature, he collected fine books and avant-garde little magazines such as *transition*, *The Egoist*, and *The Criterion*. He loved the work of the Yellow Period, was particularly fond of Oscar Wilde, Walter Pater, Baudelaire, Arthur Rimbaud, and Paul Verlaine, as well as Alfred Jarry and J. K. Huysmans. He was very familiar with modernist and contemporary writing—Guillaume Apollinaire, James Joyce, Gertrude Stein, Ezra Pound, William Carlos Williams, and Wallace Stevens—and was particularly influenced by Fitzgerald. He was also very knowledgeable about modern visual arts.

His self-education shows impeccable avant-garde credentials. His formal education was founded on fraud, which in itself might be considered another impeccable avant-garde credential. "Dada bloomed on the campus," according to his biographer, Jay Martin (1970), when in 1922 he transferred from Tufts College to Brown University, using the superior grades of another student also called Nathan Weinstein. He also passed himself off as a veteran of the U.S. Navy. At Brown he met and befriended S. J. Perelman. And in the same year he published some accomplished Beardsleyesque cartoons in Brown's humor magazine, *The Brown Jug*. In 1923, under the name of Nathaniel W. Weinstein, he published the hoax essay "Euripides—A Playwright," in *Casements*, the university magazine, followed by some apprentice poems.

Finding himself, as a Jew, excluded from the university's fraternities, he founded the Hanseatic League, a society satirically named after the Baltic provinces where his ancestors had flourished until the czarist oppression of the 1880s. His biographer notes: "West regarded himself and his friends as similar to the free towns, centers of enlightenment and modernism set in the midst of the medieval barbarism of the Bacchanalian sensualists." And Martin characterizes the esoteric interests and activities, the mystical, ritual, and magical obsessions of this self-styled intellectual elite in terms of West's "dadaist willingness to experiment with the absurd." His sexual adventurism led him to contract gonorrhea, the treatment for which left him with recurrent prostate problems. West graduated in June 1924 and went to work in his father's construction business, as he had done during his vacations.

PARIS AND NEW YORK CITY

In October 1926 West went to Paris for a few months, financed by his relatives, and there began his first novel, *The Dream Life of Balso Snell*. It was in anticipation of this trip that he officially changed his name, on 16 August 1926, to Nathanael West. He chose "West" as a surname, he told William Carlos Williams, because "Horace Greeley said, 'Go west young man.' So I did." He did not, however, go West geographically until 1933. Going to Paris was the launch of his identity as a writer and a pilgrimage to the shrine of his modernist and avant-garde heroes. He stayed near Montparnasse; bought copies of Joyce's *Ulysses* (1922) at Sylvia Beach's legendary bookshop, Shakespeare and Company; toured the cafés, bars, and brothels of the literary and bohemian scene; and was able to boast of having glimpsed or rubbed shoulders with the likes of Jean Cocteau, André Gide, Ernest Hemingway, and T. S. Eliot. He met the surrealists Philippe Soupault (who befriended him), Max Ernst, and Louis Aragon as well as the American writer Henry Miller, who was introduced to West by his closest companion in Paris, the painter Hilaire Hiler. Typically, West in later accounts fantastically exaggerated the length of time he spent in Paris as well as the sort of life he led there, sometimes embroidering on true experiences, sometimes plain inventing others. He both celebrates and satirizes such subterfuge in the unpublished story "The Impostor," which gives an account of Paris in the 1920s and of Beano, a young man who has no artistic talent except for his ability to masquerade as a brilliant avant-garde sculptor: "Here was a man who could talk a whole gallery full of art works and looked like a genius yet couldn't draw worth a damn." Like most of West's short stories, "The Impostor" was not published in his lifetime,

but as Martin observes, "parts of it West later told as true stories about himself." He was enticed home from Paris in January 1927 by his anxious family, whose fortunes, like those of many others, were taking a turn for the worse.

Over the next few years West worked in the hotel business in New York City, first on the night desk of a cheap hotel, the Kenmore Hall, where he would entertain and offer free accommodation (on unchanged beds) to fellow writers such as S. J. Perelman, Michael Gold, and Dashiell Hammett. Perelman at this time introduced West to his writer colleagues on *The New Yorker*: George S. Kaufman, Dorothy Parker, and Alexander Woollcott. West continued his hospitality when, in the fall of 1930, he became manager of the Sutton Club Hotel, which at the height of the Depression became a refuge for writers, including Perelman (who by then was married to West's sister, Laura), Hammett, Lillian Hellman, James T. Farrell, and Edmund Wilson. At this time West worked on a series of short stories for which he was unable to secure publication, and some remained unfinished. A thinly fictionalized sampling of the Sutton clientele populate West's later novels.

THE DREAM LIFE OF BALSO SNELL (1931)

It was at this time that William Carlos Williams took an interest in West and recommended *The Dream Life of Balso Snell* to Contact Editions, the prestigious small press established in Paris by Robert McAlmon and the esteemed publisher, in the 1920s, of the best experimental writing by authors such as Gertrude Stein and Ernest Hemingway. The press had been recently taken over by David Moss and Martin Kamin, and West's novel was published in August 1931 in a deluxe edition of five hundred.

The Dream Life of Balso Snell is a fast-moving, scatological, collagistic narrative that begins with the entrance of the protagonist, Balso, into the anus of the Trojan horse, followed by his tour of the horse's intestine. According to "Through the Hole in the Mundane Millstone" (1931), West's leaflet advertising the novel, Balso finds the intestine to be "inhabited solely by authors in search of an audience" whose numerous "tales are elephantine close-ups of various literary positions and their technical methods." The novel ends with an account of Balso's onanistic orgasm, brought on by a combination of literary and sexual excess. West's advertisement boasts his surpassing the maverick dadaist Kurt Schwitters's "definition, 'Tout ce' que l'artiste crache, c'est l'art' ": "Everything the artist expectorates [or spits or spews or gobs up] is art." (He also acknowledges his debt to French avant-garde sources, declaring himself "much like Guillaume Apollinaire, Jarry, Ribemont-Dessaignes, Raymond Roussel, and certain of the surrealists."

In the novel, on entering the "foyer-like lower intestine" of the Trojan horse, Balso—to "keep his heart high and yet out of his throat"—sings a song that parades many of West's avant-garde sources:

Round as the Anus
Of a Bronze Horse
Or the Tender Buttons
Used by Horses for Ani. . . .

Here we find parodied, among other things, the sparse syntax of imagism, the compressed lyric symbolism of W. B. Yeats, the perverse somatic humor of James Joyce, and the cryptic poetics of Gertrude Stein's volume of cubist poetry, *Tender Buttons* (1915). Balso encounters further down the digestive tract of the Trojan Horse parodies of Dostoyevsky, the Marquis de Sade, Rainer Maria Rilke, Rimbaud, J. K. Huysmans, Yeats, Joyce, Proust, William Carlos Williams, Pound, Perelman, Hammett, Maxim Gorky, James Branch Cabell, Rabelais, Voltaire, Aldous Huxley, and D. H. Lawrence. West's model for his eponymous hero, however, was his college basketball coach, Walter Snell.

MISS LONELYHEARTS (1933)

While still at his hotel desk, West began work on the novel *Miss Lonelyhearts*, but he also began to expand into other literary activities. At Williams's invitation he became an associate editor of a new version of *Contact* magazine, which Williams had previously coedited with McAlmon. West also contributed to the magazine *Americana*, edited by George Grosz, under the sobriquet of "the laughing morticians of the present." As in his novels, West's editorial and magazine work was concerned primarily with adapting European avant-garde techniques to American traditions for distinctively American use. *Contact*'s mission, according to West and Williams, was "to cut a trail through the American jungle without the use of a European compass." West told Williams in 1932, however, that their work would be "not only in but against the American grain and yet in idiomatic pain." *Contact* saw itself in 1931 as the "legitimate successor" to Eugène Jolas's Paris-based journal, *transition*, possibly the most important and influential little magazine of the period. West published extracts from *Miss Lonelyhearts* in *Contact* as well as work by Williams, Perelman, E. E. Cummings, and others. And in the October 1932 issue of *Contact*, he published his own important credo, "Some Notes on

Violence," which defended the excessive violence in his work as an accurate reflection of American experience:

In America violence is idiomatic. Read our newspapers. To make the front page a murderer has to use his imagination, he also has to use a particularly hideous instrument. Take this morning's paper: FATHER CUTS SON'S THROAT IN BASEBALL ARGUMENT. It appears on the inside page. To make the first page, he should have killed three sons and with a baseball bat instead of a knife. Only liberality and symmetry could have made this daily occurrence interesting.

Miss Lonelyhearts is a short, darkly funny, and highly polished satire on the newspaper media of the 1930s, and is punctuated with scenes of excessive violence. The very form of this novel is based on the popular newspaper genre of the comic strip cartoon, as West explains in his "Some Notes on Miss L." (1933), where he reveals his initial subtitle, "A Novel in the Form of a Comic Strip," and his first conception of the chapters as

squares in which many things happen through one action. The speeches contained in the conventional balloons. I abandoned this idea, but retained some of the comic strip technique: Each chapter instead of going forward in time, also goes backward, forward, up and down in space like a picture. Violent images are used to illustrate commonplace events. Violent acts are left almost bald.

This novel's searing, comedic exploration of the life of the newspaper columnist has certainly not become dated. Miss Lonelyhearts, the novel's antihero, is in fact a man, whose real name is never disclosed. He masquerades in print as a woman and a Christian. West calls him "a priest of our time" in "Some Notes on Miss L." Miss Lonelyhearts is obviously unhappy with his professional assignment, and the novel ends with his demise at the hands of an aggrieved correspondent, who shoots the columnist through a newspaper. There have been any number of critical responses to this novel, from recognition of an absurd and nihilistic vision, to readings based on Jewish mysticism, and even to naive Christian interpretations. It has been savaged, too, by feminist criticism for its apparent misogyny and its inscriptions of violence. But it has stood the test of time, not only because of its brilliant humor and style, its beautifully taut, well-honed satirical bite, not only because the norms of the print media it savages in the 1930s have remained little changed in the twenty-first century, but also because it offers a refreshingly modern insight into the politics of gender and may even offer glimpses of alternative models for gender and sexuality. Exercising an, at times, devastating black humor, West uses the experiences of Miss Lonelyhearts with his colleagues, his readers, and his long-suffering girlfriend to explore the gender politics promoted by the Hearst newspapers at the time of the Depression.

West's pointed references to the printed media's power of escapism suggest Miss Lonelyhearts' failure as a latter-day messiah: "He saw a ragged woman with an enormous goiter pick a love story magazine out of a garbage can and seem very excited by her find." Doyle, the crippled man cuckolded by Miss Lonelyhearts (and who later assassinates the columnist), appears as an assemblage of disparate elements from the press, "like one of those composite photographs used by screen magazines in guessing contests." His identity is described as if it were actually constructed out of popular journalism. West is here employing and adapting an avant-garde technique perfected by such modernist writers as James Joyce, who in the famous Nausikaa episode of his great modern novel *Ulysses* (1922), represents the consciousness of a woman, Gerty Macdowell, as if it were a collage of popular magazine and romantic fiction clichés. Not only does this technique suggest how identity in general might be socially constructed and in continual process, rather than unified and somehow already naturally given, but it also suggests the same about our gender. And it is also in this arena of gender politics that West's novel makes some important and highly amusing explorations.

It was not, however, the novel's engagement with gender politics that struck a chord with West's contemporary reviewers so much as the depiction of Miss Lonelyhearts's readers, who are found largely among the urban poor and who are represented by their letters collaged into the text. It is of no small significance that the letters from "Sick-of-it-all," "Desperate," "Broken-hearted," "Disillusioned-with-tubercular-husband," "Broad Shoulders," and so on are not actually, or perhaps not entirely, the inventions of Nathanael West. They are, apparently, real letters, according to his biographer Jay Martin, which were sent to the "Susan Chester" column of the *Brooklyn Eagle* and came into West's hands via his brother-in-law, S. J. Perelman. This disturbing information makes the reading of them even more shocking. But whether authentic or not, they offer a grotesque insight into urban experience in Depression America.

In "A New American Writer," an article originally published in Ezra Pound's literary page of *Il Mare* (21 January 1931), William Carlos Williams sums up West's achievement in *Miss Lonelyhearts* firstly in terms of his choice of subject matter: "He takes seriously a theme of great importance so trite that all of us thought there would be no life in it; I mean the terrible moral impoverishment of our youth in the cities." But Williams also points to the new literary method West has devised to achieve this, a method that involves appropriating and reorganizing the language of journalism, which is "the dialect natural to such a condition":

> Since the newspapers are the principal corruptors of all that has value in language, it is with this very journalistic "aspect" and everyday speech that language must be regenerated. West has taken as his material the idiom of the reporters, the tough men of the newspapers, and has counterpointed it with the pathetic letters and emotions of the poor and ignorant city dwellers who write to the newspapers to obtain counsel for their afflictions and poverty.

Williams identifies West's brilliant combination of powerful political satire and erudite avant-garde experimental technique as the factors that mark out this work as significant:

> After all, what is the urban population made up of? Of seduced and corrupted, nothing more. They have been gathered together so that they may be better exploited, and this is West's material. But no, his "material" is writing itself—he has invented a new manner.... "Don't be deceived" could be West's motto. Don't think yourself literate merely because you write long books and use correct English. Here are the problems, do something with them that will not be a lie. Don't deceive yourself: you don't see because you don't look. These things are there just the same. And if you think you can write poems while you live in a sewer, and at the same time think you're lying in a bed of roses—well go ahead and be happy!
> The cities are rotten and desperate—so is most polite, "literary" literature.

West himself, however, sends up serious, dogmatic, and socially concerned readings that may be in danger of turning his stunning fiction into mere allegory or political parable. In the episode "Miss Lonelyhearts Attends a Party," his editor, the hideous and cruel (and aptly named) Shrike has got hold of "a batch of letters" and goes "among his guests" distributing them "as a magician does cards":

> Here's one from an old woman whose son died last week. She is seventy years old and sells pencils for a living. She has no stockings and wears heavy boots on her torn and bleeding

feet. She has rheum in her eyes. Have you room in your heart for her?

This one is a jim-dandy. A young boy wants a violin. It looks simple; all you have to do is get the kid one. But then you discover that he has dictated the letter to his little sister. He is paralyzed and can't even feed himself. He has a toy violin and hugs it to his chest, imitating the sound of playing with his mouth. How pathetic! However, one can learn much from this parable. Label the boy Labor, the violin Capital, and so on . . . " [ellipses in original]

Miss Lonelyhearts stood it with the utmost serenity; he was not even interested. What goes on in the sea is of no interest to the rock.

The boy's toy violin, the absent desired violin, the boy's letter in which all are described, Shrike's reading of the letter, and West's representation of Shrike's reading of the letter in his novel are all themselves, of course, capable of being allegorized—not least as allegories of art or of allegory itself. As Williams says, West's " 'material' is writing itself." But his novel is also asking questions about the politics and power of writing, about where and how the voices of "the seriously injured of our civic life" (in Williams's words) are produced, and where and how they find their way into the public realm of print. West communicates these questions with considerable eloquence, humor, and humanity. The following is his three-line credo for any aspiring novelist, the coda to his brief reflection on *Miss Lonelyhearts*:

I was serious therefore I could not be obscene.
I was honest therefore I could not be sordid.
A novelist can afford to be everything but dull.

By the time *Miss Lonelyhearts* was published in April 1933 as a book, West's father had died and his fiancée, Alice Shepard, the dedicatee of his first novel, had broken off their engagement (over West's infidelity with Lillian Hellman). Although constantly complaining of poverty, he was able to buy, along with the Perelmans, a farm in Erwinna, not far from his friends the novelists Josephine Herbst and John Herrmann. His ill luck continued when Liveright, the publisher of *Miss Lonelyhearts*, went bankrupt, with only a few hundred copies of the novel surviving the printer's seizure of stock. It was republished in June by Harcourt, Brace, but the disruption slowed up sales considerably. Nevertheless, West sold the movie rights to Twentieth Century Pictures for $4,000 and soon after his novel appeared on screen in an unrecognizable form as *Advice to the Lovelorn* (1933). In July 1933 West joined the Perelmans in Los Angeles, having been

contracted as a writer to Columbia Pictures, but after intensive labor on a number of unproduced scripts, he was out of work and back hunting in Erwinna by the fall.

A COOL MILLION (1934)

A Cool Million was published by Covici-Friede in 1934, and the movie rights went this time to Columbia Pictures. In this novel West's target was the all-American rags-to-riches fantasies of Horatio Alger. His protagonist literally falls apart in his attempt to become president. Toothless, eyeless, thumbless, bald, and one-legged, Lemuel Pitkin eventually dies a fascist martyr. During one episode American consumerism is memorably scourged by the scathing invective of Chief Israel Satinpenny, who—shortly before scalping Lemuel Pitkin—itemizes some basic materials of the collagist:

The land was flooded with toilet paper, painted boxes to keep pins in, key rings, watch fobs, leatherette satchels . . . . The day of vengeance is here. The star of the paleface is sinking and he knows it. Spengler has said so; Valéry has said so; thousands of his wise men proclaim it.

O, brothers, this is the time to run upon his neck and the bosses of his armor. While he is sick and fainting, while he is dying of a surfeit of shoddy.

Satinpenny leaves a young brave to loot his "bloody head of its store teeth and glass eye." West's satire attempts to transform America's "surfeit of shoddy," or as he phrases it elsewhere, "the apocalypse of the Second Hand." But the timing of his antifascist gesture was premature and the novel failed to please reviewers, as West recalled in a 1939 letter to Saxe Commins on the later reprinting of *A Cool Million*:

Did you ever read a book called "A Cool Million" . . . ? A lot of people think it is a pretty good one and that the reason it flopped is because it was published much too soon in the race toward Fascism. It came out when no one in this country, except a few Jeremiahs like myself, took seriously the possibility of a Fascist America . . . . I feel that at the present time it might have a very good chance of arousing some interest.

HOLLYWOOD

West's season of failures continued. His collaborative attempt with Perelman, in 1934, at a play, *Even Stephen*, bombed, as did his application for a Guggenheim Fellowship, although Fitzgerald was a referee. In 1935, after a disastrous love affair with a married woman, West threw himself into political activities. Along with other writers such as Edward Dahlberg, he was arrested and jailed for picketing with strikers at a department store, and he joined the newly formed League of American Writers, whose revolutionary manifesto he signed. Back in Los Angeles, unemployed and suffering another bout of gonorrhea, he was supported by the Perelmans until January 1936, when he got a decent contract with Republic Productions. And for the remaining years of his life he worked as a screenwriter. West's screenplay for Lester Cole's story, "I Stole a Million," was his first major solo credit for Republic. For RKO he worked on *Five Came Back* (1939) and had solo credits for *Men Against the Sky* (1940) and *Let's Make Music* (1940). In *The Thirties* (1980), his journal of the period, Edmund Wilson wrote an entertaining sketch of West at work in Hollywood:

> They told West they wanted a scenario with a little perversity in it—he had written them a sentimental reminiscence (he supposed) of some old movie he had seen and had carefully stuck in so many clichés as to make it practically unreadable, so that the movie man had said, I want you to write it so that if we don't use it, you can print it as a short story.—His idea for scenario involving D. H. Lawrence stallion (shot of white arms around his neck), clean scientific steely doctor whom woman corrupts (she dances the lewd Martinique dance and beat beat of drum repeats hoof-beats of stallion—she is in dope ring to keep up stud farm because she loves the stallion so) but finally the doctor's son turns up, the only lover who has been able to compete with the stallion, she saves the doctor on account of him (wonderful photo montage of hypodermic, the machine, against her white leg)—stallion finally tramples her to death.—West tolerant.—Perelman intolerant.—West had sold movie rights of *Lonelyhearts* for $4,000.—Their names!—Gimfel—Lastvogel—West had gotten in wrong for saying to him, And the Lastvogel shall be Firstvogel.

THE DAY OF THE LOCUST (1939)

West was politically active in Hollywood. He spoke on "Makers of Mass Neuroses" at the Western Writers' Congress of 1936; in 1937 and 1938 he worked for the Spanish Refugee Relief Campaign. In 1939, when Hollywood hosted a fund-raising exhibition of Picasso's *Guernica* (1937), West was a sponsor, and he pays homage to that painting in his last novel, *The Day of the Locust*, published in May 1939. Often compared with F. Scott Fitzgerald's *The Last Tycoon* (1941), this coruscating satire on the Hollywood dream factory (originally titled "The Cheated") follows the unpromising career of an artist,

Tod Hackett and closes with his (visionary) execution of a painting. The subjects in this painting also form the focus of the novel, a seedy panorama of the grotesque, displaced, and marginalized—the losers at Hollywood's fringes rather than the success stories at its center. They were in the "the innumerable sketches he had made of the people who come to California to die; the cultists of all sorts, economic as well as religious, the wave, airplane, funeral and preview watchers—all those poor devils who can only be stirred by the promise of miracles and then only to violence." This is the California of prostitution, violence, and sleaze, where middle-class pleasure seekers "discover sunshine isn't enough":

> They don't know what to do with their time. They haven't the mental equipment for leisure, the money nor the physical equipment for pleasure.... If only a plane would crash once in a while.... Oranges can't titillate their jaded palates. Nothing can be violent enough to make taut their slack minds and bodies. They have been cheated and betrayed. They have slaved and saved for nothing.

Like Eliot's *The Waste Land*, West's description of the cultural "dumping ground" of a Hollywood film lot is a kind of avant-garde collage:

> There were bridges which bridged nothing, sculpture in trees, palaces that seemed of marble until a whole stone portico began to flap in the light breeze. And there were figures as well. A hundred yards from where Tod was sitting a man in a derby hat leaned drowsily against the gilded poop of a Venetian barque and peeled an apple. Still farther on, a charwoman on a stepladder was scrubbing with soap and water the face of a Buddha thirty feet high.

West has transformed here the traditional American list, as itemized by Emerson and Whitman, for example, into a catalogue of detritus.

The machismo of Hemingway's fiction is sent up in one of the most violent scenes in the book, where a cockfight is described in terms that also suggest the surrealist violence of a Luis Buñuel film: "The red thrust weakly with its broken bill. Juju went into the air again and this time drove a gaff through one of the red's eyes into its brain. The red fell over stone dead.... Juju pecked at the dead bird's remaining eye." Such bloody scenes are woven into the story of Tod Hackett's courtship of Faye Greener, whose name takes a swipe at Daisy Fay (she of the green light at the end of her dock) in *The Great Gatsby*. West continues his undermining of gender categories in his moving depiction of a transvestite singer who had a soft, throbbing voice and his gestures were matronly, tender and aborted, a series of unconscious caresses. What he was doing was in no sense parody; it was too simple and too restrained. It wasn't even theatrical. This dark young man with his thin, hairless arms and soft, rounded shoulders, who rocked an imaginary cradle as he crooned, was really a woman.

When he had finished, there was a great deal of applause. The young man shook himself and became an actor again. He tripped on his train, as though he weren't used to it, lifted his skirts to show he was wearing Paris garters, then strode off swinging his shoulders. His imitation of a man was awkward and obscene.

In the final, apocalyptic chapter, the artist-hero Tod Hackett, in the midst of a mindless and bloody mob riot, imagines completing his painting, "The Burning of Los Angeles." Intertextual links between Tod's painting and West's poem, "Burn the Cities" (1933), a strange celebration of the ascendancy of Marxism over Christianity, have been acknowledged, but their significance for readings of West's work remains a vexed point of debate. The first part of the poem was published as "Christmass Poem" in *Contempo* in 1933, but it was only published in its entirety after West's death.

In the final mob scene, West offers not a vision of all humanity, but a depiction of a certain social sector. West himself acknowledges this as a deliberate satiric strategy: his target is the protofascist middle-class mob. He confessed to the impossibility of including in his new novel the activities of Hollywood's left-wing progressive movement with which he sympathized, stating "I tried to describe a meeting of the Anti-Nazi League, but it didn't fit and I had to substitute a whore-house and a dirty film. The terribly sincere struggle of the League came out comic when I touched it and even libelous." And the novel was, indeed, criticized by the left because it did not directly show any of the Hollywood political forces opposed to fascism. But to do so would have skewed West's selective satiric method, as he explains in his letter to Malcolm Cowley:

I'm a comic writer and it seems impossible for me to handle any of the "big things" without seeming to laugh or at least smile.... Out here we have a strong progressive movement and I devote a great deal of time to it. Yet, although this new novel is about Hollywood, I found it impossible to include any of those activities in it. I made a desperate attempt before giving up.... Take the "mother" in Steinbeck's swell novel—I want to believe in her and yet inside myself I

honestly can't. When not writing a novel—say at a meeting of a committee we have out here to help the migratory worker—I do believe it and try to act on that belief. But at the typewriter by myself I can't.

West met Eileen McKenney in October 1939 and they were married in April 1940. In the following months his career as a screenwriter was on the up, and by the spring of 1940 he was talking about a new book: "I have the entire story clearly in my mind and know just what I intend to do with it," he told Bennett Cerf. "The more I think about it, the more certain I am that it can be a hell of a book." West's initial attempt at this project may well be constituted in the "Untitled Outline" published by Sarcan Bercovitch in his collection of West's writings, *Novels and Other Writings* (1997). It sketches "a story about a racket"—the friendship clubs found in personal columns of newspapers. On 22 December 1940, returning from a hunting trip in Mexico, West and his wife died as a result of a car crash at an intersection near El Centro, California.

AFTERLIFE

West himself thought of his work as "moral satire" but his writing eluded acclaim during his lifetime because it defied ready critical categorization. He was original but not bankable. "I seem to have no market whatsoever," he wrote to Edmund Wilson in 1939, "and while many people whose opinion I respect are full of sincere praise, the book reviewers disagree, even going so far as to attack the people who do praise my books, and the public is completely apathetic." His work was misunderstood and rejected in the 1930s, which produced a generation of writers pressed by the Soviet Union and its American supporters to follow the dogmatic principles of socialist realism. His writing did not please his communist friends, many of whom were avid exponents of socialist realism. The Marxist writer Michael Gold explained: "His writing seemed to me symbolic rather than realistic, and that was, to me, the supreme crime." West certainly recognized he was doomed to be misunderstood by his contemporaries on the left and right alike: "The radical press, although I consider myself on their side, doesn't like my particular kind of joking, and think it even Fascist sometimes, and the literature boys whom I detest, detest me in turn. The high brow press finds that I avoid the big significant things and the lending library touts in the daily press think me shocking."

By the 1950s West was gaining a notable posthumous reputation and wider readership, but his work was further traduced as absurd and nihilistic by a strand of American

Cold War criticism following W. H. Auden's lasting diagnosis of "West's Disease" in 1957: "a disease of consciousness which renders it incapable of converting wishes into desires. . . . There have, no doubt, always been cases of West's Disease, but the chances of infection in a democratic and mechanized society like our own are much greater than in the more static and poorer societies of earlier times." Norman Podhoretz, in an essay of 1957, typifies cold warrior criticism of West in finding his humor "profoundly unpolitical" and West himself so "anti-radical" as to be "almost un-American" (a novel use of the term in the era of Senator Joseph McCarthy). West's uneasy relationship with his Jewish background, and his lack of focus on specifically Jewish-American life, have encouraged some critics to denounce him as self-hating and others, like Daniel Walden, to attempt more constructively to read subtexts in West's work relating to Jewish prophetic traditions. Accusations of misogyny were leveled against West during the 1970s and during the rise of feminist criticism, when his depiction of violence or violent intent toward women was questioned. In their influential feminist work, *No Man's Land: The Place of the Woman Writer in the Twentieth Century* (1988–1989), Sandra M. Gilbert and Susan Gubar found West a misogynist and homophobic.

But there have since been readings that offer more positive explorations of West's subversive accounts of cross-dressers, homosexuals, and androgynes, his glorious disruption of gender boundaries and categories. And critics such as Rita Barnard (1995) and Matthew Roberts (1996) have moved beyond the previous despondency over West's bleak and absurd vision and dark irony to offer more sophisticated readings of his negative critique of consumerism and the culture industry. Roberts, Robert I. Edenbaum (1986), Jonathan Veitch (1997), and Deborah Wyrick (1979) have very fruitfully explored his engagement with European and American dadaism and surrealism. And there has also been an increasingly rich seam of criticism exploring his film work, his Hollywood experiences and material, and the various film adaptations of his writing, as in the work of J. A. Ward and Nancy Pogel. More importantly, West's brief oeuvre has been recognized for its enormous impact on later twentieth-century writing. Each generation, it seems, discovers him anew. His influence has been acknowledged by a diverse range of American writers, including Carson McCullers, Flannery O'Connor, Joseph Heller, Saul Bellow, Thomas Pynchon, and Ishmael Reed. And Soupault's 1946 French edition of *Miss Lonelyhearts*, translated by Marcelle Sibon, is also considered a significant landmark in European postwar fiction. Continuities with West in O'Connor's gothic grotesque and in the comedic Jewish-American writing of Heller have been explored by critics, but there has been little response to the acknowledgment by the African-American writer, Ishmael Reed, of West as his primary, most formative, literary influence. West's work is the focus of growing and renewed critical interest. His four novels were republished by the Library of America in a volume, edited by Sacvan Bercovitch, that includes an extensive selection of his short stories, scripts, and letters. The first-time reader of West is to be envied for the enormous pleasure in discovering such a talent, but as with all classic writing, repeated re-reading brings rich reward as well. It is a good time to go West.

SELECTED WORKS

The Dream Life of Balso Snell (1931)
Miss Lonelyhearts (1933)
A Cool Million (1934)
The Day of the Locust (1939)
Novels and Other Writings: The Dream Life of Balso Snell; Miss Lonelyhearts; A Cool Million; The Day of the Locust; Other Writings; Unpublished Writings and Fragments; Letters (1997)

FURTHER READING

Abrahams, Roger D. "Androgynes Bound: Nathanael West's *Miss Lonelyhearts*." In *Seven Contemporary Authors: Essays on Cozzens, Miller, West, Golding, Heller, Albee, and Powers*, edited by T. D. Whitbread. Austin, Tex., and London, 1966. One of the first essays to consider androgyny in West's novel.

Barnard, Rita. *The Great Depression and the Culture of Abundance: Kenneth Fearing, Nathanael West, and Mass Culture in the 1930s*. Cambridge, 1995. An intelligent, cultural studies–based treatment of West's work in the context of American consumerism and mass culture.

Bloom, Harold, ed. *Modern Critical Views: Nathanael West*. New York, 1986. Very useful sampling of a range of scholarship on West. Includes extracts from Stanley Edgar Hyman, W. H. Auden, James F. Light, Alvin B. Kernan, Daniel Aaron, and others.

Bloom, Harold, ed. *Modern Critical Views: Nathanael West's* Miss Lonelyhearts. New York, 1987. An excellent sampling of a range of scholarship on *Miss Lonelyhearts*. Useful introduction.

Daniel, Carter A. "West's Revisions of *Miss Lonelyhearts*." *Studies in Bibliography* 16 (1963): 232–243. Fascinating reading on the differences between early and final versions of each chapter.

Edenbaum, Robert I. "Dada and Surrealism: A Literary Instance." *Arts in Society* 5 (1986): 114–125.

Goldman, Jane. " 'Miss Lonelyhearts and the Party Dress': Cross-dressing and Collage in the Satires of Nathanael West." *Glasgow Review* 2 (Autumn 1993): 40–54.

Goldman, Jane. "Dada Goes West: Re-Reading Revolution in *The Day of the Locust*." *Imprimatur* 2, nos. 1–2 (Autumn 1996): 20–36.

Jackson, Thomas H., ed. *Twentieth Century Interpretations of Miss Lonelyhearts*. Englewood Cliffs, N.J., 1971.

Long, Robert Emmet. *Nathanael West*. New York, 1985.

Madden, David, ed. *Nathanael West: The Cheaters and the Cheated: A Collection of Critical Essays*. Deland, Fla., 1973.

Martin, Jay. *Nathanael West: The Art of His Life*. New York, 1970. Excellent. Probably the first book to read after reading West. Indispensable both as a biography and as a sound critical introduction to the work.

Martin, Jay, ed. *Nathanael West: A Collection of Critical Essays*. Englewood Cliffs, N.J., 1971. Excellent. Includes Perelman's superb portrait of West, as well as Podhoretz's Cold War demolition job and many other gems.

Pogel, Nancy, and William Chamberlain. "Humor into Film: Self-Reflections in Adaptations of Black Comic Novels." In *Black Humor: Critical Essays*. Edited by Alan R. Pratt. New York, 1993.

Roberts, Matthew. "Bonfire of the Avant-Garde: Cultural Rage and Readerly Complicity in *The Day of the Locust*." *Modern Fiction Studies* 42, no. 1 (Spring 1996): 61–90.

Ross, Alan. "The Dead Centre: An Introduction to Nathanael West." *Horizon* 106 (1957): 284–296. Ross was responsible for introducing West to a British readership after World War II. This essay introduces his best-selling edition of West's novels, *The Complete Works of Nathanael West* (1957).

Siegel, Ben, ed. *Critical Essays on Nathanael West*. New York and Oxford, 1994.

Strychacz, Thomas. *Modernism, Mass Culture, and Professionalism*. Cambridge, 1993.

Vannatta, Dennis P. *Nathanael West: An Annotated Bibliography of the Scholarship and Works*. New York, 1976.

Veitch, Jonathan. *American Superrealism: Nathanael West and the Politics of Representation in the 1930s*. Madison, Wisc., 1997. An excellent, well-written, and engaging exploration of West's avant-gardism, which extends discussion of the relevance of West's work to the era of the Los Angeles riots and the O. J. Simpson trials.

Ward, J. A. "The Hollywood Metaphor: The Marx Brothers, S. J. Perelman, and Nathanael West." In *S. J. Perelman: Critical Essays*, edited by Steven H. Gale. New York, 1992.

White, William. "Unpublished Faulkner: Reply to a Nathanael West Questionnaire." *American Book Collector* 17 (September 1966): 27.

Wilson, Edmund. *The Thirties*. Edited by Leon Abel. New York, 1980.

Wisker, Alistair. *The Writing of Nathanael West*. Basingstoke, U.K., 1990. A very useful and accessible introduction to West's novels for new readers and students. It includes an appendix of some of West's brief essays and short stories.

Wyrick, Deborah. "Dadaist Collage Structure and Nathanael West's *Dream Life of Balso Snell*." *Studies in the Novel* 11 (1979): 349–359.

WEST COAST SCHOOL

by Catherine Daly

Thousands of writers on the West Coast have made important contributions to arts and letters, and beyond that, to environmental writing, political writing, experimentalism, and performance. Under the rubric "West Coast School," this essay surveys writers living on the West Coast during the twentieth century. The work of the West Coast School writers is characterized by eroticism, spirituality, nature writing, and autobiography. San Francisco supports more poetry publishing, performance, and education than any U.S. city except New York. Most major West Coast writers have lived near San Francisco at one time.

The label "West Coast School" emphasizes characteristics many writers in this group share with New York School writers, which include participation in homosexual subculture; use of postmodern collage as a technique; concern with forming an immediate, intimate, and sincere relationship to the audience; distrust of materialism; and interest in linguistics. The term "San Francisco Renaissance" is often used to distinguish local writers and writers who were already on the West Coast in the mid-1950s, particularly those who were part of the "Berkeley Renaissance" in the 1940s, from the Beats, who migrated from New York to San Francisco in the mid-1950s but had left San Francisco by the 1960s Vietnam era. The term "San Francisco Renaissance" can refer to either of two groups: one consisting of Lawrence Ferlinghetti (also associated with the Beats and publisher of City Lights Books), Kenneth Rexroth, Gary Snyder, Joanne Kyger, and Philip Whalen, and another consisting of Kenneth Rexroth, Robert Duncan (who was at Black Mountain), Jack Spicer, Madeleine Gleason, Helen Adam, and Robin Blaser. "West Coast School" deemphasizes the tenuous relationships Kenneth Rexroth and Yvor Winters had to the earlier Chicago Renaissance.

Like the New York School, the West Coast School is perhaps not a school. It may be one or more feuding lineages of writers that have nevertheless influenced each other and have participated in the same geography and economy. The West Coast School must encompass writers as diverse as the poet and playwright Robinson Jeffers and the poet, critic, and publisher Lyn Hejinian. It must illuminate differences among Michael Palmer and Rae Armantrout, Leslie Scalapino, the West Coast Language poets, writers of the analytic lyric, and writers who use traditional forms. More than one group of writers and artists have called themselves the West Coast School. The West Coast School of surrealists is loosely associated with Philip Lamantia, a surrealist poet who met André Breton when Breton was in New York during World War II, and with the super-realist legacy, which is part of the nexus of influences on Language poetry. Lamantia, in turn, has been associated with both the Beats and the San Francisco Renaissance. The West Coast School of language poets includes Lyn Hejinian, Bob Perelman, Kit Robinson, and poets, playwrights, fiction writers, and critics no longer living on the West Coast: Ron Silliman, Barrett Watten, and Carla Harryman.

Robert Duncan, Jack Spicer, and Robin Blaser are associated with the West Coast School of abstract expressionist painters, just as New York School poets are associated with the New York School of abstract expressionist painters. Robert Duncan collaborated with his partner, the painter and collage artist Jess Collins, and Jack Spicer with his friend the collage artist Fran Herndon. Also like the New York School, the Berkeley Renaissance poets Robert Duncan, Jack Spicer, and Robin Blaser were a self-described "coterie" only secondarily interested in publishing outside their circle. Robin Blaser's long poem *The Holy Forest* was not published until 1993. Robert Duncan wrote open-ended long poems and abstained from publication for fifteen years; Jack Spicer specified that his poems should not be published or distributed outside the Bay Area during his lifetime. All three were homosexual men who wrote about their experiences before the Stonewall protests.

Spicer taught poetry writing at the San Francisco Institute of Art, where New York School writer Bill Berkson has also taught. The second-generation New York School poet Ted Berrigan, quintessential postmodern collage poet, was a teacher at the Iowa Writers Workshop while West Coast Language poets Bob Perelman and Barrett Watten were students there. He was also teaching at Yale while Kit Robinson was at Yale. Second-generation New York School poets Lew Welch and Anne Waldman were among those in attendance at the 1965 Berkeley Poetry Conference.

HISTORY

The story of West Coast School writing is that of a regional literature becoming a national literature. The 1960 *New American Poetry, 1945–1960*, anthology edited by Donald Allen, which brought many West Coast writers to national attention, was a regionalist anthology. It divided postmodern poets into groups by region. The Allen anthology split West Coast School writers into two groups: San Francisco Renaissance and "other." Poems by Helen Adam, William Everson, Madeleine Gleason, Lawrence Ferlinghetti, Jack Spicer, and Philip Lamantia were included in the San Francisco Renaissance section, separate from the Beat section of more nomadic writers but also separate from Philip Whalen, Gilbert Sorrentino, Gary Snyder, Michael McClure, and David Meltzer in the unlabeled section. Many West Coast School writers never embraced modernism and postmodernism, such as Robinson Jeffers and Yvor Winters, while almost all West Coast School writers continue the group's idiosyncratic nonconformity.

Several events were key to the relationships among the poets and to their presentation to a national audience. Two of these events are associated with the Beats: the 1955 Six Gallery reading, when Kenneth Rexroth introduced performances by Philip Lamantia, Gary Snyder, Philip Whalen, Michael McClure, and Allen Ginsberg, and the 1957 publication of Kenneth Rexroth's "San Francisco Letter" in the "San Francisco Scene" issue of *Evergreen Review*. Duncan, Spicer, Blaser, Snyder, Kyger, Welch, and Beat poets Ginsberg and Lenore Kandel read at the 1965 Berkeley Poetry Conference sponsored by UC Berkeley Extension. It was Jack Spicer's last public appearance.

Several institutions are associated with West Coast School writing. Duncan, Spicer, and Blaser met at Berkeley, and the latter two studied there with Josephine Miles. Robert Hass and Thom Gunn were students of Yvor Winters at Stanford. Madeleine Gleason helped found the Poetry Center at San Francisco State University with a donation from W. H. Auden. Duncan and Miles founded its reading series. The West Coast poets are interested in performance poetry. Shunryu Suzuki, who popularized

Zen Buddhism for a Western audience, including Snyder, Kyger, and Whalen, opened the San Francisco Zen Center in 1959. Philip Whalen served as abbot of the Hartford Street Zen Center in San Francisco.

Small presses and institutions in the 1970s gave rise to contemporary West Coast School writing. These presses include The Figures, Lyn Hejinian's Tuumba and Atelos, and Leslie Scalapino's O Books. West Coast writers have founded schools including the New College of California Poetics program, where Tom Clark, Lyn Hejinian, David Meltzer, and the late Robert Duncan taught. Black Sparrow, originally located in Santa Barbara, published West Coast writers Tom Clark, William Everson, David Meltzer, Venice Beat poet Charles Bukowski, and the second-generation New York School poet Aram Saroyan. Sun & Moon/Green Integer Press in Los Angeles publishes works by New York School, West Coast School, and Language writers as well as its translations of international experimental writing. Lawrence Ferlinghetti's bookstore and press, founded in 1953 and 1955 respectively, has published New York School poets, the Beats, and West Coast poets including Philip Lamantia and Carla Harryman.

CHARACTERISTICS

The writers of the West Coast School are primarily poets but most have written important works in other genres. Robinson Jeffers's modernization of *Medea* (1946) was his most successful play. William Everson continued his fine-press and hand-press printing from his time in a camp for conscientious objectors, through his printing of a Psalter during his period of religious vocation to his Lime Kiln Press at UC Santa Cruz. Lyn Hejinian wrote an influential autobiography, *My Life* (1978) until the 1980s. Gilbert Sorrentino was primarily associated with New York writing; since the 1980s he has taught fiction at Stanford. Many West Coast writers have published influential translations of Japanese, Chinese, Russian, and Native-American literatures.

West Coast writers display their political convictions in their writings. Robinson Jeffers spoke out against World War II, although his sons served in the military. Kenneth Rexroth, a political organizer and anarchist, and William Everson were conscientious objectors during World War II. Robert Duncan was given a psychiatric discharge from the military because he was homosexual. His 1944 essay "The Homosexual in Society" openly discussed his homosexuality and creativity. In the 1960s Gary Snyder led protests against the Vietnam War and was active in ecology movements. Duncan also protested this war. Language poetry is a political poetry based in socialism. Hejinian's and Scalapino's work is feminist. Because some West Coast School writing is politically exigent, it is sometimes forgettable after a particular moment has passed.

Most West Coast writing has a spiritual dimension. Yvor Winters searched for a morally responsible writing opposed to transcendentalism, Jeffers was a post-Protestant pantheist, Rexroth was an Anglican fascinated by mysticism who converted to Catholicism late in life, and William Everson became known as "the Beat friar" during his long period as a Benedictine lay monastic. Zen Buddhism has had a diffuse effect on the querying of self, narration, perception, and phenomenology of Kyger, Snyder, Whalen, Welch, and Leslie Scalapino. This influence is different from that of Tibetan Buddhism on the Beat writers. Michael Palmer's attempt to purify the lyric is also an attempt to correct the immorality of modernism. This focus on purification has spiritual and political aspects.

Both mythology and psychology have been important aspects of this spirituality: Jeffers's writing is Freudian, both Everson and the younger Beat poet Diane Di Prima use Jungian symbolism. The spiritualism of Duncan, Spicer, and Blaser and the cross-cultural mysticism of the surrealists after Lamantia were in many ways alternatives to the mythical structures and stories used by Jeffers, Everson, and Snyder. Helen Adam, Joanne Kyger, and Diane Di Prima reinterpreted myths and fairy tales in their early poetry. Use of myths and mysticism relate some West Coast work to that of the deep-image writers Robert Bly, James Wright, and Diane Wakoski, who was born in southern California, but also to the ethnopoetics of Jerome Rothenberg and Nathaniel Mackey, who now teach in California. David Meltzer, Diane Di Prima, Jerome Rothenberg, and Nathaniel Tarn have used kabala in their writings. Snyder has incorporated Native-American spiritual practices, oral culture, and mythology into his writing. Brenda Hillman continues the more hermetic tradition of Robert Duncan by exploring the dualities of neo-gnosticism within the history and symbolism of California. Some of this spiritually based work relies on an outside system of belief to complete or close a poem in a transcendent manner. No matter how sympathetic Western use of Native-American and Pacific Rim cultural values and characteristics, it remains distinct from use in works by Native Americans or by West Coast writers from other Pacific Rim countries.

The frank eroticism West Coast writing displays sometimes grounds the investigations of esoteric religious philosophies or plays out symbolic narratives. Incest is part of the plots of Jeffers's plays and longer narrative poems. In the cases of Everson's *River-Root* (1976) and Beat poet Lenore Kandel's *The Love Book* (1966), the erotic work is not widely available or has been censored. Leslie Scalapino and Lyn Hejinian have written erotica. Works by Rexroth, Everson, Duncan, Snyder, Kyger, Whalen, Lamantia, McClure, and others have sexual subject matter. Robert Hass's first book, *Field Guide* (1978), compares the careful observation and writing of poets to that of pornographers.

West Coast writers translate poetry: Rexroth was a self-taught translator, and his books *100 Poems from the Chinese* (1971) and *100 Poems from the Japanese* (1964) introduced this poetry to a wide audience. Gary Snyder translates from the Chinese. Snyder and Joanne Kyger lived in Kyoto, Japan, during the 1960s. During their period in residence they associated with a group of American émigré poets and translators including Clayton Eshleman and Cid Corman. Jane Hirshfield, a Zen Buddhist, and Robert Hass have continued this tradition by translating poems from the Japanese.

The West Coast of the United States is the eastern edge of the Pacific Rim, and it is geologically distinct from the remainder of the United States. Even when nature is not the subject of West Coast writing, the writing presents a complex and interesting relationship to place or landscape. Jeffers had a sense of nature overwhelming the individual. Everson addressed the violence of nature as its inscape or revelation and considered it the violence of the self. Both Everson and Snyder insisted nature was autonomous. Snyder sought cultural continuity through landscape. Robert Hass's poetry of place, derived from Kenneth Rexroth's, establishes an allegorical relationship between place, history of place, and thought.

Snyder and Whalen discovered analogues to their poetics techniques in their early menial jobs. "Riprap" is Snyder's famous comparison of collage poetry to piecing together mortarless mountainside horse trails. Whalen describes his journal collage technique as a "graph of a mind moving," a poetic that has much in common with that of New York School poet John Ashbery early in his career. Jack Spicer evolved his poetic from his academic work as a linguist.

Robert Duncan viewed region as an accident. By the 1970s, poets associated with the second generation of the New York School—Clark Coolidge, Tom Clark, Bill Berkson, and Lewis MacAdams, among them—had moved to the West Coast, where they associated with the poets and institutions supporting the younger West Coast School writers. Before moving west Clark Coolidge edited a journal with Michel Palmer. For a time Coolidge, Clark, Berkson, and MacAdams lived in Bolinas, a small town on the California coast north of San Francisco, as did Joanne Kyger, Philip Whalen, and Robert Creeley. MacAdams later relocated to Los Angeles, where he founded an advocacy organization for the Los Angeles River. In 1975 Ron Silliman edited a collection of nine "Language-centered" poets in Jerome Rothenberg's journal of ethnopoetics. Silliman's later anthology, *In the American Tree* (1986), published West Coast school experimental poets together with East Coast experimental poets.

INDIVIDUALS

Robinson Jeffers came to California as a student in Los Angeles at a time when California regionalist writers such as Ina Coolbrith, Edwin Markham, and George Stanley were dominant voices in West Coast writing. W. B. Yeats's symbolism and heightened diction, but not Yeats's spiritualism, infused Jeffers's writing. His subjects are Carmel, where he lived; violence and eroticism inherent in nature; and classical mythology. His work had a diverse influence on the writing and criticism of Everson and Lamantia and, through them, their students. Yvor Winters was opposed to Jeffers's pantheist antihumanism.

As a student at the University of Chicago, Yvor Winters met the poets of the Chicago Renaissance. The orientalism of imagism influenced his early poetry. He moved to New Mexico at a time when poets were creating a regional writing of the desert Southwest. He married the poet and novelist Janet Lewis and the couple relocated to Palo Alto. Winters taught generations of poets, including proponents of the New Formalism, at Stanford. Winters was the West Coast critic who practiced New Criticism.

Kenneth Rexroth had contact with the Chicago Renaissance writers early in his life. During his first marriage he was a painter interested in the Bauhaus artists and cubism as well as a poet. His early work is a precursor to Jack Spicer's "thing language." He began a correspondence with Yvor Winters when Winters was still an imagist poet and appreciated his verse even after they had a falling out over Winters's literary criticism. While Louis Zukofsky published Rexroth's poetry in *"An Objectivists" Anthology* in 1932, Rexroth is not an Objectivist. He became involved in radical politics as an anarchist anti-Stalinist. He worked for the precursor to the Works Progress Administration on murals in San Francisco's Coit Tower. Rexroth, opposed to Ezra Pound's fascism and anti-Semitism, was a self-taught translator. He translated the cubist poetry of Pierre Reverdy, whose work was to become so useful to the

New York School writers. Like Everson, Reverdy was a Benedictine lay monastic. Rexroth's means of translating by comparing verse and prose translations in many languages has become a common practice among poets. His literary "at homes" after World War II brought together the "Berkeley Renaissance" writers, Duncan, Spicer, and Blaser, with Everson, Lamantia, and Snyder. He introduced the poets at the famous Six Gallery reading, and his "San Francisco Letter" launched the Beat movement. Like the Beats and the poets of the New York School, he performed his poetry to jazz accompaniment.

William Everson was a farmer, conscientious objector, then Benedictine lay monastic during the Beat period, when he became known under his adopted name, Brother Antoninus. After reading Robinson Jeffers's poetry in the 1930s, he dropped out of college, bought a vineyard, and began writing. He published his first book, *These Are the Ravens*, in 1935. Everson's writing would gradually evolve away from Jeffers's, encompassing plain speech in his final autobiographical poem, *Dust Shall Be the Serpent's Food*. Everson was an informal student of Rexroth's after the war. In 1968 he wrote a critical work on Jeffers. After leaving his vocation he taught poetry, literature, and fine printing at UC Santa Cruz. Everson's critical work *Archetype West: The Pacific Coast as a Literary Region* (1976) names a regional West Coast school of writers ranging from Edwin Markham through Rexroth to many writers considered in this essay, but his focus on archetype and violence led him to overlook female poets such as his onetime wife Mary Fabilli. His poetry uses religious symbolism and free verse with heightened diction to write about sex, nature, religion, and other erotic-mystical topics. He also writes about the occult; he cast horoscopes for poems he was composing, and the signs of the zodiac became part of his symbol set. Stanford professor Albert Gelpi, a younger colleague of Winters, edited Everson's selected poems, *The Blood of a Poet* (1993), and wrote the afterword to *The Veritable Years* (1978). The Everson biographer Lee Bartlett includes Everson, Michael McClure, Kenneth Rexroth, Robert Duncan, Gary Snyder, Thom Gunn, Nathaniel Tarn, Michael Palmer, and the West Coast language poets in his West Coast School.

Robert Duncan was a self-described romantic adopted and raised in the theosophist communities of Southern California. After meeting the other Berkeley Renaissance poets, Jack Spicer and Robin Blaser, at Berkeley, he attended Black Mountain, where he later taught. His poetry makes free use of ornament, archaic diction and spelling, and grandiose rhetoric making information correspond and cohere. Under the influence of Pound, Duncan's writing is intertextual: his close reading of texts by Pindar, Homer, the metaphysical poets, and West Coast contemporaries often initiated his composition. Duncan's *The H. D. Book* is part of a legacy of eccentric texts about literature written by poets: Charles Olson's *Call Me Ishmael* (1966), Susan Howe's *My Emily Dickinson* (1985), and Louis Zukofsky's *Bottom: On Shakespeare* (1963). The poet Helen Adam's work is perhaps more like Robert Duncan's in tone and form than like the other West Coast School poets, since it adopts and twists the ballad form and traditional mythology of ballads. Duncan used traditional forms occasionally as well. Robin Blaser, because he relocated to Vancouver, British Columbia, in the 1960s, became a major voice in West Coast Canadian poetry.

Jack Spicer's serial poems are arguably the most important of the 1960s-era West Coast writings of experimental poets. Like William Everson, he viewed the West Coast as a landscape that demanded extreme writing. He viewed poets as individuals who would receive and communicate messages that were not necessarily intended for them. Like many of the West Coast School poets, he was interested in performance. He started an improvisation and nonsense-speech open mike night called "Blabbermouth." He engaged this community by converting local lore and gossip into an ideal city.

The Beat poets introduced readers to West Coast School writing through Lawrence Ferlinghetti's City Lights Publishers, the former Black Sparrow Press, and through the venerable national New Directions Press and international Sun & Moon/Green Integer Press. West Coast School writing ranges from Robinson Jeffers's modernization of classical myths to Carla Harryman's critique of those master narratives. It illuminates the extreme geography of the region through its spiritual and political positions, erotically charged abandonment, and personal performance.

[*See also* Beat Movement, The; Black Mountain Poetry; Gay Literature: Poetry and Prose; Jeffers, Robinson; *and* New York School of Poets.]

FURTHER READING

Allen, Donald M., ed. *The New American Poetry*. New York, 1960. Groundbreaking anthology.

Bartlett, Lee. *The Sun Is But a Morning Star: Studies in West Coast Poetry and Poetics*. Albuquerque, N.Mex., 1989.

Blaser, Robin. *The Holy Forest*. Toronto, 1993.

Davidson, Michael. *The San Francisco Renaissance: Poetics and Community at Mid-century*. Cambridge and New York, 1989.

Duncan, Robert. *Selected Poems*. Edited by Robert J. Bertholf. New York, 1993.

Everson, William. *Robinson Jeffers: Fragments of an Older Fury*. Berkeley, Calif., 1968.

Everson, William. *Archetype West: The Pacific Coast as a Literary Region*. Berkeley, Calif., 1976.

Everson, William. *The Crooked Lines of God: A Life Trilogy. The Residual Years (1934–1948), The Veritable Years (1949–1966), The Integral Years (1966–1994)*. Santa Rosa, Calif., 1997–2000.

Hejinian, Lyn. *My Life*. Los Angeles, 1978.

Jeffers, Robinson. *The Selected Poetry of Robinson Jeffers*. Edited by Tim Hunt. Palo Alto, Calif., 2001.

Rexroth, Kenneth. *The Collected Shorter Poems of Kenneth Rexroth*. New York, 1966.

Rexroth, Kenneth. *The Collected Longer Poems of Kenneth Rexroth*. New York, 1968.

Silliman, Ron. *In the American Tree*. Orono, Maine, 1986.

Snyder, Gary. *No Nature: New and Selected Poems*. New York, 1992.

Spicer, Jack. *The Collected Books of Jack Spicer*. Edited by Robin Blaser. New York, 1975.

Whalen, Philip. *Overtime: Selected Poems*. Edited by Michael Rothenberg. New York, 1999.

WESTERN FICTION: GREY, STEGNER, McMURTRY, McCARTHY

by William R. Handley

The vast and complex region called the American West—large parts of which Europeans and Americans once called Spanish Territory, Louisiana Territory, Mexico, the Great American Desert, and Deseret—has historically seen the clash and confluence of many cultures, ethnic groups, nations, and traditions. Such cultural crosscurrents have been among the distinctive features of the region's literary history since the sixteenth century. Even the American West's most popular genre, the formula Western, and the figure of the often gun-totin' cowboy that it celebrates, show the influence, respectively, of the Scottish borderlands made famous in the Waverly novels of Sir Walter Scott and of the figure of the Spanish *vaquero*. Nothing in this region's collective literary history is quite what it may at first seem. It was a storied landscape centuries before it became American, and it was never "the West" for Spanish explorers, some of whom arrived before the Pilgrims landed at Plymouth. It was later the North for Mexicans and the East for Asians who came there. Depending on what images the two terms call to mind, "the West" can seem older and culturally larger than "America," and certainly older than the image that the Western has propagated around the world.

The broadest chronology of this region's literature would begin with early Spanish explorers such as Cabeza de Vaca. But the literary American West arguably begins with the Lewis and Clark expedition (and its journals) from 1804 to 1806. Even from the point of view of American national boundaries, however, much of the East was once western territory, which in part qualifies the Leatherstocking Tales of James Fenimore Cooper as western fiction. Regardless of when western literature is thought to have begun, it is often divided roughly into that written before and after the end—official, at least—of the frontier in 1890. Once the West was settled, the literature of the American West shifted from being a frontier literature to a postfrontier literature that became more retrospective, nostalgic, and revisionist. The region's literary history can also be organized according to the shifting prominence of various literary genres. First came the exploration and travel narratives of much of the nineteenth century. Then came dime novels and formula Westerns in the late nineteenth and the twentieth centuries. A third genre is the more "highbrow" or "serious" western fiction, nonfiction, and poetry of a long list of writers that includes the novelists A. B. Guthry Jr., Frederick Manfred, Vardis Fisher, and D'Arcy McNickle; the poet Gary Snyder; and the (often autobiographical) essayists Edward Abbey and Richard Rodriguez. Western literature can also be categorized according to the ethnicity of writers and to their particular language cultures. These include Indian oral traditions and early autobiographies, such as Sarah Winnemucca Hopkins's *Life among the Piutes: Their Wrongs and Claims* (1883), the first autobiography and tribal history by an Indian woman. Also included are writings in Spanish and English by Spanish, Mexican, and later Chicano writers, from the eighteenth-century Pedro Font to the novelists Rudolofo Anaya and Sandra Cisneros. Their novels *Bless Me, Ultima* (1972) and *The House on Mango Street* (1994), respectively, are classics of both Chicano/a and southwestern literature. There is also a significant body of Asian and Asian-American literature written in the West, including Maxine Hong Kingston's novel *Tripmaster Monkey* (1989), which brings together both Chinese and western American literary traditions and Hisaye Yamamoto's short stories, *Seventeen Syllables* (1988), which are intricate negotiations of the Japanese-American experience, including the legacy of forced relocation during World War II. Adding to the richness of western American literature are African-American writers such as the California novelist Al Young, the poet Ishmael Reed, and Nat Love, whose 1904 autobiography tells of how a child born in the slaveholding South became a successful cowboy.

The literary West can also be broken down by region. Included in the Midwest and the Great Plains regions is the work of Willa Cather, Wright Morris, and Mari Sandoz (all Nebraska writers). The Rocky Mountains have produced such writers as Ivan Doig, Jean Stafford, and James Welch. Other western regions are Texas and the Southwest (Larry

McMurtry and Dorothy Scarborough, for example); the Pacific Northwest (where the Native American writers Sherman Alexie and Barry Lopez live); and California, which has produced a large body of literature, including the fiction of John Steinbeck, Raymond Chandler, Charles Bukowski, Joan Didion, and Octavia Butler and the poetry of Ann Stanford, Robinson Jeffers, and Kenneth Rexroth, to name just a few. There are numerous anthologies of literature from and about California, the Southwest, and the Great Plains, but also anthologies of Montana, Utah, and Great Basin fiction. Have these writers all seen themselves first or even second as western writers? Is Louise Erdrich, for example, fruitfully thought of as a Wyoming novelist or as a Native American writer? Some may not consider themselves western writers (and certainly not writers of Westerns), but the influence of western places and histories is clearly discernible in these and hundreds more writers from the West.

Subdividing the region into the "regions" of historical period, genre, ethnicity, and geography is helpful in making a map of the literature, and the bibliographies in the books edited by Thomas Lyon (1987, 1997) and Michael Kowalewski (1996) are particularly helpful in this regard. An equally fruitful way to approach western American literature is to explore a common set of topics, problems, and influences that extend beyond and across these subdivisions of time, place, and ethnic cultures. From the early nineteenth century to the beginning of the twenty-first, several important factors have shaped the development of western literature. Among them is the legacy of American conquest and settlement and the encounters among different ethnic groups, particularly whites and Indians, but also among Asians, Spanish, Mexicans, Mormons, and other immigrant groups from Europe. As a result of this history, western literature—even the popular, formula Western—is marked by an ongoing demand among readers and writers that western writing address the historical past. This demand has produced a wide scale of historical verisimilitude and often imbued western literature with both a retrospective glance and a nostalgia for authenticity. Another important characteristic of western literature is how human experience in new environments "roughed up" and redefined literary genres and conventions, as in travel and exploration narratives; nineteenth-century journalism; and the culture of tall tales, dime novels, and Indian autobiography. Throughout the last two hundred years, writers have searched for a new vocabulary and style to capture what has often seemed like hyperbolic social and natural landscapes that leave the belles lettres in tatters. The meaning of literature has changed as a result; western American literature gathers both fiction and non-fiction, "highbrow" and "lowbrow" into its geographical reach, as if in imitation of the federal consolidation of far-flung western territories.

The central orientation to and influence of landscape, place, and nature have also been hallmarks of much western literature, particularly among Native American writers but also among white American writers who have, in western settings, had a major influence on nature writing and the more recent development of ecocriticism (the study of the relation between literature and the environment). Whether or not a western writer adopts an environmentalist approach, however, the power of place is undeniable in western fiction and poetry—even when nostalgically longed for by a culture of mobility. The Kiowa writer N. Scott Momaday's Pulitzer Prize–winning *House Made of Dawn* (1968), for example, which had a major influence on the renaissance of Native American writing, shuttles between rural and urban western settings—from Oklahoma to Los Angeles—in its protagonist's gradual reconciliation with his place of origin. It thereby offers a countermodel to western American narratives of what it means to be "on the road." Finally, western literature demonstrates the long-standing clashes among romantic, realist, and naturalist genres and styles, through which the claims of history and the allure of the romantic western myth collide. Each of these literary tendencies has addressed the question of just how free, self-reliant, and self-determining Americans really have been out West. By revealing the often brutal reality and necessary limitations of the demanding western environment, writers such as Frank Norris, Jack London, Willa Cather, John Steinbeck, Wallace Stegner, Joan Didion, Larry McMurtry, and Cormac McCarthy have revised the nineteenth-century faith in the significance of the West for Americans, particularly the prevalent nineteenth-century faith in individual freedom and the nation's providential destiny.

HISTORICAL CONQUEST, MYTH, AND "AUTHENTIC" LITERATURE

In a region so diverse as to call into question whether it is a unified region, why should one even talk about literature of the American West as a discrete body of literature, cordoned off (or subsumed within) that seemingly larger body of literature called American? In part because there has always been such a complicated relationship between western regions and the American nation. A regional literature of many faces, western American writing has also borne the burden of an often monochromatic national mythology—the myth of the frontier, of westering, the idea that the process of conquering and settling the West made Americans American (self-reliant, idealistic) in popular belief. Indeed, writers such as the historian Frederick Jackson Turner, the historian and U.S. president Theodore Roosevelt, and the novelist Owen Wister (whose *The Virginian* [1902] helped to spawn iconic images of the cowboy) helped to render this belief as a kind of national dogma in the early twentieth century. This myth owed its spirit to the nineteenth-century belief that the West was America's (providentially made) Manifest Destiny. That term was coined in 1845 by John L. O'Sullivan, a now-obscure editor, forty years after Lewis and Clark explored the western half of the continent in order to develop cross-continental commercial routes and peaceful trade relations with Indians, but also to extend the nation's borders. Extend they did, rapidly and with disruptive, violent consequences for Indian peoples from the 1820s to the 1890s. Especially after the end of the Mexican-American War in 1848 and the discovery of gold in California one year later, the United States gained not only a huge amount of territory (much of it ceded by Mexico in the 1848 Treaty of Guadelupe Hidalgo), but also a sanctimonious sense of the rightness of having done so.

These and subsequent historical events in the settlement and conquest of the West had a tremendous impact on the literature that emerged from what has often seemed to easterners and foreigners as the West's culturally arid ground. The effect of the gold rush, for example, is difficult to overestimate; "the world rushed in," as the saying went, and turned the sleepy town of San Francisco into a bustling, prosperous, and polyglot city in which the writers Bret Harte (in short stories such as "The Luck of Roaring Camp" in 1868) and Mark Twain (in his 1872 *Roughing It*), and the equally flamboyant (and self-named) Joaquin Miller, honed their divergent literary skills. Through the literary magazines *Golden Era* and *The Overland Monthly* (the latter intended as the western counterpart to the *Atlantic Monthly* and as a means of proclaiming that not just ore but also literary gold could be mined in California), western writers created and quickly parodied a new western idiom and folklore that tried to understand an unusual society dominated by young men of many cultures, brought together by greed and idealism. One of the gold rush era's small literary gems is the *Shirley Letters* (1854–1855) of Louisa Clappe (or Dame Shirley) to her sister in Massachusetts, which offer a vivid and distinctive portrait of life in the mining camps.

No group suffered more from the Americanization of California than its more than one hundred Indian tribes. But for increasingly displaced and dispossessed Mexican Californios who had been promised the full rights of U.S. citizenship, the Mexican-American War and the gold rush also had damaging effects. Making this neglected story central to their art (with varying degrees of romance and historical mindedness) were writers such as the half-Cherokee John Rollin Ridge (or Yellow Bird), in his *The Life and Adventures of Joaquín Murieta, the Celebrated California Bandit* (1854) (the first novel written by an Indian); María Ampara Ruiz de Burton, whose *The Squatter and the Don* (1885) was the first novel published in English from the perspective of the Mexican Californios; and Helen Hunt Jackson, in her popular *Ramona* (1884). In some ways ahead of their time, these writers warned Californians and the nation of the dangers of race prejudice; despite their melodramatic prose, their works can have surprising contemporary resonance.

While it was nonwhite groups, especially Mexicans, Indians, and Chinese, who were materially dispossessed and culturally dislocated in the nineteenth century (if they survived), they were not the only groups for whom the facts of history bore heavily upon their writing. Long before the end of western settlement in the 1890s, when western lands became consolidated under the federal government, writing in English by Anglo-Americans that emerged from western settings often reveal a sense of disorientation—away from the familiarity of eastern literary conventions and culture and in a landscape of such vastness and novelty that a writer accustomed, say, to the pastoral mode often failed to render the surprise of western encounters to eastern readers. When they did succeed, and often with great imagination, travel writers and explorers helped to establish the role of the western author as an authentic renderer, rather than a creative genius in the romantic or Emersonian sense. In some important traditions of western writing, that demand to render—one created, at first, by eastern readers who had never been out West and who wanted to know what it was like, and later reinforced by easterners and westerners alike who grew nostalgic for an older, imagined West—has never entirely vanished. To capture "the real West" is one of the impulses of much western writing past and present, and to do so has often involved a shifting negotiation between the historical and the mythic. The literary West is not entirely either one of those Wests—and for this reason, the aesthetic complexity and interest, indeed the many-sided "truth" of the West of words, has often been critically overlooked.

ROUGHING UP GENRES

The burden to render the West in authentic and accurate detail—and the resulting roughing up of literary genres that marks western literature—began with President Thomas Jefferson's instructions to Meriwether Lewis and William Clark. Part of those instructions were to record and map the rivers, geographic features, flora and fauna, and Indian tribes they encountered. But their *Journals* (1806) are much more than a botanical, zoological, or ethnographic record. They have been called an Enlightenment epic because of their story of human survival in difficult circumstances. They have also even been regarded as an allegory of multiculturalist American identity because the cooperative company included a black servant; a young Shoshone woman named Sacagawea, whose role proved critical; and her French husband. The *Journals* are also about the failure of Enlightenment presumptions to master geography; the expedition discovered there was no continuous water passage to the Pacific that Jefferson's rational model imagined.

Written by two men of markedly different sensibilities and styles (Lewis's is the more literary one), the *Journals* invite literary interpretations not only about the almost novelistic dialogue of these two writers' accounts but about how Lewis's sometimes romantic language creates rather than merely records the "facts" of their experiences. That there was no consensus in their time on whether there even was an American literature is twin to the later problem of saying what kind of literature the *Journals* even are. To call them an exploration narrative is somewhat to simplify matters, to make assumptions about the status of literature in and about the West. Later explorers and travelers, like Francis Parkman in his *The Oregon Trail* (1849), would "decorate" the record of their experiences (drawing mostly on European sources). This invites questions about what it means to "see" new environments without recourse to literary models and about how the West changed Americans' sense of what the role of literature (in its broadest sense) can be in creating a national identity in relation to the landscapes and indigenous peoples of the West.

Exploration narratives were the first instance of the roughing up of literary genres in the West. Twain's *Roughing It* does not refer in its title to this literary question, but it literarily demonstrates it. Part autobiography, satire, travel narrative, and journalism, this novel "novel" self-consciously and often hilariously falls through the breach between fact and fiction. In that breach and book Mark Twain fashioned his voice. Today, many western writers, such as Terry Tempest Williams, employ memoir, fiction, and the political essay to render life in the West (often with less irony and wit than Twain if with more savory political attitudes) both as it is imagined to be and as it is reimagined by writers' experiences of the West.

The "real" West has always been a place where stories shape history and where historical experience alchemically turns into myth, literature, and folklore. Books of fiction and religious faith, oral stories passed through generations, exaggerated travel accounts and the tall tales of boosterism, feverish fantasies of speculation and geographic mastery, and persistent Old World myths and allegories have all directly affected human experience and writing in the West. Much western American literature tells the story of this often fraught sibling relationship between the historical and the imaginative—and between a region with extraordinary differences and artistic energies and a national myth that has simplified and sold them to a world audience.

THE WESTERN

That national myth is most personified in the gunslinging cowboy, who took shape in the dime novels published by the House of Beadle and Adams in New York City; the one hundred twenty-one Buffalo Bill novels by Edward Judson (under the pseudonym Ned Buntline) in the 1870s and the 1880s; and later the formula Western, two of whose most popular writers are Zane Grey and Louis L'Amour, whose numerous books have sold, collectively, close to half a billion copies. Two of the most influential and popular Westerns ever written—Zane Grey's *Riders of the Purple Sage* (1912) and Owen Wister's *The Virginian* (1902)—bear, in certain respects, very little resemblance to the cowboy and Indian Westerns (particularly in film) that they helped to formulate. For one thing, there are no represented Indian characters in the novels. Instead, the "bad" men against whom the central male protagonists fashion their heroism are bad white men—in Wister's case, cattle thieves, and in the case of Grey, a Mormon polygamist. Both of these figures were inspired by historical events, and indeed, Wister and Grey wanted their readers to feel that their novels had authentically captured a time and place—Wyoming and southern Utah, respectively, in the 1870s.

Zane Grey. (© *Underwood & Underwood/Corbis*)

Many Westerns similarly stage their dramatic action in areas not yet under federal control and at a time, after the Civil War and before the end of the frontier era, when struggles over the future of the identity of the American and of the nation had yet to be resolved. Grey wrote his best-selling novel over two decades after the Mormon church had given up polygamy (and after Utah had become a state in 1896), and Wister wrote of a Wyoming and cowboy figure that by 1902, he told his readers, had "vanished." This demonstrates in part how the Western formula distilled, simplified, and preserved a sense of the past for a reading public. Readers were increasingly nostalgic for those times and places that American interests had transformed—and for a morally clear-cut landscape untouched by the confusions of urbanism, monopoly capitalism, and a rapidly changing demography. Wister's bitter nostalgia for the vanished West proved too much for him, and he never again wrote a Western novel. Zane Grey, in contrast, wrote fifty-six Westerns, becoming for a time the best-selling fiction writer in early twentieth-century America. In novels such as *Heritage of the Desert* (1910) and *The Vanishing American* (1920), Grey was fascinated with Mexican, and, even more, Indian ethnicity, and simultaneously bemoaned the fate of Native Americans

and proclaimed their demise. His novels often represent an eastern man who goes West to seek rejuvenation (as Grey and so many western writers did) and who finds salvation in a mysterious woman of the western desert and a solace in western landscapes that Grey's dramatic (and often purple) prose instills with a sacred power.

NATURE'S PLACE

The grandeur of western landscapes seemed to confirm for Americans in the nineteenth century that the designs of the nation were providentially sanctioned. Treating landscape allegorically in the interests of Americans' Manifest Destiny out West, however, is to treat nature not so much as nature as it is to treat nature as nation. Against the use of landscape as national symbol (or, in the Western, plot device) is an important tradition in western American writing that seeks to value nature for its own sake through close observation of it. In the process, nature writing has often displaced the sense of American significance and importance. Moreover, it has revealed how, for the sake of survival, human beings must understand the land's limits, and their own. Like many Native American spiritual beliefs, which have often shaped it, nature writing in the American West places

338

human beings, animals, plants, and landscape on an equal plane of shared being and stresses the need for adaptability and humility. American nature writing is not confined to the West, but Western writers have had a major influence on the genre.

The work of John Muir effected a new perception about natural interrelationships in the rugged California Sierras and particularly Yosemite Valley. Imbued with a transcendentalist sense of one being from which the human eye does not stand apart, Muir's writing shows the influence of Thoreau and Emerson (with whom Muir camped out under the stars in Yosemite toward the end of Emerson's life). Muir's writing is highly literary yet scientifically sound; he was the first to discern that Yosemite was formed by glaciers, for example. The record of Muir's often ecstatic immersion in the wilderness can be found in *The Mountains of California* (1894), *Our National Parks* (1901), and *My First Summer in the Sierra* (1911).

Displaying the influence of Indian spiritualism more than American transcendentalism is the work of Mary Austin, one of the most important American nature writers, who wrote about the Mojave Desert and other areas of the Southwest. Austin's patient, observing eye is everywhere apparent in her writing, yet so is her admiration of Indian peoples (whom Muir virtually ignored) in their ability to adapt to and understand their environments. Toward the beginning of her first and perhaps most well-known book (in which she pays tribute to Muir), *The Land of Little Rain* (1903), Austin writes, "Not the law, but the land sets the limit." Describing her sense of the importance of adaptation, her dictum also sets the stage for what are often jaundiced, wise, bemused, and critical perspectives on the latecomers to the desert, the Americans, whose tendency is to exploit, litter, and move on. In her work *Lost Borders* (1909), Austin explores both white and Indian women's experiences in the desert and seeks to understand how they, like the land, have survived hardships and the betrayal of men. Throughout her work, the imperative to see clearly into things as they are and live, is enacted in prose that often has both a scientist's sense of accurate detail and a Keatsian richness of sound. With these qualities she aims to call her readers to observe for themselves the natural and social worlds she writes about and to create, ultimately, a new culture in the Southwest.

A similar sense of aesthetic contemplation of and communion with the natural world characterizes the work of John Charles Van Dyke. In such works as *Nature for Its Own Sake* (1898), *The Desert* (1903), and *The Grand Canyon of the Colorado* (1920), Van Dyke's vision, while less mystical than Austin's, is no less critical of a civilization that puts human perspectives and needs above all others. The rich tradition of western nature writing continued with such writers as Aldo Leopold, whose *Sand County Almanac* (1949) is a minor classic of its kind; Barry Lopez, in such books as *Of Wolves and Men* (1978) and *Arctic Dreams: Imagination and Desire in a Northern Landscape* (1986); Edward Abbey, who denied the label "nature writer" but whose dazzling book *Desert Solitaire* (1968) lends comparison to Thoreau's *Walden* (1854); and Terry Tempest Williams, whose first book, *Refuge: An Unnatural History of Family and Place* (1991), is both memoir and natural history along with an environmentalist critique. With dozens of other environmentalist writers in the West, these writers have profoundly revised the optimistic national story of frontier settlement and revealed both the costs that come with progress and the rewards that come with observing nature without the lens of nation.

COUNTER-WEST

After the early twentieth century, and gaining greater energy and influence beginning shortly after World War II, there has emerged what we might call a counter-West, a body of literature that has revised both the kinds of stories told about the West in popular fiction and film and Americans' nationalist myths about the region. Western writers in the twentieth century have countered the romanticized West of clear moral choice and resolution with a realistic West of tough choices, hardship, and disappointment. They have done this by examining not only the legacies of western settlement and migration but also the legacies of a myth that more often than not created expectations that could not be fulfilled in western settings. The masculine individual was replaced by the bonds of kinship; hard work replaced gunslinging; tragedy was the tenor, not optimism; celebrations of American expansion were followed by critical evaluations of a western past that, rather than seeming divided from the present, was sometimes painfully continuous with it. Hamlin Garland's *Main-Travelled Roads* (1891) is an early example of this reevaluated western literature; for Garland, the determinations of capitalism deeply qualified illusions of western freedom. Though not considered a western writer, Stephen Crane's western stories from the late 1890s, "The Bride Comes to Yellow Sky" and "The Blue Hotel," offer a satiric and ironic look at how the illusory expectations engendered by popular western myth take on a reality-effect with deflating and even dangerous consequences. In an even more naturalist vein, Frank Norris wrote of an epic California that was part romance but salted through with a sense of the severe limitations placed on human freedom by class inequities and industrialism. His novel, *McTeague* (1899), was the first western novel with an urban setting (San Francisco) and his great "epic of the wheat," *The Octopus* (1901), pitted ranchers against powerful railroad interests in the San Joaquin Valley. Jack London's work is difficult to characterize in a western context. At times indulging a western romance and a core of mysticism, his work is also interesting for its understanding of scientific farming and his critique of Social Darwinist ideas in books such as *The Sea-Wolf* (1904) and *The Valley of the Moon* (1913), which is set in Sonoma County, California.

Two other important and prolific naturalist writers who powerfully shaped the development of western literature are Willa Cather and John Steinbeck. The distinctiveness of Cather's fiction, particularly that set in the West beginning with *O Pioneers!* (1913), belies the way in which her work is an often subtle and ironic commentary not only on romantic popular fiction (particularly of the West) but on prevalent American beliefs in progress and capitalism, the homogenizing effects of Americanization (which sought to stamp out linguistic and cultural differences among immigrant groups), and the Western's version of (Anglo) masculine heroism. In Cather's fiction, many immigrant settlers are neither assimilated nor fluent in English and they suffer homesickness. Moreover, men have no monopoly on success. (Alexandra Bergson in *O Pioneers!*, for example, is more successful than her brothers.) Cather's claim that before her 1913 novel, no Swedes had ever appeared in American fiction, was somewhat misleading. Nevertheless, in returning to the Nebraska of her youth, she found original literary material. In *My Ántonia* (1918), the heroine is the daughter of Bohemian (Czech) immigrants, is not well educated, has a child outside of marriage at age twenty-four, and suffers many hardships, including the suicide by gunshot of her violin-playing father, who could not adapt to the new life on the Plains.

What makes the popular embrace of Cather's fiction so remarkable is how little it resembles the American formula for the West. Everything in Cather's country is ambiguous, success comes at a cost, and settlement involves the loss of non-American cultures. Moreover, in creating her heroines, Cather decoupled their fates from marriage, as with Marian Forrester in *A Lost Lady* (1923), whose first husband is connected to the Burlington railroad and for that reason seems to embody the old pioneer West for the bachelor Neil Herbert, who loses his aestheticizing regard for her once she is no longer married to Captain Forrester. As with so many of Cather's male narrators or protagonists, however, their perspective is qualified by gaps, other stories, and the sense of other realities that go unnarrated, which opens her novels up to ironic readings about what it means to tell a necessarily incomplete story of the past. In this regard, as in the fact that violence in her fiction is divorced from masculine heroism, Cather's work is not only artistically complex while remaining deceptively straightforward, but also represents a revision of western history long before there were professional revisionist western historians. In her masterful novels *The Professor's House* (1925) and *Death Comes for the Archbishop* (1927), Cather took a long and often antimodernist view of the history of conquest on the North American continent and of the relative latecomers, the Americans. Cather did not transcend regionalism; she found a universe in it.

John Steinbeck's uneven but rich collection of fiction reveals with sober but heartbreaking clarity the lives of the dispossessed and the economically dislocated—most famously, the migrant workers who come to California during the Depression in *The Grapes of Wrath* (1939)—and the incommensurability of western and American dreams and experience. His short story cycle, *The Pastures of Heaven* (1932), which was inspired by the work of Sherwood Anderson, is in part a series of fables about the often tragic consequences of the Edenic fable of California, from the Spanish missions to the twentieth century, and for Spanish, Indian, Mexican, and Anglo inhabitants of various classes. (Steinbeck is the only western American writer to have won the Nobel Prize in literature.)

Cather had an important influence on another of the twentieth century's most important western writers, Wallace Stegner, whose work includes over a dozen novels and an equal number of nonfiction books of western history and biography. Like Cather, Stegner was interested in how experience and myth, expectation and reality collide in demanding western environments. A historian second and a novelist first, Stegner found facts too constraining and, like Cather, treated historical fact in his fiction as the occasion for ruminating on how storied lives, like the myths of western boosterism, are themselves historical agents. In *The Big Rock Candy Mountain* (1943), Stegner revised the nineteenth century's optimistic faith in frontier progress. The peripatetic man in search of the next big thing reappears in his Pulitzer Prize–winning novel, *Angle of Repose* (1971), which reconstructs the history (based on actual sources) of the fictional narrator's grandparents, who moved all over the West in the late nineteenth century in search of success, only to fall upon tragedy and failure. The narrative structure of the novel negotiates between the 1960s, when the curmudgeonly historian-narrator is writing, and his grandparents' time, creating a sense not so much of discontinuity between frontier and postfrontier Wests but of their deep dialogic entanglement in each other. The present that the historian is escaping by writing his history comes closer to him the more history he unearths.

The braiding of western history and familial history continues in Stegner's novels *The Spectator Bird* (1976), which won the National Book Award, and *Recapitulation* (1979) and in his memoir of growing up for a time in Saskatchewan, *Wolf Willow: A History, a Story, and a Memory of the Last Plains Frontier* (1963). In his essays—collected in *The Sound of Mountain Water* (1969), *The American West as Living Space* (1987), and *Where the Bluebird Sings to the Lemonade Springs: Living and Writing in the West* (1992)—Stegner is conservationist, cultural critic, and western thinker. Alternately revered and reviled (the latter mostly by the eastern establishment and some Native American writers), Stegner's work, while of national importance, is at times as misunderstood as the West he loved, regretted, and protected. His sense of how the "geography of hope" is also a geography of failure and loss emerges in his hard-earned realism.

Larry McMurtry's varied and extensive output of western fiction—including *Horseman, Pass By* (1961), *Lonesome Dove* (1985), and *Streets of Laredo* (1993)—also revises the western myth, but with less attention to history than Stegner's. His often darkly comic work, some of it set in dusty rural outposts in his home state of Texas and later in more cosmopolitan settings, proclaims the death of the Old West and strips the western myth of masculine heroism, leaving behind only a vestigial violence that is overcome when women but particularly men learn from each other's gendered ways. McMurtry's work, while of the postfrontier category, also reveals how—in proclaiming the death of the Old West and the birth of the New—there is more continuity than disjunction between the past and a present West always haunted by it.

With at times a Faulknerian and Gothic sense of the past's tangled relationship to the present, Cormac McCarthy's fiction is as naturalist a revision of notions of frontier free-individualism as any that exist and makes the history of the American West part of a broader history of the borderlands between the United States and Mexico. In *Blood Meridian; or, The Evening Redness in the West* (1986) and in his border trilogy—*All the Pretty Horses* (1992), *The Crossing* (1994), and *Cities of the Plain* (1998)—McCarthy's Southwest is a blood-soaked existential drama about what it means, in the broadest sense, to be a self in a world of obliterating violence, profound illusion, and determining forces. In prose of often strange gorgeousness and at others of plain strangeness, McCarthy has established himself—again, like Faulkner—as the creator of a historically layered, regional literary universe. James Ellroy's crime fiction, set in Los Angeles, is another such literary world that serves as a dark upending of the Los Angelean version of the western dream of a better place. Indeed, Los Angeles has inspired numerous noirish anti-versions of its boosterized image, such as Nathanael West's *The Day of the Locust* (1939), which describes the lost people who have come to California "to die." Joan Didion's novels, *Run River* (1963), *Play It As It Lays* (1970), and essay collections, *Slouching towards Bethlehem* (1968) and *The White Album* (1979), render the aborted hopes, self-delusions, and sense of prickly dread that underlie the frontier promise in California.

These various counter-Wests are, not accidentally, by white writers; it was white Americans, after all, who invested in the frontier myth. For Native American writers in the West, such as Leslie Marmon Silko in *Ceremony* (1977) or Sherman Alexie in *The Lone Ranger and Tonto Fistfight in Heaven* (1993), revising the myth is less their tendency than reclaiming what was lost to it in Native American cultural history, particularly a sense of the ancestral past and Indian spiritual beliefs. The flourishing of Native American literature in the West in the last third of the twentieth century demonstrates not only that the West is no longer the domain of white male heroes and writers, but that western fiction is moving beyond the supposed divide between frontier and postfrontier Wests, a divide determined by a particular national story that is increasingly being supplanted by an ethnically more diverse and transnational literature (that also includes more women). The playwrights Luis Valdez and David Henry Hwang, the novelists and critics Gerald Vizenor and Louis Owens, the novelist Judith Freeman, the poet Lorna Dee Cervantes, the nature writer Ann Zwinger, and the performance artist Anna Deavere Smith are among an ever-expanding body of western writing. The contemporary literary West is what history has always shown the region to be: an extraordinary crossroads where distinct national cultures (beginning with hundreds of Indian cultures) have encountered and become transformed by each other, producing new stories and literary legacies.

[*See also* Cather, Willa; Crane, Stephen; Garland, Hamlin; Kingston, Maxine Hong; London, Jack; Lopez, Barry; McCarthy, Cormac; Momaday, N. Scott; Norris, Frank; Silko, Leslie Marmon; Stegner, Wallace; Steinbeck, John; Twain, Mark; *and* Williams, Terry Tempest.]

FURTHER READING

Allmendinger, Blake. *Ten Most Wanted: The New Western Literature.* New York, 1998. Looks at idiosyncratic Westerns in order to expand the region's canon, from the novel *Ben-Hur* to the television show *Twin Peaks.*

Bold, Christine. *Selling the Wild West: Popular Western Fiction, 1860–1960.* Bloomington, Ind., 1991. An influential study of how western writers after James Fenimore Cooper marketed and narrated the popular, mythic West.

Brumble, David. *American Indian Autobiography.* Berkeley, Calif., 1988. One of the best books on the subject.

Campbell, Neil. *The Cultures of the American New West.* Edinburgh, 2000.

Cawelti, John G. *Adventure, Mystery, and Romance: Formula Stories as Art and Popular Culture.* Chicago, 1976. Cawelti's work (also in *The Six-Gun Mystique*) was among the earliest and most influential in its understanding of the cultural work of formula Westerns.

Comer, Krista. *Landscapes of the New West: Gender and Geography in Contemporary Women's Writing.* Chapel Hill, N.C., 1999. Expanding the canon of western literature beyond the masculinist myth, this study of contemporary western women's writing argues for the centrality of place to a feminist and postmodernist western sensibility.

Etulain, Richard W. *A Bibliographical Guide to the Study of Western American Literature of the U.S.A.* 2d ed. Albuquerque, N.Mex., 1995.

Fussell, Edwin. *Frontier: American Literature and the American West.* Princeton, N.J., 1965. An early and influential study of how much canonical American literature, including the writing of Thoreau, responded to and was influenced by the westering experience.

Handley, William R. *Marriage, Violence, and the Nation in the American Literary West.* Cambridge, 2002. Twentieth-century western fiction revises readings of the West as America's destiny through scenes of violence among whites, surrounding marriage and family.

Johnson, Michael K. *Black Masculinity and the Frontier Myth in American Literature.* Norman, Okla., 2002.

Kolodny, Annette. *The Land before Her: Fantasy and Experience of the American Frontiers, 1630–1860.* Chapel Hill, N.C., 1984. A groundbreaking feminist study of the relation between a masculinist gaze, women's experience, and the western landscape.

Kowalewski, Michael, ed. *Reading the West: New Essays on the Literature of the American West.* New York, 1996. A broad-ranging collection of essays on facets of western literature and culture, including the power of place and Native American writing, with a comprehensive bibliography of all aspects of western writing.

Lamar, Howard. *The New Encyclopedia of the American West.* New Haven, Conn., 1998. A revised version of a standard reference book for students and scholars of the American West.

Lewis, Nathaniel. *Unsettling the American West: Authenticity, Authorship, and Western American Literature.* Lincoln, Nebr., 2003. A study of the rise of the western author and the demand for authenticity in western writing in the nineteenth century and beyond.

Lyon, Thomas et al., eds. *A Literary History of the American West.* Fort Worth, Tex., 1987.

Lyon, Thomas et al., eds. *Updating the Literary West.* Fort Worth, Tex., 1997. This and Lyon's volume above constitute the most comprehensive collection of essays on individual writers and general articles on the geographic, generic, and historical range of western American literature.

Milner, Clyde A., II, Carol O'Connor, and Martha A. Sandweiss, eds. *The Oxford History of the American West.* New York, 1994. Contains a fairly comprehensive essay on western American literature by Thomas Lyon.

Mitchell, Lee Clark. *Westerns: Making the Man in Fiction and Film.* Chicago, 1996. An excellent cultural analysis of the often paradoxical ways in which Westerns construct the masculine hero.

Mitchell, Lee Clark. *Witnesses to a Vanishing America: The Nineteenth-Century Response.* Princeton, N.J., 1981. This study argues that nostalgia for a vanishing West was pervasive from the beginning of western American conquest, as rendered in such genres as travel and exploration narratives and early ethnography.

Robinson, Forrest G. *Having It Both Ways: Self-Subversion in Western Popular Classics.* Albuquerque, N.Mex., 1993. A study of how western writers such as Owen

Wister and Zane Grey act in bad faith by presenting value systems by which their heroes are measured that are inherently contradictory.

Rosowski, Susan J. *Birthing a Nation: Gender, Creativity, and the West in American Literature.* Lincoln, Nebr., 1999. Revising the individual figure of the male western American, this study argues for another tradition in western women's writing—of mutuality, creativity, and an American nation not beholden to the violent frontier myth.

Slotkin, Richard. *Regeneration through Violence: The Mythology of the American Frontier, 1600–1860.* Middletown, Conn., 1973. Encyclopedic in scope, this and the succeeding two Slotkin volumes offer a generally Marxist approach to how the frontier and its economic and social violence have helped consolidate American nationalism.

Slotkin, Richard. *The Fatal Environment: The Myth of the Frontier in the Age of Industrialization, 1800–1890.* New York, 1985.

Slotkin, Richard. *Gunfighter Nation: The Myth of the Frontier in Twentieth-Century America.* New York, 1992.

Smith, Henry Nash. *Virgin Land: The American West As Symbol and Myth.* Cambridge, Mass., 1950. A foundational work in American studies, this study includes explorations of Erasmus Beadle's dime novels and other western writings in the nineteenth century.

Thacker, Robert. *The Great Prairie Fact and Literary Imagination.* Albuquerque, N.Mex., 1989.

Tompkins, Jane. *West of Everything: The Inner Life of Westerns.* New York, 1992. A reader-response look at how and why Westerns seem to reject what women stand for, such as domesticity and religion.

Wyatt, David. *The Fall into Eden: Landscape and Imagination in California.* New York, 1986. An elegant study of California writers from Mary Austin to John Steinbeck and of the Edenic myth that has shaped perceptions of the place where Americans run out of continent.

EDITH WHARTON

by Carol J. Singley

Edith Wharton, a literary realist, was a prolific writer of fiction, poetry, and nonfiction whose work helped to define a major intellectual and aesthetic movement at the turn of the twentieth century. As a chronicler of society manners and mores, Wharton was adept at portraying male and female characters in stifling social situations, variously of their own and others' making. She was especially interested in ways that society's standards shape women's choices, and she boldly articulated characters' longings for roles that give fuller rein to the range of women's emotional and sexual needs. During her literary career, which spanned over fifty years, Wharton published twenty-five novels, including the Pulitzer Prize–winning *The Age of Innocence* (1920), eighty-six short stories, and numerous volumes on travel, interior design, and the theory of fiction, earning popular and critical acclaim. Many of her works have been successfully adapted for stage and film. From the 1940s until the 1970s, Wharton's reputation suffered from a persistent comparison of her work with that of Henry James and from the misperception that she was a writer of high society—and therefore "narrow"—fiction. Subsequently, however, she has been uniformly hailed as one of the finest American writers.

Edith Wharton.
(*Courtesy of the Library of Congress*)

CHILDHOOD

Edith Newbold Jones was born on 24 January 1862 into an affluent and privileged New York City society that was to become the subject of much of her fiction. The stately brownstone where she lived was in a genteel, insular neighborhood populated by members of an elite social group known as Old New York. Wharton was descended from Dutch and Belgian settlers who had since the seventeenth century congregated in the southern section of Manhattan. They were a tight-knit group, the remnants of an American aristocracy whose wealth was derived passively from interest on municipal real estate holdings rather than from profits made in industry, as was the case with newer generations of wealthy Americans, including the Rockefellers and Vanderbilts.

Born rather late in her mother's life—her brothers were already sixteen and twelve years old—Edith may have been a surprise, even an inconvenience, to her family. George Frederic Jones and Lucretia Rhinelander Jones were a socially prominent couple; her mother was especially so and had a keen sense of fashion that, it was rumored, gave rise to the expression, "keeping up with the Joneses." Perhaps ambivalent about sacrificing her social calendar to return to the nursery, Lucretia was by most accounts a distant and disapproving mother who little understood her daughter's artistic and intellectual leanings. The young Edith found greater rapport with her father, whose temperament more resembled her own. She recalls in autobiographical writings her joyful walks with him on New York City avenues and their mutual love of poetry.

Despite growing up in an active social world, Edith was often alone as a child. Denied a formal education—as were many bright female children of her time and class—she eavesdropped on the threshold of her father's library as her brothers were tutored. She also stole surreptitiously into the library where she immersed herself in the leather-bound volumes that lined her father's shelves. Her reading was circumscribed, however, by her mother's prohibition against novels, which, it was felt, might fill her head with inappropriate romantic fantasies. The family was also suspicious of American writers of the era such as Edgar Allan Poe, deemed dissolute, and Walt Whitman, thought too bohemian. Wharton, in contrast to her family, became a fan of Whitman; she borrowed from him for the title of her autobiography, *A Backward Glance* (1934), and once prepared notes for an essay about his poetry. Edith's parents directed her to the eighteenth-century classics and noncontroversial choices such as those that Wharton later associated with the mother-daughter pair, Mrs. Archer and Janey, in her novel, *The Age of Innocence*. An obedient child, Edith followed her mother's instructions as best she could, all the while nurturing a passionate desire to read and make up stories.

Circumstances conspired to lift the young Edith out of what may have become a stultifying educational environment. A post–Civil War recession made it financially advantageous for the Jones family to live abroad, so in order to economize, Frederic and Lucretia relocated to Europe. From ages four to ten, Edith basked in the rich histories and cultures of France, Spain, Italy, and Germany. This experience, marred only by a severe case of typhoid fever in 1870, awakened her to worlds of beauty and art unavailable to her in New York City. Europe, a haven from Old New York mundanity, profoundly influenced her outlook. Exposure to European art, architecture, and landscape awakened her aesthetic sensibilities, helped her develop a visually detailed literary style, and provided the basis for the international settings in many of her novels. Wharton returned to Europe many times in fiction as well as life and eventually became an expatriate in France.

After her family returned from Europe in 1872, Edith experienced a predictably patterned childhood consisting of winters in the New York City brownstone on West Twenty-third Street and summers at Pencraig Cottage in fashionable Newport, Rhode Island. At age thirteen she became friends with Emelyn Washburn, daughter of the rector of Calvary Episcopal Church, where her family were members. At the rectory, the two friends wrote notes on the Reverend Washburn's typewriter and read books in the library. She regularly attended Episcopal services and was moved by the rich cadences of the Bible and the Book of Common Prayer. Religious in a social rather than a sacred sense, her parents nevertheless provided a framework from which Edith later launched serious inquiries into the nature of faith and reason. Wharton also began a lifelong friendship with Mary (Minnie) Cadwalader Jones, who married her brother Frederic. Their daughter, Beatrix Jones Farrand, who became a noted landscape architect, was also a close friend.

In Newport, Edith reveled in fresh air and sea breezes, watched catboats sail in Narragansett Bay, and rode her pony. If New York City was constraining, Newport freed Edith's pent-up energies and allowed her to enjoy the pleasures of childhood. She found intellectual stimulation at the home of Lewis Rutherfurd, a distinguished astronomer, and learned languages and literature from their family governess, Anna Bahlmann, who later became her governess. She also studied the behaviors of fashionable ladies and gentlemen who strolled across Newport lawns and participated in archery club events. Her keen eye took in all manner of their dress and speech; these personages, like gods and goddesses to a young child, became prototypes for characters who peopled her fiction.

Although Wharton would later praise Old New York society for the value it placed on the use of good English and on probity in business affairs, she also criticized its social complacency, lack of imagination, and resistance to change. Old New York, she observed in *A Backward Glance*, was a vessel into which into no new wine would be poured. Good breeding and good manners were insufficient for a bright, creative girl aspiring to authorship. Wharton needed models, encouragement, and a nurturing artistic environment. Despite its affluence and privilege, then, her closed society deprived her of an essential education. Throughout her childhood and young adulthood, Wharton struggled with conflicting sensibilities: an allegiance to the world into which she was born and a drive to exceed the boundaries of this narrow realm and explore art, literature, philosophy, and science. These tensions characterized her life and also became central themes in her fiction.

APPRENTICESHIP

Despite pressure to follow in the footsteps of her socially minded mother and devote her energies to fashion and leisure, Edith found ways to begin literary experimentation. Her first juvenile effort met with maternal disapproval. She began a story with dialogue between two society ladies in which one greets the other and apologizes for the unkempt condition of the drawing room. When the aspiring writer showed her masterpiece to her mother, Lucretia dampened her daughter's enthusiasm with the icy response that drawing rooms are always tidy. Wharton discloses in her autobiography, *A Backward Glance*, that, provided with no writing paper, she was driven to scribbling on wrappings of packages delivered to her house. Family indifference to her writing continued throughout her life. Even when she became an acclaimed novelist, only one relative ever spoke to her of writing.

In 1876 she tentatively penned a novella, *Fast and Loose*, under the pseudonym David Olivieri. Diffident about her abilities, she also composed reviews of the work calling the writer amateurish. The heroine, Georgie Rivers, forsakes romance in order to marry for security and wealth; when Lord Breton dies, she contracts a fatal case of pneumonia and cannot be reunited with her true love. Not published until forty years after Wharton's death, this early fiction contains the seeds of future work, recounting how a combination of social pressures and circumstance work against a character's hopes, resulting in pain and resignation. Wharton also began to write poems at this time. Indulging their daughter's desire for publication, and perhaps hoping to dissuade her from future literary pursuits, her parents arranged for private publication of a collection of twelve poems, *Verses* (1878). In 1879 she received help from outside the family. Her brother's friend, Allen Thorndike Rice, wrote to poet Henry Longfellow on her behalf; he, in turn, sent her poems to the editor William Dean Howells, who published them in the magazine *Atlantic Monthly*. The year 1879 also marked Edith's social debut. She made her entrance into New York society one year earlier than usual at the insistence of her mother, who was concerned that her daughter's shyness and seriousness might hinder her marriage prospects. Old New Yorkers frequently intermarried; Edith, it was expected, would do the same. She was briefly affianced to Harry Stevens, but his mother broke the engagement, reportedly because of alarm over Edith's intellectuality. The hurtful effects of this rejection were compounded by the death of Edith's father, at age sixty-one, in Cannes, France, in 1882. The following year marked the beginning of two significant relationships, one with Walter Berry, a lawyer who became her confidant and adviser, and the other with a sporting and wealthy Bostonian, Edward (Teddy) Wharton, who became her husband in 1885.

Although the couple shared a taste for travel and pets, the notable feature of the Wharton marriage was the couple's incompatibility. Indeed, Teddy may have been more Lucretia's choice than Edith's, a fact glaringly suggested by the wedding invitation that was engraved and sent without mention of the bride's name. Critics generally believe the marriage was not consummated for at least several days. Disharmony was exacerbated by the fact that Wharton entered marriage without knowing even the basic facts of life. Good girls, her mother had told her, did not ask about such things. Teddy was not Wharton's intellectual equal, nor was he interested in science, philosophy, history, art, or literature, all subjects that fascinated her. He suffered, moreover, from emotional instability, a condition perhaps inherited from his father, who had been institutionalized. Teddy's condition worsened as Edith's career took hold.

In the early years of her marriage, Wharton followed the patterns established by her family. From 1885 to 1888 the couple divided their time between New York City and Newport, at first settling in the Jones family cottage, Pencraig, the fictional setting for Newland and May Archer in *The Age of Innocence*. In 1888 they splurged on an Aegean cruise that was more than paid for, they discovered en route, by an inheritance bequeathed by a distant relative of Edith's. In 1889 they moved to a small house on Madison Avenue. Highlighting this period was stimulation Wharton received from a friend, Egerton Winthrop, who introduced her to the writings of Charles Darwin and other evolutionists.

Wharton continued to write, publishing poems in *Century*, *Harper's*, and *Scribner's*, leading magazines of the time. Her first short story, "Mrs. Manstey's View," appeared in *Scribner's* in 1891. About an old woman whose one pleasure—looking out a window—is destroyed when a building goes up next door, the story, as well as two other early tales ("Friends" and "April Showers"), recalls the sentimental and local color fiction associated with Wharton's predecessors such as Louisa May Alcott, Sarah Orne Jewett, and Mary Wilkins Freeman. But Wharton's realistic tales differ from theirs. She insists, as she says in her autobiography, on looking at life through clear lenses rather than the pastel-colored ones of the nineteenth-century domestic writers. Her use of imagery in this story—vistas blocked by city buildings—also expresses the sense of confinement Wharton felt in her marriage and in New York society. About this time she began to suffer bouts of nausea, fatigue, and breathing difficulties, which were diagnosed as asthma. These ailments, later thought to be psychological as well as physical, persisted throughout the decade and robbed her of vital energies during a productive time of her life.

In 1891 Wharton also composed "Bunner Sisters," a bleak tale of two sisters who scrape together a living by keeping shop in New York City. One marries a man later known to be a drug taker and returns to her sister ill and dying. The story introduces a character type frequently found in her novels: that of the unreliable suitor. Scribners rejected the story on the grounds that it was too strong for middle-class readers, sounding a note that would reverberate throughout Wharton's career. Readers wanted stories with happy endings, but Wharton portrayed characters, especially women, in dire circumstances, and she rarely rescued them from their fates. As a popular writer, she had to balance her own high literary standards with the tastes of readers she did not always respect but upon whom she relied for sales.

Wharton's early accomplishments were impressive: she published thirty short stories in widely read magazines from 1893 to 1904. She nevertheless still lacked mentors and a sure sense of herself as a writer. Edward Burlingame, her first editor at Scribners, suggested a short story collection, but he also rejected "Something Exquisite" (later "Friends") and fables, including the "The Valley of Childish Things," a subsequently much-respected allegory about an intellectual woman's frustrated search for a soul mate. In order for the writer in her to take hold, Wharton needed to separate from New York society, a step she made in 1893 with the purchase of Land's End in Newport, a seaside house far from her mother's home and spots frequented by the fashionable set. Wharton was now beginning to select houses, always important clues to the personalities of characters in her fiction, to match her own temperament. In 1894 she traveled in Tuscany, making original art discoveries described in an article for *Scribner's*. There she met the art critic Vernon Lee and developed a friendship with the French writer Paul Bourget. In 1897 she published *The Decoration of Houses*, one of her few collaborative projects. Written with architect Ogden Codman Jr., whose career she helped launch through introductions to the Newport set, this book blended architecture, traditionally a male domain, with interior design, traditionally a female one. Arguing for clean, classical, and elegant principles of design, the book helped shift taste away from Victorian clutter. A century later it remains a valued resource.

Wharton continued to write and revise stories despite a severe illness in 1898, for which she sought the rest cure made famous by Dr. S. Weir Mitchell. This cure, undertaken by other notable writers such as Virginia Woolf and Charlotte Perkins Gilman, involved a bland diet, excessive rest, and enforced passivity—frustrating as much as curative for intellectually active women. Each year resulted in a new success. Her first collection of short stories, *The Greater Inclination*, appeared in 1899, with good sales and reviews. It was followed by *The Touchstone* (1900), a novella about a deceased writer whose lover betrays her by selling her letters. A second volume of short stories, titled *Crucial Instances*, appeared in 1901. Wharton's two-volume historical novel set in eighteenth-century Italy, *The Valley of Decision*, was published in 1902, bringing her a great sense of accomplishment. A second novella, *Sanctuary*, appeared in 1903. It describes a mother who sacrifices for her son, only to realize the young man's selfishness and potential for deceit. Two volumes came out in 1904: a short story collection, *The Descent of Man, and Other Stories*, the title of which alludes to Wharton's interest in Darwinian theories of competition and natural selection, and a travel book, *Italian Villas and Their Gardens*.

Wharton's literary circle was expanding and now included writer Henry James, who became an intimate friend; Sara Norton, daughter of Harvard professor Charles Eliot Norton; and art critic Bernard Berenson, as well as Walter Berry. Her mother's death in 1901 severed a crucial tie to New York society. Wharton further loosened these bonds with the construction of a majestic summer home in Lenox, Massachusetts, called The Mount, where she entertained, gardened, and wrote according to her own designs. The Mount was truly, to adapt Virginia Woolf's phrase, "a home of her own." Wharton was at the beginning of a dazzling career, officially inaugurated with the success of her first best-seller, *The House of Mirth*, in 1905.

MAJOR PHASE

Edith Wharton wrote *The House of Mirth* for serial publication at the invitation of William Brownell, an editor at Scribners. The project was daunting—the first installment was due to appear before she had written the ending of the novel—but she later acknowledged that firm deadlines gave her a structure for writing. The novel confirms that embedded in Wharton's elite society was a rich mine of fictional material, a point James made when he robustly encouraged her to write about New York City.

The House of Mirth describes the eighteen-month downward spiral of society maiden Lily Bart as she attempts to make a good marriage. Without income of her own, Lily must marry. However, lacking both support from family and friends and the instincts necessary to survive in a competitive social environment, Lily is doomed to failure and, eventually, death. The novel's interest derives in great part from Wharton's equivocal portrayal of Lily, a woman of beauty and intelligence who cannot create a role for herself outside the narrow realm designed for women of her class and time. Lily hopes to marry for love, but aside from the tepidly interested Lawrence Selden, she can find no suitable mates among the attenuated, narrow-minded elitists and greedy Wall Street materialists who people her world. Clever enough to manipulate others but not ruthless enough to profit from her calculations, Lily is both a victim of the society that produces her and a participant in her own fate. She is too morally scrupulous to use incriminating letters against characters who malign her, but she is ill-equipped to live without accustomed social supports.

The House of Mirth is unmistakably deterministic, demonstrating Wharton's achievement in literary naturalism, also practiced by American writers such as Stephen Crane, Frank Norris, and Theodore Dreiser. But Wharton departs from naturalism in a important way: she shows that wealth and position, as well as war or poverty, can be entrapping. Trained to be little more than a sexual object or ornament in her society, with expensive bracelets whose links "seemed like manacles chaining her to her fate," Lily is destined to fail. Wharton wrote in *A Backward Glance* that the novel's tragic significance lay in the destructive powers of a frivolous society. If Lily herself does not rise to the level of tragedy—her fate is at points overly determined—Wharton succeeds admirably in articulating the weight of expectations and conditions that circumscribed women's lives at the turn of the twentieth century.

Sales of *The House of Mirth* were immediate and strong, affording Wharton a new feeling of mastery over her writing. The book appeared in October 1905; by early 1906 it was at the top of the best-seller list, surpassing sales of Upton Sinclair's muckraking novel, *The Jungle* (1906). Now at home in both Paris and Lenox, Wharton wrote with greater confidence and fervor, although familiar self-doubts lingered. She had dreamed, she commented about *The House of Mirth*, of an eagle and had given birth to a hummingbird. She plunged into her next novel, *The Fruit of the Tree* (1907), set not in New York City but in New England. Foregrounding social and moral issues around economic conditions in the textile mills, *Fruit* resembles the fiction of writers such as Sinclair and Jack London. Although Wharton does not entirely succeed in her attempt to interweave several themes, including labor reform, euthanasia, and marital distrust, she vividly portray two female characters in relation to each other and to John Amherst, the mill owner both women marry. Bessy Westmore is an indulged, high-spirited woman whose excessive energies lead to a tragic crippling; Justine Brent is a well-born, sensitive woman succeeding at a nursing career thrust upon her by circumstance. The novel turns upon Justine's decision to grant Bessy's wish

to be euthanized and upon the effect that disclosure of this action has upon her marriage to Amherst. *Fruit of the Tree* introduces contrasting pairs of female characters, a device Wharton uses in many novels, including *Ethan Frome* (1911), *The Reef* (1912), and *The Age of Innocence*.

The year 1907 is personally important in Wharton's life because it marks the beginning of a passionate love affair with the *London Times* journalist Morton Fullerton. The affair reached its height in 1908; Wharton writes about the experience of one of their trysts in a fifty-two line, Whitmanlike poem she titled "Terminus." Fullerton proved to be an exciting but inconstant lover. His lively romantic history included relationships with both men and women; he was reportedly engaged to his cousin when he began seeing Wharton. When Fullerton's attentions began to wane in 1910 or shortly thereafter, Wharton struggled with feelings of desire and abandonment, eventually constructing a friendship with him that continued through the 1930s.

The affair coincided with the disintegration of Wharton's marriage to Teddy, who was showing signs of mental imbalance. In 1909 Wharton learned that he had embezzled her trust funds; that same year he suffered an emotional breakdown. Teddy also strayed from his marriage vows, on one occasion checking into a hotel with a woman registered as Mrs. Wharton. Mounting marital pressures led Wharton to sell her beloved Lenox home, The Mount, in 1912. The couple lived increasingly apart and Wharton continued her expatriation to France. In 1912 she took up permanent residence in Paris, on rue de Varenne in the conservatively fashionable neighborhood of Faubourg St. Germain. Like so many American writers, especially women, Wharton found validation for her literary work in France. She did not, however, immerse herself in the Left Bank literary culture of writers such as Gertrude Stein, Ernest Hemingway, and F. Scott Fitzgerald. By nature shy and of an earlier generation, she remained aloof from these youthful artists. Her marriage over, she quietly obtained a divorce in a French court in 1913.

If early generations of scholars held an image of Wharton as a literary grande dame with an equally cool and distant personal life, critics revised this estimation when in 1980 more than three hundred of her letters to Fullerton were sold to the University of Texas at Austin. Wharton had asked Fullerton to destroy the correspondence, but he ignored her request. The letters describe a woman in her forties fully awakened to the powers of sexual desire. Knowledge of Wharton's midlife affair also affected critics' interpretation of her fiction. Believing her to be exempt from the vagaries of passion, readers missed the intensity with which Wharton depicts characters' sexual desires and frustrations. In this respect her fiction differs from that of Henry James, with which it is frequently compared. Although both choose international themes and render their subjects with a shared sense of irony and aesthetic sensitivity, Wharton subjects her characters more directly and harshly to the vicissitudes of desire and repression; her characters take risks with love and marriage that James's only contemplate.

Wharton's published work during the five-year period from 1907 to 1912 shows a writer firmly in charge of her literary powers, at home in both the United States and Europe. She developed a coterie of close friends and associates. She made numerous transatlantic crossings, the pace of her travels dizzying to her more sedentary associates, including James, who felt caught up in a whirlwind when in her presence. She was producing work at an astonishing rate. The novella, *Madam de Treymes* (1907), set in Paris, describes the plight of an American, Denham, foiled in his attempt to marry a countrywoman who becomes entangled in a web of European romantic and legal customs. Wharton tells the story from Denham's point of view, giving the work a tight narrative focus. The novella also explores relations between the sexes in French culture, a topic Wharton later addressed in a book praising French life, *French Ways and Their Meanings* (1919). She also published two collections of short stories, *The Hermit and the Wild Woman, and Other Stories* (1908) and *Tales of Men and Ghosts* (1910); a travel book, *A Motor-Flight through France* (1908); and a book of poems, *Artemis to Actaeon, and Other Verse* (1909). She returned to a New England setting with her stunning novella, *Ethan Frome* (1911), although not to reform issues.

Ethan Frome is a searing tale about a lonely New Englander, Ethan Frome, married to a querulous hypochondriac, Zeena. Ethan falls in love with his wife's cousin, Mattie Silver, and dreams of making a new life with her. Desperate when Zeena sends Mattie away, the lovers make a suicidal sled run that results not in death but in Mattie's paralysis and Ethan's crippling. The novel concludes with Zeena, Mattie, and Ethan locked in a ménage à trois as frozen and barren as the New England landscape in which the narrative is set. Climate and New England Calvinism enhance Wharton's theme of unredeemed love and insufficiency of human will. She also employs a narrative frame: an engineer visits the region and both witnesses and imagines Ethan's

suffering. This technical device, unusual in Wharton's fiction, allows her to depict the experiences of a largely inarticulate protagonist. With its subjective point of view, thematic refusal of compromise, and rendering of extreme psychological states, *Ethan Frome* shows Wharton's proficiency in the school of literary modernism as well as realism. In its depiction of a tortured marriage and thwarted extramarital romance, *Ethan Frome* also comments upon Wharton's own domestic dilemmas.

Wharton's next novel, *The Reef* (1912), which she described as *Ethan Frome*'s successor, continues the drama of romantic intrigue, but from a European perspective. Thought to be her most Jamesian work, *The Reef* unfolds through the points of view of two of its three main characters: George Darrow and Anna Leath, the widowed old flame he plans to marry. En route to Anna, Darrow impulsively engages in an affair with a young woman named Sophy Viner. Sophy, as fate would have it, has been hired as Anna's daughter's governess and is engaged to marry Anna's stepson. The plot centers on Darrow's guilt and Anna's sense of betrayal once she discovers the affair, as well as on Anna's obsessive fixation on her rival, Sophy Viner. Sophy is an elusive, sexually powerful woman determined, in contrast to Anna, to control her destiny. Her name alludes to the ancient Sophia, embodiment of feminine wisdom and spiritual strength, who was subsumed over the course of western religion by a masculinized Christ and deity. With the Sophia figure, Wharton delivers a critique of patriarchal social and sexual standards that limit women's roles. Sophy is Wharton's vision of a free-spirited female alternative; however, her disappearance from the text at the end of the novel—reminiscent of Ellen Olenska's absence in *The Age of Innocence*—also suggests Wharton's difficulty articulating new roles for women.

The year 1913 saw the publication of *The Custom of the Country*, a novel Wharton had begun in 1908. The novel develops a theme introduced in the 1905 masterpiece, *The House of Mirth*: damages done by a materialistic and commercially corrupt society that has lost all sense of tradition and restraint. Readers follow the exploits of one of Wharton's most magnificent creations, the aggressive, egocentric Undine Spragg. Undine moves to the East from the Midwest with her crude but exorbitantly wealthy parents, intent on acquiring more wealth, status, and husbands. She contrives to marry Ralph Marvell, whom she abandons for a wealthier Peter Van Degen. Abandoned by him, she snares a French aristocrat, Raymond de Chelles, but failing to make inroads in his traditionally structured family and society, she turns instead to Elmer Moffatt, the mogul to whom she was once briefly married. Undine, true to her name, which means "wave," is all energy and no substance. Driving but soulless, she rapaciously pursues her own ambitions, leaving behind a trail of human wreckage. The novel reflects Wharton's disenchantment with early-twentieth-century American society. In the year it was published, she returned to New York City to attend the wedding of her niece, Beatrix Jones, and was overwhelmed by the city's rootlessness.

The outbreak of World War I in 1914 threatened the French people and civilization that Wharton loved so much. The crisis provided her with an opportunity for philanthropic service on a magnitude rarely achieved by any individual during wartime, especially by one not a citizen of the nation in which she worked. Wharton immersed herself in war relief efforts. She raised money through letters home—she strongly and early on advocated United States involvement—and through the publication of *The Book of the Homeless* (1916), a collection of fiction, nonfiction, poetry, and art contributed by her contemporaries. With her friend Elisina Tyler, she also organized dozen of charities, including workrooms and hostels for displaced women and children and hospitals for tuberculin soldiers. Her work placed her near combat; she was reportedly the first civilian, with her friend Walter Berry, to go the front. Wharton's relief charities were so extensive that when the United States entered the conflict in 1917, the American Red Cross faced a challenge in absorbing them. She complained about its inefficiency and disregard of French manners and customs. For her work, the government awarded her the Legion of Honor, the highest French decoration.

Although driven by a sense of purpose and necessity, Wharton found war relief work exhausting. She was now in her mid-fifties and she was juggling her charities with an ambitious schedule of writing. She wrote war essays for *Scribner's* magazine that appeared as a book, *Fighting France, from Dunkerque to Belfort*, in 1915. She published a collection of short stories, *Xingu and Other Stories*, in 1916, which includes the title story, about an group of socially prominent women too vain to admit intellectual deficiencies. She also gathered material for two war novels, *The Marne*, which appeared in 1918, and *A Son at the Front*, which was published in 1923. Wharton also took time from the pressures of the war to write a novel set in New England, which she titled *Summer* (1917) and dubbed a heated counterpart to *Ethan Frome*. Writing the novel, she commented, gave her a brief, joyful reprieve from the destruction all around her.

Summer is a complex bildungsroman about a girl in a small New England town. It traces the summer of Charity's initiation into the wonders and perils of romance with a young visitor from the city, Lucius Harney. Charity's adolescent crises are complicated by the fact that she is adopted—she had been rescued at age five from a community known for its squalor and lawlessness—and lives alone with her widowed adoptive father, a prominent though largely idle lawyer. Pregnant but unwilling to obligate Lucius to marriage, Charity contemplates abortion and then returns to her birthplace. The novel ends with an ambiguous rescue: marriage to her guardian-father. Wharton conveys the innocence and abandon of youth through Whitmanlike descriptions of the beauties of nature and sensual abandon. But she also reveals a more troubled side of human nature. Charity's incestuous marriage and her resigned life in the stifling town of North Dormer signal Charity's defeat in a battle for love and personal autonomy.

The war finally over, Wharton attempted to regroup physically and emotionally. World War I had shattered for her and countless others the Victorian sense that human civilization was, like an escalator, steadily moving forward and upward. She struggled to make sense of the war's devastation and to salvage remnants of the culture she had known before its start. In addition to the casualties of war, she was counting other losses. Her dear friend Henry James had died in 1916; because of difficulties traveling during wartime, she had not made the trip to his bedside. Friend Egerton Winthrop also died. She availed herself of a welcome distraction by touring Morocco with Walter Berry in 1917 and, through political connections, visited harems and other sites closed to western visitors. The trip stimulated her anthropological interests in comparative cultures and resulted in the travel book, *In Morocco* (1920). Dissatisfied with recent sales and with the marketing of her books, she stunned Scribners by terminating her long association with the firm and by contracting with Appleton. She also purchased an estate called Pavillon Colombe in St. Brice-sous-Forêt, a suburb north of Paris, and set about decorating the house and refurbishing the gardens. In addition, she began work on her next novel, *The Age of Innocence*.

In *The Age of Innocence*, Edith Wharton reflects nostalgically but also critically and ironically on the Old New York society of her youth. Set in the 1870s, the novel describes a genteel bachelor, Newland Archer, caught between duty toward his conventional fiancée, May Welland, whom he marries, and his passion for her unconventional cousin, who has just returned from Europe and an unhappy marriage. Firmly entrenched in Old New York ways, Archer fancies himself immune from society's strictures and yearns for a life of intellectual and artistic stimulation so antithetical to his complacent, insular group. Such things, he thinks, might be possible with Ellen, who touches his soul, but not with May, whose eyes "look out blankly at blankness." With every gesture, however, he binds himself closer to May and her world. Believing he and Ellen are lovers, New York society mobilizes forces to send Ellen back to Europe. At age fifty-seven in the novel's final chapter, Archer looks back on what he has lost. One of the novel's many ironies is that Archer allows himself to be constrained by social codes that are all but extinct by the time his children reach maturity. Readers are left to ponder the competing demands of personal desire and social well-being.

After some controversy—the committee originally voted for Sinclair Lewis's *Main Street* (1920) but decided his descriptions of small-town life were too uncomplimentary—Wharton received the Pulitzer Prize for *The Age of Innocence* in 1921. (Judges apparently missed the barbs Wharton aimed at her own social group.) However contentious, the prize acknowledged the strength of Wharton's achievement. The plot progresses through a series of visually beautiful, detailed scenes that Wharton writes with technical precision. Each scene works seamlessly with the one before to reveal characters in relation to one another and their social environment. Wharton not only brings to life a bygone era in American culture; she also produces a timeless study of individuals and cultural change.

LATE PHASE

Critics differ on the aesthetic value of Wharton's work after *The Age of Innocence*. Older generations of critics maintained that, out of touch with the American scene, her fiction became old-fashioned and shrill in tone. Reevaluations around the turn of the twenty-first century point not only to Wharton's tremendous productivity during the 1920s and 1930s, but also to her interest in tackling new social issues and literary styles, which aligns her with modernism as well as with realism. Wharton herself mused over her long-term critical reputation. Perplexed over adverse reviews of her work, she wondered to a friend, Daisy Chanler, in 1925 whether her work was either nothing or much more than readers knew. Whatever

her misgivings, Wharton's importance to American letters was validated by several awards. In 1923 she received an honorary doctor of letters degree from Yale University, the first woman so honored by an American university. She sailed to New Haven to receive the award, the last time she would visit the United States. She also was the first woman to receive the Gold Medal from the National Institute of Arts and Letters in 1925. She was elected to the National Institute in 1926. She received another Gold Medal from the American Academy of Arts and Letters in 1929 and became the second woman elected to the American Academy in 1930.

Wharton was always involved in the business aspects of her career and enjoyed considerable financial success. Increasingly, however, she depended on literary earnings to support her households and a number of dependents, including her former sister-in-law, servants, and Belgian refugees she had supported since the war. She was especially pleased by revenues brought in by *The Age of Innocence*. The success of the novel, she quipped to Bernard Berenson, allowed her to erect garden walls and plant orchards at her new home on the French Riviera. She had in 1919 leased Ste. Claire du Vieux Château in Hyères and had begun dividing her time between Pavillon Colombe and this seaside villa. She once again established a routine that balanced privacy, sociability, and writing. She continued to gather with close friends but also mourned the deaths of friends Howard Sturgis and Sara Norton and brother Harry. Travel remained a delight. Strong income allowed her, along with Robert Norton, Daisy Chanler, and others, to commission a yacht and cruise the Aegean Sea in 1926, retracing the path she had taken in her 1888 voyage. In 1927 she purchased the château at Hyères. Her joy was marred, however, by the death of Walter Berry. Describing her desolation to Gaillard Lapsley, who became her literary executor, she wrote that Berry had been everything to her in love, friendship, and understanding.

Despite advancing years, Wharton wrote and published fiction at a steady rate. In 1922, at age sixty, she published *The Glimpses of the Moon*, a social comedy about a young American couple—well-born but broke—who sail to Europe, live off their wealthy friends, and experience life while trying to keep their relationship intact. The novel resembles *The House of Mirth* in its portrayal of a rootless, materialistic culture and anticipates F. Scott Fitzgerald's portraits of the Lost Generation. Although sales were strong, the novel falls short of the mark of excellence she reached with *The Age of Innocence*. Wharton made a last fictional visit to her parents' generation with a quartet of novels, *Old New York* (1924), set in sequential decades. *False Dawn*, which takes place in the 1840s, satirizes the poverty of American aesthetic taste, a common theme in her fiction. *The Old Maid* explores illegitimacy, adoption, and female rivalry. The tale was first rejected by the *Ladies' Home Journal* because its subject matter was deemed offensive to middle-class readers, but it was eagerly snatched up by *Red Book* after the Pulitzer Prize increased Wharton's literary cachet. The third book of the quartet, *The Spark*, set in the 1860s, brings in Walt Whitman and alludes to Wharton's mother in its condemnation of Old New York morality. *New Year's Day* indicts society's treatment of women through the theme of upper-class prostitution.

Of psychological interest is *The Mother's Recompense* (1925). The plot involves incest, a topic that fascinated Wharton and appears in several novels, including *Ethan Frome*, in which Ethan marries a mother substitute; *Summer*, about a woman who marries her adoptive father; "Beatrice Palmato," a pornographic fragment written sometime after the war about sexual relations between a father and daughter; and *The Children* (1928), in which the protagonist fantasizes marriage to a teenage child in his care. In *The Mother's Recompense*, Kate Clephane returns to New York City from Europe, hoping to reunite with the daughter she abandoned years ago when she fled her marriage to be with a lover. When she discovers that her daughter's fiancé is another man with whom she has had an affair, she renounces maternal claims and returns to Europe. As with Ellen Olenska in *The Age of Innocence*, Wharton imbues her main character, in exile from American society, with aspects of herself. Unlike Kate, Wharton was not a mother, but the novel demonstrates Wharton's interest in mother-daughter bonds. *The Mother's Recompense* was on the best-seller list for two months, displaced by F. Scott Fitzgerald's *The Great Gatsby* (1925).

Wharton continued to be productive across a wide range of genres. She collected thoughts on the theory of literature in a book titled *The Writing of Fiction* (1925). The book clarified her distaste for modernist experimentation such as practiced by James Joyce and argued instead for clarity of expression and form. Wharton cited the examples of writers such as Balzac and Stendhal to express preference for fiction that probes the moral dimensions of characters in their social environments. Human nature, she argued, is inseparable from its social context. This late phase also saw work in poetry and short fiction.

Wharton published a book of verse, *Twelve Poems* (1926), and four short story collections: *Here and Beyond* (1926), *Certain People* (1930), *Human Nature* (1933), and *The World Over* (1936). She wrote ghost stories throughout her career, excelling in this genre. Her collection, *Ghosts*, which appeared posthumously in 1937, includes period pieces as well as stories of her era that convey a modern sense of mystery and the unknown.

In 1927 Wharton published the novel *Twilight Sleep*, a satire of wealthy New Yorkers devoted to fads and trivia. The novel's title alludes to anesthesia administered to women in childbirth and suggests that modern Americans seek to eradicate pain at any cost. Wharton, with a measure of Calvinist austerity, always maintained that pain was a requisite price for pleasure. Wharton also addresses childhood in her 1928 novel, *The Children*, which criticizes fun-loving, self-indulgent parents who virtually abandon a group of siblings and half siblings. The protagonist, Martin Boyne, who becomes the brood's ad hoc caretaker, finds himself enamored of the oldest child, Judith Wheater. As a consequence of his confused attraction, he loses the trust of both Judith and his fiancée. The book was a commercial success, but Wharton complained about reviewers, who she felt had missed the novel's essential vision. In 1928–1929 a dramatized *The Age of Innocence* had a successful run on Broadway.

Immediately after completing *The Children*, Wharton began work on what became a two-volume novel, *Hudson River Bracketed* (1929) and *The Gods Arrive* (1932). While composing the first volume, she became ill with pneumonia and nearly died. The novel traces the artistic development of Vance Weston, a midwesterner who comes east to find himself and develop his craft as a writer. Undirected and naïve, Vance stumbles through a series of romantic mishaps, realizes the giddiness of success among New York literati, and eventually finds direction through his relationship with Halo Tarrant, an intelligent woman who teaches him the value of tradition and dedication to his vocation. Halo, one of Wharton's most memorable characters, forgoes her own ambitions to serve as Vance's muse and moral guide. Some critics, noting Halo's strength of character, place her in a mythic tradition of the Great Mothers. Others see in Wharton's portrayal of Halo a growing conservatism about gender roles, similar to her tendency throughout her career to express class anxiety, anti-Semitism, and cultural elitism. However out of step Wharton may seem from a contemporary perspective, it is important to appreciate that her writing was by early-twentieth-century standards ahead of its time. Major magazines, for example, refused to publish *The Gods Arrive* because it depicted an unmarried couple living together.

Wharton continued to write, travel, and expand her social circle. Beginning in 1930 she developed a close friendship with art critic Kenneth Clark. She also met Aldous Huxley and anthropologist Bronislaw Malinowski. Wharton visited England in 1931 and reunited for a time with Morton Fullerton. She toured the National Gallery of London under Clark's guidance in 1934. During this time, Wharton's religious interests took a new turn. Raised Episcopalian, she had always been interested in religion and the history of Christianity; her library contained more volumes on these subjects than on any other. She became involved with Roman Catholicism, attending masses during a trip to Rome with friend Nicky Mariano in 1931 and reading church histories and lives of the saints. By friends' accounts, her fervor fell just short of conversion.

Wharton also began to feel the financial effects of the Great Depression. Magazine prices for short fiction decreased drastically and she prodded editors to bring the highest possible fees for her work. In 1933 Wharton began her last novel, *The Buccaneers*, about young American women on romantic adventures in Europe. She was still working on the novel at the end of 1934 but never finished it; it was published in 1938 under the directorship of her literary executor, Gaillard Lapsley. Her memoir, *A Backward Glance*, appeared in 1934. Critics praised the book but also found it circumspect and uniform in style; sales were slow. Appleton editor Rutger Jewett placed her short story, "Roman Fever," in *Liberty* magazine the same year, but dissatisfied with her earnings at Appleton, she threatened to sever her relationship with the press. Successful runs of New York theatrical productions of *The Old Maid* and *Ethan Frome* in 1935 and 1936, respectively, temporarily eased her financial concerns.

In April 1935 Edith Wharton suffered a mild stroke, which temporarily impaired her sight. Later that year Mary Cadwalader Jones, the last person connecting her to Old New York, died. Although weakened from her illness, Wharton made last trips to England and Italy in 1936. She worried, along with the rest of Europe, about growing political instability and the rise of the Nazi Party. The year 1937 was marked by uneven health. She suffered a heart attack in June while visiting architect Ogden Codman outside of Paris. She was transported by ambulance to Pavillon Colombe, where she was attended by her friend Elisina Tyler. Visited by other friends and surrounded by the beauty of her gardens, she died on 11 August 1937. She was buried in Versailles, in a plot adjacent to that of Walter Berry.

Wharton's reputation rests on her work as a literary realist, but her fiction pushes the limits of realism to include naturalism and modernism. She has a sharp eye; a sophisticated aesthetic sensibility; and an incisive, often satiric, intelligence. A self-made female artist, she achieved unprecedented critical and popular success in her lifetime, setting standards for future generations of writers. Although particularly sensitive to the cultural position of women, Wharton is also sympathetic to plights of men. She articulates the challenges facing both sexes as they seek to reconcile personal desire with larger social demands. Her fiction conveys the weight of circumstance without being overly deterministic, and it explores the moral as well as social significance of conflict without being overtly polemical. Wharton's ability to document a specific time period and social milieu, and to extend this subject to more universal themes about individuals' tension with their environment, ensures her place in American literature.

[*See also* Crane, Stephen; Dreiser, Theodore; Howells, William Dean; James, Henry; Naturalism and Realism; Norris, Frank; *and* Writing as a Woman in the Twentieth Century.]

SELECTED WORKS

The Greater Inclination (1899)
The Touchstone (1900)
Crucial Instances (1901)
The Valley of Decision (1902)
Sanctuary (1903)
The Descent of Man, and Other Stories (1904)
Italian Villas and Their Gardens (1904)
Italian Backgrounds (1905)
The House of Mirth (1905)
Madame de Treymes (1907)
The Fruit of the Tree (1907)
The Hermit and the Wild Woman, and Other Stories (1908)
A Motor-Flight Through France (1908)
Artemis to Actaeon, and Other Verse (1909)
Tales of Men and Ghosts (1910)
Ethan Frome (1911)
The Reef (1912)
The Custom of the Country (1913)
Fighting France, from Dunkerque to Belfort (1915)
Xingu and Other Stories (1916)
Summer (1917)
The Marne (1918)

French Ways and Their Meanings (1919)

In Morocco (1920)

The Age of Innocence (1920)

The Glimpses of the Moon (1922)

A Son at the Front (1923)

Old New York: False Dawn (The 'Forties), The Old Maid (The 'Fifties), The Spark (The 'Sixties), New Year's Day (The 'Seventies) (1924)

The Mother's Recompense (1925)

The Writing of Fiction (1925)

Twelve Poems (1926)

Here and Beyond (1926)

Twilight Sleep (1927)

The Children (1928)

Hudson River Bracketed (1929)

Certain People (1930)

The Gods Arrive (1932)

Human Nature (1933)

A Backward Glance (1934)

The World Over (1936)

Ghosts (1937)

The Buccaneers (1938)

FURTHER READING

Ammons, Elizabeth. *Edith Wharton's Argument with America*. Athens, Ga., 1980. Wharton as feminist; her use of fairy-tale elements.

Bauer, Dale M. *Edith Wharton's Brave New Politics*. Madison, Wis., 1994. Wharton as a political writer.

Bell, Millicent. *Edith Wharton and Henry James: The Story of Their Friendship*. New York, 1965. Points of commonality and difference.

Bell, Millicent, ed. *The Cambridge Companion to Edith Wharton*. New York, 1995. Original essays on a range of works.

Bendixen, Alfred, and Annette Zilversmit, eds. *Edith Wharton: New Critical Essays*. New York, 1992. Essays on a variety of works.

Benstock, Shari. *Women of the Left Bank: Paris, 1900–1940*. Austin, Tex., 1986. Wharton in a female modernist literary tradition.

Benstock, Shari. *No Gifts from Chance: A Biography of Edith Wharton*. New York, 1994. Important critical biography emphasizing Wharton's modernism and professionalism.

Bentley, Nancy. *The Ethnography of Manners: Hawthorne, James, Wharton*. New York, 1995. Wharton's interest in sociology and anthropology.

Colquitt, Clare, Susan Goodman, and Candace Waid, eds. *A Forward Glance: New Essays on Edith Wharton*. Newark, Del., 1999. Essays on a range of works.

Donovan, Josephine. *After the Fall: The Demeter-Persephone Myth in Wharton, Cather, and Glasgow*. University Park, Pa., 1989. On mother-daughter relations.

Dwight, Eleanor. *Edith Wharton: An Extraordinary Life—An Illustrated Biography*. New York, 1995. Pictorially engaging and comprehensive.

Dyman, Jenni. *Lurking Feminism: The Ghost Stories of Edith Wharton*. New York, 1996.

Erlich, Gloria C. *The Sexual Education of Edith Wharton*. Berkeley, Calif., 1992. Psychological study of family and sexuality.

Fedorko, Kathy A. *Gender and the Gothic in the Fiction of Edith Wharton*. Tuscaloosa, Ala., 1995. Comprehensive treatment of this genre.

Fryer, Judith. *Felicitous Space: The Imaginative Structures of Edith Wharton and Willa Cather*. Chapel Hill, N.C., 1986. Wharton's literal and metaphoric uses of interior and exterior space.

Goodman, Susan. *Edith Wharton's Women: Friends and Rivals*. Hanover, N.H., 1990. Female friendships in Wharton's life and fiction.

Goodman, Susan. *Edith Wharton's Inner Circle*. Austin, Tex., 1994. Focuses on Wharton's male relationships.

Goodwyn, Janet Beer. *Edith Wharton: Traveller in the Land of Letters*. New York, 1990. Wharton's fictional use American and European topographies.

Howe, Irving. *Edith Wharton: A Collection of Critical Essays*. Twentieth Century Views Series. Englewood Cliffs, N. J., 1962. Important early essays that helped establish Wharton's literary reputation.

Joslin, Katherine. *Edith Wharton*. Women Writers Series. New York, 1991. Useful introduction emphasizing Wharton's feminism.

Joslin, Katherine, and Alan Price, eds. *Wretched Exotic: Essays on Edith Wharton in Europe*. New York, 1993. Wharton's international and expatriate themes.

Killoran, Helen. *Edith Wharton: Art and Allusion*. Tuscaloosa, Ala., 1996. Wharton's literary allusions across a range of topics.

Lewis, R. W. B. *Edith Wharton: A Biography*. New York, 1975. Pulitzer Prize–winning biography emphasizing Wharton's social world and marriage themes.

Lindberg, Gary. *Edith Wharton and the Novel of Manners*. Charlottesville, Va., 1975. Incisive treatment of manners.

Lubbock, Percy. *Portrait of Edith Wharton*. New York, 1947. Early, judgmental treatment by an associate.

McDowell, Margaret B. *Edith Wharton*. Boston, 1976. Useful introduction and overview.

Montgomery, Maureen E. *Displaying Women: Spectacles of Leisure in Edith Wharton's New York*. New York, 1998. Wharton, women, and upper-class settings.

Nettels, Elsa. *Language and Gender in American Fiction: Howells, James, Wharton, and Cather*. Charlottesville, Va., 1997. Speech and language as keys to character, theme, and plot.

Nevius, Blake. *Edith Wharton: A Study of Her Fiction*. Berkeley, Calif., 1953. Wharton as literary naturalist.

Preston, Claire. *Edith Wharton's Social Register*. New York, 1999. On characters' social inclusion and exclusion.

Price, Alan. *The End of the Age of Innocence: Edith Wharton and the First World War*. New York, 1996. Biography of Wharton's war-relief efforts.

Singley, Carol J. *Edith Wharton: Matters of Mind and Spirit*. New York, 1995. Wharton as moral writer; fictional uses of religion and philosophy.

Tuttleton, James W., Kristin O. Lauer, and Margaret P. Murray, eds. *Edith Wharton: The Contemporary Reviews*. New York, 1992.

Vita-Finzi, Penelope. *Edith Wharton and the Art of Fiction*. London, 1990. Stylistic analyses of the fiction.

Waid, Candace. *Edith Wharton's Letters from the Underworld*. Chapel Hill, N.C., 1991. Female writing as theme in the fiction.

White, Barbara. *Edith Wharton: A Study of the Short Fiction*. New York, 1991. Useful chronological overview.

Wiser, William. *The Great Good Place: American Expatriate Women in Paris*. New York, 1991.

Wolff, Cynthia Griffin. *A Feast of Words: The Triumph of Edith Wharton*. New York, 1977. Insightful psycho-literary biography.

Wright, Sarah Bird. *Edith Wharton's Travel Writing: The Making of a Connoisseur*. New York, 1997. Wharton as a major contributor to this genre.

Wright, Sarah Bird. *Edith Wharton A to Z: The Essential Guide to the Life and Work of Edith Wharton*. New York, 1998. On wide-ranging topics.

See also the article on *The Age of Innocence*, immediately following.

EDITH WHARTON'S
THE AGE OF INNOCENCE

by Carol J. Singley

Edith Wharton's Pulitzer Prize–winning novel, *The Age of Innocence* (1920), is set in 1870s upper-class New York City, the society of Wharton's youth. The novel follows the romantic entanglements of Newland Archer, who is torn between the conventional May Welland and the exciting Ellen Olenska. Written as a retrospective when Wharton was middle-aged, the novel is both a nostalgic reminiscence and an incisive satire of Old New York manners and mores. With its complex characterization, visually beautiful detail, and well-paced plot, *The Age of Innocence* is one of Wharton's finest novels.

SUCCEEDING SYSTEMS OF CONVENTION

Edith Wharton composed *The Age of Innocence* at the height of her literary powers. Her previous achievements included the best-selling *The House of Mirth* (1905); the New England novels, *Ethan Frome* (1911) and *Summer* (1917); *The Reef* (1912); and *The Custom of the Country* (1913). For many critics, the novel marks the pinnacle of Wharton's career even though she continued to publish novels until her death in 1937. *The Age of Innocence* re-creates a bygone era in nineteenth-century New York society. Wharton presents and dissects rigid social hierarchies of an elite group of upper-class Americans whose customs are extracted from those of the European aristocracy. The fact that Old New Yorkers meticulously follow conventions according to age-old patterns makes the novel seem timeless and unchanging. However, Wharton wrote *The Age of Innocence* in 1919, in the tumultuous aftermath of World War I. An expatriate in France, she had become deeply involved in war relief efforts, organizing and administering shelters, workrooms, and hospitals for needy refugees and soldiers. Fatigued from her efforts and distraught over the destruction she had witnessed, she composed the novel, as she explains in her autobiography, *A Backward Glance* (1934), as a form of escape. *The Age of Innocence* reflects the impact of the war upon Wharton's psyche, in particular, her sense that the world had irreparably changed and that civilization itself was in jeopardy. When she turns to the stable setting of Old New York, then,

she both captures a time of lost innocence and demonstrates the futility of any such static model of culture.

Wharton is remarkably precise in her re-creation of 1870s upper-class New York City. She drew on an outstanding memory and research by her niece, Beatrix Jones Farrand, to accurately depict houses, decor, streets, fashions, theaters, and other markings of the leisure class, making her novel a valuable sociological as well as literary study. Wharton also brings a larger understanding of cultural change to bear in the novel, incorporating recent developments in anthropology to produce her own ethnography of her native group. She likens New York City to a primitive tribal culture with ritual customs and taboos, in which taste has the force of law and characters carry out ascribed roles without question or deviation. Lawrence Lefferts and Sillerton Jackson, the self-appointed arbiters of social taste, point out misdemeanors and purvey gossip. The van der Luydens rule with "ancestral authority" on members' inclusion or exclusion. Newly moneyed interlopers such as Julius Beaufort and Mrs. Struthers jockey for social position and prim families like the Wellands and Archers fret over dangerous "trends" that these invaders introduce.

Wharton's plot develops from a tension between two branches of New York families: the staid Wellands, who produce the well-trained, circumspect May, and the maverick Mingotts, from whom the orphaned Ellen descends, cared for by an eccentric aunt. Connecting the two women is Mrs. Manson Mingott, an iconoclast who rules New York with an iron hand but who also goads family members to be independent like herself. Wharton ascribes to Mrs. Mingott the central question facing Archer: "Now, why in the world didn't you marry my little Ellen?"

The novel's first book opens with Newland Archer, one of New York's most eligible bachelors, arriving fashionably late at the Academy of Music, where Old New Yorkers enjoy, with religious regularity, the annual performance of Goethe's *Faust*. Archer's attention is arrested not by the demure May Welland, to whom he is to be engaged, but by her cousin, Ellen Olenska, newly arrived from Europe and fleeing an unhappy marriage to a Polish count. Archer, fancying himself a sophisticated Faustian figure who will soon enlighten May about life's mysteries, instead finds himself seduced by Ellen's beauty in a dress that reveals "a little more shoulder and bosom than New York was accustomed to seeing." He struggles with a growing love for Ellen and a sense of duty toward May. Each vacillation, however, binds him closer to May. Wishing to protect May from gossip about Ellen's colorful past, he insists on announcing their engagement early. After mouthing platitudes about women's rights to personal freedom, he becomes the family spokesperson arguing against Ellen's divorce. Overwhelmed by increasing intimacy with Ellen, he visits May in Florida and is aghast when their rendezvous results in an advanced wedding date.

Book 2 begins on the day of Archer's wedding, which he experiences at an emotional remove. Going through the motions of married life, he still pursues Ellen, hoping she will become his mistress. But if Ellen has the power to inflame his soul, she also has the strength to ground him in realities. When Archer pleads to run away with her to a place free of society's rules, she answers with age-old wisdom, "Oh, my dear—where is that country?" The impossibility of their love is sealed when New York society, believing that Archer and Ellen are already lovers, marshal forces to expel Ellen from their midst. The occasion is marked by a ceremonious dinner party given, ironically, by May and Newland Archer. Without discussion or debate, New York, like some ancient tribal culture, purges itself of a foreign threat. Ellen returns to Europe, the acquiescent scapegoat in a ritualized exclusion.

Wharton advances the action some thirty years in the final chapter of the novel. At age fifty-seven—Wharton's age when she wrote the novel—his wife deceased and his two children grown, Newland Archer looks back on the choices that he has made and that have been made for him. With characteristic ambivalence, he affirms that "there was good in the old ways" and "there was good in the new order too." On a trip to Paris with his son, he has a chance to visit Ellen, whom he has not seen since she left New York City decades ago. He imagines her living a richly cultured life, full of art, literature, and conversation. However, preferring the image of Ellen he has created in his mind to the reality that might await him, he slowly rises from the park bench outside her apartment and walks away.

Archer reflects on his life with a mixture of regret and rueful acceptance. Certainly, there are compensations for having missed "the flower of life": chiefly, the satisfaction of knowing that he has been a steady husband, loving

father, and "good citizen." But the novel's great irony is that the values for which Archer has renounced Ellen are no longer relevant by the time his children grow up. Quite the contrary. With full social approval, his son Dallas now plans to marry the illegitimate daughter of Julius Beaufort, the crass outsider who once violated New York's social borders. Like relics in the museum that he and Ellen visit during their last private moment together, Old New York standards have become obsolete. Wharton shows, however, that change brings with it new sets of social expectations. Although the younger generation enjoys relaxed social and sexual mores, Archer's son is driven by a different set of pressures, such as wishing to acquire the latest new music and follow the newest architectural trends. Archer sacrifices individual desire for greater social good, but how, Wharton asks, is this sacrifice to be measured given constantly changing social values?

THE WOMEN

Although Archer makes peace with himself, he never fully understands and at times even seriously misjudges the women with whom he is involved. From Archer's limited perspective, May is naïve, reassuring, and predictable; Ellen, in contrast, is exotic, dangerous, and exciting. However, Wharton portrays complex female characters who are complements as well as rivals and who possess strengths that represent different aspects of American womanhood.

Although Wharton's preference lies with Ellen—the character she herself most resembles—readers should not underestimate or dismiss May. May appears in the beginning of the novel as a disingenuous maiden. She is athletically vigorous rather than voluptuously beautiful, with girl-like femininity. Dressed in white, carrying lilies of the valley, and associated with ice or cool shades of blue, she is also compared to Diana, the virginal goddess of the hunt. Wharton shows, however, that May's factitious innocence is more cultural myth than reality. Behind May's elaborate innocence is a strong will and clear goal. She wants marriage and children and she knows how to mobilize New York society to help realize her dream. Although she at first mistakes the true object of Archer's affection, May is a fierce competitor once she knows her target, as suggested by her victory on the archery range. She correctly judges that offering to set Archer free will only bind him to her more closely. She also lies without hesitation about her pregnancy, calculating rightly that telling Ellen the news will persuade her to go back to Europe. Claiming the roles of wife and mother, May is procreative in a traditional sense. Her powers are self-replicating, learned from her mother and passed on to her daughter Mary.

If May is likened to fertile Diana or Civic Virtue, Ellen evokes the ancient Helen, with sensual beauty powerful enough to launch ships and start wars. Ellen is associated with the vibrant colors red and yellow; she frequently receives roses, the flower of romantic love; and she brings a rich, complicated European culture to her Americanized New York society. Like May, Ellen is creative, but in a broad artistic sense. Alive to the powers of literature, painting, dance, and music, she shapes her life without the benefit of blueprint or pattern. She lacks a solid, traditional family structure that May takes for granted. Nevertheless, she is loving and generous, as shown by the aid she extends to a neighbor's child and by her surrogate mothering of Fanny Beaufort. Ellen embodies love in a Platonic as well as erotic sense. Her probing questions challenge Archer's complacent view of New York and lead him to examine society's hypocritical standards. She also leads him, with unshakable integrity, to honor commitments to others. Ellen is Wharton's most fully drawn female character. Like Wharton herself, she cannot be contained by the narrow conventions of New York society but rather needs a sophisticated culture like that of France in order to thrive.

ASSESSMENT

Wharton wondered, after completing *The Age of Innocence*, whether a modern audience would find her novel relevant, commenting to her friend Walter Berry that the two of them may be the only ones who would remember Old New York or find it interesting. She need not have worried. *The Age of Innocence* became a best-seller and in 1921 won the Pulitzer Prize, although after some controversy. The committee originally voted for Sinclair Lewis's *Main Street* (1920), but deeming his exposé offensive to midwestern townspeople, selected *The Age of Innocence* instead. Friendly with Lewis and embarrassed to win at his expense, Wharton acknowledged the honor with a mixture of pride and bemusement. Reviewing criteria for the prize, she chuckled and despaired that judges had selected her novel, with its scathing indictment of New York society, as the one to "best present the wholesome atmosphere of American life and the highest standards of American manners and manhood."

The Age of Innocence endures as a powerful story about love, loss, and resignation. Archer loses his dream because he is too rigidly tied to the rules of his society. The novel thus demonstrates, as does much of Wharton's fiction, the force of environment on character. Wharton also shows how following one's own course can lead to personal freedom but also to social or romantic exile, as it does for Ellen. Finally, Wharton addresses larger themes of time, timelessness, and social expectation. All societies, no matter how insulated and powerful, are subject to change. Given that reality, Wharton explores how to live well by balancing social and personal commitments.

FURTHER READING

Ammons, Elizabeth. "Cool Diana and the Blood-Red Muse: Edith Wharton on Innocence and Art." In *American Novelists Revisited: Essays in Feminist Criticism*, edited by Fritz Fleischmann. New York, 1982. Insightful study of Wharton's treatment of "the woman question" and her indictment of American womanhood.

Gargano, James. "Tableaux of Renunciation: Wharton's Use of *The Shaughran* in *The Age of Innocence*." *Studies in American Fiction* 15 (1987): 1–11. Cogently analyzes how Archer's response to *The Shaughran*, a sentimental play, illuminates his personality.

Price, Alan. "The Composition of Edith Wharton's *The Age of Innocence*." *Yale University Library Gazette* 55 (1980): 22–30. Excellent review of manuscripts, including Wharton's early plan for Archer and Ellen to marry.

Saunders, Judith. "Becoming the Mask: Edith Wharton's Ingenues." *Massachusetts Studies in English* 8 (1982): 33–39. Describes May's false innocence and Wharton's critique of a social system that encourages such masks.

Singley, Carol J. "Bourdieu, Wharton, and Changing Culture in *The Age of Innocence*." *Cultural Studies* 17.3/4 (2003). Uses French sociological theory to explain Archer's social entrapment and Wharton's awareness of cultural change.

Tintner, Adeline. "Jamesian Structures in *The Age of Innocence* and Related Stories." *Twentieth Century Literature* 26 (1980): 332–347. Articulates Wharton's and James's intersecting views of art, sensibility, and manners.

Van Gastel, Ada. "The Location and Decoration of Houses in *The Age of Innocence*." *Dutch Quarterly Review of Anglo-American Letters* 20 (1990): 138–153. Detailed analysis that relates characters to their houses and decor.

See also the article on Edith Wharton, immediately preceding.

PHILLIS WHEATLEY

by David L. Dudley

In July 1761, John Wheatley, a prosperous Boston merchant, purchased an African girl as servant for his wife, Susanna. The child was named Phillis, probably after the vessel that brought her to America, and was surnamed after her owners. Thus, Phillis Wheatley came to a new world where she would achieve fame as a poet. The first African American to write a published book, Wheatley has been hailed by some as the founding mother of the African-American literary tradition but excoriated by others as not sufficiently proud of her blackness or militant enough in the struggle against slavery. The critical response to Wheatley's work has been divided from the beginning, often reflecting the assumptions, prejudices, and agendas of her readers. In the late twentieth century Wheatley began to receive her due as a poet of genuine, if modest, gifts, one whose accomplishment is all the more remarkable given the difficult circumstances of her short life. Scholarship of that time helps us to see that Wheatley's poetry reveals not only her profound faith and trust in God—what some would call otherworldly concerns—but also her commitment to the affairs of this world, centering, as one critic asserts, on the issue of spiritual and political freedom.

Within sixteen months of joining the Wheatley household, Phillis—about eight at the time of her purchase—had "attained the English Language" to the degree that she could read the Bible. She was also learning Latin. Judging from allusions in her poetry, she also knew Horace, Virgil, Ovid, Terence, and Homer. Among English poets, John Milton and Alexander Pope were favorites; Pope's heroic couplets became her most frequently used verse form.

Wheatley's first known writing was a letter dated 1765. Her first published poem, "On Messrs. Hussey

Phillis Wheatley.
(Courtesy of the Library of Congress)

and Coffin," appeared in a Rhode Island newspaper on 21 December 1767; it celebrates the safe return of two men caught in a storm off Cape Cod. Three years later, Wheatley wrote "On the Death of Mr. Snider Murder'd by Richardson," commemorating the death of eleven-year-old Christopher Snider, killed by a royalist shooting into an anti-British mob. But it was a third poem that established Wheatley's reputation on both sides of the Atlantic. George Whitefield, perhaps the most famous evangelist of his day, died in September 1770. Phillis, who may have heard him preach, wrote an elegy, "On the Death of the Rev. Mr. Whitefield, 1770," addressing it to Selina Hastings, the countess of Huntingdon, for whom Whitefield was chaplain.

WHEATLEY'S POETRY

These three early poems in some important ways typify Wheatley's subject matter, themes, and style. All are in rhyming couplets in iambic pentameter. They use biblical and classical allusions. All are occasional pieces and they deal with death and eternal life, two of Wheatley's most common themes. In her elegy George Whitefield, though dead to this world, now dwells in heaven, "Possest of glory, life, and bliss unknown." Like other Puritan elegies, this poem praises the pious good works of the deceased, offers comfort to the bereaved through the assurance that the dead man is now with God, and encourages the living to emulate his faith and life.

Beginning in February 1772, proposals appeared for subscriptions to fund the publication of a book of Phillis Wheatley's poems. After the proposals were rejected in Boston (apparently for racist reasons), the Wheatleys sent their poet to London to improve her health, promote her book, and meet the countess of

Huntingdon, to whom the volume was dedicated. In London, Phillis met many well-known people, saw the famous sights, and (given the antislavery atmosphere in England) perhaps became determined to obtain her freedom. Called back to Boston to help nurse Susanna Wheatley, now terminally ill, Phillis was not in London when *Poems on Various Subjects, Religious and Moral*, printed by Archibald Bell, appeared in September 1773. It contains thirty-eight poems, fourteen of which are elegies. It also features two subsequently famous elements: a portrait (apparently lifelike) of the poet and a page titled "To the Publick," signed by eighteen of the most prominent white men of Boston. They attest that they have "examined" "PHILLIS, a young Negro Girl, who was but a few Years since, brought an uncultivated Barbarian from *Africa*" and have determined her "qualified" to write the works published in her name. In an age when many doubted the ability of any black African to attain literacy, let alone master poetry, the certification of white men was deemed necessary to validate the poet's identity.

Among the elegies, poems on abstract subjects ("On Recollection, on Imagination"), two long narrative poems ("Goliath of Gath" and "Niobe in Distress for Her Children Slain by Apollo"), and other works, *Poems on Various Subjects* includes two pieces in which the poet refers to herself. In "On Being Brought from AFRICA to AMERICA," Wheatley asserts that it was "mercy brought me from my *Pagan* land" and revealed to her the truth about God and Jesus her Savior. The short poem ends with an ironic comment to those who see in the dark skin of black Africans a sign of God's curse on Cain, their supposed primogenitor: "Remember, *Christians*, *Negros*, black as *Cain*, / May be refin'd, and join th' angelic train." Some critics have faulted the poet for seeing the merciful hand of God at work in her abduction from Africa, but all the evidence suggests that for Wheatley, faith in God and her resulting salvation were supreme values, even above freedom in her native home.

This does not mean, however, that Wheatley accepted slavery as right—either for herself or for others. In her other self-referential poem, "To the Right Honourable WILLIAM, Earl of DARTMOUTH," Wheatley predicts that soon America will no longer

> dread the iron chain,
> Which wanton *Tyranny* with lawless hand
> Had made, and with it meant t'enslave the land

She then relates how she herself was "by seeming cruel fate...snatched from *Afric's* fancy'd happy seat." Recalling the pain her parent must have felt at her loss and the pitilessness of the one who separated father and child, the poet asks, "And can I then but pray / Others may never feel tyrannic sway?" Given that Wheatley lived in a society in which most people—even devout Christians—accepted slavery as part of the ordained order of things, and given that most of her readers were white, it appears that far from being insensible to the plight of slaves, Wheatley spoke out against enslavement as forcefully as she could. She herself was manumitted by her master after her return from London.

Poems on Various Subjects received largely favorable reviews, although Thomas Jefferson called the poems "below the dignity of criticism." The French writer and philosopher Voltaire, on the other hand, wrote that Wheatley wrote "de très-bons vers anglais" (very good English verse). Despite the success of her book, Wheatley now entered a difficult time. Susanna Wheatley's death in March 1774 was a keenly felt loss. The Revolutionary War brought upheaval. John Wheatley, who was pro-British, moved his household to Providence, Rhode Island, to escape Boston's strongly anti-British atmosphere. Wheatley apparently went with the family.

Despite the loyalties of her former master, Phillis Wheatley—now free—wholeheartedly supported the American cause. She wrote a poem honoring George Washington and enclosed it in a letter wishing him success as leader of the Continental forces. The general responded warmly and may have met the poet personally, although the matter is uncertain.

As the war dragged on, Wheatley's circumstances grew worse. John Wheatley died in March 1778, followed by his daughter Mary in September. Her brother Nathaniel Wheatley was by then living in London; he died in 1783. Phillis Wheatley, free and responsible for looking after her own needs, kept writing poetry and seeking subscriptions for a second book of verse and letters, but the book never became a reality. On 1 April 1778 she wed John Peters, a free black man about whom little is known for certain. He appears to have been ambitious and capable of doing various trades, but for unknown reasons was unable to provide adequate financial support for his wife. Wheatley bore him three children, all of whom died in infancy. She herself died in poverty on 5 December 1784, followed a few hours later by her third child, buried with her in an unmarked and now unknown grave. John Peters, from whom Phillis may have been separated at the time, was apparently not with his wife at her death. Wheatley's last poem to be published during her lifetime had appeared in September 1784, although it was written before her marriage in 1778. It is an elegy written to comfort unnamed parents on the death of their infant son.

At the start the twenty-first century, sixty-one of Phillis Wheatley's poems are extant, as well as twenty variants of poems. We know from her proposals that she penned many other poems now lost or waiting to be discovered. ("Ocean" came to light in 1998.) Additionally, there are twenty-two letters. This is not a large body of work, nor is it—in the opinion even of Wheatley's staunchest admirers—writing of the highest quality. "A good poet but not a great poet" sums up the critical view at the twentieth century's end. Had Phillis Wheatley been a free-born white American man writing occasional verse in the years before and during the American Revolution, the poems and letters might not be remembered at all. But she was a black woman, brought as a slave directly from Africa to America, where she quickly attained not only basic literacy but also mastery of the most popular poetic style of her time. During her lifetime and ever since, Wheatley and her work have been used to argue and illustrate various sides of a complex argument involving racism, slavery, and gender issues. As a result, Wheatley's poetry often has not been allowed to stand on its own merits and defects. Late-twentieth-century critics, however, stopped focusing on what Wheatley could have done or should have done in the furtherance of various causes and sought to evaluate the poet on what she did do, which was create a body of work that expresses her most deeply held values and beliefs and through which she defines herself as a free individual amidst the turmoil and upheaval of social and political revolution.

[*See also* Colonial Writing in America.]

SELECTED WORK

Poems on Various Subjects, Religious and Moral (1773)

FURTHER READING

Carretta, Vincent, ed. *Phillis Wheatley: Complete Writings*. New York, 2001. Includes all of Wheatley's known poems, variants, letters, and proposals. The introductory essay discusses the probable importance of Wheatley's trip to London as a turning point in her decision to attain her freedom one way or another. Carretta does a fine job of situating the poet and her work within the political issues of her times. An essential study.

Richmond, M. A. *Bid the Vassal Soar: Interpretive Essays on the Life and Poetry of Phillis Wheatley (ca. 1753–1784) and George Moses Horton (ca. 1797–1883)*. Washington, D.C., 1974. Examines Wheatley's life according to its various phases and discusses the critical heritage, dating from Wheatley's own day.

Robinson, William H. *Phillis Wheatley in the Black American Beginnings*. Detroit, 1975. A short biography of the poet and an analysis of her poetry.

Robinson, William H. *Phillis Wheatley: A Bio-bibliography*. Boston, 1981. Provides a chronological listing of writings about Wheatley between 1761 and 1979.

Robinson, William H., ed. *Phillis Wheatley and Her Writings*. New York, 1984. The introductory chapter, "On Phillis Wheatley and Her Boston," provides essential information about the cultural and political setting of the poet's life and work. Also included is a facsimile of *Poems on Various Subjects* as well as other poems, letters, and variants.

Shields, John C., ed. *The Collected Works of Phillis Wheatley*. New York, 1988. A volume in the highly respected Schomburg Library of Nineteenth-Century Black Women Writers, this book includes a facsimile of *Poems on Various Subjects* plus all of Wheatley's other known writings. Shields is perhaps the staunchest defender of Wheatley's poetry and provides a lengthy biographical and critical essay, arguing persuasively that the quest for freedom—spiritual and earthly—lies at the heart of all of Wheatley's poetry. With Carretta's book, one of the two essential studies of Wheatley.

E.B. WHITE

by Arnold E. Sabatelli

Without E. B. White, there would be no *Stuart Little* (1945), no *Charlotte's Web* (1952) (and quite possibly no film *Babe*). But while the bulk of White's work was not children's literature, everything he wrote—poems, editorials, and especially essays—sustained that exuberance, innocence, and clarity of rhetoric. White's prose is at once concise, gentle, humorous, and forceful. Many consider him to be the master nonfiction prose stylist of the century, and his collaboration on *The Elements of Style* with William Strunk (1959) has helped generations of writers hone their craft.

A BRIEF BIOGRAPHY

Elwyn Brooks White was born in 1899 in Mount Vernon, New York. His father, Samuel White, was a prosperous piano manufacturer. White was the youngest of a large family. After graduating from Cornell University in 1921, he worked in a range of reporting jobs before joining the staff of the recently established *New Yorker* magazine. He married the magazine's literary editor, Katharine Sergeant Angell, in 1929. He wrote for the magazine for the rest of his career and befriended many of the literary figures of his time who were associated with the magazine, such as Dorothy Parker and James Thurber. His first major success came from a collaboration with humorist James Thurber, *Is Sex Necessary?* (1929). In 1941, he published *A Subtreasury of American Humor* with his wife. In 1939, White moved to a farm in rural Maine and then wrote his columns and books from home. From 1938 to 1943, he also wrote a column for *Harper's* magazine, "One Man's Meat," which focused primarily on White's experiences in rural Maine. These essays were collected in the book, *One Man's Meat*, in 1942 to very high critical acclaim. After World War II, White's essays became increasingly more political, and he became an ardent supporter of the United Nations. *The Wild*

E. B. White. (*Colby Library*)

Flag (1946) dealt broadly with issues of internationalism, the problem of peace, and segregation. Starting in 1945 with *Stuart Little*, White wrote fiction for children. His novels, *Charlotte's Web* and *The Trumpet of the Swan* (1970), winner of the Laura Ingalls Wilder Award for children's literature, followed, and all three books are hailed as classics of children's literature. White received the gold medal for essays and criticism of the National Institute of Arts and Letters, and a special Pulitzer Prize citation in 1978. Seven U.S. colleges granted him honorary degrees. White died in 1985 of Alzheimer's disease.

ESSAYS

In all of White's essays, his quiet, urging, insistent voice ultimately makes significant discoveries. Frequently a mundane event, the death of a pig, needing to move out of an apartment, observing a raccoon, is subtly transformed into a much more far-reaching contemplation. Yet, the move to speculation and insight is always handled quite delicately. White's essays do not spend a lot of time in the abstract realm. First he spends a considerable amount of time noticing and dwelling on certain images: how the clutch engages on a Ford Model T, and how it feels when it shifts from its one low gear to its one high gear. He pays close attention to the minutiae of experience. Then, a line or two comes toward the end of the essay that turns the whole enterprise up a notch, that makes you aware that you are involved with something more complex than the retelling of an event, the description of a place. Or he will just let an image do the work for him, as in "Goodbye to Forty-Eighth Street," where he is having difficulty figuring out how to rid himself of an old trophy too bulky for the trash and with his name clearly affixed to it. Here, the weighty thing that he cannot shed, the thing that bears his name, illuminates much about White's desire to retreat to a more humble existence, to shed the too-weighty trappings of human vanity and fame.

White's nonfiction was always at the core of what he wrote, grounding and guiding his fiction. In *The Second Tree from the Corner* (1954), he collected his more admittedly "strange" pieces, some of which are remarkably experimental ad-mixtures of drama, poetry, and fiction. In one of these essays, a man arrives in a bar carrying a chess-playing machine that drinks rye and insults the other clientele of the bar. These pieces seemed aimed at finding a way into peculiarities of human behavior, and, as with his fiction, show his playfulness and tendency toward the odd or even the surreal. The bulk of his essays grew out of the writing he did for *Harper's* in his column "One Man's Meat," and from *The New Yorker*. His essays for *The New Yorker* were published in *Writings from* The New Yorker, *1927–1976* (1990).

"Once More to the Lake" is quite possibly the most often-read and commented-on essay in both high school and college writing classes. The essay, a description of returning years later with his own son to a beloved inland lake where White used to summer, the memories the trip evokes, and the unshakable sensation that time has not changed—that somehow he has become his own father—exemplifies all of the elements that make White such a great essayist. At the primary level, White's descriptions are simply wrought, but they are also charged, complex, and suggestive—as you might expect in a piece of fiction. Whether it is the sound of a summer thunderstorm coming through the rusty screens, a squirrel rushing away, or the new outboard motors making a sound so much more jarring than the inboards of his youth, White stitches together the imagery and event with an ease and understatement so that the last sentence, "As he buckled the swollen belt, suddenly my groin felt the chill of death," sneaks up and hits full force. With that final gesture, the essay moves out of the realm of simple memoir and anecdote. Watching his son pull on a wet swimsuit in order to join the others in a swim in the rain, something White remembers doing as a youth, causes this sudden realization of mortality to descend. It is as if the double wetness of rainwater falling and immersion in the lake echo the doubleness of the entire event up to now. The simple detail of his son pulling on his swimsuit is the final straw; it sharpens and focuses the emotion to such an extent that he realizes he has moved beyond youth, has almost literally, magically become his father, and is moving inexorably toward death. Yet none of this is stated. White leaves it up to the cascading imagery and that famous final line to do the work.

WORKS OF FICTION

Perhaps best known for his three novels, *Stuart Little*, *Charlotte's Web*, and *The Trumpet of the Swan*, White's children's literature is rich with the themes and issues that he came back to again and again in his many essays. In *Charlotte's Web*, for example, we find a young girl who retreats to her uncle's barn just to sit and watch the animals interact. She alone can hear the animals speaking to each other; she alone understands how it is the magical words "Some Pig" appear in Charlotte's web in a selfless effort to save the pig from the slaughterhouse. Her solitary world of the barn, in which so much happens that so few see, is a perfect metaphor for all of White's many and varied reflections on life, from the most mundane to the most global. Not only did White literally retreat to his farm (and barnyard of his own) in Maine, at first driving along old Highway 1 and eventually along the bigger highway that sadly bypassed the things he loved to see upon getting close to home—church steeples, houses nestled next to each other—he consistently moves toward the minute, often overlooked details of life and vividly reminds us of their critical importance. He takes the small roads, so to speak, journeying with us into those solitary places where mystery and awe reside. *Charlotte's Web* is, as much as anything, an invitation to retreat, to read the writing in the web, to exile oneself to a life of sublime contemplation—the life of an essayist. The more the little girl goes to the barn just to sit and watch, the more her mother is convinced something must be wrong with her. White, too, was a keen observer, withdrawn but also more intimately in tune with life.

In *Stuart Little*, Stuart, a mouse, is the natural child of an adult human, Mrs. Little. This, of course, was quite controversial at the time—considered by some to be too gross a perversion for a man of White's stature. It was even too problematic for Hollywood, which chose to have Stuart adopted in the film version of the novel. But for White, this magical, strange event is a critical part of the whole artistic expression of the book. The first thing we are forced to contend with, to accept, is this bizarre, magical event. We are forced to turn off our logical brain and turn on our symbolic or mythologic brain. Stuart is both human and mouse, both small and large; he is from the outset a paradox, as are we all. His difficulty in dealing with the most mundane tasks—grooming, dressing, getting from one place to the next—juxtaposed to his quest for his lost love, a once-caged bird, evoke powerful themes of the human yearning for transcendent, fleeting beauty, even while stranded in the daily duty of our lives. And in *The Trumpet of the Swan*, White's last major work, he more overtly contends with these themes, and offers some of the most memorable characters in children's literature: the cob Swan and his "dumb" son Louis. One of the more impressive aspects of White's children's literature is that the animal characters are such richly complex human characters at heart that they speak in recognizable voices, that the magic of their speech is not dwelt upon at all. They are simply characters. They are ultimately human. They just happen to be swans and spiders and rats and pigs.

FAMILIARITY AND EPIPHANY

Upon reading E. B. White, the reader comes away with a sense of closeness to the author. His quiet and insistent voice feels like that of a close friend or relative. For decades he shared intimate details of his personal life, reflected on his political views, and demonstrated his quirky and intense imagination in his children's novels, his essays, and his poems. To read E. B. White is to move—without quite knowing how you got there—from pleasantry, mild amusement, and fun, to deep epiphany. His works again and again throw a familiar arm around us, invite us in, coax us along, and then hit with forceful and deeply insightful impact.

[*See also* Children's Literature *and* Essay in America, The.]

WORKS

The Lady Is Cold (1929)
Is Sex Necessary? (1929)
Ho-Hum: Newsbreaks from The New Yorker (1931)
Another Ho-Hum: More Newsbreaks from The New Yorker (1932)
Alice through the Cellophane (1933)
Everyday Is Saturday (1934)
The Fox of Peapack, and Other Poems (1938)
Quo Vadimus? (1939)
A Subtreasury of American Humor (1941)
One Man's Meat (1942)
Stuart Little (1945)
The Wild Flag (1946)
Here Is New York (1949)
Charlotte's Web (1952)
The Second Tree from the Corner (1954)
The Elements of Style (1959)
The Points of My Compass (1962)
An E. B. White Reader (1966)
The Trumpet of the Swan (1970)
Letters of E. B. White (1976)
Essays of E. B. White (1977)
Poems and Sketches of E. B. White (1981)
Writings from The New Yorker, *1927–1976* (1990)

FURTHER READING

Agosta, Lucien L. *E. B. White: The Children's Books.* New York, 1995. Offers a thorough reading of his children's novels. Especially strong is the chapter on *Charlotte's Web.*

Root, Robert L., Jr., ed. *Critical Essays on E. B. White.* New York, 1994. An excellent selection of critical essays on all of White's major works. Of special note are James Thurber's "E.B.W." and John Updike's "Remarks."

Root, Robert L., Jr. *E. B. White: The Emergence of an Essayist.* Iowa City, Iowa, 1999. A close study of White's rhetorical and formal technique as a master prose stylist. A bit dry and clinical in places, but fascinating, passionate, and thorough.

EDMUND WHITE

by Jerry Phillips

In Edmund White's first novel, *Forgetting Elena* (1973), the narrator reflects that ordinary conversation is so constrained by mores and manners that little is expressed. The narrator of *The Beautiful Room Is Empty* (1988) describes the novel as a conversation in which one person—the writer—does all the talking. White suggests that whatever a writer's ostensible theme, the ulterior and more basic theme is always the nature of one's own experiences; and the ways those experiences might be shaped into an artistic vision reveal something about the human condition. The protagonist-narrator of the *The Farewell Symphony* (1997) notes that the old ambition of fiction is to communicate the most private, complex things in the most compellingly public way. He also observes that the writer is involved in an ongoing conversation with other writers in the tradition. In his novels and short stories, Edmund White converses with readers about love, sex, death, friendship, art, and power, among other themes. But his predominant theme is always the self's quest for an integrated identity in a world that is volatile, ambiguous, and difficult. Thus, Gabriel in *Caracole* (1985) comes to see that sexual desire is a cross one must bear; Austin Smith in *The Married Man* (2000) discovers the pains of love in the era of AIDS. These and others among White's characters are made to reflect on the mysterious depths of their own selfhood by the ecstatic or traumatic experiences they undergo. Indeed, White most often uses the dramatis personae of the child and the lover because he believes (as he states in *The Farewell Symphony*) that love and childhood are states wherein the self is intensely aware of its own uncanny existence.

AUTOBIOGRAPHICAL FICTIONS AND LIFE EXPERIENCES

In his aesthetic sensibility, White is to be associated with writers such as Vladimir Nabokov, Christopher Isherwood, Jean Genet, Colette, Marcel Proust, Joseph Conrad, and Henry James. For White, as for Henry James, the novelist is a participant-observer of the human comedy: he looks on and listens in while standing away from others. The writer is first a sort of conversationalist. He makes himself a student of experience by rendering his material—in the crucible of his imagination—into a considered, meaningful form. For example, *Nocturnes for the King of Naples* (1978) is written in the form of a devotional letter, so that the reader is never quite certain who is being addressed—God or the narrator's former lover. The ambiguity of the devotional object allows White to explore the links between sexuality and spirituality: at one level, the novel is a meditation on lost love and the work of memory; at another level, it is a meditation on the self's desire for oneness with a transcendent God. As a narrative artist, White commits himself to the language of subjective experience rather than empirical realism, hence his aesthetic interest, strongly revealed in *Caracole*, in the dramatic possibilities of exotic fantasy, in which subjectivity comes into its own.

In terms of narrative content, White's childhood experiences and his mature adventures in love and life provided much of the raw material for his novels. His autobiographical fictions are neither direct transcripts of his own experiences nor pure imaginative flights from them. In the last analysis, they are aesthetic designs that carve out their own space between these two polarities.

Edmund White was born in 1940 in Cincinnati, Ohio. He grew up in Cincinnati and Chicago in a conservative middle-class society. The philistine aspects of this culture—its materialism and dull complacency—are set against the burgeoning poetic sensibility of the narrator in *A Boy's Own Story* (1982). The novel indicates that the adolescent White regarded his world with the eyes of an outsider. In later years, White recalled that he consciously disavowed the white racist stance toward African Americans that was normative in his community. He attributes his antiracist sensibility to his self-discovery as a gay man.

In keeping with the conservative mores of 1950s America, the adolescent White conceived of homosexuality as both a sin and a pathology; and yet he could not deny the sexual feelings that seemed to come to him naturally.

In order to be cured of his homosexuality, at the age of fifteen White entered into Freudian psychoanalysis, which conceived of same-sex desire as a reversible neurotic perversion. *The Beautiful Room Is Empty* explores White's initial experiences with psychoanalysis in tragicomic terms. White was to remain in analysis, on an intermittent basis, over a period of twenty years.

In 1958 White became a student at the University of Michigan, where he majored in Chinese. His academic studies gave him a lasting interest in Buddhism, yet another venue (along with psychoanalysis) for considering the pressing problem of the self. White was also drawn to socialism. As his political sensibilities developed, he saw much that was attractive in feminism and gay liberation, for both proposed a radical rethinking of the relationship between the individual and society, particularly in regard to the social repression of adventurous sexual desires.

NEW YORK TO PARIS

After graduating from the University of Michigan in 1962, White moved to New York City, his home for the next twenty years. The social possibilities offered by the city clarified for White the existential challenges posed by homosexuality. Enveloped in a heterosexual world that considers him diseased, sinful, or criminal, the gay individual has to make of himself what he will, fully accepting the nature of his desires. White recognized that the problem of gay identity heightens one's awareness that the self is a unique project undertaken in the face of the world. His participation in the gay subculture of New York City eventually freed him from the pangs of self-hatred and helped him to arrive at the idea, developed in *States of Desire* (1980), that gay life is inherently philosophical in that it foregrounds the general human concern with the problem of values.

From 1962 until 1970, White worked as a writer for Time-Life Books. With the aid of the eminent translator Richard Howard, he published his first novel, *Forgetting Elena*, in 1973. The novel is less a continuous narrative than a mosaic of intensely rendered dramatic scenes. Through the consciousness of an unnamed narrator, the novel explores the spiritual motives that make for meaningful experience in a world of wondrous but painful physicality. In 1977 White co-authored *The Joy of Gay Sex* with his psychotherapist, Charles Silverstein. A second novel, *Nocturnes for the King of Naples*, appeared in 1978. Written in a densely impressionistic style that foregrounds the sensuousness of observed experience, *Nocturnes* shows the influence of the Jamesian/Conradian principle of narrative art, which is to make the reader see the events depicted.

Throughout the 1970s, White participated in a gay writers' group called the Violet Quill. More generally, he was personally acquainted with many important figures in the New York cultural scene, including Robert Mapplethorpe, the photographer. White's work drew the critical notice of established writers such as Vladimir Nabokov and Gore Vidal. In 1980 White became executive director of Columbia University's New York Institute for the Humanities, where he met the cultural theorists Susan Sontag, Roland Barthes, and Michel Foucault, among others. Barthes and Foucault strongly influenced White in his thinking about language and sexuality, culture and power. At the suggestion of the publisher of the magazine *Christopher Street*, White wrote a series of articles on gay life across the United States. These articles led to the book-length travelogue *States of Desire: Travels in Gay America* (1980). In 1982 White published *A Boy's Own Story*, which is both a "coming out" novel, a *bildung* narrative that charts the making public of one's gay identity, and a *Kunstlerroman*, a story about the development of the artist.

In 1983, with a Guggenheim Fellowship in hand, White left New York for Paris, his home for the next seven years. In 1985 he published the erotic fantasy *Caracole*, his only work that centrally concerns heterosexual characters. Through a wide range of characters, *Caracole* explores the relationship between political power and sexual freedom. In the story of Mathilda and her various lovers, the novel also explores the games of aspiration and vanity that characterize a fashionable cultural world, like the New York scene that White knew well.

White returned to the mode of autobiographical fiction in *The Beautiful Room Is Empty* (1988), the sequel to *A Boy's Own Story*. With *The Farewell Symphony* (1997) and *The Married Man* (2000), he completed the series of novels that focus on his own life. More broadly, the last two works, along with his volume of stories, *Skinned Alive* (1995), explore the meaning of love, sex, and friendship in the era of AIDS. White has been diagnosed HIV-positive. He has spoken of AIDS as a "collapse in meaning," but he also observes that the AIDS epidemic has made gay men more reflective on the cardinal values of love, friendship, and personal honor that are the concern of great art, and that make life worth living. The vast shadow cast by AIDS on the gay individual has paradoxically illuminated the value of being open to experience, which rests finally on the foundation of what White views as the joy in living. Both *The Farewell Symphony* and *The Married Man* are elegiac novels about how one should proceed in the face of tremendous loss. In the former novel, White uses a broad canvas to portray the many worlds of 1980s New York that the AIDS epidemic devastated. In the latter, his focus is more intensely personal as he imaginatively reflects on his tragic relationship with Hubert Sorin, who had died of complications related to AIDS.

The Farewell Symphony and *The Married Man* might also be read as White's mature meditations on his own career as a writer—in particular, on how he has managed to translate his private obsessions into public statements. His repeated themes are the search for ecstasy in art, love, and sex; the search for the meaning of selfhood in Buddhism and psychoanalysis; the existential value of the city in making possible the art of the self; the controversy of gay identity as experienced in the period between the Stonewall demonstration in New York City and the era of AIDS; and the writer's singular quest to capture in words the particular quality of a given experience. He has explored these matters both in his fiction and in his theoretical essays, which have been collected as *The Burning Library: Writings on Art, Politics, and Sexuality, 1963–93* (1994). Also a fine critic of literature and the arts, White has written studies of Jean Genet (1993) and Marcel Proust (1999). His book on Genet received the National Book Critics Circle Award and the Lambda Literary Award.

THE IMPORTANCE OF IDEALS

The novelist, as an archaeologist of experience, is concerned to render the imperceptible, the indeterminate, and the nearly ineffable qualities of the human world. Ambiguities are legion in love, sex, friendship, and the personal values one embraces. However, as White sees it, the characteristic impulse of the individual is to fix experience within conventional social forms that promise to cancel out the unfamiliar and the unexpected. White contends that one should not become too comfortable with the terms of one's experience, because the self must always be about the business of avoiding the unexamined life. In this regard, he stands in the tradition of American writing that originated in the transcendentalist emphasis on the project of self-reliance.

White views art as the preeminent means of reflecting on the irreducible ambiguity of experience: the self always exceeds what is said about it; a mystery resides in being here rather than there, this rather than that; and life is always in transition between formlessness and form. Art makes life meaningful by bringing it under the sway of the ideal. According to White, art, like sexual passion, is an end in itself; it cannot be measured in utilitarian

terms. Art has only one true vocation—to explore the range of human feelings, the blessings and burdens of being human. The artist delves deep into experience and makes clear to readers that life on the surface is not, and never can be, humanly satisfying. White's aestheticism is not antipolitical, but it is politics by another name.

Philosophically considered, White's novels investigate the tension between material facts and ideal values as played out in an individual's experiences, particularly in his sexual desires. Sexual concourse involves physical contact between physical beings, yet ideal values surround the complex of sex to the degree that sex elicits an ecstatic sense of selfhood. In *Caracole*, Gabriel is simply astonished at the bodily presence of his lover, Edwige. The narrator of *The Beautiful Room Is Empty* speaks of spiritually pouring himself into the objects of his sexual desire.

Love is the preeminent ideal value informing the ontology of sex. White proposes that love is the first ecstatic state, the summit of experience. He views love and friendship as two important ways in which the self tries to escape from the cave of its own isolation. In this regard, love and friendship are attempts to solve the mystery of individual identity, the fact that one is simply oneself and can never know from within the selfhood of another. Thus in *Caracole*, Mateo, the aging Romeo, is beset with fears about how he seems to younger women, the objects of his desire. In *The Married Man*, Austin Smith recognizes that some part of Julien, his lover, had always escaped him.

The lover, in White's novels, always runs up against the mystery of the beloved. The evanescent, fleeting quality of the other person poses a perennial problem for the self. The other's body presents itself as an enigma. The other as a sexual object stands away from the self at an erotic distance. But even in sexual congress there is a tragic dimension, in that physical intimacy does not guarantee real spiritual contact between persons. White's narrators invariably learn that the unique mystery of each individual sex partner is finally unresolvable.

LANGUAGE AND THE BEAUTIFUL

The self and the other remain mysteries to the end because they cannot be reduced to neat substances to which one can affix names. White's analysis of experience conducts itself through language, but it is also aimed at language, particularly language that has become flat or stale. White's characteristic style is intensely poetic: his language has the formal texture of the baroque aesthetic, with occasional hints of surrealism in certain marvelous images. White's language has a Whitmanesque concern to render the ecstatic moment when the self knows itself to be fully alive. Even before he became familiar with Roland Barthes's concept of *jouissance*, White aimed at capturing the sensual quality of experience through an erotics of language.

White's style represents his quest for ideal beauty. Beauty has long been associated with mutability and thus has definite ties to melancholy and death. Edmund White has conducted his search for beauty in full awareness of its transitory quality. Thus his tone tends toward the elegiac; however, in his affirmation of the value of experience, he seeks to reconcile the reader to the woes and wonders of life.

[*See also* Gay Literature: Poetry and Prose.]

WORKS

Forgetting Elena (1973)
The Joy of Gay Sex (1977)
Nocturnes for the King of Naples (1978)
States of Desire: Travels in Gay America (1980)
A Boy's Own Story (1982)
Caracole (1985)
The Beautiful Room Is Empty (1988)
Genet: A Biography (1993)
The Burning Library: Writings on Art, Politics and Sexuality, 1963-93. (1994; edited by David Bergman)
Skinned Alive: Stories (1995)
The Farewell Symphony (1997)
Proust (1999)
The Married Man (2000)
The Flaneur: A Stroll Through the Paradoxes of Paris (2001)

FURTHER READING

Barber, Stephen. *Edmund White: The Burning World*. New York, 1999. An insightful critical biography. Barber reads White as a late modernist writer whose central metaphors of experience are the Island and the City; especially effective at placing White in relation to larger cultural movements.

Canning, Richard. "Edmund White." In *Gay Fiction Speaks: Conversations with Gay Novelists*. New York, 2000. White speaks of his views of the self and his approach to narrative point of view.

WALT WHITMAN

by Jerome Loving

"I greet you at the beginning of a great career, which yet must have had a long foreground somewhere for such a start," Ralph Waldo Emerson told Walt Whitman on 21 July 1855. Emerson had greeted a number of poets at the beginning of their great careers, including Delia Bacon, the crazy Shakespearean who sought to dig up the bard's body to prove that "Shakespeare" was really Francis Bacon. Ellery Channing II was another "poet" Emerson had discovered. But with Whitman it was different—for the next decade at least. Whitman must have seemed the personification of Emerson's Central Man in "The Poet," an essay in which the former Unitarian minister defined the qualities of the peculiarly American bard. The poet, Emerson wrote, had first to be a transcendentalist and believe that nature is the last thing of the soul, or the only empirical evidence of God. Whitman called nature, or the grass in his first *Leaves of Grass* (1855), "the handkerchief of the Lord," dropped to attract our attention to the daily miracles of life. He—or she, Emerson might have added—had to be representative of all the folk, even the slaves and the "cleaner[s] of privies" as identified in the New York poet's coarse descriptions of the "divine average." Finally, this poet would have to celebrate America as (in Whitman's translation of Emerson) "essentially the greatest poem."

We know that Whitman was familiar with the ideas in "The Poet," for in 1842 he heard the lecture on which the essay would be based when it first appeared in Emerson's *Essays: Second Series* (1844). On one of his early lecture tours outside New England, Emerson came to New York in March to give a series on "The Times." In the audience for at least one lecture on "The Poet"—then called "Nature and the Powers of

Walt Whitman.
(*Courtesy of the Library of Congress*)

the Poet"—was young Walter Whitman, at age twenty-two editor of the *New York Aurora*, a two-penny press off Broadway. Later Whitman allegedly declared that he had been "simmering, simmering, simmering; Emerson brought me to a boil." But curiously, we have relatively little evidence of Whitman's direct use of Emerson other than the 1842 lecture and an allusion to the essay "Spiritual Laws" in 1848 when Whitman was editor of the *Brooklyn Daily Eagle*. The latest biography has tracked him to several of Emerson's lectures in the late 1840s and early 1850s, the immediate "foreground" for the first *Leaves of Grass*.

But Emerson was nevertheless a major influence on the author of America's "language experiment" in poetry, if only in giving the American bard the transcendentalist self-reliance to write in the face of British and Continental greatness. (It was not uncommon for European critics and editors to ask rhetorically who had ever read an American book.) The other major influences, along with journalism, were the Bible and opera: the one for its spiritual appeal and flowing prose and the other for the miraculous sound of the human voice in an age long before recorded music. Some liken a reading of parts of *Song of Myself*, Whitman's most important poem, to the Sermon on the Mount; indeed, in his own time Whitman himself, a former carpenter, was compared to Christ (Whitman's "elder brother," one disciple noted) for his attention to the poor, the lame, and the sick. In section 10 of *Song of Myself*, the poet-narrator washes the feet of a fugitive slave. Furthermore, most readers of this epic poem and many others in *Leaves of Grass* (a collective title that grew from twelve poems in 1855 to more than four hundred by 1892) are persuaded that they must be read aloud to capture the sound of the human voice that Whitman intended as part of their effect. As an opera reviewer for several newspapers in the 1840s, he was thrilled time and again by the bel canto ("beautiful singing") style, especially in his favorite opera by Donizetti, *Lucia di Lammermoor*, with its many arias. When the great contralto Marietta Alboni came to New York in the spring of 1853, Whitman bragged that he was on hand for every one of her performances.

A NOT SO GREAT BEGINNING

Of Dutch and English ancestry, Walter Whitman was born at West Hills, near Huntington, Long Island, to a carpenter and his wife on 31 May 1819. Walter Whitman Sr. soon afterward moved his expanding family to Brooklyn and built houses. This is the city Whitman is most immediately identified with today, along with Manhattan. Whitman's father was a better builder than he was a businessman, and the family moved repeatedly around the city as he went in and out of debt. Walter and Louisa Whitman had nine children, one of whom died soon after birth. A listing of the poet's surviving brothers and sisters sounds like one of Whitman's own poetic catalogs, for the Whitman children represented in their various successes and failures a microcosm of the America he would celebrate in *Song of Myself* and elsewhere. The impoverished family produced a famous poet, a syphilitic sailor, a hypochondriac, a decorated Civil War soldier, an unemployed alcoholic, the wife of another alcoholic, a successful civil engineer, and a mentally and physically handicapped son. Jesse, the oldest, joined the merchant marine. Around 1848 he was either hit over the head in a sailors' melee or fell from a mast. In either case, it eventually affected his sanity. In his youth, however, he apparently showed much promise. Jesse appears in Whitman's early fiction of the 1840s as the preferred elder brother. In adulthood, the younger brother eventually had the elder committed to an insane asylum in Brooklyn, where he died in 1870.

Mary Elizabeth, born two years after Walt, married an alcoholic shipwright and lived out her life in Greenport at the tip of Long Island. She is the only source of Whitman heirs today. Whitman's other sister, Hannah Louisa Whitman, married the Vermont painter Charles Lewis Heyde and became a hypochondriac. Hannah, who outlived all her siblings, was for some unknown reason Walt's favorite sister, but he was tormented by her marital complaints and her husband's not-so-clandestine attempts to criticize *Leaves of Grass*. The next three children were named for American heroes by their patriotic father: Andrew Jackson, George Washington, and Thomas Jefferson. Andrew married a streetwalker and died an alcoholic of throat cancer during the Civil War. George became a Union hero who survived the war's worst battles and confinement as a prisoner of war. And Jeff became a civil engineer in St. Louis, where he oversaw the laying of the city's waterworks. Edward, the youngest, suffered from a crippled left hand and a paralyzed leg. Also mentally retarded, he was the only member of the family who subscribed to conventional religion. He was the ward of his mother until her death and then of Walt. He died eight months after Whitman in 1892. In the poem "Faces," Whitman speaks of "the agents that emptied and broke my brother."

Whitman attended a so-called poverty school in Brooklyn. This was before state-supported public schools in New York, when those educated beyond a few grades attended private school and looked down on those who did not. Whitman left off his formal education after the sixth grade and became a printer's apprentice. Later an earnest advocate of school reform, he never spoke very much of his own schooling, for it was a time in which the awkward and prematurely tall youth was whipped for his clumsiness and shamed for his poverty. After reaching the state of "jour printer," or the journeyman stage of his trade, Whitman became a schoolteacher on Long Island for several years. At one point he founded a newspaper (the *Long Islander*, which lasted into the 1970s), and this activity led him into journalism in both Brooklyn and Manhattan. While working at the offices of the *Brooklyn Eagle* overlooking the East River, he daily rode the ferry back and forth, an experience that would contribute to one of his most famous poems, "Crossing Brooklyn Ferry."

Following his firing as editor of the *Eagle* in 1848 for his antislavery views, Whitman took a job with the *New Orleans Crescent*. He was accompanied by his fourteen-year-old brother Jeff, who of all Whitman's siblings clearly became the most sympathetic reader of the then experimental poetry in *Leaves of Grass*. The rest of the family was respectfully mystified, his mother saying of her favorite son's work that if Longfellow's *Hiawatha* (also published in 1855) was poetry, Walt's book must be, too. George, who became both conventionally respectable and rich after the war, privately thought some of the poems were of "the whorehouse order." Whitman had come to New Orleans, the military staging area, at the height of the Mexican War, which eventually brought into the Union Texas, California, Arizona, and New Mexico, following a U.S. expansionist policy that Whitman favored. Even though it added another slave state, Texas, to the Union,

Whitman's faith in democracy was so great that he thought slavery and all such evils would ultimately be absorbed and eradicated by the common good. Yet once again, because of his basic opposition to slavery, he lost his position at the *Crescent* after only three months and returned to join the ranks of the unemployed in New York.

BEGINNING OF A GREAT CAREER

Within months of his return, Whitman founded and edited the *Brooklyn Freeman*, a Free Soil newspaper. The Free Soil movement was primarily concerned with the effect of black slavery on the white working experience and thus opposed the expansion of slavery into the western territories. Many Americans then thought that slavery denigrated white labor by forcing blacks to do for no wages the same work whites did for pay; the widely held belief was that this would have a deleterious impact on American democracy, which thrived upon the individuality (real or imagined) cultivated in capitalism. The office building housing Whitman's newspaper was burned down after one issue, possibly by Copperhead proslavery advocates. Following this (his last full-time employment as a journalist), Whitman largely disappears from the biographical map until 1855, when he published the first edition of *Leaves of Grass*. We know that in the interim he speculated in house building, and he may have operated a bookstore in Brooklyn for a time. He published several antislavery poems in 1850 following passage of a strengthened Fugitive Slave Law. At least one of the poems was written in the free verse (as opposed to the traditional rhyme and meter) he would develop in his first *Leaves*.

The immediate "foreground" for Whitman's book, therefore, may have been either a bookstore or a construction site. It was in Fort Greene Park, not far from his parents' house in Brooklyn, where he later told disciples he may have had a mystical experience in 1854 while lying face up in the sun. Afterward he could never recapture the same state of mind that had produced the first *Leaves of Grass*. Emerson, after all, had felt himself a transparent eyeball through which the currents of the universe ran when he wrote his first great book, *Nature* (1836). Other writers since Whitman, especially American writers for some reason, have indicated mystical influences. The United States was almost entirely Christian in the nineteenth century, and both Emerson and Whitman identified at times with Christ as the "Central Man." It was not a conventionally religious attraction but one in which Christ was viewed as the first man to discover a personal divinity that all possessed. Emerson once said he didn't doubt that there had been a Christ; nor did he doubt there had been afterward a thousand Christs, or individuals who saw their greatness in the idea that nature was the emblem of God. Whitman celebrates all the different religions of the world in *Leaves of Grass*, both ancient and modern, exotic and conventional.

There are six distinct editions of *Leaves of Grass*: 1855, 1856, 1860, 1867, 1871, and 1881. The other "editions" are actually issues with the same pagination as the previous edition but with material added at the end—namely, the 1876, 1889, and 1892 issues. The first edition is an octavo of ninety-five pages. It presents twelve untitled poems, the opening one covering the first fifty-six pages. This poem became *Song of Myself* in the sixth edition. Following a ten-page, double-column preface in which Whitman attempts to define American poetry along Emersonian lines, this poem bursts onto the page with the words:

I celebrate myself,
And what I assume you shall assume,
For every atom belonging to me as good belongs to you.

Later, "and sing myself" was added to the first line. By celebrating himself as a representative singer, he celebrates all humankind as divine because everyone is a part of nature, or the emblem of God. This was Emerson's message too, but Whitman gives it a most important twist. For Whitman valued the emblem, or the body, as much as he did the soul it was supposed to represent. This earthiness is seen first in the poet's colloquial, indeed slangy, language. As a former printer and newspaper editor, Whitman was well aware that it was unidiomatic to "sing" oneself, that "sing" as a synonym for "celebrate" was an intransitive verb requiring a preposition as in "I sing of thee." He also knew the difference between an adjective ("good") and an adverb ("well") when he wrote that every atom of the earth belonged to himself as "good" (instead of "well") as it did to everyone else in the world. Whitman sought a language that was direct, with words so full of life that if cut, as Emerson once observed, they would bleed. He wanted a language of the body, so much so that he could proclaim, "The scent of these arm-pits aroma finer than prayer." Everything in nature, including the low and unsightly, proved the existence of God.

Whitman became a transcendentalist in a literal sense that extended beyond even Emerson's brand of New England prudery. If nature was a symbol of God, and humankind part of that nature, then all of it could and should be celebrated in the country that was "essentially the greatest poem." That included all parts of the body and its sexual uses. But the 1850s in Victorian America was an era of heavy censorship in which virtually everything was covered, even at times piano legs. He grew bolder in later editions, especially in his "Children of Adam" poems, but in the first edition he already saw the body as a lightning rod to enlightenment in a poem later entitled "I Sing the Body Electric."

> There is something in staying close to men and women and
>   looking on them and in the contact and odor of them
>   that pleases the soul well,
>   All things please the soul well, but these please the
>   soul well.

In *Song of Myself* he declared that he was both the poet of the body and the poet of the soul. Lack one, he said, and both are lacking.

In what became section 5 of *Song of Myself* he celebrated that union in sexual imagery. The body beckons the soul and embraces it:

> Loafe with me on the grass. . . . loose the stop from
>   your throat,
> Not words, not music or rhyme I want. . . . not custom or
>   lecture, not even the best,
> Only the lull I like, the hum of your valvèd voice.

Whitman recalls how he and his soul "lay in June" on a transparent summer morning, how afterward he experienced the "peace and joy and knowledge that pass all the art and argument of the earth."

Song of Myself was ultimately divided into fifty-two sections, and there are nearly as many different theories as to its thematic organization and structure. Probably the most satisfying is one of the simplest: that the poem is analogous to a symphony with a musical cycle full of crescendos and climaxes. In one of the more complex theories, the poet merges mystically with all life and experience during the first eighteen sections, then defines the self in transcendentalist terms in which parts of nature are seemingly insignificant but actually every bit a part of the divine macrocosm, and so on until the larger questions of life are mystically affirmed. All through this journey down the "open road" of life, the poet stands in for all humankind in its quest for spiritual understanding. Whitman is the Emersonian poet who will report back our daily conversations with nature and thus with God. As Emerson remarked in "The Poet," all poetry had been written "before time was." In other words, just as Whitman had noted that America was essentially the

greatest poem, the world is God's poem and therefore the source of all poetry.

Once the poet has merged his body and soul and explained the transcendental nature of the grass, he proceeds to identify and thus to represent and include all aspects of humanity. He celebrates city life, country living, and the sights of the West. As a former journalist, Whitman had seen the best and certainly the worst of city life. As a native of the Long Island countryside, he knew intimately farm life as well. He had yet to go beyond the Mississippi River, but as an inveterate reader and reviewer of many volumes in the 1840s, he knew the area of America's inevitable expansion thoroughly if vicariously. In depicting the marriage of the trapper and the "red girl" in the West in section 10, for example, he relied upon a painting by the famed artist of western scenes Alfred Jacob Miller.

Whitman relates to everybody, even the abolitionist whose extreme political position for the day he otherwise resisted. (Many an abolitionist would have overthrown the Union to rid the country of the curse of slavery, but to Whitman the United States was sacred. Like Lincoln during the Civil War, he considered the integrity of the Union more important than anything else, even slavery.) He relates even to the sexually frustrated woman, at twenty-eight years of age either still unmarried or unhappily wed. Voyeuristically she observes twenty-eight young men swimming in the nude. From her "fine house by the rise of the bank," she experiences sexual fantasies:

> Where are you off to, lady? for I see you
> You splash in the water there, yet stay stock still in
>   your room.
>
> Dancing and laughing along the beach came the
>   twenty-ninth bather,
> The rest did not see her, but she saw them and loved them.

The Whitman persona merges with the butcher boy at the market or the freed black driving a wagon or the wild gander whose "*Ya-honk*" comes to him as a personal invitation from God. He sees in lower nature and himself the same old law—"What is commonest and cheapest and nearest and easiest is Me." He goes on to catalog all human life in America: the singer in the organ loft, the carpenter dressing his plank, the duck shooter, the deacon, the spinning girl. No one is left out of this celebration, for the table of American democracy is "equally set"—not the slave, not the opium eater, not even the prostitute who "draggles her shawl, her bonnet bobs on her tipsy and pimpled neck." Later, in "To a Common Prostitute" (1860), he addresses this woman who in the nineteenth century was often rejected not only by society but her own family out of shame: "Not till the sun excludes you do I exclude you, / Not till the waters refuse to glisten for you and the leaves to rustle for you, do my words refuse to glisten for you."

"Of every hue and caste am I, of every rank and religion," Whitman declares (in the revised and improved version of *Song of Myself*), "A farmer, mechanic, artist, gentleman, sailor, quaker, / Prisoner, fancy-man [pimp], rowdy, lawyer, physician, priest." "The greatest poet," he declared in his preface, "does not moralize or make applications of morals . . . he knows [only] the soul."

Which was to say that this poet transcends normal time with its materialistic concerns to keep time with the cosmos: "The clock indicates the moment," he says in section 44 of *Song of Myself*, then asks, "but what does eternity indicate?" Just as Whitman considers the body equal to the soul (since in his time matter could not be destroyed), he extends this equality to the sexes as "the poet of the woman the same as the man." By the same token, America is now equal to other nations, indeed initially superior to most in its democratic design. And Walter Whitman, poverty school dropout and failed journalist, is now

> Walt Whitman, an American, one of the roughs, a kosmos,
> Disorderly fleshy and sensual . . . . eating and drinking
> and breeding,
> No sentimentalist . . . . no stander above men and women or
> apart from them . . . .
> no more modest than immodest.

The series of periods in this case, incidentally, are not ellipses to indicate material missing from a quotation but Whitman's oratorical marks common in the nineteenth century for the pacing of a speech. Whitman originally hoped to become an orator, then the most admired profession in the country. His soldier-brother George testified that the poet wrote " 'barrels' of lectures" around 1854; they may indeed have become the basis for the first *Leaves of Grass*.

To Whitman, everything is symbolically equal because it is a microcosm of the divine.

> I believe a leaf of grass is no less than the journeywork of
> the stars,
> And the pismire is equally perfect, and a grain of sand, and
> the egg of the wren,
> And the tree-toad is a chef d'oeuvre for the highest,
> And the running blackberry would adorn the parlors
> of heaven,
> And the narrowest hinge in my hand puts to scorn
> all machinery,

> And the cow crunching with depressed head surpasses
> any statue,
> And a mouse is miracle enough to stagger sextillions
> of infidels.

This is no relativistic universe in 1855, though *Leaves of Grass* shows the influence of science, if not directly the impact of Charles Darwin, whose *On the Origin of Species* appeared four years after Whitman's first edition, but whose ideas about evolution had been on the minds of scientists since the rise of geology and astronomy in the 1830s. Although he may have doubted providence more than once in his life, Whitman was otherwise representative of his age. Like Emerson and even Melville, he was a believer in the essential or logocentric order of the universe. He believed in evolution, not creationism; but he had no doubt that God was at its fountain. He is especially relevant in the twentieth and twenty-first centuries, so dominated by science, because he places equal emphasis on body and soul. The phenomenal world and human sexuality are subjects as worthy of poetic celebration as spirituality and love.

There is also the primitive side of Whitman, where he triumphs over the Puritan guilt that Hawthorne (one of Whitman's models for his attempts at fiction writing in the 1840s) had already shown to be at the heart of the American experience. In section 32 of *Song of Myself* he brags that he "could turn and live awhile with the animals, they are so placid and self-contained":

> They do not sweat and whine about their condition,
> They do not lie awake in the dark and weep for their sins,
> They do not make me sick discussing their duty to God,
> Not one is dissatisfied . . . . not one is demented with the
> mania of owning things,
> Not one kneels to another nor to his kind that lived
> thousands of years ago,
> Not one is respectable or industrious over the whole earth.

As far as Whitman is concerned, he still carries "tokens" of the evolutionary phases he once passed through. As he says, vast cycles of time had "ferried my cradle, rowing and rowing like cheerful boatman."

It is in this state of mind that he can salute the "friendly and flowing savage" who would soon be largely exterminated during the country's westward expansion. Because he believed Native Americans were of a primitive order and thus closer to the time of creation, they held a key to the past that was now being destroyed. Yet Whitman did not disapprove of the westward movement that was the likely agent of that destruction. He had felt the same way about the Mexican War, rationalizing the national grab for land with the idea that the U.S. Army was also liberating Mexican peasants from their aristocratic masters. Democracy, which to Whitman was simply a political extension of Emerson's proclamation that all men and women were divine (as parts of nature, the emblem of God), would simply bring everything into balance and ultimately right all wrongs. He hailed democracy as "Ma femme!" in "Starting from Paumanok."

After buttressing the reader for forty-five sections in *Song of Myself*, Whitman prepares to make his departure. He has taken the reader down the "open road" of life, pointing out the everyday miracles. Now he says in section 46 that it is time for the reader to travel the road for himself and herself. In section 52 the poet departs "as air," shaking his white locks "at the runaway sun." He bequeaths himself to the dirt "to grow from the grass I love" and tells the reader, "If you want me again look for me under your boot-soles."

Whitman selected "Leaves of Grass" as the main title for all his poems because it suggested the transcendental nature of his vision. "Leaves" were not only "spears" (also called "leaves" in describing grass) but leaves or pages in a book. The grass itself was chosen as Whitman's particular emblem of nature to celebrate because it grew so democratically among rich and poor, was optimistically green, and was indeed as part of all nature "a uniform hieroglyphic." That is to say, it was uniformly green or hopeful, and nature as God's hieroglyphic was both a sacred and secret message to humankind. As noted earlier, Whitman believed with the transcendentalists that all poetry had been written before time began. It was originally contained in the mind of God, and now with the establishment of human and animal existence it flowed through nature. Its message (as in all poetry and literature in general) was never direct but consisted only of "faint clews and indirections," as Whitman writes in "When I Read the Book." Here he is talking about the probability that someone will write his biography (to date there have been at least fifteen) and wondering how anyone could know his life well enough to complete such a task since his life and all lives are grasped or understood only by fits and starts.

Besides "I Sing the Body Electric," some of Whitman's most important poems that appeared in the first edition (possibly as cuttings from the main plant, *Song of Myself*) were "A Song for Occupations," "The Sleepers," "A Boston Ballad," and "There Was a Child Went Forth." In "A Song for Occupations," Whitman added to sex in his poetry the subject of jobs—these were two topics previously banned or ignored in American (mainly New England) poems about snowy lanes and dead infants. "The Sleepers" is presciently Freudian. "A Boston Ballad" harks back to the 1854 case of the fugitive slave Anthony Burns, who was forcefully returned from New England to his masters in the South. Just as the Quaker poet John Greenleaf Whittier had tried to shame the South by reminding it of the courage of its colonial leaders in "Massachusetts to Virginia," Whitman in "A Boston Ballad" brought back the ghosts of such heroes from revolutionary days to express their disdain for what their descendants had wrought in the New World. In "There Was a Child Went Forth," Whitman tries to show how the poet as a child became intimately involved with everything he saw and touched.

THE POET OF DEMOCRACY

Whitman's lifelong theme was the "Good Cause" of democracy and freedom. In "To Thee Old Cause," he dedicates his book to the "sweet idea" of democracy: "The chants for thee, the eternal march for thee." As a poverty school graduate and later as a journalist, he came to realize that democracy was a rare opportunity for his working-class compatriots to improve their lives. We can see the origins of this reform spirit in his editorials, which argued for temperance of the working class (so that workers would not be exploited by their employers), better schools, music education, regular personal hygiene, better pay for sewing women, and so forth—all calling upon the "divine average" to exercise as much discipline and energy as was possible in a society still controlled by the wealthy and the powerful.

When he turned to his second edition of *Leaves of Grass* in 1856 (with a total of thirty-six poems), he also turned even more to an emphasis upon women as equal members with men in this new democratic society. Through his mother, he had befriended several women in Brooklyn who were advocates of female suffrage long before it was granted in the twentieth century. Democracy applied to men *and* women, if not yet black slaves who were yet to be freed. In one of the new poems in this edition of (*Leaves of Grass*), "A Woman Waits for Me" (then awkwardly called "Poem of Procreation"), Whitman imagined athletic women (in an age before there were female sports) who knew "how to swim, row, ride, wrestle, shoot, run, strike, retreat, advance, resist, defend themselves" (one here also gets a glimpse of Whitman's great capacity to catalog). He also imagined a highly sexual woman when such conduct was hardly acceptable except to streetwalkers, whom the poet himself may have visited in lower Manhattan in the 1840s. But he also envisioned that these active women would eventually become mothers who doted on their children. As he announces in section 21 of *Song of Myself*: "there is nothing greater than the mother of men."

Clearly the most important poem of this edition, and one of Whitman's best, was "Crossing Brooklyn Ferry." Entitled "Sun-Down Poem" in 1856, it dwelled on the idea that time and space ultimately mean nothing because all creation is irrevocably connected in that divine emblem, nature. The speaker addresses the readers of the future, asking what it is that is between them. Whatever it is, he insists, "it avails not, neither time nor place—distance avails not."

> I too lived, Brooklyn of ample hills was mine,
> I too walked the streets of Manhattan island, and bathed in
> the waters around it,
> I too felt the curious abrupt questionings stir within me
> . . .
> I too received identity by my body

At least one critic has remarked that it seems as if Whitman is looking over our shoulder as we read this poem.

Between 1857 and 1862 Whitman's movements are more difficult to trace. It has been assumed for years that he was editor of the *Brooklyn Times* during this period, but the evidence for this largely unexamined claim is minuscule to nonexistent. We do know, of course, that he had been definitely writing more poems because the third edition of *Leaves of Grass* in 1860 has more than one hundred, including the clusters of "Enfants d'Adam" (afterward called "Children of Adam") and "Calamus." The first group introduces Adam waking up to his sexuality and its various consummations. Heavy emphasis is put on physical attributes and carnal knowledge. In "From Pent-Up Aching Rivers" (originally "Enfants d'Adam No. 2"), the poet insists that he would be nothing without his sexuality.

This indeed was Whitman's reason for refusing Emerson's plea to exclude this particular series from the third edition. The 1860 edition was the first to have a formal publisher instead of a printer hired by Whitman. As the book was going through the press in Boston, Emerson read the proofs. He did so more than simply out of curiosity. When in 1855 Emerson wrote him the letter "at the beginning of a great career," Whitman in his excitement at being noticed by the leading literary light in America had allowed the remarks to be published in a newspaper without Emerson's permission and even went so far as to plaster in gold letters on the spine of the

1856 edition the words "I greet you at the beginning of a great career R W Emerson." It made Emerson ipso facto the champion of twenty-four poems he had never even read. No doubt he wanted to make sure nothing of his letter was to be attached to the third edition. There wasn't, but Emerson nevertheless advised him to drop the "Children of Adam" poems in order to give his book a chance to sell (which it did anyway, selling out the first edition of one thousand copies, a success interrupted only by the beginning of the Civil War). Whitman respectfully declined, saying that *Leaves of Grass* without the "Children of Adam" poems would be like a man without his virility.

Emerson had no objection to the "Calamus" poems, which were then considered by almost everybody as merely celebrations of male friendship. This was in the era before the Oscar Wilde sodomy trials of 1895 and their concern over "the love that dare not speak its name." In fact, the word "homosexual" was not even coined until the 1890s. Today the post-Freudian consensus is that the "Calamus" poems are about homosexuality and that Whitman by extension was gay. There is other textual evidence to support the theory for his homosexuality, but there are also indications of his interest in women. Whereas the "Children of Adam" poems are about sex, or "libidinous joys only," the "Calamus" poems are about tender love. In the latter, Whitman sets out

> To tell the secret of my nights and days,
> To celebrate the need of comrades.

The "Calamus" poems are also about loneliness. By reasoning backward from them, many critics have suggested that the late 1850s, the period of their composition, must have been a dark period for Whitman personally when he suffered what today would be called a midlife crisis. Whitman more or less confirms this idea by saying that the war and his hospital work had lifted him out of his emotional "slough."

The 1860 edition of *Leaves of Grass* completes a major period in Whitman's poetic career. Many critics have argued—perhaps at the undue expense of Whitman's later work, which includes his great elegy to Lincoln (discussed below)—that the first three editions of *Leaves of Grass* constitute his most powerful and original work. The 1860 volume also introduced two of Whitman's most famous seashore poems. The seashore, or the land's edge, was a great symbol for the Poet of Paumanok (the Native-American name for Long Island, meaning "fish-shaped"), for it represented the dividing line between life and death, body and soul. By far the greater of the two, and one of Whitman's two or three best poems, is "Out of the Cradle Endlessly Rocking." In "Starting from Paumanok" (in the 1860 edition as "Proto-Leaf" and a kind of twin to the more mystical *Song of Myself*), Whitman acknowledged Long Island as the place of his birth and the island from which he surveyed that greater island of America and American democracy in largely imaginary travels around the country. In the first two editions of *Leaves of Grass*, freedom was his shibboleth. But now, as he approached forty and his beloved America approached national calamity in the Civil War, his mood shifted to one of isolation and helplessness in the face of life's disappointments.

Called "A Child's Reminiscence" in its initial 1859 publication in the *New York Saturday Press* and "A Word Out of the Sea" in the 1860 edition, "Out of the Cradle Endlessly Rocking" is the poet's discovery, or rediscovery, of his true vocation as a chanter of love and death. Often readers of this poem make the mistake of identifying the speaker as a boy because the central incident related in the poem involves a boy, the young Whitman on the sands of Paumanok. But the actual speaker is an adult in the throes of an emotional crisis that evokes the greater crisis of the human condition in which love (or desire) and death (or loss) are two sides of the same coin, the one irrevocably joined to the other. The song of the speaker is a reminiscence of the time when as a boy he first became faintly aware of death. On the shores of Long Island, or Paumanok, he observes the nesting of two mockingbirds. One day the female is blown out to sea, and the boy hears the male crying in vain for the return for his mate. Now as "a man—yet by these tears a little boy again"—the narrator comes to the conclusion that "Death" is finally the "word out of the sea," the only clue to the mystery of life that he is ever to receive. This is not as morose at it might sound, however, for he also learns that death exists as well as life, that they go hand in hand. Indeed, his new knowledge of death leads to his poetic rebirth, as he tells the solitary singer on the shore, the mockingbird:

> Now in a moment I know what I am for—I awake,
> And already a thousand singers—a thousand songs, clearer,
>   louder, more sorrowful than yours,
> A thousand warbling echoes have started to life within me,
> Never to die.

The epiphany in "As I Ebb'd with the Ocean of Life" (first published in 1860 as "Bardic Symbols" in the *Atlantic Monthly*) is not quite as sanguine. Up to this point, as a transcendentalist the poet was confident that he could walk the shores of Paumanok "seeking types," that nature proved the existence of a benign and well-meaning God. At the end of *Song of Myself*, for example, he had addressed God on a familiar basis ("Listener up there! Here you . . . . what have you to confide to me?"). Now he finds that it had all been a pathetic illusion to think that he could know anything about the spiritual shore. There in fact had been no contact with the other shore at all:

> O baffled, balked,
> Bent to the very earth, here preceding what follows,
> Oppressed with myself that I have dared to open my mouth,
> Aware now, that, amid all the blab whose echoes recoil
>   upon me,
>   I have not once had the least idea who or what I am,
> But that before me all my insolent poems, the real Me
>   still stands untouched, untold, altogether unreached.

The "real Me"—in Kantian and Emersonian terms the Platonic idea of the soul—is actually

> Withdrawn far, mocking me with mock-congratulatory
>   signs and bows,
> With peals of distant ironical laughter at every word I
>   have written
>   or shall write.

With this poem, Whitman moves temporarily out of the logocentric world of the nineteenth century and into the Darwinian world of doubt. He never abandoned romanticism entirely, but he also acknowledged the realism of the second half of the nineteenth century in which emerging probability theories and evolution's emphasis on chance in the "survival of the fittest" tended to undercut the antebellum concept of a benign God.

CIVIL WAR AND ITS AFTERMATH

It has never been explained completely why Whitman's third edition enjoyed a healthy sale until the war, when his Boston publisher went bankrupt in 1861 as the nation went on a war footing. The owners of Thayer and Eldridge were Radical Republicans strongly opposed to slavery, and their list of publications catered to the progressive-minded in both politics and literature. At least two of the books on their relatively short list were devoted to the life and achievements of John Brown, recently executed and thus martyred for his raid on Harpers Ferry. Another by William Douglas O'Connor, who soon became one of Whitman's closest friends, was an antislavery novel called *Harrington*, published in the same year as the third *Leaves of Grass*. Whitman's book had also been hailed in the *Saturday Press*, which had an artistic and bohemian readership. Yet to the more general reader, Whitman's book remained an anathema—if it was known at all.

When the war began in the spring of 1861 with the Confederate attack on Fort Sumter, Whitman responded with some of the poems that would eventually make up *Drum-Taps* (1865), including "Beat! Beat! Drums!" This recruiting poem may have encouraged his brother George to enlist in the Union army as a ninety-day soldier (both Northerners and Southerners thought the war would be over in no time) and immediately afterward for three years or the duration of the war. But otherwise Whitman tried to avoid the conflict for almost two years by spending time on Long Island and writing a warmed-over history of Brooklyn for a local newspaper. He seemed to be returning to his youthful past in search of something he had lost. It may have been a delayed reaction to the loss of a lover or some other emotional eruption in the late 1850s when he was often unemployed. Possibly the patriotic poet was in denial over the northern losses during the first two years of the war.

This personal retreat from the war was brought to a dramatic halt when the Whitman family on Portland Avenue in Brooklyn (the poet's mother and Jeff and his family, the father having died in 1855) read in one of the newspapers that an officer named "George Whitmore" had been wounded at the Battle of Fredericksburg, the latest in a string of Union disasters, on 13 December 1862. The Whitman family members knew from George Whitman's letters that there was no officer by that name in the Fifty-first Regiment of New York Volunteers, the company he had subsequently joined and from which he received a battlefield commission. Once they quickly assumed "Whitmore" was a misprint for "Whitman," Walt set out for Washington, D.C., in the hope of finding and caring for his brother in one of the more than forty makeshift military hospitals in the Union capital. Once in Washington, Whitman found O'Connor, who was now working in the wartime government. After a futile search of the hospitals, O'Connor helped Whitman secure a military pass to the military front at Fredericksburg. It was shortly before Christmas when he reached Falmouth, across the Rappahannock River, where Union troops had retreated after a day and night of fighting. One of his first sights was a pile of amputated limbs outside a makeshift Union hospital.

Whitman was relieved to find George only slightly injured by a spent miniball, but his heart went out to the many soldiers who were more seriously and often mortally wounded. He remained at the Union encampment for almost two weeks, acting as a nurse and visitor to the sick and wounded. These included captured Confederate soldiers who had been wounded. Whitman admired their bravery, while opposing the causes for which they fought. It was on the battlefield, or in the Falmouth encampment, that Whitman began to write a different kind of wartime poem for his *Drum-Taps*. One day he followed the flag of truce onto the battlefield to retrieve and bury the Union dead. The excitement for Whitman of Fort Sumter now faded into the pathos of the deaths of so many young Americans, mere youths in many cases from the cities, the country, and the West. In "A Sight in Camp in the Day-Break Gray and Dim," he compared one of the dead to "the Christ himself, / Dead and divine and brother of all, and here again he lies."

In "Vigil Strange I Kept on the Field One Night," he imagined himself speeding into "the even-contested battle," but Whitman's wartime experience consisted exclusively of tending to the sick and wounded. Shortly before the New Year he volunteered to supervise the transport of injured and debilitated soldiers back to Washington. Initially he had intended to return to New York to take up his life before the war. But as he told his mother in a letter, when he found his brother George and saw the courage and suffering of so many young men he decided to remain in Washington to do what he could to help the war effort. Once there, with the help of O'Connor and William Thayer, one of his Boston publishers now serving as the army paymaster, he secured a part-time job in the paymaster's office and otherwise dedicated himself as a "hospital visitor" to the ailing soldiers in those many wartime Washington hospitals. Most of the ailing soldiers never knew he was a poet. Whitman looked more like an old sea captain or a frontier scout in his western garb and flowing gray hair and beard. He arranged for donations from New York and from friends in New England so that he could provide *his* soldiers (as he thought of them) with small gifts to ease their daily lives on the rough hospital fare. He brought in his haversack oranges, writing paper, tobacco (which the poet never used himself), ice cream to cool parched lips, and sometimes a special delicacy such as oysters for terminal patients, of which there were many.

Walt Whitman (simply and officially "Walt" after the publication of the first *Leaves*) continued this hospital schedule twice a day for almost three years, finally becoming sick himself from the malaria and other diseases that plagued the hospitals. He witnessed many amputations, often as futile last-ditch attempts to save the lives of soldiers infected from unsterilized medical instruments in an era before the knowledge of microbes and their role in infection. It has been estimated that military hospitals of both North and South killed as many soldiers as they saved. Shortly before the end of the war, Whitman found a full-time job as a clerk in the Department of the Interior, but shortly afterward he was dismissed from that federal agency by Secretary James Harlan for being the author of "a dirty book." His friend O'Connor, enraged at the dismissal, quickly arranged for his transfer into the attorney general's office. The fiery Irishman, risking his own government position, also wrote a pamphlet entitled "The Good Gray Poet," a hagiographic screed that indicted Secretary Harlan, a former professor of moral and mental science in Iowa and a close friend of the recently assassinated Abraham Lincoln, of being Cato the Censor and lauded Whitman as America's greatest poet, grown gray in the service of his country and scorned for his many sacrifices.

Whitman remained in Washington after the war and indeed until 1872, when he suffered his first and most serious paralytic stroke and was forced to move to Camden, New Jersey, to live with George and his new wife. His dear mother died there just before he left Washington. He had brought out *Drum-Taps* at his own expense in 1865 and the fourth edition of *Leaves of Grass* in 1867, but the latter work demonstrated more than anything else his emotional and physical exhaustion from the war years and their aftermath. It contained only six new poems, none of them considered among his important writings. *Drum-Taps*, of course, had been written during the war, on the go, and in and out of the hospitals as the poems recorded the whirlwind times. When Lincoln was assassinated, he stopped the binding of the book to add a "Sequel" of eighteen poems. It contained "Hush'd Be the Camps To-day," "O Captain! My Captain!," and "When Lilacs Last in the Dooryard Bloom'd."

Whitman wrote "Hush'd Be the Camps To-day" immediately following the burial of Lincoln and expressed the Union Army's grief over the loss of its commander in chief, whose death now came to represent the sacrifice of all the soldiers. "O Captain" has been unfairly criticized for its conventional rhythm and rhyme, but read in historical context it evokes the rhythms of such folksy singing groups as the Hutchinson and the Cheney family singers who often performed at political and abolition rallies in the 1850s. The narrator of "O Captain!" is not the poet but, as Helen Vendler (2000) has suggested, the common soldier who has lost his leader. When Whitman gave his lecture on "The Death of Abraham Lincoln" in the 1870s and 1880s, he usually introduced it with this poem because he always thought of Lincoln as a man of the people.

His greatest Lincoln poem—indeed, one of the three or four most important of all his poems—is the elegy "When Lilacs Last in the Dooryard Bloom'd." Written in the tradition of Milton's "Lycidas," Shelley's "Adonais," and Tennyson's *In Memoriam*, it takes a personal loss and universalizes it. Whitman was home sick in Brooklyn when Lincoln was shot, and lilacs were in bloom. Later in his Lincoln lecture, he noted that ever afterward he was reminded of Lincoln's murder by the sight and smell of lilacs. Whitman considered Lincoln the only president of his century equal to Washington and Jefferson. Before the assassination, he had written in *The New York Times* about seeing Lincoln in his carriage in Washington. Years later, when he incorporated the piece into his autobiography, he embellished the encounter to suggest that they had exchanged glances, but the fact is that they did not. These two heroes of democracy never met. There is some evidence that Lincoln read *Leaves of Grass* to his law partners in Illinois, but the story may indeed be apocryphal. In another legend, Lincoln is supposed to have asked in the East Room of the White House about Whitman as he walked down Pennsylvania Avenue on his way home from one of the hospitals. Neither of these anecdotes has ever been verified by scholars and historians.

"When Lilacs Last in the Dooryard Bloom'd" is structured upon three basic symbols—the lilacs of spring, the fallen western star, and the warbling of the hermit thrush in the many swamps around Washington at that time. The first stands for poet's love, which is as eternal as the lilacs of "ever-returning spring"; the falling star stands for the slain president; and the song (for there is operatic music in or behind most Whitman poems) is the chant of death. These are intertwined to introduce and dramatize the long journey Lincoln's coffin actually made, the nation's (and the poet's) grief, and the dead Lincoln now enshrined as a figure of reconciliation not only to the horrors of the war but to death itself:

> Nor for you, for one, alone;
> Blossoms and branches green to coffins all I bring:
> For fresh as the morning—thus would I chant a song for
>   you O sane and sacred death.

THE GOOD GRAY POET

By 1867 Whitman had published four editions of *Leaves of Grass* and one book of wartime poems, but he was still stubbornly ignored by the genteel literary establishment in America. There were a few exceptions in Emerson, Henry David Thoreau, Amos Bronson Alcott, and others, but mainly Whitman's book was condemned because it could not pass the "standard of the evening lamp," or be read in mixed company at family circles involving women and children (the phrase almost one continuous word in the nineteenth century). The objections were that it was generally written in slang and was obscene in content because of its references to sex and parts of the body. Yet its original vision of America, the vigor of its voice, and the depth of its enthusiasm for democracy recommended it to many readers in spite of the caveats. One of them was the Englishman William Michael Rossetti, who published in 1868 the first British edition of Whitman's poetry. Actually the English reader in general was almost as puritanical as the American when it came to the body, and so Rossetti's edition had to be a selection in which Whitman's main poem, *Song of Myself* (at this juncture called simply "Walt Whitman"), was completely left out. Rather than cannibalize poems, Rossetti thought it fairer to the poetry either to include or exclude poems altogether. As a result, not only *Song of Myself* was left out but also the "Children of Adam" poems. Interestingly, the "Calamus" poems were freely included. Yet even in this emaciated state, this selection from *Leaves of Grass* probably did more to promote Whitman's international renown than all the previous editions put together.

At home, except for a small but growing band of supporters that included O'Connor and the naturalist John Burroughs, the poet still struggled for acceptance. He had even learned of disparaging remarks about his long catalogs from Emerson. While still in Washington, Whitman issued the fifth (1871) edition of *Leaves of Grass* as well as another book of poems called *Passage to India* (1871). Just as *Drum-Taps* had been absorbed into the 1867 edition of *Leaves of Grass*, the *Passage to India* poems of 1871 were absorbed into the 1881 edition. The fifth edition had very few new poems because these were deposited into *Passage to India*, which contained twenty-three new poems. Now almost all poems added to Whitman's canon were first published in newspapers or magazines or read on special occasions. The title poem, "Passage to India," uses three great technological advances—the completion of the Suez Canal, the transcontinental railroad, and the transatlantic cable—to envision not only the spread of democracy and brotherhood around the world but also the soul's circumnavigation as a "passage to more than India!" The poem was pieced together from several other

compositions and does not represent the best of Whitman in terms of the spontaneity and uncertainty found in the crisis poems of the late 1850s.

If the elite refused to accept him, his own working class began to take him up to the extent that he was invited to read an original poem at the opening of the American Institute Exhibition in New York in 1871, where the latest technology was put on display. He read "After All Not to Create Only" (later entitled "Song of the Exposition") to a hall full of mechanics. Its theme, like that of "Passage to India" in part, was that these inventions would enrich the lives of the average worker. The next year Dartmouth College invited him to read an original poem, "As a Strong Bird on Pinions Free" (later "Thou Mother with Thy Equal Brood"), another celebration of and desideratum about democracy. Whitman had been brought to the Dartmouth campus by students unhappy with the traditional curriculum not only in literature but science (where botany was "studied" in the New Hampshire winter). But he was apparently unhappy himself, at least about the generally harsh treatment of his poetry in America. In "Prayer of Columbus," first published in *Harper's* in 1874, he compared himself to the neglected Columbus at the end of his life, "A batter'd wreck'd old man, / Thrown on this savage shore, far, far from home." His fear of public indifference (fueled by an American literary establishment contemptuous of his free verse and perhaps envious of his freer choice of subjects) led him in 1876 to trigger an Anglo-American debate over his treatment at home with an anonymous article entitled "Walt Whitman's Actual American Position." British supporters of Whitman (mainly Pre-Raphaelites, who approved of Whitman's attention to the body) pounced on America for ignoring one of its very own geniuses, and the Americans struck back angrily, accusing Whitman of being nothing more than a literary barbarian—though some did praise his hospital work during the war.

That year he was virtually ignored by the festivities in nearby Philadelphia celebrating the first hundred years of the United States (the organizers of the nation's centenary chose instead as their "poet laureate" the now forgotten Bayard Taylor). In response Whitman celebrated the centennial on his own terms by issuing the 1876 edition of *Leaves of Grass*, essentially an issue or impression of the 1871 edition and a companion volume—*Two Rivulets*, which was a miscellany of new poetry and prose. By the time of the publication of the sixth (1881) edition of Whitman's book, in Boston, the last as the poet finally stopped revising and rearranging

Leaves of Grass, the book was finally "full." Anything written and published afterward went into one of the two "Annexes," called "Sands at Seventy" and "Good-Bye My Fancy," attached to the final issues of *Leaves of Grass*. Whitman hoped that future readers would read the 1881 edition instead of earlier ones. (At the time, to Whitman's great irritation, someone was selling illicitly reprinted copies of the 1860 edition.) The sixth edition of *Leaves of Grass* was only the second to have an official publisher, but when it appeared, the Boston district attorney called for its withdrawal on the grounds that many of its poems were judged to be obscene—even though all of the offensive pieces had appeared without legal challenge in earlier editions. Effectively "banned in Boston," Whitman took the plates for this edition of his poems to a Philadelphia printer. Because of the scandal over the book, *Leaves of Grass* enjoyed the best sale of its lifetime, quickly selling out the first three printings.

Most of the twenty or so new poems in the edition were unremarkable, but one that had been recently published in a British magazine was distinctive. "The Dalliance of the Eagles" observes the mating of eagles high in the sky—"the rushing amorous contact high in space together"—based on his observations during a recent trip to Canada. Because the poem was also about "sex," it was an item on the district attorney's list. As the sixth edition sold out in 1882, Whitman also issued that year *Specimen Days & Collect*, an omnium-gatherum of autobiographical writings, especially on the Civil War. The following year Richard Maurice Bucke, a Canadian alienist or psychologist, published the first biography of the poet; before publication, it was heavily revised by the poet himself.

Soon afterward, with the profits from the sale of the sixth edition, Whitman purchased a row house on Mickle Street in Camden (a state-supported museum today), just across the Delaware River from Philadelphia. Once again the poet was drawn to the river and its ferries, and he traveled back and forth between the two cities as he had between New York and Brooklyn. As Whitman's international fame spread, his home became a mecca for visitors from Europe who journeyed to the American continent mainly, it was said, to see Niagara Falls and Walt Whitman. Whitman's fame grew and grew, in large part because of his exposure in Great Britain and on the Continent. His visitors included Edward Carpenter, Oscar Wilde, and Bram Stoker (future author of *Dracula*, whose main character was supposedly modeled on Whitman).

The Good Gray Poet, his hair and beard actually white now, finished his days surrounded by disciples and from time to time called upon to lighten the nation's grief or underscore its accomplishments with such occasional poems like the ones about the tragic Johnstown Flood and the completion (after almost a century of delayed construction) of the Washington Monument. In "A Voice from Death," for example, Whitman finds even amid the rubble and horror of the Pennsylvania flood the irrepressible cycle of nature in the miraculous survival of a woman and the birth of her baby ("A suffering woman saved—a baby born!").

In one of his final poems, written in his sickroom in 1890, the partially paralyzed and ailing poet wrote yet another tribute to the miracle of nature, which as that Emersonian emblem of the unseen world of God had "written" all his poems. In "To the Sun-Set Breeze," which is actually about a faint movement of cool air that passed through his sickroom one day in the hot Camden summer, Whitman wrote:

> Ah, whispering, something again, unseen,
> Where late this heated day thou enterest at my
>   window, door,
> Thou, laving, tempering all, cool-freshing, gently vitalizing
> Me, old, alone, sick, weak-down, melted-worn with sweat;
> Thou, nestling, folding close and firm yet soft, companion
>   better than talk, book, art.

As in the case of all nature, the breeze is Whitman's microcosmic connection to creation itself. Through it, he feels "the sky, the prairies vast," "the ocean and the forest."

Walt Whitman died at the age of seventy-two on 26 March 1892, following a series of minor paralytic strokes and a steady physical decline. Unlike his fellow New Yorker Herman Melville, whose literary achievements were almost forgotten for nearly twenty years after his death in 1891, Whitman's American fame was kept alive by a band of disciples, especially Whitman's "Boswell," Horace Traubel, who kept a daily record of the poet's conversations during the last four years of his life. Whitman became the subject of a Pulitzer Prize–winning biography in 1926. The Poet of Democracy finally emerged as America's most central and influential poet in the 1940s, following his rejection by the New Critics of the 1930s whose formalism and preference for T. S. Eliot rejected Whitman's more natural rhythms and loose structures. Ezra Pound, who edited Eliot's *The Waste Land* and contributed to the nation's epic tradition with his *Cantos*, also came around to Whitman, who he said had broken "the new wood" of modern American poetry. With Whitman's fame as America's most seminal poet now secure, his influence has extended beyond literature into the realms of popular culture, as demonstrated by his iconic use in American films and politics.

[*See also* Emerson, Ralph Waldo *and* Transcendentalism.]

SELECTED WORKS

Leaves of Grass (1855, 1856, 1860, 1867, 1871, 1881–1882)
Franklin Evans; or, The Inebriate (1842)
Drum-Taps (1865)
Passage to India (1871)
Two Rivulets (1876)
Specimen Days & Collect (1882)

FURTHER READING

Allen, Gay Wilson. *The New Walt Whitman Handbook.* New York, 1975.

Allen, Gay Wilson, and Ed Folsom, eds. *Walt Whitman and the World.* Iowa City, Iowa, 1995. Essays on Whitman's reception around the globe by leading critics in each country treated.

Asselineau, Roger. *The Evolution of Walt Whitman.* Iowa City, Iowa, 1999. First published in French in 1954. First biography to discuss the connection between the poet's alleged homosexuality and his poetry.

Ceniza, Sherry. *Walt Whitman and 19th-Century Women Reformers.* Tuscaloosa, Ala., 1998.

Cowley, Malcolm, ed. *Walt Whitman's Leaves of Grass: His Original Edition.* New York, 1959.

Erkkila, Betsy. *Whitman the Political Poet.* New York, 1989.

Folsom, Ed. *Walt Whitman's Native Representations.* Cambridge and New York, 1994. Discusses Whitman in terms of emerging nineteenth-century culture and technology.

Fone, Byrne. *Masculine Landscapes: Walt Whitman and the Homoerotic Text.* Carbondale, Ill., 1992.

Kaplan, Justin. *Walt Whitman: A Life.* New York, 1980. A popular life of Whitman, highly readable and accurate with a light emphasis on the poetry.

Kaplan, Justin. *Walt Whitman: Complete Poetry and Collected Prose.* New York, 1982. Includes 1855 edition of *Leaves of Grass.* Later paperback edition contains additional background material.

Killingsworth, M. Jimmie. *Whitman's Poetry of the Body: Sexuality, Politics, and the Text.* Chapel Hill, N.C., 1989.

Klammer, Martin. *Whitman, Slavery, and the Emergence of Leaves of Grass.* University Park, Pa., 1995.

Krieg, Joann P. *A Whitman Chronology.* Iowa City, Iowa, 1998.

LeMaster, J. R., and Donald D. Kummings. *Walt Whitman: An Encyclopedia.* New York, 1998.

Loving, Jerome. *Walt Whitman: The Song of Himself.* Berkeley, Calif., 1999. A critical biography, one that discusses the life and work in tandem.

Miller, Edwin Haviland. *Walt Whitman's Poetry: A Psychological Journey.* Boston, 1968.

Miller, F. DeWolfe, ed. *Walt Whitman's Drum-Taps (1865) and Sequel to Drum-Taps (1865–6).* Gainesville, Fla., 1959.

Miller, James E., Jr., *A Critical Guide to Leaves of Grass.* Chicago, 1957.

Morris, Roy, Jr. *The Better Angel: Walt Whitman and the Civil War.* New York, 2000.

Pollak, Vivian R. *The Erotic Whitman.* Berkeley, Calif., 2000.

Price, Kenneth M. *Whitman and Tradition: The Poet in His Century.* New Haven, Conn., 1990.

Reynolds, David S. *Walt Whitman's America: A Cultural Biography.* New York, 1995. Emphasizes Whitman's political and cultural development.

Reynolds, David S., ed. *A Historical Guide to Walt Whitman.* New York, 2000.

Thomas, M. Wynn. *The Lunar Light of Whitman's Poetry.* Cambridge, Mass., 1987. Discusses Whitman's poetry as absorbing the changes and challenges in the transition of capitalism from the antebellum artisanal order to the anonymity of Whitman's "divine average" in the Gilded Age.

Vendler, Helen. "Poetry and the Meditation of Value: Whitman on Lincoln." *Michigan Quarterly Review* 39 (Winter 2000): 1–18.

"*The Walt Whitman Archive.*" Available at http://www. whitmanarchive.org.

See also the article on Whitman's *Song of Myself,* immediately following.

WALT WHITMAN'S
SONG OF MYSELF

by Huck Gutman

Walt Whitman's *Song of Myself* is thought by many critics to be both the most important and the most revolutionary poem written by an American. Like T. S. Eliot's twentieth-century landmark poem *The Waste Land*, *Song of Myself* blazed new territory and shaped many of the poems that would follow it. First published in 1855 and revised by Whitman a number of times thereafter, the poem is almost as fresh today as when it was written.

Almost. What we cannot recapture is how stunningly original the poem must have appeared when it was first published, how radical it must have seemed to the few readers who encountered it in 1855. The poem appeared, without a title, in the first edition of Whitman's *Leaves of Grass*. The volume itself had a title but no listed author, only an engraved portrait of the putative poet facing the title page, standing informally and somewhat assertively, wearing a workingman's shirt, hat on his head, looking outward. One hand is in his pocket, the other bent. The poet describes himself in section 4 of the poem:

> Apart from the pulling and hauling stands what I am,
> Stands amused, complacent, compassionating, idle, unitary,
> Looks down, is erect, or bends an arm on an impalpable
>   certain rest,
> Looking with side-curved head curious what will come next,
> Both in and out of the game and watching and wondering
>   at it.

What must the first readers have thought when they browsed through this book of poems with no listed author, a long introduction consisting of endless sentences, then a poem without title that went on and on and on? (Not until the second edition in 1856 would Whitman call it "Poem of Walt Whitman, an American," later "Walt Whitman," and in 1881 "Song of Myself.")

Those readers would have seen it as obsessively self-centered—after all, it opens, "I celebrate myself"—and without any poetic form. The poem did not rhyme, nor was it in Shakespearian blank verse. Lines sprawled across the page, and if the page was not large enough, the lines continued, indented, in the next line—or two or three. The poem went on at great length, without respite

or seeming focus. (The fifty-two numbered divisions, a total corresponding to the number of weeks in a year, were a later innovation.) The control associated with poetry must have seemed absent, an impression seconded by Whitman's words on the opening page: "Creeds and schools in abeyance . . . / I harbor for good or bad, I permit to speak at every hazard, / Nature without check with original energy." This is dangerously close to gluttony.

In fact, in the opening sections of the poem Whitman seems determined to flout many of the seven deadly sins Christianity so often warns against. Pride: "I celebrate myself." Sloth: "I loafe. . . . I lean and loafe at my ease." Lust: "I will go to the bank by the wood and become undisguised and naked." Today one can see how American he is, in part because this particular poem has taught the modern world what characterizes American-ness: an absorption with self, an openness to the world, a willingness to reject the old ways and try new ways, an immense appetite for things and for experiences. What is so difficult for contemporary readers to see, though, is that the new American archetypal figure presented in the poem, so different from the types who inhabited both Europe and classic religious texts, must have appeared revolutionary to readers in the middle of the nineteenth century.

Ralph Waldo Emerson, whose essay "The Poet" (1844) Whitman came close to plagiarizing when he wrote the long introductory essay that preceded *Song of Myself* in the 1855 edition, understood that Whitman was the new American for whom he had been calling, an American who celebrated American culture instead of turning to European behavior and form as a model for what Americans should be. Emerson understood that Whitman, in *Song of Myself*, was inventing himself, accepting himself, as an American. "I greet you at the beginning of a great career," he wrote to Whitman in his excitement at the appearance of *Leaves of Grass*, "which yet must have had a long foreground somewhere, for such a start."

Yet even Emerson could not quite believe what he encountered: "I rubbed my eyes a little, to see if this sunbeam were no illusion; but the solid sense of the book is a sober certainty. It has the best merits, namely, of fortifying and encouraging." And even he was uncertain, with no name on the title page, of who the book's author was: "I did not know until I last night saw the book advertised in a newspaper that I could trust the name as real and available for a post-office."

SECTION 1: REVOLUTIONARY POEM, REVOLUTIONARY STRUCTURE

Song of Myself is often regarded as the most revolutionary poem in the history of American culture. In the "Preface" to the first edition of *Leaves of Grass*, Whitman wrote, "The old red blood and stainless gentility of great poets will be proved by their unconstraint. A heroic person walks at his ease through and out of that custom or precedent or authority that suits him not." Whitman fulfills his own injunction, deciding in the last lines of section 1 to "permit to speak at every hazard, / Nature without check with original energy."

Whitman's celebration of the self, his celebration of the body, his celebration of democracy and egalitarianism, his embrace of vernacular language, his choice to write in "free verse," his intimacy with the reader, are all made manifest in the opening section. The very beginning of the poem indicates how new, bold, radical, is Whitman's vision and his poetic practice.

"I celebrate myself," Whitman began the poem in 1855. (In later versions he changed that first line to "I celebrate myself, and sing myself," adding the second verb, as Edwin Haviland Miller (1968) has pointed out, to connect his radical poem to celebrated epics, since Homer's *Iliad*, Virgil's *Aeneid*, and John Milton's *Paradise Lost* use the verb "sing" in their opening sentence. Although the 1855 text is the most revealing—later emendations mostly made the poem less startling and more acceptable—the text usually available is from the final version of *Leaves of Grass*, published in 1892. That text is the one used here, except as noted.) "In Adam's fall /We sinned all," the *New England Primer* said, referring to the sin of pride. Yet Whitman, in these first words, does not keep his self-regard in check: instead he tells us whatever he claims for himself is ours as well.

Immediately he reveals that he is not the typical American, hard-working and focused on tasks. "I loafe and invite my soul, / I lean and loafe at my ease observing a spear of summer grass." The poem itself will seem to loaf its way along, without a clear structure or purpose; yet like Whitman loafing on the grass, it will observe the world in order that the soul—or what in more modern terms

might be called consciousness—might make a journey toward understanding the self and the world.

For *Song of Myself* is a journey, and although it seems to have little structure—many attempts have been made to press one or another formal construct upon the "loafing" poem—its structure is in fact revealed in the fourth and fifth line of the poem. At this point Whitman has already introduced himself to us, his readers: though the poem begins with "I" and half the words of the first line refer to himself, there is a "you" in the next two lines that is meant to draw the reader into a close, intimate relation to the poet. He is talking about important things—self, soul—and he is talking to *us*. To do that, he sits down on the grass. The structure of this long poem, the great American epic, is shaped by gesture. And the elemental gesture is the opposite of the one in the *Odyssey*, where Odysseus's voyage is external. Here there is an internal voyage, but it takes place in a respite, a decision to sit down and rest awhile before moving on.

This is the structure of the poem: having decided to loaf on the grass, Whitman proceeds in section 5 to tell us about an earlier experience when he sat on the grass, one that may have been the most overpowering experience of his life. Thereafter he keeps talking, pulled more and more in the middle of the poem—sections 20 through 28—into the orbit of the body's desires and appetites; indeed, he winds himself up so powerfully that he moves toward a sexual climax. As his sexual appetite mounts, two things happen. First, in the grip of sexual excitement, he finally tells us who he is. Second, he moves from activity to passivity. That passivity, in which he listens rather than talks, remains until he feels it undermining his very being, at which point—the beginning of section 39—he reasserts himself. And then in section 46 Whitman says, "It is time to explain myself—let us stand up." So the gesture that began the poem—lying on the grass—is replaced by standing up, and a long period of leave-taking commences. Having sat down and introduced himself, the poet has now stood up and begins his goodbyes. Finally he "departs," and the poem is over. Arriving and departing, sitting and standing, talking and listening and talking again—these actions give the poem its shape.

By the time five lines have passed, the poem has announced its revolutionary content, its celebration of self, its organic structure (derived from action and gesture, not imposed by traditional forms), and its intimacy with the reader. The notion that each human has a self, that all share in what the poet has to say, is reemphasized in the third stanza, where the poet speaks of "My tongue, every atom of my blood, form'd from this soil, this air, / Born here of parents born here from parents the same, and their parents the same." The commitment to an essential sameness, the basis of democracy and egalitarianism, is another radical, central theme of *Song of Myself*.

By the middle of section 1 the reader has encountered the major stylistic feature of the poem: it is written in what is usually called "free verse." Whitman was not the first poet to write free verse in English (Christopher Smart's "Jubilate Agno," ca. 1758, is often accorded that honor), but once the example of what Whitman did in *Song of Myself* was set before poets, the trend toward writing free verse grew stronger and stronger, so that it finally became, in the second half of the twentieth century, the dominant metrical form of American poetry. Likewise, the first section introduces Whitman's commitment to the vernacular, to what the British poet William Wordsworth called in 1800 "a selection of the language really spoken by men." Although there is always something of the oracular in Whitman, who wants to be the prophet of democracy, selfhood, and the body, he has too much regard for ordinary men and women to ignore their everyday language as he writes his poem.

BODIES, SOULS, DEATH, AND LONELINESS

Whitman's aim is large. In section 2, loafing on the grass, he asks us to sit beside him. "Stop this day and night with me and you shall possess the origin of all poems," he says, following with a healthy dose of Emersonian self-reliance: "You shall no longer take things at second or third hand.... You shall listen to all sides and filter them for your self."

He then proceeds in section 5 to recount an experience of great mystery and power. Wordsworth says in his long poem *The Prelude* that

> There are in our existence spots of time,
> That with distinct pre-eminence retain
> A renovating virtue, whence, depressed
> By false opinion ... our minds
> Are nourished and invisibly repaired.

The experience Whitman narrates is one which illustrates, to him, that the body is as valuable as the soul—a conclusion at odds with most of Western religion, which teaches that the lowly body should be mortified to avoid any conflict with the all-important soul. Once again, the scene is one of loafing on the grass. Two lovers—is it Whitman's soul and body, or Whitman and his lover, or Whitman and the reader?—lie beside each other, hearing

the rhythm of the beating heart. Whitman recalls, with a "we" that is ambiguous,

> how once we lay such a transparent summer morning,
> How you settled your head athwart my hips and gently
>   turn'd over upon me,
> And parted the shirt from my bosom-bone, and plunged
>   your tongue to my bare-stript heart,
> And reach'd till you felt my beard, and reach'd till you held
>   my feet.

If it is impossible to visualize the scene precisely, the tenor of its imagery is nonetheless compelling. Whitman and his lover, or alternatively his body and his soul, are together on the grass, the head of one on the hips of the other. Clothes are stripped away, and a tongue reaches out and penetrates to his heart. Whitman ends up feeling encompassed, contained both within himself and within the embrace of the other. But is this other making metaphorical love—his heart licked by the tongue of love—or is this a coded version of oral sex? Is the soul touched by the act of love, or is a bodily act ultimately a religious experience?

The questions are compelling but beside the point. What Whitman is telling us, after all, is that body and soul are equally valuable, and the one "must not be abased to the other." His experience on the grass culminates in a profound realization: "Swiftly arose and spread around me the peace and knowledge that pass all the argument of the earth, and I know ... that a kelson of the creation is love." A kelson is a term from shipbuilding, referring to that long thick piece of timber above the keel to which the boat's frame and planking are attached: love, the kelson, is what keeps the whole of creation afloat. Love is everywhere, even in drooping leaves, the burrows of ants, and the pastures slowly reverting back to the weeds and woods from which the fields were first hewn.

Having touched on the holiness of the body and all creation, Whitman proceeds to an imagined dialogue—more like a sermon—with a small child. The child asks what grass is, and despite protestations that he does not know, Whitman proceeds to tell the child. It is a hopeful flag, a memento that God is everywhere ("lawn" refers to both grass and the linen from which handkerchiefs were made), a baby, a sign of democracy, and the hair of graves. But since the grass grows out of the mouths of corpses, it is transmuted, in Whitman's imagination, into tongues, "Oh I perceive after all so many uttering tongues." What do the tongues say? Whitman asks his readers. To him the answer is clear, related to the holiness and interconnectedness he experienced in section 5. He asks, "What do you think has become of the women and children?" only to answer:

> They are alive and well somewhere,
> The smallest sprout shows there is really no death,
> And if ever there was it led forward life, and does not wait at the end to arrest it,
> And ceas'd the moment life appear'd.
> All goes onward and outward, nothing collapses,
> And to die is different from what any one supposed, and luckier.

The lines are a transcendent celebration of the continuity of life, even after death; they show, perhaps following the Indian and Egyptian religions that so fascinated Whitman, that while death may be but an illusion, life is ongoing. But one catches a glimpse of Whitman's darker side here: Can he really be as in love with life, as totally committed to it, as he maintains, when he can proclaim: "Has anyone supposed it lucky to be born? / I hasten to inform him or her it is just as lucky to die, and I know it." And now that the possibility is raised, one wonders if the wonderful opening of the poem—"I celebrate myself"—is more an assertion than a certainty, else why would Whitman feel the need to proclaim it?

There is no question that the overall sense of *Song of Myself* is celebratory, ecstatic; there is no doubt that Whitman is driven by an wild and unquenchable energy that is recognizably and perhaps quintessentially American. But he is a complex man, one possessed of and by secrets, and that complexity, while more visible in the poems of the "Calamus" sequence (1860) or "Out of the Cradle" (1860), is the "little lower layer," to use a phrase from Melville's *Moby-Dick*, that appears at moments in *Song of Myself*.

The poem turns to catalogs throughout. Catalogs are long lists, a device characteristic of epic poems, which in Homer's poems or the Old Testament give a sense of the density of history. In Whitman's hands the catalog becomes a way of presenting the rich diversity of the world, of letting the actuality of American life spring forth in his pages. Like the great French poet Charles Baudelaire (whose major work, *The Flowers of Evil*, appeared in 1857, two years after *Song of Myself*), Whitman was an inveterate walker through cities, an idler of the streets, what the French call a *flaneur*. He and Baudelaire were the first poets to celebrate the *modern* city, giving glimpses—so familiar to the city walker—of the huge array of people and things that appear to those who spend time taking in the rich diversity a city's streets have to offer. "This is the city and I am one of the citizens, / Whatever interests the rest interests me," Whitman says in section 42.

Section 11 is unlike any other in the poem, a drama directly observed by the poet. It is a lyric that can stand on its own, a description of a rich woman watching young men, probably workers, swimming in the water. The lyric is structured by oppositions: rich and ordinary, up and down, dry and wet, dressed and undressed, friendly and lonesome, contented and longing. The woman in the drama longs for the young men, longs for their camaraderie and their lovely naked bodies cavorting in the water. In her imagination she moves among them, passing her hand so that it "descended tremblingly from their temples and ribs," clasping their nakedness to her even though "they do not ask who seizes fast to them, / They do not know who puffs and declines with pendant and bending arch, / They do not think who they souse with spray."

Why is this woman in the poem? She is a figure of loneliness, of longing, of desire for sexual satisfaction. What has she to do with Whitman's "myself"? The answer may be that Whitman had yet to deal confidently with his attraction to other men. The woman may be a projection of Whitman's own unrequited need for intimacy, for sexual fulfillment, for being comfortable (and not distant) from men's bodies, for being soused with phallic spray.

SECTION 24 AND SEXUAL ECSTASY

Whitman claims in section 16 that "I resist any thing better than my own diversity." This open acceptance is by and large one of the great triumphs of *Song of Myself*. "I dote on myself, there is that lot of me, and all so luscious," he says eight sections later. In the poem we encounter prostitutes and presidents, whites and blacks and Indians, men and women. The panoply of human existence is Whitman's terrain, and he wanders freely through it, accepting it as his own. But at the end of section 19 Whitman turns inward, and his focus is not on diversity but on desire. "This hour I tell things in confidence, / I might not tell everybody, but I will tell you."

"But I will tell you." The intimacy Whitman has been developing is now sealed, a pact between poet and reader. He will tell us things he has told no one else. Whitman continues, "Who goes there? Hankering, gross, mystical, nude; / How is it I extract strength from the beef I eat?" The strange collocation of adjectives—desirous, bodily, spiritual, naked—defines him, though he claims not to understand the great mystery of human transubstantiation, in which the bodily objects we eat (meat) become activity and consciousness (strength). Girding himself for the revelation to come, he tells us he is "solid and sound . . . deathless

... august ... I exist as I am, that is enough." There is more talk in section 21 about body and soul, and then the poem shifts into what can only be called a love poem. The night calls to him, calls bodily, "mad naked summer night." The earth calls to him, and he replies, "smile, for your lover comes." But Whitman would grow embarrassed at just how sexual was his bodily relation to the physical world, so he later excised the third and fourth line of the following passage, which appeared in the 1855 edition:

> Prodigal, you have given me love! ... therefore I to you
>   give love!
> O unspeakable passionate love!
> Thruster holding me tight and that I hold tight!
> We hurt each other as the bridegroom and the bride hurt
>   each other.

Then the reader arrives at the heart of *Song of Myself*, section 24. Finally, midway through the poem, the poet identifies himself: he provides us with his name. "Walt Whitman, a kosmos, of Manhattan the son / Turbulent, fleshy, sensual, eating, drinking, and breeding." This "Walt Whitman" is immediately identified as a universe unto himself, and an American by birth; immediately after, he emphasizes just how bodily his identity is, how driven by appetites and desires. He will be completely open, he says (though he will contradict this openness within two pages). "Unscrew the locks from the doors!" he proclaims, asking for open commerce between himself and the reader. But this is not enough, so he continues, "Unscrew the doors themselves from their jambs!"

It is at this juncture, having told us who he is, that Whitman sets forth his basic creed. He tells the reader of his two most deep-seated beliefs. The first is in democracy; he holds to the principle enunciated by Thomas Jefferson in America's Declaration of Independence (1776): "We hold these truths to be self-evident, that all men are created equal, that they are endowed by their Creator with certain unalienable Rights, that among these are Life, Liberty and the pursuit of Happiness."

"Whoever degrades another degrades me," Whitman proclaims, "I speak the pass-word primeval, I give the sign of democracy, / By God! I will accept nothing which all cannot have their counterpart of on the same terms." Then he soars; to cite Randall Jarrell (in Woodress, 1983), "To show Whitman for what he is one does not need to praise or explain or argue, one needs simply to quote."

> Through me many long dumb voices,
> Voices of the interminable generations of prisoners
>   and slaves,

> Voices of the diseased and despairing and of thieves
>   and dwarfs,
> Voices of cycles of preparation and accretion,
> And of the threads that connect the stars, and of wombs and
>   of the father stuff,
> And of the rights of them the others are down upon,
> Of the deform'd, trivial, flat, foolish, despised,
> Fog in the air, beetles rolling balls of dung.

Nowhere, in the whole history of American literature, has the commitment to democracy been expressed more cogently or more eloquently. Whitman is passionate. His role as poet is to be the voice of the wretched of the earth: of those long dumb, of prisoners and slaves and thieves, "of the rights of them the others are down upon." His allegiance is to, he has told us earlier, "a word of the modern, the word En-Masse."

But if Whitman voices the needs and concerns of the democratic mass of men and women, he also articulates "forbidden voices" of another sort, "voices of sexes and lusts." In enunciating his creed (the word comes from *credo*, Latin for "I believe"), Whitman is emphatically clear that he is the poet of the body: "I believe in the flesh and the appetites, / Seeing, hearing, feeling, are miracles, and each part and tag of me is a miracle." After telling the reader that "If I worship one thing more than another it shall be the spread of my own body," he goes on to celebrate both his own body and everything that excites the body. Whitman's love of the body is so overwhelming he cannot tell where his body ends and the natural world begins. Like the infant described by Sigmund Freud, the founder of psychoanalysis, he has here no sense of a boundary between self and not-self. Just as in the preceding stanzas on democracy he had declared his allegiance to the body politic, so here he segues from his own body—the source of his identity, "That I was I knew I was of my body" as he will write in the 1856 "Crossing Brooklyn Ferry"—to the body of the natural world. Even the sunrise is erotic, sexual, "libidinous."

MOVING INTO SILENCE, PASSIVITY, EMPATHY

But something strange happens in the following section. Much as he wants to tell us all, he cannot. He is constrained by something that remains unmentioned, untouched—something many contemporary critics believe to be his unresolved feelings about men as his sexual object of desire.

> *Walt you contain enough, why don't you let it out then?*
> Come now I will not be tantalized, you conceive too much
>   of articulation,

Do you not know O speech how the buds beneath you are
    folded? . . .
My final merit I refuse you, I refuse putting from me what I
    really am,
Encompass worlds, but never try to encompass me.

Thus does Whitman retreat into silence and passivity.
"Now I will do nothing but listen." And indeed, section 26
is a catalog of sounds, ending with a virtuoso synopsis
of the multiple emotions occasioned by opera, which the
city-roaming Whitman adored.

Silent now, letting experience wash over him, Whitman
asks the kind of basic and even naive question he is
extraordinarily capable of raising to consciousness: "To
be in any form, what is that?" His answer is a play on a
phrase common to both his time and ours, "happy as a
clam." But if a clam can be happy in its "callous shell,"
what of Whitman? For,

Mine is no callous shell,
I have instant conductors all over me whether I pass or stop,
They seize every object and lead it harmlessly through me.
I merely stir, press, feel with my fingers, and am happy,
To touch my person to some one else's is about as much as I
    can stand.

Section 28 begins, "Is this then a touch," and continues
by chronicling Whitman's betrayal: he is passive, and
touch has left him "helpless to a red marauder," the
pounding of his blood as sexual excitement overwhelms
him. Critics point to the line "I went myself to the
headland, my own hands carried me there," to support
the sense that the passive, solitary Whitman is describing
the sexual act of masturbation. The sexual touching
he describes reaches a climax, not just rhetorically but
actually, in the last stanza of section 28. Section 29 seems
to describe the postcoital triste associated with a completed
sexual act; its imagery is predominantly, but not entirely
("Sprouts take and accumulate"), male.

For the next nine sections Whitman will listen and
watch and empathize. He identifies with animals, he
travels as an interstellar cosmonaut through "Space and
Time," he empathizes with "the hounded slave" and
declares "agonies are one of my changes of garments."
Whitman also shows how imaginative understanding has
enabled him to "understand the large hearts of heroes"
like those who fought bravely in the Goliad Massacre
(1836) in Texas and those who won—and those who
died—in the newborn nation's first major naval victory,
when the outgunned *Bonhomme Richard* commanded by
Captain John Paul Jones defeated the British frigate *Serapis*
in 1779. There is a powerful linkage between the heroism

he recounts, the American nation in which Whitman was
"born here, of parents born here, and their parents the
same," and the democracy the poet believes to be the
defining characteristic of both the nation and himself.

Whitman's stunning ability to shift emotional registers
is nowhere more evident than in the final lines of section 36
when he identifies with those maimed in Jones's victory:
the poet moves from piles of bodies to a seascape at night,
to the sounds of amputation, to the cries of maimed and
dying sailors.

Formless stacks of bodies and bodies by themselves, dabs of
    flesh upon the masts and spars,
Cut of cordage, dangle of rigging, slight shock of the soothe
    of waves,
Black and impassive guns, litter of powder-parcels,
    strong scent,
A few large stars overhead, silent and mournful shining,
Delicate sniffs of sea-breeze, smells of sedgy grass and fields
    by the shore, death-messages given in charge
    to survivors,
The hiss of the surgeon's knife, the gnawing teeth of his saw,
Wheeze, cluck, swash of falling blood, short wild scream,
    and long, dull, tapering groan,
These so, these irretrievable.

I AM AN ACME OF THINGS ACCOMPLISH'D

Section 37 continues the theme of identification: prisoners, mutineers, sentenced juveniles, cholera victims,
beggars. But with his mention of beggars, Whitman
reaches another of the poem's turning points. He has,
since section 25, been resigned to silence and passivity
and in reward has been granted sexual ecstasy and great
powers of identification and empathy. But these powers
have reached their limit: he cannot beg and still remain
himself, Walt Whitman—a kosmos. So in a stunning
reversal, the poet yanks himself back with the exclamatory
"Enough!"

Askers embody themselves in me and I am embodied
    in them,
I project my hat, sit shame-faced, and beg.

Enough! Enough! Enough!
Somehow I have been stunn'd. Stand back!
Give me a little time beyond my cuff'd head, slumbers,
    dreams, gaping,
I discover myself on the verge of a usual mistake.

The mistake has been one of self-deprecation: the self,
which he began by celebrating, must never be abased
before anyone. (Whitman has two reasons for insisting

that such abasement and self-humiliation are impermissible. First, it is necessary to his, and anyone's, self-esteem; second, it violates the fundamental principle of democracy, for since all humans are created equal they need never bow down before another.)

So Whitman recognizes he must resume his active part, taking on a Christlike role: "Behold, I do not give lectures or a little charity, / When I give I give myself." He relates to the gods so directly—"taking myself the exact dimensions of Jehovah"—that he assumes a godlike role, "accepting the rough deific sketches to fill out better in myself." Not for Whitman, determined to be an American original, are preestablished religions. The new American self out of which he writes this poem will always press onward. "Not words of routine this song of mine, / But abruptly to question" both the world that appears around him and the largest issues that can be imagined: "And what is reason? and what is love? and what is life?"

The restless inquiring spirit that he praises leads him, at the start of section 46, to decide that he has loafed about enough. In the last major turning point of the poem, he announces, "It is time to explain myself—let us stand up." No longer lounging on the grass, Whitman begins a leave-taking that will conclude with his departure in the final section of *Song of Myself*. Explaining, Whitman tells us how full he is, how satisfied with himself; he seems to be the culmination to which all of evolution has been heading. (The central text of evolutionary science, Charles Darwin's *Origin of Species,* was published in 1859, although Darwin had earlier published papers on the subject.) When Whitman proclaims

> I am an acme of things accomplish'd, and I an encloser of
>   things to be.
> My feet strike an apex of the apices of the stairs,
> On every step bunches of ages, and larger bunches between
>   the steps,
> All below duly travel'd, and still I mount and mount.

His belief in intellectual evolution, in the evolution of consciousness that has produced the possibility of his current existence, is similar to that found in the work of G. W. F. Hegel, the German idealist philosopher. Like Hegel, he gloried in the possibilities of the present moment as the product of a long evolution. Of himself—an American, conscious of the equal worth of his soul and his body, resident in and supporter of democracy—Whitman is able to say: "All forces have been steadily employ'd to complete and delight me, / Now on this spot I stand with my robust soul."

Yet there is more to come, for Whitman is an expansionist. (It is worth noting that the years prior to the writing of *Song of Myself* were years of American expansion westward, as the nation grew. Whitman's expansionist self has roots in American imperialism in the first half of the nineteenth century.) He proclaims in section 45 that "there is no stoppage and never can be stoppage," just as he had earlier claimed in section 5 that "all goes onward and outward." Even his sexual appetites are connected with the expansion he sees as a driving force: "Urge and urge and urge, / Always the procreant urge of the world" (section 3). Preparing to move onward, Whitman sums up what he has already told the reader.

YOU MUST TRAVEL IT FOR YOURSELF

Long before, in section 19, Whitman had asked the reader, "Do you guess I have some intricate purpose? / Well I have." In the succeeding sections it looked like his purpose was to expose himself, quite literally, as a sexual being. Then, afterward, his purpose seemed to be to show us the diversity and heroism that comprise the America in which he lives and which he so deeply loves. But now, in the concluding sections, Whitman reveals a final purpose. That purpose is to assert, to teach, the counsel of Ralph Waldo Emerson, who said in "Self-Reliance" (1841): "Trust thyself: every heart vibrates to that iron string."

"I tramp a perpetual journey," Whitman says, preparing to move onward. "My signs are a rain-proof coat, good shoes, and a staff cut from the woods."

> Each man and each woman of you I lead upon a knoll,
> My left hand hooking you round the waist,
> My right hand pointing to landscapes of continents and the
>   public road.
> Not I, not any one else can travel that road for you,
> You must travel it for yourself.

Self-reliant the reader must be: as Whitman declares himself to be, as he believes America is and must be. What is particularly noteworthy in his assertion is the generous, intimate support he extends to the reader, as he hooks his hand about our waists and points out where we should go. "If you tire," he encourages, "give me both burdens, and rest the chuff of your hand on my hip." When again he tells us to be self-reliant—"You are also asking me questions and I hear you, / I answer that I cannot answer, you must find out for yourself"—Whitman immediately follows with the nurturing proposal, "Sit a while dear son, / Here are biscuits to eat and here is milk to drink."

"Long enough have you dream'd contemptible dreams," he says, and urges us to move onward and outward as he himself is prepared to do. The poem, in essence, is over, its lesson taught, its purpose accomplished. There are final points to be inserted: a restatement of the equality of soul and body; a declaration that though he does not understand God he finds God everywhere; a reassertion that he does not fear death; a vision he cannot quite articulate of order, union, happiness. But basically there is little to do but say goodbye. When Whitman asks for a final word from us, his readers, he realizes that his statement "I stay but a minute longer" is a contradiction of his earlier assertion, "I teach straying from me, yet who can stray from me?" So he offers his last statement about who he is, one of the great moments in all of American writing.

> Do I contradict myself?
> Very well then I contradict myself,
> (I am large, I contain multitudes.)

And indeed, Whitman has revealed himself, throughout his *Song of Myself*, as a large human being, almost as large as the vital and sprawling democracy he inhabits.

In section 47 he had insisted, nearly at the end of his extremely long monologue, that he was not just idly talking, or trying to make a buck by writing poetry.

> I do not say these things for a dollar or to fill up the time
>   while I wait for a boat,
> (It is you talking just as much as myself, I act as the tongue
>   of you,
> Tied in your mouth, in mine it begins to be loosen'd)

Whitman took a huge gamble in *Song of Myself*: that in talking of himself he could be talking of us—"what I assume you shall assume," he says in the second line of the poem—and not just of us, but *for* us. Tongue-tied by an unfamiliarity with words sufficient to address either our souls or our experience, ashamed of our bodies or our sexual desires, unable to articulate just how important democracy is to our way of living, we may find in Whitman's poem our own hearts made manifest.

Was his gamble successful? Whitman has already said that each must decide for himself or herself. Meanwhile, time is passing and he will depart. The hawk flying above reminds him he must go, just as the day itself is departing into the night. The hawk is his brother, his double: "I too am not a bit tamed, I too am untranslatable, / I sound my barbaric yawp over the roofs of the world." (Whitman will not go quietly: the "yawp" is a screech, as each reader discovers in saying the line aloud.) Looking up at the hawk, at the departing day, he sees clouds and decides to leave as they do, shifting, effusing, drifting. He goes but will return, as the clouds return as rain:

> I bequeath myself to the dirt to grow from the grass I love,
> If you want me again look for me under your boot-soles.

LONG ENOUGH HAVE YOU DREAM'D CONTEMPTIBLE DREAMS

The critic Paul Zweig (1984), among others, has pointed out that Whitman's *Song of Myself* was not quite the accurate description of himself that he claimed but a blueprint for what he wanted to be. *Song of Myself* is a utopian vision for the creation of a self. Whitman imagined himself to be fully at ease with his body when he was not. He imagined his country a glorious democracy when it was rent by slavery and hovering near the precipice of civil war. He wrote of camaraderie when he was often lonely and of knowing himself when he was in the midst of what the twentieth century would term an identity crisis. He claimed to love life when he was deeply attracted to death. He celebrated himself, yet at the time of the poem's composition he was out of work, confused, and deemed a failure by his father.

Still, the immense power of *Song of Myself* is related to these contradictions. Were Whitman to be as wondrous as he claims—even though he allows the reader to share in all his good qualities—one might quickly get tired of him, feel him to be a blowhard and a braggart. But since most readers understand, on a gut level, that Whitman is striving to create a meaningful fiction about himself, that he is positing himself in the face of an emptiness that yawns beneath all human beings, asserting himself in the face of self-doubt and incipient confusion, Whitman's assertion of self has succored a century and a half of readers.

For *Song of Myself* refuses to dream contemptible dreams. It helps the reader, as it helped Whitman, to "wash the gum from your eyes" and to "habit yourself to the dazzle of the light and of every moment of your life." Whitman, so committed to moving onward and outward, would eventually grow, through his experience nursing the wounded in military hospitals during the Civil War, into the person he imagined himself as being in *Song of Myself*. The American nation would strive—in its best moments, though certainly not always—to be as energetic, as committed to justice, as willing to embrace the new, as Whitman. And generations of writers, not just in the United States but around the globe, would find in Whitman's poem the model for a poet who speaks *for* his people and not just to them, who constructs a bridge between the desires of the individual and the needs of the body politic, and who throws off the constraints that can limit art and make it stale instead of ever new.

FURTHER READING

Allen, Gay Wilson. *The New Walt Whitman Handbook.* New York, 1975.

Aspiz, Harold. *Walt Whitman and the Body Beautiful.* Urbana, Ill., 1980.

Black, Stephan A. *Whitman's Journey into Chaos: A Psychoanalytic Study of the Poetic Process.* Princeton, N.J., 1969.

Chase, Richard. *Walt Whitman Reconsidered.* New York, 1955.

Erkila, Betsy, and Jay Grossman, eds. *Breaking Bonds: Whitman and American Cultural Studies.* Oxford, U.K., and New York, 1996.

Kaplan, Justin. *Walt Whitman: A Life.* New York, 1980.

Killingsworth, M. Jimmie. *Whitman's Poetry of the Body: Sexuality, Politics and the Text.* Chapel Hill, N.C., 1989. A solid study of Whitman's homoeroticism.

Kuebrich, Karl. *Minor Prophecy: Walt Whitman's New American Religion.* Bloomington, Ind., 1989.

Loving, Jerome. *Walt Whitman: The Song of Himself.* Berkeley, Calif., 1999. The finest contemporary biography.

Marki, Ivan. *The Trial of the Poet: An Interpretation of the First Edition of* Leaves of Grass. New York, 1976.

Maslon, Mark. *Whitman Possessed: Poetry, Sexuality, and Popular Authority.* Baltimore, 2001.

Miller, Edwin Haviland. *Walt Whitman's Poetry: A Psychological Journey.* New York, 1968. Partly psychological and psychoanalytic, it is still one of the two best critical books on Whitman.

Miller, Edwin Haviland. *Walt Whitman's* Song of Myself: *A Mosaic of Interpretations.* Iowa City, Iowa, 1984. A section-by-section analysis of the poem, providing commentary from a multitude of critics.

Miller, James E., Jr., ed. Song of Myself: *Origin, Growth, Meaning.* New York, 1964. Includes 1855 and 1892 versions on facing pages and essays considering the form of the poem.

Moon, Michael. *Disseminating Whitman: Revision and Corporeality in* Leaves of Grass. Cambridge, Mass., 1991. Homoeroticism and Whitman's text.

Pollak, Vivian. *The Erotic Whitman.* Berkeley, Calif., 2000.

Reynolds, David S. *Walt Whitman's America: A Cultural Biography.* New York, 1955.

Stovall, Floyd. *The Foreground of* Leaves of Grass. Charlottesville, Va., 1974. Cultural background to Whitman's poetry.

Whitman, Walt. *Complete Poetry and Collected Prose.* New York, 1982. Contains both the 1855 and 1890 versions of "Song of Myself."

Woodress, James. *Critical Essays on Walt Whitman.* Boston, 1983. Historical reception of Whitman; includes cited essay by Randall Jarrell on Whitman.

Zweig, Paul. *Walt Whitman: The Making of a Poet.* New York, 1984. One of the two best critical books on Whitman, it considers his psychological and artistic development. More a biography of his growth as a poet than a conventional biography.

See also the article on Walt Whitman, immediately preceding.

JOHN EDGAR WIDEMAN

by Arnold E. Sabatelli

The fiction and nonfiction of John Edgar Wideman moves between worlds of language and experience that are not usually encountered side by side. He was raised in the African-American community of Homewood in Pittsburgh, was a college basketball star for the University of Pennsylvania, and graduated from Oxford University as a Rhodes scholar. His works mix the disparate forces of his life into an artistic form that is both intellectually challenging and experimental in the best sense of the word. A prolific novelist and essayist, Wideman's texts consistently blend voices and genres and challenge the reader. Responding self-consciously to contemporary jazz forms, his later work is filled with free-form ad-libbing, discontinuity, and always a rich integration of voices.

John Edgar Wideman.
(© *Bettmann/Corbis*)

LIFE

Wideman was born in Washington, D.C., on 14 June 1941, and his family moved to Homewood shortly after his birth. In 1951 the family moved to Shadyside, an upper-middle-class white neighborhood. Here he attended a prestigious high school and earned a scholarship to the University of Pennsylvania. At the university he continued to excel in both his studies and in athletics. He was a star basketball forward, winning All Ivy League status. He graduated in 1963, and was awarded a Rhodes Scholarship to Oxford University, only the second African American to receive one. In 1966 he returned to the United States to complete a year at the famed Iowa Writer's Workshop as a Kent fellow; there he completed his first novel, *A Glance Away* (1967). From 1967 to 1973 Wideman was a faculty member at the University of Pennsylvania, where he helped create and later chaired the Afro-American Studies program.

After this auspicious start as a writer-scholar, Wideman decided he needed to "go back to the woodshed" and reconnect himself with the sources of African-American writing and the African-American experience. From 1975 to 1986 he was on the faculty at the University of Wyoming. During that time he stopped writing and immersed himself in the vast and varied prose and collected oral narratives of African-American literature. He emerged with a newly honed sense of the traditions that already had intuitively informed his work, and in a short period of time he wrote the three books that constitute *The Homewood Trilogy* (1985). In 1986 he began teaching in the writing workshop at the University of Massachusetts, Amherst. In that same year his teenage son, Jacob, inexplicably killed a friend on a summer camping trip, a tragedy that found its way into his art in both subtle and direct ways. His daughter Jamilia was a college basketball star at Stanford University and has played in the WNBA. John and Jamilia were featured on the cover of *Sports Illustrated* (17 March 1997) and in an article about her basketball career.

MAJOR AWARDS

Among his many awards, he is the only writer to have won the PEN/Faulkner Award twice, for his novels *Sent for You Yesterday* (1983) and *Philadelphia Fire* (1990). In 1998 Wideman won the Rea Award for the short story. In 1990, he received the American Book Award for fiction. He was awarded the Lannan Literary Fellowship for Fiction in 1991 and the MacArthur Award in 1993. Other honors include the St. Botolph Literary Award in 1993, the DuSable Museum Prize for Nonfiction for *Brothers and Keepers* in 1985, the Longwood College Medal for Literary Excellence, and the National Magazine

Editors' Prize for Short Fiction in 1987. In 1996 he edited the annual anthology *The Best American Short Stories*.

FICTION

In his earliest novels, *A Glance Away, Hurry Home* (1970), and *The Lynchers* (1973), Wideman established the themes that would inform the body of his work. Still, in these early novels, while characters frequently wrestle with conflicts between their African ancestry and the deep influences of European culture and ideas, the novels do not take that extra step of immersion into both cultural and intellectual backgrounds as do the later works. Without the integration of voices from the streets of Homewood or Philadelphia (in both the nineteenth and twentieth centuries) that we find in the later novels—without the more playful, jazzlike rhetorical structures that allow this shifting of voices and perspective—the early novels, while well written and deeply intelligent, lack the breadth and accomplishment of the later works. After his self-imposed exile in Wyoming, where he read and studied extensively in African-American literature, Wideman emerged ready to move in a new direction with his work.

The novels and story collection that became known as *The Homewood Trilogy*—*Sent for You Yesterday, Damballah* (1981) (stories), and *Hiding Place* (1981)—begin to juxtapose more self-consciously the forces of Oxford and the language (as Wideman prefers to call it) of African Americans. Set in his old Homewood neighborhood, where his relatives had lived since the nineteenth century, and based on real histories and characters, these three works interweave and explicate the forces that shaped him as a person and as a writer and demonstrate a deep and complex understanding of the issues and tragedies that many inner-city African Americans face. Also apparent is the influence of the African legends and stories he had studied extensively in Wyoming.

It is here that we meet the character Tommy hiding out in a shed, escaping the law—an artistic manifestation of Wideman's brother, about whom he will write further in his nonfiction work *Brothers and Keepers* (1984). His feeling that his brother was living the ideas and life he merely explicated with his Afro-American Studies students at the University of Pennsylvania is taken full-on in these works. In these works is a Faulkner-like mixing of voices and narrative points of view; his Ivy League–Oxford literary background is coupled with the language and experience of the streets of Homewood.

This blending of voices, tonalities, styles, and experience is explored still more fully in the novel *Philadelphia Fire*, a fictionalized account of the bombing by the Philadelphia police department of a series of row houses in the inner city where the radical MOVE group was holed up in a standoff with police. The main character of the novel, Cudjoe, is intent on producing Shakespeare's *The Tempest* (1611–1612), and this play, itself a self-reflexive work based on the nature of art and human failings, comes to reflect the metaphoric tempest that has raged and continues to rage in inner-city Philadelphia after the literal firestorm. Obsessed with finding a mysterious boy who many claim somehow escaped the flames, Cudjoe sets out to interview witnesses and discover what happened. His quest, however, quickly becomes entangled, and in the ultimate entanglement, the narrative at one point purposefully loses itself, asking who is Cudjoe, who is Wideman, and who is Caliban (a character in *The Tempest*). A lengthy, nonfictional, essaylike passage is inserted in the middle of the narrative; in this insertion we see the author in his home Amherst, Massachusetts, struggling with the very novel we are reading.

These kinds of postmodern complexities have come to be yet another cornerstone of Wideman's work. Running the risk of leaving the common reader behind (and perhaps limiting his own fame as a writer), his fiction frequently moves into unexpected places. His fictions are not arranged sequentially and they find a form based on a range of factors—sounds, theme, imagery. At their best, Wideman's fictions follow an organic, expansive, jazzlike progression of events and reflection where one never knows what to expect around the next bend.

While *Damballah* reads less like a collection of stories and more like a novel in stories, *Fever* (1989) and *All Stories Are True* (1992) are more traditional story collections. Often poetic, musical, elliptical, or downright oblique, the stories of these two collections mark a significant development in his work, demonstrating Wideman's willingness to move in new directions as an artist. At the point where he was gaining his highest accolades as a novelist, he turned to short fiction. For the first time in his career, Wideman was focused on trying to make complete artistic expressions in a very short space. While this compression at times seems restraining for his fluid, elliptical style, stories like "Fever," "Statue of Liberty," "everybody knew bubba riff," and others demonstrate all the elements of his writing style—playful, dense, musical prose, striking dramatic events, original forms.

With *The Cattle Killing* (1996) and *Two Cities* (1998), Wideman returns to the long form, and again these works demonstrate his willingness to challenge our concept of the novel as a form and to explore and complicate issues of race and culture. *The Cattle Killing* turns to eighteenth-century, plague-ridden Philadelphia, depicting a young preacher's quest for an African girl that bears a striking resemblance to Cudjoe's quest in *Philadelphia Fire*. In *Two Cities*, Wideman returns to the multivoiced form he explored so well in the Homewood books.

NONFICTION

Before Wideman's fiction won him wide acclaim, his most popular work was *Brothers and Keepers*, a nonfiction work about his brother, who was serving a life term for murder. In the book, Wideman explores many of the themes that shaped and continue to shape the whole body of his work. It was here that he noted the stark contrast between the sterile life of an academic intellectual and a man living on the hard streets of Homewood, and here that he lays the groundwork for the course of much of his fiction and nonfiction to come. His next full-length work of nonfiction, *Fatheralong: A Meditation on Fathers and Sons, Race and Society* (1994), looks more broadly at his family history, challenging contemporary concepts of "race" and questioning the often overly simplistic categorizations that are an integral part the "racial" problem.

Later, Wideman explored the importance and complex nature of the game of basketball. Criticized by *Sports Illustrated* as overintellectualizing the game, especially in his comparisons with jazz, most who know Wideman's work have applauded that exploration as yet another example of his far-reaching intellectual interests and his writing ability. Wideman continues to write broadly for a range of mainstream and small literary journals, including *Esquire*, *The New York Times Magazine*, *Harpers*, *Callaloo*, *The New Yorker*. His essays range from interviews and commentary on Michael Jordan to the 9/11 crisis to the nature of black speech. In all of his nonfiction one finds elements of fiction, and his essays frequently shift mode and focus and integrate the range of language he is known for in his fictional works.

COMPLEXITY WITHOUT APOLOGY

In a 1995 interview, Wideman explains that he prefers the middle ground, where any concise, pragmatic, or dogmatic claim is probably missing something. He prefers writing that pays attention to itself as writing, and he says if that leaves some readers behind, then so be it. Unable to abandon his Oxford and Ivy League lineage,

he embraces them side by side with his African-American heritage. Sometimes accused by other African-American scholars and critics of not speaking out about issues of relevance to African Americans, Wideman disregards these criticisms and consistently presents the reader with complex and intellectually challenging art. To read John Edgar Wideman, one must enter a world with an open mind and a sharply tuned ear. His works often respond as much to the way words sound and bounce off each other as to what they are saying. Highly suspicious of any description of himself as a great African-American writer because he does not want to be ghettoized in that way, Wideman continues to use his deep passion and great gifts as a writer to become a great writer, period.

SELECTED WORKS

A Glance Away (1967)
Hurry Home (1970)
The Lynchers (1973)
Hiding Place (1981)
Damballah (1981)
Sent for You Yesterday (1983)
Brothers and Keepers (1984)
The Homewood Trilogy (1985)
Reuben (1987)
Fever (1989)
Philadelphia Fire (1990)
All Stories Are True (1992)
Fatheralong: A Meditation on Fathers and Sons, Race and Society (1994)
Stories of John Edgar Wideman (1992)
Identities: Three Novels (1994)
The Cattle Killing (1996)
Two Cities (1998)
Hoop Roots (2001)

FURTHER READING

Byerman, Keith E. *John Edgar Wideman, A Study of the Short Fiction*. New York, 1998. A very short but useful compilation of the author's own essays and several interviews and short pieces by other critics.

Mbalia, Doreatha Drummond. *John Edgar Wideman: Reclaiming the African Personality*. London and Toronto, 1995. A concise and sometimes critical study of the African influences on Wideman's work.

TuSmith, Bonnie, ed. *Conversations with John Edgar Wideman*. Jackson, Miss., 1998. An excellent compilation of interviews, including one conducted by the author of this article.

RICHARD WILBUR

by Gerry Cambridge

Richard Wilbur is renowned for the finesse, delicacy, and light touch of his poems, which can seem intricate as snow crystals if rather more durable. In his easy and assured use of meter and rhyme, his work has a Marvellian nimbleness; he is undoubtedly one of the foremost poetic craftsmen in American poetry today, a poet whose facility in form has been seen with mistrust in some quarters. In general he eschews personal revelation in the making of his poems and never writes in free verse; he was thus wholly outside the confessional and free-verse movements, which have dominated American poetry in and out of the academy since the 1960s. The rise of the New Formalism in the 1980s, however, has seen him co-opted as a sort of poetic champion, along with poets such as Robinson Jeffers and Robert Frost, by many of the poets associated with that movement.

Richard Wilbur. (© *Oscar White/Corbis*)

The qualities for which Wilbur's advocates admire him are also those that his detractors criticize: urbanity, moderation, lightness of touch, charm. That ferocious poet-critic Randall Jarrell, in a review of Wilbur's second book, compared reading the volume somewhat damningly to the experience of visiting an art gallery: overly poetic with not a memorable human character in sight. Among the vagaries of poetic fashions, however, and the brickbats of criticism, Wilbur has kept, with what appears a characteristic blitheness, largely to his own poetic path.

EARLY LIFE AND CAREER

That path has been a long one. Born on 1 March 1921 in New York City, he grew up in New Jersey in rural surroundings—his eye for nature has always been acute—and attended Amherst College, graduating in June 1942. Upon graduation he immediately married Charlotte (Charlee) Hayes Ward, to whom he remains married today.

Interestingly for a poet so identified with the virtues of civilized discourse and behavior, World War II turned Wilbur to the writing of poems. He trained as a cryptographer before federal investigators felt that he was a dubious proposition on account of early left-wing sympathies. Wilbur was demoted to the infantry, though as chance would have it, he replaced the cryptographer of the Thirty-sixth (Texas) Division, who had gone mad, in 1943. He began writing as a response against the turmoil of war. The conflict, however, seems to have failed to mark him indelibly as it did his near-contemporary Anthony Hecht, and by 1947 Wilbur had graduated from Harvard, intending to teach. That same year, his first book of poems, *The Beautiful Changes and Other Poems* (1947), appeared. (Although war had prompted Wilbur to begin writing, only four of its poems make explicit reference to the conflict.) The twenty-six-year-old poet proved a precocious craftsman. The poetic voice in this first book already has a refined ease and fluency. Critics were full of praise for the poems' nimble turns and diction. Since then another six collections have followed, at an average of seven-year intervals, including the poet's most feted, *Things of This World* (1956), for which he won the Pulitzer Prize, and *New and Collected Poems* (1988), which also won a Pulitzer. In a long career as a professor teaching at Harvard University, Wesleyan University, and Smith College (he retired in 1986), he has also produced masterly translations of Molière as well as written numerous children's books and occasional criticism, frequently dealing with his obsession—insofar as he can be said to be obsessed—with the work of Edgar Allan Poe. He has in fact called his own work "a public quarrel" with what he regards as the world-renouncing aesthetics of that writer.

THE POETRY'S MAIN QUALITIES

Wilbur's aesthetic, by his own admission, is against authority and "the construction of new thought systems"; he has written that the basis of his poetry is the single poem while expressing envy for poets such as Pound, Williams, and Yeats, able to take a more "programmatic" approach to their art. As exemplified by his poems, Wilbur's approach is all for modesty, for things seen clearly and observed as purely as possible. One of the central concerns in his verse is a reverence for the physical world. His "Regarding Places," a prefatory essay to a book of artworks by American landscape artists, *A Sense of Place* (1972), recounts how a visiting friend, an abstract artist from New York, walked in Wilbur's home woods yet was too caught up in his own intellectual processes to notice anything of the immediate landscape around him. Wilbur, on the other hand, has always seemed notably aware of the things of this world. If most of us are troubled by a lack of looking, by an excess of doing at the expense of being, a certain blessedness of temperament and biographical circumstance have enabled Wilbur's vision to compensate. He is an instinctive celebrator, a poet who quotes approvingly the line from the English devotional poet Gerard Manley Hopkins: "The world is charged with the grandeur of God." His poems celebrate the otherness of the natural world; there tend to be more objects and creatures in them than people, as some of his adverse critics have noted. (On the whole, he doesn't do people well: even his few dramatic monologues, spoken by assumed characters, while frequently fascinating, don't leave a lasting impression of their speakers as being markedly different from Wilbur's usual narrator.) The reader of Wilbur's poems is seldom shocked or disturbed; chaos is always held firmly at bay, albeit hinted at, as when, in the final poem of his second collection, *Ceremony and Other Poems* (1950), he intuits that, observing a ceremonious "feigning lady" in a sylvan painting by the French impressionist Frédéric Bazille, the greater the ceremony depicted in the image the more tigers there are likely to be in the wood. (It is an interesting speculation when turned upon his own writing.)

The poems intrigue and engage: if they came to dinner they would prove sparkling and at times intimidatingly learned conversationalists. They never raise their voices, put knives to their throats, drink too much, tell dirty jokes, or take their clothes off in public. (Wilbur is a remarkably chaste poet by contemporary standards.) The poems acknowledge horror but are in the main untouched by it. The best work is radiant with objects:

Wilbur has a photographer's eye for effects of light and the linguistic dexterity to evoke them. Also, despite his lack of memorable characters, he is more various than some critics have suggested; even a glance through his *New and Collected Poems* reveals that this gallery of verse, if gallery it is, can accommodate not only poems about fountains and art, relatively standard Wilburesque subject matter, but, among other things, turkeys, a thawing river compared to a prostitute, a boy at a window watching a snowman, a decaying dog, a toad with an amputated leg, laundry dipping and falling in the breeze on a drying line, October maples, a man changing into a werewolf, vampires, a juggler, and a fire truck in his poem of that title—it shocks the poet, sunk in characteristic contemplation, wryly into the immediate moment. The poems are full of the world's colors and textures, but Wilbur seldom simply presents us with things as, say, William Carlos Williams did his infamous red wheelbarrow in his poem "The Red Wheelbarrow." Wilbur's fire truck is as brilliant as Williams's wheelbarrow, but it prompts in him the ironic, jokily self-derogatory "*Thought is degraded action!*" As the fire truck disappears, it leaves the poet to carry its image into his mind, where he reflects upon its striking actuality "enshrined / In that not extinguished fire." The fire is both the actual fire and, it may be, the fire of intellection in the poet's head; outer and inner worlds are intriguingly coupled. Wilbur frequently connects an object to an idea, which prompts further reflection or a fresh look at the object; his art at its best is an engaged and engaging negotiation between, or balancing of, the spirit and the world. The ideas and abstractions in his poems stop the verse from becoming bogged down in the physical, yet his respect for the "world's weight," as his poem "Juggler" calls it, prevents his narrators' debatings, negotiatings, and ruminations from drifting off into mere airy nothings. His best pieces are successful marriages between inner and outer worlds.

WILBUR AND EXTREMISM

Nonetheless some critics have found the work, for all its achieved balance and linguistic dexterity, finally slight. There has been the damning implication that Wilbur doesn't suffer enough in the poems, as do near-contemporary poets such as Robert Lowell, Theodore Roethke, John Berryman, Anne Sexton, and Sylvia Plath—a battered, bloody, and hugely ambitious grouping plagued by psychiatric problems and alcoholism and tempted by the suicide that the last three eventually succumbed to. Among such authentically harrowed writers, so the feeling went, Wilbur appeared almost clinically sane, robust: blessed in his marriage and career and a practicing Episcopalian to boot. While A. Alvarez, in his influential British anthology *The New Poetry* (1962), was calling for a poetry of extremism that owned up to the chaos in oneself as symptomatic of a world that had produced the Nazi death camps and the atom bomb, citing Robert Lowell and Sylvia Plath as leading exemplars of this new style, Wilbur had recently published, in his *Advice to a Prophet and Other Poems* (1961), the devotional "A Christmas Hymn," unabashedly invoking the birth of Christ in perfect stanzas and exquisite naturalistic lyrics, minutely observed, such as "A Grasshopper." (Even his "Advice to a Prophet," a poem that tries to imagine the reality of nuclear war, is a shapely lyric.) A veteran of World War II, he appeared to have no interest in indulging the destructive element, having doubtless already seen it firsthand.

Wilbur addressed his relationship to the poetry of extremism with unusual directness in a poem of reminiscence in *The Mind-Reader* (1976) titled "Cottage Street, 1953," a memory of meeting Sylvia Plath at the house of his wife's grandmother, Edna Ward. The poem contrasts Edna Ward, who will die after "eight and eighty summers," an old woman of stoic grace, with Sylvia, who will die before her, after stating "her brilliant negative." While Wilbur has professed annoyance at those critics who have read the poem as an attack on Plath, the poem clearly prefers a stoic grace, an outward looking, to the terrifying inwardness of Plath's aesthetic.

It is difficult to fault Wilbur's poetry on technical grounds. His critics have confined themselves to, finally, accusing him of being fully himself—a sort of critical equivalent of the playground taunt "Your nose is too big." Notwithstanding, Wilbur himself has exhibited a winning catholicity of taste: his poem "A Wood," from *Advice to a Prophet*, celebrates variety in the species of trees, both large and small, found in a wood. One reading of his poem could be that it his response to those critics who insist on faulting him for failing in what he had, in any case, no interest in attempting. Somewhat reminiscent of the Scottish poet Norman MacCaig, who held to his own singular and idiosyncratic vision throughout a long poetic career, Wilbur celebrates the "is-ness" of things, what the medieval philosopher Duns Scotus, who influenced Gerard Manley Hopkins (one of Wilbur's prime forebears) called *haccaeitas*, that unique quality which makes one thing itself and not some other thing. Wilbur is as likely to celebrate wild thyme growing among rocks as an oak tree; in his poems, the hierarchy of size does not mean a hierarchy of importance.

LATE EXCELLENCE

Richard Wilbur's style and concerns have remained remarkably consistent for over half a century. There has been, however, a development toward a plainer diction and a more forthright utterance in the later poems, less of a need to give a balanced view. His latest collection, the ironically titled *Mayflies* (2000)—a reference to the insect that, as an adult, lives for one day to mate, then dies—was his first since his *New and Collected Poems* of 1988. It shows no falling off in quality, and one poem, "For C," is a characteristically unfashionable celebration of marital fidelity addressed to his wife of sixty years. It praises a long marriage, which, "like a good fiddle" or the starry sky, "has the quality of something made"—a quality that Richard Wilbur's poems too impressively possess.

[*See also* Berryman, John; Lowell, Robert; Plath, Sylvia; Roethke, Theodore; *and* Sexton, Anne.]

WORKS

The Beautiful Changes and Other Poems (1947)
Ceremony and Other Poems (1950)
Things of This World (1956)
Poems, 1943–1956 (1957)
Advice to a Prophet and Other Poems (1961)
The Poems of Richard Wilbur (1963)
Walking to Sleep: New Poems and Translations (1969)
The Mind-Reader: New Poems (1976)
Responses: Prose Pieces, 1953–1976 (1976, 2000)
New and Collected Poems (1988)
The Catbird's Song: Prose Pieces, 1963–1995 (1997)
Mayflies: New Poems and Translations (2000)

FURTHER READING

Butts, William, ed. *Conversations With Richard Wilbur.* Jackson, Miss., and London, 1990. A collection of nineteen interviews with the poet.

Dale, Peter. *Richard Wilbur in Interview with Peter Dale.* London, 2000. Probably the most valuable piece of recent literature on Wilbur, this includes a lengthy interview conducted by letter, a comprehensive bibliography, and a representative selection of quotations from Wilbur's critics and reviewers.

Edgecombe, Rodney Stenning. *A Reader's Guide to the Poetry of Richard Wilbur.* Tuscaloosa, Ala., 1995. A comprehensive chronological guide to Wilbur's verse that analyzes each lyric without losing sight of the overall coherence of Wilbur's oeuvre.

Hougen, John B. *Ecstasy within Discipline: The Poetry of Richard Wilbur*. Atlanta, Ga., 1995.

Michelson, Bruce. *Wilbur's Poetry: Music in a Scattering Time*. Amherst, Mass., 1991. The first full-length study of Wilbur's work for almost twenty-five years, this argues against the charge that Wilbur's work is bland and unengaged.

THORNTON WILDER

by Philip Parry

Thornton Niven Wilder—the author of *Our Town* (1938), America's most popular "popular play"—was very nearly, though he never quite became, the Grand Old Man of twentieth-century American letters. An authentic intellectual and Europhile and dilettante, very much in the tradition of Henry James and T. S. Eliot, he was saluted and fêted throughout most of his lifetime. Equally admired as novelist and playwright, there were rumors that he was denied a Nobel Prize only because of unfair accusations of plagiarism. This unfairness is easily established. *The Skin of Our Teeth* (1942), a dramatization of the whole span of human history through the varying fortunes and misfortunes of Mr. and Mrs. Antrobus of Excelsior, New Jersey, undoubtedly makes use of James Joyce's *Finnegans Wake*, whose Humphrey Chimpden Earwicker ("Here Comes Everybody") is similarly representative; but Wilder, very much an amateur expert on Joyce's work, openly acknowledged his debts. Only a harsh judge interprets a public tribute as evidence of theft.

More damaging were those critics who, in response to *The Woman of Andros* (1930), Wilder's short and elegant and elliptical but wafer-thin third novel, accused him of retreating into antiquarian irrelevancy. There was some point to such criticism—*The Cabala* (1926) details a twentieth-century innocent's imaginative re-creation of the decadent splendors of Renaissance Italy; *The Bridge of San Luis Rey* (1927) is set in early eighteenth-century Peru—and Wilder seems to have taken it to heart: three of the remaining four novels that he would eventually write—*Heaven's My Destination* (1934), *The Eighth Day* (1967), and *Theophilus North* (1973)—have American

Thornton Wilder reading from his play *Our Town*, 1952. (*Courtesy of the Library of Congress*)

settings that are more or less contemporary; are very different from Wilder's other novels; but, despite their showing clear affiliations with his plays, have yet to receive appropriate recognition.

Heaven's My Destination, as though in protest at the reception meted out to *The Woman of Andros* (from which it takes one of its introductory mottoes), is a gentle but firm satire on the small-mindedness of stay-at-home America. Its hero—"*George Brush* is my name; / America's my nation; / *Ludington*'s my dwelling place, / And Heaven's my destination"—because he sweeps aside (hence his name) the social hypocrisies that compose America's idealized image of itself, is both admirable and impossibly simple-minded. *The Eighth Day*, a late novel that is Wilder's most ambitious literary venture, is at one and the same time a naïve piece of storytelling, in which plot is generated haphazardly as the novel lurches from one narrative crisis to the next, and a complex deconstruction—a word that Wilder would never have used—of the storyteller's art: its principal hero is killed off two-thirds of the way through in a brief subordinate clause (and under a pseudonym), and the novel ends with fresh narratives that will never find room in which to develop. *Theophilus North*, Wilder's final novel, is best characterized as an autobiographical fantasia set in 1926 in Newport, Rhode Island, where T[*heophilus*] N[*orth*] (T[*hornton*] N[*iven Wilder*]), an inexperienced but resourceful schoolteacher who is taking time out, resolves a succession of social and emotional problems in his adopted community. He expels ghosts from a haunted house; breaks up a counterfeiting ring; cures the sick by laying on of hands; finds a girlfriend for a young man with no feet (who, like Brother Juniper in *The Bridge of San Luis Rey*, wants to learn "why God sends accidents to some people and not to other people" [*Theophilus North*, p. 223]); and, in a chapter that takes Wilder into an area which he very rarely enters, reinvigorates a childless and failing marriage by surreptitiously impregnating the wife (pp. 252–272). Whimsical but also clear-eyed, *Theophilus North* is deeply moving both as fabricated autobiography and as a tribute to the resolving power of art.

Although his last two novels garnered respectful and occasionally enthusiastic reviews, and his ability to acquire public honors never failed him, there was, nevertheless, clear evidence of growing indifference toward Wilder's work in the last fifteen years of his life: by the time of his death, indeed, his reputation as a writer of the first rank had faded so thoroughly that Malcolm Cowley felt able to describe him in an obituary tribute as "the most neglected author of a brilliant generation" (*New York Times Book Review*, 21 December 1975). In the quarter-century that has followed his death, this neglect has intensified. Once acclaimed for the multiplicity of his talents, he is now remembered for a single play that is, like the Statue of Liberty, as much an American icon as an American work of art. In the beginning of the twenty-first century, the time has perhaps arrived for reappraisal; even if a complete recovery of Wilder's reputation proves beyond reach, at least a better sense of where *Our Town* stands in relationship to his other work (and to his "American" novels in particular) should emerge.

LIFE AND ART

Thornton Niven Wilder was born on 17 April 1897 in Madison, Wisconsin. Richly supplied with siblings—he had an older brother (Amos) and three younger sisters (Charlotte, Isabel, and Janet), of whom Isabel (1900–1995) served both as his personal agent and as the ever-faithful custodian of his reputation and memory—he is, nonetheless, best defined in terms of his stillborn identical twin brother, from whose failure to live he acquired an abiding sense of incompleteness. Wilder, always better when writing of partings than of couplings, fills his novels and plays with a sense of a loss (through death or exile or death-in-exile) that is perhaps not a true loss at all: "We only have what we give up," the now elderly Eustacia Lansing tells herself at the end of *The Eighth Day*. In *The Bridge of San Luis Rey*, his most famous novel—though scarcely a novel as we ordinarily understand the term—and his first work to win a Pulitzer Prize, Wilder chronicles Brother Juniper's

search for evidence of spiritual completeness and repose in the lives of those who die suddenly. To Juniper it matters that the five travelers killed when a bridge near Lima collapses "live by plan and die by plan." The book's most emotionally taxing section is Part Three ("Esteban"), the story of twin boys, Manuel and Esteban, "discovered in the foundlings' basket before the door of the Convent of Santa María Rosa de las Rosas." Twice in their brief lives they are torn apart: when Manuel falls in love with an actress and when he dies from blood poisoning brought on by a knee injury. Desperate to be reunited with his brother, Esteban plans suicide but is persuaded by Captain Alvarado, an explorer and adventurer who has hired him as a crewman, to wait for God to call him home. Just a few days later he crosses the bridge of San Luis Rey (while Alvarado takes the safe route below) and, accepting his death as the fulfillment of a wish, is plunged into the waters. In her introduction to his *Journals*, Isabel Wilder quotes a letter from a middle-aged woman who had recently lost her twin sister: from what he wrote about them in this novel it was evident, the woman claimed, that Wilder clearly understood the special relationship between identical twins (*Journals*, p. xiii).

The argument, however, does not end here. Have Juniper and Wilder (the one for religious reasons, the other for artistic ones) imposed a false order upon the inherently disordered? Brother Juniper, though his celebration of providence is central to Wilder's plot, dies in the flames of the Inquisition: the manner of his dying has, through the operation of a terrible but elegant irony, a pattern and a purpose that he has been keen to locate and identify in others' deaths. Was he right to try to do so? Was the Inquisition wrong as well as cruel? Do the travelers—who clearly represent all of us as we move forward from cradle to grave—die by accident or by design? Forty years later, in the twilight of his career, Wilder returned to the theme, but with a quite different emphasis, in his most ambitious novel. The pattern-seeking goes on, but the quest is comprehensively thwarted, for no story, Wilder both maintains and seeks to demonstrate in *The Eighth Day*, can ever truly be told: every story disintegrates into its component stories in an unstoppable regression; there can be no definitive narrative because we cannot rest upon either a true beginning or a true ending. Here is how this most burgeoning and diverse of all of his novels fails to end:

> There is much talk of a design in the arras. Some are certain they see it. Some see what they have been told to see. Some remember that they saw it once but have lost it. Some are

strengthened by seeing a pattern wherein the oppressed and exploited of the earth are gradually emerging from their bondage. Some find strength in the conviction that there is nothing to see. Some

Copy editors and printers must beware: humanity's eighth day begins when the seventh has ended, but this new week will never come to a full stop; the end (or aim) of story-telling is our dawning realization that there shall never be an end of story-telling.

Completeness and incompleteness are certainly major themes in all of Wilder's works (and in his life, since he started many more projects than he finished), but invoking his dead twin brother is an exercise in metaphorical, rather than psychoanalytical, explanation. Other qualities in his work—particularly his internationalism—are, however, firmly ascribable to the conditions of his upbringing. His parents, Amos Parker Wilder and Isabella Thornton Niven Wilder, were caring, cultured, and enterprising. Their influence upon their gifted child was immense, though sometimes in unintended ways. Amos Wilder's strict Calvinism, for example, expressed itself in his son's imaginative sympathy with a Roman Catholicism that is seen always in an exotic light: this sympathy, though it did not lead to conversion, is one expression of Wilder's rejection of cultural isolationism. (A proper sense of Wilder's international cultural perspective—he spoke French, German, Italian, and Spanish—is something that readers who confine themselves to *Our Town* may fail to develop. Grover's Corners is inescapably small-town America. Its Catholic church is just one denominational meetinghouse among many and is clearly peripheral, "over beyond the tracks" like the Polish community that it serves. To these Poles, voiceless and unassimilated and unrepresented, the *our* town of the play's title is not *their* town at all.)

This broader vision was something that Wilder gained from his parents: Amos was a journalist and part-owner of *The Wisconsin State Journal*, but served from 1906 to 1910 as consul general in Hong Kong and, latterly, Shanghai. His son was briefly educated abroad, in Hong Kong in 1906 and in a British-run missionary school in Chefoo, China, in 1910. This experience helped to open up the world for his imaginative inspection: the cardinal who plays such a prominent part in *The Cabala* (1926) makes his reputation evangelizing in "the Church's most dangerous post in Western China." For most of the time, however, Wilder had the conventional American education of a well-heeled youth: he attended Oberlin College in Ohio from 1915 to 1917, and Yale (with

a year away when he joined the U.S. Coast Artillery Corps) from 1917 to 1920. After graduation he spent eight months at the American Academy for Classical Studies in Rome, where he took the notes that would eventually be worked up into *The Cabala*. Spurred on by a rather peremptory cablegram from his father—HAVE JOB FOR YOU TEACHING FRENCH LEARN FRENCH LOVE FATHER—he hurried to Paris to brush up on the language and then taught it at Lawrenceville School for Boys in New Jersey; took a master's degree in French literature at Princeton in 1925–1926; and from 1930 to 1936 taught at the University of Chicago, where he had a lectureship that allowed him to teach for only half the year, thus enabling him to continue to write both novels and plays.

Wilder spent World War II in North Africa and Italy, working in the Intelligence Branch of the U.S. Army Air Force, and was stimulated by his experiences to write *The Skin of Our Teeth*, a study of one New Jersey family's voyage through history from the onset of the First Ice Age to the (then) present day. It won him his third Pulitzer Prize, but like so much of his work was sometimes accused of being "bookish," "bloodless," and "schoolmasterish." But, viewed "in Germany soon after the war, in the shattered churches and beerhalls that were serving as theatres," it was, Wilder maintained, a genuinely moving experience and a play that spoke directly to its audience. In 1950 and 1951 he was Charles Eliot Norton Professor of Poetry at Harvard University; in 1963 was awarded the Presidential Medal of Freedom; and in 1965 he was the first recipient of the National Medal for Literature.

Wilder never married; his closest female friendship (outside his family) was with Gertrude Stein; and, with the highly qualified exception of one chapter in *Theophilus North*, he is conspicuously unconvincing whenever he sets out to write about sexual relationships. The charming courtship of George Gibbs and Emily Webb in *Our Town* makes this point well, since George and Emily are scarcely more than children when they marry. When we next meet Emily, nine years after their wedding, she is the mother of one child and has died giving birth to another. Of their sexually productive time together we are shown nothing. (This is an absence that the Wooster Group—a radical theatrical troupe who were producing subversive reworkings of American classics—highlighted in 1981–1982 with deliberate crassness when they ran a pornographic film as the last part of their adaptation of the play [Savran, 1988, pp. 43–45].)

Inevitably gossip, some of it malicious, accumulated. This gossip would be irrelevant if it did not highlight a notable deficiency in Wilder's writing. Tennessee Williams, perceptive but horribly partisan, recalls in his *Memoirs* that after the opening night of *A Streetcar Named Desire* (1947), he was invited "to the quarters of Mr. Thornton Wilder, who was in residence [in New Haven]." Wilder, clearly fearing a rival (a very vulgar and unpolished rival, but one whose powers might easily eclipse his own), was ungracious:

> It was like having a papal audience. We all sat about this academic gentleman while he put the play down as if delivering a papal bull. He said that it was based upon a fatally mistaken premise. No female who had ever been a lady (he was referring to Stella) could possibly marry a vulgarian such as Stanley. We sat there and listened to him politely. I thought, privately, This character has never had a good lay.
>
> (*Memoirs*, pp. 135–136)

Wilder, Williams is saying, knows a good deal more about class than he does about sex. Thus this unpleasant anecdote, from which neither writer emerges with credit, directly links issues of sexual inexperience and literary creativity. Wilder linked them differently: according to Gilbert Harrison (whose rather informal biography [1983] is still the standard one), he told one of his friends that there was a trade-off between the energy expended in sexual activity and what was needed for the production of works of art. By implication he preferred art to sex and thought the preference economically sound. Other friends added helpfully, though Wilder would surely have been appalled by their betrayal, that he was "basically a neuter—[because] it was easier" (Harrison, p. 169)—which suggests, a shade unflatteringly, that Wilder's proposed choice was not one that he ever had to make. His own comments to André Maurois, whom he met on a walking holiday in 1928, are at once candid and obscure: "My weakness is that I am too bookish. I know little of life...I shall not write again before I have actually observed men better" (Maurois, 1932, pp. 38–41). Remarkably, this is a theme to which Wilder returned in his very last work, *Theophilus North*. In 1926 North had resolved, he tells us, that:

> if I were to do any so-called "writing," it would not be before I had reached the age of fifty. If I were destined to die before that, I wanted to be sure that I had encompassed as varied a range of experience as I could—that I had not narrowed

my focus to that noble but largely sedentary pursuit that is covered by the word "art."

> (*Theophilus North*, pp. 1–2)

Nonetheless, Wilder (unlike North, who saves up his notes until the early seventies) continued to write, without interruption or abatement.

REPETITIONS

"In his work," Isabel Wilder wrote in her introduction to *The Alcestiad* (1977), her brother "was not afraid to repeat himself or to be influenced by the masters in the tradition of literature who had passed the torch from hand to hand." She illustrates her observation by repeating Wilder's own image: "Literature," he wrote in his preface to *Three Plays* (1957), "has always more resembled a torch race than a furious dispute among heirs" (*American Characteristics*, 1979, p. 110). Wilder's borrowings from other authors are obvious and honest: the complex genealogy of *The Matchmaker* (1954)—an adaptation of *The Merchant of Yonkers* (1939) that is itself an adaptation of an Austrian play that is adapted from an English original—is merely the clearest instance. *The Woman of Andros* parades a similar complexity of origins: the first part of the novel, an initial disclaimer reveals, "is based upon the *Andria*, a comedy of Terence who in turn based his work upon two Greek plays, now lost to us, by Menander." But within this seemingly insubstantial though haunting novel, and between it and more substantial works, there are strange echoes that defy complete explanation but that probably map out the otherwise hidden contours of Wilder's creative life. Always a self-conscious stylist, he begins *The Woman of Andros* with a sentence that he echoes at its end. Its fourth sentence:

> Triumph had passed from Greece and wisdom from Egypt, but with the coming on of night they seemed to regain their lost honors, and the land that was soon to be called Holy prepared in the dark its wonderful burden.

is picked up by its final sentence:

> And in the East the stars shone tranquilly down upon the land that was soon to be called Holy and that even then was preparing its precious burden.

Temporal dislocation, where in this case Wilder takes us back to the time of the story and then forward to the birth of Christ, is common in his work. In *Our Town* the stage manager stands firmly in the 1930s but takes his audience back to 1901, 1904, and 1913; then back to 1899; then forward to 1913 once again; and finally forward to the time of performance. The action of the theater, Wilder wrote in "Some Thoughts on Playwriting" (1941), "takes place in a perpetual present time" (*American Characteristics*, p. 115). We leave Grover's Corners at 11 o'clock in 1913 and leave the theater at the same time in whatever year we watch the play. The stage manager links both times as he *winds his watch*: "Hm . . . Eleven o'clock in Grover's Corners—You get a good rest, too. Good night."

Much more puzzling—genuinely beyond explanation—is an echo from *The Bridge of San Luis Rey* in *The Woman of Andros*. Compare:

> There was this strange and noble figure in Peru during these years, the Captain Alvarado, the traveller. He was blackened and cured by all weathers. He stood in the square with feet apart as though they were planted on a shifting deck. His eyes were strange, unaccustomed to the shorter range, too used to seizing the appearances of a constellation between a cloud and a cloud, and the outline of a cape in the rain.

with the strikingly similar description, just three years later, of the crippled Philocles:

> He was blackened and cured by all weathers. He stood in the squares of the various ports of call, his feet apart as though they were for ever planted on a shifting deck. He seemed to be too large for daily life; his eyes were strange—unaccustomed to the shorter range, too used to seizing the appearances of a constellation between a cloud and a cloud, and the outlines of a headland in the rain.

Particularly odd is that the Alvarado material has a real purpose in the "Esteban" section of *The Bridge of San Luis Rey*: the abbess, remembering her own loss, persuades Alvarado, who permanently mourns a dearly loved daughter, to distract Esteban, who has lost Manuel. Philocles, too, has lost a daughter, but the relevance of this loss to the surrounding plot is not obvious. Instead, his maltreatment in captivity looks forward eighteen years to the hideous mutilation of Caesar's friend Turrinus, recounted in Letter V, in *The Ides of March* (1948).

More ingenious, though still troublesome, is Wilder's reusing in the third act of *The Skin of Our Teeth* of the pageant of the minutes, hours, years, and planets from *Pullman Car Hiawatha* (1931). One of a number of deliberately experimental short plays at which Wilder tried his hand in the early 1930s, *Pullman Car Hiawatha* is both very brief and immensely ambitious. It tells the story of a journey by sleeping car from New York to Chicago on 21 December 1930, but this single instance of an often repeated event is meant to be representative of all such instances. In its use of a stage manager who acts as both commentator and bit-part actor, *Pullman Car Hiawatha* anticipates *Our Town*, as does Grover's Corners, Ohio—a town through which the track passes but also a character in the play ("I represent Grover's Corners, Ohio. Eight hundred twenty-one souls"). The most spectacular part of *Pullman Car Hiawatha*, however, is an elaborately camp pageant in which the position of the speeding train is "geographically, meteorologically, astronomically, [and] theologically considered." In order to do this, a system of symbolic significances is erected in which the hours of the day represent philosophers (ten o'clock is Plato, eleven o'clock is Epictetus), while midnight is both a philosopher and a theologian (St. Augustine).

Ten years later (on 2 December 1941), faced with the need to complete *The Skin of Our Teeth*—another play in which a single set of events has universal significance—Wilder noted in his *Journals* that his attempt to economize creatively by reusing the earlier pageant was not going well, principally because the earlier material was being "dragged in indigestibly"; was "insufficiently related to the surrounding material"; did not properly respect or represent the later play's different intentions; and smacked of "the *faux-sublime*" (*Journals*, p. 37). Wilder, whose practical skills as a dramatist cannot be doubted, resolved his problem with characteristic ingenuity: at the beginning of the third act of *The Skin of Our Teeth*, Sabina announces that food poisoning—a lemon meringue pie with "blue mould all over the bottom of it"—has laid low most of the cast. This forces Mr. Fitzpatrick, the stage manager, to rehearse the pageant with volunteer replacements on stage while the audience, if it wishes, "can go out in the lobby and smoke some more." Eventually, after a good deal of confusion and ineptitude, the play restarts; but when we get to its end, we discover that *Pullman Car Hiawatha*'s pageant has been reduced to the merest outline. The *faux-sublime*, at any rate, is comprehensively avoided.

The most remarkable repetition in Wilder's corpus links *The Woman of Andros* directly and memorably to *Our Town*. One evening, in order to resolve a dispute over the respective merits of poetry and real life, Chrysis tells the story of a dying hero who persuades Zeus and the King of the Dead to allow him to spend one day ("that day that in all the twenty-two thousand days of his lifetime had been least successful") back on Earth. He must do so, however, "with a mind divided into two persons—the participant and the onlooker—the participant who does the deeds and says the words of so many years before, and the onlooker who foresees the end." Thus divided within himself (both actor and Wilderian stage manager), he sees the significance of even the most insignificant actions, but sees also that this significance is entirely lost upon those to whom (unknown to them) he has returned. Faced with such a painful recognition of how life slips by the living, he renounces his gift and returns to rest among the dead. This is exactly Emily's condition: restored to life—to the day of her twelfth birthday—but with a full awareness of the future, she finds the intensity of significance of even the apparently insignificant too painful to bear: "I didn't realize. So all that was going on and we never noticed. Take me back—up the hill—to my grave." Art, for Wilder, renews the gift but removes its pain: from a kind of death, from art's vantage point on the periphery of life, we catch the significance that we otherwise miss.

THE PLAYS

Although he first came to public recognition as a novelist, Wilder had, he wrote in the foreword to *The Angel That Troubled the Waters* (1928), been writing short plays—many with a somewhat tepid religious aspect—since he was fifteen or sixteen. These are short, vary a great deal in quality, and do not suggest a great or hidden talent, but do show a commendable willingness to experiment and compress. When, three years later, he published a second volume of plays, these, though they are still short pieces unlikely to be professionally produced with any regularity, were much more substantial and are filled with genuine promise. In three of them—*The Long Christmas Dinner* (in which a single meal lasts ninety years and chronicles the rise and fall of generations), *Pullman Car Hiawatha*, and *The Happy Journey to Trenton and Camden*—he employed the staging techniques that he was to make famous in *Our Town* and *The Skin of Our Teeth*, full-length plays that brought him his second and third Pulitzer Prizes.

The best of these short plays are not idle sports, for Wilder held firm views of what theater could and should do, could not and should not do. These views were his principles, and he set them down with engaging modesty in a small handful of essays on the nature of theater; put them to experimental testing in the best of his short plays; and brought them to practical perfection in *Our Town*. These principles are easily summarized. Since all theater is collaborative, no play is complete on the page; playwrights, producers, and actors (unlike novelists) address an audience (which is a collectivity rather than an individual); theater is based upon a series

of obvious lies (nobody dies in a death scene) and is, thus, an art of deliberate and manifest pretense; theater is a performance art; performance is an art of the *here and now*; because theater represents not things themselves but "the symbols of things," it raises "the exhibited individual action into the realm of idea and type and universal" (*American Characteristics*, pp. 102, 108).

Although some of Wilder's terminology is old-fashioned, there is nothing in what he says that need surprise or puzzle a modern theatrical semiotician for even a moment. Every action on stage is both real (we have the evidence of our senses that something really does happen) and the representation of an action that we see only in the mind's eye (or upon reflection). The rules that govern symbolization differ from time to time and from place to place, so that at present in Western theater you can represent a kiss with a real kiss but must fake an act of stabbing, whereas in some Eastern theaters the kiss also must be faked. But Wilder saw that these presentational conventions are merely local expressions of a universal rule: that the art of theater is, and is ineradicably, a symbolic art.

What the individualized, local incident symbolizes, Wilder wanted to insist, is not an equivalent (but fictional and thus offstage) instance, but a generality. Oddly, perhaps—for Wilder thinks drama a greater art form than the novel—his greatest inspiration was a novelist. "The hero of *Finnegans Wake*," he wrote in the essay "Joyce and the Modern Novel" (1957), "is the most *generalized* character in all literature, but he is also completely a unique and individualized person" (*American Characteristics*, p. 178). So Wilder's Joycean hero, Mr. Antrobus in *The Skin of Our Teeth*, is meant to be both a vividly realized individual and also Adam (that most representative of all representative men) and all of Adam's descendants. And *Our Town* is nothing so small "as a picture of life in a New Hampshire village . . . for I have set the village against the largest dimensions of time and place" (*American Characteristics*, p. 109).

Not everyone accepts *Our Town* in the terms that Wilder has here set down. Though a great popular success, it has attracted sharp criticism from academic authors, who point out—reasonably enough—how much that was current in 1938 finds no mention in the play. What force this criticism has in the early twenty-first century, however, is not clear. Wilder certainly thought that he was addressing real concerns, and not always abstractly. *Our Town* may be nostalgic, but it is not sentimental: by the time the play ends, Mr. and Mrs. Webb have lost both their children, Wally to a burst appendix and Emily in childbirth. These, as any good social history of medicine and health care will confirm, were frequently encountered dangers in the early years of the twentieth century: though in the Western world they are less common now than they once were, other ways of dying young have risen to replace them. Wilder is not a flawless writer, and he can be evasive—perhaps he offers us the consolations of religion without offering us the religion that proffers these consolations—but a simple charge of irrelevance or marginality or parochialism cannot be sustained.

"I am not one of the new dramatists we are looking for," Wilder wrote in 1957 (*American Characteristics*, p. 111). He then added, with more than a touch of an entirely characteristic wistfulness, that he wished he were. This, too, has been turned against him. In an anthology of texts titled *Theater of the Avant-Garde*, in an introduction to "American Dada and Surrealism," all of the attention is given to Gertrude Stein (with whom Wilder was on excellent terms); *Our Town*, by contrast, is dismissed as an "allegedly avant-garde" work that offers "romantic nostalgia and spiritual redemption to a Depression-weary and war-wary American public, in the form of isolation—and isolationism—in a quaint New Hampshire town of the turn of the century" (Cardullo and Knopf, 2001, pp. 442–443). The political edge to this criticism is obvious, as is its academic bias. Wilder (unlike Gertrude Stein) was never a writer of the avant-garde, and he knew that he was not: "I am not an innovator," he once wrote, "but a rediscoverer of forgotten goods" (*American Characteristics*, p. 111). But even rediscoveries need to be rediscovered from time to time: when David Mamet saw Greg Mosher's Broadway revival of *Our Town*, he recognized it as "a masterpiece" and responded by "sobbing at the simple text and the simple production" (*Make-Believe Town*, 1996, p. 64). By such simple means, as Wilder might well have said, the torch passes on.

WORKS

NOVELS

The Cabala (1926)
The Bridge of San Luis Rey (1927)
The Woman of Andros (1930)
Heaven's My Destination (1934)
The Ides of March (1948)
The Eighth Day (1967)
Theophilus North (1973)

PLAYS

The Trumpet Shall Sound (1919)
The Angel That Troubled the Waters and Other Plays (1928)
The Long Christmas Dinner and Other Plays (1931)
Our Town (1938)
The Merchant of Yonkers (1939)
The Skin of Our Teeth (1942)
The Matchmaker (1954)
A Life in the Sun (1955)
The Drunken Sisters (1957)
Three Plays (1957)
Plays for Bleecker Street (1962)
The Alcestiad (1977)
The Collected Short Plays of Thornton Wilder (1997)
The Collected Short Plays of Thornton Wilder (1998)

OTHER WORKS

American Characteristics and Other Essays (1979)
The Journals of Thornton Wilder, 1939–1961 (1985)
The Letters of Gertrude Stein and Thornton Wilder (1996)

FURTHER READING

Blank, Martin, ed. *Critical Essays on Thornton Wilder.* New York, 1996.

Blank, Martin, Dalma Hunyadi Brunauer, and David Garrett Izzo. *Thornton Wilder: New Essays.* West Cornwall, Conn., 1999.

Bryer, Jackson R., ed. *Conversations with Thornton Wilder.* Jackson, Miss., 1992.

Burbank, Rex. *Thornton Wilder.* New York, 1961.

Cardullo, Bert, and Robert Knopf, eds. *Theater of the Avant-Garde, 1890–1950: A Critical Anthology.* New Haven, Conn., 2001.

Castronovo, David. *Thornton Wilder.* New York, 1986.

Edelstein, Jerome M. *A Bibliographical Checklist of the Writings of Thornton Wilder.* New Haven, Conn., 1959.

Goldstein, Malcolm. *The Art of Thornton Wilder.* Lincoln, Neb., 1965.

Goldstone, Richard H. *Thornton Wilder: An Intimate Portrait.* New York, 1975.

Goldstone, Richard H., and Gary Anderson. *Thornton Wilder: An Annotated Bibliography of Works by and about Thornton Wilder.* New York, 1982.

Haberman, Donald. *The Plays of Thornton Wilder: A Critical Study.* Middletown, Conn., 1967.

Harrison, Gilbert. *The Enthusiast: A Life of Thornton Wilder.* New Haven, Conn., 1983.

Mamet, David. "Greg Mosher." In *Make-Believe Town: Essays and Remembrances.* London, 1996.

Maurois, André. *A Private Universe.* Translated by Hamish Miles. New York, 1932. Maurois met Wilder in 1928, and records the meeting in this book.

Papajewski, Helmut. *Thornton Wilder.* Translated by John Conway. New York, 1968.

Savran, David. *Breaking the Rules: The Wooster Group.* New York, 1988. Part One—"Route 1 & 9 (*The Last Act*); The Disintegration of *Our Town*" (pp. 9–45)—gives a detailed account of the Wooster Group's radically iconoclastic reworking of Wilder's most famous play.

Walsh, Claudette. *Thornton Wilder: A Reference Guide, 1926–1990.* New York, 1993.

Williams, Mary Ellen. *A Vast Landscape: Time in the Novels of Thornton Wilder.* Pocatello, Idaho, 1979.

Williams, Tennessee. *Memoirs.* New York, 1976.

See also the article on *Our Town*, immediately following.

THORNTON WILDER'S
OUR TOWN

by Denise Larrabee

One of the most popular plays in American theater, Thornton Wilder's Pulitzer Prize–winning *Our Town* (1938) is also one of the most easily misunderstood. Audiences and critics are quick to respond nostalgically to the daily life of the inhabitants of a small New England village in 1901, and the play's exploration of the struggle to appreciate life fully is an accessible theme. But these same viewers are apt to misinterpret the theatrical innovations Wilder incorporates throughout the play or to overlook them entirely as gimmicks.

Our Town was warmly received when it first opened on 22 January 1938 in Princeton, New Jersey; did poorly in Boston; but developed into a commercial success on Broadway, culminating in a successful film version in 1940. First reviews were mixed. In *The New Republic*, Stark Young criticized its lack of "bite, the unpredictable, the deep glimpse, the divine insight." Some reviewers missed the play's full intent and described it simply as a nostalgic recreation of times past. Others, like Brooks Atkinson in *The New York Times*, understood Wilder's intent and praised its melding of form and function, admiring Wilder's theatrical innovations in developing the play's deeper themes. Wilder, Atkinson wrote, "has transmuted the simple events of human life into universal reverie.... By stripping the play of everything that is not essential, Mr. Wilder has given it a profound, strange, unworldly significance."

By the time he wrote *Our Town*, Wilder had already written several lesser-known plays. He was a teacher, critic, essayist, and accomplished novelist. His novel, *The Bridge of San Luis Rey* (1927), won a Pulitzer Prize in 1928. Unlike many of his literary contemporaries, he was optimistic and viewed humankind as essentially good. Strongly influenced by the European theater in the 1920s and 1930s, which was experimenting with audience participation, expressionism, and political themes, Wilder possessed innovative and passionate ideas about drama and what it could achieve artistically and emotionally. Many of these ideas came to fruition in *Our Town*.

Wilder believed theater was akin to ritual—if encouraged, those who attended could experience a transformation of perspective. Toward that end he attempted to engage the audience members by stimulating their imaginations. Inspired by André Obey's *Le Viol de Lucrèce* (first produced in 1931), which he translated in 1932, and by the Noh, a medieval Japanese dramatic form, Wilder abandoned the traditional box set that placed the audience outside the action looking through an invisible fourth wall. He employed minimal scenery and props, requiring the actors to pantomime actions and the audience to imagine.

Wilder carried some literary concepts from his work as a novelist over to his work as a dramatist. He believed that, like a novel, a play required an omniscient narrator. In *Our Town*, the Stage Manager assumes this role, moving freely in time, relating information about Grover's Corners and its inhabitants from the past, present, and future.

Influenced by Gertrude Stein's *Narration* (1935), for which he wrote the introduction, and the German playwright Bertolt Brecht, Wilder accepted the idea that characters are more real in the minds of audience members when imagined by them, that the characters then become a part of their emotional memory. *Our Town*'s characters are not individuals with deep psychological motivations, but types. They possess individual traits, but are essentially allegorical, leaving room for the audience's imagination to work.

Although Wilder challenges audience members to expand their notions of drama, he still adheres to the three classical unities of time, place, and action. The entire play takes place in Grover's Corners, and while it moves back and forth in time, the primary action occurs in a logical sequence from dawn until night, offering enough structure to keep the audience emotionally connected to the experience. Consequently, *Our Town* remains one of the most frequently produced American plays in the United States and abroad.

ACT 1

As written, audiences arriving at a performance of *Our Town* are met with a bare stage in half-light. "I tried to restore significance to the small details of life by removing scenery," Wilder wrote for *The New York Times* in 1938. The Stage Manager walks on; sets tables, chairs, and a bench for the coming scene; and introduces the play. He lists the characters, establishes the time (7 May 1901, just before dawn), and describes the town in which the action occurs: "Grover's Corners, New Hampshire—just across the Massachusetts line: latitude 42 degrees 40 minutes; longitude 70 degrees 37 minutes." Comments like this that impart highly specific information are a gentle satire of the realism becoming more prevalent in American theater in the 1930s, as in the dramas of Eugene O'Neill. They also illustrate a sense of universality out of what appears, on the surface, to be a very limited and specific time and place.

Throughout the play, the Stage Manager addresses the audience directly, breaking the imaginary fourth wall that usually separates the actors from the audience. He is not only the omniscient narrator of the novel, but the Greek Chorus from ancient theater, revealing facts from the past or future that the other characters do not know. The Stage Manager moves freely through time, making him somewhat godlike, except that he speaks to the audience members familiarly, like a neighbor chatting over the back fence, pulling them in and making them part of the play itself.

After the Stage Manager describes the town and shares some local gossip, a newspaper boy, Joe Crowell, delivers his papers. The Stage Manager informs us that Joe will die fighting in France during World War I. The audience is then introduced to two families, the Webbs and the Gibbses, as they start their day—eating breakfast and getting off to school. We observe the families interacting with each other and learn that George Gibbs is obsessed with baseball and Emily Webb is an exceptional student.

After the children are sent off to school, Mrs. Gibbs and Mrs. Webb set about performing some of their daily chores—feeding chickens and stringing beans. Professor Willard shares a "scientific account" of the town, and Mr. Webb, editor of the *Grover's Corners Sentinel*, gives a "political and social report," another gentle poke of fun at realism in American theater. Some questions are taken from the audience, although in reality actors are planted throughout the theater.

The Stage Manager tells us how several hours have passed and the school children are on their way home. Emily and George have a conversation, which prompts Emily to ask her mother later if she is pretty. That evening, George asks Emily through his bedroom window for

help with his algebra and later cries when reprimanded by his father for not helping his mother around the house. Meanwhile, Mrs. Webb and Mrs. Gibbs attend choir practice and on the way home gossip about the leader, Simon Stimson, who was drunk again.

The constant activity in the first act gives the impression of time passing. A train whistle blows, a school bell rings signaling dismissal, people come and go. All the while the Stage Manager carries a watch, an instrument that offers a false sense of time. Wilder plays with the human concept of time. Hours are skipped by and simultaneous events are related in separate scenes. Throughout the play, the Stage Manager jumps forward and backward in time, sharing the history of the town at one moment and a glimpse into the future the next. In this manner, Wilder urges the audience to question its ideas about time.

Act 1 closes with Rebecca, George's younger sister, telling him about a letter a friend received from her minister addressed "Jane Crofut; The Crofut Farm; Grover's Corners; Sutton County; New Hampshire; United States of America; Continent of North America; Western Hemisphere; the Earth; the Solar System; the Universe; the Mind of God." In this last scene, Wilder illustrates the idea, better than he does anywhere else in the play, that we are all ultimately connected across time and distance—we are all one.

ACT 2

During the opening of act 2, the Stage Manager clarifies the overall structure of the play: "The First Act was called Daily Life. This act is called Love and Marriage. There's another act coming after this: I reckon you can guess what that's about." Clearly, *Our Town* is an allegory; the Stage Manager's comments reinforce awareness that the characters are types, that any suggestion of a conventional plot is incidental, and that the theme expands beyond Grover's Corners and its inhabitants.

He also relates events that have occurred during the three years that have passed since act 1: "Summer and winters have cracked the mountains a little bit more and the rains have brought down some of the dirt." As he does repeatedly throughout the play, the Stage Manager places Grover's Corners within a cosmic order, reinforcing the idea of universality. He continues, "Nature's been pushing and contriving in other ways, too: a number of young people fell in love and got married." Two of these young people are Emily and George, who have graduated from high school.

We witness the couple first discovering their love for each other in a drugstore, although neither ever actually speaks the word "love." Their feelings for each other are implied in Emily's passion when she tells George how "awful conceited and stuck-up" he has become, and in George's decision to stay in Grover's Corners. The morning of the wedding, we hear George and Emily's parents reflecting on marriage; Mrs. Webb cries, admitting that she has never told Emily anything about marriage. Both Emily and George consider backing out of the wedding, but at the last moment, in a burst of emotion unusual for this play, George professes his love for Emily. The ceremony itself is perfunctory, with a neighbor, Mrs. Soames, talking throughout about how much she loves weddings, keeping the scene from stumbling into sentimentality.

A ritual familiar to most people, the wedding in *Our Town* brings the audience together, reminding us of the universality of human experience. Thus, George and Emily's wedding is not the marriage of two individuals, but the marriage of all people everywhere, illustrating the compulsion of humans to connect with one another. Wilder draws the audience in by having it become the congregation as the newly married couple runs up the center aisle of the theater at the end of the ceremony.

Wilder further encourages the imaginations of the audience in act 2 by allowing the Stage Manager to play several roles: Mrs. Forrest, whom George accidentally bumps into while tossing his baseball in the air; the druggist, Mr. Morgan, who serves George and Emily their ice cream sodas; and the minister who marries them. By having the Stage Manager play several parts, Wilder forces audience members to share in the creative process and utilize their imaginations more fully.

Throughout the play the audience must imagine the characters performing countless actions as they pantomime. Props in *Our Town* are limited to items such as a table, several chairs, a couple of ladders, and a small bench. Wilder believed props and other theatrical features distracted an audience and interfered with their experience of the moment. Consequently, every action required by the actors relies on their use of pantomime and the audience's use of imagination, from Mrs. Webb cooking breakfast to George pulling on his overshoes.

In act 1 we see two families living side by side but not intimately connected. Here, in act 2, they are brought together through marriage. In the last act, they will separate once again through death.

ACT 3

When act 3 opens the stage is set with twelve chairs, on which sit some anonymous characters and others introduced earlier in the play, such as Wally Webb (Emily's brother) and Mrs. Gibbs (George's mother). One chair is empty. We learn that this is a cemetery and that this chair is for Emily, who has died giving birth to her second child.

The Stage Manager ruminates on how things do not change much and how beautiful the view is from the cemetery and how inconsequential many human deeds are when juxtaposed against death, such as dying for a cause one does not fully understand. "Wherever you come near the human race, there's layers and layers of nonsense," he says. At this point, the Stage Manager approaches the topic of life after death: "We all know that *something* is eternal. And it ain't houses and it ain't names, and it ain't earth, and it ain't even the stars . . . everybody knows in their bones that *something* is eternal, and that something has to do with human beings."

It is not long after Emily enters the stage and joins the dead that she decides she wants to experience life again and asks to return to the day of her twelfth birthday. The Stage Manager, as well as the dead, discourage her. "You not only live it," warns the Stage Manager, "but you watch yourself living it." Still, Emily insists on returning to life, exhibiting human nature's tendency to cling to a sense of identity and time and place.

Her twelfth birthday begins as a typical morning with breakfast in the kitchen with her family. But soon Emily finds the experience painful. "I can't bear it," she says. "I can't look at everything hard enough." Emily realizes that she never fully experienced life as she lived it. Neither did she fully connect with the people around her—even those she loved most. As she leaves, she clarifies the problem: "Oh, earth, you're too wonderful for anybody to realize you." And then Emily asks the Stage Manager the question on which the thrust of the play depends: "Do any human beings ever realize life while they live it?—every, every minute?" The Stage Manager tells her that perhaps poets and saints do, but that generally people do not.

George returns to the stage and throws himself at Emily's feet, at her grave. His grief is palpable. Brought together in marriage, George and Emily are separated again through death. But the tragedy, Wilder tells us, is not that we die, but that despite our compulsive human need for connection, we remain essentially distant from each other in life.

Critics have accused Wilder of manipulating the audience with Emily's death. Indeed, he risks becoming overly sentimental in act 3. But Wilder's intention is to move the members of the audience by successfully leading them to an awareness of their mortality while they question how they are living their own lives. And so the Stage Manager, as he has done throughout the play, interrupts the action with dialogue just as the play could plummet into sentimentality. He draws a dark curtain across the scene and begins addressing the audience.

"Most everybody's asleep in Grover's Corners," he says. "There are the stars—doing their old, old crisscross journeys in the sky." He winds his watch. "Hm. . . . Eleven o'clock in Grover's Corners.—You get a good rest, too. Good night." As if the audience can rest with all Wilder has given them to contemplate about their own existence.

[*See also* Theater in America.]

FURTHER READING

Bunge, Nancy. "The Social Realism of *Our Town*: A Study in Misunderstanding." In *Thornton Wilder: New Essays*, edited by Martin Blank, Dalma Hunyadi Brunauer, and David Garrett Izzo. West Cornwall, Conn., 1999.

Haberman, Donald C. *The Plays of Thornton Wilder*. Middletown, Conn., 1967.

Haberman, Donald C. Our Town: *An American Play*. Boston, 1989. Complete analysis of the play, including the critical reception and its importance in literary history.

Harrison, Gilbert A. *The Enthusiast: A Life of Thornton Wilder*. New Haven, Conn., and New York, 1983. Authorized biography, considered the most comprehensive study to date.

Kuner, M. C. *Thornton Wilder: The Bright and the Dark*. New York, 1972. Excellent analysis of Wilder's works, including themes, techniques, and influences.

Simon, Linda. *Thornton Wilder: His World*. New York, 1979. Biography with good bibliography.

Walsh, Claudette. *Thornton Wilder: A Reference Guide, 1926–1990*. New York, 1993. Includes all criticism written from 1926 to 1990 in English concerning Wilder's works.

Wilder, Thornton. Our Town: *A Play in Three Acts*. New York, 1938. Numerous reprints exist, many with supporting material.

Wilder, Thornton. "Some Thoughts on Play Writing." In his *Our Town*. New York, 1964.

See also the article on Thornton Wilder, immediately preceding.

TENNESSEE WILLIAMS

by John A. Bertolini

Tennessee Williams.
(Photograph by Fred Ohringer. Courtesy of the Library of Congress)

While the outline of Tennessee Williams's career as a playwright falls into the most conventional pattern conceivable, his plays do not. His career followed the traditional trajectory from parental objection and the confinements of middle-class life and small-town mentality to the struggle for success, the achievement and flourishing of that success, and worldwide fame followed by drug and alcohol abuse, to less favor from his muse and finally to death in a hotel room.

The territory staked out by Williams's plays is different from that of other major American dramatists; the line that leads from Eugene O'Neill and Lillian Hellman to Arthur Miller, for example, does not also lead to Williams. Whereas O'Neill, Hellman, and Miller draw on the Shakespearean and biblical family themes of fratricidal rivalry and father-son (mother-daughter) strife in *Desire under the Elms*, *Mourning Becomes Electra*, *Long Day's Journey into Night*, *The Little Foxes*, *Another Part of the Forest*, *All My Sons*, and *Death of a Salesman*, Williams sings for the individual soul in torment and isolation. His protagonists hang desperate with loneliness, in frenzied pursuit of the carnal as a stay against aloneness and death. They use language seemingly to decorate reality but actually to protect themselves from it. They border on hysteria, loss of control, loss of self-possession. Violence lurks near them always, or menaces them; it finally destroys possibility for them, when it does not destroy their actual bodies. *Cat on a Hot Tin Roof* (1955) is almost the only one of his plays that can be related to that central strain in American drama: family strife. It was also his most popular play and a hugely successful film.

However, because Williams did not draw on family strife as a theme in the traditional way, he nevertheless drew heavily on his own family's particularities. Much

of his imaginative output, both the dramatic and the fictional, reworks material from his experience of his own family. Indeed, it was not until he dramatized his family in *The Glass Menagerie* (1944)—so closely based on his own family that he gave the character based on himself his own name, "Tom"—that he had a clear success on stage. It also matters that his family was southern, for everything that the South meant by way of traditions, codes of manners, behavior, dress and conduct, and of a way of looking at the world provided for him a whole system with which he could make his individual characters clash.

Thomas Lanier Williams was born on 26 March 1911 in Columbus, Mississippi, to Cornelius and Edwina Dakin Williams. Tom only took the name "Tennessee" later, when he was a young man; he explained that it was a nickname he received at the University of Iowa by classmates who could not remember which southern state he came from, or alternatively that it was based on his paternal grandfather's having run (unsuccessfully) for governor of Tennessee. Clerics and clerical families figure prominently in Williams's works, partly because Tom's maternal grandfather, Walter, was an Episcopal pastor, and though his religious affiliation was yet another system with which to clash for Tom, the serenity and dignity of the man in old age would inspire Tom with admiration and envy. His grandfather had not only taken him on a trip to Europe when Tom was seventeen but also on more than one occasion had come to Tom's aid financially. Tom held him in esteem and felt both gratitude and affection for him. In his 1961 play *Night of the Iguana* the Episcopal priest, Shannon, is something of a reprobate, but his portrayal is not inspired by Tom's grandfather. Another character in that play is, however: "Nonno," the ancient and serene, forever impoverished poet clearly derives in part from Walter Dakin.

THE GLASS MENAGERIE AND THE AUTOBIOGRAPHICAL IMPULSE

Aspects of Williams's mother, "Miss Edwina," show forth in various matrons in his theater, but one in particular almost replicates her, Amanda Wingfield in *The Glass Menagerie*. Deserted by her husband, she is trying to salvage something of happiness out of life while she looks after her two grown children. (Williams's father, Cornelius, because he was a traveling salesman for a shoe company, was often away from home during Tom's childhood.) Tom is a poet but works in a warehouse at a job he hates (the author's self-portrait, for his father required him to work in a shoe factory to help support himself and the family). His sister Laura walks with difficulty because of a childhood illness; as a consequence she has retreated from life into a private universe (symbolized by her collection of glass animals) and shies away from the human contact she desperately needs. The conception of Laura's character Williams owes to his sympathetic feelings toward his sister, Rose (born in 1909), who in her late twenties was diagnosed as schizophrenic and later was the subject of a prefrontal lobotomy (1943), with her mother's permission but in the absence of her brother, Tom. In many ways *The Glass Menagerie* is Williams's apologia for his not being present to protect his gentle sister. At the end of the play, "Tom," who doubles as narrator, explains how he is haunted wherever he goes and whatever he does by the memory of her. The cost of his becoming a poet is his desertion of two needful women. In Williams's prefatory notes on the characters, he apologizes for Tom in this way: "His nature is not remorseless, but to escape from a trap he has to act without pity." Rarely does a playwright act as a lawyer arguing on behalf of a character. That Williams does so in this play argues for the guilt he felt over his sister's fate and how he indelibly assigned that guilt to his selfishness in pursuing his writer's destiny.

In performance, Laura's fate generates feelings of pathos in the audience, as does the desperation of the mother, Amanda, who in the face of constant defeats keeps clinging to the delusion that if everyone makes an effort they can regain the superior community status and gracious living they enjoyed in the past. Williams himself, however, found humor in Amanda's desperate ploys to fend off unpleasant reality. During performances of the first production of the play in Chicago, Williams often laughed at one or another of Amanda's lines or bits of behavior, while the actors did not understand why he was laughing. This stance toward his character shows that part of his success as a playwright derived from his ability to be objective about his characters even while transforming his most subjective feelings into art. Even though Amanda is intensely pathetic, perhaps tragic, she is also funny in the transparency of her social stratagems, in the apparently endless stream of words she can produce to cover temporarily the hole of silence, or hopelessness.

APPRENTICE PLAYS

The crooked path Williams followed to the success of *The Glass Menagerie* when he was thirty-three years old was a particularly frustrating one because of the several flirtations with success he had along the way. From his first publication of a work of fiction, a short story in *Weird Tales* (1928), through an honorable mention for one of his plays when he was a freshman at the University of Missouri (1929), to the first production of a one-act play (1935) by the Memphis Garden Players, Williams had to struggle to support himself or to get his family to help support him while he worked at his writing as he could. He was in and out of the University of Missouri; later he attended Washington University and then the University of Iowa, where he studied with drama professors E. C. Mabie and E. P. Conkle and enjoyed something like celebrity status (or the academic equivalent) for his prowess in playwriting. When he was out of the University of Missouri, he was forced by his father to withdraw for having failed ROTC and then made to take a job working as a clerk in the company that employed his father, the International Shoe Company (1932). This experience became the basis for his namesake character, Tom, in *The Glass Menagerie*. Likewise Tom's friend, the Gentleman Caller, was named Jim O'Connor by Williams after a handsome young man known to the Williams family when they resided in St. Louis and who, according to Williams's brother Dakin (born 1919), was brought to call for Rose just as the Jim O'Connor of the play was for Laura. Williams's lack of inhibition in using such real names shows how self-conscious he was about expressing his individual experience of life through his plays. Like Oscar Wilde before him, he took the most impersonal of literary forms, the drama, and made it speak personally for him. Like Eugene O'Neill, Williams took the most intimate interactions of his family life and virtually replicated them onstage.

In 1937 a local St. Louis theater group directed by Willard Holland produced Williams's full-length play

Candles to the Sun (1937) with mixed success. When he submitted to them his next play, *Spring Storm* (1938), which he had written for his playwriting workshop at Iowa, it was rejected. The next play he wrote, *Not about Nightingales* (1939), which he based on an incident in a Pennsylvania prison where the warden punished rebellious prisoners by scalding them to death in a hot steam room, is significant for several reasons. It shows a leftist point of view, not in an ideological or even overtly political way but in the sense of having a cultural sympathy with all outsiders, misfits, nonconformists, and rebels against the restrictions of social order, community, codes of sexual behavior, or family obligations. It is also significant in depicting a community of males living in close quarters, because here savage violence makes its first appearance in his plays, as does the issue of homosexuality, if only peripherally. And finally, successful overt symbolism as a distinguishing feature of Williams's dramatic style makes its debut in this play.

The space in which the warden punishes the prisoners is Williams's symbol for the conditions of human existence. Butch, one of the prisoners, describes the "Klondike"—for so the prisoners have dubbed the steam room—as a place where the steam hissing out of the valves has hellish effects: it makes you feel you are breathing fire; it fills the room so you cannot see; and it makes the floor so hot, you cannot stand on it, "but there's no place else to stand." This is a bleak metaphor for the terms upon which we exist on earth, unable to see our future or a way out of our pain and yet with no other way or place to live. Butch goes on to explain that the only way to survive is by breathing through a small air hole at the bottom of one of the walls. Williams here extends the metaphor to show how limited, how minuscule and humiliating are our opportunities for survival. Hence life becomes a desperate struggle for survival. The men fight over the air hole, and only the strong survive. But when they do, they have overcome the worst prison existence has to offer. For Williams, this is one of God's faces: the savage God who makes men struggle with their own kind just to live. Violence preoccupies Williams because it is part of a theological argument he had with himself all his life. For besides his sense of a savage God, Williams has his protagonist Jim offer another version of God, which he equates with the imagination, or freedom of thought. A man can think himself beyond all boundaries, in a space high above the earth among the stars, and in that thought lies a shared identity with everything that lives, and "Then you get an idea of what God is." For Jim, God is a paradox,

"something big and terrible as night is, . . . and yet as soft as a woman."

Although *Not about Nightingales* cannot be valued as any kind of documentary representation of penal conditions in America during the 1930s—Williams depicts the prisoners too sentimentally as sensitive lads, all poets, dreamers, literary critics, and fantasists, not brutal criminals indifferent to the suffering they have caused to their victims—it is nevertheless notable as a compendium of themes, images, and motifs that map Williams's imagination. The imagery of the Klondike room—the steam, the violent struggle for survival—will reappear in *Suddenly Last Summer* (1958), when Williams will again take up the argument over God's nature. And *Cat on a Hot Tin Roof* will revive the image of human beings clawing for a space to stand on that is endurable. The main female character in *Not about Nightingales*, Eva, has a presentiment of impending danger when the warden threatens her with forced sex, as Blanche DuBois will later when she feels menaced by Stanley Kowalski's sexuality in *A Streetcar Named Desire* (1947).

During the period in which he wrote *Not about Nightingales* (1938–1939), Williams was beginning to be recognized for his literary talent by the literary world; he also led a peregrine existence, taking odd jobs. He moved from Iowa to the French Quarter in New Orleans, where he observed and was attracted to the unconventional social and sexual attitudes of its denizens. On his way to California he passed through New Mexico, where he stayed with Frieda Lawrence and became her friend. (D. H. Lawrence, partly because of his novels' candor in sexual matters, was one of Williams's literary heroes.) From California he returned to St. Louis and then moved to New York, after being granted $1,000 by the Rockefeller Foundation. He also acquired the agent Audrey Woods after she had read some of his plays and sought him out; she would remain with him for almost the rest of his career. His big theatrical break came in 1940 when the Theatre Guild agreed to produce *Battle of Angels*, the play with which Williams began the first volume of his collected plays published by New Directions in 1971. He did not include any of his earlier full-length plays such as *Spring Storm* (1937–1938), about two men and two women whose romantic and sexual needs and desires remain unfulfilled, or *Candles to the Sun*, about a miners' strike. Nor did he include the play he wrote between *Battle of Angels* (1940) and *The Glass Menagerie*, *Stairs to the Roof* (1941) in which Williams mixes vaguely socialist fantasy—the square business people block the idealistic workers from reaching the roof—with pacifist sentiments. The play unhappily mixes expressionist elements, such as the magical stairs to another realm, with agitprop speeches about the coming triumph of "we the people." Nevertheless, Williams's skill as a writer for the theater is in evidence, as when he ends a scene with this line for the male protagonist: "Would you care to dance with a man who used to be handsome? [They dance.] BLACKOUT."

THE MYTH OF ORPHEUS

Battle of Angels received a Boston tryout with Miriam Hopkins in the leading female role, but its religious imagery combined with intensely expressed sexuality and violence proved disturbing to the local critics, and the Guild withdrew the production. They suggested that Williams rewrite it, which he did, and the final version was presented on Broadway in 1957 as *Orpheus Descending* (filmed in 1960 as *The Fugitive Kind*). There was good reason for Williams in 1971 to set *Battle of Angels* as the first of his collected plays, for as Donald Costello suggests (in Stanton, 1977, pp. 107–122), it contains within itself nearly everything that follows in Williams's theater, which is why he returned to the play again and again to revise it as *Orpheus Descending* (1951–1957). It signals the birth of his personal mythology, revolving around the ritual sacrifice of a poet figure. Just as *The Glass Menagerie* establishes the autobiographical matrix for subsequent plays, so too does *Battle of Angels* create the mythological reservoir from which Williams generates his imaginative world. Val Xavier, the male protagonist of *Battle of Angels*—that his last name derives from a Williams ancestor, "Sevier," shows Williams's personal identification with his character—represents the poet's misfit status in the world of the real. He descends from his true realm, the air, because he longs for human connection, like Orpheus searching for Eurydice among the dead. He wants to belong to the human realm, to be like other people and live among them, but he possesses the tragic knowledge that "no one ever gets to know anybody," that we are all trapped within ourselves: "Sentenced—you might say—to solitary confinement inside our own skins." Val expresses this thought to Myra, the Eurydice of the play, married to a cruel and bitter old man, Jabe Torrance, crippled by illness. He figures as the force of death in the play and corresponds to Pluto, the god who presides over the underworld, the kingdom of the dead. And at the end of the play he claims both Val and Myra for his own: he shoots and kills her and has Val burned to death by a mob of vigilantes. Williams meant the manner of Val's death to represent the death of Orpheus, torn apart by the Maenads. The battle fought by the angels of the title is with "the enemies of light."

The secondary female in the play, Sandra, who tries to connect with Val because of his secret vitality, expresses Williams's sense of life as a desperate search for distraction from the horror of existence in the earthly realm; she calls it "jooking," by which she means driving from one bar to the next, dancing and drinking more at each one until you cannot drink anymore. She considers herself and Val the "fugitive kind." In the revised version of the play, *Orpheus Descending*, Val elaborates on her image of life with one of his own. He explains to Lady (Myra in the earlier version) that he is like the legless birds: "they live their whole lives on the wing, and they sleep on the wind." They alight on earth only to die. Lady longs to be one of them—uncorrupted by the earth. Such a longing to escape the inescapable conditions of earthly life is for Williams what makes life ironic, and the violent destruction of the poet figure is the sacrifice that recognizes the irony. But there is also a sense on Williams's part that the poet is purified by his own sacrifice, that he rises like the phoenix out of the flames of his own destruction—or sheds his skin like a snake, for Val Xavier, the savior, leaves behind him his snakeskin jacket.

Williams would rework this mythic material seven years later in *A Streetcar Named Desire*. But before that he experienced the critical and popular success of *The Glass Menagerie*, first in Chicago, then in New York, where it won the Drama Critics Circle Award as best play (1945). Having previously lived on small amounts of literary prize money and handouts from family and well-wishers, Williams suddenly found himself famous and well remunerated for his writing. He wrote about the experience in *The New York Times* in an essay called "The Catastrophe of Success." At that time he thought the danger to his talent was security, or the confusion of his public persona with his private self, the latter being the source of creativity. But he was wrong; the real threat came from his friendship with drugs and alcohol, which became a problem in 1951 and would finally if indirectly lead to his lonely death in a hotel room in 1983.

Before writing *Streetcar*, Williams attempted an experimental play, *Ten Blocks on the Camino Real* (1946; produced 1953, when the "ten blocks" dropped out of the title, but expanded to sixteen in the play itself), reminiscent of Strindberg's *A Dream Play*. The protagonist is a young American vagrant named "Kilroy": he travels the Royal Walk of the title, with one scene devoted to each of the sixteen blocks. It is a Latin-American dreamscape in that the locals seem to be conventional south-of-the-border types while the normal rules of time, space, and reality are suspended in favor of imagination and dreaming. For example, the blocks are occupied by various literary characters: Don Quixote, Marguerite Gautier, Proust's Baron de Charlus, Jacques Casanova, Lord Byron. They are always losing their papers or their money, needing to escape to someplace or looking for romance, but only failing in the end. The symbol-heavy, episodic play was a failure with critics and public alike, much to the disappointment of Williams, who thought its success would allow him henceforth some freedom from the requirements of realism in his work.

SUMMER AND SMOKE

Although Williams worked alternately in 1946 on the two plays that would soon become *A Streetcar Named Desire* and *Summer and Smoke*, the latter was produced first, in Dallas, July 1947, while the former premiered on Broadway in December. Both plays share a heroine who clearly is a projection of Williams himself as a sexual being and as a poet. *Summer and Smoke* takes such an extremely ironic view of the gap between the body's sexual needs and the soul's spiritual hunger that the play's protagonist, Miss Alma Winemiller, is turned into a tragic figure. Alma, as a singer and the daughter of a clergyman and an insane mother, represents Williams himself, grandson of a clergyman and with a mentally ill sister. She secretly loves the town rake, John Buchanan Jr., who is not only a sexually promiscuous gambler and drunkard but an atheist as well. Williams's hidden and illicit (at that time) homosexual identity seems projected onto Alma's secret and disapproved love for her symmetrical opposite. Williams structures the action in such a symmetrical way that the irony assumes the force of inevitability. In part 1 of the play, called "Summer," Alma expounds to John her view of the soul's aspirations to higher things, particularly shared love between two people, which she sees as a matter of heart and soul more than of the body. John, in taking the opposite view that the physical side of love is paramount, challenges her to show him where the soul is on an anatomy chart. And when he urges her to try sex with him, she rejects his advances as a degradation.

In part 2, called "Winter" and made up, like part 1, of six scenes, their positions are reversed so that Alma comes to see physical love as the ruling need and her spiritual yearnings as an illusion. But John, because he was indirectly responsible for his father's being killed,

has renounced his materialist philosophy, reformed, and redeemed his physician father's death by becoming a physician himself and even completing his father's work in a fever clinic. So when Alma offers her new, changed self to him, he wishes only to think of her as she was, the expression of spirit in tenderness—it was Alma's singing to his father on his deathbed that inspired John to change his own life. Her humiliation is complete when she learns that John is engaged to a young woman, one of Alma's singing pupils. Alma suddenly sees fully the irony and futility of her life: "The tables have turned, yes, the tables have turned with a vengeance." Though the expression is a cliché, the context and Alma's bitterness give it an extraordinary force. She expounds her new insight further by comparing their symmetrical but opposite courses to "two people exchanging a call on each other at the same time, and each one finding the other one gone out, the door locked against him, and no one to answer the bell." Here Williams expresses his view of human isolation and the inevitable failure of attempts to bridge the ocean between one island and another. The parallel but opposite lines Alma and John trace make up the tragic geometry of the play, mirrored in the symmetrical ordering of the six scenes in each of the play's two parts. The structure locks the two characters inside their fates.

Williams's general model for his story comes from the nineteenth-century motif of the double (or "doppelgänger"—both the word and the idea are explicitly expounded by John and Alma in the play), of the other person inside one, the second self. More particularly the play echoes Anatole France's 1890 novel *Thaïs* (subsequently turned into an opera by Jules Massenet in 1894), in which a fourth century anchorite, Paphnutius, determines to convert to Christianity the famous Alexandrian courtesan and actress, Thaïs. He succeeds only to find that he has lost his own faith in the process and fallen in love with her himself. When he reveals his passion to her at the side of her deathbed, she does not understand him, being herself enrapt in a heavenly vision. The appeal to Williams of such an ironic tale was the schematic contrast between the twin protagonists. It was so appealing to him that he used it in both *Summer and Smoke* and *A Streetcar Named Desire*. But in the latter play he achieved more distance from his heroine, Blanche DuBois, than he had with Alma, and instead of dramatizing the relationship of his two protagonists as one of missed opportunity, of two trains going in opposite directions and passing in the night, he dramatized the conflict of Blanche and Stanley Kowalski as a head-on collision. The result was an even more compelling tragedy than *Summer and Smoke* and what many regard as his greatest play; it is one of the small number of masterpieces in American drama.

A STREETCAR NAMED DESIRE

By the time Williams wrote *A Streetcar Named Desire* and saw it staged (1946–1947), he had become relatively comfortable with his own homosexuality. It was at this time that he formed his first sustained, albeit turbulent and even violent, relationship with a male lover, Pancho Gonzalez. As to sustained emotional relationships, previous ones had been with women rather than with men. In adolescence Williams had tied himself closely to a coeval neighbor, Hazel Kramer, a relationship that continued into his twenties, when, according to his *Memoirs* (1975), Williams proposed to Hazel in a letter—she turned him down gently. While he was at the University of Iowa, he had his first and only sexually active love affair with a woman, Bette Reitz. But concurrently and subsequently he sought and found male lovers, and they found him.

Williams's personal exploration of sexuality is reflected in *A Streetcar Named Desire*, where Blanche DuBois has been married to a young poet who committed suicide after Blanche had discovered him with an older man and had expressed disgust at what she had seen. But she carries with her a burden of guilt, therefore, and much of her subsequent behavior is an attempt to atone for her sexual intolerance. By her own promiscuity thereafter she puts herself in the position of needing the same sexual tolerance and understanding that she was unable to show her husband. Her own destruction by Stanley, which Williams portrays as fated, seems to be part of the play's tragic economy. Her need to atone for her transgression leads her to identify strongly with her self-destroyed husband. In a misunderstood scene in the play, Blanche seems to try to seduce a young man collecting subscription fees for a newspaper, but this is not an older woman's debauchery in sexually soliciting a much younger man; rather, as Williams once explained to the actress Roxanna Stuart, it is Blanche's imagining herself as her dead husband and acting out one of his homosexual encounters. (Londré in Roudané, 1997). From this authorial advice one can see that within Blanche, Williams has subsumed his earlier autobiographical poet-protagonists, Tom in *The Glass Menagerie* and Val in *Battle of Angels*, by making her impersonate her homosexual husband.

As literary characters, Blanche DuBois and Stanley Kowalski have entered the American psyche as much as Huck Finn or Captain Ahab or Hester Prynne not only because Williams drew on intensely personal feelings to create them but because he also imagined them thoroughly both as types and as individuals. In imagining them as individuals he lavished all his art on their respective languages. Speech for Stanley is functional; he says only as much as is needed to communicate a specific thought. What he says is an ungrammatical but entertainingly blunt and highly communicative argot all his own, though he can employ a sarcastic or aggressive tone if he feels phoniness is present. Blanche by contrast speaks in adjectives and qualifiers because she expresses an intensely and increasingly subjective apprehension of reality. She does not report or refer to the reality that surrounds her; she tells us how she feels: the light has a "merciless glare," her sister is a "precious lamb," her dead husband's letters are "yellowing with antiquity." When she puts an "adorable little colored paper lantern" over a "naked light bulb" she does to the bulb what her adjectives do to reality: she covers it over with something decorative to make it more bearable. And the paper lantern protects her from the light as feebly as her adjectives do.

As a type representing the attempted repression of instinctual life through refinement of manners and a dedication to poetry, she delivers a memorable speech in defense of civilization to her sister, Stella, in an attempt to get her to leave her husband, Stanley, after he has abused her physically. Stanley represents all the forces antithetical to Blanche's way of life. He is unashamed, revels in his commonness, takes pleasure in his own animal vitality, and has no patience with Blanche's hypocrisies, evasions, and self-dramatizing, her constant posturing and attitudinizing—all of which for Blanche are the markers of civilization. Blanche is a tragic figure, but she is also ridiculous in her transparent attempts to manipulate people, and each of these two aspects of her being, instead of canceling one another, heighten one another.

Williams's objectivity toward Blanche, like his objectivity toward Amanda, the character based on his mother in *The Glass Menagerie*, is remarkable. Elia Kazan, who directed the first production of the play (beginning the most artistically successful collaboration between an author and a director in the history of American theater) reports in his autobiography that just before the Broadway opening of the play he became worried about the audience's obvious preference for Stanley over Blanche (they had begun to laugh at Blanche) and approached Williams about doing something to redress the imbalance of audience sympathy. Williams advised doing nothing because he insisted that Stanley was not evil and that Blanche was not wholly good. Kazan should not take sides, Williams warned, nor should he try to point a moral, on the grounds that a play that does so ceases to represent the complexity of life truthfully. The play has attained the stature it has precisely because it does not take sides; it memorably formulates the conflict between Stanley's way and Blanche's way, between instinctual life and civilized life, and leaves the audience to make up its own mind.

Blanche's downfall assumes tragic dimensions partly because she seems to be undergoing a ritual punishment for her transgressions. The Orpheus myth once again underpins the story. Blanche as the reincarnation of her Orphic poet-husband goes to the dark domain ruled by Stanley Kowalski (the Pluto figure) in order to rescue her beloved sister, Stella (Eurydice), but fails and is destroyed in the attempt, for after Stanley rapes Blanche she has a mental breakdown, and Stella has her committed to an asylum where she will have to depend, as she says she always has, "on the kindness of strangers." Williams increases the mythic pattern of her destruction by associating the inevitability of her doom with her attraction to water. She constantly resorts to it in the form of long, hot baths and alcoholic drink. Her origin and end are connected with the sea. The name of her family's plantation was Belle Reve (Beautiful Dream, that is, Beau Rêve in correct French), which is a corruption of what must have been its original name, Belle Rive, or Beautiful Shore (Londré in Roudané, 1997), and she believes that she will die on the sea from eating an unwashed grape but be purified by burial at sea. Like Shakespeare's Antony, Blanche has difficulty holding on to herself: her being is in danger of dissolving.

Rarely has an American dramatist succeeded so well as Williams did here in communicating the central point of tragedy, how death defines life. Blanche herself is death-haunted. She comes to stay with Stella as a last resort from death. She had nursed their dying relatives: "The long parade to the graveyard!" as she puts it to Stella, and Blanche is bringing up the rear of that parade. She grows increasingly desperate to evade death; she knows she is one of "the soft people" who "have to shimmer and glow," but, she tells Stella, she's "fading now": "I don't know how much longer I can turn the trick." She keeps hearing a woman in the street selling flowers for the dead—and finally the woman knocks at Blanche's door.

CONTINUED SUCCESS

With Marlon Brando playing Stanley, first in the Broadway production, then in the 1951 film version (both directed by Kazan), *A Streetcar Named Desire* became enormously successful all over the world. Williams would know success for the rest of the decade. The early 1950s provided some personal stability for Williams as he was engaged with Frank Merlo in the longest-lasting of his liaisons with men. The relationship provided Williams with a sense of domesticity, peace, and contentment that he had hardly known before. And that contentment is reflected in his next two plays, *The Rose Tattoo* (1951), set among Italian Americans (the play is dedicated to Merlo, a Sicilian-American, with gratitude for Merlo's showing him Sicily), and *Cat on a Hot Tin Roof*, in which a southern family copes with the news that the patriarch is dying of cancer. Williams called it his version of *King Lear*.

In *The Rose Tattoo*, Williams dramatizes his sense that time is the most difficult dimension of life for us to bear. The heroine of the play, Serafina delle Rose, has wanted to stop time. Her husband, who bore on his chest the rose tattoo of the title and with whom she had passionate sexual relations, has been dead for several years, but Serafina refuses to accept his death. She rejects any potential new lover and tries to prevent her daughter, Rosa (who is about to graduate high school), from growing into a sexual woman. She intended to give her daughter a wristwatch for graduation, but the play ends happily when she forgets to give her the gift—happily because the wristwatch turns out not to work, and so Serafina has not passed on to her daughter the desire to stop time. Instead Serafina has sent her daughter to join her boyfriend. Serafina even accepts a new lover for herself and becomes pregnant, and by doing so she has accepted the dominion of ongoing time again, which is what makes her story a comic one.

Tennessee Williams's tragic figures can never accept time's dominion: when they are not evading it, ignoring it, pretending it does not exist, or actively fighting it, they try to escape from it, as does Brick, the male protagonist of *Cat on a Hot Tin Roof*. As the play opens Brick has kept himself numbed with alcohol and has not had sexual relations with his wife, Maggie, since Brick's best friend and football mate, Skipper, killed himself. Brick cannot acknowledge the mutual homoerotic feelings between himself and Skipper. Instead Brick has idealized those feelings into a desire for himself and Skipper to "keep on tossing—those long, long!—high, high!—passes that—couldn't be intercepted except by time." Brick envisions an eternal boyhood here that transcends earthly impurities. Like other Williams poet-protagonists, he longs to live in a zone of freedom, somewhere above the earth, suspended in space, spared the process of physical decline, on a plane where he continually exchanges a football with another male, a likeness of himself.

As in other plays, Williams uses classical mythology as an underlying metaphor for the action, in this case the myth of Echo and Narcissus. Maggie, like Echo, pines for love of Brick; but like Narcissus entranced by the reflected image of himself in the pool, Brick is attracted to his football partner, Skipper, and tries to ignore her. Williams hints at his use of the myth by naming Brick's preferred alcoholic consolation "Echo Spring." Williams also makes mirrors in the first act occasions for Brick and Maggie to regard one another indirectly. By the end of the play, Williams implies that Maggie may succeed in getting Brick back into their marriage bed by the sheer force of her will and vitality. For though she lies to Brick's father, Big Daddy, when she asserts that she is pregnant, she determines to make the lie a truth. For the first Broadway production of the play, Elia Kazan, its director, succeeded in pressuring Williams into rewriting the third act so as to make Maggie's attempt to revivify Brick's interest in her and in life seem more assured.

Before Brick and Maggie can move toward a reconciliation, however, Brick needs to see the outcome of deceiving oneself about time, and he does see that outcome when Big Daddy, having been lied to by his family about having beaten his cancer, tells Brick all the things he is going to do now that he believes he is not going to die, all the pleasure with women he will have. Essentially Big Daddy believes that he can have his life again. His refusal to face his own mortality and therefore to renounce the love of women manifests itself in the "lech" Maggie notices that he has for her (just as King Lear believes he can turn his daughter Cordelia into a substitute wife). And Brick sees that his father's protective fantasy is just as false as his own fantasy of exchanging long, high passes with Skipper forever. Brick then blurts out the truth to his father that he is indeed dying of cancer; but Brick is also speaking truth to himself about the impossibility of remaining "boy eternal." Like King Lear, Big Daddy learns that really valuing truth means accepting the knowledge that he must die.

THEOLOGY AND EVOLUTION

Williams's next significant play was *Suddenly Last Summer*, originally part of a double bill with a much shorter play, *Something Unspoken*, and had its successful first run off-Broadway. In it Williams returned to his theological concerns, which occupied his mind and imagination intermittently over the course of his career and culminated when, under the influence of his brother, Dakin, he converted to Catholicism in 1969—though it is unclear how authentic the conversion was. The autobiographical sources of the play are clear, however, for it centers on a homosexual poet, Sebastian, who has been ritually murdered and devoured by a band of impoverished boys upon whom he had preyed to slake his sexual appetites with the justification that God decreed the dominion of the powerful over the weak in nature. His mother, Violet Venable, wants the young Dr. Cukrowicz to perform a lobotomy on Sebastian's cousin and companion, Catherine, so that she will no longer report the truth of what happened to Sebastian. (Williams's sister, Rose, it will be recalled, had undergone a prefrontal lobotomy in 1943 by her mother's consent, and he felt he should have prevented it.) Besides the connection between Catherine and Williams's sister, here is yet another version of the Orpheus myth, with the poet torn apart for his sexual behavior by a band of maddened beings.

The play takes place in the Garden District of New Orleans, where Sebastian has created a jungle garden full of violent colors and the oldest plants on earth, suggestive of the primitive struggle for survival. The garden steams "*with heat after rain,*" an image that recalls the punishment steam room in *Not about Nightingales*, where survival of the strongest was at issue. Sebastian had visited the Encantadas Islands and witnessed for himself the savagery of nature when he saw flesh-eating birds swoop down on newborn baby sea-turtles to turn them over, rip open their soft undersides, and devour them. Williams sets this story in an evolutionary context in order to juxtapose two conflicting theologies, for Sebastian concludes from the spectacle of birds and baby sea-turtles that he has seen the face of God, or all that we can know of Him. Sebastian then uses this vision of God, the self-interest of the powerful, to rationalize his subsequent sexual exploitation of starving boys. Dr. Cukrowicz offers a counter-theology of a compassionate God when he balks at performing a lobotomy on Catherine, for Mrs. Venable had offered to subsidize his medical endeavors if he would perform the operation. Though the play does not end with the doctor's definite refusal, it implies that he will not exploit Catherine for self-interest.

Williams returned to his favored theme of time's dominion over humankind when he collaborated for the last time with Elia Kazan on the Broadway production of *Sweet Bird of Youth* (1959). Though the play did not achieve critical success, it had a substantial run and became a popular film a few years later. The male protagonist, a gigolo named Chance Wayne, who has ruined his own life and that of his fiancée, Heavenly, makes one last desperate attempt to achieve fame and prosperity by attaching himself to a fading Hollywood star, Alexandra Del Lago. But age defeats him, and his enemies destroy him. Just before the curtain closes, Chance addresses the audience memorably, asking not for their pity, nor their understanding, but only for their recognition of him in themselves and for their recognition of "the enemy, time, in us all."

Williams's last major play, as well as his last real stage success, *The Night of the Iguana* recapitulated almost all of his major themes: the impoverished poet at odds with his society, now grown into an old and saintly figure who meets his end serenely; the necessity for tolerance and kindness where unconventional sexual needs express themselves; the desire for human connection to overcome the confinement of the self in loneliness; the longing for freedom and transcendence of the earthly prison; the transient status of life's sojourners. The play's success was followed by two decades of personal and artistic disintegration, with Williams's dependence on drugs and alcohol leading to one crisis after another wherever he traveled across the world, to confinements in mental asylums, paranoid episodes, and the dissolution of old partnerships, such as that with his longtime agent Audrey Wood in 1971. The failure of his 1963 play *The Milk Train Doesn't Stop Here Anymore* put him into a depression, from which he emerged at intervals to write another play only to see it too fail onstage. He tried rewriting earlier plays that had been only moderately successful, such as *Summer and Smoke*, which became *Eccentricities of a Nightingale* in 1965.

WILLIAMS'S DECLINE AND DEATH

The succession of failed productions of his subsequent plays in New York, the site of his previous theatrical triumphs, could be called "the long parade to the graveyard." Only one of these plays lasted more than two months, a humiliating indication that this brilliant playwright either had lost his talent or found only unwilling auditors among the younger generation that dominated the culture of the two decades of Williams's decline. *Slapstick Tragedy* (1966), *The Seven Descents of Myrtle* (1968), *In the Bar of a Tokyo Hotel* (1969), *Small Craft Warnings* (1972—Williams himself played a small role to keep the box office open), *Out Cry* (1973), *The*

Red Devil Battery Sign (Boston, 1975), *A Lovely Sunday for Creve Coeur* (1979), *Clothes for a Summer Hotel* (1980), *Something Cloudy, Something Clear* (1981)—although they all have fine moments of drama or compassion, all suffer from a lack of structural drive and a lack of compelling characters.

On 24 February 1983, Tennessee Williams died as he might have imagined one of his characters dying, according to his idiosyncratic view and experience of life: alone, in a transient state, while staying at yet another hotel in New York City. Death came either from his taking too many sleeping pills or from accidentally getting a small plastic cap (from some sort of medicine applicator) caught in his throat and choking on it. It was the absurd, degrading, and pitiable completion of a tragic personal and professional descent into the maelstrom. Whatever wounds he gave himself both as a man and an artist by his abuse of drugs and alcohol, the plays he produced in the 1940s and 1950s, from the vantage point of the present, have not only endured but have grown ever greater in stature as we have understood and appreciated their artistry more deeply and as we have been able to compare them to the much inferior plays produced by American theater in more recent years. Thanks to film we also have the living record provided by cinematic adaptations of his plays, often by the actors and directors who prepared them first for the stage, so that we may experience for ourselves something like the powerful impact they made in performance on audiences of his time.

[See also Theater in America.]

WORKS

Candles to the Sun (1937)
Spring Storm (1938)
Not about Nightingales (1939)
Battle of Angels (1940)
Stairs to the Roof (1941; rev. ed. Allean Hale, New York, 2000)
The Glass Menagerie (1944)
27 Wagons Full of Cotton and Other One-Act Plays (1945)
Summer and Smoke (1947)
A Streetcar Named Desire (1947)
One Arm and Other Stories (1948)
The Roman Spring of Mrs. Stone (novella, 1950)
The Rose Tattoo (1951)
Camino Real (1953)
Hard Candy: A Book of Stories (1954)
Cat on a Hot Tin Roof (1955)
Baby Doll (screenplay, 1956)
In the Winter of Cities: Poems (1956)
Orpheus Descending (1957)

Garden District: Suddenly Last Summer and *Something Unspoken* (1958)
Sweet Bird of Youth (1959)
Period of Adjustment (1960)
Three Players of a Summer Game and Other Stories (1960)
Night of the Iguana (1961)
The Milk Train Doesn't Stop Here Anymore (1963)
Eccentricities of a Nightingale (1965)
Slapstick Tragedy (1966)
The Two-Character Play (1967)
Kingdom of Earth, a.k.a. *The Seven Descents of Myrtle* (1968)
In the Bar of a Tokyo Hotel (1969)
Dragon County: A Book of Plays (1970)
Small Craft Warnings (1972)
Out Cry (1973)
Memoirs (1975)
The Red Devil Battery Sign (1975)
Vieux Carre (1977)
Where I Live (essays, 1978)
A Lovely Sunday for Creve Coeur (1979)
Clothes for a Summer Hotel (1980)
The Notebook of Trigorin (1981)
Something Cloudy, Something Clear (1981)

FURTHER READING

Boxill, Roger. *Tennessee Williams*. New York, 1988. An excellent compact study of the major plays.

Devlin, Albert J., ed. *Conversations with Tennessee Williams*. Jackson, Miss., 1986.

Kazan, Elia. *A Life*. New York, 1988. An indispensable record not only of his collaboration with Williams, but a vivid account of the theatrical context in which Williams's plays appeared.

Leverich, Lyle. *Tom: The Unknown Tennessee Williams*. New York, 1995. A richly detailed, meticulously researched biography of the playwright to 1945. A second volume is forthcoming.

Miller, Jordan Y., ed. *Twentieth Century Interpretations of* A Streetcar Named Desire. Englewood Cliffs, N.J., 1971. Valuable both for the essays on the play and for reprints of the first reviews.

Roudané, Matthew C., ed. *The Cambridge Companion to Tennessee Williams*. Cambridge, 1997. A recent collection of critical articles analyzing Williams's most important plays, full of new research and valuable insights. Felicia Londré's essay on *Streetcar* stands out among many superior pieces.

Spoto, Donald. *The Kindness of Strangers: The Life of Tennessee Williams*. New York, 1997. A compact one-volume account of the life and career by a good critic.

Stanton, Stephen S., ed. *Tennessee Williams: A Collection of Critical Essays*. Englewood Cliffs, 1977. A good collection of essays by the generation of critics just preceding those in the Cambridge companion, with Donald Costello's analysis of *Orpheus Descending* of particular value.

Williams, Tennessee. *The Theatre of Tennessee Williams*. 8 Vols. New York, 1971–1992.

Williams, Tennessee. *Selected Letters, Vol. 1: 1920–1945*. Edited by Albert J. Devlin and Nancy Tischler. 2000.

Williams, Tennessee. *Tennessee Williams, Plays 1937–1955*, and *Plays, 1957–1980*. Edited by Mel Gussow and Kenneth Holdich. New York, 2000.

Yacowar, Maurice. *Tennessee Williams and Film*. New York, 1977. An insightful study of the films made from Williams's plays based on a firm understanding of the plays themselves.

See also the articles on *The Glass Menagerie* and *A Streetcar Named Desire*, immediately following.

TENNESSEE WILLIAMS'S
THE GLASS MENAGERIE

by Melissa Knox

Tennessee Williams's tragicomic drama *The Glass Menagerie* has attracted the best actors of several generations since it was first published in 1945. He referred to this work as a "memory play." Transforming memory was his life's work as a writer: he remarks at the outset that the scene "is memory," adding that it is therefore "nonrealistic," since memory "takes a lot of poetic license" and is "seated predominantly in the heart."

The play provides a window onto Williams's own memories, telling the story of his struggle to become a writer. Like Tom, the play's narrator, Williams worked at a menial job he resented because of the time and energy it took away from his writing. Like Tom, Williams felt alone in the world. And like Tom, Williams had a mentally disturbed sister of whom he was very fond and whom he wished to protect. He blamed himself for the lobotomy that was performed on her in 1943, although he was not told about it until after the operation. The final scene of *The Glass Menagerie*, in which Tom abandons his mother and sister, probably expresses both Williams's belief that he had failed his sister and his need to escape from the family in order to save himself and develop his art. Williams felt alienated from his family, whose middle-class values conflicted with his aims as an artist, and he felt alienated from the world because he was homosexual at a time when gay men had to hide their sexuality or run the risk of social condemnation or imprisonment.

Born in 1911, some seventy-eight years before the Stonewall riots inaugurated the struggle for gay rights in New York's Greenwich Village, Williams became known for prize-winning dramas about not-so-rugged individualists struggling to make their way in an unsympathetic world. *The Glass Menagerie*—one of two plays that won him the Pulitzer Prize—conforms to this pattern. Indeed, the first short story he ever wrote, at about age thirteen, was entitled "Isolated." By 1970 he felt relaxed enough about his sexuality to remark, in a televised interview with David Frost, "Geez, I don't want to be involved in some sort of a scandal, but I've covered the waterfront" (in Van Antwerp and Johns, 1984). In the same interview

he expressed his belief that the "greatest happiness" was "felt in moments of great tenderness between two people" because "we all have a great desire to escape from ourselves and to feel joined to another human being." Above all he remained self-analytical, probing his own psyche and that of others, at one point briefly undergoing psychoanalysis. His psychic explorations had literary roots as well; as Matthew C. Roudané (1997) remarks: "From Hart Crane and D. H. Lawrence [Williams] took the imagery of repressed desires." Williams's love of D. H. Lawrence is legendary—he met the writer in Taos, New Mexico, and discussed tragedy with him. A scene in *The Glass Menagerie* shows Tom in a rage because his mother confiscates his D. H. Lawrence.

The main themes of *The Glass Menagerie*, in particular Williams's escape from the loving tyranny of his mother—whose ferocious facade of cheerfulness in the face of her despair exhausts him—and from his quietly disturbed sister, are summed up in a warning Williams puts into the mouth of Amanda Wingfield, the mother in the play: "the future becomes the present, the present the past, and the past turns into everlasting regret if you don't plan for it!"

Divided into seven scenes that move between past, present, and future in relation to the wishes and conflicts of the three main characters, the play reveals the inner lives of the devoted but domineering Amanda Wingfield and her children: the pathologically shy Laura, who limps noticeably and who is lost in her world of little glass creatures; and Tom, who works at his menial job to support his mother and sister but who is always sneaking off to the men's room to write poems. The absent father whose portrait is prominently displayed in their home looms large: Tom and Amanda both refer to him as a man who worked for the telephone company and fell in love with long distances.

Scene 1 opens with Tom's introduction to the political unrest that forms the backdrop of the play, which is set in the 1930s. America is blind to its own crumbling economy, he relates, and the conditions producing revolution in Spain produce only "disturbances of labour" here.

A joyless family dinner follows, with Amanda nagging Tom throughout the meal, Tom protesting, and Laura, as usual, saying as little as possible, speaking only to announce that she will bring in the dessert. Amanda insists that Laura remain seated so that she will be "fresh and pretty" for the "gentlemen callers" who never appear. An aging Southern belle, Amanda loves to reiterate tales of her afternoons entertaining gentlemen callers and particularly of the time that seventeen of them showed up one Sunday. At the end of the scene Laura confides to her brother that their mother is afraid she'll be an old maid.

Scene 2 shows Laura washing and polishing her collection of glass animals until she hears her mother approaching on the fire escape. Nervously Laura pushes away her ornaments and pretends to be studying for her typing class. When Amanda walks in looking ostentatiously pained, Laura knows something is wrong, but it takes half the scene to discover the source of her sorrows, namely, Amanda's accidental discovery that Laura had dropped out of the typing class months earlier. Laura attended only briefly, it seems, vomiting when she was given a speed-typing test, and Amanda despairs of Laura ever being able to support herself or to marry. She begins again to fantasize that Laura might marry, asking her if she has ever liked "some boy." Laura confesses to an interest in a boy who sang in her high school production of *The Pirates of Penzance* and who jokingly called her "Blue Roses" because he misheard her when he asked why she had been absent, and she told him she had had pleurosis. She has not seen him for the six years that have elapsed since they graduated. Amanda aggressively insists that Laura will marry, and Laura begs off with: "I'm—crippled!" Amanda denies this, as she denies all unpleasantness not conforming to her desired vision of the world, and urges Laura to cultivate charm, adding that Laura's father had had plenty of charm.

Scene 3 is made up of several mini-scenes. In the first, Tom announces that his mother, after discovering that Laura had dropped out of business college, has become ever more obsessed with capturing "a gentleman caller." Then the scene shifts to Amanda. Determined to earn enough money to provide Laura with suitable clothing and a dowry, she channels her considerable energies into a telephone campaign to lure subscribers for a magazine called *The Home-maker's Companion*. With heavy-handed Southern charm she tries to bowl over potential lady readers and alienates one of them, who hangs up on her. Lights dim and the scene shifts again to Tom and Amanda in the midst of a violent argument. Amanda has discovered among Tom's possessions a library book that irritates her genteel prudery, one of D. H. Lawrence's novels, which are known for their lyrical eroticism and are now regarded as classics. She returns it. Enraged, Tom yells that there is nothing in his life that he can call his own; Amanda interferes with every aspect of it. Tom starts to walk out and she orders him to stay: "Come back here, Tom Wingfield! I'm not through talking to you!" He pleads with her; she accuses him of doing "things" that he must be ashamed of. Ultimately provoked beyond endurance when she refuses to believe he is going to the movies, where he goes every night, he concocts an elaborate pseudo-confession, mocking her with images of himself engaging in wildly illicit behavior—visiting opium dens, working as a hired assassin, carrying "a tommy gun in a violin case." Carried away by his fantasy, he imagines his mother flying on a broomstick "over Blue Mountain with seventeen gentleman callers" and then calls her an ugly witch. He throws his coat, accidentally hitting Laura's glass collection. Amanda is aghast and says she won't speak to him until he apologizes.

Scene 4 finds a drunken Tom returning home in the wee hours of the morning. Laura lets him in, he has an hour of sleep, and then his mother's alarm goes off at six, as usual, and she commences her morning chant: "Rise and Shine!" Since she is not speaking to Tom, she urges Laura to tell him to rise and shine. Laura pleads with him to apologize, and in a painful, emotional scene, he does so. Amanda reveals her love and deep fears for her children, the devotion that is usually overlaid by her aggressive anxiety. The moment of gentle communication passes, then Amanda demandingly pleads that he bring a male friend from work to dinner to provide Laura with at least a gentleman caller, if not a husband. Amanda reveals that she knows Tom is planning to desert the family and join the merchant marine. She tells him not to do so until Laura has some "clean living" young man to protect her. Tom reluctantly promises to provide a gentleman caller.

Scene 5 begins in the early evening, the family having just finished supper. Amanda henpecks Tom, urging him to comb his hair and telling him he smokes too much. Tom retires to the fire escape, contrasting the sensual atmosphere of the Paradise Dance Hall next door with the dismal state of the war-torn world. Hitler's Germany and Spain's Guernica, devastated by bombing in the Spanish Civil War and later memorialized in the famous painting by Pablo Picasso, loom in his thoughts. His inner world seems to mirror what he sees around him, divided between a dread of being attacked and a longing for erotic freedom and adventures.

Amanda joins him on the fire escape, further eroding his attempt to find a little peace. Tom casually intimates that he has invited a young man he works with home to dinner the next evening. Amanda reacts with joy and panic, wanting to polish all her wedding silver in the young man's honor and insisting that Tom make sure he isn't a drinker. In her mind the future dinner guest is already Laura's husband, and Tom tries to calm her down, knowing his attempts are futile.

In scene 6, Tom recounts how he brought home Jim, the friend he worked with, for dinner, knowing that Jim and Laura had gone to the same high school but not whether they had been acquainted. Jim was the star of his class in many areas, Laura the reverse. Friendly with Jim, who jokingly calls him "Shakespeare," Tom muses on Jim's upcoming visit. The scene changes to the Wingfield apartment, whose decor has been utterly transformed by Amanda's frantic efforts. Amanda scolds Laura for trembling; the quietly resentful Laura allows her mother to dress her, even to poke falsies into her bust. Amanda then goes offstage and reappears dressed in a "girlish frock" of her youth: the effect is almost grotesque. Capering around the room showing it off, she mentions the name of the dinner guest, Jim O'Connor, sending Laura into a state of terror. The young man is none other than the boy Laura has had a crush on since high school, thoughts of whom have in fact constituted much of her inner life ever since. She tells her mother that she will not come to dinner, and her mother grimly refuses to excuse her. The doorbell rings, and Amanda forces Laura to answer it. Immediately Laura recognizes the object of her secret dreams and hurtles back into the living room, leaving Tom to excuse her shyness. Tom and Jim discuss their own dreams; it develops that Tom, who has now secretly joined the merchant marine, using the money for the family's light bill to pay his union dues, is about to be fired.

Amanda enters in her girlish garb; the effect is that of Bette Davis in *Whatever Happened to Baby Jane*, the movie about an aging child actress who continues to dress as a young girl. Initially shocked, Jim warms to Amanda's flirtatious manner. She calls to Laura (who answers faintly from the living room) that they will not sit down to supper without her. Faint, ill at ease, Laura joins them but is so obviously out of sorts that her mother allows her to return to the living room. While she sobs silently on the sofa, the others begin dinner.

As scene 7 opens, the characters are literally as well as figuratively plunged into darkness, since Tom has not payed the light bill. The ever-resourceful Amanda lights candles and propels Jim into the living room to be with Laura, insisting that Tom remain with her and wash dishes.

A pathetically romantic scene ensues, bittersweet since the well-meaning and very decent Jim has no idea how deeply he figures in Laura's fantasies. The two renew their acquaintance; Jim is flattered to hear that Laura remembers what a good singer he was and came to see all three of his performances in *The Pirates of Penzance*. She reminds him that he nicknamed her Blue Roses and why he did so. They look at her glass menagerie together, and Laura reveals a sly wit. Admiring her shyness and prettiness he draws her out, trying to make her less self-conscious about her crippled leg. He dances with her and kisses her as a friendly gesture, only half realizing what a storm he stirs in her, and awkwardly apologizes to the lovestruck Laura that he is engaged to be married. She contains her sorrows, giving him her favorite glass creature, a unicorn whose horn he has accidentally broken. Since the unicorn is in folklore a creature who can only be captured by a virgin, Laura's gesture underscores her otherworldly, vestal character. At this painful moment Amanda rushes into the room with lemonade. Jim leaves as gracefully as he can, confessing his engagement. Family turmoil ensues: Amanda accuses Tom, and Tom leaves in a rage, violently slamming the door, making it clear that he is gone for good. As he delivers a final speech about what he did after leaving the family, Amanda is seen on the couch beside Laura, consoling her.

FURTHER READING

Roudané, Matthew C., ed. *The Cambridge Companion to Tennessee Williams*. Cambridge, 1997.

Van Antwerp, Margaret A., and Sally Johns, eds. *Tennessee Williams: Dictionary of Literary Biography Documentary Series, An Illustrated Chronicle*. Afterword by Louis Auchincloss. Detroit, 1984. Extremely useful sourcebook containing photographs of Williams as a child and as an adult along with reviews, essays, and interviews.

Williams, Tennessee. *Four Plays*. London, 1957. Includes helpful and revealing production notes by Williams.

See also the article on Tennessee Williams that precedes this article and the article on *A Streetcar Named Desire* that follows.

TENNESSEE WILLIAMS'S
A STREETCAR NAMED DESIRE

by Philip Parry

Tennessee Williams's *A Streetcar Named Desire* (1947), aided by Elia Kazan's conversion of it into a highly successful film in 1951, is probably the most widely celebrated of all American plays. Blanche DuBois and Stanley Kowalski—who, because of the film's immense influence, are not always clearly distinguished from Vivien Leigh and Marlon Brando—have achieved iconic status, and the struggle between them has escaped the confines of art to symbolize many oppositions, some ancient, others modishly contemporary: rural/urban, past/present, creative/destructive, imaginative/practical, weak/strong, male/female, gay/straight, passive/active, native/immigrant, classy/classless. The list is seemingly endless, and the immense interpretative industry and ingenuity of twentieth- and twenty-first-century criticism ensure its continued growth. The danger, indeed, is that this abundant symbolic afterlife will overwhelm the play that gave rise to it.

Success on this scale is always a mixed blessing and can be burdensome. Kazan's capturing on film of Brando's stage performance is, for example, both benign and malignant; benign because it permits inspection of a performance that would otherwise have been lost with the passage of time, malignant because, while ensuring that Kowalski remains one of the great male roles in American theater, it has set up a standard and a style against which every subsequent Stanley is judged. Some actors try to imitate Brando, fail, and are censured. Others, with purer intentions, are damned for not even trying. (It is surely significant that when Split Britches, the lesbian and feminist theater company, staged *Belle Reprieve* [1991], a gender-questioning version of *Streetcar*, Peggy Shaw played Stanley as "a butch lesbian" but deliberately set out to imitate Brando, even going so far as to replicate famous stills from the film. "You want realism?" Stella ["a woman disguised as a woman"] asks Blanche. "With Marlon Brando and Vivien Leigh?" is Blanche's response.)

CONTROVERSIES

There is no such thing as neutral summary. Modern disputes over aspects of *Streetcar*'s plot, particularly its sexual aspects, have made this uncomfortable truth stand out clearly: the following summary may seem to be neutral but inevitably privileges some interpretations and distances others. *Streetcar* records a visit that Blanche DuBois, a southern schoolteacher, pays to her married, and pregnant, sister (Stella Kowalski) and her husband (Stanley Kowalski) in their apartment in the run-down, lower-class French Quarter of New Orleans. Blanche—edgy and distraught and imperious in some of her attitudes—immediately registers disapproval of the area ("Only Poe! Only Mr. Edgar Allan Poe!—could do it justice") and of the inadequate sleeping arrangements that the Kowalskis make for her. ("What kind of bed's this—one of those collapsible things?") Her airs and graces, backed up by his suspicion that she is drinking heavily, irritate Stanley. In particular, he wonders why she has made an unannounced visit, suspects her of funding a lavish lifestyle through fraud, and resolves to make enquiries. Meanwhile Blanche meets one of Stanley's friends—Harold Mitchell (Mitch)—and, since both feel that it is time to settle down, they begin a tentative flirtation. During a date, Blanche gives Mitch a highly colored account of her past life: when a mere girl she was briefly married to a young man who killed himself when his homosexuality was discovered. This account is partially confirmed by Stella ("This beautiful and talented young man was a degenerate") as she tries to defend Blanche against Stanley's claims that she is immoral and promiscuous and has been sacked from her job and drummed out of Laurel, the small Mississippi town where she lived. Stella's defense of her sister, a plea for sympathy rather than a denial of the charges, fails to move Stanley. Choosing to make the announcement during her birthday party, he orders Blanche to leave within a week. Later that same night Stella goes into a hospital to give birth and Stanley, "who has had a few drinks on the way and has brought some quart beer bottles home with him," rapes an already tipsy Blanche. In an episode of plot that is merely reported to us, Stella—anxious to preserve her marriage and no doubt influenced by what she knows of her sister's loose living—refuses to accept Blanche's account of what has happened. ("I couldn't believe her story and go on living with Stanley.") Driven wild by drink and shame, fear, and incipient madness, Blanche is taken away to a mental hospital while Stella and Stanley (in the play more obviously than in the film) resume their married life: "Now, honey. Now, love. Now, now, love. *[He kneels beside her and his fingers find the opening of her blouse]* Now, now, love. Now, love. . . . ").

In 1945, during the earliest stages of planning *Streetcar*, Williams had determined neither its title nor its ending. The play might be called "The Moth," "The Poker Night," "The Primary Colors," or "Blanche's Chair in the Moon," and Blanche might just leave, or go mad, or (like Anna Karenina) she might throw herself in front of a train. (Trains persist in the finished play and the noise they make punctuates its action symbolically.) Later, in a more jocular mood, he imagined her escaping from her asylum by seducing an attractive young doctor. He chose, however, to adopt a grim ending, made grimmer still if one believes that Blanche—like Williams's sister Rose in 1943—is taken away to be lobotomized. But even if, for lack of evidence, one rejects this hypothesis, one cannot doubt that Blanche is being punished. Why?

As Stanley tells Blanche in *Belle Reprieve*: "The woman in this play gets raped and goes crazy in the end." Blanche replies: "I don't want to get raped and go crazy. I just wanted to wear a nice frock." Williams's depiction of the fateful outcome of the sexual conflict between Blanche and Stanley is controversial now, partly because there have been changes in society's moral outlook but also because fate, some critics insist, is just a dishonest synonym for contrivance. Blanche, an extreme form of this argument suggests, is the entirely innocent, even saintly, victim of unresolved tensions in Williams's attitude toward his own sexual (specifically homosexual) waywardness. Thus, *Streetcar* is a wish-fulfillment fantasy that fulfills by proxy its author's need to feel punished. Intimate biographical speculation of this kind is always suspect, though in Williams's case beguilingly attractive, but is scarcely necessary. Blanche's fate is not simply—still less is it mechanically—the pressure of the past upon the present. It flows, indeed, from her nature and her situation; but her situation, though not entirely of Stanley's making, is shaped by his nature and situation. That they are fatefully linked both agree. The first time she laid eyes on him, Blanche tells Mitch, "I thought to myself that man is my executioner! That man will destroy me." This prescience is shared by Stanley: "We've had this date with each other from the beginning!" is his view of things.

Belying this apparent reciprocity, there is revealed as the play unfolds a profound inequality that modern sexual liberalism stoutly resists. Blanche, a sexual predator whose victims are adolescents, is herself the victim of predation; the equally predatory Stanley, whose victim is adult, escapes without punishment or censure. There are patterns here, of biter bit and of the revenge of the exploited, that are clarified if Stanley is shown to be significantly younger than Blanche. Brando ("a gentle, lovely guy, a man of extraordinary beauty") was eight or ten years younger than Williams had meant Stanley to be and fifteen years younger than Jessica Tandy, who was the original Blanche. The effect of this casting was, Williams said in 1981, to reduce our sense of Stanley's "black-dyed" villainy. Instead, he wanted to argue (as Elia Kazan records in his autobiography) that it is misunderstanding—"a thing not a person"—that destroys Blanche. This exculpation of Stanley, through seeing him as the amoral agent of a moral purpose, is inevitably not acceptable to everyone. In *Out on Stage: Lesbian and Gay Theatre in the Twentieth Century* (1999), a self-consciously revisionist re-reading of the play in which he assumes that Blanche (like Rose Williams) is punitively lobotomized, Alan Sinfield has argued that Blanche's sexual relations with young men are not predatory. ("Her sleeping with boys was gentle and loving.") It is Stanley and Stella, the latter through her support of her husband, "who violate her, body and mind." Because victims of domestic sexual abuse are sometimes disbelieved by close relatives, there are the beginnings of an argument here, but one that is marginal to the play, for Williams does not seem at all supportive of Blanche's promiscuity or of the notion that her actions are practically victimless. Nonetheless, Williams's remarkable indulgence toward Stanley remains controversial and (though *Streetcar*, like every play, is a symbolic object) cannot be wholly or satisfactorily accounted for in symbolic terms.

PERFORMANCE

Streetcar plays an honorable role in the history of world theater, of twentieth-century cinema, of American acting and play producing, of Broadway and Hollywood. In short, it has become an American institution. But in the presence of so much critical heritage—or baggage—we need to remind ourselves that every play with a future has a present that is more important than its past. Nonetheless, one way of discounting the past is by knowing about it;

whether theater history is deadening or liberating depends upon how we use it.

Only the third of his plays to be given a professional production, *Streetcar* was an event in Williams's life that helped to shape his subsequent career. It had been in turn shaped by the two plays that preceded it. *Battle of Angels*, later reworked as *Orpheus Descending* (first produced in 1957), premiered in Boston in 1940. Its steamy brew of sex and fire-raising, religion and confectionery—set in an all-purpose store in an "old-fashioned town in the Deep South"—shocked Boston's licensing authorities, who brought its performance to an abrupt halt. Doubtless recognizing that the time for sexual candor lay thirty years ahead and willing (as he always was) to compromise in order to acquire and retain an audience, Williams drew in his horns and produced *The Glass Menagerie*, a delicate but immensely durable study of emotional impoverishment and domestic frustration, that opened in Chicago in 1944 and transferred to Broadway in March of the following year. Eventually, after a slow start, both the play and its leading actress, Laurette Taylor (ravaged by drink and soon to die), were greeted with immense acclaim, which ensured that Williams would find it easy to get *Streetcar* staged. Elia Kazan, on the strength of what he had done just a few months earlier with Arthur Miller's *All My Sons* (first produced in 1947), was chosen as director. He brought immense strength and energy to the production and transferred this energy to his filmed version, but he was unsympathetic to some aspects of what Williams had written (to the play's half-professed, half-suppressed homoeroticism most markedly). For this reason, and perhaps because his brother (and financial backer) was a psychotherapist, he imposed a rigid Freudian style of interpretation upon it by assigning specific "spines" or motivations to each character in turn. Though these are sometimes interesting (especially the claim, nowhere explicit in anything that is said, that Mitch resents the influence of his sick mother and takes up with Blanche in order to spite her), they are the rules of thumb of practical play directing, lack interpretative generosity, and are flattening and dated. Eventually, this highly interventionist style of direction would do real damage to Williams when Kazan forced him to write a palpably inferior replacement for the third act of *Cat on a Hot Tin Roof* (first produced in 1955). Their collaboration survived this atrocity, however, and Kazan was also to direct *Sweet Bird of Youth* (first produced in 1959), perhaps Williams's last unequivocal success.

Kazan and Williams then proceeded to cast the play. Brando, whom Williams admired extravagantly—describing him as "probably the greatest living actor ... greater than Olivier"—gave an excellent reading and, despite his youthful inexperience, easily landed the part. Blanche was given to Jessica Tandy, an English actress of impeccable orthodoxy who had been impressive earlier in 1947 as Lucretia Collins in Williams's *Portrait of a Madonna* (1940). The contrast in ages and acting styles between Brando, who improvised business as he thought fit, and Tandy, who valued and provided consistency, became one of the hallmarks of Kazan's production and perfectly expressed the social disparity between Blanche and Stanley. (Though her performance was widely admired, Tandy was replaced by Vivien Leigh in the film version. Leigh, also an English actress, had been Scarlett O'Hara in *Gone with the Wind*, which generated a set of associations that bore down interestingly upon her role as Williams's pasteboard southern Belle. Her slightly phony accent and actressy demeanor helped, once more, to mark out the distance between Blanche and Stanley.)

The other two major roles were given to Kim Hunter (Stella) and Karl Malden (Mitch), both of whom were retained for the film. On stage (history relates) and in the film (as we can see for ourselves), they gave moving and skillful performances which remind us that *Streetcar* is not just a play about Stanley and Blanche. Undue concentration upon the two leads fails to acknowledge the careful way in which Williams makes us realize that no relationship between two people is ever simply a relationship between just two people. Blanche's relationship with Stanley is accurately described only in terms of Blanche's relationship with her sister and of Stanley's relationship with his wife. What both binds Blanche and Stanley together and forces them apart is a rivalry for Stella's favors that is expressed in both time and space. Blanche and Stella share memories of their youth at Belle Reve, "a great big place with white columns," that puts the apartment that Stanley provides to shame. His awareness of the social distance between his family and theirs ("The Kowalskis and the DuBoises have different notions") expresses itself as a desire to snatch Stella away from her memories of her family home. ("I pulled you down off them columns, and how you loved it.") This desire, however, is coupled with another: to safeguard Belle Reve from Blanche's dishonest mismanagement so as to keep it, or the proceeds of its sale, intact for Stella and himself (hence his invoking of the inheritance sections of the Napoleonic Code). Blanche's visit he sees as an invasion of his own private space; Laurel, the town she has left, is "not in my territory," he reminds her as, in effect, he accuses her of trespassing. This mixture of sexual rivalry, social distance, and territorial hostility is very potent.

Viewing this triangular relationship from another vantage point, we can see that Stella and Stanley are also rivals. When he rapes Blanche (and the same would be as true, or even truer, had the sex been consensual), Stanley robs Stella of unsullied access to memories of a time when she was independent of him. A similar pattern imposes itself on Blanche's putative relationship with Mitch. Now it is Stanley who is the unexpressed third point of the triangle, for Mitch and he (buddies in the army) have a shared past that will be disrupted if Mitch and Blanche marry. Thus, Stanley resents Blanche's attempt to steal Mitch from him and reacts to her schemes of seduction as though she were insulting him. When asked why he is interfering, it is to his shared past with Mitch that he appeals for justification. ("We were in the same outfit together.") In short, and Kazan's film captures this aspect of the play beautifully, Stella and Mitch are essential components of Williams's plot; they both shape, and are shaped by, Blanche and Stanley.

Finally—though he never appears on stage, is misrepresented in many productions, and was all but written out of Kazan's film—there is Allen Grey, Blanche's young, dead, homosexual husband. He is the unexpressed but unexpungible element in every relationship that she has with all subsequent men—or military cadets or school pupils or newspaper boys. His death, relived by Blanche as she recounts it to Mitch in the sixth of *Streetcar*'s eleven scenes, is emotionally as well as physically at the play's midpoint, the most potent symbol of how the past reaches out to assert its sovereignty over the present. Blanche, riven by guilty regret, blames herself for the cruel way in which she upbraided him ("I saw! I know! You disgust me") and for its disastrous consequence. ("He'd stuck the revolver into his mouth, and fired—so that the back of his head had been—blown away.") Because the dead can no longer be killed, there is nothing that prevents him reaching out from the past to poison Blanche's future. Of course *Streetcar* is not a ghost story. To say that Allen destroys Blanche is merely a way of saying that she destroys herself, but one that preserves her status as a tragic heroine. Williams, haunted by his own family memories and prey to a thousand regrets, was always an acute observer of how the dead live on.

He also persistently revisited his dominant themes and images. In *Cat on a Hot Tin Roof*, one of his finest plays, he probes another emotional triangle, whose points are Brick Pollitt, his wife Maggie, and Skipper (who is in love with Brick but who sleeps with Maggie in order to deny this unacceptable truth). Skipper's death, far from reducing this triangular relationship to a straight line, ensures that he will forever remain an impediment to Brick's and Maggie's effective union. Here is additional evidence that Williams is one of the great American dramatists of the failure of love and of the crippling influence of the past.

[*See also* Theater in America.]

FURTHER READING

Bourne, Bette, et al. *Belle Reprieve*. In *Split Britches: Lesbian Practice/Feminist Performance*, edited by Sue-Ellen Case. London and New York, 1996.

Kazan, Elia. *Elia Kazan: A Life*. New York, 1988.

Kazan, Elia. "Notebook for *A Streetcar Named Desire*." In *Directors on Directing: The Emergence of the Modern Theatre*, edited by Toby Cole and Helen Krich Chinoy. London, 1964.

Kolin, Philip C. *Williams: A Streetcar Named Desire*. Cambridge and New York, 2000.

Leverich, Lyle. *Tom: The Unknown Tennessee Williams*. New York, 1995. The standard biography and a fine work of scholarship, but does not go beyond March 1945.

Manso, Peter. *Brando*. London, 1994. The two chapters devoted to the stage and film versions of *Streetcar* are immensely illuminating.

Murphy, Brenda. *Tennessee Williams and Elia Kazan: A Collaboration in the Theatre*. Cambridge, 1992. This standard work contains a very full discussion of the original production of *Streetcar*.

Rader, Dotson. "Tennessee Williams (1981)." In *The Paris Review Interviews: Playwrights at Work*, edited by George Plimpton. London, 2000. An interview, conducted by a close friend, in which Williams speaks with considerable candor.

Roudané, Matthew C. ed. *The Cambridge Companion to Tennessee Williams*. Cambridge, 1997.

Sinfield, Alan. *Out on Stage: Lesbian and Gay Theatre in the Twentieth Century*. New Haven, Conn., and London 1999. A chapter titled "Reading Tennessee Williams" gives a fascinating though controversial account of Williams generally and of *Streetcar* in particular.

Spoto, Donald. *The Kindness of Strangers: The Life of Tennessee Williams*. London, 1985.

Williams, Tennessee. *Memoirs*. Garden City, N.Y., 1975.

Williams, Tennessee. *The Selected Letters of Tennessee Williams, 1920–1945*. Edited by Albert J. Devlin and Nancy M. Tischler. New York, 2000.

Williams, Tennessee. *The Theatre of Tennessee Williams*. Vol. 1. New York, 1971. The first of eight volumes. Aside from *Streetcar*, includes *Battle of Angels* and *The Glass Menagerie*.

See also the articles on Tennessee Williams and *The Glass Menagerie* that precede this article.

TERRY TEMPEST WILLIAMS

by Andrea Ross

Born on 8 September 1955 to a fifth-generation Mormon family and raised in Salt Lake City, Utah, Terry Lynn Tempest was the first child of Diane Dixon Tempest and John Henry Tempest III. Her publications include children's books, essays, stories, and creative nonfiction, all of which focus on human interaction with the environment. A naturalist and a writer, her engagement with the natural world began when she was a child, as she hiked and identified birds with her paternal grandmother, Kathryn "Mimi" Blackett, in the Bear River Migratory Bird Sanctuary near her home by the Great Salt Lake. As a result of her early exposure to ornithology, much of her writing is populated with birds, especially *Refuge: An Unnatural History of Family and Place* (1991). Williams's grandmother also sparked her fervor for environmental preservation by introducing her to conservationist Rachel Carson's writing. Growing up Mormon helped shape Williams's sense of ritual and showed her the importance of family, notions that proved germane to her development as a writer celebrating landscape, homeplace, and spirituality. Also significant to her writing is the Mormon tradition valuing storytelling as a way of clarifying values and self-identity. At the University of Utah, Williams pursued her love of both story and of science, majoring in English and minoring in biology. During college she met Brooke Williams, who shared her deep love for nature; they married in June 1975. She also pursued a master's degree in environmental education at the University of Utah, which involved teaching Navajo children at Montezuma Creek, Utah. She was hired in 1979 as the curator of education at the Utah Museum of Natural History, a job she continued to hold when she published her first books in 1984. During her tenure as naturalist-in-residence at the museum from 1986 to 1996, she published eight more books.

In 1991, after the publication of *Refuge*, as Williams's life and writing increasingly focused on activism, *Newsweek* magazine highlighted her as "someone likely to make a considerable impact on the political, economic, and environmental issues facing the western states this decade." By 1995, the *Utne Reader* listed her as a leading visionary—"a person who could change your life." Since then, she has received fellowships from the Guggenheim and Lannan Foundations as well as a Lila Wallace–Reader's Digest Award. In 2000, Williams was a Distinguished Lecturer at the Center for the American West at the University of Colorado, Boulder.

EARLY ACCLAIM AND PUBLICATIONS

Two of Williams's earliest published works were children's books—*The Secret Language of Snow* (1984), coauthored with Ted Major, and *Between Cattails* (1985). *The Secret Language of Snow* was named best children's science book of 1984 by the New York Academy of Sciences and serves as an early example of Williams's engagement with both natural history and the power of language; it is a study in cultural ecology as it explicates the various names for different kinds of snow in Inuit culture. *Between Cattails* explores human connection with nature in another way, teaching about wetlands ecosystems and the need for their preservation.

In the essay "Labor," in *Red: Passion and Patience in the Desert* (2001), she describes her choice not to become a mother as a part of her radically individualistic thinking; she is an outspoken woman without children who practices her own earth-based spirituality in tension with the highly patriarchal Mormon religion that values progeny and has strict canons. Still, she identifies herself as a Mormon culturally and spiritually. Similar to the way Annie Dillard treats nature as a spiritual entity in her book *Pilgrim at Tinker Creek* (1974), Williams creates her particular version of Mormonism by infusing it with ecstatic communion with nature, and a radically inquisitive outlook that can, at times, resemble scientific inquiry. Her books all deeply reflect this belief system. Indeed, Williams has said that each of her books "has turned on a question."

TRADITIONS OF STORYTELLING

Like her fellow environmental author Barry Lopez, Williams values the practice of storytelling. *Pieces of White*

Shell: A Journey to Najavoland (1984) was Williams's first book for adults, an outgrowth of her master's thesis, and her exploration of the question, "What stories do we tell that evoke a sense of place?" The book, which won the 1984 Southwest Book Award for creative nonfiction, weaves traditional Navajo folklore into her stories about flora and fauna, illuminating her sense of what it is to be a storyteller in the Mormon tradition.

Coyote's Canyon (1989), represents a further evolution of her personal storytelling tradition, and serves as a testimony to Williams's interest in mining the stories of one's own culture. In her *An Unspoken Hunger* (1994), she says that the "most radical act we can commit is to stay home." Williams dedicates *Coyote's Canyon* to the Coyote Clan, "an informal following of hundreds, maybe even thousands, of people who are quietly subversive on behalf of the land," people she originally addressed in her eulogy to fellow desert conservationist Edward Abbey. Throughout her work, Williams pays tribute to the archetypal Coyote, master of the dual forces of tricksterism and creation. In fact, she has adopted Coyote as a kind of totem. Perhaps in keeping with Coyote's dualism, Williams contrasts the traditionally male portrayal of Coyote with her own distinctly feminine approach to convincing her audience of the importance of revering and preserving wilderness. The stories hint at the kinds of magic that a close relationship with the land can evoke. Whether the protagonist is a woman who leaves her family in the city to camp alone in the wilderness to regain her sense of self, or a woman who dances in the desert as a form of spiritual communion, these stories build a narrative path to the realm of those learning to care for themselves and the earth.

Refuge employs a painfully personal mode of story-telling as it deals with the connections Williams perceives between her mother's battle with ovarian cancer and the devastating flooding caused by the rising waters of the Great Salt Lake in 1983, which imperils avian habitat in her beloved Bear River Migratory Bird Refuge. The book attempts to answer the question, "How do we find refuge in change?" as it links human tragedy and environmental tragedy; each chapter is titled with the name of a refuge bird whose residence the rising waters endangers, and each chapter's subtitle lists the level of the rising lake. In this way, Williams compares and tracks the course of her mother's illness and eventual death with the desecration of a landscape sacred to her.

Refuge, which was named Book-of-the-Year by the Association for Mormon Letters, became required reading in many college courses in ecological literature. It is considered a prominent ecofeminist statement, as it explores the relationship between the oppression and degradation of women and that of the environment. The widely anthologized epilogue, "The Clan of One-Breasted Women," galvanizes the idea of a connection between the desecration of the earth and of women. Williams recounts that a year after her mother's death, she told her father of a strange recurring dream in which she saw "a flash of light at night in the desert." Her father confirms that her "dream" is based in reality, and that one night in 1957, while driving home to Utah from California, she and her family witnessed a nuclear test explosion. Williams believes that the legacy of cancer in her family is a direct result of their status as "downwinders," people exposed to radioactive fallout from nuclear tests. She interweaves this personal anecdote with facts about the 1951–1962 aboveground nuclear tests, and an account of her arrest for civil disobedience for trespassing onto the Nevada Test Site to protest nuclear testing. After her arrest, she and nine other female protesters were stranded by the police in the open desert several miles outside of a town, where, instead of feeling helpless, they were heartened, because they already felt at home in the environment, "soul-centered and strong."

POLITICS, WILDERNESS, AND FAITH

After the publication of *Refuge*, Williams continued to explore political aspects of her connection to nature. In her book of essays *An Unspoken Hunger: Stories from the Field* (1994), she looks at "how a poetics of place translates into a politics of place." These essays are similar in trope to those of *Coyote's Canyon* in their highlighting of various people, including such noted environmentalists as Aldo Leopold, Edward Abbey, Margaret Murie, and Rachel Carson. This book touches upon ways of combining art and activism and promotes the importance of creating a community of people committed to vigilance on behalf of nature.

In her following book, *Desert Quartet* (1995), Williams returns from activism to her erotic connection to the earth. The book seeks to define an erotics of place by asking how one can have reciprocal, physical communion with the land. Williams's trope of ecstatic connection is drawn out further in *Leap: A Traveler in the Garden of Delights* (2000), in which she recounts her seven-year obsession with fifteenth-century Flemish painter Hieronymous Bosch's triptych masterpiece *Garden of Earthly Delights*. Drawing upon fifty handwritten journals of notes, Williams creates a figurative hike through Heaven, Hell, and the Garden of Earthly Delights, threading into it her ideas about environmental awareness and addressing her passionate but uneasy relationship with the Mormon church. In keeping with the activist message of many of her other works, the central idea in *Leap* is that the "greatest sin is the sin of indifference."

IN DEFENSE OF REDROCK WILDERNESS

Red: Passion and Patience in the Desert (2001) is a meditation on identifying oneself by one's home landscape, as well as a call to action in support of redrock wilderness in the American Southwest. In this volume, Williams abstracts from the texts of her books *Coyote's Canyon* and *Desert Quartet*, as well as other previously published and new pieces, including a book she edited, *Testimony: Writers of the West Speak on Behalf of Utah Wilderness* (1996). In addition, *Red* provides the reader with appendices that include a copy of the Redrock Wilderness Act, a proposal to preserve America's Redrock Wilderness, and a map of the area in question. In the same way that *Testimony* is a call to action (it was sent out to legislators to convince them to preserve southern Utah's wilderness), *Red* is a sourcebook for the citizen activist. The essays in *Red* underscore her passion for Utah's wildlands. This book is a kind of Terry Tempest Williams reader; it covers her major tropes of passion for the land and for life, conservation, earth-based spirituality, and activism for preservation of the wild.

SELECTED WORKS

Pieces of White Shell: A Journey to Najavoland (1984)
The Secret Language of Snow (1984)
Between Cattails (1985)
Coyote's Canyon (1989)
Refuge: An Unnatural History of Family and Place (1991)
An Unspoken Hunger: Stories from the Field (1994)
Desert Quartet (1995)
Great and Peculiar Beauty: A Utah Reader (1995)
Testimony: Writers of the West Speak on Behalf of Utah Wilderness (1996)
New Genesis: A Mormon Reader on Land and Community (1998)
Leap: A Traveler in the Garden of Delights (2000)
Red: Passion and Patience in the Desert (2001)

FURTHER READING

Anderson, Lorraine. "Terry Tempest Williams." In *American Nature Writers*, edited by John Elder, pp. 973–988. New York, 1996. Extensive biographical information. Note especially the comparisons with other western writers.

Armbruster, Karla. "Rewriting a Genealogy with the Earth: Women and Nature in the Works of Terry Tempest Williams." *Southwestern American Literature* 22 (1995): 209–220. An excellent treatment of ecofeminism in Williams's work.

Clark, Kip, and Deb Thornton. "Terry Tempest Williams." In *Dictionary of Literary Biography*. Vol. 206: *Twentieth-Century American Western Writers*, edited by Richard H. Cracroft, pp. 303–309. Detroit, 1999.

Leuders, Edward. "Landscape, People, and Place: Robert Finch and Terry Tempest Williams." In *Writing Natural History: Dialogues with Authors*. Salt Lake City, 1999. Edited version of writers in public dialogues at the University of Utah in 1988. Terry Tempest Williams discusses her values, personal insight, techniques, and traditions. First published in 1989.

Pearlman, Mickey. *Listen to Their Voices: Twenty Interviews with Women Who Write*. New York, 1993. In her interview, Williams touches upon her religion, childhood, and choices of genre.

Siporin, Ona. "Terry Tempest Williams and Ona Siporin: A Conversation." *Western American Literature* 31 (1996): 99–113.

WILLIAM CARLOS WILLIAMS

by Huck Gutman

By the time the twenty-first century dawned, there were many—especially among the world's poets—who maintained that William Carlos Williams was the most important American poet of the twentieth century. But such recognition had not always come to Williams.

In 1933 the poet was fifty years old. A doctor of medicine with a family practice in Rutherford, the slightly down-and-out New Jersey town where he had been born, Williams had been publishing poems for over twenty years. When several younger poets agreed to publish a volume of his *Collected Poems* (1934), Williams asked his friend, Wallace Stevens, to write the introduction. Stevens, like Williams, was a poet working in the huge shadow cast by T. S. Eliot, the Anglo-American poet who dominated both the world of poetry and the world of literary criticism. In fact, along with Robert Frost (who moved in a rather different orbit), Stevens and Williams were the leading poets of the time, fully equal to Eliot, though few in those days recognized either them or the extraordinary power of their poetic practice.

William Carlos Williams had reason to believe that his friend Stevens, with whom he often shared drinks and conversation at intellectual gatherings in New York City, would provide impetus to his career, moving him toward greater public attention. But he was distressed when he encountered Stevens's introduction in the book's galley proofs. Stevens used the word "antipoetic" eight times in the three-page essay, which claimed that Williams's use of the anti-poetic was both romantic and sentimental.

It was not that Williams did not take "unpoetic" subjects as the material for his poetry. In fact, in one of his very early poems, *The Wanderer* (1914), the young poet questions what it means to be a poet in the modern day.

William Carlos Williams.
(*Courtesy of the Library of Congress*)

How, he muses, can he adequately reflect "this modernity" in which he finds himself. That question would engross him for his entire life. In part, the answer would be the famous advice propounded by his close friend of college days, the poet Ezra Pound, to "make it new." In part, *The Wanderer* would provide an answer singularly Williams's own, for in the process of becoming a poet, the wandering figure is plunged into the polluted Passaic River and thus is baptized in the common and filthy water of his own, urban, New Jersey. In his major manifesto, *Spring and All* (1923), Williams would continue to maintain that "beauty" has a greater relation to reality than to loveliness.

It would take eleven years for Williams to respond to Stevens directly, and when he finally did, it was in a poem, "To All Gentleness" (1943):

And they speak,
Euphemistically, of the anti-poetic!
Garbage. Half the world ignored . . .

Williams had never been willing to ignore that half of human existence consigned to the garbage heap of "unpoetical experiences." He had written poems about wheelbarrows, the head of a codfish drifting in wavelets at the shore, a fire engine roaring down a city street. But no one was going to push Williams around, not even Stevens. Henceforward, he would, partly in response to that introduction, write even closer to the edge of what refined readers might regard as the antipoetic, both in subject matter and in style.

Always an iconoclast, always a rebel, never willing to be pushed around, William Carlos Williams wrote in semiobscurity until he was quite old and debilitated by a series of strokes. Then, late in life, he emerged into the light of adulation by both younger poets like Allen Ginsberg, Denise Levertov, and Robert Creeley and by the literary establishment. One can confidently say that while T. S. Eliot was the figure who presided over American poetry in the first half of the twentieth century, the second half was guided by a different spirit, that of William Carlos Williams. Williams created a new metrics and a new line, a verse supple and responsive, "free" and yet shaped by what architects of the period would call organic form, in which form followed function. He helped shift poetry back toward a greater dependence on images and objects and away from serving as a vessel for the exploitation of emotion and mood. He continued the effort of Emerson and Whitman to ground American poetry in American experience; he elevated the vernacular as the only possible language for the modern poem. He insisted, as he wrote in *Spring and All*, that the poet must deal with familiar things, using the imagination to "detach" them from everyday experiences and bring them to the forefront of consciousness and also to make these familiar things into the stuff of poems.

The poet who would rise to such prominence and such importance was born in Rutherford, New Jersey, on 17 September 1883; except during his medical studies at the University of Pennsylvania and a few other occasions, he would live in Rutherford all his life. Unlike other modern poets of his generation—Frost, Stevens, and Eliot among them—the work by which he supported himself and his family financially was not less important to him than his writing. He was a doctor in family practice, and for him medicine and writing were intertwined. Most of the poems he wrote before he was forced into retirement by a stroke were short, in part because they could be written on his office typewriter in between patients. As Robert Coles (1975) has pointed out, the careful observation of details and attentive regard for human beings that are essential to the medical diagnostician were among the greatest strengths Williams would draw on as a writer. "As a writer, I have been a physician, and as a physician a writer," Williams wrote in the foreword to his *Autobiography* (1951), where he described his poetic method. He explained that at times, in the midst of doing his everyday duties, a "fit" would come upon him and he would have to write a poem. Even in a busy doctor's office, he noted, one can find ten minutes in which to raise a typewriter—Williams's was attached to a leaf in his desk that could be raised from the kneehole to the surface of the desk—and type out the draft of a short poem. If what he was writing was not finished when the next patient appeared, the typewriter would disappear, only to reappear when the patient left.

Although he lived in New Jersey, treating patients largely drawn from the working class and immigrant communities who populated the town in which he chose to reside, it would be a mistake to regard Williams as an outsider to the intellectual ferment which made New York City, along with Paris and London, one of the capital cities of modernism. The young poet often visited the famous 291 Gallery of photographer Alfred Stieglitz, where he met painters Francis Picabia, Marsden Hartley, Arthur Dove, and Georgia O'Keeffe and artist Marcel Duchamp. Williams had made friends in college with Ezra Pound, Hilda Doolittle—who would become a famous poet herself, writing as H.D.—and painter Charles Demuth. In New York City, Williams often met with Stevens and poet Marianne Moore and other writers to talk about poetry and the arts. During this time, when the shaping figures of American modernism were at work in New York City, Williams would visit there, only to leave and return to his medical practice in Rutherford—and to the growing and diverse body of writing he was producing there.

ATTENTIVENESS

There was good reason for Williams to pay attention to the work of the photographers and painters he encountered in New York City. Stieglitz in particular was immensely influential for Williams, despite claims by the poet that he was not much affected by their relationship. The images and paintings of Stieglitz that Williams saw at 291 were important, as was the photographer himself. Stieglitz once said, "We have to learn how to see. We all have to learn to use our eyes, and 291 is here for no other purpose than to give everybody a chance to see."

To a greater extent than almost any other poet, Williams's work is concerned with sight: with what is seen, with seeing, with the process of perception. In his early books, Williams tried on various voices; restless, he was already rebelling against the British tradition in favor of American subjects and American language. But it was not until the publication of *Spring and All* in 1923 that he would make the confident leap to an entirely original voice. In that book—part prose, part poetry, and radically experimental—Williams developed an aesthetic that he would follow for the rest of his life.

Early in the volume he described the deficiency of the modern reader: "The thing he never knows and never dares to know is what he is at the exact moment that he is. And this moment is the only thing in which

I am at all interested." Williams seems to have been unaware that a decade earlier, the philosopher Edmund Husserl had published *Ideas: A General Introduction to Pure Phenomenology* (1913), in which he contended that the aim of philosophy should be to bracket a moment in time so that, using the philosophical imagination, the shape of the perceptive act could be ascertained. Yet something of the spirit of the times occupied both men, for the similarities between Williams's poetry and that branch of philosophy known as phenomenology were profound.

In *Spring and All*, Williams asserted that for him, as for Husserl, it is only the imagination that can pluck people out of semiconscious existence—always looking forward, or back—so that they can engage the reality that is right before their eyes. Williams's own poetic practice had earlier been shaped by imagism, which insisted that poems be based on sense experience of the world rather than emotion and that they use economy in presentation. His early work, along with that of Amy Lowell and the early Pound, provide the best-known examples of imagist poetry.

But *Spring and All* is not about images. It maintains that the imagination must reshape the world so it can be apprehended anew. The poet, Williams claimed, does not follow the Shakespearean injunction to hold a mirror up to nature, but instead re-creates nature by the exercise of the imagination. The most famous poem in the sequence, the poem about the red wheelbarrow, takes on a life of its own, not just as a portrayal of a thing, but a thing seen, arranged, composed. That is why "so much depends" upon that wheelbarrow, glistening vibrantly red after a rain in a yard where beside it stand some white chickens. The wheelbarrow is observed with intensity. The present moment is visualized with even greater intensity in "Poem" (1930), a later work in which the poet watches a cat step carefully into a flowerpot, or in "The Yellow Chimney" (1944), where Williams looks with great attentiveness at a smokestack, encircled by steel bands, reflecting the autumn sun.

Spring and All consists of experimental prose "chapters" that alternate with untitled but numbered poems. The lack of title, the need to refer to the poems by an uncapitalized phrase, was an essential part of the experiment. The first of these radical poetic experiments is extraordinarily successful and is the key, if there is one, to the whole volume. "By the road to the contagious hospital" recounts a roadside scene. The day is cold. Both the shoulder of the road and the fields beyond are muddy and wet. The poet's gaze is drawn to the marginal area between berm and fields, were he sees brush standing lifelessly.

Ever since the British poet William Wordsworth, poets had sought nature as a source of the sublime, the terrifyingly beautiful; those poets with less power and less ambition sought nature for its calm and sentimental beauty. If ever nature were antipoetic it would be in a place such as Williams is observing: marginal to automobile traffic, untended, undifferentiated (despite a wonderful string of five adjectives, the brush is still just "stuff"), not a flower or specimen tree or even a green leaf in sight. This is the sort of territory Williams investigated over and over again, the seemingly inconsequential sights that we all hurry by as we go wherever we have to go, as we move forward to find things worth looking at.

"By the road" turns when the "leafless" vines seem "lifeless," for the connection is made through punning, yet the poet intuits that it is an erroneous connection. The scene may appear dead and lifeless, but he knows that though "sluggish" and "dazed," spring is approaching. This remarkable poem is about attentiveness, vision, consciousness. The poet sees what is before him, and by paying attention to it, he recognizes that though the world before him now appears lifeless, spring is coming:

> Now the grass, tomorrow
> The stiff curl of wildcarrot leaf
> One by one objects are defined—
> It quickens: clarity, outline of leaf

What is beginning, of course, is not just the rebirth of the vegetation in spring but the observer's concentration on "what he is at the exact moment that he is." Objects are defined, not only in and of themselves, but for the perceiver. A "profound change" is upon the lifeless world, to be sure, as in small but unmistakable ways the vegetation shifts into the new life of spring. But the change has likewise come upon the doctor-poet, on the road to the hospital. Just as the roots of the grass and wildcarrot grip down and the plants begin to awaken, so does the attentive vision—vision for, not just vision of—root the poet in the actual world and awaken him to its glories—and his own. In the words of critic James E. Breslin (1970), "In Williams's imaginative work we enter a world in which all the objects are common, but they have been lifted, by the intensity with which they have been perceived and rendered, into a sharp distinction. It is the familiar, seen *for the first time.*"

There is a third awakening. The "hospital" of the first line is not "contagious" because of communicable disease, but because the births that take place there—much of

433

Williams's practice was in obstetrics—are reflected in the rebirth of the vegetation in spring, and in the birth of the poet's new awareness of the world, his new way of seeing. The poem is about "entrance," about what Wallace Stevens in one of his poems called "the exhilaration of changes." So new is the change that all is naked: the infant, the sprouting grass, the poet's Adamic vision. But change has come, and it is an entrance to a new world, a world in which the observer, like the child and the grass, can root down and "begin to awaken."

The poems of *Spring and All* crackle with the poet's need to explore new things with a new voice. Particularly noteworthy are two which observe America with painful clarity: "The pure products of America/go crazy" (republished as "To Elsie") and "The crowd at the ball game" (republished as "At the Ball Game"). The first takes a long look at the retarded girl who worked as a nursemaid for the Williams family and sees in her condition a combination of superficial American values and American callousness, a combination that in the larger social sphere is causing America to go astray. Shallowness and callousness, it appears to the poet, destroy all of us; both our own lives and the workings of the society are unwitnessed, unguided, like a car rolling along a highway without a driver to keep it from plunging into a ditch or smashing headlong into an accident. The second poem observes the crowd at a baseball game, registering both its unconscious democratic beauty and the venomous, grim terror that lies beneath the thoughtless emotions of the massed citizens. There is often, more often than many readers acknowledge, a strong social dimension to his poetry, which is both witness to and critic of American society.

ATTENTIVENESS AND THE COMPOSITIONAL FIELD

"By the road to the contagious hospital" and the other poems of *Spring and All* counsel close attention to objects. "No ideas but in things," Williams would pronounce, famously, in a short lyric and later in his five-volume epic poem *Paterson* (1946–1958). But never, never, is the object seen solely by itself. It is always, for Williams, part of a compositional field. Since many of his friends were photographers and painters, he understood that arrangement, placement, masses, diagonals, all serve to make the visual field of a painting interesting and engrossing. For example, "Between Walls" (1938) sets up just such a compositional field, registering the space between the hospital's wings, an infertile space strewn with

discarded cinders, in the mist of which the sun strikes a luminescent glow from a piece of broken green glass.

No poem of Williams more economically reveals his radical practice than "Between Walls." There is the seemingly free verse, which in actuality follows a pattern of two-line stanzas in which the second line is shorter than the first and has (except in one instance) two syllables. There is the antipoetic landscape "where nothing will grow," the back of a building and not its front, a veritable junkyard where cinders from the hospital's coal furnace are littered along with broken glass. There is the careful shaping of the visual field—two wings to the sides, the cinder-strewn middle, and the broken green glass catching the sunlight at the composition's center. This poem is a celebration of the seemingly ordinary, the refusal to consign anything to the antipoetic; here is no wasteland (for that surely is how T. S. Eliot, or for that matter novelist F. Scott Fitzgerald, would have seen it) but a venue for "shining." Even the most mundane, the most trashy, setting has organization and may flower into beauty if we will but look attentively at it.

The visual field often serves as the shaping force in Williams's poems. In "Nantucket" (1934) he writes of the arrangement that is before the observer who enters a summer home bedroom. In "A Bastard Peace" (1938) he writes of a semi-urban lot, a sewage disposal site once again strewn with cinders, with a path down its center; in the foreground are houses and a boy walking.

There are poems in which one senses not just an object of perception in a compositional field, but also the poet's intense focus upon a brief revelation of human desire and attentiveness. A stunning example is his poem "Proletarian Portrait" (1935), about a woman standing, bareheaded, one unshod foot poised upon her toe so that she can retain her balance as she peers into the removed shoe in rapt attention. The poem is doubly about focus: the woman intent on finding the nail in her shoe, oblivious to her surroundings as she dedicates herself to the task of looking attentively, and the poet, intent on seeing and capturing the exact delineation of what is taking place in front of his eyes. Similarly, Williams focuses in "To a Poor Old Woman" (1935) on a woman who ignores her circumstantial situation in order to "give herself" to the plum she is eating and obviously enjoying. Williams, through linguistic experiment—a key line is deconstructed as he repeats it a second and third time, and put back together at the end of the poem—tries to capture just how satisfying is the experience of biting into the plum, its taste so captivating to the woman. The plum tastes good to this person seen on the street; its taste is comforting, and it brings solace to the woman who is doubly afflicted by age and economic necessity. As the old woman eats, so the poet observes, giving himself over fully to the scene before him—and to the words that are such an integral part of observing and shaping and reshaping experience.

If sight can clamp down with tight focus, it can also move, as in "Young Sycamore" (1927). In an intensely urban setting—sycamores are city trees, and this particular specimen is growing between a sidewalk and a gutter in which runoff flows—the poet's gaze is in movement, rising upward with the trunk's ever-lessening mass until it reaches the thinned upward branches and finally the two twigs that keep reaching forward into the sky. Once again, vision and what is seen have a similar form: the tree is the visible record of the trickling water rising upward and the poet's vision moves upward, as if the world before him is a painting, following forces in the field of composition.

When vision takes place not in a moment but over time, the "change" so essential to "By the road" is highlighted. Such is the case in "Burning the Christmas Greens" (1944), when the end of the holiday season leads the poet to toss the evergreen branches from his mantel into the fireplace below. Recalling in flashback the white snow in which he cut the branches of green hemlock, the poet then watches as their vital color is consumed by the flames, green turning into red fire, fire into black coal, black coal into white ash. Change transforms, and in transforming refreshes the poet; the burning greens are an emblem of the imagination's continuing capacity to transform the world into new ways of seeing and to reshape the world of experience into art.

DEFAMILIARIZATION

If we think again of Williams's poetic response to Stevens, we note how insistent he is that what the observer sees not be treated as garbage, as inconsequential, solely because it is unpoetic. In 1917 the Russian critic Victor Shklovsky claimed in a pathbreaking essay, "Art as Technique," that the function of art is to overcome the habitualization of perception by rendering objects unfamiliar: "Art exists to make one feel things . . . to impart the sensation of things as they are perceived and not as they are known." While it is unlikely that Williams, who did not read Russian, encountered the essay, its spirit was very much akin to the modern art he encountered at Stieglitz's 291 Gallery and elsewhere.

Williams, too, believed that the artist must "defamiliarize" the world as Shklovsky claimed, make it unfamiliar, so that it can be perceived afresh. In just that fashion the poet's perception is renewed in "By the road" and in staring at the flaming hemlock in "Burning the Christmas Greens." Familiar objects are seen anew, reconstructed, remade, so that they can be truly seen instead of consigned to that half of the world considered garbage (or likewise consigned to that half of the world considered "poetic," a category so permeated by the aura of "art" that, paradoxically, it is not noticed, either).

In the whole of Williams's corpus, the need for defamiliarization is made nowhere more clearly than in his poem "The Forgotten City" (1939). Once again, the poem is about roadways. The poet is returning from a vacation, driving on a New Jersey highway under hurricane conditions. The driving wind and water cause him to take another route and he loses his bearings. On a strange road in a strange place he calls what he sees "extraordinary" and "vivid," even while it is still "commonplace." Everything seems strange, "foreign." The poet, realizing he has no idea of where he is, nonetheless resolves to return to this fascinating place. Clearly, the everyday and commonplace has been ripped—by the circumstance of the hurricane—out of the habitual; the everyday has been defamiliarized so thoroughly that he is able to see it afresh, anew.

The process of defamiliarization highlighted in "The Forgotten City" is at the core of Williams's poetic method. A large part of the prose in *Spring and All* is concerned with the operation of the imagination. The poet, Williams wrote, addresses "things with which he is familiar, simple things." He does not simply record them but somehow, by using the imagination, detaches them from everyday experience. This detachment, wrought in "The Forgotten City" by the hurricane, is also achievable through the act of imaginative attentiveness. To "intensify" the moment in which we exist, the current moment, "there is but a single force—the imagination." To this assertion of the power and importance of the imagination Williams would return to thirty years later, when he wrote his last long poems, "The Desert Music" (1951), "Asphodel, That Greeny Flower" (1955), and *Paterson* (Book 5) (1958).

The reader would make a mistake, however, to see in "The Forgotten City" only a refreshment of vision. The last lines of that poem make clear a social vision as well: Williams is confronting issues of class and the failure of American democracy. The poem ends with a question: how could the people he saw, and their lives, have become invisible, "cut off" from the process of social "representation" even though they live near the centers of power, even though they are so clearly linked to the familiar? Why are these streets, these people, never in the newspapers—or even in the books that Williams reads? The implied answer indicates that it is overhabitualization that prevents us from seeing what is before our sight. But the poem also reminds us, powerfully, that what is seen is a function of the power structure in society, which runs the machines of fame, the newspapers, the modes of "communication" that operate to display some things and render others invisible.

"The Forgotten City" insists we look deeper into the categories of poetic and antipoetic, to the people and conditions made invisible by the "commonplace" American refusal to see beyond the conventions of class. In Williams's view, it is as if certain people—the majority of Americans, those who are not wealthy and educated and possessed of "poetic" sensibilities—are themselves antipoetic, ignored, invisible. Many of the poems of attentiveness cited above were written in the Depression years of the 1930s and into the early 1940s. They do more than focus attention on the world, they insist that the reader confront the reality of working men and women and of the city environments they live in. Williams always demands that an effort be made to see beyond the categories of class. This allows him to see people and settings that most other poets would regard with distaste—as T. S. Eliot does in most of *The Waste Land* (1922)—if they can be seen at all. But then, Williams as poet was always aware of what he once said about the work of his friend, the painter Charles Sheeler: "The local is the universal."

Although best known as a poet, William Carlos Williams wrote in many genres, always defamiliarizing, always bringing before consciousness those things that, without attentiveness, would be taken for granted (which is another way of saying they would be invisible). In his boldly original essays on history, *In the American Grain* (1925), Williams recreates the characters who shaped the origins of American history: Columbus, Cortés, Cotton Mather, Benjamin Franklin. The prologue announces a method familiar to readers of Williams: "In these studies I have sought to re-name the things seen, now lost in a chaos of borrowed titles . . . to draw from every source one thing, the strange phosphorous of the life, nameless under an old misappellation."

Williams also wrote a trilogy of three novels—*White Mule* (1937), *In the Money* (1940), and *The Build-Up* (1952)—based on the history of the Stecher family. (The fictional family was patterned on that of his wife, Florence

Herman.) It looks at immigrant life and the texture of American society. Williams's short fiction in *Life along the Passaic River* (1938) explores the relationship between a doctor and his working-class, immigrant patients. "It is the genius of these stories," Robert Coles (himself a physician) wrote (1975), "that they are utterly concrete, yet lend themselves, without any help of the author in the form of discursive asides, to social comment or political asides." Always, he makes the attempt to see what is not usually seen, to bring to consciousness the huge swath of life that lies beyond ordinary seeing.

PATERSON

Adjoining the town of Rutherford, Williams's lifelong home, is Paterson, a city in northern New Jersey. In 1941 Williams chose Paterson—urban, industrial, bisected by the Passaic River—as the subject of an epic poem. *Paterson* was issued serially: book 1 appeared in 1946 and book 4—intended as the last book—came out in 1951. (After the poem was completed, Williams was restless and kept writing: book 5 was published in 1958 and he began a further book.)

Paterson sprawls. It takes its structure from a city, and so consists of a congeries of things all brought together in a great collage that is also a narrative; it incorporates reference works, newspaper articles, historical and invented characters, dialogue, private musings, aesthetics, self-reproaches, interviews. Like a city, it has neighborhoods where different elements congregate; like a city, it has a history and an ongoing development. Paterson, in the poem, is both a city and a semimythic man who resides there, Noah Faitoute ("Do Everything") Paterson. Williams explains in the Preface:

the city
the man, an identity—it can't
be otherwise—an
interpenetration, both ways.

Book 1 introduces two aspects of the city: the river and the park beside it. The central feature of the book is the waterfall of the Passaic River, which is at the heart of the city. Paterson was in fact located to take advantage of the ample waterpower of the falls. Alexander Hamilton planned the city because he realized that textile and other manufacture would flourish there; it was the first factory town in the United States. The falls represent, for the poet, the failure of language that is documented again and again in book 1. The crashing of its waters are the sounds of speech, but those sounds are chaotic and indistinguishable. People cannot talk to one another, or if they do talk it is to no effect. Words do not work:

> The language, the language
> > fails them
> they do not know the words
> > or have not
> the courage to use them.

The falls are beautiful and powerful, but Williams stresses the noise and confusion of the pouring waters. The collage that makes up the text is itself a kind of waterfall, a synecdoche of the chaos and rich diversity that make up America.

In book 2 the setting is, as the subtitle informs us, "Sunday in the Park." The city-man who is the protagonist of the poem strolls for a long time through the public park that borders the falls, often reminding the reader that he is walking along. While he walks, he observes the people. He sees a boy and girl on a blanket making love but recognizes that their thoughts are shallow and pitiful. He listens to an evangelist haranguing the people taking their ease in the park. He thinks at length about Alexander Hamilton, who feared "the great beast" of democracy, who envisioned an industrial America (and foresaw that Paterson would be a place of factories), who set up the banking system that the poet, like his friend Ezra Pound, thinks robs Americans of their wealth.

The protagonist Paterson tries to engage the world around him. The book begins,

> outside myself
> > > there is a world...
> > which I approach
> concretely.

But he feels himself to be defeated. Just as the falls were a jumble of sound, the "new" reshaping the "old," so are the sounds of the park. Voices, "multiple and inarticulate," assault "the air from all sides." Even worse for Williams the poet, as the city-man Paterson walks through the park, the words that try to take shape within him are "blocked." He knows that "without invention nothing is well spaced, unless the mind change." But all he has are evangelists, dogs, people mindlessly enjoying themselves. And he also has with him Cress, a woman poet who had written Williams a series of long letters, accusing him (with some justice) of not giving her adequate support and of using her. Her letters, quoted at great length, occupy his consciousness as he walks.

But in the third part of book 2 comes a magical moment. Williams, the master of what might be called free

verse in America, had long been troubled by his inability to demonstrate that just because lines are nonmetrical, just because they do not fall into the conventional feet of British and Roman meters, does not mean that they are without measure and rhythm. In the writing of *Paterson*, Williams inscribes the failure and blockage he himself had felt as a poet into the character of Paterson. Reflecting on these failures, Williams found himself writing these lines:

> The descent beckons
> > as the ascent beckoned
> > > Memory is a kind
> of accomplishment
> > a sort of record of renewal
> > > even
> an initiation, since the spaces it opens are new places
> > inhabited by hordes
> > > heretofore unrealized. . . .
> No defeat is made up entirely of defeat—since the world it
> > opens is always a place
> formerly
> > unsuspected

Once these lines were written, Williams looked on what he had done with a sense of discovery—and relief. He had found a new measure, an indented descending triplet, that had form, that accommodated measure (later he would say each line was measured out by the breath), and that was flexible enough to accommodate the rhythms of American speech. (The lines were also about wresting victory from defeat, and they celebrated renewal and the opening of a new world, very similarly to what he had called for in *Spring and All* and demonstrated in "By the road to the contagious hospital." But these things were secondary: Williams had discovered the poetic form, the new measure, which he would investigate for the rest of his life—and which a great many later American poets would exploit as well.)

Book 3 leaves the falls and park behind for the library. Williams's view of the library is complex and even contradictory. At first the library is all that Williams hates, a collection of things enshrined and changeless; he sees the library as a place of "desolation" and says it has a smell of "stagnation and death." But the library is also the repository of Homer, who sang about the sea and about love. Paterson thinks about the burning of the great classical library at Alexandria, Egypt: beauty was lost, as in the destruction of Sappho's poems, but he also realizes that fire also purifies and transmutes. As he thinks about giving up poetry—a voice speaks in his head, telling him to abandon "the shilly-shally of art"—he also recognizes that nothing but "deathless song" can comfort men and women who face the certainty that death is the final human destination. (The relation between death and art would occupy Williams in the long poems he wrote after he completed *Paterson*.) In the course of the book, then, Williams berates the library for solidifying, entrenching; it is the physical resting place of all the established habits that his defamiliarizing poetry, ever new, has always tried to overturn. But the library is also the repository of poetry, which is for him a leading exemplar of beauty. The resolution to these opposing views of the library appears at the end of book 3. As he recognizes that all ideas have their roots in the things of the world and our experience of and in that world of things, Williams concludes—repeating the word six times—that he must write of "this" which is in front of him, observing and imagining the world anew, in his poetry. Stick to "no ideas but in things" and move out of the library.

The fourth book of *Paterson*, and the last according to his original plan, spins somewhat out of control—first with a pastoral idyll about sexuality and class, then by contrasting radium (continuously producing energy that manifests itself as luminosity) with the debilities of money and credit. So confused is the exploration that Williams asks himself, at the start of section 3, whether he has not forgotten his original purpose, "the language."

He eventually rouses himself to waken from the seductive dream of the poem, which has led Paterson from the waterfall to the park beside it; to the library; and now, finally, to the shore of the ocean into which the Passaic River flows. The ocean is an all-encompassing totality, for in it everything not only merges but ultimately submerges; it is, he recognizes, "not our home." So strong is the warning that humans cannot dwell in that ocean into which the river empties that he repeats the phrase, "the sea is not our home" five times in less than two pages. For all its concern with the catastrophic condition of language in the present era, a time when words fail everyone except on rare occasions the poet, *Paterson* is as committed to life and renewal as *Spring and All* was thirty years previously. The sea is emphatically not our home; at the end of the poem, a man with a black dog emerges from a swim in the ocean, lies down, rubs off sand, dresses, and turns his back to the ocean. Mounting a sand dune, he picks some wild fruit and heads "inland," both to the city of Paterson and its people.

THE FINAL TRIUMPH

In 1951 Williams suffered the first in a series of strokes. Over the next few years he gave up medicine but continued to write poetry. He was also beset at times by acute depression, for there was much to be depressed about. First, there was the stroke, with its debilities and its reminder of the frailty of life. Second, he had for well over thirty years written in semi-anonymity, and although this was in the process of changing, it was harder and harder for him to sustain himself as a poet without recognition. Third, he was a victim of the age of McCarthyism and militant anticommunism, for the honor of being appointed to the prestigious post of poetry consultant to the Library of Congress turned to ashes in his mouth as reactionary political forces caused the appointment to be withdrawn just after it was offered in 1952.

Williams successfully confronted his depression head-on in "The Desert Music." This ten-page poem recounts a stop on his rail journey eastward from the West Coast—he had given a successful reading at Reed College in Oregon—in the town of El Paso, Texas, where he crosses the border into Juarez, Mexico, to meet some old friends. In the poem, Williams maintains a dialogue with himself: Are you a poet? Do poems matter? What are poems? What is their relation to the world? "The Desert Music" is the record of an identity crisis suffered by a man who had always been sure of what he did and what he was. But the answers come as quickly as the questions, and he ends the poem "ashamed" that he had doubts, saying, "I *am* a poet!" He is, as he says, "reaffirmed" by the answers that have come to his questions, by his realization that poetry is connected to music, both metrically and by its intricate dance to the music of all creation.

> And I could not help thinking
> of the wonders of the brain that
> hears that music and of our
> skill sometimes to record it.

He read the poem to a Phi Beta Kappa Assembly at Harvard, to the great delight of the students and the consternation of some of the professors. (One of the central characters in the poem is an old whore doing a striptease.)

He would go on from triumph to triumph. In 1955 he published "Asphodel, That Greeny Flower," one of the greatest love poems in the English language. The poem is an attempt to reconcile himself with his wife, Florence (Floss), after a series of his extramarital relationships had put strain on their relationship. In book 1 Williams acknowledges that his time is short, that he must address Floss in a poem because his words will soon come to an end and there is much he has to say to her about death and about his love for her. In book 2 he describes the "pinnacles" of his life, three moments when his awareness seemed most alive. He contrasts this richness of perception and imagination with the "world's niggardliness" and with the blockage and failure he had recently faced, when after a lifetime of dedication he found himself "failing the poem." Love, he recognizes, can save him—in particular, the love that his wife can, as she so often has, offer him.

But as he has hurt her, that love is not easily forthcoming. "What power has love but forgiveness?" he asks at the start of book 3.

> In other words
> > by its intervention
> what has been done
> can be undone
> > What good is it otherwise?

He asks for forgiveness, leaving aside the pride that had always kept him from asking his wife for the love he needs. And as he approaches Floss with his confession of need and his moving assertion of how much he loves her, she forgives him; in response, he acknowledges that she will always, for ever, be his "queen of love." The poem would appear concluded, but Williams has more on his mind, and so he appends a coda, a musical term for an independent passage coming after the end of a work.

In the coda he confronts directly the destruction which has driven him into speech, both the recent invention and deployment of an atom bomb which threatens all humankind, and his own death, which his recent strokes have forced him to acknowledge. The coda contrasts the light and sound of thunderstorms, the light and heat of atomic blasts. Light always "takes precedence" over thunder and cataclysm. In fact, he maintains, the interval between the two—the interval in which he is living, between the announcement of forthcoming death and death itself—is a rich time when the imagination is capable of full play and love can be simple and direct. Williams is confident, in this "sweetest" of all intervals, that the imagination can conquer death—"Only the imagination is real!" he declares—just as he believes love can conquer the fear of death. Art and marriage, the imagination and love, he declares in a wonderful concluding passage, are both "a celebration of the light." And light, he maintains, always wins out over darkness.

This celebration of art and love frame his final works, "Paterson" (book 5, composed from 1952 to 1957) and *Pictures from Brueghel* (1962). In the addition to the first four volumes of *Paterson*—book 5 being a coda in the truest sense—Williams again confronts old age, here examining the survival of art in a world that is otherwise full not only of change, but mortality. Paterson, though "approaching death," finds that he is "possessed by many poems." In particular, he thinks of the Unicorn Tapestries, finely woven scenes dating from late medieval times that hang in The Cloisters, a museum in upper Manhattan. They glorify beauty, both through their portrayal of the woman who appears in them as a virgin and through the flowers that form the background of each of the tapestries. The many flowers, Williams observes, are each an example of the weaver's enchantment with the particular things of the world. This multitude of flowers, each portrayed in specific detail, is an affirmation of the truth Williams had recognized in "By the road to the contagious hospital" over fifty years earlier. Both the things of the world and consciousness itself need only root down to "being to awaken" and blossom. Art, through the exercise of the imagination, can re-create and thus preserve the flowering that characterizes the world in which we live.

The third part of book 5 begins with a consideration of Pieter Brueghel's painting of the nativity of Christ. Williams saw the sixteenth-century Flemish painter as a precursor, someone who affirmed the same values as himself: that the local is the universal; that "ordinary" people and events—attentively observed rather than dismissed as antipoetic—must be the subject of art; that the imagination can transform the ephemeral into the enduring. He explores Brueghel's paintings in the remarkable sequence of ten poems that gave the title to his final book, *Pictures from Brueghel*. Clearly delineated as a hardworking man dedicated to painting in "Self-Portrait" (the painting does not exist, except in Williams's imagination), Brueghel is revealed, in the sequence, as dedicated to the re-presentation of common sights—hunters in snow, a peasant wedding, harvesting hay or corn. Brueghel, as Williams shows, recognizes the actuality of what is seen—a bush in the foreground as hunters return to an inn, the spoon inserted into the hatband of a man serving the wedding guests, the worker sprawled as he sleeps "unbuttoned" during the noontime lunch in the fields. Time and again the painter, as the poet, is concerned with the compositional field: "There is no detail," he says of one of Brueghel's paintings, "extraneous to the composition."

Williams, who insisted in *Spring and All* that the artist must imitate the world and not just copy it, imitated Brueghel's paintings with understated skill. The world of the everyday was Brueghel's obsession, as it was for Williams, the antipoetic seen by the exercise of the attentive human imagination and by the creative powers of that agency transformed into art. His words about Brueghel's subjects and the art he made of them seem particularly apt as a summation of the work of this extraordinary poet from New Jersey, William Carlos Williams:

It was his own . . .
no one
could take that
from him.

[*See also* Eliot, T. S.; Frost, Robert; H.D. (Hilda Doolittle); Long Poem, The; Lowell, Amy; Moore, Marianne; Nature Writing: Poetry; Pound, Ezra; *and* Stevens, Wallace.]

SELECTED WORKS

Spring and All (1923)
In the American Grain (1925)
Collected Poems (1934)
White Mule (1937)
Life along the Passaic River (1938)
In the Money (1940)
Paterson (1946–1958)
The Autobiography of William Carlos Williams (1951)
The Build-Up (1952)
Selected Essays (1954)
Selected Letters (1957)
Pictures from Brueghel (1962)
Collected Poems of William Carlos Williams, 1909–1939 (1986)
Collected Poems of William Carlos Williams, 1939–1962 (1988)
The Collected Stories of William Carlos Williams (1996)

FURTHER READING

Axelrod, Steven Gould, and Helen Deese, eds. *Critical Essays on William Carlos Williams.* New York, 1994.

Bremen, Brian A. *William Carlos Williams and the Diagnostics of Culture.* New York, 1993.

Breslin, James E. *William Carlos Williams: An American Artist.* New York, 1970. A fine overall view of the poet's works.

Coles, Robert. *William Carlos Williams: The Knack of Survival in America.* New Brunswick, N.J., 1975. On Williams's fiction.

Connarroe, Joel. *William Carlos Williams' 'Paterson': Language and Landscape.* Philadelphia, 1970.

Diggory, Terence. *William Carlos Williams and the Ethics of Painting.* Princeton, N.J., 1991.

Djikstra, Bram. *The Hieroglyphics of a New Speech: Cubism, Stieglitz, and the Early Poetry of William Carlos Williams.* Princeton, N.J., 1969.

Duffey, Bernard. *A Poetry of Presence: The Writing of William Carlos Williams.* Madison, Wis., 1986.

Mariani, Paul. *William Carlos Williams: The Poet and His Critics.* Chicago, 1975. A useful survey of the historical reception of Williams's poetry.

Mariani, Paul. *William Carlos Williams: A New World Naked.* New York, 1981. A superb biography: long, complete, considered.

Miller, J. Hillis. *Poets of Reality: Six Twentieth Century Writers.* Cambridge, Mass., 1965. The final chapter, on Williams, makes a serious claim for him as the most important and advanced poet of the twentieth century. A pathbreaking study which, although many dissent from it, is central to the academic reputation of Williams.

Miller, J. Hillis. *William Carlos Williams: A Collection of Critical Essays.* Englewood Cliffs, N.J., 1966. A seminal book of critical essays.

Morris, Daniel. *The Writings of William Carlos Williams: Publicity for the Self.* Columbia, Mo., 1995. Williams's self-presentation in the fiction and in *Paterson.*

Paul, Sherman. *The Music of Survival: A Biography of a Poem by William Carlos Williams.* Urbana, Ill., 1968. On "The Desert Music."

Riddel, Joseph N. *The Inverted Bell: Modernism and the Counterpoetics of William Carlos Williams.* Baton Rouge, La., 1974. Still fruitful; one of the first examples of deconstructive criticism in America.

Sankey, Benjamin. *A Companion to William Carlos Williams's "Paterson."* Berkeley, Calif., 1971.

Tapscott, Stephen. *American Beauty: William Carlos Williams and the Modernist Whitman.* New York, 1984.

Whitaker, Thomas. *William Carlos Williams.* Rev. ed. Boston, 1989. A brief introduction to the life and work.

See also the article on *Paterson*, immediately following.

WILLIAM CARLOS WILLIAMS'S
PATERSON

by Christopher MacGowan

William Carlos Williams had been planning the long poem that eventually became *Paterson* for more than twenty years before the publication of the first of its five books in 1946. (Subsequent volumes appeared in 1948, 1949, 1951, and 1958.) He viewed it in some ways as his answer to T. S. Eliot's *The Waste Land*, which had appeared in 1922: it would be a "local" poem about American history and the American language, rather than the polyglot of languages and landscapes in Eliot's poem. For some critics *Paterson* is a belated and not very original addition to the long poems of high modernism; for others it is Williams's finest achievement, while for yet others it is brilliant but uneven. For Williams himself it was a poem he always had to come back to. Book 5 was not part of his original plan, and a few pages beginning a sixth book were found after his death. (The 1992 edition of *Paterson*, edited by Christopher MacGowan, outlines the stages of the poem's composition, in addition to annotating many of the historical and biographical allusions.)

Many of Williams's shorter poems describe the people and places around Rutherford, the small New Jersey town where he was born and where he practiced as a physician for five decades. But for his long poem he focused on nearby Paterson, a city important to the history of the colonies and early Republic, an affluent industrial center in the late nineteenth century that had seen a steep decline in the twentieth. Like Rutherford, Paterson is on the Passaic River, which eventually flows out into the Newark marshes near New York City. What made Paterson a perfect site for industry was the waterpower from its once-famous Falls, the second biggest after Niagara in the eastern United States. The area, which had been important to the Native American population, attracted early European settlers and later drew immigrant workers. It was the focus of a plan by Alexander Hamilton to use its waterpower to manufacture and distribute many essential needs of the thirteen states. All of this history, as well as the city of Williams's time, appear in the poem. "Paterson" is a character in the poem, but he has a fluid identity sometimes separate from and sometimes identified with the city, and he is addressed in both the first and third persons.

Paterson is organized like a collage, with the mix of poetry and prose that Williams had used in such earlier volumes of short lyrics as *Spring and All* (1923) and "The Descent of Winter" (1928). The prose in *Paterson* is part of the poem's intention to be a history of the American language, and to be a search for the adequate terms in which to write the poem itself. Sources for the prose include letters the poet had received, contemporary or historical newspaper accounts, records of speech, legal and industrial records, and quotations from books and pamphlets. This collage form developed in the early 1940s from a series of aborted attempts to find a format for the poem.

THE FIRST FOUR BOOKS

Before the preface, an italicized paragraph offers a series of phrases that suggest some of the central themes of the poem. The net effect is to emphasize its open-ended nature. The poem cannot be summarized in a single phrase, and the series of tentative closures in book 4 and book 5 eventually cancel each other out.

As Williams originally conceived the poem, the four books follow the Passaic River from the high ground above Paterson, where the poem opens in book 1, to Garret Mountain Park in book 2, to the Falls themselves in book 3, and out to the Newark marshes and the sea in book 4. The headings of the first four books reflect this plan. Book 1 begins with "The Delineaments of the Giants." The myths of the traditional epic form find their native parallel in the sleeping figures, male and female, embodied in the valley and mountain surrounding the Falls. The disjunction of sexual harmony, and thus fertility, is a major theme of the poem, represented through violence between the sexes and toward the land (and its original inhabitants). But in these early lines, as often in Williams's work, he suggests a potential that could be realized, a source which could heal—a role that the Falls takes on later in the poem.

Book 1 introduces some of the historical incidents and figures associated with the Falls and the surrounding area.

The crashing roar of the waters functions as a kind of ur-language that both the poet and the city's inhabitants must hear and rearticulate to produce a poem that recognizes a power more vital than Hamilton's mercenary schemes and those of the figures who followed him. The descent of the Falls promises a rebounding ascent, a creative violence that is a frequent motif in Williams's work. Two representative incidents close the first section of this book. Mrs. Cumming's fall is reported in terms that suggest that, in contrast to the fertile African woman of the verse immediately preceding, her life with her minister husband is an empty, repressed one that pulls her toward the lure of the Falls. The other incident tells the story of Sam Patch, who made his name diving from a bank of the Falls and later made a career of daredevil jumps—an example in the poem of trivial entertainment and misplaced courage.

The theme of "divorce"—both of poet and populace from the land and of archetypal male from female—opens and closes the second section. The closing letter, from fellow writer Edward Dahlberg, prefigures the accusation closing book 2 that Williams as Paterson is himself an embodiment of divorce, separating writing from its sources in lived experience and human suffering. Book 1 concludes with a glimpse of the potential fertility beneath the Falls, a mystery, and the source of the speech that must be heard.

In book 2, "Sunday in the Park," Paterson's wandering search takes him to Garret Mountain Park, above the Falls. As he watches the desultory actions of the crowd and the momentary sparkle offered by a few figures who refuse to be repressed, two voices begin to weave through the book, both finally isolated. One is the call to a prayer meeting from a preacher, Klaus Ehrens. His condemnation of money furthers the poem's economic themes (an interest that *Paterson* shares with Pound's *Cantos*) and connects again to Alexander Hamilton. The other voice comes from the letter writer that the poem identifies with "C," or Cress, the lover who is both victim and betrayer in Chaucer's *Troilus and Criseyde*. This prose is taken from the poet Marcia Nardi's furious letters to Williams when he sought to end their correspondence. Interspersed with these two narratives are further examples of the area's violent past. The repressive culture behind the violence is also associated with the dogs banned from the park, although Musty manages to get pregnant despite restrictions. This particular motif continues in book 3, when a dog is drowned in the flood, and returns at the end of book 4, when a dog accompanies the figure heading inland to a possible new beginning.

However, in book 3, "The Library," Paterson retreats to the wrong place, a museum of the past, as the motif of the trapped "Beautiful thing" makes clear. But as Paterson reads of the wind, fire, and flood that ravaged the city in the early twentieth century, these destructive forces work within his mind and the poem to help undermine the fear and the false language that keeps him from fully responding to the roar of the Falls. In section 3 the flood even visually undermines the poem's straight lines. On another level, the violence of the elements parallels the treatment of the Native Americans who originally inhabited the area and whose culture was brutally destroyed. And on a third level, the violence is figured in a girl raped and beaten, whose condition represents the grotesque contemporary response to female sexuality. The "fertile (?) mud" that the receding floods expose at the end of book 3 has more potential, the poem suggests, than the reading list offered by Ezra Pound writing from his confinement in St. Elizabeths Hospital.

Book 4, the concluding book under Williams's original plan for the poem, is "The Run to the Sea." The trio who make up the contemporary "Idyll" of the first section—a nurse from Paterson, an older patrician woman, and Paterson himself—carries on the poem's themes of sexual frustration and manipulation. In contrast, at the center of the next section is Madame Curie, who along with her husband discovered radium. Their partnership is one of the poem's examples of the male-female principle working productively and creatively to discover another kind of source material. Additionally, letters arrive from a writer in the city itself, the then-unknown Allen Ginsberg writing to Williams of his enthusiasm for the poem as its individual volumes have appeared. These letters, along with Paterson taking his son to a lecture on atomic fission, suggest the possibility of a continuity to set against the prevalent "divorce," a continuity promised in the very title of *Paterson*.

In the final section of book 4 a reflective voice recalls the life of nineteenth-century Paterson, although the calm of its long, regular lines is juxtaposed to further violence, including reports of the first and the most recent murders in Paterson. In the final pages, as the river moves out to the sea, the poem returns upon itself as a Venus-like figure comes to shore, to be transformed into a male figure accompanied by a female dog. The gender transformations suggest the possibility of some healing of the divorce that the poem has emphasized between poet and place and between the sexes. There is also a suggestion that all four books might be the dream of the sleeping giants who opened the poem, although the literary heritage is foregrounded by the girls playing on the beach, a scene recalling Homer's *Odyssey* and James Joyce's *Ulysses* (1922). The male figure walks inland, spitting out a seed that might provide an alternative future to that represented by the hanging that follows. Williams suggested elsewhere that he had Walt Whitman in mind with this figure heading inland, suggesting both an alternative history and future—the coming of an authentic American verse in a language and form upon which *Paterson* could build.

BOOK 5

By the time the fifth book appeared in 1958, Williams was in his mid-seventies and handicapped by a series of strokes. He explained that he wanted the poem to reflect the poet's present condition—older and closer to death. Paterson the city is left behind as the book foregrounds a medieval tapestry and a Renaissance painter and is dedicated to the crippled artist Toulouse-Lautrec. The first section uses the late-fifteenth- or early-sixteenth-century Unicorn Tapestries in the museum at The Cloisters in New York City to celebrate marriage and the weaving of beauty out of the violence of the phallic unicorn's wounding, a wounding also celebrated as sexual initiation. The opening of the final section praises Brueghel's *The Adoration of the Kings* (1564) for illustrating in earthly terms the mystery of the virgin birth and its promise of renewal. This fifth book, like much of Williams's poetry of the 1950s, is much more comfortable finding its themes figured in a selectively noticed European tradition than was the case with the earlier books—as if old age gives the poet a broader view of time and artistic heritage. Some of the themes in the earlier books appear in more familiar

ways: a courageous but lonely woman "in our town"; the dialogue with Ezra Pound; a letter from an aspiring writer about a brothel; and further correspondence with Dahlberg and with Ginsberg, whose persistence was about to bring him lifelong fame with the publication of *Howl*.

In its final lines the poem returns to Paterson-Williams's own history, specifically the poet's English grandmother and the boy who would become his father in the New World. The "measure" that ends the poem is at once the measure of time by history and the poem, the celebration of the body finding release in dance, and the language and movement of poetry itself. Physical and metrical feet come together in a dance upon the native ground that for Williams is the vital source of energy, authenticity, and renewal.

[*See also* Long Poem, The.]

FURTHER READING

Mariani, Paul. *William Carlos Williams: A New World Naked*. New York, 1981. The standard biography of the poet, with a full discussion of the poem's genesis, composition, and reception.

O'Neil, Elizabeth Murrie. *The Last Word: Letters between Marcia Nardi and William Carlos Williams*. Iowa City, Iowa, 1994. The surviving correspondence between the poet and the writer whose voice is central to book 2 of the poem.

Sankey, Benjamin. *A Companion to William Carlos Williams's* Paterson. Berkeley, Calif., 1981. A book-length close reading of the poem, containing much valuable background.

Weaver, Mike. *William Carlos Williams: The American Background*. Cambridge, 1971. Still the best account of the intellectual sources of the poem.

See also the article on William Carlos Williams, immediately preceding.

AUGUST WILSON

by Josef Raab

August Wilson is the best-known and most performed African-American playwright of the late twentieth and early twenty-first centuries. Awarded two Pulitzer Prizes, his drama is centrally concerned with the painful history of blacks in the United States; each of his plays identifies a certain mood or issue of one decade of the twentieth century and illustrates it through the effect it has on individual black characters. It is not historical accuracy or any kind of comprehensive account that Wilson is after; instead, he wants to make the impact of historical events felt. Rather than write agitprop plays, Wilson seeks to represent experiences that, while they are particular to blacks and while they all emanate from his own biography and his own experiences of a racist environment, also have a universal quality. He has described his literary project thus: "I'm taking each decade and looking back at one of the most important questions that blacks confronted in that decade and writing a play about it.... Put them all together and you have a history" (Bigsby, 2000, p. 292). As in the novels of Toni Morrison, the history of African Americans coping with an unequal society is central to Wilson's work. Both authors are interested in how the present is inextricably linked to the past, and both try to rewrite American history from a black, individualized perspective. The past provides the framework for our ways of thinking and the background for the images and language to which we have become accustomed, the preconceptions we live by. Morrison, Wilson, and other black writers have therefore made it their task to re-create the emotional, psychological, and spiritual history of African Americans in their texts, to identify the ways in which the individual has tried to sustain a sense of

August Wilson. (*From* American Visions, *August/September 2000. Courtesy of the New York Public Library*)

self in the face of pressures and oppression. Rewriting African-American history, these authors believe, is especially important because that history has so far been told and distorted by others—usually by whites who have had their own agendas. Rather than voice propaganda or protest, Wilson's drama tends to express pride and admiration, celebrating how the individual—who has been placed under many pressures by a racist, unequal society or by dreams that he or she can hardly make come true—manages to cope and endure. The major historical events of the decade in which a play is set are generally referred to only in passing; they merely provide the background that illustrates problems and issues that the individual characters have to confront and struggle against. As Wilson says, "The plays deal with those people who were continuing to live their lives. I wasn't interested in what you could get from the history books."

While concentrating on the lives that individual African Americans manage to live under the conditions created by historical circumstances, August Wilson has stated that his goal in writing is to explore the African-American condition as part of the general human condition: "I write about the black experience in America and try to explain in terms of the life I know best those things which are common to all cultures" (Bigsby, 2000, p. 293). As of 2003, Wilson has written eight full-length plays (ten, including his early work to which he does not plan to return), seven of which have been published. Except for *Ma Rainey's Black Bottom* (1985), they are all set in the Pittsburgh neighborhood in which the author grew up.

BIOGRAPHICAL BACKGROUND

August Wilson was born Frederick August Kittel on the Hill, an ethnically diverse neighborhood of Pittsburgh, to the white German baker Frederick Kittel and the black cleaning woman Daisy Wilson Kittel on 27 April 1945. The fourth of six children, he grew up in a two-room apartment above a grocery store. Left to their own devices by a hard-drinking father who was rarely with them, the family was struggling on the mother's small income and on welfare. August was very close to his mother, an outspoken woman who valued reading to her children. His favorite anecdote about her concerns her response to racism: she won a new washing machine in a radio contest by giving her daughter a dime to run to the nearest pay phone and call in the answer. When the station found out that she was black, however, they offered her a voucher for a used machine from the Salvation Army instead. Rather than accepting this poor substitute, the mother told the radio people what she thought of them and decided to keep using her washboard. Not getting along well with either his father or his later stepfather, August would subsequently change his name legally to August Wilson, using his mother's maiden name as his last name.

In 1959 Wilson's stepfather moved the family to a white suburb of Pittsburgh, where the fourteen-year-old August faced constant racism at school, got into many fights, and attended various high schools as well as a trade school before dropping out of school for good in tenth grade, when a teacher said that the paper on Napoleon which he had handed in must have been written by one of his older sisters. Then fifteen years old, Wilson continued his education at the local library, immersing himself especially in the section marked "Negro." He worked as a short-order cook and as a store clerk and joined the army for one year. In 1965, at age twenty, he moved out of his mother's home and into a Pittsburgh rooming house, at the same time buying his first typewriter and a used record player. He also got involved with a group of black writers and political activists who gave him a sense of direction and encouraged his poetry. Together with his writer-teacher friend Rob Penny, he founded the Black Horizons Theatre in Pittsburgh in 1968. Despite having no experience in the theater, he successfully directed a play that Penny had written. Wilson also tried to write plays for this theater himself, but he failed to write any dialogue that satisfied him. Later on he diagnosed the root of the problem: "The reason I couldn't write dialogue was because I didn't respect the way blacks talked; so I always tried to alter it."

Wilson moved to the Minneapolis–St. Paul region in 1978, where his friend Claude Purdy had become director-in-residence at the Penumbra Theatre. Purdy asked Wilson to write a play for this theater; the outcome was a musical satire titled *Black Bart and the Sacred Hills*, and its 1981 production was the first professional staging of Wilson's work. Wilson was hired by the Science Museum of Minnesota in St. Paul to write short plays for the Children's Theatre. He quit this job after three years to become a cook for a social service organization, a job that allowed him to cook half the day and write the other half. By then he had received a fellowship for writing drama and had become a member of the Minneapolis Playwrights Center, enjoying the encouragement of fellow dramatists. He had also started sending plays to the Eugene O'Neill Theater Center's Playwrights Conference in Connecticut, which accepted *Ma Rainey's Black Bottom* for a staged reading by professional actors in 1982. The conference's artistic director, Lloyd Richards, then the dean of the Yale School of Drama, directed the play at Yale Repertory Theatre in 1984. As Yvonne Shafer has written in *August Wilson: A Research and Production Sourcebook* (1998), this cooperation with Richards

> began a process which continued for the subsequent plays: a staged reading at the Conference, production at Yale, then "production sharing" at regional theatres throughout the country, allowing Wilson the time to rewrite, cut, and polish before the production opens in New York. Wilson is thus often working on two or more plays at once as he does not like to have one play open until the next is completed.

The 1984 New York City production of *Ma Rainey's* led to a Rockefeller Fellowship and helped Wilson become nationally recognized. Having been able to devote himself full time to writing since 1982, he continued to revise his manuscripts and submit plays to the O'Neill Center. His breakthrough came in 1987, when *Fences* (1985) won all major awards, including a Pulitzer Prize. The play's success was repeated by *The Piano Lesson* in 1990, which was also awarded a Pulitzer. Wilson moved to Seattle that same year, as his second marriage was breaking up. Although controversial in his separatist stance, he has been selected for membership in the American Academy of Arts and Sciences and in the American Academy of Arts and Letters. During the 1990s he was awarded numerous prizes and fellowships; became a writer-in-residence in New Brunswick, N.J., and a drama teacher at Dartmouth College; entered a third marriage; and continued his cycle of plays that explore individual decades of the twentieth century.

INFLUENCES

August Wilson has been very forthcoming in naming the influences on his artistic sensibility. In "How to Write a

Play Like August Wilson," an essay he wrote for *The New York Times* in 1991, he stated: "In terms of influence on my work, I have what I call my four B's: Romare Bearden; Imamu Amiri Baraka, the writer; Jorge Luis Borges, the Argentine short-story writer; and the biggest B of all: the blues." Wilson does not only practice these four B's, but is also very eager to explain how they have entered his work. He seems intent on teaching these elements as constituents of African-American literature.

The African-American artist Romare Bearden, like Wilson, grew up in Pittsburgh and is best known for the collages of black life that he executed in the 1960s and 1970s. Wilson recalls being overwhelmed by the ways in which Bearden manages to capture African-American life. Reading Bearden's book *The Prevalence of Ritual* (1971) seems to have been an eye-opener for the playwright:

> What for me had been so difficult, Bearden made seem so simple, so easy. What I saw was black life presented on its own terms, on a grand and epic scale, with all its richness and fullness, in a language that was vibrant and which, made attendant to everyday life, ennobled it, affirmed its value, and exalted its presence. (Elkins, 2000, p. 11)

Apart from the authenticity of Bearden's depiction, Wilson admires especially his collage technique, affirming that in his own plays composition and arrangement are equally crucial. Moreover, both Bearden and Wilson use the call-and-recall pattern of the blues in their work, and Wilson has pointed out that paintings by Bearden have been the starting point for several of his plays.

While Romare Bearden serves as an artistic model for Wilson's techniques of presentation and for his truthful depictions of African-American life, Imamu Amiri Baraka can be seen as a kindred spirit in political terms. Both Wilson and Baraka want to get beyond the white and Western domination of America and both have responded strongly to the death of Malcolm X in 1965, which confirmed their desire to assert the value of African-American culture and to put themselves in the service of black nationalism. At the Black Horizons Theatre in Pittsburgh, Wilson directed many of Baraka's plays, favoring especially those collected in the latter's *Four Black Revolutionary Plays* (1969). As Mark William Rocha has explained, both Baraka and Wilson frequently use the motif of facing the white man: "Like Baraka's, Wilson's plays are organized around these facings with the signal difference that in Wilson's plays the confrontation occurs offstage so that emphasis is placed not so much on the confrontation itself but upon how the black community invests itself in that face-to-face encounter" (Elkins, 2000, p. 7).

If Baraka is a political influence for Wilson, Jorge Luis Borges is another aesthetic one. Wilson is most interested in the kinds of narrative progression that Borges has devised: "It's the *way* Borges tells a story. In Borges, it's not what happens, but how" (Wilson quoted in Elkins, 2000, p. 13). The quest motif frequently appears in both writers, and the discovery or recovery of text tends to play an important role. Also, Wilson may have found in Borges a model for integrating the unreal in his realistic plays and for presenting the past as the result of invention and reinterpretation.

But most important among the influences that August Wilson has named is the musical tradition of the blues. He is fond of telling that in 1965 he bought a used record player and several old records, among them Bessie Smith's "Nobody in Town Can Bake a Sweet Jelly Roll Like Mine." Listening to this song twenty-two times in a row, the playwright remembers, he had a kind of epiphany, suddenly understanding the black world around him better and realizing the richness of the lives of those elderly people with whom he shared the rooming house. To Wilson, the blues is the cornerstone of his people's culture: "I think that what's contained in the blues is the African American's response to the world. We are not a people with a long history of writing things out; it's been an oral tradition. . . . The thing with the blues is that there's an entire philosophical system at work" (Wilson in Elkins, 2000, p. 9).

Since the blues often deals with suffering as a consequence of a broken promise, it is a fitting form for Wilson's representation of America and its broken promises, along with the suffering of blacks caused by America's betrayals.

That Wilson names three African-American influences and a Latin American one is not accidental. This is connected to his repeated efforts to distance himself from a (white) Western tradition. "I haven't read Ibsen, Shaw, Shakespeare," he has claimed. "I'm not familiar with *Death of a Salesman*. I haven't read Tennessee Williams. I very purposefully didn't read them" (quoted in Elkins, 2000, p. 4). While it is improbable that this statement is truthful, it is important to see that Wilson wants to deliberately "face" the Western tradition—in the sense of taking up the work of eminent white American playwrights and revising it, thus demonstrating its inapplicability to African America. He also wants to redefine America and American literature by supplanting writers who do not capture the kind of American experience that is at the heart of his own work. In 1990, when he was told that he had won a second Pulitzer Prize, Wilson's first comment was, "Well, O'Neill won four, so I guess I better get going."

THE IMPACT OF RACISM

In all of Wilson's work, the painful impact of racism on the lives of African Americans throughout the twentieth century can be felt. In his first three plays to achieve national acclaim, the suffering caused by racial inequalities seems strongest. *Ma Rainey's Black Bottom* was first performed at the Yale Repertory Theatre in 1984 and was published in 1985. Set in 1927 Chicago, it dramatizes the exploitation of black artists by white decision makers. It presents a world with a very clear division along the color line. The historical blues singer Ma Rainey and her band are expected at a recording studio, where their manager and their producer—both insensitive to African-American concerns—discuss how to handle the musicians and how to market their product. Ma arrives very late because after a car accident a taxi had refused to take her and her black companions to the studio and a policeman had tried to arrest her because of the ensuing fight with the racist cab driver. At the studio, the band members quarrel about which version of their song to record, and it becomes obvious that there is a deep resentment of whites because of past oppression and violence as well as present exploitation. Tempers continue to run high as Ma puts down her trumpet player Levee, who has artistic aspirations of his own and who flirts with the young woman Ma has brought along. Once the recording is finally completed, Ma and her companions leave, while the band waits for its pay. Levee is put down again when the producer tells him that he does not think much of the songs Levee wrote and will only pay five dollars apiece for them. When the band's piano player then accidentally steps on Levee's expensive new shoes, Levee explodes and stabs him. Horrified by his own action, he tries in vain to save his fellow band member.

The subject matters of black musicians being exploited by white executives (who are in the studio's "control room" while the artists are sent to the basement to practice), white disrespect for black art, the attempts of some blacks to succeed in a white-dominated world, and the violence of blacks against blacks appealed to audiences nationwide, as did the use of music and lyrical monologues, which has since become a trademark of Wilson's drama.

The play was followed by an even bigger success, *Fences*, which was first performed at the Yale Repertory Theatre in 1985 and published in 1986. The central character of this Pulitzer Prize–winning drama is a fifty-three-year-old former professional baseball player of the Negro leagues, Troy Maxson, who now works as a garbage collector and lives with his family in a ramshackle house with a dirt yard. There is a decaying porch and an unfinished fence. We later find out that Troy had once planned to build that fence to define his property and his individuality, but never got very far. The time for most of the action is 1957, when the civil rights movement had started to get into swing but few results were yet felt. One sign of changes to come is that Troy has just demanded that his employer change the practice of having whites drive the garbage trucks while blacks do the heavy lifting—a struggle that Troy will eventually win. To Troy, this is a health concern rather than a political one; it illustrates his bitterness about the options that were not available to him because of his skin color. Mainly he is frustrated that he never got to play in a major-league baseball team because he is black.

Troy enjoys the home life which his loving but strong-willed wife Rose provides for him, but he also finds it constricting at times. Denied respect on a daily basis at work and elsewhere, he seeks the comforts of another woman, who pampers his ego and who is carrying his daughter. He also fears that his own disappointments may be repeated by his seventeen-year-old son Cory, so he forbids Cory to play on his school's football team, and orders him instead to take a job at a grocery store. Since his own dreams of athletic success were frustrated by a racist system, he wants his son to make a living in a menial but relatively secure job. There is a fear that the frustrations of the father in the past will be paralleled by frustrations of the son in the future. On the other hand, a job for Cory would also give Troy a feeling of no longer being economically responsible for his son. The two fight repeatedly and violently until Troy throws Cory out. Troy also dislikes Lyons, his thirty-four-year-old son by another marriage, who wants to be a musician rather than do menial work and who comes to borrow money from Troy. While Troy wants to be a responsible family man—especially in caring for his illegitimate daughter—he also hurts his wife and sons. Wilson, however, wanted to portray him primarily in a positive light. "Troy Maxson is responsible. Those images are important. Every black man did not just make a baby and run off," the author told an interviewer (Bogumil, 1999, p.36). A racist society more than any character flaws prevents him from achieving his portion of the American Dream.

The play's last scene is set in 1965 on the morning of Troy's funeral. Lyons, imprisoned for forging checks, gets some time out of jail for attending his father's funeral. Cory comes home but initially refuses to attend the funeral; he then bonds with his half-sister Raynell, by now seven years old. The mourners are joined by Troy's brother Gabriel, who believes himself to be the Archangel Gabriel. A deranged World War II veteran whose disability checks Troy first collected and whom he later committed to a mental institution, Gabriel still has a special gift: his dancing and singing open the gates of heaven for Troy.

As August Wilson told an interviewer, in *Fences* he wanted to celebrate the blueslike life-affirmation of Troy and the nobility of African Americans who cope despite racism and adverse conditions:

> Blacks in America have so little to make life with compared to whites, yet they do so with a certain zest, or certain energy that is fascinating because they make life out of nothing—yet it is charged and luminous and has all the qualities of anyone else's life. I think a lot of this is hidden by the glancing manner in which White America looks at Blacks, and the way Blacks look at themselves. Which is why I work a lot with stereotypes, with the idea of stripping away layer by layer the surface to reveal what is underneath—the real person, the whole person. (Bigsby, 2000, p. 298)

The situation of the individual is then presented as symptomatic of the situation of African Americans in general. And the individual is constrained by the historical situation in which he or she lives. While no white characters appear in *Fences*, it is obvious that white America sets the framework for the options available to blacks, for the frustration of their dreams as well as for their small victories.

Another testimony to black endurance and an exploration of black dreams is *Joe Turner's Come and Gone*, first performed at the Yale Repertory Theatre in 1986 and published in 1988. In this play, which August Wilson has called his own favorite, Seth Holly, a black man in his fifties, owns a rooming house in Pittsburgh in 1911. Seth is a skilled metal worker and would like to set up a business making pots and pans, but his white employers will not loan him the money needed to do so. The white peddler Selig sells the dustpans that Seth makes. As we will find out later, Selig is from a family that brought slaves to America and captured runaway slaves. Various other characters populate the rooming house, among them the con man Bynum, who uses spells on people: two young women, one looking for adventure, one looking for love; a guitar-playing country boy; and the thirty-two-year-old Loomis with his eleven-year-old daughter.

As Mary L. Bogumil has pointed out in *Understanding August Wilson* (1999), all these characters "attempt to rediscover, repossess, and redefine themselves historically and socially as free citizens."

Loomis was separated from his wife, Martha, because for seven years he was imprisoned by Joe Turner, brother of the governor of Tennessee, who arbitrarily jailed blacks to use them as a free workforce. When Selig finally brings Martha back to Loomis, the two quarrel about who abandoned whom. As Martha tells Loomis to try to find Jesus, Loomis denounces Jesus as a grinning white man. In a symbolic act of freeing himself from bondage, he slashes his chest with a knife, rubs blood on his face, and exits.

Wilson explained in his preface to the play that he wanted to focus on characters who had been born of freed slaves, who wanted to leave the bondage of the South behind, who were separated from one another and from their cultural heritage, and who were entering an uncertain world in which new forms of dependence were awaiting them. There they seek to "reconnect" and "reassemble" themselves as free people who have "definite and sincere worth," according to the published play's preface. So most of the characters in this play are travelers who are searching for an individual as well as for a group identity. Loomis's imprisonment symbolizes slavery and the trauma suffered by blacks. As the stage directions point out, by finding his "song of self-sufficiency" he recovers his independent identity; he is "fully resurrected, cleansed and given breath, free from any encumbrance other than the workings of his own heart and the bonds of the flesh, having accepted responsibility for his presence in the world, he is free to soar above the environs that weighed and pushed his spirits into terrifying contractions." Loomis achieves his independence by discovering his African roots; in this way Wilson uses him as a figure that leads the way for the other characters. His song and that of the other characters is the blues; as Wilson writes in his preface, these songs are "both a wail and a whelp of joy."

RECLAIMING

This duality of pain and pleasure appears in all of Wilson's plays. After his initial plays there is a stronger emphasis on black characters taking some measure of control and reclaiming what is rightfully theirs. In *The Piano Lesson*, which was first performed at the Yale Repertory Theatre in 1987 and published in 1990, history and ways of dealing with it are of central importance. In this Pulitzer Prize–winning play a brother (Boy Willie) and a sister

(Bernice) fight over what to do with a piano that their father stole from the family that had owned his ancestors. The piano's legs had been decorated by their great-grandfather with images recalling the family's past. Is the piano to be preserved as a reminder of a violent legacy or is it to be sold so that the proceeds could be used to buy the land on which their father had worked as a slave? Although the play is set in 1936 Pittsburgh, the history of slavery is felt strongly.

Boy Willie and his friend Lymon have driven up to Pittsburgh from the South with a pickup truck filled with watermelons that they want to sell in the city. At 5 A.M. they arrive at the house of the widowed Bernice, her uncle Doaker, and her eleven-year-old daughter Maretha. Boy Willie announces that the Ghosts of the Yellow Dog have drowned a man named Sutter and that he wants to sell the family piano, which belongs to him and Bernice together; although she has not played the instrument in years, Bernice refuses to have any discussion on the subject. Doaker later explains that his grandfather, then a slave of the Sutter family, carved the images into the piano's legs, that the piano was later stolen by his brother, the father of Bernice and Boy Willie, who was subsequently burned, along with three other black men, in a railroad car on the Yellow Dog line as a revenge by white men. All of these white men have mysteriously died in the meantime—Sutter being the last one of the group. Since Boy Willie's arrival, Sutter's ghost is repeatedly seen around the piano. When Boy Willie and Lymon try to take the piano away against Bernice's will, Bernice threatens them with a gun and tempers run high. Just then the presence of Sutter's ghost is felt by all in the house. Boy Willie engages him in a life and death struggle while Bernice plays the piano and sings a song in which she calls for their relatives to help them. This chases away the ghost. Boy Willie decides that he should not try to sell the piano after all, but that Bernice should play it in order to keep away Sutter's ghost. Boy Willie and another uncle leave for the South while Lymon stays on in Pittsburgh.

The land on which their ancestors worked, as well as the piano, is an integral element of the family's history, and Wilson uses both to illustrate his conviction that there is a "need to re-connect yourself." He sees black culture as having been uprooted repeatedly and therefore stresses the need for continuity; in the framework of the play, such continuity can be achieved through an active engagement with the piano and by taking control of the land on which their ancestors had worked as slaves. Only such an active use of the reminders of the painful past, the play suggests, can exorcise the ghosts of oppression. Neither Bernice's initial hiding from the slavery past nor Boy Willie's desire to cash in on it are suitable approaches in Wilson's mind. What he argues for is a rewriting of African-American history in which blacks take authorial control.

This idea of reclaiming is also strong in *Two Trains Running*, first performed at the Yale Repertory Theatre in 1990 and published in 1992. Set in a Pittsburgh restaurant in 1969, the play presents a number of black characters who are demanding justice. Memphis, the restaurant owner, is planning to sell his restaurant building to the city for a good price and then intends to go to Natchez, Mississippi, to demand that his farm, from which he had been unjustly driven away, be returned to him. Sterling, who has just spent five years in prison, wants to take the waitress Risa to a rally celebrating Malcolm X's birthday, and Wolf is successfully running numbers. Meanwhile, the mentally disturbed Hambone keeps demanding a ham from the white grocer-butcher Lutz in payment for painting his fence—a demand that he has been voicing every day for the past nine and a half years. There is a general sense of the characters trying to preserve their dignity by resisting the white economic control from which they suffer.

Sterling wins playing the numbers, but the white bosses of the game want to give him only half the winnings. He successfully challenges them and gets his winnings. Hambone dies, Memphis sells his building at an excellent price and is still planning to go down to Natchez on one of the two trains running every day. The sale of Memphis's restaurant will make an urban renewal project possible but will take away the location that formed the nucleus of this black community. At the end of the play, a blood-smeared Sterling enters with a ham he has stolen from Lutz's store to put in Hambone's coffin.

The play's comedy is mixed with the death and injustice that it portrays; its action has an almost carnivalesque quality, but there is also a deep sense that community activism is necessary and that justice is possible. Hambone, Sterling, and Memphis especially demand from whites what is justly theirs. These claims are complemented by the frequent references to the Malcolm X rally. As Wilson has explained, he wanted to express the need "to live life with dignity, to celebrate and accept responsibility for your presence in the world." However, the response of reviewers and audiences to this play was mixed.

COPING

Ways of coping with racial injustice and with the legacy of oppression have continued to be a primary interest of

August Wilson's drama. *Seven Guitars*, first performed at the Goodman Theatre in Chicago in 1995 and published in 1996, is again set in Pittsburgh and, like *Two Trains Running*, explores various individual life stories. The year is 1948: in the play's first scene, the friends of the guitar player Floyd Barton talk about his life and about his funeral that day. Then the second scene takes us back to the events that led to Floyd's violent death. Floyd returns to Pittsburgh after serving a ninety-day prison sentence and is planning to go on to Chicago to record a new song. He does not have the money to get his guitar out of the pawn shop. His agent is supposed to give him an advance but is arrested for selling fake insurance. After a string of bad luck, Floyd is not seen for two days and then returns with a new guitar and a new dress for his girlfriend Vera, not saying where he got the money for those purchases. We assume, however, that he was involved in a robbery. He buries money in the garden. When his harmonica player finds it, he gets it back from Floyd at gunpoint, only to be faced by the deranged and mysterious Hedley, who has repeatedly dreamed that his father would send Buddy Bolden (generally considered to have been the first jazz bandleader) to bring him money. When Floyd refuses to give Hedley the money, Hedley kills him with a machete, believing, in his deranged state, that he is killing Buddy Bolden.

Money is the central theme of this play; it is a destructive force and its absence keeps the characters from being able to use their potential. Wilson has described this play as being "about people battling society and themselves for self-worth" and he has established similarities to the blues and its expression of both suffering and joy. But it is also a play about community, as the title suggests. Bogumil explains:

> The title *Seven Guitars* evokes the image of the players, the characters, as separate but at times convergent members in the creation of a shared, polyphonic history. So together they continue to celebrate the life of Floyd as each hears the recording of Floyd Barton singing "That's All Right," a song which permeates this elegiac atmosphere as well as each character's consciousness." (Bogumil, 1999, p. 120)

The theme of coping as an individual and as a community is continued in *Jitney*, a play that had been in the making for two decades. A first version was performed at the Allegheny Repertory Theatre in Pittsburgh in 1982, after which Wilson laid the play aside. Revised versions were then staged at the Pittsburgh Public Theatre in 1996 and at the Crossroad Theatre in New Brunswick, New Jersey, in 1997 before the play's publication 2001. Set in 1977 Pittsburgh, this drama explores again a variety of personal life stories, ways of coping with the scarcity of economic opportunity and the violence resulting from a series of disappointments. Reflecting the tenuous successes in self-determination that African Americans had achieved by the late 1970s, Wilson makes the main character of this play, Becker, a small entrepreneur. He runs a car service in the city's Hill section, where Wilson grew up—a scaled-down version of a taxi company in which the drivers use their own private cars. There is competition and quarrel among the men, as each of them is trying to fend for himself, to get some business and make some money, to have his little portion of the American Dream. One wants to make enough money to buy a house and enable his wife to go to college; another wants to save up so that he can retire. Becker would rather forget the past, especially his son, now in his mid-thirties. This son was a victim of racism twenty years earlier: he fought back and killed his white former girlfriend. Having spent about twenty years in prison, he believes that he has paid for his deed, but he proclaims that he would commit the same murder again in an instant. His father, however, cannot go along with those ethics, stressing instead the sanctity of any human life—including the life of one who has betrayed and humiliated you. There is a sense that the son eventually starts to understand how valuable a human life is and that he will follow in his father's footsteps. After Becker's death his son takes over the business at the end of the play.

A different way of coping with the scarcity of economic opportunity appears in the play that Wilson was still revising in 2003, *King Hedley II*, which was first performed at the Pittsburgh Public Theatre in 1999 and as of 2003 was not yet published. Set in Pittsburgh's Hill district in 1985, this play takes up the character Hedley from *Seven Guitars* and concentrates on the son named King, whom Hedley is expecting in that earlier play. The decade of the 1980s is presented as one characterized by violence and disorder and by the desire to participate in the country's economic prosperity. Hedley seeks to overcome the hardship and oppression he has experienced all his life and provide a better life for himself, his mother, and his wife, Tonya. Selling stolen refrigerators with his friend Mister, he tries to save enough money to make a down payment on a video store he wants to rent. The author illustrates through his protagonist that equal opportunities are still a long way off and that in the face of disappointment and injustice, ethics tend to be thrown overboard all too often.

August Wilson takes on important themes in his plays: family, responsibility, violence directed both outward and inward, community, identity, freedom, and justice. While he explores these themes through specific African-American characters at a specific time (having told an interviewer, "I am trying to write plays that contain the sum total of black culture in America, and its difference from white culture"), their treatment also speaks to American audiences outside the black community as well as to international theatergoers. His black characters display an admirable nobility in coping with racist oppression and living under adverse conditions. Like the blues, August Wilson's drama combines sadness and laughter, suffering and joy, disappointment and hope, outrage and lyricism, anger and reconciliation in its attempts to capture slices of life.

[*See also* Theater in America.]

SELECTED WORKS

Ma Rainey's Black Bottom (1985)
Fences (1985)
Joe Turner's Come and Gone (1988)
The Piano Lesson (1990)
Two Trains Running (1992)
Seven Guitars (1996)
The Ground on Which I Stand (2001)
Jitney (2001)

FURTHER READING

Bigsby, C. W. E. *Modern American Drama, 1945–2000.* Cambridge, 2000. A useful critical introduction, informative but at times careless about detail.

Bogumil, Mary L. *Understanding August Wilson.* Columbia, S.C., 1999. Offers a biographical introduction and good, basic interpretations of the six major plays published until the late 1990s that also highlight the historical context. Contains an extensive (though incomplete), usefully annotated bibliography.

Elkins, Marilyn, ed. *August Wilson: A Casebook.* New York and London, 2000. An introduction, eleven essays, and two interviews highlight different aspects of Wilson's art, ranging from influences to politics, southernness, myth, folklore, Africa, gender, and the blues.

Nadel, Alan. *May All Your Fences Have Gates: Essays on the Drama of August Wilson.* Iowa City, Iowa, 1994.

Pereira, Kim. *August Wilson and the African-American Odyssey.* Urbana, Ill., 1995. Discusses the strategies of self-invention that Wilson's characters use (up to *The Piano Lesson*) for coping with life in the industrial North.

Shafer, Yvonne. *August Wilson: A Research and Production Sourcebook.* Westport, Conn., and London, 1998. Contains a well-informed survey of Wilson's life and career as well as detailed synopses of his major published plays up until the late 1990s and of their reviews, as well as extensive primary and secondary bibliographies. Very useful for basic information on the author and his plays and for locating secondary material.

Shannon, Sandra. *The Dramatic Vision of August Wilson.* Washington, D.C., 1995. A good account of the formation of Wilson's artistic sensibility; includes an interview with Wilson.

Wolfe, Peter. *August Wilson.* New York, 1999. A comprehensive critical appraisal of Wilson's art as well as of scholarship about him. Includes an extensive annotated bibliography.

EDMUND WILSON

by Melissa Knox

Edmund Wilson was one of a small number of American men of letters who dominated the literary scene from the 1920s, when his first volume of journals appeared, until his death in 1972. He was, first and foremost, a master of the plain style. His essays and personal memoirs reveal much about his life, complicated by four marriages, one ending in the premature death of his wife, two in divorce. His literary and cultural studies examine relationships between writers and their societies. He devoted much of his life to observing interactions between society and the individual creative mind. The virile sharpness of his writings is enriched by his occasionally cruel self-analytic streak, which reveals him often in a light to be pitied, as a man frequently finding himself in unrewarding relationships. In a university setting—one which, unlike other writers of his stature, he studiously avoided, preferring to make his mark entirely on his own terms—he might be called a generalist, a term that would not do him justice. A polymath, a Renaissance man, Wilson had an enormous range of literary, intellectual interests that included literary movements, notably symbolism, and the effects of developments in psychology and history on writers; he was engaged in the psychoanalytic study of literature among other things. Pursuing various scholarly aspirations, such as learning Hebrew in order to decipher the Dead Sea Scrolls, he had plenty of energy left over for a book-length study of his own experience with the Internal Revenue Service. He made his living mainly as a book reviewer and journalist.

Wilson had an unfortunate penchant for getting involved with women who betrayed him or made him unhappy in some way, and he had a mournful tendency to remain loyal to them, letting their sometimes mediocre work blind his normally stellar literary judgment as was

Edmund Wilson, 1946.
(Courtesy of the Library of Congress)

the case with Anaïs Nin, known for her *Diaries* (begun in 1914 and published between 1966 and 1996), in which she purports to reveal for the first time a woman's complete experience. Wilson's biographer, Jeffrey Meyers (1995), remarks that Wilson "lavished unwarranted praise upon her work—not to repay friendship, but to gain sexual favors" (p. 253). Wilson was saddened by the loss of Nin's regard, not realizing how insulted she had felt by his kindly meant writing tips, and hoped to win her friendship again. She had been, however, manipulative from the start, merely using him to get a good review of her bad novel in *The New Yorker*. This combination of childlike trust in the wrong women and an acid, knowing skepticism in his literary evaluations, characterizes Wilson's oeuvre. In fact, one trait could not exist without the other. The childlike aspect of his character made him open to impressions and particularly sensitive in capturing them; he had a child's sense of newness and discovery. Nicknamed "Bunny" in infancy by his mother, who said he looked "just like a plum bun" (Meyers, p. 7), he retained the moniker among his oldest friends, even as his mind developed the steely judgmentalism and occasional bellicosity that informed his best writings.

The mental and emotional qualities that led to many disappointments in his personal life gave his literary style its satiric bite and its strong sense of the importance of the immediate experience in daily life. One critic, David Castronovo (1984), referred to Wilson as "our enlightenment figure, a *philosophe* in an age of world wars, depressions and class conflicts, rising taxes, lowering standards, intellectual bewilderment, bombs, revolutions, and bureaucracies" (p. 1). Castronovo adds that Wilson is "in the first rank of twentieth-century essayists in English" (p. 1) Unafraid of—on the contrary, quite fond of—harsh and occasionally moralistic judgments, Wilson was after all a descendent on his mother's side of Cotton Mather, the fiery seventeenth-century preacher who delivered doomsday sermons promising hellfire. Wilson is squarely in the peculiar American tradition of the literary essay disguised as a sermon, or sometimes vice versa. According to Jeffrey Meyers, "The poet Allen Tate believed that the ghost of Cotton Mather had burrowed into Wilson's conscience like a mole" (p. 1). Introspective, moralistic, Wilson renders precisely the sense of his own isolation as an intellectual in an early letter complaining about serving in the army during World War I: "You have no idea . . . how isolated and inward you become, surrounded by and dealing with people with whom you cannot talk the real language, whose habits and manners you detest. . . . This is not the absence of charity on my part, it is only the reaction of intelligence" (quoted in Meyers, p. 34).

WILSON'S CAREER

Wilson's career spans from 1919, when he started working as a freelance writer, to 1972, when he died on 12 June, a few months after suffering one of several strokes. He had been working on essays about Russia shortly before his death. Born on 8 May 1895 in Red Bank, New Jersey, to Edmund Wilson Sr., an attorney, and Helen Mather Kimball Wilson, he graduated from Princeton in 1916, where he made important literary contacts, befriending F. Scott Fitzgerald and studying with the humanist Christian Gauss. Known for his proficiency with the biographical essay and the autobiographical memoir, he has inspired contemporary masters; among those who admire him greatly are the film critic and memoirist David Denby and the essayist and critic Joseph Epstein. Wilson worked as the managing editor of *Vanity Fair* in 1920, leaving it to becoming managing editor of *The New Republic* in 1921 but returning in 1922. He went back to *The New Republic* in 1933 and stayed there until 1941. In 1943–1944 he wrote book reviews for *The New Yorker*.

Wilson' s first major critical work, *Axel's Castle: A Study in the Imaginative Literature of 1870–1930* (1931), breaks new ground in literary approaches to the following major literary figures: W. B. Yeats, Paul Valéry, T. S. Eliot, Marcel Proust, James Joyce, and Gertrude Stein. None of these writers yet had a biographer, and Wilson provided useful biographic material connected with literary analysis. Primarily he focused on symbolism in their work, defining it as "an attempt by carefully studied means—a complicated association of ideas represented by a medley of metaphors—to communicate unique personal feelings" (Meyers, p. 141). In 1961 the eminent British critic Frank Kermode remarked that *Axel's Castle* was "alive, and everybody's business."

A second major work, *The Triple Thinkers: Ten Essays on Literature* (1938) compiles essays on a variety of literary figures with no apparent relationship to one another (revised and enlarged in 1948 and published as *The Triple Thinkers: Twelve Essays on Literary Subjects*). In fact, the common theme uniting them is Wilson's view that political, social, and cultural events within an artist's life help to illuminate the meaning of his or her work. David Castronovo (1984, p. 33) observes that the title for the volume was taken from the French novelist Gustave Flaubert, who remarked in a letter that the creative artist "is a thinker three times over," having an understanding of or ability to interpret the social, cultural, and political problems of an age. At the time that he wrote it, Wilson was fresh from a trip to Russia that had begun with an idealization of communism and ended in disillusionment with Stalinism. Like all his best work, the essays are devoted to defining the role of the artist, the meaning of the artist in society. Marxism had been embraced by many American intellectuals, and Wilson was no exception, but his particular interest in these essays concerned more the importance of social class to writers, or the way in which writers' social class and awareness of their society influences what they write. Wilson did not subscribe to the idea that politics produces art or that art should be part of a political ideology.

Wilson's venture into psychoanalytic criticism, *The Wound and the Bow: Seven Studies in Literature* (1941), started a new trend in biographically based literary criticism that was in the early and mid-twentieth century significantly developed by the eminent critics Lionel Trilling and Steven Marcus, both of whom employed Sigmund Freud's theories to understand the literary development of various writers. *The Wound and the Bow* starts with the assumption that art is, among other things, a response to and compensation for a deep emotional injury. The book's title derives from the ancient Greek myth of Philoctetes as dramatized by Sophocles. Wilson suggests that Philoctetes is a "parable of human character . . . [t]he victim of a malodorous disease which renders him abhorrent to society and periodically degrades him and makes him helpless is also the master of a superhuman art which everybody has to respect and which the normal man finds he needs" (*The Wound and the Bow*, 1941, p. 263). What is refreshing in Wilson's psychological interpretations, whether one agrees with them or not, is their thoughtful, detailed connections to events in the lives of the literary figures he discusses. Before his observations in this study, much of psychoanalytically oriented criticism had rather crudely discovered symbols and psychic defenses in the work of artists, without demonstrating any real connection between the symbol and the work or integrating the psychoanalytic theory with the artist's life and work. *The Wound and the Bow* extends Wilson's earlier work on the relation of the artist to society, since the ways in which artists struggle within themselves or attempt to resolve personal conflicts may correspond with the ways in which they respond to social conflicts.

WILSON'S VENTURE INTO COMMUNISM

To the Finland Station: A Study in the Writing and Acting of History (1940) is one of Wilson's most important works, because it deals substantially with a topic that fascinated him all his life, namely, the relationship between the individual and history. In all his works, he studies not the isolated artist or historian or scientist, but the interaction between these figures and their culture, their society, and the forces of history surrounding and being shaped by them. Wilson begins with the French scholar Jules Michelet's discovery in 1824 of the eighteenth-century Italian scholar Giambattista Vico, whose works had at that time fallen into obscurity. Vico, now widely known and read by students of history, had in his major work of 1725, *Principi di una Scienza Nuova d'intorno alla commune natura delle nazioni* (Principles of a New Science Dealing with the Nature of Nations), decided, in Wilson's words, "that it ought to be possible to apply to the study of human history methods similar to those proposed by [Francis] Bacon for the study of the natural world" (*To the Finland Station*, p. 3). Bacon was the first English essayist, who, like Wilson, is greatly indebted to the sixteenth-century French essayist Michel Eyquem de Montaigne for the idea of the essay as an attempt to explain a particular idea or problem, the word "essay" in fact deriving from the French verb "to try." Like the great French evolver of the essay, Montaigne, Wilson was primarily concerned with exploration and explanation of personalities and phenomena within history. *To the Finland Station* opens with Wilson's excitement about the possibilities considered by Michelet, for instance, studying a history "of the race considered as an individual" and on "the character of peoples as revealed by their vocabularies" (p. 3). Wilson adds that it is "strange and stirring" to find in Vico's writings "the modern sociological and anthropological mind awakening amid the dust of a provincial school of jurisprudence of the end of the seventeenth century." Adding that human history had before Vico consisted mainly in "biographies of great men" or chronicles "of remarkable happenings," or as "a pageant directed by God" (p. 4), Wilson looks forward to writing history instead as the result of a collaboration between human beings and the environments and cultures that surround them; "like individual human beings," he asserts, societies also pass "through regular phases of growth" (p. 4).

To the Finland Station falls into four sections subdivided into chapters treating individual historical figures, culminating in the fathers of Russian communism: Karl Marx, Friedrich Engels, Vladimir Lenin, and Leon Trotsky. The final chapters detail the ways in which these individuals saw themselves as historical figures. In "Trotsky Identifies History with Himself," for instance, Wilson discusses Trotsky's assertion that reading Marx and Engels provided "proof on every page that I was bound to these two by a direct psychological affinity" (p. 431). Lenin, Wilson observes, came into history at a moment when he had "no fear of Roman Pope or Protestant Synod," and stood "on the eve of the moment when for the first time in the human exploit the key of a philosophy of history was to fit an historical lock" (p. 469). The ultimate results of Lenin's idealism were a disaster, and one that shocked Wilson. In the 1971 edition of *To the Finland Station*, Wilson added an introduction in which he wrote that he had "no premonition that the Soviet Union was to become one of the most hideous tyrannies that the world had ever known."

WILSON'S JOURNALS

Apart from Wilson's innovative criticism, his journals—*The Twenties* (1975), *The Thirties* (1980), *The Forties* (1983), *The Fifties* (1986), and *The Sixties* (1993)—are founts of personal and political gossip, lively observation, and personal exposure. They capture the mood of these decades. Like James Joyce leaving an anthropologically accurate rendering of Dublin in his major novel *Ulysses*, Wilson in his journals renders with photographic and indeed phonographic precision, and with a great deal of wit, America's cultural progress in those decades. In *The Twenties*, he presents thumbnail sketches of such Algonquin Roundtable figures as Dorothy Parker and Robert Benchley, as well as portraits of prominent individuals such as the journalist and wit H. L. Mencken. He records some witticisms of Parker, known to have been one of the funniest women of the twentieth century, writing that when he sat with her at an Algonquin table that was "too narrow to have anyone across from you, so that one sat on a bench with one's back to the wall," Parker quipped, "This looks like a road company of the Last Supper" (p. 48). He captures her love of puns, as in, "Hiawatha nice girl till I met you" (p. 45).

The Thirties concerns the decade in which America plunged from prosperity to desolate poverty. When the stock market crashed in October 1929, the Roaring Twenties, the decade of frivolity and burning one's candle at both ends, descended precipitously into the years of the Great Depression. In his section on New York and Chicago, Wilson summons up the social despair of those years with this portrait from a piece entitled "Unemployed":

> In schools, factories, warehouses, old jails…yellow school walls soiled, blackboards punched through, thin blankets and a sheet, men in holey socks and slit union suits tattooed with fancy designs and with the emblems of services they no longer served, with fallen arches taken out of their flattened shoes and done up with bandages of adhesive tape, or lying wrapped up in their blankets on their backs, their skin stretched tight over their cheekbones and jawbones almost like the faces of the dead. (*The Thirties*, 1980, pp. 278–279)

The Forties concerns extremely productive years—Wilson published seven books and over one hundred essays and articles during this period. The exuberant *Memoirs of Hecate County* (1946), a fictional treatment of the sex lives of the rich and famous, or at least the comfortably upper middle class, remained a best-seller for some years until would-be censors dragged the book into court. The fact that it was out of print in 2003 is perhaps suggestive of the tame nature of its sexual content by later standards. *The Forties* offers little about World War II but much about Wilson's life and love affair with the woman who would become his fourth and final wife, Elena. In 1946 he writes: "Passion for her: blaze-up in taxi, as on both our sides it had been smoldering a long time without our paying attention to it: she would say, this is getting bad!—this is strong! My night of agony, couldn't sleep…"

The Fifties begins with an elegiac tone: "Nothing but deaths!" Wilson titles the first section, mourning the loss of, among others, the poet Edna St. Vincent Millay. "She died about dawn," he relates, reminiscing about the time he saw her in Truro, Cape Cod, and how his own decision to live there probably resulted from that visit. He observes that the night before he heard of her death he had a dream about her that was erotic, but with literary elements. In this, as in other journals, his emotional tenor

fluctuates exhilaratingly: within the same page and a half he excoriates the poet W. H. Auden as having hair that looks like "a yellow wig" and becoming "rather portly and old-man-of-the-world," then dwells on making love to his wife, Elena, at the Algonquin hotel, and finally confesses that Elena told him she hated him, that he was "a scorpion that wants to destroy." (*The Fifties*, 1986, pp. 604–605)

In the final volume of journals, *The Sixties*, Wilson observes and reminisces with the same verve as in earlier journals, but ill health and advanced age somewhat blunt his critical powers. In a letter of 26 April 1966 to his friend Elizabeth Huling, an editor, he jests, "I am feeling rather old myself, and even a pint of Scotch is likely to enfeeble me the next day."

THE EPISTOLARY WILSON

Not to be forgotten is the enormous variety of Wilson's letters over the decades, a few of which should be touched on, since they offer a lively response to controversies that engaged him in the course of his long life. Of his *Memoirs of Hecate County*, he remarked in a 1952 letter to the literary critic Mario Praz: "Hecate County was intended as a suburban inferno" (*Letters on Literature and Politics, 1912–1972*, 1977, p. 433). A cartoon of 1946 included in his letters shows a conventional-looking couple discussing the book with dubious expressions, and is captioned: "Poor Edmund Wilson—Hasn't He Any Nice Friends?" (*Letters*, p. 435). Particularly enjoyable in these letters are his quick literary reactions, as in this note to Vladimir Nabokov: "I have just read Gogol's Viy, which is certainly one of the greatest stories of the kind ever written. That little wooden church out on the edge of town with the dogs howling around it is wonderful" (*Letters*, p. 379). A letter of 1948 to George Orwell reveals Wilson's witty sense of the need for accuracy in writing:

> In *The English People*, by the way, I see that you persist in the error that I tried to dispel when I saw you in London: that the various kinds of insects in America are indiscriminately known as "bugs." of the list you give, it is true that a cockchafer is known over here as a June bug and that a ladybird is sometimes called a ladybug, but a cricket or a daddy longlegs couldn't possibly be referred to as a bug. As for wild flowers, they all have separate names. (*Letters*, p. 451)

To James Thurber, he complained of a critic expecting "to find me something different from what I'm like: that is he expected to find me a cloistered and mellow old man of letters—and kept asking me questions about books—a kind of thing that bores me, especially when I haven't read the books" (*Letters*, p. 570).

Wilson is slighted by the term "minor" writer, and might better be classed, as Somerset Maugham once said about himself, "in the very front row of the second-raters," that is, next in line after the literary giants Shakespeare, Goethe, Dante. Wilson's range of interests—from intellectual considerations of writers and politicians, to the translation and interpretation of the Dead Sea Scrolls, to the nature and study of history, all need to be reconsidered in the light of his very personal and private revelations. The confessional and autobiographical Wilson reveals the sensibility that shaped his critical perspectives, and the ability to reveal so much personally contributed to his appetite for literary and cultural study in ways that yet need to be studied.

[*See also* Algonquin Round Table.]

SELECTED WORKS

Axel's Castle: A Study in the Imaginative Literature of 1870–1930 (1931)
The Triple Thinkers: Ten Essays on Literature (1938)

To the Finland Station: A Study in the Writing and Acting of History (1940)
The Wound and the Bow: Seven Studies in Literature (1941)
Memoirs of Hecate County (1946)
The Shores of Light: A Literary Chronicle of the Twenties and Thirties (1952)
The Twenties: From Notebooks and Diaries of the Period (1975)
Letters on Literature and Politics, 1912–1972 (1977)
The Thirties: From Notebooks and Diaries of the Period (1980)
The Forties: From Notebooks and Diaries of the Period (1983)
The Fifties: From Notebooks and Diaries of the Period (1986)
The Sixties: The Last Journal, 1960–1972 (1993)

FURTHER READING

Castronovo, David. *Edmund Wilson*. New York, 1984. Clear, helpful guide to Wilson's writings.

Castronovo, David. *Edmund Wilson Revisited*. New York, 1998. Update of a thorough study, containing useful biographical information and criticism.

Meyers, Jeffrey. *Edmund Wilson: A Biography*. New York, 1995. Excellent biography containing psychologically penetrating interpretation of Wilson's life.

THOMAS WOLFE

by Mark Royden Winchell

At one point in J. D. Salinger's *The Catcher in the Rye*, Holden Caulfield remarks: "What really knocks me out is a book that, when you're done reading it, you wish the author who wrote it was a terrific friend of yours and you could call him up whenever you felt like it." Few American novelists of the twentieth century can match Thomas Wolfe in having such an effect on readers. At least since the dawn of modernism, there has been a growing polarization between the sort of writers embraced by a mass audience and those revered by scholars and critics. Wolfe is one of the few who has managed to bridge this gap. Academic studies of his work indicate that he is still one of the most respected American novelists of the twentieth century, while annual meetings of the Thomas Wolfe Society suggest that his work is loved by people who read no other canonical writer. It is one of the ironies of Wolfe's career that a novelist so often criticized for being autobiographical and self-indulgent should continue to attract such a passionate and diverse readership decades after his death.

Thomas Wolfe, 1937.
(Photograph by Carl Van Vechten. Courtesy of the Library of Congress)

EARLY LIFE

Thomas Wolfe's career as a published writer lasted for less than nine years—from the time that his first novel, *Look Homeward, Angel*, appeared, within days of the stock market crash of October 1929, until his death in September 1938. He was born in Asheville, a small but growing town in the mountains of western North Carolina, on 3 October 1900. His father, William Oliver Wolfe, was a stonecutter from York Springs, Pennsylvania, who migrated to the South following the Civil War. After burying one wife and divorcing a second, W. O. Wolfe settled in Asheville, where he set up a tombstone shop. Also, in what the

biographer Andrew Turnbull (1965) calls "an epic misalliance," the bombastic and hard-drinking Wolfe married for a third time. He and his third wife, a "mountain puritan" named Julia Westall, bred eight children (seven of whom survived birth) and a lifetime of unhappiness for all involved (p. 7).

As the youngest child, Thomas Wolfe witnessed the conflicts among other members of the family, while receiving preferential treatment himself. Because of his precocious intelligence, Wolfe was taken out of public school at the age of twelve and enrolled in a private school run by J. M. and Margaret Roberts. (Wolfe would later call Mrs. Roberts "the mother of my soul.") Just before turning sixteen, he entered the University of North Carolina at Chapel Hill. As an undergraduate, Wolfe developed a love for the theater and began writing and appearing in plays. Upon graduation in 1920, he entered George Pierce Baker's graduate workshop in playwriting at Harvard. Although he showed promise as a dramatist and earned an M.A. in 1923 (making him one of the most formally educated writers of his time), Wolfe had difficulty cutting his work to a length suitable for performance. He secured a job teaching English at New York University in 1924, while continuing to write at night.

Upon returning by boat from a trip to Europe in 1925, Wolfe met the prominent theatrical designer Aline Bernstein. Although she was nearly eighteen years his senior, the wife of a New York stockbroker, and the mother of two grown children, Wolfe began a tumultuous love affair with Mrs. Bernstein, which lasted for the next five years. She used her influence in the theater on his behalf, and later, when Wolfe turned his attention to fiction, she helped support him while he worked on his first novel. After it was rejected by several other publishers, Wolfe's manuscript, titled "O Lost," was finally accepted by the prestigious firm of Charles Scribner's Sons in 1928.

YEARS OF TRIUMPH

Maxwell Perkins, senior editor at Scribner's, had discerned in the eleven hundred typed pages of "O Lost" a brilliance that other publishers had not seen, but he also realized that the ill-formed narrative was not publishable in its present form. When Wolfe proved incapable of cutting the book on his own, Perkins guided him through the process. After the manuscript had been reduced by approximately 20 percent and substantially revised, it was retitled *Look Homeward, Angel* (a line from Milton's "Lycidas") and published to general critical acclaim. When Sinclair Lewis became the first American to win the Nobel Prize in literature in 1930, he declared that *Look Homeward, Angel* was "worthy to be compared with the best of our literary production" (as quoted in Turnbull, p. 149).

The one place where Wolfe's novel was not well received was his own hometown. Thinly disguised as Altamont, Asheville is the obvious setting of *Look Homeward, Angel*. The story focuses on the lives of the Gant family—stonemason W. O. Gant, his penurious wife, Eliza, and their seven children. Not content with her improvident husband's income, Eliza invests every spare dime in real estate. When her youngest child, Eugene, is seven, she opens a boardinghouse called Dixieland on one of the properties she owns. (Julia Wolfe had run a boardinghouse called the Old Kentucky Home.) The various boarders at Dixieland constitute a cross-section of society and provide the novel with much of its realism. From the establishment of the boardinghouse on, Eliza and her husband live mostly in separate residences, and their children are torn by conflicting loyalties. The one Gant offspring who seems indifferent to the feuds is Eugene's older brother Ben, a local newspaperman.

Although the other members of the family are vulgar philistines, Eugene harbors intellectual and literary ambitions. After winning a five-dollar prize for a composition he has written in school, he is enrolled in a private academy run by the sensitive and kindly Margaret Leonard. Told from a third-person perspective, the tale is infused with a spirit of romanticism through Eugene's role as the central consciousness. Through his eyes, his Dionysian father is more to be admired than his abstemious penny-pinching mother. Virtually all the characters are trapped by the spell of the mountains. None, however, is more pathetic than Ben Gant. After

being judged physically unfit for military service, he dedicates himself to saving Eugene from the horrors of a small-town existence.

Largely through Ben's urging, the Gants agree to finance Eugene's college education. After an awkward first year at the state university, he comes home for the summer and immediately falls in love with one of his mother's boarders, a young woman who is five years his senior. When she finally jilts him to return to her fiancé in Virginia, Eugene vainly follows her trail. Dropping out of school and taking a job of hard physical labor to forget his disappointment, he receives a telegram informing him that Ben is dying of pneumonia. Ben's extremely moving deathbed scene provides the impetus for Eugene to tell the rest of the family members what he thinks of them. Finally ready to make something of himself, he returns to school, graduates, and prepares to leave Altamont forever. Upon his final departure from the town square, he sees the ghost of his brother Ben standing next to a stone angel their terminally ill father had made.

Although Wolfe is generally considered a major figure in southern literature, *Look Homeward, Angel* more closely resembles Sherwood Anderson's *Winesburg, Ohio* and Sinclair Lewis's *Main Street* than it does the work of William Faulkner. (Crushed by bourgeois materialism, Eugene is the prototypical artist as a young man in modern American society.) Part of the reason lies in the fact that the Appalachian region of North Carolina has little in common with the Deep South. In Faulkner's mythic Yoknapatawpha County, the community itself is such a strong presence that it seems like another character in the fiction. For Eugene Gant, the primary social institution is not the town of Altamont but his own family.

If the influence of both society and geography in determining one's destiny are hallmarks of literary naturalism, the rancor of the Gant family and the isolation of the mountains make Wolfe's novel at least marginally naturalistic. Ben Gant seems to become a loser in life largely because he gets lost in the horde of children born to the family. (In his old fat lady friend Mrs. Pert, he may be looking for the maternal comfort Eliza has never given him.) The ambition of his sister Helen to become a professional singer is thwarted by her role as caregiver for their ailing father. Like their neighbors, the Gants are trapped by the constricting environment in which they live. Only Eugene beats the pattern of determinism by breaking free of family obligation and the geographical confinement of the mountains. For him, the ultimate adaptation is not to conquer his environment but to change it by moving on.

Part of Wolfe's great popularity is due to the accessibility of his style. Although he had read James Joyce and employs interior monologues in *Look Homeward, Angel*, he avoids the fragmented and discontinuous narrative style of Faulkner's *The Sound and the Fury*. Moreover, the poetry of his language resembles romantic and Victorian verse more than it does anything as distinctively modernist as T. S. Eliot's *The Waste Land*. If the writers of the Lost Generation distrusted rhetoric and sought to purify the dialect of the tribe, Wolfe gloried in the very excesses of language. At times, the cadences of his prose achieve a musical quality that has nothing to do with the literal sense being communicated. If he has a literary progenitor in the American tradition, it is the bardic Walt Whitman. Like Whitman, he set out to sing a song of himself and to speak for an entire nation in doing so.

Scribner's was understandably eager to capitalize on the success of *Look Homeward, Angel* with another novel by Wolfe. But the effort to produce one went slowly. The problem was the opposite of writer's block. Wolfe wrote so much and so compulsively that it was often difficult to prune and shape the resulting abundance into the facsimile of a well-made novel. Throughout 1933 and 1934 Wolfe and Perkins tried to make a book out of a box of autobiographical manuscript containing some five million words. When Wolfe left to attend the Chicago World's Fair in 1934, he assumed that the labor was still a work in progress. Upon his return, however, he was shocked to discover that Perkins had shipped the manuscript off to the printer. It appeared the following March under the title *Of Time and the River* (1935).

Wolfe's second novel follows Eugene Gant from Altamont to graduate study at Harvard to literary apprenticeship in New York. Completely divorced from the southern setting of *Look Homeward, Angel*, this book is more concerned with what it means to be an aspiring writer in urban America during the 1930s. As an instructor at a university in New York City, Eugene encounters a range of personality and ethnic types. In the 1950s, when an increasing number of American writers were also university professors, the academic novel became a fixture in American literature. *Of Time and the River* anticipates this trend by two decades. One of Wolfe's biographers, David Herbert Donald (1987), believes that this novel is the best literary treatment we have of life in graduate school. As the critic Joseph Schotchie (2001) notes,

Eugene's friendship with his Jewish student Abe Jones reminds us that southern writers and Jewish intellectuals constituted two of the most important literary subcultures in the United States between the 1930s and the 1950s.

Because of its sheer prolixity, *Of Time and the River* seemed to vindicate those critics who had thought *Look Homeward, Angel* to be overwritten. (In an unscientific but revealing survey the *Saturday Review of Literature* took in December 1935 to determine the best and worst novels of the preceding year, *Of Time and the River* received the most votes in both categories.) What these critics often failed to acknowledge was Wolfe's ability as a writer of short fiction. The effectiveness of the novella and short stories he published in *From Death to Morning* (1935) suggest that Wolfe's full-length novels might be better viewed as inflated collections of short fiction rather than as pared-down versions of some grander saga. In *The History of Southern Literature* (1985), Louis D. Rubin Jr. argues that the literary form that came most naturally to Wolfe was "the novella or short novel of from fifteen thousand to thirty thousand words" (p. 346).

Perhaps the most troubling aspect of his early career was the perception that Wolfe was some kind of idiot savant, reliant on Maxwell Perkins to transform his incoherent narratives into literature. This charge was made in "Genius Is Not Enough," a savage article by Bernard DeVoto, published in the *Saturday Review of Literature* in 1936. Still rankled over the premature publication of *Of Time and the River*, Wolfe severed his relations with Scribner's and signed on with Edward C. Aswell of Harper and Brothers for a $10,000 advance in December 1937. In an apparent effort to make a fresh start, Wolfe dispensed with Eugene Gant and created a new protagonist named George Webber. Although Webber's name and physical appearance differed from Gant's, his sensibility still marked him as his creator's alter ego. True to form, Wolfe produced a cornucopia of episodes amounting to several hundred thousand words. Before departing for a trip to the West in May 1938, he composed an outline for a novel and began serious revision. Wolfe was hospitalized in Seattle in July and brought back by train to the Johns Hopkins Hospital in Baltimore. After surgery for a tubercular infection of the brain, he died on 15 September 1938.

POSTHUMOUS PUBLICATIONS

Although the manuscripts Wolfe left at his death were incomplete and unformed, Harper's still needed to show a return on its advance and its short-lived connection with

Wolfe. Aswell, Wolfe's literary agent Elizabeth Nowell, and his reluctant literary executor Max Perkins went to work on Wolfe's literary remains. After massive reshuffling, rewriting, and outright invention, Aswell produced two "novels," which were published as *The Web and the Rock* in 1939 and *You Can't Go Home Again* in 1940. The first of these deals with George "Monk" Webber's childhood in a town called Libya Hill, his subsequent life as a college student, and his career as a young writer in New York. After a sudden transition that puts him on the same boat where we left Eugene Gant at the end of *Of Time and the River*, the rest of the novel tells of Webber's love affair with Esther Jack, an older Jewish woman who greatly resembles Aline Bernstein. *You Can't Go Home Again* depicts Webber's early literary career, including reactions to his first novel. Despite several memorable episodes (including more explicit satire than in his previous work), neither book is more than a preliminary fragment rushed into print to exploit the public appetite for Wolfe's work. This appetite has remained so constant that, between 1940 and 2001, Wolfe was listed as the author of at least forty additionai books, most of which contain previously unpublished material.

Wolfe's critical reputation has inevitably ebbed and flowed as literary standards have changed, but among his fellow writers, his standing has always been high. Joseph Schotchie argues that one need only look at some of the first novels produced immediately after World War II to glean a sense of Wolfe's influence. The titles of James Jones's *From Here to Eternity*, Norman Mailer's *The Naked and the Dead*, Jack Kerouac's *The Town and the City*, and William Styron's *Lie Down in Darkness* all "carry Wolfean overtones" (Schotchie, 2001, p. 64). On the fiftieth anniversary of the publication of *Look Homeward, Angel* in 1979, a diverse group of contemporary novelists paid tribute to the inspiration they had derived from Wolfe. The reason for that inspiration and the source of Wolfe's greatness had been identified a generation earlier, when Faulkner had rated his fellow southerner first among contemporary novelists. "We had all failed," Faulkner noted, "but Wolfe had made the best failure because he had tried hardest to say the most" (quoted in Walser, 1979, p. 176).

SELECTED WORKS

Look Homeward, Angel (1929)
Of Time and the River (1935)
From Death to Morning (1935)

The Story of a Novel (1936)
The Web and the Rock (1939)
You Can't Go Home Again (1940)
The Hills Beyond (1941)
Thomas Wolfe's Letters to His Mother (1943)
A Stone, A Leaf, A Door: Poems (1945)
The Portable Thomas Wolfe (1946)
The Mannerhouse: A Play (1948)
A Western Journal (1951)
Correspondence with Thomas Andrew Watt (1954)
Letters of Thomas Wolfe (1956)
The Short Novels of Thomas Wolfe (1961)
The Thomas Wolfe Reader (1962)
Thomas Wolfe's Purdue Speech: Writing and Living (1964)
The Mountains: A Play (1970)
The Notebooks of Thomas Wolfe (1970)
The Autobiography of an American Novelist (1983)
Welcome to Our City: A Play in Ten Scenes (1983)
K-19: Salvaged Pieces (1983)
Beyond Love and Loyalty: The Letters of Thomas Wolfe and Elizabeth Nowell; Together with "No More Rivers": A Story (1983)
My Other Loneliness: Letters of Thomas Wolfe and Aline Bernstein (1983)
Thomas Wolfe Interviewed, 1929–1938 (1985)
The Complete Short Stories of Thomas Wolfe (1987)
The Good Child's River (1991)
The Starwick Episodes (1994)
The Party at Jack's (1995)
O Lost: A Story of the Buried Life (2000)
To Loot My Life Clean: The Thomas Wolfe–Maxwell Perkins Correspondence (2000)

FURTHER READING

DeVoto, Bernard. "Genius Is Not Enough." *Saturday Review of Literature* (25 April 1936): 3–4, 14–15. Charges that Wolfe needed "Mr. Perkins and the assembly line at Scribner's" to shape his prose into novels for him.

Donald, David Herbert. *Look Homeward: A Life of Thomas Wolfe*. Boston, 1987. The definitive biography of Wolfe by a Pulitzer Prize–winning historian.

Holman, C. Hugh. *The Loneliness at the Core: Studies in Thomas Wolfe*. Baton Rouge, La., 1975. Seven previously published essays by one of the giants of southern literary scholarship. Some of these essays helped to establish Wolfe as a major American writer.

Idol, John L., Jr. *A Thomas Wolfe Companion*. New York, 1987. Although superseded by Idol's 2001 research guide, this is still an indispensable resource for serious students of Wolfe.

Idol, John L., Jr. *Thomas Wolfe.* Literary Masters. Vol. 13. Detroit, 2001. The most recent and valuable companion for nonspecialists undertaking scholarly study of Wolfe.

Johnston, Carol Ingalls. *Thomas Wolfe: A Descriptive Bibliography.* Pittsburgh, 1987. The standard primary bibliography of Wolfe.

Johnston, Carol Ingalls. *Of Time and the Artist: Thomas Wolfe, His Novels, and the Critics.* Columbia, S.C., 1996. A perceptive and detailed account of the critical response to Wolfe's work.

Kennedy, Richard S. *The Window of Memory: The Literary Career of Thomas Wolfe.* Chapel Hill, N.C., 1962. A biographical and critical study. Particularly good on Wolfe's relationship with Edward C. Aswell.

Klein, Carole. *Aline.* New York, 1979. Definitive biography of Aline Bernstein. Good treatment of her relationship with Wolfe.

Nowell, Elizabeth. *Thomas Wolfe: A Biography.* New York, 1960. The work of his literary agent, this is the first major biography of Wolfe. Stronger on his career in New York than on his earlier life.

Rubin, Louis D., Jr. *Thomas Wolfe: The Weather of His Youth.* Baton Rouge, La., 1955. A detailed critical examination of Wolfe as southern writer by the dean of southern literary studies.

Rubin, Louis D., Jr. "Thomas Wolfe." In *The History of Southern Literature.* Edited by Louis D. Rubin Jr. et al. Baton Rouge, La., 1985. A brief overview of Wolfe's career and his place in southern literature.

Schotchie, Joseph. *Thomas Wolfe Revisited.* Alexander, N.C., 2001. An excellent brief introduction to Wolfe for nonspecialists.

Turnbull, Andrew. *Thomas Wolfe.* New York, 1965. An extremely well written account of Wolfe's life. Particularly strong on his relationship with Maxwell Perkins, Scott Fitzgerald, and Ernest Hemingway.

Walser, Richard. "On Faulkner's Putting Wolfe First." *South Atlantic Quarterly* (Spring 1979): 172–181. Account of Faulkner's rating of Wolfe as the writer of his generation who "tried hardest to say the most."

TOBIAS WOLFF

by Pauls Toutonghi

Tobias (Jonathan Ansell) Wolff was born on 19 June 1945 in Birmingham, Alabama. The other facts of Wolff's early life are set down in his notable autobiography, *This Boy's Life* (1989), which begins with his parents' divorce and chronicles his subsequent move from the age of ten with his mother across the United States to the West Coast. He and his mother settled in Washington State, at first in Seattle and then in the small town of Concrete. The town is remarkably consistent with its name; Wolff paints it as a drizzly landscape, rainy and full of deprivations and the cruelties of an abusive stepfather. *This Boy's Life* has been widely recognized as one of the most powerful contemporary expressions of the genre of memoir.

Tobias Wolff. (*Photograph by Jerry Bauer. Courtesy of New York State Writers Institute*)

The facts of Wolff's young life are largely encapsulated in this book and his other nonfiction. What is not covered, perhaps, is Wolff's time at Oxford University, as a Wallace Stegner Fellow at Stanford University, and his subsequent twenty-year employment in the creative writing department at Syracuse University. While at Syracuse, Wolff taught both creative writing and literature classes, offering an array of courses to a diverse student population. In 1998, Wolff returned to Stanford, where, as of 2003, he teaches both fiction and nonfiction.

Wolff has received critical acclaim as both a fiction writer and a nonfiction memoirist. In 1993, *This Boy's Life* was made into a film starring Robert De Niro and Leonardo DiCaprio, a film that enjoyed both commercial and critical success.

Wolff's memoir of his days a soldier in the Vietnam War, *In Pharaoh's Army: Memories of the Lost War* (1994), recalls the deprivations and dangers of a life in the armed forces in the 1960s. His three book-length short story collections—*In the Garden of the North American Martyrs* (1981), *Back in the World* (1985), and *The Night in Question* (1996)—have been the subjects of much scholarship and casual reading. His novella, *The Barracks Thief* (1984), was awarded the PEN/Faulkner Award. Wolff is rare in that his published work has consistently veered between the genres of fiction and nonfiction. For this reason, even a brief study of his writing life cannot help but mention the parameters of his childhood.

A BOY'S LIFE

When it was first published, *This Boy's Life* took its place as a member of a noticeably languishing literary genre. In his introduction to the *Norton Book of American Autobiography* (1999), Jay Parini writes that while autobiography has always been "the essential American genre," it experienced a somewhat moribund period in the post-Vietnam era. Wolff's book can be credited for revitalizing a genre and giving it a new home on the lists of major publishers. It was reviewed on the front page of *The New York Times Book Review*, and received a great deal of coverage in major newspapers and media outlets in America and abroad.

What appealed to numerous readers was Wolff's essentially simple style—a straightforward presentation of words that recalls both George Orwell's 1946 essay "Politics and the English Language" as well as the spare, precise diction of Ernest Hemingway and Raymond Carver. In a 1986 interview with the academic James Hannah, Wolff listed those writers—as well as Anton Chekhov and Flannery O'Connor—among his influences, but continued from there, saying that "the list has no end, so I'd better stop." What gives Wolff's books their buoyant, irrepressible style is precisely this bubbling energy, as well as the author's sharp sense of irony. This ironic detachment is perhaps best exemplified by the conclusion of the acknowledgments page of *This Boy's Life*. "My first stepfather used to say that what I didn't know would fill a book," Wolff writes. "Well, here it is."

The memoir itself moves through the process of self-discovery, as a young boy bounces from stepfather to stepfather, tied to a mother whom he deeply loves, but who has a talent for finding a string of abusive or otherwise unstable men. Wolff's own father is a compulsive liar and convict; he shuttles in and out of prison for most of the book. Wolff's writing style enlivens the sad but mundane facts of a bleak childhood; and the reader—like the reader of any classic bildungsroman—follows Wolff to maturity. Yet unlike many memoirs with child-protagonists, Wolff does not reach a pinnacle of maturity by the conclusion of the text. Instead, he has lied his way into an East Coast boarding school—where he becomes the "school wildman . . . a drinker, a smoker, a make-out artist at the mixers we had with Baldwin and Shipley and Miss Fine's." He has suffered abuse and—many years later—come to a point where he wishes to tell the story. But the process of healing comes partially from telling an honest rendition of the (not always appealing) facts of his own actions.

WAR

If Wolff's childhood is characterized by the partial and occasionally compromised triumph over abuse, then his young adulthood is characterized by violence. Like numerous other men of his generation, Wolff served in Vietnam. He was not drafted, however; instead, he seeks out the army as a solace from the difficulties of making his way in the world. Some psychoanalytical critics have linked Wolff's own lack of a stable father to his desire for the order and stability of the army. As a child, his role models varied, but were united—one and all—by a single commonality: "The men I'd respected when I was growing up had all served, [as had] most of the writers I looked up to—Norman Mailer, James Jones, Erich Maria Remarque, and of course Hemingway, to whom I turned for guidance in all things." He entered the army to find a discipline and an order that was lacking from his life—an equal discipline given out to all, not calculated to abuse him and make him suffer.

The result of this desire, however, was a tour in Vietnam, where Wolff encountered the absurdities and terrors of war. For the most part, Wolff's time in-country was spent under the burden of the fear of dying. The facts of the war are mitigated somewhat by his appointment to a position behind the front lines. Nonetheless, the dangers were still quite real. In the fourth section of his memoir *In the Pharaoh's Army*—a section entitled "Close Calls"—Wolff details the various times that he nearly died. These range from encounters with unseen enemies in a local marketplace to an engine that falls from a helicopter and nearly crushes him. Much of the writing is driven by the humor and keen sense of observation that characterizes *This Boy's Life*. It also bears the constant awareness of Wolff's mortality, which makes the prose crackle with a buried power.

THE BARRACKS THIEF

Although it was preceded by *In the Garden of the North American Martyrs*, Wolff's novella *The Barracks Thief* is a remarkable piece of fiction, and one that stakes out a territory similar to that of *In the Pharaoh's Army*. The novella is set in an army training facility within the United States—in a depot for both soldiers and would-be-soldiers. The plot involves a young private who is tormented by his repressed homosexuality, and who steals the wallets of his fellow soldiers to pay for his sexual encounters with a local hooker. The point of view shifts drastically from character to character, a device that can engender equally drastic shifts in the sympathies of the reader. Although Wolff insists that he is not comfortable with the longer form, his approach to *The Barracks Thief* is both productive and insightful. The text works as a longer work of fiction.

THE SHORT FICTION

It is in the genre of short fiction that Wolff has received the most plaudits. His first collection drew together stories that had appeared in national magazines in the late 1970s, drawing from smaller publications such as *Antaeus* and *Willowsprings*, as well as commercial fiction magazines such as *Vogue*, *Mademoiselle*, and the *Atlantic Monthly*. The stories in this collection make up a diverse and variegated tapestry of approaches to the art of writing. Stories such as "Next Door," "Wingfield," and "In the Garden of the North American Martyrs," are relatively short, and pursue little narrative complexity. They are sharply observed and memorable, however, and tend to portray difficult situations with a slightly ironic and somewhat detached tone.

The longer stories in the collection, particularly the story "Hunters in the Snow," consider difficult questions with a light and subtle touch. In "Hunters," three friends go on a hunting trip in a rural area. They are men in their late twenties or early thirties—and they all have their separate, isolated problems. One is having an affair with his daughter's babysitter, another is terribly overweight, another is chronically irritable and boorish. Through an intricate series of events, one man shoots the other. In order to cover up the shooting, the two remaining men avoid taking their friend to the hospital; he dies from shock and hypothermia in the back of their truck: "As the truck twisted through the gentle hills the star went back and forth between Kenny's boots, staying always in his sight. 'I'm going to the hospital,' Kenny said. But he was wrong. They had taken a different turn a long way back."

This is a story of common people who—at critical moments in their lives—make terrible, cruel choices. This is, of course, a major theme in Wolff's writing on the Vietnam War; indeed, it is a broad theme of much war writing from twentieth-century America.

The early to mid-1980s were a remarkably productive time for Wolff, during which he released numerous books, including a second collection of stories, *Back in the World* (1985). The title is derived from the phrase that soldiers from Vietnam used for the experience of making it back to the United States. Returning to America was immersing oneself "back in the world," and adjusting to its concomitant cultural environment. It is for this reason, perhaps, that these stories have little to do with the soldier's experience and more to do with contemporary American society. With this collection, Wolff turns his eye toward stories of domestic conflict, of a quarrel between brothers. Perhaps the most memorable story in the book, "The Missing Person," deals with a priest's search for love and his internal struggles with the celibacy that accompanies his vocation. The collection shows Wolff's versatility as a writer, as well as the thematic breadth of his short fiction.

Wolff's suite of stories, *The Night in Question*, was published after a ten-year hiatus from issuing book-length fiction. By the time of its release in 1996, Wolff's reputation as a writer was well established. The collection has the feeling of a writer reaching for the upper limits of his genre—probing questions of mortality and considering the role of death in American society. Many of the stories deal explicitly or implicitly with death, as characters lose loved ones, or work at the obituaries desk of an urban newspaper, or die in violent bank robberies. Of these stories, several received major awards: "The Other Miller," "Smorgasbord," and "Firelight" were selected for the Best American Short Stories series, and "The Life of the Body" received a Pushcart Prize in 1991. "The Other Miller," in particular, has been widely anthologized. It easily ranks among Wolff's most remarkable pieces, and is a take on the ways in which pride can corrupt love, and consume the intimacy of even a mother-son relationship. Its ending is quite powerful; it surprises and astounds the reader in a way that recalls some of the early work of Hemingway.

CONCLUSION

Wolff can be approached as an author working at the peak of his creative powers. Several book-length critical studies of his writing were published in the 1990s. James Hannah's *Tobias Wolff: A Study of the Short Fiction* (1996), is widely recognized as an authoritative and informative work. Wolff's contributions to the field of American literature—in both fiction and nonfiction—are among the most crucial of the second half of the twentieth century.

SELECTED WORKS

In the Garden of the North American Martyrs (1981)
The Barracks Thief (1984)
Back in the World: Stories (1985)
This Boy's Life (1989)
In Pharaoh's Army: Memories of the Lost War (1994)
The Night in Question (1996)

FURTHER READING

Hannah, James. *Tobias Wolff: A Study of the Short Fiction.* New York, 1996. The only book-length study of Wolff's fiction. Quite lucid.

Scofield, Martin. "Winging It: Realism and Invention in the Stories of Tobias Wolff." In *Yearbook of English Studies.* Vol. 31. London, 2001. A careful consideration of the role of truth in Wolff's short fiction.

CHARLES WRIGHT

by Henry Hart

In an interview published in 1992, Charles Wright told David Young, the editor of *Field* magazine: "There are three things, basically, that I write about—language, landscape, and the idea of God." Behind much of Wright's poetry is the Emersonian idea, which in turn derives from a long line of Platonic and Christian thinkers, that the universe resembles a text authored by God—a God who inhabits us. When Ralph Waldo Emerson contended in his essay "Nature" that "words are signs of natural facts" and "Nature is the symbol of spirit," he was drawing on the old concept of "the book of nature." In this "book," language represents nature and nature represents the spirit or mind that created it—in other words, God.

Charles Wright.
(Photograph by Nancy Crampton)

Throughout his essay Emerson argued for a poetic use of language that would renounce "rotten diction and fasten words again to visible things; so that picturesque language is at once a commanding certificate that he who employs it is a man in alliance with truth and God." By employing a "natural" language (a vocabulary that adhered to the principle "no ideas but in things"), the writer could recapitulate the divine act of creation, duplicating, as it were, the book of nature in his or her own book.

The idealistic Emerson believed the best writers were perfectly capable of reincarnating Nature and God (or what he sometimes called the Oversoul) in the text. By tapping into the "universal soul within or behind his individual life," the author transported readers into "a firmament . . . of Justice, Truth, Love, Freedom, . . . Reason." Words were rungs in a ladder guiding the reader from text to nature and ultimately to Platonic and Christian ideals. If one wanted to bypass words and books, one could simply read nature. When Emerson recounted going out into a "tranquil landscape" and becoming a "transparent eyeball"—"I

am nothing; I see all; the currents of the Universal Being circulate through me; I am part or parcel of God"—he was describing his feelings of sublime transport into a firmament of Platonic and Christian ideals brought about by a contemplative reading of the landscape as God's text. Having climbed the ladder from thing to idea, from nature to Creator, he communed with the Author-God with all the self-forgetfulness, fear, and ecstasy of a reader whose eyes have been transfixed by a good book.

Charles Wright approaches landscape with Emerson's attitudes, but not his idealistic beliefs. Where Emerson detected a harmony between language, landscape, and God, Wright detects dissonance. For Wright, the transcendentalist's ladder connecting word to thing and spirit has collapsed. The faith that bound together the rungs of signifier and signified has been deconstructed; the signifier, "God," has been stripped of its transcendental meanings. What distinguishes his poetry from much other postmodernist poetry is its enduring preoccupation with Emerson's idealism and the Christian and Platonic traditions that propped it up. While many of his peers have accepted, celebrated, or simply ignored the demise of the transcendentalist's cosmos in which language, landscape, and God were intimately connected, Wright returns to it repeatedly like an elegist who cannot forget the death of a loved one. Much of the grief, nostalgia, bitterness, sardonic humor, and stoicism in his poetry arise from his backward look at a religious world that has been dismantled by twentieth-century empiricism.

In his essay "Improvisations: With Father Hopkins on Lake Como," Wright elaborates on the lost belief in a unity between language, landscape, and God (here the triumvirate appears as word, world, and Word) that pervades his poetry. Reading the *Journals* of Gerard

Manley Hopkins, the High Anglican poet who converted to Roman Catholicism in 1866 and soon after became a Jesuit, Wright comments:

> It's his reverence that strikes you, reverence for the minutiae as well as the miraculous. . . : a photo-realism from the insect to infinity. The spiritual eye that sees God's fingerprint and face on everything. . . . When he decides to describe something—a leaf, a wave or series of waves, a bird, a landscape sweep—minutely or particularly, he is able to transcend it, through language, and enter whatever it is he is describing; that the inscape is knowable and tactile through language. That the heart of the mystery, the pulse at the very unspeakable center of being, is apprehensible through writing about it. Thus the lovingly, intricately laid down musical strings of language. One no longer believes this is possible. One more often now knows that the only answer to inscape is silence. How marvelous, however, to see how the world once seemed, how Adamic it all was before the word and the world became separate. And the Word and the world became separate.

Much of Wright's poetry laments the death of that "marvelous" Eden in which words, nature, and God were bound together by faith, whether that faith belonged to Emerson, Hopkins, or Wright himself.

The first poem in his book *The Other Side of the River* (1984) highlights the way Wright yearns nostalgically for a former time of belief while recognizing that the time is forever lost. The poem, appropriately titled "Lost Bodies," opens with a typical meditative moment at night in which he remembers words carved on a concrete cross that once represented the Word. Having acknowledged how the cross overshadowed his early life in one of his Tennessee hometowns, he momentarily pines for the Christian securities of his past and his culture's past. But then, pulling himself back to the present, he says with his characteristic lighthearted sarcasm: "Something's for sure in the clouds, but it's not for me." If that something is God, He speaks and appears to others rather than to him.

Wright obsessively takes meditative journeys on dark nights to examine his past and search for divinity, but he almost always comes up with little to show for his efforts except moving poems about his endless search. In the middle of "Lost Bodies," he approaches Jesus again as if performing a formal spiritual exercise *in imitatione Christi*. Again, he is disappointed, confessing: "Still, a piece of his heart is not a piece of your heart, / Sweet Jesus, and never will be." Because of Wright's tug-of-war with Christianity, his meditations turn into elegies

that, unlike traditional elegies, offer little in the way of consoling resurrections. The dead enjoy an apotheosis in memory, but they typically come back to remind him of death's finality. Wright's elegies are also for himself—for his childhood faith in orthodox views of redemption and resurrection—and in these poems he also admits that the past endures as a reminder that it is inexorably gone, that its presence in memory is a distortion, a simulacrum, a re-presentation. "What *does* one do with one's life?" he asks in a companion poem, "Lost Souls." Surveying a room full of his publications and photographs—the words and images that represent his past—he concludes: "Nothing's like anything else in the long run. / Nothing you write down is ever as true as you think it was." Having fallen—or grown up—from that Adamic world of Emerson and Hopkins, where words mirrored reality and reality mirrored God, he now lives in a "land of unlikeness," where doubts and differences are the norm. If he once saw God face-to-face, now, altering Paul in Corinthians, he sees Him and everything else through a glass darkly.

Wright's obsessions have remained remarkably consistent throughout his career, even while his ambition has grown and his writing has developed in complexity. "In the Midnight Hour," a poem that exemplifies the minimalist style of his *The Grave of the Right Hand* (1970), Wright traces the meditator's traditional dying away from the everyday world into a visionary "dark night of the soul." He begins the poem by stipulating that the death he recounts is figurative, purgative. It is a "death-in-life," a baptism by "the waters of darkness," as he calls them, a cleansing of the eyes (those traditional windows of the soul). To the entranced meditator, the life meditated on may appear to have "substance," but Wright reminds us in his final line that this "risen" life is more vision than substance, more wishful prayer than actual fact. It is "not like water and not like darkness, but / Like smoke, like prayer." It is also important to note that, unlike the sort of traditional Christian meditations outlined by St. Ignatius of Loyola or St. John of the Cross, Wright's "dark night of the soul" has no final colloquy or communion with God. The point of Wright's spiritual exercise is to obtain a clearer vision of one's life, not one's God. Clarification and illumination are merely "like prayer"; they are not part of a prayer in any orthodox sense.

Meditational motifs can be found scattered throughout Wright's work. In a later poem, "Via Negativa" (Negative Way), in *A Short History of the Shadow* (2002), he characteristically draws on traditions of Christian meditation only to deny their traditional boons. His title refers to the mystic's "negative way" of approaching God through a negating of senses that focuses the mind on divine as opposed to worldly matters. Wright takes his epigraph—"If a man wants to be sure of his road, he must close his eyes and walk in the dark"—from St. John of the Cross, the sixteenth-century Spanish mystic who provided a detailed map of the "via negativa" in his treatise *The Dark Night* (1964). Wright begins his poem with a "composition of place" that dwells on the landscape of southwest Virginia rather than any traditional Christian site such as the crucifixion. Because the season is fall, he imagines himself undergoing a purgative falling or dying away from life that leads, paradoxically, to a spiritual ascent. How consoling it would be to have perfect transcendence, he surmises, to rise above the past and all its sins and crimes, to exist in a vacuum where he could be weightless. But when he says, "How pretty to think that gods abound, / and everything stays forgotten," his use of the overused, sentimental word "pretty" reveals how ridiculous he considers the possibility. Although he can envision resurrection and immortality, as in "Lost Bodies," he soberly acknowledges that his prayers will vanish, like his body, into nothingness—what he calls "not-ness."

Wright usually uses season and landscape as objective correlatives for his sense of fallenness, of being exiled from a Platonic and Christian Eden where word, world, and Word were unified. He strives to bring his trinity together, but the gaps remain unbridged, his linguistic and religious desires unfulfilled. In "Via Negativa" he admits:

> The verbal hunger, the narrowness
> Between the thing itself and the naming of the thing
> Coils like a tapeworm inside us
> and waits to be filled.

Once again he orchestrates a moving elegy for his losses—past, present, and future—documenting the demise of his hopes in vivid language that partly redeems them. Surrounded by what Wallace Stevens called, in a late poem, "the stale grandeur of annihilation," Wright's autumnal words take on a poignant grandeur even while bearing witness to their own, and to their maker's, annihilation.

JOURNEYS OF AN APPRENTICE

In one of his improvisational essays, Wright stated: "Poems are not just *about* journeys, of course, they *are* journeys—surreptitiously, silently, staying in one place the way plants do.... At the heart of every poem is a journey of discovery." He was alluding to the poet's meditative journeys, which are silent and stationary, but also to his own physical journeys in the United States and Europe that he frequently memorializes in his work.

Born on his father's thirty-first birthday, 25 August 1935, in a Tennessee Valley Authority hospital located in Pickwick Dam, Tennessee, Wright began his journeys early because of his father's numerous civil engineering jobs at different dam sites. His first trips were in the South, partly because his great-grandfather, Charles Ferdinand Penzel, who originally came from minor landowning nobility in Asch, Bohemia, had fought for the South in the Civil War after emigrating from Europe to Little Rock, Arkansas, as a teenager. (Wright remembers his participation in the Battle of Chickamauga in his poem "Arkansas Traveller" and obliquely in "Chickamauga.") Wright's maternal ancestors also hailed from the South; many had worked as farmers, ministers, and ferrymen in northern Virginia since the eighteenth century. His mother, Mary Winter, was born on the Mississippi Delta after her mother left Virginia to become a governess near the end of the nineteenth century. Wright inherited some of his literary interests from his mother, who—as a student at the University of Mississippi—had written short stories and dated William Faulkner's younger brother, Dean. His mother's family also had musical talents, which were passed on to his first cousins, the legendary rock musicians Johnny and Edgar Winter. Although he was one of the few in his family who could not play an instrument or carry a tune, his love of music would inspire some of his best poems.

Wright's nomadic life commenced when he was six months old. He moved with his family from Pickwick Dam to Knoxville, Tennessee, so his father could work on the Cherokee Dam. A year later, when his father got a job at the Mussel Shoals Dam in Alabama, the Wrights moved to Corinth, Mississippi, which was within commuting distance to the dam site. Before long they returned to Knoxville. In 1941 they moved again, this time to Hiwassee Village, North Carolina (it consisted of a commissary, a school, and a community hall), where Wright's father worked on the Fontana Dam. After two years in rural Hiwassee, they were uprooted again when the top-secret Manhattan Project in Oak Ridge, Tennessee, hired his father to help build the first nuclear weapons. In 1945 his father bought a house in Kingsport, Tennessee, and—World War II having ended—took a new job with a construction company. (Later he began his own construction company.)

It was in Kingsport that Wright cultivated his passion for country music. The Carter Family, one of his favorite singing groups, lived only ten miles from his house. He also enjoyed the music of Earl Scruggs, Lester Flatt, Roy Acuff, and Merle Travis. Although the melodramatic subject matter of country music—adultery, divorce, heartbreak, revenge—exerted little influence on his poetry, he was deeply attracted to the genre's concerns with death, loss, resurrection, and salvation; its bluesy tones; and its tendency to address Christian themes in a colloquial way. He commemorated its importance for him as a poet by entitling his first selected poems *Country Music* (1982).

As a boy, Wright received his formal religious training at a pioneer camp in Sky Valley near Hendersonville, North Carolina, that was run by Anne Perry, the evangelical daughter of the Episcopal bishop of South Carolina, and her husband, Jim. He spent summers when he was twelve, thirteen, and fourteen at the Perrys' camp. In 1950–1951 he and eight other students attended their school. Unwilling to spend his last two years of high school in such a small place, from 1951 to 1953 he attended an Episcopal boarding school, Christ School, in Arden, North Carolina. The school, nicknamed Jesus Tech, was larger (it enrolled 143 students), but was strict and conservative in its religious indoctrination. His experiences at the two Episcopal schools led directly to such poems as "Sky Valley Rider," "Northhanger Ridge," "The Other Side of the River," and "Blackwater Mountain." Reflecting on this formative religious period, Wright acknowledged: "I was formed by the catechism in Kingsport, the evangelical looniness at Sky Valley Community in North Carolina, and by the country songs and hymns...I kept hearing on the radio back in Tennessee." Wright graduated from Christ School in May 1953, convinced he no longer wanted to be a part of organized religion and only vaguely convinced he wanted to be a writer.

Wright got his first taste of professional writing in the summer of 1953 as a police reporter for the *Kingsport Times-News*. Each evening he scouted the police blotter for drownings, shootings, and automobile accidents. On his breaks from newspaper work he played a lot of golf and, at his mother's urging, read nearly all of Faulkner's novels and two collections of Eudora Welty's stories. He also read Ernest Hemingway, whose pared-down evocations of landscapes and characters contrasted with Faulkner's gothic embellishments. Wright would eventually fuse the two contrasting styles in his poetry.

His stint as a cub reporter over, Wright attended Davidson College, where—from 1953 to 1957—he partied at his fraternity, played more golf, went on road trips to women's colleges, took ROTC, and maintained a B average in his courses. His main undergraduate interest was history, but he also wrote what he later dismissed as "mood pieces...on the model of Thomas Wolfe." His writing as a senior, however, was good enough to win a literary prize—a collection of Hemingway's stories. During the summer after graduation, he earned a diploma and a commission from the U.S. Army Intelligence Corps at Fort Benning, Georgia, with the experience afforded by the commission having a more direct bearing on his literary future than his diploma. On his way to Fort Holabird, Maryland, for more training, he happened to go to New York City and buy the book that would change his life—the 1957 New Directions edition of the *Selected Poems of Ezra Pound*.

Although Wright put off reading Pound's poems, his interest in poetry intensified at another military outpost—the Presidio's Army Language School in Monterey, California. Here he studied Italian in preparation for overseas duty and diligently wrote in a notebook. He finally got around to reading Pound's *Selected Poems* in 1959, after he had traveled to Verona, Italy, to join the 430th CIC Detachment on security for military installations. He loaned the book to his friend Harold Schimmel, a former Cornell University English major, who encouraged Wright to read the poems and then visit one of the sites in Italy that Pound had written about—Catullus's legendary villa on Lake Garda's peninsula of Sirmione. Wright dutifully read Pound's "Blandula, Tenulla, Vagula" and in March 1959 made his momentous visit. He later recalled that he had been overwhelmed by the beauty of "the late March sun pouring through the olive trees, reflecting off their silver and quicksilver turns in the lake wind, the lake itself stretched out below me and into the distance, the pre-Alps above Riva cloud-shouldered and cloud-shadowed." He also spoke of "the whole weight of history and literature suddenly dropping through the roof of my...world in one of those epiphanic flashes that one is fortunate enough to have in one's lifetime now and then if one is ready. I was ready." In "Blandula, Tenulla, Vagula," Pound had questioned orthodox ideas of heaven and outlined his quest for an earthly paradise:

> What hast thou, O my soul, with paradise?
> Will we not rather, when our freedom's won,
> Get us to some clear place wherein the sun
> Lets drift in on us through the olive leaves
> A liquid glory?

Although Pound's diction was archaic, his poem launched Wright's own poetic quest for Sirmione-like paradises.

Ignoring Pound's harebrained political and economic theories, Wright relished the visual and auditory splendors of the great modernist's poems. He moved on from Pound's early imagistic lyrics to the epic sprawl of *The Pisan Cantos* (1948), enjoying them partly because he knew the places in Italy that Pound wrote about. For the next couple of years, Wright wrote imitations of *The Pisan Cantos*. Later in his career he acknowledged Pound's many flaws, but nevertheless praised him for recording his heroic—albeit erratic—"Dantean-Joycean voyage" through history and culture in *The Cantos*: "It remains one of the most spectacular and gorgeous literary wrecks, in English, of the century, and the lyrical songs that continue to rise from the wreckage, and the incredible music and visions of many of its parts continue to seduce us toward that same shore and those same shoals." Pound's enchanting free-verse rhythms and lyrical imagery became enduring models for Wright. Pound, who conceived of his *Cantos* as a modern-day *Divine Comedy* (c. 1308–1321), a quixotic journey through hell and purgatory to paradise, also inspired Wright to work on a long, three-part sequence that would take a lifetime to complete.

Following his four years of army intelligence work, three of which were spent in Italy, Wright traveled to the University of Iowa in 1961 to study poetry. He was twenty-six. The creative writing workshop, one of the most prestigious in the country (Robert Lowell and John Berryman had taught in it), provided him with the most intense educational experience of his life. Huddled in a group of World War II–vintage Quonset huts, his teachers Paul Engle and Donald Justice taught him to appreciate an eclectic group of writers from John Cage and William Carlos Williams to Wallace Stevens, W. H. Auden, Gerard Manley Hopkins, and John Crowe Ransom. Because "it was the era of the Great Schism, the Academics versus the Beats," as Wright recalled, the generally conservative students guided him away from Pound and Beat writers like Allen Ginsberg and Jack Kerouac toward such poets as Elizabeth Bishop, James Wright, James Merrill, Philip Larkin, Richard Wilbur, W. D. Snodgrass, John Berryman, and Robert Lowell. Wright, however, never acquiesced to the Academics' New Critical principles, which favored allusive poems written in traditional stanzaic and metrical forms. Mark Strand, a recent graduate who became a professor at Iowa in 1962 and a lifelong friend, acted as a kind of mediator for Wright between the two aesthetic camps, encouraging him to compose prose poems and

translate the Italian poet Eugenio Montale, who was known for his obscure juxtapositions of finely honed images. Wright included some of his prose poems in his first book and translated Montale's "Motteti" (a sequence of twenty poems to a mysterious lover), followed by Montale's book *La bufera et altro* (1956; *The Storm and Other Things*, 1978). He also translated Montale's fellow hermeticist, Dino Campana, whose longer prose pieces offered one model for Wright's lengthy poetic sequences.

After receiving his M.F.A. degree in 1963, Wright returned to Italy for two years as a Fulbright scholar. (Experiences from his second Italian sojourn appeared in "The Southern Cross," "Roma I," and "Roma II.") At the University of Rome he studied Dante and Montale and decided to go back to the University of Iowa for a Ph.D. degree in English. An offer to teach English at the University of California, Irvine, cut short his doctoral plans but brought him into contact with the photographer Holly McIntire, whom he married in 1969. A year earlier, restless to return to Europe, he embarked for Italy again, this time as a Fulbright lecturer on Thoreau, Emerson, and Melville at the University of Padua. It was on this trip that he and his friend, the poet James Tate, arranged to meet Ezra Pound, who unfortunately had left Italy to receive an honorary degree from his alma mater, Hamilton College, in upstate New York.

Wesleyan University Press published *The Grave of the Right Hand* after Wright returned to California. Although he later repudiated it as a warm-up volume for his Dantesque trilogy, the poems in verse and prose introduce many of the themes that resonate through his later work. In these early poems, he evokes landscapes from the American South he knew as a boy and from the European South and American West he knew as an adult. He traces journeys along a "via negativa" toward illumination. (At the end of one of the final poems, he writes: "The path will open, the Angel beckon, / And he will follow. For light is all.") The typical quester in these poems struggles through a shadowy wasteland full of fog, graves, owls, bats, moonlight, cold winds, and the ghosts of dead or mad writers. Pound and Montale are tutelary presences, but Wright seems more determined to echo the gloomy tones and stark atmospheres of his teachers, Justice and Strand, or other poets from the American South such as Edgar Allan Poe and T. S. Eliot.

A TRILOGY OF TRILOGIES

Wright may have shrugged off his first book's soft-spoken, hermetic lucubrations because they lacked ambition. (He included only five prose poems from the volume in his selected poems, *Country Music*.) In *Hard Freight* (1973), the first collection he liked well enough to consider as part of a trilogy, he grappled with his literary mentors, his Christian upbringing, and his present agnosticism in a more forthright way. He paid homage to Ezra Pound, Arthur Rimbaud, Baron Corvo, Dino Campana, and other artists, acknowledging them as guides who—like Virgil for Dante—had to be abandoned so he could find his own voice and his own *paradiso*. After literally following Pound through Venice, in one poem he addresses the hoary master as a "Cold-blooded father of light," a contradictory mix of malice and brilliance. His "Homage to Arthur Rimbaud" is similarly double-edged. "For almost a hundred years," he says, "We've gathered outside your legend and been afraid / Of what such brilliance affords." Wary of the inflammatory imaginations of artist-gods, Wright bows and moves on, just as he bows and moves on from the fervor of his early devotions to Christian gods. In "Northhanger Ridge" he recalls a candlelit vigil at the Perrys' Bible Camp when he was fourteen, mocking his and his peers' meditative intensity. "The children talk to the nothingness," he says, rather than to a verifiable God. For Wright, the fiery, youthful longing for communion ends with ash and exhaustion. Disillusioned, he portrays God and His promised redemption as insubstantial, illusory, dead as "a skull in the hard ground." A glimmer of hope flickers in the possibility that God and salvation, though asleep, will wake, but there is little in the poem that predicts such an auspicious event.

In "The New Poem," which became a popular and controversial anthology piece, Wright offers an aesthetic manifesto that endorses the sort of disillusionment he wrote about in "Northhanger Ridge." Its list of nine directives amounts to a "via negativa" that, unlike the Christian's negative journey in a traditional meditation, ends with further negations. Of his proposed "new poem," he says:

> It will not resemble the sea.
> It will not have dirt on its thick hands.
> It will not be part of the weather.

These purgatorial renunciations of the physical, however, lead to nothing spiritual or redemptive. His last stanza declares that the "new poem" will offer no consolation or help of any kind. Written partly as a tongue-in-cheek response to 1960s poets who denounced the aesthete's "art for art's sake" principles and called for sociopolitical engagement, Wright seems to be donning the mask of an Oscar Wilde-like contrarian or, in Robert Lowell's term, "a Christian atheist." But the poem also expresses Wright's genuine attachment to the meditative "via negativa" and his sorrowful belief that, at the end of the mystic's dark road, he will not find any Christian consolation.

In *Bloodlines* (1975), the second book in the first trilogy, Wright focuses more on family ghosts than artistic ghosts. His goal, however, is the same: to track down his roots, his "bloodlines," that offer clues to his identity. In "Tattoos," a sequence of twenty reminiscences, and "Skins," a sequence of twenty unmetrical sonnets, he elegizes grandparents, parents, and his childhood in an attempt to explain what experiences "tattooed" his "skin" or created his identity. Throughout these sequences, Wright shows how biology and environment determine why he is the way he is and why others are the way they are. His prayers for self-transcendence continually butt up against the hard facts of life and death.

> What you are is what you will be
> Until the end, no matter
> What prayer you answer to

he says in the first section of "Skins." In the last poem of the sequence, Wright portrays himself as an erratic, bewildered pilgrim who is doomed to roam the earth like Samuel Taylor Coleridge's Ancient Mariner. Wright's self-consciousness—especially his consciousness of himself as a frustrated quester—is the shirt of fire or tattooed skin he fails to slough off. In "Rural Route," the final poem in *Bloodlines*, his perplexed identity haunts him like the memory of his twelve-year-old face reflected on a window in Tennessee. He yearns for metamorphosis, a new self, a happier mood, but the image of his face and the personality behind it follow him wherever he goes:

> I leave the back yard, and the front yard, and the face stays.
> I am back on the West Coast, in my studio
> My wife and my son asleep, and the face stays.

Wright completed *China Trace* (1977), the last installment of his first trilogy, in November 1976. Conceived of as a unified sequence, the book traced Wright's autobiography in poems that bore the trace or tattoo of their Chinese models—namely, poems from the T'ang Dynasty translated by Pound and Arthur Waley. The "trace" also referred to Wright's conception of his life as a pilgrimage along a road ("trace" can mean road or path) that zigzagged toward Christian and Buddhist ideals. Imitating the imagism, brevity, and spiritual concerns of Chinese lyrics, Wright limited himself to twelve lines in which to convey "one man's relationship to the endlessness, the ongoingness, the everlastingness of what's around him . . . in the natural world." If he emphasized the Oriental's preoccupation with this world rather than the Christian's with the next, his relationship with both views remained quixotic. He could have been thinking of the eastern trace in his sequence when he spoke in an interview with David Young about his interest in the Buddhist's quest for inner and outer peace. "It is a search that appeals to me," he said, but admitted, "I cannot find that still, small center in my self or in the world that will make me at one with my world. But I look for it. In fact I look for that more than I would look for . . . Christian resolution. . . . I would think, as I get older, my steps would be in the service of something more along the line of a Buddhistic journey than a Dantesque journey." Like Eliot in *The Waste Land* (1922), Wright in *China Trace* travels down both Christian and Buddhist roads, and like Eliot he finds only intimations of a paradisiacal "still point" at the center of the turning world.

Wandering through remembered landscapes in Italy, his native South, and California, Wright typically describes tenebrous atmospheres symbolic of a "dark night of the soul" on the verge of illumination. Moonlight and starlight are harbingers in these night scenes of a divine enlightenment, whether Christian or Buddhist, that never comes. In "Clear Night" he begins with a characteristic scene—in a contemplative mood he surveys the moonlit landscape outside his house—and then proceeds to thoughts about God. He interrupts the quiet melancholy of the first stanza, in which "Moon-fingers lay down their same routine" as if playing a soft blues melody on his porch, with the second stanza's stentorian call for violent mystical communion. He echoes John Donne's passionate pleas in the Holy Sonnets for God to "o'erthrow me, and bend / Your force, to break, blow, burn, and make me new." He could be thinking of the sort of ecstatic woundings by God that St. Teresa, St. John of the Cross, and other contemplatives experienced at the end of their spiritual exercises when he declares: "I want to be bruised by God. / I want to be strung up in a strong light and singled out." In the final stanza, Wright depicts the natural universe of wind, vegetation, and stars as indifferent and uncomprehending. The cyclical, ongoing cosmos resembles the cars Wright hears from his porch that pass him by with no understanding of his passionate spiritual yearnings.

Some reviewers criticized *China Trace* for what they considered to be its lack of ambition, accessibility, and narrative coherence. Although Wright continued to write fragmentary narratives that blended realistic and surrealistic imagery, he enlarged his canvas in later books. In 1983, one year after publishing his first trilogy in *Country Music* and shortly after accepting a position at the University of Virginia (in 1988 he would become that university's Souder Family Professor of English), he began composing *Zone Journals* (1988), a book-long sequence that reflected his move from California to Virginia as well as his stylistic move toward the discursive expansiveness of prose. Like other modern sequences, Wright's "journals" mapped out zones that were geographical as well as psychological. Remembered landscapes continued to act as catalysts for meditations on language and God, on the world and its relation to words and the Word. The critic Helen Vendler found in his new poems a "deepening concentration that aims at either obliteration or transcendence, blanks or mysticism," arguing that Wright "remains bound to the materiality and the temporal rhythm of language, whereas both Eastern nothingness and Western transcendence, at their utmost point, renounce as meaningless both materiality and time." For Wright, mystical concentration was cyclical: it moved through the nothingness of a "dark night" to spiritual transcendence and then back to a fresh vision of the material world, "the world of the ten thousand things,"—borrowing a phrase from the *Tao Te Ching*—as he called the collection of his next three books (*The Southern Cross*, 1981; *The Other Side of the River*; and *Zone Journals*).

In the last trilogy of books, (*Chickamauga*, 1995; *Black Zodiac*, 1997; and *Appalachia*, 1998), which he collected in *Negative Blue* (2000), Wright continued to trace his pilgrimage along an eastern and western "via negativa" that culminated in a melancholy appreciation of earth's splendors as they flare and falter. His meditative obsessions are all at work in a poem with the Wallace Stevensish title "An Ordinary Afternoon in Charlottesville." His first lines marry Chinese script and Virginia peach tree, Buddhism (one thinks of Buddha under the Bo Tree of Enlightenment) and Christianity, darkness and light:

> Under the peach trees, the ideograms the leaves throw
> Over the sun-peppered grass read
> *Purgatio, illuminatio, contemplatio.*

Keenly observant as ever, Wright reads the leaf shadows that resemble Chinese ideograms and translates them into a Christian language that is both enticing and offputting, beautiful and frightening. The sounds of the Italian words, like the scents and scenes around the peach tree, are pleasant, but what the words signify is the harrowing "dark night of the soul." And what does the world think of Wright's ruminations on language, landscape, and divinity? "Meanwhile," he says breezily, shifting perspectives,

> the afternoon
> fidgets about its business,
> Unconcerned with such immolations.

Despite the indifference expressed by his surroundings, Wright keeps meditating and writing, undaunted by the world's everyday "business."

Throughout Wright's trilogies, his whimsical sense of humor, enchantment with words, love of natural beauty, and passion for metaphysical ideas offset his penchant for melancholy. His stylistic panache transforms his gloomier thoughts into song. If he envisions a *paradiso* at the end of his long journey, it resembles Pound's more than Dante's, a Buddhist's more than a Christian's.

> Do not move.
> Let the wind speak.
> That is Paradise,

Pound wrote in a draft for one of his final *Cantos*. At the end of his "Appalachian Book of the Dead III," Wright says:

> Surely some splendor's set to come forth,
> Some last equation solved, declued and reclarified.
> South wind and a long shine, a small-time paradiso. . . .

The space signified by the ellipses implies that there is still an absence waiting to be filled, a heaven that has not arrived, when in fact Wright has filled his spaces for forty years with the only paradise he really believed in—a poetic one. Ever since he went on his pilgrimage to Sirmione and glanced at the sun angling through olive trees and shimmering on Lake Garda's waves, he has diligently assembled a *paradiso* from words. Although Dante's *paradiso* may have vanished along with the Christian superstructure that propped it up, Wright's epic of glittering fragments—his trilogy of trilogies with all their infernal glooms and naturalistic splendors—is a worthy modern substitute.

[*See also* Berryman, John; Eliot, T. S.; Justice, Donald; Lowell, Robert; Pound, Ezra, and his *Pisan Cantos*; Stevens, Wallace; *and* Strand, Mark.]

SELECTED WORKS

The Voyage (1963)
6 Poems (1965)
The Dream Animal (1968)
Private Madrigals (1969)
The Grave of the Right Hand (1970)
The Venice Notebook (1971)
Backwater (1973)
Hard Freight (1973)
Bloodlines (1975)
China Trace (1977)
Colophons (1977)
Dead Color (1980)
The Southern Cross (1981)
Country Music: Selected Early Poems (1982)
The Other Side of the River (1984)
Halflife: Improvisations and Interviews, 1977–87 (1988)
Zone Journals (1988)
The World of the Ten Thousand Things: Poems, 1980–1990 (1990)
Chickamauga (1995)
Quarter Notes (1995)
Black Zodiac (1997)
Appalachia (1998)
Negative Blue (2000)
A Short History of the Shadow (2002)

FURTHER READING

Andrews, Tom. *The Point Where All Things Meet: Essays on Charles Wright*. Oberlin, Ohio, 1995. A helpful introduction to Wright's poetry that includes many of the important reviews of his work.

Contemporary Authors. Vol. 62. Detroit, Mich.,1998. New Revision Series. Contains a brief account of Wright's career.

Contemporary Authors Autobiography Series. Vol. 7. Detroit, Mich., 1988. Contains an essay by Wright about his life that illuminates the background to much of his poetry.

Contemporary Literary Criticism. Vol. 146. Detroit, Mich., 2002. Contains a substantial collection of reviews and articles about Wright, written both by admirers such as Helen Vendler and detractors such as William Logan.

Parini, Jay. *Some Necessary Angels*. New York, 1997. Offers one of the most insightful overviews of Wright's career.

Stitt, Peter. *Uncertainty and Plenitude: Five Contemporary Poets*. Iowa City, Iowa, 1997. Provides an astute discussion of some of the philosophical ideas that inform Wright's work.

Upton, Lee. *The Muse of Abandonment: Origin, Identity, Mastery in Five American Poets*. Lewisburg, Pa., 1998.

JAMES WRIGHT

by Gerry Cambridge

"The Flying Eagles of Troop 62" is a touching prose poem and reminiscence of one Ralph Neal, a scoutmaster of James Wright's Ohio boyhood. In wondering why Neal never escaped the conditions of the valley in which he was born, but worked with forbearance with his group of acned, unhappy adolescents, the poet recounts a story from the Hindu Vedantas. It is of a saint who, after a thousand lives filled with human folly and suffering, realizing that his scabby mongrel will not be allowed to enter Nirvana with him, refuses it for himself. It is not surprising that this seems to have had a considerable resonance for Wright. He is one of America's poets of the outcast, the socially marginalized, and the sometimes brute realities of an Ohio which, though he left it, never left him. Though Wright did escape, at least physically, his work is one long attempted reconciliation with some of those realities.

James Wright.
(© *Bettmann/Corbis*)

BEGINNINGS

James Arlington Wright was born on 13 December 1927 in Martins Ferry, Ohio, an industrial valley town of the Ohio River with, however, sometimes beautiful surrounding landscape. His father, Dudley, worked for some fifty years for the local Hazel-Atlas glass factory, though because of the Great Depression, which began before Wright was three, he was frequently laid off. The realities of Depression Ohio—its prostitutes, tramps, old men—would people a good deal of Wright's work later. The middle son of three, he appears to have been a sensitive child: he was a fluent writer of sonnets by tenth grade and in 1943, in his mid-teens, had a nervous breakdown which led to his missing an entire school year. Two teachers in particular encouraged his development: Helen McNeely Sheriff (one dedicatee of a book of his poems almost thirty

years later), who taught English literature, and his Latin teacher, Elizabeth Willerton Esterley. In 1946 the young poet graduated and joined the U.S. Army. He served in Japan in 1946 and 1947 with U.S. occupation forces. Paradoxically, Wright heard there from a fellow soldier about Kenyon College, Ohio, where John Crowe Ransom was a prestigious presence on the English faculty as well as editor of the influential *Kenyon Review*. Under the terms of the G.I. Bill, Wright matriculated at Kenyon in January 1948. Four years later he completed his degree. His honors thesis, interestingly, was on Thomas Hardy, whose poetry is widely peopled by a disparate crowd of characters, many in positions of despair. This may well have influenced Wright in his approach to his own material.

All this time he had been writing his own poetry. Beginning with two poems published in the *Kenyon Review* in the autumn of 1951, he achieved nationwide publication as a poet over the next three years in such leading venues as *Poetry* (Chicago) and *The New Yorker*. It was a busy time in his personal life, too; on 10 February 1952 he married a nurse and high school classmate, Liberty Kardules, and with his new wife spent 1952 and 1953 on a Fulbright Fellowship at the University of Vienna. There, he studied the poetry of George Trakl, a German World War I poet who would later prove influential in Wright's work. In March 1953 his first child, Franz, was born.

Beginning in the fall of 1953, Wright undertook graduate studies at the University of Washington in Seattle, again under distinguished teachers: Theodore Roethke and, in Roethke's absence through illness, Stanley Kunitz. He was awarded a Ph.D. in 1959, and his dissertation was titled "The Comic Imagination of Charles Dickens." Meantime, in 1954 he had submitted a book-length manuscript for the Yale Series of Younger Poets competition. A letter from W. H. Auden, the selector, on 2 July 1956 from Italy, informed him that he had won. The book was published the following year as *The Green Wall* (1957), with a curiously bland introduction by Auden which, however, picked out for especial notice Wright's concern with social outsiders.

EARLY BOOKS

The Green Wall was well-received; for example, J. E. Palmer, in the *Sewanee Review*, called Wright "one of the Elect, a young poet of great gifts," high praise for a book which now seems relatively dated, narcotized by its iambic meters. Though Wright claimed in his earlier work to have been influenced by Robert Frost and E. A. Robinson, there is little of the distinction of the best of their work. Wright's language is elevated, "poetic," sometimes with echoes of Dylan Thomas: "The fruits of summer in the fields of love," goes a line from "Eleutheria." There are verbs like "forebodes" (to rhyme with "roads") and, often, a lack of a specific situation in some poems; the fundamental question "where?" often goes begging. When we read in "On the Skeleton of a Hound" that the decaying throat of the beast "declines from summer," following on from a noun like "declivities," we know we are in the presence of a poet schooled in the New Critical awareness of the interesting, somewhat mannered, ambiguities of the verb. Elegies and laments are frequent, even in titles such as "Elegy in a Firelit Room," "Lament for My Brother on a Hayrake," and "To a Defeated Savior." The young poet seems to have a fascination with rebirth: there is a poem about Lazarus, "Come Forth," while "The Angel" is spoken by the angel on its way to open Jesus's tomb.

Among the volume's strongest poems are "The Fisherman," with its memorable descriptions of "the driftwood faces" of old men, and "Girl in a Window," who, by simply being, for the male onlookers, "gave, and did not know she gave." "To a Defeated Savior" is addressed to a god taunted as impotent to resurrect a "skinny swimmer" drowned, while "A Song for the Middle of the Night," rather more modestly, is addressed to the poet's young son, who "turns the household upside down." Written in a lilting ballad meter, alternating four- and three-stress lines, it is, for Wright, unusually humorous. Wright balanced this, though, with the grimly earnest "A Poem about George Doty in the Death House." Doty murdered a young woman; Wright calls him, sentimentally, "one for wonder," and mourns, he tells us, "no soul but his," not even that of the girl. While a noted Wright advocate such as Peter Stitt (1990) claims this is justifiable hyperbole,

Wright's sheer dismissal of feeling for the girl damages the veracity of the poem. Doty is sentimentalized—somewhat akin to the "lady with an assumed name" memorialized by Wright in his elegy for a prostitute, when his narrator asks: "how could she love so many, / Then turn away to die as though for none?" That "love" seems, perhaps ironically, an inaccurate verb in this context.

Saint Judas (1959), which had been solicited by Donald Hall for the Wesleyan University Press's new poetry series, by its very title made explicit Wright's empathy for outcasts shown in his first book. While it largely continued the style and manner of *The Green Wall*, Wright had begun attempting to purge his rhetoric, a circumstance aided by a review by the poet James Dickey of Donald Hall's *New Poets of England and America* (1957). Dickey slammed the anthology, which included work by Anthony Hecht, Thom Gunn, and Reed Whittemore, among others, for a sort of bland homogeneity; he deprecated Wright, represented by five poems from *The Green Wall*, as "ploddingly sincere." Wright was initially outraged, quite possibly because there was some basis to Dickey's criticism and also because he had seldom been subjected to adverse comment. He and Dickey exchanged a series of initially vituperative letters. The criticism, however, struck home. By the time "At the Executed Murderer's Grave"—which returned to the matter of George Doty—appeared in *Saint Judas*, it had been radically reworked following its first appearance in *Poetry* in August 1958. High-flown rhetoric ("smitten dumb / Under the vengeance of a lily's bloom") had been replaced by a blunt forthrightness which remains effective. The poem opens: "My name is James A. Wright, and I was born / Twenty five miles from this infected grave." The poem was, interestingly enough, dedicated to James Dickey.

"At the Executed Murderer's Grave" is strangely preoccupied with Doty, though it never explains that preoccupation except insofar as, in that Wright feels guilty, he and Doty are linked. It is intriguing how closely Wright identifies with the murderer: "I do not want to die," he writes, "even to keep Belaire, Ohio, safe." The poet's imaginative identification with the murderer is so close that he is alarmed. A more than usual empathy with outsiders and criminals would remain a feature of Wright's work.

Saint Judas's strongest poems continued this new, blunt manner. The book is in three sections: "Lunar Changes," "A Sequence of Love Poems" (something of a misnomer), and "The Part Nearest Home." The volume opens impressively with "Complaint"—a title which captures the bellicose nature of the speaker, for this is a bullish elegy for a dead wife, the speaker's "lost hag," full of convincing details. He asks who will "feed the hogs / And pitch the chicken's heads to hungry dogs?" The woman is mourned in terms of what practicalities she is no longer able to carry out. Written in muscular rhyming couplets, the poem is followed immediately by "Paul," which strongly echoes in tone some of the character poems of E. A. Robinson. It is spoken by an onlooker: "Paul" appears to be the narrator of "Complaint." We are given a view of the devastated widower far more subdued than in the previous piece; it helps confirm the reader's suspicion that the harsh tone of "Complaint" is a cover-up for its speaker's devastation. The book's third poem is "An Offering for Mr. Bluehart," an elegy for an orchard owner who used to chase the poem's narrator for stealing apples when a boy. Now mature, the poem's speaker better understands Bluehart, "who lost his labored wealth to thieves"; coming across fine unpicked apples as an adult, he leaves them untouched to honor the dead man's memory.

The brief middle section of love poems is mainly notable for "The Accusation," a poem elucidating its narrator's erotic attraction to ugliness, the "scarred truth of wretchedness," exemplified by the lover's scarred face. The narrator loves it because it "was broken," a sentiment one of the two strongest pieces at the book's close, its title poem, seems to buttress. While the other poem, "Devotions," is a venomous tirade against a "lost mocker" of the narrator's childhood, and of considerable power, the famous "Saint Judas," a sonnet monologue, is a poem of despair. Going out to commit suicide, Judas happens on a gang beating up a man. He runs to help, and so doing forgets his preoccupation with his own sin to help the victim. But as he does so, remembrance returns, and realization of the impossibility of salvation. The poem closes: "flayed without hope, / I held the man for nothing in my arms." The poem may well have been stronger in the third person; in the first person Judas sounds, at the sonnet's close, self-concerned. He perhaps lacks the self-abnegation of the genuine saint. The last line can also, arguably, be misread, in the sense of "I did this for nothing, it was a waste of time," rather than in what was surely the poet's intended sense of "even though this was for no purpose, I still held the man." The genuine saint would surely not be concerned that his holding the man was "for nothing," in either sense, yet this occurs to Saint Judas with such force that he must recount it.

THE NEW STYLE

The four years that would pass before Wright's third collection—the groundbreaking *The Branch Will Not Break*

(1963), which marked a radical stylistic development from his first two books—were accompanied, as changes in a poet's work often are, by considerable changes in Wright's private life. By 1959 his marriage was seriously troubled; in 1962 he was divorced. Around the end of the 1950s he came across Robert Bly's idiosyncratic and influential little magazine *The Fifties* (later *The Sixties*); Wright wrote to Bly and was invited out to his Minnesota farm. Here, Wright made numerous literary friends, including Louis Simpson, and established a long-lasting association with Bly. Wright's exposure to the rural realities of the farm, and Bly's urging him to adopt more instinctive ways of feeling, all bore fruit with his third book.

Like many poets in the 1960s who had started out writing in formal stanzas—including Robert Lowell, W. S. Merwin, and Louis Simpson—Wright, with *The Branch Will Not Break*, moved to a rhythmically looser, less orotund style. While still writing in formal stanzas occasionally, he would retain elements of this new style to the end of his life. The book also marked Wright's use of the so-called deep image, which verged upon surrealism and owed something to the European and Latin American poets Wright had been translating. The new work was rich in images and with sudden, often apparently incongruous statements, interspersed among or concluding poems. Ohio begins to appear more frequently—Wright had discovered the poetic resonance of place names—and much of the rhetoric driven by meter is gone. Conversely, however, some of the poem's titles are now, no doubt deliberately, elaborate. Examples are "Depressed by a Book of Bad Poetry, I Walk Towards an Unused Pasture and Invite the Insects to Join Me" and "As I Step over a Puddle at the End of Winter, I Think of an Ancient Chinese Governor." Each yokes, intriguingly, two dissimilar clauses incongruously together. Sometimes the poems' images are overblown; in "The Jewel," the narrator's bones, when he stands up, "turn to dark emeralds." While one could work up some sense for this, there seems no aesthetic reason for this particular image—it could as well be "dark rubies," "dark diamonds," or "dark sapphires."

Wright's most successful pieces are those in which the images are not so unusual as to be incomprehensible; not those, as in the portentously titled "Having Lost My Sons, I Confront the Wreckage of the Moon: Christmas, 1960," in which he describes the moon "walking down hallways / of a diamond." Far more powerful is one of the book's earliest successes, "Autumn Begins in Martins Ferry, Ohio," notable for its linguistic and imagistic economy. The poem deals with the considerable sporting tradition in the poet's home valley. Wright had observed in an interview that sport was regarded by those of his contemporaries with athletic ability as a potential escape route to another lifestyle. The poem's narrator, who is in Shreve High Football Stadium, thinks of the deprived, drinking Polacks and of laboring "Negroes in the blast furnace of Benwood." It is a world in which a hero archetype still exists, personified by major athletes, and in which the sons of "proud fathers," and of their women, who are "dying for love," "gallop terribly against each other's bodies." Sport becomes here less a recreation than a gladiatorial contest for self-advancement. The football players become animal—they "gallop," as horses do, and "terribly" carries a genuine weight. The mothers are "dying for love" not just literally, as part of the biology of birth and death, but colloquially; they desire the love they do not have. In twelve lines Wright paints a picture of savage necessities without a trace of sentimentality.

One of Wright's most discussed poems, "Lying in a Hammock at William Duffy's Farm in Pine Island, Minnesota," shows how far he had come from his earlier rhetorical style. A thirteen-line free verse lyric, influenced by translations of Chinese naturalistic poetry by Arthur Waley and others, its first dozen lines consist almost entirely of pure description of the natural world before the poet—among it a "bronze butterfly" and old horse droppings that "blaze up into golden stones" in the sunlight. The poem closes with the flat declaration, "I have wasted my life." Numerous critics have debated on the meaning of this statement in the poem's context; that it was so, for instance, because he had spent too much time writing in iambic meter, or had spent too much time lying in hammocks, watching the world pass. On the contrary, Wright in an interview said he intended to convey that he had "wasted" his life because he has spent too little of it in the sort of pure looking the poem exemplifies. A related piece, "Depressed by a Book of Bad Poetry," also of thirteen lines, begins with the narrator abandoning the book in line one and escaping into the natural world of grasshoppers, crickets, and ants in the concluding dozen lines. Bar one beautiful description of the shadows of ants—"So frail that I can see through them"—the poem has a similar plainness of style. In organization, it is like the previous poem turned on its head.

WRIGHT AND NATURE

The extensive portrayal of nature in *The Branch Will Not Break* is also new. Nature for Wright here offers a saving humor and otherness; its insouciant sassiness is well evoked. Wright's is a rather generous bestiary. The book's title comes from the closing line of "Two Hangovers": the poem's narrator watches a blue jay using a branch as a kind of avian trampoline, knowing that it "will not break." His poem "March," a description of a hibernating female bear—Wright often feminizes, or prefers to write about female, nature—shows a delicate humor and empathy. Sparsely written free verse, it is almost perfect of its kind. Such generosity is evoked, too, in Wright's famous "A Blessing," a lyrical description of an encounter which just skirts sentimentality. The poet and his "friend" (who was Robert Bly) step into a pasture to meet "two Indian ponies," which "bow shyly as wet swans." In an epiphany at the end, the poet is so delighted by this encounter that he realizes, as he tells us, that if he left his body he "would break / Into blossom." While some readers may find the sentiment not especially convincing, stylistically the line break at "break" sets up a moment of semantic uncertainty before puffing out, like the action described, "Into blossom." Wright's "A Blessing" is interesting for the poet's idealizing of the animals and, again, he makes one of them feminine, this time girl-delicate and therefore lacking for the narrator the implicating complications of sexuality. The poem's basic situation recalls Robert Frost's "Two Look at Two," another human-animal encounter between a pair of deer and a man and his wife. Wright's poem lacks the element of surprise and decided strangeness of the encounter in the Frost piece; to Wright, the otherness of the ponies is occasion for joy, not for reflection. There is a Franciscan extension of humanity toward the animals, though the poem might be stronger without the self-reflecting reference in the last three lines.

MIDLIFE BLEAKNESS

It would be five years before the publication of perhaps Wright's bleakest volume, the ironically titled *Shall We Gather at the River* (1968). In the interim, despite a Ph.D. and three distinguished collections of poetry, Wright was denied tenure at the University of Minnesota in 1963; excessive drinking had caused him to miss classes, and his superiors, who included the poet-critic Allen Tate, felt he was not a reliable prospect. Hired by Macalester College in St. Paul, Minnesota, for 1963–1964, he was awarded a Guggenheim Fellowship for 1965–1966 and spent it with his parents in Ohio; visiting his children, then in California; and with the Blys. These must have been lonely years for Wright, but things were soon to look up. Moving to New York City in the spring of 1966 to take up a position at Hunter College in the autumn, he soon met Edith Anne Runk—the beloved "Annie" of many later poems. They were married on 29 April 1967.

When *Shall We Gather at the River* was published the following year, it showed a poet obsessed with death and unhappiness. The book's ironic title is taken from the popular hymn; here, however, the river is not the hymn's redeeming river of salvation, but the Ohio, or the Styx. Suicide or drowning in the river is a frequent motif in the book, which is also ghosted by the presence of Jenny, who died young, a former love in the adolescence of the poet. "I sing of flat defeat / In a flat voice," a narrator in one piece tells us, flatly, and we hardly need to suspend our disbelief. To call the book despairing is to describe it optimistically. Stylistically, Wright's move to free verse had been sustained and it led him at times to a flaccidness which is a concomitant problem in the writing of free verse for the opposite reason than when employing formal stanzas. When writing badly, a poet pads out formal stanzas to fulfill the requirements of meter and rhyme; in free verse, on the contrary, the lack of formal restraints requires extra vigilance to avoid wordiness. Wright could end such a poem as "The Life," blandly, confirming loneliness, with the emphasis.

It is.
And it is
The last time.

Wright's liking for the obscure and impressive image, finally impenetrable without special pleading, also continues, sometimes complemented by inapt personifications. In the loquaciously titled "A Poem Written under an Archway in a Discontinued Railroad Station, Fargo, North Dakota," which fairly trumpets its claim to dispossessed authenticity, locomotives "sometimes . . . leap and cry out, skitterish." And in "Confession to J. Edgar Hoover," an exercise in Wright's political-surreal mode, "last evening," the poem's narrator tells us, "I devoured the wing of a cloud." The problem with surrealism is that it is strong on the illogic of the unconscious but weak on aesthetic logic. Such images by Wright communicate vaguely, but they are too easy. It is difficult to distinguish them from mere poetic sleights of hand.

Of course, a poetry of despair can be curiously cheering. The art and the lack of pretense can be affirming even when the poem's content seems negative. Wright's best poems in *Shall We Gather at the River* are often the plainest. In pieces like "Willy Lyons," "Youth," and "Two Postures beside a Fire"—the first an elegy for an uncle, "a craftsman of hammers and wood," and the others about the poet's father, Dudley—the diction is generally straightforward and the poems' contents documentary in tone. Such pieces exemplify the power of the calm, level voice of a poet speaking, as John Berryman would say, of what matters. Wright's father worked for half a century in an Ohio factory. In "Youth," which is an elegy for the man's unfulfilled dreams, the poet wonders, "Did he shudder with hatred in the cold shadow of grease?" Whether he did or not, Wright remembers that his return to his sons was "quiet as the evening." Wright's father is to him a "strange bird," whose "song remains secret." In "Two Postures beside a Fire," on a visit home Wright finds that his father has the nobility of a worker; he, conversely, is a worn intellectual, the lines of "an ugly age" marking his face. The age is not just his own chronological age, but that of modernity, the age itself. In this construction Wright merely reflects what he has experienced. His father, however, seems to have transcended the bleakness of his own experience.

CONSOLIDATION

The publication of *Shall We Gather at the River* garnered a $4,500 Rockefeller Foundation Grant for Wright in 1969, augmented by an Ingram Merrill Foundation award of $3,500. With this financial aid he was able to spend time preparing the manuscript of an early *Collected Poems* (1971) and spend the summer of 1970 with Annie in Italy and France. The *Collected Poems* was not only well received, but won Wright a Pulitzer Prize in 1972 as well as the $10,000 Fellowship of the Academy of American Poets. The book appended thirty-one new poems to Wright's first four collections (with the exception of five weaker poems dropped from *The Green Wall*); these included the outstanding "Small Frogs Killed on the Highway" and the graceful lyric "Written in a Copy of Swift's Poems, for Wayne Burns." The former is a bleak paean to doomed energy, exemplified by the frogs trying to reach wet pasture by crossing a highway. They are the amphibian equivalents of people aspiring to escape the Ohio in which Wright was born. Understandably, he identifies with them. The scenario delineated in the poem provides powerfully what T. S. Eliot called "an objective correlative" for Wright's own biographical context. The second outstanding piece among the new poems, a paean for the eighteenth-century Irish satirist Jonathan Swift's lacerating art and its "nobilities," is an implicit defense of satire.

The volume was, perhaps precipitately, followed in 1973 by *Two Citizens*—these being Wright and his wife.

It was widely criticized and Wright later seems to have regretted its publication. Many poems read like jottings rather than the finished article, and in tone it veers dramatically between vitriol against America and an at-times unabashed sentimentality about his wife. It did, however, set a new pattern in Wright's books: from now on they would mingle poetry with prose poems, and each had a strong European component. The poet becomes an artist abroad, recording local scenes with the fresh outlook of the traveler and reflecting on his native America from his new perspective. *Two Citizens* was redeemed by *To a Blossoming Pear Tree* (1977), one of Wright's strongest collections and the last to appear in his lifetime. It is a volume of attempted reconciliation with America that opens and closes with poems set there; paradoxically, these tend to be the book's strongest work. The title poem closes the volume; it contrasts a blossoming pear tree in its innocent beauty with an old man the poem's narrator recalls meeting in Minneapolis, who begs him for sex for money. Addressing the pear tree, the narrator concedes its beauty, but common humanity has him finally identifying himself with the old man. He writes of himself that his body's "dark blood" pulls him down with his "brother"; the poem's subtext is "there but for the grace of God go I." The piece exemplifies one of Wright's most durable qualities, his constant awareness of a fundamental humanity. In this poem, nature's innocence and humanity's culpability contrast powerfully.

Wright had by now reached a style of settled plainness; the earlier surrealistic element is largely absent. "Hook," for instance, is a street poem about a young Sioux man with a hook for a hand who gives the narrator money for a bus fare. Apart from its striking description of the hook "raised into the terrible starlight," the poem is so stripped of conventional poetic technique that it has to rely on the power of its content. One tends to remember the poem for its situation rather than its matter. Elsewhere in the book Wright pens a lyrical elegy for W. H. Auden, proving he could still write formally when he chose, while his "Discoveries in Arizona" is a poem of astonishment about the natural world's otherness, as manifested by a female tarantula, an ancient arachnid less amenable to Wright's anthropomorphism, perhaps, than Indian ponies, bears, and blue jays. A fourteen-year-old in the desert is showing the poem's narrator the hole where the spider lives. When the narrator confesses he has yet to see a tarantula "turn her face / away from me," the fourteen-year-old, with unself-conscious irony, reassures him that it is not important: "Maybe she's never seen you either."

The narrator is dislodged from a habitual human-centered vision; he glimpses the ahuman reality of a world in which he is both as important and as unimportant as the spider.

To a Blossoming Pear Tree was generally considered to be a return to Wright's usual standard. Two years after its appearance, however, back in New York City after a summer in Italy on another Guggenheim Fellowship, Wright developed a chronic sore throat that failed to respond to antibiotics. It was tragically diagnosed as cancer of the tongue in December 1979. James Wright died four months later, at Calvary Hospital in The Bronx on 25 March 1980. He was just fifty-two years old.

POSTHUMOUS WORKS

Wright's career, however, was not over. A posthumously published volume, *This Journey* (1982), bears some comparison with its predecessor, again being a mix of prose vignette and poetry and with a view of Ohio from the perspective of Italy. The poet remembers characters from his Ohioan childhood in pieces like "Old Bud" and "A Flower Passage," while the bitterly titled "Ohioan Pastoral" paints a world in which discarded condoms are, strikingly, "the cold balloons of lovers"; uplift and the pleasure of sexuality in this context are held to be no more significant than party balloons. Yet critics commented too on the reconciled autumnal tone of the volume, the sense of acceptance and transcendence in some of the poems. The poet celebrates the smaller creatures of earth in, for instance, "The Cicada" and "Lightning Bugs Asleep in the Afternoon"; the volume has at times a Franciscan radiance. In "The Journey" a spider—which Wright depicts, as often, as feminine—is seen to poise in the middle of her dusty web "while ruins crumbled on every side of her"; those ruins are both her own dead prey and the remains of her web. She, however, is "free of the dust." James Wright's last poems at times lightly achieve a similar freedom, if one not arrived at lightly. His *Above the River: The Complete Poems* followed in 1992, with a touching and at times harrowing memoir about Wright by his friend and fellow poet Donald Hall. The volume reveals his stature as an important twentieth-century American poet, an artist who did not flinch from the realities life had shown him. The gritty particularities of Wright's best work are matched with a rare generosity. The impression left by the experience of reading him is best summed up by the Latin noun *caritas*, a charity which is not diminished by its lapses into bitterness or by its straying towards the sentimental.

[*See also* Auden, W. H.; Dickey, James; Kunitz, Stanley; Lowell, Robert; Merwin, W.S.; New Critics, The; Ransom, John

Crowe; Robinson, Edwin Arlington; Roethke, Theodore; *and* Tate, Allen.]

SELECTED WORKS

The Green Wall (1957)
Saint Judas (1959)
The Lion's Tail and Eyes: Poems Written out of Laziness and Silence (1962)
The Branch Will Not Break (1963)
Shall We Gather at the River (1968)
Collected Poems (1971)
Two Citizens (1973)
Moments of the Italian Summer (1976)
To a Blossoming Pear Tree (1977)
This Journey (1982)
Collected Prose (1983)
Above the River: The Complete Poems (1992)

FURTHER READING

Dougherty, David C. *James Wright*. Twayne's United States Authors Series 494. Boston, 1987. A short biography in the opening chapter is followed by an account of each of the poet's major collections. A number of close readings of individual poems are offered, as well as a chronology of the poet's life and a bibliography of primary and secondary items.

Elkins, Andrew. *The Poetry of James Wright*. Tuscaloosa, Ala., 1991. One of the most significant scholarly books on Wright (though published before *Above the River: The Complete Poems*), it features close readings from each of Wright's single books.

Graziano, Frank, and Peter Stitt, eds. *James Wright: A Profile*. Durango, Colo., 1988. A miscellany, including letters, photographs, extracts from interviews, and memoirs about Wright. One of the best introductions to the poet and his work.

Smith, Dave, ed. *The Pure Clear Word: Essays on the Poetry of James Wright*. Urbana, Ill.,1982. Fifteen essays written mainly by fellow poets, and including Smith's extended interview with Wright (which also appears in Wright's *Collected Prose*). Useful mainly for a number of essays which do not appear elsewhere.

Stein, Kevin. *James Wright: The Poetry of a Grown Man: Constancy and Transition in the Work of James Wright*. Athens, Ga., 1989. With Elkins's work, above, probably the most valuable scholarly work on Wright, featuring in-depth chronological examinations of the poetry and making use of the collection of Wright's manuscripts and papers at the University of Minnesota.

Stitt, Peter, and Frank Graziano, eds. *James Wright: The Heart of the Light*. Ann Arbor, 1990. Forty-four reviews and essays, in addition to Stitt's biographical introduction, published during the course of Wright's career, offering a chronological survey of the reception and evaluation of Wright's work. Excellent as an overview.

RICHARD WRIGHT

by Mark Richardson

It all began with a fire: the one Richard Wright himself set when he was four years old. He had wondered, he tells us at the start of his autobiography, *Black Boy* (1945), "just how the long fluffy white curtains would look if I lit a bunch of straws and held it under them." They looked splendid, terrifying; and it is a wonder no one was killed. As it turned out, the little boy Wright still was at the time came closer to death than anyone, and not from the fire itself, but from the beating his mother gave him in the aftermath. "I was lashed so hard and long that I lost consciousness," he recalls. For years he was "chastened," as he dryly puts it, when he remembered that his mother "had come close to killing" him.

Richard Wright.
(*Courtesy of the Library of Congress*)

At about that time his father abandoned the family and Wright, the oldest child, underwent an ordeal of initiation. When some local boys beat him and stole the money his mother sent with him to market, she simply gave him more money, a heavy stick, and then locked him out of the house. "I am going to teach you this night to stand up and fight for yourself," she said. And so he went back out, almost paralyzed with fear: "I was alone upon the dark, hostile streets and gangs were after me. I had the choice of being beaten at home or away from home." When the gang set upon him he "let the stick fly, feeling it crack against a boy's skull," and striking out again and again. His fury horrified the boys: "They had never seen such frenzy." There were many more beatings, but now they came only from his guardians: his mother, his grandmother, his grandfather.

And there were mystifying events, too, as when the young boy awoke once to a commotion in the next room; his aunt's lover had stolen money from a woman—Wright never learned exactly who—knocked her unconscious, and set her house ablaze. He fled in the night with Wright's aunt and a pistol; the white men were after him. Another aunt, Maggie, had been married to Silas Hoskins, with whom the family briefly lived in Elaine, Arkansas, when Richard Wright was nine—that is, until Hoskins was killed by whites who "coveted his flourishing liquor business." This time the whole family fled. "Why had we not fought back?" Wright asked his mother. But "the fear that was in her made her slap [him] into silence." The little boy was learning what it meant to "limp through days lived under the threat of violence." Later, he heard a tale about a black woman who shot four white men to death—they had murdered her husband—and the story "gave form and meaning" to feelings that had long been "sleeping" in him: violent "fantasies," as he puts it, were no longer merely "a reflection of his reaction" to the ominous white world beyond; these fantasies had become for him "a culture, a creed, a religion." And when a young schoolmistress whispered to him the bloody story of Bluebeard, who married seven women and murdered them all, Wright was enchanted. Hearing that story was the first experience in his life, he reports, that elicited from him "a total emotional response." "I vowed that as soon as I was old enough I would buy all the novels there were and read them to feed that thirst for violence that was in me, for intrigue, for plotting, for secrecy, for bloody murders." Buy them he did, when he was old enough and had the money; but what is more important, he composed novels himself, almost all of them written about, and out of, his American experience of violence.

Reading and writing offered Wright a way to sublimate his violent fantasies, a way to redirect them toward socially useful ends, a way to redeem them. And acts of violence are always, in Wright's books, creative, expressive, or transformative. That is why his protagonists—Bigger

Thomas chief among them—inevitably decide to own their violent acts, even when these seem forced upon them by circumstance or by chance. And if violent acts can be expressive, then expressive acts can, in some sense, be violent; words do hurt us. Obscenity fascinated Wright for exactly this reason, well before he was old enough really to understand why. For this reason, too, he was electrified when he first read that most pugilistic of American critics, H. L. Mencken. "This man was fighting, fighting with words," Wright felt at once when he peeked into *A Book of Prefaces* (1917), a book he had obtained at the whites only public library in Memphis with a forged library pass. ("Dear Madam: Will you please let this nigger boy have some books by H. L. Mencken?" it had read). Wright was "jarred and shocked by the style, the clear clean, sweeping sentences." He "pictured the man as a raging demon"—and here the book became, for Wright, a kind of prospective mirror—"slashing with his pen, consumed with hate, denouncing everything American," and "mocking God, authority." Mencken "was using words as a weapon, using them as one would use a club." Richard Wright had found his calling. Writing emancipated him, and what is more, it laid before him an instrument of retribution against a world that seemed unwilling to allow him even to exist. In the novel of violence Wright would find redemption from the violence that had, since earliest youth, laid claim to him, when it had all begun with a fire.

THE EARLY YEARS, THE EARLY WORKS

Richard Wright was born on 4 September 1908 on a farm near Roxie, Mississippi, the son of Nathan Wright, an illiterate sharecropper, and Ella Wilson Wright, a sometime schoolteacher. The parents of his parents had been born in slavery, and one of them, his maternal grandfather, had served in the Union navy during the war. Mississippi in 1908 had for some twenty years been sitting in darkness; the state was among the first to disenfranchise the slaves whom the war had freed, and whom the Fourteenth and Fifteenth Amendments to the Constitution had made citizens and, at least in the case of men, voters. White supremacy was firmly fixed in Mississippi and would remain so at least until the mid-1960s, by which time Wright, for years an expatriate, had been buried in a cemetery in Paris.

When Wright was five his father deserted the family; this initiated a period of drifting. He lived in Natchez and Jackson, Mississippi; in Memphis, Tennessee; in Elaine and West Helena, Arkansas; in Jackson again; in Greenwood, Mississippi; in Jackson a third time; and ultimately, again, in Memphis—all of this by the time he was sixteen. Most of the time Wright lived with his mother, but at one point he was consigned to an orphanage, and for a while he lived with relatives. When he was ten, his mother suffered an incapacitating stroke, whereupon his grandmother, a strict Seventh Day Adventist, took charge of the impoverished family. In schools in a number of towns, Wright managed an itinerant sort of education, attending, in the end, Smith-Robertson Junior High in Jackson, from which he graduated valedictorian. For two years thereafter he worked in Memphis doing odd jobs at an optical company and washing dishes; it was at this time that he discovered H. L. Mencken, and through Mencken, introduced himself to novels by Theodore Dreiser, Sinclair Lewis, Sherwood Anderson, and Alexandre Dumas. In 1927 he moved to Chicago, following the path many southern-born African Americans took during the period of the Great Migration and afterwards. He took work in a delicatessen, sent for his mother and brother, and eventually landed a job at the central post office. During his early months in Chicago, Wright continued his self-education, reading voraciously, and by 1930 he had begun a novel of his own, tentatively titled "Cesspool," which appeared posthumously in 1963 under the title *Lawd Today*.

Lawd Today chronicles one long day in the life of Jake Jackson, a hapless black employee of the central post office in Chicago. In it Wright adopts certain elements of the documentary style developed by John Dos Passos in his *U.S.A.* (1937) trilogy. The novel is set on Lincoln's birthday, and extracts from a patriotic commentary on the life of the Great Emancipator and on the Civil War, taken from a radio broadcast, punctuate the narrative. The counterpoint is of course ironic. Some sixty years after the war, Wright's black protagonist runs out the course of his life in what Wright figures as a "squirrel cage" (the subtitle of one section of the novel); the meaning of emancipation remained, in 1935 (when the novel was finished), obscure.

The plot of the novel is simple: we follow Jake from dawn to deep midnight as he argues with his wife, plays the numbers, cuts up with his friends, reports for work, struggles to keep his job, and has his pocket picked at a roughhouse of a midnight party. The novel ends with a bitter, drunken, bloody fight between Jake and his wife Lil. "Lawd, I wish I was dead," she says to herself, weeping, while outside "an icy wind" sweeps around the corner of the building, "whining and moaning like an idiot in a deep black pit." The echo in that last phrase of the bleak passage in *Macbeth* (1605–1606), from which William Faulkner took the title of his 1929 novel, *The Sound and the Fury*, is no doubt deliberate. Also intentional is the echo of T. S. Eliot's *The Wasteland* (1922) in the subtitle of the concluding section of *Lawd Today*, "Rats' Alley." Wright's novel adapts both the techniques and the characteristic themes of the high modernists to a new purpose: a study of the alienation peculiar to American blacks in the great cities of the twentieth century. The novel succeeds admirably in this ambitious project, but it is also, more immediately, an indispensable record of African-American life in the era of the Great Depression; here Wright captures better than he ever would again the idioms, the vitality, and the great range of black American English. (The long, rambling conversation of Jake and his friends over a casual game of bridge is a tour de force in vernacular writing.)

Wright had, in 1931, become interested in communism—the party was active in Chicago, especially among blacks—and in 1933 he joined the local chapter of the John Reed Club, a national organization of left-wing writers and artists associated with the Communist Party; the following year he joined the party itself. His poetry began to appear in *Left Front*, *The Anvil*, and *New Masses*—the leading organs of the literary left, which was, in those days, a formidable element in American intellectual life. In 1937 Wright moved to New York City, where he began to distance himself from the party, whose discipline now seemed to him quite possibly inimical to his private interests as a writer. Although he continued to publish in its journals and to endorse its general aims, he never submitted to its discipline again. (He officially withdrew from the party in 1944.)

Lawd Today is a novel of Wright's apprenticeship to writers like Dos Passos, Faulkner, Eliot, and James Joyce. His second book, *Uncle Tom's Children: Four Novellas*, published by Harper and Brothers in 1938, forthrightly reflects his engagement with the Communist Party. It is, among other things, an experiment in socialist realism. With intoxicating optimism, and despite its often bleak and violent content, the book points toward a resolution of racial conflict in class solidarity. As the last of the four novellas, "Fire and Cloud," concludes, a black preacher named Dan Taylor leads a march of white and black poor folks on city hall, demanding fair distribution of food to the Depression-starved masses: "A baptism of clean joy swept over Taylor," we read.

> He kept his eyes on the sea of black and white faces. The song swelled louder and vibrated through him. This is the way! he

thought. Gawd ain no lie! He ain no lie! His eyes grew wet with tears, blurring his vision: the sky trembled; the buildings wavered as if about to topple; and the earth shook.... He mumbled out loud, exultingly: *"Freedom belongs to the strong!"*

As the title "Fire and Cloud" suggests, the novella, and the book as a whole, is a powerful reworking of the Mosaic story of the Exodus, which of course African-Americans had long made use of in their literature and song. The passage of the Israelites out of the wilderness of bondage and exile, and their crossing into the Promised Land, are here adapted to the transracial (and secular) dream of a socialist revolution.

Uncle Tom's Children was a commercial success; a second edition, to which a fifth story and a searing essay on "The Ethics of Living Jim Crow" were added, appeared in 1940. And yet the book left Wright unsatisfied; its warm reception troubled him. "I found that I had written," he confessed in a 1940 essay titled "How Bigger Was Born," "a book which even bankers' daughters could read and weep over and feel good about. I swore to myself that if I ever wrote another book, no one would weep over it; that it would be so hard and deep that they would have to face it without the consolation of tears. It was this that made me get to work in dead earnest." The book he produced is *Native Son* (1940), and in it we can see a sublimation, a redemption, of the aggressive motive that underlay its composition—the desire to deal his readers a blow so bitter and so hard as to deny them the cathartic consolation of tears. He would at last realize his ambition to make weapons out of words, and words out of weapons. And as for sentimental bankers' daughters, his need to hurt them, to make them feel the pain of the dispossessed, insofar as they were able, and insofar as novels would suffice to do the job, finds expression in symbolic action. For it is Mary Dalton, a banker's daughter of sorts—a naively leftist young woman who surely would have wept over *Uncle Tom's Children*—that Bigger Thomas kills.

NATIVE SON

It is hard now rightly to estimate the force of *Native Son*, though the book retains the power to shock us. In 1940 it was utterly unprecedented in its terrifying violence (two killings, the first horribly brutal in its aftermath, the second singularly brutal in its execution); in its embrace of a wounded and sociopathic hero; and in its candid exploration of sexuality, a feature of the novel muted in the somewhat bowdlerized first edition of 1945. (For details of the novel's textual history, see the "Note on the Texts" in the Library of America 1991 edition of *Native Son*.)

The plot of the novel is brisk and has something of the momentum of a thriller. The opening section immerses us in Bigger Thomas's milieu, in the poverty-stricken environment of Chicago's South Side that produced him, and of which he is, in certain respects, the perfect expression. We follow him next into the home of Mr. Dalton, to whom Bigger has been recommended as a chauffeur by a relief organization. Dalton is a robber baron who has turned liberal philanthropist, and his daughter, Mary, is a fellow traveler in Chicago Communist Party circles and the lover of a Party organizer, Jan Erlone. Mary and Jan embrace Bigger with a solicitude that is at once condescending and oppressive, and which the novel satirizes effectively.

The killing itself is, on the face of it, an accident. Mary drinks herself into semiconsciousness during a date with Jan on this, Bigger's first night as the family chauffeur. On their return to the Dalton house, Bigger faces a dilemma: how can he get Mary into her bedroom without waking Mr. and Mrs. Dalton, who would then discover that Mary has not been, as she was supposed to be, attending a lecture? He cannot simply leave her in the car, but neither can he wake the Daltons and reveal that he has ignored their instructions—even if he did so at Mary's insistence—to drive her to a lecture. So he hauls Mary upstairs on his own—a tantalizing, painful ordeal during which, as the unbowdlerized 1991 edition makes clear, Mary clumsily comes on to Bigger. As he attempts to tuck her into bed—whether or not he intends to respond to her drunken sexual advances is not clear—Mrs. Dalton appears in the doorway like an apparition. She is blind and cannot see Bigger, who in desperation covers Mary's face with a pillow to prevent her from answering her mother's call. For, should he be found at Mary's bedside, no account he might give of how he got there would prevent his being fired; or so, anyway, he fears—and with good reason after all. Before he realizes it, Mary is dead from suffocation; her mother, approaching the bed, gets a whiff of whiskey and cigarette smoke, concludes that the girl is drunk, and leaves her to sleep it off. Bigger stuffs the body into the furnace—he has to sever the head in order to make it fit—and cooks up a scheme to mislead police into believing that Mary has been kidnapped by local communists.

When a reporter, quite by chance, discovers fragments of bone in the ashes, Bigger flees; murders his black girlfriend, Bessie Mears, out of fear that she will betray him; and hides out among the dilapidated buildings of the South Side—the very buildings that absentee landlords like Mr. Dalton fail to develop so as artificially to inflate the rents they charge black tenants. Bigger is captured, charged with capital murder and rape—a crime he did not, in fact, commit—and tried. The Communist Party provides Bigger with an attorney, Boris Max, who, in the course of a long argument before the jury, offers an analysis of American racism that he hopes will account for Bigger's actions in such a way as to mitigate his responsibility and thereby save him from execution. But the effort fails; Bigger is convicted and sentenced to die.

In "How Bigger Was Born," his account of the writing of the novel, Wright sets out a theory of authorship. The novelist's imagination, as he sees it, is an intersection of the "public" and "private"—by which he means an intersection of the "socially" determined and the "personally" directed. "An imaginative novel," Wright explains, "represents the merging of two extremes; it is an intensely intimate expression on the part of a consciousness couched in terms of the most objective and commonly known events." Associated with this idea is Wright's acknowledgement that much of the meaning of *Native Son* simply seemed to "happen" to him as he wrote; he did not "intend" so much as "discover" the meaning of the book.

> I say frankly that there are phases of *Native Son* that I shall make no attempt to account for. There are meanings in my book of which I was not aware until they literally spilled onto the paper. I shall sketch the outline of how I *consciously* came into possession of the materials that went into *Native Son*, but there will be many things I shall omit, not because I want to, but simply because I don't know them.

It is through the action of forces beyond the management of the author—Wright calls these "public" as opposed to "private" materials—that his "internal" and "personal" motives actually unfold. Writing is the experience both of acting and of being acted upon; it is in fact the experience of being unable to distinguish between acting and being acted upon.

Once we set the terms of the matter in this way, it becomes apparent that Bigger Thomas in some sense "represents" the situation of his author, and not merely because Wright "identifies" with his violent rebellion (although in "How Bigger Was Born," he says that he does). *Native Son* situates Bigger precisely at the intersection of "external" compulsion and "internal" motivation, of "necessity" and "free will." Nowhere is this better achieved than in the first murder scene. Wright constructs a scene wherein his protagonist is essentially compelled to commit a crime: circumstance, not Bigger's own volition, is the agent here. Bigger seems to have no true "agency"—no genuinely "personal" motivation—in committing this crime. But though the killing is, in fact, an "accident," the novel shows how it is also what the critic Kenneth Burke, in another connection, has called a *"representative* accident." The act may be "motivated" by necessity. But it unfolds, or allows to emerge, what Bigger himself comes to recognize as his own "true" motivation, his own will: he did have murder in his heart. Bigger discovers himself in the killing. "What I killed for, I *am*," he says to his lawyer. "What I killed for must've been good! . . . I didn't know I was really alive in this world until I felt things hard enough to kill for 'em." In taking responsibility for the act—even to the point of acknowledging to his lawyer that he had been, with Mary Dalton, a party to the erotic flirtation that preceded it—he makes his existence meaningful; he creates himself in the act. For the first time, he realizes that he is himself an agent—"a person acting," not merely "a thing in motion" buffeted about by forces he cannot control. (Again, the terms are adapted from Kenneth Burke.)

In short, in *Native Son*, Wright depicts an act that is at once "accidental" and a "murder," something that our legal code, nuanced though it may be, is unable to recognize. And indeed this is Boris Max's argument in his plea on behalf of Bigger: the occurrence at the Dalton home that night did in fact somehow represent Bigger's character, which had been hardened and tempered by oppression. And yet that occurrence was also predetermined, and Bigger's role in it cast long ago. Because our culture is organized by assumptions of white supremacy, and because white supremacy had for generations been so violent and brutal in its operations, the killing of Mary Dalton had about it an air of inevitability.

The whole interest of the novel is in how Wright plays through the paradoxical implications of Bigger's situation. In killing Mary Dalton, Bigger was both volunteer and draftee, both actor and pawn. To what extent did he act that night? To what extent was he only acted upon? *Native Son* brilliantly explores these questions. And in so doing, it uniquely equips the reader to understand Wright's remarks about authorship in "How Bigger Was Born." In suffering the happy "accidents" of authorship, the novelist comes more deeply to feel his own, strictly private powers. And that, finally, is the situation of Bigger Thomas—to have his own purposes, his own meaning,

revealed by accident. The moment of the killing is the moment where he seems least in control of his own fate, and most a mere cipher compelled by circumstance; but that moment precisely marks the point at which, for the first time in his bewildered life, he becomes meaningfully creative, the first time he ever comes into possession of himself. The killing, in fact, marks the moment of Bigger Thomas's birth, and we may take it, in light of what Wright says in "How Bigger Was Born," as peculiarly emblematic of the new "birth" of freedom any author undergoes in risking so transgressive and original a novel as *Native Son*.

THE 1940s AND *BLACK BOY*

The publication of *Native Son* was a landmark; it brought to discussions of American race relations a candor as refreshing as it was unnerving. In the first three weeks of its release in 1940, the novel sold more than 200,000 copies and made Wright a literary star. (A successful stage adaptation, directed by Orson Welles, ran on Broadway from 1941 through 1943). For the first time in his life Wright felt financially secure, and his private affairs, too, began to fall into order. In 1941, after his first brief marriage to Dhima Rose Meadman ended unhappily, Wright married Ellen Poplar, a Communist Party organizer of Polish-Jewish extraction; the couple would remain together, bearing two daughters, Julia and Rachel.

On 9 April 1943 Wright delivered a lecture at Fisk University in Nashville, taking as his subject, as he put it later, "what I felt and thought about the world; what I remembered about my life, about being a Negro." In this experience lay the impetus to begin his autobiography, and its complicated textual history bears looking into not simply for what it reveals about Wright's purposes, but for what it can tell us about the difficult situation of the African-American writer in the mid-twentieth century.

In December 1943 Wright was able to deliver the manuscript of "American Hunger," as it was then called, to his agent in New York City. As it then stood, "American Hunger" was divided into two sections: "Southern Night," which treats Wright's experiences in the South, up until he fled Memphis for Chicago in 1927, and "The Horror and the Glory," which for the most part concerns Wright's experiences as a member of the Communist Party in Chicago, and which brings the narrative up to 1937, when he moved to New York City. The book was accepted in January 1944 by Edward Aswell, Wright's editor at Harper and Brothers. Within a month, the revised typescript was at the manufacturing department, and by May, Aswell was sending out bound galleys of "American Hunger" to other authors for statements he could use as advertising copy. But in June the Book-of-the-Month Club—at that time a formidable force in American publishing—expressed interest in the memoir, and thus began the exchange that ultimately led to the publication of only section 1 of the book—the section titled "Southern Night," and known ever since as *Black Boy*. (The rest of the autobiography, about one-third again the length of *Black Boy*, remained unpublished until 1977, when Harper and Row released it as *American Hunger*, the title Wright had originally chosen for the work as a whole.)

Correspondence in the Harper and Brothers archive at Princeton makes clear that it was the Book Club's request that only the first part of the memoir be published. The book now was to end as Wright fled to Chicago, with the stark summary that closes section one of "American Hunger": "This was the culture from which I sprang. This was the terror from which I fled." Wright supplied, also at the suggestion of the Book Club, several pages of new material to round out this conclusion; these followed the two sentences quoted above after a type break. Dorothy Canfield Fisher, one of the Club's officials, acted as liaison between the Club and Wright, working with the author on these final revisions, sometimes suggesting changes, which Wright followed or ignored as he saw fit.

At one point, Fisher suggested a new way to end the book, putting it to Wright in the form of a question. What (she wondered) had inspired the young Richard Wright to suppose that life could, in fact, be lived with dignity? Must it not have been our fundamental political traditions? Had it not been the case (she hopefully asked) that from the "Bastille" of racial oppression, Wright had caught "a glimpse of the American flag?" Of course, Wright was no such believer in American promises; he closed *Black Boy* without a patriotic benediction. Still, it is only fair to Fisher to add that she was not suggesting this particular change as a condition of the book's acceptance by the Club. Instead, she was asking Wright, as one who should know, to confirm her belief in the democratic promise of America—a promise that simply must, she supposed, transcend cultural, racial, and geographical boundaries. And as for that "glimpse of the American flag," when Fisher wrote this letter, the Normandy invasion was in its third week; she simply had to believe that the white supremacists were chiefly on the Nazi side of the lines. Wright knew better, and he could not offer her this consolation. He explained to Edward Aswell that he could make no such change as Fisher

suggested and still remain faithful to his sense of what American realities actually were. From 1945 until 1991 readers knew Wright's autobiography as *Black Boy* and read the text that reflected his compromise with the Book Club. In 1991, however, the Library of America published *Black Boy (American Hunger)* in the form it would have taken had the Book Club never intervened; that text is now the standard.

Black Boy (American Hunger) is a narrative of captivity and of escape; it is, like Frederick Douglass's great autobiographies, the narrative of a fugitive. And there is always something rootless, something restless, about Wright's life and work; we can see this even in the constantly changing style of his prose. The modernist experiment of *Lawd Today*, his first book, gave way to an exercise in socialist realism, *Uncle Tom's Children*. After that came *Native Son*, an almost sociological novel undertaken in the tradition of Dreiser's great works of literary naturalism. Then came the autobiography; an existentialist novel, *The Outsider* (1953), written in France; travel books; books on politics; his last novel, *The Long Dream* (1958), which owes so much to psychoanalysis and which is set, as are no other of Wright's novels, in his native Mississippi; and, perhaps most startling of all, a series of some four thousand haiku, written toward the end of his life. Wright never once settled into a style, into a form, or even into a language; his diction, from book to book, is unsure and eclectic. Doubtless this has something to do with the fact that Wright was an autodidact, but it is associated as well with an essentially fugitive quality in his temperament. But from what is he a fugitive—from what is he always in flight?

The best answer to the question lies in a description Wright gives, in *Black Boy (American Hunger)*, of his father as he saw him for the last time, after a separation of twenty-five years. The aged man stood "alone upon the red clay of a Mississippi plantation, a sharecropper, clad in ragged overalls, holding a muddy hoe in his gnarled, veined hands." "My mind and consciousness had become so greatly and violently altered," says Wright, "that when I tried to talk to him I realized that, though ties of blood made us kin . . . we were forever strangers." "I was overwhelmed," he recalls,

> to realize that he could never understand me or the scalding experiences that had swept me beyond his life and into an area of living that he could never know. I stood before him, poised, my mind aching as it embraced the simple nakedness of his life, feeling how completely his soul was imprisoned by the slow flow of the seasons, by wind and rain and sun,

how fastened were his memories to a crude and raw past, how chained were his actions and emotions to the direct, animalistic impulses of his withering body.

His father was, and would always remain, a "creature of the earth," a "peasant" held back from what Wright calls the "alien and undreamed of shores of knowing." The logic underlying this remarkable passage is binary: "animality"-humanity, past-future, "rawness"-refinement, nature-culture, body-mind, "nakedness"-civility, peasantry-cosmopolitanism, and so on, and the terms of each pair are opposed to one another as father is to son. Wright sees in his father a man locked in what the existentialists he would soon be moving among might call a life of immanence: he is bound down by the fate of the body and by the inhuman claim of nature (by the seasons, by the weather, by physical appetites, and so on). His father dwells on the plane of what Wright later calls mere "physical living," a level at which, in fact, there can be no existence "worthy of being called human."

Slavery and its aftermath had inculcated in white folks—and colonialism tended to do the same everywhere white Europeans undertook it—a habit of assimilating the opposition black-white to the oppositions body-mind, savagery-civility, and animality-humanity. This assimilation accounts in part for the often morbid fascination with which white men and women contemplate the sexuality of people of color: color, in this context, comes to mean sexuality as such, or pure embodiedness. A life devoted to sensualism of a sort, a life led, as had been his father's, according to "direct, animalistic impulses," always haunts Wright as the terrible possibility somehow marked out for him by white supremacy. Toward the end of his time in the South, when he was living in Memphis and painfully educating himself, often by subterfuge, he considered giving up the hard struggle to transcend the merely physical plane of existence on which his father had lived. "I could, of course, forget what I had read," he writes, "thrust the whites out of my mind, forget them; and find release from anxiety and longing in sex and alcohol. But the memory of how my father had conducted himself made that course repugnant. If I did not want others to violate my life, how could I voluntarily violate it myself?" There is something chaste in this line of reasoning, something a little ascetic: violation and self-violation are fates worse than death.

Above all, Wright resisted the reduction of men to bodies, or of persons to things, as the foregoing discussion

of *Native Son* perhaps indicates. And this humiliating reduction clearly underlies the "violation" Wright recalls having suffered at the hands of a white co-worker in the following passage from *Black Boy*:

> "Richard, how long is your thing?" he asked me.
> "What thing?" I asked.
> "You know what I mean," he said. "The thing the bull uses on the cow."
>
> I turned away from him; I had heard that whites regarded Negroes as animals in sex matters and his words made me angry.
>
> "I heard that a nigger can stick his prick in the ground and spin around on it like a top," he said, chuckling. "I'd like to see you do that. I'd give you a dime if you did it."

At the request of the Book-of-the-Month Club, who worried that it might be judged obscene, Wright cut this passage from the first edition of *Black Boy*. Obscene it surely is, but the obscenity is intrinsic to white supremacy; this is the characteristic gesture of a regime that would, and at the cost of much more than a dime, lock more than half of humanity into the "crude," "raw," "naked," "animalistic" prison house of the body. *Black Boy (American Hunger)* is a record of Wright's flight from precisely this fate, and the image of his broken father hangs behind the narrative like an admonition; it is an unsettling, ambivalent experience when Wright sees "the shadow of his own face" in his father's, as he puts it, and when he hears in his father's voice "an echo of his own." This flight would soon lead Wright, together with his new family, into exile. *Black Boy* rose to the top of the best-seller list—in no small part owing to the marketing strategies of the Book-of-the-Month Club—and earnings from its sale allowed Wright to resettle in Paris in 1947, where he hoped to put behind him for good the racism he still daily faced even in relatively liberal New York City.

THE OUTSIDER

Wright began work on *The Outsider*, the first of his books to be written abroad, in 1948. He had moved with his family into apartments on the Rue de Lille in Paris, had embarked on extensive readings in Continental philosophy, and had formed close relationships with Jean-Paul Sartre and Simone de Beauvoir, the two leading exponents of French existentialism. *The Outsider* is a forthrightly philosophical novel, built upon the existentialist proposition, as its hero explains, that "man is nothing in particular." The novel opens in Chicago, where Cross Damon, a black postal worker of a bookish turn of mind, finds himself trapped: his estranged wife demands child-support payments he can barely manage; his pregnant lover insists that he obtain a divorce and marry her, and, for leverage, hatches a plot to accuse him of statutory rape. (She had lied to him about her age.) When his wife, on discovering this new entanglement, reports his behavior to the Chicago postmaster, Damon's job is put in peril. Depressed, and drinking almost constantly, he considers suicide, finds himself unable to commit the deed, and descends into utter despair—only to be presented with a way out entirely by chance: a subway accident leaves him shaken, but alive, and when the body of a man who had been riding next to him is found mutilated beyond recognition with Cross's coat tangled about his body—it had gotten hung up as Cross made his escape from the wreck—the police conclude that he is dead. He assumes a false identity, resolves to create a new destiny for himself, and moves to New York City. There he is drawn into the intrigues of a group of Communist Party activists and commits four murders, partly to protect himself from discovery, but partly out of contempt for what the communists represent.

The novel's philosophical argument emerges from lengthy conversations between Cross Damon and Ely Houston, the Manhattan district attorney who ultimately uncovers his true identity, and from a protracted exchange between Damon and an official of the Communist Party who is suspicious of his intentions. The argument has two phases. First, Wright puts forward the Nietzschean view that behind all of the esteemed institutions that constitute Western culture—the church, political parties, so-called enlightened colonialism, and so on—lies a blind struggle of will. Self-sacrifice, altruism, the good of humanity, the white man's burden, the emancipation of the working class: these ideals are simply masks, impostures—instruments by means of which men, acting always in bad faith, dominate the lives of other men. Working through everything is a will to power that is itself amoral. This truth is hateful, which is precisely why we have succeeded so splendidly in deceiving ourselves about the nature of our own most cherished institutions; we do not want to think of ourselves as mere animals struggling for domination. However—and here is the second phase of Wright's argument—capitalist industrial development had, in the nineteenth and twentieth centuries, eroded the authority and prestige of religious, political, and philosophical institutions to the point that man will soon be compelled to confront himself as he "really" is. The "sentimental illusions" that used to "bind man to man," as Marx and Engels put it in the *Communist Manifesto* (1848), had—one by one—been drowned in the "icy waters" of cold, calculating power, as the West consolidated its grip on the productive capabilities of the entire globe. Humanity had been stripped bare. As Wright sees it, this is at once a curse and an opportunity: it is a curse because humans have been set adrift, have come unmoored from the ideals that used to anchor their enterprises and now find themselves disoriented; it is an opportunity because humans have for the first time acceded to the responsibility, which can be terrifying, to define themselves honestly. *The Outsider* is well suited to examine these problems; when he is mistakenly identified as among the dead in that subway wreck, Cross Damon stumbles upon precisely the opportunity, and also the burden, of self-creation. And what he discovers both exhilarates and horrifies him; namely, as we have seen, that "man is nothing in particular."

The Outsider, on its appearance in 1953, confused some of Wright's readers and disappointed others; reviews were ambivalent. His years abroad, his dabblings in philosophy, his fascination with Parisian intellectual life—all this had caused him to lose touch, it was claimed, with his real subject matter; all of this had led him to attempt a kind of novel for which he was unprepared. To be sure, the writing in *The Outsider* is often awkward, so much so that it strikes many readers as pretentious. Wright's editors at Harper and Brothers required that he make extensive revisions to the manuscript, and they struck scores of phrases, sentences, and even entire paragraphs from the typescript as it went into production.

Wright does appear to have lost the surefootedness that kept the diction of *Black Boy (American Hunger)* so forceful and clear. One encounters in *The Outsider* hundreds of such ungainly sentences as this: "His face was the living personification of stupefied surprise." Or this: "Imprisoned he was in a state of consciousness that was so infatuated by its own condition that it could not dominate itself; so swamped was he by himself with himself that he could not break forth from behind the bars of that self to claim himself." Or this: "The assumptive promises he had welched on were not materially anchored, yet they were indubitably the things of this world, comprising as they did the veritable axis of daily existence." The colloquial vigor of "welched" blends uncomfortably with such starched, bookish phrases as "assumptive promises" and "veritable axis" and with words like "indubitably"; the counterpoint hardly seems intentional or controlled. And why, one wonders, should Wright favor inversions like "imprisoned he was," which one usually encounters in poetry, and then only when necessities of meter or rhyme require the distortion?

Still, the strange language in which *The Outsider* is written is actually quite fitting: it is an index of Wright's own restlessness as a man and as a writer—the restlessness that led him, as has been pointed out, to reinvent himself with every new book, and which drew him, at last, into exile. This is the prose of an "outsider," the prose of a man who never felt quite at home, of a man who was forever a resident alien. *The Outsider*, precisely because it is a tortured and awkward book, is central to Wright's career. It is perfectly natural that he should compare Cross Damon's struggle to reinvent himself to the work of authorship. Cross, we are told, "would have to imagine this thing out, dream it out, invent it, like a writer constructing a tale." And neither Cross in *The Outsider*, nor Wright in his life and work, would ever find a language quite adequate to this purpose.

The difficulty of Wright's style in *The Outsider* is that of a man who is never entirely master of the language he uses. And his situation is realized allegorically in the situation of Cross Damon—a figure who, more than any other character in Wright's fiction, speaks for his author. Damon tries to stand apart from the fates that would determine him—the fates of the past, of family, and of race. But neither he nor Wright nor any of us can really stand as though humans were authors of themselves and knew no other kin, to adapt a line from Shakespeare's *Coriolanus* (1607–1608). No human can ever truly possess himself or herself, or so anyway *The Outsider* seems to argue. And the matter was of peculiar interest to Richard Wright, owing to his own effort to emancipate himself from the past—from the nightmare of American history—and to reinvent himself through writing. This was an effort to the transcend the "animalistic" fate to which his father had been consigned by a racist culture he could neither combat nor ignore; this was a struggle to outrun the fate of the body itself—the fate of lapsing from personhood into mere thing-ness. Cross, we are told, "was despairingly aware of his body as an alien and despised object over which he had no power, a burden that was always cheating him of the fruits of his thought, mocking him with its stubborn and supine solidity." His appetites always ruin him and are in the end untameable. To the extent that he thinks of himself as a body, to the extent that he allows his body to determine him—especially in a white supremacist culture that sees in the black body the flesh as such—to that extent precisely has he ceased to be a person. To that extent precisely has he been "chained," as Wright's own father had been, to the "direct, animalistic impulses" of the body. Wright had nothing less than this great problem in mind when he dedicated *Black Power: A Record of Reactions in a Land of Pathos* (1954)—his book about the West African Gold Coast that was, at the time, emerging from British colonial domination and would become the nation of Ghana—to "the unknown African who, because of his primal and poetic humanity, was regarded by white men as a 'thing' to be bought, sold, and used as an instrument of production; and who, alone in the forests of West Africa, created a vision of life so simple as to be terrifying, yet a vision that was irreducibly human." This "unknown African" is the father he would remember in all his life's work—the father America had denied him. And at last, *The Outsider* sets before us a challenge: how can we, now that all our illusions about humanity have been shattered by slavery and war and empire, begin at last to create a mode of living that truly deserves to be called human?

RICHARD WRIGHT'S ORDEAL

In the last moments of *The Outsider*, Ely Houston asks Cross Damon a question: "How was it with you?" Some indication as to how Wright himself might answer this question if it were put to him is to be found in the Book of Job. It is hardly insignificant that Wright should have set passages from Job, that greatest and most baffling of Western meditations on suffering, at the head of no fewer than four of his books: *Native Son* ("Even today is my complaint rebellious, and my stroke is heavier than my groaning"); *Black Boy* ("His strength shall be hunger-bitten, and destruction shall be ready at his side"); *The Outsider* ("Mark me, and be astonished, and lay your hand upon your mouth"); and *Savage Holiday* ("And, behold, there came a great wind from the wilderness and smote the four corners of the house").

So, how was it with Richard Wright? Apparently as it had been with Job in the midst of his own ordeal. The world seemed to him a place of inscrutable suffering—a place where punishment is administered without regard to justice, and prosperity bestowed without regard to merit. The Communist Party, at least as Wright knew it, attempted a nuanced and ultimately redemptive account of this suffering: it gave suffering meaning and indicated how it all would someday end. Evil was to the party no mystery. But for Wright evil appears to have remained precisely that—which may be one reason why he could not, at the end of the day, be satisfied with communism. He had, in the "southern night" of which he speaks in *Black Boy*, seen too much of motiveless malignity ever to suppose it might really be overcome; his American books are a chronicle of savage beatings, sadistic laughter, and acts that chill the blood.

Wright's work, especially the fiction, suggests that he had seen something truly unspeakable in his fellow men. And as he aged he found his satisfactions, it may be, where he could, and expected relatively little from the world—much less than he expected when he concluded the first edition of *Uncle Tom's Children* with an exhilarating promise of socialist revolution. Out of his later years come the ephemeral, often whimsical, pleasures of the haiku, a form hardly suited to the ambitious, totalizing analyses of political problems he had attempted in *Native Son* and *The Outsider*. And out of the same years come such scenes as the one in *Pagan Spain* (1957) that tells the charming, though melancholy, story of a meal he once shared with a Spanish family in Madrid, laughing into the dawn, cutting up, singing, and staging a mock bullfight. These are the good hours, Wright seems to suggest, when the world is somehow redeemed: a fugitive from Mississippi; a Spanish family left fatherless and widowed by Franco and the fascists; an hour or two of mirth set over against a Job-like world of torment; and a promise on Wright's part—for this is what he gave his new Spanish friends as he parted from them at the station—to tell what he had seen.

Still, from the time he published *The Outsider* until his death seven years later, Wright would never again find an audience like the one that bought copies of *Native Son* and *Black Boy* by the hundreds of thousands. Several nonfiction books followed over the next few years: *Black Power: A Record of Reactions in a Land of Pathos*, about the Gold Coast (later Ghana), which he visited in 1953; *The Color Curtain* (1956), a book about the 1955 conference of nonaligned nations in Bandung, Indonesia, which Wright had attended; *Pagan Spain*, the study of Spanish culture just discussed; and *White Man, Listen!* (1957), a collection of essays. Wright's last major novel, *The Long Dream*, which revisits his native Mississippi, appeared in 1958 to bad reviews. The following year the Wrights began preparations to resettle in London;

Wright had grown estranged from the literary culture of his adopted Paris and was an outsider once again. But the move was never completed. Wright suffered a series of illnesses, ultimately dying of heart failure in a Paris clinic on 28 November 1960, at the young age of fifty-two—leaving the rest of us to mark him, lay our hands upon our mouths, and be astonished at his violent and redemptive imagination.

[*See also* Harlem Renaissance *and* Mencken, H. L.]

SELECTED WORKS

Uncle Tom's Children (1938)
Native Son (1940)
Black Boy: A Record of Childhood and Youth (1945)
The Outsider (1953)
Black Power: A Record of Reactions in a Land of Pathos (1954)
Savage Holiday (1954)
The Color Curtain: A Report on the Bandung Conference (1956)
Pagan Spain (1957)
White Man, Listen! (1957)
The Long Dream (1958)
Eight Men (1961)
Lawd Today (1963)
American Hunger (1977)
Richard Wright. Vol. 1, *Early Works.* Vol. 2, *Later Works.* (1991)

FURTHER READING

Aaron, Daniel. *Writers on the Left: Episodes in American Literary Communism.* New York, 1972. This book is not devoted to Wright, but it does offer the best portrait we have of the left-wing literary culture of the 1930s in which Wright first found his voice.

Fabre, Michel. *The Unfinished Quest of Richard Wright.* Translated from the French by Isabel Barzun. New York, 1973. A biography; especially valuable for its treatment of Wright's years in France.

Gates, Henry Louis, Jr., and K. A. Appiah, eds. *Richard Wright: Critical Perspectives, Past and Present.* New York, 1993. A useful anthology of reviews and essays; contains an extensive bibliography of secondary material.

Kinnamon, Kenneth. *The Emergence of Richard Wright: A Study in Literature and Society.* Urbana, Ill., and Chicago, 1972.

Rampersad, Arnold, ed. *Richard Wright: A Collection of Critical Essays.* Englewood Cliffs, N.J., 1995. An important reassessment of Wright by a number of scholars.

Rolwey, Hazel. *Richard Wright: The Life and Times*. New York, 2001. The first new biography to be published since Margaret Walker's appeared in 1988.

Walker, Margaret. *Richard Wright, Demonic Genius: A Portrait of the Man, a Critical Look at His Work*. New York, 1988.

Webb, Constance. *Richard Wright: A Biography*. New York, 1968.

See also the article on *Native Son*, immediately following.

RICHARD WRIGHT'S
NATIVE SON

by William R. Nash

Richard Wright's *Native Son* (1940) chronicles the life of Bigger Thomas, a black youth whose efforts to cross the lines of race and class in Depression-era Chicago bring deadly results. Picked by the Book-of-the-Month-Club as a main selection (a first for a novel written by an African American), *Native Son* initially sold well to an audience expecting a mystery. They got much more than they bargained for, as Bigger murders first his white employer's daughter and then his own girlfriend. However, even as Wright demonstrates Bigger's brutality, he emphasizes the impact of racist socioeconomic forces on his character's development. This orientation, which shows the influence of American naturalist authors like Theodore Dreiser and of the Chicago school of sociology, suggests an almost exculpatory lack of agency on Bigger's part. At the same time, though, Wright shows that Bigger has the capacity for mental growth, which comes through his understanding the consequences of his actions to his family and community. In the process of telling Bigger's story and raising questions about collective and personal moral responsibility, Wright produces a scathing indictment of American racial injustice that remains pertinent.

FEAR

Told in three books ("Fear," "Flight," and "Fate"), *Native Son* covers a few crucial days in Bigger's life. Book 1, "Fear," establishes the main conflicts of the story. As a condition of his family's maintaining its public assistance income, Bigger takes a job as chauffeur to the wealthy Dalton family. Mr. Dalton, a successful businessman whose holdings include Bigger's slum tenement, and his blind wife see themselves as philanthropists, although they actually do little to help African Americans. Their daughter, Mary, dallies with communism and with a particular communist organizer named Jan Erlone. At the time when he was composing the novel, Wright was also wrestling with his feelings about the American Communist Party, from which he had become at least partially estranged. Throughout *Native Son*, he presents alternating portraits of communists as first ineffectually paying lip service to an ideal of egalitarianism and then as powerfully committed to ending racial inequality.

Mary and Jan's misguided attempts to befriend Bigger immediately take a tragic turn. The white couple insists on eating with Bigger in a Southside restaurant, Ernie's Kitchen Shack, insensitively overlooking the fact that Bigger had many friends there who would not understand his actions. Afraid to violate the social order but even more afraid of losing his job, Bigger goes along with Jan and Mary. To cover his discomfort, Bigger also drinks most of a bottle of rum with Jan and Mary. Later, he drops off a sexually satisfied Jan and takes Mary home. Because she is too drunk to stand, Bigger must carry her up to her room. Once again frightened, but also aroused, Bigger takes Mary upstairs, places her on her bed and fondles and kisses her. When her blind mother enters the room, Bigger is terrified that she will find him and accuse him of raping her daughter. He covers Mary's mouth with a pillow to keep her quiet, accidentally killing her. Then, to avoid detection, he burns her corpse in the Daltons' furnace.

FLIGHT

Book 2 describes Bigger's flight through Chicago's slums and his eventual capture by the police. His flight begins when reporters discover small pieces of Mary's bones in the ashes of the furnace. Afraid that the ashes might reveal evidence of his crime, Bigger has consistently resisted clearing the hopper. The first time that someone else removes the ashes, Bigger's fears are realized. This occurrence proves that the bonds of socialization that regulate Bigger's behavior are nearly impossible to escape. Although Bigger believes himself to be a new man because he has killed Mary, his refusal to clear the ash hopper demonstrates the limitation of Bigger's actual transformation.

In addition to its role as the engine of Mary's immolation, the Daltons' furnace occupies an important place in the symbolic structure of *Native Son*. Throughout the novel, Wright links Bigger with the furnace. At one point, when the newsmen discover Mary's remains in the furnace, the author explicitly equates the man with the machine. Other important parallels between Bigger and the furnace are less obvious; one notes, for instance, that coal spreads out "fanwise" when Bigger stokes the fire. When Bigger realizes how much he is at risk, Wright notes that fear spreads out "fanwise" in Bigger's stomach.

This equation of Bigger with the furnace reflects Wright's debt to determinism; seen in this light, Bigger is little better than a machine. Although he possesses terrifying physical force, he can only react to others. In this way, Bigger also resembles the dreaded rat with which he does deadly battle in the novel's first scene. And this parallel reinforces Bigger's real position in American society as the hunter of the rat becomes himself the hunted. This inversion of Bigger's position in the hierarchy of power strongly reinforces Wright's ironic commentary on the possibilities for self-realization that are open to African Americans in his era.

Faced with imminent capture, Bigger flees. Unfortunately, in the period between committing the crime and being discovered, Bigger and his girlfriend, Bessie Mears, have tried to collect ransom for a supposedly kidnapped Mary and to shift suspicion for the crime onto the communists. When he runs, therefore, Bigger must either bring Bessie along or risk betrayal if she is captured. He drags her along with him into an abandoned building, where he rapes her and then batters her almost to death with a brick. With these actions, Bigger actually becomes the things that he has feared the white world will label him as. Overcome with horror at what he has done, he impulsively dumps her body down an airshaft without remembering that she was holding all of the money that he had gotten out of Mary's purse. Suddenly destitute once again, Bigger must flee through the abandoned buildings of the snow-covered Southside if he is to survive.

Bigger's flight emphasizes several of the more important symbols in book 2. First, his entire experience as a fugitive coincides with a snowstorm that blankets Chicago in whiteness. This pervasive symbol reminds the reader of who controls Bigger's world. Although one sees the Southside as segregated space in the first book of the novel, a place where blackness rules, the snow shows that whiteness can overcome any boundaries it chooses to its own advantage. Against the backdrop of the snow, Bigger's blackness makes him more of a target for the white mob.

The target imagery extends into the description of the newspaper map that shows the progress of the mob's search for Bigger. Ironically, however, Wright now uses black shading to represent the segments of the map that have been covered and leaving the rest white. This inversion of the novel's conventional color scheme emphasizes the falseness of color designation, as one can arbitrarily assign positive or negative attributes to colors like black and white. In the accounts of Bigger's action, his blackness represents his demonic characteristics; in the map that shows the search's progress, black represents the swift, sure encroachment of white justice. This modification of symbols in the newspaper also reminds the reader that members of the dominant, read "white," society are the only ones who have redefinition at their disposal. Black in the Black Belt clearly means power only when the whites say it does.

The newspaper, which is the vehicle for these definitions, further reinforces these notions. From after the night he murders Mary until he has been jailed for his crime, Bigger obsessively seeks out and reads newspapers. In going consistently to the *Tribune*, though, Bigger effectively makes the paper the authority on who and where he is. In the court of public opinion, the paper tries and convicts him immediately, thereby shaping how the general public sees him as well. In the process of detailing his saga, the paper also relies on racist formulations of identity that shape perceptions of Bigger that are often contrary to reality. Although he did not rape Mary, for instance, the paper brands him as "rapist" and "Negro sex-slayer." From this point on, his reality is determined entirely by the impact of that terminology. His view of self is also largely shaped by this source; it is only when he comes to terms with himself as he awaits execution that he can escape from this particular bind.

Before he is fully free from the pervasive power of these white definitions, Bigger can still see the fundamental injustice of the black community's circumstance. His efforts to find food and an empty flat in which to hide afford Wright the opportunity to present sociological evidence about racism in Chicago. Bigger reflects on the inflated prices that blacks must pay for food in the Black Belt stores, stores that incidentally rarely have black owners. He also recalls his mother's efforts to find a new flat as he looks for shelter. Noting that the housing crunch is driven by rental practices that restrict black movement, Bigger realizes that the whites confine his community as if blacks were beasts. Wright's message to readers in these passages is unmistakable: forcing people to live under these conditions prepares the way for the rise of Bigger Thomas.

It also threatens any sense of African-American community. As Bigger hides in an empty flat, he overhears two black men discussing what they would do if they knew where he was. One of the men, Jim, argues that he would die before he would surrender Bigger, reasoning that black solidarity is the best defense against racism. Jim's opponent, Jack, counters that he has lost his job because his white boss assumes he is like Bigger. In his view, the economics of the situation demand that he focus only on his individual needs.

Wright uses the final moments of Bigger's flight to illustrate the realities of both Jim's and Jack's positions. The white mob thundering through the building where Bigger hides violates everyone and everything it comes across, subjecting a young black woman to unwanted sexual advances and destroying what property occupants of the building have gradually amassed. Faced with this kind of destruction, one can easily understand why a resident might choose self-protection. On the other hand, given what the mob does to Bigger once he is caught, one can reasonably say that solidarity is an ideal for which to strive. When Bigger lies in the snow with his arms spread and his wrists pinned it is clear that he will be crucified by this mob. Why would or should anyone turn him in to face that? The only possible good that can come out of these circumstances arises if Bigger has learned enough from his experiences to have something redemptive to die for. This raises the questions that Wright addresses in book 3, "Fate."

FATE

One of the most striking contrasts between "Fate," which is easily the most didactic section of the novel, and the first two sections is the absence of movement. Now that the question of physical escape from the forces that threaten Bigger is moot, Wright explores the notion of liberation on several other levels. First, he considers what, if anything, Bigger has learned from his experiences; second, he forces the readers to confront what they have learned from reading the novel. In pursuing these twin themes, Wright also extends his discussion of the potential help and harm that black Americans can derive from the Communist Party.

After his capture, Bigger retreats into a trancelike state, refusing to eat, drink, or even speak for three days. He is jolted out of his trance by the appearance of a parade of visitors that includes his family, his gang, the Daltons, state's attorney Buckley, his mother's minister, and Jan. Jan brings along a friend, Boris Max, who offers his legal services to Bigger free of charge. A communist like Jan, Max takes the case because he believes that Bigger is the victim of pervasive societal oppression. This important

scene, which Wright acknowledges as stretching the boundaries of credibility, establishes the deep tension between organized Christianity and communism, as Bigger witnesses a verbal battle between Jan and his mother's minister. It also, in Wright's words, elicits "a certain important emotional response from Bigger." It is only here, in the presence of his suffering family and his worried friends, that Bigger realizes the full impact of his actions. Having survived in his world for so long by holding everyone else at a distance, Bigger finds the idea of his being connected to others, and of his actions having an effect on his family, staggering. Shaken by his new insight, Bigger moves in an instant from utter nihilism to grief and wonder, a fear of his own death that is tempered somewhat by his sadness at having harmed his family with his crimes.

This nascent awareness suggests some development in Bigger's consciousness, some individual growth that takes him beyond the brutality of his earlier life. One sees further evidence of this change when Bigger has an extended conversation with Max about his life and his crimes. In talking to Max, Bigger finds a sense of strength and purpose that he has never known before. This evolution in his character suggests his maturation; it also raises questions about the justifiability of executing him. Given that he has shown a capacity for growth, one cannot simply label him an animal, as one might well be tempted to do after the events of the first two books. This does not excuse his actions; however, it does complicate the process of judging him, which seems to be Wright's purpose throughout the novel.

It also enriches the picture of the communists; whereas Jan and Mary seem ineptly good-hearted in the first section, Jan shows himself to be more or less enlightened here. He appears in Bigger's cell and makes a speech about social justice and his own complicity in Mary's death; he then introduces Max, who seems to have an ability to reach Bigger on a deeper level than anyone else has to date. Wright extends the impact of this new view of the communists in Max's powerful defense argument, which stands as essentially an indictment of white America for everything that it has inflicted on Bigger and his community. Building on the sociological data about conditions in black Chicago from book 2, Max's passionate speech extends the evidence of profound social injustice and strengthens the novel's message to readers about their own complicity in Bigger's crimes. With this chain of events and motifs, Wright apparently sets up a stinging social critique in the last book of his novel.

But one cannot rest with that reading, as Wright once again complicates the issues with additions that make simple judgment impossible for the reader. Bigger's compassion for his mother in the jail cell scene quickly gives way to shame that "amounted to hate" when she begs the Daltons to spare him. He might feel connected to his community for a moment, but that connection cannot last. Similarly, he attacks the minister that his mother has sent, rescinding his (admittedly empty) promise to pray by knocking the minister to his knees and throwing away the cross that the preacher had left with him. In these moments, the Bigger of the double murders reappears. With this, one might well conclude that Bigger cannot change in any meaningful way, a conclusion that would justify his impending execution and situate him firmly in the reader's mind as a monster.

One cannot easily sustain that interpretation, given what the reader sees Bigger endure in these last days. In the incident with his mother, for instance, Bigger does everything in his power to shield himself and his family from humiliation in front of a white audience. Mrs. Thomas's abject groveling represents the antithesis of that effort, an action that under the circumstances makes Bigger's reaction not unreasonable. With regard to the cross, one must read that passage in the context of Bigger's having just seen a burning cross hoisted outside his jail cell. The equation of the cross that is supposed to represent his salvation with the mob that howls for his destruction is more than Bigger can bear. When he casts away the cross, he is not so much rejecting salvation as he is recognizing that what truth he can find will come not from symbols, but rather from meaningful connections with individuals. To some extent, he achieves such a connection with Max, although the lawyer cannot fully face the final reality of Bigger's life; he achieves a more powerful connection with Jan, who becomes the first white man Bigger can refer to without adding a "Mister" to his name. His ability to assert this equality, which comes only

in the last lines of the novel as the prison doors clang shut on him, marks the moment of escape and of what freedom Bigger is able to attain. It also reinforces the bitter irony of Wright's story.

In "How Bigger Was Born," the explanatory essay that Wright composed the same year his landmark novel was published, he notes that his intention in writing *Native Son* was to create a book that was "so hard and deep" that an audience "would have to face it without the consolation of tears." *Native Son* is certainly such a book; readers rarely weep over Bigger Thomas's fate, regardless of where they stand on the issue of what degree of accountability he bears for his actions. More often than not, though, readers do agonize over how to view Bigger; as they struggle to balance the brutality of his actions with the harsh reality of his life, they must reframe their perceptions of American society. By creating this monumental narrative and detailing Bigger's horrific experiences as racial victim and victimizer, Wright makes a crucial contribution to our understanding of the struggle for racial justice in the United States.

[*See also* Naturalism and Realism.]

FURTHER READING

Fabre, Michel. *The Unfinished Quest of Richard Wright.* 2d ed. Urbana, Ill., 1993. The authoritative biography.

Gates, Henry Louis, Jr., and K. A. Appiah, eds. *Richard Wright: Critical Perspectives Past and Present.* New York, 1993. A comprehensive collection of essays and reviews treating all of Wright's major publications.

Kinnamon, Keneth, and Michel Fabre. *Conversations with Richard Wright.* Jackson, Miss., 1993. A collection of interviews with Wright conducted throughout his career.

Miller, Eugene E. *Voice of a Native Son: The Poetics of Richard Wright.* Jackson, Miss., 1990.

Rampersad, Arnold, ed. *Richard Wright: A Collection of Critical Essays.* New York, 1994.

See also the article on Richard Wright, immediately preceding.

WRITING AS A WOMAN IN THE TWENTIETH CENTURY

by Wendy Martin and Sharon Becker

During the Progressive Era, roughly spanning 1890 to 1920, the American woman struggled to change the definition of womanhood in profound ways. At issue was the right to vote, to wear bloomers, to be free from corseting, to work outside the home, and to have a place in the world beyond the domestic sphere. By 1900 the "new woman" had emerged; these modern women were attending college, getting jobs, agitating for the right to vote, rejecting traditional domesticity, proudly asserting themselves in public, and in general, becoming an integral part of American popular culture and invading its literature as well.

At the end of the nineteenth century, writers such as Rebecca Harding Davis, Elizabeth Stuart Phelps, and Charlotte Perkins Gilman were already writing about women seeking lives outside traditional feminine norms. It is impossible, indeed, to trace developments in twentieth-century women's writing without considering one of the most important texts produced by an American woman in the late nineteenth century: Kate Chopin's *The Awakening* (1899). Chopin's protagonist, Edna Pontellier, is dissatisfied with marriage, children, her home, and the stifling codes of a society that refuses to acknowledge women as creative, sexual beings. In response to her confining world, Edna is driven on a quest for autonomy, solitude, and self-discovery. This radical pursuit ultimately leads Edna to swim into the ocean until her strength leaves her. Because nineteenth-century writing, and by extension society, offered no effective narrative solutions to Edna's struggle to achieve selfhood, Chopin's protagonist drowns.

Although Edna's search for autonomy in a society hostile to women's independence ends with her drowning, each successive generation of women writers push Edna further and further to the shore of self-discovery. As the twentieth century progresses, the voices of women become louder and more artistically innovative. Women of color join the chorus, making American stories more vigorous, complex, and inventive. In the twentieth century, women's writing travels a course in which each generation of female

characters progresses toward vital and independent lives, free from society's traditional limitations. From Lily Bart's death, hastened by her resistance to society's marital expectations, in Edith Wharton's *House of Mirth* (1905) to Sethe's escape from slavery into selfhood in Toni Morrison's *Beloved* (1987), women writing fiction in the twentieth century created textual reflections of women's positions in American culture.

WRITING THEIR LIVES IN THE NEW CENTURY

The suffrage movement, and the involvement of women in surrounding political movements such as socialism and the temperance movement, inspired a particular genre of writing that included both creative and political texts which examined the issues and problems facing women at the turn of the century. In "The Traffic in Women," an essay published in *Anarchism and Other Essays* (1917), Emma Goldman views prostitution as a larger trope for the oppression of women in a capitalistic society. Elizabeth Robins's play *Votes for Women* (produced in 1907) and her novel *The Convert* (1907) portray heroines rejecting marriage proposals and undergoing abortions at a time when abortions were both scandalous and illegal, thus refusing domestic expectations for women to maintain their separate and equal place in the world. The autobiography also became a popular form of writing for women. Written by women such as Elizabeth Cady Stanton and Alice James, autobiographies exposed the private thoughts and feelings of women at a time when the public expression of dissatisfaction by women was taboo. Other women writers interested in exploring the social situation of women did so through utopian fiction, often envisioning women living in a world free from gender constrictions. Charlotte Perkins Gilman expressed her yearnings for women's equality in *Herland* (1915), a utopian novel in which an all-female society is capable of reproducing without men and of building and maintaining a complex community.

Through the genres of regionalism and realism, women writers concentrated on the domestic details of women's lives in order to explore the powerful relationship between women's development and the society that created them. In regionalism, women established a congruous, and sometimes utopistic, relationship with the land as their thoughts, feelings, and struggles were reflected in the natural world around them. Heroines in realist novels were often set adrift in cityscapes, their fates tied to the whims of capitalism and patriarchal control. Women writers of regionalism and realism commonly used romantic and domestic plots to explicate not only women's position in the home, but in the world at large.

Writers of realism attempted to depict life in an objective manner and created stories that often focused on the details of everyday life. Edith Wharton's novels concentrate on upper-class women confined by the expectations imposed on them by a materialistic and acquisitive society. In her novels *The House of Mirth* (1905), *Custom of the Country* (1913) and *The Age of Innocence* (1920), Wharton portrays wealthy New York City society and how, at the turn of the century, this society created a generation of women, indulged and sheltered, who are disconnected from the world beyond tea parties, balls, and dressmakers. Wharton condemns the society for making these women ornamental and useless, while she simultaneously depicts them as sabotaging themselves through an acceptance of the definition of women as decorative objects.

As America became an increasingly large and complicated nation, interest grew in how Americans living in different parts of the country talked, ate, and lived. Women regionalist writers, whether their narratives focused on the South, East, or West, wrote of women's domestic lives with a specificity and complexity that has been overlooked. Both Sarah Orne Jewett's *The Country of the Pointed Firs* (1896) and Mary E. Wilkins Freeman's *A New England Nun and Other Stories* (1891) capture the New England landscape in exquisite detail, rendering a world of stoic women who live in a chosen state of often blissful isolation. Kate Chopin, Ellen Glasgow, and Grace King were all southerners who anchored their stories in the southern landscape. Both King and Chopin, in the subtle and complex stories, "The Little Convent Girl" (1892) and "Desiree's Baby" (1892), respectively, confront the issues of race and gender by delineating the convoluted nature of miscegenation, racial categories, and self-definition in the Deep South. Ellen Glasgow's novels, such as *Virginia* (1912) and *Barren Ground* (1925), capture the South on the cusp of change from a rural, agriculturally based society to a modern, mechanized one. Glasgow dramatizes southern women's struggle to escape the claustrophobic, patriarchal social code that historically dominated southern life. In *The Land of Little Rain* (1903), Mary Austin recounts her experiences in the Owens Valley desert. Austin rejects the names given to the places she visits, creating her own names for these sites and thus personalizing the landscape and symbolically blending herself inextricably with the earth. The heroines of Willa Cather's *O Pioneers!* (1913) and *My Ántonia* (1918) thrive in the harsh beauty of the Nebraskan prairie and embody a pioneer spirit essential, in Cather's view, to the human character, but one that is lost in modern America.

WOMEN OUTSIDE THE MAINSTREAM

African-American women at the turn of the twentieth century were also involved in writing about the world around them. Alice Dunbar-Nelson's short stories, published at the turn of the century, helped establish the short story genre within the tradition of African-American literature. Francis Ellen Watkins Harper's novel, *Iola Leroy* (1892), delineates the African-American experience through the Civil War and Reconstruction. In 1900 Pauline E. Hopkins published *Contending Forces: A Romance Illustrative of Negro Life North and South*. Though the novel's framework is based on the traditional tropes of domestic and historical romance, Hopkins provides a startling account of bourgeois African-American life and offers the domestic drama, long the staple of white women writers, as a model of resistance to racism.

Women of other ethnicities and races also wrote at the turn of the twentieth century. Asian-American Edith Maud Eaton, who as Sui Sin Far published stories in a volume titled *Mrs. Spring Fragrance* (1912), explored the lives of Chinese families living in Seattle and San Francisco. Gertrude Bonnin, a Native American writer who used the pen name Zitkala-Sa, authored collections of traditional Indian stories, *Old Indian Legends* (1901) and *American Indian Stories* (1921). Bonnin combined American storytelling techniques, such as the romantic plot, with Native American legends and contemporary native culture at a time when Indians were largely absent from the American cultural landscape. Mary Antin, a Jewish immigrant from Czarist Russia, introduced an important addition to American ethnic minority women's fiction: the assimilation story. Antin's *From Plotzk to Boston* (1899) and *The Promised Land* (1912) both present the experiences of a woman eager to integrate herself successfully into American culture and offer stories of resistance to typical constructions of femininity. Antin writes passionately of the importance of higher education and self-reliance for all American women.

Gertrude Stein states in her book, *Everybody's Autobiography* (1937), "In the nineteenth century men were confident, the women were not." If Stein's observation is accurate, then it is in the twentieth century in which women gained their confidence. As the writing in the last decades of the nineteenth and the first decades of the twentieth century shows, women were no longer content to remain silent about their dissatisfaction with their roles in the world. Political tracts, realistic renderings of New York City society, and carefully crafted depictions of the Nebraskan prairie often covertly express women's desires for sexual equality, social recognition, and self-determinism. As America inched closer to World War I, writing women became more experimental in style and subject, thus breaking the last tie to the nineteenth century's long-suffering "angel of the house."

WOMEN, MODERNISM, AND THE AGE OF ANXIETY

The first decade of the twentieth century was marked by the tumult of technological and industrial innovation. Many Americans hailed these revolutions as the push the country needed to truly come alive as a nation. However, some American artists and writers saw a dark side to this mechanical modernity. For these writers the assembly line, mechanized industrial machinery, and the ability to record and play back music and human voices, project images on a screen, and traverse huge distances were the result of technological innovations that had the power to permanently disconnect human beings from each other. Indeed, the era between the beginning of World War I in 1914 and the advent of World War II in 1939 has been termed the "Age of Anxiety." The devastating repercussions of modern warfare employed during World War I left a generation of men overwhelmed with feelings of disillusionment, disappointment, and uncertainty towards the world in general. Many women, in contrast, faced changes in the world with enthusiasm.

Miss Gertrude Bonnin, whose Indian name was Zitkala-Sa. (© *Bettmann/Corbis*)

The genre of writing deemed modernism emphasized a radical redefining of literary style, syntax, and subject matter. Modernists sought to unhook language from its traditional meanings and definitions and to push the form of storytelling beyond its traditionally rigid constructions. Because this new genre demolished traditional cultural hierarchies and artistic assumptions, it allowed women to rise to the fore of literary creation. Long left out of mainstream American culture, women writers anxiously embraced newly emerging forms of poetry and fiction as a way to best capture the unique experience of being a woman in modern America. The stylistic innovations of modernism became the method through which, as the English writer Virginia Woolf expressed it, "a woman's sentence" was contemplated. This woman's sentence was not only created through the fresh construction of language but also through newly discovered subjects. Modernist women wrote of lesbianism and sexual freedom while rejecting domesticity, and in the process shattered all traditions in women's writing.

POETRY OF THE MODERN WOMAN

Women embraced a new poetic ideal, infusing their poems with challenging language and using form itself as a medium in which to express literary and cultural resistance. The poets Louise Bogan and Amy Lowell dedicated much of their poetry to the issues of modern womanhood. In her poem, "Women" (1922), Bogan exhorted women to stop living as if they had no "wilderness" in them. One of Amy Lowell's most striking poems, "The Sisters" (1925), is a long meditation on the silence that surrounds female poetics:

> Taking us by and large, we're a queer lot
> We women who write poetry. And when you think
> How few of us there've been, it's queerer still.

Hilda Doolittle, better known as H.D., rose to poetic prominence as a member of the imagist school of poetry, and her work often relies upon an intricate play among Greek mythology, psychological connections between nature and humanity, and the structure of the poem itself: short lines, free verse, and concise imagery. Her poem, "Eurydice" (1917, 1925), considered to be one of H.D.'s most personal poems, twists the familiar myth to formulate an accusation against egocentric men who recklessly wield power over women.

Elinor Wylie's poetry, the most successful of which was collected in *Nets to Catch the Wind* (1921), strikes a balance between the modernist austerity of technique and a delicate evocation of the natural world. Wylie's pessimistic stance on the modern world is marked by her recurrent attention to the theme of feminine alienation and exile. Wylie influenced poets like Edna St. Vincent Millay, whose poetry often takes a backseat to the mythology surrounding Millay herself. Her ethereal beauty, red hair, and green eyes embodied the mythical flapper of the Jazz Age. Millay's poetry, though at times dark and reflective, nonetheless most often celebrates sexual and personal independence. Her collection of poetry, *Second April* (1921), features Millay's most innovative contributions to modernist verse: the reinvention of the sonnet. Millay revitalized the traditional sonnet by removing the female muse as subject and replacing her with a male beloved who becomes the focus of sensual love.

Standing in opposition to Millay's sensuality are the poems of Marianne Moore, whose poetic aesthetic is marked by a dedication to compression of language and image and an extraordinary attention to a singular object. Moore often focused on animals, as in the poem "The Jerboa" (1932), emphasizing the vast lessons couched in a tiny, particular entity. Incorporating already-published materials into her poems—magazine articles, newspaper clippings, advertising slogans—through the use of quotation marks, Moore creates a powerful pastiche in which a world of writing speaks both to and through her. Using quotation and endnotes as a poetic technique, Moore successfully engages the readers in the text, casting them as cocreators of the poem. Thus, Moore's work represents a communal or meeting space where Moore dually instructs the reader while exposing the construction behind her lessons.

THE FICTION OF MODERNISM

Women who wrote modernist prose experimented with language as much as their sisters who wrote poetry. Their new literary approaches stand in stark contrast to the novels written by women at the beginning of the century, which often featured a standard, linear narrative and presented women mostly in domestic and romantic entanglements that could only covertly express women's issues and desires. Modernist fiction freed the female character from operating only in this domestic sphere. No longer bound by its constraints, modernist women writers used the newly emerging literary forms to critique directly domesticity, traditional love relationships, and the trap capitalism often set for the women who decided that being modern meant being a consumer.

Gertrude Stein is cited more often than any other woman writer as the leader of the female branch of the modernist movement. She eschewed all literary expectations as she sought to release language from its common meanings, remove linear time from the narrative, and reinvent the reader's relationship to the text. Stein's writing, including the novel *Three Lives* (1909) and the autobiography, *The Making of Americans* (1925), is often constructed through a repetition of simple words and phrases, a technique meant not only to free language from its roots but to erase the hierarchal structure of "high" and "low" language. Stein's prose poems in *Tender Buttons* (1914) fracture the totems of domesticity (teapots, cakes, freshly washed laundry) into multifaceted word pictures, symbolically deleting the domestic simplicity of these items and infusing them with feminine sensuality, thus redefining these common words and images for her readers.

The most significant work of Djuna Barnes, a reclusive yet influential member of the modernist movement, is *Nightwood* (1937), which explores a turbulent love affair between two women. It is also a dense and complicated text redolent with grotesque imagery, metaphysical speculation about the relationship between body and spirit, and an exuberant exploration of language. Thus, in *Nightwood*, Barnes explodes the traditional romantic plot, modernizing it not only by focusing on lesbian characters but also by narrating this transgressive love story in experimental language and narrative form.

Katherine Anne Porter's short stories often deal with women who are torn between a desire for traditional domesticity and a yearning for an independent life. The stories of *Pale Horse, Pale Rider* (1939) highlight the elegant and controlled style of Porter that embodies a tension between the author's ironic distance and her close connection with her characters, who struggle for personal freedom. Dorothy Parker's short stories, poems, and criticism are often remembered for their humor and dark, sardonic edge. Like Porter, Parker exposes the moment of discovery of self, but for Parker this moment is more often disappointing than revelatory. Her story, "The

Big Blonde" (1929), best represents Parker's interest, often comically rendered, in the disjunction between outward appearances and inward feelings.

Eudora Welty combined a sharp sense of humor with a precise evocation of her native Mississippi landscape. Her first collection of fiction, *A Curtain of Green, and Other Stories* (1941), is marked not only by humor but also by the precision of metaphor, a perfect rendering of southern idiom, and a simplicity of language that often belies the complicated undercurrents running below the text. The women of Welty's stories, such as the protagonists in "Why I Live at the P.O." and "Petrified Man," often search for individuality while clinging to the small towns that repress them. Like turn-of-the-century regionalist writers, Welty often used the domestic drama as a starting point of her critique of American culture; however, her mythological symbols, the often nonlinear shape of her narrative, and her focus on the underdogs of society allows her work to resonate beyond the borders of her region.

Women writing modernist fiction pushed the genre of women's fiction beyond previously established boundaries. The change was not only in form, but also content. As women in American society were leading increasingly public lives, the size and shape of women's worlds began to expand. Women's writing reflected these expansions, and writers captured these changes through challenging narratives and the use of inventive language.

AMERICAN DRAMA AND THE EARLY TWENTIETH CENTURY

While women writers were pushing traditional boundaries of "women's fiction," women were also reshaping the form and content of the theater, often in response to social changes. Susan Glaspell wrote both fiction and drama, most of which involve women searching for the meaning of life isolated from success, money, or even happiness. Glaspell's play, *Trifles* (produced in 1916), presents her recurrent theme of the new woman who seeks her dreams despite the hostility of the conservative, repressive world. Lillian Hellman's tough, lively, and ironic writing forced the social and psychological concerns of women to the American stage with such plays as *The Children's Hour* (produced in 1934), the story of a lesbian schoolteacher in love with her colleague and best friend, and *The Little Foxes* (produced in 1939), a tale of a woman who craves both power and money, both of which helped redefine the direction of modern theater. Clare Booth Luce's *The Women* (produced in 1936) examined the competitive, and often vicious, interactions of wealthy, pampered

wives, and bitter divorcées. Other playwrights, such as Shirley Graham, Hallie Flanagan, and Margaret Ellen Clifford, used the stage as a forum for issues such as racism and the plight of workers during the Great Depression.

WOMEN AND THE HARLEM RENAISSANCE

The Harlem Renaissance, though concurrent with the modernist literary movement, stands as a distinct literary endeavor. Though its roots stretch back to the beginning of the century, the movement did not truly flower until the late 1910s and early 1920s. New York City, already established as a center of publishing, became a haven for African Americans wishing to leave the South after Reconstruction. Harlem became a center of African-American life in which jazz and blues music became prominent attractions, numerous magazines and newspapers gave voice to African-American concerns, and an African-American literary renaissance bloomed.

The writers of the Harlem Renaissance were determined to focus a lens on their unique experience of American life and culture. African-American writers' work was charged with different issues than those that preoccupied white writers of the same period. African-American writers, though they experimented with narrative form and language like white modernists, were committed to using those techniques to explore black life and black issues. Additionally, a revision of narrative forms and of language allowed black writers to capture the unique rhythms of black language and culture.

Women writers such as Angelina Weld Grimké and Anne Spencer made early inroads into the Harlem Renaissance movement through the publication of poetry. Gwendolyn B. Bennett wrote poetry in a traditional form, but addressed as her subjects black women and girls, figures often left out of the poetic world. Helene Johnson also used a traditional poetic form, as in "Sonnet to a Negro in Harlem" (1927), but rejected typical sonnet subjects for the world of modern, urban blacks. Women's biggest contribution to the Harlem Renaissance came with fiction. Some of these writers, such as Jessie Redmon Fauset and Nella Larsen, wrote about the complexities of race and gender through the framework of the lives of everyday African-American women. Jessie Redmon Fauset's novel, *Plum Bun: A Novel without a Moral* (1929), tells of a middle-class, light-skinned African-American woman who passes as a white woman not only because she can, but because being "white" allows her access to the worlds of money and power that would normally be inaccessible to black women. Nella Larsen's novel, *Passing*

(1929), contrasts the lives of two women, one who has passed for white daily and one who has passed for white occasionally. The novel, however, is about more than the question of race, as Larsen also addresses the complexities of female friendship and sexuality.

Although published at the end of the Harlem Renaissance, Zora Neale Hurston's complex fiction is considered to be the some of the finest work of the movement. Trained as a folklorist at Columbia University under the tutelage of Franz Boas, Hurston infuses her fiction with black idiom, overtones of African myths and legends, and the details of modern African-American life. Generally acknowledged as Hurston's best novel, *Their Eyes Were Watching God* (1937) is the story of Janie Crawford, her three tumultuous marriages, and most important, the discovery of Janie's own voice. Introduced as a romantic young girl repressed by prevalent racism, sexism, and poverty, Janie grows into a woman with a greater understanding of the complexities of self-definition. Hurston's story stands as a testament to the strength of a generation of African-American women striving for a place in the world.

The Great Depression and the rumblings of World War II signaled the end of modernism and of the Harlem Renaissance as cohesive literary movements. Although modernists and the writers of the Harlem Renaissance sought to create languages and forms that delineated the modern experience, the world continued to change, necessitating new forms of literature and creating new genres of writing that reflected America's changing relationship with the categories of race, gender, class, and ethnicity.

THE LITERATURE OF CHANGE, 1940–1980

The marketing of the American family as a perfect unit began in the 1930s, after the heady 1920s and the beginning of the Great Depression. The promotion of family togetherness became a safety line, enabling Americans to pull through hard times. During World War II the family served as an important reminder of the perfection of American life and was set as a beacon of hope for "our boys" overseas. However, the 1950s were truly the golden age of the family. America, reborn after the scrimping and saving of World War II, was a shiny, plasticized, boomeranged, and tail-finned world in which television and advertising packaged the perfect family alongside gelatin salads and pink refrigerators. Nevertheless, as this myth of familial perfection was being constructed, it was simultaneously being destroyed by

women writers who resisted the lie of domesticity and the figurehead of the perfect housewife that stood in the center of that lie.

In the poem "Snapshots of a Daughter-in-Law," (1958–1960), poet Adrienne Rich looks to the future when women rise,

> at least as beautiful as any boy
> or helicopter,
> poised, still coming, her fine blades making the air wince.

Rich goes on to describe a woman mindlessly polishing teaspoons, her shaved legs gleaming like tusks, her mind as blank as a "wedding cake." Tillie Olsen's recurrent theme of women silenced through poverty and domesticity coalesces in her novella, *Tell Me a Riddle* (1961), as a dying grandmother, once a revolutionary political speaker, regains her voice after years of domesticated silence. Eva's deathbed speech counters the silence the 1950s placed on women as well as immigrant communities and the poor. Thus, Eva's act of speaking becomes one of resistance to the cultural norms. Southern writer Flannery O'Connor exploded the genre of Southern Gothic into one that spoke not only of loneliness and isolation but also offered a radical revision to the very fabric of American life. A female graduate student's jettisoned artificial leg becomes symbolic for her own loss of innocence and hope in "Good Country People" (1955), a family on a mundane road trip is brutalized by bandits in "A Good Man Is Hard to Find" (1953), and a mentally disabled young woman is left sleeping in a diner by her new husband in "The Life You Save May Be Your Own" (1953). O'Connor's women are defined not by their perfection but by the very flaws that make them vulnerable to seduction, violence, or disappointment. Her women stand as a testament to the terrible beauty of faults and foibles, and O'Connor clearly values these very women who fall short of expectation.

In 1963, Betty Friedan's *The Feminine Mystique* exploded the myth of the contented suburban housewife. This explosion resounded across the country, revolutionizing not only what women wanted from their lives, but also what women wrote. Mary McCarthy's novel, *The Group* (1962), a best-seller, follows a set of female friends from their time together in college into their lives as independent women. McCarthy explores a number of taboo subjects, such adultery, abortion, divorce, and insanity, while also exposing the American marriage to be an institution fraught with misogyny. McCarthy positions the women who resist the boundaries of traditional femininity—marriage, a ladylike appearance, heterosexuality—as the only successful women of the novel. In the years between the publication of *The Group* and the advent of the 1970s, the women's movement as an organized and powerful force came to the attention of the wider American public. Writers and activists such as Jo Freeman, Nancy Chodorow, Casey Hayden, Mary King, and Caroline Bird all brought the issues of women's equality to the page, signaling that women were serious about ending the construction of woman as housewife. Joyce Carol Oates's frequently anthologized story, "Where Are You Going, Where Have You Been?" (1966), explores the life of Connie, an ordinary high school student who is seduced into a relationship with an ominous "friend." Connie's vulnerability to Arnold Friend and the violence that is suggested at the end of the story stand as powerful symbols of the failure of the traditional interpretation of femininity. Through Connie, Oates locates the innocent, primed-for-domesticity girl as an anachronism, one that will be forced completely out of the house through the coming decades.

The literature of African-American women reflected a resistance not necessarily to suburban domesticity but to a culture that often ignored them. Ann Petry's novel, *The Street* (1946), focuses on the daily degradation faced by black Americans of both genders. However, Petry's female protagonist simultaneously resists and succumbs to this degradation as she murders the man who attempts to rape her. The blunt examination of rape, and the issues of power that surround rape, was a revolutionary topic at the time, particularly as written by an African-American woman. Other African-American writing, like Paule Marshall's *Brown Girl, Brownstones* (1959), also speaks of African-American women and girls who enact resistance to American cultural repression simply by their very existence. Gwendolyn Brooks was the first African-American woman to receive the Pulitzer Prize for poetry for her collection, *Annie Allen* (1949). In her poetry, Brooks uses black idiom and slang as a vehicle to express black rage and oppression. *A Street in Bronzeville* (1945) and *Bronzeville Boys and Girls* (1956) concentrate on the boredom of poor youth and the sadness of mothers who have lost their children and men to violence and the streets. At a time when poetry was often self-consciously intellectual, Brooks's use of casual language in combination with a close attention to poetic form was a revolution in style.

POETIC VOICES, POETIC SUBJECTS

Poetry written after the apex of modernism reflects a more simplified approach to the poetic project. Though writers continued to experiment with language and form, poetry in general began to reflect an individualized and personal viewpoint that was absent in modernism. The assertion of the individual, that is, the poet, into the poem was perhaps a reaction against the oppressive quest for sameness that enveloped the country at mid-century.

Sylvia Plath and Anne Sexton are perhaps the two best-known women of the confessional school of poetry, which emphasized the use of poetry as a mode to explore the universal through personal failings and desires. Sylvia Plath's poems are a study in opposition: dark yet playful, intensely rhythmic and carefully rhymed, yet far from traditional. Plath utilizes simple language and repetition to craft poems about the most difficult of subjects: the hatred for her father, her uncertainty as a mother, and her own delicate mental state. Yet she also writes poems of breathtaking beauty, elevating beekeeping and nature walks to moments of divine transcendence. Plath's poems begin in the personal but, through the use of myth and often the metaphysical symbolism of the natural world, they become universal statements about the quest for a place in the universe.

Anne Sexton's collections, *To Bedlam and Part Way Back* (1960), *All My Pretty Ones* (1962), *Live or Die* (1966), *Love Poems* (1969), *Transformations* (1971), *The Book of Folly* (1972), and *The Death Notebooks* (1974), reveal not only Sexton's psychological travails but her physical trauma—menstruation, abortion, incest, drug abuse—that remained largely silenced in women's poetics before the woman's movement. Sexton's direct language, repetition of words and phrases, and alternation of short, concise lines with long, languid stanzas help create a unique poetry that is at once light on the page but heavy in the mind of the reader.

Although confessional poetry revolutionized women's poetics, other poets like Elizabeth Bishop, working from a more traditional vein, examined women's lives in profound ways. Bishop's tropes of exile and travel, her precise language and brilliant images, reflect a woman finding her self through a close examination of the world around her. Other poets, such as Marilyn Chin, Pat Parker, Judy Grahn, June Jordan, Marge Piercy, Pat Mora, and Rita Dove, revolutionized poetics through topic by focusing on Latina, Native American, African-American, and lesbian lives and politics. Adrienne Rich's poems reflect these changing concerns while also mirroring the transformations in Rich's personal life from wife and mother to lesbian and political activist. Rich's early poetry is relatively traditional with standard line breaks and rhythmical stanzas. However, by the 1970s her poetry incorporates stylistic innovations such as punctuation suggested only by spaces within the stanzas, along with traditionally taboo poetic subjects such as pornography explored in rigidly constructed couplets in order to reflect the changing place of women in the world. Though Rich commonly addressed woman as subject, poems of hers such as "Diving into the Wreck" (1973) are more political and the poetic process becomes a way for Rich to redress the wrongs of the contemporary world.

THE FINAL DECADES OF THE TWENTIETH CENTURY

The civil rights movement, women's liberation movements, and protests against the Vietnam War, and the accompanying social reverberations throughout the final decades of the twentieth century, helped to redefine the trajectory of American literature. As African-American activists recovered a long-suppressed and forgotten African-American literary tradition, women writers like Adrienne Rich were calling for a recovery of "foremother" writers such as Virginia Woolf and Marianne Moore. In breaking through the wall of domination built by the hegemony of male literary precursors, women writers of the late twentieth century had a unique challenge. Texts such as Tillie Olsen's *One out of Twelve: Writers Who Are Women in Our Century* (1972) and poems like Denise Levertov's "Hypocrite Women" openly sought to redefine the scope of women's literature and the way in which this literature spoke directly to women and excluded masculine influence.

The proliferation of literary styles in African-American writing from the 1960s through the end of the twentieth century can be attributed to the interest of African Americans in reframing black history as well as in recovering long-ignored black literary traditions. African-American writers reactivated the painful ghost of slavery in order to understand the contemporary configuration of black American life. Additionally, writers like Alice Walker and Paule Marshall published stories about black life in a language uniquely crafted to convey the sounds of black English, which also dovetailed with the recovery of African-American oral storytelling traditions. This language allowed African-American writers to shape a picture of life that existed outside the boundaries of white language and experience.

Sonia Sanchez's first volume of poetry, *Homecoming* (1969), set the tone for poetry by African Americans in

the 1970s and 1980s. Sanchez's conversational style and black slang, set to a jazzy rhythm, was at once exuberant and political. Nikki Giovanni's assured and controversial stance of black militancy as the answer to white repression made her an instant subject of magazine articles and news reports. Audre Lorde's first book of poetry, *The First Cities*, published in 1968, turns the rage African Americans felt about racism into a medium of positive self-definition. Lucille Clifton's poetry also takes on the project of racism in America, but Clifton does so by reanimating her own past as well as the history of Africans and African Americans. Clifton uses spare language and short, concise lines to convey small moments of dignity in the lives of urban blacks.

The year 1970 was a landmark in African-American women's writing as Maya Angelou's autobiography, *I Know Why the Caged Bird Sings*, broke open the silences of African-American women about their lives in mid-nineteenth century America. Toni Cade Bambara's collections of short stories—*The Black Woman* (1970), *Tales and Stories for Black Folks* (1971), *Gorilla, My Love* (1972), and *The Sea Birds Are Still Alive* (1977)—were also groundbreaking publications in the 1970s. Bambara dedicates herself to the exploration of the African-American past and present through the use of black idiom and slang, both of which are used as a form of resistance to the hegemony of Western language and an affirmation of African-American culture. Asserting through her stories that African-American women, in particular, have, "a certain way of being in the world" that is determined as much by gender as it is by education, political outlook, and class, Bambara creates heroines who are independent, tough-minded, and above all, survivors.

In Alice Walker's essay, *In Search of Our Mothers' Gardens: Womanist Prose* (1983), the growth of art and literature by African-American women is explored. Walker asserts that though black women were not always allowed access to education, they nonetheless learned to express themselves artistically through crafts such as cooking, sewing, and oral storytelling. Walker's *The Color Purple* (1982) was the first novel by an African-American woman to win the Pulitzer Prize for literature. Though she faced criticism for her portrayal of black men as violent and sexually deviant, the novel was most often praised for its unflinching look at black life. Walker's work is indicative of the changes present in literature by African-American women in the 1980s. Though still political, writing by African-American women became more grounded in the richness of the individual experience and spoke of African-American lives not only in their extraordinariness, but also in their ordinariness.

Toni Morrison, author, teacher, and critic, saw her first novel, *The Bluest Eye,* published in 1970. In the decades since its publication, Morrison has become a household name, and she enjoys the unique status of being both critically respected and widely read. Though her novels *Sula* (1973), *Song of Solomon* (1977), and *Tar Baby* (1981) were all best-sellers, her greatest achievement in fiction is considered to be *Beloved* (1987), for which she won the Pulitzer Prize in 1988. The story of Sethe, a former slave who kills one of her children to prevent them from being taken into slavery, is told through a complicated narrative structure. The story weaves back and forth in time, creating a complex narrative quilt that raises Sethe's particular struggles both within and without slavery to a more general story about the ravages of slavery on African Americans as a community and the need to move forward with life. While the past needs to be honored, it cannot be permitted to entrap future generations. By claiming her life for herself, Sethe symbolically embodies a level of freedom and self-possession available to black women courageous enough to embrace it.

Native American intellectuals and writers created and enjoyed a cultural renaissance throughout the 1970s, publishing books that offered a revisionist view of Native American history and creating novels, short stories, and plays that spoke dually of the Native American past and the dissatisfaction Indians felt in the twentieth-century world. By the 1980s, writers like Joy Harjo and Louise Erdrich further challenged American readers by focusing on the struggle of Native American women to reside in a space between both old and new worlds. In her work, which includes the novels *Love Medicine* (1984), *The Beet Queen* (1986), and *Tracks* (1988), Erdrich crafts unflinching visions of Native peoples who occupy increasingly complicated worlds. Using traditional Native American stories, a nonlinear narrative, and characters that border on being magical, Erdrich etches an indelible portrait of Native Americans living in a modern America while simultaneously trying to maintain ties to tradition. Joy Harjo's poetry provides a unique perspective on Native American life as she recovers the lost voices of her ancestors through her use of lyrical language and the rhythms of Native American speech and song. Leslie Marmon Silko's quiet style reflects an oral storytelling tradition that relies on repetition and simple language,

as exemplified in her frequently anthologized story, "Lullaby" (1975), which encompasses the complexities of Native American life. Her characters, like Erdrich's, are caught between the ghosts of the past and the bleak landscape of the future.

The cultural visibility of another group of Americans, Latinos, increased in the mid-1960s when activists, recovering the label of "Chicano" (once a title of derision), began demonstrating on college campuses over a variety of issues. These Chicano activists sought to revitalize their community's connection to their historic past, while writers, musicians, and artists reclaimed Aztec roots, the use of Spanish, and traditional Mexican handiwork. Gloria Anzaldúa's landmark text, *Borderlands/La Frontera: The New Mestiza* (1987), reflects not only this absorption of the Mexican past but also the incorporation of the feminist tradition. This interplay of texts is a physical manifestation of the cultural, social, and linguistic borderland contemporary Chicanas occupy. Sandra Cisneros's two collections of short stories, *The House on Mango Street* (1984) and *Woman Hollering Creek and Other Stories* (1991), both participate in Anzaldúa's effort to use Mexican myth while presenting Latinas as continuously creating a vital, contemporary culture. Cisneros's straightforward style, use of Spanglish, and commitment to telling stories about ordinary people offer an essential portrait of Latina life and culture in the larger context of American culture.

Asian-American voices have also become an integral part of the landscape of American literature. Maxine Hong Kingston's *The Woman Warrior: Memoirs of a Girlhood amongst Ghosts* (1976) is at once an autobiography, a retelling of Chinese myths, and a fictionalized account of Kingston's family history. Kingston deftly criticizes the patriarchal traditions of Chinese culture while also indicting America's racism as having a devastating effect on Chinese-American women. Amy Tan's *The Joy Luck Club* (1989) continues Kingston's project of using traditional Chinese mythology to explicate the lives of contemporary Chinese-American women. The novel unfolds through stories told by eight women, four Chinese and four Chinese American, reflecting Kingston's use of "talkstories" as a the backbone of Chinese culture. Bharati Mukherjee prefers to categorize herself as an American writer, not a South Asian writer of Indian descent. Indeed, her novels—*The Tiger's Daughter* (1971), *Wife* (1975), *Jasmine* (1989), and *Holder of the World* (1993)—are narratives not only of assimilation by Indian characters to American culture, but also the general quest by human beings for acceptance, love, and a constantly shifting definition of self.

If Edith Wharton's *House of Mirth* crystallized the plight of women at the turn of the twentieth century, then Toni Morrison's *Beloved* is a testament not only to the strength of African-American women, but is symbolic of the journey made by American women through the twentieth century. From a life begun in complete submission, Sethe not only endures, but claims her energy and life on her own terms, an accomplishment that Wharton's Lily Bart strove for but never reached. As bookends of the twentieth century, *House of Mirth*'s Lily Bart and *Beloved*'s Sethe represent the beginning and the end of the journey begun by *The Awakening*'s Edna Pontellier. Each of the many texts written by women in the years between *House of Mirth* and *Beloved* is a tiny island upon which Edna could rest, gain strength, and move forward. Standing so close to the end of the twentieth century makes it impossible to define the trends, themes, and writers who will endure the test of time. However, one can say with assurance that women in the late twentieth century occupy literary spaces not open to women at the beginning of the century. Contemporary fiction, poetry, and drama written by women no longer fit neatly into categories such as realism, regionalism, or modernism. Instead, women's writing now encompasses a much larger range of experiences and is a more vivid and accurate reflection of American women's place in the twentieth century.

[*See also* Asian American Literature; Autobiography: White Women during the Civil War; Barnes, Djuna; Morrison's *Beloved*; Bishop, Elizabeth; Brooks, Gwendolyn; Cather, Willa; Chopin, Kate; Erdrich, Louise; Glasgow, Ellen; H.D. (Hilda Doolittle); Harlem Renaissance; Hellman, Lillian; Hurston, Zora Neale; Jewett, Sarah Orne; Jewish-American Fiction; Kingston, Maxine Hong; Latino/Latina Fiction in America; Levertov, Denise; Lowell, Amy; McCarthy, Mary; Millay, Edna St. Vincent; Moore, Marianne; Native American Literature; Oates, Joyce Carol; O'Connor, Flannery; Plath, Sylvia; Poetess in American Literature; Porter, Katherine Anne; Rich, Adrienne; Sexton, Anne; Silko, Leslie Marmon; Stein, Gertrude; Hurston's *Their Eyes Were Watching God*; Walker, Alice; Welty, Eudora; *and* Wharton, Edith.]

FURTHER READING

Ammons, Elizabeth. *Conflicting Stories: American Women Writers at the Turn into the Twentieth Century.* New York, 1991. Ammons's work encompasses the often ignored and maligned writing by women from the early 1890s through the late 1920s. Authors featured include Sarah Orne Jewett, Kate Chopin, Edith Wharton, Willa Cather, Alice Dunbar-Nelson, Ellen Glasgow, Charlotte Perkins Gilman, Pauline Hopkins, Sui Sin Far, Gertrude Stein, Mary Austin, Jessie Redmon Fauset, and Nella Larsen.

Barstow, Jane Missner. *One Hundred Years of American Women Writing, 1848–1948: An Annotated Bio-Bibliography.* Pasadena, Calif., 1997. A good reference guide for beginning scholars of American women writers. Each chapter provides a general essay on the time period, an annotated list of books and articles, biographical and critical information about the sixty-six featured authors, and a list of selected and featured writings by the authors discussed.

Cahill, Susan Neunzig, ed. *Writing Women's Lives: An Anthology of Autobiographical Narratives by Twentieth Century American Women Writers.* New York, 1994. Excerpts from the autobiographies and memories of such American luminaries as Edith Wharton, Ellen Glasgow, Lillian Hellman, Tillie Olsen, Denise Levertov, and Maya Angelou.

Carby, Hazel. *Reconstructing Womanhood: The Emergence of the Afro-American Woman Novelist.* New York, 1987. Focuses on African-American women authors of the nineteenth and early twentieth century through political, literary, and social lenses. The novelists discussed include Frances Harper, Pauline Hopkins, Ida Wells, Anna Cooper, Jessie Fauset, and Nella Larsen.

Cutter, Martha J. *Unruly Tongue: Identity and Voice in American Women's Writing, 1850–1930.* Jackson, Miss., 1999. Cutter argues that the goal of late-nineteenth- and early-twentieth-century American women writers was to free language and storytelling from its masculine origins.

Drake, William. *The First Wave: Women Poets in America, 1915–1945.* New York, 1987. Provides biographical information on twenty-seven American women poets active in the early twentieth century, including Marianne Moore, Amy Lowell, and Louise Bogan.

Gilbert, Sandra M., and Susan Gubar. *No Man's Land: The Place of the Woman Writer in the Twentieth Century.* 3 vols. New Haven, Conn., 1988–1989. A landmark study of women writers in which Gilbert and Gubar provide a thorough outline of the literary, historical, and social forces that shaped the writing of women in the twentieth century.

Gould, Jean. *Modern American Women Poets.* New York, 1984. Gould presents biographical studies of women poets writing in the second half of the twentieth century, including Elizabeth Bishop, Sylvia Plath, Anne Sexton, Gwendolyn Brooks, Adrienne Rich, Audre Lorde, and Nikki Giovanni.

Kubitschek, Missy Dehn. *Claiming the Heritage: African-American Women Novelists and History*. Jackson, Miss., 1991. An examination of African-American feminine identity in novels by twentieth-century black women writers. Novels discussed include Zora Neale Hurston's *Their Eyes Were Watching God*, Paule Marshall's *Brown Girl, Brownstones*, Jesse Redmon Fauset's *Plum Bun*, and Nella Larsen's *Quicksand*. Also includes discussion of Toni Morrison, Alice Walker, and other late-twentieth-century writers.

Lumsden, Linda J. *Rampant Women: Suffragists and the Right of Assembly*. Knoxville, Tenn., 1997. Communicates the approaches of early-twentieth-century suffragettes through newspaper accounts, autobiographies, and creative writing by women deeply involved in the movement.

Reynolds, Guy. *Twentieth-Century American Women's Fiction: A Critical Introduction*. New York, 1999. Reynolds views writing by women as inextricably linked to historical and social issues as well as the literary concerns pervasive throughout the twentieth century.

Stansell, Christine. *American Moderns: Bohemian New York and the Creation of a New Century*. New York, 2000. Stansell is primarily interested in how the modernist movement played itself out among New York City writers, poets, political activists, and artists. A good overview of the movement as a whole that makes an argument for feminism as the central focus of both male and female modernists.

Walker, Cheryl. *Masks Outrageous and Austere: Culture, Psyche, and Persona in Modern Women Poets*. Bloomington, Ind., 1992. Walker attempts to recover and canonize women poets of the late nineteenth and early twentieth century left behind because of the restrictive construction of femininity during the modernist period.

Wheeler, Kathleen M. *A Guide to Twentieth-Century Women Novelists*. Oxford, 1997. Wheeler examines writing by women in English through four periods: realism and the rise of early modernism, from 1895 to 1925; high modernism and the development of the social-moral novel, from 1918 to 1945; neorealism, the postwar novel, and early postmodernist innovations, from 1944 to 1975; and internationalism, diversification, and experimentation, from 1970 to 1995. Also includes a section on feminist theory and a bibliography of research resources.

TOPICAL OUTLINE OF ARTICLES

The entries in *The Oxford Encyclopedia of American Literature* are conceived according to the general conceptual categories listed in this topical outline. Some entries are listed more than once because the conceptual categories are not mutually exclusive. Entries in the encyclopedia proper are organized alphabetically.

AUTHORS

Adams, Henry
Agee, James
Aiken, Conrad
Albee, Edward
Alcott, Louisa May
Alger, Horatio
Algren, Nelson
Alvarez, Julia
Ammons, A. R.
Anderson, Sherwood
Angelou, Maya
Ashbery, John
Auden, W. H.

Baldwin, James
Banks, Russell
Barnes, Djuna
Barth, John
Barthelme, Donald
Beattie, Ann
Bellow, Saul
Benét, Stephen Vincent
Berry, Wendell
Berryman, John
Bierce, Ambrose
Bishop, Elizabeth
Bradstreet, Anne
Brodkey, Harold
Brooks, Gwendolyn
Buck, Pearl S.
Bukowski, Charles
Burroughs, William S.

Capote, Truman
Carruth, Hayden

Carver, Raymond
Cather, Willa
Cheever, John
Chesnutt, Charles W.
Chopin, Kate
Collins, Billy
Cooper, James Fenimore
Crane, Hart
Crane, Stephen
Creeley, Robert
Crèvecoeur, J. Hector St. John de
Cummings, E. E.

Dana, Richard Henry
DeLillo, Don
Dickey, James
Dickinson, Emily
Didion, Joan
Dillard, Annie
Doctorow, E. L.
Dos Passos, John
Douglass, Frederick
Dreiser, Theodore
Du Bois, W. E. B.
Dunbar, Paul Laurence

Edwards, Jonathan
Eliot, T. S.
Elkin, Stanley
Ellison, Ralph
Emerson, Ralph Waldo
Erdrich, Louise

Faulkner, William
Fitzgerald, F. Scott
Ford, Richard
Franklin, Benjamin
Freneau, Philip
Frost, Robert

Gardner, John
Garland, Hamlin
Ginsberg, Allen
Gioia, Dana
Glasgow, Ellen
Glück, Louise
Gunn, Thom

Hacker, Marilyn
Hapgood, Hutchins
Harte, Bret
Hawthorne, Nathaniel
Hayden, Robert
H.D. (Hilda Doolittle)
Hecht, Anthony
Heller, Joseph
Hellman, Lillian
Hemingway, Ernest
Henry, O.
Hoagland, Edward
Howard, Richard
Howells, William Dean
Hughes, Langston
Hugo, Richard
Hurston, Zora Neale

Irving, John
Irving, Washington

Jackson, Laura Riding
James, Henry
Jarrell, Randall
Jeffers, Robinson
Jewett, Sarah Orne
Jong, Erica
Jordan, June
Justice, Donald

Kazin, Alfred
Kees, Weldon
Kennedy, William
Kerouac, Jack
Kincaid, Jamaica
King, Stephen
Kingston, Maxine Hong
Kinnell, Galway
Kunitz, Stanley
Kushner, Tony

Lardner, Ring
Lazarus, Emma
Levertov, Denise
Levine, Philip
Lewis, Sinclair
Lindsay, Vachel
London, Jack
Longfellow, Henry Wadsworth
Lopez, Barry
Lowell, Amy

Lowell, Robert
Loy, Mina

Mailer, Norman
Malamud, Bernard
Mamet, David
Masters, Edgar Lee
Mather, Cotton
Matthews, William
Matthiessen, Peter
McCarthy, Cormac
McCarthy, Mary
McClatchy, J. D.
McCullers, Carson
McNally, Terrence
McPhee, John
Melville, Herman
Mencken, H. L.
Merrill, James
Merwin, W. S.
Millay, Edna St. Vincent
Miller, Arthur
Miller, Henry
Momaday, N. Scott
Moore, Marianne
Morrison, Toni

Nabokov, Vladimir
Naylor, Gloria
Norris, Frank

Oates, Joyce Carol
O'Brien, Tim
O'Connor, Flannery

O'Hara, John
Olds, Sharon
O'Neill, Eugene
Ostriker, Alicia
Ozick, Cynthia

Paley, Grace
Parker, Dorothy
Pinsky, Robert
Plath, Sylvia
Poe, Edgar Allan
Ponsot, Marie
Porter, Katherine Anne
Pound, Ezra
Prose, Francine
Proulx, Annie
Pynchon, Thomas

Ransom, John Crowe
Reed, Ishmael
Rich, Adrienne
Robinson, Edwin Arlington
Roethke, Theodore
Roth, Henry
Roth, Philip
Rukeyser, Muriel

Salinger, J. D.
Sandburg, Carl
Schwartz, Delmore
Sexton, Anne
Shepard, Sam
Silko, Leslie Marmon
Simic, Charles

Simms, William Gilmore,
    and Antebellum
    Southern Literature
Sinclair, Upton, and
    the Muckrakers
Singer, Isaac Bashevis
Smith, Dave
Snyder, Gary
Soto, Gary
Stafford, Jean
Stafford, William
Stegner, Wallace
Stein, Gertrude
Steinbeck, John
Stern, Gerald
Stevens, Wallace
Stevenson, Anne
Stone, Robert
Stowe, Harriet Beecher
Strand, Mark
Styron, William
Swenson, May

Tarkington, Booth
Tate, Allen
Tate, James
Taylor, Edward
Taylor, Peter
Thoreau, Henry David
Thurber, James
Tocqueville, Alexis de
Trilling, Lionel
Twain, Mark

Updike, John

Very, Jones
Vidal, Gore
Vonnegut, Kurt

Walcott, Derek
Walker, Alice
Warren, Robert Penn
Welty, Eudora
West, Nathanael
Wharton, Edith
Wheatley, Phillis
White, E. B.
White, Edmund
Whitman, Walt
Wideman, John Edgar
Wilbur, Richard
Wilder, Thornton
Williams, Tennessee
Williams, Terry Tempest
Williams, William Carlos
Wilson, August
Wilson, Edmund
Wolfe, Thomas
Wolff, Tobias
Wright, Charles
Wright, James
Wright, Richard

WORKS

---

*Adventures of
    Huckleberry Finn*
Age of Innocence, The
All the King's Men
Ambassadors, The
American Buffalo
As I Lay Dying
*Autobiography of Malcolm X,
    The*
Ballad of the Sad Café, The
"Bartleby the Scrivener"

Bell Jar, The
Beloved
Catcher in the Rye, The
Death of a Salesman
Four Quartets
Glass Menagerie, The
Gone with the Wind
Grapes of Wrath, The
Great Gatsby, The
Lolita

*Long Day's Journey
    into Night*
"Lottery, The"
Moby-Dick
Native Son
*Notes toward a
    Supreme Fiction*
On the Road
Our Town
Paterson
Pisan Cantos, The

Portrait of a Lady, The
Raisin in the Sun, A
Red Badge of Courage, The
Scarlet Letter, The
Slaughterhouse-Five
Song of Myself
Sound and the Fury, The
Streetcar Named Desire, A
Sun Also Rises, The
Tender Is the Night

THEMES

Academic Novels
Algonquin Round Table
Asian American Literature
Autobiography:
    General Essay
Autobiography:
    Slave Narratives
Autobiography: White
    Women during the
    Civil War
Beat Movement, The
Black Arts Movement
Black Mountain Poetry
Chicago Renaissance
Children's Literature
Colonial Writing in America
Confessional Poetry
Detective Fiction

Essay in America, The
Fireside Poets, The
Fugitives and Southern
    Agrarianism, The
Gay Literature: Poetry and
    Prose
Harlem Renaissance
Imagism and American
    Poets
Italian-American
    Literature
Jewish-American Fiction
Latino/Latina Fiction
    in America
Literary Theory in America
Little Magazines
Long Poem, The
Metafiction

Native American
    Literature
Naturalism and Realism
Nature Writing: Poetry
Nature Writing: Prose
New Critics, The
New Formalism, The
New Journalism, The
New York School
    of Poets
Objectivism (Reznikoff,
    Zukofsky, Oppen)
Poetess in
    American Literature, The
Popular Fiction
Proletarian Literature
Puritanism: The Sense of an
    Unending

Romanticism in America:
    The Emersonian
    Tradition
Science Fiction
Sentimental Literature
Short Story in America,
    The
Theater in America
Transcendentalism
Vietnam in Poetry and
    Prose
War Literature
West Coast School
Western Fiction: Grey,
    Stegner, McMurtry,
    McCarthy
Writing as a Woman in the
    Twentieth Century

DIRECTORY OF CONTRIBUTORS

Joy Arbor
University of Nebraska, Lincoln
Barnes, Djuna; Didion, Joan; Lowell,
Amy; Parker, Dorothy; Swenson, May

Scott Ashley
University of Newcastle, United Kingdom
Imagism and American Poets

James P. Austin
University of California, Irvine
Carver, Raymond; O'Hara, John; *On the
Road*; *Separate Peace, A*;
Slaughterhouse-Five

Charles Robert Baker
Independent Scholar, Dallas, Texas
Capote, Truman; Cooper, James
Fenimore; *Great Gatsby, The*;
Hemingway, Ernest; Irving, Washington;
Sun Also Rises, The; Tarkington, Booth

Cates Baldridge
Middlebury College
Stone, Robert

Susan Balée
*Independent Scholar, Wyncote,
Pennsylvania*
Autobiography: General Essay;
Longfellow, Henry Wadsworth;
O'Connor, Flannery

Rachel Barenblat
*Executive Director, Inkberry,
Williamstown, Massachusetts*
Ostriker, Alicia

Michael Barsanti
Rosenbach Museum, Philadelphia
Little Magazines

Jane Beal
University of California, Davis
Edwards, Jonathan

Sharon Becker
Clairmont Graduate University
McCarthy, Mary; Welty, Eudora; Writing
as a Woman in the Twentieth Century

Alfred Bendixen
California State University, Los Angeles
Hawthorne, Nathaniel; *Scarlet Letter, The*

John A. Bertolini
Middlebury College
Williams, Tennessee

Ian Bickford
*Independent Scholar, Mountain View,
California*
Barth, John; Barthelme, Donald; Dillard,
Annie; Kerouac, Jack

Pegge Bochynski
Salem State College, Salem, Massachusetts
Thurber, James

Alicia Borinsky
Boston University
Latino/Latina Fiction in America

H. W. Brands
Texas A & M University
Franklin, Benjamin

Daniel G. Brayton
Middlebury College
Bradstreet, Anne

Cornelius Browne
*Oregon State University Cascades, Bend,
Oregon*
Crane, Hart; *Walden*

Christopher Buck
Michigan State University
Hayden, Robert

Christopher Buckley
University of California, Riverside
Levine, Philip

Philip Bufithis
*Shepherd College, Shepherdstown,
West Virginia*
Brodkey, Harold

Nancy Bunge
Michigan State University
Anderson, Sherwood

John Burt
Brandeis University
All the King's Men; Warren, Robert Penn

Ronald Bush
St. John's College, Oxford
Four Quartets; *Pisan Cantos, The*;
Waste Land, The

Susan Butterworth
*Salem State College, Marblehead,
Massachusettes*
Hurston, Zora Neale; *Their Eyes Were
Watching God*

Matthew J. Caballero
Albancy, California
Lindsay, Vachel; Masters, Edgar Lee;
Matthews, William

Gerry Cambridge
*Independent Scholar and Poet, Glasgow,
Scotland*
Hecht, Anthony; Jeffers, Robinson;
Millay, Edna St. Vincent; New
Formalism, The; Ransom, John Crowe;
Roethke, Theodore; Very, Jones; Walcott,
Derek; Wilbur, Richard; Wright, James

Chuck Carlise
Davis, California
Beat Movement, The; Burroughs,
William S.; Ginsberg, Allen

Steven R. Carter
Salem State College, Salem, Massachusetts
Raisin in the Sun, A

Janice E. Cavoto
Independent Scholar, Glenside, Pennsylvania
Ambassadors, The; To Kill a Mockingbird

Laurie Champion
San Diego State University, Imperial Valley, California
Irving, John; Short Story; America, The

Maile Chapman
Hamburg, Germany
Oates, Joyce Carol

William Bedford Clark
Texas A & M University
Fugitives and Southern Agrarianism, The

Lorinda B. Cohoon
University of Texas, El Paso
Stowe, Harriet Beecher

Kate Cone
Topsham, Maine
Cummings, E. E.

Mark Conway
College of Saint Benedict and Saint John's University
Bukowski, Charles; Carruth, Hayden; Collins, Billy

Christopher Jane Corkery
College of the Holy Cross, Worcester, Massachusetts
Stafford, Jean

Peter Coviello
Bowdoin College, Brunswick, Maine
Transcendentalism

Michael Coyle
Colgate University
Pound, Ezra

Catherine Daly
Independent Scholar, Los Angeles
New York School of Poets; West Coast School

Joseph Dewey
University of Pittsburgh
DeLillo, Don

Morris Dickstein
Graduate Center, City University of New York
Jewish-American Fiction

Aaron K. DiFranco
University of California, Davis
Ammons, A. R.; Berry, Wendell; Nature Writing: Poetry; Snyder, Gary

Lynn Domina
State University of New York, Delhi, New York
Autobiography: White Women during the Civil War

Scott Donaldson
Scottsdale, Arizona
Cheever, John; Robinson, Edwin Arlington

Robert M. Dowling
U.S. Coast Guard Academy
"Bartleby the Scrivener"; Chesnutt, Charles W.; Dos Passos, John; Hapgood, Hutchins; Henry, O.; Proulx, Annie; Sandburg, Carl

David L. Dudley
Georgia Southern University, Statesboro, Georgia
Dunbar, Paul Laurence; Wheatley, Phillis

Joseph Duemer
Clarkson University
Vietnam in Poetry and Prose

Stefanie K. Dunning
Miami University of Ohio
Angelou, Maya; Walker, Alice

John Elder
Stewart Professor of English and Environmental Studies, Middlebury College
Nature Writing: Prose

Richard Everett
San Francisco Maritime National Historical Park
Dana, Richard Henry

Dina Ripsman Eylon
Independent Scholar, Toronto
Stein, Gertrude

Thomas J. Ferraro
Duke University
Italian-American Literature

Amanda Fields
University of Minnesota
Buck, Pearl S.; Erdrich, Louise; Gone with the Wind; Naylor, Gloria; Silko, Leslie Marmon

Annie Finch
Cincinnati, Ohio
Poetess in American Literature, The

Frederick Ethan Fischer
Shepherd College, Shepherdstown, West Virginia
Schwartz, Delmore

Edward Halsey Foster
Stevens Institute of Technology, Hoboken, New Jersey
Adams, Henry; Gay Literature: Poetry and Prose; Tate, Allen

Jonathan Freedman
Middlebury College
James, Henry

Angela M. Garcia
Escuela Americana, El Salvador
Alcott, Louisa May

John Gatta
University of Connecticut
Colonial Writing in America

Stephen K. George
Brigham Young University
Steinbeck, John

Dana Gioia
National Endowment of the Arts, Washington, D.C.
Kees, Weldon; Longfellow, Henry Wadsworth

Jan Goggans
Sacramento, California
Grapes of Wrath, The; McPhee, John; Norris, Frank

Jane Goldman
University of Dundee, Scotland
West, Nathanael

Susan Goodman
University of Delaware
Glasgow, Ellen; Howells, William Dean

Arielle Greenberg
Bentley College, Dedham, Massachusetts
Bell Jar, The

Emily R. Grosholz
Pennsylvania State University
Justice, Donald; Stevenson, Anne

David L. Gunton
Independent Scholar, New York, New York
Objectivism (Reznikoff, Zukofsky, Oppen)

Huck Gutman
University of Vermont
Song of Myself; Williams, William Carlos

Lisa J. Hacken
New York, New York
Chronology

Marilyn Hacker
The City College of New York
Ponsot, Marie

Mary Hadley
Georgia Southern University, Statesboro, Georgia
Detective Fiction

William R. Handley
University of Southern California, Los Angeles
Western Fiction: Grey, Stegner, McMurtry, McCarthy

Charles Hannon
Washington and Jefferson College, Pennsylvania
Faulkner, William

Henry Hart
College of William and Mary
Dickey, James; Lowell, Robert; Simic, Charles; Wright, Charles

Thomas S. Hart
Concord-Carlisle Regional High School, Concord, Massachusetts
Thoreau, Henry David

Burton Hatlen
University of Maine, Orono, Maine
Long Poem, The

Patricia B. Heaman
Wilkes University, Wilkes-Barre, Pennsylvania
As I Lay Dying; Updike, John

Kathleen A. Heininge
University of California, Davis
King, Stephen

Glenn Hendler
University of Notre Dame
Alger, Horatio

Brian Henry
University of Georgia
Ford, Richard; Salinger, J. D.

Danielle Hinrichs
Claremont Graduate University, Madison, Wisconsin
New Journalism, The

Jen Hirt
University of Idaho
Garland, Hamlin; Lardner, Ring

Philip Hobsbaum
Glasgow, Scotland
Auden, W. H.; Berryman, John; Confessional Poetry; Eliot, T. S.; Jarrell, Randall; New Critics, The; Notes toward a Supreme Fiction

Tyler Hoffman
Rutgers University–Camden
Bishop, Elizabeth; Frost, Robert

Patrick Colm Hogan
University of Connecticut
Literary Theory in America

Benjamin Ivry
New York, New York
Howard, Richard; Melville, Herman

Tanya E. C. Jarvik
University of California, Davis
Gardner, John; Winesburg, Ohio

Anett Jessop
University of California, Davis
Jackson, Laura Riding; Loy, Mina

Judith E. Johnson
Albany, New York
Kizer, Carolyn

Paul Johnston
State University of New York, Plattsburgh
Benét, Stephen Vincent; Fireside Poets, The; Lopez, Barry

Elaine M. Kauvar
Baruch College, City University of New York
Ozick, Cynthia

Kathryn W. Kemp
Clayton College & State University, Morrow, Georgia
Crèvecoeur, J. Hector St. John de; Tocqueville, Alexis de

Robin Kemp
Hambidge Fellow, Atlanta
Chopin, Kate; Stafford, William

Mary Louise Kete
University of Vermont
Sentimental Literature

Claire Keyes
Salem State College, Massachusetts
Rich, Adrienne

Karen L. Kilcup
University of North Carolina, Greensboro
Jewett, Sarah Orne

Janna King
Bryn Athyn, Pennsylvania
Glück, Louise

Judith Kitchen
State University of New York, Brockport
O'Brien, Tim; Tender Is the Night

Jerome Klinkowitz
University of Northern Iowa
Metafiction; Vonnegut, Kurt

Melissa Knox
University of Bielefeld, Westphalia, Germany
Death of a Salesman; Glass Menagerie, The; "Lottery, The"; Portrait of a Lady, The; Wilson, Edmund

Erik Kongshaug
San Pedro, California
Sinclair, Upton, and the Muckrakers

Denise Larrabee

Independent Scholar, Philadelphia
Our Town; Porter, Katherine Anne

J. Michael Lennon

Wilkes University, Wilkes-Barre,
Pennsylvania
Mailer, Norman

Jan Heller Levi

New York, New York
Rukeyser, Muriel

James A. Lewin

Shepherd College, Shepherdstown, West
Virginia
Singer, Isaac Bashevis

Kimberly Lewis

University of Chicago
McCarthy, Cormac; Smith, Dave; Stern,
Gerald

Sheldon W. Liebman

The Feltre School, Chicago
Emerson, Ralph Waldo

Richard Lingeman

Editor, New York
Lewis, Sinclair

James Longenbach

University of Rochester, New York
Pinsky, Robert; Stevens, Wallace

Jerome Loving

Texas A & M University
Dreiser, Theodore; Whitman, Walt

Margo Lukens

University of Maine, Orono, Maine
Native American Literature

Christopher MacGowan

College of William and Mary
Paterson

Edward A. (Sandy) Martin

Middlebury College
Mencken, H. L.

Wendy Martin

Claremont Graduate University,
Claremont, California

McCarthy, Mary; Welty, Eudora; Writing
as a Woman in the Twentieth Century

Janet McCann

Texas A & M University
Olds, Sharon

John McCardell

Middlebury College
Simms, William Gilmore, and
Antebellum Southern Literature

Sean McDonnell

University of California, Davis
Kinnell, Galway; Merwin, W. S.

Molly McQuade

Independent Scholar, Baltimore
Bierce, Ambrose; Chicago Renaissance;
Dickinson, Emily

John McWilliams

Middlebury College
Puritanism: The Sense of an Unending

Adam Scott Miller

Villanova University
Mather, Cotton; Taylor, Edward

Greg Miller

University of California, Davis
Baldwin, James; Kincaid, Jamaica

Brett C. Millier

Middlebury College
Kunitz, Stanley; Moore, Marianne

Rob Morris

Babson College, Wellesley, Massachusetts
Academic Novels; Algonquin
Round Table

Brenda Murphy

University of Connecticut
Theater in America

William R. Nash

Middlebury College
Black Arts Movement; Brooks,
Gwendolyn; Ellison, Ralph; Harlem
Renaissance; *Native Son*

Robert Niemi

St. Michael's College, Colchester, Vermont
London, Jack; Proletarian Literature

Caitriona O'Reilly

Trinity College, Dublin
Plath, Sylvia

Louis H. Palmer III

Castleton State College, Castleton,
Vermont
Ballad of the Sad Café, The; McCullers,
Carson

Jay Parini

Middlebury College
Vidal, Gore

Philip Parry

The University of St. Andrews, Scotland
Miller, Arthur; O'Neill, Eugene; Shepard,
Sam; *Streetcar Named Desire, A*; Wilder,
Thornton

Donald Pease

Dartmouth College
Romanticism in America: The
Emersonian Tradition

Jerry Phillips

University of Connecticut
White, Edmund

Sam Pickering

University of Connecticut
Children's Literature

Ellen Pifer

University of Delaware
Nabokov, Vladimir

Sanford Pinsker

Franklin & Marshall College Lancaster,
Pennsylvania
Bellow, Saul; Malamud, Bernard;
Trilling, Lionel

Ron Powers

Middlebury, Vermont
Twain, Mark

William H. Pritchard

Amherst College
Roth, Philip

Josef Raab

University of Bielefeld, Germany
Kushner, Tony; *Long Day's Journey into*
Night; Wilson, August

Mark Richardson

Western Michigan University
Crane, Stephen; Douglass, Frederick; Du Bois, W. E. B.; H.D. (Hilda Doolittle); *Red Badge of Courage, The*; Wright, Richard

Zack Rogow

University of California, Berkeley
Jordan, June; Kazin, Alfred

Michael Rosovsky

Emerson College, Boston
Hoagland, Edward

Susan J. Rosowski

University of Nebraska, Lincoln, Nebraska
Cather, Willa

Andrea Ross

University of California, Davis
Williams, Terry Tempest

Joyce A. Rowe

Fordham University
Moby-Dick

David Ryan

Independent Scholar, New York
Elkin, Stanley; Miller, Henry; Pynchon, Thomas

Arnold E. Sabatelli

Writer, Bethany, Connecticut
Aiken, Conrad; Momaday, N. Scott; Tate, James; White, E. B.; Wideman, John Edgar

Bill Savage

Northwestern University
Algren, Nelson

Gary Scharnhorst

University of New Mexico
Naturalism and Realism

Steven P. Schneider

University of Texas–Pan American
Soto, Gary

Susan M. Schultz

University of Hawaii at Manoa
Ashbery, John

Lacy Schutz

New York City
Black Mountain Poetry; Creeley, Robert; Hugo, Richard; Levertov, Denise

Lynn Orilla Scott

Michigan State University
Autobiography: Slave Narratives; Reed, Ishmael

J. D. Scrimgeour

Salem State College, Salem, Massachusetts
Autobiography of Malcolm X, The; Hughes, Langston

Donna Seaman

American Library Association, Chicago, Illinois
Agee, James; Beattie, Ann

Sylvia Bailey Shurbutt

Shepherd College, Shepherdstown, West Virginia
"Yellow Wallpaper, The"

Carol J. Singley

Rutgers University, Camden
Age of Innocence, The; Wharton, Edith

Ellen McGrath Smith

University of Pittsburgh
Jong, Erica; Paley, Grace; Sexton, Anne

Patrick A. Smith

Bainbridge College, Georgia
Doctorow, E. L.; Matthiessen, Peter

Willard Spiegelman

Southern Methodist University, Dallas, Texas
Merrill, James

Jenny Spinner

University of Connecticut
Essay in America, The

Vincent Standley

Writer, Lincoln, Rhode Island
Science Fiction

Heather Stephenson

Independent Scholar, Cambridge, Massachusetts
McClatchy, J. D.

Yerra Sugarman

New York University
Hacker, Marilyn; Lazarus, Emma

Paul Sullivan

Columnist, New York
Fitzgerald, F. Scott; Styron, William

Victoria D. Sullivan

Saint Peter's College, Jersey City
Albee, Edward

John Sutherland

University College, London
Popular Fiction

Kella Svetich

University of California, Davis
Asian American Literature; Kingston, Maxine Hong

Pauls Toutonghi

Cornell University
Adventures of Huckleberry Finn; Chronology; Heller, Joseph; *Things They Carried, The*; War Literature; Wolff, Tobias

Kathrine Varnes

University of Missouri, Columbia
Alvarez, Julia

Karma Waltonen

University of California, Davis
McNally, Terrence

Ted Weesner Jr.

Tufts University and Emerson College
Catcher in the Rye, The

Theresa M. Welford

Georgia Southern University, Statesboro, Georgia
Freneau, Philip; Gunn, Thom

J. Chris Westgate

University of California, Davis
American Buffalo; Mamet, David

Robert Wilson

Independent Scholar, Manassas, Virginia
Taylor, Peter

Mark Royden Winchell

*Independent Scholar, Clemson,
South Carolina*
Gioia, Dana; *Sound and
the Fury, The*;
Wolfe, Thomas

Nicolas S. Witschi

Western Michigan University
Harte, Bret

Lani Wolf

University of California, Davis
Banks, Russell; Kennedy,
William; Prose, Francine;
Roth, Henry; Stegner,
Wallace

William Wright

Pipersville, Pennsylvania
Hellman, Lillian

Thomas Wright

Independent Scholar, London, England
Poe, Edgar Allan

Kristine Yohe

Northern Kentucky University
Beloved; Morrison, Toni

Andrew Zawacki

The University of Chicago
Lolita; Strand, Mark

COPYRIGHT NOTICES

517

INDEX

Page numbers in **boldface** indicate article titles

Snyder, Gary, (*continued*)

San Francisco Renaissance and, **4:**329

sequence long poem and, **2:**504

translations from Chinese, **4:**331

Vietnam War and, **4:**330

West Coast School and, **4:**330, 331, 332, 334

Zen Buddhism and, **1:**143, 144, **2:**504, **4:**331

Snyder, Ruth, **4:**171

"Soap" (Stern), **4:**105

Soares, Lota de Macedo, **1:**181, 184, 186, 188

So Big (Ferber), **1:**39, **3:**390

Social Darwinism, **3:**26

Alger's popular fiction and, **3:**389

literary naturalists and, **3:**213–215, 216

as London influence, **2:**469, 472, 473, **4:**340

Norris's critique of, **3:**341

socialism

Language poets and, **4:**331

Lewis and, **2:**434, 436–437, 439

London and, **2:**471, 474, **3:**421

proletarian literature and, **3:**420, 421

Sandburg and, **3:**527

Sinclair and, **4:**46, 47

Steinbeck and, **4:**100

White (Edmund) and, **4:**366

socialist realism, **3:**289, **4:**326, 483, 486

"Society" (Emerson), **1:**482

Sociology for the South (Fitzhugh), **4:**36

Socrates, **1:**422, **2:**98

"Sofegietto" (Rich), **3:**467

Soft Machine, The (W. S. Burroughs), **1:**225

Sogliadatai (Nabokov). *See Eye, The*

"So Help Me" (Algren), **1:**43

Solar Storms (Hogan), **3:**204

Solataroff, Ted, **2:**329

Soldier Boy, The (W. Adams), **2:**347

Soldier Boy, The (W. T. Adams), **1:**272–273

"Soldiers Home" (Hemingway), **2:**205

Soldiers' Pay (Faulkner), **2:**3, 4, 14, 18, 214, **4:**288

"Soldier Walks under the Trees of the University, The" (Jarrell), **2:**316

Sole Survivor, A (Bierce), **1:**176, 178, 179–180

Sollors, Werner, **1:**262, 263, **2:**278

Solomon, Andrew, **1:**98

Solomon, Carl, **1:**142, 146, **2:**110, 111

Solomons, Leon, **4:**81

Solstice (Oates), **1:**4

"Solution" (Oppen), **3:**289

Solzhenitsyn, Aleksandr, **3:**125

Some Account of the Fore-Part of the Life of Elizabeth Ashbridge, **1:**296

Somebody in Boots (Algren), **1:**43, 44, **3:**425

Some Imagist Poets (anthology series), **2:**259–260, 263, 264

Lowell (Amy) editorship, **2:**514, **3:**405

"Some Notes on Miss L." (West), **4:**319, 322

"Some Notes on Organic Form" (Levertov), **2:**423

"Some Notes on Violence" (West), **4:**322

Some of the Dharma (Kerouac), **2:**369

"Some Reflections on American Manners" (Tocqueville), **4:**197

Somerville, Jane, **4:**104

Something Cloudy, Something Clear (T. Williams), **4:**418

Something Happened (Heller), **1:**4, **2:**193, 194

"Something Is There" (Singer), **4:**55

Something Said (Sorrentino), **3:**127

Something to Declare (Alvarez), **1:**48

Something to Remember Me By (Bellow), **1:**159

Something Unspoken (T. Williams), **4:**417

Some Thoughts Concerning Education (Locke), **1:**277

Some Thoughts Concerning the Present Revival of Religion in New England (Edwards), **1:**434

"Some Thoughts on Playwriting" (Wilder), **4:**402

Some Trees (Ashbery), **1:**63–64, 69, **3:**266

"Somthing Pure" (Reed), **3:**458

"So Much Water So Close to Home" (Carver), **4:**19

Son, Diana, **1:**78

"Sonatina in Yellow" (Justice), **2:**351

Son at the Front, A (Wharton), **3:**216, **4:**350

Sondheim, Stephen, **3:**52

Sone, Monica, **1:**75

"Song" (Creeley), **1:**337

"Song" (Rich), **3:**465

Song, Cathy, **1:**71, 73

Song Flung Up to Heaven, A (Angelou), **1:**62

"Song for a Dark Girl" (Hughes), **2:**150

"Song for Baby-O, Unborn" (DiPrima), **1:**145

"Song for Occupations, A" (Whitman), **4:**374

"Song for Simeon, A" (Eliot), **1:**448

"Song for the Middle of the Night, A" (J. Wright), **4:**474

Song of Hiawatha, The (Longfellow), **2:**25–26, 478, 480, 481, 510, **3:**285, 486

challenged as American epic, **2:**492

as most widely read long poem, **2:**485, 491

Song of Myself (Whitman), **2:**485, 491, 497, **4:**138, 371–377, 380, **382–390**

Song of Roland, The (Merwin transl.), **3:**119

Song of Solomon (Morrison), **3:**167, 169, 170, 172–173, 174, **4:**503

Song of the Andoumboulou series (Mackey), **2:**503

Song of the Cicadas (Mong-Lan), **1:**80, **4:**260

"Song of the Exposition" (Whitman), **4:**379

Song of the Indians Wars, The (Neihardt), **2:**492

Song of the Lark, The (Cather), **1:**241, 244–245, 249

"Song of the Law Abiding Citizen" (Jordan), **2:**349

"Song of the Taste" (Snyder), **4:**63

Song of Yvonne (Brainard), **1:**74

Songs and Sonnets (Masters), **3:**29

Songs for Jadina (Lau), **1:**73

Songs of a Semite: The Dance to Death, and Other Poems (Lazarus), **2:**414

Songs of Gold Mountain: Cantonese Rhymes from San Francisco Chinatown (Hom, ed.), **1:**72

sonnet

Alvarez and, **1:**46

Auden and, **1:**86, 87, 88

Berryman and, **1:**172, 173

Brodkey and, **1:**208

Collins and, **1:**288

Frost and, **2:**80

Hacker and, **2:**131, 132

Kees and, **2:**357

Lazarus and, **2:**415

Lowell (Robert) and, **2:**521

McClatchy and, **3:**52

Merrill and, **3:**111, 113

Millay and, **3:**130–135

New Critics on, **3:**246

Ransom and, **3:**455–456

Sonnet (Ashbery), **1:**63, 64

Sonnets, The (T. Berrigan), **2:**505, **3:**268, 269

"Sonnets for an Ungrafted Tree" (Millay), **3:**132, 133

"Sonnet to a Negro in Harlem" (H. Johnson), **4:**499

"Sonnet—To Science" (Poe), **3:**367

"Sonny's Blues" (Baldwin), **1:**120, 121, 123, **4:**17

Son of Royal Langbrith, The (Howells), **2:**233, **3:**214

Son of the Forest, A (Apess), **3:**200

Son of the Middle Border, A (Garland), **2:**96

Son of the Wolf, The (London), **2:**472

Sonoma County, Calif., **2:**473, 474, **4:**340

Sons of the Sheik, The (Hull), **3:**390

Sontag, Susan, **1:**498, **4:**366

Soonest Mended (Ashbery), **1:**65, 66

Sophie's Choice (Styron), **3:**395, **4:**143

Sophist, The (Bernstein), **2:**500

Sopranos, The (television series), **2:**284

Sordello (Browning), **3:**407

Sorin, Hubert, **4:**367

Sorrell and Son (Deeping), **3:**390

Sorrentino, Gilbert, **2:**282, **3:**126–127, **4:**330

"Sorrow" (Millay), **3:**130

Sorrow Dance, The (Levertov), **2:**423

Soto, Gary, **2:**426, **3:**228, **4:66–69**

Sot-Weed Factor, The (Barth), **1:**135, 136

"Sot-Weed Factor, The; or, a Voyage to Maryland, &c." (Cooke), **1:**294

Soul of an Immigrant, The (Panunzio), **2:**277

"Souls Belated" (Wharton), **4:**15

Souls of Black Folk, The (Du Bois), **1:**419–423, 426

"Souls of White Folks, The" (Du Bois), **1:**419

Sound and the Fury, The (Faulkner), **2:**1–2, 4–5, 9, 10, 14, **18–22**, **4:**459, 482

French translation of, **2:**12

Sound of Mountain Water, The (Stegner), **4:**341

Sounds of Poetry, The (Pinsky), **3:**352

Soupault, Philippe, **4:**321

For Reference

Not to be taken from this room